IRISH PEDIGREES.

VOL. I.

ABBREVIATIONS.*

Arm. (Armiger),	...	...	...	Stands for	Bearing Arms.
A.T.	...	...	,,	Armée Territoriale.
b.	...	...	,,	born.
bur.	...	...	,,	buried.
C.L.H.	...	...	,,	Knight of the Legion of Honour.
Col.	...	...	,,	Colonel.
cont.	...	...	,,	contemporary.
C.T.	...	...	,,	Chief of Tirconnell.
Cust. Pac. (custos pacis)	...	...	,,	Custodian of the Peace.
d.	...	...	,,	died.
dau.	..	...	,,	daughter.
D.C.	...	...	,,	District of Columbia.
d.s.p.	...	...	,,	died without offspring.
G.C.L.H.	...	...	,,	Grand Cross of the Legion of Honour.
La.	...	...	,,	Louisiana.
L.H.	...	...	,,	Legion of Honour.
Lieut.-Col.	...	...	,,	Lieutenant-Colonel.
m.	...	...	,,	married.
Mass.	...	...	,,	Massachusetts.
Milés	...	...	,,	A Soldier.
Mo.	...	...	,,	Missouri.
N.C.	...	...	,,	North Carolina.
ob.	...	...	,,	he died.
ob. v.p.	...	...	,,	he died in his father's lifetime.
O.L.H.	...	...	,,	Officer of the Legion of Honour.
p.	...	...	,,	page.
Pa.	...	...	,,	Pennsylvania.
plenæ ætatis ...	...	...	,,	of man's age.
pp.	...	...	,,	pages.
s.p. (sine prole)	...	...	,,	without offspring.
s.p.m.	...	...	,,	without male offspring.
temp.	...	...	,,	in the time of.
unm.	...	...	,,	unmarried.
U.S.A.	...	...	,,	United States, America.
Va.	...	...	,,	Virginia.
v.p.	...	...	,,	in his father's lifetime.
Vit.	...	...	,,	living.
W. I.	...	...	,,	West Indies.

* *Abbreviations:* It is only the less obvious Abbreviations employed in this Work, and which might not be intelligible to the general reader, that are here given.

very sincerely yours,

John O'Hart.

IRISH PEDIGREES;

OR,

THE ORIGIN AND STEM

OF

THE IRISH NATION.

BY

JOHN O'HART,

ASSOCIATE IN ARTS, QUEEN'S UNIVERSITY IN IRELAND ; FELLOW OF THE ROYAL
HISTORICAL AND ARCHÆOLOGICAL ASSOCIATION OF IRELAND ; MEMBER
OF THE HARLEIAN SOCIETY, LONDON ; AUTHOR OF "IRISH
LANDED GENTRY WHEN CROMWELL CAME TO
IRELAND," ETC.

" Where are the heroes of the ages past ?
Where the brave chieftains, where the mighty ones
Who flourished in the infancy of days ?
All to the grave gone down."
—HENRY KIRKE WHITE.
"Man is but the sum of his Ancestors."
—EMERSON.

FIFTH EDITION.

IN TWO VOLUMES.
VOL. I.

Fifth Edition
Originally Published
Dublin, 1892

Reprinted
Genealogical Publishing Co., Inc.
1001 N. Calvert St., Baltimore, Md. 21202
1976, 1989, 1999

Library of Congress Cataloging in Publication Data

O'Hart, John.
  Irish pedigrees.

  Reprint of the 1892 ed. published by J. Duffy, Dublin.

  Bibliography: p.
  1. Ireland—Genealogy. 2. Ireland—History—To 1172. I. Title.

CS483.05 1976   929'1'09415   76-12097

ISBN 0-8063-0737-4 (set number)

ISBN 0-8063-1259-9 (Volume I)

Made in the United States of America

PREFACE.

In this Edition we have inserted all the Genealogies contained in the Third Edition of IRISH PEDIGREES, as well as those given in our IRISH LANDED GENTRY WHEN CROMWELL CAME TO IRELAND; and, wherever we could do so, we have given a description of the Armorial Bearings* of each family whose genealogy we have traced.

From the large quantity of *additional* matter collected therefor, this Edition became so voluminous, that it had to be divided into two Volumes.

In this Vol. we give the "ORIGIN AND STEM OF THE IRISH NATION," and, so far as we could collect them, the genealogies of the families which branched from that ancient stem; together with the territories possessed by the ancient Irish families in the twelfth century; a Chapter on the "English Invasion," and another on the "Cromwellian Devastation," of Ireland.

In Vol. II. we give the "Families in Ireland from the twelfth to the end of the sixteenth century," with the counties in which they, respectively, were located; the Names of the Settlers in Ireland under the "Plantation of Ulster;" the Names of the Adventurers who came into Ireland with the Cromwellian Settlement, or with the Revolution; the Names of the Huguenot and Palatine families which settled in Ireland; the "Most important families in Ireland, and the counties in which they were located, at the beginning of the seventeenth century;" the Genealogies of Anglo-Irish and other families which settled in Ireland since the English invasion; the Irish Brigades in the service of foreign nations; the papers contained in the Appendix to the Third Edition of our IRISH PEDIGREES, and in the Appendix to our IRISH LANDED GENTRY; the "Opinions of the Press," from Newspapers and Periodicals in the Old and New World, etc.

A careful perusal of the Work will show that, in the wide field of our genealogical research, we have been unable to collect *all* the Irish and Anglo-Irish Pedigrees; but, we are satisfied that we have collected all of them that are preserved in our public archives, or that escaped the ravages of the Elizabethan Wars,† and the Strafford and Cromwellian devastations, in Ireland.

---

* *Bearings :* A drawing or illustration of any of those Armorial Bearings can, at a moderate charge, be procured from Mr. William T. Parkes, of 12 Fleet-street, Dublin.

† *Wars :* For a description of the state of Ireland in the reign of Queen Elizabeth, see Sir Charles Gavan Duffy's " *Bird's-Eye View of Ireland.*"

During the Wars of Queen Elizabeth some of the "new comers" settled in Ireland; many of them, in the time of Sir William Petty;* others of them, during the Ulster Plantation; others, during Strafford's Viceroyalty; others, during the Cromwellian, and others, during the Williamite, Confiscations.

The old Irish genealogies which are collected in this Work are carried down to the lineal representative of each family living when such family was deprived of its patrimony, to make room for the new settlers, according as each foreign migration† landed in Ireland; and some of them down to the present time; but most of the Anglo-Irish and Anglo-Norman genealogies by us recorded are brought down to the Commonwealth period, when the estates of those families were confiscated.

Members of many of the present Irish families will see, in one or other of the Lists given in No. 1, or No. 2 Appendix, contained in Vol. II. of this Edition, the names of their ancestors who first settled in Ireland:

> And oh ! it were a gallant deed
> To show before Mankind
> How every race and every creed
> Might be by love combined;
> Might be combined, yet not forget
> The *fountains* whence they rose ;
> As, filled by many a *rivulet*
> The stately SHANNON flows.

While O'Clery brings most of the Irish genealogies contained in his Book down to A.D. 1636; MacFirbis, to 1666; and O'Ferrall's *Linea Antiqua*, to 1708, it is only in a few cases that, in any of those great works, the *locality* of any representative of an Irish family living at those respective periods is mentioned: possibly, because, under the Laws of Tanistry, the locality in which was situate each family patrimony in Ireland was in those times well known. To MacFirbis, however, we may look, so far as their genealogies are contained in his Book, for the lineal

---

* *Petty :* It may interest our readers to know that Sir William Petty was the first to introduce into Ireland what is known as *Quit Rent :* that is, one penny per acre (or 10s. per quarter or 120 acres) of land held by each of the then Irish Proprietors, to be paid to Queen Elizabeth "for ever," in consideration for which each Proprietor was made to believe that he would be confirmed in his possessions, and protected by the Government against all breakers of the law. When, however, through Petty's Survey, the Government became cognizant of the extent of land possessed by each Irish Catholic Proprietor, there was almost in every case a wholesale confiscation of their Estates ; the rulers of provinces, counties, or districts in Ireland largely sharing in the result of those confiscations.

† *Migration :* The first English migration came into Ireland in 1168, in the reign of King Henry II. From that period down to the end of the reign of Henry VIII. there were seventy-eight such migrations.—See Sections 3 and 4, under the heading "New Divisions of Ireland, and the New Settlers," in the Appendix, No. 1, in Vol. II.

representatives of the Irish, Anglo-Irish, and Anglo-Norman families living when the Estates of the Irish " Papist Proprietors" and of the Irish " Delinquent Protestants"* were confiscated, under the Cromwellian Settlement of Ireland.

For the information respecting the Irish Brigades serving in France, Spain, Austria, the Spanish Netherlands, etc., contained in either Appendix to Vol. II., we are indebted to the courtesy of Mr. J. Casimir O'Meagher, of Mountjoy-square, Dublin ; which, with untiring energy, Mr. O'Meagher compiled in the Archives† of the several countries to which they relate : in whose services the Irishmen mentioned in those Papers brought renown on their own native land. To the present representatives of those families, in whatever clime their lot is cast, those Papers will afford interesting information.

But, while in the Spanish Netherlands, and other European countries, Irishmen have shed lustre on their native country, we venture to say that nowhere and under no circumstances have they displayed more heroism, magnanimity, dauntless enterprise, genius, dignity, burning zeal, good citizenship, unsullied fidelity, and administrative power, than in the Service of America.‡ As to them in exile the Land of the " Stars and Stripes" had been a refuge and a home, for that Land our countrymen have with willing hearts fought, and bled, and died. Whenever disaster seemed to threaten the Great Western Republic, either from foreign power, or internal discord, Irishmen were the first to grasp their swords, in her defence, and the last to sheathe them; until her foes had been vanquished, and the smiles of peace had returned to brighten and beautify her, once more, through the length and breadth of her vast and God-favoured Empire. It is therefore that we in Ireland should feel proud of their exploits; and it is therefore that we ourself feel pleasure in herein recording the names mentioned in the Paper in the Appendix No. 2, headed " The Irish Brigades in the Service of America." In that Paper we give a List of the Officers in the Irish-American Brigades during the American War of 1861-1865, between the Northern and Southern States,

---

* *Delinquent Protestants :* By this designation were known the loyal Protestants who sided, or were suspected of sympathy, with their King, the unfortunate Charles I.

† *Archives :* The papers, above mentioned, treat on the "Irish Brigade in the Service of France ;" "The Irish Legion ;" "Irish Endowments in Austria ;" "Irishmen who served in Austria: Old Army Lists;" "Irishmen serving in Austria ;" "Modern Army Lists ; a "List of Irishmen who have served in the Spanish Army ;" and a "List of Persons of Irish Origin, enjoying Honours and Emoluments in Spain," in 1881.

‡ *America :* For the "Early Irish Settlers in America," see the *Celtic Magazine* (New York : Halligan and Cassidy,) for April and May, 1883 ; which will well repay perusal.

on the Slave-Emancipation question; when, unhappily, the Federal Army*
of the North was pitted against the Confederate Army of the South.
That Federal Army was, it will be remembered, chiefly composed of
Meagher's Irish Brigade and of Corcoran's Irish Legion (two distinct
Brigades), besides several Regiments and many Companies in the "Union"
Volunteers, coming from certain States of the Union, all of whom served
in the Federal Army; but in the Confederate Army in that War were
many distinguished Officers,† *Irish* by birth or descent, whose names, if we
knew them, we would also herein gladly record. Among those were
General "Stonewall" Jackson, General Patrick Ronayne-Cleburne;
General (now United States Senator) Mahone, etc. In a future edition,
however, we hope to be able to give the names of all the Irish Officers in
the Confederate Army; together with the names of any Irishmen (by birth
or descent) who at any time filled the Office of President of the United
States of America, or of Governor of any State in the Union; or who in
any other position in any of our Colonies shed lustre on their Nation and
their Race.

And if God spares us, we shall give, in a future Edition of our "IRISH
LANDED GENTRY WHEN CROMWELL CAME," the names of *all* the Irish
Landed Gentry in Ireland, A.D. 1641; and the names of the persons who
in every county in Ireland succeeded to those Estates, or to any portions
of them.

In the fervent hope that (see No. 81, p. 40, *infra*,) the relation which
the *lineal descent* of the present Royal Family of England bears to the
ancient Royal Stem of Ireland, would conduce to a kindly feeling on behalf
of Her Gracious Majesty towards *ourself* and our bleeding country; we
humbly forwarded to Queen VICTORIA a presentation copy of the Third

---

* *Army* : Besides the Irish Brigade and the Irish Legion in the Federal Army,
there were several Regiments distinctively *Irish* in different States, and many Irish
Companies; besides many Irish Officers whose Companies were partly Irish, such as :
> The 37th New York Volunteers ("Irish Rifles").
> The 40th do. do. ("Tammany Regiment").
> Colonel Cass's Pennsylvania Regiment.
> Colonel Mulligan's Chicago Regiment; etc.

So that the names of the Irish Officers in the service of America would, even with
their brief records, fill a good-sized volume; not to speak of the Irish Officers who
held command in the "Rebel" or Confederate Army. We might observe that every
full Regiment had about thirty-five officers.

† *Officers* : The names of the Officers in Meagher's Irish Brigade are taken from
Captain Conyngham's "Irish-American Brigade and its Campaigns," published in
1866; and the names of the Officers in Corcoran's Irish Legion are taken from the
Official Report of the Adjutant-General of the State of New York. If in either Return
it be found that we omitted any name which ought to be inserted, we beg to say that
such omission was unintentional.

There is, we find, a large number of *Irish* Officers at present in the Regular Army
of the United States of America.

Edition* of this Work; in pp. 40-44 of which that "lineal descent" is carefully traced, as it also is in pp. 37-41 of this Volume. It is needless to say that Her Majesty graciously accepted and acknowledged the presentation.

As the Book of Genesis and the Writings of the Apostles contain expressions and conceptions respecting the Creation, which cannot be clearly interpreted unless by the latest results of Geological Science, we give in pp. 1-32 of this Volume, a Chapter† on "THE CREATION," in which, guided by Geological laws, we have humbly ventured to interpret those expressions and conceptions without conflicting in any manner with the account of the Creation contained in the Sacred Volume! In our dutiful veneration for the Visible Head of the Church to which we belong, we respectfully forwarded another presentation copy of that Edition also to Pope LEO XIII., for his gracious acceptance ; earnestly requesting the consideration by His Holiness, not only of the views which we humbly propound in that Chapter, but also of the Chapter headed "The English Invasion of Ireland," in which it was stated, on the authorities therein mentioned, that Pope Adrian‡ IV., in the exercise of his Temporal Power, granted Ireland to King Henry II. of England. The chapter on "The English Invasion of Ireland" is also given in pp. 792-799 of this Volume. It was

* *Edition:* A copy of that as well as a copy of this edition, may be seen in the Library of the House of Commons, and in the Library of the House of Lords, London ; as well as in the Library of Congress at Washington, D.C. ; etc.

† *Chapter*: It may interest our readers to look through that chapter in its entirety ; for, without entering into any religious controversy whatever on the subject, we venture to say that it will help to throw light on the *Edenic* period of Man's existence before his first sin !

‡ *Adrian* : On the vexed question of Pope Adrian's Bull, which was dated from Rome, A.D. 1155, it is sometimes urged that the said Bull was a *forgery :* because, it is alleged, Pope Adrian IV. was *not* at all in Rome in that year, for that he was in exile at Beneventum, on account of a revolt caused by the arch-innovator Arnold of Brescia. But it will be seen by reference to the following authorities, which a friend of ours has brought under our notice, that Adrian IV. was, in the plenitude of his tem poral power, in Rome, A.D. 1155 : In a life of this Pope, written by Cardinal Aragonius, which is to be found in Muratori's "*Rerum Italicarum Scriptores,*" Tom. III., Part I., p. 441, it is stated that, so far from Arnold being able to drive the Pope out of Rome, his Holiness laid an interdict on the city in the very middle of Holy Week. The Romans were so terrified that they drove Arnold out of the city. Frederick Barbarossa then seized him, and sent him back a prisoner to the Pope, who condemned him to be hanged. An account of his execution, in the month of May, will be found in Sismondi's "*Republiques Italiennes,*" T. I., p. 316, Ed. Brussels, 1826. Aragonius gives an account of the Pope's proceedings during the summer of 1155 : as, for instance, his crowning, as Emperor, Frederick Barbarossa, the celebrated Hohenstaufen, which took place in the month of June. In the autumn of 1155, Adrian IV. went to Beneventum for the purpose of absolving William, King of Sicily, from his excommunication, and receiving his homage (see page 445, *Muratori,* above mentioned). In fact, Pope Adrian IV. was never so powerful at Rome as he was in that year ; having the support of the Emperor, as well as that of his own troops. For further information, the reader is referred to the great Benedictine Work : "*Histoire des Gaules et de la France,*" T. xv., p. 661.

our privilege to receive from the Holy Father, per the Right Rev. Doctor Kirby, Bishop of Lita, and Rector of the Irish College in Rome (through whom the Presentation was made), the following kind and courteous reply :

"Rome, 30th December, 1881.

"DEAR SIR,

"I had the pleasure to receive your esteemed letter of the 25th instant, which was followed by your Work on the 'Irish Pedigrees,' a day or two after. I hasten to inform you that I had the honour of an audience with the Holy Father on yesterday, and I availed myself of the occasion to present him with your Work, which he graciously received. I explained to him its object. He looked over it with interest, and said that he would have it placed in the Library. He was pleased to authorize me to send to you, together with his thanks for the Work, his Apostolic Benediction, which I trust will be a help and an impulse to you to continue to employ your superior talents for the advantage of our holy religion and country, in the production of works useful to both ; thus meriting for yourself at the proper time the encomium and promise of Divine Wisdom : ' *Qui elucidant me vitam æternam habebunt.*' Wishing you every success in your most laudable undertaking, and all the blessings and graces of this holy season,

"I am, yours sincerely,

"✠ T. KIRBY, Bishop of Lita, etc.

"John O'Hart, Esq.,
"Ringsend, Dublin."

It only remains for us to express our grateful acknowledgments to the late Sir Samuel Ferguson, LL.D., Q.C., and the Officers in his Department with whom we came in contact in the Public Record Office ; to John K. Ingram, Esq., LL.D., the Librarian of Trinity College, and his obliging Assistants; to the Rev. M. H. Close, M.A., Major MacEniry, John T. Gilbert, Esq., F.R.S., and J. J. MacSweeney, Esq., all in the Royal Irish Academy, Dublin : for the uniform kindness and courtesy which we experienced from each and every of them during our tedious researches in their respective Institutions.

For other literary aid (see the Preface to Vol. II.) received from Alfred Webb., Esq., Dublin ; Thomas O'Gorman, Esq., Sandymount, Dublin ; C. J. Hubbard, Esq., United States, America; Rev. C. A. Agnew, Edinburgh ; S. Smiles, Esq., London ; Rev. George Hill, late Librarian, Queen's College, Belfast; William J. Simpson, Esq., Belfast; and James M'Carte, Esq., Liverpool, our best thanks are also due, and here respectfully tendered.

As this Work unveils the ancestors of many of the present Irish, Anglo-Irish, and Anglo-Norman families, of various shades of religious and political opinions, we have endeavoured in its pages to subserve no sect or party. And we beg to say that, while our IRISH PEDIGREES and our IRISH LANDED GENTRY are necessarily *national* in character, there is nothing in them to wound the feelings of Celt or Saxon, Catholic or Protestant, Liberal or Conservative.

Hardinge (see his "Epitome" *MS.*, in the Royal Irish Academy, Dublin), in his "*Circumstances attending the Civil War in Ireland in* 1641-1652," truly says:

"In the rise and progress of Empires, as naturally as in the lives of men, there are events concerning which the biographer or historian would willingly remain silent, did not the salutary lessons to be derived from them demand publication."

That sentence we freely adopt, and we heartily endorse the sentiment it contains. We shall rejoice that we did not remain "silent," if the publication of the facts which we record in this Work will conduce to the removal of the causes for *discontent* which have long distracted our afflicted country:

> While History's Muse the memorial was keeping,
> Of all that the dark hand of Destiny weaves,
> Beside her the Genius of ERIN stood weeping,
> For *hers* was the story that *blotted* the leaves.

JOHN O'HART.

RINGSEND SCHOOL, RINGSEND,
DUBLIN : *December*, 1887.

FROM THE PREFACE TO THE FIRST EDITION.

As accounting for the appearance of this Work I should mention that, from a certain family tradition, conveyed to me in my boyhood, it was my life's ambition to meet with some ancient Irish Manuscript that would throw light on my family pedigree. It was, therefore, that I hailed with pleasure the publication, in 1846, of the *Annals of the Four Masters** (Dublin : Geraghty, 8, Anglesea Street), which Owen Connellan, Irish Historiographer to their late Majesties George the Fourth and William the Fourth, translated into English, from Irish Manuscripts preserved in the Libraries of Trinity College and the Royal Irish Academy, Dublin. From the same Manuscripts the late John O'Donovan, LL.D., M.R.I.A., also translated and edited the "*Annala Rioghachta Eireann ;* or, The Annals of the Kingdom of Ireland," by the Four Masters, from the Earliest Period to the Year A.D. 1616. Dublin: Hodges and Smith, Grafton Street, 1851.

Those "Annals of the Kingdom of Ireland" I need not say I read with care ; from them I derived a large fund of valuable information which I freely employed in the compilation of this Volume.

For other information in connection with my subject, I am also indebted to "The Tribes and Customs of the district of Hy-Maine,"† published by the Irish Archæological Society; "The Book of Rights ;" Celtic Society ; "The Topographical Poems by O'Dugan and O'Heerin :"‡

---

* *Four Masters* : The " Four Masters" were so called, because Michael O'Clery, Peregrine O'Clery, Conary O'Clery, together with Peregrine O'Duigenan (a learned antiquary of Kilronan, in the county Roscommon), were the *four* principal compilers of the ancient Annals of Ireland in the 17th century. Besides the above-named authors, however, two other eminent antiquaries and chroniclers assisted in the compilation of the Annals—namely, Ferfassa O'Mulconry and Maurice O'Mulconry, both of the county Roscommon.—CONNELLAN.

† *Hy-Maine* : " Hy-Maine" was the principality of the O'Kellys ; a large territory comprised within the present counties of Galway and Roscommon, and extending from the river Shannon, at Lanesborough, to the county Clare, and from Athlone to Athenry in the county Galway ; these O'Kellys were of the Clan Colla. The O'Kellys in the ancient Kingdom of Meath, who were one of the families known as the "Four Tribes of Tara," were descended from the Clan Colman of the southern Hy-Niall.

‡ *O'Dugan and O'Heerin* : Shane O'Dugan, the author of "O'Dugan's Topography," was the chief poet to O'Kelly of Hy-Maine ; and died A.D. 1372. Giolla-na-Neev O'Heerin, who died A.D. 1420, wrote a continuation of O'Dugan's Topography : these Topographies give names of the Irish Chiefs and Clans in Ireland from the twelfth to the fifteenth century.—CONNELLAN.

Irish Arch. and Celt. Society; "Rollin's Ancient History:" Blackie and Son, Glasgow; Yeatman's "Early English History:" Longmans, Green, and Co., London; Miss Cusack's "History of Ireland:" National Publication Office, Kenmare; "Irish Names of Places," by P. W. Joyce, LL.D.: M'Glashan and Gill, Dublin; O'Callaghan's "History of the Irish Brigades:" Cameron and Ferguson, Glasgow; Haverty's "History of Ireland:" Duffy, Dublin; The Abbé MacGeoghegan's "History of Ireland;" Keating's "History of Ireland," etc.

But the work to which I am most indebted for the IRISH PEDIGREES is that portion of the Annals of Ireland known as "O'Clery's Irish Genealogies;" *so* called because compiled by Michael O'Clery, who was the chief author of the "Annals of the Kingdom of Ireland," above mentioned.

Actuated by the consideration that, should I neglect to publish this Work or consign it to a future time, another opportunity for collecting materials reliable as those now in my possession might never again present itself, I have ventured to unveil the Irish Genealogies. In doing so I beg to say that I had no sect or party to subserve; for, in the IRISH PEDIGREES are given the genealogies of families of various shades of religious and political opinions.

J. O'HART.

RINGSEND SCHOOL, DUBLIN,
December, 1875.

FROM THE PREFACE TO THE SECOND EDITION.

At all times the subject of genealogies must command the respect and attention of both rich and poor; on account of the intimate bearing it has upon the individual, together with the tribes, people, nation, and family to which he belongs. So it was in the past; and so it ever shall be. The ancient Romans were fond of having the statues of their illustrious ancestors in prominent places, so as to animate themselves to deeds of virtue and valour; and also that the memory of them would shed lustre on their descendants. Even our blessed Saviour would condescend to have his genealogy, according to the flesh, traced up and left on record: the Evangelist St. Matthew traces it back to Abraham; the Evangelist St. Luke, back to our first parents. And we are told by St. Jerome that, in his own day, the boys in the very streets of Jerusalem could name their ancestors up to Adam.

The ancient Irish were not behind other nations in this respect; for, according to O'Donovan, in the *Miscellany of the Celtic Society* (1849)—

> "Those of the lowest rank among a great tribe traced and retained the whole line of their descent with the same care which in other nations was peculiar to the rich and great; for, it was from his own genealogy each man of the tribe, poor as well as rich, held the charter of his civil state, his right of property in the cantred in which he was born, the soil of which was occupied by one family or clan, and in which no one lawfully possessed any portion of the soil if he was not of the same race as the chief."

Up to the end of the sixteenth century—or as long as the "Tanist Law"* remained in force in Ireland, collections of authentic Irish pedigrees existed; in one or other of which was carefully registered, the birth of every member of a sept, as well of the poor as of the rich, and by which was determined the portion of land to be allotted for the sustenance of each head of a family and of those dependent on him. All those local records have disappeared: when, by the conquest of Ireland, they ceased to be useful for their own special purpose, they would naturally be neglected; and, in all probability, have most of them perished. But, before they disappeared, they doubtless formed the *basis* of the genealogical collections made by O'Clery, MacFirbis, Keating, and O'Ferrall, etc.

"A time came," writes the author of *The Life and Letters of Florence MacCarthy Mór*, "when it was of importance for the conquerors of Ireland to know something of

---

* *Tanist-Law*: See "The Laws of Tanistry," in No. 1 Appendix, of Vol. II.

the native families from whom they must expect irreconcilable hostility, or might hope for allegiance ; and out of this necessity arose a new value for all genealogical records, present and past, which had not yet perished.   The attention of English official personages in Ireland, towards the close of the sixteenth century, was, in a marked manner, directed towards the recovery of such documents ; and able statesmen like Sir George Carewe, then President of Munster ; Lord Burgley, and Sir Robert Cecyll ; Irish supporters of the Government, like the Earl of Thomond ; official legal persons, as Richard Hadsor ; and, as Dr. O'Donovan asserts, paid spies, employed by the lord deputies, greatly contributed to the preservation of Irish pedigrees, and, truth to say, greatly also to the inaccuracies and confusion in which so many collections abound.   From wills and lawsuits—customary sources of genealogical evidence, little information could be expected amongst a people who had no power of disposing of the portion of sept-lands which they held during life, and whose contentions when not settled by the sword, were pleaded and decided orally by Brehons on hill-sides under the open heavens, and which were little likely to be placed on permanent record : hence the more diligence would be needed by spies, or official persons, for acquiring the information, past or present, desired by the English Government."

In preparing the materials for this Edition I saw the great help it would render to the Science of Comparative Philology, were I to give in its correct orthography* each Irish proper name mentioned in the Work. With that view I revised, *de novo*, all my Notes ; and, mistakes and errors excepted, have written the personal names and sirnames therein recorded as they were spelled in the Irish language.   To the Philologist and Ethnologist the study of these Irish proper names will disclose a mine of antiquarian wealth more precious, in my opinion, than any of the rich antiquities lately discovered in Assyria, Mycenæ, or the Troad.

Up to the eleventh century every Irish personal name was significant, and was sometimes rendered more so by the application of some additional sirname or epithet.   The English meaning of the Irish name or epithet, from which each Irish sirname is derived, is, in almost every instance, here given ; and, in some cases, I trace the epithet or its cognate in others of the ancient languages, to show that the Gaelic Irish speech is connected in sisterhood with the most venerated languages in the world.

The reader who looks through the "Index of Sirnames" will find in the body of the work (where I give the derivation of the names), that many families are of Irish descent who have long been considered of foreign extraction : for, dispossessed in former times of their territories in Ireland, by more powerful families than their own, or by the Danish, or English, invasion, members of some Irish families settled in Great Britain, or on the Continent; and, from time to time afterwards, descendants of

---

* *Orthography* : It may be well to mention that the word in [bracket] in any page in this work is meant to approximate the pronunciation of the Irish word which precedes it.

such persons, with their sirnames so twisted, translated, or disguised, as to appear of English or Anglo-Norman origin, came to Ireland in the ranks of its invaders—in the hope that, if they succeeded in its conquest, they would, as many of them did, receive from the conquerors some of the Irish estates confiscated in those unhappy times in Ireland.

It may be asked—Why trace in this Work the genealogy of the present Royal Family of Great Britain and Ireland ; since Queen VICTORIA'S immediate ancestors were German Princes who were in no way connected with Ireland. I would reply that, as Queen VICTORIA is of *Irish lineal descent*, I have traced in IRISH PEDIGREES Her Majesty's Lineage. And it is satisfactory to me to have to record that the Queen's Irish lineal descent, as I trace it down from Heremon, son of Milesius of Spain (a quo the *Milesian Irish* Nation), is the same as that compiled by the Rev. A. B. Grimaldi, M.A., and published* within the last month or two in London.

Scholars who are best acquainted with them contend that the *Annals of the Kingdom of Ireland*, compiled by the " Four Masters," are more reliable than even those of Greece, which have been accepted because of the accident of the Greek language having been studied and encouraged by the Romans, who led the mind of Europe so long before and after the Christian era. Therefore it was that, through conquest, most of the countries of Europe, including Britain and Gaul, were forced to receive the Roman civilization. But, with Pagan Rome Ireland had no dealings : " She was," writes De Vere, " an eastern nation in the West; her civilization was not military, it was patriarchal—whose type was the family, and not the army; it was a civilization of Clans." Claudian, speaking of the battles of the Roman general Stilico with the Britons and Picts, and the Scots of Ireland, in the latter end of the fourth century, says :

—— Totam cum Scotus *Iernem*,
Movit et infesto spumavit remige Tethys ;

which may be translated, as follows :

When the Scot moved all *Ireland* against us, and the ocean foamed with his hostile oars.

" Leagued with their countrymen in Scotland, and with the Picts," continues De Vere, " the ancient Irish had repeatedly driven back the Romans behind their further wall, till they left the land defenceless."

---

* *Published* : The Leaflet in which Queen VICTORIA's lineal descent is traced by the Rev. Mr. Grimaldi, M.A., is published in London by W. H. Guest, 29, Paternoster Row.

Therefore it was that Pagan Rome hated Ireland and its belongings; and, following in the footsteps of their masters, the Roman-conquered nations learned to frown not only on the language of Ireland, but on Ireland's admirable Philosophy:

> Long, long neglected Gaelic tongue,
>   Thou'st died upon our Irish plains,
> Save some lingering sounds that stay,
>   To tell us that a wreck remains.
> Our "hundred hills" each bears a name—
>   An echo from each vale is wrung
> Upon our ears—these bring with shame
>   Remembrance of our native tongue.

JOHN O'HART.

RINGSEND SCHOOL, DUBLIN,
    August, 1878.

FROM THE PREFACE TO THE THIRD EDITION.

In the priceless volumes of O'Clery's and MacFirbis's great MS. Works, which are written in the Irish language, and deposited in the Royal Irish Academy, I found pedigrees which are not recorded in O'Farrell's *Linea Antiqua*, nor in the Betham Genealogical Collections, both of which are preserved in the Office of Ulster King-of-Arms, Dublin Castle; while in Ulster's Office some of the ancient Irish Genealogies are more fully recorded than they are in either of the former volumes.

In the Works of O'Clery and MacFirbis are—1. The lineal descent of the Spanish Royal Family, from Adam down to King Philip V.; 2. The Genealogy of St. Patrick, the Apostle of Ireland; 3. The Genealogy of St. Brigid, the Patron Saint of Ireland; 4. An account of Ceasair, who came to Ireland before Noah's Deluge;* 5. Of Partholan, the first *planter* of Ireland; 6. Of Neimhidh; 7. Of the Firbolgs; 8. Of the Tuatha de Danans; 9. Of the Gaels; 10. Of the Milesians; 11. Irish Pedigrees; 12. Anglo-Irish and Anglo-Norman Genealogies; 13. The Irish Saints, etc. Those here numbered 1, 2, 3, 4, 6, 9, 10, 11 and 12 are given in this Edition; and some of No. 13.

MacFirbis, who wrote his Work A.D. 1666, records more of the Irish Genealogies than does O'Clery, who brings his work down to 1636. But even MacFirbis does not give all the *Irish* Genealogies. The wonder is, however, that he had any to record; for, the Cromwellian devastation which occurred in his time, was (see pp. 799-802, *infra*), intended to exterminate the Irish race out of Ireland; and it is certain that, during that devastation, many of the Irish Genealogies were lost or destroyed!

By the Statute of 5 Edward IV., c. 3. (A.D. 1465) it was enacted, that every Irishman dwelling within the Pale (then comprising the counties of Dublin, Meath, Louth, and Kildare) should take an English surname . . . "of some towne, as *Sutton, Chester, Tryme, Skryne, Corke, Kinsale;* or colour, as *White, Blacke, Browne;* or art or science, as *Smith* or *Carpenter;* or office, as *Cooke, Butler;* and that he and his issue shall use this name under payne of forfeyting of his goods yearly till the premises be done, to be levied two times by the yeare to the King's warres, according to the discretion of the Lord Lieutenant of the King or his Deputy."—*Statutes at Large, Ireland.* Vol. I., p. 29.

*₁*Deluge* : See Note (†), p. 7, *infra*.

Among the other authorities which we consulted in our latest researches are "Dana's Geology;" the "De la Ponce MSS." (in two vols.); and the "Book of Howth," which is comprised in the Carew Manuscripts, printed by order of the Master of the Rolls, England, and a copy of which is contained in the vol., styled "Calendar of State Papers, Carew, Book of Howth, Miscellaneous." The two latter works may be seen in the Library of the Royal Irish Academy, Dublin. De la Ponce gives the names and, in many cases, the genealogies of gentlemen from Ireland, of Irish, Anglo-Irish, and Anglo-Norman descent, who, after the violation of the Treaty of Limerick, retired to, or entered the service of France. And, from an English standpoint, the "Book of Howth" affords much curious information in relation to the English invasion of Ireland; and to the Prince and Princess of Brefni or *Mithe*, as "Brefni" is strangely called in the Carew and other State papers (purporting, perhaps, to mean *Midhe* [mee] which was the ancient name of the Kingdom of Meath).

For other information bearing on our subject we are largely indebted to Prendergast's "Cromwellian Settlement of Ireland."

Among the MSS. volumes which are preserved in the Library of Trinity College, Dublin, and which I carefully studied, are those mentioned in the Paper under that heading in the No. 1 Appendix to Vol. II. Some of those volumes have enabled us to give the names of the families who settled in Ireland from the English invasion down to the middle of the 17th century. And, with his usual courtesy, Mr. Prendergast has kindly permitted us to give from his great work the names of the Cromwellian Adventurers for Land in Ireland, at that period of unhappy memory to the Irish people.

As other family names came into Ireland at the time of the Revolution, it may interest our readers, who have seen Dalton's "King James's Army List," to also see a list of "King William and Queen Mary's Forces in Ireland, in 1690." That List, together with the names of the persons in whom the civil power vested in Ireland, in 1689, is also given in the No. 1 Appendix to Vol. II. of this Edition. Dalton's "King James's Army List," published in Dublin in 1855 (and which is classed in Trin. Coll. Lib. "Gall. Z. 2. 204"), was compiled from the MS. Vol. in that Library classed F. 1. 14, which gives the Muster Roll of the Army* of King James II. in Ireland in 1689; while the List of William and Mary's forces in Ireland, in 1690, was compiled by us from the MS. Vol. F. 4. 14, in the same Library.

---

* *Army :* King James's Army in Ireland then consisted of eight regiments of Horse, seven of Dragoons, and fifty-six of Infantry.

In the MS. Vols. in Trin. Coll., Dublin, classed E. 3. 2, F. 3. 23, F. 3. 27, and F. 4. 18, are fragments of the pedigrees (from two to three or more generations) of most of the English families whose names are mentioned in those volumes. A few of those fragments are given in this work; brought down to the first half of the 17th century.

F. 3. 16 is full of curious information. The writer of a paper in p. 188 of that Vol. says :

"Before I enter into discourse of the present affaires of Ireland and the benefitt that may be made thereof, I will under your Lopps (Lordships') favour make bould to premise and give a light touch by way of digression of ye flourishing state of that Iland in ancient tyme : though now it be in least repute of any land of Europe. I finde that about the yeare of our Lord's Incarnacion, 450, at which tyme the Romaine Empire being overrunne by barberous nacions, Pietie and good letters through Christendome lay overwhelmed by the invndacion of those sauages. Ireland flourished soe noteable in all manor of Litterature and Sancttity as the common and received proverbe then ranne :

> Exemplo patrum Commotus amore Legendi ;
> Fuit ad Hibernos Sophia mirabile Claros.

And St. Barnard witnesseth as much :

Confluxerunt omni parte Europæ, in Hibernia : discendi causa tanquam ad mercatū. bonari artium . . . Flocuerunt sancti in Hibernia quasi stellæ in cœlo ; et aræne in littore maris ffestus auirnus . . . "

E. 2. 14 (or *Codices MSS. in Bibl. Lambethana*) mentions the many manuscripts relating to Ireland which are deposited at Lambeth; among which are "Bulla Joan. Papæ 22, Ed. 2. Regi Angl. an. 4. Pontificatus;" "The Pope's Letter to Tyrone, dated 20th January, 1601;" "A Brief of the Articles of the Plantation of Mounster (Munster) in 28 Elizabeth;" etc.

It may be said that some Celtic families whose genealogies are given in this work more properly belong to England, or Scotland, than to Ireland. But it will be seen (by following up their lineages) that they are of Milesian *Irish* extraction. And, to those who think that "Nothing good can come out of Nazareth," it will, no doubt, appear strange, that the present Royal Family of England derives its *lineal descent* from the Royal stem of Ireland.

It will be observed that some of the ancient Irish pedigrees are traced down only to the English invasion of Ireland; some, to the reign of Queen Elizabeth; some, to the Plantation of Ulster; some to the Cromwellian, and others to the Williamite confiscations; and some down to A.D. 1887. It will also be seen that, of those Irish families whose pedigrees are traced in this work, some contain more generations than others, for the same period of time. But this may be accounted for by the fact, that many of the personages whose names are recorded in the ancient Irish Genealogies were *Chiefs* of Clans, and that the chiefs of dominant Irish families in the past were often slain in early manhood: because, in war, the Irish Chief headed his clan, and, thus in *front* of the battle, was always exposed to the onslaught of his foe. Hence the average age of the generations is low in the pedigrees of those families which longest continued dominant; which accounts for the greater number of generations.

With reference to the origin of *sirnames* in Ireland it may be mentioned that, in the eleventh century, the Irish Monarch Brian Boroimhe [Boru] made an ordinance that every Irish family and clan should assume a particular sirname (or *sire*-name); the more correctly to preserve the history and genealogy of the different Irish tribes. Each family was at liberty to adopt a sirname from some particular ancestor, and, generally, took their names from some chief of their tribe who was celebrated for his valour, wisdom, piety, or some other great qualities. And the members of a family, each in addition to his own proper name, took, as a common designation, the name of their father, or their grandfather, or of some more remote ancestor : in the first case prefixing the " Mac," which means *son ;* and, in the other two cases, " Ua" (modernized *O'*), which signifies *grandson* or *descendant of ;* and, in all instances, the genitive case of the progenitor's name followed the "Mac,"* or the " O'" :

" In the early ages," writes Dr. Joyce, " individuals received their names from epithets implying some personal peculiarities, such as colour of hair, complexion, size, figure, certain accidents of deformity, mental qualities—such as bravery, fierceness, etc.: and we have only to look at the old forms of the names, to remove any doubt we may entertain of the truth of this assertion."

By tracing any sirname to the page or pages to which the Index refers, the reader will, as a rule, find whether such sirname is of *Milesian Irish,* or of foreign origin.

I need not say that in my research I felt it a duty as well as a "labour of love," to collect the *Irish* Genealogies contained in this Volume; and to preserve them in book-form for the information of posterity.

J. O'HART.

RINGSEND SCHOOL, DUBLIN,
    October, 1881.

---

* *Mac :* See Joyce's *Irish Names of Places.* Some Irish families have adopted the prefix *Fitz* instead of *Mac ;* but it is right to mention that these two prefixes are synonymous.

REFERENCES,

AMONG the Authorities consulted in the compilation of this Work are the following:

1.—Annals of the Four Masters.
2.—Archdall's *Monasticon Hibernicum.*
3.—Burke's "Landed Gentry."
4.—Carte's "Duke of Ormond."
5.—Collins's Peerage.
6.—Dalton's "King James's Irish Army List."
7.—De Burgh's "Landowners of Ireland."
8.—De Burgo's *Hibernia Dominicana.*
9.—Fiant's Elizabeth.
10.—Freeman's "Norman Conquest."
11.—Hanmer's "History of Ireland."
12.—Hardiman's "West Connaught."
13.—Hardinge on the "Circumstances attending the Civil War in Ireland, 1641-1652."
14.—Harris's *Hibernica.*
15.—Inquisitions in Chancery.
16.—Jackson's "Curwens of Workington Hall."
17.—Jacob's Peerage.
18.—Journal of the Irish Arch. Society.
19.—Lodge's Peerage.
20.—Magee's "History of Ireland."
21.—Mill's "History of the Crusades."
22.—Murphy's "Cromwell in Ireland."
23.—Nicholson's "History of Westmoreland."
24.—O'Conor's "Military Memoirs of the Irish Nation."
25.—O'Laverty's "Historical Account of the Diocese of Down and Conor, Ancient and Modern.
26.—Patent Rolls, *temp.* James I.
27.—Tribes and Customs of Hy-Many.
28.—Ware's "Antiquities of Ireland."
29.—Wright's "History of Ireland."
　　Etc.

We are also indebted to the valuable labours of the Rev. Dr. Slaughter, whose "History of St. Mark's Parish, Virginia," contains much genealogical information; and to the labours of Col. J. Chester; Messrs. Atkinson, of Whitehaven; William Murray Robinson; George W. Hanson, of Maryland; Gough, Nicols, etc.

DEDICATION.

THE RIGHT HONOURABLE THE EARL OF ABERDEEN.

My Lord,

Desirous, in common with my countrymen, of paying a well-merited tribute of respect to the Earl of Carnarvon on his retirement, in January, 1886, from the Irish Viceroyalty, I requested his Lordship's acceptance of the Dedication of the enlarged Edition* of my Irish Landed Gentry when Cromwell came to Ireland, which I was then preparing for the press ; for, during Lord Carnarvon's short sojourn in Ireland, his Lordship governed this country with that mild sway which endeared him and his amiable Countess to the Irish people, irrespective of Class or Creed. With his uniform courtesy, Lord Carnarvon kindly accepted the Dedication. That Work, however, is so laborious, that, in my scanty leisure time, I cannot possibly have even the first volume of it ready for the press sooner than two or three years more.

Meantime, the Third Edition of my "Irish Pedigrees" being exhausted, there was such a demand for a Fourth Edition of the Work, that I had at once to engage in its preparation ; and thus postpone the compilation of the enlarged Edition of my Irish Landed Gentry when Cromwell came.

Satisfied that, no matter how humble the tribute, your Lordship would not look with indifference on any work which treats of the sad story of my suffering country since its annexation to England; I respectfully asked your Lordship, on your retirement in June, 1886, from the Irish Viceroyalty, to accept the Dedication of this Edition of my Irish Pedigrees. In accepting the Dedication, your Lordship has but given a proof of the

---

* *Edition :* To include the names of *all* the Irish landed gentry, in every county in Ireland, whose estates had been confiscated under the Cromwellian Settlement ; and the names of the persons to whom, respectively, those estates were then in whole, or in part, conveyed.

kind and conciliating spirit which also characterised *your* Administration, during the pleasing sojourn in Ireland of your Lordship and the amiable Countess of Aberdeen.

In this Edition are given the " Origin and Stem of the Irish Nation ;" the Genealogies of the Irish families which branched from that Stem ; and the Names of the families of Danish, Anglo-Norman, English, Welsh, Scottish, Huguenot, and Palatine extraction which, from time to time, settled in Ireland. It is needless to say that, to make room for each migration of these foreign families into this country, many of the "*Mere Irishrie*" were, by the English Authorities of those times in Ireland, cruelly deprived of their patrimonies. But the greatest ruin sustained by the Irish people was in the Commonwealth period, when the Protestant Irish landlords who sympathised with King Charles I., and the Catholic Irish landlords of that period who escaped Strafford's spoliation, were reduced to the ranks of the peasantry !

Of the ruin which the English connection has produced in Ireland, my own family, my Lord, is a sad instance. At the time of the English invasion of Ireland, one of my ancestors, who is No. 106 on my family pedigree (see p. 672, *infra*), was the Prince of Tara ; and Murcha O'Melaghlin was King of the ancient Kingdom of Meath. In the Chapter headed " The English Invasion of Ireland," pp. 792-799, *infra*, it will be seen that the names of the last King of Meath and the last Prince of Tara were not amongst the signatures of the States (*Ordines*), Monarch, Kings, and Princes of Ireland, which were sent to Rome, A.D. 1172 (*Chartis subsignatis oraditis, ad Romam transmissis*) ; notifying Pope Adrian IV., under their Signs Manual, of their assent to his transfer of their respective sovereignties to King Henry II. of England, and of all their Authority (*Imperium*) and Power. But, while second to none in their veneration for the Supreme Pontiff, the King of Meath and his Nobles could not recognise in Pope Adrian IV. any authority to transfer to King Henry II., of England, or to any foreign Potentates, the sovereignty of their Kingdom, and, with their sovereignty, the power of dispossessing themselves and their people of their ancient patrimonies !

But Henry II. had his revenge : one of his first public acts in Ireland was (contrary to his solemn promise that he desired only the *annexation* of the country to England, but in no instance to disturb or dispossess any of the Irish Kings, Princes, Chiefs, or people,) to depose the King of Meath,*

---

* *Meath :* The Kingdom of Meath afterwards formed the principal portion of the English Pale.

and confer his Kingdom on Hugh de Lacy, as a *nucleus* for the first English Plantation of Ireland :

> No more to chiefs and ladies bright
> The harp of Tara swells ;
> The chord alone that breaks at night
> Its tale of ruin tells.
> Thus Freedom now so seldom wakes,
> The only throb she gives
> Is when some heart indignant breaks,
> To show that still she lives.

Thus deprived of his family patrimony in the Kingdom of Meath by Henry II., the last Prince of Tara received from the then Prince of Tirconnell* a territory in North Sligo, where, up to the Viceroyalty of the Earl of Strafford, *temp.* Charles I., my family ranked as Chieftains. There, at Ardtarmon,† and at Ballinfull (anciently called *Dun Fuil*), near Lisadill, the seat of Sir Henry William Gore Booth, Bart., are the ancient remains of the O'Hart castles in the county Sligo. But in the beginning of the 17th century the Castle of *mBotuinn* (corruptly anglicised "Newtown"), on the shore of Lough Gill, near Dromahair, was (see under No. 116, on our family pedigree, pp. 673-675) built in the Tudor style, by Aodh (or Hugh) Mór O'Hart; another, by his brother Brian O'Hart, on the site of the family old castle at Ardtarmon ; and a third, by another brother Teige O'Hart, at North Grange or Drumcliffe. The remains of these once splendid castles at Ardtarmon and Newtown are in tolerable preservation ; but, it is worthy of remark that, the stone which was imbedded in the front wall immediately over the entrance to the Newtown Castle has been removed therefrom, and, strange to say, is said to have been "buried in Mr. Wynne's garden at Hazlewood," near the town of Sligo, and (see pp. 674-675) thence removed to Lisadill by the Gore-Booth family, who were, in the female line, the lineal descendants of the Captain Robert Parke, who, according to the Civil Survey, was the recognised owner of Newtown, A.D. 1641. But *why* the said stone was removed from its place over the Newtown Castle entrance, or by whose orders it was taken away, I have not ascertained. Possibly the Family Arms of the person who built said Castle, and the date of its erection, have been engraved on said stone. If so, it would explain, perhaps, why the said stone has been so mysteriously removed.

* *Tirconnell :* At that period the northern portion of the present county Sligo belonged to the Principality of Tirconnell.

† *Ardtarmon :* Or, more properly, "Art-tarmon :" *Art* being the root or name *a quo* the sirname "O'Hart ;" and *tarmon* being the Irish for "sanctuary" or "protection," and sometimes meaning "church-lands."

The last of my ancestors who lived in the Castle of Newtown, above mentioned, was (see Note ‡ " Newtown Castle," pp. 676-677) Donoch (or Donogh) O'Hart, who (see the same pages) is No. 120 on my family pedigree ; this Donoch was, under the Cromwellian Settlement, dispossessed on the 3rd of June, 1652.

Up to the time of the Earl of Strafford, who was the Irish Viceroy *temp.* Charles I., my family held their estates in the county Sligo ; but that Viceroy ruthlessly dispossessed (particularly in the Province of Connaught) almost all the Catholic Proprietors, especially the Proprietors of the *old Irish race,* in his time in Ireland.

Of Strafford's Government we read in Darcy M'Gee's *History of Ireland,* Book VIII., p. 93 :

"The plantation of Connaught, delayed by the late King's (James I.) death and abandoned among the new King's ' Graces,' was resumed. The proprietary of Connaught had in the 13th year of the late reign paid £3,000 into the Record Office, Dublin, for the registration of their Deeds ; but the entries not being made by the Clerk employed (for that purpose), the title to every western county, five in number, was now called in question. The Commissioners to inquire into defective Titles were let loose on the devoted Province, with the noted Sir William Parsons at their head ; and the King's title to the whole of Mayo, Sligo, and Roscommon was found by packed, bribed, and intimidated Juries. The Grand Jury of Galway refused to find a similar verdict, and were in consequence summoned to the Court of Castle-Chamber, and sentenced to pay a fine of £4,000, each, to the Crown. The Sheriff who empanelled them was sentenced to pay a fine of £1,000 ; even the Lawyers who pleaded for the actual proprietors were stripped of their gowns ; the Sheriff Darcy died in prison ; and the work of spoliation proceeded."

The latest member of my family who held landed property in the county Sligo, was Charles O'Hart, who, up to about A.D. 1735, owned Cloonamahon Beg and Cloonamahon Mór, thereout of which he paid ten shillings *per annum* to the King ; but, like the rest of the barony of Tirerill, Cloonamahon belonged in the Middle Ages to the MacDonoughs, and up to the close of the 16th century. In 1641, O'Connor Sligo* was the owner of Cloonamahon ; but, under the Cromwellian Settlement, it had fallen by lot to Robert Brown, a Cromwellian dragoon, from whom Cornet Cooper bought it as a debenture ; but the Cornet had to relinquish

* *O'Connor Sligo :* "The O'Harts," says Archdeacon O'Rorke, in his very interesting volume, *Ballysadare and Kilvarnet,* "were always loyal to the O'Connors, by whom they were singularly trusted and favoured. Most probably it was while O'Connor Sligo owned Cloonamahon that the ancestor of Bishop O'Hart came to live there." In support of this opinion it may be observed that, as the name *Charles* does not, before that period, appear among those mentioned in the "O'Hart" pedigree, it is reasonable to suppose that said Charles O'Hart was, through gratitude, so called after Charles O'Connor, who was The O'Connor Sligo at that period.

it in favour of the then Earl of Strafford, who claimed and obtained it from
the Commissioners for executing the Act of Settlement. On the 2nd July,
1666, Charles II. made grants, under the Acts of Settlement and Explanation, of most of the county Sligo, including Cloonamahon, to William,
Earl of Strafford, and Thomas Radcliffe, Esq. And in the *Tripartite Deed
of Partition* of the County Sligo, made on the 21st July, 1687, the third
year of James II., between William, Earl of Strafford, first part; Rev.
John Leslie, D.D., second part; and Joshua Wilson, of the City of Dublin,
third part, we read that Clooonamahon Beg and Cloonamahon Mór were
then owned by Charles O'Hart (or Hart) above mentioned.

Said Charles O'Hart was brother of the Right Rev. John O'Hart,
Bishop of Achonry, who lived in Cloouamahon till he and his brother
were, in the reign of George II., deprived of their property, about the
year 1735,* in a way that illustrates the iniquity of those times:

"The brothers Charles and Bishop O'Hart having refused to take the oath
of supremacy, they had to look about for some Protestant friend to serve
secretly as Trustee of the estate for them—a service which kind-hearted and
high-minded Protestants frequently performed at the time for Catholic
owners of property, to enable them to evade the Penal Laws! There lived
then on the townland of Cartron, which adjoins Cloonamahon, a Protestant
gentleman named Laurence Betteridge, with whom Dr. O'Hart and his
brother were on terms of constant social intercourse and the closest friendship; and this man they pitched upon to act for them. On being applied
to, the obliging neighbour was only too happy, he said, to be able to do a
good turn for friends whom he so loved; but, having received all the
powers and papers from the O'Harts, Betteridge proceeded to Dublin
Castle and there treacherously took the property to himself, in reality as
well as in form. The wretch was not proof against the temptation of
robbing friends by due form of law; and, when taunted with the villany,
coolly replied that he himself had a son, for whom he felt more love and
concern than for the children or the brother of Charles O'Hart. But
neither father nor son was anything the better for the ill-gotten estate.
On the contrary, the acquisition seemed only to bring them bad luck; for,
in a very short time, they quarrelled with one another, and old Betteridge,
in order to spite the son, and get himself away from a place where he was
detested and despised, resolved to dispose of the property. With this
view he offered it privately for sale to a Mr. Thomas Rutledge, who then
kept a shop in Collooney, and who, not having money enough to make the

* *1735:* In Dr. W. Maziere Brady's *Episcopal Succession in England, Scotland, and
Ireland.* Vol. II., p. 191, we read—"1735: John O'Harte, succeeded by Brief, dated
September 30th, 1735. He died before May, 1739."

purchase, borrowed from Joshua Cooper, of Markrea Castle, what was wanted ; giving that gentleman, in return, a lien on the property of 4s. 6d. per acre, a burden which it still bears.

"The three daughters of the said Thomas Rutledge were respectively married—one to Mr. Meredith, another to Mr. Phibbs, and another to Mr. Ormsby, and received as their marriage portions the Cloonamahon estate, which included Lisaneena, Ballinabull, and Knockmullen : to Mr. Meredith his wife brought Lisaneena ; to Mr. Phibbs his wife brought Ballinabull ; and Mr. Ormsby, as his portion, received Knockmullen, which he soon afterwards sold.

"At that period, in Ireland, Catholic owners of landed property frequently held their estates in the names of Protestant trustees, who honourably fulfilled all the conditions of the trust. O'Connell used to tell of an humble, but high-spirited tailor who acted as trustee for half the Catholic gentlemen of Munster. Betteridge, in his legalized robbery, probably proceeded under a law of 1709, which enacted :

'That all leases or purchases in trust for Papists should belong to the first Protestant discoverer ; and that no plea or demurrer should be allowed to any bill of discovery, relative to such trusts, but that such bills should be answered at large.'

"The Catholics regarded the encouragement given to discoverers and informers as an intolerable grievance, and, in an Address and Petition (written by the immortal Edmund Burke) to George III., refer to it thus:

'Whilst the endeavours of our industry are thus discouraged (no less, we humbly apprehend, to the detriment of the national prosperity, and the diminution of your Majesty's revenue, than to our particular ruin,) there are a set of men, who, instead of exercising any honest occupation in the commonwealth, make it their employment to pry into our miserable property ; to drag us into the courts ; and to compel us to confess on our oaths, and under the penalties of perjury, whether we have, in any instance, acquired a property in the smallest degree exceeding what the rigour of the law has admitted ; and in such case the informers, without any other merit than that of their discovery, are invested (to the daily ruin of several innocent, industrious families), not only with the surplus in which the law is exceeded, but in the whole body of the estate and interest so discovered ; and it is our grief that this evil is likely to continue and increase, as informers have, in this country, almost worn off the infamy which in all ages, and in all other countries, has attended their character, and have grown into some repute by the frequency and success of their practices.'

"In the reign of Queen Anne, the Irish House of Commons passed a Resolution :

'That the prosecuting and informing against Papists was an honourable service ;' thus endeavouring to exalt a class of men from whom common humanity recoils with loathing, and who have found no apologist in history except the infamous and inhuman Tiberius Nero; even his vile senate, as Tacitus implies, evincing a reluctance to descend with him so low:

"Ibaturque," says the historian, "in eam sententiam, ni durius contraque morem suum, *palam pro accusatoribus*, Cæsar irritas leges, rempublicam in præcipiti conquestus esset: subverterent potius jura quam custodes eorum amoverent. *Sic delatores, genus hominum publico exitio repertum et pœnis quidem nunquam satis coercitum, per premia eliciabantur.*"—TACITUS, *Annal.*, lib. IV., c. 30.

"The good Bishop O'Hart, before his eviction from Cloonamahon, was famous for hospitality. Turlough O'Carolan, the last of the eminent Irish Bards,* often visited the O'Harts, and showed his admiration of the Bishop's genial nature and many virtues, by composing two songs in his honour, only one of which has been preserved, and is given in Hardiman's *Irish Minstrelsy*, Vol. I., p. 28, with an English translation by Thomas Furlong, of which the following is a stanza:

'In this hour of my joy, let me turn to the road,
To the pious one's home let me steer;
Aye! my steps shall instinctively seek that abode,
Where plenty and pleasure appear.
Dear Harte, with the learned thou art gentle and kind;
With the bard thou art open and free,
And the smiling and sad, in each mood of the mind,
Find a brother's fond spirit in thee.'

"The celebrated Owen (or Eugene) O'Hart, Bishop of Achonry, was not only present at the Council of Trent, but took a leading part in the deliberations of that august assembly. This distinguished Bishop was consecrated in 1562, died in 1603 at the great age of 100, and was buried in his own cathedral at Achonry. He received special faculties from the Pope in 1575, for the whole ecclesiastical province of Tuam; signed in 1585 the Indenture of Composition between Sir John Perrott and the Chieftains of the County Sligo, *temp.* Queen Elizabeth;† took part in the Provincial Synod that assembled in Ulster, in that year, to promulgate the decrees of the Council of Trent, and enjoyed all through life the confidence and favour of the Holy See. The consummate prudence with which this Prelate steered his course through the difficult times in which he lived, was on a par with his great learning."‡

* *Bards*: According to Walker's *Historical Memoirs of the Irish Bards* (Dublin, 1818), Turlough O'Carolan (or Carolan) died in March, 1738, in the sixty-eighth year of his age; and was buried in Kilronan, in the county of Roscommon.

† *Elizabeth*: See the names to that Indenture, in Note† "*Ardtarmon*," p. 673, under No. 116 on the "O'Hart" (No. 1) pedigree.

‡ *Learning*: For further valuable information respecting Sligo families, see *History of the Parishes of Ballysadare and Kilvarnet*, by the Venerable Archdeacon O'Rorke, D.D., P.P. (Dublin: James Duffy and Sons, 1878).

In October, 1873, it was permitted me, through the courtesy of Sir Bernard Burke, Ulster King-of-Arms, to compare my Genealogical Notes with O'Farrell's *Linea Antiqua*, preserved in the Office of Arms, Dublin Castle: to see if the pedigrees which I had collected from O'Clery's and MacFirbis's ancient Irish and Anglo-Irish Genealogies, agreed with those recorded in the *Linea Antiqua*. With that flowing courtesy for which he is proverbial, Sir Bernard not only granted me that permission, but also the permission to inspect Sir William Betham's enlarged edition of the *Linea Antiqua*, and any other record in the Office of Arms bearing on my subject.

In the *Linea Antiqua* I found that the " O'Hart" pedigree agreed with the family genealogy as I had traced it, down to Donoch O'Hart, who (see p. 676, *infra*) is No. 120 on my family pedigree ; and who held possession of the family castle at Newtown, on the shore of Lough Gill, up to the 3rd of June, 1652. And it was from the *Linea Antiqua* that I carefully compiled the earlier portion of "The Lineal Descent of the Royal Family of England" (see pp. 37-41, *infra*), and ascertained the strange fact that the ancient Irish Monarch ART, who is No. 81 on that *lineal descent*, was the ancestor of my family :

> Thus shall memory often, in dreams sublime,
> Catch a glimpse of the days that are over ;
> Thus, sighing, look through the waves of time
> For the long-faded glories they cover.

With great respect, I am,

My Lord,

Your very faithful servant,

J. O'HART.

RINGSEND SCHOOL,
RINGSEND, DUBLIN,
December, 1887.

CONTENTS.

* *Settlers :* In the former Editions of this Work the new settlers in Ireland, after its invasion by the English in the twelfth century, were entered as " Anglo-Norman," or " English" Families. But we have found that many families whose names were so entered, are of *Irish* descent. It is, therefore, in our opinion, more correct to enter them as " New Settlers," than as " Anglo-Norman or English.

PART I.

I.—THE CREATION.

In the Book of Genesis the six successive days of Creation part themselves into two grand divisions, namely :—(1) Life under cosmic light, and (2) Life under the light of the sun. On the third day we have vegetation of the earth under cosmic light, which fully answers to the period of the *coal plants* of the carboniferous era. On the fourth day (Gen. i. 14) God made the sun and the moon, to be "for signs, and for seasons, and for days, and for years." The sun, then, is the standard for our computation of time ; and the first "year" of the world, as we understand the word *year*, must have commenced with the creation of the sun. According to our system of astronomy the earth revolves round its own axis once in twenty-four hours, producing day and night; and round the sun once in the year, producing the four seasons : therefore, before the creation of the sun, the days of twenty-four hours each had no existence.

THE COSMIC DAY OF THE BOOK OF GENESIS.

But while the "day" by which we compute our year consists of twenty-four hours, nearly, Geology supplies unerring testimony, that the pre-solar or cosmic days mentioned in the Sacred Volume in connection with the Creation, were, each, a period of vast duration ! Geology also clearly teaches, that the lowest forms of vegetable and animal life were first called into existence, which were gradually followed by other and higher organizations; and confirms the truth of divine revelation, that man was the last created animal, and that a comparatively recent period only has elapsed since his first appearance on the surface of our globe.

On the fifth day God made the birds : and ordered the swarming of the waters with living creatures, among which are specified "the great Taninim" or "Dragons" belonging to the class *Reptilia*, of which the crocodile of Egypt is an example. These serpent-monsters of the deep answer perfectly to the Reptilia of the *Saurian* period. On the sixth day Man is created in connection with the land animals, domestic and wild, and with the fishes and vegetation of the modern type, or those of the present era.

At the close of the Carboniferous or *Coal* period the atmosphere became so far purified as to admit of the appearance of animal life of the order of the Reptilia of the seas, with which the waters swarmed during the Saurian period.

The closing era of the Reptilian age was the Cretaceous or *Chalk* period. In the Cretaceous period, which closed the pre-Tertiary, the atmosphere, which was previously incapable of sustaining the high-class, warm-blooded

A

animals, became sufficiently purified to admit of their appearance. With the opening of the Cretaceous period we find a great change in vegetation : then appeared the oak, palms, maple, willow, etc., and the ordinary fruit-trees of temperate regions, adapted to Man's needs.

THE CREATION OF MAN.

After the Creation of Man, and before his first sin, there intervened a sabbatical day or period of cosmic rest, during which the Lord God pronounces all things good. Two cosmic days, therefore, or periods of indefinite length, are indicated in the Genesis account of the Creation, as that portion of the *Edenic* period of Man in which he existed before his first sin ; blessed and perfect in the companionship of God, and under the injunction :

"Be fruitful and multiply, and replenish the earth and subdue it."

In the beginning of the Tertiary era the British Isles were a land of palms, with species of fig, cinnamon, etc. ; a vegetation* like that of India and Australia at the present time. At the end of the Tertiary period, Europe was an Archipelago ; and the sea, which we now call the Arctic Ocean, was the Mediterranean of that period. The late discoveries of Professor Nordenskiold bring to our view the remains of the Tertiary period in the Arctic regions. In a letter† from him recently published in the *London Standard*, he calls attention to the New Siberian Islands, which, from a scientific point of view, are very remarkable.

THE GARDEN ERA OF MAN'S EXISTENCE.

Guided by geological laws we can, therefore, assign the *Garden* era of the Edenic period of Man's existence to the close of the pre-Tertiary. We have an indication of the duration of the Garden period, in the climatic conditions under which Man is described as there existing during a period of indefinite length ; before the close of which those conditions were essentially changed. A period of cold came on which necessitated the wearing of fur clothing. It is a curious circumstance how perfectly this agrees with the climatic changes which introduced the Tertiary period, as laid down by modern geologists. The Garden period, then, closed with the coming on of the cold of the Tertiary ; during which era, however, the climate and all other conditions were favourable for the distribution of Man over the globe.

---

* *Vegetation:* "Such a vigorous growth of trees," says Lyell, "within twelve degrees of the pole, where now a dwarf willow and a few herbaceous plants form the only vegetation, and where the ground is covered with perpetual snow and ice, is truly remarkable."

† *Letter:* "These (the New Siberian) islands," says the Professor, "open the book of the history of the world at a new place. The ground there is strewn with wonderful fossils. Whole hills are covered with the bones of the mammoth, rhinoceros, horses, uri, bison, oxen, sheep, etc. The sea washes up ivory upon its shores. In this group is possibly to be found the solution of the question of the ancestry of the Indian elephant, and important facts with regard to the vertebrates which existed at the time of Man's first appearance upon the earth."

It will be noted that in the Eden* narrative the driving from the Garden took place gradually : Man is first sent forth ; is then clothed in fur ; is then driven out, excluding him for ever from a return to his primitive home. The Garden spot was left behind, and Man went forth to till the ground whence he was taken, and to which he must return.

At the close of the Tertiary era occurred the Deluge, which, in the period of Mammal life, was the first continental convulsion of a universal character which changed the face of the inhabited world. That convulsion introduced the Quaternary (Glacial or Drift) period, which answers the conditions of the Genesis account as to the era of Noah's Flood.

THE HEBREW LAND SYSTEM.

In the Quaternary period the distribution of the three Noetic families from their respective centres took place over vast portions of the earth ; formed the second dispersion of the human race from Central Asia ; and the first great distribution of the Ethnic races, as laid down in the race-table of the sons of Noah.

The Babel or third dispersion mentioned in Genesis is related of a people who came from the East to the Plain of Shinar, and dwelt there. The tower which these people attempted to build was, by them, to be dedicated to their false god Bel, and called *Babel:* the narrator in Genesis stating that the Lord God did at that spot confuse the universal language, so that Babel (the "gate of Bel") became *Balal*, the "city of confusion." That account directly introduces the genealogy of Arphaxad, who was son of Shem, and ancestor of Eber or Heber a quo the *Hebrews.*

As Magog, son of Japhet, who was the favourite son of Noah, was the ancestor of the *Gaels*, it is a strange coincidence that the very ten generations from Adam down to Noah, which are given by the Semitic writers, are the very ten generations given by the narrators of the early genealogy of the Gaels !

THE GAELIC LAND SYSTEM SAME AS THAT OF THE HEBREWS.

Even in the matter of the Gaelic System of allotting a portion of land to each head of a family for the sustenance of himself and those dependent on him (and which obtained among the Gaels in Ireland down to the seventeenth century, in the reign of King James I., of England), how

---

* *Eden :* The first migration from Eden mentioned in the Genesis accounts, is that of the Cainites, eastward. The northern portions of the Asiatic, European, and American continents would seem to have been the area of the first dispersion of mankind ; which, going on through the Tertiary period, we may suppose, gradually overspread the then habitable portions of the globe. Remains of the human race belonging to the Tertiary period have been discovered in North America and in Europe : and announced as the latest result of modern geological science in respect to the age of Man upon the earth. Although it is stated that in this period the arts of metallurgy and music were well advanced at the civilized centre of Eden, it is not to be supposed that the migratory nomads of the Cainite dispersion would have made use of any other than the rudest implements of stone and flint in their wanderings to the uttermost parts of the then habitable globe.—MacWHORTER.

strangely coincident was that Gaelic System with the Land System of the Hebrews :

"Ye shall divide the land by lot for an inheritance among your families; to the more ye shall give the more inheritance, and to the fewer ye shall give the less inheritance; every man shall be in the place in which his lot falleth."—*Numbers* xxxiii. 54. See also *Numbers* xxvi. 54-56; and *Joshua* xi. 23, and xiv. and xvi., etc.

This similarity between the Land System of the Irish Gaels and that which obtained among the Hebrews is the more extraordinary, when we consider the intimacy which existed between Moses and Gaodhal [Gael]. But we are unable to say which (if either) of these two ancient peoples gave their Land System to the other.

GEOLOGY SUSTAINS THE GENESIS ACCOUNT OF THE CREATION.

Because of recent geological discoveries, some persons imagine that the Science of Geology conflicts with the Genesis account of the Creation. Among those discoveries is that of a man whose photograph is given in the revised edition of Dana's Geology, and who lived in the South of France, on the shores of the Mediterranean Sea, in the Quaternary era, which was the geological period next preceding our own. In its relation, therefore, to those discoveries the period of Man's existence upon the earth has become a subject of great interest; for, it must be admitted that the truths established by geological science are, at least, as worthy of acceptance as was the Copernican theory of Astronomy, in its time, as opposed to the Ptolemaic system.

As a sincere Christian of the Roman Catholic Communion, we entertain profound veneration for the Bible. But, as everywhere throughout the Sacred Books of the Hebrews and the Writings of the Apostles appear expressions and conceptions framed upon the standpoint of the Creation, as recorded in Genesis, which can only be interpreted by the latest results of geological science, we are satisfied that our readers, who calmly and dispassionately consider the subject, will find with us that nothing could be more absolutely coincident with the Genesis account of the Creation than are the discoveries of Geology.

The first eleven chapters of Genesis give in brief outline a history of Man, from the Creation of our First Parents to the time of the migration of Abraham from the valley of the Euphrates to the shores of the Mediterranean Sea; and constitute an introduction to the religious history of a special branch of the Semitic* family. This general introductory history is composed of a number of separate fragments or statements arranged in consecutive order, without chronology; and embodies a selection from the traditions and records of the ages preceding Abraham of what was considered in his family to be historic concerning the creation of the Universe and of the first Man. We may reasonably presume that these records, carefully selected and carefully preserved, were brought by Abraham from the valley of the Euphrates into the land of Palestine; and con-

---

* *Semitic :* See the (New York) "Princeton Review," for July, 1880, under the heading "The Edenic Period of Man": an article written by the late Professor MacWhorter, one of the most eminent of the Semitic scholars of his day.

stituted his Family Bible—the beginning of the Sacred Books of the Hebrews.

SEMITIC IDEA OF A GENEALOGY.

But with the Semitic writers the idea of a *Genealogy* was not so much that of a succession of persons or of individual lives, as a *period of time ;* to be filled out with a record of the more prominent events of that period, and the persons connected with them. Great leaps, therefore, often occur from the record of some historic character to his successor, who is called his *son*, even if a very remote descendant in point of time. This mode of forming a genealogy has, perhaps, its most striking illustration in the opening of the Gospel of St. Matthew, beginning : " The book of the generation of Jesus Christ, the son of David, the son of Abraham ;" and the closing of the genealogy, with the statement, that the generations from Abraham to Christ are three times fourteen or forty-two generations, whereas St. Luke gives fifty-six generations as covering this period. But this involves no discrepancy from the point of view of the two narrators ; for, the three double sevens of St. Matthew are used as indefinite numbers,* not intended to be taken as literal, but simply as representative of a complete time—of the idea that the full period had arrived for the appearance of the " Son of David, the son of Abraham :" *seven* being a sacred number with Semitic writers ; and multiples of seven, the highest expression of completeness of God's time that could be used in connexion with the advent of the Messiah.

In the filling out of the history in the time between Adam and Noah, very long periods are attributed to special human lives, and required for the consistency of the narrative ; but this filling out of an indefinite period by *ten* generations is analogous to, and illustrated by, the filling out by St. Matthew of the period between Abraham and Christ by forty-two generations.

The post-Noetic Sethite succession in the line of Shem filling out the period from Noah to Abraham with *ten* lives of decreasing periods in the length of life assigned to each, is also, no doubt, formed upon the principle

---

* *Numbers :* The use of definite numbers as representative of indefinite time is an oriental mode of presenting historic events, which does not in the least interfere with the truthfulness of the record for the purpose held in view by the writers. It is, however, very difficult for western minds to adapt themselves to the point of view of such methods of computation. The Christian religion has come to us from the East, founded upon a series of historical facts, and we must seek those facts through an understanding of their surroundings, and the methods employed to convey them. In the time when they took shape their form was adapted, to be understood by all who heard them. It is only the lapse of ages and our own ignorance which have obscured them. The inhabitants of Mesopotamia or the Tigro-Euphrates basin were, from the earliest period, a mixed population, representing every branch of the human family of the Noetic dispersion ; who, together, developed and used a common *time-notation,* called the " Chaldean System." It has been customary to consider as mythical the enormous length assigned in the Chaldean records to the development of the human race, and the Chaldean early civilization ; but late discoveries and researches show that the history of the development of the material civilization of the Euphrates valley goes back to a far earlier period than has ever before been held possible.— MacWhorter.

of the pre-Noetic succession of *ten;* to convey the same idea of indefinite time, but of a complete succession of the sacred line.

It is a curious fact that in the Chaldean records the period corresponding to the pre-Noetic era of Man's existence is filled out with *ten* Kings; whose united Reigns covered a cycle of ten cosmic days. These ten days were used by the Chaldeans, after the oriental mode, as representative of a great time-cycle, not of definite but of indefinite length; which was thus conceived by them in placing it as an introduction to their historic annals. And these ten time-periods or cosmic days also appear in the early histories of all the most ancient civilizations; including those of the Eberite branch of the Semitic family. In these Eberite records not only is no limitation intended to be expressed of the pre-Noetic period of Man's existence; but, on the contrary, the use of the representative number *ten,* as the number of generations of that period, is designed to convey an idea of *indefinite* time. In this view, therefore, these early Semitic records of the house of Eber take their place by the side of the early histories of all the most ancient peoples of the earth; and both explain them and are explained by them. We have then some data of comparison of the cosmic day of the Book of Genesis with the time-measures of modern Geology; especially with those related to the life of Man upon the earth.

THE COSMIC DAY OF THE CHALDEANS.

A *cosmic* day or period with the Chaldeans was a great cycle of forty-three thousand two hundred years; and of the Chaldeans Lenormant says:

"They were the first to divide the day into twenty-four hours, the hour into sixty minutes, and the minute into sixty seconds. Their great periods of time were calculated on this scale. The great cycle of 43,200 years, regarded by them as the period of the precession of the Equinoxes, was considered as *one* day in the life of the Universe."

In the Chaldean account of the Creation these cosmic days and years were used representatively for great periods; and all the time-divisions of the Hebrews were the same as those in use by the Chaldeans. The relation of these time-periods or cosmic days of the Chaldeans, to the discoveries of modern geology, is therefore plainly seen.

The Eden narrative, commencing Genesis ii. 4, says:

"These are the generations of the heavens and the earth in the day when they were created, in the day that the Lord God made the heavens and the earth."

Here is a *day* spoken of, which shows that the term is there used for indefinite periods of time.

THE DELUGE.

The chroniclers of Sacred History fix the date of the building of Nineveh as one hundred and fifteen years after the Flood; the Tower of Babel as one hundred and forty years; and the reign of Belus, son of Nimrod, in Babylon, as about two hundred and fifteen years.* According

* *Years:* According to Dr. O'Connor, in his *Rerum Hibernicarum Scriptores Veteres,* the year of the Pagan Irish was luni-solar; consisting, like that of the

to the Four Masters, Partholan was the first *planter* of Ireland, one hundred and eighty-five years after the building of Nineveh, or three hundred years after the Deluge.*

THE DIVISION OF THE WORLD BY NOAH.

When the Flood had subsided, and that Noah and his sons, Shem, Ham, and Japhet, had come out of the Ark, God blessed them and said: "Increase and multiply, and fill the earth." (Gen. ix.)

Noah divided the world amongst his three sons: to Shem he gave Asia within the Euphrates, to the Indian ocean; to Ham he gave Syria, Arabia, and Africa; and to his *favourite*, Japhet, he gave the rest of Asia, beyond the Euphrates, together with Europe to Gades (now Cadiz): " May God

Phœnicians and Egyptians, of 365 days and six hours. But while it is certain that the ancient Irish had four seasons in their year, the fact is, that, according to the "Book of Rights," we cannot yet determine the season with which the Pagan Irish year commenced.

* *The Deluge :* According to the Four Masters, a colony reached Ireland before that of which Partholan was the *planter*. Ceasair came to Ireland " forty days before the Deluge," with a colony of fifty damsels and three men—" Bith, Ladhra, and Fintan their names." On this subject some humorist has written—

> " With fifty damsels in her train,
> Came Ceasair o'er the Eastern main;
> Three heroes with her crossed the water,
> Attendants on Bith's roving daughter."

Ceasair is reputed to have been a daughter of Bith, who was a son of Noah, and a half brother of Shem, Ham, and Japhet. Because Bith and Ceasair abandoned the true God, Noah refused them a place in the Ark; and the narrative goes on to say that, thus refused, they, with Ladhra and Fintan consulted together, and by Ceasair's advice applied to an idol, who told them to build a ship, but the idol could not tell them at what time the Deluge was to take place. They accordingly built a vessel, and having well stored it with provisions, Bith, Ladhra, and Fintan, together with three ladies, Ceasair, Barran, and Balva, accompanied by their handmaids, then put to sea; and, after some time, on the fifteenth day of the Moon, and forty days before the Deluge, they landed near Bantry, in the county Cork, and from thence proceeded to where the rivers Suir, Nore, and Barrow join, below Waterford, where they parted : Fintan taking Ceasair and seventeen of the damsels; Bith took Barran and seventeen more; and Ladhra took Balva and the remainder of the damsels to *Ard-Ladhra* (" and from him it was named"), now the hill of Ardmine, county Wexford, where he died, being " the first that died in Ireland." After his death Balva and her handmaids returned to Ceasair, and Fintan and Bith divided them between them; but Bith having soon after died at *Sliabh-Beatha* (now know as " Slieve Beagh"—a mountain on the confines of the counties of Fermanagh and Monaghan, "and from him the mountain is named"), Fintan became so alarmed at the prospect of the large family left in his charge, that he deserted them and fled to the territory of *Aradh* [Ara], near *Loch Deirgdheire* (now " Lough Derg"—an expansion of the river Shannon, between Killaloe, in the county Clare, and Portumna in the county Galway), where he died; and from Fintan is named *Feart Fintain*, i.e., " Fintan's Grave." Thus abandoned, Ceasair and her band of women retired to *Cuil Ceasra*, where she died of a broken heart, and was buried in *Carn Ceasra*, on the banks of the river Boyle, in Connaught, near *Cuil Ceasra*.

In a poem which some wag has attributed to this Fintan he is made to say that he survived the Flood; and that he continued alive till the sixth century of the Christian era, when he died. No doubt the narrative, that a colony reached Ireland "forty days before the Deluge," seems very apocryphal; but, as the Four Masters mention the circumstance, we thought it right to here give the foregoing details.

enlarge Japhet, and may he dwell in the tents of Shem, and Canaan be his servant." (Gen. ix. 27).

Japhet had fifteen sons ; amongst whom he divided Europe and the part of Asia that fell to his lot. The Bible gives the names of seven of those sons, namely : Gomer, Magog, Madai, Javan* (or Iauan), Thubal, Mosoch, and Thiras. The nations descended from these seven sons are known ; but we know not the names of the other sons, from whom the Chinese and other nations of Eastern Asia are descended.

The sons of Shem were Cham, Assur, Arphaxad, Lud, and Aram. This Assur was the founder of Nineveh : from him "Assyria" was so called. The sons of Ham were Chus (or Cush), Mesram, Phut, and Canaan ; and Cush begot Nimrod.

From Madai, son of Japhet, came the Madeans, whom the Greeks called "Medes ;" from Javan, son of Japhet, were descended the Greeks and Ionians ; from Thiras, son of Japhet, came the Thracians ; from Thogarma, son of Gomer, son of Japhet, came the Phrygians and Armenians ; from Iber, son of Thubal, son of Japhet, came the Iberians, who were afterwards called Spaniards.

Javan was the fourth son of Japhet. Although the Hebrews, Chaldeans, Arabians, and others gave no other appellation than that of "Ionians" to all the Grecian nations, yet from the fact that Alexander the Great, in the prediction of Daniel (Dan. viii. 21), is mentioned under the name of "Javan," or "Ion," it is evident that Javan was not only the father of the Ionians (who were but one particular Greek nation), but also the ancestor of all those nations that went under the general denomination of "Greeks." The sons of Javan were Elishah, Tharsis, Cetthim, and Dodanin. Elisha : the ancient city of Elis (in Peloponnesus), the Elysian fields, and the river Elissus contributed to preserve his memory. Tharsis is believed to have settled in Achaia, or the neighbouring provinces of Greece, as Elishah did in Peloponnesus. Cetthim (or Chittim) was, according to the first book of the Maccabees,† the ancestor of the Macedonians ; for (I. Macc. i. 1), it is there said that Alexander, the son of Philip the Macedonian, went out of his country (which was that of Chittim), to make war against Darius, king of Persia. And Dodanin was, no doubt, the ancestor of the "Danai" of the Greeks, and of the Tuatha-de-Danans of ancient Ireland.

Homer calls the Grecians "Hellenes," "Danai," "Argivés," and "Achaians ;" but, from whomsoever the Grecians derive their name, it is strange that the word *Græcus* is not once used in Virgil. Pliny says that the Grecians were so called from the name of an ancient king, of whom they had but a very uncertain tradition.

---

* *Javan* : In fol. 3 of O'Clery's Irish Genealogies the lineal descent of King Philip V. of Spain is carefully traced down from Adam, through this Javan (or Iauan), son of Japhet.

† *Maccabees* : The derivation of this name seems to be the same as that of the Irish sirname *MacCabe* ; namely *caba*, which is the Irish for a cape, a cap, or hood ; while the Hebrew *Kaba* has the same meaning.

THE MILESIAN IRISH NATION.

Magog was the son of Japhet, from whom the Milesian Irish Nation is descended; he was contemporary with the building of Nineveh, and his son Baoth was contemporary with Nimrod.

Upon the division of the earth by Noah amongst his sons, and by Japhet of his part thereof amongst his sons, Scythia came to Baoth's lot; whereof he and his posterity were kings. Thus in Scythia, in Central Asia, far from the scene of Babel, the Valley of Shinar (the *Magh Senaar* of the ancient Irish annalists), it is considered that Baoth and his people took no part with those of Shem and Ham in their impious attempt at the building of that Tower; that therefore, on that head, they did not incur the displeasure of the Lord; and that, hence, the lasting vitality of the Celtic language!

According to the Four Masters, the Celtic language was the Scythian; which was, from Gaodhal, who "refined and adorned it," afterwards called *Gaodhilg* or "Gaelic."

There is reason to believe that the *Scythian* was the language of our First Parents. As the Celtic, Teutonic, and Slavonic nations were of Scythian origin, so was the Scythian language the parent stock of all the dialects* spoken by those nations. The Celtic or Gaelic† was the language of Ireland; in which were written the ancient Irish records, annals, and chronicles.

Phœniusa Farsaidh, son of Baoth, son of Magog, son of Japhet, was the inventor of *Letters;* after him his descendants were called *Phœnicians.* His name is sometimes rendered "Feniusa Farsa;" and his descendants were called *Feiné* and Phœné. The ancient Irish were also called *Feiné:* a proof of identity of origin between the Phœnicians and the ancient Irish.‡

* *Dialects:* There are at present no less than 3,642 languages and dialects spoken throughout the world.

† *Gaelic:* It is to the Gaelic language that the following stanza, translated from a poem written in the third century by the Irish Monarch Carbre Liffechar, refers—

Sweet tongue of our Druids and bards of past ages;
Sweet tongue of our Monarchs, our saints, and our sages;
Sweet tongue of our heroes, and free-born sires,
When we cease to preserve thee our glory expires.

‡ *Ancient Irish:* In Connellan's *Four Masters* we read—"The great affinity between the Phœnician and Irish language and alphabet has been shown by various learned antiquaries—as Vallancey, Sir Laurence Parsons, Sir William Betham, Villaneuva, and others; and they have likewise pointed out a similarity between the Irish language and that of the Carthaginians, who were a colony of the Tyrians and Phœnicians. The Phœnician alphabet was first brought to Greece from Egypt by Cadmus. And Phœnix, brother of Cadmus the Phœnician who first introduced *letters* amongst the Greeks and Phœnicians, is considered by O'Flaherty, Charles O'Connor, and others, to be the same as the celebrated *Phœniusa* (or Feniusa) *Farsaidh* of the old Irish historians, who state that he was king of Scythia, and ancestor of the Milesians of Spain who came to Ireland; and that, being a man of great learning, he invented the Irish alphabet, which his Milesian posterity brought to Ireland; and it may be further observed that the Irish, in their own language, were, from Phœniusa or Feniusa, called *Feiné:* a term latinized *Phœnii*, and signifying *Phœnicians*, as shown by Charles O'Connor and in O'Brien's Dictionary."

In Asia Minor, the Phœnicians founded the cities of Miletus and Mycalé, in Mæonia, on the shore of the Ægean Sea—the ancient Lake Gyges (*gigas:* Greek, *a giant*). The people of Miletus were called "Milesians," on account of their heroism (*mileadh:* Irish, a hero), even before the time of Milesius of Spain.

According to Mariana and other Spanish historians, the "Brigantes" (a people so called after Breoghan, or Brigus, the grandfather of Milesius of Spain), were some of the Brigas or Phrygians of Asia Minor; and were the same people as the ancient Trojans! Brigus sent a colony from Spain into Britain; and many of the descendants of that Gaelic colony, who settled in England and in Ireland since the English Invasion, are erroneously considered as of Anglo-Saxon, or Anglo-Norman descent.

Brigantia (now Corunna), a city in Galicia (where the Gaels settled), in the north of Spain, was founded by that Breoghan or Brigus; and from Brigantia the Brigantes came to Ireland with the Milesians. According to Ptolemy's Map of Ancient Ireland, the Brigantes inhabited the territories in Leinster and Munster, now forming the counties of Wexford, Waterford, Tipperary, Kilkenny, Carlow, and Queen's County; and the native Irish of these territories, descended from the Brigantes, were, up to a recent period, remarkable for their *tall* or gigantic stature.

Homer,* the most ancient author in the heathen world, names the "proud Miletus" as among the Trojan forces mentioned in the "Catalogue," Book II. of the *Iliad:*

> " Of those who round Mæonia's realms reside,
> Or whom the vales in shade of Tmolus hide,
> Mestles and Antiphus the charge partake;
> Born on the banks of Gyges' silent lake.
> There, from the fields where wild Mæander flows,
> High Mycalé and Latmos' shady brows,
> And *proud Miletus.*" . . . . . —POPE's *Homer.*

" If we look upon this Catalogue with an eye to ancient learning," says Pope, " it may be observed that, however fabulous the other part of Homer's poem may be according to the nature of Epic poetry, this account of the people, princes, and countries is purely historical, founded on the real transactions of those times; and by far the most valuable piece of history and geography left us concerning the state of Greece in that early period. Greece was then divided into several dynasties, which Homer has enumerated under their respective princes; and his division was looked upon so exact, that we are told of many controversies concerning the boundaries of Grecian cities, which have been decided upon the authority of this piece (the ' Catalogue'):·the city of Calydon was adjudged to the Ætolians notwithstanding the pretensions of Æolia, because Homer had ranked it among the towns belonging to the former. When the *Milesians* and people of Priene disputed their claim to Mycalé, a verse of Homer (that above given) carried it in favour of the Milesians."

Spain was first peopled after the Deluge by the descendants of Iber, who were called Iberes and Iberi; the country, Iberia; and its chief river, Ebro. The Phœnicians in the early ages settled in Iberia, and gave it the

---

* *Homer:* According to some of the ancients, Homer was a native of Mæonia—the old name of Lydia, in Asia Minor, and was therefore called *Mæonides.* As a Mæonian, then, his language must not have been very different, if at all, from that spoken by Cadmus the Phœnician, or Cadmus of Miletus, as he was also called: "Miletus" having been a city in Mæonia. The name "Homer" was only an epithet applied to Mæonides, because he was *blind* ("homeroi:" Gr., *blind men.*)

name of Spania, from " Span," which, in their language, signified a *rabbit*—as the place abounded in rabbits ; by the Romans the country was called Hispania ; and by the Spaniards, Espana, which has been anglicised Spain. The city of Cadiz (the ancient *Gadhir*) was founded by the Phœnicians ; who were celebrated for their commercial intercourse with various ancient nations, as Greece, Italy, Spain, Gaul, Britain, and Ireland. In Ree's *Cyclopedia*, in the article on Ireland, it is said :

"It does not appear improbable, much less absurd, to suppose that the Phœnicians might have colonized Ireland at an early period, and introduced their laws, customs, and knowledge, with a comparatively high state of civilization ; and that these might have been gradually lost amidst the disturbances of the country, and at last completely destroyed by the irruptions of the Ostmen" (or Danes).

Dr. O'Brien, in his Irish Dictionary,* at the word *Fearmuighe*, considers that the ancient territory of " Fermoy," in the county of Cork, derived its name from the Phœnicians of Spain who settled there, and were in Irish called *Fir-Muighe-Feiné*, which has been latinized *Viri Campi Phœniorum*, meaning the "Men of the Plain of the Phœnicians." The Phœnicians were, as above mentioned, celebrated for their commercial intercourse with other nations : hence they were by some of the ancient Irish historians confounded with the Fomorians (*fogh :* Irish, plundering, and *muir*, the sea ; hence signifying *Pirates*)—a name by which, on account of their piratical expeditions, the Scandinavians were, according to O'Donovan's Four Masters, known to the ancient Irish ; and because of their having come from Getulia, or Lybia (the Gothia of the Gaels), in the north of Africa, where Carthage was afterwards built, the Feiné or Phœnicians, were considered by others "to have been African or Phœnician pirates, descendants of Ham." These Feiné are represented as a race of giants ; and from them the *Fiana Eireann* (*feinné :* Irish, " the troops' of the ancient militia of Ireland ;" Arab, *fenna*, "troops,") are considered to have been so called : the appellation "*Fiana Eireann*" being, on account of their great strength and stature, given to that ancient military organization which flourished in the reign of King Cormac MacArt, Monarch of Ireland in the third century ; and which, before it became disaffected, was the prop and protection of the Monarchy.†

* *O'Brien's Dictionary* : The Right Rev. John O'Brien, Roman Catholic bishop of Cloyne, was the author of that Irish-English Dictionary ; which is a very learned and valuable work, not only on the Irish language, but also on the topography of Ireland and the genealogies of its ancient chiefs and clans. That work was first published at Paris, A.D. 1768 ; and a new edition of it was published in Dublin, in the year 1832, by the Right Rev. Robert Daly, late Protestant bishop of Cashel.

† *Monarchy* : In the reign of King Cormac Mac Art, or Cormac Ulfhada, the one hundred and fifteenth Monarch of Ireland, flourished the celebrated military organization called the *Fiana Eireann*, or " Irish Fenians," who (like the Red Branch Knights of Ulster) formed a militia for the defence of the throne. Their leader was the renowned Finn, the son of Cumhail (commonly called "Finn MacCoole," whose genealogy see in the " O'Connor Faley pedigree"), who resided at the hill of Allen in Kildare. Finn and his companions-in-arms are to this day vividly remembered in tradition and legend, in every part of Ireland ; and the hills, the glens, and the rocks of the country still attest, not merely their existence—for that, no one who has studied the question can doubt—but also the important part they played in the government and military affairs of the Kingdom. One of the principal amusements of these old heroes, when not employed in war, was *hunting ;* and after their long sporting excursions, they

At an early period in the world's history the Gaels, moving west-wards, reached Gaul, whence, in after ages they crossed the Alps (*ailp* : Irish, "a huge heap of earth"), into Italy, where they possessed the territory called by the Romans *Gallia Cisalpina*, or "Gaul this side of the Alps ;" and others of them proceeding now eastwards penetrated into Greece, and settled on the banks of the Ister, where they were called "Istrians." From Gaul they crossed the Pyrenees, and settled in Iberia or Spain ; and, there mixing with the Iberians, they were called "Celto-Iberi."

The Celts were the first inhabitants of Europe after the Deluge. They inhabited those parts on the borders of Europe and Asia, about the Euxine sea, and thence spread over Western Europe and the countries afterwards called Germany, Gaul, Italy, Spain, Britain, and Ireland. The western part of the European continent, comprising parts of Gaul, Germany, Spain, and Italy, was, by ancient geographers, denominated *Celtica*, or the "Land of the *Celts*"—a name afterwards applied to Gaul, as the land of the *Gaels*. Southern Italy was peopled by a mixture of Celts and Greeks.

The Celts were of the Caucasian race—a race which included (with the exception of the Lapps and Finns) the ancient and modern Europeans and Western Asiatics, such as the Assyrians, Babylonians, Medes, Persians, Scythians, Parthians, Arabs, Jews, Syrians, Turks, Afghans, and Hindoos. To these must also be added the European colonists who have settled in America, Australia, and other parts of the world. But, notwithstanding all the variations in colour and appearance which are observable in the Caucasian, Mongolian, Ethiopian, Malayan, and American races, God has made of *one* blood all nations of men ; and the most positive identity exists among them all !

In his Irish Dictionary, Dr. O'Brien derives from the Celtic many names of countries terminating in *tan :* as, Britan or Britain ; Aquitain, in Gaul ; Lusitan or Lusitania, the ancient name of Portugul ; Mauritan or Mauritania, the land of the Moors ; Arabistan, the land of the Arabs ; Turkistan, the land of the Turks ; Kurdistan, the land of the Kurds ; Farsistan, Luristan, etc., in Persia ; Caffristan and Afghanistan, the lands of the Caffres and the Afghans ; Hindostan, the land of the Hindoos ; etc.

A great affinity between the Celtic and the Sanscrit languages has also been shown by many etymologists ; and the word "Sanscrit," itself, has been derived from the Celtic word *Seanscrobhtha* [sanskrivta], which signifies "old writings," and has the same signification in the Irish language. As the Sanscrit is one of the most ancient of languages, we can therefore form an idea of the great antiquity of the Celtic.

had certain favourite hills on which they were in the habit of resting and feasting during the intervals of the chase. These hills, most of which are covered by cairns or moats, are called *Suidhe Finn* [Seefin]—"Finn's seats," or resting places ; and they are found in each of the four provinces of Ireland. Immediately under the brow of the mountain "Seefin," near Kilfinane, in Limerick, reposes the beautiful vale of Glenosheen, whose name commemorates the great poet and warrior, Oisin [Osheen], the son of Finn.—*See* JOYCE's "*Irish Names of Places.*"

THE CELTIC, TEUTONIC, AND SLAVONIC NATIONS.

The principal Celtic nations were the Gauls, the Celtæ, the Belgæ, and the Gauls of Northern Italy ; the Galatians or Gauls of Asia Minor, and of Gallicia, in the north of Spain ; the Boii and Pannonians of Germany, who are branches of the Gauls ; the Celtiberians of Spain ; the Cimmerians of Germany ; the Umbrians ; the Etrurians or Etruscans ; the Samnites and Sabines of Italy ; the Thracians, Istrians, and Pelasgians of Greece ; the Britons, the Welsh, and the Manx ; the Caledonians, and the Irish, etc.

The Teutonic nations were the Goths and Vandals, who overthrew the Roman empire, and conquered parts of France, Spain, Italy, and Africa ; the Franks and Burgundians, who conquered France ; the Longobards, who conquered Northern Italy, now known as "Lombardy ;" the Suevi, Alemmanni, and other powerful nations of ancient Germany ; the Anglo-Saxons, who conquered England ; and the Scandinavians or people of Sweden, Norway, and Denmark. In modern times, however, the Teutonic nations are the Germans, Danes, Swedes, Norwegians, Dutch, Swiss, English or British, the Anglo-Irish, and the Anglo-Americans, etc.

The name "Teuton" is derived from the Gothic *teut*, which signifies "a god ;" and the term "Teutons" has been applied to various nations of Scythian origin, speaking cognate dialects of one great language—the Celtic.

The Sclavonic or Slavonic nations were sometimes called "Sclavonians ;" and were descended from the Slavi or Sclavi of the Roman writers—a Scythian race who dwelt in Germany. The name is derived from *slava*, which signifies "glory." The Sarmatians were also of Scythian origin, and settled in the territory from them called by the Romans, " Sarmatia ;" which comprised the country now called Poland, and parts of Russia, Prussia, and Austria.

As it was Cadmus the Phœnician that introduced the use of *letters* into Greece, about the time that Moses is considered to have written the Pentateuch (or first five books of the Bible), the knowledge of "letters" must have therefore existed among the Phœnicians and their colonies long before Homer wrote ; and there can be no doubt that " letters" and their use were then known in Cadmus's own city of Miletus, and the other cities of Asia Minor, for, according to Herodotus, who is believed to have written about four hundred and fifty years before Christ, the Ionians of Asia Minor preceded the other Greeks in acquiring the art of *writing ;* and used skins on which to write, before they had the "papyrus." It would therefore appear that the Feiné or Phœnicians were the first people who were acquainted with the art of writing by letters : hence they were able to *record* their genealogies and the leading events of their race down from the Deluge.

THE SCYTHIAN FAMILY.

As the Milesian or Scotic Irish Nation is descended from the Scythian family, it may not be out of place here to give a brief sketch of Scythia.

Japhet, son of Noah, was the ancestor of the Scythians. The name "Scythian" was applied to those nations who displayed skill in *hunting*

and the *use of the bow*. In his Dictionary, Dr. O'Brien states that the word
"Scythian" is derived from the Celtic word *sciot*, which, in the Irish
language signifies a dart or arrow; and this derivation seems probable, as
the Scythian nations, particularly the Parthians, were all famous archers.
The Greek colonists on the north of the Euxine or Black Sea, hearing
their Scythian neighbours frequently call archers, shooters, and hunters
(who were very numerous among them), by the names of "Scuti,"
"Scythi," "Shuten," or "Schuten"—each of which signifies *Scythians*,
applied that name to the whole nation. This word, or rather its ancient
primary signification, is still preserved in the English, German, Lithuanian,
Finnish, Livonian, Courlandish, Lapponian, Esthonian, and Prussian
tongues: a fact which goes to prove that all these nations are of Scythian
origin.

The Scythians were among the most warlike and valiant people of
antiquity, and fought chiefly in war-chariots. They worshipped the sun,
moon, and winds, and their chief deity was their god of war, called by the
Greeks 'Ares; and Odin or Wodin, by the Goths, Germans, and Scandinavians. The Sacæ, ancestors of the Saxons; the Sarmatæ, progenitors
of the Sarmatians; the Basternæ, the Goths, the Vandals; the Daci or
Dacians; the Scandinavians, the Germans; the Franks, who conquered
France; the Suevi, Alans, Alemanni; the Longobards or Lombards;
and many other tribes, were all powerful nations of the Scythian family.
The Huns of Asia, who, under Attila in the fifth century, overran the
Roman empire, are stated by some writers to have been Scythians; but
that opinion is incorrect, for the Huns were of the Mongol or Tartar,
while the Scythians were of the great Caucasian race. The name
"Tartar,"—the modern appellation of the pastoral tribes of Europe and
Asia—was unknown to the ancients; and the opinion that "Tartarus,"
the name of the infernal regions, was borrowed from the word "Tartar,"
on account of the *gloomy* aspect of the country about the Cimmerian
Bosphorus, has no just foundation, as that word is a modern corruption:
the genuine names being "Tatars" and "Tatary," not *Tartars* and
Tartary.

Scythia was divided into two large portions—European and Asiatic:
the former extending along the north of the Danube and the Euxine; the
latter, beyond the Caspian Sea and the river Jaxartes (now Siboon).
Scythia in Asia was divided by the chain of the Imaus mountains or
Beloor Tag—a branch projecting north from the Indian Caucasus, now
the Hindoo Cush or western part of the Himalayas. These divisions
were distinguished by the names of Scythia *intra*, and Scythia *extra*, Imaum
(or Scythia *inside*, and Scythia *beyond*, Imaus). Ancient Scythia included
all the country to the north of the Ister (or Lower Danube), and east of the
Carpathian mountains; extending north to the Hyperborean or Frozen
Ocean, and eastwards as far as the Seres, on the west of China: an immense
region, but still not commensurate with the whole of what is now called
"Tartary," which extends to the north and west of China as far as the
mouth of the Amoor.

Moving to the west, the Scythians settled in Scythia in Europe—that
vast tract of couutry north of the Danube and Black Sea, and embracing
what is now known as "European Russia." At a later period it was

called *Getæ* or *Gothi;* and, in a more advanced stage of geographical knowledge, " Sarmatia Europæa."

The term " Getæ" is evidently a generic designation given to various tribes of Scythians, such as the *Massa-Getæ*, the *Thyssa-Getæ*, the *Tyri-Getæ*, etc. ; as, in later times, we read of the *Meso-Gothi*, the *Visi-Gothi*, the *Ostro-Gothi:* hence, as in the latter case, "Gothi" or "Goths" was the primary appellation, so in the former case was the term " Getæ."

The " Getæ" of the Gaels dwelt in *Getulia* or Lybia, in the north of Africa, where afterwards stood the city of Carthage : these Getæ and the Carthaginians were identical in origin ; but the " Getæ" of Herodotus dwelt to the south of the Danube, and were by him classed as Thracians, while he extended Thrace to the Danube : thus making it include what in subsequent times was called Mœsia, now known as Bulgaria. In the expedition of Alexander the Great, however, to the Danube, the Getæ inhabited the north side of the stream. The Thyssa-Getæ were located on the Volga ;* the Tyri-Getæ, on the Tyras or Dniester ; and the Massa-Getæ, on the Jaxartes, etc. The Scythia invaded by Darius, and described by Herodotus, extended in length from Hungary, Transylvania, and Western Wallachia, on the west, to the Don, on the east ; and included the countries now known as Eastern Wallachia, the whole of Moldavia, and the Buckowina, Bessarabia, Boudjack, Little Tartary, Podolia, Wolhynia, Ukraine Proper, the province of Belgorod, and part of the country of the Don Cossacks. But, besides these countries, the ancient Scythia in Europe included the whole of European Russia, Poland, Scandinavia, Wallachia, stretching east from the Norwegian and Kiolin mountains, to the Uralian range. In the account of European Scythia given by Herodotus the peninsula of the "Tauri"—or *Taurica Chersonesus* (Crim. Tartary), as it was called—is not included. The Tauri were a savage, cruel, and inhospitable people ; from this savage tribe and others of similar dispositions along its coast, it is not improbable that the Euxine acquired among the ancients the epithet of the "Inhospitable Sea."

Historians, in the accounts they have left us of the manners and character of the Scythians, relate things of them that are entirely opposite and contradictory. At one time they represent them as the justest and most moderate people in the world ; at another, they describe them as a fierce and barbarous nation, which carried its cruelties to such excesses as are shocking to human nature. This contrariety is a manifest proof that those different characters are to be applied to different nations in that vast family ; and that, although they were all comprehended under one and the same general denomination of "Scythians," we ought not to confound them or their characters together. According to Justin, they lived in great simplicity and innocence. They did not give the name of goods or riches to anything but what, humanly speaking, truly deserved that title : as health, strength, courage, the love of labour and liberty, innocence of life, sincerity, an abhorrence of all fraud and dissimulation, and, in a word,

---

* *Volga :* The ancestors of these Thyssa-Getæ of Herodotus were, no doubt, the "Firbolgs" or " Firvolgians" (the *men* from the banks of the *Volga*), who, according to the Four Masters, invaded Ireland before the Tuatha-de-Danans.

all such qualities as render man more virtuous and more valuable. If to these happy dispostions we could add the knowledge of the true God, without which the most exalted virtues are of little value, they would have been a perfect people.

" When," says Rollin, " we compare the manners of the Scythians with those of the present age, we are tempted to believe that the pencils which drew so beautiful a picture of them were not free from partiality; and that Justin and Horace have decked them with virtues that did not belong to them. But all antiquity agrees in giving the same testimony of them; and Homer, in particular, whose opinion ought to be of great weight, calls them the most just and upright of men."

GAODHAL [GAEL] CONTEMPORARY WITH MOSES.

Objections have been advanced against the accuracy of the Irish Genealogies; because it is difficult to reconcile a point of chronology on the subject of Gaodhal, who, according to the Pagan Irish chroniclers, was fifth in descent from Japhet, and contemporary of Moses, who, according to the Book of Genesis, was of the fourteenth or fifteenth generation after Shem. Granting the genealogy of Moses, as recorded, to be correct, the anachronism which here presents itself may easily be accounted for; on the supposition that the copyist of the Milesian Manuscripts may have omitted some generations between Japhet and Gaodhal. In the histories of those times so far remote, there are other things, besides, hard to be reconciled. For instance, the learned differ about the king who reigned in Egypt in the time of Moses, and who was drowned in the Red Sea: some pretend that it was Amenophis, father of Sesostris; others say that it was Pheron, son of Sesostris; whilst the Pagan Irish chroniclers say it was Pharaoh Cincris. The Hebrews, the Greeks, and the Latins disagree concerning the number of years that elapsed from the time of the Creation to the coming of the Messiah; whilst on this point, the *Septuagint* agrees with the Pagan Irish chroniclers! These differences, however, do not affect the truth of the events recorded to have happened in the interval between the Creation and the birth of our Redeemer—for instance: the Deluge, the birth of Abraham, the building of the Temple of Jerusalem, etc.; nor ought a similar anachronism with respect to Gaodhal and Moses destroy the truthfulness of the Irish Genealogies.

It has also been objected, that Navigation was unknown in those early periods, and that it therefore cannot be believed that the Gaels (or descendants of Gaodhal above mentioned) had been able to make such distant voyages by sea, as that from Egypt to Crete, from Crete to Scythia, from Scythia to Africa, from Africa to Spain, and from Spain to Ireland. This difficulty will vanish if we but consider that the art of sailing had been at all times in use, at least since the Deluge. We know that long before Solomon, the Phœnicians, Egyptians, and Greeks possessed the art of navigation:

"The Phœnicians," says Herodotus, "who traded to all countries with the merchandise of Egypt and Assyria arrived at Argos, a trading city in Greece; and, after disposing of their merchandise, they carried off the wives of the Greeks, together with Io, daughter of King Inachus, who reigned at Argos, about the year of the world

3,112; after which some Greeks trading to Tyre carried away, in their turn, Europa, daughter of the King of Tyre, to be revenged for the insult their countrymen sustained by the carrying off of their wives from Argos."

It may be asked, Why did not the early Gaels (or the Gadelians as they were also called) establish themselves in some part of the continent, rather than expose themselves to so many dangers by sea? The answer is obvious: The Scythians (from whom the Gaels are descended) had neither cities nor houses; they were continually roving, and lived in tents, sometimes in one country, sometimes in another; for, in those early ages, society had not been sufficiently settled, and property in the possession of lands was not then established as it since has been. This accounts for the taste for voyages and emigrations which prevailed in the primitive ages of the world. The Egyptians, Phœnicians, Greeks, and Carthaginians (who were themselves a colony of Phœnicians) sent colonies into different countries; and Carthage herself, after having founded three hundred cities on the coast of Africa, and finding herself still overcharged with inhabitants, sent Hanno with a fleet and thirty thousand volunteers, to make discoveries on the coast of Africa, beyond the Pillars of Hercules, and to establish some colonies there. But, whatever truth may be attached to the Irish Annals in regard to the genealogies of the Irish Nation, and the voyages and transmigrations of the Gaels in different countries, it appears at all times indisputable that these people, while claiming the glory of having come originally from Egypt, derived their origin from the Scythians: the accounts of foreign authors confirm it; among others, Newton (Chron. Dublin edit., page 10) says, that—

" Greece and all Europe had been peopled by the Cimmerians or Scythians from the borders of the Euxine Sea, who, like the Tartars, in the North of Asia, led a wandering life."*

So careful, however, were the Milesian colonists of their genealogies, that they maintained a class of men to record and preserve them; for, with them a man's right of inheritance to property depended on his genealogy, except where "might" took the place of "right." Our

MILESIAN IRISH GENEALOGIES,

records, and chronicles were therefore at certain periods carefully examined, in order to have them purged of any errors which might from time to time have crept into them; and, thus revised, those state documents formed the materials from which, in the third century of the Christian era, was compiled by order of the celebrated Monarch, King Cormac Mac Art, the history of the Irish Nation, from the earliest period, which was called the *Psalter of Tara;* from which and other more recent records was written in the ninth century by Cormac MacCullinan, the bishop-king of Munster, the noble work known as the *Psalter of Cashel*—the original of which is deposited in the Library of the British Museum, London.

In the fifth century, St. Patrick, St. Benignus, and St. Carioch were, according to the Four Masters, three of the nine personages appointed by

* *Life :* See the Abbé MacGeoghegan's *History of Ireland.*

B

the triennial parliament of Tara, in the reign of Laeghaire,* the 128th Monarch of Ireland: "to review, examine, and reduce into order all the monuments of antiquity, genealogies, chronicles, and records of the Kingdom." These monuments of antiquity, genealogies, chronicles, and records so revised, examined, and reduced into order, by St. Patrick and his colleagues on that occasion, were carefully preserved in our national archives up to the Danish and Anglo-Norman invasions of Ireland : after which some of the Irish Manuscripts were ruthlessly destroyed by the invaders; some were conveyed to Belgium, Denmark, England, France, Rome, etc. ; some were preserved in public and private libraries in Ireland; and some were deposited for safe-keeping in Irish and Scotch Convents and Monasteries.

THE ANNALS OF THE FOUR MASTERS.

In his search for authentic records from which to compile the *Annala Rioghacta Eireann* (or "The Annals of the Kingdom of Ireland") now known as the *The Annals of the Four Masters*, Michael O'Clery, their chief author, and a monk of the Order of St. Francis, appears to have found the most important of the ancient Irish records ; for, he states that he compiled the Irish Genealogies " from the ancient and approved chronicles, records, and other books of antiquity of the Kingdom of Ireland."

Addressing his friend Fargal (or Farrell) O'Gara, lord of Moy-O'Gara and Coolavin ("one of the two knights elected to represent the county Sligo in the Parliament held in Dublin, this present year of our Lord, 1631"), to whom the Annals of the Four Masters were inscribed, Michael O'Clery says in his Dedication page:

"On the 22nd January, A.D. 1632, this work was undertaken in the Convent of Donegal, and was finished in the same Convent on the 10th day of August, 1636 ; being the eleventh year of the reign of Charles, King of England, France, Scotland, and Ireland."

O'Clery proceeds :

" In every country enlightened by civilization, and confirmed therein through a succession of ages, it has been customary to record the events produced by time.   For sundry reasons nothing was deemed more profitable and honourable than to study and peruse the works of ancient writers, who gave a faithful account of the chiefs and nobles who figured on the stage of life in the preceding ages : that posterity might be informed how their forefathers employed their time, how long they continued in power, and how they finished their days."

O'Clery continues :

" In consequence of your uneasiness on the general ignorance of our civil history, and of the monarchs, provincial kings, lords, and chieftains, who flourished in this country through a succession of ages; with equal want of knowledge of the synchronism necessary for throwing light on the transactions of each, I have informed you

* *Laeghaire*: Ware begins his "Antiquities of Ireland" with the reign of this Monarch, and the apostleship of St. Patrick ; and he assigns as a reason for doing so, that much of what had been written concerning the predecessors of that Monarch was mixed with fables and anachronisms.   As this is a fault common to all ancient histories, no doubt Ware's criticism is just.   Two things in it, however, are worthy of notice, namely—first, that Laeghaire had predecessors in the monarchy, and monuments which speak of them ; and second, that these monuments were mixed with fables and anachronisms.—*MacGeoghegan*.

that I entertained hopes of joining to my own labours the assistance of antiquaries I held most in esteem for compiling a body of Annals, wherein those matters should be digested under their proper heads; judging that, should such a compilation be neglected at present, or consigned to a future time, a risk might be run that the materials for it would never again be brought together."

And O'Clery adds:

"In this idea I have collected the most authentic Annals I could find in my travels (from A.D. 1616 to 1632) through the kingdom; from which I have compiled this work, which I now commit to the world under your name and patronage." ¡

The Annals so collected by O'Clery were digested as follows: One portion of them is an historical abridgment of the Irish Kings, their reign and succession,* their genealogies and death; another portion is a tract on the genealogies of the Irish saints, called *Sanctilogium Genealogicum;* the third treats of the first inhabitants and different conquests of Ireland, the succession of her Kings, their wars, and other remarkable events from the Deluge until the arrival of the English in the twelfth century; another of the works was called the Annals of Donegal; and another, the Irish Genealogies.

From O'Clery's Irish Genealogies, and other sources, O'Ferrall, who was Irish Historiographer to Queen Anne, translated into English, A.D. 1709, his *Linea Antiqua:* a Manuscript copy of which was deposited in the Office of Arms, Ireland, and another in the Royal Library at Windsor; but which does not contain all the Irish pedigrees given by O'Clery. It would appear that it gives the pedigrees of those families only who were of note in Ireland in O'Ferrall's time. In Sir William Betham's edition of the *Linea Antiqua,* however, many Irish genealogies are given which are not mentioned by O'Ferrall, but which are contained in O'Clery's Book of Irish Pedigrees, and recorded by Mac Firbis.

PATRONYMIC PREFIXES.

In all ages and in all nations some families were more distinguished than others: some were known by the prefix *De, Von,* or *Don;* the *Mac* was peculiar to Scotland, while Ireland retained the *O'* and *Mac.* Without *O'* and *Mac* the Irish have no names, according to the old verse:

> "Per *O'* atque *Mac,* veros cognoscis Hibernos;
> His duobus demptis, nullus Hibernus adest."

Which has been translated thus—

> "By *Mac* and *O'* you'll always know
> True Irishmen, they say:
> But, if they lack the *O'* or *Mac,*
> No Irishmen are they."

Many of the old Irish families omit the *O',* and *Mac;* others of them,

---

* *Succession*: It may be reasonably asserted that the people who were able to appreciate the importance of recording the names of their kings, their reign and succession, and who possessed a *written* language to enable them to do so, cannot be said to have been "uncivilized."

from causes over which they had no control, have so twisted and translated their sirnames, that it is often difficult to determine whether those families are of Irish, English, or French extraction. By looking for the sirname, however, in the page of this Work to which the " Index of Sirnames" refers, the descent of the family bearing that name may, as a rule, be ascertained.

Other families are considered as of English, or Anglo-Norman descent; but some of those families can be easily traced to Irish origin. For example : "Hort" can be derived from the Irish proper name *O'h-Airt ;* "Ouseley" and "Wesley," from *Mac Uaislaidh* [Mac Oossley]; "Verdon" and " De Verdon," from the Irish *fhear-donn* [fhar-dun], signifying the " brown man ;" "Vernon" and "MacVernon," from the Irish *fhear-nuin* (*nuin :* Irish, the ash tree); etc.

This volume also contains the names of the Irish Chiefs and Clans in Ireland, from the twelfth to the fifteenth century, and where the territories they possessed were located; the names of the leading families of Anglo-Norman, English, and Scotch descent, who settled in Ireland from the twelfth to the seventeenth century; and of the modern Irish Nobility. Under these several heads Connellan's "Four Masters" contains very full information—more than, in case of the Irish Chiefs and Clans, is given in O'Dugan's and O'Heerin's Topographies: Connellan we have therefore adopted, save, in a few instances where we found that some of the Irish families were, inadvertently perhaps, mystified.

Some Irish sirnames are now obsolete, and some extinct; the following are the modern forms of a few of the obsolete sirnames : *MacFirbis* has become "Forbes ;" *MacGeough*, "Goff," "Gough," and "MacGough ;" *MacRanall,* "Reynell" and "Reynolds ;" *MacTague,* "Montague;" *Mulligan,* "Molyneux ;" *O'Barie,* "Barry ;" *O'Bearra,* "Berry" and "Bury ;" *O'Caoinhan,* "Keenan ;" *O'Donocho,* "O'Donoghue" and "O'Donohoe ;" *O'Gnieve,* "Agnue" and "Agnew ;" *O'Rahilly,* "O'Reilly" and "OReilly ;" etc.

THE IRISH LANGUAGE A KEY TO THE MODERN LANGUAGES OF EUROPE.

On the importance that should attach in our schools and colleges to a knowledge of the Irish language,[*] the late lamented Mr. Patrick McMahon, M.P., for New Ross, writing to us on the subject, says :

"I think it a great pity that Irish is not more studied as a Key to Greek and Latin and the modern dialects of Latin. One who knows Irish well will readily master Latin, French, Spanish, Italian, and Portuguese. Our Carthaginian forefathers were famed for their knowledge of languages: *Carthago Bilinguis.* An effort should be made to have it taught more generally in the Irish schools and colleges ; not through antiquarian sentimentality, but as the readiest means of enabling our youths to master modern languages. I am very glad to see that you know it so thoroughly."

[*] *Irish Language :* Of that language Archbishop Ussher, Protestant Primate of Armagh, wrote—" Est quidem lingua Hibernica, et elegans cum primis, et opulenta; sed ad eam isto modo excolendam (sicuti reliquas fere Europæ linguas vernaculas intra hoc sæculum excultas videmus), nondum exstitit hactenus qui animum adjiceret; nullum adhuc habemus hujus linguæ Lexicon, sive per se factum, sive cum alia lingua comparatum."—*Epist. Usser.*

To the Irish-speaking people the Irish language is rich, elegant, soul-stirring and expressive; and, for figurative or ornamentation purposes, can favourably compare with any other language in the world.

In the reign of Queen Elizabeth the Irish language was proscribed. But, now, that linguists have found that the Celtic is the "Key" to the modern languages of Europe; and that some European Universities have already established Chairs for the cultivation of Celtic learning, let us hope that the State, which has undertaken to preserve from decay "Celtic Antiquities" in Great Britain and Ireland that are not so ancient as the Celtic language, will, for its intrinsic value to Philology, if not for its great antiquity, revive* and foster the rich, expressive, and mellifluous language of the Gaels.

Many were the revolutions of empires, states, and nations, since the days of Gaodhal, a quo the GAELS : The Assyrian† made way for the Babylonian empire; the Babylonian, for the Medo-Persian; the Medo-Persian, for the Macedonian; the Macedonian, for the Roman; and in its turn also, the Roman empire ceased to have existence : so, in Ireland, the Tuatha-de-Danans conquered the ancient Firblogs (or Firvolgians); so the Milesian or Scotic Nation conquered the Tuatha-de-Danans; and so, in its turn, was the Milesian Irish Nation ultimately subdued by the Anglo-Normans; as were the De-Danans by the Milesians; as were the ancient Britons by the Saxons; and as were the Saxons by the Normans. But we must not forget that the course of events, the progresses and retrogressions of the world's history are from God. His writing is upon the wall whenever and wherever it is His holy will.

THE SEAT OF THE GARDEN OF EDEN.

Eminent German Geologists and Ethnologists maintain that the locality of Man's primitive origin, the seat of the Garden of Eden—the so-called "Paradise"—was in the Pacific Ocean, south of the present continent of Asia, westward to Africa, and eastward to Australia.   When the great

* *Revive :* That the Irish language shall revive, may be hoped from the untiring labours in that direction of the Societies for its preservation, lately established in Dublin and in the United States of America; and from the fact that, since 1878, it has formed a portion of the *curriculum* in the Irish National Schools, and in the schools in connexion with the Board of Intermediate Education in Ireland.   More lately still, the Royal University of Ireland was established, on whose *curriculum* also the Irish language forms a subject for examination.

† *Assyrian :* The following Table shows how long each of the five great empires of antiquity existed, compared with the Milesian Irish Dynasty :

Empires of Antiquity.

1. The Assyrian empire	lasted 1,413 years.	
2. „ Babylonian	222	„
3. „ Medo-Persian	222	„
4. „ Greek or Macedonian	187	„
5. „ Roman	1,229	„

But, according to the Four Masters, the *Clann-na-Milidh* (as the Milesians were called) sailed from Galicia in Spain and invaded Ireland, Before Christ 1698 years.   The Milesian Dynasty therefore existed in Ireland, from B.C. 1698 to A.D. 1172, or during a period of 2,870 years.

Pacific continent* slowly sank, so that the ocean commenced filling up the
valleys, Man retreated to the mountains, which, by continued sinking, were
transformed into islands ; and now form the many groups of Polynesia.
If this theory could be reconciled with the narrative in the Sacred
Volume (see Genesis, ii. 10, 11, 12, 13, 14)—and Scripture Commentators
confess that the sites of some countries, cities, and places mentioned in
the Bible are even yet unascertained—it would explain the origin of the
ancient temples and other buildings found in America after its discovery
by Christopher Columbus, A.D. 1492; and proclaim the great civilization
of the inhabitants of the Pacific continent before its submersion. It is
not, however, difficult to understand that, civilized as those people may
then have been, the insular position of the races thus preserved should,
in the absence of intercourse with other civilized nations, have, in the
course of ages, conduced to a savage condition—savage in some instances
even at the present day ; nor is it difficult to see that their insular
position should also have conduced to the preservation of their language—
whatever it may have been.

Writing of the Pyramids of Egypt—"those stupendous monuments of
human labour and engineering skill," Canon U. J. Bourke says :

"Egypt stands in her Pyramids a perennial landmark in the domain of the world's
history, connecting the period of the Deluge with the present. Take away the records
written by the pen of Moses, there still remain the Pyramids, raising their heads above
all passing mists, and proclaiming the story of the knowledge and the skill, and the
practical power of the immediate posterity of Noah and his children."

THE FIRST INHABITANTS OF EUROPE.

The first inhabitants of Europe after the Deluge were the Celts, who
were descended from Japhet. But the Celts and the Gaels were identical
in origin ; for, according to Liddell (in his "History of Rome"), *Celt* is
strictly the same as *Gael*, and the Greek *Keltai* and *Gallatai* and the Latin

---

* *Continent :* It is a well-known fact that the whole Pacific coast (especially
California) with all its mountains, is perpetually rising, and that at a comparatively
rapid rate. The land containing on its bosom the great American lakes is slowly
sinking ; while Southern Indiana, Kentucky, and the surrounding States are rising.
Geological investigations prove that those great lakes, except Ontario, had formerly a
southern outlet ; until, by gradual northern depressions and southern upheavals, a
northern outlet was formed from Lake Erie into Lake Ontario, about forty thousand
years ago ! This outlet—the Niagara river—is still wearing its channel. The division
line of the watershed south of the lakes and the Mississippi Valley has since that time
been steadily travelling southward ; and when Chicago recently turned the water of Lake
Michigan through the Chicago river into the Mississippi Valley, the old state of affairs
was artificially re-established. New Jersey is sinking, with New York City and Long
Island, at the estimated rate of about sixteen inches per century. The coast of Texas
is ascending at a comparatively very rapid rate—some observers stating that it is as
much as thirty or forty inches in the last half century. Combining these observations
with the results of the recent deep-sea soundings of the United States steamer
"Tuscarora," in the Pacific Ocean, we find that the bed of that ocean is evidently a
sunken continent ; abounding in volcanic mountains some twelve thousand feet high,
many of them not reaching the surface of the ocean, and others, which do so, forming
the numberless islands of the Pacific. The study of coral rocks proves that this sinking
has continually been taking place during several centuries ; and observations of the
coast reveals the fact that it has not ceased.

Galli are all one. Heretofore, however, the Celts and the Gaels were considered as two distinct nations : the Celts as descended from Gomer ; the Gaels, from Magog—two of the sons of Japhet.

According to O'Brien's "Irish Dictionary," that portion of the posterity of Japhet, which peopled the south and south-west parts of Europe, must, after the Deluge, have first proceeded from the centre of the dispersion of mankind (Genesis xi. 8,) towards the straits of the Thracian Bosphorus, and those of the Hellespont, which they crossed by means of boats ; whose construction was, doubtless, familiar to them from the traditional knowledge they had of the Ark. Those tribes which passed over the Hellespont first inhabited the south parts of Thrace,* as also Macedonia or ancient Greece; and those which crossed the Thracian Bosphorus (now called the straits of Constantinople) must have been the first inhabitants both of the northern parts of Thrace and of Lower, and Upper, Mesia, and also of Dacia when some of them had crossed the Danube.† In process of time a portion of the tribes which first settled in the two Mesias and the northern parts of Thrace proceeded towards Illyricum and Pannonia ; from which regions, where they were separated into two different bodies, it is natural to conclude (from the situation of those localities) that they proceeded towards the west by two different courses : those of Pannonia going towards Noricum (now called Austria), Stiria, Carniola, and Upper Bavaria—from which countries it would appear that all the western parts of Germany were first peopled, as the east and north-east of that country were probably peopled from Dacia; and those of Illyricum taking their course towards Istria, from which point of the Adriatic coast they poured down into the regions of Italy, whence, in after ages, some of them proceeded to Gaul, speaking the very same language as that spoken by those of their nation whom they left in Italy, and who, by the ancient authors, were called *Indigenæ* or *Aborigines :* meaning that they were the original or primitive people who first inhabited that land. Those people were the Siculi, the Ausones, the Umbri (and all their descendants of different names mentioned by Cluver in his Geogr., *Liber* 3, c. 33, p. 332). Some of the ancient authors rank the Aborigines with the Umbrians, whom Pliny (*Lib.* 3, c. 14) represents as the most ancient people of Italy : "Umbrorum gens Antiquissima Italiæ existimatur ;" and Florus calls them "Antiquissimus Italiæ populus." But it is conceded that the Aborigines were a tribe of the first inhabitants of Italy and, consequently, of the same stock of people of whom the first planters of Gaul were only a detachment ; as the Umbri are acknowledged by some of the ancient authors to have been of the same stock as the old Gauls. The Sabini, who, as well as the Umbri and the Aborigines, formed a portion of

---

* *Thrace:* The ancient name of Adrianople, in Thrace, was, according to Ammianus, *Uscudama* ("uisge" : Irish, *water*, and "daimh," *a house*, more correctly "domh," Lat. "dom-us"), meaning "the watery residence :" showing an affinity in language between the Thracians and the ancient Irish !

† *Danube:* The name of the river "Danube" is, in the old Celtic, *Danou* ("dana :" Irish, *bold* ; "obha" or "obhuin," an old Irish word for *river*), and signifies "the bold impetuous river." See the Irish epithet *Gharbh*, in Note under the "O'Mahony" pedigree, for the root of the Latin river *Garumna* and the French *Garonne ;* each of which literally means "the boisterous river."

the people afterwards called Latins, were but a tribe of the Umbri, and consequently of the same stock as the primitive Gauls. That the primitive inhabitants of the above-mentioned regions had originally but one and the same language, Cluver, in his German. Antiq., c. 6, 7, 8, produces clear vestiges in Gaul, Germany, Spain, Italy, and Illyricum; he might have added Thrace, Macedonia, and Greece:

"I am much inclined," says the Right Rev. Dr. O'Brien, "to believe that the near agreement which the ancient writers have remarked between the old Latin and Greek was, in greater measure, owing to this original identity of the European languages, than to whatever mixture might have been introduced into the Latin from the dialects of the Greek adventurers that came to Italy from time to time. Nor do I doubt but that the Gauls who repassed the Alps and settled in Upper Italy in the earliest times of the Romans, found the language of that country very nearly agreeing with their own : in the same manner and by the same reason that the people of Ireland and those of the Highlands of Scotland easily understand each other's dialects, though it be now near twelve hundred years since the Scots of Scotland parted from those of Ireland."

That the Iberno-Celtic or Gaelic-Irish language is the best preserved dialect of the old Celtic, and therefore the most useful for illustrating the antiquities of all the Celtic nations, was the opinion of the great Leibnitz, who, in his *Collectan. Etymol.* vol. i., p. 153, writes:

"Postremo, ad perficiendam, vel certe valde promovendam litteraturam Celticam diligentius Linguæ Hibernicæ studium adjungendum censeo, ut Lhudius egregie facere cæpit. Nam, uti alibi jam admonui, quemadmodum Angli fuere Colonia Saxonum, et Brittanni emissio veterum Celtarum, Gallorum, Cimbrorum ; ita Hiberni sunt, propago antiquiorum Britanniæ habitatorum, colonis Celticis, Cimbricisque nonnullis, ut sic dicam, medus anteriorum. Itaque ut ex Anglicis linguæ veterum Saxonum, et ex Cambricis veterum Gallorum ; ita ex Hibernicis vetustiorum adhuc Celtarum, Germanorumque, &c., ut generaliter dicam. accolarum Oceani Britannici Cismarinorum antiquates illustrantur. Et si ultra Hiberniam esset aliquæ insula Celtici sermonis, ejus filo in multo adhuc antiquiora duceremur."

And the learned Welshman,[*] Edward Lhuyd, mentioned by Leibnitz in the foregoing extract, acknowledges that the roots of the Latin are better and more abundantly preserved in the Irish than in the Welsh, which is the only Celtic dialect that can pretend to vie with the Gaelic Irish, as regards purity or perfection. Addressing the Irish nation, Lhuyd says :

"Your language is better situated for being preserved than any other language to this day spoken throughout Europe ;"

meaning, no doubt, that languages are best preserved in *islands* and in mountain-countries, as being the most difficult of access for strangers ; and especially because the Roman arms never reached Ireland, which, up to the Danish invasion, received no colonies but from Celtic countries. But, addressing the Welsh, the candid Lhuyd gives the preference to the Irish, not only for purity and perfection, as well as for priority of establishment in the British Isles, but also for its utility in illustrating the remote antiquities of Great Britain ; he says :

"It is impossible to be a complete master of the ancient British, without a competent knowledge of the Irish language."

* *Welshman:* See Lhuyd's "Irish Vocabulary;" and his *Archæologia Britannica,* published in English by Dr. Nicholson, in his "Irish Library."

And he fully establishes the fact that the Gaels* had been

THE PRIMITIVE INHABITANTS OF GREAT BRITAIN,

before the Cymri or ancient Britons (who were the ancestors of the Welsh) arrived in that island ; and that the dialect of those Gaels was then the universal language of the whole British Isle.†

The Island of Great Britain was called by the Gaels, *Alban, Albain,* ("aill" : Irish, *a rock* or *cliff ;* and "ban," *white :* because, it is thought, of the chalky or white cliffs of Dover, as seen from the direction of Gaul), and, more lately, *Albion ;* and when the Gaels were driven by the Britons to the northern portion of the Island, that part only was called *Alba, Alban,* or *Albain,* while the southern portion of the Island, now known as England, was called Britain or Albion.

According to Ussher, in his *Antiquit. Eccl. Brit.,* page 378, "Albion" was the name under which Great Britain was known to the Greeks, not only in the time of Ptolemy, Marcianus Heracleota, Eustachius, etc., but also in the much more ancient time of Aristotle and of Theophrastus : a very natural name for it by a Gaul placed on the continent or near Calais, where the first and only knowledge he may have of the British Isle consists in the bare sight of the *white cliffs* of Dover ; and this Gaul, having crossed the channel and observed the situation and shape of the land above Dover, naturally calls it *Ceantir‡* ("ceanntir :" Irish, *headland*), which the Romans latinized *Cantium,* now "Kent." A numerous colony of the Gaels having afterwards crossed over from Gaul to Britain, which by degrees they peopled from one end to the other, they gave names to all the remarkable objects of nature and art throughout the whole country—such as rivers, mountains, headlands, towns, etc. ; and, accordingly, we find these Gaelic names everywhere in England and Wales, from Dover to York, namely, from *Ceantir* (or Kent) to the river *Isc,* now called the "Ouse," which passes through York ; and from the river *Isca* (which passes through the town of *Caer-Leon-ar-Isc,* in Monmouthshire), to *Longdion* ("now London"), and its river *Tamh-isc* or *Thamisis,* now the "Thames."

In his *Mona Antiqua,* Roland observes that the remains of old habitations still to be seen on the tops of high places in Anglesea, are called to this day *Ceitir Guidelod,* which he anglicises "the Irishmen's

---

* *Gaels :* Baxter, in his *Glossario Antiquæ Britanniæ,* considers that the Brigantes (who were a part of the Gaelic colony which went from Spain to Ireland) were the first inhabitants of Britain ; and Lhuyd shows that the Brigantes were the first inhabitants of all that part of Great Britain which now comprehends England and Wales.

† *Isle :* When the Cymri (see "Cimbrians and Britons," in the Appendix,) settled in Britain, they forced the Gaels to the northern part of the Island ; and the name *Alban* or *Albain,* which the Gaels had first given to it, followed them, so as to be appropriated to whatever tract they inhabited. Hence it is that the term *Albanach* is the Irish for a native of Alba or Scotland, or North Britain, even at the present day.

‡ *Ceantir :* This word is compounded of the Irish *ceann,* the head ; and *tir* (Lat. *ter*-ra), a land, a country, a nation ; and this *ceann* makes *cinn,* in the genitive case. Hence the Anglo-Saxon word *king ;* because the "King" is the *head* of his people or subjects : the Irish C being equivalent to the English letter K ; and the final double *n,* to the English *ng.*—See O'Brien's Irish Dictionary, under the word "Cinn."

cottages,"* but which should more properly be rendered " the habitations
of the Gaels ;" and he justly observes that those are vestiges of the first
habitations that were made by the first planters of the island, because the
valleys were then covered with woods, which were the haunts of wolves
and other wild beasts. Two other objects, whose names are plain Irish,
are living evidences that the Gaels were the ancient inhabitants of
Anglesea, before the Welsh : The landing-place of the ferry or passage
from North Wales to Anglesea is, in Welsh, called *Port-aeth-wy*, which is a
corruption of the Irish *Port-ath-bhuidhe*, meaning " the bank or landing-
place of the yellow ford"—the water of that arm of the sea being of a
yellowish colour. It is also remarkable that *Tin-dath-wy*, the name of the
territory adjacent to *Port-aeth-wy*, is pure Irish ; for *tyn*, in Welsh, signifies
" a country or territory," as *tain* does in Irish : so that originally the name
was *Tain-ath-bhuidhe*, meaning "the territory of the yellow ford."

Even the name of the very capital of Britain, as used in the time of
the Romans (who added the termination "um" to it) was mere Irish ; for,
long [lung] is still the only word in common use in Irish to signify "a
ship," as *din* or *dion* has been used to express " a place of safety or protection" : so that *Longdin* or *Longdion*, which the Romans changed to
Londinum (now " London"), literally means " a place of safety for ships."
It is also worthy of remark that the name of the river on which London
is built was plain Irish. Cæsar calls it *Isis*, which is only latinizing the
Irish word *Isc* (" water)," which was the Gaelic name of that river before
the Romans invaded Britain ; and whether the word *Tam* was always
prefixed to *isc* or *isis*, either as an epithet, or as being the name of the
river "Tame," which joins its water, in either case the Irish word *Tamh*,
which signifies " still" (or quiet, gentle, smooth), was a natural epithet
for the river " Thames," as well as being a very significant name for the
river " Tame," on account of the *stillness* of its water.

According to the ancient Irish historians, and to Nenius, the Briton, the
Gaelic colony which came to Ireland from Spain, and brought a mixture of
the old Spanish or Cantabrian into the Irish language, was called the
"Milesian or Scotic Nation." They were also called " Scots." That
Milesian colony never inhabited Britain before their arrival in Ireland, but
came directly by sea to this country ; whence, after a long process of time,
the Irish Monarch Cormac Mac Art in the third century established a
colony, then known as Dalriada, in the north-west coast of Great Britain,

---

* *Cottages* : The ancient Irish had four sorts of habitations, viz.—1. *Caithir*, a city
(the Welsh *ceitir*) ; 2. *Baile*, a town (Lat. *villa*), called *Baile mor*, if a large town ;
3. *Dun*, a strong or fortified habitation ; 4. *Bruighean*, a palace, a royal residence, a
grand house or building. *Bruighean* is like the *Prain* of the Welsh, which means a
King's court ; they also call it *Priv-lys* (" primh-lios" : Irish, a *chief fort*), meaning a
principal residence. The Irish word " brug" or " brog" is the root of *Bruighean*, here
mentioned ; and is the same in meaning as the German, Gaulish, and Spanish *bruiga*,
briga, and *broga*. The Thracian *bria* (acc. *brian*) signified a town or habitation ; and
the Irish *bruighean* is pronounced " bruian," the same as the Thracian *brian*—both
words having the same signification.

Strabo observes that the Phryges were formerly called *Bryges*, or as the Greeks
wrote it, *Bruges* (Irish, *Brugeis*), and were of the Thracian kind : " Phryges antiquitus
Bryges Thracum genus ;" which goes to prove that the Phrygians, Thracians, and
the ancient Irish dwelt in houses and in cities, and were thus distinguished from the
Nomads.

and, in the fifth century of the Christian era, another Irish colony went there under the command of Fergus Mor MacEarca, the founder of the Scottish Monarchy in North Britain.*

The Gaelic-Irish bears a striking affinity not only to the old British in its different dialects, the Welsh and Armoric, besides the old Spanish or Cantabrian language preserved in Navarre and the Basque provinces, but also to the Greek, the Latin, the Hebrew, the Phœnician, the Chaldee, the Syriac, the Arabic, etc. Instances of this affinity are given throughout this Work. Dr. O'Brien shows that the *Lingua Prisca* of the Aborigines of Italy (from which the Latin of the twelve tables, and afterwards the Roman language, were derived) could have been nothing else than a dialect of the primitive Celtic;† and I venture the opinion that, if Philologists investigate the matter, they will find that the Aborigines of America and of the Polynesian Islands speak dialects of the ancient Celtic !

The Problem—" What was the language of our First Parents"—has long been a disputed question. Some say it was the Pelasgian, which was another name for the Japhetic ; and some say that the Japhetic was the Scythian, which was another name for the Celtic or Gaelic.

In a Scottish Gaelic poem by Allister MacDonald, in reference to the Gaelic language, the following jocose passage occurs :

> " Si labhar Adhamh a b-pairthas fan,
>   S'ba snasmhar Gaelig a n-beul aluin Eabha,"

which may be interpreted :

" The expressive Gaelic language was that which Adam spoke in Paradise, and which flowed from the lips of the fair Eve."

Or, divested of its adjectives, the passage may be reduced to the following proposition :

THE CELTIC WAS THE LANGUAGE OF EDEN.

Let us seriously examine this proposition. Of the Gaelic speech the Very Rev. Canon Bourke writes :

" In its plastic power and phonetic fecundity Irish-Gaelic possesses like its primitive Aryan parent tongue, not only the virtual but the formal germinal developments of dialectic variety."

And Canon Bourke also says :

" The science of Comparative Philology has, without direct reference to revelation, enabled men of literary research to discover the most convincing proofs, to show that before the dispersion of the human family there existed a common language, admirable in its raciness, in its vigour, its harmony, and the perfection of its forms."‡

That common primeval language of Man, which some call by the name " Aryan," I prefer to call the *Scythian* ; for the following reasons :

Phœniusa Farsaidh (or Fenius Farsa : see No. 14, on the " Lineal

---

* *Britain* : See No. 90 on "The Lineal Descent of the Royal Family of England."

† *Celtic*: For further valuable information on this subject, see Dr. O'Brien's " Irish Dictionary."

‡ *Forms* : See BOURKE's *Aryan Origin of the Gaelic Race and Language*. In the same strain writes Adolphe Pictet, of Geneva, in his *Les Origines Indo-Europeennes, ou les Aryas Primetife* (Paris, 1859).

Descent of the Royal Family," Part I., c. iv.), son of Baoth, son of Magog, son of Japhet, was, according to the Four Masters, the inventor of *Letters;* he was also the grandfather of Gaodhal, a quo the GAELS. This Phœniusa Farsaidh was king of Scythia, and was the ancestor of the Phœnicians : after him the Scythian language was called the "Phœnician." It is worthy of remark that Cadmus* the Phœnician, who is mentioned by O'Flaherty in his *Ogygia*, as brother of Phœniusa Farsaidh, was, according to the ancient Irish annalists, contemporary with Joshua, and it is a curious coincidence that the Alphabet† of the Gaels consisted of *sixteen* letters—the very number of letters as in the Phœnician Alphabet, and the very number brought by Cadmus to Greece, from Egypt, where the Gaels were first located, and whence they made their first migration, namely— that to the Island of Creta (now called Candia), in the Mediterranean Sea.

According to the Four Masters, the Scythian language was the Celtic ; which, after Gaodhal [gael] who "refined and adorned it," was called *Gaodhilg* or *Gaelic.*

THE GAELIC, THE MOST PRIMITIVE ALPHABET.

The ancient Alphabet of the Gaels contained sixteen letters; the Phœnician, sixteen ; the modern Gaelic, eighteen ; the Burmese, nineteen ; the Italian, twenty; the Indians of Bengal, twenty-one; the Chaldee, Hebrew, Latin, Samaritan, and Syriac, twenty-two each ; French, twenty-three ; English, twenty-four (it has now twenty-six) ; Greek, twenty-four ; Dutch and German, twenty-six ; Slavonic and Spanish, each twenty-seven ; Arabic, twenty-eight ; Welsh, twenty-eight ; Persian, thirty-one ; Coptic, thirty-two ; Turkish, thirty-three ; Georgian, thirty-six ; Armenian, thirty-eight ; Russian, forty-one ; Muscovite, forty-three ; Sanscrit and Japanese, each, fifty ; Ethiopic and Tartarian, each, two-hundred-and-two ; the Chinese have, properly speaking, no Alphabet, except we call their whole language by that name : their letters are words, or rather hieroglyphics, amounting to about eighty thousand.

In the primitive Gaelic Alphabet H and P were not included.

The letters of the Gaelic Alphabet were named after shrubs and trees : the name of the letter, in every instance, save that of the aspirate H, begins with the letter itself ; to preserve, as it were, its proper sound or power.

---

* *Cadmus* : This name may be derived from the Irish *Cadhmus* [caw-mus], which means "pride." Some persons, however, advance the opinion that there was no such person as Cadmus ; while others maintain that there was such a man, for that he founded a colony in Bœtia, and that the town of *Cadmea*, in that colony, was called after him !

† *Alphabet* : This circumstance regarding the Gaelic alphabet is the more remarkable, as its whole natural and primitive stock of letters is but sixteen in number ; the same as that of the first Roman or Latin alphabet which, according to Tacitus (*Anal.* ii) and Pliny (*Lib.* 7, c. 56), Evander, the Arcadian, brought from Greece to the Aborigines of Italy, and which was the original Phœnician set of letters communicated by Cadmus to the Greeks. And yet our sixteen letters of the primitive Irish alphabet were sufficient for all the essential purposes of language ; each preserving its own sound or power, without usurping that of any other letter.—*See O'Brien's Irish Dictionary.*

The sixteen letters of the ancient Gaelic Alphabet were arranged in the following order: B L F S N D T C M G R, and A O U E I. The H and P have since been added; so that the modern Gaelic Alphabet consists of eighteen letters, arranged as follows: A B C D E F G H I L M N O P R S T U.

Beginning with A, the names of the letters of the modern Gaelic Alphabet are: *Ailm*, which means the fig or palm tree; *Beith*, the birch tree; *Coll*, the hazel tree; *Dair*, the oak tree; *Eadha*, the aspen tree; *Fearn*, an alder tree; *Gort*, the ivy; (H) *Uath* (the name of the aspirate *h*), the white thorn; *Ioga*, the yew tree; *Luis*, the wild ash; *Muin*, the vine tree; *Nuin*, the ash tree; *Oir*, the broom tree; *Peith*, the dwarf elder; *Ruis*, the bore tree; *Suil*, the willow tree; *Teine*, the furze or whin bush; *Ur*, the heath shrub.

There is no K in the Gaelic Alphabet, ancient or modern; nor had the ancient Latins any character like that letter: they gave the sound of K to C, as in the word *sacra* (pronounced "sakra"), where the *c* has the sound of the English letter *k*. The Latin name *Cæsar* is now in English pronounced "Seasar" (where *c* has the sound of *s*); in German, however, it is pronounced "Kaiser;" but in no case can C, in Gaelic, be sounded like S. Nor have the Greeks the letter C in their Alphabet; but K (the Greek letter "kappa") corresponds to the Gaelic and Latin C, which has or should have the sound of the English letter K.

Baoth, son of Magog, son of Japhet, was contemporary with Nimrod, of whom, according to an ancient Irish poem, it is said:

One was at first the language of mankind,
Till haughty Nimrod, with presumption blind,
Proud Babel built; then, with confusion struck,
Seventy-two different tongues the workmen spoke.

That *one* language was the language of Mankind down from Adam to the building of the Tower of Babel, when (Genesis xi. 1) "the whole earth was of one language and of one speech."

Upon the division of the Earth by Noah amongst his sons, Shem, Ham, and Japhet; and by Japhet of his part thereof amongst his sons, Scythia came to Baoth's lot. Thus in Scythia, in Central Asia, far from the scene of Babel, the "Valley of Shinar"—the *Magh Senaar* of the ancient Irish annalists, Baoth and his people, we are told, took no part with those of Shem and Ham in the building of the Tower of Babel; and that hence the lasting vitality of the Celtic language!

If Baoth and his people took no part in the building of the Tower of Babel, it may be affirmed that they did not on that head incur the displeasure of the Lord; and, that, therefore, their language was not confused. But the language of Baoth and his people was the Scythian: *ergo*, the Scythian language was not confused. If, then, the Scythian language was not confused; and that *one* was the language of mankind, from Adam down to the building of the Tower of Babel, "when the whole earth was of one language and of one speech," it would follow that the *Scythian* was that *one language*—was, in fact, the language of Eden. But it has been above shown that the Scythian language was the Celtic : therefore, it may be affirmed that " The Celtic was the language of Eden."

Some persons consider that, because the Hebrew* was the language of the Jews, who were the chosen people of God, it therefore was the language of our First Parents ; but, if the ancient Gaelic Alphabet had only sixteen letters, while the Hebrew had twenty-two, it would appear that, of the two languages, the Gaelic is the more primitive—is in fact more ancient than any of the languages above enumerated, save the Phœnician, with which it was identical!

THE INVENTOR OF LETTERS.

After the confusion of tongues at the Tower of Babel, Phœniusa Farsaidh, king of Scythia, and the inventor of *Letters*, as above mentioned, employed learned men to go among the dispersed multitude to learn their several languages ; who, when those men returned well-skilled in what they went for, opened a " school" in the Valley of Shinar, near the city of Æothena, where, with his younger son Niul, he remained teaching for twenty years. On account of Niul's great reputation for learning, Pharaoh invited him into Egypt ; gave him the land of Campus Cyrunt, near the Red Sea, to inhabit ; and his daughter Scota in marriage.

THE RIVER "NILE" SO CALLED.

The ancient Irish historians tell us that the river " Nile" was so called after this Niul ; and that Scota, his wife, was the daughter of Pharaoh, who (Exodus ii. 5) rescued the infant Moses from drowning in the Nile : hence, it is said, the great interest which Niul and Scota took in the welfare and education of Moses ; the affection which Moses entertained for them and their son Gaodhal ; and the friendship which long afterwards existed between the Feiné and the Israelites in the land of Promise. Such was the intimacy between Moses and Niul, that, we are told, Moses invited him to go on board one of Pharaoh's ships on the Red Sea, to witness the miracle (Exodus xiv. 16, 17, 18) to be performed by the Great I AM, the God of the Israelites, in their deliverance from Egyptian bondage ; but, on account of his being the son-in-law of Pharaoh, Niul, while sympathising with the Israelites in their great affliction, asked Moses to excuse him for declining the invitation. Then Moses held Niul excused.

* *Hebrew*: The Druidic Irish had Hebraic customs to a great extent: for instance—the Druidic judges were of a priestly caste, and wore each a collar of gold. Buxtorf states that this collar was called *Iodhan Morain ;* and "Iodhan Morain" is Chaldee for *Urim and Thunmim* (see Exodus, xxviii. 30). Whether it was the Gaels who borrowed that Mosaic badge from the Israelites, or that it was the Israelites who borrowed it from the Gaels, we cannot say ; but *Iodhan Morain* is also Gaelic, and as such is said to be so called after a celebrated Irish Brehon who lived in the first century of the Christian era. (See " Brehon Families," in the Appendix.)

As showing an affinity between the Irish and the Hebrew languages, it may be remarked that the Irish pronoun *se* signifies " he," " him," and that the Hebrew pronoun *se* also means " he," " him ;" that the Irish pronoun *so*, which means "this" or " that," is like the Hebrew *so*, which has the same meaning ; and that the Irish pronoun *isi*, always expressed to signify " a female," is analogous to the Hebrew *isa*, which means " a woman."—*See* BUXTORF's *Hebrew Lexicon.*

The Egyptians were the most learned nation on the face of the earth; and the Bible tells us that Moses was instructed in all the learning of Egypt. It does not however appear that, before the time of Moses, the Egyptians had any knowledge of *Alphabetical* writing. If, then, it was the Celtic Alphabet which Cadmus the Phœnician brought from Egypt into Greece, we may infer that the Celtic language and Alphabet were at that time known in Egypt; and that it was in the school conducted by Niul and his father in the Valley of Shinar, or from Niul and his colony in Egypt, that the Egyptians received their knowledge of *Letters*, and probably much of the knowledge for which ancient Egypt was so renowned. But, wherever the Feiné (or Phœnicians) and the Egyptians received their education, it was they who had the honour of instructing, civilizing, and polishing the Grecians, by the colonies they sent among them : the Phœnicians taught them navigation, writing, and commerce; the Egyptians, by the knowledge of their laws and polity, gave them a taste for the arts and sciences, and initiated them into their mysteries.

For three successive generations the descendants of the Feiné, who, under the chieftaincy of Niul here mentioned, settled in Egypt, possessed and inhabited the territory near the Red Sea which was granted to him and his people by Pharaoh. Because, however, of the sympathy which Niul and his colony had manifested for Moses and the Israelites in bondage, the Egyptians forced Sruth, son of Asruth, son of Gaodhal, son of the said Niul, to leave Egypt, himself and his colony; when, after some traverses at sea, Sruth and the surviving portion of his people (who were known as *Phœné* or *Feiné*, as well as *Gaels*,) reached the island of Creta, where he died. We learn that some of Sruth's colony remained in Creta; some of them migrated thence to Getulia, in the North of Africa, where Carthage* was afterwards built; and some of them sailed towards the Land of Canaan, where on the island of Sor, off its coast, they founded the city of "Tyre :" this colony of the Gaels was called *Tyrians*. Grateful for the sympathy which their forefathers in Egypt had experienced from Niul and his people, the Israelites, after they had been some time settled in the Land of Promise, allotted to the Tyrians that tract of country on the north-west of Palestine, which had been inhabited by the Canaanites; and that territory was, from the name "Phœné," called *Phœnice* and, more lately, *Phœnicia.*

---

* *Carthage :* This name is derived through the Latin *Cartha-go*, from the Phœn., Chald. and Syr. *Kartha*, "a walled city;" which word "Kartha" seems to be derived by metathesis from the genitive case *cathrach*, of the Irish *cathair* [cawhir], "a city." The Irish *Maol Carthach* means the hero or king of the city; and *Mel Kartha* (meaning the King of the city) was the title of the Phœnician Hercules—the reputed founder of Tyre. *Mel Kartha* is evidently derived from the Irish or Celtic *Maol Carthach.* The sirname *MacCarthy* is derived from *Carthach*, who is No. 107 on the "MacCarthy Mór" Pedigree; and, judging from the meaning of the name, we are inclined to think that the said Carthach was the founder of the *city* of Cashel, which was formerly the royal seat of the Kingdom of South Munster—Compare *cathair* with the British *kaer;* the Scythian *car;* the ancient Saxon *caerten;* the Goth. *gards;* the Cantabr. *caria;* the Breton *ker;* the Heb. *kariah* or *kiriah* and *karth;* the Syr. *kari-tita;* and the Gr. *karak.* Compare also the Phœn., Chald., and Syr. *kartha*, the Punic *Cartha*, the Heb. *kyria*, and Pers. *car*—each of which means a walled city ; the Heb. *chader*, a city, and *kyr*, a wall.

THE ROUND TOWERS OF IRELAND.

As the Phœné while in Egypt were familiar with the motives which actuated the Egyptians in building their Pillar-Towers along the Nile (similar to those in Babylon and other Eastern nations), it is considered that, from the same motives, the Phœnician leaders who settled in Ireland in those early times, did there erect those mysterious " Round Towers," concerning the origin of which there have been so many conflicting opinions ; for, at that early period in the world's history, a colony of the Feiné, who are represented as good navigators, a race of giants, and " great builders in stone," discovered and settled in Ireland.

II.—ANCIENT IRISH PROPER NAMES.

AT this stage it may be well to give for the reader's information the follow-ing Irish proper names and adfixes :—

Aodh [ee], anglicised *Hugh*, was one of the most frequent names of Kings and Chiefs among the Irish ; the word signifies *fire*, the Vesta of the Pagan Irish, and was probably derived from the religious worship of the Druids. This name has been latinized Aedus, Aedanus, Aidus, Aidanus, Hugo, and Odo ; and is the root of *Hughes, MacHugh, Hodson, Hudson,* etc.

Aongus, or Æneas, derived from *Aon,* excellent, and *gus,* strength, is the root of *Guinness, MacGuinness, Innes, Ennis, Hennessy,* etc.

Ardgal may be derived from *ard,* exalted, and *gal,* valour ; and *Artgal,* from the proper name *Art,* and *gaol* [geel], a relative of.

Art signifies noble, great, generous, etc. ; and is the root of *O'Hart,* etc.

Blosgach implies great strength ; and is the root of the sirname *MacBlosgaidh,* anglicised *MacCloskey.*

Brandubh, from *bran,* which here means a raven, and *dubh,* black. This name was applied to a person whose hair was of a very dark colour.

Brian is derived from *bri,* strength, and *an,* very great, meaning a warrior of great strength ; or *brian* may be derived from *bran,* a mountain torrent, which implies powerful strength. *Bran,* in this meaning of the term, is the root of the sirnames *Brain, Brian, Brien, Bryan, Bryant, Byrne, Byron, O'Brien, O'Byrne,* etc.

Cairbre, from *corb,* a chariot, and *ri,* a king ; signifying the " ruler of the chariot."

Cathair [cahir], from *cath,* a battle, and *ar,* slaughter.

Cathal [cahal] signifies " a great warrior :" and is derived from *cath,* a battle, and *all,* great.

Cathbhar [cah-war] signifies a " helmeted warrior :" from *cathbhar,* a helmet ; but some derive it from *cath,* a battle, and *barr,* a chief. This was a favourite name with the chiefs of the O'Donnells of Tyrconnell ;

CHAP. II.]   ANCIENT IRISH PROPER NAMES.   33

because, it is thought, of their lineal descent from Conn of the Hundred Battles (in Irish called *Conn Ceadcatha*), the 110th Monarch of Ireland, who lived in the second century   It is, however, probable that they assumed the adfix *cath*, in commemoration of that illustrious ancestor.

Conall means friendship ; or it may be derived from *con*, the genitive of *cu*, a hound (as applied to a swift-footed warrior), and from *all*, great, or mighty.

Conchobhar signifies the "helping warrior ;" and is derived from *cu* or *con*, as above, and *cobhair* [cowir] aid. The name has been anglicised "Conn," and latinized "Cornelius" and "Conquovarus ;" and the root of the sirname *Connor, O'Conor* and *O'Connor*. Wherever *cu*, a hound, commences the name of any chief, it means, figuratively, "a swift-footed warrior ;" as, *Cuchonnacht, Cuchullan* (*Ulladh* [ulla], sometimes inflected *Ullain :* Irish "Ulster"), *Cumidhe* (*Midhe* [mee] : Irish, "Meath"), *Cu-Ulladh :* meaning, respectively, "the warrior of Connaught," "the warrior of Meath," "the warrior of Ulster," etc. It may be here observed that *Ulladh*, meaning the province of Ulster," but now represented by the counties of Down and Antrim, was so called because it was the territory into which the ancient *Ulla* were driven by the three Collas, in A.D. 333. The name *Cuchonnacht* has been anglicised "Connor" and "Constantine."

Conn (latinized "Quintus," and anglicised *Quinn*) is derived from *conn*, wisdom. It is by some derived from *cu* (genitive *con*), a hound or swift-footed warrior.

Cormac signifies "the son of the chariot," etc. ; and is derived from *corb*, a chariot, and *mac*, a son.

Diarmaid signifies the "god of arms ;" and is derived from *dia*, a god, and "*armaid*" (the genitive plural of *arm*) of arms. As an epithet, it was applied to a warrior, and was equivalent to one of Homer's heroes—*Dios Krateros Diomedes*, or "The god-like fighting Diomede." The name has been anglicised Darby, Dermod, Dermot, and Jeremy or Jeremiah ; and became a sirname, as *MacDiarmada*, anglicised *MacDermott*, in Ireland, and *MacDiarmid*, in Scotland.

Domhnall [donal] is derived from *domhan* [dowan], the world, and *all*, mighty ; and is the root of the sirnames *MacDonald, MacDonnell, Daniel, MacDaniel*, and *O'Donnell*.

Donoch, Doncha, or *Donchu* is the root of *MacDonough*, and *O'Donohue ;* and is by some considered to be derived from *donn*, brown, and *cu*, a warrior. This name is more properly derived from the *Clann Domhnaigh* (see the "MacDonough" pedigree), and is anglicised Donogh and Denis, in Ireland ; and Duncan, in Scotland.

Eachmarcach [oghmarchagh] and *Eachmilidh* [oghmili] have almost a similar signification : the former is derived from *each*, a steed, and *marcach*, a rider ; the latter, from *each*, a steed, and "*mileadh*," a hero.

Eigneachan [enehan] is derived from *eigean*, force, and *neach* [nagh], a person ; and may signify "a plundering chief."

Eochaidh is derived from *each* or *eoch* [och], a steed ; and signifies "a knight or horseman." It is pronounced "Eochy," "Ohy," and "Ahy." This name has been latinized Achaius.

Eoghan signifies "a young man," or "youthful warrior;" and as a personal name has been anglicised Eugene and Owen.

Feargal is derived from *fear* [fhar], a man (lat. *vir*), and *gal*, valour; and signifies "a valiant warrior." This Irish word is the root of the Latin proper name "Virgil," and of the surnames *O'Farrell*, *O'Ferrall*, and *Freel*; it also became a Christian name in some families, as "Farrell O'Rourke," etc.

Feidhlim or *Feidhlimidh*, signifies "great goodness." It is pronounced "Felim," and "Felimy;" is anglicised Felix, and latinized Fedlimius; it is derived from the Irish *feile*, hospitality.

Fergus signifies "a strong warrior;" and is derived from *fear*, a man, and *gus*, strength.

Fiacha or *Fiach*, is derived from *fiacha*, a hunter; and is a frequent name of Kings and Chiefs, from the earliest ages: probably from the occupation or amusement of *hunting*, so prevalent in early times.

Fionn means fair-haired, and was a favourite adfix to the names of many Kings and Chiefs.

Flaithbheartach [flahertagh] is derived from *flaith*, a chief, and *bearthach*, cunning; and means "a clever or cunning chief,"

Flann, blood, signifies "of a red complexion."

Gearrmaide signifies "the chief with the short cudgel;" and is derived from *gearr*, short, and *maide*, a stick.

Giolla means "a servant or disciple;" as *Giolla-Iosa* (anglicised Giles, and latinized Gelasius), "the servant of Jesus;" *Giolla-Chriosd*, "the servant of Christ;" *Giolla-Muire*, "the servant of Mary;" *Giolla-Paidraig*, "the servant of St. Patrick," etc. This name *Giolla* is latinized "Gulielmus," and anglicised "William."

Guaire signifies "noble or excellent."

Maol was prefixed chiefly to the names of ecclesiastics; and signifies a "bald or tonsured person," who became the spiritual servant or devotee of some saint: as *Maol-Iosa*, "the servant of Jesus;" *Maol-Peadair*, "the servant of Peter;" *Maol-Poil*, "the servant of Paul;" *Maol-Colum* (contracted to "Malcolm,") "the servant of St. Columkille." This word *Maol* is the root of the sirname *Moyles*.

Maolmordha is derived from *mordha*, proud, and *maol* (as above); it is anglicised *Myles*.

Maolseachlainn, signifying "the servant of St. Seachnal" (or Secundinus), the nephew of St. Patrick, was a name frequent amongst the Chiefs and Kings of Meath; it is contracted to *Melachlin*, which is the Irish for the Christian name Malachy or "Malachi;" and has been applied as a sirname to the latest Kings of Meath and their descendants—namely, *O'Melaghlin*. *Muircheartach* is derived from *muir*, the sea, and *ceart*, a right; and may signify "a naval warrior," or a chief who established his rights *at sea*. This name is the root of the sirname *Murtagh*, *Moriarty*, *Mortimer*, etc.

Muireadhach (the root of the sirname *Murdoch*), may be derived from *muir*, the sea, and *eadhach*, a protector; it is a name equivalent to that of "admiral," and has been anglicised *Maurice* and *Murray*.

Niall (genitive *Neill*) signifies a "noble knight" or "champion;" this name is the root of the sirname *O'Neill*, etc.

Ruadhraige or *Rudhraighe* has been anglicised Rory, Roderick, and Rogers; and may be derived from *ruadh*, valiant, or *ruadh*, red, and *righ*, a king: signifying " the valiant, or red-haired king."

Tadhg (modernized *Teige*) originally meant " a poet ;" it is the root of the sirnames *Teague, MacTague, Tighe, Montague*, etc.

Tighearnan [tiarnan] is derived from *tighearna*, a lord; and is the root of *Tierney MacTernan*, etc.

Toirdhealbhach [torlogh] is derived from *tor*, a tower, and *dealbhach*, shape or *form:* signifying " a man of tower-like stature." This name has been anglicised Terence, Terrie, Terry, etc.

Tomaltach is derived from *tomailt* provisions; and hence came to signify, " a man of hospitality." The root of the word is "*tomhas*," a measure; and from "*tomhas*," by metathesis, comes " Thomas."

Torloch (from *tor*, a tower, and *leac*, a stone) signified a man possessed of " great strength and stature."

Tuathal [tool] comes from *tuatha*, territories—meaning one possessed of "large landed property;" it is the root of the sirnames *Toole, O'Toole, Tootal, Tolan*, etc.

Ualgarg meant " a famous and fierce warrior ;" it is derived from *uaill*, famous, and *garg*, fierce.

(*a*.) CHRISTIAN NAMES OF MEN.

The following are a few of the ancient Irish *Christian* names of Men, which have been anglicised :

The Name in Irish.	Anglicised.
Berach,	Barry.
Brian,	Bernard, Barney, Barnaby.
Conn,	Constantine, Corney, Cornelius.
Cosnava,	Constantine,
Cuconnacht,	Constantine, Connor.
Cumaighe,	Quintin.
Dathi,	David.
Dubhalethe,	Dudley.
Dubhaltach,	Dudley.
Dubhdara,	Dudley.
Ferdorach,	Frederic, Frederick, Ferdinand.
Giolla-Padraic,	Patrick.
Heremon,	Irwin (now nearly obsolete).
Lughaidh,	Lewy, Lewis.
Melaghlin,	Malachy, Malachi.
Ruadhri,	Rory, Roderick, Roger.
Tomoltach,	Timothy, Thomas.

(*b*.) NAMES OF WOMEN.

A few ancient Irish names of Women are here given ; but, for fuller information on the subject, the reader is referred to *Ban-Seanchus* (meaning "History of Remarkable Women"); which forms a curious tract in the Book of Leacan, fol. 193—

Name in Irish.	Anglicised.
Aine,	Hannah.
Brighid,	Bridget.
Finola or Finnghuala, meaning " of the fair shoulders."	Nuala, and Penelopé.
Graine,	Grace.
Lasairfhina,	Lassarina.
Meadhbh [meave],	Maud, Mab, Mabby.
Mor [more], majestic,	Martha, Mary.
Sadhbh [soyv],	Sabina, Sally.
Sorcha,	Sarah, Sally, Lucy, Lucinda.
Una,	Winnifred, Winny.
Sheela,	Celia, Sibby.

To these may be added :—

Dearforgail or *Dearvorgal*,* which signifies " a purely fair daughter ;" and is derived from *dear*, a daughter, and *forgil*, purely fair.

Dubhdeasa or *Dudeasa*, signifies " a dark-haired beauty ;" and is derived from *dubh* [duff], dark, and *deas*, beautiful. This word is the root of the sirnames *Dease* and *Deasy*.

Flanna signified " a rosy-complexioned beauty."

III.—IRISH ADFIXES.

THE following are some of the leading prefixes and affixes employed in the formation of Irish proper names :—

Beag or *Beg*, small.

Cineal or *cinel*, signifies " kindred, race, and descendants ;" as *Cineal Eoghain*, " the descendants of Owen ;" *Cineal Connaill*," the descendants of Connell," etc.

Clann (or *Clon*) means " children, descendants, race ;" as *Clan-na-Mile* [meel], "the descendants of Milesius;" *Clan-na-Gael*, " the descendants of Gaodhal," etc.

Fear [fhear], a man, *fhear*, the man, *fir*, *feara*, men, as *feargaol*, a relative ; *fir tire*, " the men of the country": from which word " Vartry," a river in the county Wicklow, is derived.

Lis, a fort; as, *Listowell*, " the fort of *Tuathal* :" *Lisburn*, *Lisdoonvarna*, etc.

Mac, the son or descendant of; as *Cormac MacAirt*, "Cormac the son of Art ; *MacDonnell*, "the descendants of Donall," etc.

Muintir, the people of. By this word, " Muintir," people, and " Cin," kindred, all families in Ireland were known before the introduction of

---

* *Dearvorgal*: See No. 112 on the " O'Rourke" pedigree, for Dearvorgal, the wife of Tiernan O'Ruarc, Prince of West Brefni; to whom, in "The Song of O'Ruarc," Thomas Moore alludes in his *Irish Melodies*.

sirnames; as *Cin Airt* or *Muintir Airt,* "the people or kindred of Art," the 112th Monarch of Ireland; *Muintir Eoghain,* "the people of Owen," etc.

Ne, progeny; as *Carrow-ne-kin-Airt,* the Irish name for "Kinnaird"— a townland in the parish of Crossmolina, barony of Tyrawley, and county of Mayo : which means the (*carrow* or) quarter of land where settled some of the (*ne* or) progeny of the (*kin* or) offspring of the Monarch *Art,* who was called Art-Ean-Fhear, or, as it is contracted, "Art-Enear," the 112th Monarch, as above. And the name "*Tiernaar,*" (or Tir-Enear), a barony in the west of Mayo, is, no doubt, similarly derived.

O',Ui, Hy, descendants of ; as *O'Brien, Ua-Hairt* (or "O'h-Airt"), now *O'Hart ; Ui-Laeghaire,* now *O'Leary ; Hy-Niall,* "the descendants of Niall," etc. It may be observed that *Hy* is the plural of *Ua* or *O,* and is more correctly written *Ui.* The plural form denotes, therefore, the *Clan,* or the whole body of the descendants.

Og [oge], young; as Conchobhar (or Connor) og, meaning *young* Connor.

Rath, a fort stronghold; as *Rathmore,* etc.

Ruadh [rooa], red; this word is the root of the sirnames *Roe* and *Rowe.*

Tir or *Tyre,* a district, or territory ; as *Tyrawley,* a barony in the county Mayo, which means "Awly's district ;" *Tirowen* [tyrone], "Owen's district ;" *Tyrconnell,* "Connall's district"—now the county Donegal.

Tullagh, a hill or green; as *Tullaghoge,* "the hill of the youths," now called "Tullyhawk," and situate in the parish of Desertcreaght, and barony of Dungannon. Tullaghoge was a green eminence in Tirowen, in the immediate territory of the O'Hagan's, who were the lawgivers of O'NEILL, and were known as "Cineal-Owen of Tullaghoge :" where since the destruction of the palace of Aileach, A.D. 1101, the stone chair upon which The O'Neill was proclaimed, was preserved up to the year 1602, when it was demolished by Lord Mountjoy, then lord deputy of Ireland. "In the year 1602," writes Fynes Moryson, "the Lord Deputy Mountjoy remained here (at Tulloghoge) for five days, and brake down the chair wherein the O'Neills were wont to be created, being of stone planted in the open field."—*See* FYNES MORYSON'S *Rebellion of Hugh Earl of Tyrone, Book iii., c.* I.

IV.—THE LINEAL DESCENT OF THE ROYAL FAMILY OF ENGLAND.

FORMAN, who wrote in the eighteenth century, says :

"The greatest antiquity which the august House of Hanover itself can boast, is deduced from the Royal Stem of Ireland."

The following Table carefully exhibits the "Royal Stem of Ireland," from which the present Royal Family of England derives its *lineal descent* :

136. VICTORIA ALEXANDRINA, Queen of Great Britain and Ireland, living in 1887 : Daughter of

135. Edward, Duke of Kent: son of

134. George the Third : son of

133. Frederick Louis, Prince of Wales : son of

132. George the Second : son of

131. George the First: son of

130. Princess Sophia ; married to Ernest Augustus, Duke of Brunswick and first "Elector of Hanover," A.D. 1658 ; died at Hanover on the 8th June, 1714 : daughter of

129. Elizabeth, Queen of Bohemia : daughter of

128. James the First of England and Sixth of Scotland : son of

127. Mary, Queen of Scots : daughter of

126. James the Fifth of Scotland : son of

125. Margaret : daughter of

124. Elizabeth of York : daughter of

123. Edward the Fourth : son of

122. Richard Plantagenet : son of

121. Lady Anne Mortimer : daughter of

120. Roger Mortimer : son of

119. Lady Philippa ; married to Edward Mortimer, Earl of March, from which marriage descended the House of York, or "The White Rose ;" born, 16th August, 1335 : only child of

118. Lionel, Duke of Clarence : son of

117. Edward the Third : son of

116. Edward the Second: son of

115. Edward the First* : son of

114. Henry the Third : son of

113. John : son of

112. Henry the Second : son of

111. The Princess Maude : daughter of

110. Queen Matilda (in whom the *lineal descent* continues: who was the wife of Henry the First of England, the youngest son of William the Conqueror) : only daughter of Malcolm III. (d. 1093).

109. Malcolm the Third, of Scotland : son of Duncan (d. 1041).

108. Duncan : son of Beatrix.

Malcolm the Second left no issue but two daughters, named Beatrix (or Beatrice) and Doda.   Beatrice, the elder daughter, got married to Crinan,†

---

* *Edward the First* : King Edward the First was twice married : first to Eleanor, sister of Alphonso XI., king of Castile, in Spain ; and secondly to Margaret, daughter of Philip III., king of France.   Of this second marriage were born Thomas Plantagenet at Brotherton (a small village in Yorkshire), A.D. 1300, who, in consequence, was called *De Brotherton* ; who was created Earl of Norfolk, and made " Marshal of England."   This Thomas Plantagenet left two daughters, from one of whom came— 1. The Mowbrays and Howards,[1] Dukes of Norfolk.   2. The Earls of Suffolk.   3. The Earls of Carlisle.   4. The Earls of Effingham.   5. The Lords Stanford.   6. The Lords Berkely.   7. The Marquises of Salisbury.

From the other daughter of Thomas Plantagenet the *Ord* family is descended. See the " Ord" pedigree.

Edmund, the second son of King Edward the First, by the second marriage, was created Earl of Kent.

† *Crinan*: According to some authorities Beatrix was twice married : first, to

[1] *Howards :* For the ancestors of the " Howard" family, see No. 104, on the " MacDowall" pedigree.

lord of the Isles, and by him had a son named Duncan, the father of Malcolm the Third; while Doda, the younger daughter, got married to Synel, lord of Glammis, and by him had a son named MacBeatha or MacBeth (d. 1057). Before the accession to the throne of Scotland, of Malcolm the Third or Malcolm Ceann Mor (*cean mor :* Irish, large head), as he was called, on account of the *large* size of his *head*, the lineal descent continued in the following:

108. Duncan, who d. 1041 : son of
107. Beatrix (or Beatrice): daughter of
106. Malcolm the Second, who d. 1040: son of
105. Cenneth, who d. 994 : son of
104. Malcolm the First, who d. 958: son of
103. Donald, who d. 903 : son of
102. Constantine, who d. 878: son of
101. Cenneth (known as " Kinneth MacAlpin"), who d. 854 : son of
100. Alpin, who d. 834: son of
99. Eochaidh (or Eochy) Rinnamail : son of
98. Aodh (or Hugh) Fionn : son of
97. Donart : son of
96. Donald Breac : son of
95. Eochaidh Buidhe* (*buidhe* : Irish, yellow) : son of
94. Ædhan : son of
93. Gabhran.

The Scotch historians differ in some particulars from the ancient Irish annalists : for instance, they record this Gabhran (No. 93) as the *son* instead of the grandson, of Donart, No. 91.

93. Gabhran : son of
92. Eochaidh : son of
91. Donart : son of
90. Fergus Mor Mac Earca.

"In A.D. 498, Fergus Mor Mac Earca, in the twentieth year of the reign of his father, Muredach, son of (Eugenius, or) Owen, son of Niall of the Nine Hostages, with five more of his brothers, viz., another Fergus, two more named Loarn, and two named Aongus (or Æneas), with a complete army, went into Scotland to assist his grandfather Loarn, who was king of Dalriada, and who was much oppressed by his enemies the Picts, who were in several battles and engagements vanquished and overcome by Fergus and his party. Whereupon, on the king's death, which happened about the same time, the said Fergus was unanimously elected and chosen king, as being of the Blood Royal, by his mother ; and the said Fergus was the first absolute king of Scotland, of the Milesian Race : so the succession continued in his blood and lineage ever since to this day."—*Four Masters.*

According to the Scottish chroniclers, it was A.D. 424, that Fergus Mor Mac Earca went from Ireland to Scotland. Before him, the Milesian kings in that country were kings only of that part of it called "Dalriada," of which Loarn, the grandfather of Fergus Mor Mac Earca (*Mac Earca :* Irish, son of Earca, daughter of Loarn) was the last king (see Part IX., c. iv. under "The Genealogy of the Kings of Dalriada").

Crinan who was Lay Abbot of Dunkeld, and the son of Duncan, who was Abbot of Dunkeld ; and, secondly, to the Lord of the Isles. By Crinan, Beatrix had Maldred, Cospatrick, and Duncan I. (d. 1041), King of Scotland, who is No. 108 on the foregoing Lineal Descent.

* *Buidhe* : From this Eochaidh Buidhe the *Boyd* family derives its sirname.

90. Fergus Mor Mac Earca, the brother of Murchertach (or Murtogh Mor Mac Earca, the 131st Monarch of Ireland :* son of

89. Muredach: son of

88. Eoghan [Owen]: son of

87. Niall Mor (known as Niall of the Nine Hostages), the 126th Monarch: son of

86. Eochaidh Muigh Meadhoin (or Eochy Moyvone), the 124th Monarch : son of

85. Muredach Tireach [teeragh], 122nd Monarch : son of

84. Fiacha Srabhteine, the 120th Monarch : son of

83. Cairbre Liffechar, the 117th Monarch : son of

82. Cormac Ulfhada (commonly called "Cormac Mac Art"), the 115th Monarch : son of

81. Art-Ean-Fhear (or Art-Enear), the 112th Monarch : the ancestor* of O'h-Airt, anglicised O'Hart : son of

80. Conn Ceadcatha (or Conn of the Hundred Battles), the 110th Monarch : son of

79. Felim Rachtmar (or Felim the Lawgiver),'the 108th Monarch : son of

78. Tuathal Teachdmar, the 106th Monarch : son of

77. Fiacha Fionn Ola (or Fiacha of the White Oxen), the 124th Monarch : son of

76. Feareadach [Feredach] Fionn Feachtnach (or Feredach the True and Sincere), the 102nd Monarch : son of

75. Crimthann Niadh-Nar (called Crimthann the Heroic), the 100th Monarch, who reigned when CHRIST was born : son of

74. Lugaidh Sriabh-n Dearg, the 98th Monarch : son of

73. Breas-Nar-Lothar : son of

72, Eochaidh Feidhlioch, the 93rd Monarch : son of

71. Fionn : son of

70. Fionnlaoch : son of

69. Roighean Ruadh : son of

68. Asaman Eamhnadh : son of

67. Enda Agneach, the 84th Monarch : son of

66. Aongus (or Æneas) Turmeach-Teamrach, the 81st Monarch (from whose younger son, Fiacha Fearmara, the kings of Dalriada, in Scotland, down to Loarn, the maternal grandfather of Fergus Mor Mac Earca, No. 90 on this stem, were descended): son of

65. Eochaidh Altleathan, the 79th Monarch : son of

64. Olioll Casfiacalach, the 77th Monarch : son of

63. Conla Caomh, the 76th Monarch : son of

62. Iarn Gleo-Fhathach, the 74th Monarch : son of

61. Melg Molbhthach, the 71st Monarch : son of

---

* *Monarch of Ireland:* For the period during which each of the Irish Monarchs mentioned in this Table, reigned, see the " Roll of the Monarchs of Ireland since the Milesian Conquest."

* *Ancestor* : See the pedigree of " O'Hart ;" carefully traced from this Monarch, who reigned in the second century of our era, down to the present time (A.D. 1887). It is a curious fact that no other name than No. 81 on the foregoing Table is the origin of any other Irish sirname on record !

60. Cobthach Caol-bhreagh, the 69th Monarch : son of
59. Ugaine Mor, the 66th Monarch : son of
58. Eochaidh Buidh : son of
57. Duach Ladhrach, the 59th Monarch : son of
56. Fiachadh Tolgrach, the 55th Monarch : son of
55. Muirerdhach [Muredach] Bolgach, the 46th Monarch : son of
54. Simeon Breac, the 44th Monarch : son of
53. Aodh Glas : son of
52. Nuadhas Fionnfail, the 39th Monarch : son of
51. Giallchadh, the 37th Monarch : son of
50. Olioll Olchaoin : son of
49. Siorna Saoghalach, the 34th Monarch : his son ; lived 250 years,
and reigned 150 years.
48. Dein : son of
47. Rotheachta, the 22nd Monarch : son of
46. Maon : son of
45. Aongus Ollmuchach, the 20th Monarch : son of
44. Fiachadh Lamhraein, the 18th Monarch : son of
43. Simorgoill : son of
42. Eanbrotha , son of
41. Tighearnmas, the 13th Monarch : son of
40. Falach (or Fallain) : son of
39. Eithriall, the 11th Monarch : son of
38. Irial Faidh, the 10th Monarch : son of
37. Heremon, the second Monarch of Ireland, of the *Milesian* line ;
son of Galamh [galav], otherwise called Milesius of Spain.
36. MILESIUS of Spain : son of
35. Bile : son of
34. Breoghan (or Brigus) ; a quo the "Brigantes;" son of

33. Brath : son of
32. Deagh : son of
31. Arcadh : son of
30. Alladh : son of
29. Nuadhad : son of
28. Nenuall : son of
27. Febric Glas : son of
26. Agnan Fionn : son of
25. Heber Glunfionn : son of

24. Lamhfionn : son of
23. Agnan : son of
22. Tait : son of
21. Oghaman : son of
20. Beouman : son of
19. Heber Scutt [Scott] : son of
18. Sruth : son of
17. Asruth : son of

16. Gaodhal, a quo the *Clann-na-Gaodhail* or the GAELS : son of

15. Niul : son of
14. Phœniusa (or Fenius) Farsaidh, the inventor of *Letters :* son of
13. Baoth (*baoth :* Irish, simple;
Heb. *baath*, to terrify) : son of
12. Magog : son of
11. Japhet : son of
10. Noah : son of
9. Lamech : son of

8. Methuselah : son of
7. Enoch : son of
6. Jared : son of
5. Mahalaleel : son of
4. Cainan : son of
3. Enos : son of
2. Seth : son of
1. ADAM, who (Genesis i.) was
the first Man.

V.—THE LINEAL DESCENT OF KING PHILIP V., OF SPAIN.

IN O'Clery's Irish Genealogies is the following pedigree ; the names being spelled as by O'Clery; and the descent being from father to son—from Adam down to King Philip V. :

1. ADAM.
2. Seth : his son.
3. Henos : his son.
4. Cainan : his son.
5. Malaleel : his son.
6. Iared : his son.
7. Henoch : his son.
8. Mathusalam : his son.
9. Lamech : his son.
10. Noe : his son.
11. Iapeth : his son.
12. Iauan : his son.
13. Dodanin : his son.
14. Hercules : his son.
15. Thusco : his son.
16. Altheo : his son.
17. Blascon : his son.
18. Cambo Blascon : his son.
19. Dardano : his son.
20. Ericthonio : his son.
21. Troe : his son.
22. Illo : his son.
23. Loomedonte : his son.
24. Priamo : his son.
25. Heleno : his son.
26. Genger : his son.
27. Franco : his son.
28. Esdron : his son.
29. Gelio : his son.
30. Basabiliano : his son.
31. Plaserio : his son.
32. Plesron : his son.
33. Eliacor : his son.
34. Gaberiano : his son.
35. Plaserio : his son.
36. Antenor : his son.
37. Priamo : his son.
38. Heleno : his son.
39. Plesron : his son.
40. Basabiliano : his son.
41. Alexandre : his son.
42. Priamo : his son.
43. Getmalor : his son.

44. Almadion : his son.
45. Diluglio : his son.
46. Heleno : his son.
47. Plaserio : his son.
48. Diluglio : his son.
49. Marcomiro : his son.
50. Priamo : his son.
51. Heleno : his son.
52. Antenor : his son.
53. Marcomiro : his son.
54. Antenor : his son.
55. Priamo : his son.
56. Heleno : his son.
57. Dioclés : his son.
58. Basano : his son.
59. Clodomiro : his son.
60. Nicanor : his son.
61. Marcomiro : his son.
62. Clodio : his son.
63. Antenor : his son.
64. Clodomiro : his son.
65. Merocado : his son.
66. Casandre : his son.
67. Antario : his son.
68. Franco : his son.
69. Clogion : his son.
70. Marcomiro : his son.
71. Clodomiro : his son.
72. Antenor : his son.
73. Paterio : his son.
74. Richimero : his son.
75. Odemara : his son.
76. Marcomiro : his son.
77. Clodomiro : his son.
78. Faraberto : his son.
79. Sunon : his son.
80. Hilderico : his son.
81. Baltero : his son.
82. Clodio : his son.
83. Valter : his son.
84. Dagoverto : his son.
85. Clogion : his son.
86. Genebaldo : his son.

87. Dagoverto : his son.
88. Clodion : his son.
89. Marcomiro : his son.
90. Faramundo : his son.
91. Clodion : his son,
92. Merobeo : his son.
93. Childerico : his son.
94. Clodoreo : his son.
95. Clotario (or Olotario): his son.
96. Sigisberto : his son.
97. Thoeberto : his son.
98. Bebo : his son.
99. Roperto : his son.
100. Amprinto : his son.
101. Gontramo : his son.
102. Luthardo : his son.
103. Betgon : his son.
104. Rapoto : his son.

105. Berengario : his son.
106. Othon : his son.
107. Vernero : his son.
108. Alberto Elrico : his son.
109. Alberto, 2 : his son.
110. Rodulpho : his son.
111. Alberto, 3 : his son.
112. Alberto Elsabio : his son.
113. Leopoldo : his son.
114. Ernosto : his son.
115. Federico : his son.
116. Maximiliano : his son.
117. Don Philipe, 1 : his son.
118. D. Charolus : his son.
119. D. Philipe, 2 : his son.
120. D. Philipe, 3 : his son.
121. D. Philipe, 4 : his son.
122. D. Philipe, 5 : his son.

VI.—THE PEDIGREE OF SAINT PATRICK APOSTLE OF IRELAND.

In MacFirbis's Genealogies the pedigree of St. Patrick, the Apostle of Ireland, is given, as follows :

1. Patrick or Padraic, Apostle of Ireland : son of
2. Calpinn (or Alpin) : son of
3. Potit : son of
4. Odais : son of
5. Connudh : son of
6. Leobut : son of
7. Merc : son of
8. Oda : son of
9. Orc : son of
10. Muric : son of
11. Orc : son of
12. Leo : son of
13. Maxime : son of
14. Othrag : son of
15. Enciede (or Ere) ; son of
16. Erise : son of
17. Piliste : son of
18. Pherine (or Farine) : son of
19. Briottan Maol (a quo *Britain*) : son of
20. Fearghus Lethderg : son of
21. Nemhidh, a quo the *Nemidians;* descended from Magog, son of Japhet.

VII.—THE PEDIGREE OF ST. BRIGID, VIRGIN,
The Patron Saint of Ireland (1 Feb. 523).

1. St. Brigid, Virgin : daughter of
2. Dubhtach :, son of
3. Demri : son of
4. Bresal : son of
5. Den : son of
6. Conla : son of
7. Art Corb : son of
8. Cairbre Niadh : son of
9. Cormac : son of
10. Aongus Meann : son of
11. Eochaidh Finn Fothart, who was brother of Conn of the Hundred Fights, the 110th Monarch of Ireland. (See No. 80 on the " O'Hart" pedigree.")

PART II.

I.—THE STEM OF THE IRISH NATION, FROM ADAM DOWN TO MILESIUS OF SPAIN.

"GOD THE FATHER, SON, AND HOLY GHOST, who was from all eternity, did, in the beginning of Time, of nothing, create Red Earth; and of Red Earth framed ADAM; and of a Rib out of the side of Adam fashioned Eve. After which Creation, Plasmation, and Formation, succeeded Generations, as follows."—*Four Masters.*

1. ADAM.
2. Seth.
3. Enos.
4. Cainan.
5. Mahalaleel.
6. Jared.
7. Enoch.
8. Methuselah.
9. Lamech.

10. Noah* divided the world amongst his three sons, begotten of his wife Titea: viz., to Shem he gave Asia, within the Euphrates, to the Indian Ocean; to Ham he gave Syria, Arabia, and Africa; and to Japhet, the rest of Asia beyond the Euphrates, together with Europe to Gades (or Cadiz).

11. Japhet was the eldest son of Noah. He had fifteen sons, amongst whom he divided Europe and the part of Asia which his father had allotted to him.

12. Magog: From whom descended the Parthians, Bactrians, Amazons, etc.; Partholan, the first *planter* of Ireland,† about three hundred years

---

* *Noah*: This allusion to his wife "Titea" would imply that Noah had other children besides, Shem, Ham, and Japhet. The Four Masters say that he had a son named Bith.—See Note, "The Deluge," page 7.

·† *Ireland*: According to the Four Masters, "Ireland" is so called from *Ir*, the second son of Milesius of Spain who left any issue. It was known to the ancients by the following names:—

To the Irish as—1. *Inis Ealga,* or the Noble Isle. 2. *Fiodh-Inis,* or the Woody Island. 3. *Crioch Fuinidh,* the Final or most remote Country. 4. *Inis-Fail,* or the Island of Destiny. 5. *Fodhla,* learned. 6. *Banba* (from the Irish *banabh,* a sucking pig.) 7. *Eire, Eri, Eirin,* and *Erin,* supposed by some to signify the Western Isle. 8. *Muig Inis,* meaning the Island of Mist or Melancholy.

To the Greeks and Romans as—9. Ierne, Ierna, Iernis, Iris, and Irin. 10. Ivernia, Ibernia, Hibernia, Juvernia, Jouvernia, Hiberia, Hiberione, and Verna. 11. Insula Sacra. 12. *Ogy-gia,* or the Most Ancient Land. (Plutarch, in the first century of the Christian era, calls Ireland by the name *Ogy-gia;* and Camden says that Ireland is justly called *Ogy-gia,* as the Irish, he says, can trace their history from the most remote after the Flood ; and also the rest of the colonies* that planted there, viz., the Nemedians, who planted Ireland, Anno Mundi three thousand and forty-six, or three hundred and eighteen years after the birth of Abraham, and two thousand one hundred and fifty-three years before Christ. The Nemedians continued in Ireland for two hundred and seventeen years ; within which time a colony of theirs went into the northern parts of Scotland,

antiquity : Hence O'Flaherty has adopted the name "Ogy-gia" for his celebrated work, in Latin, on Irish history and antiquities.) 13. Scotia. 14. Insula Sanctorum.
To the Anglo-Saxon as—15. Eire-land.
To the Danes as—16. Irlandi, and Irar.
To the Anglo-Normans as—17. Irelande.

* *Colonies* : According to some of the ancient Irish Chroniclers, the following were the nations that colonized Ireland :—

1. Partholan and his followers, called in Irish *Muintir Phartholain*, meaning "Partholan's People." 2. The Nemedians. 3. The Fomorians. 4. The Firbolgs or Firvolgians, who were also called Belgæ or Belgians. 5. The Tuatha-de-Danans. 6. The Milesians or Gaels. 7. The Cruthneans or Picts. 8. The Danes and Norwegians (or Scandinavians). 9. The Anglo-Normans. 10. The Anglo-Saxons (or English). 11. The Scots from North Britain.

1. *Partholan* and his followers came from Scythia, and were located chiefly in Ulster at *Inis-Saimer*, in Donegal, and in Leinster at *Ben Edair* (now the Hill of Howth), in the county Dublin. After they had been in Ireland some thirty years, nearly the whole people perished by a plague ; thousands of them were buried in a common tomb, in Tallaght, a place near Dublin : the name "Tallaght" meaning *Tam-Laght* or the Plague Sepulchre.

2. *The Nemedians* came from Scythia in Europe, and were located chiefly in Ulster at Ardmacha (or Armagh), and in Derry and Donegal ; and in Leinster at the Hill of Uisneach, which is situated a few miles from Mullingar, in the county Westmeath.

3. *Fomorians* : According to the Annals of Clonmacnoise, the Fomorians (*fogh* : Irish, plundering ; *muir*, the sea) were a "sept descended from Cham, son of Noah, who lived by pyracie and spoile of other nations, and were in those days very troublesome to the whole world ;" and, according to O'Donovan's "Four Masters," the name "Fomorians" was that given by the ancient Irish to the inhabitants of Finland, Denmark, and Norway ; but, according to Connellan, those people are considered to have come from the north of Africa, from a place called Lybia or Getulia, and to have been some of the Feiné or Phœnicians, whose descendants afterwards there founded the city of Carthage ; and in Spain the cities of Gahdir or Gades (now Cadiz), and Kartabah (now Cordova). As Sidon in Phœnicia was a maritime city in the time of Joshua, and its people expert navigators ; and as the Phœnicians, Sidonians, and Tyrians, in those early ages, were celebrated for their commercial intercourse with Greece, Italy, Gaul, Spain, and Britain, there is nothing whatever improbable in a colony of them having sailed from Africa to Ireland : whose coming from *Africa* may have led to the belief that they were "descended from Cham (Ham) ; as their commercial intercourse with other nations may have led to their being considered "pirates." Possibly, then, the Fomorians here mentioned were the Erithneans, who were Phœnicians, and a colony of whom settled in Ireland at a very early period in the world's history. The Fomorians are represented as a race of giants, and were celebrated as having been great builders in stone. They were located principally along the coasts of Ulster and Connaught, mostly in Antrim, Derry, Donegal, Leitrim, Sligo, and Mayo, and had their chief fortress (called *Tor Conaing* or Conang's Tower) on *Tor Inis* or the Island of the Tower, now known as "Tory Island," which is off the coast of Donegal ; and another at the Giants' Causeway, which in Irish was called *Cloghan-na-Fomoraigh* or the Causeway of the Fomorians, as it was supposed to have been constructed by this people, who, from their great strength and stature, were, as above mentioned, called *giants :* hence the term "Giants' Causeway"—a stupendous natural curiosity of volcanic origin, situated on the sea-coast of Antrim, and consisting of a countless number of basaltic columns of immense height, which, from the regularity of their formation and arrange-

under the conduct of their leader Briottan Maol,* from whom *Britain* takes its name, and not from " Brutus," as some persons believed. From Magog were also descended the Belgarian, Belgian, Firbolgian or Firvolgian colony that succeeded the Nemedians, Anno Mundi, three thousand two hundred and sixty-six, and who first erected Ireland into a Monarchy.† [According to some writers, the Fomorians invaded Ireland next after the Nemedians.] This Belgarian or Firvolgian colony continued in Ireland for thirty-six years, under nine of their Kings ; when they were supplanted by the Tuatha-de-Danans (which means, according to some authorities, "the people of the god Dan," whom they adored), who possessed Ireland for one hundred and ninety-seven years, during the reigns of nine of their kings ; and who were then conquered by the Gaelic, Milesian, or Scotic Nation (the three names by which the Irish people were known), Anno Mundi three thousand five hundred. This Milesian or Scotic Irish Nation possessed and enjoyed the Kingdom of Ireland for two thousand eight

ment, have the appearance of a vast work of art ; and hence were supposed to have been constructed by giants.

After the Fomorians became masters of the country, the Nemedians (*neimhedh :* Irish, dirt, filth of any kind), were reduced to slavery, and compelled to pay a great annual tribute on the first day of winter—consisting of corn, cattle, milk, and other provisions ; and the place where these tributes were received was named *Magh Ceitne,* signifying the Plain of Compulsion, and so called from these circumstances. This plain was situated between the rivers Erne and Drabhois (*drabhas :* Irish, dirt, nastiness), between Ballyshannon and Bundrowes, on the borders of Donegal, Leitrim, and Fermanagh, along the sea-shore.—See Connellan's " Four Masters."

Three bands of the Nemedians emigrated with their respective captains : one party wandered into the north of Europe ; others made their way to Greece, where they were enslaved, and obtained the name of " Firbolgs" or *bagmen,* from the leathern bags which they were compelled to carry ; and the third section took refuge in England, which obtained its name *Britain*, from their leader " Briottan Maol."—*See* Miss Cusack's *" History of Ireland."*

4. The *Firbolgs* or *Firvolgians,* who were also Scythians, divided Ireland amongst the five sons of their leader Dela Mac Loich : " Slainge [slane] was he by whom Teamor (or Tara) was first raised." (Four Masters). One hundred and fifty Monarchs reigned in Tara from that period until its abandonment in the reign of Diarmod, son of Fergus Cearrbheoil, who was the 133rd Monarch of Ireland, and King of Meath. The Firvolgians ruled over Connaught down to the third century, when King Cormac Mac Art, the 115th Monarch of Ireland, attacked and defeated the forces of Aodh or Hugh, son of Garadh, King of Connaught, who was the last King of the Firbolg race in Ireland ; and the sovereignty of Connaught was then transferred to the Milesians of the race of Heremon—descendants of King Cormac Mac Art. The Firbolg race never after acquired any authority in Ireland, being reduced to the ranks of farmers and peasants ; but they were stil very numerous, and to this day a great many of the peasantry, particularly in Connaught, are considered to be of Firbolg origin.

5. The *Tuatha de Danans,* also of the Scythian family, invaded Ireland thirty-six years after the plantation by the Firbolgs. According to some annalists, they came originally from Persia, and to others, from Greece ; and were located chiefly at Tara in Meath, at Croaghan in Connaught, and at Aileach in Donegal. The Danans being highly skilled in the arts, the Round Towers of Ireland are supposed to have been built by them. The light, gay, joyous element of the Irish character may be traced to them. They were a brave and high-spirited race, and famous for their skill in what was then termed *Magic :* hence, in after ages, this wonderful people were considered

* *Briottan Maol :* See No. 19 on " The Pedigree of St. Patrick, Apostle of Ireland," Part I., c. vi., p. 43.

† *Monarchy :* Mac Firbis shows that Ireland was a Monarchy, before and after Christ, for a period of 4,149 (four thousand, one hundred and forty-nine) years !

hundred and eighty-five years, under one hundred and eighty-three Monarchs; until their submission to King Henry the Second of England, Anno Domini one thousand one hundred and eighty-six.*

13. Baoth, one of the sons of Magog; to whom Scythia came as his lot, upon the division of the Earth by Noah amongst his sons, and by Japhet of his part thereof amongst his sons.

14. Phœniusa Farsaidh (or Fenius Farsa) was King of Scythia, at the time that Ninus ruled the Assyrian Empire; and, being a wise man and desirous to learn the languages that not long before confounded the builders of the Tower of Babel, employed able and learned men to go among the dispersed multitude to learn their several languages; who sometime after returning well skilled in what they went for, Phœniusa Farsaidh erected a school in the valley of Senaar, near the city of

to have continued to live in hills or raths, as the "good people" long so commonly believed in as *fairies*, in Ireland. But their "magic" consisted in the exercise of the mechanical arts, of which those who had previously invaded Ireland were then ignorant. It is a remarkable fact, that weapons of warfare found in the carns or gravemounds of the Firbolgs are of an inferior kind to those found in the carns of the Tuatha-de-Danans: a proof of the superior intelligence of the latter over the former people. The inventor of the *Ogham* [owam] Alphabet (*ogham*: Irish, "an occult manner of writing used by the ancient Irish") was Ogma, father of one of the Tuatha-de-Danan Kings. In McCartin's Irish Grammar it is stated that there were no less than thirty-five different modes of writing the Ogham, which has hitherto defied the power of modern science to unravel its mysteries. But the truth of our ancient history is strangely confirmed by the fact that the letters of this Alphabet are all denominated by the names of trees and shrubs indigenous to Ireland! According to the "Book of Leinster," it was "Cet Cuimnig, King of Munster, of the royal line of Heber, that was the first that inscribed Ozam [or Ogham] memorials in Erinn." This extract gives a clue to the period when *Ogham* stones were first erected, and why the most of them are to be found in the Province of Munster; for, according to the *Septuagint* system of chronology, that King of Munster reigned about the year 1257 before the birth of Christ!

6. The *Milesians* invaded Ireland one hundred and ninety-seven years later than the Tuatha de Danans; and were called *Clan-na-Mile* [meel], signifying the descendants of Milesius of Spain.

7. The *Cruthneans* or *Picts* were also Scythians, and, according to our ancient historians, came from Thrace soon after the arrival of the Milesians; but, not being permitted by the Milesians to remain in Ireland, they sailed to Scotland and became the possessors of that country, but tributary to the Monarchs of Ireland. In after ages colonies of them came over and settled in Ulster; they were located chiefly in the territories which now form the counties of Down, Antrim, and Derry.

8. The *Danes* and *Norwegians* (or *Scandinavians*), a Teutonic race of Scythian origin, came to Ireland in great numbers, in the ninth and tenth centuries, and were located chiefly in Leinster and Munster, in many places along the sea-coast: their strongholds being the towns of Dublin, Wexford, Waterford, Cork, and Limerick.

9. The *Anglo-Normans* came to Ireland in the twelfth century, and possessed themselves of a great part of the country, under their chief leader, Richard de Clare, who was also named Strongbow. They were a Teutonic race, descended from the Normans of France, who were a mixture of Norwegians, Danes, and French, and who conquered England in the eleventh century. The English invasion of Ireland was accomplished ostensibly through the agency of Dermod MacMorough, King of Leinster; on account of his having been driven from his country by the Irish Monarch for the abduction of the wife of Tiernan O'Ruarc, Prince of Breffni. For that act, Roderick O'Connor, the

* *A.D.* 1186: It was, no doubt, in that year, that, weary of the world and its troubles, Roderick O'Connor, the 183rd Monarch of Ireland, retired to a Monastery, where he died, A.D. 1198. But, see No. 184 on the "Roll of the Monarchs of Ireland since the Milesian Conquest," and the Note "Brian O'Neill," in connection with that Number.

Æothena, in the forty-second year of the reign of Ninus; whereupon, having continued there with his younger son Niul for twenty years, he returned home to his kingdom, which, at his death, he left to his eldest son Nenuall : leaving to Niul no other patrimony than his learning and the benefit of the said school.

15. Niul, after his father returned to Scythia, continued some time at Æothena, teaching the languages and other laudable sciences, until upon report of his great learning he was invited into Egypt by Pharaoh, the King; who gave him the land of Campus Cyrunt, near the Red Sea to inhabit, and his daughter Scota in marriage : from whom their posterity are ever since called *Scots*; but, according to some annalists, the name "Scots" is derived from the word *Scythia*.

It was this Niul that employed Gaodhal [Gael], son of Ethor, a learned and skilful man, to compose or rather refine and adorn the language, called *Bearla Tobbai*, which was common to all Niul's posterity, and afterwards called *Gaodhilg* (or Gaelic), from the said Gaodhal who composed or refined it ; and for his sake also Niul called his own eldest son "Gaodhal." [The following is a translation of an extract from the derivation of this proper name, as given in Halliday's Vol. of Keating's Irish History, page 230 :

" Antiquaries assert that the name of *Gaodhal* is from the compound word formed of 'gaoith' and 'dil,' which means a *lover of learning;* for, 'gaoith' is the same as *wisdom* or *learning,* and 'dil' is the same as *loving* or *fond.*"]

Monarch of Ireland, invaded the territory of Dermod, A.D. 1167, and put him to flight. King Dermod was obliged, after many defeats, to leave Ireland, in 1167; throw himself at the feet of King Henry the Second, and crave his assistance, offering to become his liegeman. Henry, on receiving Dermod's oath of allegiance, granted by letters patent a general license to all his English subjects to aid King Dermod in the recovery of his Kingdom. Dermod then engaged in his cause Richard de Clare or Strongbow, to whom he afterwards gave his daughter Eva, in marriage ; and through his influence an army was raised, headed by Robert Fitzstephen, Myler Fitzhenry, Harvey de Monte Marisco, Maurice Prendergast, Maurice Fitzgerald, and others ; with which, in May, 1168, he landed in Bannow-bay, near Wexford, which they reduced, together with the adjoining counties—all in the kingdom of Leinster. In 1171, Earl Strongbow landed at Waterford with a large body of followers and took possession of that city. He then joined King Dermod's forces, marched for Dublin, entered the city, and made himself master.

King Dermod died in his castle at Ferns, county Wexford, A.D. 1175, about the 65th year of his age. Of him Holingshed says—" He was a man of tall stature and of a large and great body, a valiant and bold warrior in his nation. From his continued shouting, his voice was hoarse ; he rather chose to be feared than to be loved, and was a great oppressor of his nobility. To his own people he was rough and grievous, and hateful unto strangers; his hand was against all men, and all men against him."

10. The *Anglo-Saxons* or *English,* also a Tuetonic race, came from the twelfth to the eighteenth century. The *Britons* or *Welsh* came in the twelfth and thirteenth centuries. These English colonies were located chiefly in Leinster, but also in great numbers in Munster and Connaught, and partly in Ulster.

11. The *Scots,* who were chiefly Celts of Irish descent, came in great numbers from the tenth to the sixteenth century, and settled in Ulster, mostly in Antrim, Down, and Derry ; but, on the Plantation of Ulster with British colonies, in the seventeenth century, the new settlers in that province were chiefly *Scotch,* who were a mixture of Celts and Saxons. Thus the seven first colonies that settled in Ireland were a mixture of Scythians, Gaels, and Phœnicians ; but the four last were mostly Teutons, though mixed with Celts ; and a compound of all these races, in which Celtic blood is predominant, forms the present population of Ireland.

16. Gaodhal (or Gathelus), the son of Niul, was the ancestor of the *Clan-na-Gael*, that is, "the children or descendants of Gaodhal." In his youth this Gaodhal was stung in the neck by a serpent, and was immediately brought to Moses, who, laying his rod upon the wounded place, instantly cured him : whence followed the word "Glas" to be added to his name, as Gaodhal Glas (*glas :* Irish, green ; Lat. *glaucus ;* Gr. *glaukos*), on account of the *green scar* which the word signifies, and which, during his life, remained on his neck after the wound was healed. And Gaodhal obtained a further blessing, namely—that no venemous beast can live any time where his posterity should inhabit ; which is verified in Creta or Candia, Gothia or Getulia, Ireland, etc. The Irish chroniclers affirm that from this time Gaodhal and his posterity did paint the figures of Beasts, Birds, etc., on their banners and shields,* to distinguish their tribes and septs, in imitation of the Israelites ; and that a "Thunderbolt" was the cognizance in their chief standard for many generations after this Gaodhal.

17. Asruth, after his father's death, continued in Egypt, and governed his colony in peace during his life.

18. Sruth, soon after his father's death, was (see page 31) set upon by the Egyptians, on account of their former animosities towards their predecessors for having taken part with the Israelites against them ; which animosities until then lay raked up in the embers, and now broke out in a flame to that degree, that after many battles and conflicts, wherein most of his colony lost their lives, Sruth was forced with the few remaining to depart the country ; and, after many traverses at sea, arrived at the Island of Creta (now called Candia), where he paid his last tribute to nature.

19. Heber Scut (*scut :* Irish, a Scot), after his father's death and a year's stay in Creta, departed thence, leaving some of his people to inhabit the Island, where some of their posterity likely still remain; "because the Island breeds no venemous serpent ever since." He and his people soon after arrived in Scythia ; where his cousins, the posterity of Nenuall (eldest son of Fenius Farsa, above mentioned), refusing to allot a place of habitation for him and his colony, they fought many battles wherein Heber (with the assistance of some of the natives who were ill-affected towards their king), being always victor, he at length forced the sovereignty from the other, and settled himself and his colony in Scythia, who continued there for four generations. (Hence the epithet *Scut*, "a Scot" or "a Scythian," was applied to this Heber, who is accordingly called Heber Scot.) Heber Scot was afterwards slain in battle by Noemus the former king's son.

20. Beouman; 21. Ogaman; and 22. Tait, were each kings of Scythia, but in constant war with the natives ; so that after Tait's death his son,

23. Agnon and his followers betook themselves to sea, wandering and coasting upon the Caspian Sea for several (some say seven) years in which time he died.

24. Lamhfionn and his fleet remained at sea for some time after his

* *Shields :* This shows the great antiquity of *Gaelic* Heraldry.

D

father's death, resting and refreshing themselves upon such islands as
they met with.   It was then that Cachear, their magician or Druid,
foretold that there would be no end of their peregrinations and travel
until they should arrive at the Western Island of Europe, now called
Ireland, which was the place destined for their future and lasting abode
and settlement ; and that not they but their posterity after three hundred
years should arrive there.   After many traverses of fortune at sea, this
little fleet with their leader arrived at last and landed at Gothia or Getulia
—more recently called Lybia, where Carthage was afterwards built ; and,
soon after, Lamhfionn died there.

25. Heber Glunfionn was born in Getulia, where he died.   His
posterity continued there to the eighth generation ; and were kings or
chief rulers there for one hundred and fifty years—some say three hundred
years.

26. Agnan Fionn ; 27. Febric Glas ; 28. Nenuall ; 29. Nuadhad ;
30. Alladh ; 31. Arcadh ; and 32. Deag : of these nothing remarkable is
mentioned, but that they lived and died kings in Gothia or Getulia.

33. Brath was born in Gothia.   Remembering the Druid's prediction,
and his people having considerably multiplied during their abode in
Getulia, he departed thence with a numerous fleet to seek out the country
destined for their final settlement, by the prophecy of Cachear, the Druid
above mentioned ; and, after some time, he landed upon the coast of Spain,
and by strong hand settled himself and his colony in Galicia, in the north
of that country.

34. Breoghan (or Brigus) was king of Galicia, Andalusia, Murcia,
Castile, and Portugal—all which he conquered.   He built Breoghan's
Tower or *Brigantia* in Galicia, and the city of *Brigansa* or *Braganza* in
Portugal—called after him ; and the kingdom of Castile was then also
called after him *Brigia*.   It is considered that "Castile" itself was so
called from the figure of a *castle* which Brigus bore for his Arms on his
banner.   Brigus sent a colony into Britain, who settled in that territory
now known as the counties of York, Lancaster, Durham, Westmoreland,
and Cumberland, and, after him, were called *Brigantes ;* whose posterity
gave formidable opposition to the Romans, at the time of the Roman
invasion of Britain.

35. Bilé was king of those countries after his father's death ; and his
son Galamh [galav] or Milesius succeeded him.   This Bilé had a brother
named Ithe.

36. Milesius, in his youth and during his father's life-time, went into
Scythia, where he was kindly received by the king of that country, who
gave him his daughter in marriage, and appointed him General of his
forces.   In this capacity Milesius defeated the king's enemies, gained
much fame, and the love of all the king's subjects.   His growing greatness and popularity excited against him the jealousy of the king; who,
fearing the worst, resolved on privately despatching Milesius out of the
way, for, openly, he dare not attempt it.   Admonished of the king's
intentions in his regard, Milesius slew him ; and thereupon quitted
Scythia and retired into Egypt with a fleet of sixty sail.   Pharaoh
Nectonibus, then king of Egypt, being informed of his arrival and of his
great valour, wisdom, and conduct in arms, made him General of all his

forces against the king of Ethiopia then invading his country. Here, as in Scythia, Milesius was victorious ; he forced the enemy to submit to the conqueror's own terms of peace. By these exploits Milesius found great favour with Pharaoh, who gave him, being then a widower, his daughter Scota in marriage ; and kept him eight years afterwards in Egypt.

During the sojourn of Milesius in Egypt, he employed the most ingenious and able persons among his people to be instructed in the several trades, arts, and sciences used in Egypt ; in order to have them taught to the rest of his people on his return to Spain.

[The original name of Milesius of Spain was, as already mentioned, " Galamh" (*gall :* Irish, a stranger ; *amh*, a negative affix), which means, *no stranger :* meaning that he was no stranger in Egypt, where he was called " Milethea Spaine," which was afterwards contracted to " Milé Spaine" (meaning the Spanish Hero), and finally to " Milesius" (*mileadh :* Irish, a hero ; Lat. *miles*, a soldier).]

At length Milesius took leave of his father-in-law, and steered towards Spain ; where he arrived to the great joy and comfort of his people, who were much harasssed by the rebellion of the natives and by the intrusion of other foreign nations that forced in after his father's death, and during his own long absence from Spain. With these and those he often met ; and, in fifty-four battles, victoriously fought, he routed, destroyed, and totally extirpated them out of the country, which he settled in peace and quietness.

In his reign a great dearth and famine occurred in Spain, of twenty-six years' continuance, occasioned, as well by reason of the former troubles which hindered the people from cultivating and manuring the ground, as for want of rain to moisten the earth ; but Milesius superstitiously believed the famine to have fallen upon him and his people as a judgment and punishment from their gods, for their negligence in seeking out the country destined for their final abode, so long before foretold by Cachear their Druid or magician, as already mentioned—the time limited by the prophecy for the accomplishment thereof being now nearly, if not fully, expired. To expiate his fault and to comply with the will of his gods, Milesius, with the general approbation of his people, sent his uncle Ithe, with his son Lughaidh [Luy], and one hundred and fifty stout men to bring them an account of those western islands ; who, accordingly, arriving at the island since then called Ireland, and landing in that part of it now called Munster, left his son with fifty of his men to guard the ship, and with the rest travelled about the island. Informed, among other things, that the three sons of Cearmad, called Mac-Cuill, MacCeacht, and MacGreine, did then and for thirty years before rule and govern the island, each for one year, in his turn ; and that the country was called after the names of their three queens—Eire, Fodhla, and Banbha, respectively : one year called " Eire," the next " Fodhla," and the next " Banbha," as their husbands reigned in their regular turns ; by which names the island is ever since indifferently called, but most commonly " Eire," *

---

* *Eire :* Ancient Irish historians assert that this Queen was granddaughter of Ogma, who (see *ante*, page 47, in Note No. 5, under "Tuatha de Danans,") invented

because that MacCuill, the husband of Eire, ruled and governed the country in his turn the year that the Clan-na-Milé (or the sons of Milesius) arrived in and conquered Ireland. And being further informed that the three brothers were then at their palace at Aileach Neid,* in the north part of the country, engaged in the settlement of some disputes concerning their family jewels, Ithe directed his course thither; sending orders to his son to sail about with his ship and the rest of his men, and meet him there.

When Ithe arrived where the (Danan) brothers were, he was honourably received and entertained by them; and, finding him to be a man of great wisdom and knowledge, they referred their disputes to him for decision. That decision having met their entire satisfaction, Ithe exhorted them to mutual love, peace, and forbearance; adding much in praise of their delightful, pleasant, and fruitful country; and then took his leave, to return to his ship, and go back to Spain.

No sooner was he gone than the brothers began to reflect on the high commendations which Ithe gave of the Island; and, suspecting his design of bringing others to invade it, resolved to prevent them, and therefore pursued him with a strong party, overtook him, fought and routed his men and wounded himself to death (before his son or the rest of his men left on ship-board could come to his rescue) at a place called, from that fight and his name, *Magh Ithe* or "The plain of Ithe" (an extensive plain in the barony of Raphoe, county Donegal); whence his son, having found him in that condition, brought his dead and mangled body back into Spain, and there exposed it to public view, thereby to excite his friends and relations to avenge his murder.

And here I think it not amiss to notify what the Irish chroniclers, observe upon this matter, viz.—that all the invaders and planters of Ireland, namely, Partholan, Neimhedh, the Firbolgs, Tuatha-de-Danans, and Clan-na-Milé, where originally Scythians, of the line of Japhet, who had the language called *Bearla-Tobbai* or *Gaoidhilg* [Gaelic] common amongst them all; and consequently not to be wondered at, that Ithe and the Tuatha-de-Danans understood one another without an Interpreter— both speaking the same language, though perhaps with some difference in the accent.

The exposing of the dead body of Ithe had the desired effect; for, thereupon, Milesius made great preparations in order to invade Ireland— as well to avenge his uncle's death, as also in obedience to the will of his gods, signified by the prophecy of Cachear, aforesaid. But, before he could effect that object, he died, leaving the care and charge of that expedition upon his eight legitimate sons by his two wives before mentioned.

Milesius was a very valiant champion, a great warrior, and fortunate and prosperous in all his undertakings: witness his name of "Milesius,"

the *Ogham* Alphabet; and that it is after that Queen, that Ireland is always personated by a *Female* figure!

* *Aileach Neid:* This name may be derived from the Irish *aileach*, a stone horse or stallion, or *aileachta*, jewels; and *Neid*, the Mars of the Pagan Irish. In its time it was one of the most important fortresses in Ireland.

given him from the many battles (some say *a thousand*, which the word
" Milé" signifies in Irish as well as in Latin) which he victoriously fought
and won, as well in Spain, as in all the other countries and kingdoms he
traversed in his younger days.

The eight brothers were neither forgetful nor negligent in the execution
of their father's command; but, soon after his death, with a numerous
fleet well manned and equipped, set forth from Breoghan's Tower or
Brigantia (now Corunna) in Galicia, in Spain, and sailed prosperously to
the coasts of Ireland or *Inis-Fail*,* where they met many difficulties and
various chances before they could land : occasioned by the diabolical arts,
sorceries, and enchantments used by the Tuatha-de-Danans, to obstruct
their landing; for, by their magic art, they enchanted the island so as
to appear to the Milesians or Clan-na-Milé in the form of a Hog, and no
way to come at it (whence the island, among the many other names
it had before, was called *Muc-Inis* or "The Hog Island"); and withal
raised so great a storm, that the Milesian fleet was thereby totally dispersed and many of them cast away, wherein five of the eight brothers,
sons of Milesius, lost their lives. That part of the fleet commanded
by Heber, Heremon, and Amergin (the three surviving brothers), and
Heber Donn, son of Ir (one of the brothers lost in the storm), overcame
all opposition, landed safe, fought and routed the three Tuatha-de Danan
Kings at Slieve-Mis, and thence pursued and overtook them at Tailten,
where another bloody battle was fought; wherein the three (Tuatha-de-
Danan) Kings and their Queens were slain, and their army utterly
routed and destroyed : so that they could never after give any opposition to the Clan-na-Milé in their new conquest; who, having thus

---

* *Inis-Fail :* Thomas Moore, in his *Irish Melodies*, commemorates this circumstance
in the " Song of Inisfail " :

> They came from a land beyond the sea
> And now o'er the western main
> Set sail, in their good ships, gallantly,
> From the sunny land of Spain.
> " Oh, where's the isle we've seen in dreams,
> Our destined home or grave?"
> Thus sang they, as by the morning's beams,
> They swept the Atlantic wave.
>
> And lo ! where afar o'er ocean shines
> A spark of radiant green,
> As though in that deep lay emerald mines,
> Whose light through the wave was seen.
> " 'Tis *Innisfail*—'tis *Innisfail!* "
> Rings o'er the echoing sea ;
> While, bending to heaven, the warriors hail
> That home of the brave and free.
>
> Then turned they unto the Eastern wave,
> Where now their Day-god's eye
> A look of such sunny omen gave
> As lighted up sea and sky.
> Nor frown was seen through sky or sea,
> Nor tear o'er leaf or sod,
> When first on their *Isle of Destiny*
> Our great forefathers trod.

sufficiently avenged the death of their great uncle Ithe, gained the possession of the country foretold them by Cachear, some ages past, as already mentioned.

Heber and Heremon, the chief leading men remaining of the eight brothers, sons of Milesius aforesaid, divided the kingdom between them (allotting a proportion of land to their brother Amergin, who was their Arch-priest, Druid, or magician ; and to their nephew Heber Donn, and to the rest of their chief commanders), and became jointly the first of one hundred and eighty-three* Kings or sole Monarchs of the Gaelic, Milesian, or Scottish Race, that ruled and governed Ireland, successively, for two thousand eight hundred and eighty-five years from the first year of their reign, Anno Mundi three thousand five hundred, to their submission to the Crown of England in the person of King Henry the Second ; who, being also of the Milesian Race by *Maude*, his mother, was lineally descended from Fergus Mor MacEarca, first King of Scotland, who was descended from the said Heremon—so that the succession may be truly said to continue in the Milesian Blood from before Christ one thousand six hundred and ninety-nine years down to the present time.

Heber and Heremon reigned jointly one year only, when, upon a difference between their ambitious wives, they quarrelled and fought a battle at Ardcath or Geshill (Geashill, near Tullamore in the King's County), where Heber was slain by Heremon ; and, soon after, Amergin, who claimed an equal share in the government, was, in another battle fought between them, likewise slain by Heremon. Thus, Heremon became sole Monarch, and made a new division of the land amongst his comrades and friends, viz. : the south part, now called Munster, he gave to his brother Heber's four sons, Er, Orba, Feron, and Fergna ; the north part, now Ulster, he gave to Ir's only son Heber Donn ; the east part or *Coigeadh Galian*, now called Leinster, he gave to Criomthann-sciath-bheil, one of his commanders ; and the west part, now called Connaught, Heremon gave to Un-Mac-Oigge, another of his commanders ; allotting a part of Munster to Lughaidh (the son of Ithe, the first Milesian discoverer of Ireland), amongst his brother Heber's sons.

From these three brothers, Heber, Ir, and Heremon (Amergin dying without issue), are descended all the Milesian Irish of Ireland and Scotland, viz. : from Heber, the eldest brother, the provincial Kings of Munster (of whom thirty-eight were sole Monarchs of Ireland), and most of the nobility and gentry of Munster, and many noble families in Scotland, are descended.

From Ir, the second brother, all the provincial Kings of Ulster (of whom twenty-six were sole Monarchs of Ireland), and all the ancient nobility and gentry of Ulster, and many noble families in Leinster, Munster, and Connaught, derive their pedigrees ; and, in Scotland, the Clan-na-Rory—the descendants of an eminent man, named Ruadhri or Roderick, who was Monarch of Ireland for seventy years (viz., from Before Christ 288 to 218).

From Heremon, the youngst of the three brothers, were descended one hundred and fourteen sole Monarchs of Ireland : the provincial Kings and

* *Three:* We make the number to be 184 : see p. 62, *infra*.

Hermonian nobility and gentry of Leinster, Connaught, Meath, Orgiall, Tirowen, Tirconnell, and Clan-na-boy; the Kings of Dalriada; all the Kings of Scotland from Fergus Mor MacEarca down to the Stuarts; and the Kings and Queens of England from Henry the Second down to the present time.

The issue of Ithe is not accounted among the Milesian Irish or Clan-na-Milé, as not being descended from *Milesius*, but from his uncle Ithe; of whose posterity there were also some Monarchs of Ireland (see Roll of the Irish Monarchs, *infra*), and many provincial or half provincial Kings of Munster: that country upon its first division being allocated to the sons of Heber and to Lughaidh, son of Ithe, whose posterity continued there accordingly.

This invasion, conquest, or plantation of Ireland by the Milesian or Scottish Nation took place in the Year of the World three thousand five hundred, or the next year after Solomon began the foundation of the Temple of Jerusalem, and one thousand six hundred and ninety-nine years before the Nativity of our Saviour Jesus Christ; which, according to the Irish computation of Time, occurred Anno Mundi five thousand one hundred and ninety-nine: therein agreeing with the *Septuagint*, Roman Martyrologies, Eusebius, Orosius, and other ancient authors; which computation the ancient Irish chroniclers exactly observed in their Books of the Reigns of the Monarchs of Ireland, and other Antiquities of that Kingdom; out of which the Roll of the Monarchs of Ireland, from the beginning of the Milesian Monarchy to their submission to King Henry the Second of England, a Prince of their own Blood, is exactly collected.

[As the Milesian invasion of Ireland took place the next year after the laying of the foundation of the Temple of Jerusalem by Solomon, King of Israel, we may infer that Solomon was contemporary with Milesius of Spain; and that the Pharaoh King of Egypt, who (1 Kings iii. 1,) gave his daughter in marriage to Solomon, was the Pharaoh who conferred on Milesius of Spain the hand of another daughter Scota.]

Milesius of Spain bore three Lions in his shield and standard, for the following reasons; namely, that, in his travels in his younger days into foreign countries, passing through Africa, he, by his cunning and valour, killed in one morning *three Lions ;* and that, in memory of so noble and valiant an exploit, he always after bore three Lions on his shield, which his two surviving sons Heber and Heremon, and his grandson Heber Donn, son of Ir, after their conquest of Ireland, divided amongst them, as well as they did the country: each of them bearing a *Lion* in his shield and banner, but of different colours; which the Chiefs of their posterity continue to this day: some with additions and differences; others plain and entire as they had it from their ancestors.

II.—ROLL OF THE MONARCHS OF IRELAND,

Since the Milesian Conquest.

NAMES of the one hundred and eighty-four Kings* or Monarchs of Ireland, from the conquest thereof by the Milesian or Scottish Nation, Anno Mundi, 3,500, down to Roderick O'Connor, the Monarch of Ireland, A.D. 1186 : a period which embraces two thousand eight hundred and eighty-five years. The date opposite each name tells the year in which the Monarch began to reign:—

Before Christ.

1. H. Heber and Heremon, jointly, began to reign A.M. 3,500 ; or	1699
2. E. Heremon, alone, ...	1698
3. E. Muimne ⎫	
4. E. Luighne ⎬ Three Brothers, ...	1683
5. E. Laighean ⎭	
6. H. Er ⎫	
7. H. Orba ⎬ Four Brothers, ...	1680
8. H. Feron ⎥	
9. H. Fergna ⎭	
10. E. Irial Faidh, ...	1680
11. E. Eithrial, ...	1670
12. H. Conmaol, ...	1650
13. E. Tighearnmas, ...	1620
14. L. Eochaidh Edghothach, ...	1543
15. I. Cearmna ⎫ Brothers, ...	1532
16. I. Sobhrach ⎭	
17. H. Eochaidh Faobhar-glas, ...	1492
18. E. Fiacha Lamhraein, ...	1472
19. H. Eochaidh Mumha, ...	1448
20. E. Aongus (or Æneas) Ollmucach, ...	1427
21. H. Eanna Airgthach, ...	1409
22. E. Rotheacta, ...	1382
23. I. Seidnae, ...	1357
24. I. Fiacha Fionn-Scothach, ...	1352
25. H. Munmoin, ...	1332
26. H. Fualdergoid, ...	1327
27. I. Ollamh Fodhla, A.M. 3882, ...	1317
28. I. Finachta Fionn-sneachta, ...	1277
29. I. Slanoll, ...	1257

* *Kings:* As the kings descended from Heber, Ir, and Heremon (the three sons of Milesius of Spain who left any issue), as well as those descended from their relative Lughaidh, the son of Ithe, were all eligible for the Monarchy, the letter H, E, I or L, is employed in the foregoing Roll of the Monarchs of Ireland, *before* the name of each Monarch there given, to distinguish his lineal descent. Thus H, E, and I refer to the three brothers Heber, Heremon, and Ir, respectively : H, is placed before the names of the Monarchs who were descended from Heber ; E, before those descended from Eremon or Heremon ; I, before those descended from Ir ; and L, before those descended from Lughaidh.

Before Christ.

30. I. Gead Ollghothach, ...	1240
31. I. Fiacha (3), ...	1228
32. I. Bergna, ...	1208
33. I. Olioll, ...	1196
34. E. Siorghnath Saoghalach ; lived 250 years, and reigned 150 years, ...	1180
35. H. Rotheacta (2), ...	1030
36. H. Eiliomh, ...	1023
37. E. Giallcadh, ...	1022
38. H. Art Imleach, ...	1013
39. E. Nuadhas Fionnfail, ...	1001
40. H. Breas Rioghachta, ...	961
41. L. Eochaidh Apach, ...	952
42. I. Fionn, ...	951
43. H. Seidnae Innaraidh, ...	929
44. E. Simeon Breac, ...	909
45. H. Duach Fionn, ...	903
46. E. Muireadach Bolgach, ...	893
47. H. Eanna Dearg, ...	892
48. H. Lughaidh Iardhonn, ...	880
49. I. Siorlamhach, ...	871
50. H. Eochaidh Uarceas, ...	855
51. E. Eochaidh (Brother of No. 53), ...	843
52. H. Lughaidh Lamhdearg, ...	838
53. E. Conang Beag-eaglach, ...	831
54. H. Art (2), ...	811
55. E. Fiacha Tolgrach	805
56. H. Olioll Fionn, ...	795
57. H. Eochaidh (7), ...	784
58. I. Argethamar, ...	777
59. E. Duach Ladhrach, ...	747
60. H. Lughaidh Lagha, ...	737
61. I. Aodh Ruadh, ⎫	
62. I. Dithorba, ⎬	730
63. I. Cimbath. ⎭	

These three, Nos. 61, 62, and 63, were grandchildren of Argethamar, No. 58; and they mutually agreed to reign by turns, each of them for seven years. They accordingly ruled until each of them reigned three times seven years; and Aodh Ruadh (No. 61), before it came to his fourth turn to reign, was drowned at *Eas Ruadh* [Easroe], now Ballyshannon, in the county Donegal (*eas:* Irish, a cataract; Heb. *eshed*, a pouring of water), leaving issue one daughter named Macha Mongrua, who succeeded to the Monarchy.

Before Christ.

64. I. Macha Mongrua (that daughter), ...	667
65. H. Reacht Righ-dearg, ...	653
66. E. Ugaine Mor (Hugony the Great), ...	633
67. E. Bancadh (survived his elevation to the Monarchy only one day), ...	593

Before Christ.

68. E. Laeghaire Lorc, ...   593
69. E. Cobthach Caoil-bhreagh, ...   591
70. E. Labhra Longseach, ...   541
71. E. Melg Molbhthach, ...   522
72. H. Moghcorb, ...   505
73. E. Æneas Ollamh, ...   498
74. E. Iarn Gleofathach, ...   480
75. H. Fearcorb, ...   473
76. E. Conla Caomh, ...   462
77. E. Olioll Casfiacalach, ...   442
78. H. Adhamhair Foltchaion, ...   417
79. E. Eochaidh Altleathan, ...   412
80. E. Fergus Fortamhail, ...   397
81. E. Æneas Turmeach-Teamreach, ...   384
82. E. Conall Collaimrach, ...   324
83. H. Niadhsedhaman, ...   319
84. E. Eanna Aigneach, ...   312
85. E. Crimthann Cosgrach, ...   292
86. I. Ruadhri Mor (a quo " Clan-na-Rory "),   ...   288
87. H. Ionadmaor, ...   218
88. I. Bresal Bodhiobha, ...   209
89. H. Lughaidh Luaighne, ...   198
90. I. Congall Clareineach, ...   183
91. H. Duach Dalladh-Deadha, ...   168
92. I. Fachna Fathach, ...   158
93. E. Eochaidh Feidlioch, ...   142
94. E. Eochaidh Aireamh, ...   130
95. E. Edersceal, ...   115
96. E. Nuadhas Neacht, ...   110
97. E. Conaire Mor, ...   109

After the death of Conaire Mor, there was an *Interregnum* of five years.

98. E. Lughaidh Sriabh n-Dearg, ...   34
99. E. Conchobhair, ...   8
100. E. Crimthann Niadh-Nar, ...   7

In the seventh year of this Crimthann's reign, our LORD JESUS CHRIST
was born.

Anno Domini.

101. — Cairbre Cean-cait* (of the Firbolg race),   ...   9
102. E. Feareadach Fionnfeachtnach, ...   14
103. E. Fiatach Fionn (a quo " Dal Fiatach "),   ...   36
104. E. Fiacha Fionn-Ola, ...   39
105. I. Eiliomh MacConrach, ...   56
106. E. Tuathal Teachtmar, ...   76
107. I. Mal MacRochraidhe, ...   106

---

* *Cean-cait :* This word *cean-cait* (" cat," gen. " cait :" Irish, *a cat ;* Gr. Vulg.
" kat-is," " gat-as," and " kat-a ;" Lat. " cat-us ;" It. and Span. " gat-o ;" Fr. " chat ;"
Bel. " kat-te ;" Russ. " kot-e ;" Arm. " kas ;" Wel. and Cor. " kath ;" and Turk.
" ket-i ") means *cat-headed.*

Anno Domini.

108. E. Felim Rachtmar, ... 110
109. E. Cathair Mor, ... 119
110. E. Conn Ceadcatha, ... 123
111. E. Conaire MacMogha Laine, ... 157
112. E. Art Eanfhear* (ancestor of *O'Hart*), ... 165
113. L. Lughaidh Maccon, ... 195
114. E. Fergus Dubh-Dheadach, ... 225
115. E. Cormac Mac Art (or Cormac Ulfada), ... 226
116. E. Eochaidh Gunta, ... 266
117. E. Cairbre Liffechar, ... 267
118. L. Fothadh Airgtheach ⎱ Brothers, ... 284
119. L. Fothadh Cairpeach ⎰
120. E. Fiacha Srabhteine (ancestor of *O'Neill*), ... 285
121. E. Colla Uais (ancestor of *MacUais*), ... 322
122. E. Muireadach Tireach, ... 326
123. I. Caolbadh, ... 356
124. E. Eochaidh Muigh Meadhoin, ... 357
125. H. Crimthann (3), ... 365
126. E. Niall Mor (or Nial of the Nine Hostages), ... 378
127. E. Dathi, ... 405

All the foregoing Monarchs were Pagans; but some authors are of opinion that Nos. 112, 115, and 126 were enlightened by the Holy Spirit in the truths of Christianity. Others are of opinion that the Monarch Laeghaire, son of Niall Mor, and who is No. 128 on this Roll, died a Pagan, although reigning at the time of the advent of St. Patrick, in Ireland.

Anno Domini.

128. E. Laeghaire MacNiall, ... 428
129. E. Olioll Molt, son of Dathi, ... 458
130. E. Lughaidh; son of Laaeghaire, ... 478
131. E. Muirceartach Mor MacEarca, brother of Fergus
      Mor MacEarca, the Founder of the Milesian
      Monarchy in Scotland, ... 503
132. E. Tuathal Maolgharbh, ... 527
133. E. Diarmid, son of Fergus Cearrbheoil, ... 538
134. E. Donall (1) ⎱ Brothers—both died of the Plague
135. E. Fergus (3) ⎰ in one day, ... 558
136. E. Eochaidh (13) ⎱ Nephew and Uncle, ... 561
137. E. Boitean (1) ⎰
138. E. Anmire, ... 563
139. E. Boitean (?) 566

* *Art Eanfhear:* It is stated in the "History of the Cemeteries," that this Monarch believed in the Faith, the day before the battle (of *Magh Mucroimhe,* near Athenry, where he was slain by Lughaidh Maccon, A.D. 195), and predicted the spread of Christianity. It would appear also that he had some presentiment of his death; for, he directed that he should not be buried at Brugh on the (river) Boyne, the Pagan cemetery of his forefathers, but at a place then called *Dumha Dergluachra* (the burial mound of the red rushy place), "where Trevait (*Trevet,* in the county Meath) is at this day," (see Petrie's "Round Towers," page 100).—*Irish Names of Places.*

Anno Domini.

140. E. Aodh (2), ...   567
141. E. Aodh Slaine, ...   594

Some annalists state that this Aodh Slaine was a brother of Lochan
Dilmhain, who, according to the "Book of Armagh," was ancestor of
Dillon; but (see the "Dillon" pedigree) Lochan Dilmhain was brother
of Colman Rimidh, the next Monarch on this Roll, who reigned jointly
with Aodh Slaine, for six years.

Anno Domini.

142. E. Colman Rimidh, ...   —
143. E. Aodh Uar-iodhnach, ...   600
144. E. Mallcobh, ...   607
145. E. Suimneach Meann, ...   610
146. E. Donall (2), ...   623
147. E. Ceallach, ...   639
148. E. Congall (3)   652
149. E. Diarmid (2) ⎫
150. E. Bladhmhac   ⎬ Reigned jointly, ...   656
151. E. Seachnasach, ...   664
152. E. Ceanfail, ...   669
153. E. Finachta Fleadhach, ...   673
154. E. Longseach, ...   693
155. E. Congall (4), ...   701
156. E. Fergall, ...   708
157. E. Foghartach, ...   718
158. E. Ceneth, ...   719
159. E. Flaithertach, ...   722
160. E. Aodh Olann, ...   729
161. E. Donall (3), ...   738
162. E. Niall Frassach, ...   758
163. E. Doncha (1), ...   765
164. E. Aodh Ornigh, ...   792

In this Monarch's reign the Danes* invaded Ireland.

---

* *The Danes* : "Ten years with four score and seven hundred was the age of Christ
when the pagans went to Ireland." The Vickings (or Danes) having been defeated
in Glamorganshire in Wales, invaded Ireland, in the reign of the monarch Aodh
Ornigh. In A.D. 798, they ravaged the Isle of Man, and the Hebrides in Scotland ;
in 802, they burned "Hi Colum Cille ;" in 807, for the first time in Ireland, they
marched inland ; in 812 and 813, they made raids in Connaught and Munster. After
thirty years of this predatory warfare had continued, Turgesius, a Norwegian Prince,
established himself as sovereign of the Vickings, and made Armagh his head quarters,
A.D. 830. Sometimes the Danish Chiefs mustered all their forces and left the island
for a brief period, to ravage the shores of England, or Scotland ; but, wild, brave, and
cruel, they soon returned to inflict new barbarities on the unfortunate Irish. Turgesius
appropriated the abbeys and churches of the country ; and placed an abbot of his own
in every monastery. A Danish captain was placed in charge of each village ; and
each family was obliged to maintain a soldier of that nation, who made himself master
of the house, using and wasting the food, for lack of which the children of the lawful
owners were often dying of hunger. All education was strictly forbidden : books and
manuscripts were burned and "drowned ;" and the poets, historians, and musicians,
imprisoned and driven to the woods and mountains. Martial sports were interdicted,
from the lowest to the highest rank ; even nobles and princes were forbidden to wear

Anno Domini.

165. E. Conchobhair (2),	...	...	...	817
166. E. Niall Caille,	...	...	...	831
167. E. Malachi I.,	...	...	...	844
168. E. Aodh Fionnliath,	...	...	...	860
169. E. Flann Sionnach (ancestor of *Fox*),	...	...	876
170. E. Niall Glundubh (aquo *O'Neill*)	...	...	914
171. E. Doncha (2),	...	...	...	917
172. E. Congall,	...	...	...	942
173. E. Donall (4),	...	...	...	954
174. E. Malachi II. (ancestor of *O'Melaghlin*),		...	978

Malachi the Second was the last absolute Monarch of Ireland. He reigned as Monarch twenty-four years before the accession to the Monarchy of Brian Boroimhe [Boru], and again after Brian's death, which took place A.D. 1014, at the Battle of Clontarf.

175. H. Brian Boroimhe (ancestor of and aquo *O'Brien*),   1001
Brian Boru reigned sixty-six years, twelve of which as Monarch; he was eighty-eight years of age when slain at the Battle of Clontarf.

After Brian's death—

Malachi II. was restored to the Monarchy, 1014. After nine years' reign, Malachi died a penitent at *Cro Inis* (or the "Cell on the Island"), upon Loch Annin in Westmeath, A.D. 1023; being the forty-eighth Christian King of Ireland, and accounted the last absolute Monarch of the Milesian or Scottish line: the provincial Kings and Princes always after contesting, fighting, and quarrelling for the sovereignty, until they put all into confusion, and that the King of Leinster brought in King Henry the Second to assist him against his enemies.

Those and such as our histories mention to have assumed the name and title of Monarchs of Ireland, without the general consent of the major part of the Kingdom, are as follows:—

176. H. Doncha (or Donough)   1022
This Doncha was son of Brian Boru, and was King of Munster till the death of the Monarch Malachi the Second. He then assumed the title of Monarch, till defeated and banished from Ireland by Dermod, son of Donough, called "Maol-na-Mho," King of Leinster, who is accounted by some to succeed Doncha in the Monarchy; yet is assigned no years for his reign, but that he contested with the said Doncha until he utterly defeated and banished him, A.D. 1064: from which time it is likely that Dermod reigned the rest of the fifty-two years assigned for the reign of Doncha, who died at Rome, A.D. 1074.

177. E. Diarmid (3), or Dermod, ...   ——
By the Irish historians this Dermod, son of Doncha or Donough, King of Leinster, is assigned no date for his accession to the Monarchy.

178. H. Tirloch O'Brien, ...   1074

their usual habilaments: the cast-off clothes of the Danes being considered sufficiently good for slaves! In A.D. 948, the Danes were converted to Christianity; and at that time possessed many of the sea-coast towns of Ireland—including Dublin, Limerick, Wexford, and Waterford.—*Miss Cusack.*

Anno Domini.

This Tirloch was the son of Teige, eldest son of Brian Boru; and was styled Monarch of Ireland from his uncle's death at Rome, A.D. 1074.

179. E. Donall MacLoghlin, son of Ardgal, King of Aileach, was styled Monarch, and ruled alone for twelve years; began to reign, ... 1086

180. H. Muirceartach O'Brien, King of Munster, was, from 1098 up to his death, A.D. 1119, jointly in the Monarchy with Donall MacLoghlin; began to reign, ... 1098

Donall reigned alone, after the death of Muirceartach O'Brien, to his own death, A.D. 1121; began to reign alone the second time, and reigned two years, ... 1119

From Donall's death, A.D. 1121, to A.D. 1136, though many contested, yet, for fifteen years, none assumed the title of Monarch, ... 1121

181. E. Tirloch Mor O'Connor, King of Connaught for fifty years, and Monarch from A.D., ... 1136

182. E. Muircearth MacLoghlin, grandson of Donal (No. 179, above), was styled Monarch from A.D. ... 1156

183. E. Roderick O'Connor,* 1166

184. (E. Brian O'Neill,† No. 113 on the O'Neill" pedigree 1258)

---

* Roderick O'Connor, King of Connaught, was the last undoubted Monarch of Ireland from his predecessor's death, A.D. 1166, for twenty years, to the year 1186 ; within which time, by the invitation of Dermod-na-n-Gall, King of Leinster, the English first invaded Ireland, A.D. 1169. The Monarch Roderick, seeing his subjects flinch and his own sons turn against him, hearkened to and accepted the conditions offered him by King Henry II., which being ratified on both sides, A.D. 1175, Roderick continued in the government (at least the name of it), until A.D. 1186, when, weary of the world and its troubles, he forsook it and all its pomp, and retired to a Monastery, where he finished his course religiously, A.D. 1198.

† *Brian O'Neill :* It is worthy of remark that, at A.D. 1258, the Four Masters mention that "Hugh, the son of Felim O'Connor, and Teige O'Brien, marched with a great force to Caol Uisge (near Newry), to hold a conference with Brian O'Neill, to whom the foregoing chiefs, after making peace with each other, granted the sovereignty over the Irish." And, two years later, at the Battle of Down, this Brian gallantly laid down his life in defence of the Kingdom of Ireland, which he claimed to govern. (See D'Arcy McGee's History of Ireland, Vol. I., p. 208.) Again, the Four Masters, at A.D. 1260, in giving the names of the killed at the Battle of Drom Deirg, mention Brian O'Neill as "Chief Ruler of Ireland." In his letter to Pope John XXII., Donal, the son of the said Brian, says he is "Donald O'Neill, King of Ulster, and by hereditary right lawful heir to the throne of Ireland."—*See* CONNELLAN'S *"Four Masters,"* p. 722.

PART III.

I.—THE LINE OF HEBER.

*In Munster.**

1.—THE STEM OF "THE LINE OF HEBER."

THE Stem of the Irish Nation, from Milesius of Spain (who is No. 36, page 50), down to No. 94 Aodh Dubh, King of Munster, from whose two sons respectively descended the illustrious families of *O'Sullivan,* and *MacCarthy.*

The three sons of Milesius who left any issue were—1. Heber Fionn, 2. Ir, and 3. Heremon. Heber being the eldest of those three sons, the descent from him is here first given:

36. MILESIUS.

1	2	3
37. Heber Fionn.	37. Ir.	37. Heremon.

This Heber Fionn was the first Milesian Monarch of Ireland, conjointly with his brother Heremon. Heber was slain by Heremon, Before Christ, 1698.

38. Conmaol: his son; was the twelfth Monarch.

(The year in which any of the Monarchs began to reign can be ascertained in the "Roll of the Monarchs of Ireland," in the last preceding chapter.)

* *Munster*: A short time before the Christian era, Eochy Feidlioch, the 93rd Milesian Monarch of Ireland, divided the Kingdom into five Provinces, namely— Ulster, Connaught, Leinster, and the two Provinces of Munster. In Irish the name of a Province is *Coigeadh* [coo-gu], which signifies "a fifth part."

Tuathal Teachtmar (or Tuathal the Legitimate), the 106th Monarch, made, in the beginning of the second century, a new division of Ireland into five provinces; and having taken a portion from each of the Provinces of Leinster, Munster, Ulster, and Connaught, formed the new Province or Kingdom of Meath. This division continued for many centuries, and even long after the Anglo-Norman Invasion. Thus the Irish Government was a *Pentarchy*: a supreme Monarch being elected to preside over all the Provincial Kings, and designated *Ard-righ* or High King (*righ*: Irish a king; Hind. *raja*; Lat. *rex*; gen. *regis*; Fr. *roi*). The Kingdom of Munster (in Irish *Mumha*, *Mumhan,* and *Mumhain*) derived its name, according to O'Flaherty's "Ogygia," from Eochaidh Mumha, who was King of Munster, and the 19th Monarch of Ireland. Munster is latinised "Momonia." Ancient Munster comprised the present counties of Tipperary, Waterford, Cork, Kerry, Limerick, and part of Kilkenny; to which, in the latter part of the third century, was added the territory now forming the County of Clare, by Lughaidh Meann, King of Munster, of the race of the Dalcassians, who took it from Connaught and added it to Munster.

Ancient Munster is mentioned under the following divisions, namely—*Tuadh Mumhan* or North Munster, anglicised "Thomond;" *Deas Mumhan* or South Munster, rendered "Desmond;" *Urmhumha, Oirmhumha* or East Munster, rendered "Ormond;" and *Iar Mumhan* or West Munster.

Thomond, under its ancient Kings, extended from the Isles of Arran, off the coast of Galway, to the mountain of *Eibline,* near Cashel in Tipperary; thence to

39. Eochaidh Faobhar Glas: his son; the 17th Monarch.

40. Eanna Airgthach: his son; was the 21st Monarch; and the first who caused silver shields to be made.

41. Glas: his son.

42. Ros: his son.

43. Rotheacta: his son.

44. Fearard: his son.

45. Cas: his son,

46. Munmoin: his son; was the 25th Monarch; and the first who ordained his Nobles to wear gold chains about their necks.

47. Fualdergoid: his son; was the 26th Monarch; and the first who ordered his Nobility to wear gold rings on their fingers.

48. Cas Cedchaingnigh: his son. This Cas was a learned man; he revised the study of the laws, poetry, and other laudable sciences (which were) much eclipsed and little practised since the death of Amergin Glungheal, one of the sons of Milesius, who was their Druid or Archpriest, and who was slain in battle by his brother Heremon soon after their brother Heber's death.

49. Failbhe Iolcorach: his son; was the first who ordained that stone walls should be built as boundaries between the neighbours' lands.

50. Ronnach: his son.

51. Rotheachta: his son; was the 35th Monarch.

52. Eiliomh Ollfhionach: his son.

53. Art Imleach: his son; the 38th Monarch.

54. Breas Rioghacta: his son; the 40th Monarch.

55. Seidnae Innaridh: his son; was the 43rd Monarch; and the first who, in Ireland, enlisted his soldiers in pay and under good discipline. Before his time, they had no other pay than what they could gain from their enemies.

Cairn Feareadaigh, now Knock-Aine in the County Limerick; and from *Leim Chucullain* (or Cuchullin's Leap), now Loop-Head, at the mouth of the river Shannon in the county of Clare, to *Sliabh Dala* mountains in Ossory, on the borders of Tipperary, Kilkenny, and Queen's County; thus comprising the present counties of Clare and Limerick, with the greater part of Tipperary; but, in after times, Thomond was confined to the present county of Clare.

Ormond was one of the large Divisions of ancient Munster. Ancient Ormond extended from *Gabhran* (now Gowran) in the county of Kilkenny, westward to *Cnamhchoill* or *Cleathchoill*, near the town of Tipperary; and from *Bearnan Eile* (now Barnanelly), a parish in the county of Tipperary (in which is situated the Devil's Bit Mountain); and from thence southward to *Oilean Ui-Bhric* or O'Bric's Island near Bonmahon, on the coast of Waterford; thus comprising the greater part of Tipperary, with parts of the counties of Kilkenny and Waterford. The name of Ormond is still retained in the two baronies of "Ormond," in Tipperary.

Desie or *Desies* was an ancient territory, comprising the greater part of Waterford, with a part of Tipperary; and got its name from the tribe of the Deisigh, also called *Desii*. These Desii were descended from Fiacha Suidhe, a brother of the Monarch Conn of the Hundred Battles; who, in Meath, possessed a large territory called from them *Deise*, or *Deise Teamrach*, that is, "Deise of Tara"—because situated near Tara; and the name of this ancient territory is still retained in the two baronies of "Deece," in the county Meath. In the reign of Cormac Mac Art, the 115th Monarch, Aongus or Æneas, Prince of Deise in Meath, and grandson of Fiacha Suidhe, resenting the exclusion of his own branch of the family from the Monarchy, waged a rebellion against Cormac Mac Art; and with a body of forces broke into the palace of Tara, wounded

56. Duach Fionn: his son ; died B.C. 893.

57. Eanna Dearg: his son ; was the 47th Monarch. In the twelfth year of his reign he died suddenly, with most of his retinue, adoring their false gods at *Sliabh Mis*, B.C. 880 years.

58. Lughaidh Iardhonn : his son.

59. Eochaidh (2) : his son.

60. Lughaidh : his son; died B.C. 831.

61. Art (2): his son ; was the 54th Monarch ; and was slain by his successor in the Monarchy, who was uncle to the former Monarch.

62. Olioll Fionn: his son.

63. Eochaidh (3) : his son.

64. Lughaidh Lagha : his son; died B.C. 730.

65. Reacht Righ-dearg: his son ; was the 65th Monarch ; and was called "Righ-dearg" or the red king, for having a hand in a woman's blood: having slain queen Macha of the line of Ir, and (see No. 64, on the "Roll of the Monarchs," page 60), the only woman that held the Monarchy of Ireland. He was a warlike Prince and fortunate in his undertakings. He went into Scotland with a powerful army to reduce to obedience the Pictish nation, then growing refractory in the payment of their yearly tribute to the Monarchs of Ireland ; which having performed, he returned, and, after twenty years' reign, was slain in battle by his Heremonian successor, B.C. 633.

66. Cobthach Caomh : son of Reacht Righ-dearg.

67. Moghcorb : his son.

68. Fearcorb : his son.

69. Adhamhra Foltcain : his son ; died, B.C. 412.

70. Niadhsedhaman : his son ; was the 83rd Monarch. In his time the wild deer were, through the sorcery and witchcraft of his mother,

Cormac, and killed his son Ceallach ; but Cormac, having quelled the rebellion in seven successive battles, drove Aongus and his accomplices into Munster, where they got settlements from Olioll Olum, then king of Munster, who granted them the lands extending from the river Suir southward to the sea, and from Lismore to *Cean Criadain*, now Creadon Head : thus comprising almost the whole of the territory afterwards called the county Waterford ; and they gave to that country the name of *Deise* or *Nandesi*, which, in Munster, was called *Deisi*, to distinguish it from *Deise*, in Meath. The Desians becoming numerous and powerful in Munster, Aongus, King of Munster in the fifth century, conferred on them additional lands, and annexed to their territory *Magh Feimin*, which extended north of the river Suir as far as *Corca Eathrach*, comprising the country called *Machaire Caisil* (or the plain of Cashel), and districts about Clonmel ; forming the present barony of Middlethird, with part of Offa, in Tipperary. The territory comprised in this grant of King Aongus was distinguished by the name of *Deise in Tuaisceart* or North Desie, and the old territory in Waterford was called *Deise Deisceart* or South Desie. The name *Desie* is still retained in the two baronies of " Decies," in the county Waterford.

Desmond : The territory called " Desmond " comprised, according to Smith in his Histories of Cork and Kerry, the whole of the present county of Cork, and the greater part of Kerry, together with a portion of Waterford, and also a small part of the south of Tipperary, bordering on Cork, called the *Eoghanact Caisil :* thus extending from Brandon Mountain, in the barony of Corcaguiney, county Kerry, to the river Blackwater, near Lismore, in the county Waterford ; but, in after times, under the Fitzgeralds, Earls of Desmond, this territory was confined to the baronies of Bear and Bantry, and other portions of the south-west of Cork, together with that part of Kerry south of the river Mang.

West Munster : The north-western part of Kerry, with a large portion of Limerick,

E

usually driven home with the cows, and tamely suffered themselves to be milked every day.

71. Ionadmaor: his son; was the 87th Monarch.

72. Lughaidh Luaighne: his son; the 89th Monarch.

73. Cairbre Lusgleathan : his son.

74. Duach Dalladh Deadha: his son; was the 91st Monarch, and (except Crimthann, the 125th Monarch, was) the last of thirty-three Monarchs of the line of Heber that ruled the Kingdom; and but one more of them came to the Monarchy—namely, Brian Boroimhe, the thirty-first generation down from this Duach, who pulled out his younger brother Deadha's eyes (hence the epithet *Dalladh*, " blindness," applied to Deadha) for daring to come between him and the throne.

75. Eochaidh Garbh: his son.

76. Muireadach Muchna: his son.

77. Mofebhis: his wife. [In the ancient Irish Regal Roll the name of Mofebhis is by mistake entered after that of her husband, instead of the name of their son, Loich Mór; and, sooner than disturb the register numbers of the succeeding names, O'Clery thought best to let the name of Mofebhis remain on the Roll, but to point out the inaccuracy.]

78. Loich Mor: son of Muireadach and Mofebhis.

79. Eanna Muncain : his son.

80. Dearg Theine : his son. This Dearg had a competitor in the Kingdom of Munster, named Darin, of the sept of Lugaidh, son of Ithe, the first (Milesian) discoverer of Ireland ; between whom it was agreed that their posterity should reign by turns, and when (one of) either of the septs was King, (one of) the other should govern in the civil affairs of the Kingdom; which agreement continued so, alternately, for some generations.

extending to the Shannon, and comprising the present baronies of Upper and Lower Connello, was called *Iar Mumhan* or West Munster. This territory is connected with some of the earliest events in Irish history. Partholan, who planted the first colony in Ireland, sailed from Greece through *Muir Toirian* (the ancient Irish name of the Mediterranean Sea), and landed on the coast of Ireland at *Inver Sceine*—now the Bay of Kenmare, in Kerry.

The Milesians of the race of Heber Fionn possessed the greater part of Munster ; but the descendants of Ithe, the uncle of Milesius of Spain, also possessed in early times a great part of that province. The race of Heber furnished most of the Kings of Munster, and many of them were also Monarchs of Ireland. The Ithians or the race of Ithe also furnished many Kings of Munster, and some of them were also Monarchs of Ireland. By the old annalists the Heberians were called *Deirgtheine*, after one of their ancient Kings of that name ; the Ithians were also called *Dairiné*, from one of their Kings so named.

The *Clan-na-Deaghaidh* settled in Munster a short time before the Christian era. They were named "Degadians," from Deagadh or Deadha their chief; and "Ernans," from Olioll Earon, a Heremonian prince in Ulster, and an ancestor of Deag (see No. 68 in the "Genealogy of the Kings of Dalriada.")

The Degadians or Ernans being expelled from Ulster by the race of Ir (or the Clan-na-Rory), went to Munster, where they were favourably received and had lands allotted to them by Duach, King of Munster, of the race of Heber, and the 91st Monarch of Ireland.

According to Keating, O'Flaherty, O'Halloran, and other historians, the *Clan-na-Deaghaidh* or Ernans became very powerful, and were the chief military commanders of Munster, and masters nearly of the entire country: some of them became Kings of Munster, and three of them also Monarchs of Ireland—namely, 1. Edersceal, 2. Conaire Mor, 3.

81. Dearg (2) : son of Dearg Theine.

82. Magha Neid : his son.

83. Eoghan Mor [Owen Mor], or Eugene the Great : his son. This Eugene was commonly called "Mogha Nuadhad," and was a wise and politic prince and great warrior.   From him *Magh-Nuadhad* (now "*Maynooth*") is so called ; where a great battle was fought between him and Conn of the Hundred Battles, the 110th Monarch of Ireland, A.D. 122, with whom he was in continual wars, until at last, after many bloody battles, he forced him to divide the kingdom with him in two equal parts by the boundary of Esker Riada—a long ridge of Hills from Dublin to Galway ; determining the south part to himself, which he called after his own name *Leath Mogha* or Mogha's Half (of Ireland), as the north part was called *Leath Cuinn* or Conn's Half ; and requiring Conn to give his daughter Sadhbh (or Sabina) in marriage to his eldest son Olioll Olum.   Beara, daughter of Heber, the great King of Castile (in Spain), was his wife, and the mother of Olioll Olum and of two daughters (who were named respectively), Caomheall and Scothniamh ; after all, he was slain in Battle by the said Conn of the Hundred Battles.

84. Olioll Olum : son of Eoghan Mor ; was the first of this line named in the Regal Roll to be king of both Munsters ; for, before him, there were two septs that were alternately kings of Munster, until this Olioll married Sabina, daughter of the Monarch Conn of the Hundred Battles, and widow of Mac Niadh, chief of the other sept of Darin, descended from Ithe, and by whom she had one son named Lughaidh, commonly called "Luy Maccon;" who, when he came to man's age, demanded from Olioll, his stepfather, the benefit of the agreement formerly made between their ancestors ; which Olioll not only refused to grant, but he also banished Maccon out of Ireland ; who retired into Scotland, where, among his many friends and relations, he soon collected a strong party, returned with them

Conaire the Second, who were respectively the 95th, 97th, and the 111th Monarchs of Ireland. This King Conaire the Second (or Conaire Mac Mogha Laine) was married to Sarad, sister of King Art Eanfhear, his successor in the Monarchy: of this marriage was Cairbre Riada, from whom were descended the Dalriadians, Princes of Dalriada in Ulster ; and who was the first King of Dalriada in Scotland, of which Loarn, the maternal grandfather of Fergus Mór Mac Earca—the founder of the Milesian Monarchy in Scotland, was the last.

About the beginning of the Christian era, Eochaidh Abhra Ruadh (or Eochy of the Red Brows or Eyelids), of the race of Heber, and a man of gigantic stature, was King of South Mun ster ; and Conrigh Mac Dairé, one of the chiefs of the Deagas or Ernans, was Prince of North Munster, and was succeeded by Cairbre Fionn Mór, son of the Monarch Conaire Mór, as King of Munster. In the second century, Eochaidh, the son of Daire, succeeded as King of both Munsters. In the same century, Eoghan Mór, the celebrate d King of Munster (also called Eoghan Taidleach or Owen the Splendid), of the race of Heber, and maternally descended from the *Clan-na-Deaga*, was a great warrior. The Clan-na-Deaga or Ernans becoming so powerful at the time, as nearly to assume the entire sovereignty of Munster—to the exclusion of the race of Heber—they were attacked and conquered by Eoghan Mór, who expelled them from Munster, except such families of them as yielded him submission.

Conn of the Hundred Battles, having succeeded Cahir Mór as (the 110th) Monarch of Ireland, had long and fierce contests with the above-named Eoghan [Owen] Mór for the sovereignty of the country ; but they at length agreed to divide the Kingdom between them, by a line drawn direct from Dublin to Galway : the northern half, consisting of the Kingdoms of Meath, Ulster, and Connaught, being Conn's share, and to Ireland, and with the help and assistance of the rest of his sept who joined with them, he made war upon Olioll; to whose assistance his (Olioll's) brother-in-law, Art-Ean-Fhear, then Monarch of Ireland, came with a good army; between whom and Maccon was fought the great and memorable battle of Magh Mucromha (or Muckrove), near Athenry, where the Monarch Art, together with seven of Olioll's nine sons, by Sabina, lost their lives, and their army was totally defeated and routed. By this great victory Maccon not only recovered his right to the Kingdom of Munster, but the Monarchy also, wherein he maintained himself for thirty years; leaving the Kingdom of Munster to his stepfather Olioll Olum, undisturbed.

After the battle, Olioll, having but two sons left alive, namely Cormac-Cas and Cian, and being very old, settled his kingdom upon Cormac, the elder son of the two, and his posterity; but soon after being informed that Owen Mór, his eldest son (who was slain in the battle of Magh Mucromha, above mentioned), had by a Druid's daughter issue, named Feach (Fiacha Maolleathan as he was called), born after his father's death, Olioll ordained that Cormac should be king during his life, and Feach to succeed him, and after him Cormac's son, and their posterity to continue so by turns; which (arrangement) was observed between them for many generations, sometimes dividing the kingdom between them, by the name of South, or North Munster, or Desmond, and Thomond.

From these three sons of Olioll Olum are descended the Hiberian nobility and gentry of Munster and other parts of Ireland; viz., from Owen Mór are descended *M'Carthy, O'Sullivan, O'Keeffe,* and the rest of the ancient nobility of Desmond; from Cormac-Cas are descended *O'Brien, MacMahon, O'Kennedy,* and the rest of the nobility and gentry of Thomond; and from Cian [Kian] are descended *O'Carroll* (of Ely-O'Carroll), *O'Meagher, O'Hara, O'Gara,* etc.

thence called *Leath Cuinn,* signifying "Conn's Half" (of Ireland); and the southern portion, or Kingdoms of Leinster and Munster, being allotted to Owen Mór, or Mogha Nuadhad, as he was called, and hence named *Leath Mogha,* or "Mogha's Half"; and this division of Ireland was long recognized in after times, and is often mentioned in the Annals of the Four Masters. But Owen Mór was afterwards defeated and forced to fly to Spain, where he lived for some time in exile; and there entering into a confederacy with Fraoch, his brother-in-law, who was Prince of Castile, they collected a powerful army with which they landed in Ireland, to recover the sovereignty from Conn of the Hundred Battles; and both armies fought a tremendous battle on the Plain of Moylena, in which Conn was victorious, and Owen Mór was slain. According to O'Flaherty, this battle was fought in the ancient barony of Fircall, in the King's County, where there are still to be seen two hillocks or sepulchral mounds, in one of which was buried the body of Owen Mór, and in the other that of Fraoch, the Spaniard, who was also slain in that battle.

Olioll Olum, son of Owen Mór, having refused to grant to Lugaidh Maccon the portion of Munster to which he was by a former arrangement entitled, Lugaidh [Luy] contended with Olioll, who defeated him and Nemeth, Prince of the Ernans, in a great battle; after which Olioll became sole King of Munster.

Lugaidh Maccon having been expelled from Munster by Olioll Olum, and banished to Britain, projected an invasion of Ireland; and, assisted by the Britons and other foreign auxiliaries under the command of Beine Briot (or Beine the Briton), who was one of the most famous warriors of that age, and son of the King of Wales, landed a powerful army in Galway. Olioll's cause was espoused by his brother-in-law Art-Ean-Fhear (then Monarch of Ireland, and the uncle of Lugaidh Maccon), and by Forga, King of Connaught; who collected their forces and fought a great battle with the

85. Owen Mór (2) : son of Olioll Olum.

86. Fiacha (or Feach) Maolleathan : his son.

87. Olioll Flann-beag : his son.   This Olioll, King of Munster for thirty years, had an elder brother, Olioll Flann-mór, who, having no issue, adopted his younger brother to be his heir ; conditionally, that his name should be inserted in the Pedigree as the father of this Olioll ; and so it is in several copies of the Munster antiquaries, with the reason thereof, as here given.

88. Lughaidh : son of Olioll Flann-beag ; had two younger brothers named Main Mun-Chain, and Daire (or Darius) Cearb ; and by a second marriage he had two sons—1. Lughach, 2. Cobthach.

89. Corc : eldest son of Lughaidh.   This Corc, to shun the unnatural love of his stepmother, fled in his youth to Scotland, where he married Mong-fionn, daughter of Feredach Fionn, otherwise called Fionn Cormac, King of the Picts (who, in Irish, are called Cruithneach or Cruithneans), by whom he had several sons, whereof Main Leamhna, who remained in Scotland, was the ancestor of "Mor Mhaor Leamhna," i.e., *Great Stewards of Lennox ;* from whom were descended the Kings of Scotland and England of the *Stewart* or *Stuart* Dynasty, and Cronan, who married Cairche, daughter of Leaghaire MacNiall, the 128th Monarch of Ireland, by whom he got territory in Westmeath, from her called "Cuircneach," now called *Dillon's Country.*

This Corc, also, although never converted to Christianity, was one of the three Kings or Princes appointed by the triennial parliament held at Tara in St. Patrick's time, "to review, examine, and reduce into order all the monuments of antiquity, genealogies, chronicles, and records of the kingdom ;" the other two being Daire or Darius, a Prince of Ulster, and Leary the Monarch.   With these three were associated for that purpose St. Patrick, St. Benignus, and St. Carioch ; together with Dubhthach,

---

foreigners, in the county of Galway, where the latter were victorious ; and after which Lugaidh Maccon became Monarch of Ireland, leaving Munster to his stepfather Olioll. In this battle the Monarch Art was slain ; and his head cut off near a brook or pool, which, from that circumstance, was called *Turloch Airt*—situated between Moyvola and Killornan in the county of Galway.   According to Connellan, the Irish kerns and galloglasses generally decapitated the chiefs they had slain in battle, as they considered no man actually dead until his head was cut off.

Olioll Olum had three sons named Eoghan, Cormac Cas and Cian [Kian] ; and by his will he made a regulation that the kingdom of Munster should be ruled alternately by one of the posterity of Eoghan (or Eugene) Mór and Cormac Cas.   This Cormac Cas was married to Oriund, daughter of King of Denmark, and by her had a son named Mogha Corb.   From Cormac Cas, king of Munster, or according to others, his descendant Cas, who was king of Thomond in the fifth century, their posterity got the name *Dal Cais,* anglicised "Dalcassians ;" the various families of whom were located chiefly in that part of Thomond which forms the present county of Clare ; and the ruling family of them were the O'Briens, Kings of Thomond.   From Eoghan, the eldest of the sons of Olioll Olum, were descended the *Eoghanachts* or "Eugenians," who were, alternately with the Dalcassians, Kings of Munster, from the third to the eleventh century.   The Eugenians possessed Desmond or South Munster.   The head family of the Eugenians were the MacCarthys, princes of Desmond.   From Cian, the third son of Olioll Olum, were descended the *Clan Cian,* who were located chiefly in Ormond ; and the chief of which families were the O'Carrolls, princes of Ely.   In the latter part of the third century, Lugaidh Meann, King of Munster, of the race of the Dalcassians, took from Connaught the territory afterwards called the county of Clare,

Fergus, and Rosse Mac Trichinn, the chief antiquaries of Ireland (at the time). From Corc, the City of *Cork* is called, according to some authors.

90. Nathfraoch : son of Corc ; had a brother named Cas.

91. Aongus or Æneas : his son. This was the first Christian King of Munster. He had twenty-four sons and twenty-four daughters, whereof he devoted to the service of God one-half of both sexes.

When this King was baptized by St. Patrick, the Saint offering to fasten his Staff or Crozier in the ground, accidentally happened to pierce the foot of Æneas through, whereby he lost much blood ; but thinking it to be part of the ceremony (of Baptism), he patiently endured it until the Saint had done. He ordained three pence per annum from every person that should be baptized throughout Munster, to be paid to St. Patrick and the Church in manner following : viz., five hundred cows, five hundred stone of iron, five hundred shirts, five hundred coverlets, and five hundred sheep, every third year. He reigned 36 years, at the end whereof he and his wife Eithne, daughter of Crimthann-Cas, King of Leinster, were slain.

92. Felim, his son ; was the second Christian King of Munster. His eleven brothers that did not enter into Religious Orders were—1. Eocha, third Christian King of Munster, ancestor of *O'Keeffe ;* 2. Dubh Ghilcach ; 3. Breasail, from whom descended the great antiquary and holy man Cormac Mac Culenan, the 39th Christian King of Munster, and Archbishop of Cashel, author of the ancient Irish Chronicles called the "Psalter of Cashel;" 4. Senach ; 5. Aodh (or Hugh) Caoch (Eithne was mother of the last three); 6. Carrthann ; 7. Nafireg ; 8. Aodh ; 9. Felim ; 10. Losian ; and 11. Dathi ; from all of whom many families are descended.

and added it to Thomond. In the seventh century, Guaire, the 12th Christian King of Connaught, having collected a great army, marched into Thomond, for the purpose of recovering the territory of Clare, which had been taken from Connaught ; and fought a great battle against the Munster forces commanded by Failbhe Flann and Dioma, Kings of Munster, but the Conacians were defeated. In the third century, Fiacha Maolleathan, King of Munster, and the grandson of Olioll Olum, had his residence at Rathnaoi, near Cashel, now called Knockraffan ; and this Fiacha granted to Cairbre Musc, son of the king of Meath, and a famous bard, as a reward for his poems, an extensive territory, called from him, *Muscrith Tire*, comprising the present baronies of "Ormond," in the county of Tipperary. The Kings of Desmond of the Eoghan or Eugenian race, were also styled Kings of Cashel, as they chiefly resided there.

The name "Cashel" (in Irish *Caisiol* or *Caiseal*) signifies *a stone fortress or castle ;* or, according to others, *a rock ;* or, as stated in Cormac's Glossary, is derived from *Cios*, rent, and *ail*, a rock, signifying the rock of tribute : as the people paid tribute there to their Kings. This Fortress of the Kings was situated on the great rock of Cashel ; and Corc, King of Munster, of the Owen Mór or Eugenian race, in the fourth century, was the first who made Cashel a royal residence. This Corc, residing sometimes in Albany, married Mongfionn, daughter of Fearadach, King of the Picts—the Princes descended from this marriage were progenitors of the earls of Lennox and Marr, who were "Great Stewards" of Scotland, and a quo the surname *Stewart.* Aongus (or Æneas), who was the first Christian King of Munster, was the grandson of this Corc. In the ninth and tenth centuries the Danes overran different parts of Ireland, and made settlements, particularly in the sea-ports of Dublin, Wexford, Waterford, Limerick, and Cork. In the middle of the tenth century, Ceallachan, King of Cashel, who was of the Eugenian race, and a celebrated warrior, carried on long and fierce contests with the Danes ; whom he defeated in many battles. Ceallachan died, A.D. 952.

93. Crimthann : his son.

94. Aodh Dubh [Duff] : his son ; reigned 15 years.

95. Failbhé Flann : his son ; was the 16th Christian King of Munster, and reigned 40 years. From this Failbhé Flann the *MacCarthy* families are descended. He had a brother named Fingin,* who reigned before him, and who is said by the Munster antiquaries, to have been the elder; this Fingin was the ancestor of *O'Sullivan*. As the seniority of these two families has been a disputed question, we here go no further in the descent of the House of Heber : we commence the " MacCarthy " genealogy with this (No. 95) Failbhé Flann ; and the " O'Sullivan " genealogy with Fingin, his brother. Each of these genealogies can be seen, *infra*, in its alphabetical order.

BRADY.

Lord Chancellor of Ireland.

Arms: Az. a saltire engr. or. betw. four martlets ar. on a chief gu. three dishes, each holding a boar's head couped of the second. *Crest:* A martlet or. charged on the breast with a trefoil slipped vert. *Motto:* Vincit pericula virtus.

SIR DENIS O'GRADY, *alias* O'BRADY, of Fassaghmore, co. Clare, who is No. 124 on the " O'Grady " genealogy, was an ancestor of this branch of that family. He had a grant from King Henry the Eighth, by Patent, in 1543, of Tomgrany, Finnagh, Killachullybeg, Killachullymor, Seanboy-Cronayn, Killokennedy, Clony, Killchonmurryan, Enocheim, Parchayne, and Kiltulla, in the county Clare ; d. in 1569. Sir Denis had four sons :

I. Edmond, who d. s. p. in 1576.

II. Donal, who also d. s. p.

III. John, who surrendered his estates to Queen Elizabeth, and from her had a regrant by Patent, in 1582. This John m. Catherine Bourke, and had :

    I. Donogh O'Grady, of Fassaghmore, from whom descended the O'Gradys of the county Limerick, and elsewhere.

IV. Right Rev. Hugh *Brady*, lord bishop of Meath, was the first of the family that omitted the sirname " O'Grady " : his descendants have since called themselves " Brady."

125. Right Rev. Hugh Brady first Protestant Bishop of Meath: fourth son of Sir Denis ; b. at Dunboyne, county Meath. Was twice m. : by his first wife Hugh had no issue ; his second wife was Alice, dau. of Sir Robert Weston, Lord Chancellor of Ireland, by whom he had three sons and a daughter :

    I. Luke, who m. Agnes Evans, and had one son and one daughter :

---

* *Fingin:* If we look to the Roll of " The Kings of Munster " (in the Appendix), under the heading " Provincial Kings," we find that Fingin, son of Hugh Dubh, is No. 14 on that Roll, while his brother Failbhe is No. 16 thereon. The MacCarthy's, in our opinion, owed the prominent position they held in Desmond at the period of the English invasion of Ireland, not to primogeniture, but to the disturbed state of Munster during the Danish wars, in which their immediate ancestors took a prominent and praiseworthy part.

I. Luke, b. at Rosscarbery.
I. Alice, who m. Laurence Clayton, of Mallow, brother of Sir Randall Clayton.
II. Nicholas, of whom presently.
III. Gerald, who m., but d. s. p.
I. Elizabeth, d. unm.

126. Nicholas, second son of Hugh; was "Escheator" of Connaught in 1606; m. and had :

127. Major Nicholas Brady, of Richmond, in Surrey; and of Bandon, co. Cork; m. Martha, dau. and heiress of Luke Gernon, Esq., of Cork (who was Second Justice of the Presidency Court of Munster, 1618—1660), and had two sons :

I. (   ), whose descendants have long been settled in England.
II. Rev. Nicholas Brady, D.D.; b. at Bandon, co. Cork, on 28th October, 1659; d. at Richmond, Surrey, on the 22nd May, 1726. This Doctor Brady published, in conjunction with Mr. Tate (Poet Laureate) the version of the Psalms which first appeared in 1698, and which still remains in the Books of Common Prayer; of him more presently.

128. Rev. Nicholas Brady, D.D. : second son of Major Nicholas; m. on the 29th June, 1690, Letitia Synge, and had four sons and four daughters :

I. Nicholas, LL.B., was Vicar of Tooting, in Surrey, d. 11th Dec., 1768, and was bur. at Clapham. He m. Martha, dau. of William Lethulier, Esq., of Clapham, and had an only son :
I. William, of Sydenham, who m. Susannah Le Keux, and d. s. p. on 12th Sept., 1773.

II. George, b. 26th July, 1705.
III. (   ) Name unknown.
IV. Thomas, of whom presently.
I. Elizabeth, m. a Mr. Morgan.
II. Letitia, m. a Mr. Woodhouse.
III. Mary, m. a Mr. Paton.
IV. Martha, d. unm.

129. Thomas Brady, of Richmond, Surrey; fourth son of Rev. Nicholas, D.D.; m. Eleanor, dau. of Rev. Dr. Cheyne, of Clapham, and had a son and a daughter :

I. Nicholas, of whom presently, b. at Richmond in 1734; and d. 18th May, 1808.
I. Letitia, who m. John Collins, Esq., of Woolmers, Herts, England.

130. Nicholas-William, the son of Thomas; m. on 4th November, 1758, Dorothea Creighton (d. 2nd Feb., 1824), of Penrith, in Cumberland, and had, with other children :

131. Francis Tempest Brady (d. 11th April, 1821), who m. on the 9th March, 1789, Charlotte (died 10th July, 1822), dau. of William Hodgson, Esq., of Castle Dawson, co. Antrim, and had three sons and eight daughters :

I. Sir Nicholas William Brady, of Willow Park, co. Dublin; b. 16th Feb., 1791; d. 28th Nov., 1843; Alderman and Lord Mayor of Dublin (1839-1840); Knighted by King George IV.; in Oct., 1815, m. Catherine-Anne-Emily (d. 12th July, 1839); dau. of Peter-Jacob Hodgson, Esq., Comptroller of the Customs, Dublin, and had four sons and two daughters :
I. Hodgson-Tempest-Francis.
II. Cheyne.
III. George.
IV. Rev. William Maziere,* D.D., formerly Rector of Newmarket, co. Cork, who,

---

* *Maziere*: Rev. William Maziere Brady, D.D., Author of " Clerical and Parochial Records of Cork, Cloyne, and Ross" (Dublin: Alexander Thom. 1863).

in 1851, m. Frances, widow of Hugh O'Reilly, Esq., of New Grove, and daughter of William Walker, Esq., of High Park, co. Dublin.

I. Elizabeth; who m. in 1852, J. H. Wharton, M.B., of Dublin.

II. Amelia.

II. Maziere, created a Baronet, and of whom presently.

III. Rev. Francis-Tempest (d. 1873), Rector of St. Mary's, Clonmel, co. Tipperary; b. 2nd Mar., 1808; m. Frances (d. 2nd June, 1854), and had two sons and five daughters:

I. Horace-Newman, b. 1843.

II. Frances-Tempest.

I. Susannah-Frances.

II. Charlotte-Isabella, who m. Ven. Archdeacon Richard John Thorpe.

III. Letitia-Dorothea, who m. Rev. W Hamilton Oswald.

IV. Anne-Frances.

V. Harriett, who, in 1879, m. Christopher J. H. Johnson, Esq., of Kirkby Overblow, in Yorkshire.

Of the eight daughters of Francis-Tempest-Brady were : 1. Elizabeth-Mary, who d. in 1789 ; 2. Dorothea, who d. in 1793 ; 3. Mary, who d. in 1793 ; 5. Charlotte, who d. in 1799 ; 6. Mary-Anne, who d. in 1817 : these five daughters d. young. The seventh and eighth daughters* were:

VII. Dorothea (d. 1874), who on the 1st June, 1842, m. the Rev. David Carlyle Courtney, Rector of Glenarm, co. Antrim, and had issue.

VIII. Charlotte (d. 1876), who on the 21st Sept., 1825, m. John Mollan, M.D., of Fitzwilliam square, Dublin.

132. Sir Maziere Brady, Bart., Lord Chancellor of Ireland : second

son of Francis-Tempest; b. 20th July, 1796. Was twice m.: first, on the 26th July, 1823, to Elizabeth-Anne (d. 15th June, 1858), dau. of Bever Buchanan, Esq., of Dublin, and had two sons and three daughters:

I. Francis-William, the present Baronet, of whom presently.

II. Maziere-John, Barrister-at-Law ; b. 28th Sept., 1826 ; m. in 1853 Elizabeth, youngest dau. of Rev. Robert Longfield, of Castlemary, co. Cork, and had:

I. Robert-Maurice, Lieutenant, in Royal Artillery ; b. 13th Dec., 1854.

II. William-Longfield, b. 16th July, 1863.

I. Emily-Augusta-Mary, who on 4th Nov., 1879, m. H. C. Philpotts, Esq., R.H.A., eldest son of Lieut.-General Philpotts, R.H.A., and grandson of Henry Philpotts, Bishop of Exeter.

II. Maud-Cherry-Elizabeth.

The three daughters of Sir Maziere Brady, Bart., were :

I. Eleanor, who on the 20th July, 1853, m. the Rev. Benjamin Hale Puckle, Rector of Graffham, Huntingdonshire.

II. Charlotte-Louisa, who in 1864, m. the Rev. John Westropp Brady, Rector of Slane, county Meath.

III. Eliza-Anne.

Sir Maziere Brady, m. secondly, on 15th Dec., 1860, Mary, second dau. of the Right Honbl. John Hatchell, of Fortfield, Terenure, co. Dublin ; and was created a Baronet on the 19th Jan., 1869 ; he d. 13th April, 1871.

133. Sir Francis-William Brady, Q.C., D.L., County Court Judge for the county of Tyrone, and living in 1887 : elder son of Sir Maziere ;

---

* *Daughters :* We have not ascertained the fourth daughter's name.

m. on the 7th Nov., 1847, Emily-Elizabeth, youngest dau. of the Right Rev. Samuel Kyle, Bishop of Cork, and has had issue:

I. Maziere-Kyle, b. 25th Mar., 1849.

I. Marion-Eleanor.

134. Maziere-Kyle Brady, Capt. R.E.: son of Sir Francis William; b. 25th March, 1849, and living in 1887.

BRENAN.

Of O'Brenan, County Kerry.

Arms: Gu. two lions ramp. combatant supporting a garb or. in chief two swords in saltier, and one in fesse ppr. *Crest:* An arm in armour embowed, the hand grasping a dagger, all ppr. *Motto:* Virtute et operibus.

1. JOHN BRENAN, of O'Brenan, co. Kerry, interred in the churchyard of St. Michan's, Dublin, in 1699; father of:

2. Daniel Brenan, married to Mary Anne O'Sullivan; will proved, 1721; father of:

I. James Brenan, Doctor of Physick, born 1635, old style; married to a daughter of the Hon. Richard Barnewell, of Turvey. By his will, proved 1738, he directs his mortal remains to be "interred in his family's burial place, St. Michan's Churchyard, in the *Suburbs of Dublin.*" He left a daughter, Anne, who d. young.

II. John Brenan, born 1700, O.S.; interred in St. Michan's, 1732, O.S.

III. Daniel Brenan, born 1702, O.S.; died s.p.

IV. Catherine, born 1703, O.S.

V. Peter Brenan, Chirurgeon, born 1705, O.S.; founder, in 1738, of St. Catherine's Hospital, Meath Street, which was united with St. Nicholas's Hospital, Francis Street, in 1765. Living in Kennedy's Lane, 1763 (Gilbert's History of Dublin);

will proved 1767. He left a dau. Jane, who died young.

VI. Rev. Thomas Brenan, S.J., born 1708, O.S., entered the Roman Province of the Society of Jesus, 1725; returned to Ireland 1744; employed in one of the Parish Churches of Dublin for nearly ten years, and gained distinction as a preacher; Superior of the Irish Seminary at Rome, 1754; Rector of a Jesuit College in Derbyshire, 1769, and died there in 1773, shortly after the suppression of his Order.

3. Charles Brenan, born 1707; will proved 1767; father of:

I. Martha, born 1741, who m., in 1762, Nicholas Keatinge, who died in 1767, leaving Maurice Keatinge, Q.C., who was father of the Right Hon. Richard Keatinge, Judge of the Probate Court, and a Privy Chancellor of Ireland; b. 1793, d. 1876.

II. Mary-Anne, a spinster, born 1750, will proved 1825.

III. Eleanor, married in 1785, to Quin Braughall; will proved 1824.

4. Catherine Brenan, born 1757,

died 1832 ; married in 1780, to Don. John Brett, of Coltrummer, Brevet-Colonel of the Regiment of Hibernia in the Spanish Service, who left issue :

I. Jane, born 1783, died 1853 ; married to Mark Monsarrat, and left issue.

II. Catherine, born 1785, died 1834 ; married to William Allen, and left issue.

III. Alicia, born 1786 : married to Joseph O'Meagher, in 1827, died 1867 : had issue :

I. John William O'Meagher, born 1829; died 1854, un-married.

II. Joseph Casimir O'Meagher, born 1831, living 1887.

III. Alicia (living in 1883); married to Michael John O'Grady, Esq.

CARROLL. (No. 1.)

Of Maryland, United States, America.

Arms : Gu. two lions ramp. combatant ar. supporting a sword point upwards ppr. pommel and hilt or. *Crest :* On the stump of an oak tree sprouting, a hawk rising all ppr. belled or.

IN the "Journal of the Royal Historical and Archæological Association of Ireland," for October, 1883, No. 56 (Vol. VI., 4th Series), is given a very interesting paper, communicated by the learned Frederick John O'Carroll, A.B., Barrister-at-Law, and entitled " *Stemmata Carrollana*, being the true version of the Pedigree of Carroll of Carrollton, and correcting that erroneously traced by Sir William Betham, late Ulster King-of-Arms." That Pedigree commences with Fionn (slain 1205), who is No. 114 on the " O'Carroll" (Princes of Ely) Pedigree ; and proceeds, as follows :

114. Fionn, King of Ely (slain 1205), who had :

115. Teige, Chief of Ely, who had (Maolruanaidh and) Donal who settled at Litterluna.

116. Donal, Chief of Ely, who had :

117. Donough Dhearg (d. 1306), Chief of Ely, who had :

118. William Alainn (the Hand-some), chief of Ely, who had :

119. Donough (d. 1377), Chief of Ely, who had :

120. Roderic, who had :

121. Daniel, who had :

122. Roderic,* who had :

123. Donough,* who had :

124. Teige, who had :

125. Donough, who had :

126. Daniel, who had :

127. Anthony, who had :

128. Daniel of Litterluna, who had four sons : I. Anthony ; II. Charles ; III. Thomas ; IV. John, who d. in 1733.

I. Anthony, of Lisheenboy, in the co. Tipperary (will proved 1724), who had four sons :

I. Daniel.

II. Michael.

---

* *Roderic and Donough :* Omitting these two names, this pedigree corresponds exactly with the *Linea Antiqua*, and, says Mr. F. J. O'Carroll, " it is actually so given in another part of the Carrollton MS. A comparison of the dates with the number of generations, however, corroborates the accuracy of the version given in this text."

III. James, a Captain in Lord Dongan's Regiment of Dragoons, from whom descend : Anthony R. Carroll, and Redmond F. Carroll, of Dublin ; and Alfred Ludlow Carroll, of New York.

IV. Charles (will proved 1724).

II. Charles: second son of Daniel ; settled in Maryland, in 1688. (See No. 129.)

129. Charles: second son of Daniel ; received a large grant of land in Maryland, and arrived there 1st Oct., 1688, with a commission constituting him Attorney-General. He m. a dau. of Colonel Henry Darnall, a Kinsman of Lord Baltimore, and was appointed by that nobleman his Agent and Receiver-Gen.

130. Charles : son of Charles.

131. Charles, who d. 1833: his son ; was the last survivor* of the Signers of American Independence,† in 1776.

This Charles left one son and two daughters,—1. Mary, married to Richard Caton‡ of Maryland ; 2.

---

* *Survivor:* This is the Charles Carroll, Maryland's "First Citizen," who was the only Signer that fearlessly wrote his address on the Declaration of American Independence ; " as became him, he was the most earnest and active in every measure taken in opposition to the encroachments of the British Government." His latest words were :

" I have lived to my 96th year, I have enjoyed continued health, I have been blessed with great wealth, prosperity, and most of the good things which the world can bestow—public approbation, esteem, applause : but what I now look back on with the greatest satisfaction to myself is, that I have practised the duties of my religion."

The line of Carroll of the Caves, expired, says Mr. F. J. O'Carroll, in the male line in the person of Charles, son of Charles Carroll, of Annapolis (the descendant of the celebrated Ferganainm O'Carroll) . . . " and is now represented, through the female line, by General John Carroll of ' The Caves,' Baltimore, the name ' Carroll' having been assumed in compliance with the will of the last male representative in bequeathing his vast estates and possessions."

† *Independence :* The following were the Signatories to the " Declaration of American Independence," in Congress, on the 4th July, 1776 :—1. John Adams. 2. Samuel Adams. 3. Josiah Bartlet. 4. Carter Braxton. 5. Charles Carroll, of Carrollton (the Charles Carroll above-mentioned). 5. Samuel Chase. 6. Abra. Clarke. 7. George Clymer. 8. William Ellery. 9. William Floyof. 10. Elbridge Gerry. 11. Button Gwinnett. 12. Lyman Hall. 13. John Hancock. 14. Benjamin Harrison. 15. John Hart. 16. Joseph Hewes. 17. Stephen Hopkins. 18. Fras. Hopkinson. 19. Samuell Huntington. 20. Th. Jefferson. 21. Thomas M. Kean. 22. Francis Lightfoot Lee. 23. Richard Henry Lee. 24. Faans. Lewis. 25. Phil. Livingston. 26. Thomas Lynch, jun. 27. Thomas Mayward, jun. 28. Arthur Middleton. 29. Lewis Morris. 30. Robert Morris. 31. John Morton. 32. Thos. Nelson, jun. 33. Wm. Paca. 34. Robert Francis Paine. 35. George Read. 36. Casar Rodney. 37. George Ross. 38. Benjamin Rush. 39. Edward Rutlidge. 40. Roger Shearman. 41. James Smith. 42. Richard Stockton. 43. Thos. Stone. 44. Geo. Taylor. 45. Matthew Thornton. 46. Geo. Walton. 47. Wm. Whipple. 48. Wm. Williams. 49. James Wilson. 50. Jns. Withinpoole. 51. Oliver Wolcott, and 52. George Wythe.

‡ *Richard Caton :* This Richard Caton had by his wife Mary Carroll four daughters —Marianne, Elizabeth, Louisa, Katherine, and Emily. Marianne married Robert Patterson, and afterwards, on Oct. 25, 1825, Richard Colley, Marquis of Wellesley, the eldest son of Garrett, the first Earl of Mornington. The Marquis was Lord Lieutenant of Ireland, Governor-General of India, and the elder brother of Arthur Wellesley, the Duke of Wellington. Elizabeth married Baron Stafford, and Louisa Katherine married first Sir Felton Bathurst Hervey, Baronet, and after his death, in 1828, she wedded Francis Godolphin D'Arcy, the seventh Duke of Leeds. Emily married John Mactavish, for a long time the British Consul in Baltimore, and father of Charles Carroll Mactavish, who married a daughter of the late Lieutenant-General Winfield Scott.

Catherine. m. to General Robert Goodloe Harper,* of South Caroline.

132. Charles Carroll of Carrollton Manor: only son of Charles of Carrollton ; m. Harriet, dau. of the Hon. Benjamin Chew, Chief Justice of Pennsylvania; had four daughters —Mary Carroll, who married Richard H. Bayard ; Louisa Carroll, who married Mr. Jackson ; Harriet Carroll, who married the Hon. John Lee ; and Elizabeth Carroll, who married Dr. Richard Tucker.

133. Charles Carroll: son of Charles ; in October, 1825, married Mary Diggs Lee, a granddaughter of the Hon. Sim Lee, the second Governor of Maryland. This Charles Carroll had several children, viz.—Mary, Charles, Thomas-Lee,

the Hon. John Lee, Louisa, Oswald, Albert-Henry, a second Thomas-Lee Carroll, Robert Goodloe, Harper Carroll, and Helen-Sophia. Thomas-Lee Carroll and Oswald Carroll died young. Mary Carroll, in 1866, married Dr. Acosta, and resides in Paris. Governor John-Lee Carroll, April 24th, 1856, married Anita Phelps, the daughter of Royal Phelps, a prominent merchant of New York. She died March 24th, 1873, and Governor Carroll, in April, 1877, married Miss Mary Carter Thompson, the daughter of the late Judge Lucas P. Thompson, of Staunton Va, and a sister of the wife of his brother Charles. Louisa Carroll, in 1858, married George Cavendish Taylor.

CARROLL. (No. 2.)

Of Ely O'Carroll.

Arms: Ar. two lions ramp. combatant gu, supporting a sword point upwards ppr. pommel and hilt or.   *Crest:* On the stump of an oak-tree sprouting, a hawk rising, all ppr. belled or.   *Motto ;* In fide et in bello forte.

DANIEL CARROLL, of Litterluna, who is No. 128 on the pedigree of "Carroll of Maryland," United States, America, had four sons: 1. Anthony of Lisheenboy ; 2. Charles, who settled in Maryland in 1688 ; 3. Thomas (of whom presently) ; and 4. John, who d. 1733. [For the descendants of (1) Anthony of Lisheenboy, and of (2) Charles, who settled in Maryland in 1688, see " Carroll of Maryland " pedigree.]

129. Thomas: third son of Daniel of Litterluna ; was Lieut.-Colonel in King James's Army, Commander of Carroll's Dragoons, was killed at the battle of the Boyne on 1st July, 1690 ; m. and had :

I. Thomas, of whom presently.
II. John.

130. Thomas: son of Thomas ; m. and had :

I. John (b. 1708), m. Sarah, dau. of Henry and Sarah Greer, of Lisacurran.

II. Edward, of whom presently.

131. Edward (b. 1715), who in 1738 m. Sarah, dau. of Archibald and Jane Bell, of Trummery, and had five sons and five daus.   Of the sons were :

I. John, of whom presently.

------

* *Harper* : Three children by his wife Catherine Carroll survived General Harper, viz. :—Charles, who married Miss Chafelle, of South Carolina ; Robert, who died on board of one of the packets returning from Europe ; and Emily.

II. Edward (b. 1750), who in 1775 m., and went to and settled in America in 1801. Had five sons and one dau.; his fourth son Thomas, M.D., of Cincinnati, m. and had among other children, Robert-William, Counsellor-at-law, now of Cincinnati, who m. and has three sons and two daus.

132. John, of Hyde Park, Cork: son of Edward (131); b. 1740; on the 19th April, 1776, m. Sarah, dau. of Charles and Deborah Corfield, and had five sons and two daus. Of the sons were:

I. Joshua, of whom presently.

II. Thomas (b. 1784), m. in 1816 Mary Hatton, and had three sons and one dau. Of these sons, Joseph the second son, now of Cork, m. his cousin Caroline Hatton, and has three sons.

133. Joshua: son of John (132); b. 1777; on the 6th June, 1805, m. Sarah, dau. of John Barcroft, and Sarah Haughton, of Cleve Hill, Cork, and had three sons and four daus. The sons were:

I. John (b. 1807), m. in 1832 Janetta Hargrave, and had two sons and two daus.

II. Barcroft Haughton, d. unm.

III. William (b. 1814), m. his cousin Susan Eliza Grubb, of Cahir Abbey, and had one son and one dau. The daus. of Joshua were:

I. Helena, of whom presently.

II. Susan, m. Alexander Lawe.

III. Elizabeth, m. Henry Olliffe, brother of Sir Joseph Olliffe.

IV. Mary Anne, m. Thomas Manly.

134. Helena: eldest daughter of Joshua (133); b. 1811; on the 19th May, 1836, m. Alfred Greer, J.P., Dripsey House, Co. Cork, and had five sons, the eldest of whom was Thomas, No. 135 on this pedigree.

135. Thomas Greer (b. 4th April, 1837), of Sea Park, Carrickfergus, J.P., and late M.P. for Carrickfergus; m. 28th July, 1864, Margaret, only child of John and Jane Owden, of Sea Park, Co. Antrim, and niece of Sir Thomas Scambler Owden; living in 1887. (For the children of this Thomas Greer see the "Greer" Pedigree).

CASEY. (No. 1.)

Of Munster.

Arms : Ar. a chev. betw. three eagles' heads erased gu.   *Crest :* A hand fesseways issuing from a cloud.   *Motto ;* Per varios casus.

CORMAC, a brother of Conla, who is No. 87 on the "O'Carroll Ely" pedigree, was the ancestor of *O'Cathasaigh, i.e.,* Na Saithne; anglicised *Casey.**

87. Cormac: son of Tadhg (or Teige).

88. Gailineach ("gailineach": Irish, *flattering*)*:* his son; a quo *O'Gailineigh,* anglicised *Galinagh.*

89. Glasaradh: his son.

90. Faghad: his son.

91. Ionrosa: his son.

92. Beag: his son.

93. Brogan: his son.

* *Casey :* The patrimony of this family was at Coiltemabhreenagh, in the parish of Mitchelstown, barony of Brigown, and county of Cork.

94. Fionnachtach: his son.
95. Lulagh (or Lulgach): his son.
96. Echtbran: his son.
97. Feargus: his son.
98. Broghurban: his son.

99. Corcran: his son.
100. Maolmichil: his son.
101. Cathasach (" cathasach " : Irish, *brave*)*:* his son ; a quo *O'Cathasaigh.*
102. Gairbith: his son.

CASEY. (No. 2.)

Of Dublin, Westmeath, and Longford.

Arms : Ar. a chevron between three falcons' heads erased, gu. *Crest :* A hand fesseways, issuing from a cloud.

ROBERT CASSE married Margaret Caddle, and had:

2. William, who married Joanna, daughter of —— Blanchfield, and had:

3. Stephen, who m. Anastace Young, and had:

1. Stephen, of whom presently;
2. Symon, who married Margaret, daughter of —— Cleere, and had two children — one of whom was John, who married Honora White, and had a daughter Anastasia.

4. Stephen (2): the elder son of Stephen ; m. Kath. Morphee, and had: 1. John, of whom presently;

2. Patrick, who had William, who had Margaret.

5. John : the elder son of Stephen (2); m. Rose, dau. of —— Cantwell, and had:

6. John, who m. Alsona Swaine, and had:

7. Stephen (3), who m. Lucia Walsh, and had: 1. Lawrence, of whom presently ; 2. Joanna, who m. George Burke.

8. Lawrence : son of Stephen (3); was Supervisor of the Port of Dublin ; m. Joanna Andrews, and had:

9. William Casey, of Ballygaveran.

This family is descended from the same ancestor as "Casey" No. 1. These O'Caseys were lords of Saithne, in the County of Dublin (a territory which was co-extensive with the barony of Balrothery, West), of which they were dispossessed by DeLacy at the time of the Anglo-Norman Invasion :

O'er Saithne of Spears (here Delvan rolls his flood),
O'Casey rules, whose sword is stained with blood.—*O'Dugan.*

The O'Caseys were also styled lords of Magh Breagh or Bregia, which comprised five of the thirteen Triocha Ceads of the ancient principality of Meath. Saithne was a subdivision of Bregia of which the O'Caseys assumed sovereign authority. Bregia extended from Dublin City to Beallach Brec, west of Kells, and from the Hill of Howth, to the mountain of Fuad on the south of Ulster. We read in the Irish Annals, that :

A.D. 1018. Oisin O'Casey, lord of Saithne and Fingal, was slain.
1023. Ainbeth, lord of Saithne, was slain.
1049. Torloch O'Casey was put to death.

1045-1061. Mention is made of Garvey O'Casey, "lord of Breagh."

1066. Mulcarn O'Casey, lord of Bregia, was slain.

1073. Maolmora O'Casey, lord of Breagh, and his kinsman Ruark O'Casey, were killed in a domestic feud.

1140. Donal, lord of Saithne, died, and was succeeded by his brother Flatherty.

1146. Cathasach O'Casey; and Cormac O'Casey, Archbishop of Leinster, died.

1153. Donal O'Casey, lord of Saithne, was slain.

1171. Ivar O'Casey's wife died, she was named Tailté, and was dau. of O'Melaghlin, King of Meath.

1179. Ivar died.

1323. Giolla Airnin O'Casey, erenach of Cluan-da-rath, died. This place is now named Clondra, barony of Longford.

1381. Thomas *Casey*, Governor of Athlone Castle, for the English.

1388. Thomas *Casey*, Governor, died; his son John succeeded him.

1367. William O'Casey was consecrated Bishop of Ardagh.

1370. William, Bishop of Ardagh, died; was interred in his Cathedral.

1542. Thomas *Casey* obtained from Henry VIII. a grant of the Carmelite Monastery of Athboy, Co. Meath, with all the appurtenances, including a Castle. The country around Athboy was called *Leuighne;* it forms and gives name to the now barony of "Lune," Co. Meath.

CLANCY.

Of Munster.

Arms : Ar. two lions pass. guard. in pale gu.   *Crest :* A hand couped at the wrist erect, holding a sword impailing a boar's head couped all ppr.

NIALL or Neal, brother of Menmon who is No. 106 on the "Macnamara" pedigree, was the ancestor of *MacFlancha,** which is anglicised *Clanchy, Clancie, Clancy, Mac Clancy, Clinch,* and *Glancy.*

106. Niall: son of Aodh (or Hugh) odhar; a quo the Hy-Niall (or *O'Neill*), of Munster.

107. Flancha: his son; a quo *MacFlancha.*

108. Donal: his son.

109. Gilloilbhe ("oilbheim": Irish, *a reproach*) : his son.

110. Flaitheamh : his son.

111. Gilloilbhe (2) : his son.

112. Flaitheambh (2) : his son.

113. Flathrigh (*flath :* Irish, " a chief", and *righ,* "a king"; Corn. *ruy ;* Arm. *rue ;* Hind. *raj-a ;* Lat. *rex ;* Fr. *roi*) : his son; a quo *O'Flathrigh,* anglicised *Flattery.*

---

* *MacFlancha :* The root of this name is the Irish word "Flann," genitive, "flainn" [floin or flin], *blood ;* and the name itself means "the descendants of the red-complexioned man." Besides *MacFlancha* the following surnames are derived from the same prolific root: Flanagan, Flannagan, Flinn, Flynn, Glenn, Glynn, Linn, Lynn, Macklin, Maglin, Magloin, McGloin.

114. Diarmaid (or Dermod) : his son.

115. Lacneach : his son ; had two brothers—1. Hugh, and 2. Donal.

116. Hugh : son of Lacneach.

117. Donal : his son.

118. Hugh (2) : his son.

119. Murtagh : his son.

120. Baothach (latinized Boetius) : his son.

121. Hugh (3) : his son.

122. Baothach (2) : his son.

123. Baothach (3) Clancy : his son.

COGHLAN.

Lords of Delvin.

Arms : Gu. two lions pass. counter pass. ar.   *Crest* : A fret or.

DEALBHA* (or Dealbhaoth), a brother of Blad who is No. 92 on the "O'Brien" (of Thomond) pedigree, was the ancestor of *MacCoghlain;* anglicised *Coghlan, Coghlen*, and *MacCoghlan*.†

92. Dealbha : the ninth son of Cas.

93. Aedhan : his son ; had a brother named Gnobog, who was the ancestor of *O'Curry*.

94. Bilé (or Beg) : his son.

95. Anbhile : his son.

96. Sioda : his son.

97. Trean : his son.

98. Treachar : his son.

99. Dathal (or Dathin) : his son.

100. Lorcan : his son.

101. Cochlan ("cochal" : Irish, *a cowl* or *hood*) : his son ; a quo *MacCochlain*.

102. Maol-Michil : his son.

103. Cochlan (2) : his son.

104. Fionn : his son.

105. Fuathmaran : his son.

106. Fogartach : his son.

107. Anbheith : his son.

108. Gormogan : his son.

109. Laithgheal : his son.

110. Cochlan MacCoghlan : his son ; the first who assumed this sirname.

111. Murtach : his son.

112. Longseach : his son.

113. Aodh (or Hugh) : his son.

114. Conchobhar (or Connor) mór: his son.

115. Conor oge : his son.

116. Amhailgadh [Awly] : his son.

117. Melachlin : his son.

118. Donal : his son.

119. Conor (3) : his son.

120. Shane (or John) : his son.

121. Melachlin (2) : his son.

122. Felim : his son.

123. Melachlin (3) : his son.

124. Cormac : his son.

125. Art : his son.

126. John (2) : his son.

127. John oge MacCoghlan : his son.

128. Torlogh : his son ; the last lord of Delvin ; living in 1620.

---

* *Dealbha* : From this Dealbha the territories of the "seven Dealbhnas" (part of the King's County) are so called ; and now go by the name of *Delvin* : whereof his posterity were Lords, until dispossessed, during the Commonwealth, by Oliver Cromwell.

† See the "MacCoghlan" pedigree.

F

COGHLAN.

Of Drym, County Roscommon.

Armorial Bearings: Same as "Coghlan," lords of Delvin.

DERMOD COGHLAN, of Drym, county Roscommon, had:

2. Richard, who had:

3. John, of Drym, who d. 28th Feb., 1637. He m. Kath. dau. of Edmond Malone, of Buolynchoan, gent., and had:

I. Tibot, of whom presently.

II. Richard, who m. Anne, dau. of Melaghlin Dalaghan, in the co. Roscommon.

4. Tibot Coghlan: son of John; m. Anne, daughter of John Leigh O'Molloy, of Ahadonoh, county Roscommon, gent.

CONNELL.

Of Desmond.

Arms: Ar. a chev. gu. betw. two spurs in chief, and a battle-axe in base az. shaft or. *Crest*: A bee erect ppr. *Motto*: Non sibi.

FAOLGURSA, a brother of Daologach who is No. 98 on the "MacCarthy Mór" pedigree, was the ancestor of *Cineal Connaill*; anglicised *Connell*, *Connelly*, and *MacConnell*.

98. Faolgursa: son of Nathfraoch.

99. Dongeallach: his son.

100. Sneaghra: his son.

101. Conall (" conall": Irish, *love*): his son; a quo *Cineal Con. naill.*

102. Domhnall: his son.

103. Artgal: his son.

104. Cuirc: his son.

105. Corcran: his son.

106. Cudlighean: his son.

107. Lorcan: his son.

CONROY.

Of Munster.

Arms: Gu. three bends ar. on a chief or, as many cinquefoils az. *Crest*: A lion ramp. vert supporting a pennon gu.

DEALBHAOTH, a brother of Blad who is No. 92 on the "O'Brien" (of Thomond) pedigree, was the ancestor of *MacConroi* of Munster; anglicised *Conroy*, *Conry*, and *MacConry*.

92. Dealbhaoth: son of Cas, *i.e.*, Tal.

93. Gno Mór: his son.

94. Mothan: his son.

95. Maoltuile: his son.

96. Saraan: his son.

97. Comhghal: his son.

98. Dungallach: his son.

99. Dongus: his son.

100. Innealach: his son.

101. Lorcan: his son.

102. Luighdheach: his son.

103. Cas: his son.

104. Sioda: his son.

105. Baodan: his son.
106. Luighdheach: his son.
107. Amhalgadh: his son.
108. Cu-Ri: his son.
109. Conchobhar: his son.
110. Diarmaid: his son.
111. Feargus: his son.
112. Donchadh: his son.
113. Cu-Ri ("cu," gen, "con:")

Irish, *a warrior;* "Ri," *a King*):
his son; a quo *MacConroi.*
114. Feargus: his son.
115. Donchadh: his son.
116. Donchadh: his son.
117. Conchobhar: his son.
118. Donchadh: his son.
119. Conchobhar: his son.

CORMAC.
Of Munster.

Arms: Az. three bezants in pale betw. two palets ar. a chief or.   *Crest*: A hand couped in fesse holding a sword in pale on the point thereof a garland of laurel all ppr.

NATHI, a brother of Felim who is No. 92 on the "MacCarthy Mór" pedigree, was the ancestor of *Cineal Cormaic;* anglicised *Cormac, Cormack,* and *Cormick.*

92. Nathi: son of Aongus.
93. Feareadhach: his son.
94. Cabhsan: his son.
95. Cormac (" cormac :" Irish, *a brewer*): his son; a quo *Cineal Cormaic.*

96. Ronan: his son.
97. Cucearthach: his son.
98. Cudruin: his son.

CULLEN.
Of Munster.

Arms: Gu. on a chev. betw. three dexter hands erect couped at the wrist ar. a garb betw. two trefoils slipped vert.   *Crest*: A mermaid with comb and mirror all ppr.

DONN, brother of Brian who is No. 93 on the " Keely" pedigree, was the ancestor of *O'Coilean;* which has been anglicised *Colin, Collin, Collins, Culhane, Cullen,* and *O'Cullen.*

93. Donn: son of Caolluighe.
94. Dunaghach: his son.
95. Ainnir: his son.
96. Coilean an Catha (" coilean :" Irish, *a young warrior*), meaning "the young war dog:" his son; a quo *O'Coilean.*
97. Conor: his son.
98. Dermod: his son.
99. Teige O'Cullen: his son; who settled in Carbery and first assumed this surname.

100. Coilean-caonra: his son.
101. Donall: his son.
102. Conor mór: his son.
103. Conor oge: his son.
104. Teige Mhaighe o-Nagrain: his son.
105. Giolla Lachtghi: his son.
106. Niall: his son.
107. Randall: his son.
108. Randall (2): his son.
109. Dermod O'Cullen: his son.

CURRY.

Arms : Az. a lion pass. guard. or. *Crest :* An arm in armour embowed, holding a spear, all ppr.

GNOBOG, brother of Aedhan who is No. 93 on the "Coghlan" pedigree, was the ancestor of *O'Curaidh ;* anglicised *Corey, Cory,* and, more lately, *Curry, Currie, O'Curry,* and *O'Corra.**

93. Gnobog : son of Dealbha.

94. Baodan : his son.

95. Maithan : his son.

96. Maoltuile : his son.

97. Saraan : his son.

98. Aodh : his son.

99. Dungal : his son.

100. Dungus : his son.

101. Innealach : his son.

102. Luachan† : his son.

103. Lughaidh : his son.

104. Cas : his son.

105. Sioda : his son.

106. Baodan (2) : his son.

107. Lughaidh (2) : his son.

108. Amhailgadh (or Awly) : his son.

109. Curadh (" curadh,"‡ Irish, *a valiant champion*) : his son ; a quo *O'Curaidh.*

110. Conor : his son.

111. Diarmaid (Dermod) O'Corey : his son : the first who assumed this sirname.

112. Fergus : his son.

113. Donoch (Donogh) : his son.

114. Curadh (2) : his son.

115. Fergus (2) : his son.

116. Donogh (2) : his son.

117. Donough (3) : his son.

* *O'Corra :* Of this family was *John Curry,* M.D., a distinguished Catholic physician and writer, who was born in Ireland early in the 18th century. He was descended from the O'Corra family, of Cavan, who lost their estates in the wars of 1641-1652, and 1689-1691. His grandfather, a cavalry officer in James's army, fell at the battle of Aughrim. Disqualified by his religion from obtaining a degree in Ireland (on account of the stringency of the Penal Laws against Catholics), Doctor John Curry went to Paris, there studied medicine for several years, and took his diploma at Rheims. Returning to practise in Ireland, he rose to eminence as a physician ; and took up his pen in defence of his co-religionists. The incident that impelled him to do so is thus related by his editor, Charles O'Connor : " In October, 1746, as he passed through the Castle-yard on the memorial day of the Irish rebellion of 1641, he met two ladies, and a girl of about eight years of age, who, stepping on a little before them, turned about suddenly, and, with uplifted hands and horror in her countenance, exclaimed—*Are there any of those bloody Papists in Dublin?* This incident, which to a different hearer would be laughable, filled the Doctor with anxious reflections. He immediately inferred that the child's terror proceeded from the impression made on her mind by the sermon preached on that day in Christ Church, whence those ladies had proceeded ; and having procured a copy of the sermon, he found that his surmise was well founded." He combated such bitter prejudices in a *Dialogue,* the publication of which created a great sensation, and it was replied to by Walter Harris. Dr. Curry rejoined in his *Historical Memoirs.* In 1775, he published anonymously *An Historical and Critical Review of the Civil Wars in Ireland.* With Mr. Wyse, Mr. O'Conor, and a few more, Dr. Curry was one of the founders of the first Catholic Committee, which in March, 1760, met privately at the Elephant Tavern in Essex-street, Dublin—the forerunner of the powerful Catholic Associations which seventy years afterwards, under O'Connell, achieved Emancipation. He died in 1780. Two of his sons were officers in the Austrian service.—For further information on this subject, see Webb's valuable work—*Compendium of Irish Biography* (Dublin : Gill and Son, 1878).

† *Luachan :* A quo *O'Luachain* ("luach" : Irish, *price*), anglicised *Price.*

‡ *Curadh :* This word is derived from the Irish obsolete substantive *cur,* "power," "manliness"; and from it some genealogists incorrectly derive *Conry* (see "Conroy").

118. Donal: his son.
119. Conor (2): his son.

120. Donal (2): his son.
121. Conor O'Curry: his son.

DALLAN.

CUIRC, a brother of Macbroc who is No. 92 on the "Lyons" pedigree, was the ancestor of *O'Dallain,* anglicised *Dallan.*

92. Cuirc: son of Eachdhach Liathan.
93. Corbaire Cul: his son.
94. Dallan ("dallan": Irish, *one who is blind*): his son; a quo *O'Dallain.*
95. Aonghus: his son.

96. Ceannfoda: his son.
97. Cairbre Sionach: his son.
98. Fiacha: his son.
99. Crunmaol: his son.
100. Aigneach: his son.
101. Cuan: his son.

DORAN.

Arms: Per pale sa. and ar. a boar pass. counterchanged, on a chief az. three mullets of the second. *Crest*: Out of a ducal coronet or, a lion's head proper.

CATHAL, a brother of Maccraith who is No. 109 on the "O'Sullivan Vera" pedigree, was the ancestor of *O'Dheorain* ("deor": Irish, *a tear*; "an," *one who*); anglicised *Doran.*

109. Cathal: son of Buadhach.
110. Giolla Padraic: his son.
111. Niall: his son.
112. Conchobhar: his son.
113. Maolfhionnan: his son.
114. Saorbreathach: his son.

115. Domhnall: his son.
116. Uilliam Dearg: his son.
117. Seaan: his son.
118. Uilliam: his son.
119. Muircheartach Buidhe: his son.

DOWNS.

Arms: Ar. three palets gu. *Crest*: A wolf's head erased ppr. charged on the neck with a mullet ar.

BROCAN, a younger brother of Lughaidh who is No. 88 on the "O'Hara" (No. 1) pedigree, was the ancestor of *O'Duana*; anglicised *Doan, Downs, Duaine, Duane, Devan, Dwain,* and *Hooke.*

88. Brocan ("brocan": Irish, *a little badger*): third son of Cormac Galeng; a quo *O'Brocain,* anglicised *Brogan.*
89. Talglaine: his son.
90. Gosda: his son.
91. Finghin: his son.

92. Blathmac: his son.
93. Baodan: his son.
94. Crunmaol: his son.
95. Maoinach: his son.
96. Colgan: his son.
97. Crunmaol (2): his son.
98. Robartach: his son.

99. Ruadhrach : his son.

100. Aonachan ("aonach" : Irish, *a fair*) : his son ; a quo *O'h-Aonaghain*, anglicised *Hanagan, Hinnegan, Henaghan,* and *Henehan*.

101. Airgead : his son.

102. Aongus : his son.

103. Tuileagna : his son.

104. Tuileagna (2) : his son.

105. Cormac : his son.

106. Crunmaol (3) : his son.

107. Diognadha : his son.

108. Crimthann : his son.

109. Oisein : his son.

110. Alla ("alla :" Irish, *a hall*) : his son ; a quo *O'h-Alla* anglicised *Ally* and *Hall*.

111. Siodhal : his son.

112. Eochagan : his son.

113. Dubhan ("_dubhan") [duan] : Irish, *a dark-complexioned man ; a fishing hook*) : his son ; a quo *O'Duana*.

114. Searragh : his son.

115. Ceallach O'Duana ; his son ; first assumed this sirname.

116. Giolla-Chriosd : his son.

117. Tuileagna O'Duana : his son.

DURKIN.

SINEALL, brother of Carthann who is No. 93 on the " Macnamara" (No. 1) pedigree, was the ancestor of *O'h-Dobharcon ;* anglicised *Durkin*.

93. Sineall : son of Cassan.

94. Cillin ("cillin" : Irish, *a little cell*) : his son ; a quo *O'Cillin*, anglicised *Killeen*.

95. Aodh : his son.

96. Banbhan ("banbh :" Irish, *a sucking pig*) : his son ; a quo *O'Banbhain*, anglicised *Hogg* and *Hogge*.

97. Dubhlaoidh : his son.

98. Dobharchu ("dobharcu :" Irish, *an otter*) : his son ; a quo *O'h-Dobharchon*.

99. Luchodhar : his son.

100. Orghus : his son.

101. Menmon Odhar : his son.

102. Cathan : his son.

103. Gormghal : his son.

104. Ceilceann (" ceil :" Irish,_to eonceal ; Heb. " chele," *a prison*)_: his son.

105. Padraic (Patrick) : his son.

106. Donal : his son.

107. Donoch O'h-Dobharcon : his son.

EARK.

CAIRBRÉ, a brother of Daire who is No. 91 on the " O'Connell" pedigree, was the ancestor of *O'Eirc ;* anglicised *Eark* and *Ercke*.

91. Cairbre : son of Brian.

92. Earc (" earc" : Irish, *speckled*) : his son ; a quo *O'Eirc*.

93. Oilioll Ceannfoda : his son.

94. Macearc : his son.

95. Greillean : his son.

96. Conall (or Amhalgadl) : his son.

97. Cuan : his son.

98. Maoltuile : his son.

99. Muirt : his son.

100. Tuathal : his son.

EUSTACE.

(*Ginel Iusdasach.*)

Lords Portlester and Viscounts Baltinglass.*

Arms : Or, a saltire gu.   *Crest* : A stag statant, betw. the horns a crucifix, all ppr
Supporters : Two angels ppr.   *Motto* : Cur me persequeris ?

DONCHADH, a brother of Tadhg [Teige] who is No. 106 on the " O'Brien"
(of Thomond) pedigree, was the ancestor of *MacIusdais ;* anglicised
Eustace.

106. Donchadh : a son of Brian
Boroimhe, the 175th Monarch of
Ireland.

107. Pór (or Pur) of Raithear
Pueuruigh : his son; a quo *O'Poir*
or *O'Puer* (" pór," gen. " poir" :
Irish, *seed, race,* or *clan*), which became *Le Poer,* modernized *Power.*

108. Bened of Raithear Beneudaigh : his son.

109. Iusdas (i.e., Lucas) : his son;
a quo *MacIusdais* (" ios" or "fios" :
Irish, *knowledge,* and " das," *a desk*),
and *MacLucais* (" luach" : Irish,
reward, and " cas," *hasty ;* Heb.
" chush"), anglicised *Lucas.*

110. Muiris : his son.

111. Nioclas : his son.

112. Risdeard : his son.

113. Tomhas : his son.

114. Alasder : his son.

115. Uilliam : his son.

116. Sheon : his son.

117. Sir Eadbhard : his son.

118. Tomhas : his son.

119. Risdeard : his son.

120. Margreagach : his son ; had
three brothers — 1. Eamon, 2.
Builter, 3. Tomhas.

121. Robeard (or Robert) Eustace :
his son; had four brothers — 1.
Alaster. 2. Sheon. 3. Risdeard.
4. Another Robeard.

---

* *Portlester* : This family was, according to MacFirbis, descended as here stated. In
Webb's *Compendium of Irish Biography,* it is stated that—" Sir Roland Eustace, or
Fitz Eustace, Lord Portlester, was descended from a branch of the Geraldines to whom
Henry II. had granted the country round Naas. In 1454 he was appointed Deputy to
Richard, Duke of York; and again in 1462 he filled the same office for the Duke of
Clarence. Subsequently he was tried for plotting with the Earl of Desmond, and
acquitted. Created Portlester, he married Margaret, daughter of Janicho d'Artois, by
whom he had two daughters ; the elder married Gerald, 8th Earl of Kildare. He held
the office of Treasurer of Ireland for many years, and was in 1474 appointed to the
custody of the great seal, which six years afterwards he refused to surrender when the
King granted the post to another. This was for a time a great hindrance to public
business, until the King authorized the construction of a new great seal for Ireland by
Thomas Archbold, Master of the King's Mint in Ireland, and that in Eustace's hands
was 'damned, annulled, and suspended,' while his acts as Treasurer were also
repudiated . . . Eustace refused to give up the seal ; his son-in-law Kildare positively
declined to admit a new Lord Deputy, Lord Grey ; James Keating, Constable of Dublin
Castle, broke down the drawbridge, and defied the Deputy and his three hundred
archers and men-at-arms to gain admittance ; and the Mayor of Dublin proclaimed that
no subsidy should be paid the Earl ; while a parliament held at Naas repudiated Lord
Grey's authority; and one summoned at Trim declared the proceedings of Kildare's
parliament at Naas null and void. Lord Portlester died 14th December, 1496, and was
buried at Cotlandstown, County of Kildare. Two monuments were erected to his
memory—one in the new abbey, Kilcullen, which he had founded in 1460 ; the other in
St. Audeon's Church, Dublin, where he had built a chapel to the Virgin."

FENNESSY.

Arms : We are unable at present to give the Arms of this family ; but the *Crest** is a mailed arm holding a halbert.   *Motto :* Recte adhibito Deus adjuvat.

THIS is a Munster family of purely Irish origin ; descended from Fiangus, who, according to the learned Professor O'Looney, was "Chief of a district of country near Cashel of the Kings," in the County Tipperary ; and a quo *O'Fianngusa* ("fiann" : Irish, *a soldier of the ancient Irish militia ;* and "gus," *strength*), anglicised *O'Fennessy,* and *Fennessy.* Fiangus, as the name implies, must have been a strongly-built man and a brave warrior. Commencing with Richard Fennessy, who died A.D. 1747, the following is the pedigree of this ancient family :—

1. Richard Fennessy† and Cathe-rine his wife held a large farm at Ballynattin, near Clerihan, and a few miles south of Cashel, in the co. Tipperary ; also farmed the adjoining townland of Shanbally. He died in 1747, leaving one son.

2. Richard (d. 1779): son of Richard ; established a Nursery at Ballynattin, the first of the kind in Ireland ; m. and had eight sons and four daughters : one of these daugh-ters m. Bourke of Rouscoe, co. Tipperary ; and another dau. m. Nicholas White of Kilcarone. The sons were :

I. John, a Nursery-man at Bally-nattin, who m. Miss Murphy of Ballinamona, near Cashel, co. Tipperary, and had no issue.

II. William, of whom presently.

III. David, who was an Army-Surgeon, d. in Waterford, unm.

IV. Richard, who was by his uncle William, of Limerick, established in the Nursery in Waterford which had been pre-viously occupied since 1712 by his uncle Nicholas, the VI. son of Richard (No. 2) who d.

1779. This Richard m. Miss Carey of the co. Kilkenny, and dying at the age of 96 (worth some £30,000), left four sons, besides a daughter Catherine (or "Kitty") who m. Timothy Lundrigan of Castle Grace, near Cloheen. The four sons were : 1. Edward, 2. Richard, 3. David, 4. John.

I. Edward (d. 1873), who was a Nursery-man in Waterford, m. Mary Belcher of Water-ford, and had three sons :

I. William-Henry (living in 1887), a Nursery-man in Waterford ; was High Sher-iff of Waterford in 1874 ; m. Lilian Agnes, dau. of Major Rance, and has, be-sides one daughter, two sons :

I. Edward, and II. Arthur —both living in 1887.

II. Edward, a Nursery-man at Kilkenny, was High Sheriff of that city in 1886.

III. Thomas, living in 1887.

II. Richard, m. Miss Jones of London, and had a Nursery

* *Crest*: On a tombstone over the grave of Richard Fennessy, in the churchyard of Tullamelan, near Knocklofty, co. Tipperary, is an inscription, and a crest which is a mailed arm holding a halbert.

† *Fennessy :* In Lenehan's History of Limerick we find amongst the names of those who, in 1747, under the Act 13 Charles II., took the oaths of allegiance, the name of Richard *Fenecy* (and his wife Catherine), farmer of Shanbally, co. Tipperary.

at Islington; emigrated to Australia, and died there.

III. David, was an Attorney in Waterford; m. Miss O'Brien of Waterford; emigrated to America, and d. s. p.

IV. John, who was a Nursery-man in Kilkenny, m. Miss Waring of that county, and d. s. p.

V. Thomas: fifth son of Richard (No. 2); was a Nursery-man at Clonmel; m. Miss Daniel of Powerbee, and had two sons and three daughters. The sons were:

I. Richard.

II. Hugh (alive in 1865), a Nursery-man at Limerick, who m. the widow of Mr. Sargent, and had, besides five daughters, three sons, one of whom, Thomas, was for some time Manager of the Great Southern and Western Railway (Ireland). This Thomas Fennessy emigrated to America, whither his brothers had preceded him.

The three daughters of Thomas (No. V.) were:

I. Ellen; II. Mary; and III. Anne, who m. Mr. O'Sullivan, of Limerick.

VI. Nicholas: the sixth son of Richard (No. 2); alive in 1732; established in 1712 the Nursery in Waterford; m. Margaret Power of Castle Blake, near Ballynattin, and had two sons:

I. Thomas, who emigrated to America.

II. Richard (b. 1719), who m. and also went with his wife and child to America in 1831; that child was a daughter, Nancy, who m. Henry Wilkinson (alive in 1876),

Inspector of Light Houses at Charleston, U. S. A.

VII. Michael: seventh son of Richard (No. 2); went to the North of Ireland, married, and settled on the estate of Lord Londonderry; had one son Robert (b. 1791, d. 1847), who joined the Army and was appointed Foreign Service Messenger to the King, m. an Irish lady and had three daughters (married), and four sons: three of the sons d. s. p., the youngest Rodney is m. and living in London in 1887.

VIII. Edward (or Ned), a Nurseryman at Ballynattin; alive in 1831; m. Miss Maher of Cloneen; having no issue he willed the place to one of his nieces, who m. Michael O'Donnell (d. 1855), of Seskin, near Carrick-on-Suir.

3. William: second son of Richard (No. 2); was a Nursery-man at Limerick and Castleconnell; m. Margaret Ryan of Bilboa Court, co. Limerick, and had, besides eight daughters, two sons:

I. Edward, who m. and d. in Limerick, s. p.

II. Richard (alive in 1835), of whom presently.

The eight daughters of William, of Limerick, were:

I. Ellen, who d. unm.

II. Mary, m. her cousin Richard Bourke, and with him emigrated to America. In 1856 this Richard Bourke was Clerk of the Court of Common Pleas in Cincinnati.

III. Amelia, m. James Cooney, and with him emigrated to Australia, where they died s. p.

IV. Catherine, m. — MacCarthy, and with him emigrated to America, where they died, leaving one son William (d. in San Francisco, 7th March, 1877), who m. and left two children.

V. Anne, m. — MacInerney, of the co. Clare, and with him emigrated to America, where they died, leaving a son Thomas who, in 1876, represented the 9th ward of his city (San Francisco), in the Legislature. This Thomas m. an American lady of Irish descent and has (1887) two sons—1. Thomas Fennessy, 2. Daniel Fennessy; and three daughters: 1. Mary, 2. Kate, 3. Anne—all taking the name *Fennessy* before that of Mac-Inerney.

VI. Susan, m. a Mr. Considine, and had a son.

VII. Eliza, m. a Mr. Ryan; left no issue; she d. Dec. 1879.

VIII. Margaret, m. another Mr. Ryan; and d. at Nenagh, co. Tipperary, April 1880, leaving no issue.

4. Richard (alive in 1835): second son of William (No. 3); established a Nursery in Tralee; m. Anne Beary of Derk, co. Limerick, and had two sons and one daughter:

I. William, of whom presently.

II. Edward (alive in 1887), a farmer at Ballybrood, Pallas green, co. Limerick; m. Maria Mulrenin, of Limerick, and had two daughters—1. Angelina (d. 1880), 2. Ada; and a son, Claude, living in 1887.

I. Maria, only dau. of Richard (No. 4), m. Robert Smithwick, of Cottage, near Tipperary, and had two sons and five daughters. The sons were:

I. John, living in 1887, and managing his father's lands.

II. Richard, a Civil Engineer, and B.A., living in 1887 at Gordon, Sheridan County, Nebraska, U. S. A.

The five daughters were: 1. Annie, 2. Georgina, 3. Cornelia, 4. Alexandra, 5. Florence.

5. William F. R. Fennessy (alive in 1887): elder son of Richard (No. 4); is a Civil Engineer; migrated to America, and lives at Avon, Fulton County, Illinois; was twice married: first, to Cornelia Woods, of New York State, by whom he has had (besides two daughters—1. Sophia, 2. Euphemia), six surviving sons:

I. William-Barton, of whom presently.

II. Ernest, a stock-farmer, living in 1887 at Avon, Illinois; m. Minnie Bliss, and has a daughter, Ethel-Cornelia.

III. Edward-Clinton, who is Chief Clerk in the Office of the P. P. C. Co., St. Louis, Mo.

IV. Maurice, Clerk in the Office of the P. P. C. Co., St. Louis, Mo.

V. Effie. VI. Florence.

William F. R. Fennessy married, secondly, in 1881, Lucy Robertson of St. Louis, Mo.

6. William-Barton Fennessy, of Lichfield, Illinois: eldest son of William; alive in 1887; is a Cigar and Tobacco Manufacturer; m. Bella Harry of Charleston, Illinois, and has a son Clinton-Lloyd, aged two years.

HAGERTY.*

Arms : An oak tree eradicated ppr. on a chief gu. three birds ar. beaked and legged sa. *Crest :* An arm in armour embowed, the hand grasping a scymitar all ppr. *Motto :* Nec flectitur nec mutat.

SNEAGHRA, a brother of Daolagach who is No. 98 on the " MacCarthy Mór" pedigree, was the ancestor of *O'h-Eigeartaigh ;* anglicised *O'Hegarty, Hegarty, Hagerty, Haggerty.*

98. Sneaghra : son of Nadfraoch.
99. Conall : his son.
100. Domhnall : his son.
101. Artgal : his son.
102. Maolfhionnan : his son.
103. Cearbhall : his son.

104. Ceallachan : his son.
105. Cormac : his son.
106. Egeartach ("eig-ceart :" Irish, *injustice) :* his son : a quo *Oh-Eigearteigh.*

HALLY.

THE *O'h-Ailche* family (" ailce :" Irish, *manners, behaviour*), anglicised *Halley*† and *Hally*, is a branch of the O'Kennedys of Ormond, descendants of Cormac Cas. Tuatha-Fearalt, a district in the county of Tipperary (the exact situation of which cannot now be ascertained), was the lordship of the family, whom O'Heerin mentions in the following lines :

> "Tuatha-Fearalt, of the fair-woods,
> Is the lordship of O'Ailche;
> A plain of fair fortresses, and a spreading tribe ;
> The land resembling Teltown of rivulets."

From the topographical description here given, it would appear to have been that portion of Hy-Fogharty, in Tipperary, lying between Lyttletown, in that county, and Urlingford, in Kilkenny. *Tuatha-Fearalt* signifies "the country of hardy men ;" from *tuatha*, "a district," or "country," and *Feara-alt*, "hardy men," or "men of sinew." Or, it

* *Hagerty :* Of this family was William Stuart Hagerty of London, whose ancestors for some 200 years were settled in England. His daughter, Maria Henrietta Stuart Hagerty, m. Thomas J. Leary, who was connected with the building trade, and with a slate quarry in the vale of Avoca. Their only surviving son was the late Doctor William Hagerty O'Leary, M.P. for Drogheda, who resumed the prefix *O'* to his patronymic; was born at Dublin in 1836; and died in London on the 15th Feb., 1880. Wm. H. O'Leary, M.P., m. Rosina Rogers, of Dublin, and left nine children. Of him, Sir Charles A. Cameron, in his *History of the Royal College of Surgeons in Ireland* (Dublin : Fannin and Co., 1886), says : " Mr. O'Leary spoke very eloquently, though somewhat floridly. In stature he was very short; three Irish members (of Parliament) were, in his time, the shortest, tallest, and stoutest members in the House—namely, W. O'Leary, Mr. O'Sullivan (co. Limerick), and Major O'Gorman."

Mr. O'Leary died while attending his Parliamentary duties in London, from congestion of the lungs ; his remains were brought to Ireland, and interred in Glasnevin Cemetery, Dublin.

† *Halley :* It is worthy of note that the celebrated astronomer, Halley, was a descendant of this family, who were hereditary physicians in Ireland.

may signify "the possession of *Fearalt*," who may have been some remarkable progenitor of the family under notice. Few, if any, of the name are to be met with at this day, either in Kilkenny or Tipperary.

HALY.
Of Ballyhaly, Co. Cork.

Arms : Vert. three bars wavy ar. in chief a mullet pierced or. *Crest :* A mermaid with comb and mirror all ppr. *Motto :* Sapiens dominabitur astris.

THE *O'h-Algaith* or *O'h-Algaich* ("algach :" Irish, *noble, brave*), anglicised *O'Haly* and *Haly*, are descended from Cosgrach, son of Lorcan, who is No. 103 on the "O'Brien" (Kings of Thomond) pedigree; and are to be distinguished from the *O'Ailches*, who, although of the same descent, are a distinct family. (See the "Healy" pedigree.)

The O'Halys are of old standing in the county of Galway, as appears from the Four Masters, under A.D. 1232. The representative of the senior branch of the sept, in 1730, was Simon Haly, Esq., of Ballyhaly, who m. Eleanora, dau. of Teige O'Quinn, Esq., of Adare, an ancestor of the Earl of Dunraven.

HAMILTON.
Duke of Abercorn.

Arms : Quarterly, 1st and 4th, gu. three cinquefoils pierced erm., for HAMILTON ; 2nd and 3rd, ar. a ship with sails furled and oars sa., for ARRAN ; in the point of honour over all an escutcheon az. charged with three fleurs-de-lis or. and surmounted by a French ducal coronet, for CHATELLERAULT. *Crest :* Out of a ducal coronet or. an oak fructed and penetrated transversely in the main stem by a frame-saw ppr. the blade inscribed with the word "Through," the frame gold. *Supporters :* Two antelopes ar. horned, ducally gorged, chained, and hoofed or. *Mottoes :* Through ; and Sola nobilitas virtus.

WALTER (the *Mór Mhaor Leamhna* or "Great Steward of Lennox"), lord high steward of Scotland, who is No. 115 on the "Stewart" pedigree, was the remote ancestor of *Hamilton,** duke of Abercorn. This Walter, lord steward, married Margery, the only daughter of Robert Bruce (called "King Robert the First"), King of Scotland; upon whose issue by the said Walter the crown was entailed by the Scotch Parliament, in default of male issue of the said Robert Bruce's only son, David, King of Scotland, who died without issue, A.D. 1370.

115. Walter, lord "Steward" of Scotland : son of John of Bute; ancestor of *Stewart* and *Stuart*.

116. Robert Stewart or Robert the Second, King of Scotland : his son.

117. Robert the Third, King of Scotland : his son ; his first name was John.

118. James the First, King of Scotland : his son.

---

* *Hamilton :* This sirname is derived from the Irish "amhail" (Gr. "omal-os," Lat. "simil-is") *like,* and "thonn," *a wave ;* and implies that the ancestor of the family was as *impetuous* in battle as the billows are at sea."

119. James, the Second, King of Scotland : his son ; had a brother named Ninion.

120. Princess Mary of Scotland : his daughter, who married James, the first lord Hamilton.

121. James Hamilton, first earl of Arran : their son.

122. James, second earl of Arran : his son.

123. Claud, the first lord Paisley : his son.

124. James, first earl of Abercorn : his son.

125. Sir Geoege Hamilton : his son : created a baronet, A.D. 1660.

126. James : his son ; who died in his father's lifetime.

127. James : his son ; the sixth earl of Abercorn.

128. James, the seventh earl : his son.

129. Hon. John Hamilton : his son.

130. John-James, the ninth earl of Abercorn : his son ; was created " marquis of Abercorn."

131. James, viscount Hamilton : his son.

132. James Hamilton, marquis of Abercorn : his son ; created in 1868, " marquis of Hamilton and duke of Abercorn," in the Peerage of Ireland ; living in 1885 ; was Lord Lieutenant of Ireland, in 1876 ; had a brother named Claud.

133. James, marquis of Hamilton : his son ; living in 1887. This James had 7 sisters, named—1. Lady Harriet. 2. Lady Beatrice. 3. Lady Louisa. 4. Lady Catherine. 5. Lady Georgina. 6. Lady Alberta Frances Anne. 7. Lady Maud Evelyn ; and five brothers, named— 1. Claud John. 2. George Francis. 3. Ronald Douglas. 4. Frederick Spencer, and 5. Ernest William.

134. James Albert Edward Hamilton, lord Paisley : his son ; born in 1869, and living in 1887.

HANRAHAN.

Of Munster.

AEDH (or Hugh), brother of Anluan who is No. 100 on the " O'Brien" pedigree, was the ancestor of O'h-Anraghain ; anglicised Hanrahan.

100. Hugh : son of Nathun.

101. Fionn : his son.

102. Foghmail : his son.

103. Aongus : his son.

104. Muireadhagh : his son.

105. Eoghan (owen) : his son.

106. Cu-Ultagh : his son.

107. Faolan : his son.

108. Donghaile : his son.

109. Seagha : his son.

110. Maithan : his son.

111. Teige na Lann (" lann :" Irish, the blade of a sword ; Lat. " lan-io," to cut) : his son ; a quo O'Laine, anglicised Lane, and Laney.

112. Ricard Mór : his son.

113. Ricard Oge : his son.

114. James : his son.

115. Murtogh : his son.

116. Donogh : his son.

117. Brian : his son.

118. Shane (or John) : his son.

119. Donall : his son.

120. Donall Oge : his son.

121. Thomas : his son.

122. John (2) : his son.

123. William Mór an Racan (an racan : Irish, " the rake"), called William O'h-Anraghain (or William the Rake) ; his son ; who lived in Ballyna-Ccroidhe.

124. William Oge O'Hanraghan : his son.

    125. Teige : his son.

    126. Donall (3) : his son.

127. Rory : his son.

128. Brian (2) : his son.

129. Denis O'Hanraghan : his son.

HEFFERNAN.*

AONGUS (or Æneas) Ceannattin, brother of Blad who is No. 92 on the "O'Brien" pedigree, was the ancestor of *O'h-Iffernain;* anglicised *Hefferan, Heffernan,* and *Heyfron.*

92. Æneas Ceannattin : son of Cass.

    93. Conall : his son; had a brother named Baoth ("baoth :" Iriah, *simple*), a quo *Booth.*

    94. Colman : son of Conall.

    95. Geimhdealach : his son.

    96. Culen (or Ulen) : his son.

    97. Cathbharr (or Abhartach) : his son.

    98. Conor (also called Corc) : his son.

    99. Iffernan ("ifearn :"† Irish *hell ;* Lat. "infern-us") : his son ; a quo *O'h-Iffernain.*

    100. Faolchadh : his son.

    101. Conligan : his son.

    102. Sioda : his son.

103. Donoch : his son.

104. Conn : his son. Some annalists make this Conn the ancestor of *Muintir Cuinn* or *Quin,* of Munster.

105. Meil (or Neal) : his son.

106. Faolach : his son.

107. Corc : his son.

108. Moroch (or Mortogh) his son.

109. Donoch (2) : his son.

110. Giollaseana : his son.

111. Donoch (3) : his son.

112. Donall : his son.

113. Thomas : his son.

114. Donall : his son.

115. Donal Oge : his son.

116. Conor O'Heffernan : his son.

HEHIR.

THE *O'h-Aichir, O'Haithchir, O'Hehir, Hehir,* and *Hare,* are all one family, of the Dal-Cas sept. They were formerly chiefs of Magh-Adhair, a district in the County Clare, lying between Ennis and Tulla ; but, having been driven thence by the Hy-Caisin in early times, they settled in the country

---

    * *Heffernan :* Of this family was Paul Heffernan, M.B., who was born in Dublin in 1719, and who, as a poet, associated with Foote, Garrick, and Goldsmith. Intended for the Catholic priesthood, he was sent to study in France, and lived there seventeen years. On his return to Dublin he took the degree of Bachelor of Medicine (M.B.), and in 1750 conducted the *Tickler,* a periodical paper in opposition to Lucas and his friends. He died in June 1777. In *Notes and Queries,* 2nd and 3rd Series, will be seen references to him ; and a full memoir, with lists of his works, is given in *Walker's Magazine* for 1794.

    † *Ifearn :* Some genealogists derive "Heffernan" from the Irish *afrionn,* the Mass or Eucharistic offering.

now forming the barony of Islands, where they became possessed of the districts of Hy-Cormac and Hy-Flanchada, according to O'Heerin :—

> " Of the race of Eoghan of Orior-Cliach,
> Are the Hy-Cormac of the smooth fair plain ;
> The fertile land is the lordship of O'Hehir,
> The ancestor of powerful chiefs.
> The head of many a powerful house
> Are of the noble clan of O'Haithchir ;
> They govern Hy-Flanchadha of hospitable mansions,
> And are valiant and well-armed Fenians."

The district of Hy-Cormac, comprised the ،Callan mountains, and extended to the town of Ennis. In A.D. 1094, Amhlaobh O'Hehir was slain ; and, in 1099, Donogh O'Hehir, lord of Magh-Adhair, died. This Magh-Adhair was the place of the inauguration of the O'Briens as princes of Thomond, and the O'Hehirs always assisted at the ceremony.

In 1197, died, Gilla-Patrick O'Hehir, Abbot of Innisfallen, in the 79th year of his age; and, in two years afterwards, Auliffe O'Hehir, a religious of the same establishment. By the late Dr. O'Donovan, the "O'Hares" are set down as a tribe of the Hy-Feigeinte, of the race of Eoghan-Mór.

We believe this family is now (1887) well represented by various gentlemen in the County Clare.

HICKEY.*

(*Ireland.*)

Arms: Gyronny of eight sa. and or. on the first four acorns, and on the last as many oak leaves counterchanged. *Crest:* A lamb reguard. holding over the dexter shoulder a flag, charged with an imperial crown.

EINSIODA, brother of Maolclochach who is No. 101 on the " MacNamara" pedigree, was the ancestor of *O'h-Iocaigh*, and *MacIocaigh* anglicised *Hickey*, and *Hickie.*

---

* *Hickey :* Rev. William Hickey ("Martin Doyle"), well known for his efforts to elevate the condition of the peasantry of Ireland, was eldest son of Rev. Ambrose Hickey, rector of Murragh, co. Cork. He was born about 1787, graduated at St. John's College, Cambridge, and subsequently took the degree of M.A. in the University of Dublin. He was ordained a clergyman of the Established Church in 1811, and appointed to the curacy of Dunleckny, co. Carlow. In 1820 he was inducted into the rectory of Bannow, co. Wexford ; in 1826 was transferred to that of Kilcormick, in 1831 to Wexford, and in 1834 to Mulrankin, where he ministered the remainder of his life. As a parochial clergyman he was esteemed alike by Catholics and Protestants. He commenced his career as a writer in 1817, his first work being a pamphlet on the *State of the Poor in Ireland.* Afterwards followed a series of letters under the pseudonym of "Martin Doyle," under which he continued to write. He wrote numerous works ; his latest production, published a few years before his death, was *Notes and Gleanings of the County Wexford.* In all his writings he took the broadest philanthropic views, studiously avoiding religious and political controversy. He was awarded a gold medal by the Royal Dublin Society, in recognition of his services to Ireland, and enjoyed a pension from the Literary Fund. He was a man of an eminently charitable and feeling nature, and died comparatively poor, 24th October, 1875, aged 87.

101. Einsioda : son of Cuilean.
102. Ainiochadagh : his son.
103. Iocaigh (" ioc :" Irish, *a payment*) : his son ; a quo *O'h-Iocaigh* and *MacIocaigh.*
104. Michliagh : his son.
105. Erc : his son.
106. Donall O'Hickey : his son ; first assumed this sirname.
107. Deagbadh : his son.
108. Aedh : his son. •

109. Cormac : his son.
110. James : his son.
111. Cormac (2) : his son.
112. Teige : his son.
113. Owen : his son.
114. Muireadhagh : his son.
115. John : his son.
116. Aedh (or Hugh) : his son.
117. John (2) : his son.
118. John (3) O'Hickey : his son.

The O'Hickeys were formerly Chiefs of a district in the vicinity of Killaloe, County Clare, also of a cantred in the barony of Upper Connello, in the County of Limerick. They were hereditary physicians to the O'Briens, Kings of Thomond; to the MacNanamaras, lords of Hy-Caisin; and to the O'Kennedys of Ormond; and several of them are said to have compiled and translated valuable medical works, amongst others Nichol O'Hickey, the translator into Irish of a Latin Medical Work, called "The Rose," known also as the "Book of the O'Boulgers." The O'Hickies possessed a copy of "The Lily," a celebrated Medical Work, compiled in A.D. 1304, of which several transcripts are known to exist.

1. James Hickie, Esq., of County Clare, whose estates were seized on by the English in 1652.
2. William ; his son.
3. William (2) : his son.
4. Michael : his son.
5. William (3) : his son.
6. William (4) : his son.
7. William Creagh Hickey, Esq., J.P. : his son; the representative of this family, living at Killelton, County Kerry, in 1864.

HOGAN.*

Arms†: Gu. three lions pass. in pale or. each holding betw. the forepaws an esquire's helmet ppr. *Crest :* A dexter arm in armour embowed, the hand grasping a sword all ppr.

COSGRACH, brother of Cineidh [kenneth or kenneda] who is No. 104 on

---

* *Hogan :* Of this family was the late celebrated sculptor, John Hogan, who, in 1800, was born at Tallow, in the County of Waterford. Shortly after his birth his father, who was a builder, removed to Cork. His mother, Frances Cox, was great-granddaughter of Sir Richard Cox, the Chancellor. Exhibiting in his youth a strong taste for art, some friends who were attracted by his works, raised sufficient funds to enable him to sojourn at Rome for a few years. Hogan reached Rome on Palm Sunday, 1824. His best friend was Signor Gentili, then a lawyer, and afterwards a popular Catholic priest and preacher in Dublin. In 1838, Mr. Hogan married an Italian lady, and in 1848 returned to Dublin. He died on the 27th March, 1858, aged 57 years.

† *Arms :* The ancient arms of this family were—Sa. on a chief or. three annulets of the field (another the tinctures reversed).

the "O'Brien" pedigree, was the ancestor of *O'h-Ogain*, of Munster; anglicised *O'Hogan, Hogan, Ogan,* and *Ougan.*

104. Cosgrach : son of Lorcan : a quo *Cosgrave,** of Munster.

105. Aitheir : his son.

106. Ogan (" ogan :" Irish, *a youth*): his son ; a quo *O'h-Ogain.*

107. Teige : his son.

108. Conor : his son.

109. Teige (2) : his son.

110. Giolla Padraic : his son.

111. Aodh : his son.

112. Edmond : his son.

113. Edmond (2) : his son.

114. Edmond (3) : his son.

115. Diarmod : his son.

116. Conogher : his son ; who died A.D. 1635.

117. Conogher (2), *alias* Giall-garbh † [gilgariv], O'Hogan, of Cranagh, county Tipperary : his son ; a quo *Kilgarriff*. This Giall-garbh had a brother named Der-mod ; living in 1657.

KEARNEY.

(*Of Cashel*).

Arms : Ar. a chev. betw. three buglehorns stringed sa.   *Crest :* A swan's head and neck erased, in the bill an annulet.

AONGUS, brother of Eochaidh Ball-dearg who is No. 94 on the "O'Brien's pedigree, was the ancestor of *O'Cearnaigh* (Chaisil); anglicised *Kearney, O'Kearney, Carney, Kerny, O'Carney,* and *Carnie.*

94. Aongus : son of Carthann Fionn.

95. Ronan : his son.

96. Dioma : his son.

97. Ainleach : his son.

98. Cearnach (" cearnach :" Irish, *victorious*) : his son ; a quo *O'Cearnaigh* (chaisil).

99. Torpa : his son.

100. Domhnall Na Catha ar Fhocht : his son.

101. Cathal : his son.

102. Donchadh : his son.

103. Donchadh : his son.

104. Cu-ar-phairc : his son.

105. Murchadh : his son.

106. Bran : his son.

107. Seaan : his son.

108. Bran : his son.

109. Conchobhar : his son.

110. Bran : his son.

111. Conchobhar : his son.

112. Seaan : his son.

113. Donchadh : his son.

114. Uilliam : his son.

115. Donchadh : his son.

116. Giolla Padraic Mór : his son.

117. Domhnall : his son.

118. Donchadh : his son.

119. Pilip : his son.

120. Risteard : his son.

---

* *Cosgrave :* The Irish *Cosgar,* " victory," is the root of the sirname *O'Cosgrighe :* anglicised Cosgrave, M'Coscry, MacCusker, Lestrange, and L'Estrange.

† *Giallgarbh :* This name (" giall," Irish, *a hostage*, and " garbh," *fierce*) means the " fierce hostage."

G

KEELY.

CONN, brother of Cairbre Eadhbha who is No. 91 on the " O'Donovan " pedigree, was the ancestor of *O'Caoile* and *MacCaoile ;* anglicised *Keely, Keily, Kiely,* and *Cayley.*

91. Conn: son of Brian.

92. Caoile ("caoile : Irish, *leanness*): his son; a quo *O'Caoile* and *MacCaoile*, chiefs of *Hy MacCaoile*, now the barony of " Imokilly," county Cork.

93. Brian : his son ; had a brother named Donn, who was the ancestor of *Cullen*, of Muster.

94. Conn (2): son of Brian.

95. Donall: his son.

96. Direach (" direach :" Irish, *straight :* Heb. " derech," *a way*): his son ; a quo *O'Dirighe*, anglicised *Derry* and *Deering.*

97. Donn O'Caoile : his son ; first assumed this sirname.

98. Maccon : his son.

99. Cairbre: his son.

100. Flann : his son.

101. Cumhal : his son.

102. Mathun : his son.

103. Dermod na Glaice : his son.

104. Donagh Nimhneach ("nimhneach :" Irish, *peevish*): his son ; a quo *O'Nimhnighe*, anglicised *Neeny.*

105. Mathun Gharbh : his son.

106. Muirceartagh : his son.

107. Maolseaghlainn : his son.

108. Donogh O'Keely : his son.

KELLEHER.

THE family of *Kelleher* or *Keller*, in Irish *O'Ceileachair* (" ceileach" : Irish, *wise, prudent*), derive their sirname from Ceileachar, son of Donchuan, brother of Brian Boroimhe [Boru], the 175th Monarch of Ireland, who is No. 105 on the " O'Brien" (Kings of Thomond) pedigree. In the twelfth, and even so late as the sixteenth century, the O'Kellehers were possessed of lands in Munster ; but the pedigree of the family is, we fear, lost. " Donogh O'Kelleher," successor of St. Kieran of Saiger, *i.e.* Bishop of Ossory, died, A.D. 1048. The late Rev. —— Kelleher, P.P. of Glanworth, county Cork, represented the senior branch of this Sept. A younger branch of the family is represented by Alderman Keller, of Cork.

KENNEDY.

(Of Munster).

Arms : Sa. three helmets in profile ppr. *Crest :* An arm embowed vested az. holding a scymitar all ppr.

DONCHUAN, a brother of the Monarch Brian Boru who is No. 105 on the " O'Brien" pedigree, was the ancestor of *O'Cinnidh ;* anglicised *Kennedy.*

105. DonchaCuan: son of Cineadh.

106. Cineadh (" cineadh :" Irish, *a nation* or *kind*, Gr. " gen-os ;"

Lat. " gen-us "): his son ; a quo *O'Cinnidh.*

107. Aodh : his son.

108. Donchuan : his son.

109. Mahoun O'Kennedy : his son; first assumed this sirname.

110. Teige : his son.

111. Giollacomin (or Giollaca-oimhghin) : his son.

112. Donall-Cathaleitreach : his son.

113. Teige : his son; had a brother named Giollacomin.

114. Giollacomin (2) : his son.

115. Giolla Padraic : his son.

116. Aodh : his son.

117. Donall : his son.

118. Gillcomin : his son ; had two brothers—1. Patrick, and 2. Donall Gall.

119. Padraic (or Patrick) : his son.

120. Philip : his son.

121. Dermod : his son.

122. Maithan : his son ; a quo " Clann Maithan Donn O'Kennedy."

123. Teige : his son; had three brothers.

124. Rory : his son.

125. Dermod O'Kennedy : his son ; had four brothers.

KILROY.*

Chiefs in the Barony of Clonderlaw, County Clare.

WHEN the county Clare, like the other parts of Ireland, was devastated under the Commonwealth Government of Ireland, to make room for the Cromwellian Settlement, the old Irish families who were dispossessed and who escaped transportation as " slaves " to the Sugar Plantations of America, had to seek homes and refuges wherever they could, for themselves and their families. It was at that unhappy juncture in the history of Ireland, in the year 1653, that, according to tradition, a son of the last Chief of this family, settled in Keenagh—one of the mountain fastnesses in the proximity of Mount Nephin, in the barony of Tyrawley, and county of Mayo ; from whom the following branch of that ancient family is descended :

1. ( ) A son of Riocard ; had three sons : 1. Michael, 2. Peter, 3. Mark :

I. Michael, married and had : 1. Patrick ; 2. Mary, who m. and had a family.

I. This Patrick married and had : 1. Peter, 2. Edward. I. This Peter, m. and had : 1. Thomas ; 2. Patrick— both these sons living in Keenagh, in August, 1871.

II. Edward : the second son of Patrick, son of Michael, had a son named Peter— also living in Keenagh, in August, 1871.

II. Peter, the second son of No. 1 ; m. and had Bridget, who m. and had a family.

III. Mark, the third son of No. 1, of whom presently.

2. Mark : the third son of No. 1 ; m. and had : 1. Peter ; 2. Bridget.

I. This Peter, of whom presently.

II. Bridget, m. —— Gill, of Glenhest, also in the vicinity of Glen Nephin, and had : I. Denis Gill (living in 1871), who m. Anne Hagerty (also living in 1871), and had issue.

3. Peter : son of Mark ; m. Mary Geraghty, of Kinnaird, in the parish of Crossmolina, and had surviving

---

* *Kilroy :* This genealogy is by mistake here entered. The " Kilroy " pedigree is given in full, *infra*, among the " Ir Genealogies."

issue four daughters: 1. Norah: 2. Mary; 3. Bridget; 4. Margaret; I. This Norah, of whom presently. II. Mary, who married Michael Geraghty (or Garrett), of Kinnaird, above mentioned, and had: 1. Michael, who m., and emigrated to America in 1847; and had issue; living (1887) in Deerpark, Maryland, U.S.A. 2. Patrick, of Kinnaird, who m. Mary Sheridan, and had issue; this Patrick and his family emigrated to America, in the Spring of 1883, and is living (1887) in Deerpark, Maryland. 3. John, who emigrated to America with his brother Michael, in 1847. 4. A daughter, who d. unm. 5. Mary, who m. Michael Gilboy, and had issue.

III. Bridget, who was the second wife of Patrick Walsh of Cloonagh, in the parish of Moygownagh, in the said barony of Tyrawley, and had: 1. Margaret, who m. Thomas Fuery, and with him emigrated to America. 2. Walter, who also emigrated to the New World.

IV. Margaret, who m. Thomas Regan, of Moygownagh, above mentioned, and had two children—1. Mary, 2. Patrick: 1. This Mary (d. 1881), m. John (died in 1886), eldest son of Martin Hart, of Glenhest, and had issue. 2. Patrick, who d. young.

4. Norah Kilroy: eldest daughter of Peter; m. John O'Hart, and (see No. 124 on the "O'Hart" genealogy) had:

I. Michael; II. Michael: both of whom d. in infancy.

III. Rev. Anthony, a Catholic Priest, of the diocese of Killala, who d. 7th Mar., 1830.

IV. Mary, who d. unm. in 1831.

V. Anne (d. 1841), who m. James Fox (d. 1881), of Crossmolina, and had: 1. Mary (living in 1887), who m. J. Sexton, of Rockfort, Illinois, U.S.A., and had issue; 2. Anne, who d. unm.

VI. Bridget (deceased), who m. John Keane, of Cloonglasna, near Ballina, Mayo, and had issue—now (1887) in America.

VII. Patrick (d. in America, 1849), who married Bridget Mannion (d. 1849), and had two children, who d. in infancy.

VIII. Catherine (d. in Liverpool, 1852), who m. John Divers, and had: 1. Patrick, 2. John.

IX. John, of whom presently.

X. Martin, who d. in infancy.

5. John O'Hart (living in 1887), of Ringsend, Dublin: son of said Norah Kilroy; who (see No. 125 on the "O'Hart" pedigree) m. Eliza Burnet (living in 1887), on the 25th May, 1845, and had: 1. Fanny; 2. Patrick; 3. Mary (d. 1880); 4. Margaret; 5. Eliza; 6. Nanny; 7. John-Anthony (d. in infancy); 8. Louisa; 9. Hannah; 10. Francis-Joseph, who d. in infancy.

6. Patrick Andrew O'Hart, of 45 Dame Street, Dublin: son of John; living unm. 1887.

LAWSON.

(Ireland).

Arms: Ar. on a bend betw. two trefoils slipped sa. three mascles or.

LABHRAS (" labhras :" Irish, *a laurel tree*), brother of Philip who is No. 112 on the " O'Sullivan Beara" pedigree, was the ancestor of *Clann Labhrais* or *MacLabhrais;* anglicised *Lawson.*

LOUGHNAN.

Arms: Vert a dexter hand couped apaumée, and in chief an arrow fessways ar.
Crest: A castle triple-towered ppr.

FIONNACHTACH, a brother of Iomchadh Uallach who is No. 88 on the " O'Carroll Ely" pedigree, was the ancestor of *O'Lachtnain* Ele ; anglicised *O'Loughnan,* and *Loughnan,* of Ely O'Carroll, and modernised *Loftus.*

88. Fionnachtach : son of Conla.
89. Eachdach : his son.
90. Tighearnach : his son.
91. Cu-Maighe : his son.
92. Maolfabhal : his son.
93. Crunmaol : his son.
94. Breasal : his son.
95. Dungallach : his son.
96. Maolfabhal : his son.
97. Ruadhrach : his son.
98. Aongus : his son.
99. Cuanach (" cuanach :" Irish, *deceitful*) : his son ; a quo *O'Cuanaighe,* anglicised *Cooney;* had a brother Lachtnan (" lachtna :" Irish, *tawny;* or a *kind of coarse gray apparel*), a quo *O'Lachtnain* Ele.

LYNCH.*

Arms: Sa. three lynxes pass. guard. ar. *Crest:* On a ducal coronet or, a lynx, as in the arms.

THE O'Lynch family derives its origin from Aongus, the second son of

---

* *Lynch:* John Lynch, D.D., Archdeacon of Tuam, author of *Cambrensis Eversus* and other works, was born in Galway *circa* 1600, of a family which claimed descent from Hugh de Lacy. His father, Alexander Lynch, was at the period of his son's birth, one of the few schoolmasters left in Connaught. John Lynch was ordained priest in France about 1622. On his return to Ireland he, like his father, taught school in Galway, and acquired a wide reputation for classical learning. Essentially belonging to the Anglo-Irish party, he could not endorse any policy irreconcilable with loyalty to the King of England. On the surrender of Galway in 1652 he fled to France. Besides minor works, he was the author of *Cambrensis Eversus*, published in 1662, under the name of " Gratianus Lucius." It was dedicated to King Charles II. That great work written in Latin, like all his other books, was an eloquent defence of Ireland from the strictures of Giraldus Cambrensis. About the same period appeared his *Alithonologia*, which, as a history of the Anglo-Irish race, especially of their anomalous position under Queen Elizabeth, has no rival. In 1669, he published a life of his uncle, Francis Kirwan, Bishop of Killala, edited with a translation and notes by the Rev. C. P. Meehan, in 1848.—WEBB.

Carthan Fionn Oge Mór, who is No. 93 on the "O'Brien Kings of Thomond" pedigree.

They were lords of Owny-Tir, a territory on the border of the county of Tipperary, and they are mentioned as follows by O'Heerin :—

> "The O'Lynches, estated chiefs,
> Inhabit the wood in front of the foreigners."

The settlement of the Galls or Foreigners, here alluded to, is the City of Limerick, which as early as the ninth century became the principal maritime station of the Danes; and the estate of the Lynches was, in all probability, the country lying around Castleconnell, in the barony of Owny and Ara, with a portion of the lands comprised in the county of the City of Limerick.

In A.D. 1061. Malcolm O'Lynch, priest of Clonmacnoise, died.
     A.D. 1080. Eochy O'Lynch, lord of Owny-Tir, died.
     A.D. 1109. Flaherty O'Lynch, successor of St. Kieran of Clonmacnoise, died.
     A.D. 1151. The grandson of Eochy, lord of Owny Tir, died.
     A.D. 1159. Maolmuire O'Lynch, Bishop of Lismore, died.
     A.D. 1325. Thomas O'Lynch, Archdeacon of Cashel, died.
     A.D. 1540. John Lynch, the last prior of the Franciscan Friary of Waterford, was forced to surrender, to the Inquisitors of Henry VIII., this house with its appurtenances, which were then granted to Patrick Walsh of Waterford, at the annual rent of £157 13s. 4d., Irish money.

LYONS.*

Arms : Ar. a chev. sa. betw. three lions dormant cowarded gu.

MAIN MUN-CHAIN, a brother of Lughaidh who is No. 88 on the "Line of Heber," *ante,* was the ancestor of *O'Liathain ;* anglicised *Lyons, Lehan, Lehane,* and *Lyne.*

88. Main Mun-chain : son of Olioll Flann-beag.	90. Daire (or Main) Cearb : his son.
89. Cirb : his son.	91. Eachdhach Liathan ("liat-

---

* *Lyons :* The late Doctor Robert Spencer Dyer Lyons, Physician, of Merrion Square, Dublin, was of this family. His father, Sir William Lyons, was a merchant of the City of Cork, where Dr. Lyons was born on the 13th of August, 1826 ; and was twice Mayor and High Sheriff of that city. His mother was Harriet, daughter of Spencer Dyer, of Garus, Kinsale. In 1859, Dr. Lyons investigated the causes of the unsanitary state of Lisbon (in which at the time yellow fever raged), and submitted to King Pedro V. suggestions for their removal, which were approved of. Upon that occasion Dr. Lyons received the cross and insignia of the Ancient Portuguese Order of Christ. He served in Parliament as member for Dublin fron 1880 to 1885. Dr. Lyons married, in 1856, Maria, daughter of the late Right Honourable David Richard Pigot, Lord Chief Baron of the Exchequer in Ireland ; he died in 1886.

han :" Irish, *one who is greyhaired*) : his son ; a quo *O'Liathain.*

92. Macbroc : his son.
93. Maccaille : his son.
94. Caillean Dubh : his son.

95. Feareadhach Dhorn-mór : his son.
96. Feargus Tuile : his son.
97. Ronan Diocholla : his son.
98. Dunchadh : his son.
99. Anmchadh : his son.

LYSAGHT.*

Baron Lisle.

Arms : Ar. three spears erect in fesse gu. on a chief az. a lion of England.   *Crest :* A dexter arm embowed in armour, the hand brandishing a dagger all ppr.   *Supporters :* Two lions or.   *Motto :* Bella ! horrida bella !

THIS family of *Lysaght* or *MacLysaght* is descended from Donal Mór, King of Cashel, who is No. 110 on the " O'Brien" Kings of Thomond pedigree. The sirname is a corruption of *Giolla-Iosa,* as derived from Giolla Iosa Mór O'Brien, whose posterity were of note in the vicinity of Ennistymon, county Clare, from the 13th to the 17th century. Several respectable families of the name may be met with in that county at the present day.

1. John Lysaght, of Ennistymon, had :

2. John Lysaght (2), who was a cornet in Lord Inchiquin's army ; m. Mary, the dau. of Nicholas MacDermod O'Hurley, of Knocklong, co. Limerick. Was engaged fighting against his country at Knock-na-Ness, 13th November, 1647.

3. Nicholas : son of John (No. 2) ; was Captain of a troop of horse, and was mortally wounded at the Boyne ; died in September following. This Nicholas m. Grace, dau. of Colonel Holmes, of Kilmallock.

4. John : son of Nicholas ; was M.P. for Charleville ; and was created " Baron Lisle," on the 18th September, 1758 ; m. Catherine, dau. of Chief Baron Deane, of the Irish Court of Exchequer ; and d. in 1781.

5. John : son of John ; m., in 1778, Mary Anne, dau. of George Connor, of Ballybricken House, co. Cork.

6. George : son of John (No. 5) ; m. Elizabeth, dau. of Samuel Knight.

7. John-Arthur, of Mount North, co. Cork, the fifth Baron : son of George ; Chief of the sept in 1865.

* *Lysaght :* Edward Lysaght, a poetical writer, was born in the county of Clare, on the 21st December, 1763. He was educated at Cashel, and at Trinity College, where he became a B.A. in 1782. In 1784 he took his degree of M.A. at Oxford ; and four years afterwards was called both to the English and Irish Bar. He is best known for his songs, such as " The Sprig of Shillelagh," and " The Man who led the Van of the Irish Volunteers." He must have died shortly before 1811, at which date a small collection of his *Remains* was published in Dublin.

MACAULIFFE.*

Of Duhallow; or Lords of Clanawly.

Arms: Ar. three mermaids with combs and mirrors in fess az. betw. as many mullets of the last. *Crest:* A boar's head couped or.

TEIGE, brother of Cormac who is No. 109 on the "MacCarthy Mór" pedigree, was the ancestor of *MacAmhailaoibh* (anglicised *MacAwliff*, and *MacAuliffe*), of Eallo or Duhallow, in the county Cork.

109. Teige : son of Muredach.

110. Donogh : his son.

111. Amhailgadh ("amhail:" Irish, *like,* and "gad," *a twisted osier*) : his son ; a quo *MacAmhailgaidh*—meaning "the son of the withe-like man."

112. Conor MacAwliff : his son.

113. Conor Oge : his son.

114. Maolseaghlainn : his son.

115. Conor (2) : his son.

116. Conor (3) : his son ; had issue —Owen, Maurice, and Murtogh. Maurice had a son, Thomas, who was father to Connor Don, head of the *MacAuliffes Don.*

117. Murtogh : his son ; had a brother Owen.

118. David : his son.

119. Cealla : his son ; had two sons, Murtogh and Teige.

120. Murtogh Mac Auliffe : his son.

The last lord of Clanawly, Florence MacAuliffe, was attainted in 1641, by Oliver Cromwell (See our *Irish Landed Gentry, p.* 285), with Mac-Donogh MacCarthy, lord of Kanturk, who was nephew of MacAuliffe; and their lands were given to the Aldworths, and other English families.

The head of this family was, in 1840, weighmaster in the market-house of Kenmare.

"How are the mighty fallen ! ! !"

MACBRODY.

THE *MacBruaideaghea* family, anglicised *MacBruodin, MacBrodin,* and *MacBrody,* derive their descent and sirname from Bruadeagha, son of Aongus Cinathrach (*clan Arach*), the fifth son of Cas, who is No. 91 on the "O'Brien, Kings of Thomond" pedigree. The MacBrodys were one of the most learned families of Munster, and they became in very early times hereditary historians to several of the dominant tribes of Thomond, by whom they were rewarded with large grants of land in that principality.

Among the many distinguished writers produced by this family, may be mentioned Cormac MacBrody, whose approbation of the *Annals of Donegal,* the Four Masters procured in 1636 ; and Anthony MacBrodin, a Franciscan friar, Jubilate Lecturer on Divinity in the Irish College at Prague, and author of the celebrated work entitled, *Passio Martyrum Hiberniæ,* and other works on Theology.

The Book of the MacBruodins (or MacBrodys), in which was chronicled events, which occurred between the years 1588 and 1602 (See Appendix), was compiled by Maolin Oge MacBrody, in the last mentioned year. It

* *MacAuliffe :* The chief residence of the head of this sept was Castle-MacAuliffe, near Newmarket, in the barony of Duhallow, on the banks of the river Dalloo, to the left of the road leading from Newmarket to Millstreet, and about a mile from the former. Modern vandalism has left scarcely a trace of this once strong building ; Caislean-an-Cnock and Curragh castle also belonged to the MacAuliffe family.

was used in the compilation of the Four Masters, and considered a most trust-worthy record.

In A.D. 1563, Dermod MacBrody, son of Conor, son of Dermod, son of John, chief professor of Ibrackan, in Clare, died, and he was succeeded by his kinsman, Maolin MacBrody.

In 1582, Maolin, who was the son of Conor, son of Dermod, son of John, professor in History to the O'Briens, died, and his brother Giolla-Bride, succeeded him in the professorship.

In 1427, Dermod, son of Maolin, died. This Maolin was chief professor of Poetry and History to the O'Quins of Cinel-Fermaic, in the barony of Inchiquin, co. Clare; and he was succeeded, at his death, by his son, Dermod, above mentioned. Maolin, son of Dermod, died 1438; and John, son of Maolin, in 1518.

In 1531, Conor, son of Dermod, son of John, son of Maolin, son of Dermod, son of Dermod, son of Maolin, son of Dermod, Chief Historian and Bard to the O'Quins, died.

In 1570, Donal MacBrody, a very learned man, flourished; he was author of a poem consisting of forty-two verses or stanzas, of four lines each, which he wrote for James Fitzmaurice Fitzgerald of Desmond.

In 1602, Maolin Oge MacBrody, son of Maolin, son of Conor, son of John, died on the 31st of December. He was an excellent Historian and epic poet, the compiler of the "Book of the MacBrodys," and author of the poems, commencing, "Give ear to me, *O Inis an Laogh;*" "Know me O MacCoghlan;" "Let us make a visit to the children of Cais;" "Strangers here are Cahir's race;" "From four the Gadelians have sprung;" and also the following verse or stanza, composed on the occasion of the restoration of his property which had been seized on by the forces of Hugh Ruadh O'Donnell, Prince of Tirconnell, in 1599:—

> "It was destined that in revenge for Oileach,
> O Hugh Roe, as foretold by the prophet,
> That your forces would come to Magh Adhair;
> In the north the needy seeks assistance."

This was the Maolin MacBrody, who assisted in making the Irish translation of the New Testament, published by Ussher, in Dublin, in 1602.

The celebrated "Contention of the Bards" (about 1604) was carried out by one Teige MacBrody of Clare, and Lughaidh O'Clery of Donegal.

The last record we have of this family is in 1642, when Conor Mac-Brody, of Letter-Maolin, son of Maolin Oge, above mentioned, died.

MacCARTHY MOR. (No. 1.)

Arms: A stag trippant, attired and unguled or. *Crest:* A dexter arm in armour ppr. cuffed ar. erect and couped at the wrist, holding in the hand a lizard, both also ppr. *Supporters:* Two angels ppr. vested ar. habited gu. winged or, each holding in the exterior hand a shield, thereon a human head affronted erased. *Motto:* Forti et fideli nihil difficile.

FAILBHE FLANN, son of Aodh Dubh, who is No. 94 on the "Line of Heber" (*ante*), was the ancestor of "MacCarthy Mór." From him the pedigree of the family is as follows:

95. Failbhe Flann (d. A.D. 633): son of Aodh Dubh; was the 16th | Christian King of Munster, and reigned 40 years. He had a brother

named Fingin,* who reigned before him, and who is said by the Munster antiquaries to be the elder; this Fingin was ancestor of *O'Sullivan*. (See the "Vera-O'Sullivan" pedigree.)

96. Colgan: his son; was the 21st Christian King of Munster, for 13 years. He is styled, in O'Dugan's "Kings of the Race of Heber," *Colga McFalvey the Generous Chief.*

97. Nathfraoch; his son; King of Munster A.D. 954.

98. Daologach: his son; had two brothers—Faolgursa and Sneaghra.

99. Dungal: his son; from whom are descended the Clann Dunghaile or *O'Riordan*,† who was antiquary to O'Carroll Ely; had a brother Sneidh.

100. Sneidh: son of Dungal. This Sneidh had five brothers—1. Algenan, the 32nd Christian King of Munster; 2. Maolguala, the 33rd King; 3. Foghartach; 4. Edersceol; and 5. Dungus, from all of whom are many families. Maolguala here mentioned had a son named Maolfogartach, who was the 34th Christian King of Munster, who was taken prisoner and stoned to death by the Danes who were then invading Ireland.

101. Artgal: son of Sneidh.

102. Lachtna: his son. This prince lived during the seven years' reign of his kinsman, the celebrated Cormac, King of Munster.

103. Bouchan: his son; left, besides other children, Gormflath, who married Donal, King of the Desii, to whom she bore Mothla O'Felan, who fell at Clontarf.

104. Ceallachan Cashel: his son; was the 42nd Christian King of Munster; reigned ten years; was a great scourge to the Danes, and at length routed them totally out of Munster. In one battle (Knock-Saingal, co. of Limerick) with a single stroke of his battle-axe he cleft the skull of Aulaf, the Danish general, through his heavy brass helmet.

105. Doncha or Duncan: his son; was the first "Prince of Desmond."

106. Saorbhreathach or Justin: his son; had two brothers—1. Foghartach or Maolfoghartach, the 43rd King of Munster after Christianity was planted there; and 2. Murcha, who was ancestor of *O'Callaghan* of Cloonmeen.

---

* *Fingin:* According to O'Dugan and O'Heerin, who lived in the 14th century, we find that Fingin was the elder son. He was elected joint King of Munster, with Cairbre, upon the death of Amalgaidh and in the lifetime of Failbhe. His name also appears on the Regal Roll before that of his brother; and he represented his native province in the Assembly at Dromceat (the Mullogh, in Roe Park, near Limavady, in co. Derry), convened by Hugh, Monarch of Ireland, and honoured by the presence of St. Columbcille.

The MacCarthys owned the prominent position which they held in Desmond at the time of the Anglo-Norman invasion not to *primogeniture*, but to the disturbed state of the province during the Danish wars, in which their immediate ancestors took an active and praiseworthy part; to the impartial exercise of the authority enjoyed by those ancestors by usurpation and tanistic right; the possession of that authority at an eventful period, namely the arrival in Ireland of Henry II., by whom MacCarthy, upon his submission, was acknowledged as King of Desmond; and the prostrate condition to which the Danish wars had brought the collateral branches of the family, who had, at least, an equal claim on the allegiance of the inhabitants of South Munster. O'Sullivan Mór always presided at meetings of the Munster chiefs, even when MacCarthy attended; and it was he whose voice made MacCarthy—"THE MACCARTHY MÓR."

† *O'Riordan:* This name has by some of the family been lately rendered *Ritherdan.*

107. Carthach,* Prince of Desmond : son of Justin ; a quo *MacCarthaigh*, anglicised *MacCarthy*, and *MacCaura* ;† was a great commander against the Danes ; was A.D. 1045, burned to death, with a great number of his kinsmen, in a house in which he had taken shelter after a conflict with some Dalcassian troops, by the son of Lonargan, the grandson of Donchuan who was brother to Brian Boroimhe. It is right to observe that *MacCarthy* has, in some branches of the family, become *Maccartney*, *McCarthy*, *McCartie*, *McCarty*, and *Carter ;* and that there was in Ireland an *O'Carthaigh* family, which was anglicised O'Carthy, and modernized *O'Carry,* *Carté*, *Cartie*, and *Carty*.

THE MacCARTHYS.

"Come, Clan MacCarthy, honours look for you."
—ROMAN VISION.

" The chiefs of Munster, of the fortress of the Shannon,
Are of the seed of Eoghan, the son of Oilliol ;
MacCarthagh, the enforcer of the tributes,
Is like a storm-lifted wave lashing the shore."
—O'HEERIN.

THE MacCarthys, who were the dominant family in Desmond from the period of the establishment of sirnames, down to the reign of Conn

*Carthach :** This word may be derived from *cartha* or *carrthadh*, a pillar ; or from *cathrach*, the gen, case of *cathair*, a city. In the latter case the word *carthach* would imply that this Prince of Desmond was "the founder of a city."—See Note "Carthage," p. 31.

MacCaura :† The following Stanzas respecting the Clan of MacCarthy or MacCaura are here given, as the author's tribute of respect to the memory of the late lamented D. F. MacCarthy, one of the sweetest of Ireland's poets :

THE CLAN OF MacCAURA.

By *Denis Florence MacCarthy.*

I.

Oh ! bright are the names of the chieftains and sages,
That shine like the stars through the darkness of ages,
Whose deeds are inscribed on the pages of story,
There for ever to live in the sunshine of glory—
Heroes of history, phantoms of fable,
Charlemagne's champions, and Arthur's Round Table—
Oh ! but they all a new lustre could borrow
From the glory that hangs round the name of MacCaura !

II.

Thy waves, Manzaneres, wash many a shrine,
And proud are the castles that frown o'er the Rhine,
And stately the mansions whose pinnacles glance
Through the elms of old England and vineyards of France
Many have fallen, and many will fall—
Good men and brave men have dwelt in them all—
But as good and as brave men, in gladness and sorrow,
Have dwelt in the halls of the princely MacCaura.

Baccach, Prince of Ulster, when they fell into comparative insignificance, branched from time to time into the following Houses :—The MacCarthys Mór ; the Clan Teige Roe ; the MacCarthys of Duhallow, called Mac-Donogh Carties ; Clan Donal Fionn ; Clan Dermod Oge ; MacCarthy na Mona ; MacCarthy Clough-Roe ; MacCarthy Aglish ; MacCarthy Rath-duane ; MacCarthy Drishane ; MacCarthy of Carrignavar ; MacCarthy Riabhach ; MacCarthy Rabagh ; Clan Dermod Reamhar ; MacCarthy Duna ; MacCarthy Glas ; MacCarthy of Muscry ; MacCarthy of Spring-house ; MacCarthy of Ballynoodie ; MacCarthy of Minnesota ; etc.

108. Muireadach : son of Carthach; the first who assumed the sirname " MacCarthy ;" was lord of Eogh-anacht Caisil ; born 1011 ; became ruler of his country in 1045, and d.

1092. He had a brother named Teige, who, on the death of said Muireadach succeeded to the crown of Munster, and who d. in 1123, leaving a dau. Sadhbh (Saiv) ; this

III.

Montmorency, Medina, unheard was thy rank
By the dark-eyed Iberian and light-hearted Frank,
And your ancestors wandered, obscure and unknown,
By the smooth Guadalquiver, and sunny Garonne—
Ere Venice had wedded the sea, or enrolled
The name of a Doge in her proud " Book of Gold ;"
When her glory was all to come on like the morrow,
There were chieftains and kings of the clan of MacCaura !

IV.

Proud should thy heart beat, descendant of Heber,
Lofty thy head as the shrines of the Guebre.
Like *them* are the halls of thy forefathers shattered,
Like *theirs* is the wealth of thy palaces scattered.
Their fire is extinguished—*your* flag long unfurled—
But how proud were you both in the dawn of the world !
And should both fade away, oh ! what heart would not sorrow
O'er the towers of the Guebre—the name of MacCaura !

V.

What a moment of glory to cherish and dream on,
When far o'er the sea came the ships of Heremon,
With Heber, and Ir, and the Spanish patricians,
To free *Inis-Fail* from the spells of magicians !
Oh ! reason had these for their quaking and pallor,
For what magic can equal the strong sword of valour?
Better than spells are the axe and the arrow,
When wielded or flung by the hand of MacCaura.

VI.

From that hour a MacCaura had reigned in his pride
O'er Desmond's green valleys and rivers so wide,
From thy waters, Lismore, to the torrents and rills
That are leaping for ever down Brandon's brown hills ;
The billows of Bantry, the meadows of Bere,
The wilds of Evaugh, and the groves of Glencare—
From the Shannon's soft shores to the banks of the Barrow—
All owned the proud sway of the princely MacCaura !

lady m. Dermod O'Brien (See "O'Brien Lords Inchiquin" Pedigree, No. 108.) Muireadhach left three sons—1. Cormac, 2. Donogh, and 3. Teige.

109. Cormac Magh-Tamnagh, bishop-King of Caisil: his son; succeeded to the throne on the death of his uncle Teige in 1123. This Prince m. Sadhbh, the widow of Dermod O'Brien, and his uncle Teige's daughter, by whom he had, besides other children, Dermod; Teige who d. s. p.; and Finghin who was called "Lic-Lachtna," and

who was killed in 1207. This Cormac, "King of Desmond" and "Bishop of the Kings of Ireland," .... was by treachery killed in his own house by Tirlogh, son of Diarmaid O'Brien, and by Dermod Lugach O'Conor "Kerry." Sometime before this Cormac, the ancient division of South and North Munster (or Desmond and Thomond) was renewed: this family retaining that of Kings of South Munster (or Desmond), and the progeny of Cormac Cas, second son of Olioll Olum, that of North Munster (or

VII.

In the house of Miodhchuart, by princes surrounded,
How noble his step when the trumpet was sounded,
And his clansmen bore proudly his broad shield before him
And hung it on high in that bright palace o'er him;
On the left of the Monarch the chieftain was seated,
And happy was he whom his proud glances greeted,
'Mid monarchs and chiefs at the great *Feis of Tara*—
Oh! none was to rival the princely MacCaura!

VIII.

To the halls of the Red Branch, when conquest was o'er,
The champions their rich spoils of victory bore,
And the sword of the Briton, the shield of the Dane,
Flashed bright as the sun on the walls of Eamhain—
There Dathy and Niall bore trophies of war,
From the peaks of the Alps and the waves of the Loire
But no Knight ever bore from the hills of Iveragh
The breast-plate or axe of a conquered MacCaura!

IX.

In chasing the red-deer what step was the fleetest,
In singing the love-song what voice was the sweetest—
What breast was the foremost in courting the danger—
What door was the widest to shelter the stranger—
In friendship the truest, in battle the bravest,
In revel the gayest, in council the gravest—
A hunter to-day, and a victor to-morrow?
Oh! who, but a chief of the princely MacCaura!

X.

But oh! proud MacCaura, what anguish to touch on
That one fatal stain of thy princely escutcheon—
In thy story's bright garden the one spot of bleakness—
Through ages of valour the one hour of weakness!
Thou, the heir of a thousand chiefs sceptred and royal—
Thou, to kneel to the Norman and swear to be loyal—
Oh! a long night of horror and outrage and sorrow
Have we wept for thy treason, base Diarmuid MacCaura!

Thomond; to which they were trusting during the reigns of fifty Kings of this Sept over all Munster, from Fiacha Maolleathan down to Mahoun, son of Cenneadh, and elder brother of Brian Boromha [Boroo], who was the first of the other Sept that attained to the sovereignty of all Munster; which they kept and maintained always after, and also assumed that of the whole Monarchy of Ireland for the most part of the time up to the Anglo-Norman Invasion, and the submission of Dermod to Henry the Second, King of England.

110. Dermod-Mór-na-Cill-Baghain,

Prince of Desmond, and King of Cork, A.D. 1144 to A.D. 1185: his son; was the first of the family that submitted to the Anglo-Norman yoke, A.D. 1172; was b. A.D. 1098; and m. twice, the second wife being a young Anglo-Norman lady named Petronilla de Bleete (or Bloet), "dame issue d'une noble famille d'Angleterre," with whom the family of *Stack* came to Ireland, and through whose influence they obtained from Dermod MacCarthy extensive possessions in the county of Kerry. Dermod was 75 years old when he contracted this second marriage.

By his submission to the English King, Dermod alienated the affections of his subjects (or clansmen), and his own children even rose against him. Cormac Liathanach, his eldest son, was proclaimed King of Munster, by the constitutional party of his people, and collected a numerous force for the expulsion of the strangers with whom his degenerate father was in alliance.

XI.

O! why, ere you thus to the foreigner pander'd,
Did you not bravely call round your Emerald standard
The chiefs of your house of Lough Lene and Clan Awley,
O'Donogh, MacPatrick, O'Driscoll, MacAuley,
O'Sullivan Mór, from the towers of Dunkerron,
And O'Mahon, the chieftain of green Ardinteran?
As the sling sends the stone, or the bent-bow the arrow,
Every chief would have come at the call of MacCaura!

XII.

Soon, soon, didst thou pay for that error, in woe—
Thy life to the Butler—thy crown to the foe—
Thy castles dismantled and strewn on the sod—
And the homes of the weak, and the abbeys of God!
No more in thy halls is the wayfarer fed—
Nor the rich mead sent round, nor the soft heather spread—
Nor the *clairseach's* sweet notes—now in mirth, now in sorrow—
All, all have gone by but the name of MacCaura!

XIII.

MacCaura, the pride of thy house is gone by,
But its name cannot fade, and its fame cannot die—
Though the Arigideen, with its silver waves shine
Around no green forests or castles of thine—
Though the shrines that you founded no incense can hallow—
Nor hymns float in peace down the echoing Allo—
One treasure thou keepest—one hope for the morrow—
True hearts yet beat of the clan of MacCaura!

Dermod was taken prisoner and put into confinement so as to place him beyond the possibility of rendering any assistance to the Anglo-Normans who invaded Desmond. Cormac was murdered in 1177, by Conor and Cathal O'Donoghue for the killing of Maccraith O'Sullivan ; his father was released, and slaughtered all those who questioned his authority and who would not submit to him ; in this murdering he was aided by Raymond le Gros, to whom, in consideration of such services, he granted the whole country forming the now barony of ClanMaurice in the county of Kerry. According to the then established law of Ireland the Chief of any tribe had it not in his power to alienate any portion of the tribe lands, so Dermod was legally guilty of treason against the Constitution, and of the robbery of his people. This Raymond le Gros had a son, Maurice, from whom his descendants have been named Fitzmaurice, the head of which family is at present called " Marquis of Lansdowne." This Dermod was slain in 1185 near the City of Cork, by Theobald Fitzwalter (Butler), and the English of that place, whilst holding a conference with them :—

> " And thus did he pay for his error in woe,
> His life to the Butler, his crown to the foe."

Dermod had five sons—1. Cormac, above mentioned, whose descendants are given in the Carew Collections of MSS., from 1180 to 1600 ; 2. Donal, who succeeded him ; 3. Muircheartach, who was slain by the O'Driscolls, in 1179 ; 4. Teige Roe na-Scairte ("na-scairte :" Irish, *of the bushes*, and a quo *Skerrett*), from whom are descended the *Clan Teige Roe ;* and 5. Finin, a future Prince of Desmond, who, in 1208, was slain by his nephews.

111. Donal Mór na-Curra* ("na curra" : Irish, *of the planting ;* "cur" : Irish, *a sowing ;* Heb., "cur," *to dig*), Prince of Desmond from 1185 to 1205 : his son. Born 1138. Donal defeated the Anglo-Normans in Munster, and drove them out of Limerick, in 1196 ; and again, in 1203, he defeated them when upwards of one hundred and sixty of these free-booters were slain. He left three sons, viz.: 1. Dermod of Dun-Droghian, who d. in 1217, leaving two sons, Teige and Finin, who were killed by their uncles—Teige in 1257, and Finin in 1235 ;

2. Cormac Fionn ; and 3. Donal Oge, alias Donal Goth† ("goth" : Irish, *straight*), who was lord of Carbery, and ancestor of *MacCarthy Glas*, and *MacCarthy Riabhach*. From this Donal Mór the word "Mór" (or Great) was added to the sirname of the elder branch of this family, to distinguish them from the younger branches spread from this ancient stock.

112. Cormac Fionn : his son ; born A.D. 1170. This prince founded the Abbey of Tracton, near Kinsale. He was earnestly solicited by the English King Henry III. to aid him

* *Donal Mór na-Curra :* From whom is derived the title *MacCarthy Mór.* It may be here observed that, according to Windele, the MacCarthy Mór was inaugurated at Lisban-na-Cahir, in Kerry ; at which ceremony presided O'Sullivan Mór and O'Donoghoe Mór. His Captains of war were the O'Rourkes, probably a branch of the O'Rourkes, princes of Brefney ; the MacEgans were his hereditary Brehons (or Judges) : and the O'Dalys and O'Duinins were his hereditary poets and antiquaries.

† *Goth :* Some descendants of this Donall Goth have called themselves *Gott.*

in his Scottish wars. He died in 1242, and left six sons—1: Donal Roe, of whom below; 2. Donn, of Inis-Droighan, who was ancestor of *MacCarthy of Acha-rassy;* 3. Dermod, who was the ancestor of *Mac-Donough,* and the *MacCarthys, of Duhallow;* 4. Donal Fionn, who was the ancestor of the MacCarthys called "Clann Donal Fionn," of Evenaliah; 5. Doncha-an-Drumin (or Doncha the Drummer), who was the ancestor of *MacDonnell of Barrotto,* and a quo *O'Druim,* anglicised *Drum, Drumin,* and *Drummond;* and 6. Donoch Cairtneach, a quo the *Viscounts MacCartney,* barons of Lisanoure. This Donoch, who became King of Desmond, left two sons: 1. Donal, who joined Edward the Bruce in his invasion of Ireland, and afterwards served under the standard of his brother, Robert King of Scotland, from whom he obtained a grant of lands in Argylshire, whence some of his descendants removed into Galloway, out of which a branch of the family removed into the county of Antrim, where it received a title from the English government, in the person of George Macartney, who, in 1776 was created *Viscount Macartney* and Baron of Lisanoure; the second son of Donoch was Teige of Dun Mac Tomain, who had a daughter Sadhbh (*anglicé* "Sarah"), who married Turlogh O'Brien, Prince of Thomond, who is No. 109 on the "O'Brien of Thomond" pedigree. This Cormac had a dau. Catherine, m. to Murtogh Mór O'Sullivan Mór.

113. Donal Roe MacCarthy Mór, Prince of Desmond: his son, b. 1239; d. 1302; he m. Margaret, the dau. of Nicholas Fitzmaurice, third lord of Kerry, by his wife Slaine, the dau. of O'Brien, prince of Thomond. He left, besides other children—Donal Oge; and Dermod Oge, of Tralee, who was slain in 1325 at Tralee, by his own cousin, Maurice Fitz-Nicholas Fitz-Maurice, 4th lord of Kerry; this Dermod Oge was ancestor of the *Mac-Finghin Carthys* of Cetherne and Gleneroughty, who was in 1880 represented by Randal Mac Finghin Mór—the Very Rev. Dr. MacCarthy, then Catholic Bishop of Kerry.

114. Donal Oge MacCarthy Mór: son of Donal Roe; b. 1239, d. 1307. This prince entered Carbery in A.D. 1306, and took his father's cousin-german, Donal Maol MacCarthy, prisoner; he released him soon afterwards, however, and in the close of the same year, both princes led their united forces against the Anglo-Normans, in Desmond. He left a daughter, Orflaith, who m. Turlogh Mór O'Brien, who is No. 114 on the "O'Brien of Thomond" pedigree.

115. Cormac MacCarthy Mór, Prince of Desmond: his son; b. 1271; d. 1359. This Prince m. Honoria, the dau. of Maurice Fitz-Maurice, 6th lord of Kerry, by his wife Elizabeth Condon, and had issue:—1. Donal; 2. Dermod Mór, created "Lord of Muscry," in 1353, and who was the ancestor of Mac-Carthy, lords of Muscry (or Muskerry) and Earls of Clancarty; 3. Feach (or Fiacha), ancestor of MacCarthy of Maing; 4. Donoch, ancestor of MacCarthy of Ardcanaghty; 5. Finghin (or Florence); 6. Eoghan; 7. Donal Buidhe (*pr. bhwee);* 8. Teige of Leamhain; and a daughter Catherine, m. to O'Sullivan Mór.

116. Donal MacCarthy Mór, Prince of Desmond: his son; b. 1303, d. 1371. He m. Joanna, the dau. of Maurice Oge Fitzgerald, 4th earl of

Kildare (d. 1391); and left issue :—

1. Teige; and 2. Donal, who d. s. p., in 1409. This Donal's wife Joanna, was usually styled the "Countess of Desmond."

117. Teige na Manistreach ("na manistreach": Irish, *of the Monastery*) : his son; b. 1340; d. 1413, in the City of Cork, and was interred there in the Franciscan Monastery, which he richly endowed.

118. Donal an Daimh ("an daimh" : Irish, *the poet*) : his son; b. 1373. This distinguished prince rebuilt the Franciscan abbey of Irrelagh or Muckross, on the borders of Lough Lene, the foundation of his ancestor, Cormac MacCarthy Mór, and dedicated it to the Holy Trinity. He died at an advanced age, leaving, besides other children, Eleanor (Nell), who m. Geoffrey O'Donoghue, chief of Glenflesk.

119. Teige-Liath : his son; born, 1407. He was slain in a battle between his own forces and those of the Earl of Desmond, in 1490.

120. Cormac Ladhrach : his son; b. 1440; d. 1516. This prince m. Eleanor, the dau. of Edmond Fitzmaurice, 9th lord of Kerry, by his wife, Mora, the dau. of O'Connor-Kerry.

121. Donal an Drumin : his son; b. 1481. This prince concluded a peace in 15— with Leonard Grey, Lord deputy of Ireland, into whose hands he delivered Teige and Dermod O'Mahony, his kinsmen, as hostages for his future fealty. He left issue :—1. Donal; 2. Teige, whose dau. Catherine, m. Thomas Fitzmaurice, lord of Kerry; 3. Catherine, who m. Finghin MacCarthy Reagh; and 4. Honoria, the 4th wife of James Fitzgerald, 15th Earl of Desmond.

122. Donal MacCarthy Mór: his son; b. 1518, d. 1596. This prince m. Honoria, the dau. of his brother-in-law, James, Earl of Desmond. He was, in 1565, created by Queen Elizabeth, Earl of Clancare (or Glencare), in the "Kingdom of Kerry," and Viscount of Valentia in the same county. Glencare or Clancare is a corrupted form of "Clan Carthy"—the English Court at that time being ignorant of the language or usages of the Irish. In 1568, this Donal was looked upon by his countrymen as "King of Munster." The "honours" heaped on him by the "virgin queen" expired with him, as he left no male legitimate issue. He left an illegitimate son, Donal, who proclaimed himself "The MacCarthy Mór," but did not succeed in his designs. His only legitimate child, the Princess Elana, married the celebrated Finghin MacCarthy. At A.D. 1596 the Four Masters say of this Donal:—

" MacCarthy Mór died, namely Donal, son of Donal, son of Cormac Ladhrach, son of Teïge; and although he was called MacCarthy Mór, he had been honourably created earl (of Clancare in Cork), before that time, by command of the sovereign of England ; he left no male heir after him, who would be appointed his successor; and only one daughter (Elana or Ellen), who became the wife of the son of MacCarthy Riabhach, namely Fingin or Florence, and all were of opinion that he was heir to that Mac-Carthy, who died, namely Donal."

123. Elana : dau. and heiress of Donal The MacCarthy Mór, Prince of Desmond; m. in 1588 Fingin (or Florence) MacCarthy Riabhach ("riabhach;" Irish, *brindled, swarthy*), Prince of Carbery and a quo *Rea*, *Ray*, and *Wray*), and had issue :—1. Teige who d. s. p., in the Tower of

H

London; 2. Donal; 3. Florence;* and 4. Cormac. This Florence, the husband of Elana, and son of Sir Donogh MacCarthy Riabhach, was b. in Carbery, 1579, d. in London, Dec. 18th, 1640; his burial is thus registered in St. Martin's-in-the-Fields, London:—

"MARKARKEY,
Decr. 18, 1640,
Dms. Hibernicus."

He was twice in captivity in London: the first period lasted eleven years and a few months; his second lasted thirty-nine years. His first offence was marrying an Irish Princess without Queen Elizabeth's permission; his second was "for reasons of state;" in neither case was he brought to trial. In 1600, in The O'Neill's camp at Inniscarra, near Cork, Florence was solemnly created *The MacCarthy Mór*, with all the rites and ceremonies of his family for hundreds of generations; which title and dignity was formally approved of by Aodh (or Hugh) O'Neill, the then virtual *Ard Righ*, or Ruler of the Irish in Ireland.**

124. Donal :† son of Elana and Fingin; m. Sarah, the dau. of Randal McDonnell, earl of Antrim, and widow of Nial Oge O'Neill of Killelah, and of Sir Charles O'Connor Sligo. Issue—two sons— 1. Flo-

rence, who m. Elinor, dau. of John Fitzgerald, Knight of Kerry, and died without issue; and 2. Cormac.

125. Cormac MacCarthy Mór : son of Cormac ; m. Honoria, dau. of John, Lord of Brittas ; and was a Colonel in the army of King James II.

126. Fingin (or Florence) MacCarthy Mór : his son ; m. Mary, dau. of Charles MacCarthy of Cloghroe. Issue : — 1. Randal ; 2. Cormac ; 3. Donal ; 4. Eliza ; and 5. Anne.

This (1) Randal, conformed to the late Established Church in Ireland; m. Agnes, eldest dau. of Edward Herbert, of Muckross, by Frances Browne, youngest dau. of Nicholas, the second lord and sister to Valentine the third lord Kenmare. Issue :—
1. Charles (d. s. p. 1770), who was called *The Last MacCarthy Mór*, and was an officer in the Guards ; 2. a dau. Elizabeth, m. to Geoffrey O'Donoghue of the Glen.

127. Cormac: the second son of Fingin ; lived along the Blackwater, and at Cork ; married Dela, the dau. and heiress of Joseph Welply (or Guelph), who emigrated from Wales, and settled in Cork, possessing a tract of land betwen the North and South Channel, with other portions of the confiscated estates of the

* *Florence :* This Florence, the third son of Elana and Fingin, married Mary, dau. of O'Donovan, and had issue—Donogh (or Denis). This Donogh m. Margaret Finch, "an English lady of distinction," and by her had two sons, viz: 1. Florence, his eldest son, who followed James II. to France, and was there father (of other children as well as) of Charles MacCarthy, living in 1764, and then in the French service ; and 2. Justin, his second son, who remained at Castlelough : and by his second wife Catherine Hussey, dau. of Colonel Maurice Hussey, of Cahirnane, said Donogh had Randal of Castlelough, who sold his estate to Crosbie in the reign of Geo. II. Randal had several sons who became very poor ; and some of his descendants are now living.

** See Life and Letters of *Florence MacCarthy Mór*, by Daniel MacCarthy Glas (London: Longmans, Green, Reader and Dyer ; Dublin : Hodges and Smith).

† *Donal :* This Donal succeeded as *MacCarthy Mór*, and he inherited nearly all of his grandfather Donal's estates; together with those of his father Finin, in Carbery. In Munster this Donal and his brothers were still styled "THE ROYAL FAMILY."

Muscry MacCarthys, which were purchased for him. Cormac succeeded to Welply's possessions, assumed the name of his father-in-law, and was generally called "Welply Mac-Carthy." He died about 1761. Issue:—John, Dela, Samuel, and James.

128. John MacCarthy Mór (alias Welply): son of Cormac; married Elizabeth Minheer, by whom he had issue three sons, and eight daughters. The sons were—1. William, who is 129 on this pedigree; 2. John,* of Bengour, parish of Murragh, co. Cork, who married a Miss Norwood; 3. Joseph, who died unmarried. Of the daughters, one was married to Alderman Sparks; one to Alderman Penlerrick, of Cork, one to— Baldwin, of Ballyvorney; one (Abigail, who d. 20th Sept., 1722) to John Nash (d. 1725), of Brinney, near Bandon; one to Sir John Crowe; one to—Bellsang of Bandon; and another to Walter Philips of Mossgrove, Kilnalmeaky.

129. William:† son of John Mac-Carthy Mór (alias "Welply"), The MacCarthy Mór; m. Anne Harris of Bandon. On the death of his parents, in Cork, he removed to one of his possessions called Crahallah, barony of Muscry, and subsequently to Lower Bellmount, parish of Moviddy, where, in 1833, he died aged 91 years, divested of nearly all his property; his wife died in 1836, aged 81 years; both buried at St. Helen's, Moviddy. Issue, three sons and six daughters:—I. John (No. 130 on this stem); II. Marmaduke; III. William; IV. Elizabeth V. Mary; VI. Jane; VII. Catherine; VIII. Anne; and IX. Sadhbh (or Sarah).

(II.) Marmaduke: second son of William; m. Jane Uncles of Carbery, resided in Cork city, and d. s. p.; interred at Moviddy.

(III.) William of Crookstown: third son of William; m. twice; 1st, to Ellen, dau. of John and Joanna Holland his wife; 2ndly, to Ellen Collins of Mitchelstown (d. Feb., 1873). Issue only by 1st wife:—1. Annie, b. 15th March, 1833, m. 4th March,

---

* John : This John of Bengour had by his wife, amongst other children, Samuel (d. 1885) of Kilronan, near Dunmanway. The distinguished J. J. Welply, Esq., M.D., Bandon, co. Cork, is (1887) son to this Samuel; he is m. to Miss Jagoe, and has issue

† William : Old Sam Welply of Macroom was a brother's son of this William. This Sam had four sons and three daughters. The sons were James, Daniel, John, Sam. James was married to Mary Collins, sister of Bishop Collins, of Limerick; Daniel was married to a Miss Fegan. Samuel was married to Dorcas, daughter of Major Crowe, of Limerick. John's wife was a Miss Richardson, sister-in-law of the Rev. Simon Davis, Rector of Macroom, and aunt of William Hutchinson Massey, of Mount Massey, Macroom. Of the three Miss Welplys, two were married to two first cousins—Patrick, and Charles Riordan, of Macroom; and the third to a Mr. Hennessy, of Mill Street.

Another cousin to No. 129, also named William, lived at Prohurus, near Macroom, and was married to a Miss Scriviner, from Kerry. Of their children, Henry, the eldest, was married to a Miss Slattery, of Thurles; Ellen, to a Mr. White, of Thurles; Anne, to Mr. Lynch, of Kilmurry, Barony of Muskerry; Jane, to the late James Baldwin, of Macroom; Eliza, to a Mr. Murphy, of Macroom; and Samuel, to a Miss D'Esmond, of Cork.

One of these Mrs. Riordans, had two daughters—Mary Anne, and Catherine; Mary Anne married a Mr. Feely, Bank Manager in Tramore, co. Waterford, and had a son Maurice, a Barrister-at-Law; Catherine married her cousin, Daniel O'Connell Riordan, Q.C. This Catherine died in June, 1879.

1850, to John Spence, has two sons, and six daus., some of them married, they reside in London, Canada West, North America.

2. Elizabeth-Jane; second daughter of William; b. 12th April, 1835, m. 10th June, 1860, at St. Luke's Church, Chelsea, London, to James Howell. Issue :—three children—1. James-Philip-Edward, b. 24th June, 1861; 2. Arthur-William, b. 22nd Feb., 1864; and 3. Elizabeth Ellen (Bessie), b. March 8th, 1866. James Howell, d. 21st Feb., 1870, and this Elizabeth-Jane, m. secondly James Lidbetter, of Buckland, near Hastings, Sussex, August 13th, 1877, at St. Peter's Church, Pimlico, London; he died s. p. May 11th, 1881, buried at Fulham Cemetery. This Elizabeth-Jane and her three children are alive in London in 1887.

3. Mary Anne; third dau. of William; b. Nov. 11th, 1842, m. Feb. 9th, 1862, Joseph Topley, at St. Philip's Church, Kensington, London. Issue :—One dau., Elizabeth-Jane, b. August 13th, 1864, d. Jan. 24th, 1874. Joseph Topley d. Jan. 3rd, 1871. This Mary-Anne m. secondly to Richard Cole of Nighton, Radnorshire, at St. Paul's Church, Hammersmith, Feb. 4th,

1873. Issue :—One son—Charles Alfred, b. April 7th, 1874. This Richard Cole d. July 28th, 1874. Mrs. Cole and her son are living at Old Brentford, Middlesex, in 1887.

William ("Welply") MacCarthy Mór; died May 12th, 1873, aged 73 years, and was buried at Hammersmith cemetery.

(IV.) Elizabeth, m. twice; 1st, to George Good (or O'Guda), of Reen, parish of Murragh, co. Cork; issue extinct, the last being Anne of Crookstown, d. 5th Nov., 1881, and buried at Moviddy. This Elizabeth m. 2ndly, to John Payne, only son of Thomas Payne,* of Garryhankard, near Bandon: surviving issue being Jane-Elizabeth, m. John Curran of Coothill, who was subsequently teacher in Fermoy College, more lately Manager of the Turkish Baths of Bray, and lastly of Lincoln Place Baths, Dublin, where he d. in 1886, leaving no issue; this Jane-Elizabeth lives (1887) at Rathcore Rectory, Enfield, co. Meath.

(V.) Mary, m. William Rose, of Ballincollig, near Cork, both

---

* *Payne :* Thomas Payne was married to Rebecca, daughter of the Rev. Mr. Harrison, of Limerick, and Rector of Kilbrogan, Bandon. This Thomas had a brother named George, who had issue two sons. The late Rev. Somers Payne, of Upton, was this Thomas Payne's uncle's son. The Rev. Somers Payne's mother was sister of John and Henry Shears, Merchants, in the City of Cork, who perished on the scaffold for alleged "high treason" at the opening of the present century.

This family of "Payne" is, we understand, now represented by John-Warren Payne, Esq., J.P., Beach House, Bantry; James Henry Payne, Esq., J.P., Beachmount, Upton; and the Rev. Somers H. Payne (Vicar Gen., Kilaloe), Upton. A few others reside in parts of West Cork, and in Bandon, as farmers and shop-keepers. About forty years ago Richard, son of John, son of Thomas Payne, emigrated, and now lives in Cincinnatti, Ohio, U.S. America.

The ancestors of the gentlemen here alluded to were natives of the south-east of England; and, as early as A.D. 1400, settled in Ireland. "Seon Pauint" (John Payne), was bishop of Meath in 1500. On the confiscation of the lands of The O'Mahony and MacCarthy Riabach, portions were purchased by the ancestors of this family. The head of the name is Sir Coventry Payne, Bart., Wootton House, Essex, England. There are various gentlemen of the name in the south of England, and in London.

d., leaving issue : Alexander, and Mary : Alexander (d. 1879), m. 'twice: 1st, to a Miss Lee, by whom he had a numerous issue; by his 2nd wife, Miss Kelleher, he had no issue : Mary, m. Cornelius Sporle, of Essex, England ; only surviving issue is Louisa, m. to Joseph Rainsbury.

(VI.) Jane, m. Richard, son of Walter De Val (or Wall) of Lower Bellmount; d. leaving an only dau. Jane-Anne, who m. Robert O'Neill, *alias*, "Payne,"—See the "O'Neill" Prince of Tyrone pedigree, No. 133.

(VII.) Catherine d. unm.

(VIII.) Anne, m. Michael Cunningham, of Bantry, subsequently of Lower Bellmount :—Issue —1. Michael, who m. three times: 1st, to Mary Lynch, 2nd to Mary Healy, and 3rd to Mary Broe; issue by the first marriage extinct; by the 2nd marriage he had :

1. John (in Boston), m. and has issue ; (2.) Maria (d.), m. a Mr. Kelly. Issue:—Annie, Frederick, Cecilia ; 3. Annie (d), m. a Mr. Graham. Issue :—Arthur - John-George ; 4. Marmaduke, d. an infant; 5. Patrick (in Boston), unm. in 1887 ; 6. Nora (in Chicago), unm. in 1887 ; issue by the 3rd marriage —7. Nelly (or Eleanor), b. 3rd Sept., 1865 ; 8. Edward, b. 8th June, 1876 ; 9. Sadhbh (or Sarah) d. an infant; and 10. Alexander, b. 12th Dec., 1871; these three with

their mother live at Lr. Bellmount, 1887. 2. William, the second son of Anne, m. a Miss Jeffers, of Waterford; lives (1887) in Dublin, and has issue. 3. Daniel, the third son of Anne, lives in England. 4. Margaret, d. unm.

IX. Sadhbb (or Sarah), m. Richard Swords, of Bandon; lived and died in Cork; buried at St. Finn Barr's. Issue— William, Robert, Edward, Joseph, Mary-Anne, Sarah, Elizabeth, and Jane ; Richard Swords, d. in Cork ; Mary-Anne (1887) lives in Cork; the others reside in Washington, U.S. America.

130. John : eldest son of William ; m. Anne O'Crowly, of Kilbarry, barony of Muskerry; d. leaving issue—

I. John; of whom presently; II. Joseph; III. Duke ; IV. Margaret; V. Anne.

II. Joseph, is unm.

III. Duke has been a Captain in the U.S. Army ; resides at Oxford, Ohio, U.S.A., and is married.

IV. Margaret, m. and d. leaving a dau. Maggie.

V. Anne, m. Thomas Walsh, of Kilmurry ; alive in Cincinnatti, 1886, no issue.

131. John MacCarthy Mór,* *alias* "Welply :" his son ; m. a Miss Lane a native of Moss Grove Commons, co. Cork, and emigrated to America about forty-six years ago ; living in Cincinnatti in 1887; has six surviving children.

---

† *MacCarthy Mór:* There is now (1887) in Hanley, Staffordshire, England, a Mr. MacCarthy, a Wine Merchant, who claims to be the lineal descendant of " *The MacCarthy Mór* ;" he is the son of Thomas, son of Justin, son of Donall, but we regret that we are at present unable to trace the lineage back any farther.

MacCARTHY REAGH. (No. 2.)

Prince of Carbery.

Arms and *Crest :* Same as MacCarthy Mór. *Motto :* Fortis, ferox, et celer.

DONAL GOTH ("goth," Ir., *straight*), second son of Donal Mór-na-Curra, King of Desmond (see No. 111 on the "MacCarthy Mór" pedigree), was the ancestor of *MacCarthaigh Riabhach* ("riabhach" : Irish, *swarthy*, etc.), anglicised *MacCarthy Reagh.*

112. Donal Goth; son of Donal Mór-na-Curra ; known also (see MacFirbis) as Donal Glas; lord of Carbery, A.D. 1205 to 1251. This Donal dethroned Dermod Fitz-Mahon O'Mahony, lord of Iveagh, after the sanguinary engagement of Carrigdurtheacht, in which the three sons of The O'Mahony, and O'Coffey (or O'Cowhig), chief of Coillsealvy were slain. Donal, who was in 1251 slain by John Fitzthomas Fitzgerald, commonly called "John of Callan," left six sons, viz. ; 1. Dermod Don, who succeeded his father, and whose descendants, known as the "Clan Dermod," possessed an extensive district in Carbery, and the Castles of Cloghane and Kilcoe ; 2. Teige Dall, ancestor of the "Clan Teige Dall ;" 3. Cormac, of Mangerton, so called from having defeated the English at the foot of that mountain, in 1259 ; 4. Finghin Raghna-Roin, so called from his having been slain at this place by the attendants of John de Courcy, in 1261 ; 5. "The Aithcleirach ;" and 6. Donal Maol.

113. Donal Maol: his son ; became lord of Carbery, 1262 to 1310; defeated the de Courcys of Kinsale in several engagements, and liberated Donal and Teige MacCarthy, who were kept in close confinement by their Kinsman Dermod Mac-Carthy Mór of Tralee. Donal Maol left two sons—Donal Caomh, and Cormac.

114. Donal Caomh (or the Handsome) : his son ; upon the death of his father became, in 1311, Prince of Carbery ; he died in 1320, leaving, besides other children, Donal Glas ; Cormac Donn, the ancestor of *MacCarthy Glas ;* and a daughter married to Dermod FitzConnor O'Mahony, by whom she had Donogh O'Mahony of Iveagh. Donal Caomh married the widow of Dermod O'Mahon, and daughter to Robert de Carewe, "Marquis of Cork," who settled in Carbery, having built a castle near the Abbey of Bantry, called "Carewe Castle," *alias* Downi-marky.

115. Donal Glas: eldest son of Donal Caomh ; Prince of Carbery from A.D. 1326 to 1366. This Prince rebuilt the Abbey of Timoleague upon the ruins of the ancient abbey of the same saint (St. Molaga), and in this abbey he was buried in 1366, leaving by his wife—a daughter of O'Cromin—two sons, Donal Reagh, and Dermod ; and a daughter Mary, who married Bernard O'Sullivan Bere.

116. Donal Glas, MacCarthy Reagh, Prince of Carbery : son of Donal Glas ; married Joanna Fitzmaurice, by whom he had Donogh of Iniskean ;* Dermod an-Dunaidh ;

* *Donogh of Iniskean:* From this Donogh descended the "Slught Dermod" of Iniskean (in Carbery, west of Bandon), and the MacCarthys "Rabach,"—many of whom still live around Bandon. From Dermod, son of Finin, son of Cormac, son of *Donogh,* are descended the former ; and from Finin, son of Donal "Rabach," son of Cormac, son of same *Donogh,* the latter branch.

Donal Glas* (d. s. p. 1442); Eoghan, slain 1432 ; and Cormac na-Coille. This Donal was sirnamed *Riabhach* or "swarthy," on account of his appearance; from him the family has been named "Reagh;" he died 1414.

117. Dermod an Dunaidh Mac-Carthy Riabhach: his son; Prince of Carbery in 1452 ; married Ellen, the daughter of Teige, lord of Muscry, and had issue: Finghin ; Donal, who predeceased his father ; and Dermod, who had a son Fing-hin.

118. Finghin MacCarthy Reagh, Prince of Carbery: his son ; married Catherine, daughter of Thomas Fitzgerald, the 8th "Earl of Des-mond," who was beheaded at Dro-gheda ; he left issue : Donal, Dermod, Donogh, and Cormac.

This Finghin was in high favour with Henry VII., King of England, who "authorized" him, in con-junction with Cormac MacTeige, lord of Muscry, to get the homage of the independent Irish chiefs.

119. Donal MacCarthy Reagh, Prince of Carbery: his son ; go-verned Carbery for twenty-six years ; assisted Cormac Oge Laidir, lord of Muscry, against the English in Munster, in 1521. He married twice : first, to the daughter of Cormac Laidir, lord of Muscry, by whom he had two sons and one

daughter—the sons were : 1. Der-mod, who was slain by Walter Fitz-gerald, son of the Earl of Kildare ; and 2. Donal, who died s. p. ; the daughter was Ellen, who married Teige Mór O'Driscoll. Donal Mac-Carthy Reagh married secondly to Eleanor Fitzgerald (daughter of Gerald Fitzgerald, 8th Earl of Kil-dare), whose sister Alice was wife to Conn O'Neill, Prince of Ulster : the issue of this marriage was four sons, who were successively (by usage of tanistry) "Princes of Car-bery :"—1. Cormac na-Haine ; 2. Finin, married Catherine, daughter of Donal an-Drumin, Prince of Des-mond, he left no male issue ; 3. Donogh (d. 1576), married Joanna, the daughter of Maurice Fitzgerald, by whom he had *Finin*, who married Elana, Princess of Desmond, and who was made *The MacCarthy Mór* by Aodh O'Neill, Prince of Ulster ; Donogh had also Dermod Maol, who m. Ellen, the dau. of Teige O'Donoghue of Glenflesk ; and Julia, who married Owen O'Sullivan Mór. Donogh married, secondly, to a dau. of John, lord Power, by whom he had Donogh Oge, who m. Graine, the dau. of Dermod, lord Muscry ; was interred at Timoleague ; 4. Owen (" of the Parliament") d. 1593; m. Ellen, dau. of Dermod O'Cal-laghan, by whom he had two sons and six daughters:—the sons were

* *Donal Glas :* This Donal left illegitimate sons, the founders of the "Slught Glas;" these possessed most of the parishes of Ballinadee and Ballymoney, on the Bandon. Their chief residence was the Castle of Phale, in 1601, the stronghold of the brothers, Donogh, Donal, and Finin Mac Carthy, the acknowledged heads of the Slught Glas. Finin fled to Spain in 1601, and Donogh died soon after, leaving his brother Donal the head of the *Phale Carties.* Owen, son of Donogh, was "attained" (attainted) in 1642. His son Owen-Roe-Glaughig MacCarthy is still remembered, and the site of the gallows, on which he hanged evil disposed people, is yet pointed out. The Old Castle of Phale was standing some seventy years ago; its stones were used to build Ballyneen Village and Ballymoney Protestant Church, and not a vestige of it now exists. Superintendent MacCarthy, who presided some years ago over the Dublin Metropolitan Police, was the Head of this tribe. For a time Kilgobban Castle also belonged to the Slught Glas. Some of them settled as farmers at Kilnacronogh, where their descendants may still be found.

—Finin, who m. Eleanor, the dau. of Edmond Fitzgibbon, the White Knight, and widow of his cousin Cormac ; and had by her several children : one of these, Catherine, m. Dermod MacCarthy, younger son of Teige an-Duna; Ellen, who married Finin O'Driscoll; Julia, who m. Dermod, son of Donal O'Sullivan Mór ; Eleanor, who m. Finin M'Owen Carragh Carthy of Kilbrittain ; Joanna, who m. Donal O'Donovan ; Honoria, who married Edmond Fitzgerald, Knight of the Valley; Graine, who m. twice, first, Barry Oge of Buttevant, and, secondly, Cormac, son of Cormac MacTeige, of Muscry.

120. Cormac na Haoine, Prince of Carbery : son of Donal ; married Julia, dau. of Cormac, lord of Muscry, and had by her a son called Donal-na-Pipi.

121. Donal-na-Pipi, Prince of Carbery (d, 1612) : his son ; became Prince on the death of his uncle Owen ; he married Margaret Fitzgerald, dau. of Sir Thomas Roe Fitzgerald, and had by her a numerous issue :—1. Cormac ; 2. Donough (proprietor of Kilbrittain, d. s. p.); 3. Teige, chief of Kilgobane, d. s. p. ; 4. Donal ; 5. Owen ; 6. Julia, who m. Edmond, Lord Barry ; 7. Ellen, who m. Teige MacCarthy, of Ballikay (co. Cork), by whom she had three sons who died young, and two daughters ; 8. Finin, of Bandubh, who left a son Donal, who married Honoria, dau. of Owen O'Sullivan Bere, by whom he had a son, Finin of Bandubh, who became a lieutenant-colonel in the Regiment of Donal MacCormac MacCarthy Reagh, in the service of James II.

122. Cormac : son of Donal; m. Eleanor, dau. of Edmund Fitzgibbon, the White Knight, and who afterwards married Finin Mac-

Carthy, of Iniskean, and had by him a son Donal. This Cormac died before his father.

123. Donal, Prince of Carbery : son of Cormac No. 122 ; m. Ellen, dau. of David Roche, lord Fermoy, and had by her a son Cormac.

124. Cormac MacCarthy Reagh, Prince of Carbery : son of Donal ; m., before his father's death, Eleanor, dau. of Cormac Oge, Lord Muscry ; was commander of the Munster Clans in 1641, his lieutenant being Teige an-Duna. This Cormac (or Charles) had by his wife issue :—1. Finin ; 2. Donal (who raised a regiment of Foot for James II.), m. Maria, dau. of Colonel Richard Townsend, of Castletown, and dying in 1691 was interred at Timoleague; 3. Donogh, who m. Margaret de Courcy, by whom he had :—1. Alexander, who served on the side of James II. at the Boyne and Aughrim ; 2. Donal, who died in the French Service ; and 3. Eleanor-Susanna, who m. Baron de Hook of the French Service; 4. Ellen, who m. John, Lord Kinsale ; and 5. Catherine, who m. Pierre St. John, of Macroom, by whom she had a son and three daughters. This Cormac was alive in 1667. Most of his estates were confiscated by Cromwell (1652), but at the Restoration, he got back a portion. After the taking of Kilbrittain Castle, he led a wandering life in Carbery, in Bere, and in Bantry,

125. Finin MacCarthy Reagh, Prince of Carbery : his son ; born in 1625 ; went to France in 1647 ; married there the dau. of a French Count ; had by her two sons—1. Cormac ; and 2. Dermot (b. 1658), m. in France and d. *circa* 1728, there leaving a son Donal. This Donal MacCarthy Reagh was b. in France 1690, came to Ireland, and

lived near Dunmanway, where he m. Kate O'Driscoll, by whom he had :—1. Margaret, who m. Richard O'Neill, Hereditary Prince of Ulster (see the "O'Neill Princes of Tyrone" pedigree, No. 131); 2. Cormac; 3. Donal; 4. Owen; and another son and a daughter.

126. Cormac: son of Finin; Prince of Carbery; returned to Ireland, married there, and died leaving one son Owen.

127. Owen: Hereditary Prince of Carbery; married, and died in 1775, leaving issue a son.

128. Cormac (or Charles) MacCarthy Reagh: his son; born about 1721, married Catherine, daughter of Charles Bernard* of Palace-Anne (near Iniskean). This Cormac, who was a solicitor, was Seneschal of the Manor of Macroom, Recorder of Clonakilty, and Clerk of the Crown for the County. His wife died in Bandon, aged 104 years.

129. Francis-Bernard MacCarthy Reagh: his son; Hereditary Prince of Carbery; in 1793 married Elizabeth (who d. January 1844) daughter of William Daunt of Kilcascan, by his wife Jane Gumbleton of Castle Rickard. She was sister of the late Captain Joseph Daunt of Kilcascan, who died 1826: issue of Francis Bernard—five sons and four daughters.

130. William MacCarthy Reagh: his son; Hereditary Prince of Carbery; born 7th October, 1801; married on 10th February, 1827, to Margaret-Foster, daughter of the Rev. Mountiford Longfield, of

Churchill, Co. Cork, and sister of the Right Hon. Judge Longfield. Her mother was a Miss Lysaght. This William and his wife, in 1848, or thereabouts emigrated to Wisconsin, U.S., America; died, leaving issue, all settled in America :—1. Francis-Longfield MacCarthy; 2. Grace-Lysaght, b. 5th March, 1829; d. 12th July, 1839; 3. Elizabeth, b. 15th October, 1830; m. 1852, to Arthur ·Beamish Bernard, son of Samuel Beamish, of Maghmór (near Bandon); heir of Entail of Palace Anne, which he sold, and is now settled in America; 4. Margaret-Anne, b. 4th March, 1833; m. on 9th June, 1852, to George, son of the late Dr. Beamish: Issue, one son and two daughters; 5. Mountiford-Longfield, b. 4th June, 1835; m. Elizabeth, dau. of Samuel Beamish, of Maghmór, niece of Arthur Beamish-Bernard, of Palace-Anne, who, in 1855, died in America (she died on the 15th Jan., 1862, leaving two sons); 6. William-Henry, b. 27th Oct., 1837; 7. Henry-Longfield, b. 24th March, 1839; d. 14th April, 1840; 8. Mary-Caroline, b. 16th May, 1840; 9. Robert-Longfield, b. 30th August, 1842; living in 1880; 10. Grace-Patisnee, b. 16th June, 1845, at Palmyra, Wisconsin.

131. Francis-L. MacCarthy Reagh: son of William; Hereditary Prince of Carbery; born 30th December, 1827; married a widow, by whom, issue, one son, whose name we have not learned.

* *Bernard:* "Beamish" was his patronymic. His mother was a Bernard of the same family as the "earls of Bandon." On the death of his uncle Tom Bernard, in 1795, he adopted the sirname *Bernard*, as a condition of inheriting Palace Anne. The house (on the Bandon) is now (1887) in ruins; and the place occupied by a dairyman

MacCARTHY. (No. 3.)

Lords of Muskry.

Armorial Bearings : Same as those of the " MacCarthy Mór."

CORMAC MACCARTHY MOR, Prince of Desmond (see the MacCarthy Mór Stem, No. 115,) had a second son, Dermod Mór, of Muscry ("now "Muskerry") who was the ancestor of *MacCarthy, lords of Muscry,* and *earls of Clan Carthy.*

116. Dermod Mór : son of Cormac Mór, Prince of Desmond ; b. 1310 ; created, by the English, in A.D. 1353, "Lord of Muscry;" issue :— 1. Cormac; 2. Felimy; who was ancestor of *MacCarthy of Tuonadronan ;* and Donoch, whose descendants are called *Carthy* (modernized "Cartie"), *of Cluanfada.* This Dermod was taken prisoner by MacCarthy of Carbery, by whom he was delivered up to his (Dermod's) mother's brother the Lord Fitz-Maurice, who put him to death, A.D. 1368.

Another authority states he was slain by the O'Mahonys in 1367.

117. Cormac, lord of Muscry : his son; b. 1346. This Cormac was slain by the Barrys in Cork, and interred in Gill-Abbey, in that city, on the 14th of May, 1374. From his youngest son Donal are descended the *Carthies of Sean Choill* (Shanakiel).

118. Teige (or Thadeus), lord of Muscry : his son ; b. 1380, d. 1448 ; governed Muscry thirty years ; issue :—1. Cormac ; 2. Dermod, ancestor of the *MacCarthys of Drishane,* and founder of the castle of Carrigafooka ; 3. Ellen, who married Dermod-an-Duna MacCarthy, Prince of Carbery ; and Eoghan,* of Rathduane.

119. Cormac Laidir : his son ; b. 1411 ; married to Mary, dau. of Edmond Fitzmaurice, lord of Kerry, by whom he had Cormac Oge, and a dau. who married Donal Mac-Carthy-Reagh, of Carbery. This Cormac, in 1465, founded the Franciscan Monastery of Kilcredhe or *Cill-Credhe* (now "Kilcrea"), in the parish of Kilbonane, dedicated to St. Bridget, founded five additional churches ; and also built the donjon of Blarney Castle, together with the castles of Kilcrea, and Ballymaccadan. The *Four Masters* record his death as follows, under A.D. 1494 :

"Cormac, *i.e.* the MacCarthy, the son "of Tadg, son of Cormac, lord of Mus-"kerry, was killed by his own brother "Eoghan, and by his (Eoghan's) sons. "He was a man who raised and revered "the church, and was the first founder of "the monastery of Kilcrea ; a man that "ordained that the Sabbath should be "kept holy in his dominions as it ought "to be ; and he was succeeded by Eoghan, "son of Tadg."

He was buried in Kilcrea, in the middle of the choir ; the inscription on his tomb runs thus :—

"Hic jacet Cormacus, fil. Thadei, fil. Cormac fil. Dermidii Magni MacCarthy, Duns de Musgraigh-Flayn, acistius conventus primus fundator. an. Dom. 1494."

120. Cormac Oge, lord of Muscry :

* *Eoghan :* From this Eoghan descended Donogh MacCartie, who lived *temp.* James II., and married Eva O'Donoghue, of Glenflesk, by whom he had a son, Charles, who married a Miss Barrett, of Barretts. By this lady Charles had a son, Charles, who married Mary O'Leary, daughter of Art. O'Leary (and niece of Col. MacCarthy

son of Cormac Laidir ; b. A.D. 1447 ; d. in 1537 ; buried at Kilcrea. Married to Catherine Barry. Issue :— Teige ; and Julia, who was married thrice : first, to Gerald Fitzmaurice, lord of Kerry ; secondly, to Cormac MacCarthy Reagh, of Kilbrittain Castle ; and thirdly, to Edmond Butler, lord Dunboyne. This Cormac defeated the Fitzgeralds in several engagements ; fought the battle of "Cluhar and Moor" (Mourne Abbey), where he, assisted by MacCarthy Reagh and other chieftains, defeated James Fitzgerald —earl of Desmond—who ravaged Munster in 1521. This Cormac attended Parliament in 1525, as "lord of Muscry." He had a dau. Ellen, m. to James Barrett ; and another, Mary, married to O'Sullivan Mór.

121. Teige, lord of Muscry : his son ; born, A.D. 1472 ; died in A.D. 1565 ; buried at Kilcrea. This Cormac married Catherine, the daughter of Donal MacCarthy Reagh, prince of Carbery, and by her had issue :—1. Dermod ; 2. Sir Cormac MacTeige, lord of Muscry, who was ancestor of the families of Courtbreack, Bealla, Castlemór,* and Clochroe ; 3. Owen, who was slain at Dromanee ; 4. Donal-na-Countea,† who died in 1581 ; 5. Ceallachan, who was ancestor of the *Carthys of Carricknamuck ;* 6. Donoch, who was ancestor of the *Carthys of Carew ;* 7. Eleanor.

122. Dermod, lord of Muscry : his son ; born A.D. 1501 ; m. Elana, dau. of Maurice Fitzgerald, and niece of James, the 15th earl of Desmond ; died in 1570, buried at Kilcrea. Issue :—Cormac ; Teige, ancestor of the *MacCarthys of Insirahell* (near Crookstown, co. Cork) ; Julia, married to John de Barry, of Laisarole ; and Grainé, who married Donogh Oge MacCarthy Reagh, of Carbery In 1563, this Dermod fought and defeated Sir Maurice Dubh (duff) Fitzgerald, his father-in-law, who was beheaded by his guard.

123. Cormac Mór, lord of Muscry : his son ; born, A.D. 1552 ; married to Maria Butler. Issue :—1. Cormac ; 2. Teige, ancestor of the *MacCarthys of Aglish ;* Donal, ancestor of the *MacCarthys of Carrignavar ;* and Julia, who married twice : first, David Barry of Buttevant ; and, secondly, Dermod O'Shaughnessy of Gort, in the county of Galway. This Cormac Mór attended parliament in 1578 as "Baron of Blarney ;" conformed to the Protestant church ; died in 1616 ; and was buried at Kilcrea. He also contested with Florence MacCarthy Reagh for the dignity of "MacCarthy Mór," but did not succeed. Acted as Sheriff of Cork ; and on the memorable 21st October, 1601, when all his kinsmen were ranged under the O'Neill, the *Red Hand of Ulster,* at Kinsale, this Cormac assisted the

of Drishane), by whom he had a son Denis, who married Joanna O'Donoghue Dubh, and had Charles, who married Mary O'Donoghue of Killaha (niece to the O'Donoghue of the Glens), and Jeremiah, who was the father of Denis MacCarthy of Woodview, co. of Cork. Charles, the eldest son of Denis, had by his wife, Mary O'Donoghue, a son Denis, who married Catherine, daughter of D. O'Connell, of Tralee (by his wife Ellen, sister of Daniel O'Connell, M.P.) ; and a son Daniel MacCarthy, of Headford Castle, in the county of Kerry.

* *Castlemór* : This castle is now a ruin near the Bride, on a limestone rock ; built by the MacSweeneys. It was possessed by Phelim MacOwen MacCarthy, who was driven from it by Oliver Cromwell in the Commonwealth period.

† *Donal-na-Countea* : This epithet *na-Countea* means "of the county." In the State Papers, *temp.* Elizabeth, this Donald is styled "Donyll ny-Countie."

English against the Irish, who were there commanded by O'Neill and O'Donnell. For this act he received many "honours" from the English.

124. Cormac Oge, 17th lord of Muscry : his son ; born A.D. 1564 ; married Margaret, the daughter of Donogh O'Brien, by his wife Elena Roche ; and died in London, on the 20th of February, 1640. This Cormac was educated at Oxford (England), and on the 15th of November, 1628, was created " Baron of Blarney" and " Lord Viscount Muscry." Issue :—1. Donogh ; 2. Maria, who married Sir Valentine Brown, ancestor of the Earls of Kenmare ; 3. Ellen, who married Colonel Edward Fitzmaurice, only son of Thomas, 18th lord of Kerry ; and 4. Eleanor, who was the first wife of Cormac MacCarthy Reagh.

125. Donoch MacCarthy, lord Viscount Muscry : son of Cormac ; born A.D. 1594 ; created " Earl of ClanCarthy" by Charles II., in 1658 ; was confederate chieftain and commander of the Munster forces in the civil wars in Ireland of 1641-52 ; exiled to the Continent, and his property conferred on his second wife Ellen (a sister of the first Duke of Ormond) and her issue ; returned to Ireland at the " Restoration" of Charles II. ; contested the right of Florence and Donal to the dignity of MacCarthy Mór (See Appendix, Annals of the Four Masters") ; died in London (England), July, 1665. By his first marriage this Donoch had a son named Donall, who was known as the *Buchaill Bán* (or " the

fair-haired boy"). By his second marriage he had three sons :—1. Cormac ; 2. Ceallachan, who conformed to the Protestant religion ; 3. Justin,* created " Lord Mountcashel" by King James II., in 1689 ; and died in France, 1st July, 1694, at Barrege, of the effects of wounds.

Cormac, lord Muskerry, above mentioned (who d. 24th Dec. 1675), was, in 1665, engaged in a sea fight with the Dutch off Harwich, whilst in the same ship with the Duke of York, afterwards James II. ; he (Cormac) died on the 22nd of June, 1665, of wounds received in this action. He married Margaret, the daughter of Ulick de Burgo, 1st Marquis and 5th Earl of Clanrickard, and 2nd earl of St. Albans, by whom he had two children :—1. Charles-James, b. 1663, who died young ; and 2. Francis, born 1664.

126. Ceallachan MacCarthy : second son of Donoch ; married Elizabeth Fitzgerald, sixth daughter of George Fitzgerald, the 16th earl of Kildare ; had issue by her one son, Donoch ; and four daughters, one of whom, Catherine, married Paul Davis, who was created "lord Viscount Mountcashel," by whom she had a daughter, who was married to Justin, son of Donoch, 4th earl of ClanCarthy. This Ceallaghan, who died in 1676, was being educated in France, for Holy Orders, but when the news of his brother's death reached him, he quitted his monastery, became a Protestant, and married.

127. Donoch MacCarthy, the 4th Earl of Clan Carthy : son of said Ceallaghan ; born 1669 ; was edu-

* *Justin :* This Justin married Arabella, second daughter of Thomas Wentworth, Earl of Strafford, and had issue : Margaret, married to Luke, Earl of Fingal, who died in 1693 ; and Ellen, who married William de Burgh, Earl of Clanrickarde, by whom she had a daughter Honoria (or Nora), who married twice : first, to the celebrated Patrick Sarsfield, Earl of Lucan ; and, secondly, on the 26th of March, 1695, to James Fitzjames (Stuart), Duke of Berwick, natural son of King James II.

cated in Oxford, and having, like his father, conformed to the Protestant religion, was, before he was sixteen years of age, privately married to Elizabeth Spencer, second daughter of Robert Spencer, earl of Sunderland. In 1688, he received and entertained King James II., on his arrival in Ireland, having become a Catholic when James II. became King. In 1690, on the taking of Cork, he was taken prisoner by John Churchill, Earl of Marlborough, and confined in the Tower of London, from which, in 1694, he escaped to France; in 1698, he returned to England, was arrested, and exiled on a pension of £300 a year; his estates, worth over £200,000 a year, were confiscated, and sold in violation of the "Treaty of Limerick;" he died at Prals-Hoff, in the territory of Hamburg, on the 19th September, 1734. By his wife, who accompanied him into exile, and died abroad in June, 1704, he left issue :—1. Robert ; 2. Charlotte, who married John West, Lord Delaware ; and 3. Justin, who married his own first cousin, the Hon. Miss Davis, dau. of Paul, lord viscount Mountcashel.

128. Robert, hereditary Lord of Muscry, earl of Clan Carthy, Baron of Blarney, etc. : his son ; born 1686, and died in a chateau near Boulogne, A.D. 1770 ; married twice : by his first wife, Jane Plyer, daughter of Captain Plyer, of Gosport, Southampton, he left no issue ; at the age of 63 years he married a young wife, who brought him two sons :—1. Dermod ; 2. Cormac. This Robert was a Commodore in the English Navy. Having failed to regain his father's estates, he threw up his commission and joined the "Pretender." At length he settled at Boulogne-Sur-Mer, in France, and obtained from the French King an annual pension of £1,000. His estates were seized by the English, and sold to the Hollow Swords Blade Company ; Chief Justice Payne ; the Very Rev. Dean Davis, of Cork; General Sir James Jeffries ; and others. Blarney Castle and surrounding estate is now (1887) possessed by Sir George Colthurst, who married a Miss Jeffries.

129. Dermod : son of Robert ; an officer in the French service, at the time of the Revolution in France ; threw up his commission, and with his family (having married in France, in 1772, to Rose, youngest daughter of Nial O'Neill, Prince of Ulster), returned to Ireland ; died in 1815, and was buried in the family vault in Kilcrea. Left issue three sons and four daughters.

130. Cormac, hereditary Earl of Clan Carthy, etc. : his son ; resided in comparative obscurity in the City of Cork ; married there to Nora, dau. of William O'Neill, of Ulster (see "O'Neill, Prince of Tyrone" Pedigree, No. 130), and died in 1826, leaving issue :— Donogh, Dermod, Teige, and Ada (or Adelaide). Buried at Moviddy.

131. Donogh, hereditary Earl of Clancarthy, etc.: his son ; married Eva MacLoughlin, granddaughter to Mary O'Neill, who was dau. to Nial, Prince of Ulster ; died in 1871 ; buried at Kilcrea ; left issue four sons :—1. Justin ; 2. Robert ; 3. Cormac ; 4. Finghin ; and three daughters :—Elana, Elizabeth, and Ada. Eva died in 1874, and was buried at Moviddy.

132. Justin MacCarthy, hereditary Earl of Clan Carthy, etc. : his son ; married Margaret O'Daly, in Cork, prior to leaving thence in 1878 ; had issue :—1. Teige ; 2. Cormac ; and 3. Charlotte ; living in St. Louis, America, in January, 1887.

MacCARTHY REAGH. (No. 4.)

Of Spring House ; and Counts of Toulouse, France.

Armorial Bearings : Same as those of the "MacCarthy Reagh."

THIS family is descended from Donal na-Pipi MacCarthy Reagh, Prince of Carbery, who is No. 121 on the "MacCarthy Prince of Carbery" Stem.

122. Owen: son of Donal na-Pipi; married Honoria, daughter of Taige-an-Duna MacCarthy, of Dunmanway (see "MacCarthy Glas" Stem, No. 122).

123. Donal : his son; proprietor of Knocknahinsy; m. Honoria, dau. of John O'Hea, of Corably, co. Cork; died 16th December, 1666.

124. Donogh : his son; proprietor of Spring House, co. Tipperary, which he purchased in his father's lifetime. Married 27th July, 1660, Elizabeth, daughter of Edmond Hackett, of Ballyskillan, county Tipperary; died in 1713; interred at Bansha, in that county. His children were :—1. Justin; 2. James ; 3. Charles (of Laganstown), m. Clara O'Ferrall, d. s. p.; 4. Denis, m. a Miss Herringman; 5. Alexander ; 6. Elizabeth, married to Michael Kearney, proprietor of Fethard and Kilbrogan ; 7. Honoria, m. James Fox, of Kilmalchy, King's County ; 8. Joanna, m. John Therry, of Castle Therry, co. Cork ; 9. Margaret ; 10. Catherine, married to Francis Kearney, of Knockinglass, co. Tipperary ; 11. Eleanor, m. to Jeremiah O'Donovan, of Kinograny,

co. Cork ; 12. Maria, m. to Daniel O'Mahony, of Dunloe Castle, co. of Kerry.

125. Justin MacCarthy : his son ; b. 28th February, 1685 ; m. on 14th February, 1709, Marie, dau. of John Shee, of Ballylogue, co. Tipperary ; died in April, 1756 ; buried at Bansha. By his wife (who d. 15th Nov. 1744), he left issue :—1. Denis; 2. John,* b. 6th April, 1725 ; m. Anne, dau. of Thomas Wyse, of Waterford, by whom he had four sons and four daughters; 3. Maria, m. James Mandeville, of Ballydine ; 4. Elizabeth, m. Daniel Ryan, of Inch, in the co. Tipperary ; and 5. Margaret, who d. unm.

126. Denis of Spring House : son of Justin ; b. 21st June, 1718; m. on the 29th September, 1743, Christine, dau. of Robert French, of Rahasane, near Craughwell, co. Galway ; died 13th September, 1761, at Argenton, Berry, in France.

127. Justin: son of Denis ; born at Spring House, 18th August, 1744 ; m., on the 16th September, 1765, Maria Winifred, dau. of Nicholas Tuite, of Tuitestown, Westmeath ; d. in 1812, leaving issue :—1. Denis-

---

* *John :* This John's descendants are here traced—

126. John : the second son of Justin ; b. 6th April, 1725 ; m. Anne Wyse, of Waterford, in 1747 ; issue:—James, b. 1749 ; Charles, b. 1752 ; Justin, b. 1755 ; Dermod, b. 1756 ; Anne, b. 1750 ; Eliza, b. 1751 ; Maria, b. 1754 ; and Christine, b. 1755. This John d. 1779.

127. Charles : his son ; m. (1776) Miss Morrogh, co. Cork ; was a Lieutenant in the Bengal Navy ; had issue : Joseph, b. 1777 ; Charles, b. 1778 ; Robert, b. 1780 ; and Anne, b. 1779 ; besides other children.

128. Charles ; his son : b. 1778, d. *circa* 1846 ; m. a Miss Tuite, and had many children ; was a Civil Engineer, and a Lieutenant in the Tipperary Militia.

129. Rev. Charles F. MacCarthy, D.D.: his son ; b. 1818, d. 1877. Resided in Dublin.

Joseph, b. 18th July, 1766; 2. Nicholas-Tuite (the Abbe Mac-Carthy), b. in Dublin, 19th May, 1769; d. at Annecy (France) on the 3rd May, 1833; 3. Robert-Joseph; 4. Joseph-Charles, b. 1777; 5. Joseph-Patrick, b. 1799, m. 1818, and left issue :—1. Nicholas-Francis-Joseph (b. 1833); 2. Winifred (b. 1819); 3. Anna-Maria (b. 1825); 4. Maria-Theresa (b. 1828); 5. Justin, b. 1785; 6. Anna-Maria, b. 1767; 7. Christine-Maria, b. 1772; and 8. Maria, b. 1780.

This Justin was only seventeen years at the time of his father's death, who was obliged to leave Ireland on account of the penal laws. Immediately on the death of his father Justin hastened to realize all that his family had been able to preserve of the débris of an immense

fortune, and selected for the future home of himself and his posterity the city of Toulouse, in France.

In September, 1766, this Justin became the Count MacCarthy Reagh, of the City of Toulouse, in the Department of the Haute Garonne, receiving letters patent from Louis (Capet) XVI., the French King, and on the 25th of February, 1767, formed a part of the Court of Paris.

128. Robert-Joseph MacCarthy Reagh, Count of Toulouse: his son; born June 30th, 1770. On the 9th of May, 1809, he married Emilia-Maria de Bressac, and died at Lyons, on the 11th July, 1827.

129. Justin-Marie-Laurent-Robert MacCarthy Reagh, Third Count of Toulouse: his son; born May 6th, 1811.

MacDONOGH-CARTIE. (No. 5.)

Prince of Duhallow.

THIS is the senior of the various Scions of the "MacCarthy Mór" family, being descended from Cormac Fionn, who is No. 112 on that Stem, and the fifth in direct descent from Carthach, a quo the sirname *MacCarthy*.

113. Dermod: third son of Cormac Fionn MacCarthy Mór.

114. Donogh: his son.

115. Cormac: his son.

116. Donogh: his son.

117. Donogh Oge: his son; d. 1501.

118. Cormac: his son; lived in 1520.

This family possessed *Duthaidh*

Ealla, i.e. "The estate on the river Allo," which territory forms and gives name to the present barony of "Duhallow." Mac-Donogh's Castle of Kanturk was a fortress so strong and extensive, that the "Lords of the Council" in England (*temp.* Elizabeth) transmitted an order to Ireland to have the work stopped.

MacCARTHY GLAS.* (No. 6.)

Armorial Bearings : Same as those of " MacCarthy Reagh."

DONAL* CAOMH who is No. 114 on the " MacCarthy Reagh " pedigree, was the ancestor of *MacCarthy Glas.*

115. Cormac Donn : son of Donal Caomh, Prince of Carbery ; obtained from his father for himself and his descendants the territory of *Gleanna-Croim*—the country for miles around Dunmanway. This Cormac became Chieftain of Carberry, and was slain in 1366. He left issue :— 1. Dermod, who was taken prisoner by his cousin MacCarthy of Carberry ; given over to the English, and by them murdered in 1368 ; 2. Felim ; 3. Donal ; 4. Eoghan ; 5. Tadhg; 6. Finghin ; 7. Cormac ; and 8. Donogh, who had a son Finghin, who had a son Cormac, whose dau. m. Donogh O'Crowly.

116. Felim : his son ; a quo *Sliochd Feidhlimidh*—the tribe name of the MacCarthys of Glean na-Croim ; was chieftain of his family ; had two sons— 1. Tadhg ; and 2. Finghin.

117. Tadhg of Dunmanway : his son ; succeeded his father as chieftain.

118. Finin : his son ; lord of Glenna-Croin.

119. Cormac : his son ; had issue : 1. Finin ; and 2. Dermod na-n Glac. (1) Finin succeeded his father as chieftain ; m. Ellen, dau. of O'Sullivan Bere, and had issue Cormac (who was killed by his cousin Cormac Donn in a quarrel respecting the succession to the chieftaincy) : this Cormac m. More, dau. of Dermod Oge O'Leary, by whom he had a son Finin, who petitioned Queen Elizabeth in the matter of his father's inheritance. The other sons of this Cormac were :—Felim, slain in 1641; and Cormac Reagh ; and a dau. m.

to Dermod O'Crowly, of Coillsealbhach.

120. Dermod na-n Glac : second son of Cormac ; was known as " Dermod of the conflicts;" m. in 1563, Eleanor, dau. of Teige, the 11th lord of Muscry ; left issue two sons—1. Cormac Donn ; 2. Finin ; 3. Teige an-Fhorsa. (1) Cormac Donn, who slew his cousin Cormac, son of Finin, and who was murdered in Cork by the English. This Cormac Donn m. More, dau. of Connor O'Leary, by his wife, a dau. of MacFinin Dubh, by whom he had a son Felim, and a dau. who m. Art O'Crowly. (2) Finin d. s. p. And (3) Teige an-Fhorsa.

121. Teige : his son ; called "Teige an-Fhorsa" (or Teige of the forces); chieftain, 1578 to 1618. Died in Cork City, 3rd July, 1618. Was twice married : first, to the widow of Torlogh Bacchach MacSweeney, Constable of Desmond, and dau. of Donal MacFinin of Ard Tully ; and, secondly, to Eleanor, dau. of Rory MacSheehy (this lady survived him), by whom he had issue :—1. Tadhg ; 2. Dermod, of Dyreagh, and proprietor of Togher Castle, and the lands of Shanacrane, etc., near Dunmanway ; and a dau., who m. Randal Oge O'Hurley, of Ballinacarrig Castle.

122. Tadhg-an-Duna (or " Teige the Hospicious"): eldest son of Tadhg an-Fhorsa ; b. A.D. 1584; chieftain from 1618 to 1648; second in command of the Munster forces in 1641. This Tadhg was twice married : first, to a dau. of Brian Mac-

* *Glas :* This word in Irish means a lock, lamentation, the sea, green, pale, poor, etc. This Donal possessing a *sea* coast, was naturally called "Donal Glas."

Owen MacSweeney of Cloghda Castle : by this lady, who was granddaughter to Owen MacSweeney, of Mishanaglas, he had two sons, viz. : —1. Tadhg-an Fhorsa ; and 2. Dermod, ancestor of *MacCarthy Glas.* He married, secondly, Honoria, dau. of Donal O'Donovan, lord of Clan Cahill (by his wife Joan, dau. of " Sir " Owen MacCarthy Reagh), by whom he had : 3. Honoria, who m. Owen, fourth son of Donal " Pipi ;" 4. Joan, who m. Cormac MacTadhg MacCarthy, of Ballea, and grandson of Sir Cormac MacTadhg, lord of Muscry ; 5. Eoghan, founder of the Ballynoodie Family ; and 6. Ceallaghan, living in Dunmanway Castle, 1652. Tadhg-an-Duna, d. 24th May, 1649, and was the last chieftain of this clan who exercised the rights of his position.

123. Dermod (called in English official documents " Jeremy Cartie, Esq.") : second son of Tadg-an-Duna ; restored to the lands of Glean-na-Croim (1684), under the " Commission of Grace," by Charles II. ; m. Catherine, dau. of Finin MacCarthy, of Iniskean (son of Sir Owen MacCarthy Reagh), by his wife Eleanor, dau. of Edmund Fitzgibbon, the White Knight, by whom he had Felim, and a dau. Elizabeth, who m. Edmond Shuldham, crown solicitor, to whom she brought the lands regranted to her father in 1684, together with the lands of Ardtully, and three townlands near Kenmare. This Dermod died in 1685. The lands and Castle of Togher, comprising 1,419 acres, were not restored to Dermod ; these were left in possession of the " patentees," Edward and William Hoare, whose descendants are (1887) in possession to this day.

124. Felim : his son ; had no inheritance but the sword ; was a Captain in the Irish Army ; fought on the side of James II., both before and after the King's arrival in Ireland, 22nd March, 1689 ; he left Ireland with the " Wild Geese," was in France at the time of his sister's marriage, upon hearing of which he hurried back, but was shot (assassinated) before he reached his native glen. By his wife Mary, dau. of Tadhg MacCarthy, of Knocktemple, Felim left three sons :—I. Dermod an-Duna ; II. Owen ; and III. Cormac Glas. (I) Dermod an-Duna, m. Ellen, dau. of Ceadach O'Donovan, by his wife Margaret, dau. of Sir Finin O'Driscoll, by whom he had two sons :—1. Charles ; and 2. Teige na-Feile. This (1) Charles (called " of Butler's Gift") married Kate O'Donovan, of Balleedown, great aunt to Timothy O'Donovan, of Donovan's Cove, and sister to Timothy the " Swordsman." By this marriage said Charles had two sons, who d. (s. p.) before himself ; and four daus. :—1. Ellen, m. O'Sullivan of Carriganass ; 2. Mary, m. Maurice Hennigan, who had a dau. Ellen, m. to her cousin Charles, son to Jerry an-Duna ; and two other daus., one m. to Timothy O'Leary, of Glasheens, and the other to Daniel Callanan, of Caheragh. And this (2) Teige (called " na-Feile") m. Elizabeth O'Donovan, and had issue : Jerry an-Duna, and Charles (who d. s. p.). Jerry an-Duna m. a Miss Calanan of Kinsale, and had issue two sons and one dau. —the eldest son, Charles, d. s. p. ; the younger emigrated to Canada many years ago ; and the dau. Mary died unm. This Jerry an-Duna lived during the end of his life with Timothy O'Donovan, of Donovan's Cove, and died in 1826, aged 84 ; interred at Kilbarry, one mile west of Dunmanway.

125. Owen : second son of Felim ; m. Faby O'Herlihy, and had by her

I

two sons :—I. Donogh (or Denis); and II. Florence. (I.) Donogh m. a dau. of O'Leary, of Ive Leary, and had issue:—Donogh Oge, a noted man remembered still in Glean na-Croim; and Angel, who m. Owen Calanan, the father of Dermod Mac-Owen, a celebrated physician, who resided at Clonakilty, and who is still remembered in Carbery. Owen Calanan had also issue by his wife Angel, a dau. Mary, m. to Cornelius MacCarthy (Clan Dermod), brother to the then Parish Priest of Inishannon, and by whom he had a dau. Nora, m. to John MacDonald, of Dunmanway, by whom he had a dau. Mary, who m. Eugene MacFinin MacCarthy, (brother to the Very Rev. Dr. MacCarthy, Vice-President of Maynooth College, who subsequently became the Right Rev.

Bishop of Kerry): the issue of this marriage was a son Randal Mac-Finin MacCarthy.

126. Florence MacCarthy Glas: son of Owen; had two sons—I. Donogh, and II. Charles, and a daughter. III. Angel. This (II.) Charles had a son Denis, and a dau. Angel: Denis was father of Mrs. Shorten of Kilnacronogh, parish of Kinneigh, who was b. 1791. (III.) Angel was mother to Daniel O'Leary, of Shanlarig, parish of Kilmichael; b. 1796.

127. Donogh: son of Florence.

128. Owen: his son; known as "The Old Root;" m. Julia, sister to Dean Collins of Cork.

129. Eugene MacCarthy Glas of Dunmanway (*The Old Root*): son of Owen; b. 1801; living in Dunmanway, 1871.

MacCARTHY GLAS. (No. 7.)

Of Dunmanway.

Armorial Bearings : Same as those of " MacCarthy Reagh."

CORMAC GLAS, third son of Felim, who is No. 124 on the "MacCarthy Glas" pedigree, was the founder of this branch of that family :

125. Cormac Glas: third son of Felim.

126. DONAL (or Daniel), of Dunmanway: elder son of Cormac Glas ; m. Catherine Collins.

127. Donogh (or Denis) : their son ; m. Ellen the dau. of Florence, son of Dermod MacCarthy, heir of Millane, and grand-daughter of Timothy O'Donovan of Loghernth.

128. Daniel: their son ; m. Eleanor MacCarthy of Muires. This Eleanor is (1887) living in Dunmanway, and is dau. of Charles MacCarthy of Muires, by his wife Ellen, dau. of Owen, whose father was Charles of Cloghroe. Owen's wife was a Miss Coghlan.

This Daniel Glas, died leaving a numerous posterity.

129. Justin : his son; living in 1887.

We understand that Messrs Denis and Eugence MacCarthy, National Teachers, residing (in 1887) in Dunmanway, are cousins to this Justin, son of Daniel Glas.

MacCARTHY DUNA. (No. 8.)

Or MacCarthy Dooney.

Armorial Bearings : Same as those of "MacCarthy Glas."

THIS Family was descended from Tadhg-an-Duna, who is No. 122 on the " MacCarthy Glas" Stem.

123. Tadhg an-Fhorsa (2): eldest son of Tadhg an Duna; was living at Togher Castle, in 1641. Married, on the 22nd October, 1641, Gennet Coppinger, the widow of Nicholas Skiddy of Cork, by whom she had one son. This Tadhg died in 1650; he possessed in fee the town and lands of Fearlaghan, known by the names of Tullagh Glas, Gortnidihy, Maulcullanane, and Carrigatotane, in the parish of Kilmeen, barony of Carbery, co. Cork; and the town and lands of Curryboy, Coolmontane and Tullagh, lands in Inchigeela. Those possessions were seized on by English adventurers and his widow and son expelled therefrom.

124. Tadhg an Duna (2): only son of Tadhg an-Fhorsa (2) ; known as " Nominal lord of Glean na-Croim ;" was only eight years old on the death of his father, who secured the possessions by obtaining a " Decree of Innocence," so that although the lands of Togher were confiscated after the war of 1641-52, those of Dunmanway were then saved. But, after the 3rd of October, 1691, in conformity with the terms of the " Violated Treaty" of Limerick, Tadhg's patrimony was seized by the Williamites, so that in 1696, he died situated as the National Poet describes :—

" Ni Tadhg an-Duna d'ainim !
" Acht Tadhg gan dun, gan daingean ;
"Tadhg gan bó, gan capall,
" I m-bothainin isiol deataigh,
"Tadhg gan bean gan leanbh !" etc.

Interpreted :

Not Teige of the Dunthy name !
But Teige without Dun, without Daingean ;
Teige without cow, without horse,
In a low smoky cabin—
Teige without wife, without child ! &c.

And again :

" Crioch a bheatha sa marbh a aonar (an aovacht),
" A n-aras cumhang a luib chnuic sleibhe."

Interpreted :

The end of his life, and death together,
In a narrow dwelling in the curved ridge of a mountain.

This exactly describes the fate of the last lord of Glean-na-Croim. Married Honora, dau. of Donal O'Donovan, lord of Clancahill. Tadhg left issue two sons ; one, it seems was of weak intellect, and " no better than no son at all."

125. " Captain Jacques (James) MacCarthy Duna or *Dooney :* his son ; an officer in the service of France, of whose fate we learn that he fought and fell at Landen, 1693. We know not whether he had issue.

MacCARTHY DUNA. (No. 9.)

Of Ballyneadig and Lyradane.

TADHG AN-DUNA of Dunmanway Castle, who is No. 122 on the " Mac-Carthy Glas" Stem, was the father of the founder of this Family.

123. Eoghan; son of Tadhg an-Duna; b. 1601; d. 20th of October, 1691.

124. Tadhg: his son; was captain of a Kerry regiment of infantry, which James II. imported to England as "men on whom he could rely." After the attainder of Donagh, Earl of ClanCarthy, in 1691 and 1696, this Tadhg administered, to his father, a leasehold interest in the town and lands of East Ballyneadig, co. Cork, which claim was adjudged within the Articles of Limerick. This Tadhg was buried in the choir of Kilcrea abbey.

125. Cormac of Leyradane: his son; m. a dau. of Radly, of Knockrour, and had issue :—Tadhg; Cormac; Callaghan; Dorothy, m. to George Fitton; Catherine, m. to Owen MacCarthy, "Maister na-Mona," who d. 1790.—See "MacCarthy na-mona" Family No. 126.

126. Tadhg: son of Cormac; b. 1714, d. January, 1763; m. Joanna, dau. of Denis MacCarthy, of Dooneen, leaving issue by her :—Cormac; Callaghan, who m. a Miss Hennessy; Tadhg; Mary, m. to O'Leary, of co. Kerry; and Ellen, m. to Nagle, of Mallow. By his will, dated 11 November, 1763, this Tadhg bequeathes all his estate, right, title, and interest of, in, and to, the lease and lands of Rathduff to his eldest son Cormac, who is to lose a pecuniary legacy "if he should at any time intermarry with any daughter of Eliza O'Donoghue, widow of O'Donoghue, late of the county of Kerry;" his interest in the lands of Monalaby, Lisavoura, and Lyredane to Callaghan; and Ballymartin to his two sons Cormac and Callaghan, equally.

127. Cormac of Kilbane (White Church) and Lyredane: son of Tadhg; b. 1738; m. in 1764 Mary eldest dau. of Geoffrey O'Donoghue of the Glen, by Elizabeth, dau. of Randal MacCarthy Mór, (See "MacCarthy Mór" Stem, No. 126.) She died in childbirth with her infant son. Cormac m. secondly, 12th November, 1766, Mary, eldest dau. of Michael Finucane, M.D., of Ennis; and by this lady had fifteen children, of whom only two survived him: 1. Michael-Stephén-Joseph; and 2. Bridget-Ellen, m. to Francis Lord Morgan. She d. 18 May, 1818, leaving issue :—1. Elizabeth-Frances, m. to Robert Mahon, of Ashline Park, co. Clare; and 2. Sarah, d. unm. 1837. This Cormac, on the 14th May, 1796, conformed to the Protestant Religion, and died 25th January, 1807.

128. Michael: his son; b. at Ennis, December 26th, 1771; m. 24th Jan., 1791, Mary, dau. of Capt. Samuel Meade, R.N., and by her (who d. 30th Dec., 1837, aged 71), he had issue :—1. Charles-Edward; 2. Richard-Moore (b. 1802), lieutenant in second Regt. of Foot; 3. Rev. Francis-Michael, A.M. (b. 1804), who m. Frances-Mary, dau. of William Robinson, LLD., barrister-at-law, by whom he had six sons :—1. Revd. Egerton-Francis Meade, A.M., m. Laura-Margaret, dau. of Hedley Vicars, barrister-at-law, and had with other issue Egerton-Hedley-Desmond; Walter-Emilius; Alfred-Finucane, d. unm.; Herbert-Charles; Ernest-Gambier, d. unm.; Arthur Stephen Noel; Frances-Mary, m. to Rev. Charles Baker; Ellen-Augusta, d. unm.; Florence-Caroline; Constance-Amelia, m. to Albert Hartshorne. The daus. of Michael were :—Mary, m. to Capt. Charles Harvey Bagot; Margaret-Elizabeth, m. to Mark Ranclaud, M.D.; Charlotte, m. to Col. Robert

Owen ; Elizabeth, d. unm. ; Sophia. This Michael died 19th June, 1829.

129. Charles-Edward : his son ; b. 7th March, 1800 ; appointed Ensign in the 22nd Regt. of Foot, 16th Dec., 1815 ; m. 4th August, 1831, Elizabeth-Augusta, second dau. of John Goldsborough Ravenshaw, a Director of the East India Company, and by her (who d. 1871) had issue :—1. Charles-Desmond ; and 2. Henry-Mead, b. 1834, d. 1851. This Charles-Edward died 31st July, 1861.

130. Charles Desmond MacCarthy, M.A.: his son ; born 13th December, 1832 ; educated at Rugby, and Trinity College, Cambridge ; living in 1887.

MacCARTHY. (No. 10.)

Of Cloghroe.

Armorial Bearings : Same as those of " MacCarthy, Lords of Muscry."

TEIGE, lord of Muscry, who is No, 121 on the " MacCarthy Lords of Muscry" Stem, was ancestor to the Cloghroe MacCarthy family.

122. Cormac MacCarthy, of Ballea, Castlemore, Courtbreac, and Cloghroe, usually styled " Sir Cormac MacTeige" : son of Teige lord of Muscry ; had three sons, viz. :—1. Teige ; 2. Donogh MacCarthy na-Mona, commonly called the "Master of Mourne ;" and 3. Charles.

123. Charles of Cloghroe : third son of Cormac.

124. Charles : his son ; his estate was confiscated in 1641 under the Cromwellian settlement.

125. Cormac Oge of Cloghroe : his son ; living in 1677. Married a sister of Teige of Aglish, by whom he had issue :—1. Denis ; 2. Alexander ; 3. Margaret ; 4. Nelly ; 5. Mary, married to Florence Mac-Carthy Mór (see MacCarthy Mór Stem, No. 126) ; 6. Catherine ; and 7. Ellen, married to a Mr. Anketell,

126. Denis MacCarthy : his son ; married Mary, the daughter of Sir J. Meade (by his wife, the Hon. Lady Elizabeth, and sister of Sir Richard Meade, afterwards Earl of Clanwilliam), by whom he had issue :—Elizabeth who married Joseph Capell, by whom she had a daughter Jane, who married Robert MacCartie of Carrignavar ; and a son Justin, who died *sine prole*, in 1762. This Denis died on the 2nd of April, 1739, at Ballea, in the 45th year of his age ; and was interred in the Monastery of Kilcrea, where the following inscription may be seen on his tomb :—

" Let honour, valour, virtue, justice mourn,
  Cloghroe's MacCarthy, lifeless in this urn ;
Let all distressed draw near and make their moan,
  Their patron lies confined beneath this stone."

MacCARTHY. (No. 11.)

Of Aglish.

Armorial Bearings : Same as those of "MacCarthy, Lords of Muscry."

CORMAC, Lord of Muscry, was the ancestor of this Family.—See Stem of the "MacCarthy (Muscry)" Family, No. 123.

124. Tadhg MacCarthy of Aglish : son of Cormac, lord of Muscry.

125. Dermod : his son ; died at an advanced age, leaving two children, —a son, and a daughter who married Charles of Cloghroe.

126. Tadhg of Aglish : his son ; suffered for his adherence to the Stuarts, by having his lands of 4,005 Irish acres seized on by the Williamites, and himself expelled from his home.

127. Charles : his son, of whose career very little is known : many of his descendants still live at or near the old lands. This Charles had a sister Joanna, who m. John O'Connor "Kerry," who, in 1652, was cruelly put to death by the followers of Cromwell.—See the O'Connor Kerry pedigree, No. 122.

MacCARTHY GLAS. (No. 12.)

Of England.

Armorial Bearings : Same as "MacCarthy Glas."

125. CORMAC GLAS (otherwise "Charles of Lorraine"): third son of Felim, who is No. 124 on the "MacCarthy Glas" pedigree ; was a captain of the Royal Irish Regiment of Foot Guards to King James II. He m. Angel, dau. of Randal Oge O'Hurley, of Ballinacarriga Castle, by whom he had two sons :— I. Donal of Dunmanway, and II. Donogh.

126. Donogh Glas : son of Cormac ; m. Catherine, dau. of Malachy O'Crowly, by whom he had three sons :—I. Donogh, II. Cormac (these two left no male issue), III. Donal ; and a dau. Angel, who m. O'Donovan of Banlahan, by whom she had three sons—the youngest of whom Thomas, was a celebrated Irish poet.

127. Donal Glas : third son of Donogh ; m. Mary Kelleher, by whom he left issue :—I. Donogh, II. Donal, III. Thomas, IV. Justin. This (I) Donogh m. Mary Mac-Carthy and had issue :—Sir Charles Justin MacCarthy, Knt., Governor of Ceylon, who m. Sophia, dau. of Sir B. Hawes (Under Secretary of State for War), by whom he had two sons :—Felix, a Member of Council at Bermuda, and Police Magistrate, who d. s. p. ; and William, a Registrar-general of lands at Ceylon, who was alive in 1871, but had no issue. This (III) Thomas (*Montalto*) died of yellow-fever, at St. Domingo, left no issue. (IV) Justin, d. s. p.

128. Donal Glas (2) : second son of

Donal; m. Mary Ward, by whom he left an only son, Donal (No. 129).

129. Donal Glas, of Glean-na-Croim: son of Donal; m. Harriet Alexandrina Bassett, youngest dau. of the late Admiral Sir Home Popham, K.M., G.C.B., by whom he had issue:—I. Henry Popham Tenison, a captain in the Royal Artillery, who died unm. aged 28 yrs.; II. Elizabeth Radcliff, who d. at Bath, aged 15 yrs.; and III. Florence Strachan. This Donal Glas, d. at Southampton, England, in 1884. He was a gentleman of refined taste and high literary attainments; author of the *Siege of Florence, Massaniello*, the *Free Lance,*

Life and Letters of Florence Mac-Carthy Mór, and *Historical Pedigree of the Sliochd Feidhlimidh.*

130. Florence Strachan MacCarthy Glas: his son; m. Alice, youngest dau. of the late Rev. James Linton, of Heningford House, Huntingdon-shire, England (by his wife Eliza-beth, dau. and co-heiress of the Rev. Thomas Maria Wingfield of Torking ton), by whom he has had issue:— I. Finin, II. Charles, III. Donal, IV. Eugene, V. Kathleen, VI. Mary, VII. Aileen (or Eibhlin), all living in 1887. This Florence Strachan, residing in 1887, at Clydesdale, Sur-biton Road, Kingston-on-Thames, Surrey, England.

MacCARTHY. (No. 13.)

Of Carrignavar.

Arms : A buck trippant, attired and unguled or.   *Crest* : A dexter arm in armour couped below the elbow, grasping a lizard. *Motto* : Same as MacCarthy Mór.

124. DONAL: son of Cormac Mór MacCarthy, lord of Muscry, by his wife Maria Butler, was ancestor of this family; he had two sons—1. Donal, and 2. Cormac Spainach.

125. Donal (2): his son, died at an advanced age, leaving a son Cormac who forfeited Carrignavar, etc., for the part he took in the Revolution of 1688-9. His estates were put up for sale in 1702 at Chichester House, in Dublin, and subsequently came into the possession of the family by purchase. This Cormac died with-out issue, whereupon the estates reverted to the descendants of the second son of Donal No. 124.

126. Donal (3): son of Cormac Spainach, the second son of No. 124; died at Carrignavar in 1692, leaving two sons:—Donal, and

Cormac (or Charles) called of "Carrignavar," who in 1718 became a Protestant; he was thus able to purchase his estates.

127. Donal (4): son of Donal.

128. Donal Oge (5): his son; had two sons:—1. Justin, who pre-deceased his father in 1762; and 2. Robert. This Donal's will bears date 23rd of August, 1763.

129. Robert: his son; m. in Octo-ber, 1784, Jane, the dau. of Joseph Capell, of Cloghroe (see "MacCarthy of Cloghroe" Pedigree, No. 126), and his wife Elizabeth, dau. of Denis MacCarthy of Cloghroe. They had issue:—1. Justin MacCartie; 2. Joseph Capell MacCartie; and 3. Elizabeth.

130. Justin MacCartie: his son.

MacCARTHY NA-MONA. (No. 14.)

Armorial Bearings : Same as those of " MacCarthy, Lords of Muscry."

THE founder of this family was Sir Cormac MacTeige, lord of Muscry, who is No. 121 on the "MacCarthy, lords of Muscry" Stem.

122. Donoch MacCarthy, called "Maister-na-Mona": son of Sir Cormac MacTeige by his first wife Ellen Barrett, who was daughter of James Barrett, by Ellen, sister of Teige (No. 121), and consequently his (Sir Cormac's) first cousin. He got the name *Na-Mona* from the preceptory of Mourne and the lands around this religious establishment, which his father willed to him. This Donoch m. Ellen. dau. of Donal MacOwen MacTeige Illoyghie Mac-Sweeney, Chief Warder of Blarney Castle. He died in February, 1605, leaving a son Cormac, then twelve years old.

123. Cormac MacDonoch Mac-Carthy: said son; born 1593; m. a dau. of Donal O'Donovan, of Rahine, by his wife Joan, dau. of Sir Owen MacCarthy Reagh; left issue:—1. Donoch; and 2. Teige, whose dau. Mary m. Donoch O'Donovan, of Castlehaven.

124. Donoch MacCarthy, "Maister na-Mona": his son; had by his wife Catherine (living in 1700) twelve children: the eldest named Charles; another, Daniel, d. 1766. This Donoch died in February, 1683, intestate, leaving to his widow and his children the management of his estate. Under a lease of 99 years, at a yearly rent of £56 11s. 3¾d., granted by Ellen Countess Dowager of Clancarthy, and Donoch, earl of Clancarthy, dated 30th October, 1677, he entered into the lands of Courtbrack, Ballmarypeak, Claune-

ballycullen, and Lahackaneen, in the Barony of Muscry, which lands were in 1641 the ancient property and inheritance of his ancestors.

125. Charles MacCarthy, "Maister na-Mona": his son; he had sixteen sons, thirteen of whom emigrated; in 1700 he claimed and was allowed the benefits of above lease, the reversion of which was forfeited by the attainder of Donoch, earl of Clancarthy; which claim was adjudged within the "Articles of Limerick."

126. Owen MacCarthy, the last "Maister na-Mona": his son; born 1706; married Catherine (living in 1764), dau. of Charles MacCarthy, of Lyredane; died 5th November, 1790; was interred in Kilcrea Abbey, leaving an only son, and three daughters, residents in Cork: 1. Mary, married to Barry; 2. Anne, died aged 76; and 3. Catherine died in 1832, all buried in Kilcrea, "pursuant to their dying wishes."

127. Charles MacCarthy: his son; entered the service of the King of Portugal, was colonel of a regiment of horse, and Governor of Miranda, in 1790. He died in Portugal in 1792, leaving an only daughter, who d. s. p. in 1832; and was buried in Kilcrea.

(Mourne Abbey passed through the Encumbered Estates Court, and was purchased about the middle of the present century by a Colonel Beamish, of Lota Park, Cork.)

MacCARTHY. (No. 15.)

Of Minnesota.

Armorial Bearings : Same as those of " MacCarthy, Lords of Muscry."

DONAL, eldest son of Donoch, who is No. 125 on the "MacCarthy" (lords of Muscry) pedigree, was the ancestor of *MacCarthy* of St. Paul, Minnesota, U. S. America.

125. Donoch, the eighteenth lord Muscry, Baron of Blarney, the first " earl of Clancarthy," Confederate Chieftain and Commander of the Munster forces, in the wars of 1641-52.

126. Donal, popularly styled the *Buachaill Ban :* his eldest son ; married a daughter of MacCarthy Derreacha of Glean-na-Chroim.

127. Donal-Cormac, of Drinshane Castle : his son.

128. Fingin (or Florence), of Coom : his son ; had four daughters.

129. Fingin Mór : his son ; took an active interest in the Irish Insurrection of 1798, and was by his followers acknowledged the "MacCarthy Mór ;" died imprisoned in Cork jail, A.D. 1818, aged 98 years ; had issue by his wife, Margaret O'Connor, five sons* and five daughters †

130. Donal Mór‡ : his son ; a

---

* *Sons :* The sons were—1. Donal Mór ; 2. Fingin Oge ; 3. John ; 4. Cornelius ; 5. Charles ; and the daughters were—1. Margaret ; 2. Ellen ; 3. Catherine ; 4. Mary ; and 5. Johanna. Fingin Oge, here mentioned, married Mary O'Crowley, by whom he had issue who migrated to America ; John married a MacCarthy (Tullig), and had issue who died in Ireland without issue ; Cornelius married Kate Forbish, by whom he had issue who went to America and settled in Vermont ; and Charles married Nancy O'Donovan, and emigrated to Canada. Margaret married Owen O'Connor (Cathal), who took part in the Irish Insurrection of 1798 ; the issue of this marriage was Ellen, married to Timothy Collins, also a " '98" man ; John, father of John O'Connor, C.E., Ottawa, Canada ; Timothy, father of the Rev. John S. O'Connor, P.P., of Alexandria, Canada ; and Owen, father of Eugene and Edward O'Connor, of St. Paul, Minnesota. Of the other daughters of Fingin Mór, Ellen married Samuel Beamish ; Catherine married John Callanan ; Johanna married John Beamish ; and Mary married Hurlihy, the chief of his sept, by whom she had a son named Denis, who removed to America.

† *Daughters :* The four daughters were married—one to O'Mahony (Coin) ; another to O'Connor (Cathal), of Coom, a descendant of Cathal-craobh-dearg O'Connor, King of Connaught ; another to O'Sullivan, of Curragh ; and another daughter to O'Leary, of Ive-Leary, called "Teige-na-Post." The issue of this last marriage was Professor Arthur O'Leary ; Jeremiah O'Leary, father of Professor Jeremiah O'Leary of Lindsay, Ont., Canada, living in 1877, and father of Arthur and Hugh O'Leary of the same place Barristers, etc. ; and a daughter, Nancy, who was married to Jeremiah O'Brien, of Dunmanway, county Cork. Of the children of this last marriage were the late Very Rev. Canon O'Brien, P.P., of Bandon, County Cork, and his brother Dr. O'Brien.

‡ *Donal Mór :* His sons were—1. John ; 2. Cornelius ; 3. Charles ; and his daughters—1 Mary ; 2. Ellen ; 3. Johanna. Mary, his eldest child, born A.D. 1790, married Hayes, by whom she had two children—John and Johanna ; Mary survived her children, and was in 1877 living in Canada. John and Cornelius, sons of Donal Mór, went to Canada, where they died without issue ; Ellen married Martin Donovan, of Dunmanway ; and Johanna went to Canada, where she married Joseph DeFoe, by whom she had a son, surviving, named Daniel MacCarthy DeFoe, Barrister, etc., of Toronto, and a daughter Eliza, married to Paul Whyte.

captain in the Insurrection of 1798; and commanded the Irish forces in the battle of Ballynascarthy; rescued General Roger O'Connor from a troop of horse, and received the French fleet at Bantry; left Ireland, and died in America A.D. 1828. By his wife Mary O'Callaghan-Richeson, this Donal Mór had four sons and three daughters.

131. Cormac (Charles): his son; b. 2nd February, 1808; left Ireland in 1828, living in St. Paul, Minnesota, United States, America, in 1880; sole male representative of his family; by his wife Ellen O'Connor-Collins, had issue living three sons, and two daughters Mary and Johanna.

132. Cornelius Mór MacCarthy: his son; b. 6th October, 1846; Counsellor and Attorney-at-Law, St. Paul, Minnesota. This Cornelius has two brothers — 1. Daniel-Francis * MacCarthy, 2. John-Collins MaCcarthy—the names of whose children are given below, in the Note under " Daniel-Francis."

MacCLANCY.

Of Munster.

As in page 80, we give the genealogy of this family, it only remains for us here to observe that the *MacFlanchada* or *MacFlancha* a quo *MacClancy, Clancy*, etc., were chiefs of the district called Flaith-Ui-Hallurain, situated between Tulla, in the barony of Tulla, and Clare-on-Fergus, both in the county Clare.

In 1192, Raghnail (or Reginald) MacClancy was promoted to the See of Emly, from the position of erenachship; he died in five years afterwards, and was interred in the Church of Beallach-Conglais. In 1483, Conor Oge MacClancy, head professor of poetry in Thomond, died; and he was succeeded by his Kinsman, Hugh MacClancy. The Hugh here mentioned was chief historiographer, poet, and professor of Brehonism (or Law) in Thomond; he died in 1492.

In 1575, Hugh, son of Boetius MacClancy, professor of Brehonism and poetry, in Thomond, and "one of the most upright of Irish Brehons," died; and, in the year following, his kinsman, Boetius Oge, son of Murtogh MacClancy, chief professor of Brehonism to the Dal-Cas; and keeper of a Biatach, or house of hospitality, died.

A.D. 1578, John, son of Donal, son of Thomas, son of Teige MacClancy, chief professor in Brehonism, to the Earl of Thomond, died; " and there

---

* *Daniel-Francis:* This Daniel-Francis MacCarthy, of St. Paul, Minn., married Elizabeth, daughter of Joseph Allen, by whom he had issue— Charles-Allen, Catherine-Louise, Joseph-Pius, Ellen-Frances, and Daniel. His brother, John-Collins MacCarthy, of St. Paul, Minn., married Anne-Eliza, daughter of John H. Grindall, by whom he had issue—Charles-Grindall, Daniel-Francis, Mary-Agnes, John-Edward, and Annie-Florence.

was not a Brehon in Ireland who had a more extensive estate or a nobler
mansion than he."

A.D. 1585, Boetius, son of Boetius MacClancy, represented the county
of Clare in Perrott's Parliament. This chieftain died at his residence at
Knock-Fionn, now Knockfinn Hill, parish of Killileagh, co. Clare, in the
month of April, 1598.

A.D. 1641, the Clan Teige O'Brien, commanded by Boetius Clancy, a
celebrated chieftain, and "a man of great property and influence in Clare,"
made a descent on the Isles of Arran, but was defeated with some loss, by
the united forces of the Lords Thomond and Clan Ricarde. This Boetius
had his residence at Knockfinn, now known as St. Catherine's, in the
barony of Corcumroe, but no vestiges of his once well-defended and
hospitable mansion now remain. The stones were long since used for
building purposes, and a large mound of earth marks its site.

MacCOGHLAN.

Of Cloghan, King's County.

Arms : Gu. three lions pass. guard in pale ar. *Crest* : A dexter arm embowed,
vested gu. holding in the hand a sword, both ppr.

> "MacCoghlan now deserts his lime-white towers."
> *Roman Vision.*

ACCORDING to some genealogists, the MacCoghlans derive their descent
and sirname from Coghlan, son of Flatile, of the race of Cormac Cas; as
we are informed by O'Cleary in his dedication of the *Reim-Rioghraidhe* (or
succession of Irish Kings) to Torlogh MacCoghlan, Chief of his name, in
the second quarter of the seventeenth century.—See "Coghlan," which is
taken from the *Linea Antiqua.*

92. Dealbha, 9th son of Cas.	107. Uathamaran : his son.
93. Aindealaig : his son.	108. Faghartagh : his son.
94. Sithe : his son.	109. Anbith : his son.
95. Blad : his son.	110. Gormagan : his son.
96. Comghal Breac : his son.	111. Flatile : his son.
97. Braccan : his son.	112. Coghlan : his son.
98. Saraan : his son.	113. Murtogh : his son.
99. Comghal : his son.	114. Longsidh : his son.
100. Clochcon : his son.	115. Hugh : his son.
101. Dougosa : his son.	116. Connor : his son.
102. Caindighe : his son.	117. Awly : his son.
103. Coghlan : his son.	118. Melaghlin : his son.
104. Mulvihill : his son.	119. Awly : his son.
105. Coghlan : his son.	120. Melaghlin : his son.
106. Fionn : his son.	121. Fergus : his son.

* *Arms* : Another branch of this family had : Arms—Gules three lions passant-
combatant argent. *Crest* : A fret or.

122. Donagh: his son.
123. Torlogh: his son.
124. Felim: his son.
125. James: his son.

126. James (2): his son.
127. James (3): his son.
128. James (4): his son.
129. Torlogh: his son.

In 1498, Cormac MacCoghlan, son of Eoghan, son of the Bishop, an official, of Clonmacnoise, died; and in 1533, Cormac MacCoghlan, lord of Delvin (*i.e.* of *Clan Conor*), and Cahir MacCoghlan, died; in 1585, John, son of Art, son of Cormac, Lord of Delvin, attended Perrott's Parliament; he died in 1590, and was succeeded by his son, John Oge. This John Oge, who is the last chief of the sept mentioned by the Four Masters entered into an alliance, offensive and defensive, with Hugh O'Neill, Prince of Ulster, in 1598. His son Torlogh was lord of Delvin, in 1620. In 1622, Mathew de Renzie* obtained a grant of 1,000 acres of the forfeited estates of the MacCoghlan, on the condition that he should not take the name or title of O'Rourke, O'Mulloy, Fox, MacCoghlan, or O'Doyne, "nor receive, nor pay any Irish rent, taxes, or services, nor divide his land according to the Irish custom of gavelkind." Sir Arthur Brundell, had also a grant of a large portion of the MacCoghlan estates; and several burgesses of Banagher obtained districts or cantreds.

The Rev. Charles MacCoghlan, vicar-general of Leighlin, John MacCoghlan, of Garrycastle, Terence MacCoghlan, of same place, and Teige MacCoghlan, of Kilcolgan Castle, were the representatives of the borough of Banagher in James's Parliament.

In 1790, Thomas MacCoghlan, the last independent representative of this once illustrious family died, leaving no legitimate male representative to inherit his name. None of his descendants were suffered by the "Ma"† [*Maw*] to use the prefix *Mac*, or to claim any relationship with himself. His great estates passed at his decease to the Right Hon. Denis Bowes Daly, who likewise had no children, and who shortly before his death, in 1821, sold the MacCoghlan Estates to divers persons; the chief purchaser being Thomas Bernard, Esq., M.P. The last MacCoghlan represented the King's County in several Parliaments.

---

* *De Renzie:* Mathew de Renzie died on the 29th August, 1634; as appears by the following epitaph, copied from the tomb of the family, in the Church of Athlone:—
"This monument was erected by the Right Worshipful Mathew de Renzie, Knight, who departed this life, August 29th, 1634, aged 57 years. Born at Cullen, in Germany, and descended from the renowned warrior, George Castriot, *alias* Seanderberg, who in the Christian wars fought 52 battles, with great conquest and honour, against the Turks. He was a great traveller and general linguist, and kept correspondence with most nations, in many weighty affairs, and in three years gave great perfection to this nation, by composing a Grammar, Dictionary, and Chronicles in the Irish tongue; in Accounts most expert, and exceeding all others in his great applause. This work was accomplished by Mathew de Renzie, his son, August 29th, 1635."

† *Ma:* This was a title by which *The* MacCoghlan was then generally known.

MacCOULAHAN.*

Of Banagher.

Motto : Snadh na Sean.

IN p. 184 of " Tribes and Customs of Hy-Many " is a pedigree of this family :

1. Carroll MacCuolahan, had :
2. Donogh Keogh MacCuolahan (living in 1602), who had :
3. Brian, who had :
4. Hugh, who had :
5. Hugh (d. 1667), who had :
6. Hugh (d. 1686), who had :
7. Daniel, a Lieutenant in the service of James II., who had :
8. Doctor John (d. 1761), who became a Protestant, and who had :
9. Hugh, who had :
10. Daniel† (d. 1841), who had :
11. Henry, b. 1817 ; living in 1843.

MacELLIGOTT.

County Kerry.

Arms : Az, a tower triple-towered ar.

THE earliest anglicised forms of this family name that we meet with were *McEllycudd, McEllycuddy,‡ McKelgol, McEillgodd, McLeod, McKelgol, McEllcole, McEligot, McEligott ;* and more lately *MacElligott, Elliott,* and *Archdeacon.*

In 1259, the forces of Mary McEllycudd, of Galey, co. Kerry, invaded Scotland with the Army of Edward the First. She brought to Maurice Fitzmaurice, the Second Lord of Kerry, five Knight's fees, about Listowel and Tralee. Most of those Estates were confiscated about 1559 and 1613.

In 1653, Edmund McElligott, of Galey parish, of Coolceragh, was transplanted with four of his household. This Edmund was the grand-father of :

* This Daniel MacCuolahan (who d. in 1841) m. Frances Antisel, of Arbour Hill, co. Tipperary, and by her had issue—1. Hugh (d. s. p. in 1828) ; 2. Henry, living in 1843.

† *MacCuolahan :* In p. 183 of the "Tribes and Customs of Hy-Many," the *MacUallachains* and *O'Uallachains* are mentioned as of the same family.

‡ *MacEllicuddy or MacGillicuddy :* Some Irish scholars derive these names from "MacGillgocuddy," which they say means *the devotee of the saintly.* For our derivation of "MacGillicuddy," see that family genealogy *infra.*

According to Miss Hickson's "Kerry Records," the blood of the MacElligotts is inherited by nearly every respectable family in the counties of Cork, Kerry, and Limerick ; and is also to be found in almost every Court in Europe.

The *Motto* of the MacElligotts was :

"Nulla manus tam liberalis et generalis
Atque universalis quam *Sullevanus.*"

1. John McElligott, of Limerick, who (see the "Evans" pedigree) m. Elizabeth, grandaunt of the late Sir de Lacy Evans. and granddaughter to Colonel Griffiths Evans, and had :

2. Richard Pierce McElligott (1756), of Limerick, who was twice married: first, to Miss Loftus (a descendant of Loftus, Mayor of Limerick, in 1425, and " Bailiff " of Limerick, in 1422—31—41—44), and by her had three sons and four daughters :
I. John.
II. Richard.
III. Pierce.

I. Alice.
II. Elizabeth.
III. Mary.
IV. Another Alice.
Richard Pierce MacElligott's second wife was Jane, daughter of Captain William Craig, of Cork, 2nd Foot Regiment ; the issue of the second marriage were two sons and two daughters :
I. Charles.
II. Ulysses.
I. Anne.
II. Jane, who (see the "Ryding" pedigree), m. Stephen Nathaniel Ryding, L.D.S., and had issue.

In connexion with the foregoing Motto, it may be observed that the families of MacElligott and MacGillicuddy were branches of the *O'Sullivan Mor* family.

Some of the Castles and places of the MacElligotts were : Carriganess, Dunboy, Reendeshart, Ardea, Dunkerron, Carrnebeg, Cappanacuss, Dunloa, Bodenesmeen, Castlecurrig, Ballymacelligot, Carrignafeela, Ardballa, Ballynagrillagh, O'Brennan, Tullygaron (now "Chute Hall,") Lisardbouly, Glandovellane, Tourreagh, Carrick, Glogbanmackin, Rathanny, Glaunageenta, Galey parish, Coolceragh ; and Ballyelegot, co. Waterford.

In 1590 were lost, in the barony of Trughanacmy (or Trughenacking), parish of Ballymacelligott, the following four castles: 1. Ballymacelligott ; 2. Carrignafeala ; 3. Ardballa ; 4. Ballnagrillagh.

In 1595, the Lord of the Reeks of Bodevysmine was slain in the Desmond Wars.

In 1598, his territory was given to Barrett ; but some of it was restored.

In 1604 John MacElligott was pardoned by King James the First, who, in 1605, gave Theobald Bourk of Castleconnell a parcel of the estates of MacDermott O'Sullivan, otherwise called "MacGillicuddie," who died in rebellion.

In 1613 the lands of Ulic MacElligott were given to Sir T. Roper.

In 1624 an Inquisition on Maurice MacElligott's Estates.

In 1625 he was pardoned and allowed to grant to his nephew and heir, John MacGillicuddy, Tullygaron, Lisardbouly, Glandovellane, and Toureagh, all of which passed per a Miss MacElligott to the "Chute" family.

In 1630, Connor MacGillicuddy, of Carrig Castle, co. Kerry, drowned (shipwrecked).—*MSS.* Trinity College, Dublin.

In 1631, Inquisition on John MacGillicuddy's Estates.

In 1645, Miss MacGillicuddy, in the Castle of Ballingarry in Clanmorris when taken from the Parliamentary party.

In 1646, two cousins, namely, Colonel MacGillicuddy and Colonel MacElligott, at the Seige of Ballybriggan Castle, near Tralee.

In 1652, MacGillicuddy, taken prisoner at the battle of Knocknicloghy.

In 1653, Edmund MacElligott above-mentioned was transplanted, and in the same year Maurice (or "Morrice") MacElligott forfeited O'Brennan Castle.

In 1656 he forfeited Ballymacelligott, Rathanny, and Glaunageenta, and was transplanted. In the same year Richard MacElligott was in Donoghue's Regiment, and taken prisoner at the then siege of Limerick.

In 1673, Colonel MacElligott and Teige MacElligott lost part of Culenagh and Garrinagh, which was given to Robert Marshall.

This Richard Pierce MacElligott was a scholar of great eminence; his MSS, were full of interest to the soldier, the mathematician, and the linguist. Some of those MSS. have since his death been deposited in the Library of the Royal Irish Academy, and other places, in Dublin, and elsewhere; some taken by friends; and some borrowed by others, who, without any acknowledgment, have published their contents as their own work. Even in fortifications and Military Art our newest systems were to him already old. As a Tribute to the memory of Mr. MacElligott, the following poem on him, by one of his descendants, the elder brother of the late Sir de Lacy Evans, is here worthy of record:

> " Where are those days as beauteous and sublime
> As those of the original Paradise,
> When angels missioned from above came down,
> To teach the Deity's infinite wisdom, love
> And all His glorious attributes to man!
> Where are those days of beauty, gifted man?
> When, in the original power of genius, thou
> Led'st forth thy pupil through the blooming fields
> Of Art, of Science, and of Classic lore!
> Then Archimides' self and Euclid taught,
> From thy clear brain, and fire-touched eloquent lips. •
> There Homer sped his music of the soul.
> Demosthenes again sent forth, through Greece
> Those thunders which struck tyrants pale, of you;
> Whose very echoes in our modern day
> Have taught the Turkish despot wretch to bend
> His recreant knee to mind, and own the power
> Which from on high rebukes the tyrant, and
> In blushes paints the visage of the slave!
> To reach, to feel, to teach those nobler points
> In morals, wisdom, in eternal truth,
> In Art, in Science, or in Classic lore:
> All this was thine. But higher, nobler, still,
> 'Twas thine to teach the youthful mind to rise
> Above the sordid level of the crowd,
> To build its own foundations deep and strong,
> And raise the superstructure to the stars!

In 1687 Colonel MacGillicuddy, called Denis, was Sheriff of the county Kerry, and got estates under an assumed name.

In 1688 Colonel Roger MacElligott with his Regiment was in Hampton Court, and in Chester; and with it returned to Ireland.

In 1689 Col. Roger MacElligott and his cousin Col. Cornelius MacGillicuddy, of the Reeks (who was Governor of Kinsale), were both in Parliament as Members for Ardfert. Two MacGillicuddys, one of whom was an Ensign, and the other a Lieutenant, were both in Lord Kenmare's Regiment.

In 1690 Col. MacGillicuddy war Governor of Cork when it was taken by the future Duke of Marlborough.

In 1697 Col. Roger MacElligott was released from the Tower of London, after four years' incarceration therein. He then joined the Irish Brigade in France, as Colonel, with three of the MacGillicuddys.

In 1733 we find James Mason, grandfather of Robert Emmett, in Ballymacelligot; and, in

1778, his descendant a general in Austria.

Like the DeLacys and other Irish families, the history of Europe at that period is full of the exploits of the MacElligotts.

> To scorn each petty tyrant, as he crawls
> In reptile slime on the dishonour'd earth—
> To cherish in the heart each worthy man—
> And court assiduously that converse pure,
> Which is the prototype, foretaste, of Heaven !
> Where are those days ?   Yes, yes, they yet will live
> Immortal e'en on earth, for they belong
> To Heaven's own atmosphere ; and the rich seed
> Of glorious mind, cultured by thee, shall bloom
> And fructify throughout th'embellished land !
> Oh ! may thy sons, and theirs, ascend to that
> High and immortal tone of sentiment,
> That vigour made of fire and sprung from Heaven !

" *Ollis est ignea vigor et celestis origo.*

"GLIN (co. Limerick), 11th May, 1844."

Richard Pierce MacElligott, the subject of the foregoing Poem, having been a political prisoner in Limerick Jail, in 1798, the following is an extract from a letter by him sent out, pasted with a piece of potato to the bottom of a plate :

" What shall I suffer walking up and down this dismal place from light to light, with no companion but a man, who (three times flogged) lies dying in a corner a still breathing corpse ; and legions of rats of all ages, which have forgotten the timidity of their species, and lord it here with hereditary sway :

> "Hail ! solitude, all gloomy horrors hail !
> For Truth has led me to thy dismal shrine.
> In her bright face all earthly glories pale ;
> Thy darkest den is filled with light divine.

> "What shall I suffer ?
> After this, Nothing.

.   .   .   .   .   .

" There were three happy fellows on every lamp on the bridge, as I was crossing here ; the lantern hoops were breaking ; so I must wait till some kind friend drops off. They nearly took up (or occupied) all the little footpath, and the toes of some of them were touching it.

"As I passed, I thought what a splendid and economical plan for *lamp-lighting ;* for, by its piercing rays, the whole earth could see into the dark hearts of a distant people, and follow its each individual to the world's ends while he carries one grain of pride.   In the glory of such bright eternal light, who would not wish to burn?   Not Typhus, not Smallpox ; No! No !"

Mr. MacElligott was, however, reprieved.

MacENIRY.

Lord of Connello, Co. Limerick.

Arms : Ar. an eagle displ. vert.   *Crest :* A falcon close belled ppr.

ACCORDING to the Genealogical Tables compiled by Dr. O'Donovan from the Book of Leacan, and O'Cleary's and MacFirbis's Genealogies, this ancient family is descended from Sedna the fourth son of Cairbre Aedhbha (ancestor of *O'Donovan*), the tenth in descent from Olioll Olum,

King of Munster, who died A.D. 234. The sirname in Irish is *Mac-Ineirghe*.*

The territory of the MacEnirys originally formed part of that of the Ui-Cairbre Aedhbha, and at one time extended from the river Maig to Abbey Feale on the borders of Kerry. It subsequently comprised that portion of the barony of Upper Connello formerly called Corca-Muichet, now the parish of Corcomohid, or Castletown MacEniry.

Up to the period of the Cromwellian Settlement of Ireland, the MacEnirys held considerable estates in the county of Limerick.

There are numerous references to members of this family in the Annals of the Four Masters and other authentic records:

Kennith MacEneiry, King of Conallo, slain in battle, A.D. 1029.

MacAngheiree, lord of Conaille (Connello), slain at the battle of Fermoy, near Thurles, A.D. 1081.

MacEineiry, erected a castle in Kilmoodan (Castletown MacEniry) in 1349.

William Oge McKynery of Ballyaudley, co. Limerick, an adherent of Desmond, slain at Aherb, 7th August, 1585.

John McEniry of Castletown McEniry, co. Limerick, "chief of his nation;" Gerald McEniry, his cousin, and Shane McThomas McEniry, of Kilmorie, co. Limerick, his brother-in-law, surrendered the lands possessed by them and their ancestors for 200 years in Cork and Limerick; receiving a re-grant thereof from the Crown, A.D. 1607.

Connor McEnnrey, Petitioner in "Court of Claims" (1666), under a decree to his father (a transplanter) at Athlone, in 1656.

Symon MacEneiry, forfeited (1641) the lands of Castletown, &c., in Connelloe, co. Limerick; and in the same year John MacEneery, Donagh MacEnery, Mortogh MacEniry, and Andrew MacEniry, Garret and Bryan McEnery, and Thomas McWilliam McEniry also forfeited estates in the same county.

Antoine Macenery, Lt.-Colonel of Dillon's regiment, Irish Brigade, in the service of France, in 1696.

Arthur Macenery, Brigadier-General in the French army, in 1748-61.

Dons Malachias and Juan MacEnery, Lieutenants in the regiment of Ultonia, in the Spanish service, in 1718.

The following is the pedigree of a branch of this ancient family:

1. McEneiry of Castletown, co. Limerick.
2. Thomas: his son; born *circa*

1672; will dated 1745.
3. Philip: his son; will dated 1752. Had two sisters, one named

---

* *MacIneirghe :* This sirname ("eirghe :" Irish, *a rising*) is distinct from *O'h-Ainnerraidh* or *O'h-Ainnearaigh* ("an :" Irish, the definite article; "nearach," *lucky, happy*), chiefs of Cuilleanntrach, and a quo *O'h-Inneirghe*, anglicised *O'Henery* and *MacHenery ;* and has been variously rendered as follows: MacInneirghe [Innery], MacAneiridh, MacAngheire, MacEineiry, MacEneiry, *MacEniry*, and *MacInerny*, (which now obtain in the family). MacEnrigh, MacIndereighe, MacInnerigh, McEndrie, McEnery, McEnnery, and M'Kynery ; and in France, Mannery. From the spelling and pronunciation of "MacIneirghe" we are satisfied that it is the sirname from which *Irwin, Irvine, Irving, MacNair, MacNeir, MacNeary,* and *Neary* are derived. It was therefore our mistake to derive any of these sirnames from *O'Conaire* or *MacConaire.*

K

Bridget; and two brothers—John and Thomas.

4. Thomas : his son, died in 1807; will dated 1807. Had a brother John and two sisters, m.; the youngest, Elinor, d. in 1826.

5. Thomas : his son ; a merchant in Dublin; d. 1852; will dated 1852. Had a brother Francis, who d. young; and two sisters, m.— Anne (d. 1812), and Elizabeth (d. 1861).

6. Lieutenant Henry - Francis MacEniry : son of Thomas ; d. 1873, leaving issue, a son Thomas ; had five brothers and five sisters. The elder brothers were : 1. Thomas,

who d. young ; 2. Charles-James, who died in 1822. The younger brothers were : 1. Major Robert-John, living in 1887 ; 2. George, who d. young; 3. Edmund Paul, who died in 1872, leaving issue a dau., Mary Marcella, living in 1887. The sisters were : 1. Margaret ; 2. Anne; 3. Mary, who all died young ; 4. Elizabeth Anne, who was married, and who d. in 1878, s. p.; 5. Harriette-Susanna, married, d. in 1854, leaving issue, Frederick Thomas Goold, living in 1887.

7. Thomas Robert MacEniry ; son of Henry-Francis, living in 1887.

MacGILLICUDDY. (No. 1.)

Chiefs in Dunkerron, Co. Kerry.

Arms : Gu. a wyvern or. *Crest :* A representation of MacGillicuddy's Reeks, co. Kerry, ppr. *Motto :* Sursum corda.

GILLE MOCHODH, brother of Murtogh who is No. 113 on the "O'Sullivan Mór" pedigree, was the ancestor of *MacGiolla Mochodha ;* anglicised *MacGillicuddy, MacElligott, MacLeod, Elliott,* and *Archdeacon.*

113. Gille Mochodh (" moch :" Irish, *early ;* " odh," gen. " odha," *music*): son of Dunlang; a quo *MacGiolla Mochodha.*
114. Conchobhar : his son.
115. Gille (or Giolla) Mochodh : his son.

116. Conchobhar : his son.
117. Donchadh : his son.
118. Domhnall : his son.
119. Conchobhar : his son.

MAGILLICUDDY. (No. 2.)

Of the Reeks—continued.

1. THE Magillicuddy (A.D. 1580) m. Joan, dau. of Bishop Crosbie, and had issue :
I. Donogh, of whom presently.
I. Sheela.
2. Donogh : son of the Magillicuddy ; m. a Spanish lady, and had :
I. Cornelius, who m. the dau.

of MacCarthy Mór, but had no issue.
II. Donogh, of whom presently.
3. Donogh : son of Donogh ; m. Lucretia, dau. of Derryick Van Dachelor, and·had :
I. Donogh, of whom presently.

I. Inez, who m. —— Anketell.

4. Donogh: son of Donogh; m. Anne Blennerhassett of Killorglin Castle, and had:

   I. Cornelius, of whom presently.

   II. John (d). III. Philip (d).

   I. Mary, who m. —— Fitzmaurice of Duagh; but whose descendants are dead.

   II. Kate, who m. Fitzgerald of Glynn; had no issue.

   III. Elizabeth, who m. Denis Sugrue.*

5. Cornelius: son of Donogh; m. Catherine Chute of Chute Hall, and had:

I. Denis (deceased).

II. Richard, who m. the Honourable Arabella de Moleyns; no issue.

III. Frank, of whom presently.

6. Frank: third son of Cornelius; m. Catherine Mahony, and had:

7. Richard, who was twice m.: first, to Margaret Bennet, and had issue, but the sons died young. Richard's second wife was Anna Johnson, by whom he had:

   I. Richard-Patrick, The MacGillicuddy.

MacGRATH. (No. 1.)

Chiefs in the County Waterford.

Arms: Quarterly, 1st, ar. three lions pass. gu.; 2nd, or. a dexter hand lying fessways, couped at the wrist ppr. holding a cross formée fitchée az.; 3rd, gu. a dexter hand lying fessways, couped at the wrist ppr. holding a battle axe or.; 4th, ar. an antelope trippant sa. attired or.

CRAITH, brother of Roger who is No. 117 on the "O'Sullivan Mór" pedigree, was the ancestor of *MacCraith:* anglicised and modernized *MacGrath*, *McGrath*, *Magrath*, *MacCrae*, *Macrae*, and *Creeth*.

117. Craith ("craith:" Irish, *to weave*): son of Dunlong; a quo *MacCraith*, implying "the son of the weaver."

118. Donall MacCraith: his son.

119. Conor: his son.

120. Owen: his son.

121. Buadhach: his son.

122. Dermod: his son.

123. Conor (2): his son.

124. Owen MacGrath: his son.

125. Thomas MacGrath of Glenaboy, Tallow, co. Waterford: his son. Had by his wife five children of whom three were sons, namely—1. Edward, 2. Daniel, 3. Thomas.

126. Daniel of Lismore,† county Waterford: second son of Thomas; b, 21st January, 1751; d. in Montreal, Canada, in 1860—at the advanced age of 109 years. This Daniel married Ellen, daughter of

---

* *Denis Sugrue;* See No. 7 on the "O'Connor" ("of Carrig-a-Foyle) pedigree.

† *Daniel of Lismore:* The marriage of this Daniel with his wife Ellen (b. 1772), was the first union of the Clanaboy McGraths with those of Clanabawn. Instances of the large stature of many of the ancient Irish families are recorded. It may be mentioned that this family was particularly remarkable in that regard; for, not only was this Daniel McGrath a tall, strong, and handsome man, but his wife was a tall, handsome and majestic woman; they certainly were noble specimens of the ancient Irish race.

Thomas MacGrath* of Ardagh, near Youghal, co. Cork, and by her had four sons and twelve daughters: one of the sons died young, the others grew up and were married, viz.— Alderman Thomas MacGrath of Montreal (who d. in 1864); Denis MacGrath of New York, U.S. (who d. in 1846) ; and Daniel, who is No.

127 on this Stem. Ellen. a dau. of Denis MacGrath here mentioned, and niece of Thomas Murphy, Esq., of New York, m. Terence Murtagh of that city.

127. Daniel MacGrath, of Lachine, Province of Quebec, Canada: son of Daniel; living in 1887, "a childless widower."

MACGRATH. (No. 2.)

Of Ballynagilty, County Waterford.

PHILIP MACGRATH, of Ballynagilty, co. Waterford, Chief of the Clan of Sleveguor, had:
  2. Donal, who had:
  3. Philip, who had:
  4. John MacGrath, of Ballynailty, gent., who died 4 May, 1639.

He m. Eleanor, daughter of James Butler, of Derryloskan, county Tipperary, and had one son and three daughters :—
  I. Philip.
  I. Ellen, II. Anne, III. Margaret.
  5. Philip MacGrath : son of John.

MACMAHON. (No. 1.)

Lords of Corca Baisgin, County Clare.

Arms : Ar. three lions pass. reguard. in pale gu. armed and langued az. *Crest :* A dexter arm in armour embowed ppr. garnished or. holding in the hand a sword both ppr. pommel and hilt gold. *Motto ;* Sic nos sic sacra tuemur.

TURLOGH MÓR, the 178th Monarch of Ireland, who died A.D. 1086, and is No. 107 on the "O'Brien" (of Thomond) pedigree, had two sons: 1. Mathghabhuin†;

---

* *Thomas McGrath :* This Thomas was descended from the Ulster M'Graths of Clanaboy, who were of the race of Clan Colla ; and who as late as the 17th and 18th centuries were men of influence in the county Waterford. He had by his wife Ellen (dau. of —— Ahern of Shanakill, county Waterford) six children, of whom two were sons, viz. :—1. Parson Denis M'Grath, near Dundalk ; 2. Thomas McGrath, of Kilcalf, county Waterford. The Rev. Denis M'Grath here mentioned married a dau. of General McNeill, and by her had one dau., and two sons—1. Thomas *Magrath,* who was mar. to a dau. of the late Judge Lefroy, and 2. James Magrath : these two sons were for many years members of the East India Company, and the-latter (James) was the owner of a large estate near Liverpool, England, on which he resided in 1836.

† *Mathghabhuin :* This name means "the bear of the plain," or a "wild calf ;" for a bear is strictly a kind of *wild calf.* From this word is derived the surnames *Mahon, MacMahon, Mahony,* and *O'Mahony ;* but it may be here observed that the "Mahon" and "*MacMahon*" families of Munster are distinct from the "Mahon" and "MacMahon," of Ulster.

2. Dermod : this Mathghabhuin was the ancestor of *MacMathghamhna* anglicised *MacMahon.*

108. Mathghabhuin ("magh :" Irish, *a plain ;* "gabhuin," *a calf*) : son of Turlogh Mór; a quo *Mac-Mathghamhna* (of Munster).

109. Morogh : his son.

110. Dermod MacMahon : his son ; first of this family who assumed this sirname.

111. Morogh` na Mongnach : his son.

112. Donogh : his son.

113. Dermod : his son.

114. Rory Buidhe [boy] : his son.

115. Donogh na Glaice : his son.

116. Teige Roe : his son ; had a brother named Donogh.

117. Teige (2) : his son.

118. Turlogh (or Terence) : his son.

119. Teige (3) : his son. This Teige had two brothers—1. Brian ; and 2. Donogh (or Donatus), who (there is reason to believe) was the ancestor of "MacMahon" of France.*

120. Morogh : son of Teige.

121. Teige (4) : his son.

122. Turlogh Roe : his son.

123. Sir Teige : his son.

124. Sir Turlogh MacMahon, of *Corca Baisgin* (now the barony of "Moyarta," in the county Clare : his son.

MacMAHON. (No. 2.)

Marshal of France.

Armorial Bearings : Same as those in the preceding ("MacMahon") genealogy.

TERENCE (or Turlogh) MACMAHON, ancestor of this family, who died in 1472, must have been contemporary with Turlogh who is No. 118 on the "O'Brien" pedigree, and who died in 1459. This fact leads us to believe that this Terence (or Turlogh) MacMahon was the same person as the Turlogh (or Terence) who is No. 118 on the (foregoing) "MacMahon" (of Munster) pedigree, whose son, Donogh (latinized "Donatus") was the

---

* *MacMahon of France :* Patrick MacMahon of Torrodile, in the county Limerick, having espoused the cause of King James the Second, settled in France after the Treaty of Limerick, A.D. 1691. His son, John MacMahon of Autun, in France, was created "Count de Equilly;" who, in order that his children and his posterity might have sufficient proof of "the proud fact that they were of Irish descent," applied on the 28th September, 1749, to the Irish Government (accompanying his application with necessary facts, etc., for the Officers of Ulster King of Arms), to have his genealogy, together with the records, etc., of his family duly authenticated, collected, and recorded, with all necessary verification. All this was accordingly done, the various requisite signatures affixed thereto, and countersigned by the then Lord Lieutenant of Ireland. In these records, preserved in the Office of Arms, Dublin Castle, Count de Equilly is described as of "the noble family, paternally, of 'MacMahon,' of Clondeas (in the county Clare), and maternally, of the noble family of 'O'Sullivan Beara.'" This John MacMahon (Count de Equilly) was the grandfather of Marshal MacMahon of France, Duke of Magenta, President of the French Republic; born A.D. 1808, and living in 1887.

"Donatus MacMahon" who is mentioned in the Count de Equilly's genealogy (see No. 119), in this pedigree.

118. Terence (or Turlogh) Mac-Mahon, proprietor of Clondiralla, (modernized "Clonderlaw"), who died A.D. 1472, married Helena (daughter of Maurice Fitzgerald, earl of Kildare) by whom he had a son, named Donogh or Donatus.

119. Donatus, who married Honora O'Brien : their son.

120. Terence, married to Johanna, daughter of John Macnamara, of Dohaghtin — commonly called "Macnamara Reagh" : their son.

121. Bernard, who was married to Margaret, daughter of Donogh O'Brien, of Daugh : their son.

122. Murtagh, whose wife was Elonora, daughter of William O'Nelan (or O'Nealan), of Emri, who was colonel of a regiment of horse in the army of King Charles the First: their son.

123. Maurice, who was married to Helena, daughter of Maurice Fitzgerald, of Ballinœ, Knight of Glyn : their son.

124. Murtagh, whose wife was Helena, daughter of Emanuel Mac-Sheehy, of Ballylinan : their son.

125. Patrick, of Torrodile, in the county Limerick: their son, who married Margaret, daughter of John O'Sullivan of Bantry, in the county Cork ; and who, after the Treaty of Limerick, A.D. 1691, first visited France in the suite of the exiled King James the Second of England, and there settled.

126. John MacMahon (or Jean Baptiste de MacMahon) of Autun, in France, but born in Ireland : their son; who, in 1750, was ennobled by the French Government, and created "Count de Equilly."

127. Maurice De MacMahon : his son: was faithful to the Bourbon cause, and was therefore, during the reign of Loüis XVIII., King of France, created a Lieutenant-General, and Commander of the Order of St. Louis.

128. Marshal Patrick MacMahon, President of the French Republic, Duke of Magenta, etc. : his son ; born in 1808, and living in 1887.

MACNAMARA. (No. 1.)

Lords of Bunratty, County Clare.

Arms : Gu. a lion ramp. ar. in chief two spear heads or.

CASIN, a younger brother of Bladd, who is No. 92 on the "O'Brien" (of Thomond) pedigree, was the ancestor of *Macconmara;* anglicised *Macnamara, MacNamara,* and *McNamara.*

92. Casin : son of Cas.

93. Carthann : his son. This Carthann had three brothers—1. Eocha, who was ancestor of *O'Grady* etc. ; 2. Sineall, ancestor of *Durkin,* of Munster ; and 3. Cormac, ancestor of *Clann Eocha.*

94. Ardgal (also called Fergal): his son.

95. Athluan : his son.

96. Conn : his son.

97. Eoghan : his son.

98. Dungal : his son.

99. Urthuile ("ur ;" Irish, *recent,*

"tuile," *a flood, a torrent*) : his son; a quo *O'h-Urthuile*, anglicised *Harley, Hurly, Herlihy, Flood* and *Torrens.*

100. Cullin : his son; a quo the Macnamaras are called *Clan Cullin.*

101. Maolclochach ("cloch" : Irish, *a stone*): his son : a quo *O'Maolcloiche,* of Munster, anglicised *Stone* and *Stoney*; had a brother named Einsioda, who was the ancestor of "*Hickey.*"

102. Sioda an Eich-bhuidbe (or Sioda of the yellow horse) : his son.

103. Assioda : his son.

104. Enna (or Sedna) : his son.

105. Aedh Odhar ("odhar" : Irish, *palefaced*): his son; a quo *Siol Aedha* of Munster ("aedh or aodh" : Irish, *fire;* Sanscrit, "edhas," *firewood*); anglicised *Hay* and *O'Hay.*

106. Menmon : his son; had a brother named Niall, who was the ancestor of *Clancy,* of Munster.

107. Donal : son of Menmon.

108. Cu-mara ("cu," gen. "con," *a warrior;*" "muir," gen. "mara," *the sea*; Lat. "mar-e;" Arab. "mar-a"): his son; a quo *Macconmara,* meaning the descendants of the sea protector.

109. Donal **Macnamara** : his son ; first assumed this sirname; d. A.D. 1099.

110. Cu-mara (2) : his son.

111. Neal (or Niall) : his son.

112. Cu-meadh Mór : his son.

113. Lochlann : his son.

114. Maccon : his son.

115. Cu-meadh (2) : his son.

116. Maccon (2): his son; had two brothers—1. Donoch, and 2. Lochlann.

117. John an Ghabhaltuis (or John the Conqueror) : his son ; had two brothers—1. Sioda, 2. Mahon, and 3. Lochnann.

118. Donal an-Marcsluaigh (or "Donal the Horse of the Army"): his son.

119. John : his son.

120. Cumeadh (3) Mór : his son.

121. Rory (or Roger) Carragh : his son.

122. Cumeadh (4) : his son.

123. Donoch : his son.

124. Cumeadh (5) Liath : his son.

125. Donald Riabhach : his son.

126. Donald Oge : his son.

127. Teige Macnamara : his son.

MACNAMARA. (No. 2.)

From the De La Ponce MSS.

MACCON, a brother of Donal an Marcsluagh who is No. 118 on the foregoing pedigree, was the ancestor of this branch of the *MacNamara* family.

118. Maccon : son of John an Ghabhaltuis.

119. Sioda : his son.

120. Maccon : his son.

121. Sioda : his son.

122. Mathew : his son.

123. Denis : his son.

124. Mathew : his son.

125. Jean (or John) : his son.

126. Jean, Chev. de St. Louis : his son ; m. D. Catherine St. Jean.

127. Claude-Mathieu : his son ; m., 18 April 1732, D. Henriette Concand.

128. Jean Baptiste : his son ; b. 9 Feb., 1738 ; a Page in 1752.

MACNAMARA FIONN. (No. 3.)

Armorial Bearings : Same as those of "Macnamara," Lords of Bunratty.

SIODA, brother of John an Ghabhaltuis (or John the Conqueror) who is No. 117 on the "Macnamara" pedigree, was the ancestor of *Macnamara Fionn.*

117. Sioda : son of Maccon.
118. Maccon : his son.
119. John Macnamara Fionn ("fionn,": Irish, *fair*): his son.
120. Cu-mara : his son.
121. Cumeadh : his son.

122. Teige : his son.
123. John : his son.
124. Donal : his son.
125. Donoch Macnamara Fionn : his son.

MACNAMARA.* (No. 4.)

Arms : A lion rampant ducally crowned, or. in the chief two spear-heads of the last. *Crest :* Out of a ducal coronet, a hand and arm holding a gold-hilted sabre.

MAHON, a brother of John an Ghabhaltuis who is No. 117 on the (No. 1.) "MacNamara" pedigree, was the ancestor of this branch of that family.

117. Mahon : son of Maccon.
118. Donal Ballach : his son.
119. John : his son.
120. Mahon : his son.
121. Rory : his son.
122. Donogh : his son.
123. Teige : his son.

124. Teige Oge : his son.
125. Donogh : his son.
126. Mahon : his son.
127. John : his son.
128. Teige : his son ; representative of this family, A.D. 1721.

MACNAMARA. (No. 5.)

CONMARA, a brother of Aedh Odhar, who is No. 105 on the "MacNamara" (Lords of Bunratty) pedigree, was the ancestor of this branch of that family.

105. Conmara : son of Enna.
106. Donal : his son.
107. Conmara : his son.
108. Niall : his son.
109. Conmeadha : his son.
110. Maccon : his son.
111. Conmeadha : his son.

112. Maccon : his son.
113. Sioda Com : his son.
114. Flann : his son.
115. Lochlan : his son.
116. Flan : his son.
117. Flan : his son.
118. Sioda : his son.

---

* *Macnamara :* Of this family was Rawdon Macnamara, who, in 1831, was President of the Royal College of Surgeons in Ireland ; and who was born at Ayle, in the co. Clare. His father was Teige (or Thady) Macnamara, and his mother was Narcissa, dau. of Dr. Dillon, physician to Colonel Rawdon, who subsequently became

MOLONEY.*

Arms: Azure on the dexter side a quiver erect holding three arrows, on the sinister a bow erect all ppr. *Crest:* An arm embowed, holding a scimitar ppr.

THE *O'Moloneys* derive their descent from Brenan Bán, the second son of Blad, son of Cas, who is No. 91 on the "O'Brien Kings of Thomond" Stem. They were chiefs of Coiltenain (now Kiltannon), a district in the barony of Tulla, co. Clare, and had castles at Rinnua and Coolistigue. The representative of this family in 1864 was James Molony, Esq., of Kiltannon House.

1. James O'Moloney, of Kiltannon.
2. James: his son.
3. James: his son.
4. James: his son.
5. James, of Kiltannon: his son; living at Kiltannon House in 1864.

MORIARTY.

Chiefs of Eoghanacht of Loch Leine.

Arms: Ar. an eagle displ. sa. *Crest:* An arm embowed in armour holding a dagger, the blade environed with a serpent.

CAIRBRE LUACHRA (also called Cairbre Cruithneach), son of Corc, who is No. 89 on the Line of Heber, *ante*, was the ancestor of *O'Muircheirtaigh*, anglicised *Moriarty, Muriarty* and *Murtagh.*

89. Corc, King of Munster.
90. Cairbre Luachra: his son.
91. Maine Munchaoin ("mun:" Irish, *urine;* "caoin," *to weep;* Heb. "kun," *to lament*): his son; a quo *O'Munchaoin,* anglicised *Minchin.*
92. Duach Iarfhlaith: his son; had two sons: 1. Cobhtach; and 2. Fiachra Garve, who had a son Fiachna, whose son was Cuimen

Fodha, Bishop of Clonfert, b. A.D. 590, d. 658.
93. Cobhtach: his son.
94. Crimthann: his son.
95. Aodh Bennan: his son; d. 619.
96. Muldoon: his son; had a brother named Cathal.
97. Conaing: his son.
98. Aodh (2): his son.
99. Muldoon (2): his son.

Lord Moira. The strong friendship existing between Thady Macnamara and the Colonel caused the former to name his son "Rawdon"—a cognomen ever since retained in the family. In 1818 Macnamara married Mary, eldest daughter of George Symmers of Dangan Park, co. Galway; and died in York-street, Dublin, on the 2nd November, 1836. Dr. Rawdon Macnamara, second son of the aforesaid Rawdon Macnamara, was born at 28 York-street, Dublin, on the 23rd Feb., 1822. In 1846 this Doctor Macnamara married Sarah, only child of Patrick Blanchard, of Eagle Lodge, Brompton, London, and has had issue.

* *Molony:* Of this family was Dr. Michael Molony, who, in the (second) Charter granted by King George IV. to the Royal College of Surgeons in Ireland, is named as one of the "body politic and corporate" of that Institution.

100. Cathan : his son.
101. Muriartach or Muircheartach ("muir:" Irish, *the sea,* and "ceart," *just;* Lat. "cert-us") : his son ; a quo *O'Muircheirtaigh.*
102. Aodh (3) : his son.
103. Muldoon (3) : his son.
104. Murtogh : his son.
105. Muldoon (4) : his son.
106. Muirceardoig : his son ; King of Loch Leine, A.D. 1068.

107. Tadhg : his son.
108. Eoghan : his son.
109. Muldoon (5) : his son.
110. Eoghan (2) : his son.
111. Eoghan (3) : his son.
112. Eoghan (4) : his son.

In A.D. 1107, O'Moriarty, King of Eoghanacht of Loch Leine, was expelled from his lordship by Mac-Carthy, King of Desmond.

O'BRIEN. (No. 1.)

King of Thomond.

The Armorial Bearings of the "O'Brien" (of Thomond) family are :
Arms : Gules three lions, passant, guardant, per pale, or and argent.
Crest : On a wreath issuing out of clouds, a naked arm, embowed, the hand grasping a sword, all ppr.
Motto : Lamh Laidir an Uachdar.

THE following is the *Stem** of this family, from Cormac Cas, who was the ancestor of *O'Briain* of Thomond (anglicised *O'Brien, Bernard, Brien, Bryan,* and *Bryant*), and a younger brother of Owen Mór, who is No. 85 on the "Line of Heber;" down to Henry O'Brien, the eighth Earl of Thomond, who d. in 1741.

85. Cormac Cas : second son of Olioll Olum, King of Munster, by his wife Sabh or Sabina, daughter of Conn of the Hundred Battles, and relict of MacNiadh ; he was one of the most distinguished champions of his time, and " remarkable for strength of body, dexterity, and courage." He defeated the Lagenians (or Leinster men) in the battle of Iorras Damhsa, Carmen (or Wexford), Liamhan (or Dunlaven), Tara, Teltown, and Samhna Hill ; and the Conacians in the famous battle of Cruachan, in the county Roscommon. Cormac d. at *Dun-tri-Liag,* (or the Fort of the Stone Slabs), now " Duntrileague," in the county Limerick, of wounds received in the battle of Samhna Hill, from the spear of Eochy of the Red Eye-brows, King of Leinster. He was m. to Samer, dau. of Fionn Mac-Cumhal (Fionn MacCoole), and sister of the poet Oisin, by whom he left, with other children :

86. Mogha Corb (or Mogha of the Chariots), who was b. A.D. 167, and attained a very old age. This Prince, who became King of Munster, which he governed for the space of twenty years, fought the memorable battle of Gabhra or

* *Stem* : Along with the Stem, the genealogies of the following branches of this family are also contained in this Volume : 1. *O'Brien,* of America ; 2. of Ara ; 3. of Dough ; 4. of England ; 5. of Ennistymon ; 6. of Lords of Inchiquin ; 7. of Marquises of Thomond ; 8. of O'Brien of Newtown ; and of Viscounts Clare, etc.

Garristown, near Dublin, against the Monarch Cairbre Liffechar, A.D. 284.

87. Fear Corb: his son; b. 198; governed Munster for seven years; fought the battles of Tlachtga and Teltown against the Lagenians, in the latter of which he slew Tinne the son of Triun, a distinguished warrior; and defeated the Conacians in the battles of Ceara, Corann, and Rathcruaghan, with great slaughter.

88. Æneas Tireach: his son; b. 232; was distinguished for his patriotism and courage, particularly in the battle of Cliodhna, near Clonakilty; and was remarkable for the strictness of his laws, as well as for his impartial judgments.

89. Lughaidh Meann: his son; b. 286; dispossessed the Firbolgs of the tract now known as the county Clare (which had in his time formed part of Connaught), and attached it to Munster.

90. Conall Each-luath ("each:" Irish, Lat. " eq-uus," Gr. "ik-kos" a horse; " luath :" Irish, agile, Welsh " lludw," nimble), or Conall of The Swift Steeds: his son; b. 312. Had two sons—1. Cas; 2. Eana Arighthach.

91. Cas: the elder son; a quo the Dal Cais or " Dalcassians ;" b. 347. Had twelve sons :—1. Blad, 2. Caisin, 3. Lughaidh, 4. Seana, 5. Aengus Cinathrach, 6. Carthann Fionn, 7. Cainioch, 8. Aengus Cinaithin, 9. Aodh, 10. Nae, 11. Loisgeann, and 12. Dealbheath.

92. Blad ("bladair :" Irish, to coax ; Lat. " blater-o," to flatter) : the eldest son of Cas; a quo O'Bladair, anglicised Blair, Flattery, and Blood (of Munster); b. 388; left four sons :—1. Carthann Fionn Oge Mór; 2. Carthann Dubh; 3. Eochaidh ; 4. Brennan Ban, ancestor

of O'Brennan (of Thomond), Glinn, Glynn, Maglin, Magan, Muldowney (now "Downey"), O'Hurley, etc.

93. Carthann Fionn Oge Mór: eldest son of Blad. Had two sons : 1. Eochaidh Ball-dearg ; 2. Aongus, who was the progenitor of O'Curry, O'Cormacan, O'Seasnain, etc.

94. Eochaidh Ball-dearg : son of Carthann Fionn Oge Mór. Received Baptism at the hands of St. Patrick, and d. at an advanced age, leaving two sons: 1. Conall, 2. Breacan, a quo "Ibrickan," a barony in the county Clare.

95. Conall: the elder son. Died vita patris, and left issue: 1. Aodh Caomh; 2. Molua Lobhar, or St. Molua the Leper, founder of the church of Killaloe, co. Clare.

96. Aodh Caomh ("caomh :" Irish, gentle ; Arab. "kom," noble ; Lat. "com-is"): the elder son; a quo O'Caoimh, anglicised Coombe. Was King of Cashel. Of him Lodge says : "He was the first Christian King of this family, that became King of all Munster; and his investure with the authority and title of King of that Province was performed at his own Court, in the presence of St. Breanan of Clonfert, and of his domestic poet MacLemein, who afterwards became first bishop of Cloyne ; and also by the concurrence of Aodh Dubh, son of Criomthan, then chief representative of the Eugenian race." He had two sons: 1. Cathal; 2. Congall, the ancestor of O'Noonan, of Thomond and South Connaught.

97. Cathal: the elder son.

98. Turlogh: his son; b. 641. Had—1. Maithan ; 2. Ailgeanan, who was the ancestor of O'Meara, Scanlan and MacArthur.

99. Maithan : son of Turlogh; b. 683.

100. Anluan : his son.

101. Corc : his son.

102. Lachtna: his son. Had his residence at a place called *Grinan Lachtna*, near Killaloe: he d. at an advanced age.

103. Lorcan (also called Fingin): his son; was King of the Dalcassians; d. 942. Had three sons:— 1. Cineidi; 2. Cosgrach, the ancestor of *Cosgrave* of (Munster), and *O'Hogan ;* 3. Lonargan, a quo *Lonergan ;* 4. Congal; 5. Bran Fionn, a quo *Slioght Branfionn*, in Wexford: a sept who took the permanent sirname of *O'Brien*, from this Bran, when sirnames were introduced into Ireland.

104. Cineadh (or Cineidi), King of Thomond* : the son of Lorcan ; m. Babhion, dau. of Arcadh, son of Murrough O'Flaherty, lord of *Iar Connacht* or West Connaught.

105. Brian† Boroimhe [Boru], the 175th Monarch of Ireland : a younger son of Cineadh ; b. 926, at Kincora, the royal seat of his ancestors ; and fell by the hand of Brodar, the Danish admiral, at the Battle of Clontarf, on Good Friday, the 23rd April, 1014, in the 88th year of his age. This Brian ("Brian:" Irish, *very great strength*), was the ancestor of *O'Brien*, Kings of Thomond. He had eleven brothers, of whom only four left issue, viz.— 1. Mahoun, the eldest brother, who was King of Munster, before Brian, and a quo many families. II. Donchuan, who was the ancestor of, among other families, *Eustace*, *O'Kennedy*, *O'Regan*, (of Thomond), *O'Kelleher*, *O'Beollan* (or "Boland"), *O'Casey*, *Power*, *Twomey*, etc. III. Eichtigern (a quo *Ahearne*, *Hearne*, *Heron*), who was ancestor of *MacCraith*, (or *MacGrath*), of Thomond, etc. IV. Anluan, who was the ancestor of *Quirk*, etc.

Brian Boroimhe was four times m. ; his first wife was Mór (more), dau. of Flan O'Hyne, Prince of Hy-Fiachra Aidhne, in Galway, by whom he had three sons of whom

---

* *Thomond* : The place of inauguration of the O'Briens, as Kings and Princes of Thomond, was at Magh Adhair, a plain in the barony of Tullagh, county of Clare ; and their battle-cry was *Lamh Laidir An Uachdar*, or "The Strong hand Uppermost." On their armorial ensigns were three lions rampant, which were also on the standards of Brian Boroimhe, borne by the Dalcassians at the battle of Clontarf. In modern times the O'Briens were Marquises of Thomond, Earls of Inchiquin, and Barons of Burren, in the county of Clare ; and many of them were distinguished commanders in the Irish Brigades in the service of France, under the titles of Earls of Clare, and Counts of Thomond.

† *Brian* : Brian Boroimhe is represented by our old annalists as a man of fine figure, large stature, of great strength of body, and undaunted valour ; and has been always justly celebrated as one of the greatest of the Irish Monarchs, equally conspicuous for his mental endowments and physical energies ; a man of great intellectual powers, sagacity, and bravery ; a warrior and legislator ; and, at the same time, distinguished for his munificence, piety, and patronage of learned men : thus combining all the elements of a great character, and equally eminent in the arts of war and peace ; a hero and patriot, whose memory will always remain famous as one of the foremost of the Irish Kings, in wisdom and valour. Brian lived at his palace of *Cean Cora* (Kincora), in a style of regal splendour and magnificence, unequalled by any of the Irish Kings since the days of Cormac MacArt, the celebrated Monarch of Ireland in the third century—the glories of whose palace at Tara were for many ages the theme of the Irish bards.—Connellan's *Four Masters*.

Oh, where, Kincora! is Brian the Great ?
And where is the beauty that once was thine ?
Oh ! where are the Princes and Nobles that sate
At the feast in thy halls, and drank the red wine.
Where, oh, Kincora !

Murrough, who fell at the Battle of Clontarf, was one. Brian was secondly m. to Eachraidh, dau. of Cearbhall, son of Olioll Fionn, and had: 1. Teige ;* 2. Donal, who distinguished himself at Clontarf, and was slain by the Siol Murray in a battle fought by the Dalcassians against the Conacians. His third wife was Gormliath, the "Kormloda" of Icelandic history; sister of Maolmora, King of Leinster: and relict of Aulaf, the Danish King of Dublin, to whom she bore the celebrated Sitric, who succeeded his father as King of the Danes of Dublin. By Gormliath Brian had Donogh, the 176th Monarch of Ireland, who was the ancestor of *Plunkett*, and of the O'Briens of Coonagh, in Limerick, and of Aherlow, in Tipperary; and a daughter Sabh, who m. Cian, who is No. 109 on the "O'Mahony" pedigree, by by whom she had Mathgabhuin, the founder of the family of *O'Mahony*, in the county Cork. Brian's fourth wife was Dubhcobhla, who d. s. p. 1009; she was dau. of Cathal O'Connor, King of Connaught.

106. Teige: younger son of Brian Boroimhe; m. Mór, dau. of Gilla-Brighid O'Mulloy, Lord of Fircall, in the King's County. (Another authority gives Mór as being the dau. of Melaghlin, son of Maolmora the 51st Christian King of Leinster). Teige was killed in 1022 by his brother Donogh, who thus became King of Munster. Donogh was m. to Driella, dau. of Godwin, Earl of Kent, and sister of Harold II., the last Saxon King of England; after a reign of forty-nine years Donogh abdicated; went on a pilgrimage to Rome, and took the habit of a

Monk in the monastery of St. Stephen where he soon after died.

107. Turlogh Mór (d. in 1086, aged 77 years), became King of North Munster on the abdication of his uncle Donogh; m. Mór, the dau. of O'Hyne, of Kilmacduagh, in the co. Galway, by whom he had four sons and a daughter. The sons were—1. Teige, who d. at Kincora, leaving two sons, Murrogh and Daniel. 2. Murtogh, who succeeded his father; carried fire and sword, in A.D. 1101, through Conacht and Tir Conal; marched to Aileach Neid which he burned; and after a reign of 30 years he retired (1116) to the monastery of Lismore to repent of his sins—especially of his violation of the sacred soil of Aileach; he died at Lismore in 1119, leaving: Donal, the Shorthand (whose sons Connor and Lewy fell in battle in 1151); Mahon, ancestor of *MacMahon* of Corca Bascin, and Cineidi Ochar. 3. Dermod, of whom presently. 4. Donogh, slain in 1103 at the battle of Magh Coba. And the dau. was Mór, who m. Roderic O'Connor the 183rd Monarch of Ireland.

108. Dermod: son of Turlogh Mór; in 1116 succeeded his brother, Murtogh, as King of North Munster; m. Sadhbh, dau. of Teige MacCarthy Mór, Prince of Desmond (see "Mac-Carthy Mór" pedigree, No. 108), by whom he had issue—two sons, 1. Connor-na-Catharach, and 2. Turlogh. The Princess Sadhbh, on the death of Dermod, m. her cousin Cormac Magh-Tamnagh MacCarthy Mór. Dermod, in 1116, was defeated by the Hy-Niall and their Conacht relatives at Ruadh-Bheithach, near Dunkellin, co. Galway; he d. in A.D. 1120, was interred in

* *Teige*: In O'Farrell's *Linea Antiqua*, on the "Roll of the Monarchs of Ireland," at No. 178, this Teige is mentioned as the "eldest" son of Brian Boroimhe.

Killaloe, and was succeeded by his son Connor, who, dying in 1142, was succeeded by his brother, Turloch.

109. Turlogh: son of Dermod; became Klng of North Munster in 1142 ; he m. twice—first, to a dau. of MacCarthy Mór, who d. s. p.; and secondly, to Narait or Ragnait, the dau. of O'Fogarty, lord of Ely-Deisceart (or Eliogarty), in Tipperary, by whom he had five sons: —1. Donal Mór; 2. Murtogh, who d. s. p.; 3. Brian of the Mountain, lord of Ormond; 4. Dermod; 5. Consaidin or Constantine ("Saidh :" Irish, *mildness, gentleness* ; "in," *little*), bishop of Killaloe (d. 1194), ancestor of the *MacConsidine* of the co. Clare.

Teige, uncle of Turlogh, contended with him for the Sovereignty of Munster, and a bloody battle was fought at *Cluan-na-Catha*, near Ardfinan, in Tipperary, in which Teige was defeated. In the year after, another terrible battle was also fought between Turlogh and Teige and his allies, at Barrymore in Cork, in which Teige was again defeated ; upwards of seven thousand fell on both sides, A.D. 1152.

Turlogh, after a reign of 25 years, died and was interred at Killaloe, 7th Nov., 1167, leaving his son Murtogh King of Munster, who was slain in 1168, by the people of Clare, at the instigation of Connor O'Brien; for which his brother Donal, on his accession, fined them 3,000 *cows.*

110. Donal Mór (d. 1194): son of Turlogh ; the last King of North Munster ; was m. to Orlacan, dau. of Dermod *na Gall* MacMorough (by his wife, the dau. of O'Moore, Prince of Leix), and had Mór, who married Cathal Craobh Dearg O'Connor (d. 1224), the 51st Christian King of Conacht, with nine sons: 1. Donogh Cairbreach ; 2. Murtogh *Dall*, an-

cestor of the *Clan Murtogh Dall O'Brien*, of Hy-Bloid, in the northeast of the co. Clare ; 3. Connor *Ruadh ;* 4. Murtogh Fionn, ancestor of the *Clan Turlogh Fionn* of the same territory; 6. Donal Conachtach, ancestor of *Clan Donal Conaghtaigh*, of Echtge, and subsequently of Ara, in the county Tipperary ; 7. Brian (surnamed " of Burren"), ancestor of *Clan Bhriain Boirnigh ;* 8. Connor, ancestor of *Clan Connor Guasanaigh ;* 9. Dermod *Fiodhnuich*, ancestor of the *Clan Dermod Fiodhniagh.* In 1169, this Donal Mór founded a religious house, afterwards the cathedral church on the site of the existing edifice in Cashel; in 1171, he founded a nunnery in the City of Limerick, but not a vestige of it remains. In 1172, following the example of Dermod MacCarthy Mór, King of South Munster, he made Henry II., King of England, a tender of his submission on the banks of the Suir :—

" Woe worth that hour, woe worth that day,
    That cost the freedom of the Gael ;
    And shame to those who broke the trust,
    In them reposed by Inis Fail."

In 1175, Donal, blinded Dermod, son of Teige O'Brien, and Mahon, son of Turlogh, his kinsmen, which act caused the death of Dermod soon after at Castleconnell. In 1176, Donal expelled the Anglo-Normans from the City of Limerick, putting most of Henry II's garrison to the sword. In 1192, he drove the English out of Upper Ormond, Ara, and Coonagh, where they established themselves; and stripping them of the booty they took from the native chieftains.

111. Donogh Cairbreach O'Brien: eldest son of Donal Mór ; d. 1242. Was the first of the family that assumed this sirname, and the title

of "Prince." Was surnamed "Cair-breach," from his having been nurtured in *Hy-Cairbre-Aobha*. He erected the palace of Clonroad, near the town of Ennis, and m. Sabia, dau. of Donogh O'Kennedy, lord of Muscry Tire, by whom he had Sabina* (who married Geoffrey O'Donoughue of Killarney), and six sons: 1. Connor; 2. Turlogh; 3. Murtogh; 4. Dermod; 5. Teige Dall; 6. A daughter Slainé, who d. Abbess of Killowen, in the barony of Islands, co. Clare—the foundation of her father in 1190. This Donogh Cairbreach O'Brien founded the abbeys of Corcomroe, in the barony of Burren, co. Clare; Killcooley, in the parish of Slievearadh, county Tipperary; Galbally, in the parish of Galbally, barony of Costlea, co. Limerick; and the Franciscan Monastery at Ennis, co. Clare.

112. Connor-na-Siuddine: eldest son of Donogh; slain at the Wood of Siudan, in Burren, county Clare, in 1268: hence the epithet affixed to his name, and a quo *Sidney*.† He m. Mór, dau. of MacNamara, lord of Hy-Coileann, and left issue: 1. Teige; 2. Brian Ruadh, ancestor of *O'Brien of Arra;* 3. Murtogh, who died without legitimate male issue.

113. Teige (d. 1259): the son of Connor; surnamed *Caol Uisge:* so called from his having (see No. 113 on the "O'Neill," Princes of Tyrone pedigree) attended there to hold a conference with Brian Catha Duin O'Neill, to whom this Teige O'Brien and Hugh O'Connor "granted the sovereignty over the Irish," in 1258, or constituted him Monarch of Ireland. This Teige m. Finola, dau. of Kennedy, son of Kennedy, son of Murtogh O'Brien, and had: 1. Turlogh Mór; 2. Donal, who defeated Mahon, grandson of Donal Conachtach, at the Abbey of Clare, in 1276.

114. Turlogh Mór, the hero of MacGrath's "Wars of Thomond:" the son of Teige; d. at his residence *Insi-an-Lasi* in 1306. Was m. three times: first, to Sabina (d. s. p.), dau. of Teige MacCarthy, of Dun-Mac-Tomain; secondly, to Orflath, (or Aurnia), dau. of Donal Oge MacCarthy Mór, by whom he had— 1. Brian (ancestor *of Siol Bhriain na Geall*, of Glen Cean), 2. Murtogh (founder of the houses of Thomond and Inchiquin), 3. Dermod (who left no issue); and the third marriage of Turlogh was to Sabina O'Kennedy, of Muscry Tir, by whom he had two sons—1. Connor, and 2. Donal.

115. Murtogh: second son of Turlogh Mór; d. 1343. Was twice m.: first, to Sarah (d. s. p.) dau. of O'Kennedy, of Ormond; and, secondly, to Edaoin or Edina, dau. of his standard bearer, MacGorman, of Ibrackan, by whom he had three

---

* *Sabina:* This Sabina, her husband, his brother, and three of Sabina's sons, were burned in their own house at the "Green Ford," by Fingin Mac Donal MacCarthy.

† *Sidney:* From another authority we learn that the cognomen of this Connor should be written *Suiderly*, or "of the spittles;" and the fact of his effigy having a short pipe in its mouth gives support to this conjecture: hence it is clear that the Irish *smoked* in the twelfth century!

It is also stated that Connor was slain by his own Kinsman, Dermod, son of Murtogh O'Brien, whereupon Brian, son of Connor, was nominated "The O'Brien." Connor was interred in the north end of the abbey of Corcomroe, where the peasantry still point out the site of his tomb. On the tomb in bas-relief is the effigy of a mailed warrior in the usual recumbent posture, wearing the round tunic of the 13th century, and a short *pipe* in his mouth.

sons : 1. Maithan ; 2. Turlogh Maol, ancestor of *O'Brien* of Bun-Cumeragh, in the county Waterford ; 3. Teige.

116. Maithan Maonmaighe, who d. 1369 : the son of Murtogh. The epithet applied to him means that he was fostered in "Maonmaighe," near Loughrea. Was m. to Winifred, dau. of O'Connor Corc., by whom he had seven sons : 1. Brian ; 2. Connor (who m. Mary, dau. of Teige O'Brien, lord of Coonagh, by whom he had—1. Dermod; 2. Donal, bishop of Limerick ; 3. Brian Dubh, the progenitor of *O'Brien* of Carrigagunnel and Glin, in the county Limerick) ; 3. Teige Baccach, ancestor of *O'Brien*, of Ballygarridan ; 4. Turlogh ; 5. Murtogh ; 6. Dermod; 7. Donal.

117. Brian Catha-an-Aonaigh (or Brian of the Battle of Nenagh) who d. 1399: son of Maithan. Was twice m. : first to Slaine, dau. of Lochlan Laidir MacNamara, by whom he had three sons : 1. Teige na Glaoidh Mór (d. s. p.) ; 2. Mahon Dall, who had Turlogh, who had Brian, the progenitor of *Siol Bhriain Debriortha* (or the exiled); 3. Turlogh. Secondly, to Margaret, dau. of James Fitzgerald of Desmond, by whom he had Brian Udhar Catha, who was the ancestor of *O'Brien*, of Eachdroma.

118. Turlogh Bog : a younger son of Brian of the Battle of Nenagh ; d. 1459. Was the hero of Glen Fogarty and Ballyanfoil ; married Catherine, dau. of Ulick FitzWalter Burke, by whom he had issue : 1. Teige ; 2. Donogh-Teige, bishop of Killaloe, who was called "Terence," by Ware ; 3. Connor Mor na-Shrona, ancestor of *O'Brien*, of Sealhendhe, in Clare; 4. Turlogh Oge, who, from his dark complexion, was called "Gilla Dubh," and who was the progenitor of *O'Brien*, of Ballymac-

doody ; 5. Mahon, of Kilclaney; 6. Kennedy ; 7. Brian Ganeagh ; 8. Murtogh Beg.

119. Teige an-Chomhaid, or Teige of the Castle of Chomhad, in Burren, which he erected in 1459 in his father's lifetime : son of Turlogh Bog; d. 1466. He m. Annabella, dau. of Ulick Burke, son of "Ulick of the Wine," of Clanrickard, and had six sons : 1. Turlogh Donn ; 2. Donal, whose sons Brian, Connor, and Murtogh possessed the estates known as *Tir Briain Cacthnava, Dubh*, and *Dun-Hogan*, all in the co. Clare ; 3. Donogh, of Drom-fion-glas, who had four sons— Murtogh, Teige, Dermod, and Brian-na-Corcaidh (who divided his estates of Cahir-Corcrain, and Castletown, amongst his sons: I. Mahon, II. Murrogh, III. Connor, IV. Dermod, V. Murtogh, and VI. Teige-an-Comain) ; 4. Murtogh Garbh ; 5. Murrogh; 6. Dermod Cleireach, of Cacthnava-na-Madara, who had six sons—I. Donall-na-Geall, II. Murrogh-an-Tarman, III. Brian-an Comhlach, IV. Mahon, V. Donogh, VI. Torlogh.

120. Turlogh Donn, who d. 1528 : son of Teige-an-Chomhaid ; married twice : first, to Joan, dau. of Thomas, eighth Lord Fitzmaurice (see No. 13 on the "Fitzmaurice" pedigree) ; and, secondly, to Raghnait, dau. of John MacNamara, of Clan Coilcain, and by her had: I. Connor; II. Donogh; III. Murrough, first Earl of Thomond and Baron of Inchiquin ; IV. Teige, slain by Pierce, Earl of Ormond ; V. Dermod ; VI. Margaret, m. to Owen O'Rourke, of the county Leitrim ; VII. Slaine, m. to Henry Oge O'Neill, son of Henry, Prince of Ulster; VIII. Fionala, who m. Manus O'Donnell, Chief of Tirconnell

121. Connor, who d. 1540: eldest

son of Turlogh Donn ; was twice m.:
first, to Anabella, dau. of Ulick
Ruadh [Roe] de Burgo, of Clan
Ricarde, and had :

   I. Donogh Ramhar (or Donogh
     the Fat).

   II. Sir Donal, ancestor of *O'Brien*
     of Dough, Newtown, and
     Ennistymon.

Connor m. secondly, Alice, dau.
of Maurice Fitzgerald, Earl of
Desmond, by whom he had four
sons :

   I. Sir Turlogh, lord of Ibrackan.

   II. Teige, of Ballinacorrig, whose
     dau. Amory m. John, Knight
     of Kerry.

   III. Murrogh, of Cahironanane,
     whose only son, Dermod, died
     young.

   IV. Murtogh, of Dromtyne,
     whose two sons d. s. p.

122. Donogh Ramhar, the second
Earl of Thomond : eldest son of
Connor ; m. Helena, dau. of Pierce,
Earl of Ormond, and had :

   I. Connor.

   II. Donal, ancestor of *O'Brien* of
     Ballincorran, in the co. Clare,
     represented in 1741 by William
     O'Brien, son of Murrogh-na-
     Buile.

   I. Margaret, who m. Dermod,
     Lord Inchiquin.

   II. Honoria, who m. Teige Mac-
     Namara of Clan Coilcain.

   III. Mór, who m. Theobald, son
     of William, the first Lord
     Castleconnell.

123. Connor, the third Earl: the
son of Donogh Ramhar; was twice
m.: first, to Joanna, dau. of Thomas,
the 16th Lord Kerry, and had a
dau., who d. s. p. ; and, secondly, to
Winifred, dau. of Turlogh O'Brien
of Ara, by whom he had :

   I. Donogh, of whom presently.

   II. Teige, who m. Slania, dau.
     of Teige, son of Murrough,
     Earl of Inchiquin, the pro-
     prietor of Smithstown Castle
     otherwise called Ballygowan,
     and had :

     I. Turlogh, of Ballyslattery,
      who m. the dau. of Donogh
      O'Brien, of Leamanagh, and
      had a son Connor.

     II. Col. Murtagh, who m.
      Joanna, dau. of Turlogh
      MacMahon, of Clena, but d.
      s. p.

   III. Dermod, who m. Una, the
     dau. of Donogh O'Brien, of
     Newtown, and d. s. p.

   III. Sir Donal, from whom des-
     cended the Viscounts Clare ;
     the third son of Connor.

   I. Honoria : the eldest daughter
     of said Connor, the third Earl
     of Thomond ; who m. Thomas,
     the 18th Lord Kerry.

   II. Margaret, who m. James, the
     second Lord Dunboyne.

   III. Mary, who m. Turlogh Ruadh
     MacMahon.

124. Donogh :* the eldest son of
Connor, the third Earl of Thomond ;
was the fourth Earl, who was com-

---

* Donogh : In 1601, this Donogh O'Brien, the fourth Earl of Thomond, assisted the
English against the Irish and Spaniards at Kinsale. He commanded a thousand men,
chiefly English, and the defeat of the native Chiefs and Princes was owing in a great
measure to the bravery which he displayed. It is stated by Carew, in the *Pacata
Hibernia*, that Donogh had often told him that an Irish prophet, whose writings he had
often read, foretold the defeat of the Irish at Kinsale ; and Fynes Morison says that the
Manuscript containing the said "prophecy" was shown to Mountjoy on the day of that
engagement. On the 6th May, 1605, Donogh was appointed President of Munster ; and
Commander-in-Chief of the English forces in that Province, on the 25th of the same
month, in that year. He died on the 5th of September, 1624, and was interred in the
Cathedral Church of Limerick, where a handsome monument, exhibiting a Latin inscription, was erected to his memory.

L

monly called the "Great Earl;" d.
Sept., 1624; m. Elizabeth, dau. of
Gerald, the eleventh Earl of Kil-
dare, and had:

I. Henry, the fifth Earl, who m.
Mary, dau. of Sir William
Brereton, Baron of Leighlin,
and dying in 1639, left:

I. Mary, whose first husband
was Charles Cockaine, first
Viscount Cullen.

II. Margaret, who was the
second wife of Edward
Somerset, Marquis of Wor-
cester.

III. Elizabeth, who was the
second wife of Dutton, Lord
Gerard, of Bromley.

IV. Anne, who m. her cousin-
german Henry, the seventh
Earl of Thomond.

V. Honoria, who m. Henry,
Earl of Peterborough.

II. Brian, the sixth Earl, of whom
presently.

125. Brian, the sixth Earl of
Thomond: the second son of
Donoch.

126. Henry, the seventh Earl:
his son; m. twice: first, his cousin-
german, Anne, as above mentioned,
and had:

I. Henry, Lord of Ibrackan, who
m. Catherine Stuart, sister of
the last Duke of Richmond and
Lennox, of that House, and
had:

I. Donogh, who m. Sophia, dau.

of Thomas Osborne, Duke of
Leeds, but d. s. p.

II. George.

I. Mary, who m. Robert, the 17th
Earl of Kildare.

II. Catherine, who m. Edward
Hyde, Earl of Clarendon.

Henry, the seventh Earl of Thomond, was secondly m. to Sarah,
daughter of Sir Francis Russell, of
Chippenham, and had:

III. Henry, who d. young.

IV. Another Henry.

III. Elizabeth, who d. s. p.

IV. Finola, who was the first
wife of Henry Howard, Earl of
Suffolk.

V. Mary, wife of Sir Mathew
Dudley, of Clopton.

127. Henry Horatio, Lord O'Brien,
and Baron of Ibrackan: youngest
son of Henry, the seventh Earl; d.
1690, *vita patris;* m. Henrietta, dau.
of Henry Somerset, Duke of Beau-
ford, and had:

I. Henry, of whom presently.

I. Mary.

II. Elizabeth.

128. Henry O'Brien: the son of
Henry Horatio; succeeded his
grandfather as the eighth Earl of
Thomond. He m., in 1707, Eliza-
beth, dau. of Charles, Duke of
Somerset; was created an English
Peer by the title of "Viscount of
Tadcaster," in 1714; and d. without
legitimate male issue, on the 20th of
April, 1741.

O'BRIEN. (No. 2.)

Marquises of Thomond.

MURROUGH, the third son of Turlogh Donn, who is No. 120 on the "O'Brien" (Kings of Thomond) pedigree, was the ancestor of this branch of that family:

121. Murrough:* son of Turlogh Donn; d. 1551; was the first "Earl of Thomond" and "Baron of Inchiquin; m. Eleanor, dau. of Thomas FitzGerald, Knight of the Valley, and had three sons and three daughters; the sons were:

I. Dermod of whom presently.

II. Teige, of Smithstown Castle, who m. Mór, dau. of Donal O'Brien, and had:
  I. Turlogh, who d. s. p.
  I. Honoria, who m. Richard Wingfield, an ancestor of the Viscounts Powerscourt.
  II. Slaine, who m. Teige, son of Connor, the Third Earl of Thomond.
  III. Hannah, who m. Donogh O'Brien.

III. Donogh, from whom descended O'Brien of Dromoland.

The daughters were:

I. Margaret, b. 1535, who m. Richard, the second Earl of Clanricard.

II. Slaine, whose second husband was Sir Donal O'Brien, of Dough.

III. Honoria, who m. Sir Dermod O'Shaughnessy, of Gort, and had issue.

122. Dermod, who d. 1557; eldest son of Murrough; inherited the Barony of Inchiquin, only—the Earldom of Thomond having been conferred on his cousin Donogh Ramhar, who is No. 122 on the "O'Brien" (Kings of Thomond) pedigree. Dermod m. Margaret, dau. of said Donogh, and had:

123. Murrough, who d. in 1573; was the third Baron of Inchiquin; m. Anabella (or Mable), dau. of Christopher Nugent, the ninth Lord Delvin, and had:

124. Murrough, the fourth Baron, who d. in 1597; m. Margaret, dau. of Sir Thomas Cusack, Knt., Lord Chancellor, and Lord Justice of the "Pale," and had:

I. Dermod, of whom presently.

II. Teige, who m. Slaine, dau. of Murrough O'Brien, of Ara.

I. Slaine, who m. William Dongan, Recorder of Dublin.

125. Dermod, who d. 1624: the elder son of Murrough; was the fifth Baron; m. Ellen, dau. of Sir Edward Fitzgerald, of Ballymaloe and Cloyne, Knt., and had four sons and three daughters:

I. Murrough, of whom presently.

II. Henry, a Lieutenant-Colonel in the Army of Charles I., King of England.

III. Christopher, who d. in infancy.

---

* *Murrough*: This Murrough O'Brien, having, A.D. 1543, dispossessed his nephew, Donogh, of the principality of Thomond, repaired to England and made his submission to King Henry VIII., to whom he resigned the principality, and was created therefor "Earl of Thomond," and Baron of Inchiquin: the conditions being, that he should utterly forsake and give up the name *O'Brien*, and all claims to which he might pretend by the same; and take such name as the king should please to give him; and he and his heirs and the inheritors of his lands should use the English dress, customs, manners, and language; that he should give up the Irish dress, customs, and language, and keep no kerns or gallowglasses.—CONNELLAN.

IV. Christopher (2), a Lieutenant-Colonel in the Irish
Confederate Army, who was
created "Baron of Inchiquin,"
by the Supreme Council of
the Catholic Confederation at
Kilkenny ; m. Honoria, dau.
of Turlogh MacMahon of
Clonderala.

I. Honoria, who m. Anthony
Stoughton of Rattoo, in the
co. Kerry, and had, besides
other children, Elizabeth
Stoughton, who m. Colonel
Roger Moore, of Johnstown,
near Dublin, and had Elizabeth, who m. Colonel Henry
Edgeworth, and had :

I. Henry Edgeworth, of Lizard,
near Edgeworthstown, in
the co. Longford.

II. Robert.

III. Rev. Essex Edgeworth of
Templemichael, in the said
county, who, in Nov., 1719,
m. Elizabeth, dau. of Sir
Robert King, Bart., from
whom the Earls of Kingston
and the Viscounts Lorton
descended.

I. Maria,

II. Elizabeth.

II. Mary : the second dau. of
Dermod, m. His Grace, the

Most Rev. Dr. Boyle, Protestant
Archbishop of Armagh.

III. Anne : the third dau. d.
unm.

126. Murrough-an-Toitean :* son
of Dermod, d. in 1674 ; was the
sixth Baron and the first *Earl of
Inchiquin :* m. Elizabeth, dau. of Sir
William St. Leger, Knt., President,
of Munster, and had :

I. William, of whom presently.

II. Charles, slain at the siege of
Maestricht.

III. John, who served as a Captain in the United Provinces
under the Prince of Orange.

I. Elizabeth, whose second husband was John MacNamara, of
Cratloe.

II. Honoria, who m. Theobald,
the third Lord Brittas (outlawed in 1691), by whom she
had two sons and one dau. :

I. John, fourth Lord Brittas,
a Captain in the French
Army, who had a son, also
a Captain in that Army,
and known as the fifth Lord
Brittas (and likewise Lord
Castleconnell, a title forfeited by his grandfather in
1691, for his adherence to
King James II.) ; another
son, Thomas, a Benedictine

---

* *Toitean :* Murrough-an-Toitean ("toitean :" Irish, *a burning*, or *conflagration*)
or Murrough of the Conflagrations, was appointed President of Munster, where he is
well remembered for his cruelties, and always mentioned with an imprecation ; so
cruel, that in Munster it is commonly said of a person who appears to be frightened ;
Do chonnairc se Murcadh no an tur b-fhoisge do, "He has seen Murrough or the
clump next to him." This Murrough, in 1642, at the head of 1,850 foot and 400
horse, attacked the Irish under Lord Mountgarret, at Liscarroll, and defeated them
with great slaughter. He sided with the Parliament, in 1644, against King Charles
the First, and was by that Parliament appointed President of Munster. In 1647, he
reduced several fortified places in the county of Waterford ; besieged Cahir, in
Tipperary, which surrendered to him ; and took " Cashel of the Kings" by storm :
"The inhabitants of Cashel," says "Lewis, "took refuge in their church on the
rock which was well fortified and garrisoned. Inchiquin proposed to leave them
unmolested on condition of their contributing £3,000, and a month's pay for his army.
This offer being rejected, he took the place by storm, with great slaughter, both of
soldiers and citizens : among them twenty of the clergy were involved ; and, having
secured the immense booty of which he obtained possession, he dispersed his forces
into garrison."

monk, who d. at Perugia in 1722; and Elizabeth, who m. James (FitzTheobald) Mathew, of Thurles.

III. Mary, whose first husband was Henry Boyle, of Castle-

martyr, father of Henry, first Earl of Shannon.

IV. Finola, who d. s. p.

127. William: eldest son of Murrough - an - Toitean; was the second Earl of Inchiquin; d. at

Murrough-an-Toitean defeated the Irish under Lord Taaffe and Sir Alexander MacDonnell (commonly called "Alastrum Mór," who was the eldest son of Sir James, of Eanagh and Ballybannagh, No. 118 on the "MacDonnell," of the County Clare pedigree), at the Battle of Knocknaness, on the 13th of November, 1647; for which the Parliament sent him a letter of thanks, with a present of £1,000. In 1648, he reduced Nenagh, as appears by the following letter which he wrote to his friend, Colonel David Crosbie, Governor of Kerry:

"I have reduced Nenagh, and am this day marching after Owen Roe (O'Neill), either to the Boyne or Borris-in-Leix. Preston is before Athy, and being possessed of part of it three days since, it is confidently believed he is Mr. (Master) of it by this tyme. I have now only to advise you to use your best care in keeping ye country in good order, remayneing

"Yor affectionate friend,
"INCHIQUIN.

"Ballynekill,
17th Sept., 1648."

Of Murrough-an-Toitean we read in De Vere's *Wail of Thomond:*

"Can it be? Can it be? Can O'Brien be traitor?
    Can the great House Dalcassian be faithless to Eire?
The sons of the stranger have wrong'd—let them hate her!
    Old Thomond well knows them; they hate her for hire!
Can our Murrough be leagued with the rebels and ranters
    'Gainst his faith and his country, his king and his race?
Can he bear the low wailings, the curses, the banters?
    There's a scourge worse than these—the applause of the base!

"Was the hand that set fire to the churches descended
    From the band of the King that uprear'd them, BOROIMHE?
When the blood of the priests and the people ran blended,
    Who was it cried, 'Spare them not?' Inchiquin, who?
Some Fury o'er-ruled thee! some root hast thou eaten!
    Twas a demon that stalked in thy shape! 'Twas not thou!
Oh, Murrogh! not tears of the angels can sweeten
    That blood-stain; that Cain-mark erase from thy brow!"

Soon after the reduction of Nenagh, Murrough-an-Toitean changed sides: Early in 1649, he openly espoused the cause of Charles II., who in a letter from the Hague appointed Murrough President of Munster; and on the 14th of April of same year he was pronounced a traitor by the Commonwealth Parliament. On the 1st of June following he sent the subjoined communication:

"To the Officer commanding in Cheeffe, Castlemaine.
"By the Lord President of Maunster:

"You, and the rest of the Warders of Castlemaine, are hereby required to be obedient to the directions and commands of Coll. David Crosbie uppon all occasions, and to deliver him, if occasion shall require for his Maties. (Majesty's) service, admonition (ammunition) out of the said Castle; thereof you may not faile at yor pill (peril); and for yor soe doeing this shall be yor Warrant.

'INCHIQUIN.

"Dated the first of June, 1649."

his castle of Rostellan, near Cloyne, in 1691. Married Mary, dau. of Edward Villiers, Knt., and sister of Edward, Earl of Jersey, and had:

I. William, who d. 1719, m. Anne, Countess of Orkney, and had:
I. William, Lord O'Brien, who d. s. p.
II. George, Lord O'Brien.
III. Augustus, d. s. p.
IV. Murrough, d. s. p.
I. Mary, who married Murrough, the fifth Earl of Inchiquin.
II. Anne.
III. Frances.
IV. Elizabeth.
II. James, of whom presently.
III. Charles, who d. unm.
IV. Donal, who d. 1768.
I. Mary: the elder daughter of William; married Robert (died 1744), 19th Earl of Kildare.
II. Henrietta.

128. James (died 1771), M.P. for Youghal: second son of William (d. 1691); married Mary, dau. of Very Rev. William Jephson, Protestant Dean of Kilmore, and had:

I. Murrough (d. 1808), the fifth Earl, who was created *Marquis of Thomond;* m. the Lady Mary O'Brien, but d. without male issue: in default of which the remainder was to the issue of his brother Edward, who d. in 1801, in the lifetime of Murrough.
II. Edward, of whom presently.
III. John, who was a Lieutenant in the English Navy.

I. Mary.
II. Anne, who m. the Most Rev. Dr. Cox, Protestant Archbishop of Cashel, and had a son:
I. Richard Cox.
III. Henrietta, whose first husband was Teige O'Loughlin, of Burren, in the co. Clare.

129. Edward: the second son of James; d. 1801; married Mary, daughter of —— Carrick, and had:

I. William, the second Marquis of Thomond, who d. 1846; succeeded to the title on the death of his uncle, Murrough, in February, 1808; married Elizabeth, daughter of Thomas Trotter, Esq., of Duleek, by whom he had four daughters.
II. James, of whom presently.
III. Edward, R.N.

130. James; the third Marquis: second son of Edward; was the seventh Earl, and the twelfth Baron. Was an Admiral of the White G.C.H., and commanded the "Emerald" at the capture of St. Lucia and Surinan. Married twice: first, in 1800, to Miss Bridgeman —— Willyams; and secondly, to Jane, daughter of Thomas Ottley, Esq., but died in 1855, without surviving male issue, and on his death the *Marquisate of Thomond,* and *Earldom of Inchiquin* became extinct. The "Barony" devolved on the Dromoland branch of the *O'Brien* family, in the person of Sir Lucius O'Brien, who is No. 131 on the "O'Brien" (Lords of Inchiquin) pedigree, *infra.*

O'BRIEN. (No. 3.)

Viscounts Clare

SIR DONAL, the third son of Connor O'Brien, the third Earl of Thomond, who is No. 123 on the "O'Brien" (Kings of Thomond) pedigree, was the ancestor of this branch of that family :

124. Sir Donal: son of Connor; Lord of Moyarta and Carrignoulta (now Carrigaholt); created *Viscount Clare* by King Charles II., in 1662 ; m. Catherine, dau. of Gerald, Earl of Desmond, and d. in 1662, leaving :

I. Connor of whom presently.

II. Donogh, who d. 6 August, 1638.

III. Murrough : who left issue.

IV. Teige, who m. Mary, dau. of Gerald Fitzgerald of Ballighane.

125. Connor, the second Viscount : son of Sir Donal ; d. in 1670 ; m. Honoria, dau. of Donal O'Brien, of Dough Castle, and had one son and six daughters :

I. Daniel, of whom presently.

I. Margaret, who m. Hugh (Fitz-Philip) O'Reilly, Lord of East Brefni.

II. Ellen, who married Roger O'Shaughnessy of Gort.

III. Honoria, who m. John Fitz-Gerald, Knight of Kerry.

IV. Catherine, whose second husband was John MacNamara, of Moyreisk.

V. Sarah, who m. Donal O'Sullivan Beare.

VI. Anne, who d. unm.

126. Daniel, the third Viscount : son of Connor ; fought and fell at the Battle of the Boyne, in 1690, in the cause of King James II. ; m. Philadelphia, eldest dau. of Francis Leonard, the Lord Darce, and sister to Thomas, Earl of Sussex, and had :

I. Daniel, the fourth Viscount, who d. unm. in 1697.

II. Charles, the fifth Viscount.

127. Charles, the fifth Viscount Clare* : son of Daniel ; was mortally wounded on "*Ramillies' Bloody Field,*" on the 11th of May, 1706, and dying at Bruxelles was interred in the Irish Monastery in that city. He m. the dau. of Henry Buckley, and had :

I. Charles, of whom presently.

I. Laura, who m. the Count de Bretuil.

128. Charles, the sixth Viscount, who d. 1761 : the son of Charles ; was presented by his cousin Henry, Earl of Thomond, to King George the First, who assured the said Charles of pardon of the outlawry in which he continued by the attainder of his grandfather in 1691,

---

* *Viscount Clare* : This is the Lord Clare to whom the following lines refer :

　When, on Ramillies' Bloody Field,
　The baffled French were forced to yield,
　The victor Saxon backward reeled
　　Before the charge of Clare's Dragoons.

• • • • •

CHORUS.

Viva la, for Ireland's wrong !
　Viva la, for Ireland's right !
Viva la, in battle throng,
　For a Spanish steed, and sabre bright !

provided he (No. 128) conformed to the Protestant Religion; but Charles declined, and joined the Irish Brigade in the service of France. He commanded at *Fontenoy** (1745), and distinguished himself at the head of the Irish Troops in that well-contested field; and on the eve of that Battle was promoted to the rank of Lieutenant-General, and Marshal of Thomond, Governor of New Brisack (in Alsace); and Captain-General of the Province of Languedock, for his distinguished services at Laufeldt, in 1747. In 1755, he m. Mary-Genevieve-Louisa Ganthier de Chiffreville, Marchioness de Chiffreville, in Normandy, and had a son and a daughter:

I. Charles, of whom presently.
I. Antonietta-Maria - Septimanie, who m. the Duke de Choiseuil-Praslin, and had issue.

129. Charles, seventh Viscount, who d. s. p. at Paris, 29th Dec., 1774; since which time the title has remained in abeyance.

O'BRIEN. (No. 4.) (OF ENGLAND.)

Branch of Viscounts Clare.

MURROUGH, the third son of Sir Donal, the first Viscount Clare, who is No. 124 on the "O'Brien" (Viscounts Clare) pedigree, was the ancestor of this branch of that family.

124. Sir Donal, created Viscount Clare by King Charles II., in 1662.
125. Murrough: his third son; was called Murrough-en-Casa; to escape persecution, he migrated to Kerry under the protection of his relative The MacCarthy Mór.
126. Murrough: his son.
127. Murrogh Oge: his son; m. a dau. of O'Rourke.
128. Brian Ban: son of Murrough Oge; m. Ellen Moriarty, and had:
I. Teige, of whom presently.
II. Murrough.

III. Donogh.
129. Teige: eldest son of Brian Ban; m. Joanna, sister of Silvester Moriarty, Rear-Admiral of the Blue.
130. Bryan, of the co. Kerry: son of Teige; b. 1740; m., 20th Nov., 1797, Ellen, dau. of Justin Mac-Carthy (by Joanna Conway, his wife), and had:
I. Richard, who d. unm. in Jan., 1861.
II. Lucius, who d. unm. in America, in March, 1865.
III. Turlogh-Henry, author of the

---

* *Fontenoy :* At Fontenoy the Irish saved France from defeat when the battle was almost won by the English. As a last resource, Marshal Saxe ordered up his last reserve, the Irish Brigade, of which this Viscount Clare held the command:

" Lord Clare," he says, " you have your wish ; there are your Saxon foes !"
The Marshal almost smiles to see, so furiously he goes !
How fierce the look these exiles wear, who're wont to be so gay :
The treasured wrongs of fifty years are in their hearts to-day :
The Treaty broken, ere the ink wherewith 'twas writ could dry,
Their plundered homes, their ruined shrines, their women's parting cry,
Their priesthood hunted down like wolves, their country overthrown ;
Each looks as if revenge for all were staked on him alone.
" On Fontenoy, on Fontenoy ;" nor ever yet elsewhere
Rushed on to fight a nobler band than these proud exiles were.

. . . .

"Round Towers of Ireland," who d. unm. in 1835.

IV. Rev. Edward, Vicar of Thornton, Curtis, Ulceby, Lincolnshire, England.

V. Rev. John, M.A., Vicar of Henfield, Sussex, England,'who m. in 1843, Elizabeth, dau. of J. Hunt, Esq., and has issue.

VI. Rev. James, D.D., of Mag-

dalen Hall, Oxford, England; Incumbent, Founder, and Patron of SS. Patrick and James, Hove, Sussex, England; m. in August, 1844, Octavia, second dau. of Charles Hopkinson, of Wotton Court, Gloucester, and of Cadogan Place, London.

O'BRIEN. (No. 5.)

Barons and Earls of Inchiquin.

DONOGH, the youngest brother of Dermod, who is No. 122 on the "O'Brien" (Marquis of Thomond) pedigree, was the ancestor of this branch of that family :

122. Donogh ; the third son of Murrough, the first Earl of Thomond ; d. 1582. His father assigned to him the Castles and lands of Dromoland, Leamanagh, Ballyconnelly, Corcumroe, etc. ; m. Slaine, dau. of John MacNamara Fionn, of Crathloe, and had one son and two daughters :

I. Connor, of whom presently.

I. Margaret.

II. Finola, who m. Uaithne O'Loughlin, of Moyrin, in Clare.

123. Connor (who d. in 1603), of Leamanagh : son of Donogh ; m. Slaine, dau. of Sir Turlogh O'Brien, of Dough Castle, and had a son :

124. Donogh (2), who was knighted by King Charles I., and who d. in 1634. This Donogh m. Honoria, dau. of Richard Wingfield, an ancestor of the Viscounts Powerscourt, and had three sons and one daughter :

I. Connor, of whom presently.

II. Donogh, of Tobbermaile.

III. Murrough, who m. Hannah, dau. of his kinsman Turlogh O'Brien of Cluonan, and had a son named Teige.

I. Margaret, who m. Turlogh, son of Teige O'Brien of Dromore.

125. Connor (2), of Leamanagh, who d. 1651 : the eldest son of Donogh ; m. Mary, dau. of Sir Turlogh MacMahon, and had two sons and two daughters :

I. Sir Donogh, of whom presently.

II. Teige, who m. the dau. of Captain Edward Fitzgerald, of Carrigowrane.

I. Honoria, who married Donogh O'Brien, of Dough.

II. Mary, who m. Donogh MacNamara.

126. Sir Donogh, of Leamanagh and Dromoland : son of Connor ; d. 1717.- Was created a Baronet on the 9th of Nov., 1686. He was twice married : first, to Lucia, dau. of Sir George Hamilton, by whom he had a son Lucius, of whom presently ; and secondly, to Eliza, dau. of Major Deane, by whom he had :

II. Henry.

I. Honoria.

II. Elizabeth.

127. Lucius : son of Sir Donogh by his first marriage ; d. (before his father) in 1717 ; m. Catherine, dau.

of Thomas Keightley, of Hertford-shire, and had two sons and two daughters :

I. Sir Edward, of whom presently.
II. Thomas.
I. Anne.
II. Lucia.

128. Sir Edward, of Dromoland, M.P. : son of Lucius : was the second Baronet ; d. 1765. Sir Edward m. Mary, dau. of Hugh Hickman, of Fenloe, and had :

I. Sir Lucius-Henry, of whom presently.
II. Donogh.
III. Edward.
I. Henrietta.
II. Anne.
III. Mary.
IV. Catherine, who m. Charles MacDonnell, of New Hall, near Ennis.
V. Lucia.

129. Sir Lucius-Henry, of Dromo-land, M.P., the third Baronet : son of Sir Edward ; d. 1795 ; m., in 1768, Nichola, dau. of Robert French, of Monivea Castle, in the co. Galway, M.P., and had :

I. Sir Edward, of whom presently.
II. Lucius.
III. Robert.
IV. Donogh.
V. Henry.
I. Nichola.
II. Henrietta.
III. Catherine.
IV. Lucy.
V. Anna-Maria.
VI. Charlotte.

130. Sir Edward, of Dromoland, the fourth Baronet, who d. in 1837 ; son of Sir Lucius-Henry ; m. in 1799, Charlotte, dau. of William Smith, of Cahirmoyle, Newcastle West, in the county Limerick, and had :

I. Sir Lucius, of whom presently.
II. William Smith O'Brien, M.P. (b. 17th Oct., 1803 ; d. 18th

June, 1864), heir to the estates of his maternal grandfather William Smith ; the "Wallace" of his country, who, on the 19th Sept., 1832, m. Lucy-Caroline (d. 13th June, 1861), eldest dau. of Joseph Gabbett, Esq., of Limerick, and, besides a daughter Charlotte-Grace (living in 1887), the good and philanthropic Miss C. G. O'Brien, of Emigration fame in Ireland, had Edward-William, J.P., (b. 23rd Jan., 1837, and living in 1887), of Cahirmoyle, co. Limerick. William Smith O'Brien d. in Wales, but his remains were brought to Ire-land and interred at Rath-ronan, co. Limerick.

III. Edward.
IV. Robert.
V. Henry.

Sir Edward's daughters were :
I. Granna (or Grace).
II. Anne.
III. Harriet.
IV. Catherine.
V. Leney.

131. Sir Lucius, of Dromoland, the fifth Baronet, and thirteenth Baron of Inchiquin : son of Sir Edward ; b. 1800, d. 1872 ; m. twice : first, Mary, dau. of William Fitzgerald, Esq., of Adelphi, co. Clare, by whom he had one son and three daughters :

I. Edward-Donogh, of whom pre-sently.
I. Juliana-Cecilia, b. 1839.
II. Charlotte-Anne, b. 1840.
III. Mary-Grace, b. 1848.

Sir Lucius was secondly m. (on 25th Oct., 1854) to Louisa, dau. of James Finucane, Esq.

132. Edward Donogh O'Brien, of Dromoland, the sixth Baronet, and the fourteenth " Baron Inchiquin" : son of Sir Lucius ; b. 1837 ; living in 1887.

O'BRIEN. (No. 6.)

Of Ara, in the County of Tipperary.*

BRIAN RUADH [roe], second son of Connor-na-Siuddine, who is No. 112 on
the "O'Brien" (Kings of Thomond) pedigree, was the ancestor of this
branch of that family.

113. Brian Ruadh, who was murdered at the Castle of Bunratty, by
Thomas le Clare, had:
    I. Donogh, who was drowned in
    the Fergus, leaving five sons:
    1. Dermod, 2. Mahon, 3. Teige,
    4. Connor-na-Feasoige, 5. Mur-
    togh Gharbh.
    II. Donal, of whom presently.
    III. Murtogh.
    IV. Teige Roe.
    V. Brian.
    VI. Turlogh.
114. Donal: second son of Brian
Ruadh; married Margaret, dau of
Turlogh Dubh MacMahon, of Clon-
darala, and had:
    I. Bryan, of whom presently.
    II. Donogh.
    III. Donal.
115. Brian: the son of Donal;
settled in Ara, in the county of
Tipperary, and m. the dau. of
Henry de Burgo, by whom he had:
116. Murrough-ra-Ranaighe, who
m. Mór, dau. of O'Kennedy, of
Ormond, and had:
117. Turlough, who m. Honoria,
dau. of De Barry Oge, of Buttevant,
and had:
118. Teige, who had:
119. Donal Mór, who had:
120. Murtogh Caoch, who had:
121. Turlogh, who m. Mór, dau. of

Donogh (FitzJohn) O'Carroll, and
had five sons and one dau.:
    I. Murtogh, of whom presently.
    II. Donogh, who died in his
    father's lifetime.
    III. Turlogh Carrach, the pro-
    prietor of the Castles of
    Bealanath and Cnockan-an-
    Enfin.
    IV. Teige-na-Buile, who possessed
    the Castle of Kilcolman.
    V. Murrough-an-Tuath, of the
    Castle of Aos-Greine.
    I. Winifred, who m. Connor, the
    third Earl of Thomond.
122. Murtogh: eldest son of Turlogh; possessed the Castles of
Monroe, Pallas, Cahirconnor, and
Castletown. This Chieftain conformed to the Protestant Religion,
entered into Holy Orders, and was
appointed to the See of Killaloe.
He d. in 1613, leaving two sons and
four daughters:
    I. Sir Turlogh, of whom presently.
    II. John, who d. s. p.
    I. Slaine, m. to Teige (Fitz-
    Murrough) O'Brien, Baron of
    Inchiquin.
    II. Honoria.
    III. Mór.
    IV. Margaret.
123. Sir Turlogh: the son of Murtogh; m. a sister of Donal O'Brien,
of Annagh, and d. s. p. in 1626.

* *Ara:* See the Pedigree of "*MacUi-Brien Ara,*" in Vol. H. 1. 7, MSS. Lib.,
Trinity College, Dublin. "Ara" is a small mountain tract, south of Lough Dearg,
and north of the Keeper Hills.

O'BRIEN. (No. 7.)

Of Dough, Newtown, and Ennistymon.

SIR DONAL, the second son of Connor, who is No. 121 on the "O'Brien" (Kings of Thomond) pedigree, was the ancestor of this branch of that family :

122. Sir Donal: son of Connor; m. his cousin, Slaine, dau. of Murrough, first Earl of Thomond, and relict of Patrick, the twelfth Lord of Kerry, and had :

I. Sir Turlogh, of whom presently.

II. Murtogh, who m. Mary French.

III. Connor, who m. Mary, dau. of Teige MacMahon, of Carrigan-Ultach ("Carrigaholt"), and had Mary, who m. Teige MacNamara; and a son Daniel.

I. Mary, who m. Turlough Ruadh MacMahon, and had two daughters, of whom one m. O'Donnell, "Earl" of Tirconnell; and the other m. Mathew Maol MacMahon, of Clynagh.

II. Sarah, who m. O'Sullivan Beare.

III. Finola, whose second husband was Anthony O'Loughlin, of Burren, co. Clare.

123. Sir Turlogh: eldest son of Sir Donal ; m. Annabella, dau. of Sir —— Lynch, of Galway, Knt., and had :

I. Donal, of whom presently.

II. Donogh, of Newtown Castle, who m. Margaret, dau. of Sir John Burke, of Derrymaclaghna, Knt., and had :

I. Slaine, who m. Connor O'Brien, of Leamanagh ; and

I. Connor, who m. Elena, dau. of Sir Dermod O'Shaughnessy, Knt., of Gort, in the county Galway, and had Donogh, who m. Martha, dau. of Henry Ivers, of Dough.

124. Donal: son of Sir Turlogh ; m. Ellen, dau. of Edmond Fitzgerald, Knight of Glin, and had :

I. Teige, of whom presently.

II. Murtogh, who m. Slaine, dau. of John MacNamara, of Moyriesk.

I. Mary, who m. Sir James MacDonnell.

II. Honoria, who m. Connor, the the second Lord Clare.

125. Teige, of Dough, the son of Donal ; m. Mor, dau. of Murtogh O'Brien, of Arra, and had :

I. Donogh, of whom presently.

II. Murtogh, who m. Mary, dau. of Turlogh O'Neill.

126. Donogh, of Dough : son of Teige ; m. Honoria, dau. of Connor O'Brien, of Leamanagh, and had :

127. Christopher, who removed to Ennistymon, and was twice m. : first, to Elizabeth, dau. of Theobald Matthew, of Thomastown, co. Tipperary, and by her had :

I. Donogh, who d. young.

I. Elizabeth, who m. twice : first, to Charles MacDonnell, and secondly to Thomas Keane.

Christopher, of Ennistymon, secondly m. Mary, dau. of Randal MacDonnell, and by her had :

II. Edward, of whom presently.

III. James.

128. Edward, of Ennistymon : second son of Christopher ; m. Susanna, dau. of Henry O'Brien, of Stone Hall, and had one son and three daughters :

I. Christopher, of whom presently.

I. Mary.
II. Anne.
III. Harriett.

| 129. Christopher : son of Edward ; living in the early part of the nineteenth century.

O'BRIEN. (No. 8.)

Of Ballynalacken, County Clare.

Arms : Gu. three lions pass. guard. in pale per pale or. and ar. *Crest :* An arm embowed, brandishing a sword ar. pommelled and hilted or. *Motto :* Viguer de dessus.

DONAL, a younger son of Turlogh Donn (d. 1528), who is No. 119 on the " O'Brien" (Kings of Thomond) pedigree, was the ancestor of this branch of that family ; and possessed the territories there mentioned.

120. Donal, who was known as Donal Bacach (" bacach :" Irish, *lame*): second son of Teige-an-Chomhaid : m. Saibh, dau. of O'Loghlin, Prince of Burren, and had four sons :
  I. Brian.
  II. Teige.
  III. Connor, of whom presently.
  IV. Mortogh.
  Brian, Teige, and Mortogh left no issue ; but their brother Connor inherited their lands.
121. Connor, of Carruduff: third son of Donal Bacach ; m. Celia, dau. of O'Dea, Prince of Ive-Fermaic, and had :
122. Donogh, of Carruduff, who m. Honora, dau. of O'Hehir, lord of Ive-Cormaic, and had two sons :
  I. Dermod, of whom presently.
  II. Connor, a quo Donal Cam and his issue :
123. Dermod, of Carruduff: son of Donogh, m. Eleanor, dau. of Teige MacMahon, of Dangan-an-Elly, in the barony of Moyarta, co. Clare, and had :
  I. Donal, of whom presently.
  II. Morrogh.
124. Donal, of Carruduff: son of Dermod. In 1652, (see the "Book of Survey and Distribution") this Donal lost his estate by the Crom-

wellian Settlement of Ireland ; he m. Honora, dau. of O'Connor of Corcomroe, and had :
125. Brian, of Leitrim, who, under the Act of Repeal passed by King James II. in the Parliament held in Dublin, A.D. 1689, possessed himself of the Estate of Carruduff, aforesaid. This Brian m. Mary, dau. of Lochlin MacConsidine of Lac, in the co. Clare, Chief of his name, and had four sons :
  I. Dermod, Knt. of the Military Order of St. Louis; was in the Regiment of Lord Clare; and d. s. p.
  II. Torlogh, of whom presently.
  III. Teige, of Lanna, who d. s. p.
  IV. Morrough (or Morgan), who d. in 1774. He was a Captain in Lord Clare's Regiment ; Knight of the Military Order of St. Louis, in Oct., 1736, married at Landrecies, Maria Louisa de Thomak (a French lady), and had :
    I. Brian (or Bernard), who was an Aid-Major, in Lord Clare's Regiment, and died at Vitre in Brittany in 1758.
    II. Florence Dermod (or Darby), born at Landrecies, 3rd October, 1743 ; Captain in Clare's Regiment ; Knight

of Royal and Military Order of St. Louis; and Commandant of St. Germain de Calberte in the Sevennes. On the 6th September, 1774, at Bogny, in the diocese of Reims, he married Dame Maria Theresa de Covarruviasde Leyva, dau. of Charles, Marquis of Covarruvias de Leyva, Colonel of the Life Guards of the Duke of Modena, and Inspector-Genl. of his forces; and had: Marie-Theresa-Thadeé O'Brien, b. at Bogny, aforesaid, on the 9th October, 1780.

126. Torlogh, of Leitrim: second son of Brian of Beatath-Corick, Esq. (by Catherine, dau. of Jeoffry O'Connell, of Breantry, Esq., and sister of Colonel Maurice O'Connell, who d. s. p.), and had two sons and one daughter:

I. Torlogh, of whom presently.
II. John, who m. Miss Foster, of Kells, and had:
Terence, who d. unm. in Oct., 1829.
I. Catherine, a professed Nun at Limerick.

127. Torlogh, of Cross or Elmvale: son of Torlogh; m. Eleanor, dau. of Mortogh O'Hogan, of Cross (by Eleanor Butler, niece of Sir Toby, Butler, Knt., M.P., Chief Commissioner of the Inch, at the Capitulation of Limerick), and had two sons and one daughter:

I. John, of Limerick, who m. Margaret, dau. of ———— Macnamara, Esq., of London; and d. s. p. in 1792 (Will dated 1st Feb., 1792; and proved 20th Dec., 1792).
II. James, of whom presently.

128. James, of Limerick (d. 21st

Feb., 1806): second son of Torlogh; in Feb., 1791, m. Margaret* (d. 6th April, 1839), dau. of Peter Long, Esq., of Waterford, and had four sons:

I. John (died 1855), of whom presently.
II. Peter (b. Sept., 1799), of Limerick, who m. Emily, dau. of Edward Shiel, Esq., and sister of the Right Honble. Richard Lalor Shiel, M.P. In Sept., 1855, this Peter d. s. p.
III. Terence, b. Dec., 1802; d. unm. in March, 1820.
IV. James, b. 27th Feb., 1806; dead. Was called to the Bar in 1830; made Q.C., in 1841; Serjeant in 1848; Judge in 1858; was M.P. for Limerick, from Oct., 1854, to Jan., 1858. In July, 1836, this James m. Margaret, dau. of Thomas Segrave, Esq., and had one son and five daughters:

I. John, b. 25th Feb., 1855.
I. Anne, a Nun, b. 1837.
II. Margaret, a Nun, b. 1839.
III. Mary, b. in 1845.
IV. Clara, b. in 1847.
V. Emily, b. in 1849.

129. John (d. 6th Feb., 1855; bur. in Francis-street burial ground, Dublin), of Elmvale, J.P., afterwards of Ballinalacken, in the co. Clare; was High Sheriff of that county; M.P. for the City of Limerick, from 1841 to 1852. This John m. Ellen (d. Dec., 1869; bur. in Francis-street, Dublin), dau. of Jeremiah Murphy, Esq., Hyde Park, Cork, and had six sons and four daughters:

I. James, of whom presently.
II. Jerome, in the 28th Regt.
III. John, a Cistercian Monk.
IV. William (d.), I.A.H. Artillery.
V. Peter, of 41 Merrion square,

---

*Margaret: This lady was dau. of Peter Long, by Anne, his wife, elder dau. of Stephen Roche, Esq., of Limerick, and sister of John Roche, Esq., of Dublin. Margaret m. secondly Cornelius O'Brien, Esq., M.P., co. Clare.

Dublin, called to the Bar in 1865; made Q.C. in 1880; Senior Crown Prosecutor for Dublin in 1883; and appointed Her Majesty's Third Sergeant-at-Law, in 1884. This Peter, in Aug., 1867, m. Annie, dau. of Robert Clarke, Esq., J.P., of Bansha, co. Tipperary and had:

I. Annie-Georgina.

II. Eilen-Mary.

VI. Terence.

I. Margaret, who m. James Martin, Esq., J.P., of 99 Fitzwilliam square, Dublin.

II. Ellen, who m. Robert Daniell,

Esq., J.P., of Newforest, co. Westmeath.

III. Catto, a Nun.

IV. Anna.

All these sons and daughters of John (No. 129), except William, living in 1884.

130. James O'Brien, of Ballynalacken, co. Clare, J.P., D.L.: eldest son of John; b. in the City of Limerick, on the 9th Jan., 1832; was High Sheriff of the co. Clare: in 1858; m. in 1865 Georgina, widow of Francis McNamara, Calcutt, Esq., J.P., M.P., of St. Catherine's, co. Clare; living in 1884.

O'BRIEN. (No. 9.)
Of Ballyetragh, County Waterford.

TURLOGH MAOL, second son of Murtagh, who is No. 115 on the "O'Brien" (Kings of Thomond) pedigree, was the ancestor of "O'Brien" of Bun-Cumeragh, in the county Waterford. The O'Briens of Ballyetragh are a branch of that family. Several other branches* of the O'Briens of Thomond settled from time to time in the county Waterford, and there held large tracts of land. We can trace the Ballyetragh branch as far back as Anthony O'Brien, of Comeragh, who in 1549 obtained a pardon from the Government: and who was contemporary with Connor, who is No. 121 on the same pedigree. In 1598 Terlagh O'Brien, son of said Anthony, lived in Comeragh† Castle, at the foot of the Comeragh Mountains; in 1619 that Castle was unsuccessfully besieged by eleven knights of the Furlong family. According to the "Book of Survey and Distribution" for the co. Waterford, Derby O'Brien, son of said Terlagh, was the proprietor of Comeragh, in 1641; and, according to Exchequer Inquisitions taken at Dungarvan, on the 9th October, 1656, said Derby O'Brien‡ was dead in that year.

* *Branches :* Of those branches we find that Daniel O'Brien, of Ballyknocke, in 1632, was the son of Teige (d. 1620), who was the son of a Donagh O'Brien; that Murtagh O'Brien, of Cottir, in 1641, was the son of Mahon (d. 1623), who was son of a Donagh O'Brien; and that Donagh O'Brien of Jemybrien, in 1641, was the son of a Brian O'Brien. There are several Inquisitions in the Chancery Records for the co. of Waterford, in the reign of Charles I., regarding the O'Briens.

† *Comeragh :* Salterbridge near Cappoquin, on the river Blackwater, also belonged to this family.

‡ *Derby O'Brien :* As this Derby was dead in 1656, it may be supposed that the Mary Brien of Kilcomeragh, who was transplanted from the co. Waterford, in 1653, was his wife. Among the O'Briens who in that year were also transplanted from the co. Waterford were Terlagh O'Brien, of Cottin; Donagh O'Brien, of Kilnafahane; and Brian O'Brien, of Ballyathin (or "Boullyattin")—See "Transplanters' Certificates," in the Public Record Office, Dublin; and "Persons Transplanted," in p. 349 of our *Irish Landed Gentry when Cromwell came to Ireland.* (Dublin: Duffy and Sons, 1884).

After a fierce resistance by the five sons of Derby O'Brien, Comeragh Castle was taken by Cromwell, who hanged four of them; the fifth son, John, of Kilnafrahane, escaped to the sea-coast and settled near Helvick Head. From said John are descended the O'Briens, of Ballyetragh, co. Waterford.

Commencing with Anthony, and with (121) the number of Connor, both above mentioned, the following is the pedigree of this family:

121. **Anthony** of Comeragh, who was pardoned by the Government in 1549, had:

122. **Terlagh**, living in 1598, who had:

123. **Derby**, of Comeragh Castle, living in 1641, who had:

124. **John**, who had:

125. **Matthew**, who had:

126. **John**, who had:

127. **Matthew**, who m. Mary, dau. of Mr. Keating, of Tubrid, co. Tipperary, one of the family of the eminent Irish historian Jeoffrey Keating.* One of that lady's brothers was Parish Priest of Kilgobinet; it was, therefore, that this Matthew O'Brien came to reside at *Ballyetragh*, near his brother-in-law. Of the issue of that marriage was:

128. **Michael**, who m. Miss Rogers, of Coolroe, co. Waterford (whose family is mentioned in Smith's History† of Waterford, as among the Landed Gentry residing near Suir), and had four sons and five daughters:

I. Pierse, of whom presently.

II. Matthew Rogers O'Brien (d.), of Coolroe, above mentioned; who m. Ellen, dau. of James Connolly, Barrister-at-Law (a descendant of the famous Harry Flood), and had three sons and three daughters:

I. Gerald,
II. Thomas,   } All three living
III. Michael, }   in 1884.

The daughters were:

I. Anne, who m. Doctor Walsh, of New York.

II. Helen, who m. Doctor Dutt, of Calcutta.

III. Mary, who (see the "Ryding" pedigree, *infra*), m. Frederick Ryding, L.D.S., R.C.S.E.; both living in 1887.

III. Thomas, of Kilnafrahane; third son of Michael.

IV. Michael: the fourth son.

The five daughters of Michael (No. 128) were:

I. Mary, who m. M. Hudson, Esq.

II. Anne, who m. a Mr. Barry.

III. Ellen.

IV. Eliza.

V. Kate.

129. **Pierse** O'Brien, of Ballyetragh, co. Waterford: eldest son of Michael, living in 1887; is the present representative of the Ballyetragh family.

* *Keating :* There were four brothers Keating, all Priests, who had studied at the then famous University of Coimbra, in Portugal. They were near relatives of the Rev. Father Sheehy, of famous memory, who was arrested in the house of Mr. Keating of Tubrid, above mentioned.

† *History :* Published in 1750.

O'BRIEN OF AMERICA. (No. 10.)

Branch of the Marquises of Thomond.

DONAL, a younger brother of James, who is No. 128 on the " O'Brien" (Marquises of Thomond) pedigree. was the ancestor of this branch of that family : whose descent from said Donal down to the Rev. Matthew Patrick O'Brien, Rector of St. Vincent de Paul's R.C. Church, in Minersville, Schuylkill County, Pennyslvania, United States, America, and living in 1883, is as follows :

128. Donal : a son of William, the second Earl of Inchiquin ; settled in the county Waterford, and d. 1768.

129. James : son of Donal ; b. 1730 ; d. 1800.

130. John : his son ; b. 1765 ; d. 1840. Married Catherine (d. 25th Dec., 1860), dau. of Matthew Carroll, of Lahardown, near Portlaw, co. Waterford (a descendant of the Carrolls of Littalouna, King's County, Ireland, the parent stock and home of the Carrolls of Carrollton, Maryland, U.S.A.), and had seven sons and four daughters.

131. Martin : son of John ; d. 1858. Married in 1828, Honora Mullen (a descendant of Connor, brother of Dathi, who is No. 102 on the " Concannon" pedigree), and had four sons and two daughters— all of whom emigrated to the United States, America :

I. John, of whom presently.
II. Thomas, who in 1857, m. Ann Dean, a native of the county of Mayo, and had one son and four daughters :
I. Martin. I. Mary-Anne.
II. Cecilia. III. Clara-Amelia.
IV. Annie.

III. Michael A. O'Brien: the third son of Martin ; living unm. in 1883.
IV. Rev. Matthew Patrick O'Brien (b. 3rd Sept., 1837), ordained Priest in St. Charles' Seminary, Philadelphia, on the 5th April, 1869, and was in March, 1883, Rector of St. Vincent de Paul's R. C. Church, in Minersville, Schuylkill County, Pa., U.S.A.

Martin's two daughters were :
I. Mary, who in 1868, in Philadelphia, m. Michael Cahill (d. 24th July, 1881), and had one son and two daughters, living in 1883 :
I. John Cahill. I. Mary Cahill.
II. Honora Cahill.
II. Bridget O'Brien, the second dau. of Martin, living unm. in 1883 :

132. John O'Brien (b. 1829, d. 1865) : eldest son of Martin ; m. in Camden, New Jersey, Margaret Cusack (d. 1864), a native of the co. Cavan, Ireland, and had :
133. Thomas O'Brien, b. 1861 ; and living in Philadelphia, in 1887.

M

O'CALLAGHAN.*

Of Duhallow.

Arms : Ar. in base a mount vert, on the dexter side a hurst of oak trees, there-from issuant a wolf pass. towards the sinister, all ppr.

CEALLACHAN, who is No. 104 on the "MacCarthy Mór" pedigree, was the ancestor of *O'Ceallaghain*, of Munster; anglicised *Callaghan* and *O'Callaghan ;* and *Colquhoun*, in Scotland.

104. Ceallachan ("ceallach": Irish, *war*): son of Buochan; a quo *O'Ceallaghain.*

105. Doncha (or Donoch) : his son.

106. Murcha (or Morogh) : his son.

107. Domhnall (or Donall) O'Callaghan : his son ; first assumed this sirname.

108. Ceallachan (2) : his son ; died A.D. 1092.

109. Cenede : his son.

110. Morogh : his son.

111. Aodh : his son.

112. Mahoun : his son.

113. Maccraith : his son

114. Lochlann : his son.

115. Melaghlin : his son.

116. Maccraith (2) : his son.

117. Cenede (2) : his son.

118. Donogh, of Dromine : his son.

119. Conor : his son.

120. Teige Ruadh : his second son.

121. Donogh (2), of Dromine : his son ; died 1578.

122. Conor (2) : his son.

123. Ceallachan (3) : his son.

124. Cathaoir Modartha ("modartha" : Irish, *surly*) : his son.

125. Donogh (3) : his son ; had three brothers.

126. Teige O'Callaghan : his son. This Teige had four brothers—1. Donogh; 2. Cathair; 3. Ceallachan; and 4. Morogh:

The Chief of this Sept was transplanted into the County Clare by Oliver Cromwell.

O'CARROLL. (No. 1.)

Princes of Ely O'Carroll.

Arms : Sa. two lions ramp. combatant or. armed and langued gu. supporting a sword, point upwards ppr. pommel and hilt gold.

CIAN, the youngest brother of Eoghan [Owen] Mór who is No. 85 on the "Line of Heber," *ante*, was the ancestor of *O'Cearbhaill* Ele ; anglicised *O'Carroll*† Ely, *Karwell, Carvill, Garvill*, and *MacCarroll.*

* *O'Callaghan :* Of this family are the Viscounts Lismore. There was an "O'Callaghan" family, chiefs in Oriel (or co. Louth), who were a branch of the Clan Colla ; and another "O'Callaghan" family, chiefs in Erris, co. Mayo, who were a branch of the Hy-Fiachrach, of Connaught.

† *O'Carroll :* There were several distinct "O'Carroll" families, for instance—1. O'Carroll, chiefs of O'Carroll Ely ; 2. O'Carroll (now *Carroll*), who was chief lord of Ossory, from A.D. 845 to 885 ; 3. O'Carroll, a family in the barony of Magunihy, co. Kerry ; 4. O'Carroll, Princes of Oriel, etc.

85. Cian: third son of Olioll Olum, King of Munster.

86. Teige: his son.

87. Conla: his son; had a brother named Cormac Galeng.

88. Iomchadh Uallach: his son; whose brother Finnachta was ancestor of *Meagher*, and *Maher*.

89. Sabhrann: son of Iomchadh.

90. Iomdhun: son of Iomchadh; whose brother Fec was ancestor of *O'Flanagan*,* of Ely, and of *O'Conor*, of Ciannacht (or Keenaght), in the county Derry.

91. Earc: son of Iomdhun.

92. Eile righ dhearg ("eiligh": Irish, *to accuse*), or "Eile, the red king": his son; after whom the territories possessed in Leinster by this sept, were called *Duiche Eiligh*, i.e., "The Estates of Ely," whereof his posterity were styled "Kings," there being no other title of honour then used in Ireland, save that of "Prince" and "Lord," until the English introduced the titles of "Duke," "Marquis," "Earl," "Viscount," and "Baron." This Eile was the ancestor of *O'h-Eiligh* (of Ely-O'Carroll), anglicised *Healy*, and *Hely*.

93. Druadh: his son.

94. Amruadh: his son; a quo *O'h-Amridh;* was ancestor of *O'Corcrain* ("corcra": Irish, *red*), anglicised *Corcoran*, and *Coghrane*.

95. Meachar: his son.

96. Tal: his son.

97. Teige: his son.

98. Inne: his son.

99. Lonan: his son.

100. Altin: his son.

101. Ultan: his son.

102. Cnamhin ("cnaimh": Irish,

a bone): his son; a quo *O'Cnaimhin*, anglicised *Nevin*, *MacNevin*, *Bone*, *Bonass*, and *Bowen*.

103. Dubhlaoch: his son.

104. Aodh (or Hugh): his son.

105. Cearbhall ("cearbhall": Irish, *massacre, slaughter*): his son; a quo *O'Cearbhaill* Ele.

106. Monach O'Carroll: his son; was the first of this family that assumed this sirname.

107. Cu-Coirneach (also called Cu-Boirne): his son.

108. Riogbradan: his son.

109. Donal: his son.

110. Fionn: his son.

111. Maolruanaidh: his son.

112. Donoch: his son.

113. Goll an-Bheolaigh ("beolach": Irish, *talkative*): his son.

114. Fionn (2): his son.

115. Teige: his son.

116. Maolruanaidh: his son; and Donal, the ancestor of "Carroll," of Carrollton, Maryland.

117. William: his son.

118. Roger: his son.

119. Teige, of Callen: his son.

120. Teige Aibhle Magh Glaisse: his son.

121. Maolruanaidh na Feisoige (or Mulroona of the Beard): his son; was the ancestor of the Birræ: ("birra:" Irish, *standing water*), a quo the name of the town of "Birr," in the King's Co.

122. John O'Carroll, prince of Ely: son of Maolruanaidh na feisoige.

123. Donogh: his son; chief of Ely in 1536; m. dau. of O'Connor Faley; had a brother named Maolruanaidh, who was the ancestor of

---

* *O'Flanagan:* There were also several families of "O'Flanagan" in Ireland. 1. in Ely O'Carroll; 2. in Connaught; 3. in Fermanagh; 4. in Oirgiall; 5. in *Uactar Tire*, now the barony of "Upperthird," in the north-west of the county Waterford. The O'Flanagans of Upperthird were dispossessed shortly after the English Invasion by the family of Le Poer (now "Power"), who still possess a large portion of that territory; etc.

O'Carroll of Maryland, United States of America.

124. Teige : his son ; m. to Sara, dau. of O'Brien.

125. Cian : his son ; m. to dau. of O'Melaghlin.

126. Donogh of Buolebrack (Bally-brack*), parish of Roscrea, barony of Clonlisk, King's county : his son ; transplanted to Beagh, co. Galway, by Oliver Cromwell.

127. Donal (or Daniel): his son; an officer in the service of King Charles II.

128. John of Beagh : his son.

129. Redmond of Ardagh, co. Galway : his son.

130. Redmond of Ardagh : his son.

131. John of Turlogh, co. Galway : his son.

132. Frederick-Francis, of Kil-tevna, Dunmore, co. Galway: his son ; living in 1887 ; whose eldest brother Redmond O'Carroll, men-tioned in Burke's " Vicissitudes of Families," was the father of—1. Rev. John-James O'Carroll, S.J., of Milltown Park, near Dublin, and 2. Rev. Francis-Augustine O'Carroll, of the Oratory, South Kensington, London—both living in 1887.

133. Frederic-John O'Carroll, A.B, Barrister-at-Law, 67 Lower Leeson street, Dublin : son of Frederick-Francis ; living in 1887.

O'CARROLL. (No. 2.)

Of Gort, County Galway.

DONOGH, who is No. 126 on the " O'Carroll" (Princes of Ely) pedigree, married Dorothy, dau. of O'Kennedy of Ormond (by his wife Margaret, dau. of O'Brien of Ara), and had a dau. Mór, who m. her kinsman Robert O'Carroll ; and thirty sons whom he presented " in one troop of horse (all accoutred in habiliments of war) to the Earl of Ormond, together with all his interest for the service of King Charles the First."

127. Donal (or Daniel) : one of those sons.

128. John : his son.
   According to some authorities,

this was the member of the family who was transplanted to Beagh, in the county Galway, by Cromwell. He m. Margaret Bermingham, dau.

---

* *Ballybrack :* The property of this Donogh O'Carroll, when he was transplanted, included, according to the Down Survey Map, the present townlands of Ballybrack, Ballyclery, Glascloon, and Clonbrennan.

In 1641 O'Carroll's castle of Kinnity, in the barony of Ballybrit, King's County, was granted to Mr. Winter, by whom it was held for Charles I. William Parsons, son of Lawrence, and nephew of Sir William, Lord Justice of Ireland, was constituted Governor of Ely-O'Carroll, and Constable of Birr Castle, which he garrisoned with his followers. His father, Surveyor-General, obtained in 1620, from James I., a grant of the castle, fort, village and lands of Birr. This castle of Birr was besieged by the O'Carrolls in 1642 ; but Sir Charles Coote, father of the first Earl of Montrath, who came to its relief, obliged them to raise the siege. It was taken by general Preston in 1643, and held by him for the Confederate Catholics, until 1650, when it was taken for the Commonwealth, by Henry Ireton, Oliver Cromwell's son-in-law.

of Lord Athenry, and had two sons: 1. Redmond of Ardagh, 2. Daniel.

129. Daniel: second son of John of Beagh; became a Colonel of horse in the service of Queen Anne, by whom he was Knighted. He m. Elizabeth, dau. of Thomas Jervis, Esq., of Southamptonshire, and had two sons:—1. Daniel, 2. John.

130. John: second son of Daniel; from whom descended the O'Carrolls of Gort, represented in 1798 by —— Carroll, whose dau. Mary, m. a man named Kennedy, and was living at Tierneevan, near Kilmacduagh, county Clare, in 1850.

O'CARROLL. (No. 3.)

Of Coologe, County Roscommon.

THIS, also, is a branch of "O'Carroll" of Ely.

DONOGH O'CARROLL, of Coologe (known as Donogh "Killiagh"), Esq., had:

2. Ony, who had:

3. Donogh "ne Killy," who had:

4. William, of Coologe, who d. 15 April, 1636. He m. Honora, dau. of John Meagher of Cloone, co. Tipperary, gent., and had:

I. Donogh, of whom presently.

II. Kedagh.

III. John.

IV. Teige.

V. Carle.

VI. Ony.

5. Donogh: eldest son of William m. Katherine, dau. of Walter Bourke, of Borrisoleigh, county Tipperary, Esq.

O'CARROLL. (No. 4.)

Of Desmond.

SNEAGHRA, brother of Daologach who is No. 98 on the "MacCarthy Mór" pedigree, was the ancestor of *O'Cearbhaill* of Desmond; anglicised *O'Carroll.*

98. Sneaghra: son of Nadfraoch.

99. Conall: his son.

100. Domhnall: his son.

101. Artgal: his son.

102. Maolfhionnan: his son.

103. Cearbhall ("cearbhall": Irish, *massacre, carnage*): his son; a quo *O'Cearbhaill.*

104. Ceallachan: his son.

105. Cormac: his son.

106. Egeartach ("eig-ceart": Irish, *injustice*): his son; a quo *O'h-Ei-geartaigh*, anglicised *Hegarty*, and *Hagerty*. (See the "Hagerty" pedigree).

O'COLLINS.

Lords of Lower Connello, County Limerick.

Arms* : Az. on a chevron ar. betw. three bezants as many birds sa., on a chief or, a griffin pass. per pale gu. and sa. *Crest*: A griffin pass. gu. *Another Crest* : On a chapeau gu. turned up erm. a griffin pass. per pale sa. and gu.

THE *O'Cuileann* family (" cuileann :" Irish, *a whelp*, meaning *a young fear-less warrior*), anglicised *O'Collins* and *Collins*, is distinct from the *O'Coilean* (" coilean :" Irish, *a whelp*, also), anglicised *O'Cullen* and *Cullen* (see the " Cullen " pedigree, *ante*) ; and derives their descent from Fiacha Fighinte, son of Daire Cearb, son of Olioll Flann Beag, who is No. 87 on the " Line of Heber" (*ante*). They were lords of Eighter Conghalach or Lower Con-nello, in the county of Limerick, until deprived of their possessions by Maurice Fitzgerald, second "lord of Offaly," in the second quarter of the thirteenth century. They were also chiefs of a portion of Eoghanacht Ara, now a barony in the same county ; as we are informed by O'Heerin :

> " O'Collins, a distinguished chief,
> Rules over the Eoghanacht of Aradh."

When the " war loving O'Collins's" were deprived of their estates by Fitzgerald in 1228, they removed to Carbery, in co. Cork, where they obtained lands from their kinsman Cathal, son of Crom O'Donovan, a powerful prince in that country. From one of these settlers in Carbery descended John Collins, author of a *MS. History of the O'Donovans*, written in Myross, March, 1813 ; *Lines on the Ruins of Timoleague Abbey ; An Irish Translation of the Exile of Erin, by Reynolds,* etc. He attended school at Kilmacabee, near Myross, about the middle of the last cen-tury, with Jerry an-Duna, to whom he was related. When they parted, Jerry commenced a life of projects and peregrinations ; Collins remained at home, and occupied himself with the collection of the tradi-tions, history, and genealogy of the reduced local Irish families. Dr. O'Donovan pronounced John Collins to be " the last of the bards, genealogists, and historiographers of Munster." As his pursuits were not of a lucrative nature, like many others of late years, he was compelled to supplement any slender resources he may have derived from them, by other means : he taught school in the townland of Cappagh, in Myross, up to the year 1817 ; after that in the town of Skibbereen, until 1819, when he died there at the age of between 70 and 80 years. He was buried in Kilmeen—between Dunmanway and Clonakilty. One daughter of his lived at Skibbereen in 1874. Many old people in the locality knew him, and all have a high respect for his memory.

In A.D. 1109, Maolisa O'Collins, Bishop of Leath-Cuin (Conacht and Ulster), died. In 1126, Murray O'Collins, erenach or manager of the church lands and revenues of the religious establishments at Clogher, was killed. In A.D. 1266, Mahon O'Collins, lord of Claonglas, was killed by

---

* *Arms* : The ancient Arms of this family were—two swords in saltire, the blades streaming with blood.

his wife, with a thrust of a knife, in a fit of jealousy. Claonglas was a district in Hy Conal Gabhra, in the barony of Upper Connello, south-east of Abbeyfeale; it was sometimes called Hy Cuileann, a name by which the more extensive territory of Hy Conal Gabhra was also known. In A.D. 1832, we learn that Michael Collins, Bishop of Cloyne and Ross, died.

There are in the present day several highly respectable families of this name and race in the counties of Cork, Limerick, Louth, Down, Tyrone, Dublin, Clare, and Tipperary; those in the latter two counties, we regret to add, are with few exceptions in narrow circumstances.

William Collins, "the finest English poet which England has produced," was, though a native of England, of *Irish* extraction; he was the son of a poor hatter in Chichester, being born there on the 25th of December, 1720; he died a lunatic in his sister's house, in that town in 1756.

This family is (1887) represented in the Antipodes by C. MacCarthy Collins (or O'Collins), Esq., Barrister, &c., Brisbane; and in co. Cork by Mr. Daniel Collins, Clouncallabeg, Kilbrittan.

There is another family of this name descended from Cullean, son of Tuathal, according to the following pedigree compiled by Cathan O'Dunin:—

Corc, No. 89 on the "Line of Heber," *ante*.
Criomthan : his son.
Laoghaire : his son.
Flanlaoi : his son.
Tuathal : his son.
Culean (a quo *O'Collins*) : his son.

Very few notices of *this* family or of their possessions are preserved by the annalists; one in particular may be mentioned:—John Collins, a native of Kilfenora, a Dominican Friar, suffered martyrdom for his faith, in 1657, at the hands of Oliver Cromwell's troopers.

O'CONNELL.*

Arms : A stag trippant betw. three trefoils countercharged. *Crest :* A stag's head erased, charged with a trefoil. *Motto :* Cial agus neart.

DAIRE CEARB, brother of Lughaidh, who is No. 88 on the "Line of Heber," *ante*, was the ancestor of *O'Conaill ;* anglicised *O'Connell.*

88. Daire Cearb : son of Olioll Flann-beag.
89. Fiacha : his son ; had four brothers, one of whom named Fiachra was ancestor of *O'Donovan.*
90. Brian : his son ; had a brother

---

* *O'Connell :* There was another *O'Conaill* family in the county Limerick; another in the territory between the river Grian, on the border of the county Clare, and the plain of Maenmoy—comprising parts of the barony of Leitrim in the county Galway, and of Tullagh in the county Clare; another in Londonderry; and another in Hy-Maine. But the pedigrees of these families are, we fear, lost.

named Cairbre, who was the ancestor of *Ua-Cairbre* (anglicised "O'Carbery)," etc.

91. Daire (or Darius) : son of Brian.

92. Fionnliath : his son.

93. Conall ("conall:" Irish, *friendship*) : his son ; a quo *Ua-Conaill* or *O'Conaill.*

1. Aodh O'Connell of the race of Daire Cearb, and descended from Conall No. 93 above, m. Margaret, dau. of Maithan Maonmaighe O'Brien, Prince of Thomond, by whom he had issue.

2. Geoffry : his son; lived in 1370; m. Catherine, daughter of O'Connor-Kerry.

3. Donal : his son ; m. Honoria, dau. of O'Sullivan Bere.

4. Aodh : his son ; was Knighted by Sir Richard Nugent, then lord lieutenant of Ireland. He m. Mary, a dau. of Donal MacCarthy Mór (No. 116 on the MacCarthy Mór Stem).

5. Maurice : his son ; m. Juliana, dau. of Rory O'Sullivan Mór. This Maurice declared for Perkin Warbeck, but obtained pardon from the English King, through the influence of The MacCarthy Mór, on the 24th of August, 1496.

6. Morgan : his son ; m. Elizabeth, dau. of O'Donovan, lord of Clan-Cathail, in Carbéry.

7. Aodh : his son ; m. Mora, dau. of Sir Teige O'Brien, of Balle-na-Carriga, in Clare.

8. Morgan : his son ; called " of Ballycarberry;" was High Sheriff of the county of Kerry; he m. Elana, dau. of Donal MacCarthy.

9. Richard : his son ; m. Johanna, dau. of Ceallaghan MacCarthy, of Carrignamult, in the county of Cork. This Richard assisted Queen

Elizabeth's generals against the Great Geraldine ; surrendered his estates, and obtained a re-grant thereof through the influence of the lord deputy.

10. Maurice : his son ; was High Sheriff of Kerry ; he m. Margaret, dau. of Conchobhar O'Callaghan, of Clonmeen, in the county of Cork.

11. Geoffry : his son ; High Sheriff of Kerry ; m. Honoria, dau. of The MacCrohan, of Lettercastle.

12. Daniel, of Aghagabhar : son of Geoffry ; m. Alice, d. of Christopher Segrave, of Cabra, in the county of Dublin.

13. John, of Aghagower and Derrynane : his son ; m. Elizabeth, dau. of Christopher Conway, of Cloghane, in the county of Kerry.

14. Daniel : his son ; m. Mary, dau. of Dubh O'Donoghue, of Amoyss, in the county of Kerry.

15. Morgan, of Cahireen, in the barony of Iveragh : his son ; m. Catherine, dau. of John O'Mullane, of Whitechurch, by whom he had issue :—1. Daniel ; 2. James (of Tralee); and 3. Ellen, who m. D. O'Connell, of Tralee.

16. Daniel : his son ; styled "The Liberator," who was M.P., and also Lord Mayor of Dublin. He m. his cousin, Mary O'Connell, by whom he had issue :—1. Morgan ; 2. Maurice ; 3. John ; and 4. Daniel. This Daniel, The Liberator, was b. in 1775, and d. at Genoa, on the 15th May, 1847 ; his heart was sent to Rome, and his body interred in the Prospect Cemetery, Glasnevin, Dublin, where a round tower of Lucan granite, 173 feet high, surmounted by a granite cross 7 feet in height, has been erected to his memory. A splendid statue of The Liberator,* in O'Connell Street,

---

* *Liberator*: Daniel O'Connell, "The Liberator," was born 6th August, 1775, at Carhen, near Caherciveen, co. of Kerry. His father was Morgan O'Connell; his mother,

Dublin, forms one of the chief attractions of one of the grandest streets in Europe.

17. Morgan: the eldest son of The Liberator; had three brothers —1. Maurice; 2. John; 3. Daniel;

and three daughters—1. Ellen; 2. Catherine; 3. Elizabeth.

18. Daniel O'Connell, of Derrynane Abbey, co. Kerry: son of Morgan; living in 1887.

O'CONNOR.*

Keenaght, Co. Londonderry.

Arms : Ar. on a mount in base, an oak tree all ppr.

THIS family was driven out of their territory of Glean-Geimhin and Cianachta (now the barony of "Keenaght," co. Derry), by the O'Cahans, before the English invasion.

Fionnchan, a brother of Conla who is No. 87 on the "O'Carroll Ely" pedigree, was the ancestor of *O'Conchobhair*, Cianachta; anglicised *O'Connor*, of Keenaght, in the county Derry.

87. Fionnchann : son of Tadhg.

88. Fec : his son.

89. Fionnchann : his son.

90. Eathchin : his son.

Kate O'Mullane, of Whitechurch, near Cork. They were poor, and he was adopted by his uncle Maurice, from whom he eventually inherited Derrynane. At thirteen he was sent, with his brother Maurice, to a Catholic school near Cove (now Queenstown), near Cork, the first seminary kept openly by a Catholic priest in Ireland since the operation of the Penal Laws. A year later the lads were sent to Liege; but were debarred admission to the Irish College, because Daniel was beyond the prescribed age. After some delay they were entered at St. Omer's. There they remained from 1791 to 1792, Daniel rising to the first place in all the classes. They were then removed to Douay, but before many months the confusion caused by the French Revolution rendered it desirable for them to return home. In 1794, O'Connell was entered as a student of Lincoln's Inn. We are told that for a time after his return from France he believed himself a Tory; but events soon convinced him that he was at heart a Liberal. His first public speech was made on 13th January, 1800, at a meeting of Catholics held in the Royal Exchange, Dublin, to protest against the Union. O'Connell married a cousin in 1802. His biographies abound in racy anecdotes of his wonderful readiness and ability at the Bar. The Whig Party attained to power in 1806 under Lord Granville; they were the supporters of Catholic Emancipation, and the Catholics were elated thereat, but divided as to their proper course of action. John Keogh, the old and trusted leader of the party at the time, maintained that dignified silence was their true policy; while O'Connell advocated a course of constant agitation, and his opinions were endorsed by 134 votes to 110, at a conference of the party. He soon became the undisputed leader of the Irish people. A Repeal agitation was inaugurated in 1810 by the Dublin Corporation, then a purely Protestant body; and at a meeting of the freemen and freeholders in the Royal Exchange, O'Connell repeated the sentiments he had enunciated in 1800 : "Were Mr. Percival to-morrow to offer me the Repeal of the Union upon the terms of re-enacting the entire Penal Code, I declare it from my heart, and in the presence of my God, that I would most cheerfully embrace his offer." The Centenary of O'Connell's birth was celebrated with great enthusiasm in Dublin and elsewhere, in 1875. Some writers would give O'Connell an *English* ancestry : See *Notes and Queries*, fourth Series.—WEBB.

* *O'Connor*: There were several "O'Connor" families in Ireland.

91. Erc : his son.
92. Cormac : his son.
93. Cnidhceann : his son.
94. Suibhne : his son.
95. Ceannfaola : his son.
96. Tadhg : his son.

97. Tomaltach : his son.
98. Conchobhar (" conchobhar :" Irish, *the helping warrior*) : his son ; a quo *O'Conchobhair*.
99. Ruadhri : his son.

O'CORCORAN.

THIS family derives its origin from Amruadh, who is No. 94 on the " O'Carroll Ely" pedigree; and were in Irish called *O'Corcrain* (" corcra :" Irish, *red*), which has been anglicised *O'Corcoran*, *Corcoran*, and *Coghrane*. They were formerly chiefs of Munster Corcrain, in the county of Tipperary, co-extensive with the parish of Killenaule, in the barony of Slieveardagh ; of the district of Clare Ruaine, in North Tipperary ; and also of the territory lying around Cleenish, in the barony of Clan-Awly, county of Fermanagh. Several members of the house of Cleenish gave superiors to the famous abbey of Daimhinis (or Devenish), on Lough Erne.

In 1001. Cahalan O'Corcoran, abbot of Devenish, died.
1040. O'Corcoran, abbot of Iniscaltra, " the most celebrated ecclesiastic of Western Europe, both for religion and learning," died at Lismore, and was interred in the church of St. Carthagh.
1045. Cathasagh O'Corcoran, coarb of Glen-Uissin, in Hy-Bairche, the territory of the Mac Gormans, in the county of Carlow, died.
1095. The bishop O'Corcoran, successor of St. Brennan, of Clonfert, died.
1055. Fiacha O'Corcoran, died.
1163. Maolisa O'Corcoran, successor of St. Comghaile, died.
1487. Brian O'Corcoran, Vicar of Cleenish, died.

The O'Corcorans sank into obscurity at the period of the Anglo-Norman Invasion, and several branches of the sept removed into the counties of Cork, Kilkenny, and Waterford. In Kilkenny they obtained a settlement from the FitzWalters (or Butlers), who were in possession of their ancient patrimony. And a senior branch of these settlers was represented by the late Most Rev. Michael Corcoran, Bishop of Kildare and Leighlin, in the commencement of this century ; and by the Corcorans of Enniscorthy, in co. Wexford.

The co. Cork branch of the family settled in Carbery, and are now (1887) represented by Jeremiah (Dan) O'Corcoran, of Bengowe, Parish of Murragh, who has a son, the Rev. Daniel O'Corcoran, a Catholic clergyman in the city of Cork.

O'COTTER.

Of Rockforest, Mallow, County Cork.

Arms :* Quarterly, 1st and 4th, ar. a chev. gu. betw. three serpents ppr., for COTTER ; 2nd and 3rd, az. a fess betw. a fleur-de-lis in chief and a mullet in base or., for ROGERSON.　*Crest :* A dexter arm embowed armed ppr. grasping a dart.　*Motto :* Dum spiro spero.

THE Irish patronymic of this family is *Ua-Coiteoir* or *O'Coiteoir* (" coiteoir :" Irish, *a cottager, a boat-builder*).　In Gibson's *History of Cork*, this family is stated to be of Danish origin.　The name " Cotter," also spelled " Kotter," is common through Denmark and Northern Europe ; and, so far as this family was concerned, was in Ireland anciently written " MacCottyr," " MacCotter," and " McCottir."　Sometimes the name was in Irish written *McCoithir*, as well as *MacCoithir*.　The head of the family in the Commonwealth period was William, son of Edmond *Cotter*, of Coppingerstown Castle, near Midleton, in the co. Cork.　That William forfeited his Estates under attainder, consequent on his taking part in the Irish War of 1641. It would appear (see p. 274 of our " Irish Landed Gentry") that, for the same cause, William Catter, of Gearigh, in the barony of Imokilly, co. Cork, then also forfeited his Estates : which inclines us to believe that the two Williams were identical ; as there is no other William Catter or Cotter mentioned in the List of the " Forfeiting Proprietors in Ireland, under the Cromwellian Settlement."

Edmond *Cotter* (son of Garrett *Cottir*, of Innismore ; son of William *Cottyr*, of Innismore, co. Cork ; son of William Cottyr, *temp.* King Edward IV.), the kinsman and contemporary of the above mentioned William Cotter, of Coppingerstown Castle, was the ancestor of this branch of the family.　That Edmond Cotter held considerable property, chiefly Anngrove, which was his principal residence, and situate near Carrig-twohill ; he also had property in Innismore, where he held a great part of the site of Queenstown (or "The Cove of Cork"), and land in other districts.　While, however, the said Edmond was possessed of considerable wealth, it appears by his Will, that he held his Estates for the most part subject to head rents.

1. Edmond Cotter, of Innismore and Anngrove, co. Cork ; son of Garrett Cottir ; was twice m. : first, to Elizabeth, dau. of John Connell, Esq., of Barry's Court, and by her had three sons and three daus. :

I. Garrett, who d. unm.

II. Sir James, of whom presently.

III. John, who m. and had two sons and one daughter.

I. Ellen, who m. John Evans, Esq.,

II. Mary, who m. William Barry, Esq.

III. Catherine, who m. John Gwinn, Esq.

Edmond's second wife was Ellen

---

* *Arms :* The Arms of Cotter (Ireland) are : Az. three evetts in pale ppr.　*Crest :* A lion pass. reguard ppr.

The prefix *Ua* or *O'* of this " Cotter" family clearly shows that it is of *Irish* extraction ; for, while some Danish and other foreign families that settled in Ireland assumed the prefix *Mac*, they never ventured to assume the prefix *O'*.

Sarsfield (of Lord Kilmallock's family), and by her he had three sons and three daughters:

IV. Edmond.

V. William.

VI. Patrick.

IV. Anne.

V. Eleanor.

VI. Alice.

"He d. in 1660, as is recorded on the monument surmounting the ancient vault in Carrigtwohill Abbey."

2. Sir James Cotter (d. 1705), of Anngrove, Knt., and M.P.: son of Edmond; was twice m.: first, to Mary (d. s. p.), dau. of Sir William Stapleton, Bart.; and, secondly, on the 30th July, 1688, to the Honble. Eleanora Plunkett, eldest dau. of Matthew, the seventh Lord Louth, and by her had two sons and two daughters:

I. James, of whom presently.

II. Laurence, who d. aged 88 years, unm.

I. Mary, who m. Wm. Mahony, Esq., Barrister-at-Law.

II. Alice-Monica, who d. young. This Sir James was Commander-in-Chief of King James's Forces, in the Counties of Cork, Limerick, and Kerry.

3. James Cotter, of Anngrove: son of Sir James; b. 4th Aug., 1689; was, for his devotion to the cause of the Stuarts, executed on the 7th May, 1720; m. in 1706 Margaret (d. 1725), eldest dau. of Major George Mathew, of Thurles, and had two sons and two daus.:

I. James, who was created a Baronet, on the 11th Aug., 1763, and of whom presently.

II. Edmond, who m. a Miss O'Brien, of the co. Clare, and had two sons and two daus.:

I. George, a Captain in the Army, who d. s. p.

II. Edmond, a Major in the Army.

I. Ellen, who m. Michael Galwey, Esq., of Rockspring, in the co. Cork.

II. Elizabeth, who m. Kean Mahony, Esq., M.D.

4. Sir James Cotter, Bart. (d. 9th June, 1770), of Rockforest: son of James; b. 1714, and in 1746, m. Arabella, dau. of Rt. Honble. John Rogerson, Lord Justice of the Court of Queen's Bench, and had four sons:

I. Sir James-Laurence, of whom presently.

II. Edmond, who d. unm.

III. Rogerson, M.A., and M.P. for Charleville, who m. and had issue.

IV. Rev. George-Sackville, M.A., who also married and had issue.

5. Sir James-Laurence Cotter, Bart., of Rockforest, M.P., who d. 9th Feb., 1829: eldest son of Sir James; b. in 1748; was twice m.: first, to Anne (d. s. p. in 1773), only dau. of Francis Kearney, Esq., of Garretstown, near Kinsale; and secondly, to Isabella, dau. of the Rev. James Hingston, of Aglish, in the co. Cork, by whom he had six sons and four daus.:

I. Sir James-Laurence, his heir, of whom presently.

II. Rev. John-Rogerson, who was thrice m., and d. without surviving issue.

III. Rev. George-Edmond (d. 6th Aug., 1880), who m. and had issue.

IV. Richard-Baillie, who d. unm. in 1843.

V. Henry-Johnson, who d. unm. in 1830.

VI. Nelson-Kearney (d. in 1842), M.D., who m. and had issue.

The four daughters were:

I. Isabella, who m. James-Digges La Touche, Esq., of Dublin, and had issue.

II. Henrietta, who m. John Wise, Esq., of Cork, and had issue.

III. Catherine.

IV. Thomasine, who m. Arundel Hill, Esq., of Graig, co. Cork, and had issue.

6. Sir James-Laurence, Bart. (d. 31st Dec., 1834), of Rockforest, M.P. for Mallow: eldest son of Sir James; m. on 1st Jan., 1820, Helena (d. 1st June, 1876), dau. of James Lombard, Esq., of Lombardstown, in the co. Cork, and had an only child:

7. Sir James-Laurence, Bart., of Rockforest, Mallow, in the co. Cork; b. 4th April, 1828, and living in 1884; m., first, on 14th June, 1851, Julia-Emily (d. 5th Feb., 1863), dau. of Frederick-Albert Loinsworth, Esq., M.D., and had two sons and one daughter:

I. Sir Ludlow, Knt., who d. in 1882.

II. James-Lombard, b. 1st Sept., 1859; an Officer in the 28th Foot; of whom presently; living in 1884.

I. Jane-Louisa, who d. 26th Aug., 1883.

Sir James-Laurence Cotter m., secondly, on 30th April, 1864, Jane Vergette, dau. of W. K. Maughan, Esq., of Sedgwick House, in Middlesex, England, and by her had:

III. Guy, b. in 1865, but who d. in infancy.

8. James - Lombard Cotter: second son of Sir James-Laurence, Bart., m. in May, 1884, Clare, Mary, dau. of the late Captain Segrave, 14th Regiment.

O'CRONAN.

THE *O'Cronain* family (" cron": Irish, *ready*; " an," *one who*), anglicised *O'Cronan* and *Cronan*, are, according to some writers, descended from the celebrated Druid Mogh Raith, who assisted Simon Magus with the Riotha Ramhar; but O'Dunin, who wrote in the beginning of the 14th century, gives, from older annals, the following as the family pedigree:

95. Carbery: a younger son of Aodh Dubh, who is No. 94 on the " Line of Heber," *ante.*

96. Conor Clarinach: his son.

97. Salbhuidhe; his son.

98. Duibhlaing: his son; had a brother Flathniadh, a quo *O'Flathniadh.*

99. Ealathach Ard: his son; had a brother Flathimh, a quo *O'Flathimh;* and another brother Flan, a quo

O'Flainn of Munster, anglicised *O'Flynn.**

100. Ealathan: his son.

101. Maoluir: his son.

102. Cronan: his 4th son; a quo *O'Cronain ;* had a brother Cathalan, a quo *O'Cahalan* and *Cahalan ;* another brother Buadhach, a quo *O'Beddy* and *Beddy ;* and another brother Maolin, a quo *O'Maolin.*

* *O'Flynn :* It is worthy of remark that the *O'Flainn* of Munster have anglicised their name *O'Flynn* and *Flynn ;* while the *O'Flainn* of Connaught and Ulster have anglicised their name *O'Flinn* and *Flinn.*

O'CULLEN.

Of Leinster.

THE *O'Cuilin* ("cuil": Irish, *a couch*; "in," *little*) family, anglicised *O'Cullin, O'Cullen, Cullin,* and *Cullen,* derive their descent from Cuilin, son of Dubh, son of Eochy Mór, son of Corc, who is No. 89 on the "Line of Heber" (*ante*) ; and were possessed of a tract of land in the barony of Dunkerron, co. Kerry, which they held under the O'Sullivans. A branch of this family formerly occupied the barony of "Kilcullen," in the co. Kildare, and were chiefs of Coille-Cullin. Prior to the thirteenth century this family held also the romantic country around Glencullen, in the co. Wicklow; in the thirteenth century the O'Cullens were expelled from this locality by the O'Byrnes and O'Tooles. Other members of this tribe were chiefs of Arra, in Tipperary, and of part of Conello, co. Limerick.

Patrick Cullen, an Augustinian hermit, one of the compilers of the Registry of Clogher, was consecrated bishop of that See in 1519; he died in the Spring of 1534, and was interred in his own cathedral.

O'Cullen, a religious of the convent of Athenry, in the co. Galway, suffered death for his faith, in 1652. His head was fixed on one of the spikes of the gates of Athenry !

The late Cardinal Paul Cullen, Lord Archbishop of Dublin, was of this family.

Members of this family are now located in Ulster, one of whom is Mr. William Cullen, Teacher of the Eliza-street National School, Belfast; and another, Joseph Cullen of Belfast, whose pedigree is as follows:

MURTAGH CULLEN, of Eskragh, co. Tyrone, who was b. *circa* 1747, was the first of this family that settled in Ulster. He m. Bridget, daughter of Mark Devlin, of Glenoe, co. Tyrone, and had six sons and one daughter :

I. Patrick.
II. John.
III. James.
IV. Charles.
V. Hugh, of whom presently.
VI. Michael.
I. Nancy.

The said Murtagh d. at Belfast, and was bur. at Donoughmore, co. Tyrone.

2. Hugh: fifth son of Murtagh; b. at Eskragh in 1790; d. at Belfast in 1853. He m. Esther, daughter of Thomas Carbery, of Eskragh, and had six sons and three daughters :

I. John.
II. James.
III. Hugh.
IV. Bernard, of whom presently.

V. Joseph.
VI. Matthew.
I. Esther.
II. Catherine.
III. Margret.

3. Bernard, of Belfast : fourth son of Hugh; b. 1829; living in 1884; m. on 15th December, 1850, Anne, daughter of William Curless, of Clogher, co. Tyrone, and had five sons and one daughter :

I. Joseph, of whom presently.
II. Zachary, b. 30th June, 1856, and living in New York in 1884.
III. Bernard, born 10th Sept., 1858.
IV. Paul, b. 28th April, 1861.
V. John, b. 3rd March, 1864.
I. Mary. All these children,

save Zachary, living in Belfast in 1884.

4. Joseph Cullen, of Belfast:

eldest son of Bernard; b. 29th Oct., 1851, and living in 1887.

O'DALY.

Of Munster.

THIS *O'Dalaigh* family, anglicised *O'Daly*, is descended from Enda (or Eanna), son of Aongus (who is No. 91 on the " Line of Heber," *ante*), by his wife Eithne, daughter of Criomthan, son of Eanna Ceannsalach, King of Leinster.

These O'Dalys were chiefs of Muintir Bhaire (now *Bere*), in the south-west of co. Cork; also of Noghubhal-Ui-Dalaigh, or Noghoval-Daly, a parish in O'Keeffe's Country, in the north-west of the same county. This family gave birth to several eminent ecclesiastics, and to many poets of no mean reputation; many of whom were hereditary bards to Mac-Carthy and O'Mahony.

The late Father Daly, P.P. of the united parishes of Kilbonane, Aghinagh, Moviddy, and Kilmurry, in Muscry, was, we believe, a native of Kinneigh, in Carbery; and one of the most illustrious representatives of this family in this century: a family now (1887) represented by James O'Daly, of Maghbeg, situate to the west of Bandon-Bridge.

O'DEA.

Chiefs of Dysart O'Dea, County Clare.

Arms : Ar. a dexter hand lying fessways, couped at the wrist, cuffed indented az. holding a sword in pale, all ppr. in chief two snakes embowed vert.   *Crest :* A hind statant ppr.

ÆNEAS (or Aongus) Ceannathrach, a brother of Blad who is No. 92 on the " O'Brien" (of Thomond) pedigree, was the ancestor of *O'Deadhaichd ;* anglicised *Day, O'Day, O'Dea, Dee,* and *Deady.*

92. Æneas Ceannathrach : son of Cas.

93. Rethach : his son.

94. Seanach : his son.

95. Diomma : his son.

96. Dunsleibh : his son.

97. Cuallta (" cuallta": Irish, *a*

wolf) : his son ; a quo *O'Cualltaigh,* anglicised *Kielty* and *Wolf.*

98. Fermac : his son.

69. Fercionn (" cionn," gen. " cinn :" Irish, *a head, a cause*): his son : a quo *O'Fercinn*, by some anglicised *Perkin* and *Perkins.**

---

* *Perkins :* According to MacFirbis, " Perkins" and " Perkinson" were in Gaelic rendered *MacPiaruis,* and sometimes *MacPeadhair,* which are by him classed among Saxon families (*Sloinnte Saxonta*) settled in Ireland.

100. Flann Scrupuil : his son
101. Flancha : his son.
102. Dubhsalach : his son.
103. Donn : his son.
104. Donal : his son.
105. Deadha (" deadhachd :" Irish, *godliness*) : his son ; a quo *O'Dead-haichd.*
106. Donoch : his son. This Donoch had an elder brother named Conn Mór, who was ancestor of *Muintir Cuinn* or *Quinn* of Munster ; and Donoch's younger brother, Flaithertach, was the ancestor of *Roughan.*
107. Aichear : son of Donoch.
108. Giall-gaire : his son.
109. Muredach : his son.
110. Flaithertach : his son.

111. Lochlann : his son.
112. Flaithertach (2) Fionn : his son.
113. Padraic : his son.
114. Rory : his son.
115. Donoch : his son.
116. Lochlann (2) : his son.
117. Donal : his son.
118. Edmond : his son.
119. Conor : his son.
120. Lochlann (3) : his son.
121. Shane (or John) : his son.
122. Lochlann Riabhagh : his son.
123. Conor Cron (or Swarthy Conor) : his son.
124. Michael : his son.
125. Michael Oge O'Deadha : his son.

The O'Deas were formerly chiefs of Triocha Cead Cinel Fermaigh, *i.e.*, the cantred of the tribe of the plain, otherwise Triocha Uachtarach, or the upper district, and of Dysart-ui-Deadhadh, now the parish of Dysart, called also *Dysart O'Dea*, in the barony of Inchiquin, co. of Clare, comprising 24,000 statute acres :

> " With due respect we first treat
> Of the elevated lands of Triocha Uachtar ;
> O'Dea is the lawful inheritor
> Of these brown-nut producing plains."
>
> —O'HEERIN.

We are informed that in very early times a branch of this sept removed into the county of Tipperary, and became possessed of an extensive estate in the barony of Slivearadh, as O'Heerin says :—

> " Slieve Aradh of the fair lands
> O'Dea enjoys as his estate."

The O'Deas had several castles in the barony of Slivearadh, and also in their original territory of Cinel Fermaic (the tribe name of the Family)— where some remains of the castle of Dysart may be seen at the present day.

Amongst the most noted of this family in ancient times we find that :—
In A.D. 1106, Raghnal O'Dea, lord of Dysart, died.
A.D. 1151, Flaherty O'Dea, lord of Dysart, was slain at the battle of Moin-Mór.
A.D. 1311. Laghlin Riabhach O'Dea, was slain by Mahon, son of Donal Conachtach O'Brien.
A.D. 1403. Cornelius O'Dea, Archdeacon of Kilaloe, was consecrated bishop of Limerick ; he resigned his sacred charge in 1426, and lived a secluded life till his death, 27th July, 1434.

He was interred in the cathedral, where a monument of black marble was raised to his memory by his worthy successor, John Mottell, Canon of Kells.

1588. Mahon O'Dea, son of Loghlin, son of Rory, son of Murrogh, son of of Mahon Buidhe, lord of Cinel Fearmaic, died.

1589. Dermod Oge O'Dea, son of Dermod, son of Denis, son of Dermod, son of Connor, *i.e.*, the bishop of Limerick (see above A.D. 1403), son of Murrogh *an Dana* O'Dea, died, and was interred in the church of Dysart-Tola, in the town of Dysart.

1598. Dermod, son of Edmond, son of Rory O'Dea, of Tulla O'Dea, was slain in July.

O'DONOGHUE. (No. 1.)
Of Cashel.

THE *O'Donoghue* family of Cashel, co. Tipperary, was the stem whence sprung the several branches of this family in Kerry and in Ossory, and was descended from Cas, son of Corc, who is No. 89 on the "Line of Heber" (*ante*).

These O'Donoghues were Princes of the Eoghanacht of Cashel, a territory in the co. Tipperary, extending from Cashel to Clonmel:

Eoghanacht Cashel is in the plain of Cian,
O'Donoghue is its lineal inheritor;
Its name in other days was Feimhin,
Which extended to the border of the brown-nut plain.
—O'HEERIN.

Hence we learn from this extract that Magh Feimhin was the ancient name of this extensive district.

A.D. 1010. Flan, son of The O'Donoghue, of Cashel, successor of St. Enda, of Ara, in the co. Tipperary, died.

A.D. 1014. Dungal O'Donoghue, King of Cashel, flourished. This prince fought at Clontarf, and died about 1026.

A.D. 1028. Art, son of The O'Donoghue, of Cashel, erenach of Mungret in county of Limerick, died.

A.D. 1043. Magrath O'Donoghue, Lord of Eoghanacht-Cashel, died.

A.D. 1038. Cuduligh O'Donoghue, heir to the lordship of Cashel, was slain.

A.D. 1057. Donchadh O'Donoghue, Lord of Eoghanacht-Cashel, was killed.

A.D. 1078. Connor O'Donoghue, heir of Cashel, died.

These O'Donoghues fell into decay at a very early period, and very few of their descendants are to be met with in Tipperary, at the present day.

O'DONOGHUE. (No. 2.)
Of Ossory.

THE O'Donoghues of Ossory were a branch of the O'Donoghues of Cashel; they were chiefs of an extensive district of Ossory, given by the people of

N

Leinster to the Kings of Cashel as *eric* (or fine) for the death of Ederscoil, King of Munster, who was slain at the Hill of Allen, in the county of Kildare, by Nuadha-Neacht, King of Lagenia (or Leinster). This property which extended from Gowran, in Kilkenny, to Dun-Grianan, in Tipperary, subsequently came into the possession of this family, who held it till the end of the 12th century, when it was seized on by some Anglo-Norman adventurers, some of whose descendants still hold it. The chief seat of the O'Donoghue, Prince of Ossory, was at Gowran, and the name of this district was Magh Mail or the plain of Mal, as we read:—

> "The man who is elected to govern Magh Mail,
> Is O'Donoghue of the fair Gabhrain."

Jerpoint Abbey was founded by one of these O'Donoghues in 1178.— See "O'Donoghue" (No. 5) pedigree.

O'DONOGHUE MOR.* (No. 3.)
Princes of Lough Lein, Co. Kerry.

Arms : Vert two foxes ramp. combatant ar. on a chief of the last an eagle volant sa. *Crest :* An arm in armour embowed holding a sword, the blade entwined with a serpent all ppr.

CAS, brother of Nathfraoch, who is No. 90 on the "Line of Heber," was the ancestor of *O'Donchada* or *O'Donchu ;* anglicised *O'Donocho*, and modernized *O'Donoghue*, *O'Donohoe*, *O'Donoghy*, *Donoughue*, *Donaghy*, and *Dunphy*.

90. Cas: son of Corc, King of Munster.

91. Eochaidh : his son.

92. Crimthan : his son.

93. Laeghaire : his son; had a brother named Hugh (or Aodh) Gharbh : this Hugh was the ancestor of *O'Mahony*.

94. Aodh Oraidh ("oraid:" Irish, *an oration, a prayer :* Lat. "oro," *to pray*): son of Laeghaire.

95. Cairbre Riosthran : his son.

96. Cloranach : his son.

97. Dunlong Breac (or Brone): his son.

98. Eladhach : his son.

99. Dunlong (2) : his son.

100. Altan : his son.

101. Flaithrigh : his son.

102. Æneas : his son.

103. Dubhd'abhoireann ("dubh:" Irish, *dark,* Heb. "dobh-i;" "d'a :" Irish, *of the ;* and "boireann," *a large rock*), signifying "the dark complexioned man of the large rock:" his son; a quo *O'Dubhoireainn* [daverin], anglicised *Davoren.*†

104. Donal Mór : his son.

105. Donal Oge : his son.

106. Cathbha : his son.

107. Conor : his son.

108. Dubhd'abhoireann (2) [duff-daverin]: his son.

* *O'Donoghue Mór :* The chief of this sept lived at Ross Castle, on an island in the Lakes of Killarney, up to the reign of Queen Elizabeth.

†*Davoren :* As above shown, *Dubhd'abhoireann*, the ancestor of this family, signifies "the dark featured man of the rock:" meaning, no doubt, the large rock at Ballyna-lackin ("the village or district of the rocks"), on the sea-shore near Lisdoonvarna, in the county Clare, where stand the remains of the once strong castle of the "Davoren" family.

109. Donal (3) : his son.

110. Donoch or Donnchu ("donn :" Irish, *brown*, and "cu," a *warrior*), meaning "the brown haired warrior :" his son ; a quo *O'Donchada* or *O'Donchu*. This Donoch died A.D. 1057.

111. Conmhighe : his son.

112. Cathal O'Donocho : his son ; first assumed this sirname ; died 1063.

113. Donoch : his son.

114. Æneas : his son.

115. Amhailgadh Mór : his son.

116. Cathal : his son. This Cathal (who was an ancestor of *O'Donoghue*, of Lough Lein), had a younger brother named Connor, who was the ancestor of " *O'Donoghue* of the Glen," county Kerry.

117. Dubhd'abhoireann (3) : his son.

118. Amhailgadh [awly] : his son.

119. Thomas : his son.

120. Amhailgadh (3) : his son.

121. Teige : his son ; died 1320.

122. Aodh (or Hugh) : his son.

123. Shane (or John) : his son.

124. Teige (2) : his son.

125. Rory : his son.

126. Rory (2) : his son.

127. Rory (3) : his son.

128. Goffrey (or Jeoffrey) : his son ; died 1759.

129. Donall (or Daniel) : his son ; died A.D. 1790. This Donall had an elder brother named Timothy, who died, unmarried, in 1768.

130. Cathal (or Charles) : son of Daniel (or Donall) ; died 1808.

131. Charles O'Donocho, of Lough Lein, county Kerry : his son ; born 1806 ; had a brother named Daniel.

O'DONOGHUE.* (No. 4.)

Lords of Glenfesk.

CONNOR O'DONOCHO, a younger brother of Cathal, who is No. 116 on the foregoing (" O'Donoghue of Lough Lein") pedigree, was the ancestor of *O'Donoghue* of the Glen.

116. Conor : son of Amhailgadh Mór.

117. Aedh (or Hugh) na Midhe : his son.

118. Jeoffrey an Tigh (or Jeoffrey of the Mansion) : his son.

119. Conor (2) : his son.

120. Donall : his son.

121. Jeoffrey (2) : his son ; died 1520.

122. Donall (2) : his son.

123. Jeoffrey (3) : his son.

124. Rory : his son.

125. Donall (3) : his son.

126. Jeoffrey (4) : his son.

127. Teige : his son.

128. Jeoffrey (5) : his son.

129. Teige (2) : his son.

130. Jeoffrey O'Donocho, of the Glen, county Kerry : his son.

O'DONOGHUE. (No. 5.)

ANNALISTS are not clear as to the origin of this family, or the nature of its connection with the great sept of the same name in Kerry, or with any of

---

* *O'Donohgue :* There was another family of this name in ancient Meath ; and another in Connaught.

the same name within the Pale, or in the county Tipperary; but that this was of an intimate character may be judged from the preceding No. 1, No. 2, and No. 3 (" O'Donoghue") genealogies.

In a Manuscript History of Holy Cross Abbey, co. Tipperary, written A.D. 1640, by Father Malachy Harty (now in the possession of the Most Rev. Dr. Croke, Archbishop of Cashel), the following entry occurs at p. 64, in reference to the Cistercian Abbey of Jerpoint, co. Kilkenny:

"*Ieriponte.* Fundator hujus Abbatiæ fuit Donatus O'Donoghe, Regulus, qui magnis redditibus illam locupletavit anno Incarnationis Verbi Divini 1180."

Translated:

"*Jerpoint.* The Founder of this Abbey was Donogh O'Donoghe,* King, who enriched it with great revenues in the year of the Incarnation of the Divine Word 1180."

O'DONOVAN. (No. 1.)

Lords of Clancahill.

Arms : Ar. issuing from the sinister side of the shield a cubit dexter arm vested gu. cuffed of the first, the hand grasping a skein or old Irish sword in pale, the blade entwined with a serpent all ppr. *Crest :* On a chapeau gu. turned up erm. a falcon alighting ar. tips of wings and tail sa. *Motto:* Vir super hostem.

OLIOLL Flann-beag, who is No. 87 on the "Line of Heber," *ante,* was the ancestor of *O'Donamhain ;* anglicised *O'Donovan, Donovan,* and *Mac-Donovan.*

87. Olioll Flann-beag: son of Fiacha Muilleathan ; was King of Munster.

88. Daire Cearb: his second son ; ancestor of *O'Connell.*

89. Fiachra Finnghinte (or Fiacha Fidhgeinte): his son.

90. Brian: his son; was contemporary with Niall of the Nine Hostages.

91. Cairbre Aedhbha: his son ; had a brother named Conn, who was the ancestor of *Keely.*

92. Erc : son of Cairbre Aedhbha.

93. Olioll Ceannfhada: his son ; living A.D. 489.

94. Laipe : his son ; had a bro-ther named Caoinealadh, who was the ancestor of *Trasey* and *Tracey,* of Munster, and of *Kenealy.*

95. Aongus : son of Laipe.

96. Aodh (or Hugh) : his son.

97. Cruinnmhaol : his son.

98. Eoghan (or Owen) : his son ; living A.D. 667.

99. Roin : his son.

100. Hugh (2): his son.

101. Dubhd'abhoireann : his son ; a quo, according to some genealogists, *Davoren.*

102. Ceannfaola : his son.

103. Cathal : his son.

104. Uamhach : his son.

105. Cathal (2): his son.

* *O'Donoghe* : See Note "O'Donoghue," under the *O'Donoghue* (No. 4) pedigree. Rory O'Donocho, a scion of the "O'Donoghue" family, ancient lords of Glenfesk, in the county Kerry, settled in the county Meath, in the Commonwealth period, and there married Edith Rothwell, and had issue.

106. Amhailgadh : his son.

107. Donamhan : his son ; a quo *MacDonamhain ;** but for euphony sake anglicised *O'Donovan ;* m. a dau. of Ivor, King of the Danes of Limerick ; was defeated in a battle fought A.D. 977, between his own forces assisted by Amhlaff, the Dane, and the Dal-Cais, commanded by Brian Boroimhe and his two elder brothers. He was afterwards slain at the battle of Croma, by Donchuan, son of Cineadh, and brother of Brian. Collins of Myross relates :—" Mahon, son of Cineadh, brother of Brian Boroihme, and Maolmoradh, son of Bran, son of Cian, of the Eugenian line, and ancestor of O'Mahony, were candidates for the throne of Munster. Mahon defeated Maolmoradh in two different battles, and Maolmoradh despairing to succeed by open force, had recourse to treachery; the Bishop of Cork and the other principal clergy of the province interposed, in consequence of which it was agreed that both princes should meet with a few friends at both sides at Donamhan's house in Kerry. Mahon came there on the appointed day accompanied by only 12 of his nobles. In the interim Maolmoradh tampered with Donamhan, and came to his house with a strong party of horse, on which Mahon was made prisoner, hurried off to the county of Cork, and there basely murdered at a place called Leacht Mahon near Macroom. Maolmoradh was thereon proclaimed King of Munster, and Donamhan for his services received nine score townlands in Carbery, in the south of the county of Cork, afterwards as it happened by the law of gavel-kind, divided among his descendants, as follows : —*Glean-na-Chroim*, or the parish of Fanlobish ; *Clan Loghlin*, or the parish of Kilfoghmabeg; *Gleana-Mhuilin*, or the parish of Kilmeen ; *Garruidhe-O'Gearbe*, or the parish of Myross ; *Clancathail*, or the parish of Drimoleague, and part of the parish of Drinagh."

108. Cathal O'Donovan :† his son; was the first who assumed this sirname.

109. Amhailgadh (2) : his son ; fought at Clontarf in the division commanded by Cian, Prince of Kinalmeaky, and husband of Sadhbh, dau. of Brian Boroimhe.

110. Murcha: his son; lord of Hy-Fidginte.

111. Aneisleis‡ (" aneis :" Irish, *a hide ;* " leis," *with him*)*:* his son ; from whom the family of *Mac-Aneslis* derive their descent and sirname. This chieftain assisted

---

* *MacDonamhain :* According to some genealogists this name is derived from the Irish "*dona*," *froward* (Pers. "doon," *vile*)*;* and "amhain :" Irish, *alone* or *only*. Thus derived, the name would imply that this Donamhan was the *only* one of the family who was *refractory*.

† *Cathal O'Donovan :* In another genealogy of this family which we have seen, the names, after this Cathal, are as follows :—

109. Amhailgadh (2) : son of Cathal.
110. Morogh : his son.
111. Ainisleis : his son.
112. Ranall (also called Maolruanaidh) : his son.
113. Maolra : his son.
114. Ancrom : his son.
115. Lochlann : his son ; had a brother named Cathal.

116. Donogh, of Loughcrow: son of Lochlann.
117. Cathal : his son.
118. Dermod : his son.
119. Donogh (2) : his son.
120. Conor : his son.
121. Hugh (3) :. his son.
122. Dermod (2) : his son.
123. Donogh O'Donovan : his son.

‡ *Aneisleis :* This name is now rendered Anesley, Standish, and Stanislaus.

Donogh, son of Brian, to obtain possession of the government of Leath-Mogha, and defeated the Danes of Limerick in several engagements.

112. Raghnall (Randal, Ranulf or Reginald): his son. (This name "Reginald" bespeaks a Danish alliance). This Raghnall was the ancestor (according to MacFirbis) of the MacRaghnalls, or *Reynolds* of Carbery and Kinalea, in the county of Cork.

113. Maolruanaidh: his son.

114. Crom: his son; built the Castle of Crom, on the river Maigue, in the county of Limerick, in which he received and entertained Torlogh O'Connor, King of Conacht, in 1146. It is from this Crom that the territory of *Glean-na-Chroim*, in the parish of Fanlobush, in Carbery, has its name; which his descendants held down to the year 1290, when they were dispossessed by the Mac-Carthys, whereupon the then O'Donovan gave them a district in the parish of Kilmacabea, containing seven townlands, which they held till the time of Oliver Cromwell; the title *Mac-an-Croim* was hereditary in this branch of the family. According to the *Annals of Innisfallen*, Crom was killed in, or immediately before, the year 1254, at *Inis-an-bheil* (now "Pheale") near Iniskean, to the west of Bandon in the county of Cork, by O'Mahony's people. This Crom was ancestor of all the septs of the O'Donovan family in the baronies of Carbery, in the county of Cork, and of several others in Leinster.

115. Cathal: the eldest son of Crom; in his father's lifetime held the entire of his lands in the county of Cork; settled in the parish of Drimoleague, in Carbery, which from him and his posterity was called *Clan Cathail*, which is defined

by an Inquisition taken at Cork on the 6th of October, 1607, as containing two manors, viz., "the manor of Castell O'Donyvane containing twenty and one ploughlands, and the manor of Rahyne." The territory of Clancahill contained, in all, three score and seven ploughlands, and extended "from the sea on the south to the river Myalagh, and was bounded on the north with the lands of Clandonell Roe, and the lands of *Glean-na-Chroim*, and with the lands of Clandoghlin on the east, and the lands of Clandermodie and Clanteige revoe on the west." This Cathal lived to a very great age, and his principality in the county of Limerick which was overrun, and his strong Castle of Crom were wrested from him by Maurice Fitzgerald, second Lord Offaly, who was the first of that family who came to Munster, and was made Lord Justice of Ireland in the year 1229, in the reign of Henry III. of England. Hence the said family of Fitzgerald took the motto "*Crom-a-bū*" (Crom Aboo), from the victory obtained at Crom.

Cathal never had any possessions in the original territory (see No. 89 on this genealogy), of *Ui-Fidhgeinte*, or (see No. 91) *Ui-Cairbre Aedhbha*, in the present county Limerick; but he had acquired a large tract of mountain territory in *Corca Luighe*, the original principality of the O'Driscolls, etc.; to which newly acquired district he transferred the tribe-name of his family, viz., "Cairbre"—a name which, by a strange whim of custom, was afterwards applied to a vast territory now forming four baronies in the county of Cork. This extension of name looks strange, as it was transferred since the year 1200, and as the race who transferred it did not remain the dominant family in the district. The fact seems to have been that when MacCarthy Reagh got possession of a part of this territory in the latter end of the thirteenth century, the *Ui-Cairbre Mór* were the most important tribe within it; and that he and his descendants applied the name to the O'Donovan territory and to all the minor cantreds annexed by him from time to time.

Cathal left two sons, viz., Ivar of Castle Ivor, now Castle Ire, in the parish of Myross, which he erected in 1220, and of which his descendants kept possession down to the time of Donal na-g-Croiceainn, and Tadhg.

116. Tadhg (or Teige): son of Cathal; had two sons, Murcha ; and Lochlin, sirnamed "Tancuste," who obtained from his father, 36 ploughlands between the river Roury and Glandore harbour ; and who became the ancestor of the *Clan Loghlin O'Donovans*, who held their possessions down to the time of Oliver Cromwell.

117. Murcha (Morogh or Morgan): his son ; had a second son Aongus, who possessed 28 ploughlands of Gleanamhullin, which are comprised in the parish of Kilmeen, and who had his residence at Clais-a-Rusheen, of which extensive ruins remain.

118. Concobhar (Conor, or Cornelius): his son.

119. Raghnal (or Randal): his son; had a son named Dermod, who was ancestor of the subsequent chiefs of the O'Donovans; and another named Tioboid (or Toby), the ancestor of a sept of the O'Donovans, called *Sliochd Tioboid*, who possessed a tract of land near the town of Skibbereen, where they built the castle of Gortnaclogh—the ruins of which still remain, and are shown on the Ordnance Map on a detached portion of the parish of Creagh.

120. Dermod: son of Raghnall ; lord of Clan-Cathal, was nominated " Prince of Carbery," by MacCarthy Reagh.

121. Teige, of Dromasta: his son ; m. Ellen, the daughter of Denis O'Donovan, of Meeny, in the parish of Drimoleague ; he was slain by the O'Donovans of Meeny at a place called, from the circumstance, *Deereen Tadhg*, on the bank of the river Ilen, which separates Meeny from Dromasta ; and his murderers on the same night killed the inhabitants of thirteen houses (the O'Donovans of Gurteen Flur), to the east of Meeny, only one man, Timothy O'Donovan, escaped.

122. Donal, called *Na-g-Croiceainn* (or *of the hides*), from his having been wrapped up in a cow-hide when an infant by his mother, to hide him from the claimants to the chieftainship of Clan-Cathal, who had conspired to murder him: son of Teige and Ellen, his wife ; was made chief of Clan Cahill by MacCarthy Reagh, about 1560 ; was fostered by O'Leary, of Carrigacurra (now called Castle Masters), parish of Inchageelah, in Ibh-Leary, having, with his mother, taken refuge there when his father was murdered ; with the assistance of O'Leary, Denis Meeny O'Donovan, MacConnolly, and their followers, he slew Diarmaid (Dermod) an-Bhairc (or *of the bark*, from being bred at sea), at Rosscarbery, in presence of MacCarthy Reagh, when the straight white wand was put in his right hand, and he was saluted " *O'Donovan.*" It was he who built Castle Donovan in 1560, but it is supposed he only improved an older structure. He was married to Ellen, dau. to O'Leary, at the Church of Drumali, after having had by her Dermod (slain in 1581 at *Lathach na-nDamh*, by Donal O'Sullivan, who afterwards became

The O'Sullivan Beare), and other sons, who were declared "illegitimate" by the Lord Chancellor, Adam Loftus, in 1592. His "lawful" sons were Donal and Teige ; he died in 1584.

123. Donal (2): son of Donal; m. Ellen, dau. of William Barry of Lislee, in Barry Roe, who was the son of James FitzRichard Barry, Lord Ibane and Viscount Buttevant, and had issue. This Donal built Rahine Castle in 1607 ; and burned to the ground the Protestant Bishop's house at Ross, which had been a short time before built by William Lyon, Protestant Bishop of Cork, Cloyne, and Ross. In February, 1592, his brother Teige attempted to depose this Donal on the score of "illegitimacy," but failed. He died in 1639. He had four sons : —Donal, Teige, Richard, and Edmund.

124. Donal (3) : his son ; was a man distinguished both in peace and war, admired by his friends and respected by his enemies. During the Cromwellian wars he joined the Stuart side, with the Earl of Castlehaven. His principal seat was at Rahine Castle in Myross. He was present at the taking of Mallow, and Doneraile, in 1645, and assisted Lord Castlehaven to take the castles of Milton, Connagh, and Rostellan, in the same year.

In 1652 he was dispossessed of large portions of his patrimony which were partitioned among the officers and soldiers of Cromwell in lieu of pay ; many of these settled on the plots assigned them, others sold their shares to monied adventurers for a trifle.

The parish of Drimoleague was divided amongst Colonel Sandford, Major Tonson, Captain Butler, Lieutenant Gilkes, Ensigns White, Wood, &c. ; and Sampson Trige,

Samuel Jervois, and Henry Beecher had lands assigned to them in the parish of Myross. This Donal married Joanna, daughter of Owen MacCarthy Reagh (see No. 119 on the MacCarthy Reagh pedigree) and left by her five sons and a daughter :— 1. Donal; 2. Denis, of Fortnaught, in the parish of Castlehaven, who m. Mary, dau. of Cormac MacDonoch MacCarthy-na-Mona (see MacCarthy-na-Mona pedigree No. 123), by whom he had a son Donal, whose great-grandson, Philip of Cooldorcha, in the parish of Myross (who m. Elizabeth, dau. of Rickard MacKeadagh O'Donovan), represented this branch of the family in the first quarter of the present century ; 3. Keadagh Mór, ancestor of the O'Donovans of Crook Haven, Knockduff and Kinligh, represented in 1813 by Keadagh O'Donovan of Inchiclogh, near Bantry, and by Richard O'Donovan of Phale, on the Bandon, son of Richard, son of Donal, son of Keadagh ; 4. Teige, who had a son Donal, who had a son Teige, otherwise "Captain Timothy O'Donovan," who with O'Driscoll and Mac-na-Crimeen MacCarthy were killed at the taking of Castletownsend in 1690; 5. Philip, who had a son Donal, who had a son Donal of Dunamarke, near Bantry ; and 6. Honoria, married to Tadhg an-Duna-MacCarthy of Dunmanway. This Donal died in 1660.

125. Donal (4) : his son ; possessed none of the family estates at his father's death. He petitioned Charles II., King of England, to restore them to him. The King wrote to the government in Dublin directing their attention to the matter; the result being that a portion of the Manor of Rahine was restored to him, but no part of the Manor of Castle Donovan, which the King, by patent, in the 18th year of

his reign, granted to Lieutenant Nathaniel Evanson. A copy of the King's letter was preserved at Banlahan, and lay in the possession of Edward Powell. In 1684 O'Donovan was put on his trial for "High Treason," but was acquitted. He afterwards became a Colonel of a Regiment of Foot in the service of James II., and was Deputy-Governor of Charles-Fort at the mouth of the Bandon, in 1690, under Sir Edward Scott, when it was attacked by John Churchill (Duke of Marlborough) and forced to surrender. This Donal married twice, first, Victoria, dau. of Captain Coppinger, by whom he had a dau. m. to Conn O'Donovan, ancestor of O'Donovan of Lisard; and, secondly, Elizabeth, the dau. of Major Tonson, by his wife Elizabeth, the sister of Henry Beecher, above mentioned, by whom he had :—1. Richard ; 2. Conor, otherwise *Conchobhar-na-Bhuile* (or "of the madness"), who had his residence at Achres, in the parish of Drimoleague, and had besides other children, Rickard; 3. Sarah, who m. Samuel Morris of Skibbereen, by whom she had Daniel Morris, Counsellor-at-law, and a dau. Honoria, who m. Michael O'Driscoll of Ballyisland ; 4. Elizabeth, m. to Daniel O'Leary of Glassheen, near Cork ; and 5. Catherine, m. to Rickard, son of Tadhg O'Donovan. This Donal died in 1703.

126. Captain Richard O'Donovan: son of Donal (4); m. in 1703, Eleanor Fitzgerald, daughter of the Knight of Kerry, by whom he had, amongst others :—1. Donal ; 2. Richard, who d. unm. ; and some daughters, the eldest, of whom, Elizabeth, m. Sylvester O'Sullivan, head of the sept called *MacFineen Duff*, of Direen-a-Vuirrig, in the county of Kerry, by whom he had a numerous issue.

127. Donal (5): son of Captain Richard; m., in his 18th year, Anne, dau. of James Kearney of Garrettstown. He m. secondly, in 1763, in the 60th year of his age, Jane, dau. of John Beecher, of Holleybrook, near Skibbereen (she was 15 years old), by whom he had four children : —1. Richard, of whom below ; 2. John, a Captain in the English Army ; Ellen, m. John Warren of Codrum, d. s. p. 1840 ; 4. Jane, d. unm. in 1833. Donal, in his Will dated December, 1778, in case of failure of issue, male and female, in his sons, left the reversion of his estates to Morgan O'Donovan, Esq., then living in the City of Cork, who was grandfather of O'Donovan of Montpelier, and of O'Donovan of Lisard, near Skibbereen. His second wife died in 1812, and he (Donal) died in 1778—both were buried in the church at Myross.

128. Richard (2): his son ; b. in 1764, d. s. p. in 1829. Married in 1800 Emma-Anne Powell (d. 1832), a Welsh lady ; he was Colonel in the Enniskillen Dragoons, and afterwards a General in the English Army; he was an intimate acquaintance of the English Prince Regent, and saved the life of the Duke of York during the retreat of the English Army from Holland. This Richard upset his grandfather Donal's Will " by levying fines and suffering a recovery" of the property, which he willed to his wife. At her death she willed the estate to her brother Major Powell, one of whose sons—Colonel Powell—now (1887 enjoys its possession.

By Richard's death the senior branch of the O'Donovan family became extinct. But from Teige, son of Donal (2) who is No. 123 on this pedigree, the Genealogy is brought down to this year, 1887.

O'DONOVAN. (No. 2.)

Of Lisard, County Cork.

Arms : Same as " O'Donovan," Lords of Clancahill.

124. Teige : son of Donal, No. 123 on the " O'Donovan," lords of Clancahill pedigree, No. 1.

125. Morogh : his son.

126. Conn : his son ; m. to a dau. of Donal O'Donovan (4).

127. Morgan : his son.

128. Morgan (2) : his son.

129. Rev. Morgan (3) : his son.

130. Morgan-William : his son ; d. 1870. Had two brothers—1. William-James, who d. unm. ; 2. Henry-Winthrop, of Lios Ard, Skibbereen, county of Cork, living in 1887, and known as " O'Donovan, Lord of Clancahill."

O'DONOVAN. (No. 3.)

124. EDMUND O'DONOVAN : son of Donal, who is No. 123 on the " O'Donovan" Lords of Clancahill (No. 1.) pedigree ; m. a Miss Burke ; d. 1643, being slain in the battle of Ballinvegga, fought on the 18th of March of that year between Ormond and General Preston.

125. Richard : his son.

126. Conn (or Cornelius) : his son ; m. Rose Cavanagh, sister of Brian-

na-Stroice ("of the strokes"), who fought at the Boyne.

127. William : his second son.

128. Richard : his son.

129. Edmond : his son ; d. 1817.

130. Dr. John O'Donovan* (d. 1861) : his son ; Barrister-at-Law ; and honoris causa, LL.D., T.C.D., in consideration of his translation, etc., of the Annals of the Four Masters ; had a brother Michael.

* ODonovan : Webb, in his great work, the Compendium of Irish Biography, writes :—" John O'Donovan, a distinguished Irish scholar, was born at Atateemore, in the co. Kilkenny, 9th July, 1809. The death of his father in 1817 caused the dispersion of the family, and John was brought to Dublin by his elder brother Michael, who, although in poor circumstances, procured for him the rudiments of a sound education. He often ascribed his taste for historical pursuits to the narrations of his uncle, Patrick O'Donovan, who was well versed in the Gaelic lore of the county of his birth. In 1826 O'Donovan began to apply himself to archæological investigations and to the philosophical study of the Irish language. Through James Hardiman he was engaged to transcribe legal and historical documents in the Irish Record Office ; and, with some slight assistance from his brother, was enabled to support himself until he obtained a situation on the Ordnance Survey of Ireland, in the historical department, under George Petrie, left vacant on Edward O'Reilly's death in 1829. To him was confided the examination of the ancient manuscripts in the Irish language in the Royal Irish Academy, and elsewhere, for the purpose of fixing the nomenclature on the maps, and extracting the local information they contained. Already acquainted with modern Gaelic, in the course of these labours he gradually acquired a knowledge of the language in its ancient and obsolete forms. Working in company with Petrie, O'Curry and Mangan, after researches in all parts of Ireland, the names of 62,000 townlands were satisfactorily fixed. . . . His first important essays appeared in the Dublin Penny Journal, to which he was a frequent contributor, until the fifty-sixth number, in July, 1833, when the paper passed out of the management of John S. Folds. . . . . . Several

O'FLANAGAN.

Chiefs of Kinelargy,* in Ely O'Carroll.

Arms : Ar. on a mount in base an oak tree ppr. a border vert.

FEC, a brother of Iomdhun who is No. 89 on the "O'Carroll Ely" pedigree, was the ancestor of *O'Flannagain*, Ele; anglicised *O'Flanagan*, of Ely O'Carroll.

89. Fec : son of Iomchadh Uallach.

90. Fionnachtach : his son.

91. Neachtan : his son.

92. Maolfabhal : his son.

93. Donsleibhe : his son.

94. Arga : his son ; a quo *Cineal nArga.*

95. Aongus : his son.

96. Flannagan ("flann :" Irish, *red*) : his son ; a quo *O'Flannagain* Ele.

97. Ceanfaoladh : his son.

98. Lorcan : his son.

99. Domhnall : his son.

100. Macniadh : his son.

101. Mughron : his son.

102. Diarmaid : his son.

103. Cucalma O'Flannagain : his son.

O'GARA.

Chiefs of Coolavin aad Sliabh Lugha.

Arms : Three lions ramp. az. on a chief gu. a demi lion ramp. or. *Crest :* A demi lion ramp. erm. holding betw. the paws a wreath of oak vert. acorned or. *Motto ;* Fortiter et fideliter.

BEICE, who is No. 101 on the "O'Hara" pedigree, had two sons—1. Eadhradh, and 2. Saorgus : this Saorgus was the ancestor of *O'Gadhra ;* anglicised *O'Gara, Geary,* and *Gerry.*

102. Saorgus : son of Beice.

103. Claonachan ("claon" : Irish, *prejudiced*) : his son ; a quo *MacClaonachain*, anglicised *MacClanaghan* and *MacClenaghan.*

104. Gadhar (" gadhar :" Irish, *a mastiff*, which means that in battle he was fierce as a mastiff) : his son ; a quo *O'Gadhra.*

105. Rorc O'Gara : his son ; first assumed this sirname.

106. Conor : his son.

107. Dunsleibhe : his son.

108. Dunsleibe Oge : his son.

of his papers will also be found in the *Irish Penny Journal*, 1840-1841. In 1836 he commenced the compilation of an analytical catalogue of the Irish manuscripts in Trinity College, Dublin. . . . He was called to the Bar in 1847. He was now engaged on the great work of his life—the translation, annotating and editing of the first complete edition of the *Annals of the Four Masters*, for Hodges and Smith, the Dublin Publishers. . . . . O'Donovan may be said to have been the first historic topographer that Ireland ever produced. He died in Dublin, 9th December, 1861, aged 52, and was buried in Glasnevin Cemetery.

* *Kinelargy :* This ancient territory corresponds with the present barony of Ballybrit, in the King's County.

109. Roger : his son.
110. Dunsleibhe (3) : his son.
111. Congal : his son.
112. Ragnach : his son.
113. Dermod (3) : his son.
114. Tumaltach (or Timothy) : his son.
115. Timothy Oge : his son.
116. Eoghan : his son.
117. Dermod (2) : his son.
118. Olioll : his son.
119. Teige : his son.

120. Fargal O'Gara : his son. This is the Fargal O'Gara, lord of Moy-O'Gara and Coolavin, to whom Michael O'Clery, their chief author, dedicated the *Annala Rioghacta Eirionn*,* and who was one of the two knights elected to represent the county Sligo in the Parliament held in Dublin, A.D. 1634. The family was, in 1648, dispossessed, consequent on the war of 1641-1652.

The O'Garas were lords of the territory of Luighne, now forming and giving name to the barony of Leyney or Lieny, in the county of Sligo, whence they were expelled by the MacSurtains (or Jordans,—known in the co. Cork as *Lordans*) and MacCostelloes, families of Anglo-Norman descent; and they were obliged to remove into *Cuil-Ui-Fionn*, now the barony of Coolavin, in the same county. They are sometimes styled lords of Sliabh Lugha, a district on the confines of the counties of Sligo and Mayo, comprising, besides lands in the former, a large portion of the barony of Costello in. the latter county. Sliabh Lugha, as well as the country of Luighne, derives its name from Luigh, son of Cormac Galeng, son of Teige, son of Cian, the third son of Olioll Olum, King of Munster, who is No. 84 on the "Line of Heber." From Cormac Galeng, here mentioned, the Gailenga derive their descent and tribe-name. O'Dugan says :

> " Let us proceed into the Lienys,
> Let us leave the country of Carbury,
> Let us treat of the race of Cian,
> In the warlike Lienys of trenchant blades.
> The princes of Lieny of wide-spread fame,
> Are O'Hara and O'Huathmaran ;
> Let us visit Lieny of sword-armed heroes,
> And bear O'Kearnahan in memory,
> Good is each mansion of that tribe—
> Of these is O'Gara."

The following notices of this family are collected from various sources :—

A.D. 964. Tiachleach O'Gara was slain; he was lord of South Leyney.
1056. Rory O'Gara, tanist of Leyney, was slain.
1059. Rory O'Gara, heir presumptive of the lordship of Leyney, died. His uncle, Conal, died, 993.
1067. Donlevy O'Gara, lord of Leyney and Magh-Ui-Gadhra, was killed by Brian O'Hara.
1128. O'Gadhra, lord of Leyney, was slain on an expedition into Leinster. His kinsman, O'Gara of Moy-Gara, was slain at the battle of Ardee.
1206. O'Gara, lord of Sliabh-Lugha, died.

* *Annala Rioghachta Eirionn :* This name means " The Annals of the Kingdom of Ireland ;" now known as the *Annals of the Four Masters.*

1207. Connor O'Gara, lord of Leyney, flourished.

1217. Donal O'Gara, died.

1226. Ferghail O'Teighe, Captain of the House of Cathal of the Red Hand O'Connor, and Aodh, son of the said Cathal, were slain by Dunlevy O'Gara, lord of Leyney; and Dunlevy himself was slain in the year following, by his own nephew, the Giolla-Roe O'Gara; and Giolla-Roe was slain soon afterwards at the instigation of Hugh O'Connor.

1228. The sons of Teige O'Gara slew Murtogh O'Flanagan.

1237. A prey was taken by Connor MacCormac O'Gara, whose brother was killed on that occasion.

1241. Teige, son of Rory O'Gara, died.

1254. Manus O'Gara was killed.

1256. Rory O'Gara, lord of Sliabh Lugha, was slain by David FitzRickard Cuisin; but Hugh, son of Felim O'Connor, plundered the murderer's lands, demolished his castle, seized his possessions, and slew himself in revenge for the murder of his friend.

1260. Teige, son of Cian O'Gara, was slain at the battle of Dromderg, at *Dun-da-Leath-glas* or Downpatrick, fought between the English, commanded by Stephen, Earl of Salisbury, and the Irish Nation under the command of King Brian O'Neill; Hugh O'Connor being second in command. In this sanguinary struggle the Irish King lost his life in defence of his people.

1285. Rory O'Gara, lord of Sliabh Lugha, was slain by De Bermingham on Lough O'Gara, in the barony of Coolavin.

1325. Brian O'Gara, of Coolavin, died.

1328. Donogh Roe O'Gara and five of his name were slain. Dermod O'Gara slew Teige O'Connor.

1435. O'Gara was killed by his own people on Inis Bolg, an island in Lough Techet, now Loch O'Gara; his own brother, Connor Cam, was the principal in the murder. This Connor Cam was slain in the year following, in an attempt to repel the MacDonoghs from Coolavin. Felim O'Connor preyed the country of O'Gara; and the latter in revenge preyed the people of Ballymore-O'Flynn.

1461. Fergal O'Gara, tanist of Coolavin, was killed by MacCostelloe.

1464. Tomaltach O'Gara was killed in a nocturnal attack on Sliabh Lugha, by Maurice MacCormac MacDermott Gall, and by Edmund MacCostelloe of the Plain.

1469. Eoghan O'Gara, son of Tomaltach Oge, son of Tomaltach Mór, lord of Coolavin, died between the two Lady-days, in Autumn; and his son, Eoghan, died soon afterwards; and Dermod, son of Eoghan, son of Tomaltach, succeeded to the lordship.

1478. The son of Fergal O'Gara, above mentioned, and Manus, son of David, were slain.

1495. Teige, son of Donal, son of Eoghan O'Gara, and Cian, son of Brian O'Gara, were slain. Cian, son of Eoghan, son of

Tomaltach Oge O'Gara, was "rhymed to death" by a bard. Dermod, son of Eoghan, son of Tomaltach Oge, lord of Coolavin, was taken prisoner by O'Donnell, at the battle of Bel-an-droichet, near Sligo. His son, Eoghan, died in 1537.

1648. FARGAL O'GARA, the last name on this family pedigree, lord of Moy O'Gara and Coolavin, to whom Brother Michael O'Clery dedicated the Annals of Ireland (the Four Masters), was M.P. for the county of Sligo, from 24th March, 1628, till 30th May, 1640. He was educated at Trinity College, Dublin; and he was the first of the family who conformed to the Protestant religion.

1716. Bernard O'Gara, a native of Sligo, was appointed to the archiepiscopal see of Tuam. He died in 1740, and was succeeded by his brother Michael O'Gara, who died between 1752 and 1755.

This is the last entry we find of this family.

A friary was erected at Knockmore, in the 14th century, by O'Gara, of which the doorways and windows are in good preservation; and it is still a favourite burial place. Here are also the ruins of Gara Castle, the residence of that O'Gara whose descendant, Colonel O'Gara, left Ireland, after the battle of Aughrim, and entered the Austrian service.

O'GRADY.* (No. 1.)

Chiefs of Cinel Dunghaile.†

Arms : Per pale gu. and sa. three lions pass. per pale ar. and or. *Crest* : A horse's head erased ar. *Motto* : Vulneratus non victus.

EOCHA (or Eochaidh), a younger brother of Carthann, who is No. 93 on the "Macnamara" pedigree, was the ancestor of *O'Gradhaighe‡* or *O'Gradha ;* anglicised *O'Grady*, *MacGrade*, and *O'Brady*.

93. Eocha : son of Caisin.	95. Finan : his son.
94. Breannan : his son.	96. Foranan : his son.

* *O'Grady* : Of this family is Dr. Edward Stamer O'Grady (b. 23rd Nov., 1838, in Baggot Street, Dublin, and living in 1887), who is the son of the late Edward Stamer O'Grady, 4th Dragoon Guards, by his wife Wilhelmina, daughter of the late Richard A. Rose, of Ahabeg, county of Limerick. Dr. O'Grady became, in 1883, a member of the College of Physicians. He is married to Minnie, eldest daughter of the late John Bishop, of Galbally, county of Limerick, and has had issue three sons and two daughters.

† *Cinel Dunghaile* : This territory comprised the present parish of Tomgraney, co. Clare ; and Iniscaltra and Clonrush, co. Galway.

‡ *O'Gradhaighe* : This sirname was also called *O'Bradaighe*, anglicised "O'Brady." The two forms of sirname seem to be synonymous ; for, while *O'Gradhaighe* ("gradh" Irish, *love ;* Lat. "grat-ia") means "the descendants of the love-making man," *O'Bradaighe* ("bradaich ;" Irish, *roguish*) means "the descendants of the roguish man :" roguish here meaning "lovemaking."

97. Tiobraid : his son.

98. Dungal: his son ; a quo *Cineal Donghaile.*

99. Fodalbha : his son.

100. Rodgus : his son.

101. Flaithreach : his son.

102. Seachnadhseach : his son.

103. Cormac : his son.

104. Collachtach : his son.

105. Conn : his son.

106. Conn Oge : his son.

107. Art : his son.

108. Treassach : his son ; had a brother named Artagan (meaning "little Art,") a quo *O'h-Artagain,* which has been anglicised *Hartigan* and *Hartan.*

109. Gradhach (also called Bradach) : his son ; a quo *O'Gradhaighe.*

110. Maolmaith : his son.

111. Edrocht : his son.

112. Mortach : his son.

113. Aneisleis : his son.

114. Moroch : his son.

115. Dermod : his son.

116. Ceanfaola : his son.

117. Moroch (2) : his son.

118. Dermod (2) : his son.

119. Moroch (3) : his son.

*120. John O'Grady, *alias* O'Brady : his son ; died, 1332.　Had a brother named Donal.

*121. John : his son ; d., 1372.

*122. John : his son ; d., 1417.

123. John O'Grady, *alias* O'Brady, of Fassaghmore, county Clare : his son.

124. Sir Denis, of Fassaghmore : his son.　Sir Denis O'Grady, *alias* O'Brady, had a grant from King Henry the Eighth, by Patent, in 1543, of Tomgrany, Finnagh, Kilbechullybeg, Kilbechullymor, Seanboy, Cronayn, Killokennedy, Clony, Killchomurryn, Enochem, Tarchayne, and Killula, in the county Clare ; he died in 1569.　This Sir Denis had four sons—1. Edmond, who died without issue, in 1576 ; 2. Donal, who also died without issue ; 3. John, who surrendered his estates to Queen Elizabeth, and had a regrant by Patent, in 1582 ; and 4. Hugh, to whom his brother John conveyed Tomgrany and other lands.

125. Most Rev. Hugh Brady, lord bishop of Meath : son of Sir Denis. This Hugh was the first of the family who omitted the sirname of "O'Grady ;" his descendants have since called themselves *Brady.*

126. Luke : his son ; d., 1621 ; had two brothers—1. Nicholas, and 2. Gerald.

127. Luke Brady, of Tomgrany : son of Luke ; alienated Scariff by license, in 1634.

* Of the above three persons, thus (*) marked, No. 120 was archbishop of Cashel ; No. 121, archbishop of Tuam ; and No. 122, bishop of Elphin.

O'GRADY.* (No. 2.)

Of Kilballyowen.

THE O'Gradys were lords of Cineal Donghaile, a territory in the county of Clare, forming the present barony of Lower Tulla; as we learn by O'Heerin :

> " O'Grady seized the entire lands
> Of the profitable Cineal Donghaile;
> Yellow-hilted and keen his sword,
> And sledge heavy are the blows of his forces in conflict."

120. Donal, a brother of John, who is No. 120 on the "O'Grady" (No. 1.) genealogy; slain in 1309.
121. Hugh : his son.
122. William : his son.
123. Donal : his son.
124. Gilla-Duff : his son.
125. Mathew : his son.
126. Donogh : his son.
127. Dermod : his son.
128. Thomas : his son.
129. John : his son.
130. Thomas : his son.

131. John : his son; m. in 1771 Mary-Eliza De Courcy.
132. Gerald : his son; m. Eliza Waller.
133. Gerald de Courcy O'Grady, Esq., J.P., of Killballyowen, co. Limerick : his son ; commonly called THE O'GRADY, living in 1865 ; m. Anne Wise, and had :
134. William de Courcy, who had :
135. Thomas de Courcy O'Grady ; living in 1887.

O'GUNNING.

Ireland.

Arms : Gu. on a fesse erm. betw. three doves ar. ducally crowned or, as many crosses pattée of the first.

THE *O'Conaing*, or, as the name is now anglicised *O'Gunning* and *Gunning*, derive their name and descent from Conaing, son of Cineadh, son of Donchuan, brother of Brian Boroimhe, Monarch of Ireland, who is No. 105 on the " O'Brien, Kings of Thomond " pedigree ; and were Chiefs of Aos-Greine, a territory in the county Limerick which has been variously located ; and also of Crioch Saingil, or Singland, otherwise St. Patrick's, a parish in the county of Limerick, where formerly stood the principal residence of the lords of Aos-Greine, as we read :

> " Aos-Greine of the smooth fair plains,
> O'Conaing of Crich Saingil governs."

We are of opinion that Aos-Greine forms part of the present baronies

---

* *O'Grady :* Julia, only daughter of Edward O'Grady of Kilballyowen (and niece of Standish, first Lord Guillamore), m. Wellington-Anderson Rose, late of the 4th Dragoon Guards, and had a dau. Eliza-Thomasina, who m. William Cleburne, C.E. (See " Cleburne," *infra*).

of Clanwilliam and Coonagh, on the borders of which is a parish called
"Greane," and the town of Pallas-greane, the scene of a tremendous battle
in the middle of the 10th century.   Palais-Aos-Greine, which may have
been the ancient name of this territory, and now shortened to "Pallas-
greane," would signify the "Palace of the worshippers of the Sun," or "the
place of residence of the sun-worshippers;" and that a *grianan*—a palace or
summer residence—existed here, the following lines from O'Heerin go to
prove :

> "He [O'Conaing] held the *fair Grian*,
> Of the illustrious house of Eoghan."

According to O'Brien, Aos-Greine was situated in the barony of Small
County.

In A.D. 1032. Edras O'Conaing, son of Eoghan, son of Conaing, lord of
   Aos-Greine, and "heir of Munster," died.

A.D. 1125. Kennedy O'Conaing, erenach of Cill Dulua, or Killaloe,
   died.

A.D. 1137. Donal O'Conaing, Archbishop of Leath Mogha, *i.e.* Leinster
   and Munster, died.

A.D. 1195. Donal O'Conaing, bishop of Killaloe, died.

A.D. 1261. Brian Roe O'Brien, lord of Thomond, ancestor of the
   O'Briens of Ara, in Tipperary, demolished Caislean-Ui-
   Chonaing, *i.e.* the castle of O'Conaing, now *Castle-Connell*, in
   the county of Limerick, and put the garrison to the sword.

A.D. 1490. Mathamhna (Mahon) O'Conaing, vicar of the abbey of
   Lethrachta, or Latteragh, in Upper Ormond, died.

Several respectable members of this family are to be met with in the
counties of Limerick, Clare, Tipperary, and Donegal, at the present day.

O'HANRAGHAN.

Chiefs of Corcaree, County Westmeath.

(See "Hanraghan," *ante*.)

Arms : Gu. a lizard pass. in fess or, in chief a trefoil slipped betw. two holly leaves
ar. in base a garb of the second.   *Crest :* An arm erect, couped below the elbow, vested
vert, cuffed ar. holding in the hand ppr. a holly leaf vert.   *Motto*: An uachtar.

THE *O'h-Anraghain* family (anglicised *O'Hanraghan* and *Hanrahan*) were
formerly lords of Corcaraidhe, a territory in the county of Westmeath,
forming the present barony of Corcaree, to which it gave name; and
several families of this sept are to be met with in that and surrounding
districts at the present day.   They were also chiefs of a district in the
present co. Tipperary.

In 1402, Gilla-Evin O'Hanrahan, grandson of Mahon, son of Kennedy,
styled chief of Hy-Cremhthanan (the country of *O'Duff* in Leix), was
slain.

O

In 1096, Gilla-Columb O'Hanrahan, erenach of Ross-Alither (now Ros-carbery) in Cork, died.

In 1132, died, Mulbrennan O'Hanrahan, successor of St. Brendan, at Clonfert ; and, in two years afterwards, his kinsman and successor, Gilla-Brennan O'Hanrahan, a member of the house of Corcaree.

In 1580, on the 6th of April, Daniel O'Hanraghan, an aged priest, a native of Kerry, was, for his faith, martyred by a company of English soldiers, at Lislaghtan.

O'HARA* BUIDHE. (No. 1.)

Chiefs of Leyney, County Sligo.

Arms : A demi lion ramp. holding in the dexter paw a chaplet of laurel. *Crest :* A hawk's head betw. two wings. *Motto :* Try.

CORMAC Galeng,† brother of Conla who is No. 87 on the O'Carroll (Ely) pedigree, was the ancestor of *O'h-Eadhradh ;* anglicised *O'Hara* and *O'Hora.*

87. Cormac Galeng : son of Teige.

88. Lughaidh (or Luy) : his son. This Lughaidh was the ancestor of *Muintir-Cormac ;* of *Muintir Dul-chonta* (" dul :" Irish, *a snare,* " canta," *to speak ;* Lat. " cano," *to sing*), anglicised "Delahunty," "Delahunt," " Hunt," and " De-la-Hunt." This Lughaidh had two brothers—1. Galinan, who was an-cestor of *O'Casey* ; and of *Muintir Owen* (of the county Galway), angli-cised *Owens ;* 2. Brocan, who was the ancestor of *O'Duana.*

89. Niacorb (meaning " the gilded chariot") : son of Lughaidh.

90. Artcorb : his son.

91. Fiochar : his son.

92. Fidhghe : his son.

93. Natfraoch : his son.

94. Breannan : his son.

95. Fionnbar : his son.

96. Dermod : his son.

97. Taithleach (" taithleach :" Irish, *handsome*) : his son.

98. Ceannfaola : his son.

99. Taithlioch (2) : his son.

100. Flaithna : his son.

101. Beice : his son.

102. Eadhradh (" eidir :" Irish, *between,* and " tu," *you*) : his son ; a quo *O'h-Eadhradh.* This Eadh-radh had a younger brother named Saorgus, who was the ancestor of *O'Gara.*

103. Magnus : his son.

---

* *O'Hara :* Sir Charles O'Hara, Baron Tyrawley, an officer distingushed in the War of the Spanish Succession, was born in the county of Mayo, in 1640 ; he was raised to the peerage in 1706. In the following year he commanded the left wing of the allied army at the battle of Almanza, 25th April, 1707 (N.S.), and remained in the Peninsula until the conclusion of the war. On his return to Ireland he took his seat in the House of Lords. He was for some time Commander-in-chief of the Army in Ireland. He died 8th June, 1724, aged 84, and was buried in St. Mary's Church, Dublin. His son James, second Baron Tyrawley (born 1690, died 1774), was created Baron of Kilmaine in 1721, for eminent military services. He attained the rank of General, filled several impor-tant diplomatic posts, and was Governor of Minorca.

† *Galeng :* From this Cormac Galeng the barony of "Gallen, ' in the county Mayo, is so called.

104. Moroch : his son.

105. Donal : his son.

106. Murtagh : his son.

107. Taithlioch, of Ormond : his son.

108. Aodh (or Hugh) : his son.

109. Conor Gud ("guda;" Irish, *a gudgeon*) ; his son ; a quo *O'Guda**.

110. Hugh O'Hara : his son ; the first who assumed this sirname. This Hugh had three sons—1. Dermod, who was ancestor of *O'Hara* buidhe [boy] ; 2. Artriabhach (or Arthur the grey-haired), ancestor of *O'Hara* reagh ; and 3. Cuconnaght, who, some say, was the ancestor of *O'Hara* of the Route.

111. Dermod : the eldest son of Hugh ; had a brother named Artriabhach.

112. Arthur : his son.

113. Donal : his son.

114. Fergal : his son.

115. Teige : his son ; who was the ancestor of *O'Hara*, of the Route.

116. John Buidhe : his son ; had a brother named Melaghlin†.

117. Roger : his son.

118. (We could not make out this name).

119. Olioll : son of No. 118.

120. Cian : his son.

121. Cormac : his son.

122. Teige : his son.

123. Teige Oge O'Hara Buidhe [boy] : his son.

The O'Haras were Chiefs of Luighne, an extensive territory in the county of Sligo, which gave name to the present barony of Leyney, in the county Sligo ; but it is to be observed that ancient Luighne was much more extensive, comprising the whole country within the diocese of Achonry. It was also known by the name of Gailenga, and these were the tribes of the race of Cormac Gaileng between whom the country was divided ; which names are preserved in the baronies of Leyney, in Sligo, and Gallan, in the county of Mayo. The O'Haras are styled by O'Dugan :

"The Kings of Luighne of the blade-armed warriors."

In A.D. 1063. Conaing O'Hara, lecturer at Clonmacnoise, died.

1147. Durcan O'Hara, a sub-chief of Leyney, died.

1157. Connor O'Hara, tanist of Leyney, and Teige MacMurtogh O'Hara, were slain ; Donough O'Hara flourished.

1183. Bec O'Hara, lord of North Conacht, was murdered by Conor Dermody, in his own house at Loch MacFeradach.

1225. Duarcan O'Hara, Teige O'Hara, and Edina, the daughter of Dermod, son of Donal O'Hara, died.

1231. Conor Gud O'Hara, died. This Conor had a son, Hugh, whose third son (see Stem above) was ancestor of O'Hara of the Ruta or Routes, in the county of Antrim, who had his chief seat at Crebilly. This Dalriadian branch of the North Conacht O'Haras, removed to the county of Antrim, with the Red Earl of Ulster, in the beginning of the 14th century.

---

* *O'Guda* : This name has been anglicised *Good, Dudgeon* and *Gudgeon ;* and is now (1887) represented by Henry Good of Aglish, Muscry, co. Cork.

† *Melaghlin* : According to some genealogists, this Melaghlin was the ancestor of *O'Hara*, of the Route.

1234. Donogh, son of Duarcan O'Hara, slew Hugh, lord of Leyney, and assumed the government of the territory ; but he was taken prisoner soon afterwards by Teige O'Connor, and slain, on his way to a place of confinement, by the son of Hugh.

1261. Cathal O'Hara and five of his people were slain by a party under the De Bermingham, in the church of St. Feichin, at Ballisodare ; and Donal O'Hara plundered the Berminghams in revenge, and slew Sefin De Bermingham, the chief's son, with the bell which he (Sefin) stole from the church of Ballisodare.

1266. Ballisodare and Carbury of Drumcliff were plundered by the English.

1278. Brian O'Dowd and Art na-Capall O'Hara, defeated the Berminghams, and slew Conor Roe Bermingham, and the two sons of Myles Mór de Bermingham.

1298. Donogh, son of Donal O'Hara, a distinguished chief, was slain by his own kinsman, Brian Carrach.

1303. A religious house of some sort was founded on the borders of the lake of Ballymote by O'Hara, lord of Leyney.

1314. Manus MacDonal O'Hara was slain by Manus MacWilliam O'Hara.

1316. Art O'Hara, lord of Leyney, was slain at the battle of Athenry, fought on the 10th of August.

1340. Rory, son of Manus O'Hara, died.

——. Murrogh, son of Mulloy O'Hara, abbot of Boyle, and bishop elect of Leyney, died.

1396. The bishop O'Hara died.

1409. Brian, son of John O'Hara, bishop of Achonry, died.

1410. Donal, son of Cormac O'Hara, heir to the lordship of Leyney, died.

1420. Teige, son of Fergal O'Hara, tanist of Leyney, died.

14—. O'Hara Roe, bishop of Achonry, died.

1435. Donal, son of Fergal Caech O'Hara, was slain.

1448. John MacJohn O'Hara, heir to the lordship of Leyney, was slain.

1537. O'Hara Riabhach was taken prisoner by O'Donnell.

1560. Teige Buidhe O'Hara, lord of Leyney, was killed by Cathal Oge O'Connor, "and there had never been in Conacht, of the race of Cormac Gaileng, a more hospitable man than he."

1582. Felix O'Hara, a Franciscan friar, was hanged and quartered by the English, on account of his faith.

1596. The two O'Haras, lords of East and West Leyney, joined the camp of O'Donnell and Theobald Burke, on the banks of the river Robe (a quo Ballinrobe), county of Mayo.

This family maintained an independent position down to the time of Oliver Cromwell.

The O'Haras had castles at Castlelough, Memlough, and other parts of Leyney.

In the times of Anne and George I., King and Queen of England, this family received the titles of Barons of Tirawley and Kilmaine, in the county of Mayo.—See note, p. 210.

The following are the names of the "O'Haras," who were Lords of Leyney, from A.D. 1023 to 1560.

Donal, slain, 1023.	Dermod, d. 1250.
Duarcan, killed, 1059.	Donal, slain, 1266.
Brian, d. 1067.	Art na-Capall, v. 1278.
Tiachleach, d. 1095.	Donal, d. 1294.
Tiachleach, *vivens*, 1134.	Donogh, slain, 1298.
Murrogh, killed, 1134.	Art, slain, 1316.
Hugh, d. 1155.	Fergal, slain, 1323.
Rory, slain, 1157.	Donal, d. 1358.
Donal, d. 1177.	Cormac, d. 1365.
Bec, slain, 1183.	Fergal, d. 1390.
Conor Gud, d. 1231.	John, v. 1420.
Hugh, slain, 1238.	———, d. 1449.
Donogh, slain, 1238.	O'Hara Riabhach, v. 1537.
MacHugh, v. 1240.	Teige Buidhe, slain, 1560.

O'HARA REAGH. (No. 2.)

ARTHUR REAGH (or Art riabhach), brother of Dermod who is No. 111 on the "O'Hara" (No. 1) pedigree, was the ancestor of *O'Hara* Reagh (or "the grey-haired.")

111. Arthur Reagh O'Hara: second son of Hugh.

112. John : his son.

113. John Oge: his son.

114. Donoch : his son.

115. William : his son.

116. Arthur (2) : his son.

117. Corc Caisiol* (" caiseal :" Irish, *a bulwark*): his son; a quo O'Caiseil, anglicised *Cassell* and *Castles*.

118. Felim : his son.

119. Dermod : his son.

120. Dermod Reagh O'Hara Reagh: his son.

---

* *Caisiol :* This word is compounded of the old Irish *cas*, "a house" (Lat., Ital., and Span. *casa*), and *iol* or *aoil*, Irish, "lime;" so that *caisiol* signifies " a building of stone and lime mortar." Whence the house or court of the Kings of Cashel was called *Caisiol*, at least as early as St. Patrick's time : a fact which proves that the old Irish knew and practised the art of building with stone and lime mortar, before the introduction of Christianity into Ireland.

According to *Giraldus Cambrensis*, the Castle of Pembroke was, by Arnulphus de Montgomery (son of the great earl of Shropshire, and son-in-law of Mortogh Mór O'Brien, King of Ireland, who died A.D. 1119), built with sods or twigs lined about with sods of earth : " ex virgis et cespite tenui." It would therefore appear that the English people at that time knew nothing of the art of building with stone and mortar ; "since," says Dr. O'Brien, "so great and opulent a man as Arnulphus did not put it in practice with regard to his Castle of Pembroke; which was the more

O'HARA. (No. 3.)

Of the Route, co. Antrim.

TEIGE O'HARA, who is No. 115 on the "O'Hara" (No. 1) pedigree, was the ancestor of *O'Hara* of the Route.

115. Teige ; son of Fergal.

116. Melaghlin : his son ; had four brothers—1. John Buidhe (ancestor of *O'Hara* Buidhe) ; 2. Cormac ; 3. Manus, and 4. Brian.

117. Manus : son of Melaghlin.

118. Cormac : his son.

119. Rory Ballach : his son.

120. John : his son.

121. Cathal (or Charles) O'Hara, of the Route : his son.

O'HARA. (No. 4.)

Of Crebilly, County Antrim.

Armorial Bearings . Same as those of "O'Hara," of O'Hara Brook, co. Antrim ; namely—*Arms* : Vert on a pale radiant or., a lion ramp. sa. *Crest :* A demi lion ramp. pean, holding betw. his paws a chaplet of oak leaves vert, acorned ppr.

RORY-BALLACH of Dundromart, co. Antrim, Esq., who is No. 119 on the "O'Hara" No. 3 (of the Route) pedigree had :

120. John (or Shane) O'Hara.

121. Cathall* (Cahall or Charles) O'Hara (d. 1639), of the Route and of "Craigbilly" (or Crebilly), co. Antrim : son of John. This Cathal m. Margaret, dau. of "Dool Oge" MacDuffy, co. Antrim, and had two sons and five daughters. One of

the daughters, Grace, m. Arthur O'Neill of Shane's Castle ; another daughter, Sheela, m. Phelim Dubh O'Neill : both of these two husbands were brothers of Sir Henry O'Neill, and sons of Shane, son of Brian O'Neill. The two sons were— 1. Cormack, 2. Sorley.

necessary, as he designed it for the preservation of the conquest he had made of the county of Pembroke. As to the old Britons, so far were they ignorant of the art of building stone work, that when Ninian, who converted the southern Picts, built his church of stone and lime mortar, they called it *candida casa* or 'white house ;" being the first structure of the kind, as Bede observes, that was seen in Britain."

* *Cathal :* During the reigns of the Stewart Kings of England, there were frequent investigations into property tenures. These investigations are termed *Inquisitiones.* The originals of these are preserved in the Record Office, Dublin. A calendar of such as referred to Ulster was published by the Record Commissioners ; the publication was called *Inquisitiones Ultoniæ.* One of these Inquisitions taken in Carrickfergus, on the 15th August, 1640, of which the following is a translation from the original Latin, finds that :

"Cahall O'Hara was seized in fee of the manor, castle, town, and land of Crebilly, Gannanaghmagherky, Ballykeele, Tannagoe, Ballynemarlagh, Ballynelessan, Ballycrankill, Ballytullagh, Ballydonevaddin, Ballydirban, Crossneslerny, Grannagh, Slate, Tullaghgarley, Ballyoffey, Ballygregagh, Bally . . . Kildoney, and a water mill, Aghecleach, Semnenerne, Grenagh, Killgad, Tawnaghbrack, parcels of the manor of Crebilly, and two fairs at the town of Crebilly foresaid.—

"In Ballymicknilly 120 acres, Ballynegathel 120 acres, Moyawer 60 acres . . . 60 acres, Clontefenan 60 acres, Ballyviely 60 acres, in Loghgile otherwise Tullelosse and Dromheilen 30 acres, and Leganlie and Corkee 30 acres, all which last mentioned premises lie in the Tuagh (district) of Loghgyle within the barony of Dunluce. Being

I. Cormac, of whom presently.

II. Sorley (or "Surrell"), who m. Mary, dau. of John, son of Brian O'Neill (? sister of his brothers-in-law), and had three sons :—1. Owen, 2. Hugh, 3. Ceallach, of whom hereafter.

122. Cormack : elder son of Cathal ; m. Margaret, dau. of Thomas Walsh of Curnemony (? Carnmony), and had :

123. Teige, who was living in 1689. This Teige m. and had four sons :

I. John, who m. Miss Rowe, and d.s.p. ; left estates to the Rowes,

who sold their claim to Oliver and Henry O'Hara, on behalf of their nephew Henry, son of their second brother Charles.

II. Charles : second son of Teige ; of whom presently.

III. Oliver, who d. s. p., left personal estate to his nephew Bernard O'Neill of Leminary, who was ultimately sold out.

IV. Henry, of Claggin, who m. Margaret Jameison, and had two sons, 1. Henry, 2. Oliver :

I. Henry : the elder son of Henry of Claggin ; m., first,

so seized, said Cahall, on the 20th of October, in the 8th year of the present reign by his deed granted the premises to Arthur . . . Gilladuffe O'Cahan, of Doneseverioke (Dunseverick), John Oge Stewart, of Glenarm, and James McGorry McHenry, of Lochan, and their heirs, for a certain use mentioned in said deed. Foresaid Cahall O'Hara by another deed bearing date 11th August, 1638, demised to Cahall O'Hara, of Slate, his executors and assigns the office of Seneschal of Court Leet and Court Baron of foresaid manor, along with the rents of a fair and market, for the term of 99 years, as by deed appears, the tenor of which follows in the original.

"Charles the present King, by his letters patent bearing date 1st of December, in the 9th year of his reign, granted to foresaid Cahall to alienate the premises mentioned in the original.

"Foresaid Cahall by his deed dated 27th August, 1623, to Donal Boy O'Hara, of Loghgyle, his executors and assigns, one-half of the townland called by the name of Quarter . . . . &c., for a term of 41 years, as by the said deed, the tenor of which follows in the original appears.

"Foresaid Cahall O'Hara, by another deed, dated 3rd February, 1631, demised to Patrick McDonogh Boy O'Hara, his executors and assigns, parcels of the foresaid as by his deed the tenor of which follows in the original appears.

"Foresaid Cahall O'Hara, by his deed bearing date 14th April, 1638, granted to Teige O'Hara, his executors and assigns, the said townlands of Ballytullygarley, Bally-crankill, Ballynelessane, Ballylissecossane, Ballytulleghenesane, Ballecarnenck . . . . . . Ballybregagh, and . . . . , as by his deed, the tenor of which follows in the original, appears.

"Foresaid Cahall O'Hara died on the 22nd of March, 1639, Teige O'Hara is his great-grandson and heir, and foresaid Teige then was of full age and married. Foresaid are held of the King by Knights' service."

In reference to this Inquisition the reader will observe that the spelling of the townlands is very quaint, having been written by English law clerks, who did not know how to spell the Irish words. The mark . . . . indicates where in the original Inquisition the word or words are illegible. The first set of townlands mentioned are in the Crebilly manor, and most of the present names which those townlands bear occur in Laverty's, Vol. III., of *Down and Conor*.

The second set of townlands are in the manor of Loughguile which was sold under the provisions of an Act of Parliament early in last century to a Mr. McCartney, ancestor of Lord McCartney, who was ambassador to China. The modern names of the townlands in the Loughguile estate are Ballynagashel, Ballyveeley, Clontyfinnan, Moyaver, Corkey, Loughguile, Ballybradden and Tully.

Acres in the Inquisition is most misleading, as it is only a sort of approximation of extent ; frequently what is entered in an Inquisition as 30 acres, will really be 200 acres.

"Carrickfergus, 15th August, 1640, Teige O'Hara, of Crebilly, was seized in fee of he townland of Clontyfenane, the half townland of Balleville, Ballauraddan, otherwise

Charity Chichester; and, secondly, Anne Magennis, and had two sons—1. Alexander, 2. Henry:

I. Alexander m. Emma Jones, and had Henry:

    I. Henry m. Letitia Jones, and had Henry-Jones O'Hara:

        I. Henry-Jones O'Hara, d. s. p. at Torquay. His remains were removed to the family vault in the graveyard of Kells Abbey, co. Antrim ; where a monument* was in 1854 erected to his memory. This branch is now extinct.

II. Henry: second son of Henry: no issue recorded.

II. Oliver : second son of Henry, of Claggin ; married Honoria McManus, and had—1. Hester, 2. John, 3. Henry, 4. Rawdon:

    I. Hester, the last of her branch, died in advanced age, after 1854 ; it was this Hester who erected the monument above mentioned (see Note "Monument," *infra*.)

    II. John, a lieutenant in the 68th regiment of the line, d. s. p. in the West Indies.

    III. Henry, an adjutant in the East India Co.'s Service, d. s. p. in the East Indies.

    IV. Rawdon : the fourth child of Oliver ; also an adjutant in the East India Co.'s Service, fell at Kolwaga. This branch of the family is also extinct.

Renlec, and Tullymaccavill, in the barony of Dunluce, containing 60 messuages, 60 tofts, 60 gardens, 600 acres of arable land, 600 acres of pasture, 120 acres of meadow, 300 acres of moor, 300 acres of marsh, and 300 acres of underwood. So being seized raised a fine in the 15th year of the present reign, to Cahall O'Hara, of Slatte, and Tyrell O'Hara, of Townebrack (Tawnabrack), and their heirs in perpetuity. Foresaid are held of the King by Knights' service."

This Inquisition refers to the Loughguile estate, and refers evidently to a trust deed.

* *Monument :* The following is a copy of an inscription on a monument in the graveyard of Kells Abbey, co. Antrim :—

"This monument is erected in the year of our Lord 1854, by Hester O'Hara, daughter of Oliver O'Hara, and his wife, Honoria McManus, the only lineal survivor of the ancient family of O'Hara, of the Route and Crebilly. Her ancestors have been interred in this vault for several generations ; and previously at Loughguile, near where the ancient residence stood. Among these ancestors have been her grandfather, Henry O'Hara, of Claggin, youngest son of Teige O'Hara, of the Route and Crebilly, and heir presumptive of his nephew, Henry Hutchinson O'Hara, of Crebilly. Her grandmother, Margaret Jameison ; their son, Henry O'Hara, his first wife, Charity Chichester, and his widow, Ann Magennis, their son, Oliver O'Hara, his widow, Honoria McManus, also Mary O'Hara, alias O'Neill, widow of their grandson, Henry O'Hara, buried in Wexford, their grandson, Alexander O'Hara, and his wife, Emma Jones, their great-grandson, Henry O'Hara, and his widow, Letitia Jones, and Henry Jones O'Hara, son of said Henry and Letitia, who died at Torquay, and whose remains were removed hither for interment.

"John, Henry, and Rawdon O'Hara were grandsons of Henry O'Hara, of Claggin, and brothers to Hester O'Hara, who erected this monument. The first of them a lieutenant in the 68th regiment of the line, died in the West Indies ; the second, adjutant in the East India service, died in the East Indies ; the third an adjutant in the same service fell at Kolwaga. Marcus, great-grandson of the same Henry, fell at the storming of St. Sebastian.

"Verily, verily, I say, &c. . . . . John, v. 25."

This inscription is a curiosity of literary composition ; it seems to have been written by Hester O'Hara when she had arrived at senility.

124. Charles : second son of Teige, m. and had :

125. Henry: who m. Mrs. Hamilton (widow of — Hamilton, of Portglenone), daughter of Right Rev. Dr. Hutchinson, Bishop of Down and Connor. That lady had by her first marriage a son, Charles Hamilton ; to Henry O'Hara she bore Henry-Hutchinson O'Hara, who is No. 126 on this pedigree.

126. Henry-Hutchinson O'Hara: son of Henry ; succeeded his father *circa*, 1745, and d. s. p. ; leaving by his Will (dated A.D. 1759) the Crebilly and other estates to Charles Hamilton's son, John Hamilton (*i.e.* son of Charles Hamilton of Portglenone), thus passing by the O'Haras of Claggin, the descendants of his (Henry-Hutchinson O'Hara's) grand-uncle Henry, and the other collateral branches, even leaving the remainder to O'Hara, of O'Hara-Brook, whose family name was *Tate* (see O'Laverty's *Down and Connor*, Vol. III., p. 427). Said John Hamilton (b. *circa* 1755 or 1757) then added " O'Hara" to his name. He m. a young French Catholic lady, Madeleine Collet. The marriage ceremony was performed by the Rev. Hugh O'Devlin, P.P., of Ballymena, in the year 1787 ; but as under the Penal Laws this marriage was illegal—" O'Hara" being a Protestant—they were re-married in Dumfries, Scotland, according to Scotch law. The issue by this marriage was two sons who died without issue. John Hamilton " O'Hara" repudiated this wife, and, in A.D. 1791, married Miss Jackson, dau. of Right Hon. R. Jackson, niece of Lord O'Neill, and sister-in-law of the Right Rev. Dr. Alexander, Protestant Bishop of Down and Connor. This second wife of John Hamilton " O'Hara," d. in 1802 without issue. In 1819, said Hamil-

ton " O'Hara" m. Miss Duffin, dau. of Mr. Duffin, one of his tenants ; she bore him two children—1. Henry-Hutchinson - Hamilton " O'Hara," 2. Mary-Hamilton " O'Hara."

John-Hamilton " O'Hara" d. in 1822. After his death, his eldest son by the first wife—his only wife in fact—sought, on the strength of the Scotch marriage, to eject by law the son by the last marriage. The case was tried in Carrickfergus on the 26th July, 1825. He was not successful: the representative of Henry Hutchinson Hamilton " O'Hara" obtained the verdict, and he came into possession, when, in 1840, or thereabouts, he became of age ; he d. s. p., and his sister (Mrs. Genl. Wardlaw), was in 1885 in possession of Crebilly Manor and Estates.

Commencing with Sorley (or " Surrell"), the second son of Cathal O'Hara, who is No. 121 on this family genealogy, the following is the pedigree :

122. Sorley : second son of Cathal, m. Mary, dau. of John, son of Brian O'Neill, and had three sons—1. Owen, 2. Hugh, 3. Ceallach.

123. Owen m. and had Teige.

124. Teige m. and had Brian.

125. Brian m. and had Brian (or Bernard).

126. Bernard, b. *circa* 1765. In consequence of the troublous times connected with the Irish Insurrection of 1798, with which he was accused of being identified, this Bernard retired to Scotland; he afterwards returned to Ireland, and settled at Saintfield, co. Down, where he d. in 1845 ; he is buried at Kilcairn, near Saintfield. He was twice m. ; no issue by the second marriage. His children by the first marriage were—1. Patrick, 2. John, 3. Mary, 4. Bridget :

I. Patrick (b. 1793), of whom presently.

II. John.

III. Mary, who m. Mr. Hamilton.

IV. Bridget, who married Mr. MacMullen.

127. Patrick O'Hara (b. 1793): son of Bernard; was twice m., first, to Margaret McGenniss, and had:—1. Mary, living in 1885; 2. Margaret, d. 20th July, 1830; 3. Another Margaret, who died in infancy, 12th August, 1830; 4. Catherine, died 20th Oct., 1831; 5. Patrick, died 14th July, 1831; 6. Bernard. d. 13th Sept., 1832; 7. John, died 30th Aug., 1838; 8. Helen, b. at Paisley, Scotland, in 1836, d. at Montreal, Canada, in 1852. Patrick O'Hara, m., secondly, at St. Merrin's Church, Paisley, Scotland, by Rev. John Carolan, to Mary McGee, daughter of Richard McGee and Margary McBride, his wife (both of the co. Donegal), and had :

I. Catherine, d. in infancy.

II. Patrick, b. 1846, d. 1847.

III. William-Jerrold, of whom presently.

IV. Jane, b. 1850, d. 1854.

V. John-Paul, b. 29th June, 1852, living in 1885; m. Mary Wall, and had:—1. Florence-Mary-May, d. ; 2. Catherine, 3. Annie, 4. Helen-Agnes; 5. John-Paul, d. 1884.

128. William-Jerrold O'Hara, of Montreal, Canada; son of Patrick; b. 14th April, 1848, at Montreal, and living in 1887 ; m., 2nd Oct., 1877, Annie - Elizabeth, third daughter of Arthur McFaul, Esq., of Prescott, Ontario, Canada (formerly of the co. Antrim, Ireland), and had :

I. Grace - Eveleen - Annie -Marie, living in 1885.

This William-Jerrold O'Hara is the present representative of the ancient family of O'Hara of the Route and Craigbilly, co. Antrim.

O'HEA.
Chiefs of Muscry-Luachra.

Arms : A dexter arm lying fessways, couped below the elbow, vested gu. turned up of the first, grasping in the hand a sword in pale entwined with a serpent descending all ppr.

THE *O'h-Aodha* family (anglicised *O'Hea, Hay, Hayes,* and *Hughes*) derives its name and descent from Aodh (or Hugh), the ninth son of Cas, who is No. 91 on the "O'Brien, Kings of Thomond" pedigree. They were formerly Chiefs of Muscry-Luachra, a territory in the barony of Coshlea, co. Limerick, whence a branch of the sept removed into Carbry, in Cork, where they became possessed of the lands called Pobble-O'Hea. Dr. O'Donovan says that Muscry-Luachra bordered on Sliabh Luachra, in Kerry ; and that the river Avonmore had its source in this district.

O'Heerin mentions the O'Heas, thus :

> " O'Hea, the bestower of cattle,
> Enjoys the wide-extending Muscraighe-Luachra ;
> The clan of the land of sweet songs,
> Inhabit along the stream famed for salmon."

We learn that Brian O'Hea, erenach of the *Egles Beg* of Clonmacnoise, died, 986. Murray O'Hea, lord of Muscry-Luachra, died, 1009. Flan

O'Hea, successor of St. Enda of Ara, died, 1110. Felix O'Hea, a Cistercian monk, was appointed to the See of Lismore, on the death of Giolla-Chriost (or Christian) O'Conarchy, in 1179; he died in 1217, and was interred in the church of St. Carthach, at Lismore.

Timoleague is the burial place of the Carbery O'Heas, where a monument has been erected over their tomb.

The chief representative of the Desmond O'Heas in the middle of the 17th century was James O'Hea, of Gleann-a-Rouska; whose daughter, Ellen, by his wife, Joanna, daughter of William Gallwey (a descendant of the great Gallwey of Kinsale), was married to William O'Brien of Seartbarry, by whom she had a daughter, Joanna, who was grandmother (by whom the mother of Mrs. Margaret Fitzgerald) of the House of Barry of Buttevant, and who lived to the age of 125 years, retaining her faculties to within three hours of her death.

Another representative of this tribe was Cornelius O'Hea, of West Barry-Roe, living in 1720; whose daughter, Helen, married James Barry, of Mount Barry, co. Cork, son of William FitzJames Barry, by his wife, Ellen, dau. of Mathew MacThomas O'Hea, of Kilkeiran, son of James Barry, of Ballymacroheen, by his wife, Catherine, dau. of David Barry Bán, son of James Barry of Lislee (near Court MacSherry), who commanded 150 men in Barryroe in the year 1641; for which his estates were confiscated and granted to King James II. These lands were purchased from the Government, at Chichester House sale in Dublin, at the beginning of the last century, by Mr. Von Homrigh, who sold them to the Rev. Dr. Synge, by whose representatives they are now held.

We learn that the chief representatives of this ancient family are (in 1887):—

John O'Hea, Woodfield, Lisavaird, Clonakilty.
Michael O'Hea, Keelrovane, do. do.
James O'Hea, Baltinakin, Kilbrittain.
Rev. John O'Hea, The Square, Clonakilty.
James O'Hea, Lissycrimeen, Bullerstown, Bandon; and the Rev. Jeremiah O'Hea, C.C., Bantry.
Mr. Patrick O'Hea, Solicitor, 44 Grand Parade, Cork, is, we learn, also a scion of the Carbery sept of O'Hea.

O'HERLIHY.

Of Ballyworny, County Cork.

Arms: Gu. a chev. ar. betw. three owls ppr.

WILLIAM O'HIERLYHY, of Ballyworny, co. Cork, had:
2. Daniel, who had:
3. William, who had:
4. Daniel, who d. 2 Mar., 1637.
This Daniel m. twice; his first wife

was Giles, dau. of Art O'Leary, by whom he had four sons:
I. William.
II. Teige.
III. Daniel.
IV. Thomas.

The second wife of Daniel was Sheela, dau. of Maelmor Mahony, by whom he had four sons :

V. Connor.
VI. Maurice.

VII. Donogh.
VIII. David.

5. William O'Herlihy : eldest son of Daniel.

O'HOGAN.

(See "Hogan," page 96, *ante*.)

BESIDES the Armorial Bearings assigned to this family in p. 96, they had :
Arms: Ar. on a chev. sa. three martlets of the field. *Crest :* An ostrich's head betw. two feathers or.

COSGRACH, second son of Lorcan, who is No. 103 on the "O'Brien," Kings of Thomond Stem, was the ancestor of this family. They were Chiefs of Crioch Cian, a territory in the principality of Ormond, and had a fortified residence at Ardcrony, a parish in the barony of Lower Ormond ; and another at Ballylusky, in the same territory. On a stone slab in the old castle of Beechwood, is the date 1594, with the initials O. H. ; from which it would appear that this was one of the residences of the O'Hogans, princes of Crioch Cian, from whom it passed to the Tolers. It would appear that a branch of this family settled in the county of Kildare soon after the Anglo-Norman Invasion, as a Dominican friary had been founded at Athy, by some members of the family, in 1253.

O'Heerin says :—

> "O'Hogan of Crich Cian rules over
> Clan Ionmanain of the fair lands."

In 1281, Mathew O'Hogan, a native of Ballyhogan, dean of Killaloe, who was advanced to that see in 1267, died, and was interred in the Dominican convent at Limerick. He was succeeded by his kinsman, Maurice O'Hogan, who was consecrated in 1282 ; who governed his see for seventeen years ; and, dying, was interred in the cathedral. Thomas O'Hogan, canon of Killaloe, was consecrated bishop of that see in 1343. He died in the month of October, 1354, and was interred in the Dominican friary of Nenagh. Richard O'Hogan, a native of Limerick, a Franciscan friar, was consecrated bishop of Killaloe in 1525. His translation to Clonmacnoise, where he died in 1538, is the last record we have of this ancient family.

O'HURLEY.* (No. 1.)

Lords of Knocklong.

THE *O'h-Urthailé*† or *O'Hurley* family derive their sirname and descent from Urthailé Ard, son of Heber (of the race of Brenan Ban), son of Blad, son of Cas (a quo *Dal Cas* or the *Dalcassians*), son of Conall Eachluath, who is No. 90 on the " O'Brien" (of Thomond) genealogy. The O'Hurleys were formerly Chiefs of the territory forming the parish of Knocklong, in the barony of Costlea, county of Limerick, where the ruins of their castle of Knocklong, and of an old church, the foundation of this family, still exist; of the parish of Kilruane, in the barony of Lower Ormond, county of Tipperary, where the ruins of their ancient castle of Rath-Hurly may be seen; of the country forming the parish of Kilcullane, barony of Small county, county of Limerick, where they erected the castle of Kilcullane in 1464; of the parish of Kilnelonahan, in the baronies of Coshma and Pubblebrien, same county, where Dermod O'Hurley, Chief of his Clan, built a strong castle in the early part of the 15th century; and (as we are informed by Giolla na-Neev O'Heerin) of the territory of Triocha-Hy-Bloid, the situation of which cannot now be correctly ascertained.

Commencing with Dermod na Darach, the following is the family pedigree:

1. Dermod na Darach.	11. William : his son.
2. Donogh an Caladh : his son.	12. Heber : his son.
3. Donal Oge : his son.	13. Urthaile : his son.
4. Murchadh Mór : his son.	14. Tadg (or Teige) : his son.
5. John Mór : his son.	15. Donogh Airm : his son.
6. Connor an Locha : his son.	16. Cormac : his son.
7. Thomas : his son.	17. Teige : his son.
8. Raghnal : his son.	18. William Ganaig : his son.
9. Philip : his son.	19. Cormac : his son.
10. Maurice : his son.	20. Donal : his son.

* *O'Hurley* : Dermot O'Hurley, Archbishop of Cashel, was born near Limerick, about 1519. Educated for the priesthood, he resided at Louvain for fifteen years, and held the chair of Canon Law at Rheims for four years. On the 11th September, 1581, he was appointed by Pope Gregory XIII. to the See of Cashel. For two years government spies sought opportunities to seize him, but their plans were frustrated by the fidelity of his co-religionists. At length he was arrested and brought before the Privy Council for examination. He was horribly tortured. The executioners placed the Archbishop's feet and calves in tin boots filled with oil; they then fastened his feet in wooden shackles or stocks, and placed fire under them. The boiling oil so penetrated the feet and legs that morsels of the skin, and even flesh, fell off and left the bone bare. The Archbishop resolutely refused to purchase a cessation of his torments by acknowledging the Queen's supremacy in matters of religion. An end was put to his sufferings by his being hanged on a tree outside Dublin, 19th June, 1584. He was buried in St. Kevin's, Dublin.

† *O'h-Urthailé :* For an *O'h-Urthuile* family, see No. 99 on the "MacNamara" (No. 1) Genealogy. *O'h-Urthuile* also has been anglicised *O'Hurley*, etc.

From DONAL No. 20 Descended :

1. Teige O'Hurley, Chief of his name, and lord of Knocklong: father of:

2. Dermod, of Knocklong, who had a daughter Juliana (who was m. to Edmund Oge de Courcy, of Kinsale, by whom she had John, the 18th Baron of Kinsale), and two sons:—1. John; 2. Thomas.

3. Thomas, of Knocklong: younger son of Dermod ; attended Perrott's memorable Parliament of 1585. Had two sons—1. Randal, founder of Ballinacarrig Castle ; 2. Maurice.

4. Maurice of Knocklong: second son of Thomas, whose Will, dated 1634, is in the Public Record Office, Dublin. In 1601, he obtained a Patent for a weekly market to be held at Knocklong on Tuesdays ; and two fairs each year, to be held on the 28th of May and 1st of October. He m. twice : first, Racia Thornton, who d. s. p. ; and secondly, Grania, dau. of O'Hogan, by whom he had a son, Sir Thomas of Knocklong, of whom presently. This Maurice d. *circa* 1632, and was interred in the churchyard of Emly, where a slab four feet long by two and a half feet in breadth, exhibiting the inscription,* given in foot Note, was erected to his memory. The inscription is in relief; and at the lower corner of the slab is carved an old tree, in allusion to the ancient seal of Knocklong, the old name of which was *Cnoc-na-Daraigh*, i.e. the "Hill of Oaks."

5. Sir Thomas of Knocklong: son of Maurice ; m. Joanna, dau. of John Brown, of Mount Brown, county of Limerick, and had :

I. Sir Maurice, of whom presently.

II. John, who had, besides three daughters, a son John, who had a son John, who was a Colonel in the army of King James II., King of England.

I. Catherine, who m. Pierce, Lord Dunboyne.

II. Anne, who married Daniel O'Mulryan.

III. Grace, who m. Walter Bourke.

IV. Elinora, who m. David Barry, of Rahinisky, by whom she had

* *Inscription* : The following is a true copy of that inscription :

"Per illustris Dominus D. Mauritius Hurleus Armiger Monumentum, Hoc sibi sisq. charissimus conjugibus Graniæ Hoganæ et Kaciæ Thorentonæ totiq. posteritati posuit elaborariq. fecit.
An. Di. 1632.
Hic jacet Hospitii, columen, pretatis Asylum,
Ingenio clarus, clarus et eloquio,
Laus patrice, litum supssor, pacis amator,
Regula justitiæ, religiones ebur,
Hostibus Hurleus fuit hostis, amicus
Mauricius moderans tempora temporibus,
Fax fidei, fulerum miserorum, gemma vivorum,
Stemmatis antiqui gloria magna sui.
Huic decus, huic probitas, suis corporis integra mille
Naturæ dotes unicus omne capit.
Vixisti mundo, vives in sæcula vivis,
Fortuna felix prole perexinia,
Ergo vive Deo vivo cui vivere vita est
Sic tibi dante Deo vita prennis erit.
Sumptibus Hurlæi fabricarunt hoc Monumentum,
Patricius Kerryl, Nicholaus Cowly."

Edmund, Queen Anne's foster-father.

6. Sir Maurice, of Knocklong, who was a Member of the "Supreme Council" of Kilkenny, in 1647. His estates were seized by Cromwell, who transplanted the old Baronet to Galway, where he d. in 1683. His son:

7. Sir William sat in King James's Parliament, of 1689, as M.P. for Kilmallock. He m. Mary,

dau. of Colonel Blount (by his wife, the sister of Walter Bourke above mentioned), and had:

8. Sir John Hurley, who, in 1714, was arrested in Dublin, on a charge of having raised a body of troops for the "Pretender." He made his escape from prison, but of his subsequent career we know nothing. Had a son John. The descendants of this John lived at Drumacoo, near Kinvara, in 1840.

O'HURLEY. (No. 2.)

Of Ballinacarriga.

RANDAL: son of Thomas O'Hurley, who is No. 3 on the foregoing genealogy, and who attended Perrott's Parliament in 1585, erected the Castle of Ballinacarrig, near Dunmanway, in the county of Cork. He m. Catherine Collins, dau. of O'Collins, a Chief in Carbery, and had:

5. Randal Oge Dubh, who married Ellen de Courcy, dau. of John, 18th Baron of Kinsale, and had:

6. Randal Oge Beagh, who was outlawed by the English in 1641. He m. twice: first, a dau. of Teige Oursie MacCarthy, of Dunmanway, by whom he had:

I. Randal.

His second wife was the widow of Gerald, 19th Lord of Kinsale, by whom he had:

II. "Dermond," mentioned in the "Depositions" made in 1641.

III. Daniel, called "of Dromgarra."

7. Randal: the eldest son of Randal Oge Beg; m. his cousin Ellen Collins, and had issue by her six sons—two were priests, two were

killed in war by the English, and two left issue. This Randal Oge Beg was "outlawed" with his father in 1641.

8. Randal of Ballinacarriga: his eldest son; married, and had issue:— his one dau. Angelina m. to Cormac Glas MacCarthy, who is No. 125 on the MacCarthy Glas pedigree, p. 134.

9. Randal: his son; married and had issue.

10. Randal: his son; had three sons — Randal Oge, Teige, and Finghin.

11. Randal Oge: his son; married, and had issue:—

I. John, who emigrated to America with his family in or about 1810.

II. William, of whom presently.

III. Jeremiah, m. and had issue.

12. William: son of Randal Oge; m. and had issue:

I. James; and

II. Jeremiah, who married a Miss D'Esmond, and had issue, Richard, who emigrated; other sons died.

13. James: his son; m. a Miss D'Esmond, and had issue.

I. William.

II. Anne, m. to Richard Brad-field, of Kilowen, on the river Bandon, has issue.

III. Ellen, m. to Timothy O'Sul-livan, parish of Murragh, and has issue.

14. William O'Hurley, of Ballina-carriga : only son of James ; m. Miss Annie O'Crowley, living in 1887, and has issue by her:

I. James.
II. Mary.
III. Jeremiah.
IV. John.
V. Daniel.
VI. Ellen.
VII. William.
VIII. Hannah.
IX. Timothy ; and
X. Annie.

15. James : son of William O'Hur-ley of Ballinacarriga.

This family is distinguished as *Na-Carriga*, or heirs to the Ballina-carriga Castle estates.

12. Jeremiah ; the third son of Randal Oge ; m. and had issue.

13. James : his eldest son ; m. Julia D'Esmond ; lived at Murragh, and afterwards at Farranavane, north of Bandon ; had issue :

I. Jeremiah, d. s. p.

II. James, of whom below.

III. Humphry, who emigrated to America.

IV. Jeremiah of Murragh, near Palace Anne, m. a Miss But-timer, and has fourteen sons and six daus. ; living in 1887.

V. William emigrated to America.

VI. Maurice, of Farranavane, m. Joanna Canty, and has issue by her—James, Denis, Hum-phry, Julia, Mary-Anne, Mar-garet, and Joanna.

VII. Mary, m. Jeremiah O'Sulli-van (O'Sullivan *Mór* family), of Scartnamuck, north of Bandon, and has issue living in 1887—Kate, Julia, Ellen, Daniel, Mary-Anne, James, Timothy, Annie, and Jeremiah.

14. James O'Hurley, of Farrana-vane : his son ; m. Kate Kehely of Farranthomas, and has had issue by her—James (d. unm.), Mathew, Humphry, Julia, Mary-Anne, Jeremiah, Maurice, and Kate.

15. Mathew O'Hurley : his son.

(This branch of the family is also known as *Na-Carriga*.)

O'HURLEY. (No. 3.)

Of Tralee.

John O'Hurley, a younger son of Sir Thomas, who (see p. 222) is No. 5 on the Knocklong branch of this family, had:

7. John, a Colonel in the Army of King James II., who had:

8. Charles, who had :

9. Donogh, who m. Anne, dau. of Robert Blenerhassett (by his wife Avice Conway), and had five sons:

I. Charles, of whom presently.

II. Thomas, who m. the dau. of Thomas Blenerhassett.
III. John.
IV. Donogh.
V. William.
And three daughters :
I. Alice.
II. Avice.
III. Sarah.
10. Charles, who had :
11. John, who had two sons :

I. The Rev. R. C. Hurley, V.G.
II. John.
12. John: second son of John; was a Clerk of the Crown for the co. of Cork, and, at his decease (in 185—) left two sons:
   I. John, of Fenit.
   II. Robert.
13. Robert Conway O'Hurley:

second son of John. Was twice married; first, to a dau. of Arthur Blennerhassett, of Ballyseedy; and, secondly, to Miss Colleton, dau. of Sir R. Colleton, Bart. This Robert was alive in 1865, was a Barrister-at-Law, and a Member of the Munster Bar.

O'KEEFFE.* (No. 1.)

Chiefs of Fermoy, and more lately of Pobble O'Keeffe.

Arms: Vert a lion ramp. or. in chief two dexter hands couped at the **wrist** erect and apaumée of the last. *Crest:* A griffin pass. or, holding in the dexter claw a sword ppr.

ÆNEAS, the first Christian King of Munster, who is No. 91 on the "Line of Heber," p. 70, had a son named Eochaidh (or Eocha) Areamh, also called Eocha Fionn, who was the third Christian King of Munster, and the ancestor of *O'Caoimhe* (by some written *O'Cefada*); anglicised *O'Keeffe* and *Keeffe.*

91. Æneas: the first Christian King of Munster.
92. Eocha Areamh: his son; the third Christian King.
93. Criomthan-Sreabh: his son; the fourth Christian King. This Criomthan had five sons—1. Cairbre Crom, who was the seventh Christian King; 2. Aodh Crom, the tenth Christian King; 3. Cormac; 4. Fiachra; and 5. Scannall.
94. Cairbre Crom: son of Criomthan-Sreabh.
95. Aodh: his son.
96. Cathal: his son.
97. Cugan Mathair: his son.
98. Fionghin: his son.
99. Cathal Ginasth: his son.
100. Art: his son.
101. Gorman: his son.
102. Fionghin Cingegan: his son.
103. Caomh ("caomh:" Irish,

gentle; Ar. "kom," noble; Lat. "com-is"): his son; a quo *O'Caoimhe*; living in 950.
104. Cathal: his son.
105. Donogh: his son.
106. Aodh: his son; first assumed the sirname *O'Keeffe.*
107. Donal: his son.
108. Fionghin: his son.
109. Aodh: his son.
110. Fionghin: his son.
111. Mahon: his son.
112. Eoghan: his son.
113. Connor: his son.
114. Art: his son.
115. Donal: his son.
116. Art: his son.
117. Donal: his son.
118. Mahon: his son.
119. Art: his son.
120. Donal: his son.
121. Art: his son; m. Elana, dau.

---

* *O'Keeffe*: This family originally possessed the southern half of ancient *Feara Muighe* (now "Fermoy"), from which they were driven after the English invasion, when they settled at Duhallow, in the district known as *Pobble O'Keeffe.*

of Connor, son of Donogh MacTeige Roe O'Callaghan, by whom (who d. 18th Oct., 1593) he left issue :— 1. Art Oge ; 2. Manus, who m. the dau. of Sir Donogh MacCarthy Riabhach ; 3. Aodh ; 4. Donal; and a dau. who m. Murrogh na-Mort McSweeney. This Art, who died 21st March, 1582, was " seized in fee of the castle, town, and lands of Dromagh, containing one quarter of land of Cullyne, of one quarter of land of Dwargan, and one quarter of Claragh, all situate, lying, and being in the county of Cork, and barony of Duhallow, and held from the queen *in capite.*

122. Art Oge: his son; b. A.D. 1547, and d. 31st May, 1610 ; m. Honoria, dau. of Dermod MacConal MacCarthy of Inniskean, in Carbry (by his wife Eleanor, dau. of Sir Cormac MacCarthy Riabhach), by whom he left issue :—1. Manus ; 2. Donal, of Ballymacquirk; 3. Donagh, of Cuilbeggan, who died 14th May, 1614, leaving a son Donal, b. 1610.

123. Manus : son of Art Oge (of Dromagh); b. 1567; m. and left issue :—1. Donal; 2. Aodh. This Manus was styled " chief of his nacion."

124. Donal of Dromagh : his son ; married thrice : 1st, the dau. of his kinsman Art O'Keeffe ; 2ndly, the dau. of Thomas Creagh of Limerick ; and 3rdly, a dau. of Lord Viscount Roche, of Fermoy, by whom he had issue :—1. Donal ; 2. Aodh ; 3. Connor ; 4. Eleanor; 5. Caomh ; and 6. Art.

125. Donal of Dromagh : his son ; was a member of the " Catholic Convention" of 1647, and had the command of a company of Foot in the Irish army. He m. Johanna Everett, *alias* Butler, by whom he had a son :

126. Donal of Dromagh, who commanded a company of Foot in the service of James II. of England, at Aughrim, where he was slain. He m. twice; 1st, Elizabeth Roche ; and 2ndly, Anne, dau. of Dominick Sarsfield, of Cork, by whom he had a son :

127. Donal Oge, who was an ensign in Boiseleau's infantry, and distinguished himself on many a far foreign field from Dunkirk to Belgrade ; m. and had issue :—1. Denis ; 2. Caemh (of Bandon); 3. Arthur ; and 4. Mary Anne.

128. Arthur : his son : m. the dau. of Eoghan MacSweeney, by whom he had a son :

129. Daniel (of Bandon). This Daniel m. Mary, dau. of Cornelius O'Delany, by whom he had issue :— 1. Arthur, 2. Caemh, 3. Cornelius, 4. William, 5. Joseph, and 6. Francis.

130. Arthur : his son (who died Nov. 5th, 1828); married and had issue :—1. Caemh, 2. Eoghan, and 3. Arthur.

O'KEEFFE. (No. 2.)

Of Ballymacquirk.

123. DONAL (or Daniel): second son of Art Oge, who is No. 122 on the foregoing ("O'Keeffe") pedigree; commanded a company of foot in the battle of Knockinross, in 1641. He m. Mary, dau. of Eoghan Vera O'Sullivan, of Cappanacusha, in the county of Kerry, by whom he left

issue—1. Finghin; 2. Art, who followed the fortunes of Charles II., King of England, and in whose service he commanded a company of foot, and in whose Declaration of Royal gratitude he had a proviso made for him; and 3. Denis, whose son Connor became Lord Bishop of Limerick, and founded three Bourses in the College of Lombards in Paris, for the education of three Catholic clergymen.

124. Finghin: his son; m. Honoria, dau. of Brian O'Connor-Kerry; he d. in A.D. 1667.

125. Donal: his son; m. Margaret, dau. of Nicholas Hutson of Newmarket, in the county of Cork. This Donal raised a company of foot for King James II., in whose service he fought and fell at Aughrim.

126. Arthur: his son; slain at Aughrim; m. and left issue:—1. Hutson; 2. Nicholas, who followed James II. to France; and 3. a daughter.

127. Hutson: his son; settled in Religny, in the province of Campagne, in France, where he m. Reine Jacquemart, by whom he had an only dau. Jane.

128. Jane O'Keeffe: his dau.; in 1738, m. Gabriel Deville. She d. in 1768, leaving issue:

129. Captain Nicholas Gabriel Deville; born March 8th, 1741. This Nicholas, who was Secretary to his "Most Christian Majesty," m. Maria Regina Faucheux, by whom he had a son (No. 130).

130. Gabriel Denis Deville, an officer in the Swiss Guards, and afterwards a Captain in Roll's Regiment, in English pay, in 1797.

O'KELLEHER.

THE family of *O'Ceileachair* ("ceileach :" Irish, *wise, prudent*), anglicised *O'Kelleher, Kelleher,* and *Keller,* derive their sirname from Ceileachar, son of Donchuan, brother of Brian Boroimhe [Boru], the 175th Monarch of Ireland, who is No. 105 on the "O'Brien" (Kings of Thomond) pedigree. In the twelfth, and even so late as the sixteenth century, the O'Kellehers were possessed of lands in Munster: but the pedigree of the family is we fear lost. "Donogh O'Kelleher," successor of St. Kieran of Saiger, *i.e.* Bishop of Ossory, died, A.D. 1048. The late Rev. —— Kelleher, P.P., of Glanworth, county Cork, represented the senior branch of this Sept. A younger branch of the family is represented by Alderman Keller, of Cork.

O'KENNEDY.

Of Munster.

Armorial Bearings: Same as those of "Kennedy," (*ante*, page 98.)

THE *O'Cinnidha, O'Kennedys* or *Kennedys* derive their descent and sirname from Cineadh, the younger son of Donchuan (Doncha Cuan) who was brother of the Monarch Brian Boroimhe, who is No. 105 on the " O'Brien, Kings of Thomond" pedigree.

They were powerful chiefs in Ormond or North Tipperary, from the 11th to the close of the 16th century, and are mentioned in O'Dugan's toprographical poem :—

> " O'Kennedy of the crimson arms,
> Is chief of the smooth and extensive Glean-Omra."

According to Dr. O'Donovan, the district of Glean Omra was situated in the east of the county Clare, bordering on the Shannon, "whence," he says, "the O'Kennedys were driven into Ormond, in the early part of the 12th century, by the O'Briens and Clan-Coilean ;" but in this he is mistaken, as the O'Kennedys of Glen-Omra are numbered among the clans of Oir-Mumhan (or Ormond) by O'Dugan, who wrote in the 14th century, and there is no authority to show that the "principality" of Glen-Omra ever formed part of Thomond.

Frequent mention is made of the O'Kennedys by the Annalists :—

In A.D. 1110. Flan O'Kennedy, abbot of Trim, a learned poet, died.

In 1117. Two chiefs of the O'Kennedys of Ormond were slain in an engagement with the people of Conacht.

In 1159. Giolla-Kevin O'Kennedy died whilst on a pilgrimage at Killaloe ; and two chiefs of the sept, one of whom was the son of Giolla-Ciaran, lord of Ormond, fell at the battle of Ardee.

In 1198. O'Kennedy, abbot of Innisfallen, died.

In 1212. Donal O'Kennedy, bishop of Killaloe, died.

In 1240. Sadhbh (or Sabia), the dau. of O'Kennedy, and wife of Donogh Cairbreach O'Brien, died. (See "O'Brien" Stem, No. 111.)

In 1254. The monastery of Nenagh was founded by O'Kennedy, chief of Ormond.

In 1255. Donal O'Kennedy, archdeacon of Killaloe, who was raised to the episcopal dignity in 1251, dying at Limerick, was interred in the Dominican convent, in that city.

In 1371. Brian O'Kennedy, lord of Ormond, was treacherously slain by the English ; and Edmond O'Kennedy, heir to the lordship, died.

In 1464. Mór, the dau. of James O'Kennedy, and the wife of Mac-Geoghagan, of Westmeath, died. James and Donal, sons of Bryan who accompanied this lady into the territory of Moycashel, settled there, and were the founders of the name of *Kennedy*, in Westmeath.

The close of the 16th century, found the O'Kennedys fast sinking into obscurity, as appears from the fact of their not having been summoned to attend Perrott's " Conciliation" Parliament, in 1585. A branch of this family removed to Dublin in the early part of the 16th century, and gave sheriffs to the city for the years, 1591, 1601, 1631, and 1688 ; and the office of Chief Remembrancer was filled by members of this branch from 1625 to 1634.

Sir Richard Kennedy, " counsel" for Sir Phelim O'Neill, in 1652, was in 1660, appointed Baron of the Court of Exchequer ; and, having conformed to the Protestant religion, obtained large grants of confiscated land in the counties of Wicklow, Carlow, and Kilkenny. Alderman Walter Kennedy, brother to this Sir Richard, had a son, Christopher, whose son, Sir Thomas Kennedy, became *Aide-de-Camp* to Richard Hamilton, Duke of Tyrconnell ; and colonel of a regiment in the service of Charles III., King of Spain. After his death, in 1718, his family returned to Dublin, where, in 1864, this branch of the family was represented by James Marinus Kennedy of Clondalkin ; the elder line, Sir Richard's, becoming extinct in 1709.

In 1756. Hyacinth O'Kennedy, was abbot of Lorha, in co. Tipperary ; in 1758 this saintly man became a missionary to the Island of St. Croix, then a dependency of France, where he died in 1761.

In 1757. Patrick Kennedy, a friar of the Dominican Convent of Roscommon, died.

In 1836. Patrick O'Kennedy was consecrated bishop of Killaloe ; he died in January, 1857.

THE "O'KENNEDYS," LORDS OF ORMOND.

A.D.	
Fitz (or Mac) Madden, *vivens* 1088.	Philip, *d.* 1381.
Murtogh, *v.* 1112.	O'Kennedy Donn, *sl.* 1403.
Gilla-Kevin, *d.* 1159.	O'Kennedy Fionn, *d.* 1423.
Gilla-Ciaran, *v.* 1160.	MacDonal MacMahon O'K., *sl.* 1427.
Amlaobh, *v.* 1164.	Corry Roe, *d.* 1441.
Donal, *d.* 1180.	James, *sl.* 1444.
Murrogh, *slain* 1194.	Donal, *v.* 1448.
Murtogh, *v.* 1195.	Conor an-Chuam, *v.* 1558.
Brian, *sl.* 1371.	Philip MacDermod O'K., *v.* 1585.

There are several respectable families of the O'Kennedys to be met with at the present day in the counties of Dublin, Kildare, Wicklow, Wexford,* and Tipperary ; they are also numerous, but in narrower circumstances, in the counties of Westmeath, King's County, Queen's County, Waterford, and Clare.

---

* *Wexford:* Patrick Kennedy was born in the county of Wexford early in 1801. Although he was a Catholic, he came to Dublin as Assistant at the Protestant Training School, Kildare-place, in 1823. After a few years he established the small lending-library and book-shop in Anglesea-street (corner of Cope-street), where he spent the remainder of his life. He was a man of considerable ability, and contributed several articles to the pages of the *University Magazine.* The best of these : *Legends of the Irish Celts, Tales of the Duffrey,* and *Banks of the Boro,* were afterwards published separately. In the graphic delineation of Irish rural life, as he experienced it when a boy in the county Wexford, he has seldom been surpassed. His works are singularly pure, and he cramped his prospects in trade by declining to lend or deal in works that he considered of an objectionable tendency. Mr. Kennedy was widely known and respected by the literary world of Dublin. He died 28th March, 1873, aged about 72, and was buried at Glasnevin.

O'LEARY.*

Arms: Ar. a lion pass. in base gu. in chief a ship of three masts sa. sails set ppr. from the stern the flag of St. George flotant. *Crest:* Out of a ducal coronet or. an arm in armour embowed, holding a sword ppr. pommel and hilt gold. *Motto:* (Irish) Laidir isé lear Righ. *Another Motto:* Fortis undis et armis.

LAOGHAIRE, a brother of Brian who is No. 90 on the "O'Connell" pedigree, was the ancestor of *O'Laoghaire,†* of the Line of Heber; anglicised *O'Leary,* *Leary,* and *O'Learie.*

90. Laoghaire: son of Fiacha.
91. Aodh: his son.
92. Trean: his son.
93. Sedna: his son.
94. Sinell (or Singil): his son.

95. Aodhan: his son.
96. Ronan: his son.
97. Cuamhla: his son.
98. Sneadgal: his son; had a brother Eladach.

O'LENEHAN.

Chiefs of Upper Third, County of Waterford.

Arms: Ar. on a mount vert a buck trippant gu. attired or, in the mouth a trefoil slipped of the second, a chief az. charged with a castle having on each tower an obtuse spire surmounted by a weathercock, and on an arch over the curtain wall a cross flory all of the field. *Crest:* A buck trippant gu. attired or, holding in the mouth a trefoil slipped vert, and resting the forefoot on an escutcheon of the BURKE arms, viz., or, a cross gu. in the first quarter a lion ramp. sa. and in the second a hand of the last. *Motto:* Patriæ infelici fidelis.

THE *O'Leineachain* family ("leine": Irish, *a linen garment*), anglicised *O'Lenehan, Lenehan,* and *Lenihan,* descended from a younger son of the House of MacEniry of Cappagh. They were formerly a family of note in the counties of Tipperary and Limerick, where the name is sometimes rendered *MacLenehan* and *MacLanaghan;* and chiefs of a district forming

---

* *O'Leary:* Arthur O'Leary, D.D., a prominent politician and writer, was born in 1729, at Acres, near Dunmanway, co. Cork. He was educated at St. Malo, in France, where he spent twenty-four years as prison chaplain. . . . . . "Although it was known," says Webb, "that Dr. O'Leary was in the receipt of a Government pension during the latter part of his life, and that this was conferred partly to restrain him from writing against the Union (it is believed that he declined the favour), it was never suspected until lately that he was in receipt of Government pay as early as 1784." In 1789 Dr. O'Leary left Ireland for ever, and took up his residence in London as one of the chaplains to the Spanish embassy. There, as in Ireland, his society was courted by leading politicians of liberal views—by Burke and Sheridan, by Fox and Fitzwilliam. Towards the close of 1801, his health began to decline, and after residing a short time in France, he returned to England, broken down in health and spirits, and died in London on 7th January, 1802, aged 72. He was burried in old St. Pancras churchyard, where a monument was erected to his memory by his friend Lord Moira.

† *O'Laoghaire:* Some genealogists derive this sirname from the Irish "laogh," *a calf,* and "gair," *an outcry* (Gr. "gar-uo"); others, from the Irish "leath," *a half,* and "gair," *a laugh;* and others, from "lear," the *sea,* and "righ," *a king,* meaning "King of the sea."

the present barony of Upper Third, in the co. Waterford, where, on the left bank of the river Suir, and where the river receives the waters of the Clodagh, they had a strong castle, of which they were dispossessed by the Purcells and the De Grandisons, who expelled them from their patrimonial inheritance. They also possessed Crota Cliach and Hy-Coonagh, a territory partly in the barony of Owney and Arra, in Tipperary, and partly in the barony of Coonagh, co. Limerick.

A worthy representative of the family is Mr. Maurice Lenihan, J.P., of Limerick, the Proprietor of the *Limerick Reporter*, and son of James Lenihan, Esq., of Waterford.

The death of Mulciaran O'Lenaghan, a religious of Tumna, county Roscommon, who died A.D. 1249, is recorded by the Four Masters, as follows :—

"Mulciaran O'Lenaghan, a dignified priest of Tumna, a man who kept a house of hospitality for the clergy and laity, died on his way to Ardcarne, to attend a sermon there, on the Friday before Lammas ; and was interred with great honour and solemnity."

O'LIDDY.

THE *O'Liddy*, or *Liddy*, or *Leddy*, as the name is sometimes anglicised, derive their descent and sirname from Lidhda, a celebrated Munster chieftain of the Dal-Cais, who fell at Clontarf, A.D. 1014. The exact situation of the O'Liddy patrimony in the co. Clare cannot now be ascertained; but it is believed that it formed part of the present barony of Tulla.

In 1058, Carbery O'Liddy, grandson of Lidhda, founder of the name, and erenach of Emly, was slain ; and in 1122, Conor O'Liddy, successor of St. Ailbe of Emly, died. In 1171, say the Four Masters, a party of the O'Connors went on a predatory expedition into Thomond ; they plundered Siartachain O'Liddy, and slew himself in battle.

The tribe-name of this family was *Muinter Dobharcan, i.e.*, "The people (or descendants) of Dobharcan, of the race of Lughaidh," the third son of Cas (No. 91 on "O'Brien, Kings of Thomond" Stem) ; from whose grandson, Durcan, the *O'Durkans* of Thomond, derive their descent and sirname.

O'LONERGAN.

Chiefs of Clar-Cahir, County Tipperary.

THE *O'Longairgain* family ("longair" : Irish, *a ship's crew ;* "gan," *without*), anglicised *O'Lonergan, Lonergan,* and *Lunergan,* derive their sirname and descent from Longairgan, son of Donchuan, son of Cineide, who is No. 104 on the "O'Brien, Kings of Thomond" pedigree. They were Chiefs of *Clar Cahir* or the plains of Cahir, the seat of the Kings and Princes of

Tipperary; and a junior branch of this sept, which removed into Hy-Many, in South Conacht, in early times, became hereditary harpers to the O'Kellys, lords of that principality.

The castle of Ballinamanaley, in the parish of Fohenagh, barony of Killconnell, is said to have belonged to this family; and, according to tradition, Lowville, the seat of the MacDonaghs, marks the site of another of the residences of the music-loving O'Lonergans.

Frequent mention is made of this sept in the Irish Annals :—

In A.D, 1099. Annadh O'Lonergan, successor of Columb, Coarb of Creevan, in Hy-Many, died. We are inclined to believe this O'Lonergan was not a descendant of Donchuan; as it seems the family did not settle in Conacht at so early a period, when the Dal-Cassian O'Lonergans were few and in affluent circumstances; it is very probable this man was a member of some Hy-Manian family.

In A.D. 1131. Connor O'Lonergan was killed.

In 1147. Donal O'Lonergan, chief of Ormond, flourished.

In 1152. Donatus O'Lonergan was appointed to the see of Cashel; he died, 1158.

In 1161. Tadgh O'Lonergan, bishop of Killaloe, styled "of Thomond," died.

In 1206. Donal O'Lonergan, called "Donal II.," a Cistercian monk, a native of Muscry-Tire, in Ormond, was advanced to the see of Cashel; being confirmed in his see by Pope Innocent III. on 5th April, 1219. This prelate assisted at the fourth Council of Lateran, or twelfth general Council, held in the Basilica of the Lateran, A.D. 1215, at which 1185 Fathers attended, and Pope Innocent III., (Lathario Conte), who excommunicated John (Lackland), King of England, presided. The Annals of Ulster, and the Four Masters, state that he died at Rome; but other authorities affirm that he died at Burgundy, returning to Ireland, and that he was interred in the convent of Citeaux, in that city.

Donal O'Lonergan III. was consecrated archbishop of Cashel, in 1216; he resigned his sacred charge in 1223, and died nine years afterwards.

Allan O'Lonergan, a Franciscan friar, was consecrated bishop of Cloyne, in 1274; he died in 1283.

Frederick O'Lonergan, a Dominican friar, was elected to the vacant see of Killaloe, in 1437. He died in 1439, in the monastery of Holy Cross, co. Tipperary. At the dissolution of the monastic institutions, *temp.* Henry VIII., Edward O'Lonergan was seized of the priory of Cahir, and 180 acres of land in the vicinity of the establishment, valued at one shilling per acre.

O'LYNCH.*

Of Thomond.

Armorial Bearings : Same as those of "Lynch" (*ante*), page 102.

AONGUS, a brother of Eochaidh Ball-dearg who is No. 94 on the "O'Brien" (Princes of Thomond) pedigree, was the ancestor of this branch of that family. The family derives its name from Longseach ("longseach :" Irish, *a mariner*), a descendant of that Aongus ; and were after him called *O'Loingsigh*, or, anglicé, *O'Lynch*, and *Lynch*. It would appear that the "O'Lynches' Country" was that portion of territory lying around Castle-connell, in the barony of Owny and Ara, with portion of the lands comprised in the county of the City of Limerick.

O'MAHONY.† (No. 1.)

Chiefs of Hy-Eachach (now the Barony of Iveagh, Co. Cork).

Arms : Quarterly, 1st and 4th, or. a lion ramp. az.; 2nd, per pale ar. and gu. a lion ramp. counterchanged ; 3rd, ar. a chev. gu. betw. three snakes torqued ppr. *Crest* : Out of a viscount's coronet or, an arm in armour embowed, holding a sword ppr. pommel and hilt or, pierced through a fleur-de lis az.

HUGH GHARBH (or Hugh the Terrible), a younger brother of Laeghaire who is No. 93 on the "O'Donoghue" (of Lough Lein) pedigree, was the ancestor of *O'Mathamhna ;* anglicised *O'Mahony* and *Mahony*.

93. Aedh (or Hugh) an Gharbh‡ [garriv] : son of Crimthann.	94. Tighearnach : son of Hugh Gharbh.

* *O'Lynch :* In the *Linea Antiqua*, it is stated that William le Petit was the progenitor of all the Lynches of Ireland ; who are mentioned as one of the families of "The Tribes of Galway." There was in Tirowen another "Lynch" family of *Irish* origin.

† *O'Mahony :* Daniel O'Mahony, Lieutenant-General, a distinguished officer in the Irish Brigade in France, brother-in-law of the Marshal Duke of Berwick, signalized himself at the Boyne, Aughrim, and Limerick, and accompanied his regiment to the Continent. In January, 1702, some of the Irish Brigade under O'Mahony, turning out in their shirts in the middle of the night, defeated Prince Eugene's attempt to capture Cremona. For their bravery and resolute refusal of the offers made by Prince Eugene to turn them from their allegiance, Louis XIV. sent his thanks to the regiment and raised their pay. O'Mahony was made a colonel, and was subsequently recommended to Philip V. of Spain, by whom he was put in command of a regiment of Irish Dragoons. He was subsequently appointed a Lieutenant-General, and created Count of Castile. He died at Ocana in January, 1714.

‡ *Gharbh :* The epithet *gharbh* ("gharbh :" Irish, *rough, terrible, impetuous ;* Lat. "grav-is") is the root of the Latin river *Garumna* and the French *Garonne* : both of which are derived from the Irish *Garbh-amhuin* ("amhuin" : Irish, *a river ;* Lat. "amnis"), meaning "the boisterous river."

95. Felim :* his son.
96. Ceannfaola : his son.
97. Fergin : his son.
98. Beice (or Becc) : his son ; a quo *Cineal mBeice*, anglicised *Beck* or *O'Beice* ("beic :" Irish, *a shout*).
99. Ferdaltach : his son.
100. Artgall : his son.
101. Connall : his son.
102. Alioll Brugha (" brugh :" Irish, *a large house*) : his son ; a quo *Burgess*.
103. Cugeiltach : his son.
104. Conor : his son.
105. Taithneach : his son.
106. Spellan : his son.
107. Cian : his son ; had a brother named Maolmoradh.
108. Braon : his son.

109. Cian (2) : his son.
110. Mathghabhuin (" maghgha-bhuin :" Irish, *a bear*, or, literally, "a calf of the plain") : his son ; a quo *O'Mathamhna* or *O'Maghghamhna* ; living 1014.
111. Brodceann O'Mahony : his son ; first assumed this sirname.
112. Cumara : his son.
113. Donoch : his son.
114. Cian (3) : his son.
115. Donoch : his son.
116. Dermod : his son.
117. Teige : his son.
118. Donoch (3) : his son.
119. Dermod Mór : his son.
120. Finghin : his son.
121. Donal : his son.
122. Dermod : his son.
123. Conor O'Mahony :† his son.

O'MAHONY. (No. 2.)

* *Felim :* According to other genealogists, the following is the pedigree of *O'Mahony*, down from this Felim—

95. Felim : son of Tighearnach.
96. Fergus : his son.
97. Beic : his son ; a quo "Cineal mBeice."
98. Firdaleithe : his son.
99. Artgall : his son.
100. Connall : his son.
101. Olioll Brughadh : his son.
102. Cucoigilt : his son.
103. Conor : his son.
104. Cathniadh : his son.
105. Cian : his son.
106. Bran : his son.
107. Maolmoradh : his son.
108. Cian (2) : his son.
109. Mathghabhuin : his son ; a quo *O'Mahony*.
110. Brodceann O'Mahony : his son ; first assumed this sirname.
111. Cumara : his son.
112. Donoch : his son.
113. Cian (3) : his son.
114. Donoch naHimirce-timchioll : his son.

115. Dermod : his son ; had a brother named Conor.
116. Teige : his son ; had a brother named Maccraith.
117. Donoch, of Rathdreon : his son.
118. Dermod Mór : his son ; had a brother named Teige an Oir, meaning "Teige of the Gold." This Teige was the ancestor of *Goold*.
119. Finghin (or Florence) : his son ; had two brothers—1. Donall ; 2. Dermod.
120. Dermod Ranntach : his son.
121. Conor Cabach : his son.
122. Conor Fionn na n-Eich : his son.
123. Conor na-Croise ("crois :" Irish, *a cross* ; Lat. "cruix ;" Fr. "croix") : his son ; a quo *O'Crosse* anglicised *Cross* and *Cruise*.
124. Conor fionn : his son.
125. Donall : his son.
126. Conor O'Mahony : his son.

† The O'Mahony family were "undisputed kings of Raithlean, and had a right to be kings of Cashel whenever that kingdom happened to be vacant ; and from whom the Kings of Cashel had no right to demand anything except a bowing of the head."— *Book of Munster.*

The O'Mahonys were for many ages sovereign princes of the countries or districts

O'MAHONY. (No. 3.)

THE following pedigree of the senior branch of this family has been copied from the Genealogical MSS. at Lambeth:

107. Maolmoradh: son of Bran; living in 1014. King of Munster in 965.

108. Cian (2): his son; married Sadhbh, dau. of Brian Boroimhe by his third wife, Gormliath.

109. Mahon: his son; a quo *O'Mahony*; had two sons—Dermod, and Donogh of Muscry.

110. Dermod; his son.

111. Conor: his son.

112. Dermod: his son; m. a dau. of Donal Caomh MacCarthy Reagh; living in 1311.

113. Donogh, of Iveagh: his son.

114. Conor: his son.

115. Dermod Mór: his son.

116. Finin: his son.

117. Donal: his son.

118. Dermod Ronsaghe: his son; had two sons—Finin; and Maolmoradh.

119. Finin: his son.

120. Donal: his son.

121. Dermod: his son; had four sons:—1. Finin; 2. Conor Kittog of Ardinterran; 3. Donogh Mór of Dunmanus; and 4. Donal of Dunbeacon, whose issue has been extinct.

(122). 1. Finin of Rosbrin, m. a dau. of O'Donoghue Mór, by whom she had Donal, and a dau. m. to Conor MacCormac O'Driscoll.

(123). Donal: son of Finin, (124) Conor: son of Donal, (125) Donal: son of Donal, (126) Teige: son of Donal.

(122). 3. Donogh Mór of Dunmanus, had a son (123) Teige; Teige

had a son (124) Donogh; and Donogh had a son (125) Donal.

122. Conor Kittog of Ardinterran: son of Dermod; m. a daughter of O'Dowd, by whom he had issue—1. Conor Fionn; 2. Finin Caol; 3. David; 4. Dermod; and 5. a dau. m. to Owen, son of Maolmuire MacSwiney.

(123). 2. Finin Caol had a son (124) Donal, who had a son (125) Conor.

(123) 3. David had a son (124) Conor, who had a son (125) Finin.

123. Conor Fionn: his son; m. Ellen, base dau. of Donal MacFinin MacCarthy Reagh; d. 1513; had issue—1. Conor Fion Oge; 2. Dermod, d. s. p.; 3. Finin of Crogan; 4. Donal Bhade; and 5. Joanna, who m. twice, first to Conor MacFinin O'Driscoll, and secondly to O'Mahony Dubh of Carbery.

3. (124) Finin of Crogan, who had a son, (125) Donal, living in 1600.

4. (124) Donal Bhade, m. a dau. of O'Mahony of Carbery by whom he had (125) Conor Bhade, who m. twice—first the dau. of O'Mahony of Carbery by whom he had (126) Conor; and secondly to the dau. of Edmond MacSwiney.

124. Connor Fionn Oge: his son; m. Ellen, dau. of O'Mahony of Carbery, by whom he had—1. Conor; 2. Dermod; 3. Maurice; 4. Finin; and 5. a dau. who was Concubine to Sir Eoghan O'Sullivan.

125. Connor, his son; attended

called *Cineal-Ædh*, *Cineal-mBeice*, *Ibh-Conlua*, and all that part of Muscry which lies southward of the river Lee; and, in later ages, of the large district called *Scull*, together with that of *Ive-eachach* [Iveagh], in the county Cork.

the memorable parliament convened by Perrott in Dublin, 1583. From this Conor descended the O'Mahony's Fionn, several of whom served in the army of the English King James II., and in the Irish Brigade in the service of the French King Louis XIV.

The O'Mahonys possessed *Hy-Eachach Mumhan*, now the barony of Iveagh, in the south-west of the county of Cork; *Cineal-mBeice*, now the barony of Kinalmeaky; *Cineal-Aodh*, now the barony of Kinalea; *Tiobrad*, in the barony of Iveragh, county of Kerry, from the chiefs of this district are descended the O'Mahonys of Dunloe, represented in 1864 by Daniel O'Mahony. The O'Mahony of Castle Quin—Myles, son of Cian, son of Myles, son of Cian—descended from Conor O'Mahony of Kinalmeaky who lost his estates in the Desmond wars, thence he removed to Kerry; and the O'Mahony of Dromore Castle—Denis, son of Richard-John, son of Denis, son of John—from Dermod O'Mahony, who fought and fell on the field of Aughrim on the side of James (Stuart) II., King of England.

We believe the present representatives (1886) of Cian, Prince of Kinalmeaky, are John (Cian) O'Mahony of Clothduff, barony of Muscry, whose brothers are Rev. Michael O'Mahony, C.C., Upper Glanmire, and Rev. Denis O'Mahony, C.C., Nucestown, Enniskean, county Cork. The eldest representative is Jeremiah O'Mahony, of Shanacloyne, parish of Templemartin, and barony of Kinalmeaky, aged 100 years, whose sons are John of Curravordy, and Bartholomew of Shanacloyne, both married and have many children.

Cian, No. 108 above, had his residence in a strongly fortified fort, now called *Cathair Mór*, in the townland of Gurranes, barony of Kinalmeaky; this fort is nearly entire, of a circular form, and surrounded by three embankments and a deep fosse; there are traces of a second fosse. A few paces to the west of *Cathair Mór* is another fort called *Lios na m-ban* or the fort of the women; here the Princess Sadhbh held her court: and to the east and south-east of *Cathair Mor*, are the remains of other forts of a smaller size, the residence of the military and civil dependants of Cian. Another fortified residence of the O'Mahonys was *Grian-na-hunic* (now Mossgrove) in Kinalmeaky, which was dismantled some few years ago for materials to erect a farm house and offices, by a farmer named Desmond. Tradition relates this fortification and surrounding country to have been possessed by a Colonel, Donal O'Mahony, a remote ancestor of the O'Mahonys of Clothduff and Shanacloyne. There are ample grounds to show that this family possessed nearly all the country occupied at a later date by the MacCarthys Reagh, Glas, Duna, and part of Muscry, together with that taken by the O'Sullivans.

The O'Mahonys had castles at Rathlin (now Lord Bandon's castle); Ardinterran (now Ardintenant); Ringmahon; Dunbeacon; Dunmanus; Rosbrin; Blackcastle (Schull); Ballydevlin (Kilmore); Dromdeely (county Limerick); and Ballymodan (East Carbery).

The last Prince of Rathlin was Connor O'Mahony of Kinalmeaky, who at the age of 23 years fought and fell on the National side in the Desmond wars: he left issue, who are now, mostly farmers on the soil of their ancestors.

O'MEAGHER

Chiefs of Ikerin, County Tipperary.

Arms: Az. two lions ramp. combatant or, supporting a sword, in pale. *Crest:* **A** falcon rising ppr.

FIONNACHTA, a younger brother of Iomchadh Uallach, who is No. 88 on the " O'Carroll" (Ely) pedigree, was the ancestor of *O'Meachair:* anglicised *O'Meagher, Meagher,* and *Maher :*

88. Fionnachta: second son of Conla.

89. Eochaidh: his son.

90. Etchon: his son.

91. Lugha: his son.

92. Feach (or Fiacha): his son.

93. Felim: his son.

94. Doncuan: his son.

95. Lugha (2): his son.

96. Fergna: his son.

97. Aodh: his son.

98. Meachar :* his son.

99. Cu-coille: his son.

100. Ceallach: his son.

101. Meachar ("meach :" Irish, *hospitality*): his son; a quo *O'Meachair.*

102. Dluthach: his son.

103. Teige Mór: his son.

104. Eigneach: his son.

105. Donal: his son.

106. Moroch: his son; first assumed this sirname, viz. *Ua-Meachair.*

107. Meachar :† his son.

108. Feach: his son; had a brother Eochaidh, a quo *Kehoe, Keogh,* and *MacKeogh,* of Munster.

109. Iarin: his son.

110. Donoch: his son.

111. Murtach: his son.

112. Melachlin: his son.

113. Fionn: his son.

114. Dermod: his son.

115. Gilla-na-Naomh: his son; had an elder brother, Gilbert.‡

116. Teige: his son.

117. Gilleneuffe [rectius Gilla-na-Neeve] O'Meagher: his son. An inquisition taken at Clonmel on the 30th of May, 1629, found that this Gillaneuffe O'Meagher on the 30th of August, 1551, executed a deed by which he covenanted to pay John O'Meagher, of Clonykenny Castle—who was then chief of his name, and father of Colonel Teige-ege O'Meagher and of Ellen, wife of Dr. Gerard Ffennell, member of the Supreme Council of Confederation —and his heirs a rent of twelve shillings; that he was father of Daniel [118], who was father of John [119]; that John was in his lifetime seized of the lands of Ballybeg Camlin, Clonyne, Cloughmurle Grange, and Gortvollin, situated in the barony of Ikerrin and county of Tipperary, which he held by knight service, and that John O'Meagher [120] was his son and heir-at-law, of full age, and married.

118. Daniel O'Meagher: his son; born 1508, died 1576.

119. John O'Meagher: his son; born 1541, died 1599.

120. John O'Meagher: his son; born 1570, died 1640.

121. Thaddeus O'Meagher: his son; born 1603, died 1650.

* *Meachar:* According to O'Clery, the name *Ua-Meachair* or *O'Meagher* is derived from this Meachar, No. 98.

† *Meachar:* And this name is rendered *Murchadh-Og,* by O'Clery.

‡ *Gilbert:* This Gilbert was father of Piers, who was father of Gilbert, who was father of Teige O'Meagher.

122. John O'Meagher: his son; born 1635, died 1705.

This John O'Meagher and his mother, Anne O'Meagher, were, on the 30th January, 1653, ordered by the Commissioners sitting at Clonmel to transplant to Connaught. By an order in Council dated Dublin Castle, the 3rd of December, 1655, their petition was referred to the Commissioners of Revenue at Loughrea.

123. Thaddeus O'Meagher: his son; born 1662, died 1732.

124. John O'Meagher : his son ; born 1706, died 1775.

125. Thaddeus O'Meagher : his son; born 1739, died 1811.

126. John O'Meagher : his son; born 1772, died 1844.

127. Joseph T. O'Meagher: his son ; born 1803, died 1882.

128. John William O'Meagher: his son; born 1829, d. s. p. 1884; had a younger brother, Joseph Casimir O'Meagher, born 1831, and living in 1887, in Dublin.

129. Joseph Dermod O'Meagher: son of Joseph Casimir; born 1864; B.A. of Dublin University, 1884; has had four brothers: (1) John Kevin, born 1866, B.A. of the Royal University, 1886; (2) Donn Casimir, born 1872, died 1874 ; (3) Malachy Marie, born 1873; (4) Fergal Thaddeus, born 1876, and a sister, Mary Nuala.

O'MEARA.*

Of Lismisky, County Tipperary.

Arms: Gu. three lions pass. guard. in pale per pale or. and ar. a border az. charged with eight escallops of the last. *Crest* : A pelican vulning herself ppr. *Motto :* Opima spolia.

DONAL O'MEARA had :

2. William, of Lismisky, county Tipperary, his son and heir, who had :

3. Teige, of Lismisky, gent., who d. 30th April, 1636, and was bur. in the Abbey of Clonmel. He m. Honora, dau. of Robert Grace, of

Corktown, co. Kilkenny, Esq., and had three sons and two daughters :
I. Daniel.
II. William.
III. Patrick.
I. Ellin.
II. Elan.
4. Daniel O'Meara : son of Teige.

THIS family derives its descent from Ailgeanan, the second son of Turlogh, who is No. 98 on the "O'Brien Kings of Thomond" pedigree. We find the O'Mearas settled in Ormond in very early times, whence a branch of

---

* *O'Meara* : Dr. Barry Edward O'Meara, surgeon to Napoleon Bonaparte at St. Helena, was born in Ireland in 1770, educated at Trinity College, and at an early age appointed Assistant-Surgeon to the 62nd Regiment. He served for some years in Sicily, Egypt, and Calabria. In consequence of a duel, he was obliged to quit the army, but soon received an appointment in the navy. He was serving in the *Bellerophon*, when, on the 14th July, 1815, Napoleon surrendered himself on board of her. His professional skill and knowledge of Italian gained the favour of the ex-Emperor, at whose request he was sent with him to St. Helena, as his medical attendant. He died in London, 3rd June, 1836, aged 66.

the tribe removed into Kilkenny, where they became hereditary physicians to the Butlers of the 16th and 17th centuries; and many of them were eminent literary men, and poets of no mean reputation.

The following were the possessions of the O'Mearas from the 12th to the close of the 16th century :—Hy-Fathaidh and Hy-Niall, districts in the barony of Upper Ormond, in the county of Tipperary, thus mentioned by Giolla-na-Neev O'Heerin, who wrote in the 15th century :—

> " O'Meara, who is a good prince,
> And chief of Hy-Fahy, obtained extensive lands;
> And the Hy-Nialls of the race of Eoghan the fair-haired,
> Are the lions of whom I treat."

Hy-Finach, otherwise Tuaim-ui-Mheara, or Toomavara, a district in Upper Ormond, adjoining Hy-Fahy and Hy-Niall, co-extensive with the parish of Aghnamadle, and deriving its name from being the burial-place of the O'Mearas—the word *Uaim*, signifying "a tomb," "a vault," or "place of interment;" Hy-Eochaidh Fion, a district adjoining Hy-Niall on the south, and other estates in Ormond, also belonged to this sept.

In A.D. 1540, Teige O'Meara, the last prior of the hospital, founded at Nenagh, A.D. 1200, for Augustinian canons, by Theobald FitzWalter, the founder of the house of Ormond, surrendered the same to the Inquisitors of King Henry VIII., and it was given to Oliver Grace of Nenagh, at the annual rent of £39, Irish money.

In A.D. 1541, 29th June, Donal O'Meara, " chief of his nacion," obtained a grant of English liberty.

In 1745, William O'Meara, bishop of Clonfert, was translated to Killaloe; he died in 1762.

Many gentlemen of this name took service in the Irish Brigade (*vide* pp. 555-6 of our *Irish Landed Gentry*); one of whom, a lieutenant in the battalion of Walsh, became General of Brigade in the French service, and Commandant of Dunkirk, as appears from the following correspondence between that officer and Frederick, Duke of York :—

Letter from General of Brigade O'Meara, dated August 23rd.

" CITIZEN-PRESIDENT,—I have the honour of addressing to you the subjoined copy of the summons just made to me on the part of the Duke of York, with a copy of my reply.

(Signed)   " O'MEARA."

Head Quarters of the combined army before Dunkirk, August 23rd.

" SIR,—I give you notice that the army I command is at your gates. Your city, destitute of any real defence, can oppose no resistance to the victorious arms which I might instantly employ against it, if I did not wish to prevent the total ruin of a flourishing city, and if humanity and generosity did not render me desirous of sparing human blood. I, therefore, summon you, Sir, to surrender the city of Dunkirk to his Britannic Majesty, before I employ against it the very considerable force at my disposal; apprising you, however, that I will listen to any proposition you make, provided they may be such as are not injurious to the consideration and the honour of the British arms, the interest of Great Britain, and those of her allies. I give you twenty-four hours to deliberate on the summons.

(Signed),   " FREDERICK, Duke of York.

" *Commander of the combined army before Dunkirk.*"

Copy of the answer to the Summons :—

" Dunkirk, August 23rd, 2nd year of the French Republic, one and indivisible.

" GENERAL,—Invested with the confidence of the French Republic, I have received your summons to surrender an important city. I answer by assuring you that I shall defend it with the brave Republicans whom I have the honour to command.

(Signed),　　　　　　　　　　" O'MEARA."

Amongst the writers of this family we may mention Dr. Dermod O'Meara, author of the *Pathologia Hereditaria Generalis*, published in Dublin, 1619 ; and reprinted in London, 1665, and in Amsterdam, 1666. This Dermod was a poet as well as a physician ; he wrote some Latin pieces to Sir Walter Butler, of Kilcash, grandfather of James, 12th earl, and 1st Marquis and Duke of Ormond.

Edmond, son of Dr. Dermod O'Meara, like his father, graduated at Oxford ; he was the author of a work entitled, *Examen Diatribæ Thomæ Willisii de Febribus cui accesserunt Historiæ aliquot Medicinæ Rariores*, published in London, 1665.

William, son of this Edmond, who flourished in the third quarter of the 17th century, wrote some Latin verses, which were published with his father's works. With some degree of probability he was the O'Meara mentioned in the following stanza, translated from the celebrated satire of Feardorcha (or Ferdinand) O'Daly, on Dr. Whalley, of Stephen's Green, Dublin :—

" Where are the ready satiric Druids?
Where is O'Meara, the prince of the literati ?
In forests are they ?　Or in mountain glens ?
Or did they fall altogether at Aughrim ?"

O'MORONEY.

Of Clare, and America.

Arms : Az. three crosses-crosslet or, betw. as many boars' heads, couped above the shoulders, ar. langued gu.　*Crest :* A lion ramp. ar. holding between the paws a sceptre or halbert, or.　*Motto :* Amicis semper fidelis.

THIS family name is one of the anglicised forms of the Irish *O'Maolruanaidh*, which is derived from Maolruanaidh (or Mulroona) Mór, a younger brother of Conchobhar (or Connor) who is No. 106 on the " O'Connor" (Kings of Connaught) pedigree. Other forms of this ancient family name were— *O'Mulrooney, O'Mulroney, O'Moroney, Moroney, Moroni, Mulrooney, Rooney, Roney, Rowney,* etc. According to O'Dugan's Topography, *O'Maolruanaidh* was one of the three chiefs of Crumthan or Cruffan, a district comprising the barony of Killian and part of Ballymoe, in the county Galway. The O'Moroney portion of the family more lately settled in the co. Clare, where many of them still remain ; and whence some members of the family emigrated to America some 120 years ago, and others more lately. Descendants of those emigrants are now located in the States of Tennessee,

North Carolina, Virginia, Kentucky, and Louisiana: among them being Mr. Timothy Moroney of New Orleans, living in 1887.

We are unable to trace the genealogy of the family farther back than Pierce Morony, of Clown Meagh, whose Will bears date 8th Dec., 1678, and who married Margaret, dau. of Theobald Butler, by whom he had (with four daughters, the youngest of whom Catherine, was wife of Thady Quin, an ancestor of the Earl of Dunraven) two sons, of whom the younger was:—

2. Pierce Morony, who m. and had issue two sons and four daughters. The elder son was Edmond.

3. Edmond, of Poulmallen, co. Clare: elder son of Pierce; was twice m. : first—to Mary-Anne, dau. of Ralph Westropp, Esq., of Maryfort, by whom he had four sons and four daughters:
I. Thomas, of whom presently.
II. Westropp. III. John. IV. Ralph.
I. Jane. II. Hannah. III. Mary-Anne. IV. Elizabeth.
He m., secondly, Blanche Vincent, of Limerick, and by her had two sons and three daughters:
V. Edmond. VI. Exham.
V. Elizabeth. VI. Blanche. VII. Susannah.

4. Thomas (d. 1832) of Milltown-House, J.P., High Sheriff of the co. Clare, in 1796: eldest son by the first marriage; m. in 1776 Frances (d. 1793), dau. of Edmond Morony, Esq., of Cork (by Mary, his wife, dau. of Francis Goold, Esq.), and left at his decease five sons and three daughters:
I. Edmond. II. Thomas-Harrison, of whom presently.
III. Francis-Goold. IV. Henry. V. John.
I. Mary. II. Anne. III. Frances.

5. Thomas-Harrison Morony (d. 13 Jan., 1854), of Milltown-House, J.P.: second son of Thomas; m., 20th March, 1809, Anna Burdett, and had issue three sons and five daughters:
I. Thomas (b. 1809), who in 1833

m. Anna-Maria, eldest dau. of George Dartnell, Esq., of Limerick, and d. leaving issue one son and three daus.:
I. Thomas, who d. in 1836.
I. Rose. II. Anne. III. Emily, who d. 1854.
II. Burdett, of whom presently.
III. Henry, b. 22nd, Nov., 1819; and d. unm. 18 April, 1841.
I. Charlotte, who in 1837 m. Thomas Barclay, Esq., of Ballyarkny, and had issue.
II. Frances, who m. the Rev. Michael Fitzgerald, rector of Kilfarboy, and vicar of Kildysart, in the co. Clare, and had issue.
III. Anna-Maria, who in 1868 m. William Duckett, Esq., J.P., of Duckett's Grove, county Carlow.
IV. Emily, who in 1851 m. Edward Griffiths, second son of Louis Griffiths, Esq., of Cheltenham, England, and had issue.
V. Louisa, who d. unm. 4th July, 1857.

6. Burdett Morony (b. 18th June, 1815, and living in 1876, but since deceased, of Milltown-House, co. Clare, J.P. and D.L., High Sheriff 1861-62: second son of Thomas-Harrison Morony; m., on 11th June, 1847, Eleanor Lucinda, dau. of George Dartnell, Esq., of Limerick. Mrs. Burdett Morony, relict of said Burdett Morony, now (1887) occupies Miltown-House, Milltown-Malbay, co. Clare.

Q

O'MULVILLE.

Of Killowen, County Clare.

Arms : Per fess ar. and gu. in chief a salmon naiant ppr. betw. two lions ramp. combatant az. supporting a dexter hand of the second, in base a harp or, between two battle axes in pale, the blades turned outwards ppr. *Crest :* A dexter cubit arm in pale ppr. grasping two battle axes in saltire ppr. the blades outwards. *Motto :* Pro aris et focis.

COMMENCING with Owen O'Maolmichil, who, in 1653, was deprived of his estate by the Cromwellian Settlement, the following is the genealogy of this branch of that family :

1. Owen, of Doon Maolmichiall and Killowen, co. Clare, living in 1653, had :

2. Hugh, who had :

3. Flan, who had :

4. Lawrence, who was twice m., first, to a Miss Stackpool; and secondly, to a daughter of O'Grady, of Cooga, lords of the O'Gonnola, on the Shannon. Lawrence had :

5. Daniel *O'Mulvihill*, of Knockanira, co. Clare, who d. in 1820. This Daniel married a Miss Lysaght* of Ballykeale, and had five sons :

I. Charles, who d. in 1847.

II. Daniel, of Kilglassy, county Clare, of whom presently.

III. George, who was an M.D.

IV. William, of Gort, co. Galway, M.D., who had :

I. The Rev. Urquhart *Mulville,* a Protestant clergyman, living in 1881, in Tramore, co. Waterford.

V. Henry Mulville, M.D.

It will be seen that the last three sons of Daniel, of Knockanira, co. Clare, were all M.D's.

6. Daniel, of Kilglassy : second son of Daniel of Knockanira ; had three sons :

I. Captain Charles Blood Mulville, of whom presently.

II. Neptune Blood Mulville, who is a merchant in the city of Sacramento, California.

III. (   )

7. Captain Charles Blood Mulville; late of the 3rd Dragoon Guards, and living in 1881 : son of Daniel, of Kilglassy; whose daughter is m. to a Captain Trench.

O'NEILL.

Of the County Clare.

THIS family, sometimes called *Nihell, Neile,* and *Creagh,* derive its origin from Neil, the son of Congal, the son of Aodh Caomh, King of Cashel, who is No. 96 on the "O'Brien Kings of Thomond" stem. *Clan*

---

* *Lysaght :* It is, perhaps, worthy of remark that Miss Lysaght's brother John was the intimate friend of Lord Edward Fitzgerald and of Lord Lisle (? Lile) ; and that George Lysaght was her first cousin. Her mother was daughter of Major Kent, of King William's Army ; and her grandmother was a Miss Moroney of Miltown-Malbay, co. Clare.

Daelbhaoi was the tribe name of this family, and the principal seat of their chief was at Finlora :—

> " The land of Clan-Daelbhaoi of the poets,
> Is governed by O'Neill, lord of Fionluaraigh ;
> To his residence come the hosts of Tradree,
> Warriors of flaxen tresses."

The domain of this O'Neill was co-extensive with the deanery of Tradree, comprising the parishes of Tomfinloe, Kilnasodagh, Kilmalaery, Kilcoury, Clonloghan, Drumline, Feenagh, Bunratty, and Killaneen.

Of this family was Lieut.-Col. O'Neill, who served in the Regiment of Lord Clare, and fell at Fontenoy ; and Sir Balthazer O'Neill, a Brigadier-General in the service of the King of Naples. In 1585, Torlogh O'Neill, a native of Tomfinloe, succeeded the martyred Dermod O'Hurley, as archbishop of Cashel. Laurence Nihell, was bishop of Kilfenora in 1791. The head of this family in 1690—down to which the sept maintained a respectable position in Clare—was married to the daughter of Thomas Coppinger, Esq., of Ballyvolane, in the county of Cork, by his wife, the daughter of Edward Galwey, Esq., of Lota, and sister of John Galway, Esq., a member of parliament for the city of Cork, in King James's Parliament, held in Dublin, 1689.

We regret being at present unable to procure the genealogy of this family.

O'SULLIVAN BEARA.* (No. 1.)

Lords of Beara (now Berehaven), County Cork.

Arms : Per pale sa. and ar. a fess betw. in chief a boar pass. and in base another counterpass. all counter changed, armed, hoofed, and bristled or.   *Crest :* On a lizard vert a robin redbreast ppr.

GIOLLA-NA-BHFLAINN, younger brother of Giolla-Mochoda [Gilmochud] who is No. 111 on the " Vera-O'Sullivan" pedigree, was the ancestor of *O'Sullivan Beara.*

111. Giolla na-Bhflainn : son of Donall Mór O'Sullivan.

112. Philip : his son.

113. Annaidh : his son.

114. Awly : his son ; had a brother named Gilmochud (who was the ancestor of *O'Sullivan Maol*, and) a quo *MacGillicuddy.*

115. Teige : his son.

116. Dermod Balbh : his son ; had two sons :—1. Donal Crone, and 2. Donogh ; this Donogh had a son, Donal, who had a son, Dermod, who had a son Eoghan, called " Sir Eoghan," to whom Queen Elizabeth, granted the chief rents of the castle,

---

* *Beara :* Of this family was the late illustrious Alexander Martin Sullivan, M.P., Barrister-at-Law, etc. ; who was better known as " A. M. Sullivan," of the Dublin *Nation*, before his brother the Right Honourable T. D. Sullivan, M.P., the present Lord Mayor of Dublin, became the Proprietor of that excellent paper.

town, and lands of Dunboy, with 57 "carrucates" of other lands, and who, in 1585, attended Perrot's Parliament, in Dublin. This Sir Eoghan had a son, Eoghan O'Sullivan Bere, to whom, and to his heirs for ever, James I., King of England, granted the chief rents of Dunboy. This Eoghan had a son, Colonel Donal O'Sullivan Bere, who lost his estates for his adherence to the Stuarts ; in 1660, those estates were restored by Charles II.

117. Donal Crone : elder son of Dermod Balbh.

118. Donal : his son.

119. Dermod an-Phudar : his son; m. to Julia, dau. of MacCarthy Reagh. This Dermod was, in 1549, burned to death in his castle of Dunbuidhe (Dunboy), by the explosion of a barrel of powder; and his brother Amhlaobh (Awly), his tanist, died the same year.

120. Donal : his son ; m. to a dau. of Sir Donal O'Brien of Thomond ; had two sons :—1. Donal ; and 2. Dermod, who died at Corunna, aged 100 years, and soon after his aged wife followed him. This Dermod had a son, Philip, author of the *Historiæ Catholicæ Hiberniæ Compendium,** who became an officer in the Spanish Navy. This Donal was slain in 1563, by MacGillicuddy.

121. Donal, Prince of Beare : his son ; defeated, in 1581, a Captain Zouch, who went to plunder his people ; leaving 300 of said plunderers slain on the field. In 1600,

he openly acknowledged Aodh O'Neill, Prince of Ulster, as the *Ard Righ* or Monarch. In 1602, his fortress of Dunbuidhe was stormed by Carew, and the garrison of 143 men slain. Soon after (in 1603)—" Berehaven's lord left his stately hall," and performed the memorable march to O'Rourke's country in Brefny. On the 2nd of January, 1602, he was proclaimed an "outlaw" by the English. In 1604, this Donal sailed for Spain, where King Philip gave him a warm reception; made him a Grandee of the Kingdom of Spain, Knight of St. Jago, and Earl of Berehaven; with a pension of 300 golden pieces monthly. His wife (who [accompanied him to Spain) was Ellen, dau. of Donal O'Sullivan Mór. He was assassinated at Madrid by an Anglo-Irishman named Bath, in the 57th year of his age.

122. Donal, Prince of Bere, Earl of Berehaven, etc. : his son; entered the army, and fell at Belgrade, fighting against the Turks; he was alive in 1615.

Unfortunately, we are unable at present to bring down the stem of this illustrious family to our times ; but we learn that in 1864, it was represented by John O'Sullivan Bere, of Keanitrenang (otherwise Coolagh), co. Cork, son of John, son of Captain Murtogh O'Sullivan, of Coolagh, of *Keim-an-Eigh* notoriety, in 1797.

* *Compendium* : Philip O'Sullivan Beara's *Historiæ Catholicæ Hiberniæ Compendium* was published in Lisbon in 1621 ; and republished with notes by Dr. Kelly of Maynooth, in 1850. It contains Topography, Pilgrimage to St. Patrick's Purgatory, the English in Ireland from the Anglo-Norman Invasion to 1588, and a history of the O'Neill's and O'Donnell's wars. Philip O'Sullivan Beara died in 1660, as appears by a letter from Father Peter Talbot (afterwards Catholic Archbishop of Dublin) to the Marquis of Ormond, dated from Madrid, the 10th of January, 1660 :—" The Earl of Birhaven," he writes, " is dead, and left one only daughter of twelve years to inherit his titles in Ireland and his goods here, which amount to 100,000 crowns."

O'SULLIVAN MÓR. (No. 2.)

Lords of Dunkerron.

Arms : A dexter hand couped at the wrist, grasping a sword erect. *Crest*: On a ducal coronet or, a robin redbreast with a sprig of laurel in its beak. *Motto :* Lamh foistenach abu.

DONAL NA SGREADAIDHE, a younger brother of Dermod, who is No. 121 on the "Vera-O'Sullivan" pedigree, was the ancestor of this illustrious branch of that family.

121. Donal na Sgreadaidhe (or "Donal of the Shriek"): son of Owen.

122. Donal of Dunkerron : his son ; m. Mary, dau. of Cormac Oge, lord of Muscry, and, dying in 1580, left issue—1. Owen ; 2. Dermod, tanist of Dunkerron, who m. Julia, dau. of Owen MacCarthy Reagh, Prince of Carbery ; 3. Broghe, who m. the dau. of O'Donovan of Carbery ; 4. Connor, who m. Una (or Winifred), dau. of Edmond Fitzgerald, Knight of the Valley ; 5. Donal, who m. the dau. of O'Leary, widow of MacGillicuddy ; 6. Ellen, m. to Donal O'Sullivan Beara ; and 7. a dau. who m. John, Knight of Kerry.

123. Owen of Dunkerron : son of Donal ; m. Julia (living 1603), dau. of Donogh MacCarthy Reagh, Prince of Carbery (and sister to Florence MacCarthy Mór) ; and, dying, in 1623, left issue—1. Donal ; 2. Owen (living in 1640), who had a son, Dermod ; 3. Dermod ; 4. Mary ; 5. Ellen ; and 6. Julia, who m. John O'Connor - Kerry. In 1585, this Owen attended "Perrott's Parliament," in Dublin.

124. Donal (d. 1633) : son of Owen ; m. twice : his first wife was Honoria (d. s. p.), dau. of Edmond Fitzgibbon ; his second wife was Jane, dau. of Patrick Fitzmaurice, the White Knight of Kerry, by

whom he had the following children :—1. Owen ; 2. Donal, married to Mary, dau. of Jenkins Conway, of Kilrolan, co. Kerry ; 3. Philip ; 4. Dominick ; 5. Ellen, who married Finin MacCarthy, of Gorgalt ; 6. Mary ; 7. Dermod ; and 8. Julia. This Donal was buried in the Abbey of Irrelah, co. Kerry.

125. Owen: son of Donal ; married Mary, dau. of Sir Edmund Fitzgerald, of Ballymalow, near Cloyne, co. Cork. This Owen styled "Owen O'Sullivan More," *alias* "The O'Sullivan, Dunkeron Castle," was one of the Forfeiting Proprietors under the Cromwellian Confiscation consequent on the war of 1641-1654.

126. Donal : son of Owen ; died about 1699.

127. Rory-Ramhar : his son ; m. Juliana, dau. of Philip O'Sullivan Beara.

128. Donal O'Sullivan Mór : his son ; m. Hester O'Sullivan, who d. on 17th Jan., 1796, and was buried in Killarney. This hereditary Prince of Dunkerron died, s. p. on the 16th April, 1754, and was the last male representative of this branch of the House of O'Sullivan Mór.

It is a lamentable fact that the O'Sullivan Mór people are in Munster, now reduced to the position of poor labourers. Such is life !

PADDEN.
Of Thomond.

Arms: See those of " O'Brien " of Thomond.

BRIAN OG, a brother of Tirloch who is No. 118 on the " O'Brien" (of Thomond) pedigree, was the ancestor of *MacPhaidin* (" Paidin :" Irish, a diminutive of *Patrick*) ; anglicised *MacFadden*, *Padden*, and *Patten*.

---

118. Brian Og : son of Brian Catha-an-Aoniagh.
119. Diarmaid : his son.
120. Brian : his son.
121. Cormac : his son.
122. Riocard : his son.

123. Diarmaid : his son.
124. Dubh : his son.
125. Donchadh : his son.
126. Daibidh : his son.
127. Sean MacPhaidin : his son.

PLUNKETT.* (No. 1.)

Armorial Bearings : For the Arms of the several branches of the " Plunket" family, see Burke's Armory.

DONOGH, brother of Teige who is No. 106 on the " O'Brien" (of Thomond) pedigree, was the ancestor of *O'Pluingceid ;* anglicised *Plunket*.

106. Donogh : son of the Irish Monarch Brian Boru.
107. Pluingcead ("planc :" Irish,

to *strike severely ;* " cead," *first,* Chald. " chad"): his son ; a quo *O'Pluingceid.*

* *Plunket :* Of this family was Oliver Plunket, Archbishop of Armagh, b. at Lough-crew, co. Meath, in 1629. In 1645 he was sent to Rome under the care of Father Scarampo, Papal Legate, to complete his education ; and next year he entered the Irish College, where he remained eight years. In 1645 he was ordained for the Irish ministry, but the state of the country at that unhappy period rendered his return impossible, and he continued to reside in Rome, where he spent altogether some twenty-five years—from 1645 to 1669. In 1668 he was appointed agent of the Irish clergy at Rome ; and about that time he composed his Irish poem, "O Tara of the Kings." On the 9th July, 1669 he was nominated Archbishop of Armagh ; and in November was duly consecrated at Ghent, it being supposed that his consecration there would be less likely to bring him into trouble with the government in Ireland, than if done in Rome . . . . . In 1674 the clergy were everywhere obliged to fly to the woods and mountains to seek a refuge. In 1678, Catholics were forbidden to reside in any corporate town. In July, 1679, he was arrested in Dundalk, and committed to Newgate, Dublin. He was charged with having compassed the invasion of Ireland by foreign powers . . . . In October, 1680, he was removed to England, and on the 3rd of May, 1681, was arraigned at the King's Bench, when he pleaded " Not Guilty." Five weeks were allowed him to procure witnesses, and on the 8th of June he was again brought up for trial. . . . . The jury after a quarter of an hour's consideration returned a verdict of "Guilty," and he was sentenced to be hanged, drawn, and quartered. He was brought to Tyburn on 1st July, 1681. Captain Richardson, Keeper of New-gate, testified to his bearing, as follows : " When I came to him this morning he was newly awoke, having slept all night without disturbance ; and, when I told him he was to prepare for execution, he received the message with all quietness of mind, and went to the sledge as unconcerned as if he had been going to a wedding." After

108. Oliver: his son; the first of the family who came to Bulin or Boilean.

109. Walter Plunket: his son; first assumed this sirname.

110. John: his son.

111. Alexander: his son.

112. Thomas: his son.

113. Richard Dubh: his son.

114. Patrick: his son. This Patrick had four brothers—1. Oliver,* who was the ancestor of *Plunket,* lords Dunsany; 2. Edward, the ancestor of *Plunket,* lords of Clannabretney; 3. Garret, the ancestor

of *Plunket,* lords of Balrath; and 4. Thomas, the ancestor of *Plunket,* lords of Rathmore.

115. Thomas (2): eldest son of Patrick; had a brother named Richard, who was the ancestor of *Plunket,* lords Louth.

116. Richard: son of Thomas.

117. Patrick: his son.

118. Redmond: his son.

119. John: his son; the first "lord of Killeen" (A.D. 1436) and "earl of Fingall."

120. James Plunket: his son; had a brother named Christopher.

PLUNKET. (No. 2.)

Lords of Fingall.

Sir Christopher, a younger brother of James, is No. 120 on the foregoing "Plunket" (No. 1) genealogy, was the ancestor of this branch of that family.

120. Sir Christopher, Lord of Killeen, Deputy to Thomas Stanley, Knt., Lord Lieutenant of Ireland, 1432, had:

121. Sir Thomas, Knt., his third son, who was Chief Justice of the

Common Pleas, *temp.* Edward IV. This Sir Thomas m. Marian, dau. and heir of —— Cruce, of Rathmore, co. Meath, and had:

122. Edmund Plunket,† of Rathmore, Knt.

making a long and dignified speech, pointing out the absurdity of the charges preferred against him, he resigned himself to the executioner. Wood says in his *Athenæ Oxonienses* that Archbishop Plunket's remains rested in the churchyard of St. Giles's-in-the-Fields, until 1683, when they were removed to Landsprug in Germany. His head, which it was permitted us to see in October, 1886, is preserved in a shrine in the Convent of St. Catherine, Drogheda. Fox, in his *History of James II.,* says: "Charles II. did not think it worth while to save the life of Plunket, the Popish Archbishop of Armagh, of whose innocence no doubt could be entertained."

* *Oliver:* This Oliver had a son named Oliver Oge Plunket, who was the ancestor of *Plunket,* lords of Loughcrew.

† *Plunket:* In the "De la Ponce MSS.," this name is spelled *Pluncket,* so late as A.D. 1788.

The only branches of the "Plunket" family now in existence, are those of the Lords of Louth, Fingal, and Dunsany; all the others are considered to be extinct, for many years—their properties were all confiscated. Loughcrew is in the hands of Mr. Naper; Mr. Wade holds Clannabretney (or Clonabrany) ; and the Blighs have Rathmore. The tomb of the Clonabranny Plunkets is in a very good state of preservation: its inscription is in Latin (with the old Roman raised letters); the date, 1525. The Fingall Plunkets have their burial-place in their old family chapel, in which none but members of the family who have a right of burial there are permitted to be interred. That venerable ruin is situate within a few yards of the hall-door of Killeen Castle, Tara, county Meath, the seat of the Earl of Fingall; the tomb of his lordship's

PLUNKET. (No. 3.)

Lords Dunsany.

JOHN Plunket, Lord of Dunsany, had:

2. Nicholas (the second son), of Clonabreney, co. Meath, who had:

3. Christopher, his heir, who had:

4. Alexander, his heir, who had:

5. Oliver, his heir, who had:

6. Christopher, his heir, who had:

7. Oliver, his heir, who had:

8. Thomas Plunket, of Clonabreney, who died at Hacketstown, co. Dublin, 1st Dec., 1640. He m., first, Margaret, dau. of Car. Moore, of Balyna, co. Kildare, and had six sons and four daughters:

I. Christopher, of whom presently.

II. Alexander.
III. Edward.
IV. Patrick.
V. Henry.
VI. John.

The daughters were:

I. Ellice, who m. William Drake, of Drakerath, co. Meath.
II. Margaret.
III. Anne.
IV. Jane.

The said Thomas, m. secondly. Jane, sister of Christopher Foster, Knt., and widow of Thomas Elliot, of Balriske, co. Meath, s. p.

9. Christopher Plunket: eldest son of Thomas; m. Jane, dau. of Edward Dowdall, of Athlumney, co. Meath.

PLUNKET. (No. 4.)

Of Baune, County Louth.

ALEXANDER PLUNKET, Lord Chancellor, had:

2. John, who had:

3. Richard, who had:

4. Edward, of Baune, county Louth, who had:

5. Alexander, of Baune, who d. 17th May, 1635, and was buried in Mandevilstown. He m. Ellen, dau. of Alexander Plunket, of Gibstown, co. Meath, Esq., and had:

1. John. II. Patrick. III. George. IV. Edward. V. James. VI. Richard.

6. John Plunket, of Baune: son of Alexander.

PLUNKET. (No. 5.)

Of Irishtown, County Meath.

ALEXANDER PLUNKET, Knt., Lord Chancellor of Ireland, who (see Monument of Rathmore) d. 1500, had:

family lies immediately in front of the altar. At the very foot of this tomb was buried in 1824 a Mr. George Plunket, who was in the sixth degree removed in relationship to the grandfather of the present Earl (living in 1887): twenty years later, that George Plunket's son was laid in the same tomb; and a few years later a daughter of the said George. That George Plunket was, we find, great-grandfather of Count George Noble Plunket, of Dublin, Barrister-at-Law, living in 1887.

I. Thomas, of Rathmore, of whom presently.

II. Christopher, of Rathmore, Knt.

III. Edward, of Rathmore, who had: 1. Thomas (son and heir), who had: 2. Sir Oliver (son and heir), who had: 3. Richard, of Rathmore (son and heir), who had: 4. Alexander, of Girly (d. 15 Jan., 1633), who m. Katherine, dau. of Jenico, Viscount Gormanstown.

2. Thomas, of Rathmore: eldest son of Alexander.

3. Gerard, of Irishtown, county Meath: his son.

4. Robert: his son.

5. Gerard: his son.

6. James, of Irishtown: his son; d. 31st Mar., 1639. He m. Eliza, dau. of Thomas Plunket, of Tiltown, co. Meath, and had:

7. Gerard (d. 1st May, 1638), who married Anna, dau. of Alexander Plunket, of Cartown, co. Louth, and had five sons and three daughters:

I. Robert, of whom presently.

II. Alexander.

III. George.

IV. Edward.

V. Christopher.

The daughters were:

I. Katherine, who m. William Darditz, of Hamplinstown, co. Meath.

II. Margaret, who married James Doyne, of Trim.

III. Joan, who m. Oliver Misset, of Dondlestown, co. Meath.

8. Robert Plunket: eldest son of Gerard; m. Tho., dau. of Edward Bath, of Sidan.

PLUNKET. (No. 6.)
Lord Chancellor of Ireland.

Arms : Sa., a bend arg. betw. a castle, in chief, and a portcullis in base or. *Crest :* A horse pass. arg., charged on the shoulder with a portcullis sa. *Supporters :* Dexter, an antelope or ; sinister, a horse arg., each gorged with a plain collar sa., pendent therefrom a portcullis, also sa. *Motto :* Festina lente.

SIR PATRICK PLUNKET, living *temp.* King Henry VIII., married a granddaughter of Sir William Welles, Lord Chancellor of Ireland. A descendant of said Sir Patrick Plunket was (see the "Conyngham" pedigree) the Rev. Thomas Plunket ; commencing with whom the pedigree of this branch of the "Plunket" family is, as follows :

1. Rev. Thomas Plunket married Mary, dau. of David Conyngham, and left two sons—1. Patrick, 2. William.

I. Patrick, who was a Physician, m. and had:

I. William, who emigrated to America, m. and had (besides sons who d. in infancy) four daus. :—1. Margaret, 2. Isabella, 3. Hester, 4. Elizabeth :

I. Margaret married Isaac Richardson and left a large family. Her eldest son was :

I. Dr. William Plunket Richardson, whose granddaughter Mary R. Chrimes was living in 1885 at 4,500 Wabash Avenue, Chicago, Illinois, U.S.A.

II. Isabella m. but left no issue.

III. Hester, who m. her cousin Robert Baxter, of Ireland, and had a dau. Margaret who married her cousin, Dr. Samuel Maclay, but left no issue.

IV. Elizabeth m. Senator Samuel Maclay, and left a large family, their descendants mostly living in Pennsylvania.

II. William-Conyngham: second son of Thomas ; of whom presently.

2. William* Conyngham Plunket, b. 1765, d. 1854: second son of Thomas ; created " Baron Plunket" in 1827 ; made Lord Chancellor of Ireland in 1830 ; m. Catherine, dau. of John Causland, M.P. for Donegal, and had six sons and four daus. The sons were :

I. Thomas, the second Baron, of whom presently.

II. John, Q.C., the third Baron ; b. in 1793, died in 1871 ; m. in 1824 Charlotte (d. Sept. 1886), dau. of the Right Hon. Charles-Kendal Bushe, Lord Chief Justice of the Court of King's Bench in Ireland, and had five sons and eight daughters ; the sons were :

I. William - Conyngham, of whom presently.

II. Charles-Bushe (b. 1830, d. 1880), who in 1860 married Emmeline, dau. of J. Morell, Esq., and had one son and four daughters : 1. David-Darley, b. in 1869 ; 1. Charlotte-Emmeline ; 2. Kathleen-Phœbe ; 3. Flora-Louisa; 4. Violet-Loe.

III. David-Robert, P.C., Q.C., LL.D., M.P. for the University of Dublin.

IV. Arthur - Cecil - Crampton, formerly in the 8th Foot ; b. 1845, d. Oct., 1884 ; m. in 1870 Louisa-Frances, only child of James Hewitt, Esq., and had four sons and five daughters. The sons were : 1. Edward-Cecil-Lifford, b. 1871 ; 2. Henry-Coote-Lifford, b. 1875 ; 3. Archibald-John-Lifford, b. 1877 ; 4. James-Pratt-Lifford, b. 1880; and the five daughters were : 1. Vivian-Charlotte-Lifford ; 2. Louisa-Frances; 3. Eleanor-Alice-Lifford ; 4. Ruby-Isa-

---

* *William :* William Conyngham Plunket, Lord Plunket, Lord Chancellor, was born at Enniskillen, 1st July, 1765. Shortly after his birth, his father, who was a Presbyterian minister, was called to officiate at the Strand Street Chapel in Dublin. Young Plunket entered college about the same time as his friends, Thomas A. Emmet and Yelverton. He became distinguished for his oratorical powers in the debates of the Historical Society, and in his third year obtained a scholarship. At his mother's house in Jervis Street (his father died in 1778), Burrowes, Bushe, Emmet, Magee (afterwards Archbishop), Tone, and Yelverton, constantly met on terms of the closest intimacy. In 1784 he entered at Lincoln's Inn, and two years afterwards was called to the Irish Bar, His progress was rapid and steady. In 1797 he was made King's Council ; and in conjunction with Curran in 1798, he unsuccessfully defended John and Henry Sheares. He was brought into Parliament by Lord Charlemont in 1798, and was one of the most strenuous opponents of the Union. in 1807 Plunket entered Parliament for Midhurst ; but in 1812 he exchanged that seat for the University of Dublin, which he represented until his elevation to the peerage. From the first he strenuously supported the claims of the Catholics for Emancipation, and worked with his friend Henry Grattan for their advancement. He died at Old Connaught, near Bray, county Wicklow, on the 4th January, 1854, aged 89, and was buried in Mount Jerome Cemetery, Dublin.

bel-Lifford ; 5. Irene-Arthur-Lifford.

V. Patrick-Henry-Coghill (twin with Arthur), late of the 70th Foot ; m. in 1878 Anne-Agnes, youngest dau. of John Murray, Esq., of Marlfield, Clonmel, and has had four daughters : 1. Charlotte-Mabel ; 2. Evelyn - Jane Ranger ; 3. Agnes-Josephine Bushe ; 4. Kathleen-Sybil.

The eight daughters of John, the second Baron, were :

I. Anna (d. 1884), who in 1851 m. Right Rev. John R. Darley, D.D., Bishop of Kilmore.

II. Katherine-Frances (d. 1881), who in 1851 m. Sir John-Jocelyn Coghill, Bart.

III. Charlotte (d. 1878), who m. in 1853 Thomas-Henry Barton, Esq., and had issue.

IV. Louisa-Lilias, who in 1852 m. Richard-Jonas Greene, Esq., 2nd son of the Right Honble. Richard-Wilson Greene, Baron of the Exchequer in Ireland, and has issue.

V. Emily-Mary.

VI. Selina-Maria, who in 1864 m. Philip-Crampton Smyly, Esq., M.D., and has issue.

VII. Josephine-Alice.

VIII. Isabella-Katherine.

III. David, a Barrister-at-Law, who in 1837 m. Louisa, dau. of Robert Busby, Esq., and died Sept., 1868.

IV. William-Conyngham, Rector of Bray ; d. 1857.

V. Patrick (d. 1859), a Judge of the Court of Bankruptcy in Ireland ; m. in 1838 Maria, dau. of John Atkinson, Esq., of Ely Place, Dublin, and had two sons and a daughter :

I. William-Conyngham, born 1839.

II. Charles-John-Cedric, born 1854.

I. Constance-Gertrude-Maria, who in 1886 m. Richard-Mayne Tabuteau, Esq., of Simmons Court, co. Dublin.

VI. Robert (d. 1867), was Dean of Tuam and Rector of Headford, m. in 1830 Mary, dau. of Sir R. Lynch-Blosse, of Castle Carra, co. Galway, and had four daughters :—1. Catherine, who in 1853 m. the Rev. Weldon Ashe, Prebendary of Tuam and Incumbent of Annaghdown, who d. in 1874 ; 2. Isabella, who in 1856 m. G. St. George Tyner, Esq., F.R.C.S.I. ; 3. Elizabeth-Louisa ; 4. Frances-Mary, who in 1857 m. Rev. George-Oliver Brownrigg, Rector of Ballinrobe, Tuam ; 4. Mary-Lynch Blosse, who in 1872 m. Robert-Vicars Fletcher, Esq., M.D., F.R.C.S.I.

The four daughters of William, the first Baron, were :

I. Elizabeth (d. 1835), m. in 1824 Rev. Sir Francis Lynch-Blosse, Bart., of Castle Carra, who d. in 1840.

II. Catherine, who d. in 1868.

III. Isabella (d. 1857), who in 1846 m. Henry Quin, Esq., of Burleigh, co. Wexford.

IV. Louisa.

3. Thomas Plunket, P.C., D.D., second Baron : eldest son of William, the first Baron ; was in 1839 consecrated Lord Bishop of Tuam, Killala, and Achonry ; b. 1792, and d. in Oct., 1866, when he was succeeded by his brother John. He m. in 1819 Louisa-Jane, dau. of John-William Foster, Esq., of Fanevalley, co. Louth, and had issue five daughters :

I. Katherine.

II. Mary-Elizabeth-Alice, who in

1862 m. Colonel Sir Thomas-Oriel Forster, Bart., C.B.

III. Frederica-Louisa-Edith, who d. unm. in Feb., 1886.

IV. Gertrude-Victoria.

V. Emily-Anna, who d. in 1843.

4. His Grace, Most Rev. The Right Honble. William-Conyngham Plunket, D.D., of Newton, county Cork, the fourth Baron : eldest son of John, the third Baron; Archbishop of Dublin, and Primate of Ireland; b. 1828, and living in 1887; m. in June 1863 Anne-Lee, only dau. of the late Sir Benjamin-Lee Guinness, Bart., of Ashford,

M.P. (and sister of Arthur, the first Lord Ardilaun), and has two sons and four daughters :

I. Honble. William Lee, of whom presently.

II. Honble. Benjamin John, born 1870.

I. Honble. Elizabeth Charlotte.

II. Honble. Olivia Anne.

III. Honble. Kathleen Louisa.

IV. Honble. Ethel Josephine.

6. The Honble. William Lee Plunket : son of the Right Honble. William Conyngham Plunket, fourth Baron ; b. 19th Dec., 1864, and living in 1887.

POWER. (No. 1.)

("*Ginel Puerach.*")

County Waterford.

Arms : Ar. chief indented sa.

THIS ancient family claims descent from Sir Robert De Poer, who, it is said, came to Ireland with Strongbow, A.D. 1172 ; but, according to Mac-Firbis, the family is of *Irish* descent.

Risdeard, a brother of Iusdas who is No. 109 on the " Eustace" pedigree, was the ancestor of *O'Poir*,* normanized *Le Poer*, and anglicised *Power*.†

109. Risdeard : son of Bened of Raithear Beneudaigh.

110. Seonin : his son.

111. Maigcin : his son.

112. Seonin : his son.

113. Daibhi : his son.

114. Nioclas : his son.

115. Risdeard : his son.

116. Piarus (Pierce) : his son.

117. Risdeard : his son.

118. Seon (or John) Power or De Poer : his son. (See Note, *infra*, " Earl of Tyrone.")

119. John Oge : his son.

120. Richard Power : his son.

As above mentioned, Robert "De Poer," whose ancestor it is said came into England with William the Conqueror, was, we are told, the first of this family that, A.D. 1172, came into Ireland with King Henry the

---

* *O'Poir :* See No. 107 on the " Eustace" pedigree, for the derivation of *O'Poir*.

† *Power :* We are indebted to the courtesy of Count Edmond de Poher de la Poer, of Gurteen, co. Waterford, for an elaborate Pedigree of " The Family of Pohar, Poer, or Power," which gives this family a *French* origin. It is but right, however, to say that the Irish origin of the family as given by MacFirbis is also that given in the MS. Vol. F. 4. 18, in the Library of Trinity College, Dublin.

Second, who, by charter, granted unto the said Robert, by the name of Robert *Puber*, the City of Waterford, with "the whole province thereabouts;" and made him marshal of Ireland. In the year 1179, this Robert De Poer was joined in commission with Sir Hugo De Lacy, as lords justices of Ireland. In the year 1177, John De Courcy, with the aid of Roger Poer (who was likely the brother or one of the three sons of the said Robert), conquered Ulidia. We read that this Roger (or Sir Roger) Le Poer was the friend and companion in arms of Sir John De Courcy and Sir Armoric St. Lawrence, and was the standard-bearer and marshal of Ireland ; of him *Giraldus Cambrensis* writes :—

"It might be said, without offence, there was not one man who did more valiant acts than Roger Le Poer, who, although he was a young man and beardless, yet showed himself a lusty, valiant, and courageous gentleman ; and who grew into such good credit that he had the government of the country about Leighlin, as also in Ossory where he was traitorously killed."

And *Cambrensis* says that Sir Roger Le Poer was "the youngest, bravest, and handsomest of all the Anglo-Norman knights." This Sir Roger married a niece of Sir Armoric St. Lawrence (ancestor of the earls of Howth), and by her had a son, John Le Poer, living A.D. 1197, whose grandson, Sir Eustace, sat in Parliament in 1295. He was succeeded by lord Arnold Le Poer, who slew Sir John Boneville in single combat; and was one of the commanders in the Army of King Edward the First of England, against Edward Bruce, in Ireland, in 1315. Lord Arnold Le Poer was succeeded by lord Robert Le Poer, seneschal of the co. Wexford, and treasurer of Ireland. To him succeeded Matthew ; after him John ; and after him, Richard, whose son Nicholas was summoned to Parliament by Writ, dated 22nd November, 1375, and "three times afterwards." Of those Writs, Lodge says : "These are the most ancient *Writs of Summons* to Parliament that remain on record in the Rolls Office of Ireland." Richard, lord Le Poer, grandson of the said Nicholas, married Catherine, second daughter of Pierce Butler, eighth earl of Ormond (and hence, probably, the Christian name *Piers, Pierse, or Pierce*, came into the "Power" family).

In 1673, Richard, lord Le Poer, was created "viscount of Decies" (or viscount De Decies) and "earl of Tyrone ;"* whose grandson had an only daughter, the lady Catherine Le Poer, who married Sir Marcus Beresford, baronet, and carried into the "Beresford" family (now represented by the marquis of Waterford) the ancient barony by "Writ of Summons" of the lords Le Poer. It may be well to observe that, among the modern nobility

* *Earl of Tyrone* : The following extract from Lodge's Peerage of the "Earldom of Tyrone" may be of interest to members of the *Power* family : "John, lord Le Poer, being only eight years and a half old at his grandfather's death, became the ward of King James the First, who, 7th December, 1606, granted his wardship to his mother ; but, 30th March, 1629, he had a special livery of his estate (he became a lunatic before the rebellion of 1641), and marrying Ruth, daughter and heir of Robert Pypho, of St. Mary's Abbey, Esq., had five sons and four daughters : viz., 1. Richard, created earl of Tyrone ; 2. Pierse, Killowan, county Waterford, who married Honora, daughter of John, the second lord Brittas (having issue Richard, who died there in February, 1635, leaving, by Ellen, daughter of William Butler, of Balliboe, county Tipperary, gent., 1. John, his heir, which John married Ellen, daughter of Daniel Magrath, of Mountaincastle, in

of Ireland, no "barony" is so much prized (because of its antiquity) as that of *Writ of Summons* to Parliament.

So early as A.D. 1368, the *Le Poers* (or *Powers*) were very numerous in the county Waterford, and in possession of a very large portion of the county called "Powers' Country;" and, besides the family of Curraghmore (the seat of the marquis of Waterford), there were those of the baron of Donisle, and the house of Kilmeaden—both of which were destroyed by Oliver Cromwell, during his "Protectorate."

Of the *Le Poer* family (which has existed in the county Waterford for the last seven centuries) there have been many branches and offshoots; one or two of which we are able to trace down to the present time. I. The following is one of them as far as we can trace it:

1. John Power, of Kilmeaden.
2. Nicholas: his son.
3. Piers: his son.
4. Sir William: his son.
5. John (2): his son.
6. David: his son; died A.D. 1696.

7. John (3): his son; had two brothers; died (before his father) in 1693.

8. David Power: his son; living in 1709; had one brother.

II. Pierce Power,* by his second wife, Grace, daughter of Sir T. Osborne, was the ancestor of the following branches of the *Power* family:

1. Pierce Power; had three younger brothers—1. Richard, of Carrigaline, county Cork; 2. Breine; 3. Robert.

2. Pierce (2): son of said Pierce; had six younger brothers—1. Milo, 2. Richard, 3. David, 4. John, 5. Thomas, and 6 Anthony.

3. Nicholas: son of Pierce; had a brother, the Rev. John, who died *s.p.*

4. Pierce, of Ballyhane, near Whitechurch, county Waterford:

son of Nicholas; had three sisters—1. Penelope, 2. Eliza, 3. Alicia; married, in 1762, Elizabeth, dau. of Valentine Browning, son of Major Browning, who came to Ireland with Cromwell. The male issue of that Major Browning having failed, the said Elizabeth Browning became the heiress of Affane, near Cappoquin; and thus the Affane property came into the possession of the said Pierce Power, who died in 1815.

5. Rev. William Power: his fifth

---

the county Waterford; Pierce, whose daughter Judith was married to Mr Ducket; James, Ellen, and Anne, and founded the family at Rathcormac, in the county Waterford); 3. Robert; 4. John, who died unmarried in Dublin; 5. David, who died there, 17th August, 1661, and was buried at St. Michan's; 1. Ellen, married to Thomas Walsh, of Piltown, sen., Esq.; 2. Catherine, married to John Fitzgerald, of Dromana, Esq. (whose only daughter, Catherine, was mother of John, late earl Grandison): 3. Margaret; and 4. Mary.

In Notes at foot of the foregoing, Lodge gives the following references: MS. Pedig. Trin. Coll., 1676; and again MS. Pedig. Trin. Coll. Plea and Ans. Villers to Poer. 14th November, 1676.

* *Pierce Power*: This Pierce was twice married: by his first marriage he had a son named Roger.

son; had four brothers—1. Samuel,* 2. Nicholas (who died young, *s.p.*), 3. John,† 4. Pierce; and three sisters —Alice, married to John Drew, Esq., of Frogmore, county Cork, 2. Catherine, married to Sir Christopher Musgrave, Bart., of Tourin, county Waterford, 3. Jane, married to Rev. George Miles. This William succeeded to Affane, in 1815; married, in 1807, Mary-Araminta, dau. of the Rev. Thomas Sandiford; and died 1825, leaving issue—1. Samuel Browning, 2. Edward, 3. Rev. Thomas.

6. Samuel Browning Power: eldest son of William; succeeded to Affane in 1825; was a J.P. for county Waterford; in 1831 married Mary, daughter of Thomas Woodward, Esq., of the Forest of Dean, Gloucestershire; died in 1867, leaving issue three sons and three daughters: the sons were — 1. William, 2. Richard-Charles, 3. Frederick-Edward; the daughters were—1. Frances-Susanna, 2. Mary-Araminta, 3. Susanna-Louisa.

7. Captain William Power, of Affane: eldest son of Samuel-Browning; in 1869 married Catherine-Mary, only surviving child of Captain Jervois, R.N., of Winifred Dale, Bath; living in 1880.

POWER. (No. 2.)

Lords Power.

RICHARD, Lord Power, had: 2. Thomas of Cullefin, county Waterford, *Arm.*, who had: 3. James, who had: 4. Thomas, who d. 15 Dec., 1637. He m. Margaret, dau. of Peter Butler of Monyhory, co. Wexford, and had four sons and four daus.:

I. Peter, of whom presently.

II. Richard, who m. Gyles, dau. of David Power, of Culroe, co. Waterford.

III. John.   IV. James.

The daughters were:

I. Joan, who d. s. p.

II. Gyles, who m. Jeffrey Fanning of Fanningstown, co. Tipperary.

III. Katherine.

IV. Margaret, who m. Richard Power, of Ballincurry, county Waterford.

5. Peter Power: eldest son of Thomas; m. Katherine, dau. of William Wale, of Clonymuck, co. Wexford.

---

* *Samuel*: This Samuel Power was married to Anne, daughter and co-heir of Sir G. Browne, by whom he had three sons and three daughters: the sons were—1. George-Beresford, married to Elizabeth Reeves, by whom she had one son (Samuel) and one daughter (Dorothea-Carttor); 2. Samuel; 3. Rev. Henry. The daughters were— 1. Anna, married to D. Blake, Esq.; 2. Elizabeth; 3. Georgina.

† *John*: This John was twice married: first to Anna Ross, by whom he had three children—1. Pierce, 2. Elizabeth, married to W. L. Ogilby, 3. Mary, married to J. Farrell; his second marriage was to Jane Bennett, by whom he had five children—1. Samuel, married to Rebecca Danver, 2. Philip, 3. John, 4. Philip, 5. Anna-Ross. The children of this Samuel Power and his wife Rebecca Danver, were—1. John-Danver, 2. Florence-Danver, 3. Frederick-Danver, 4. Arthur-Danver, 5. Lilian Danver, 6. Philip-Danver, 7. Norman-Danver, 8. Arnold-Danver.

POWER. (No. 3.)

Of Rathcormack, County Waterford.

JOHN, Lord Power, had :

2. Peter (his second son), who had :

3. Richard, of Rathcormack, Esq., who d. Feb., 1635. He m. Ellen, dau. of William Butler, of Ballybor, co. Tipperary, gent., and had issue :

4. John, who m. Ellen, dau. of Donagh McGrath, (or *Macrath*), of Mountaincastle, co. Waterford. This John had four brothers :—1. James, 2. Edmund, 3. William, 4. Peirce ; and one sister Ellen.

QUAILE.

Arms : Erm. on a canton vert. a calvary cross on three grieces or.

REACHTABRA, a brother of Fiachra an-Gaircedh who is No. 97 on the "Vera-O'Sullivan" pedigree, was the ancestor of *O'Cuill ;* anglicised *Quaile, Quill, Penfeather,* and *Pennefather.*

97. Reachtabra : son of Seachnasach.

98. Flann : his son.

99. Iondrachtach : his son.

100. Maonach : his son.

101. Bran : his son.

102. Maolfohartach : his son.

103. Donchadh : his son.

104. Flann : his son.

105. Cuill (" cuille" : Irish, *a quill*): his son ; a quo *O'Cuill.*

106. Aodh : his son.

107. Donchadh : his son.

108. Ceannfaoladh : his son.

109. Aodh : his son.

110. Mathghamhnach : his son.

111. Ceannfaoladh : his son.

112. Seaan : his son.

113. Donchadh O'Cuill : his son.

QUIN.

Earls of Dunraven,

Arms* : Quarterly, 1st and 4th, gu. a hand couped below the wrist grasping a sword ppr., on each side a serpent, tail nowed, the heads respecting each other or., in chief two crescents ar., for O'QUIN, of Munster ; 2nd and 3rd, az. a chev. betw. three lions' heads erased or. with a mullet for diff., for WYNDHAM. *Crests:* 1st, QUINN : A wolf's head erased ar. ; 2nd, WYNDHAM : A lion's head erased within a fetterlock and chain or. *Supporters* : Two ravens with wings elevated ppr. collared and chained or. *Motto:* Quæ sursum volo videre.

ÆNEAS (or Aongus) Ceannathrach,† a younger brother of Blad who is No. 92 on the "O'Brien" (Kings of Thomond) pedigree, was the ancestor of *O'Cuinn* or *Muintir Cuinn,* of Munster ; anglicised *O'Quin, Quin,* and *Quain.*

* *Arms* : The arms of O'QUIN, of Munster, were : Gu. a hand couped below the wrist grasping a sword all ppr. betw. in chief two crescents ar., and in base as many serpents erect and respecting each other, tails nowed or. *Crest* : A boar's head erased and erect ar. langued gu.

† *Ceannathrach :* This is the epithet ("ceann" : Irish, *a head ;* "atrach," *a boat*) employed in some Irish MSS. in the case of this Æneas ; while *Ceannattin* ("ceann" : Irish, *a head ;* "attin," *furze*) is the epithet in others.

92. Æneas Ceannathrach : a younger son of Cas, a quo *Dal Cais*, or *Dalcassians*.

93. Rethach : his son.

94. Seanach : his son.

95. Diomma : his son.

96. Dunsleibhe : his son.

97. Cuallta ("cuallta" : Irish, *a wolf*) : his son ; a quo *O'Cualltaigh*, anglicised *Kielty, Quilly*, and *Wolf*.

98. Fermac ("fear" : Irish, *a man;* "mac," *bright, pure, clear*) : his son ; a quo *Cineal Fearmaic*, of Thomond.

99. Fercinn ("cionn" : Irish, *head, cause, account*) : his son ; a quo *O'Fercinn*, by some anglicised *Perkin* and *Perkins*.*

100. Flann Scrupuil : his son

101. Flancha : his son.

102. Dubhsalach : his son.

103. Donn : his son.

104. Donal : his son.

105. Deadha (" deadhachd :" Irish, *godliness*) : his son ; a quo *O'Dead-haichd*, anglicised *O'Day, O'Dea,*† *Day, Dee*, and *Deedy*.

106. Conn Mór (" conn": Irish, *wisdom*) : his eldest son ; a quo *O'Cuinn* or *Muintir Cuinn*. Had a younger brother Donoch, from whom descended the *O'Dea* (of Thomond) family ; and another younger brother, Flaithertach, who was the ancestor of *Roughan*.

107. Niall : son of Conn Mór ; had a younger brother named Donal.— See the *Linea Antiqua*. This Niall was slain, A.D. 1014, at the Battle of Clontarf, fighting on the side of the Irish Monarch Brian Boroimhe [boru], against the Danes.

108. Feadleachair : son of Niall.

In this generation the sirname was first assumed in this family.

109. Corc : his son.

110. Murrogh : his son.

111. Donogh : his son.

112. Giolla-Sionan : his son.

113. Donogh : his son.

114. Donal : his son.

115. Tomhas : his son.

116. Donal : his son.

117. Donal : his son.

118. Connor O'Quin : his son ; who lived in the second quarter of the 14th century.

119. Donal : his son.

120. John : his son.

121. Donogh : his son. This Donogh had, besides his successor, another son John, who was Bishop of Limerick.

122. James, of Kilmallock : son of Donogh.

123. Donogh : his son ; mar. Miss Nash, of Ballynacaharagh, by whom he had two sons, namely—1. Donogh Oge ; 2. Andrew, mentioned incidentally in a letter from Lord Kerry to Col. David Crosbie, dated 3rd October, 1648.

124. Donogh Oge : son of Donogh ; m. a Miss O'Riordan.

125. Teige : their son. Had a dau. Elenora, who was m. to Simon Haly, of Ballyhaly.

126. Valentine, of Adare : son of Teige ; m. Mary, dau. of Henry Wyndham, of the Court, county Limerick ; d. 1744.

127. Wyndham : son of Valentine ; in 1748 m. Frances, dau. of Richard Dawson, of Dawson's Grove.

128. Valentine-Richard : their son;

---

* *Perkins :* According to MacFirbis, " Perkins" and " Perkinson" were in Gaelic rendered *MacPiaruis*, and sometimes *MacPeadhair*, which are by him classed among Saxon families (*Sloinnte Saxonta*) settled in Ireland.

† *O'Dea* : This family of " O'Dea," who are of the *Cineal Fearmaic*, of Thomond, and of the Dalcassian race, are a distinct family from *O'Dea*, of Slieveardagh, in the county Tipperary.

R

created "Earl of Dunraven and Mount Earl," on the 22nd January, 1822. He m., in 1777, Frances, dau. of Stephen, first Earl of Ilchester, by whom he left, at his decease in 1824, his successor, another son Richard-George, and a dau. Harriet, who m. Sir William Payne-Gallwey, Bart.

129. Windham-Henry Wyndham, the second Earl, who d. 1850 : son of Valentine-Richard; m., on 27th Dec., 1810, Caroline, dau. and sole heiress of Thomas Wyndham, Esq., of Dunraven Castle, Glamorganshire, and had :

I. Edwin-Richard-Wyndham, of whom presently.

II. Windham-Henry-Wyndham (d. 1865), Captain Grenadier Guards; b. 1829 ; m., in 1856, Caroline, third dau. of Vice-Admiral Sir George Tyler, K.H. (she re-married in 1867 Col. N. O. S. Turner, R.A.), and left with other issue :

    I. Windham-Henry-Quin ; b. 1857.

I. Lady Anna-Maria-Charlotte (d. 1855), who m. in 1836, the Right Hon. William Monsell (now Lord Emly), of Tervoe, co. Limerick.

130. Edwin-Richard-Wyndham,* the third Earl (who d. Oct., 1871) : son of Windham-Henry-Wyndham ; b. 1812. Was twice married : first, to Augusta, third dau. of the late Thomas Goold, Esq., Master in Chancery; and secondly, to Anne, dau. of Henry Lambert, Esq., of Carnagh (who, as the Dowager Countess of Dunraven, m. secondly, on the 26th April, 1879, Hedworth Hylton Jolliffe, second Baron Hylton). The children of Edwin-Richard-Wyndham by the first marriage were :

I. Windham-Thomas-Wyndham, of whom presently.

I. Lady Caroline-Adelaide ; b. 1838; d. 1853.

II. Lady Augusta-Emily ; b. 1839.

III. Lady Mary-Frances; b, 1844; m. in 1868 Arthur Hugh Smith-Barry, Esq., of Marbury Hall, Cheshire, and of Fota Island, Cork (who was M.P. for Cork, 1867-1874.)

IV. Lady Edith.

V. Lady Emily-Anna.

131. Windham-Thomas-Wyndham

---

* *Wyndham* : Edwin-Richard-Wyndham Quin, third Earl of Dunraven, was a prominent archæologist. At Eton he showed a strong taste for astronomy ; and he afterwards spent three years at the Dublin Observatory under Sir William Hamilton. Natural Science occupied much of his attention ; he was also deeply interested in the study of Irish antiquities, and was a prominent member of the Royal Irish Academy, the Celtic Society, and several Archæological associations. His chosen friends were men such as Graves, Stokes, Petrie, Reeves, and Todd. He accompanied the Comte de Montalembert to Scotland, when engaged upon his *Monks of the West*, one volume of which is dedicated to Lord Dunraven : "Prænobili viro Edvino Wyndham Quin, Comiti de Dunraven." Attended by a photographer, he visited nearly every barony in Ireland, and nearly every island on its coast. He made his investigations with a view to the publication of an exhaustive work on the architectural remains of Ireland, profusely illustrated with photographs, his main object being to vindicate the artistic and intellectual capabilities of the ancient and mediæval Irish. Having died before the completion of the work, the result of his labours has been given to the world, at the expense of his family—*Notes on Irish Architecture, by Edwin, third Earl of Dunraven*: *Edited by Margaret Stokes*. (London : 1875 and 1877) : two superb volumes, with 125 illustrations, most of them large photographs. What may be called the spirit of ancient Irish architecture is brought out in this book in a style never previously attempted in pictorial representations.

Quin, of Adare† Manor, Adare, co. Limerick, and of Dunraven Castle, Bridgend, Glamorganshire, late 1st Life Guards : son of Edwin-Richard- Wyndham; living in 1887; b. 12th Feb., 1841; m., 29th April, 1869, Florence, second dau. of Lord and Lady Charles Lennox Kerr; succeeded his father, as the fourth Earl, on the 6th October, 1871. Issue :

   I. Lady Florence Emid.

   II. Lady Rachael-Charlotte.

   III. Lady Aileen May.

RING.

Arms : Ar. on a bend gu. three crescents of the first.   *Crest* : A hand vested sa. cuffed or., holding a roll of paper.

DAIRE CEARB, a brother of Lughaidh who is No. 88 on the " Line of Heber," was the ancestor of *O'mBillrin ;* anglicised *Ring.*

88. Daire Cearb : son of Olioll Flann-Beag.

89. Fiacha Fidgente : his son.

90. Brian : his son.

91. Cairbre : his son.

92. Erc : his son.

93. Aill Ceannfhoda : his son.

94. Lapadh : his son.

95. Aongus : his son.

96. Aodh : his son.

97. Crunnmaol : his son.

98. Eoganan : his son.

99. Aodh Ron : his son.

100. Dubhdhabh : his son.

101. Ceannfaoladh : his son.

102. Dall ("dall" : Irish, *blind*) : his son ; a quo *O'Dhaill* Gabhra, anglicised *O'Dally, O'Dell, Odell,* and *Dale.*

103. Fursach : his son.

104. Duneadach : his son.

105. Aongus : his son.

106. Dubarthach : his son.

107. Billrian ("bill" : Irish, *small,* "rian," *a footstep*) : his son ; a quo *O'mBillrin.*

108. Ecthighearn : his son.

109. Suthan ("suth" : Irish, *soot, the weather,* "an," *one who*) : his son ; a quo *O'Suthain,* anglicised *Sutton.*

110. Maolruanadh O'mBillrin : his son.

† *Adare :*

Oh, sweet Adare ! oh, lovely vale !
   Oh, soft retreat of sylvan splendour !
Nor summer sun, nor morning gale,
   E'er hailed a scene more softly tender.
How shall I tell the thousand charms
   Within thy verdant bosom dwelling,
Where, lulled in Nature's fost'ring arms,
   Soft peace abides and joy excelling.

     ·   ·   ·   ·   ·

              —GERALD GRIFFIN.

ROUGHAN.

FLAHERTACH, the third son of Deadha who is No. 105 on the "O'Dea" pedigree, was the ancestor of *O'Roghain;* anglicised *Rowhan, Roan,* and *Roughan.*

106. Flahertach : son of Deadha.
107. Searragh Roghan ("seair-riach" : Irish, *a foal,* and "rogha," *a choice*) : his son ; a quo *O'Roghain.*
108. Faolan : his son.
109. Feach : his son.
110. Olioll : his son.
111. Eanna : his son.
112. Criomthann : his son.
113. Feareadhach : his son.
114. Foalusa : his son.
115. Donogh Claragh : his son.
116. Ainbhleithe : his son.
117. Ceallach : his son.
118. Morogh : his son.
119. Eoghan (or Owen) : his son.
120. Muireadhagh : his son.
121. Murtogh : his son.
122. Dermod O'Roughan : his son.

SHANNON.

[*Arms* : Gu. a bend or. *Crest* : A demi talbot sa.

COSCRACH, a brother of Cineadh (or Cendedach) who is No. 106 on the "Kennedy" (of Thomond) pedigree, was the ancestor of *O'Seanchain;* anglicised *Shanahan,* and *Shannon.*

106. Coscrach : son of Donchadh Cuan.
107. Flaithbeartach : his son.
108. Seanchan ("seancha" : Irish, *an antiquary,* or *genealogist*) ; his son ; a quo *O'Seanchain.*
109. Donchadh Dubh : his son.
110. Ruadhri : his son.
111. Donchadh : his son.
112. Aodh : his son.
113. Flaithbeartach : his son.
114. Taidhg : his son.
115. Ruadhri : his son.
116. Donchadh : his son.
117. Aodh : his son.
118. Flaithbeartach : his son.
119. Taidhg : his son.
120. Aodh O'Seanchain : his son.

SHEEDY.

ACCORDING to some genealogists, Sioda, who is No. 62 on the "Mac-Namara" pedigree, was the ancestor of *MacShioda;* anglicised *MacSheedy, Sheedy, Silk,* and *Silke.* But this family directly descends from Sioda,[*] a younger brother of John an Ghabhaltuis (or John the Conqueror), who is

---

Sioda : According to a description of the County Clare, preserved in the Library of Trinity College, Dublin, *Clann Coilein* (situate in the western portion of that county), the territory of the MacNamara, known as the "MacNamara Fionn," comprised the

No. 117 on the " MacNamara" genealogy : that Sioda who was the ancestor of " MacNamara Fionn."

117. Sioda ("Sioda" : Irish, *Silk*) : son of Maccon ; a quo *MacShioda*.

118. Maccon-Dal : his son.

119. Sioda : his son ; had a brother John Fionn.

120. Florence : his son.

121. Lochlan : his son.

122. Florence : his son.

123. Florence : his son.

124. Sioda : his son.

125. Daniel Sheedy : his son. Had two brothers—1. Donoch (or Denis), 2. Thade ; living in 1691.

SLATTERY.

OWEN (Eoghan), brother of John who is No. 118 on the " Hickey" pedigree, was the ancestor of *O'Slatiairaidh ;* anglicised *Slattery.*

118. Owen O'Hickey : son of John ; was called *An-Slat-Iairaidh* (" Slat" : Irish, *a rod*, and " iair," *to ask*), as if he deserved the *birch* ; a quo *O'Slatiairaidh.*

119. William O'Slattery : his son ; was the first that assumed this sirname.

120. John O'Slattery : his son.

SPELLAN.

Arms : Sa. a fess erm. a bend gu. guttée d'or ; *another :* Sa. a fess erm. a bend or, guttée de sang; *another :* Sa. ten bezants, four, three, two, and one, betw. two flaunches ar. ; and *another :* Gu. a chief erm.

THIS family is variously called *O'Spealain, Spellan, Splaine, Spollen, Spellman,* and *Spilman ;* and is descended from Mahon, son of Kennedy, the brother of Brian Boroimhe, who is No. 105 on the " O'Brien Kings of Thomond" Stem. The *O'Hanrahan* family is also descended from this Mahon or Mahoun. The tribe-name of the *O'Spellan* sept was Hy-Leughaidh, a name subsequently given to the lands of which they were possessed in the barony of Eliogarty, county of Tipperary ; and a name derived from Leughaidh, a remote ancestor of the family. O'Heerin says :

> " The chief of Hy-Leughaidh of swords,
> Is O'Spellan of the bright spurs ;
> Majestic is the march of the warrior."

Of this family was the learned author of the *Manual of Therapeutics.* A branch of the house of Hy-Leughaidh in early times settled in the following parishes : Killaloe, Aglish, Killurin, Kilkeady, Kilbrooney, Tullagh, Moynoe, Kilnoe, Killokennedy, Kiltrinanela, Feakle, Kilfinaghty, and Inishcaltragh.

As the O'Grady's were seated in Tomgrany, Scariff, and Moynoe, it may be assumed that they were tributary to the Chiefs of the MacNamaras.

After the Cromwellian Settlement the "Sheedy" family were scattered : some of them settled in the county Cork, some in Tipperary, some in Limerick, and some in West Clare ; but few, if any, of them are now to be found in their ancient patrimony of *Clann Coilein.*

barony of Galmoy in the county of Kilkenny, and gave name to "Bally-spellane," celebrated for its mineral waters; another branch settled in the barony of Barrymore, county of Cork, and gave name to "Ballyspillane," a parish in that barony.

We believe the present representative of this family is Philip Splaine, Esq., The Green, Passage West, county Cork, whose ancestors, for many generations, resided in Templemartin parish, barony of Kinalmeaky, co. Cork, their chief residence being built in the centre of an old fort in the townland of Gurranes, in that parish, and convenient to the old palace of the O'Mahony Princes.

STEWART. (No. 1.)

High Stewards of Scotland.

Arms : Or. a fess chequy az. and ar.

CORC, No. 89 on the stem of the "Line of Heber," was married to Mong-fionn, daughter of Feredach Fionn (also called Fionn Cormac), King of the Picts.   Main Leamhna, one of the sons by that marriage, remained in Scotland with his grandfather, Feredach Fionn, who gave him land to inhabit, called *Leamhain* (anglicised *Lennox*), which his posterity enjoyed ever since with the appellation or title of *Mór Mhaor Leamhna,* i.e. "Great Steward of Lennox;" and at length became Kings of Scotland and of England.   This term "Steward" is the origin of the sirnames *Stewart* and *Stuart.*

89. Corc : King of Munster.
90. Main Leamhna : his son.
91. Donal : his son.
92. Muredach : his son.
93. Alen (or Alan), the elder, first "Great Steward of Lennox :" his son ; a quo *Stewart.*

94. Alen, the younger : his son.
95. Amhailgadh [awly], the elder: his son.
96. Awly, the younger : his son.
97. Walter : his son.
98. Donogh (Doncan or Duncan) : his son.

"Here the old Irish copy of the Genealogy of this Royal Family is defective, some leaves being either torn or worn out with time, wherein the pedigree (in all likelihood) was traced down to the time of the writing of that book some hundreds of years past ; and no other copy extant to supply it.   I am (therefore) necessitated to follow the Scottish writers, where they begin to take notice of this noble and princely family, in the person of Bianco, who was lineally descended from the above-named Donogh or Duncan, who was Thane of Lochquaber ; was one of the chief nobility of Scotland ; and near Kinsman to the good King Duncan, who was murdered by the usurper Macbeth, as were this Bianco and all his children except his son Fleance."— *Four Masters.*

[As this Bianco was murdered by Macbeth, he must have been contemporary with his "near kinsman the good King Duncan," who (see p. 39) is No. 108 on the "Lineal Descent of the Royal family ;" we may therefore reckon Bianco as, at least, No. 107 on this family stem.]

107. Bianco, lineally descended from Duncan, who is No. 98 on this stem.

108. Fleance : his son.
109. Walter : his son.
110. Alan Stewart : his son.   This

Alan went to the Holy Land with Godfrey of Boloign (now "Boulogne") and Robert, duke of Normandy, A.D. 1099; where he behaved himself with much valour, for the recovery of Jerusalem.

111. Alexander: his son.

112. Walter: his son; who in the great battle of Largys, fought against the Danes, A.D. 1263.

113. Alexander (2): his son.

114. John, of Bute: his son; lord high steward of Scotland; was one of the six governors of the Kingdom during the controversy between Robert Bruce and John Baliol, for the Crown, A.D. 1292.

115. Walter: his son. This Walter, lord high steward of Scotland, married Margery,* only daughter of Robert Bruce, King of Scotland; on whom the Crown was entailed, by Parliament, upon default of male issue of the said Robert Bruce's only son, David, which happened accordingly.

116. Robert Stewart: their son; was A.D. 1370, under the name of "Robert the Second," crowned King of Scotland.

117. John: his natural son; who changed his name, and was crowned King of Scotland, under the title of "Robert the Third."

118. James the First, King of Scotland; his son; was, at the age of fourteen years, imprisoned in the tower of London, and remained there a prisoner for nineteen years. He was murdered in 1437; when his son, James the Second, was only six years old.

119. James the Second, King of Scotland: his son; was slain by the splinter of a cannon, which bursted at the siege of Roxburgh, in 1460. This James† had a brother named Ninion ("noinin:" Irish, *a daisy*), who was ancestor of *Craig* of Banbridge, and of *Stewart* of Baltimore, Maryland, United States, America.

120. James the Third, King of Scotland: son of King James the Second; slain in 1488.

121. James the Fourth, King of Scotland: his son; was slain in the battle of Floddenfield, fought against the English, A.D. 1513. This James was married to Margaret, eldest daughter of King Henry the Seventh of England.

122. James the Fifth, King of Scotland: his son; died in 1542.

123. Mary Stewart (or Stuart), "Queen of Scots:" his only daughter and heir; was proclaimed Queen of Scotland, A.D. 1542; and beheaded on the 8th February, 1587, leaving issue one son by her second husband, Henry Stuart, lord Darnley. Mary, Queen of Scots, was first married to the Dauphin of France; where the sirname "Stewart" first assumed the form of *Stuart*.

124. James Stuart, known as James the Sixth of Scotland: her son; *b.* in Edinburgh Castle, 19th June, 1566; *m.* Anne, daughter of Frederick II., King of Denmark, and had by her issue—1. Henry (*d.* 6th Nov.,

---

* *Margery:* It is recorded that King James the First of England jocosely used to say —"It was through a *lassie* (meaning this Margery) that the Stuarts obtained the crown of Scotland; and it was through a *lassie* (meaning Queen Elizabeth) that they succeeded to the crown of England."

† *James:* In his "History of Scotland" Sir Walter Scott states that James the First, King of Scotland, had two sons, one of whom died in childhood without issue; the other succeeded to the throne as James the Second. According to Collier's "History of the British Empire," James I., of Scotland, had only one son; but he had also a son named Ninion.

1612, aged 19 years), 2. Charles, and 3. Elizabeth who married in 1613, Frederick, Elector of the Palatine of Bavaria, afterwards King of Bohemia, on whose youngest daughter Sophia the succession to the English Crown was settled by Act of Parliament, A.D. 1710. This James, who (see p. 40) is No. 128 on the "Lineal Descent of the Royal Family," was King James the First of England ; where, on the death of Queen Elizabeth, who died without issue, he began to reign on the 24th day of March, A.D. 1603. He died on the 27th March, 1625, of a tertian ague, at his Palace of Theobalds, Herts, and was buried at Westminster. In his reign, as King of England, took place what is called the "Ulster Plantation" of Ireland ; meaning that the province of Ulster was seized by the English Government of that period, and parcelled out amongst English and Scotch adventurers, who were then *planted* in Ulster. See the "Flight of the Earls," in the Appendix.

————"On Queen Elizabeth's demise,
The Scottish JAMES her vacant place supplies,
Uniting into one, both crowns he claims,
And then conjunctively *Great Britain* names."
———— EGERTON.

125. Charles I. : son of King James I., of England ; b. at Dunfermline, Fifeshire, Scotland, 19th November, 1600 ; crowned at Westminster, 6th Feb., 1626, and at Holyrood, 18th June, 1633 ; m. Henrietta, dau. of Henry IV., King of France, by his wife, Mary de Medici. Issue by her— Charles ; Mary, who was married to William, Prince of Orange, father of King William the Third of England ; James ; Henry, who died in 1660 ; Elizabeth, who died in 1649 ; and Henrietta (d. 20th Jan., 1670), who was married in 1661 to Philip, duke of Orleans. This Charles was, by the Cromwellian party, beheaded, 30th January, 1648-9, in front of the Banqueting House, Whitehall, London. His body was exposed to public view in one of the apartments ; and afterwards privately buried in St. George's, Windsor. On the death of King Charles I., his son Charles II., after a period of twelve years' despotism under the "Protectorate" of Cromwell, returned from exile in France and Holland ; landed at Dover, 25th May, 1660 ; entered London on the 30th of that month—his thirtieth birthday ; ascended the throne of England, and was crowned at Westminster 23rd April, 1661. Charles II. was born at St. James's Palace, London, in 1630 ; m. Catherine, Infanta of Portugal, 20th May, 1662, by whom he had no issue. This "Merry Monarch" died 6th Feb., 1685, it is said of apoplexy ; but Burnet says, in his "History of his own Times," that there was strong suspicion that Charles II. had been poisoned.

126. James II. : second son of King Charles I. ; b. in Edinburgh Castle, in 1633 ; crowned at Westminster ; and reigned from 1685 to 1688. He was twice married : first to Anne (d. in 1671), dau. of Hyde, earl of Clarendon, by whom he had Mary, who was married to William of Nassau, Prince of Orange ; Queen Anne ; and other children ; married secondly, 30th September, 1673, a dau. of Alphonso D'Este, duke of Modena, of whom he had one son.

James II., having by the Revolution been deprived of the throne of Great Britain and Ireland, was hospitably received, himself, his family, and his friends who accompanied him to France, by Louis XIV., at the palace of St. Germain; he was in 1696 offered the Crown of Poland, which he declined. He died on the 16th September, 1701.

127. James-Francis-Edward : son of James II.; by some called "King James the Third," by others "The Pretender;" b. at St. James's Palace, London, 20th June, 1688 ; married 2nd September, 1719, the Princess Maria-Clementina Sobieski, (daughter of Prince James-Louis Sobieski, son of John Sobieski, King of Poland, who, in 1683, saved Vienna and Europe from the Turks), and had by her issue two sons. This James Stuart died at Rome, 30th December, 1765, and was there interred.

123. Charles-Edward : son of James-Francis-Edward ; commonly called "The Young Pretender;" b. at Rome 31st December, 1720 ; m. in 1772 Louisa (who d. 1824), dau. of Prince Sobieski of Gedern in Germany, and had by her issue one son. This Charles-Edward in 1745 landed in Scotland, with the view of regaining the Crown of Great Britain and Ireland ; but was ultimately defeated at Culloden, A.D. 1746. He escaped to France, accompanied by Vera-O'Sullivan and the renowned Flora Mac-Donald; d. January, 1788, at Albano, in Italy, and was buried at Rome.

129. Charles-Edward, living in 1830 : son of Charles-Edward ; m. Catherine Bruce* (at the Peak Derbyshire, England), by whom he had issue—John-Sobieski Stuart, and Charles-Edward Stuart. John Sobieski Stuart, who was called Compt D'Albanie, did on the marriage of his younger brother, resign his claim to the throne ; he died February, 1872.

130. Charles-Edward (3): second son of Charles-Edward ; married Anne De La Poer Beresford.

131. Charles-Edward (4): his son; who, on the 15th June, 1874, married Alice Hay, daughter of the late Earl of Erroll, at the Roman Catholic Church, Spanish-place, London ; living in Austria, in 1880.

STEWART of Baltimore. (No. 2.)

Ninion, a brother of James the Second, King of Scotland, who is No. 119 on the foregoing ("Stewart") pedigree, was the ancestor of *Stewart*, of Baltimore, Maryland, United States, America.

119. Ninion Stewart: a son of James the First, King of Scotland.	120. James: his son.
	121. Ninion (2): his son.

---

* *Catherine Bruce :* The Charles-Edward Stuart who married Catherine Bruce, was, for fear of assassination, brought up under an *alias* "Hay Allen ;" he was known in Scotland as *Iolar* (" iolar :" Irish, *an eagle*). An old Highlander, one of those who saw the last of "Iolar" in Scotland, uttered the following words :—

"Dhia beannachd an la ! agus Eirichibh air sgiath nam Beann Iólar oig uasal a'h-Albainn."

And the exclamation of the Highlander, who last saw "Iolar" and Catherine Bruce, his wife, was :—

"On beannachd dhuib-se uasail aillidh rothaitneach do dh' Albainn."

122. James (2): his son.
123. Christian : his son.
124. Ninion (3): his son.
125. William: his son.
126. James (3): his son.
127. James (4): his son; born near Augher, county Tyrone, Ireland, about 1706; died in Wilmington, Delaware, U.S., America, A.D. 1788: Will recorded on 5th July of that year; had a brother named Samuel, who was born in Ireland in 1704, and died in Wilmington in 1773.
128. James (5): his son.
129. Joseph James, of Baltimore: his son; born in Delaware, in 1793; living in 1877: had a bro-

ther named William, father of General Alexander P. Stewart, of Oxford, Mississippi, United States, America, Chancellor of the University of Mississippi, and living in 1880.
130. Hon Joseph-James Stewart, of Baltimore, Maryland, U.S.A : son of Joseph-James; living in 1880; married Mary, daughter of James Baynes of Woodhall Park, parish of Aysgarth, Yorkshire, by his wife Martha Burgh of Bristol, England, of the De Burgh family.
131. George C. Stewart: his son ; born in 1860 ; has a brother named James B. Stewart, born in 1862— both living in 1877.

STEWART. (No. 3.)

Lords Castlestewart.

Arms : See Burke's "Armory."

ANDREW STEWARD, Lord of Evingdale, *alias* Avandale, had :
2. Andrew, Lord Ochiltre, *alias* Oghiltre, *alias* Ughiltre, who had :
3. Andrew, who had :
4. Andrew, Lord Ochiltre, who had :
5. Andrew *Stewart*, Bart., of Nova Scotia, Lord Castlestewart, county Tyrone, who d. 30th March, 1639, and was bur. on the 3rd April. He m. a dau. of John, Earl of Atholl, who d. 15th Oct., 1635, and had :

I. Andrew.
II. Robert.
6. Andrew, Lord Castlestewart : son of Andrew ; m. Joyce, dau. of Arthur Blundell, of Blundelstown, Knt., and had one son and three daughters :
I. Josias.
I. Eliza.
II. Margaret.
III. Joyce, s. p.
7. Josias Stewart: son of Andrew.

SULLIVAN.

As a tribute of gratitude, and of our respect to the memory of the late Dr. Sullivan for his disinterested goodness and kindness to us when, in the Autumn of 1845, poor and friendless we entered the Training Department of the Board of National Education in Ireland ; we here give the following brief narrative from Webb's *Compendium of Irish Biography,* to commemorate the name of our dear and cherished friend :—

Robert Sullivan, LL.D., Barrister-at-Law, etc., the author of a number of well-known educational works, was born at Holywood, county of Down, in January, 1800. He was educated at the Belfast Academical Institution ; graduated in Trinity College, Dublin, in 1829; and, on the introduction of the system of National Education into Ireland in 1831, was appointed an Inspector. He was afterwards transferred to the Training Department, Marlboro' Street, as Professor of English Literature. His *Geography, Spelling Book Superseded, Literary Class Book, Grammar,* and *Dictionary,* have gone through numerous editions, and are constantly being reprinted. The touching expressions he received from time to time of the gratitude of those whom his sympathy had encouraged, or his generosity had aided, showed the kindliness of his nature, and his success in communicating knowledge. He died, s. p., in Dublin, 11th July, 1868, aged 68 : and was buried at Holywood.

TAVNEY.

Ros, a brother of Daire, who is No. 91 on the "O'Connell" pedigree, was the ancestor of *Fheara Tamhanaighe* or *O'Tamhanaighe* ("tamhanach :" Irish, *a dolt*) ; anglicised *Tamany,* and *Tavney.*

91. Ros : son of Brian.
92. Ece (" ece :" Irish, *clear ;* Lat. " ecce," *behold*) : his son.
93. Ros : his son.
94. Daimh Dasachdach : his son.
95. Daimhin : his son.

96. Fedhlim : his son.
97. Lonan : his son.
98. Maolochtrach : his son.
99. Cuanach : his son.
100. Aurthach : his son.

TRACEY.

Of Munster.

CAOINEALADH, brother of Laipe, who is No. 94 on the "O'Donovan" pedigree, was the ancestor of *O'Caoinealaidh,* anglicised *Coneely, Kaneely,* and *Kanelly ;* and of *O'Treassaigh,* of Munster, anglicised *Trasey, Tracey,* and *Tracy.*

94. Caoinealadh : son of Olioll Ceannfhada.
95. Feargaile : his son.
96. Treassach (" treas :" Irish, *the*

third in order): his son ; a quo *O'Treassaigh.*
97. Dermod : his son.
98. Ceadach na-Brighe ("brigh :"*

---

* *Brigh :* This Irish word seems to be the root of the sirname *Bright.* The name *Ceadach* ("cead :" Irish, *first ;* Chal d. " chad ") implies "the foremost man ;" and *Ceadach na Brighe* means "the man who was foremost for his strength."

Irish, *strength ;* Gr. " bri," *very great;*
Heb. " bri," *fruit*) : his son.

   99. Don O'Trasey (or O'Tracey) :
his son ; first assumed this sirname.

   100. Ceadach : his son.

   101. Cuinge : his son.

   102. Conor : his son.

   103. Conor Luath : his son.

   104. Edmond : his son.

   105. Edmond Oge : his son.

   106. James : his son.

   107. James Oge O'Trasey : his son.

VERA-O'SULLIVAN. (No. 1.)

Of Cappanacusha Castle, near Kenmare, co. Kerry.*

Arms :† A dexter hand couped at the wrist, grasping a sword erect. *Crest :* On a ducal coronet or, a robin redbreast with a sprig of laurel in its beak. *Motto :* Lamh foistenach an uachtar.

ACCORDING to O'Heerin's Topography, the O'Sullivans, before they settled in Kerry, were Princes of Eoghanacht Mór, Cnoc-Graffan, a territory in the barony of Middlethird, county Tipperary, which is said to have embraced the districts of Clonmel, Cahir, Clogheen, Carrick-on-Suir, and Cashel of the Kings, in the fifth and sixth centuries ; and are thus mentioned:

> O'Sullivan, who delights not in violence,
> Rules over the extensive Eoghanacht of Munster ;
> About Cnoc-Graffan broad lands he obtained,
> Won by his victorious arms, in conflicts and battles.

The Vera-O'Sullivans are believed to have traded with Cornwall, Bristol, and places in the East ; are said to have had ships, yawls, and many boats ; and some of them to have been noted sailors and commanders at sea.   The figure-head of their ships (as represented on a seal in possession of Mr. T. Murtogh Vera-O'Sullivan, in India, which has been submitted to us for inspection) was a sailor standing upright in a boat with a fish in each hand extended over his head, which are believed to have been Scripture emblems of the Christian Church.   This branch of the O'Sullivan family, it would appear, were the pioneers of the O'Sullivans, who first settled in Kerry ; the O'Sullivan Mór family following soon after.   From their bravery and prowess the Vera-O'Sullivans were by their own people styled the " No surrenders ;" and by their British neighbours they were called " Devils in fight."   They were nearly all soldiers in the service of

---

* *Cappanacusha* (or, in Irish, *Ceapa-na-Coisé*) Castle was destroyed on two or three occasions during the wars in Ireland ; on the last occasion it was not rebuilt. It is in ruins, situate in the present demesnes of Dromore Castle, Kenmare, now in possession of MacDonough O'Mahony, J.P.

† *Arms :* It is worthy of remark, in connection with the claim of the " O'Sullivan" family to be the *senior* branch of the House of Heber, who was the eldest son of Milesius, that the flag of the Milesians represented a *dead serpent* entwined round a rod ; in commemoration of the rod of Moses, by which he cured the neck of Gaodhal when stung by a serpent ; while the *ancient* Arms of this family was a dexter hand couped at the wrist, grasping a sword erect, the blade *entwined with a serpent*, &c.

Anstria, France, and Germany, in which countries they held high commands.

The territory of the Vera-O'Sullivans of Cappanacusha Castle, adjoined that of the O'Sullivan Mór; extended from the barony of Dunkerron, co. Kerry, to the present Williamstown and Millstreet; and was bounded as follows: On the north, by Williamstown and Millstreet; south by Kenmare; west by Dunkerron; and east, by Glancrought.

FINGIN, brother of Failbhe Flann, who is No. 95 on the Line of the House of Heber, was the ancestor of *O'Suilebhain;* anglicised *O'Sullivan,** and *Sullivan.*

95. Fingin : son of Aodh Dubh, King of Munster; from him descended the *O'Suilebhain* family, anglicised *O'Sullivan** and *Sullivan*; was elected joint King of Munster, in the life-time of his brother Failbhe; m. Mór Mumhain. (See No. 94 on the "Stem of the Line of Heber," *ante*).

96. Seachnasagh : son of Fingin.

97. Fiachra an Gaircedh : his son; had a brother Reachtabra.

98. Flann Noba : son of Fiachra.

99. Dubhinracht : his son.

100. Morogh : his son.

101. Moghtigern : his son.

102. Maolura : his son.

103. Suilebhan ("suilebhan:" Irish, *one eye*): his son : a quo *O'Suilebhain.*

104. Lorcan : his son.

105. Buadhach Atha-cra) "buaidh:" Irish, *victory*, Heb. "buagh," *to exult*; "atha :" Irish, *a ford*, and "cradh," *death*): his son.

106. Hugh : his son.

107. Cathal : his son.

108. Buadhach O'Sullivan : his son; first assumed this sirname.

This Buadhach is said to have gone over the sea for a Slavonic or Macedonian wife, and from her this branch of the O'Sullivan family derives the name *Vera-O'Sullivan;* "Vera" meaning *faith*, in the Sla-

vonic tongue. He had two sons— 1. Maccraith, 2. Cathal.

109. Maccraith : son of Buadhach.

110. Donal Mór : his son.

111. Giolla Mochoda (or Gilmochud): his son; had a brother, Giolla na-Bhflainn, who was the ancestor of *O'Sullivan Beara.*

112. Dunlong : son of Giolla Mochoda; in 1196 left co. Tipperary, and settled in the co. Kerry.

113. Murtogh Mór : his son; m. Catherine, dau. of MacCarthy Mór. Had a brother Gille Mochodh.

114. Bernard : his son; m. Mary MacCarthy of the House of Carbery, and had two sons, Buochan and Philip.†

115. Buochan : son of Bernard.

116. Dunlong : his son.

117. Ruadhri (or Roger): his son; had a brother named Craith, a quo *MacGrath.*

118. Donal : son of Roger.

119. Donal of Dunkerron : his son.

120. Eoghan (or Owen): his son.

121. Dermod of Dunkerron : his son; had a younger brother named Donal na Sgreadaidhe (or "Donal of the Shriek") from whom the *O'Sullivan Mór* family is descended.

122. Connor : son of Dermod.

123. Donal : his son.

124. Owen Ruadh : his son.

---

* *O'Sullivan :* The root of this sirname is the Irish *suil.* gen. *sul.* "the eye." And *suil.* "the eye," is derived from the Irish *sul*, "the sun" (Lat. *sol.*); because the "eye" is the light of the body. The old Irish called "Sunday," *Dia Suil* (Lat. *Dies Sol-is*), before the Christians called it *Dia Domhnaigh* (Lat. *Dies Dominica*), "the Lord's day."

† *Philip :* See No. 115 on the "MacCarthy Reagh" pedigree.

125. Owen* of Cappanacusha Castle : his son ; forfeited his estate in the war of 1641-1652.

126. Dermod : his son. Of the children of this Dermod the names of the following are known :
I. Murrough-Vera, of whom presently. II. Murtogh Fion. III. William-Leim-laidir. IV. Philip. V. Thige laidir (or strong Timothy). VI. John-Vera.† VII. Timothy-Murtogh.

127. Murrogh - Vera O'Sullivan : son of Dermod.

128. Thige Laidir ("strong Timothy") : his son.

129. John-Vera : his son.

130. Timothy-Vera : his son.

131. Timothy-Murtogh-Vera : his son ; an officer in the Indian Commissariat, living in Fyzabad, Oude, Bengal, Hindostan, in 1887 ; m. Ellen Fitzpatrick, and has had issue :
I. William John-Vera, of whom presently.
II. Timothy-Murtogh-Vera.
III. James-Thomas-Vera.
IV. Henry James-Vera.
V. John-Vera.
VI. Eugene-Sextus-Vera.
VII. Eoghan-Donal-Vera.
VIII. Hugh-Vera.
I. Mary-Ellen-Vera.
II. Nelly-Eleanor-Vera.
III. Eveleen (Eibhlin)-Vera.
IV. Catherine-Veronica-Vera.
V. Nora-Mary-Vera.
VI. Nesta-Lucy-Vera.
VII. Mary-Erina-Vera.
VIII. Finnola-Vera.

132. William - John -Vera O'Sulli-

---

* *Owen :* This Owen Vera O'Sullivan had a daughter Mary, who in 1641, married Daniel, son of Art Oge O'Keeffe of Ballymacquirk Castle, Duhallow, co. Cork, and had issue three sons:—1. Art Oge, who followed the hard fortunes of Charles II., 2. Denis, whose son Connor became Lord Bishop of Limerick ; 3. Daniel, who married Margaret Hudson of Newmarket, co. Cork, by whom he had a son Arthur, who along with his father were slain at the Battle of Aughrim, fighting on the side of King James II. This Arthur's son Hudson O'Keeffe fled to France, there married Gabriel Deville, had issue, and became absorbed in the French nation.

† *John Vera :* This John Vera O'Sullivan was the chief companion, and general-issimo, of Prince Charles Edward Stuart, called " The Pretender ;" he struggled hard to recover the Crown of England for the House of Stuart. He afterwards served with great distinction in the service of the King of France, where he was considered a Military-Scientist, and one of the most engaging and best bred officers in the French Army. He was specially knighted by " James the Third." On the 17th April, 1747, Sir John Vera O'Sullivan married Louisa, daughter of Thomas Fitzgerald, and left a son Thomas Herbert Vera O'Sullivan, who served in the British Army under Sir Henry Clinton at New York ; again in the Dutch service, and was the bosom friend of Prince de Figne ; he died as Field Officer in 1824, leaving two sons :—1. John-William ; and 2. Thomas-Gerald, who perished in swimming ashore with a rope to save a crew of a distressed ship. John-Lewis, son of John-William, was in 1854 United States Minister to the Court of Portugal. General Sir John Vera O'Sullivan's portrait is in the possession of his grandson : he is in the uniform of the 7th Regiment Irlandés, which shows the names of the following officers—Bulkeley, Clare, Dillon, Roth, Berwick, Lally, and Fitzjames.

General Sir John Vera O'Sullivan was educated in Paris ; and to give him the most expensive education, his parents mortgaged the little property that remained to them in Desmond, and which was held in trust for them by a kind Protestant gentle-man of that neighbourhood. After the death of Sir John's mother, he returned to, Kerry, and privately sold the Desmond property, as the Irish Catholics were then pro-scribed. He never afterwards returned to Ireland.

Thomas, son of Sir John Vera-O'Sullivan, was an officer in the Irish Brigade ; he removed to America and entered the British service, which he ultimately exchanged for the Dutch. He died a major at the Hague in 1824,

van : eldest son of Timothy-Mur-
togh-Vera O'Sullivan ; living in
India in 1887, and serving in Bengal
Commissariat Department.

VERA-O'SULLIVAN. (No. 2.)

Of Cappanacusha Castle.

Junior Branch.

Armorial Bearings : Same as those of " Vera O'Sullivan."

115. PHILIP O'SULLIVAN : second
son of Bernard, No. 114 on the foregoing pedigree ; m. Honoria (or
Nora) O'Connor Kerry.

116. Donal : his son ; m. Joanna
MacCarthy.

117. Richard (or Rory) : his son ;
m. Una, dau. of Neil Oge O'Neill,
Prince of Ulster.

118. Owen : his son ; m. to Graine
MacCarthy.

119. Donal (2) : his son ; m. to
Maedhbh O'Donnell.

120. Philip (2) : his son ; m. to
Nelly, a dau. of Owen O'Sullivan
Mór.

121. Rory : his son ; m. to Mór
Fitzmaurice.

122. Donal (3) : his son ; m. to
Julia O'Donovan.

123. Owen (2) : his son ; m. Elizabeth Fitzgerald.

124. Ruadhraidh : his son ; m.
Julia MacCarthy, of Drishane.

125. Donal (4) : his son ; m. Elana
MacAuliffe.

126. John : his son ; m. Mary
O'Keeffe, of Killeen.

127. Tadhg (or Thige) : his son ;
m. Joanna O'Callaghan, of Clonmeen, co. Cork ; had issue :—1.
Philip ; 2. Connor, b. 2nd May,
1683, d. 5th May, 1769 ; m. to

Ellen, dau. to Stepney Galwey,
merchant, Cork. This Tadhg d.
4th Aug., 1706, aged 54 years.

128. Philip (3) : his son ; b. 8th
March, 1682, d. 1754 ; m. Elizabeth,
dau. of —— Irwin, of Roscommon,
by whom he had—1. Owen, 2.
Benjamin (of Cork), and 3. Oonagh
(or Una) :

   (2). Benjamin had a son, Sir
     Benjamin, who was father of
     George James O'Sullivan of
     Wilmington, Isle of Wight
     (1867).

129. Owen : his son ; b. 1744, d.
1808 ; he remained at or about
Kenmare, where he m. a Miss
O'Moriarty, and had by her several
children, who, finding strangers in
possession of their patrimony, dis-
persed themselves to seek by hard
labour a means of subsistence.
Among other children he had—1.
Donogh (or Denis), 2. John, 3.
Donal, 4. Owen, 5. Nora, and 6.
Julia.

130. Donogh (or Denis) : his son ;
b. 1776, d. 1838 ; buried at Kilmurry, barony of West Muskerry,
co. Cork ; m. a Miss M'Auliffe, and
by her had issue :—1. John, 2.
Denis, 3. Owen, and 4. Nora.*
This Donogh led a wandering life

---

* *Nora :* This Nora m. a man named Murphy, and had by him, two sons—1.
Conn (d. s. p.) ; and 2. Denis, who m. Kate Burke, and had issue—1. Conn, 2. John, 3.
Denis, 4. Kate. This Denis resides (1887) at Douglas, near Cork.

in East and West Muskerry, generally at Shandubh, parish of
Moviddy, where he died.

131. John*: his son; b. about
1799, d. ——, buried at Kilmurry;
resided for some time at Ahandubh,
afterwards at Teeraveen, parish of
Kilmurry, where he died. He m.
Rachel, the dau. of Richard (or
Roderic) O'Neill, hereditary Prince
of Ulster, and by her had issue·—
1. Donogh; 2. Joanna; 3. John;
4. Nora; 5. Richard; 6. Donogh
(2) (or Denis); 7. Kate; 8. another
girl, and 9. Kate (2).

All of these d. s. p. except Nora,
Richard, and Denis, who are living
in 1887. (4) Nora, m. Donal
O'Cahan (or Kane), resides (1887)
at Rerour, parish of Kilbonane; has
no issue.

(6) Denis, m. Ellen,† the dau. of
William Sheehan of Killegh, by
his wife Joanna Hennessy, and
has had issue: Honora (or Nora),
b. 1861, d. 1867; Rachel, b.
25th April, 1869; Joanna, b.
14th May, 1871; John, b. 20th
May, 1873; Richard, b. 5th
June, 1875; and Denis, b.
22nd July, 1879. This Denis
with his family resides (1887)
at Curraghbeh, parish of Kilmurry.

132. Richard O'Sullivan: his son;
b. —; m. Kate O'Donovan, has by
her only one child living—Julia, b.
21st June, 1864; unm. in 1887.
This Richard resides (1887) at
Maghbeg, a few miles to the west
of Bandon, as a farm-labourer to a
man named Daly! John: eldest
son of Denis, brother of Richard
(132), is living in 1887, at Curraghbeh, near Kilmurry.

IRISH MONARCHS OF THE LINE OF HEBER.

1. Heber Fionn: son of Milesius of Spain.
2. Er
3. Orba
4. Feron   } : sons of Heber Fionn; reigned together one year.
5. Fergna
6. Conmaol: son of Heber Fionn.
7. Eochaidh Faobhar-glas: son of Conmaol.
8. Eochaidh Mumha: son of Mofeibhis, son of Eochaidh (7).
9. Eanna Airgthach: son of Eochaidh Faobhar Glas.
10. Munmoin: son of Cas, son of Fearard, son of Rotheacta, son of
Ros, son of Glas, son of Eanna (9).
11. Fualdergoid: son of Munmoin.
12. Rotheacta: son of Ronnach, son of Failbhe Iolcorach, son of Cas
Cedchaingnigh, son of Fualdergoid.

---

* *John* : We believe that the Revd. Daniel O'Sullivan, P.P., of Enniskane, west of
Bandon, was a cousin to this John. This Rev. gentleman's memory, as a zealous priest,
and a solid Irish scholar and poet, is still fresh in the memory of the people of south
and west Cork.

† *Ellen* : The other brothers and sisters of this Ellen are :—John, Mary, William,
Michael, Mark (of Lahore), Nora, James, and Robert.

13. Eiliomh : son of Rotheacta.
14. Art Imleach : son of Eiliomh.
15. Breas Rioghachta: son of Art Imleach.
16. Seidnae Innaraidh: son of Breas Rioghachta.
17. Duach Fionn : son of Seidnae Innaraidh.
18. Eanna Dearg : son of Duach Fionn.
19. Luaghaidh Iardhonn : son of Eanna Dearg.
20. Eochaidh Uarceas: son of Luaghaidh Iardhonn.
21. Lughaidh Lamhdearg : son of Eochaidh Uarceas.
22. Art : son of Lughaidh Lamhdearg.
23. Olioll Fionn : son of Art.
24. Eochaidh : son of Olioll Fionn.
25. Luaghaidh Lagha : son of Eochaidh (24).
26. Reacht-Righ-dearg : son of Luaghaidh Lagha.
27. Moghcorb : son of Cobthach Caomh, son of Reacht Righ-Dearg.
28. Adhamhair Foltchaion : son of Fearcorb, son of Moghcorb.
29. Niadhsedhaman : son of Adhamhair Foltchaion.
30. Ionadmaor : son of Niadhsedhaman.
31. Lughaidh Luaighne : son of Ionadmaor.
32. Duach Dalladh-Deadha : son of Cairbre Lusgleathan, son of Lughaidh Luaighne.
33. Crimthann : son of Felim, son of Aongus, etc., son of Duach (32). See the "Line of Heber," No. 93.
34. Brian Boroimhe : son of Cineadh, son of Lorcan, etc., son of Cormac Cas (See O'Brien Stem), son of Olioll Olum, son of Eoghan Mór, son of Dearg, son of Dearg Theine, son of Eanna Muncain, son of Loich Mór, son of Muireadach, son of Eochaidh Garbh, son of Duach (32).
35. Donough : son of Brian Boroimhe.
36. Tirloch : son of Teige, son of Brian Boroimhe.
37. Muirceartach : son of Teige, son of Brian Boroimhe.

S

CHAPTER II.

THE LINE OF ITHE.

ITHE (or Ith), brother of Bilé who is No. 35, page 50, was the ancestor of the *Ithians.* This Ithe was uncle of Milesius of Spain ; and his descendants settled mostly in Munster.

THE STEM OF THE "LINE OF ITHE."

The Stem of the Irish Nation, from Ithe down to (No. 73) Cobthach Fionn, a quo *O'Coffey,** of Munster.

35. Ithe : son of Breoghan, King of Spain.

36. Lughaidh [Luy] : his son ; a quo the Ithians were called *Lugadians.*

37. Mal : his son.

38. Edaman : his son.

39. Logha : his son.

40. Mathsin : his son.

41. Sin : his son.

42. Gossaman : his son.

43. Adaman : his son.

44. Heremon : his son.

45. Logha Feile : his son.

46. Lachtnan : his son.

47. Nuaclad Argni : his son.

48. Deargthine : his son.

49. Deagha Derg : his son.

50. Deagha Amhra : his son.

51. Ferulnigh : his son.

52. Sithbolg : his son.

53. Daire (or Darius) Diomdhach : his son.

54. Each-Bolg : his son ; had a brother named Luy, who was the ancestor of *Clancy* of Dartry, in Leitrim ; and some say, of *Mac-aulay* or *MacGawley* of Calry, in Westmeath.

55. Ferulnigh (2) : his son.

56. Daire (2) : his son ; from whom the Ithians were called *Darinians.*

57. Luy : his son.

58. MacNiadh : his son. Sabina, daughter of Conn of the Hundred Battles, was married to this Mac Niadh [Nia], by whom she had a son named Luy Mac con (*cu;* Irish, gen. *con, coin,* or *cuin, a greyhound,* also *a champion ;* Gr. *Ku-on*), to whom the *soubriquet* "Mac con" was affixed, because in his youth he was wont to suckle the teat of a favourite *greyhound.* After Mac Niadh's death, Sabina got married to Olioll Olum, king of Munster, as already mentioned. (See p. 67.)

59. Luy Mac con : his son ; the 113th Monarch of Ireland.

60. Aongus (or Æneas) : his son ; had four brothers :—1. Fothach Argthach, the 118th Monarch of Ireland jointly with his brother Fothach Cairpeach, by whom, A.D. 285, he was slain ; 2. the said Fothach Cairpeach, the 119th Monarch ; 3. Duach, ancestor of *Conell, O'Hennessy, McEirc,* etc. ; 4. Fothach Canaan, ancestor of *MacAlim*

---

* *O'Coffey :* There were other families of this name in ancient Meath and in Connaught, but not of the same stock as this fam'ly.

or *MacCalum,* Earls of Argyle, etc. From one of these brothers also descended *O'Hallinan,* etc.

61. Fergus : son of Æneas.

62. Luigheach : his son.

63. Æneas Bolg : his son.

64. Gearan : his son ; had a brother named Trean.

65. Conall Claon ("claon" : Irish, *partial ;* Gr. "klin-o") : his son.

66. Ceann Reithe ("reithe": Irish, *of a ram ;* " ceann" *a head*) : his son ; a quo *O'Reithe.**

67. Olioll : his son ; had a bro-

ther named Trean, from whom descended St. Beoardh (8 March) of Ardcarn.

68. Fergus : son of Olioll.

69. Connacille : his son.

70. Maccon : his son.

71. Olioll (2) : his son.

72. Dungal : his son.

73. Cobthach Fionn ("cobthach" : Irish, *victorious ;* " fionn," *fair,* meaning "the fairhaired victor") : his son ; a quo *O'Cobhthaigh,* anglicised *O'Coffey, O'Cowhig, Coffey, Coffy,* and *Coffee.*

ANTHONY.

Arms : Ar. a leopard betw. two flaunches sa. *Crest :* A goat's head gu.

DONGALACH, who is No. 69 on the "Needham" pedigree, was the ancestor of *O'Uaithne* ("uaithne" : Irish, *green*) ; anglicised *Anthony, Antony, Green,* and *Antonie ;* and a quo the name of the barony of " Owney" in Tipperary.

69. Dongalach : son of Fothach.

70. Foghartach : his son.

71. Flaith-im : his son.

72. Gorggal : his son.

73. Aongus : his son.

74. Dearmatha : his son.

75. Cathan : his son.

76. Cathalan : his son.

77. Cathmath : his son.

78. Ruadhri : his son.

79. Matudan : his son.

BARRY. (No. 1.)

Arms : Ar. three bars gemels gu.

FOTHACH CANAAN, the fifth son of Lughaidh Maccon, who is No. 59 on the " Line of Ithe," *ante,* was the ancestor of *O'Baire ;* anglicised *Barry,†* *Barie, Barrie,* and normanized *De Barrie,* and *Du Barri.*

* *O'Reithe :* This name has been anglicised *Ram.*

† *Barry :* Of this family was James Barry, the distinguished artist, who was born in Cork in October, 1741 ; and died in London on the 22nd February, 1806, aged 64 ; and was interred in St. Paul's, near to his friend Sir Joshua Reynolds.

Another of this family name was John Barry, Commodore, who was born near Tacumshin, co. Wexford, in 1745 ; he died in September, 1803, and was burried in Philadelphia. He went to sea at the age of fourteen ; and the colony of Peansylvania became his adopted country. When only twenty five he had risen to be the commander

59. Lughaidh (or Luy) Maccon, the 113th Monarch of Ireland : son of MacNiadh.

60. Fothach Canaan : his son.

61. MacNiadh [nia] : his son.

62. Breasal : his son.

63. Eochaidh (or Eocha) : his son.

64. Conor : his son.

65. Baire : his son.

66. Garran : his son.

67. Aodh (or Hugh) Beag : his son.

68. Echin : his son.

69. Eochaidh Aigneach : his son.

70. Baire ("baire" : Irish, *a hurling match*) : his son ; a quo *O'Baire.*

William Fitzphilip Barry got a grant and confirmation from King John, dated 8th November, 1208, of the three cantreds of—1. Olthan, 2. Muscry, 3. Dunegan and Killedy; which Fitzstephen had given his father in the "kingdom of Cork."

1. William Fitzphilip Barry; whose parentage is not mentioned.

2. David : his son ; the ancestor of *Barry,* of Barrymore ; was Lord Justice of Ireland, A.D. 1267.

3. Robert : his son.

4. Philip : his son.

5. David (2) : his son.

6. Davoc : his son.

7. William Maol : his son.

8. Lawrence : his son.

9. James : his son.

10. Richard : his son.

11. James (2) : his son.

12. Richard (2) : his son.

13. James (3) : his son.

14. David Barry : his son ; living A.D. 1170.

BARRY. (No. 2.)

Viscounts of Buttevant, County Cork.

Arms : Ar. three bars gemels, gu. *Crest :* Out of a castle with two towers, ar. a wolf's head sa. *Supporters :* Two wolves ducally gorged and chained or. *Motto :* Boutez en avant.

RICHARD, the second son of Viscount Buttevant, had :

2. Thomas, of Ballyroney, county Cork, who had :

3. Thomas, who had :

4. David, who had :

5. John, who had :

6. David, who d. 3rd Jan., 1639.

He m., first, Ellen, dau of —— Hacket, and by her had five daughters. David's second wife was Eliza, dau. of —— Suple, by whom he had :

7. John Barry, who m. Ellen, dau. of Richard Barry, of Monydonly, co. Cork, gent.

of the *Black Prince,* one of the finest traders between Philadelphia and London. Early in the War of Independence, he was given a naval command by Congress, and was one of the first to fly the United States flag at sea. In 1777 he was publicly thanked by General Washington, for his valuable services. It is stated that Lord Howe vainly endeavoured to tempt him from his allegiance by the offer of the command of a British ship-of-the-line. In 1778 and 1779, he commanded the *Relief,* and was accorded the rank of Commodore. From the conclusion of the War until his death, he was constantly occupied in superintending the progress of the United States Navy ; and has been called by some naval writers the father of the American Navy.

BARRY. (No. 3.)

Of Sandville, County Limerick.

Arms : See those of " Barry" (No. 2.)

A CADET of the " Barry" family of Buttevant got by marriage, early in the fifteenth century a considerable estate in the Clangibbon country, near Kilmallock, in the co. Limerick. A member of the family inter-married* with the family of Bourke of Clanwilliam, in the same county.

1. Donal Barry (d. in 1612), of Owney (now Abington), had :

2. " Dowle" (or Daniel), who d. in 1640, was buried in the family vault† at Abington, which he had erected in 1633. He m. Johanna Bourke, of the Bourkes (Lord Brittas) family, and had :

3. David, who succeeded his father in 1640, but lost his property in the general confiscations after 1649. This David Barry, having saved the life of a member of the Ingoldsby‡ family, was excused from transplanting, and settled under the protection of Ingoldsby on the lands of Fryarstown, in the parish of Rochestown, about 1656. This David Barry left several sons.

4. John, of Fryarstown : son of said David; d. in 1710, leaving three sons.

I. James, of whom presently.

II. David. III. Thomas. These two sons David and Thomas served in the army of King James II.

---

* *Intermarried :* The Barrys intermarried with the Bourkes; the Raleighs, of Rawleystown ; Fitzgeralds and Molonys of the co. Clare; Hartwells of Bruff; O'Shaughnessys, a branch of the Gortensignara family ; Grenes, of Cappamurra; etc. The principal seats of the Bourkes (mentioned in this genealogy) were Brittas Castle ; Bilboa Court, Caherconlish, Castle Connell, Ballybricken Court, Ballynegarde, and Kilpeacon. A large grant of the lands of Rawleystown, which was part of the Desmond Estate, was in 1609 made by King James the First to James Raleigh, uncle to Sir Walter Raleigh.

† *Vault :* The inscription on that vault is still legible, and reads as follows :—

✠

" Nobilis admodum Dulamus Barry In honorem suorum Parentum sui ipsius, Uxoris Joannæ Bourke, et filiorum suorum, hoc sepulchrum fieri curavit.

" Antiqua Genitus Barri de stirpi Dulamus
Quique Appolonea Doctus in arte viget.
Quique fide plenus nusquam languentibus agris,
Defuit et Potriam qualibet auxit ope
Hæc pius extinctis monumenta parentibus affert,
Quæ sibi quæque deinsint monumenta suis
Tu qui cernis opus mortis memor esto futuræ,
Dic præcor hac vivant qui tumulantur humo.
A.D. 1633."

‡ *Ingoldsby :* Sir Henry Ingoldsby, governor of Limerick, got large grants of the confiscated Estates of the Bourkes, in the Barony of Clanwilliam, co. Limerick ; including Ballybricken, Fryarstown, Luddenmore, Ballyhoudan, etc. Sir Henry Ingoldsby's mother was Elizabeth, daughter of Sir Oliver Cromwell, Knight of the Bath, eldest brother of the Protector's father. Lord Massy represents this family at present.

5. James (d. in 1735): son of John; had three sons:

I. Garrett, of whom presently.
II. James.
III. John.

6. Garrett: son of James; d. in 1771, leaving one son.

7. James of Fryarstown; b. 4th February, 1749; d. 1st May, 1819. This James m., on 3rd Nov., 1767, Anastasia Bourke-White, and had three sons:

I. James, of Rockstown Castle, b. 4th May, 1771; d. 25th July, 1828. This James m. on the 10th February, 1812, Dilyana Molony, of Craggs, county Clare, and had two daughters, but no son.
II. Thomas. b. 1773; d. in 1837. He m., in 1818, Miss Hartwell, of Bruff, and had issue.
III. John, of Sandville.

8. John Barry, of Sandville :* son of James; b. 20th Feb., 1779; d. 29th Aug., 1839. He m., 13th Feb., 1804, Mary, only daughter of R. O'Shaughnessy, Esq., and had issue three sons and one daughter:

I. James, of whom presently.
II. Thomas, of Caherline, b. 1809; d. 1866, leaving issue.
III. John, b. 1823; d. unm. in 1860.
I. Mary, who m. on 23rd Feb., 1843, John Ball, Esq., nephew

of the Right Hon. Judge Ball, and had issue.

9. James: eldest son of John; b. 17th Nov., 1805; d. 2nd Sept., 1856. This James was twice m. : first, on the 18th July, 1833, to Christina (d. s. p. in 1835), dau. of D. Clanchy, Esq., D.L., of Charleville; secondly, on the 29th Nov., 1837, he m. Maria, dau. of John Grene,† Esq., J.P., of Cappamurra, co. Tipperary, and by her had five sons and two daughters:

I. James-Grene, of whom presently.
II. Albert, b. 23rd May, 1842; in Holy Orders.
III. Nicholas.
IV. William.
V. John.
I. Annie, who, on the 29th Nov., 1867, m. Thomas Butler, Esq., R.M.
II. Mary.

10. James-Grene Barry, J.P. : eldest son of James; b. 20th April, 1841; and living in 1883. This James m. on 20th June, 1881, Mary, only dau. of T. Kane, Esq., of Whitehall, co. Clare, M.D., J.P., and has had :

I. James, of whom presently.
II. Gerald, b. 18th Dec., 1883.

11. James Barry: son of James-Grene Barry; b. 8th June, 1882, and living in 1883.

BARRY. (No. 4.)

Lords of Santry, County Dublin.

Arms : Barry of six ar. and gu.   *Crest :* Out of a ducal coronet or. a wolf's head erased gu. collared gold.   *Supporters :* Two wolves ar. guttée de sang collared az. *Motto :* Regi legi fidelis.

* *Sandville :* Sandville is a part of Fryarstown.

† *Grene :* The Grenes of Cappamurra are descended from a brother of Sir Thomas Grene, of Bobbing, Kent, who settled at Corstown, co. Kilkenny, in 1608. This family have retained the old spelling of the name *Grene.*

PATRICK BARRY had :
  2. James, who had :
  3. Richard, who had :
  4. Sir James, Lord of Santry, and Lord Chief Justice of the King's

Bench, who d. in Feb., 1673. He m. Kath., dau. of Sir Richard Parsons, and had :
  5. Richard Barry, the last Lord of Santry.

CLANCY. (No. 2.)

Of Dartry, County Monaghan.

Arms : Ar. two lions pass. guard. in pale gu.   *Crest :* A hand couped at the wrist erect, holding a sword impaling a boar's head couped all ppr.

LUGHACH (or Luy), brother of Each Bolg, who is No. 54 on the "Line of Ithe," was the ancestor of *MacFlanchaidhe*, of Dartry; anglicised *Clanchy, Clancie, Clancy,* Clinch,†* *Glancy,* and normanized *De Clancy.*

54. Lughach: son of Daire Diomdhach.
  55. Eochaidh : his son.
  56. Æneas : his son.
  57. Olioll : his son.
  58. Cormac : his son.
  59. Dunlang : his son.
  60. Cathair : his son.
  61. Flann : his son.
  62. Algeal : his son.
  63. Amhailgadh : his son.
  64. Eochaidh : his son.
  65. Dunlang: his son.
  66. Lughach ; his son.
  67. Conall : his son.
  68. Fiach : his son.
  69. Conall (2): his son.
  70. Fionn : his son.
  71. Cronluachra : his son.
  72. Flanchaidh ("flan" Irish, *red complexioned ;* " caidh" *chaste*) : his son ; a quo *MacFlanchaidhe.*‡

73. Aodh Cleireach : his son.
  74. Cathal na Caiirge (" cairaig" : Irish, *a rock* or *bulwark ;* Gr. " charax ;" Wel. " karreg ;" Corn. " carrag") : his son ; a quo *O'Caiirge,* anglicised *Carrick, Garrick, Craig,* and *Rock.*
  75. Giolla (or William) : his son.
  76. Teige : his son.
  77. Cathal : his son.
  78. Teige (2): his son.
  79. Teige Baccach : his son.
  80. William (2): his son.
  81. Cathal Dubh : his son ; had a brother named Fearach.
  82. Cathal Oge : his son ; had a brother named Teige Oge.
  83. Cathal Dubh [Dhu] Mac-Clancy, of Dartry : son of Cathal Oge.

---

* *Clancy :* In 1750 Michael Clancy, M.D., published in Dublin his Memoirs and Travels, and a Latin Poem—*Templina Veneris sive Amorum Rhapsodiæ.*

† *Clinch :* Of this family was the Barrister-at-Law, who in the early part of this century was known as the " great Counsellor Clinch," and who lived in Dublin. Mr. Clinch left four sons and two daughters—1. who was a Stipendiary Magistrate in Jamaica, under the Governorship of Lord Sligo ; 2. who was an Inspector of National Schools in Ireland ; 3. Bernard, who was a Sub-Inspector in the Irish Constabulary ; 4. Peter. One of the daughters was named Margaret.

‡ *MacFlanchaidhe* [MacFlancha] : see Note (*), under the "Clancy" (of Munster) pedigree, p. 80.

COFFEY.

Of Munster.

THIS family were dynasts or chief lords of that portion of the ancient territory of *Corca Luighe,** now called Barryroe-east, and Barryroe-west, in the county Cork. In Irish the family name is *O'Cobhthaigh ;* anglicised *O'Coffey, O'Cowhig,* and, more lately, *Coffey, Coffy,* and *Coffee.*

74. Donoch Mór; son of Cobthach Fionn, who is No. 73 on "The Line of Ithe," *ante.*

75. Donall Mór: his son.

76. Maccraith : his son.

77. Conchobar (or Conor): his son.

78. Maghnus (or Maighneas): his son.

79. Conor (2): his son.

80. Maithan Dall: his son.

81. Cobthach (2): his son.

82. Dermod : his son.

83. Fergal : his son.

84. Donoch : his son.

85. Aodh (or Hugh): his son.

86. Maghnus (2): his son.

87. Conor (3): his son.

88. Niocholl: his son.

89. Walter : his son.

90. Cobtach (3): his son.

91. Teige : his son ; had a brother named Niocholl, who was the ancestor of *MacNicol.*

92. Olioll (3) : son of Teige.

93. Dermod (2): his son.

94. Donall (2): his son.

95. Maghnus (3): his son.

96. Cobthach (4) : his son.

97. Conor (4): his son.

98. Maolpadraic : his son.

99. Ceannfaolla : his son.

100. Aodh (2): his son.

101. Cumumhan : his son.

102. Muireadach : his son.

103. Cathal (or Charles) : his son.

104. Donall (3): his son.

105. Brian : his son.

106. Murtoch : his son.

107. Crimthann : his son.

108. Saortuile : his son.

109. Niochall : his son.

110. Aodh (3) : his son.

111. Cathal (2) : his son.

112. Donoch (2) : his son.

113. Felim : his son.

114. Teige (2) : his son.

115. Cathal (3) : his son.

116. Donall (4) : his son.

117. Aodh (4) : his son.

118. Cormac : his son.

119. Aodh (or Hugh) : his son.

120. Cathal (4): his son.

121. Teige (3) : his son ; living in 1657.

122. Shane : his son ; living in 1701 ; held the lands of Muckross (at Killarney) under Charles Mac Carthy Mór, from A.D. 1693.

123. Dermod (or Darby): his son ; buried in Muckross Abbey, where his tomb exists.

* *Corca Luighe :* This was a territory in Carbery, in the west of the county Cork; and was so called because principally inhabited by families of the Lugadian Race, descendants of Luighaidh, son of Ithe, uncle of Milesius of Spain, and the first Milesian discoverer of Ireland. *Corcaluighe* ("corcach:" Irish, *swampy ground*) extended from Bandon to Crookhaven and to the river of Kenmare ; and was anciently possessed by the O'Baires [O'Barrys], O'Coffeys, O'Deas, O'Driscolls, O'Fihillys, O'Flains, O'Heas, O'Henegans, O'Learys, etc.

The city of "Cork" is by some derived from the Irish word *corcach,* above mentioned ; because it is built on a low marsh island, formed by the branches of the river Lee

124. Edmond: his son; living in 1807.

125. Edmond (2): his son; died in 1841. This Edmond had an elder brother named William, and a younger brother named John—both of whom died unmarried.

126. Edward Lees Coffey: son of Edmond (2); living in America in 1881, and had a family. This Edward had four brothers—1. James-Charles of Dublin, d. 1880; 2. John-William; 3. David; 4. Henry.

NEEDHAM.

Arms : Ar. a bend engr. az. betw. two bucks' heads cabossed sa. attired ar. *Crest :* A phœnix in flames ppr., etc.

MACNIADH, who is No. 58 on the "Line of Ithe," was the ancestor of *O'Niadh* or *O'Neidhe* Uaithne (or *O'Niadh* of the barony of Owney in Tipperary); anglicised *Needham, Neville,* and *Macnie.*

58. MacNiadh ("niadh:" Irish, *a mighty man,* or *champion:* son of Lughaidh or Luy; a quo *O'Niadh* or *O'Neidhe.*

59. Fothach Argthach: his son.
60. Fachtna: his son.
61. Dallan: his son.
62. Feargus: his son.

63. Maccaille: his son
64. Laisre: his son.
65. Natfraoch: his son.
66. Fionnan: his son.
67. Toman: his son.
68. Fothach : his son.
69. Dongalach: his son.

NICHOLSON. (No. 1.)

Arms : For the Armorial Bearings of the several branches of this family, see Burke's " Armory."

NIOCHOLL, brother of Teige who is No. 91 on the "Coffey" pedigree, was the ancestor of *MacNicaill,* sometimes written *NacNiocoil,* and *MacNioclais ;* anglicised *MacNichol, MacNicol,** Nicholls, Nicholas, MacNicholas, Nicholson, Nicolson, Nicols, Nicson,* and *Nixon.*

91. Niocholl ("nicaill:" Irish, "ni," *not,* and "caill," *to lose ;* Heb. "calah," *he faileth*): son of Cobthach; first of the family who settled in Scotland.

92. Ard : his son.

93. Asmain : his son.
94. Arailt: his son.
95. Turc Athcliath (*athcliath :* Irish, "Dublin) :" his son ; meaning Turc of Dublin.
96. Amlaeimh : his son.

* *MacNicol :* In a lately published work, purporting to give the " History of the Scottish Clans," it is stated that this Clan was of Norwegian orgin. No doubt the Clan, from time to time, may have made several marriage alliances with Danish and Norwegian families ; but the Clan MacNicol was of *Irish* extraction ! Gregall Mac-Nicol, who is No. 113 on this pedigree, acquired historic notability by his opposition

97. Taidg [Teige] : his son.
98. Carfin : his son.
99. Aillin : his son.
100. Poil : his son.

101. Fogail : his son.
102. Muireadach : his son.
103. Arailt (2): his son.
104. Erlile : his son.

to and defeat of the Danes and Norwegians : a fact, which in itself, would go to prove that the Clan MacNicol is *not* of Danish or Norwegian descent.

In connection with this subject we have lately been favoured with the following—

"*Notes anent Clan MacNicol.*"

By William Nicolson, of Millaquin Refinery, Bundaberg, Queensland :

1. THE badge of the Clan is a sprig of *oak*, in memory of their ancestor *Daire*. —See O'HART's *Pedigrees; Annals of the Four Masters*, &c.

2. The Daireinians or Dairinoi have been identified as the Kairinoi of Ptolemy, and as the Clan now known as MacNicol or Nicolson, *anglicé* Nicholson.

3. The adoption of the Clan name of O'Niochol or MacNicol was the result of the fealty of the Daireinians to Brian Boru, who having ordained that every sept should adopt some particular surname, in order to preserve correctly the history and genealogy of the different tribes, the majority of them adopted that of *O'Niochol*, one of their chiefs celebrated to this day for his unbounded hospitality. Niochol is No. 91 on the Stem of the Clan.

4. Clan MacNeachtain, now MacNaughten, and Clan MacNeachdail now MacNicol or Nicolson, have from time immemorial been in such close contact, that they have often had their chief in common, and their Tartan is so remarkably similar as to point out some special reason for the close affinity existing between them. O'Dugan names O'Taireceirt (Daire) as chief of Clanna Neachtain ; and in the *Annals of the Four Masters*, O'Taireceirt is given also as chief of Clanna Snedgile, otherwise Snackroll : Snackroll being Nicol or Nicolson.

5. The persistence of some Nicolsons as to Danish descent, and the equally persistent assertion of other Nicolsons as to the *Irish* lineage of the Clan can be satisfactorily accounted for, and these apparently contradictory statements reconciled : For example—Ottar Snedgile, or Snackroll, or Nicolson, an Irish prince and Earl of the Western Hebrides, became King over the Danes in Dublin, from A.D. 1146 to 1148, by choice of the Danes to whom he was allied by ties of relationship, and there are other instances of the sort ;—moreover, the settlement of Nicolsons in Cumberland and in Northumberland appears to be directly traceable to the period when Irish princes formed matrimonial alliances with the princesses of Danish lineage ;—nevertheless, in spite of the Danish affinities of some of the chiefs of Clan MacNicol or O'Niochol, the majority of the Nicolsons seem to have fought for Brian Boru at Clontarf.

6. In the year 1204, Sitrig O'Sruithen, Archineach of Congbhala, chief of Clan Congbhala, chief of Clan Snedgile, died and was buried in the church built by himself. It would appear that in him Fuileadh, No. 105 on the Stem of the Nicolsons (Fuileadh the destitute), lost a friend and protector. Giollareigh was the next chief of Clan Snedgile and of Clan Fingin, but who are Clanna Fingin ?

105. Fuileadh, the destitute, 106. Erblile, and 107. Sdacail, the Estate loser, were all contemporaries of and near of kin to the celebrated Andrew Nicolson who was, as was Ottar Snackoll, a Hebridean chief and high in authority amongst the Danish princes. Fuileadh, Erblile, and Sdacaill appear to have been on the Irish because losing side in Clan matters : hence the flight and destruction that portion of the Clan, from time to time removing from Ireland and settling in Skye, in Cumberland, in Northumberland, &c., becoming of necessity increasingly allied to the Danish party. Even the names of the members of the Stem of the Nicolsons, as traced by O'Hart, prove this solution of the Irish and Danish traditions of the Clan MacNicol to be correct.

101. Fogail the fugitive.

102. Muireadach at the time of the death of Sitrig O'Sruithen was, as his name implies, a chief of Clan MacNicol or Snedgile, who had taken to a sea-faring life, and

105. Fuileadh : his son.
106. Erbhle (or Erlerle) : his son.
107. Sdacaill (" staid :" Irish, *an estate;* " caill," *to lose*) : his son.
108. Torstan : his son.
109. Tortin : his son.
110. Torcill : his son.
111. Seaill : his son.

112. Gillemare : his son.
113. Gregall : his son.
114. Nicaill : his son.
115. Neaill : his son.
116. Aigh : his son.
117. Nicaill (2) : his son.
118. Eoin (or John): his son.
119. Eogan : his son.

was probably supporting himself and his adherents by piracy with the help of Danish allies.

103. Arailt, or Harold his son, as his name implies must have had a Danish mother, for " Harold" is *not* an Irish name ; his mother was most probably a Dublin Danish princess.

104. Erlile, his son, was probably reared in Skye ; for in his youthful days the country of the O'Niochol in Ireland was ravaged by English and Irish alike. In A.D. 1212 Giolla Fialach O'Boyle, with a party of the Kinnel Connell, plundered some of the Kinel Owen, who were under the protection of the O'Taireceirt. O'Taireceirt overtook them, and in the conflict which ensued, was slain.

105. Fuileadh, his son : of the period in which he lived the *Four Masters* write that then no man spared his neighbour, but took advantage of his misfortunes, and spoiled and plundered him ; and that many women, children, and helpless persons perished of cold and famine during the wars of this period. Nor were matters any more favourable to him and his clansmen in Syke, where the Nicolsons were appealing to Norwegians and Danes for help against the Scots of the mainland, who continually made incursions into the Western Hebrides, slaying women and children, even placing babes on the points of their spears and shaking them till they were pierced through and fell down the shaft of the spears to their hands, when they threw them away lifeless. These horrible excesses led to King Hacon's Expedition, and at Largs Andrew Nicolson, one of the most gigantic men of his day, fought at the head of a body of Danes and Norwegian and Skye men, gaining for himself renown which lasts to this day. It is recorded that prior to the battle he cut down one of his foes slicing him in halves lengthways, *i.e.* from the crown of his head to the seat in the saddle, so that his adversary dropped instantly half on one side of the horse he was riding, and half on the other side. In spite of prodigies of valour the Skyemen, Danes, and Norwegians were routed, but under Andrew Nicolson's guidance (he being in command of Hacon's fleet) they reassembled in Skye where the allies were abundantly supplied with provisions.

Here then in the history of the times we have the clue to the Irish and Danish traditions of Clan MacNicol—Fogail, the fugitive, becomes such by reason of his unsuccessful opposition to Invaders of Ireland—Muireadach, his son, seeks on the waters the safety he cannot find on land, and thenceforward the Nicolsons and Danes are closely allied.

From the time of Sdacail, the Estate loser, dates, we believe, the following proverb :—

Bumasdair de chlann Mhic Neachdaill agus amadan de chlann Mhic Cuin.

(A fool of the Nicholsons and an idiot of the McQuinn) ;

A proverb evidently fixing some event in the career of the chiefs of each Clan, whereby the Clan rights were prejudicially affected by them as representatives of the septs.

This view of the case is confirmed by the fact of the well known break, here occuring in the chiefship of Clan MacNicol, *i.e.*

108. Torstan McLeod, contemporary with 105, Fuileadh.
109. Torcin : his son ; contemporary with 106. Erlile.
110. Torcill : his son ; contemporary with 107, Sdacaill.

This Torcill is the Torcill who married the heiress of the Nicolson chiefs, whose family in the male line became, according to Fullarton, at that date extinct. And it is important to note that the son of Torcill and of this heiress is named Scaill, probably

120　Eion (2) :* his son.
121. Alexander : his son.
122. Donald : his son ; had a bro-
her named Neil.
123. Malcolm : son of Donald.
124. Donald MacNicol : his son ;
Chief of the Clan in the Isle of
Skye, in the reigns of King Charles

I. and II. ; was thrice married and
had twenty-three children ; one of
the wives was Margaret Morrison,
of Lewis.
　　125. Malcolm : his son ; Chief of
his Clan ; married the poetess Mary
MacLeod, sister of John Garbh

the original form of the name of Sdacaill the Estate loser. It is evident that the
peculiar form of the genealogy in the original Gaelic :—

*Scaill, ic Torcill, ic Totin, ic Torstain McSdacaill, ic Erlile O'Fuileadh, ic Erlile
MacArailt, ic Muireadach, ic Fogail,* is intended to convey some such solution of the
succession as this :—

　　Scaill the first then has his dynasty perpetuated in Scaill the second,—Scaill being
the true form of the name. That there is nothing far-fetched in the hypothesis above
advanced will be clear to all who are familiar with Celtic and Hebraic play upon the
pronounciation and signification of names. O'Hart gives Nicail or Nicol to be equivalent of one who "*loseth not*;" *i.e.* Scaill and Sdacaill to be equivalent to "*Estate
loser.*" Sdacaill's Heiress knew all this and named her son accordingly ;—just as in the
case of Jesus of Nazareth, those who believe him to be the Messias call him Jeschua, but
the Jews rejecting him call him Jeschu. They carefully leave out the " a," because by
so doing they indicate that he could not save himself much less save his people ;
moreover, by omitting the "a" the Cabbalists were able to give an evil significance to
the name : the remaining letters being held forth as equivalent to "His name and
remembrance shall perish."
　　Lastly, upon the foregoing basis sundry difficulties of chronology are removed, and
all the conflicting elements of the Clan history are reconciled. Moreover, the reason
for Torcill's son by the Heiress being named Scaill, as a per contra to Sdacaill, is the
more evident on comparison of Celtic land laws with the record contained in Numbers
XXXVI.
　　No. 95. Torc Athcliath : It is supposed that the Castle of Athcliath, near Sligo,
demolished in A.D. 1317, was built by Torc.
　　No. 69. Con-a-cille : From a careful comparison of dates and periods of generation,
it becomes evident that Con-a-cille was contemporary with Laeghaire McNiall, first
Christian King of Ireland ; and that he gained his name by reason of his church
building for Saint Patrick, by whose ministry he was converted.
　　73. Cobthach Fionn (fair-haired victor) probably acquired soubriquet under Fergus
Mór Mac Earca when that founder of the Milesian Monarchy in Scotland went
thither to fight the Picts. He would certainly head a substantial army of Daireinians
who could at no other date have had sufficient motive for emigrating from Ireland to
Scotland in sufficient numbers to found the colony of Dairinoi or Kairinoi, since identified as the Clan MacNicol.—See my Notes, 1, 2 & 3, *supra.*
　　88. Niochol Snackoll Snedgile : That the Clan was divided at Clontarf seems
certain. Brian Boru declined the offer of troops made by the King of Ulster in consequence of former feuds between them, but accepted the aid of Sitrig, the Dane,
against the Danes ; and as Torc Athcliath (or Torc of Dublin) was certainly one of
Brian Boru's supporters, and as Sitrig is a name not unfrequent in Nicolson genealogies,
the inference may be justifiable that this Sitrig and Torc were kinsmen.
　　101. Fogail the fugitive : Excepting that the *Four Masters* mention the O'Taireceirt heads of Clan MacNicol or Sneidgile as patriots, I have found nothing to show
which of the chiefs opposing the English Invasion Fogail could have been.

　　* *Eoin :* According to some records the three names between this Eoin and
Donald, No. 124, are as follows :—No. 121 Nicaill (3) ; No. 122, Andreas ; and No.
123, Nicaill (4). This Nicaill (4), who was called the "Outlaw," had a son No. 124,
who was called Donald Mór, who had a son William, No. 125. It would however,
appear that the members of this Clan had a great partiality for marrying into their
own families ; from which cause the names of the sons-in-law, in those three generations
may have been inserted for those of the sons, or, *vice versa :* being of the same sirname.

MacLeod, the tallest Highlander in his time. Of the brothers and sisters of this Malcolm we have ascertained the names of the following: 1. Donald; 2. William; 3. Rev. Alexander, who twice married into the family of "The MacDonald, of the Isles;" 4. Patrick, who married Grizel Frazer, a near relative of the then Lord Lovat; 5. George; 6. John, who died unmarried; 7. James; 8. Jane, who was married to MacKinnon, of Corrie; 9. Rachel, married to Ronald MacDonald; 10. Mary, married to Alexander,

McQueen; and 11. Neill, who married Kate MacDonald.

126. John: son of Malcolm: married Anne MacLean; had a brother Angus.

127. Malcolm: son of John; married Jessie MacDonald.

128. Donald: his son; married Margaret MacDonald; died 1797.

129. John: his son; married Marion Davidson; died 1850.

130. Norman Nicholson, the Chief of the Clan; his son: living in Camelford, Cambeltown, Tasmania, A.D. 1880.

NICOLSON. (No. 2.)
Of Portree.

NEIL, brother of Donald, who is No. 122 on the foregoing ("Nicolson," No. 1) pedigree, was the ancestor of *Nicolson*, of Portree, Isle of Skye, Scotland.

122. Neil: son of Alexander.

123. John: son of Neil.

124. Samhairle (Sorley or Samuel), of Drumnie: his son; married Margaret O'Donnell.

125. Alexander : his son; married a MacLean, of Borera.

126. Donald: his son; married Mary MacQueen.

127. Alexander: his son; born in 1722; married Catherine MacQueen; died 1809.

128. Samuel (2): his son; born in 1757; married in 1789 Betsey (or Elizabeth), daughter of Norman Nicolson* of Peinefiler, Portree. This Samuel died in 1832; and Betsey, his wife, died in 1853.

129. Norman :† their son; born in 1803; married Marion Bethune in 1837; living in 1878 in Peinefiler, Portree, Isle of Skye.

130. Samuel Nicolson, of Greenock: his son; born in 1838; married in June, 1873, to Jessie McDougall; living in 1877; had two brothers and two sisters: the brothers were—1. Neil; 2. Norman and the sisters were—1. Maryanne, 2. Margaret.

131. Norman Nicolson: son of Samuel; born in 1873, and living in 1878; had two sisters—1. Marion, 2. Mary.

* *Nicolson :* This Norman Nicolson was the son of John, son of Neil, son of Donald MacNicol (No. 124 on the foregoing No. 1 pedigree), the Chief of the Clan in the Isle of Skye, in the reigns of King Charles I. & II ; and this Neil with many members of the Nicolson family, migrated to America, at the end of the seventeenth, and beginning of the eighteenth, century.

† *Norman :* This Norman Nicolson, in a letter to the writer of these pages, says—" The MacDonalds, MacLeods, Nicolsons, and MacQueens (or MacQuinns) came from Ireland here (to Scotland) ages and ages ago."

NICHOLSON. (No. 3.)

In America.

WILLIAM, a younger brother (or rather brother-in-law) of Malcom who is No. 125 on the "Nicholson" No. 1 pedigree, was the ancestor of several branches of the *Nicholson* family, in America.

125. William : son of Donald Mór, and son-in-law of Donald, the Chief of the Clan ; said to have married the Chief's daughter ; and said to have perished at or near Sedgemoor at the time of the battle of that name.

126. John (commonly called " The Sailor ;" the H. P. and P. of D. of the " Stuart Papers") : his son ; signs his name *Nicolson ;* married Joanna Coke, at Dartmouth, on the 3rd December, 1695.

127. William, of Marlborough, Devon, merchant : son and only child of John, "The Sailor," and Joanna Coke ; spelled his name *Nicholson ;* married Elizabeth Trosse, on the 7th April, 1724, at South Huish, Devonshire. He d. 1781.

128. Joseph, of Kingsbridge, Devonshire : his son ; married Mary Dunsford, on 17th March, 1761 ; had a brother named Jonathan.

129. William of Plymouth : son of Joseph ; married Sarah Hewett, on 14th December, 1747 ; had brothers named Joseph, Thomas, John,* Benjamin, and a sister Mary.

130. Joseph (2) : son of William ; married Caroline Gregory, at Stoke-Damerel, on 13th December, 1826.

131. Joseph (3) : his son ; married Annie Stevens at Milwaukee, United States, America, on the 29th November, 1855.

132. Walter-Gregory : his son ; m. Ada L. Greenwood, at Milwaukee, aforesaid, on the 7th Oct., 1880. Had a brother named William-Stevens Nicholson, then living at 406, Milwaukee Street, Milwaukee, Wisconsin, U. S. A. ; and two sisters —1. Harriette-Elizabeth, 2. Sarah-Caroline—now (1880) living in England.

---

* *John* : This John was twice married—first to Mary Ball ; second to Elizabeth Luscombe. By the first marriage he had a son named John, who was married to Elizabeth Penn, a kinswoman to the founder of Pennsylvania, in the United States, America. The male line of this family has become extinct ; but there is a grand-daughter—Ellen-Octavia Nicholson (Mrs. D. Lindsay), living in Victoria, British Columbia, whose sister Emma lived (in 1880) in Devonshire, England.

This John's sister, Mary Nicholson, was, on the 29th March, 1791, married to Philip Gibbs, by whom she had twelve children, almost all of whom were (in 1877) in Canada, British America. Elizabeth Nicholson-Gibbs, one of those twelve children, was on 3rd June, 1830, married to James Dore Blake, M.D. : the issue of this marriage were—1. Philip-James, born in September, 1831, since deceased ; 2. James Gibbs-Nicholson-Blake, born in January, 1833 ; 3. Libra-Augusta, born in August, 1838 ; 4. Joseph (deceased), born in March, 1836 ; 5 Joseph Nicholson-Blake, born in May, 1838 ; 6. Elizabeth Anne, born in May, 1841 ; 7. Edward-Thomas, born in June, 1842 ; 8. Mary Anne, born in May, 1844 ; 9. Sarah-Margaret, born in July, 1847 ; 10. Samuel Hahnemann, born in July, 1850.

The Philip Gibbs here mentioned was a first cousin of Samuel Newcomen Gibbs, who was the father of Frederick Waymouth Gibbs, for many years tutor to H. R. H. Albert-Edward, Prince of Wales (1880).

NICHOLSON. (No. 4.)

Of Plymouth, England.

JONATHAN, a brother of Joseph who is No. 128 on the "Nicholson" No. 3 pedigree, was the ancestor of *Nicholson,* of Plymouth.

128. Jonathan : son of William ; married in Feb., 1762, at Kingsbridge, to Amy May.

129. Robert : his son ; married in April 1784, at Kingsbridge, to Elizabeth Poppleston.

130. Jonathan (2) : his son ; in February 1820, at the parish church of Stoke-Damerel, Devon, was m. to Jane-Anne Remfry.

131. Jonathan-Henry : his son ; married, in December 1842, at St. George's church, East Stonehouse, Devon, to Anne Hanibling. This Jonathan-Henry had a brother named Robert, who, in June, 1857, at St. Andrew's church, Plymouth, was married to Emma Philips, by whom he had five sons—1. Jonathan Henry, born in 1858; 2. Robert-Joseph, born in 1860; 3. James-Remfry, born in 1868; 4. Ernest-Charles-Remfry, born in 1871 ; and 5. Arthur-Philips, born in 1874— all living in 1877.

132. John-William : son of Jonathan-Henry ; born in Dec., 1848 ; had three brothers and four sisters —the brothers—1. Jonathan-Henry, born in June, 1851; 2. Henry-born in November, 1855 ; 3. Robert-Joseph, born in February, 1860 ; and the sisters were—1. Jane-Anne, 2. Mary-Elizabeth, 3. Emma, 4. Maria Remfry, 5. Elizabeth-Caroline-Popplestone ; all living in 1880.

NICOLSON. (No. 5.)

Of London.

JOSEPH, a brother of William who is No. 129 on the "Nicholson" No. 3 pedigree, was the ancestor of another branch of the *Nicolson* family, in London.

129. Joseph : son of Joseph, of Kingsbridge ; born in May, 1771 ; in 1793 was married to Fanny Sheppard.

130. James : his son ; married Lydia Laurie, at St. Dunstan's church, on the 7th November, 1828; living in 1877, at 34 Walbrook, Mansion House, London; had a brother named John : this John married — Church of Rochester, and had two sons, one of whom is dead ; the other, also named John, a draper, in 1880 residing at No. 341 City-road, London, E., who m. and had issue—Caroline-Sarah-Anne, b. Sept., 1856 ; Walter-Thomas, b. Feb., 1860 ; Arthur-William, b. June, 1862 ; Frank-Barclay, b. December, 1867.

131. Ebenezer : son of James ; m. at Moorfields, in Dec., 1854, to Sarah Thompson. Had three brothers, James, John, and Joseph, and two sisters : the brothers were —I. James, now (1880) of Trent-

ham House, Darnley-road, Hackney, London, who married Charlotte Abernethy, at Whitechapel, on the 25th June, 1857, and had issue six children—I. William Abernethy, b. July, 1858 ; 2. Henry-James, b. Oct., 1860 ; 3. Mary-Louisa, b. April, 1862 ; 4. Sarah-Elizabeth, b. July, 1864 ; 5. Ebenezer, b. April, 1866 ; 6. Charlotte, b. April, 1870. II. John, living (in 1880) at 113 South Pauline street, Chicago. III. Joseph, living (in 1880) also at 113 South Pauline street, Chicago ; m. and had issue Eva-Blanch, b.

1880. The two sisters are—Fanny and Mary, now (1880) living at Hackney : Fanny is m. to Major Buskin, and had children. This Ebenezer has three sons and three daughters : the sons were—1. Arthur-Ebenezer, b. in 1855 ; 2. James-Alexander, b. June, 1863; 3. Frank-Abernethy, b. in November, 1864. The daughters were—1. Ellen-Sarah, 2. Anne-Lydia, 3. Eliza-Mary—all six children living in 1877.

132. Arthur-Ebenezer, b. 1855 : son of Ebenezer.

NICHOLSON. (No. 6.)

Of Moreton-in-the-Marsh, and of Lydney, Gloucestershire, England.

129. Thomas: son of Joseph of Kingsbridge, who is No. 128 on the "Nicholson" (No. 3) pedigree ; m. Esther Birt, on 18th September, 1796.

130. Rev. Thomas, a Baptist minister : his son ; b. 13th April, 1805 ; m. Mary-Anne Miles, on the 2nd April, 1828, at Newland, Gloucestershire.

131. Thomas, now (1880) of Mynydd Isa, near Mold, Flintshire, Wales : his son ; b. 9th June, 1830 ; m. Fanny Hutchins, at Coleford, on 4th July, 1851. This Thomas had (in 1880) three brothers—(1) Isaiah, (2) John, (3) Frank. (1) Isaiah, of 79 Manor place, London, b. 7th Feb., 1833, m. Lizzie Henderson, at Lydney, Gloucestershire, on 10th March, 1853, and had four children : 1. Horace-Leonard, b. 27th Jan., 1856, and m. Millie Brewster at St. Peter's church, Deptford, on 8th Dec., 1877 ; 2. Elizabeth-Mary,

b. 5th Dec., 1859, m. William Gates of Egham, Surrey, at Old Charlton, on 20th Feb., 1878 ; 3. Isaiah-Birt, b. 5th June, 1858; 4. Ada-Gertrude, b. 6th May, 1870. (2) John, of Tullahoma, Coffee county, Tennessee, U. S. America, b. 16th Nov., 1835, m. Jane Berger Kendall, in 1856, and had ten children : 1. John-Frederick, b. 20th Jan., 1858 ; 2. Kate, b. 30th Jan., 1859 ; 3. Walter-Kendall, b. 5th April, 1860 ; 4. Frances-Mary, b. 18th August, 1862 ; 5. Harry, b. 17th Dec. 1864 ; 6. Clara-Flora, b. 10th Jan., 1867 ; 7. Alice-Jane, b. 3rd March, 1868 ; 8. Hubert-Miles, b. 14th Feb., 1871 ; 9. Ella-Grace, b. 18th Nov., 1873 ; 10. Thomas-Norman, b. 22nd July, 1875. (3) Frank, of Greenwood Terrace, St. John's Church, Road, Hackney, E., b. 4th Feb., 1842, m. Matilda Pole, at Mare street, Hackney, on 10th May, 1864 and has had two children—1.

Adelaide-Margaret, b. 9th Jan. 1867 ; 2. Arthur-Pole, b. 20th July, 1869.

132. Edgar - Thomas Nicholson : son of Thomas, of Mynydd Isa; b. 2nd Nov., 1864. This Edgar (living in 1880) had four sisters : 1. Helen-Miles, b. 21st Aug., 1858 ; 2. Flora (or Florence), b. 10th July, 1861 ; 3. Fanny-Matilda, b. 26th Nov., 1866; 4. Laura-Hutchins, b. 24th Dec., 1868.

NICHOLSON. (No. 7.)

BENJAMIN, brother of William who is No. 129 on the "Nicholson" No. 3 pedigree, was the ancestor of another branch of the *Nicholson* family, living at Plymouth.

129. Benjamin : son of Joseph ; b. in July, 1776 ; m. Anne Von Neck, in April, 1800.

130. Rev. Samuel,* of Plymouth, Baptist minister : his son ; b. in April, 1801 ; m. in March, 1824, Jane, dau. of Thomas Nicholson, who is No. 129 on the " Nicholson" No. 4 pedigree ; d. 1856.

131. Henry-Martyn Nicholson, of Windsor place, Plymouth, England: son of Samuel.

NICHOLSON. (No. 8.)

Of Coleford.

REV. WILLIAM NICHOLSON, brother of Joseph who is No. 130 on the "Nicholson" No. 3 pedigree, was the ancestor of *Nicholson*, of Laird's Hill, Coleford, Gloucestershire, England.

130. Rev. William, a Baptist minister : son of William, of Plymouth ; b. in 1805 ; m. Martha, a daughter of Thomas Nicholson (No. 129 on the "Nicholson" No. 6 pedigree), on the 8th April, 1834; living in 1877.

* *Samuel* : The children of this Samuel and Jane Nicholson were—1. Samuel-Pierce, born April 1826, died in September, 1849 ; 2. Jane Jarvis, born August, 1827, died in infancy; 3. Jane Jarvis, born Oct., 1828, d. February, 1859 ; 4. Anna, born December, 1829, d. Sept., 1877 ; 5. Eustace, b. June, 1831, d. June, 1852 ; 6. Mary, b. Nov., 1832, d. in infancy ; 7. Mary (2), b. Sept., 1834, d. March, 1859 ; 8. Lydia, b. June, 1836, and living in 1878 ; 9. Sarah, b. February, 1838, d. March, 1877 ; 10. Philip-Edward, b. June, 1839, living in 1878 ; 11. William-Carey, and 12. Henry-Martin (twins), b. Sept., 1841, and both living in 1878 ; 13. Phebe Nicholson, b. May, 1843, and living in 1878 : all the surviving members of this family being (in 1878) unmarried, save Philip-Edward, No. 10. This Philip-Edward was, on the 6th August, 1863, married to Emilie-Louise Thourneysen : their children were—1. Samuel-Arnold, born in 1865, died November 1869 ; 2. Edward-Basil, born Sept., 1867, living in 1878; 3. Marguerite, b. August, 1872, living in 1878 ; and 4. Walter-Frederick, born July, 1876, and living in 1878.

T

131. William Nicholson (Nicolson or MacNicol), of The Laird's Hill, Coleford ; now (1887) of Millaquin Refinery, East Bundaberg, Queensland : his son ; b. in Feb., 1835 ; m. Ellen Cowley, on 16th Dec., 1856 ; and living in 1887. This William, who has been commonly called "Patrick," has a sister named Eliza.*

132. Charles-Ebenezer-Thurston-Grove-Cowley Nicholson : his son ; b. in Feb., 1867. This Charles had a brother named Bertram Archibald, b. in July, 1868 ; and two sisters— 1. Ellen, 2. Lilian-Maude : all living in 1887.

NICHOLSON. (No. 9.)

Of Detroit, U.S.A.

Rev. Alexander, a brother of Malcolm who is No. 125 on the "Nicolson" No. 1 pedigree, was the ancestor of *Nicholson*, of Detroit, Michigan, U.S., America.

125. Rev. Alexander : son of Donald MacNicol, Chief of the Clan in the Isle of Skye, Scotland.

126. James :† his son ; who went to the county Down, in Ireland, and was, it is believed, ancestor of Genl. John Nicolson, who was slain at Delhi. This James seems to have been kin to Leotain Nicholson, who settled in Dublin.

127. Joseph Nicolson, or Nicholson, of Derryogue, co. Down : son of James ; m. Eliza-Sarah Blackwood of Belfast, sister of the Rev. John Blackwood, of the Rocky Quarter, Seaforth, co. Down, and

cousin to Sir John Blackwood, whose widow became Lady Dufferin.

128. Thomas Nicholson : son of Joseph ; m. Jane Small of Cranfield, at Kilkeel, county Down. Had two brothers—Robert and John.

129. Joseph : his son ; b. in co. Down on 25th Sept., 1826 ; now (1880) Superintendent of the House of Correction, Detroit, Michigan, U.S. America.

130. John Nicholson ; his son ; has two sisters—1. Frances-Jane, 2. Mary-Louise ; all of whom living in 1880.

* *Eliza* : This Eliza Nicholson (now of Rothsay, near Ravensbourne, Dunedin, Orago, New Zealand), was married to Edward Davies, of Caerleon, near Newport, Monmouthshire, England ; they had (in 1878) five children, the names of three of whom we have ascertained—1. Edward Nicholson-Davies, 2. Ernest Nicholson-Davies, 3. Arthur Nicholson-Davies.

† *James :* It is also believed that this James followed the business of a goldsmith, which he found very lucrative.

NICHOLSON. (No. 10.)

Of Philadelphia.

NEIL, a younger brother of Malcolm who is No. 125 on the " NICOLSON" No. 1 pedigree, was the ancestor of this family.

125. Neil: son of Donald Mac-Nicol, Chief of the Clan in the Isle of Skye, Scotland; m. Kate Mac-Donald.

126. John : his son; d. 5th March, 1807 ; m. Ann —— (who d. 19th May, 1783); was a friend of Benjamin Franklin, of the United States, America.

127. John; son of John ; d. 4th Feb., 1799, aged 27 years ; married Rebecca ——, who d. in 1812.

128. John : his son ; d. 28th Feb., 1833, aged 35; m. Eliza ——, who d. in 1845.

129. James Bartram Nicholson : his son; born 1820, and living in 1880.

130. Lieut.-Col. John P. Nicholson, of 146 North Sixth Street, Philadelphia, Pennsylvania: his son ; living in 1880.

NICHOLSON. (No. 11.)

Of San Francisco.

LEOTAIN, a kinsman of James who is No. 126 on the " Nicholson " (of Detroit, U.S.A.) pedigree, was the ancestor of Nicholson, of San Francisco.

127. Leotain Nicolson, or Nicholson, of Dublin ; m. Margaret ——.

128. Henry, of Dublin: his son ; m. Mary ——, of Virginia, United States, America, in 1799.

129. John-Young Nicholson, of Alexandria, Virginia, U.S.A. : his son ; m. Sarah Moody, of Virginia, 17th September, 1829.

130. John-Henry, of San Francisco, California : his son ; m. Emily Kitzmillar, of St. Louis, U.S.A., on 23rd Sept., 1857 ; living in 1880.

131. Walter-Henry Nicholson : his son ; had a brother Rishworth, and three sisters—1. Emily, 2. Maude, 3. Genevieve—all five of whom living in 1880.

NICHOLSON-SCOTT. (No. 12.)

ROBERT NICHOLSON, a brother of Thomas who is No. 128 on the " Nicholson" (of Detroit) pedigree, was the ancestor of this family.

128. Robert Nicholson : eldest son of Joseph of Derryogue; b. 1793; m. Elizabeth Gibson, at Kilkeel, co. Down, 19th Oct., 1810.

129. Anne; his daughter; b. at Kilkeel, 14th Nov., 1811 ; m. Rev. W. Anderson Scott, D.D., at Nash-

ville, Tenessee, U.S.A., in January, 1836.

130. Col. Robert Nicholson-Scott, United States Army, living in 1880: her son; b. 21st Jan., 1838; married 28th Nov., 1862, Elizabeth Goodale, second dau. of General Silas Goodale, U.S. Army, and had three children—1. Martha Hunt, b. 25th Oct., 1865; 2. Abbey-Pearce, b. 24th July, 1871; 3. Anna-Nicholson, b. 28th Oct., 1874.

NICOLSON. (No. 13.)

Of Aberdeen.

GEORGE, a younger brother of Malcolm who is No. 125 on the "Nicolson" No. 1 pedigree, was the ancestor of this family.

125. George: son of Donald; Chief of the Clan.

126. John: his son; married Jane Mathew, and by her had three sons —1. John, 2. William, 3. Thomas of Thunderton: (1) John, born at Inverveddie, m. Margaret, youngest dau. of the venerable and learned poet and historian, Rev. John Skinner, of Longside, author of the Ecclesiastical History of Scotland; (2) William, b. at Inverveddie, m. Grace, second dau. of the said Rev. John Skinner; (3) Thomas of Thunderton.

127. Thomas of Thunderton: son of John; m. Janet Robertson.

128. William: his son; b. 27th May, 1799; living (in 1880) at 125 Crown Street, Aberdeen; m. on 24th Dec., 1826, Catharine Simpson, and by her had six children—1. George, b. 4th Mar., 1828, unm.;

2. Wllliam, b. 19th Feb., 1830; 3. Very Rev. James, dean of Brechin, b. 12th March, 1832; 4. Thomas, born 9th January, 1836, unm.; 5. Margaret, b. 24th March, 1840, unm.; 6. David, medical officer in Portsmouth, b. 25th Dec., 1844, unm.

129. William, living in 1880: second son of William; b. 19th Feb., 1830; m. on 19th July, 1860, in London, Grace-Lawson Henderson, and by her had five children—1. Catharine-Jemima, b. 20th July, 1861; 2. Rachel-Amelia, b. 10th July, 1863; 3. Robert-Henderson, b. 23rd March, 1865; 4. Grace-Wilhelmena, b. 5th May, 1867; 5. William-James, b. 23rd July, 1869 —all living in 1880.

130. Robert-Henderson Nicolson: son of William; living in 1880.

NICOLSON. (No. 14.)

Of Skye, and Prince Edward's Island.

ANGUS, brother of John who is No. 126 on the "Nicolson" No. 1 pedigree, was the ancestor of this family.

126. Angus: son of Malcolm.
127. Murdoch: his son.

128. Donald: his son; m. Anne Martin, and by her had five chil-

dren : 1. Samuel, whose descendants are in Skye, in England, and in America; 2. Donald, whose family is extinct ; 3. Angus, whose descendants are in Skye and in America ; 4. Armiger, b. 1755; 5. Margaret, m. Donald M'Kay at Uig Skye.

129. Armiger : son of Donald ; b. in 1755, d. in 1855; m. in 1794 Margaret M'Kenzie, at Uig Skye, and by her had eight children—1. Murdoch, of whom presently; 2. Donald ;* 3. Margaret, b. 1801, m. in 1831 at Uig Skye, to John M'Lean ; 4. Catherine, b. 1804, m. at Uig Skye in 1830 to Donald MacDonald ; 5. Rachel, b. 1807, m. at Uig to Norman M'Pherson, and emigrated to Prince Edward's Island, North America ; 6. Malcolm, b. 1811, m. at Dundee, and emigrated to Prince Edward's Island, where (in 1880) he and his family resided; 7. Samuel, b. in 1814, m. in Prince Edward's Island, where (in 1880) he and his family resided; 8. Ann, b. 1817, d. 1842.

130. Murdoch ; son of Armiger ; b. 1795, d. Nov., 1861.   Was twice m. : first, to Janet M'Lean, at Uig Skye in 1831, and by her had five children—1. Malcolm, of whom presently ; 2. Margaret, b. 1833, d. 6th June, 1869 ; 3. Donald, b. 1835, emigrated† to Prince Edward's Island ; 4. Euphemia, b. 1840, m. at Uig Skye 30th March, 1871, to Alexander M'Leod ; 5. John.‡ Secondly, Murdoch, who d. in Nov., 1861, m. Isabella Beaton, at Kilmuir, Skye, in 1847, and by her had four children—1. Ann, born Aug., 1849 ; 2. Donald, b. 2nd Nov., 1852, living (in 1880) at 120 Thistle Street, S.S. Glasgow ; 3. Armiger, b. May, 1855; 4. Janet, b. Nov., 1858.

131. Malcolm : Eldest son of Murdoch ; b. 1832 ; m. Ann Mathieson at Snizort, Skye, on 2nd March, 1871, and by her had (in 1880) four children—1. Janet, 2. Flora, 3. Murdoch, 4. Alexander.

132. Murdoch Nicolson ; son of Malcolm ; living in 1880.

---

* *Donald* : This Donald, b. 1798, m. at Uig Skye, Isabella Lamont, in 1840, and by her had seven children : 1. Samuel, b. 1841, m. at Uig in 1869 Euphemia Lamont ; 2. Malcolm, b. 1844, d. 1860; 3. Mary, b. 1847 ; 4. John, b. 1849 ; 5. Margaret, b. 1853; 6. Armiger, b. 1856 ; 7. Rachel, b. 1857.

† *Emigrated* : This Donald, b. 1835, emigrated to Prince Edward's Island, 9th June, 1858 ; m. there Janet McLean, on 18th March, 1863, and by her had (in 1880) eight children : 1. Janet-Penelope, b. 3rd Feb., 1864 ; 2. Euphemia-Ann, and 3. Mary-Ann (Twins), b. 15th March, 1865 ; 4. Catherine-Eliza-Gillies, b. 2nd Oct., 1866 ; 5. Malcolm-Angus, b. 25th Nov., 1868; 6. Margaret-Jane, b. 5th June, 1871 ; 7. Ida-Bell, b. 20th July, 1873 ; 8. Donald-Murdoch, b. 16th Nov., 1877.

‡ *John* : This John, b. in 1843, and living in 1881, m. on 18th August, 1874, at Crosshill, Glasgow, to Margaret Carswell, and by her had three children—1. John, b. 5th Feb., 1875 ; 2. Janet-Margaret, b. 31st August, 1876 ; 3. Susan-Kate-McLachlan, b. 15th February, 1879, d. 8th April, 1880.

NICOLSON. (No. 15.)

*Of Hawkhill, Rosemarkie, Inverness, now of Pietermaritzburg,
Cape of Good Hope.*

DONALD,* a younger brother of Malcolm who is No. 125 on the "Nicolson"
No. 1 pedigree, was the ancestor of this family.

125. Donald: son of Donald.

126. Patrick: his son.

127. Malcolm: his son; m. Miss Grant.

128. Dr. Simon Nicolson, of Calcutta: his son; m. Miss Mac-Leod.

129, Major (then Lieutenant) Charles-Arthur Nicolson: his son; m. on 8th Sept., 1842, at Calcutta, Agnes-Cecilia-Adelaide Fagan, and had—1. Simon; 2. Charles-Arthur, b. in Inverness; 3. Christopher, b. in Inverness, 1845, d. 1846; 4. Isabella, b. in Calcutta, 1847, d. 1871; 5. George, b. in Dayeeling, now (1881) living in Pietermaritz-burg, Cape of Good Hope; 6. Robert, b. in Dayeeling, in 1850, d. in Gibraltar, 1880; 7. Anne, born 1851, d. 1852; 8. Malcolm, b. in Allahabad in 1853; 9. Patrick M'Lean, b. at Brighton, 1854; 10. James-Octavius, b. at Tunbridge Wells, 1856; 11. John, b. at same place, 1857; 12. Martin-Decimus, b. in London in 1858; 13. Agnes, b. in London in 1859, married in St. Alban's Cathedral, Pretoria, on 25th Dec., 1879, to Charles Muskett Spratt, Clerk in Holy Orders.

130. Simon Nicolson: eldest son of Charles-Arthur; b. in Calcutta; living in 1881.

NICOLSON. (No. 16.)

Of Australia.

ALEXANDER, another younger brother of Malcolm who is No. 125 on the
"Nicolson" No. 1 pedigree, was the ancestor of this family.

125. Alexander: son of Donald; was twice married: first, to Marion, dau. of John MacDonald of Castle-ton, grandson of Sir Donald Gorm MacDonald, of the Isles; and secondly, to Florence MacDonald, a member of the same family.

126. Donald: his son; m. Margaret,† only dau. of the Rev. Alexander MacQueen of Snizort.

---

* *Donald*: In page 108 of the first and second edition of the second series of this Work, this Donald was by mistake entered as having died unmarried; but that was not the case.

† *Margaret*: This Margaret's mother was daughter of William MacDonald (Tutor of The MacDonald), brother to Sir Donald MacDonald and Sir James MacDonald of Sleat. William MacDonald's wife (Margaret MacQueen's mother) was the eldest daughter of Sir Ewen Cameron of Lochiel; and William MacDonald was son of Sir Donald MacDonald by his wife the Lady Mary Douglas, dau. of the Earl of Moreton.

127. Alexander : his son; b. 4th April, 1766; m. late in life his cousin Susanna, eldest daughter of Donald Nicolson of Scoribreac, and had ten children : 1. Margaret, m. 28th Oct., 1842, to Rev. Angus Martin, of Snizort, and had eleven children, most of whom were (in 1881) living; 2. Jessie, m. 19th Oct., 1858, to Donald Frazer; 3. Archibald, m. to Annie MacIntyre, in Australia, who bore him four children—Susanna, Duncan, Donald, and Norman, all living in 1881 ; 4. William, m. in Australia, in 1868, to Charlotte McKillop, and by her had (in 1881) a son Alexander ; 5. Malcolm, d. young ; 6. *Malcolm-Norman, d. 25th Oct., 1861 ; 7. *Donald-Norman, d. 30th April, 1868 ; 8. Susanna-Margaret, d. 25th Aug., 1868 ; 9. Isabella-Caroline-Brownlow, living in 1881; 10. Grace-Hay, d. an infant.

NICHOLSON.† (No. 17.)

Of Stramore, Guildford, Co. Down; and of New York.

1. Robert Nicholson of Stramore had :

I. John, of whom presently.

II. Isabella, m. Henry Clibborn, Esq., of Lisanisky, co. Westmeath.

2. John Nicholson of Stramore : son of Robert; m. Isabella Wakefield, and had :

I. Robert Jaffrey Nicholson of Stramore House, co. Down.

II. Alexander Jaffrey Nicholson, M.D., who married Miss Hogg of Lisburn, and had General Nicholson of the British Army.

III. Meadows-Taylor, of whom presently.

IV. Richard.

V. Rawdon-Hautenville, who m. Miss Dixon.

VI. Christiana, who married Alan O'Brien Bellingham, and died without issue.

VII. Mary married Rev. Richard Olpherts, and had a daughter Isabella.

VIII. Charlotte, married Rev. John Beatty, and had four children—John, Thomas, Mary, and Isabella.

IX. Elizabeth, m. Mr. Williams, and had with others, a dau. Gertrude.

X. Isabella, d. unm.

3. Meadows-Taylor Nicholson, a Banker in New York : son of John ; married Amelia Guest (aunt of Commodore John Guest, U.S. Navy), and had :

4. Joshua-Clibborn Nicholson of "Buena Vista," New Rochelle, New York; who married Zaida Nelson, and had :

I. Harry-Meadows, b. 11th Oct., 1875.

II. Charles-Brighter, born 16th June, 1877.

III. Zaida Clibborn.

IV. Kathleen-Nelson.

V. Ethel-Guest.

---

* *Malcolm* and *Donald* were men of gigantic size : Malcolm stood 6 feet 7 inches, in his hose ; and Donald 6 feet 6 inches.

† *Nicholson* : See the Appendix, under the heading " Stem of the Nicholsons," for a few Notes bearing on the *Irish* origin of the *Nicholson* family.

O'DRISCOLL.

Arms : Ar. a ship or ancient galley, sails furled sa. *Crest :* A cormorant ppr.

ÆNEAS, brother of Fothach Canaan who is No. 60 on the "Barry" pedigree, was the ancestor of *O'h-Edersceoil ;* anglicised *O'Driscoll.*

60. Æneas: son of Lugach (Lughaidh or Luy) Maccon, the 113th Monarch of Ireland.

61. Nathi: his son; whose brother Fergus was the ancestor of *Coffey.*

62. Edersceal: his son; had nine sons; his brother Coleman had three sons.

63. Brandubh: his son; had eight sons.

64. Flannan: his son; had a brother named Forannan, who was father of St. Colum (27th February), St. Eltin (11th December), and St. Mochumna (7th June).

65. Columna: his son.

66. Comdhan: his son.

67. Flannan (2): his son.

68. Folachta: his son.

69. Æneas: his son

70. Dungus: his son; had a brother named Main.

71. Murghul: his son

72. Dungal: his son.

73. Nuadad: his son.

74. Fionn: his son.

75. Edersceal ("edearbh:" Irish, *false,* and "sceal," *a story*): his son; a quo *O'Edersceoil.*

76. Fothach: his son.

77. Maccon: his son.

78. Fionn: his son.

79. Fothach (2): his son.

80. Donoch Mór: his son; had a brother named Aodh (or Hugh), who was the ancestor of *O'Driscoll Bearra.*

81. Amhailgadh an Gasgoine ("gas:" Irish, *a stalk ;* "goin," *a stroke*): his son; a quo *O'Gasgoine,* anglicised *Gasgoine,* and *Gascoine.* This Amhailgadh had a younger brother named Maccraith, whose son Donoch was the father of Maccon, father of Ainach, father of Fingin, father of Conor, father of Conor Oge, father of Sir Fingin O'Drsicoll Mór, who was alive A.D. 1460, and who founded the Franciscan Abbey of Innisherkin Island.

82. Morogh: son of Amhailgadh.

83. Donoch Oge: his son.

84. Dermod: his son.

85. Murtogh: his son.

86. Fingin: his son.

87. Maccon: his son.

88. Murtogh (2): his son.

89. Donal: his son.

90. Sir Fingin O'Driscoll: his son.

O'LEARY.

FOTHACH Canaan, the fifth son of Luy Maccon, the 113th Monarch of Ireland who is No. 59 on the "Coffey" pedigree, was the ancestor of *OLaeghaire ;* * anglicised *O'Leary,* and *Leary.*

59. Luy Maccon.

60. Fothach Canaan: his son.

61. Duach: his son.

62. Treana: his son.

* *O'Laeghaire :* For the derivation of this sirname, see Note, under the "O'Leary" pedigree (Line of Heber), *ante.*

63. Eirc : his son.

64. Ros (" ros :" Irish, *a promontory*): his son ; a quo *O'Ruis*, anglicised *Ross* and *Rush.*

65. Laeghaire : his son ; a quo *O'Leary.*

66. Fiach : his son.

67. Dunlang : his son.

68. Ros (2) : his son.

69. Main : his son.

70. Aongus (or Æneas) : his son.

71. Earc : his son.

72. Conor Cliodhna : his son.

73. Teige : his son.

74. Donoch na Tuaima (" tuaim :" Irish, *a dyke or fence*) : his son ; a quo *O'Tuaima*, anglicised *Toomey, Twomey,* and *Twomey.*

75. Conamnan : his son.

76. Dermod : his son.

77. Cumumhan : his son.

78. Donoch : his son.

79. Teige (2) : his son.

80. Maolseaghlainn : his son.

81. Teige (3) : his son.

82. Maolseaghlainn (2) : his son.

83. Tomhas Mór : his son.

84. Tomhas Oge : his son.

85. Athbiadh : his son.

86. Cumumhan (2) : his son.

87. Amhailgadh : his son.

88. Dunlang (2) : his son.

89. Art : his son.

90. Teige (4) : his son ; had a brother named Luighdhach.

91. Dermod : son of Teige.

92. Conogher O'Leary : his son ; first assumed this sirname.

93. Donogh : his son ; married to Ellen, dau. of Dermod O'Crowley ; d. 4th Jan., 1637.

94. Amhailgadh (or Auliff) O Leary : his son ; had a brother named Conogher.

IRISH MONARCHS OF THE RACE OF ITHE.

1. Eochaidh Edghothach, son of Datre, son of Conghal, son of Eadamhuin, son of Mal, son of Lughaidh [*Lewy, Lewis,* or *Louis*], son of Ithe, son of Breoghan, King of Spain and Portugal, who (see page 50) is No. 34 on " The Stem of the Irish Nation." This Eochaidh was the 14th Milesian Monarch, reigned 11 years ; was, B.C. 1532, slain by Cearmna, of the " Line of Ir," who succeeded him.

2. Eochaidh Apach, son of Fionn, son of Oilioll, son of Floinruadh, son of Roithlain, son of Martineadh, son of Sitchin, son of Riaglan, son of Eochaidh Breac, son of Lughaidh, son of Ithe, called *Apach* (" plague" or " infection") on account of the great mortality during his reign (of one year) among the inhabitants of Ireland. He was killed by Fionn of the " Line of Ir," B.C. 951. This Eochaidh was the 41st Monarch.

3. Lughaidh MacCon, son of MacNiadh, son of Lughaidh, son of Daire, son of Ferulnigh, son of Each-Bolg, son of Daire, son of Sithbolg, son of Ferulnigh, etc.

This Lughaidh was called *MacCon* from the *greyhound,* Ealoir Dearg, with which he played when a delicate child ; his mother was Sadhbh, dau. of Conn of the Hundred Battles ; he was killed, A.D. 225, by Comain Eigis, at Gort-an-Oir, near Dearg Rath, in Leinster.

4. Fothadh Airgtheach }
5. Fothadh Cairpeach } : sons of Lughaidh MacCon; were both slain
during the first year of their joint reign: Fothadh Cairpeach was slain
by his brother Fothadh Airgtheach; soon after this the murderer was
slain by the Irish Militia in the battle of Ollarbha, A.D. 285, when the
House of Heremon, in the person of Fiacha Srabhteine (ancestor of *The
O'Neill*, of Tyrone), resumed its place on the Irish Throne.   These brothers
were the 118th and 119th Monarchs of Ireland, and the last of the "Line
of Ithe" who reigned.

CHAPTER III.

THE LINE OF IR.

IR was the fifth son of Milesius of Spain (who, see page 50, is No. 36 on "The Stem of the Irish Nation"), but the second of the three sons who left any issue. His descendants settled in Ulster.

THE STEM OF THE "LINE OF IR."

OR,

THE Stem of the Irish Nation, from Ir down to (No. 105) Feargal, a quo *O'Farrell,* Princes of Annaly.

36. Milesius of Spain.

37. Ir : his son. This Prince was one of the chief leaders of the expedition undertaken for the conquest of Erinn, but was doomed never to set foot on the "Sacred Isle ;" a violent storm scattered the fleet as it was coasting round the island in search of a landing place, the vessel commanded by him was separated from the rest of the fleet and driven upon the island since called *Scellig-Mhicheal,* off the Kerry coast, where it split on a rock and sank with all on board, B.C. 1700.

38. Heber Donn : his son ; born in Spain; was granted by Heber and Heremon the possession of the northern part of Ireland, now called Ulster.

39. Hebric : his son ; was killed in a domestic quarrel.

40. Artra : his youngest son ; succeeded in the government of Uladh or Ulster ; his elder brothers, Cearmna and Sobhrach, put forth their claims to sovereign authority, gave battle to the Monarch Eochaidh, whom they slew and then mounted his throne; they were at length slain : Sobhrach at Dun Sobhrach, or "Dunseverick,"

in the county of Antrim, by Eochaidh Meann ; and Cearmna (in a sanguinary battle fought near Dun Cearmna, now called the Old Head at Kinsale, in the county of Cork, where he had his residence), by his successor Eochaidh Faobhar-glas, grandson of Heber Fionn, B.C. 1492.

41. Artrach : son of Artra.

42. Sedna : his son; slew Rotheacta, son of Maoin, of the race of Heremon, Monarch of Ireland, and, mounting his throne, became the 23rd Monarch. It was during his reign that the Dubhloingeas or "pirates of the black fleet" came to plunder the royal palace of Cruachan in Roscommon, and the King was slain, in an encounter with those plunderers, by his own son and successor, who mistook his father for a pirate chief whom he had slain and whose helmet he wore.

43. Fiacha Fionn Scothach, the 24th Monarch : son of Sedna ; so called from the abundance of white flowers with which every plain in Erinn abounded during his reign ; was born in the palace of Rath-Cruachan, B.C. 1402 ; and slain, B.C. 1332, in the 20th year of his reign, by Munmoin, of the Line of Heber.

44. Eochaidh (2) : his son; better known as *Ollamh Fodhla,** i.e., "Ollamh, or chief poet of Fodhla" (or Ireland); began his reign, A.M. 3882, B.C. 1317 (according to the received computation of the Septuagint, making A.D. 1 agree with A.M. 5199). This Eochaidh was the 27th Monarch of Ireland, and reigned 40 years. It was this Monarch who first instituted the *Feis Teamhrach* (or "Parliament of Tara"), which met about the time called "Samhuin" (or 1st of November) for making laws, reforming general abuses, revising antiquities, genealogies, and chronicles, and purging them from all corruption and falsehood that might have been foisted into them since the last meeting. This Triennial Convention was the first *Parliament* of which we have any record on the face of the globe; and was strictly observed from its first institution to A.D. 1172; and, even as late as A.D. 1258, we read in our native Annals of an *Irish Parliament*, at or near Newry. (See "O'Neill" Stem, No. 113.) It was this Monarch who built Mur Ollamhan at Teamhair (which means "Ollamh's fort at Tara"); he also appointed a chieftain over every cantred and a brughaidh over every townland.

According to some chroniclers, "Ulster" was first called *Uladh*, from Ollamh Fodhla. His posterity maintained themselves in the Monarchy of Ireland for 250 years, without any of the two other septs of Heber and Heremon intercepting them. He died at an advanced age, A.M. 3922, at his own Mur (or house) at Tara, leaving five sons, viz. : 1. Slanoll; 2. Finachta Fionnsneachta (or Elim); 3. Gead

Ollghothach, and 4. Fiacha, who were successively Monarchs of Ireland; and 5. Cairbre.

45. Cairbre : son of Ollamh Fodhla; King of Uladh; d. in the 22nd year of the reign of his brother Fiacha.

46. Labhradh : his son; governed Ulster during the long reign of his cousin Oiliol, son of Slanoll.

47. Bratha : his son; was slain by Breasrigh, a prince of the Heberian race, in the 12th year of the reign of Nuadhas Fionn-Fail.

48. Fionn : his son; fought against the Monarch Eochaidh Apach at Tara, defeated him, and became the 42nd Monarch; but after a reign of 22 years was slain by Seidnae Innaraidh, his successor.

49. Siorlamh : his son; so called from the extraordinary length of his hands (*Lat.* "longimanus," or *long-handed*); slew the Monarch Lughaidh Iardhonn, and assumed the sovereignty of the kingdom, which he held for 16 years, at the expiration of which, in B.C. 855, he was slain by Eochaidh Uarceas, son of the former King.

50. Argeadmar (or Argethamar) : his son; ascended the Throne of Ireland, B.C. 777, and was the 58th Monarch; after a reign of 30 years, was slain by Duach Ladhrach. He left four sons :—1. Fiontan, whose son, Ciombaoth, was the 63rd Monarch; 2. Diomain, whose son, Dithorba, became the 62nd Monarch; 3. Badhum, who was father of Aodh Ruadh, the 61st Monarch, who was drowned at *Eas Ruadh* (or Assaroe), now Ballyshannon, in the county of Donegal, and grandfather of Macha Mongruadh, or "Macha of the Golden Tresses," the 64th Monarch, and the only queen Ire-

---

* *Ollamh Fodhla :* See the Paper in the Appendix headed "The Irish Parliaments," for further information respecting this truly celebrated Irish Monarch.

land ever has had, who laid the foundation of the Royal Palace of Emania, in the county of Armagh, where her consort Cimbath, died of the plague; the fourth son of Argeadmar was Fomhar.

51. Fomhar: son of Argeadmar; died during the reign of Cimbath.

52. Dubh: his son; was King of Ulster.

53. Ros: his son.

54. Srubh: his son.

55. Indereach: his son.

56. Glas: his son.

57. Carbre (or Cathair): his son.

58. Feabhardhile: his son.

59. Fomhar (2): his son.

60. Dubh (2): his son.

61. Sithrich: his son.

62. Ruadhri (or Rory) Mór: his son; was the 86th Monarch; died B.C. 218. From him the "Clan-na-Rory" were so called. He left, amongst other children—1. Bresal Bodhiobha, and 2. Congall Clarei-neach, who were respectively the 88th and the 90th Monarchs; 3. Conragh, the father of the 105th Monarch Eiliomh; 4. Fachna Fathach, the 92nd Monarch, who, by his wife Neasa was father of Conor; 5. Ros Ruadh, who by his wife Roigh, the father of the celebrated Fergus Mór; and 6. Cionga, the ancestor of the heroic Conal Cearnach, from whom are descended *O'Moore*, *MacGuinness*, *M'Gowan*, and several other powerful families in Ulster and Conacht.

63. Ros Ruadh: son of Rory Mór; m. Roigh, dau. of an Ulster Prince.

64. Fergus Mór: his son; commonly called "Fergus MacRoy" or "Fergus MacRoich," from Roigh, his mother, who was of the sept of Ithe; was King of Ulster for three (some say seven) years, and then forced from the sovereignty by his cousin, Conor MacNeasa, whereupon he retired into Conacht, where

he was received by Maedhbh (Maev) Queen of that Province, and by her husband Oilioll Mór, and, sustained by them, was in continual war with Conor MacNeasa during their lives.

Maedhbh was the dau. of Eochy Feidlioch, the 93rd Monarch, who gave her in marriage to his favourite Tinne, son of Conragh, son of Ruadhri Mór (No. 62 on this stem), with the Province of Conacht as a dowry. This prince was slain at Tara by Monire, a Lagenian prince, in a personal quarrel; and Maedhbh soon after married Oilioll (who was much older than she was), the son of Ros Ruadh by Matha Muireasg, a Lagenian princess. Oiliol was far advanced in years when Fergus Mór sought shelter beneath his roof at Rath-Craughan, in Roscommon, and the Queen Maedhbh, being young, strayed from virtue's path, proved with child by Fergus, and was delivered of three male children at a birth. The names of these princes were:—1. Ciar [Kiar], a quo Ciarruighe Luachra, Ciarruighe Chuirc, Ciarruighe Aoi, and Ciarruighe Coinmean; 2. Corc, a quo Corc Modhruadh (or Corcum-roe); and 3. Conmac, a quo Conmaicne-Mara (now Connemara), Conmaicne Cuile Tolaigh (now the barony of Kilmaine, co. Mayo), Conmaicne Magh Rein (the present co. Longford, and the southern half of the co. Leitrim), Conmaicne Cinel Dubhain (now the barony of Dunmore, co. Galway).

According to the native genealogists these three sons of Fergus and Maedhbh ought to stand in the following order—1. Conmac; 2. Ciar; and 3. Corc.

Fergus Mór was slain by an officer belonging to the court of Oiliol Mór, as he was bathing in a pond near the royal residence, and he was interred at Magh Aoi.

The other children of Fergus Mór were :—1. Dallan, 2. Anluim, 3. Conri, 4. Aongus Fionn,* 5. Oiliol, 6. Firceighid,† 7. Uiter, 8. Finfailig,‡ 9. Firtleachta, and 10. Binne.

65. Conmac: eldest son of Fergus Mór, by Maedhbh ; whose portion of his mother's inheritance and what he acquired by his own prowess and valour, was called after his name : "Conmaicne" being equivalent to *Posterity of Conmac.* The five Conmaicne contained all that (territory) which we now call the county of Longford, a large part of the counties of Leitrim, Sligo, and Galway ; and Conmaicne Beicce, now called "Cuircneach" or *Dillon's Country*, in the county of Westmeath, over all of which this Conmac's posterity were styled Kings, till they were driven out by English adventurers.

66. Moghatoi : his son.

67. Messaman : his son.

68. Mochta: his son.

69. Cetghun : his son.

70. Enna : his son.

71. Gobhre : his son.

72. Iuchar : his son.

73. Eoghaman : his son.

74. Alta : his son.

75. Tairc : his son.

76. Teagha : his son ; had a brother, Dallan,§ who had a son Lughdach, who had a son Lughdach, whose son was *St. Canice* of Aghaboe.

77. Ethinon : his son.

78. Orbsenmar: his son ; after whose death a great Lake or Loch broke out in the place where he dwelt ; which, from him, is ever since called "Loch Orbsen" (now *Lough Corrib*).

79. Conmac : his son ; some Irish annalists are of opinion that the territories called "Conmacne" above mentioned, are called after this Conmac, and not from Conmac, No. 65 on this Stem.

* *Aongus Fionn* : This Aongus was ancestor of the Chiefs of Owny-Beg, now a barony in the county of Tipperary :

64. Fergus Mór, King of Ulster.	72. Diochon : his son.
65. Aongus Fionn : his son.	73. Sleibhe : his son.
66. MacNiadh : his son.	74. Gofnid : his son.
67. Orchon : his son.	75. Conor : his son.
68. Foranan : his son.	76. Dermod : his son.
69. Labhra : his son.	77. Lochlan : his son.
70. Cait : his son.	78. Dubhthaig : his son.
71. Oiliol : his son.	79. Maolbrenan : his son.

† *Firceighid* : This Firceighid was ancestor of the *Eoghanacht* of *Ara-Cliach,* a district in the county of Limerick on the borders of Tipperary :

65. Firceighid : son of Fergus Mór.	74. Cuchonacht: his son.
66. Rory : his son.	75. Maonaig : his son.
67. Lawlor : his son.	76. Dinfeartach : his son.
68. Daire: his son.	77. Duibtheach : his son.
69. Conri : his son.	78. Loingsedh : his son.
70. Benard : his son.	79. Dunlaing : his son.
71. Doncha : his son.	80. Bruadar : his son.
72. Eocha : his son.	
73. Eoghan : his son ; a quo *Eoghanacht Ara-Cliach.*	

‡ *Finfailig* : This Finfailig was ancestor of O'Dugan and O'Coscridh, chiefs of Fermoy, in the county of Cork. (See the "Dugan" Stem.)

§ *Dallan* : Had a son Lughdach, who had a son, Nathi, who had a son, Baer, who had a son, Becan, whose son, was *St. Mochna* of Ballagh, sometimes called *St. Cronan.*

80. Lughach : his son.
81. Beibhdhe : his son.
82. Bearra : his son; a quo *O'Bearra*, anglicised *Berry* and *Bury*.
83. Uisle : his son.
84. Eachdach : his son.
85. Forneart : his son.
86. Neart : his son.
87. Meadhrua : his son.
88. Dubh : his son.
89. Earcoll : his son.
90. Earc : his son.
91. Eachdach : his son.
92. Cuscrach : his son.
93. Fionnfhear : his son.
94. Fionnlogh : his son.
95. Onchu : his son.
96. Neidhe : his son.
97. Finghin : his son.
98. Fiobrann : his son; had four brothers, from three of whom the following families are descended :—
1. Maoldabhreac (whose son Siriden was ancestor of *Sheridan*), ancestor of *O'Ciarrovan* (now *Kirwan*), *O'Ciaragain* (now *Kerrigan*), etc. ; 2. Mochan, who was the ancestor of *O'Moran* ; and 3. Rinnall, who was ancestor of *O'Daly* of Conmacne.
99. Mairne : his son. From this Mairne's brothers are descended *O'Canavan, O'Birren, Birney,* and *MacBirney, O'Kenney, O'Branagan, Martin, Bredin,* etc.
100. Croman : son of Mairne.

101. Eimhin : his son; had three brothers :—1. Biobhsach, who was ancestor of *MacRaghnall* (or *Reynolds*) of Connaught; 2. Gearadhan, ancestor of *Gaynor* ; 3. Giollagan, ancestor of *Gilligan* and *Quinn* of the co. Longford. From these three brothers are also descended *Shanly, Mulvy, Mulkeeran,* etc.
102. Angall : his son. From this Angall that part of Conmacne now known as the county of Longford, and part of the county of Westmeath was called the "Upper Anghaile," or *Upper Annaly ;* and the adjacent part of the county of Leitrim was called the "Lower Anghaile," or *Lower Annaly* ; and his posterity after they lost the title of Kings of Conmacne, which his ancestors enjoyed, were, upon their subjugation by the Anglo-Normans, and on their consenting that their country be made "Shire ground," styled lords of both Anghalies or Annalies.
103. Braon : his son. This Braon's brother Fingin was ancestor of *Finnegan,* etc.
104. Congal : son of Braon.
105. Feargal ("feargal" : Irish, *a valiant warrior*) : his son; a quo *O'Fergail*, anglicised *O'Farrell, O'Ferrall, Farrell, Freehill,* and *Freel*.

CAHILL. (No. 1.)

Of Corkashinny, or the Parish of Templemore.

Arms : Ar. a whale spouting in the sea ppr.   *Crest :* An anchor erect, cable twined around the stock all ppr.

CATHAL, brother of Lochlann, who is No. 103 on the "O'Conor" (Corcomroe) pedigree, was the ancestor of *O'Cathail*, anglicised *Cahill*.

103. Cathal ("cathal:" Irish, *valour*) : son of Conor Mear (also called Conor* na Luinge Luaithe) ; a quo *O'Cathail*.

* *Conor na Luinge Luaithe* : This name, anglicised, means "Conor of the Swifter-Sailing Ship" ("luath," comp. "luaithe :" Irish, *quick*) : a quo *O'Luaithe*, anglicised *Quick,* and by some *Lowe*.

104. Conor : his son.

105. Donall Dana* (" dana :" Irish, bold ; Pers. and Arab, "dana," a poet) : his son.

106. Teige O'Cahill: his son ; first assumed this sirname.

107. Brian Bearnach : his son.

108. Cathal (2): his son.

109. Murtogh : his son.

110. Edmond : his son.

111. Donall Dunn : his son.

112. Tomhas na Sealbuidhe("seal:"

Irish, *a seal*), meaning "Thomas of the Seals :" his son ; a quo *O'Seal-luidhe* or *O'Seala*, anglicised *Shelly* and *Sales.*

113. John : his son.

114. Murtogh : his son.

115. Edmund : his son.

116. Teige Laidir ("laidir :" Irish, *strong*): his son ; a quo *Lauder, Strong,*† and *Stronge.*

117. Tomhas O'Cahill: his son ; living A.D. 1700.

CAHILL. (No. 2.)
Of Ballycahill, Thurles, County Tipperary.

Arms : Ar. a whale spouting in the sea ppr.   *Crest :* An anchor erect, cable twined around the stock all ppr.

CATHAL, a younger brother of Lochlann, who is No. 103 on the " O'Connor of Corcomroe" pedigree, was the ancestor of this branch of that family. This sept originally possessed Corca Thine, now called Corkashinny, or the parish of Templemore, co. Tipperary ; and more lately Ballycahill, near Thurles.

In 1653 Daniel O'Cahill, brother of "Bogh" O'Cahill, chief of the Clan, forfeited, under the Cromwellian Settlement, his castle and lands of Bally-cahill, which were granted to Edward (or Edmund) Annesley,‡ ancestor of Lord Annesley ; and on the 28th Jan., 1654, the said Daniel§ and his family were transplanted to Ballyglass, co. Mayo. Commencing with this Daniel *Cahill* or O'Cahill, the following is the pedigree :

1. Daniel Cahill, transplanted in 1654 to Ballyglass, co. Mayo, married and had :

2. Daniel, who m. and had :

3. William, who, after the Battle of the Boyne, settled in the Queen's County, and there, in 1715, married Mary, dau. of Michael Mulhall, and had two sons—1. John, 2. Thomas ; and a daughter Elizabeth.

4. Thomas : son of William, m. Bridget, dau. of Owen Harte, and had four sons :—1. Daniel, of whom presently ; 2. Thomas ; 3. Oliver ; 4. another Daniel. The third son Oliver was a Civil Engineer, who d. in 1859, leaving three sons :

I. Patrick Cahill, LL.B.

II. John Cahill.

---

* *Dana :* This Donall was the ancestor of *Dawney,* and, it is said, of *Dane* and *Deane.*

† *Strong :* While some genealogists derive this sirname from " Strongbow," others are of opinion that *Strong* and *Stronge* are Headfordshire or Border names—derived from the Anglo-Norman *Storange.*

‡ *Annesley :* See page 452 of our *Irish Landed Gentry.*

§ *Daniel :* See p. 361, *Ibid. ;* and No. 344, fol. 62, of the *Book of Transplanters,* Clonmel.

III. Rev. Thomas Cahill, S.J., living in Melbourne.

5. Daniel : son of Thomas ; m. Catherine, dau. of Oliver Brett (a descendant of Sir Philip le Brett, governor of Leighlin). The issue of this marriage was three sons, two of whom died young, and the third was the celebrated Divine, who is No. 6 on this pedigree.

6. The Very Rev. Daniel William Cahill,* D.D., a Catholic Priest, who died in Boston, America, 28th October, 1864 ; and whose remains were in 1885 translated to Ireland, and interred in Glasnevin Cemetery, Dublin, where, in grateful recognition of Doctor Cahill's signal services to Ireland, his compatriots erected in 1887 a statue over his grave.

CAWLEY.
Of West Connaught.

Arms : Sa. a chev, erm. betw. three swans' heads, erased at the neck ar.

THE family of O'Cadhla (" cadhla :" Irish, fair, beautiful, anglicised O'Cawley, MacCawley, and Cawley), derives its name and descent from Cadhla, a descendant of Conmac, son of Fergus Mór, who (see page 301) is No. 64 on the " Line of Ir." The O'Cawleys were Chiefs of Conmacne-Mara (now Connemara), in West Galway. They were a peaceful tribe, and took little or no part in any of the many disturbances which agitated Ireland since the Anglo-Norman invasion.

1. Cadhla, a quo O'Cadhla, anglicised O'Cawley.
2. Donoch Caoch: his son.
3. Donal : his son.
4. Iomhar Fionn : his son.
5. Gilla-na-Neev : his son.
6. Gilla-na-Neev (2) : his son.
7. Doncha Mór : his son.
8. Doncha Oge : his son.
9. Aodh Dubh : his son.
10. Doncha (3) : his son.
11. Cathal : his son.
12. John (or Owen) : his son.
13. Muireadhagh : his son.
14. Muircheartagh : his son.
15. Flan : his son.
16. Muircheartagh (2) : his son.
17. Flan (2) : his son.

18. Malachy : his son.
19. Patrick : his son.
20. Melaghlin : his son.
21. Aodh (2) : his son.
22. Muircheartagh (3) : his son.
23. Muircheartagh Oge (4) : his son.
24. Malachy O'Cawley : his son. This Malachy was a native of West Conacht ; and in 1630 was appointed to the Archbishopric of Tuam-da-ghualan (now Tuam). This distinguished prelate was the last of a long line of illustrious chiefs, and the rightful owner of an extensive estate in the barony of Ballinahinch, in the county of Galway. He commanded a detachment of the Irish

* Cahill : Daniel William Cahill, D.D., a pulpit orator, and lecturer upon chemistry and astronomy, was born in the Queen's County, in 1796. After studying at Maynooth, he was ordained, and for a time was a professor in Carlow College. He is well remembered as a fluent lecturer, was the author of many pamphlets, and for a time edited a newspaper in Dublin. Removing to the United States, he died in Boston, in October, 1864, aged about 68 years.—WEBB.

U

army in 1645, and was slain* near Sligo in that year, in an unsuccessful attempt to take the town from the Parliamentarians, who held it under Sir Charles Coote.

CRONNELLY.

Princes of Crich-Cualgne, in Ulster

Arms : Two croziers in saltire.

CONNALL, who is No. 92 on the "Guinness" Stem, was the ancestor of this family.

93. Cu-Ulladh : son of Conall; b. A.D. 576.

94. Cas : his son.

95. Cu-Sleibhe : his son.

96. Conal : his son.

97. Fergus : his son.

98. Bresail : his son.

99. Cineath : his son.

100. Nial : his son.

101. Buan : his son.

102. Culenain† : his son.

103. Cronghall : his son ; d. 935 ; a quo *O'Cronnelly*, lord of Conaille.

104. Cineath (2) : his son.

105. Matadan : his son ; slain 995 ; Prince of Crich-Cualgne.

106. Cronghall (2) : his son.

107. Rory : his son.

108. Angusliath : his son.

109. Connall : his son.

110. Brian Roe : his son.

111. Gillananeev : his son.

112. Cu-Ulladh (2) : his son.

113. Cineath (3) : his son.

114. Cillachriost : his son.

115. Eoghan : his son.

116. Cathal : his son.

117. Eoghan (2) Mór : his son.

118. Eoghan (3) Oge : his son.

119. Brian (2) : his son.

120. Cosgniadh : his son.

121. Eoghan (4) ; his son.

122. John the Prior : his son.

123. Gillachriost (2) : his son.

124. Donal : his son.

125. Tadhg : his son.

126. Richard : his son.

127. Donal (2) Buidhe‡ : his son.

128. Donal (3) : his son.

129. Tadhg (2) : his son.

130. Tadhg (3) : his son.

131. Riocaird : his son.

132. Tadhg (4) : his son.

133. Riocaird (2) : his son.

134. Tadhg (5) : his son ; b. 1804, and living in 1864.

135. Richard F. O'Cronnelly (2) : his son ; a member of the Irish

---

* *Slain :* Of the "Cawley" tribe was the man by whom Gerald Fitzjames Fitzgerald, Earl of Desmond, was in 1583 mortally wounded in Gleanaguanta. That man was, as Cox states, a native Irishman, who had been bred by the English, and was serving as a kern under the English commandant of Castlemaigne, in 1583. On the 11th November, Fitzgerald was slain, his head sent to London, and his body hung in chains in Cork.— (See Ormonde's Letter, 15th Nov., 1583, in the State Paper Office.)

† *Culenain :* A quo *O'Cullenane* and *Cullenane.*

‡ *Donal Buidhe :* This Donal was head of the Galway branch of the family, was an officer in the army of King Charles I. ; was in the Battle of Edgehill, October 23rd, 1642 ; and also at Marston Moor. On the defeat of the Stuart cause at Worcester, in 1651, he returned to his ancestral home at Killeenan, near Rahasane, co. Galway, where he died *circa* 1659 ; his remains were interred in the now ruined church of Kileely, where an oblong stone slab marks his last resting-place.

Constabulary Force; and residing in the Constabulary Depôt, Phœnix Park, Dublin, Ireland, in June, 1864; b. 1833; Chief of his name and race. Author of *Irish Family History.*

Upon the defeat of the Ultonians in 1177, one of the chiefs of this family was given as an hostage for the future fealty of the sept of Conaille to De Courcy, by whom he was sent to England, where he became the ancestor of the *Cranleys* of Cranley, one of whom, a Carmelite friar, was elected Archbishop of Dublin, in 1397, at the instance of King Richard II. This prelate came to Ireland in 1398, and was appointed Lord Chancellor by Richard II., who sent him on a mission to the Continent. He died at Farrington, in England, on the 25th of May, 1417, and was buried in the New College, Oxford.

CURTIN.

Arms : Vert in front of a lance in pale or, a stag trippant ar. attired gold, betw. three crosses crosslet of the second, two and one, and as many trefoils slipped of the third, one and two.   *Crest :* In front of two lances in saltire ar. bedded or, an Irish harp sa.

FRAOCH, brother of Cubroc, who is No. 82 on the " O'Conor" (Corcomroe) pedigree, was the ancestor of *Clann Cruitin;* modernized *O'Cruitin* and *O'Cuarthain;* and anglicised *MacCurtin, Curtin, Curtain, Jordan,* and *Jourdan.*

82. Fraoch : son of Oscar.
83. Carthann : his son.
84. Lonan : his son.
85. Seanan : his son.
86. Labann : his son.
87. Brocan : his son.
88. Cruitin* File (" cruitin :" Irish, *a crooked-back person ;* " file," *a poet, bard* or *minstrel*): his son ; a quo *Clann Cruitin.*
89. Maolruana : his son.
90. Fergus : his son.
91. Saorbreitheamh† O'Cruitin :

his son; first assumed this sirname.
92. Saortuile : his son.
93. Mudhna : his son.
94. Altan : his son.
95. Conor : his son.
96. Flann : his son.
97. Aralt : his son.
98. Giolla Chriosd : his son.
99. Aodh (or Hugh) : his son.
100. Conor (2) : his son.
101. Hugh : his son.
102. Hugh Oge : his son.

* *Cruitin File :* The word *cruitin* [crutteen] is derived from the Irish *cruit,* "a lyre," "harp," or " violin" (Lat. *cythar-a*). Of the ancient Irish *Cruit* Evans wrote : " Ex sex chordis felinis constat, nec eodem modo quo violinum modulatur, quamvis a figura haud multum abludat."

† *Saorbreitheamh :* This word is compounded of the Irish *saor,* a workman, a carpenter, a builder, a joiner, a mason ; and *breitheamh,* a judge. Some of the descendants of this Saorbreitheamh were, by way of eminence, called *Mac-an-t-Saoir* (literally, " the sons or descendants of the workman"), which has been anglicised *MacIntyre, Carpenter, Freeman. Joiner, Judge, Mason,* etc. It was our mistake in the first series, page 227, to give " MacIntyre" as synonymous with " O'Mictyre," chiefs of Hy-MacCaille, now the barony of " Imokilly," in the county Cork ; for, *O'Mictyre* (" mactire :" Irish, *a wolf*) is quite distinct from *Mac-an-t-Saoir,* and has been anglicised *Wolf* and *Wolfe.*

103. Solomon : his son.
104. Conor (3) ; his son.
105. Seanchuidh (" seanchuidh :" Irish, *a chronicler*): his son ; a quo *O'Seanchuidh*, anglicised *Sanchy*.
106. Fearbiseach : his son.
107. Eolus : his son.
108. Crimthann : his son.
109. Hugh na Tuinnidhe (" na-tuinnidhe :" Irish, *of the den*): his son ; a quo *Tunney*.

110. Conor (4) : his son.
111. Conor Oge : his son.
112. Hugh Buidhe* : his son ; author of the " English Irish Dictionary" published in Paris, A.D. 1732.
William McCurtin, miller and merchant, Tipperary, was of this family. His son, Charles McCurtin, living in 1887, represents him in Springhouse Mill, Tipperary.

DUGAN.

Chiefs of Fermoy.

Arms : Quarterly, az. and erm. in the 1st and 4th quarter a griffin's head or. *Crest :* A talbot statant ppr. collared ar.

FERGUS MÓR (Fergus MacRoy), King of Ulster, who is No. 64 on the " Line of Ir," was founder of this family.

65. Fionfailig : son of Fergus Mór, King of Ulster.
66. Firglin : his son.
67. Firgil : his son.
68. Firdeicit : his son.
69. Cumascagh : his son ; a quo *O'Coscridh*, anglicé *Cosgrave*.
70. Mogh Ruith : his son. This was a famous Druid called " Mogh Ruith" (*Magus Rotœ*), from his having made a wheel, the *Ruitha-Ramhar*, by means of which he was enabled to ascend into the air, in presence of an astonished multitude.
71. Labhra : his son.

72. Dethi : his son.
73. Sarglinn : his son.
74. Suirce : his son.
75. Laiscre : his son.
76. Iolainn· : his son.
77. Magnan : his son.
78. De-Thaile : his son.
79. Congan-Gairin : his son.
80. Ceallach : his son.
81. Dailgaile : his son.
82. Muircheardoig : his son.
83. Lomainig : his son.
84. Dubhagan :† his son ; a quo *O'Dubhagain*, anglicised *O'Dugan*, *Dugan*, *Duggan*,‡ and *Doogan*.
85. Hugh : his son.

---

     * *Hugh Buidhe ;* This Hugh and Andrew MacCurtin were natives of the county Clare, and distinguished as poets in the 18th century. Hugh wrote an Irish Grammar, an English-Irish Dictionary, and an Essay in Vindication of the Antiquity of Ireland. And Manuscripts in the Library of Trinity College, Dublin, copied by Andrew MacCurtin, between 1716 and 1720, are referred to by Eugene O'Curry, who styles him " one of the best Irish scholars then living."

     † *Dubhagan*, which means a " dark-featured, small-sized man."

     ‡ *Duggan :* Of this family was Peter Paul Duggan, an artist, born in Ireland, who early in life went to the United States, America, developed a taste for art, and ultimately became Professor in the New York Free Academy. Though the crayon was his

86. Dermod : his son.
87. Melaghlin : his son.
88. Conor : his son.

89. Hugh (2): his son.
90. Donal : his son.

DUNCAN.

Arms : Sa. five eagles displ. in cross ar.

DUNCHEANN (*dunceann :* Irish, "a chief of a fort"), the second son of Naradh who is No. 97 on the "Ruddy" pedigree, was the ancestor of *O'Duncinn,* anglicised *Duncan,* and *Dunkin ;** and Tormach (*tormach,* Irish, " an augmentation or increase"), the third son of the said Naradh, was the ancestor of *O'Tormaigh,* anglicised *Tormey.*

FARRELL.

Of Waterford.

Crest : A dexter hand erect appaumée gules.   *Motto :* Prodesse non nocere.

WALTER FARRELL, married Honora Henneberry (whose sister, Margaret, m. Richard de Courcy), and had issue : 1. Patrick, 2. Peter, 3. John.

2. John Farrell, the third son, m. Alice, 3rd child of Richard Bermingham by Frances White, his wife, and had : 1. Honora, 2. Walter, 3. Richard, 4. Mary, 5. Frances, 6. Patrick, 7. Peter, 8. John.

3. Walter, the eldest son, married Bridget, dau. of John Reville by Mary O'Brien (*recté* Ni-Brien), his wife, and had eleven children, nine of whom *d. s. p.* He acquired by purchase St. Saviour's or Black Friars Abbey, Waterford, which was established by King Henry III. in 1235 at the request of the citizens for the Dominican Order; and also some house property adjoining. Part of this was subsequently demolished for city improvements. The rest remains in the family.

favourite medium, he occasionally painted a masterly head in oil. For many years an invalid, he latterly resided near London, and died in Paris on the 15th October, 1861. And of this family was Doctor James Duggan, whose name is mentioned in the Second Charter granted in 1828 to the Royal College of Surgeons in Ireland.

* *Dunkin :* William Dunkin, D.D., a friend of Swift and Delany, was probably of the family of the Rev. Patrick Dunkin, whose metrical Latin translations of some Irish "ranns" are acknowledged by Archbishop Usher. William Dunkin was ordained in 1735—in which year we find him repaying Swift's friendship and patronage by assisting him in his poetical controversy with Bettesworth. In 1737 Swift endeavoured to obtain for him an English living, writing of him : " He is a gentleman of much wit, and the best English as well as Latin poet in the Kingdom. He is a pious man, highly esteemed." This appeal was fruitless ; Dunkin was, however, placed by Lord Chesterfield over the Endowed School of Enniskillen. He died about 1746. A collected edition of his poems and epistles appeared in two Vols. in 1774.

Richard Farrell, the 2nd son, b. 1771, m. 1808 Mary Ann, 3rd child of Robert-Thomas Power (son of Thomas Power by Mary Cummins his wife), by his wife, Mary Doyle (eldest child of John Doyle by his wife, Alice Russell, née Spencer); and has : 1. Mary, 2. John, of whom presently ; 3. Robert, 4. Richard, 5. Robert, 6. Walter, 7. Edward, 8. Alicia, of whom presently ; 9. Maria, living unm. in 1887; 10. Thomas, 11. Marcus, 12. Charles, 13. Thomas.

Richard, living in 1887, youngest child of the aforesaid Walter Farrell and Bridget Reville, married Mary Downey, living in 1887, and has : 1. Kate, 2. Mary, twins; 3. Walter, 4. Annie, 5. John, 6. Gertrude, 7. Alice, 8. Richard, 9. Augustine, 10. Margaret-Mary, 11. Francis, 12. Frances, all living, unm., in 1887, in Waterford, except Annie, who is in the Sister of Mercy Convent, Rochester, N.Y.; and Francis, who died in infancy.

Alicia (b. 1817, living in 1887), 8th child of the foresaid Richard Farrell and Mary Ann Power, m. in 1848 John Flynn, of Kilkenny, widower (b. 1806, living in 1887), son of James Flynn of Limerick by his wife, Catherine O'Connor (recté

Ni-Connor) of Wexford ; and has : 1. Mary-Anne (b. 1849), living in 1887, in the Passionist Convent, Mamers, France ; 2. Alice, of whom presently ; 3. Richard, 4. Richard-Joseph, 5. Mary, 6. Mary-Agnus, 7. Robert, living in 1887 ; 8. Alphonsus, of whom presently ; 9. John-Aloysius, of whom presently.

Alice, living in 1887, the second child of Alicia, married Richard Dempsey, and has : 1. Mary-Alicia, 2. Clement-Thomas.

Alphonsus, 8th child of Alicia, m. Florence Dempsey (both living in 1887) and has had : 1. John-Archibald, who died an infant; 2. Richard-Clement, 3. Bertha, 4. Walter-Henry, the three last living in 1887, in Dublin.

John Aloysius, of Orange Grove Estate, Luckhardt, Sydney (living in 1887), 9th child, married Mary Leonard, and has : 1. Alicia-Mary, 2. Richard-Patrick.

4. John Farrell, eldest son of the aforesaid Richard Farrell by Mary Ann Power, m. his first cousin, 10th child of Walter Farrell and Bridget Reville, and has eight children, of whom four now survive (in 1887).

5. Walter Farrell, the second son of these, was b. 1865, living, unm., in 1887, in London.

GUINNESS.*

or

MacGuinness.

Lords of Iveagh, County Down.

The ancient Arms of this family were : Vert a lion ramp. or, on a chief ar, a dexter hand erect, couped at the wrist gu.

Cionog (or Cionga), brother of Ros who is No. 63 on the "Line of Ir," p. 301, was the ancestor of *MacAonghuis* [oneesh] ; anglicised *MacGuinness, Maginnis, Magennis, Magenis, MacInnes, Guinness, Angus, Ennis, Innis,* etc.

63. Cionga : son of Rory Mór.

64. Capa (or Cathbharr) : his son.

65. Fachna Fathach : his son; the 92nd Monarch of Ireland.

66. Cas : his son ; and brother of Conor MacNessa, who deposed Fergus MacRoy from the sovereignty of Ulster.

67. Amergin : his son.

68. Conall Cearnach : his son ; the famous warrior, so often mentioned in the Irish Annals as connected with the Red Branch Knights of Ulster.

69. Irial Glunmhar : his son ; King of Ulster; had a brother named Laoiseach Lannmor, who was also called Lysach, and who was the ancestor of *O'Moore.*

70. Fiacha Fionn Amhnais : Irial's son ; who, of the line of Ir, was the 24th King of Ulster, in Emania.

71. Muredach Fionn : his son ; King of Ulster.

72. Fionnchadh : his son.

73. Connchadh (or Donnchadh) : his son.

74. Gialchad : his son.

75. Cathbha : his son.

76. Rochradh : his son.

77. Mal : his son ; the 107th Monarch.

78. Firb : his son.

79. Breasal Breac : his son.

80. Tiobrad Tireach : his son ; was the 30th King of Ulster, of the Irian line ; and contemporary with Conn of the Hundred Battles, the 110th Monarch of Ireland, whom he assassinated A.D. 157.

81. Fergus Gaileoin (or Foghlas) : his son.

82. Aongus Gabhneach : his son ; a quo *O'Gaibhnaigh,* anglicised *Gowan, MacGowan,*† *O'Gowan, Gibney, Smythe, Smith,* etc.

83. Fiacha Araidhe : his son ; from whom, who was the 37th King of Ulster of the Irian line, the ancient territory of "Dalaradia" (sometimes

---

* *Guinness* : Sir Benjamin Lee Guinness, Bart., a distinguished member of this family, born 1st November, 1798, was an opulent brewer, in Dublin, and M.P. for Dublin from 1865 until his death. He is best remembered as the restorer of St. Patrick's Cathedral, Dublin, at a cost which has been estimated at £130,000 ; and as the head of a business firm that has acquired a world-wide reputation. He died possessed of a large fortune, and, besides several mansions in and near Dublin, was the owner of a beautiful estate at Cong, in the county of Mayo, on the shores of Lough Corrib. He evinced great and practical interest in Irish archæology by his tasteful preservation of the antiquarian remains upon his large estates. He died on the 10th May, 1868, aged 69, and was buried at Mount Jerome, Dublin.—Webb.

† *MacGowan :* The *Arms* are : Ar. a lion ramp. gu. between two cinque foils vert. *Crest :* A talbot pass.

called "Ulidia," comprising the present county of Down and part of the county Antrim) was so named.

84. Cas: his son; had a brother named Sodhan;* who was ancestor of *O'Manning, MacWard*, etc.

85. Fedhlim: his son; King of Ulster.

86. Iomchadh: his son.

87. Ros: his son; King of Ulster.

88. Lughdheach: his son.

89. Eathach Cobha: his son; from whom *Iveagh*, a territory in the county of Down, derived its name; and from that territory his descendants in after ages took their title as "Lords of Iveagh."

90. Crunnbhadroi: his son.

91. Caolbha: his son; the (123rd and) last Monarch of the Irian race, and 47th King of Ulster.

92. Conall: his son; had three brothers: 1. Feargan, who was the ancestor of *MacCartan*; 2. Saraan, who was the last King of Ulster, of the Irian race, and in whose time the Three Collas conquered Ulster; 3. Conla.

93. Fothach: son of Conall.

94. Main: his son.

95. Saraan: his son.

96. Mongan: his son.

97. Aodhan: his son; had a brother Foghartach, who was ancestor of *MacArtan*.

98. Feargus: son of Aodhan.

99. Breasal Beldearg: his son.

100. Conchobhar: his son.

101. Domhnall: his son.

102. Blathmac: his son.

103. Laidhne: his son.

104. Aidiotha: his son.

105. Aongus ("aon:" Irish, *excellent;* "gus," *strength*): his son; a

quo *MacAonghuis*. This Aongus was called Æneas Mór.

106. Aongus Oge (or Aodh): his son; first of the family who assumed this sirname.

107. Eachmilidh: his son.

108. Aongus: his son.

109. Eachmilidh: his son.

110. Flaitheartach: his son.

111. Aodh (or Hugh) Reamhar: his son.

112. Dubhinsi: his son.

113. Giolla Coluim: his son.

114. Ruadhrigh: his son.

115. Eachmilidh: his son.

116. Murtogh Riaganach: his son.

117. Art (or Arthur) na-Madhmainn: his son.

118. Aodh (or Hugh): his son.

119. Art: his son.

120. Hugh: his son.

121. Donall Mór: his son; had two elder brothers—1. Hugh, 2. Eachmilidh (who had a son Hugh), and seven younger brothers—1. Felim, 2. Edmond, 3. Cu-Uladh, 4. Muirceartach, 5. Brian, 6. Ruadhrigh (Rory, or Roger), 7. Glaisne.

122. Donall Oge: son of Donall Mór.

123. Hugh (also called Feardorach or Ferdinand): his son.

124. Art Ruadh [roe], or Sir Arthur *Magennis*, of Rathfriland: his son; was in 1623 created Viscount Iveagh, county Down; m. Sarah, dau. of Hugh O'Neill, Earl of Tyrone, and had issue—1. Hugh Oge, of Iveagh, who had a son named Arthur; 2. Conn, 3. Arthur, 4. Rory, 5. Daniel (who is No. 125, *infra*); 6. Rose, 7. Evelin, 8. Eliza. He was buried in Dromballybrony on the 15th June, 1629.

125. Daniel: son of Art Ruadh; m. Eliza Magennis; d. 1658.

‡ *Sodhan:* According to the *Linea Antiqua* this Sodhan was the ancestor of *O'Dugan.*

126. Bernard,* a Colonel : his son ; d. 1692. Had a brother Roger Mór, who m. N. Cavanagh.

127. Roger Oge : son of the aforesaid Roger Mór; m. Maria Magennis. Had a brother Bernard, who was a Lieutenant-Colonel,† 1703-1734.

128. Heber : son of Roger Oge ; d. 1760.

129. Arthur : his son ; a Captain ; d. 1794. (See the "De la Ponce MSS.")

HEALY.

Chiefs of Pobal O'Healy, in the County Cork.

Arms : Az. a fesse betw. three stags' heads erased in chief ar. and a demi lion ramp. in base or. *Another :* Az. three boars' heads, couped in pale ar. *Crest :* On a chapeau a lion statant, guard. ducally gorged.

ASADHMUN, a son of Fergus Mór who (see p. 301) is No. 64 on the "Line of Ir," was the ancestor of *O'h-Eilighe ;* anglicised *O'Healy‡ Healy,* and *Hely.*

64. Fergus Mór : son of Ros (known as Ros Ruadh).

65. Asadhmun : his son. Had three half brothers—1. Conmac, 2. Ciar, 3. Corc.

66. Ailsach : son of Asadhmun.

67. Oineach : his son.

68. Eoghan : his son.

69. Delbhna : his son.

70. Fiodhcuirce : his son.

71. Eachamun : his son.

72. Alt : his son.

73. Athre : his son.

74. Eachadun : his son.

75. Orbsinmhar : his son.

76. Modhart : his son.

77. Saul : his son.

78. Meascu : his son.

---

* *Bernard :* This Bernard had a son Roderic, who in 1707 was Page de . . . . and d. 1726.

† *Colonel :* This Lieutenant-Colonel Bernard Maginnis had a son Murtagh, who was a Captain, and who had a son Charles-Francis, b. 1745.

‡ *O'Healy :* Some Irish Genealogists deduce the descent of the " O'Healy" family from Cosgrach, son of Lorcan, King of Thomond, who was grandfather of **Brian Boroimhe** [Boru], who is No. 105 on the " O'Brien" (of Thomond) pedigree, and who was the 175th Monarch of Ireland ; others deduce it from the " O'Haly" family, which is an anglicised form of the Irish *O'h-Algaich* (" algach" : Irish, *noble*), while *O'Healy* is from the Irish *O'h-Eilighe,* as above shown. But (see the "Hally" and " Haly" pedigrees, respectively), the two genealogies are quite distinct, and the two families not at all descended from the same stock as " O'Healy ;" for it is the " O'Haly" family that is descended from Cosgrach, son of Lorcan, who is No. 103 on the " O'Brien" (of Thomond) pedigree, and the " O'Haly" family is descended from Donchuan, brother of Brian Boru, while the "O'Healy" family is descended from Fergus Mór, who is No. 64 on the "Line of Ir." Others again say that the O'Healys of Donoughmore are a branch of the "MacCarthy Mór" family, Princes of Desmond ; but we are unable to trace that connection. It is worthy of remark, however, that the *Arms* assigned by Keating to the " O'Healy" family, namely—Az. a fesse between three stags' heads erased in chief ar. and a demi lion ramp. in base or., are borne by the Helys, Earls of Donoughmore : which goes to show that their name was formerly " O'Healy." The founder of the House of Donoughmore was John *Hely,* Provost of Trinity College, Dublin, Secretary of State for Ireland, and Keeper of the

79. Ullamh : his son.
80. Measa : son of Ullamh.
81. Cuilean : his son.
82. Cunath : his son.
83. Mearcu : his son.
84. Arad : his son.
85. Iomchadh : his son.
86. Cathair : his son.
87. Luchd : his son.
88. Adhlann : his son.
89. Luchd : his son.

90. Luchdreach : his son.
91. Maoltoirnd : his son.
92. Bath : his son.
93. Elhe ("ele:" Irish, *a bier, a litter*) : his son ; a quo *O'h-Eilighe.*
94. Feargus : his son.
95. Felim : his son.
96. Coibhdealach : his son.
97. Conrach : his son.
98. Conmhach : his son.
99. Conn O'Healy : his son.

KILROY. (No. 1.)

Chiefs in Clonderlaw, County Clare.

TIOBRAID, a younger brother of Fiacha Fionn Amhnais who is No. 70 on the "Guinness" pedigree, was the ancestor of *MacGiolla Raibhaigh ;* anglicised *MacGillereagh, MacGilrea, MacGilroy, MacKilroy, Gilroy, Kilroy, MacGreevy, Greevy, Creevy, Gray,* * and *Grey.*

70. Tiobraid : son of Irial Glun-mhar, who was a King of Ulster.
71. Cairbre : his son.
72. Forgall : his son.

73. Mesin : his son.
74. Meinn : his son.
75. Cormac : his son.
76. Cairbre : his son.

Privy Seal in 1774, the celebrated author of *The Commercial Restraints of Ireland,* who, in 1771, married Christiana, daughter of Lorenzo Nickson, Esq., of Wicklow, and grandniece and heiress of Richard Hutchinson, Esq., of Knocklofty, in the county Tipperary, whose name the said John Hely assumed. Since then the family has borne the name of *Hely-Hutchinson.* John Hely-Hutchinson obtained a Peerage for his wife, who took the title of "Baroness Donoughmore, of Knocklofty," the seat of the present Earl. Mr. Hely-Hutchinson was subsequently offered an Earldom, and was about to become "Earl O'Hely," when he died. The Peerage created for his wife descended, according to limitation, to their son, Richard, who, after becoming "Baron Donough-more" by inheritance, was created *Earl of Donoughmore,* in December, 1806. His brother John succeeded him as Baron, and second Earl of Donoughmore ; and John, dying, was succeeded by his Nephew, John, as third Earl, who married the Hon. Margaret Gardiner, seventh daughter of Luke, first Viscount Mountjoy, by Margaret (daughter of Hector Wallis, Esq., of Dublin, and Springmount, Queen's County), mentioned in the "Wallis-Healy" Genealogy, *infra,* which see.

* *Gray :* Of this family was Sir John Gray, M.P., who was born at Claremorris, in the County of Mayo, in 1816. and died at Bath, in England, on the 9th of April, 1875, Of him, WEBB, in his *Compendium of Irish Biography,* writes :—" He studied medicine, and shortly before his marriage. in 1839, settled in Dublin as Physician to an Hospital in North Cumberland-street. He was before long drawn into politics, and in 1841 began to write for the (Dublin) *Freeman's Journal,* of which paper he eventually became proprietor. He warmly advocated the Repeal of the Union (between Great Britain and Ireland), and was one of O'Connell's ablest supporters. Full of suggestive energy and resource, he originated and organized those courts of arbitration which O'Connell endeavoured to substitute for the legal tribunals of the country. He was

77. Macniadh : his son.
78. Eochaidh : his son.
79. Fachtna : his son.
80. Eoghan : his son.
81. Dallan : his son.
82. Feargus : his son.
83. Goill : his son.
84. Glaisne : his son.
85. Nacroide : his son.
86. Fiontan : his son.
87. Fiacha : his son.
88. Bearach : his son.
89. Brogan : his son.
90. Naistean : his son.
91. Eochaidh : his son.
92. Donoch : his son.
93. Congealt : his son.
94. Longseach : his son.
95. Giolla Riabhach ("riabhach" : Irish, *gray, swarthy*,) : his son ; a quo *MacGiolla Raibhaigh*.
96. Riocard : his son.
97. Mathghabhuin : his son.
98. Riocard (2) : his son.
99. Domhnall [donal] : his son.
100. Riocard (3) : his son.

101. Conchobhar : his son.
102. Donchadh : his son.
103. Torg-reach : his son.
104. Muireadach : his son.
105. Murrogh : his son.
106. Riocard (4) : his son.
107. Donchadh (or Donoch) : his son.
108. Eochaidh : his son.
109. Tirlogh : his son.
110. Diarmaid [dermod] : his son.
111. Donoch : his son.
112. Tomhas : his son.
113. Conall : his son.
114. Mathghabhuin : his son.
115. Riocard (5) : his son.
116. Donall : his son.
117. Ruadhri : his son.
118. Tomhas : his son.
119. Conchobhar [connor] : his son.
120. Donn : his son.
121. Riocard (6) : his son.
122. Uaithne [Anthony] : his son.
123. Riocard (7) : his son.

KILROY. (No. 2.)

WHEN the county Clare, like the other parts of Ireland, was devastated under the Commonwealth Government of Ireland, to make room for the Cromwellian Settlement, the old Irish families who were dispossessed and

prosecuted in 1844 for alleged seditious language, and suffered imprisonment with O'Connell. After O'Connell's death, Dr. Gray continued to take a prominent part in Irish politics and in local affairs. It was to his energy and determination, as a member of the Dublin Corporation, that the citizens of Dublin owe their present excellent Vartry water supply. . . . . On the opening of the works, 30th June, 1863, he was Knighted by the Earl of Carlisle, then Lord Lieutenant of Ireland. At the general election of 1865 Sir John was returned M.P. for Kilkenny, a seat which he held until his death. He took a prominent and effective part in the passage of the Church and Land Bills, and supported the Home Rule movement. He died at Bath, 9th April, 1875, aged 59, and his remains were honoured with a public funeral at Glasnevin, Dublin. His fellow-citizens almost immediately afterwards set about the erection in O'Connell Street, of a Monument in appreciation of his many services to his country, and of the splendid supply of pure water which he secured for Dublin. Sir John Gray was a Protestant. . . . . . His paper, the *Freeman's Journal*, which he raised by his talents to be the most powerful organ of public opinion in Ireland, he left to the management of his son, Mr. Edmund Dwyer Gray, M.P., living in 1887."

who escaped transportation as "slaves" to the Sugar Plantations of America, had to seek homes and refuges wherever they could, for themselves and their families. It was at that unhappy juncture in the history of Ireland, in the year 1653, that, according to tradition, a son of the last Chief of this family, settled in Keenagh—one of the mountain fastnesses in the proximity of Mount Nephin, in the barony of Tyrawley, and county of Mayo; from whom the following branch of that ancient family is descended:

124. ( ) A son of Riocard, who is No. 123 on the "Kilroy" (No. 1) pedigree; had three sons :—1. Michael, 2. Peter, 3. Mark :

I. Michael, married and had: 1. Patrick; 2. Mary, who m. and had a family.

    I. This Patrick married and had: 1. Peter, 2. Edward.

      I. This Peter, m. and had : 1. Thomas; 2. Patrick—both these sons living in Keenagh, in August, 1871.

      II. Edward : the second son of Patrick, son of Michael, had a son named Peter—also living in Keenagh, in August, 1871.

II. Peter, the second son of No. 1.; m. and had Bridget, who m. and had a family.

III. Mark, the third son of No. 1, of whom presently.

125. Mark: the third son of No. 124, m. and had: 1. Peter; 2. Bridget.

I. This Peter of whom presently.

II. Bridget, m. —— Gill, of Glenhest, also in the vicinity of Glen Nephin, and had :

    I. Denis Gill (living in 1871), who m. Anne Hagerty (also living in 1871), and had issue.

126. Peter : son of Mark ; m. Mary Geraghty, of Kinnaird, in the parish of Crossmolina, and had surviving issue four daughters :—1. Norah; 2. Mary; 3. Bridget; 4. Margaret.

I. This Norah, of whom presently.

II. Mary, who married Michael Geraghty (or Garrett), of Kinnaird, above mentioned, and had : 1. Michael, who m., and emigrated to America in 1847 ; and had issue ; living (1887) in Deerpark, Maryland, U.S.A. 2. Patrick, of Kinnaird, who m. Mary Sheridan, and had issue; this Patrick and his family emigrated to America, in the Spring of 1883, and are living (1887) in Deerpark, Maryland. 3. John, who emigrated to America with his brother Michael, in 1847. 4. A daughter, who d. unm. 5. Mary, who m. Michael Gilboy, and had issue.

III. Bridget, who was the second wife of Patrick Walsh of Cloonagh, in the parish of Moygownagh, in the said barony of Tyrawley, and had : 1. Margaret, who m. Thomas Fuery, and with him emigrated to America. 2. Walter, who also emigrated to the New World.

IV. Margaret, who m. Thomas Regan, of Moygownagh, above mentioned, and had two children—1. Mary, 2. Patrick (1.) This Mary (d. 1881), m. John (died in 1886), eldest son of Martin Hart, of Glenhest, and had issue (2.) Patrick, d. young.

127. Norah Kilroy: eldest daughter of Peter; m. John O'Hart, and (see No. 124 on the "O'Hart" genealogy) had :

I, Michael; II. Michael: both of whom d. in infancy.

III. Rev. Anthony, a Catholic Priest, of the diocese of Killala, who d. 7th Mar., 1830.

IV. Mary, who d. unm. in 1831.

V. Anne (d 1841), who m. James Fox (d. 1881), of Crossmolina, and had: 1. Mary (living in 1887), who m. J. Sexton, of Rockfort, Illinois, U.S.A., and had issue; 2. Anne, who d. unm.

VI. Bridget (deceased), who m. John Keane, of Cloonglasna, near Ballina, Mayo, and had issue—now (1887) in America.

VII. Patrick (d. in America, 1849) who married Bridget Mannion (d. 1849), and had two children, who d. in infancy.

VIII. Catherine (d. in Liverpool, 1852), who m. John Divers, and had : 1. Patrick, 2. John.

IX. John, of whom presently.

X. Martin, who d. in infancy.

128. John O'Hart (living in 1887), of Ringsend, Dublin : son of said Norah Kilroy ; who (see No. 125 on the "O'Hart" pedigree) m. Eliza Burnet (living in 1887), on the 25th May, 1845, and had: 1. Fanny ; 2. Patrick ; 3. Mary (d. 1880) ; 4. Margaret; 5. Eliza ; 6. Nanny ; 7. John-Anthony (d. in infancy) ; 8. Louisa ; 9. Hannah ; 10. Francis-Joseph, who d. in infancy.

129. Patrick Andrew O'Hart, of 45 Dame Street, Dublin: son of John ; living unm. 1887.

LEAVY.

Arms: Same as those of " O'Farrell."

CUSLIABH, brother of Giolla Iosa who is No. 109 on the "O'Farrell" pedigree, was the ancestor of *MacConsleibhe ;* anglicised *Leavy.*

109. Cushliabh ("cu:" Irish, *a hound ;* "sliabh," *a mountain*), meaning " the warrior of the mountain": son of Braon O'Farrell ; a quo *Mac-Consleibhe.*

110. Cuchaille : his son.

111. Eichtighearna : his son.

112. Cucatha MacConshleibhe: his son ; first assumed this sirname.

113. Maolseaghlainn : his son.

114. Sitric : his son.

115. Giolla Chriosd : his son.

116. Maolseaghlainn (2) : his son.

117. Giolla (or William): his son.

118. Owen MacConsleibhe (or O'Leavy): his son.

LEYDON, or LIDDANE.

Chiefs in Tipperary.

Arms : Ar. three eagles' heads erased sa.

OSGAR, son of Onchu who is No. 75 on the "O'Connor" (Corcomroe) pedigree, had two sons—1. Cuerc, who was ancestor of *Quirk ;* and 2.

Fraoch, who was the ancestor of *O'Liodhain*,* anglicised *Leydon, Laydon*, etc.

75. Osgar : son of Onchu.
76. Fraoch : his son.
77. Carthann : his son.
78. Lonan : his son.
79. Seannagh : his son.
80. Laphan ("lapa": Irish, *the lap*): his son ; a quo *O'Laphain*, anglicised *Laffan*.
81. Brocan (or Breoghan) : his younger son.
82. Felim (or Filé) : his son.

83. Maolruanaidh : his son.
84. Fiangus : his son ; a quo *O'Fianngusa*, anglicised *O'Fennessy*, and *Fennessy*.†
85. Seartach : his son.
86. Saorthuile : his son.
87. Mugna : his son.
88. Liodhan ("liodhan :" Irish, *the Litany*): his son ; a quo *O'Liodhain*.

LYNCH.

Of Ulster.

Arms : Sa. three lynxes pass guard ar. *Crest :* On a ducal coronet, or, a lynx, as in the arms.

CONLA, a brother of Connall, who is No. 92 on the "Guinness" pedigree, was the ancestor of *O'Leathlabhair* (of the Line of Ir), which has been anglicised *Lawlor*,‡ and *Lalor ;* and of *Muintir Loingsigh*, or *O'Loingsigh*, of Ulster, anglicised *Linch, Lynch, Linskey*, and *Lynskey*.

92. Conla : son of Caolbha.
93. Eochaidh : his son ; King of Ulster for 26 years.
94. Baodan : his son.
95. Fiacha : his son.
96. Eochaidh Iarlaith : his son.
97. Leathlabhar : his son.

98. Inrachtach : his son.
99. Tomaltach : his son.
100. Longseach : his son.
101. Leathlabhar : his son ; King of Ulster, for 15 years ; a quo *O'Leathlabhair*.
102. Eiteach : his son.

* *O'Liodhain :* This Irish sirname has been anglicised Leyden, Laydon, Leighton, Leydon, Leyton, Lighton, Litton, Loudon, Lydon, Lyddon, Lytton, etc.

† *Fennessy :* For the derivation of this sirname see the "Fennessy" pedigree, page 88, where, because the family originally belonged to the co. Tipperary, it was our mistake to include the pedigree among the "Heber Genealogies." But in our research we have since found that FIANGUS, who is No. 84 on the "Leydon" pedigree, was the ancestor of the family, which is therefore of *Irian* origin ; and which was located in the territory now known as the barony of Ownybeg in the County Tipperary, of which territory the descendants of Aongus Fionn, son of Fergus Mór, who is No. 64 on the "Line of Ir," page 301, were chiefs.
Firceighid, another son of the said Fergus Mór, was the ancestor of the *Eoghanacht Ara-Cliach*, a district in the County Limerick bordering on Tipperary ; and Finfailig, another son of the said Fergus Mór, was the ancestor of *O'Dugan* and *O'Cosgrave*, chiefs of Fermoy, County Cork.—See the "Dugan" pedigree, p. 208.

‡ *Lawlor :* For the derivation of this sirname, see No. 104 on the "Lawlor" (of Monaghan) pedigree, in the "Heremon Genealogies."

103. Longseach ("longseach :" Irish, *a mariner*): his son: a quo *Muintir Loingsigh.*

104. Aodh : his son; King of Ulster for five years.

105. Doncha : his son.

According to another Genealogy, Nicholas, brother of James le Petito, who is No. 2 on the "Petit" pedigree, was the ancestor of *Lynch*, of the county Galway; but either that genealogy, or the pedigree of *Petit* (or "Le Petit," as the name was first spelled) must be inaccurate: the "Lynch" (which is as follows) exceeding the "Petit" pedigree by thirteen generations, in five hundred years, from the common stock.

1. William le Petito.
2. Nicholas de Linch : his son ; a quo *Linch* and *Lynch.*
3. John : his son.
4. Maurice : his son.
5. Hugh : his son.
6. David : his son.
7. Thomas : his son.
8. James : his son.
9. Thomas (2) : his son.
10. David (2) : his son.
11. Thomas (3) : his son.
12. James (2) : his son.
13. Thomas (4) : his son.
14. John Buidhe : his son.
15. Thomas (5) : his son.
16. Henry : his son.
17. Robuc : his son.
18. Arthur : his son.
19. Stephen : his son.
20. Nicholas (2) : his son.
21. Sir Henry : his son.
22. Sir Robuc Linch : his son.

MacARTAN.

Arms : Vert a lion ramp. or. on a chief ar. a dexter hand couped at the wrist gu. betw. in the dexter a crescent of the last, and in the sinister a mullet sa. *Crest :* A bear ramp. sa. muzzled or.

FOGHARTACH, brother of Aidan, who is No. 97 on the "Guinness" pedigree, was the ancestor of *MacArtain ;* modernized *MacArtan.*

97. Foghartach : son of Mongan.
98. Grontach : his son.
99. Artan ("art :" Irish, *a god, a stone, noble*): his son ; a quo *Mac Artain.*
100. Onchu : his son.
101. Crumna Crioch (" crioch :" Irish, *a country* or *perfection*): his son ; a quo *Cree.*
102. Conor Aich ("aicid :" Irish, *sickness ;* Gr. "ach-os"): his son.
103. Eachach : his son.
104. Searrach : his son.
105. Ranall : his son.
106. Ceneth : his son.
107. Gillcolum : his son.
108. Donall : his son.
109. Donoch : his son.
110. Shane (or John) : his son.
111. Tomhas Mór : his son.
112. Tomhas Oge : his son.
113. Searrach Mór : his son.
114. Giolla Padraic : his son.
115. Donall (2) : his son.
116. Gilgree Fionn : his son.
117. Gillcolum (2) : his son.
118. Eachmilidh : his son.
119. Aodh (or Hugh) : his son.
120. Tirlach : his son.
121. Felim : his son.
122. Eachmilidh (2) : his son.
123. Felim (2) : his son.
124. Patrick MacArtan : his son.

MacCARTAN.

Chiefs of Kinealarty, County Down.

Arms : Vert a lion ramp. or, on a chief ar. a crescent betw. two dexter hands couped at the wrist gu. *Crest :* A lance erect or, headed ar. entwined with a snake descending vert. *Motto :* Buallim se (I strike him).

FEARGAN, a brother of Connall, who is No. 92 on the "Guinness" pedigree, was the ancestor of *MacCartain ;* modernized *Cartan, Carton, MacCartan,* and *Macartan.*

92. Feargan : son of Caolbhadh.

93. Mongan : his son.

94. Fogartach : his son.

95. Cruinneith : his son.

96. Artan :* his son ; a quo *Mac Artain*(anglicised *MacCartan*), Lords of "MacArtan's Country," called, after him, *Kinealarty,* now the name of a barony in the county Down.

97. Cuoincon : his son ; Lord of Kinealarty.

98. Crum na Cruach ("cruach :" Irish, *a stack*) : his son ; a quo *Croke,*† *Crooke,* and *Stack.*‡

99. Concruach : his son.

100. Eochaidh : his son ; first assumed the sirname *MacCartan ;* had a brother named Eocha Oge.

101. Searran : his son.

102. Bugmaille : his son.

103. Ciannait : his son.

104. Gillcolum : his son.

105. Donall : his son.

106. Fionnach (or Donoch) : his son.

107. Shane (or John): his son.

108. Tomhas : ("tomhais :" Irish, *to measure*) : his son ; a quo *Mac Tomhais,* and *MacTamais,* anglicised *Thomas, Thom, Toms, MacThomas, Tomson, Thomson, Thompson, Tomkins,* and *Tomkinson.*

109. Tomhas Oge : his son.

110. Searran (2) : his son.

111. Giollapadraic : his son.

112. Giollapadraic Oge : his son ; a quo *Killpatrick ;* had a brother named Donal.

113. Giolgaginn : son of Giollapadraic.

114. Giollacolum ("colum :" Irish, *a dove*) : his son ; a quo *O'Gilcoluim,* anglicised *Gilcolm, Colum,* and *Columb.*

115. Eachmilidh : his son.

116. Aodh (or Hugh) : his son.

117. Torlogh : his son.

118. Felim (or Phelim) : his son.

119. Eachmilidh (2) : his son.

120. Felim (2) : his son ; had two brothers—1. Donall, and 2. Anthony; died in 1631.

121. Patrick MacCartan, of Bally-dromroe : son of Felim.

122. John : his son ; left Ireland in the service of King James the Second ; living in 1691.

123. Anthony : his son ; followed King James the Second, and became a Captain in the Irish Brigade in the French Service.

124. Antonie Joseph : his son ; a physician.

---

* *Artan* See the derivation of this name in the foregoing ("MacArtan") pedigree.

† *Croke :* While the *Croke* here mentioned is of Irish origin, there is among the *Huguenot* families given *infra,* a sirname which has been modernized "Croke."—See *Le Blount.*

‡ *Stack :* Some genealogists consider that this family is of Danish extraction.

125. Andronicus: his son; was Medical Doctor, and had a brother who was also an M.D.

126. Felix MacCartan, of Lille, in Flanders: his son.

MacGARRY.

Arms : Ar. a lion ramp. betw. four trefoils slipped vert, in chief a lizard pass. of the last.   *Crest :* A fox's head couped gu. holding in the mouth a snake ppr.   *Motto :* **Fear gharbh ar mait.**

ANBEITH, brother of Brocan, who is No. 103 on the "Shanley" pedigree, was the ancestor of *MacSeairaigh* ; anglicised *MacGarry, Magarry, Coltsman,* and *Seery.*

103. Anbeith : son of Eolus.

104. Muireadach : his son.

105. Eachmarc : his son.

106. Searrach ("seairach :" Irish, *a colt*): his son ; a quo *MacSeairaigh.*

107. Fionn : his son.

108. Luachcas ("luach ;" Irish, *wages ;* "cas," *money*): his son.

109. Maothan ("maoth :" Irish, *tender*): his son ; a quo *O'Maoithain,* anglicised *O'Meehan* and *Meehan.*

110. Matha : his son.

111. Gormgall : his son.

112. Eachmarc (2) : his son.

113. Maccraith : his son.

114. Simeon : his son.

115. Donall : his son.

116. Amhailgadh [awly]: his son.

117. Awly Oge : his son.

118. Gillchriosd : his son.

119. Maccraith (2) : his son.

120. Thomas Mór : his son.

121. Thomas Oge : his son.

122. Rory Breac ("breac :" Irish, *speckled ;* Chald. "brak-ka ;" Arab. "a-brek"): his son ; had a brother named Jeoffrey.

123. Manus Dubh : son of Rory Breac.

124. Conor : his son.

125. Rory (2) : his son.

126. Cairbre : his son.

127. Gillgrooma MacGarry : his son ; had a brother named Rory.

MacGUINNESS.

See " Guinness," page 311.

ART RUADH MacGUINNESS, who is No. 124 on the "Guinness" pedigree, and who was the first "Viscount Iveagh," was the first of the family that anglicised the name *Magennis.*

MADIGAN.

Arms : Same as those of "Manning."

FELIM, the youngest brother of Iomchadh, who is No. 85 on the "Manning" pedigree, was the ancestor of *O'Madadhgain ;* anglicised *O'Madigan,* and *Madigan.*

85. Felim : son of Sodan.
86. Fionchu : his son.
87. Ros : his son.
88. Luchta : his son.
89. Amergin : his son.
90. Ceneidh : his son.
91. Maoldubh : his son.
92. Fionngal : his son.
93. Sealbhach ("sealbh :" Irish, *possession*): his son ; a quo *Selby.*
94. Dunechar : his son.
95. Dobhalen : his son.
96. Gussan : his son.
97. Labhras ("labhras :" Irish, *a laurel tree ;* Lat. "laurus") : his son.

98. Sarcall : his son.
99. Scoileach (*scoileach :* Irish, "one who keeps a school ;" Lat. *schola ;* Greek, *schole ;* Fr. *e-cole*): his son ; a quo *O'Scoilaigh,* anglicised *Scally, Skelly, Scully,* and *Scallan.*
100. Madadhgan ("madadh :" Irish, *a dog*), meaning "a little warrior :" his son ; a quo *O'Madadhgain.*
101. Gillcira : his son.
102. Dunsliabh : his son.
103. Scoileach (2) O'Madadghgain : his son.

MANNING.

Ireland.

Arms: Ar. a chev. betw. three quarterfoils gu.

FIACHA ARAIDHE, the 37th King of Ulster, of the Irian race, who is No. 83 on the "Guinness" pedigree, had two sons—1. Cas, and 2. Sodhan ; this Sodhan was the ancestor of *O'Maoinein* [monneen] ; anglicised *Mannin, Manning, Mannion,* and *Richey.*

83. Fiacha Araidhe.
84. Sodhan : his son.
85. Iomchadh : his son.
86. Degill : his son.
87. Cas : his son.
88. Conall : his son.
89. Flann Abrad : his son.
90. Maoinin ("maoin :" Irish, *riches, wealth*), meaning "the wealthy little man :" his son ; a quo *O'Maoinein.*

91. Dubhagan ;* his son.
92. Fergus : his son.
93. Fingin : his son.
94. Tuathal : his son.
95. Manus : his son
96. Aodh (or Hugh): his son.
97. Donall : his son.
98. Maothan : his son.
99. Moroch : his son.
100. Maothan (2): his son.
101. Donall (2) : his son.

* *Dubhagan* : Some genealogists derive from this Dubhagan, the *O'Dubhagain* family, which has been anglicised *Dugan.*

102. Donoch: his son.
103. Dermod : his son.
104. Gilliosa: his son.
105. Donoch (2): his son.
106. Hugh (2): his son.
107. Melachlin : his son.
108. David: his son.
109. Donall (3): his son.

110. Melachlin (2): his son.
111. Donall (4): his son.
112. William: his son.
113. Donall (5): his son.
114. Melachlin (3): his son.
115. John: his son.
116. John Oge O'Manning: his son.

MOLEDY.

Arms : Same as the Arms of " O'Farrell" (No. 1).

MAOLANEIDIDH, a younger brother of Fergal, who is No. 105 on the " O'Farrell" pedigree, was the ancestor of *O'Maolaneididh;* anglicised *Melody, Melady, Moledy,* and *Moody.*

105. Maolaneididh (" eideadh :" Irish, *armour*): son of Congal; a quo *O'Maolaneididh.*
106. Donall: his son.
107. Dermod: his son.
108. Fingin : his son.
109. Donall (2): his son.
110. Eichtighearna : his son.
111. William (or Giolla): his son.
112. Eoghan (or Owen): his son.
113. Dermod (2): his son.
114. Eanna: his son.
115. Donall (3): his son.
116. Fingin (2): his son.
117. Eichtighearna (2): his son.
118. Owen (2): his son.

119. Robert : his son.
120. Philip : his son.
121. Cormac : his son.
122. Moroch : his son.
123. John : his son.
124. Robert (2): his son.
125. Cormac (2): his son.
126. Sir Patrick Moledy: his son; died without issue, and left his property to his younger brother's four children, namely—one daughter, and three sons: 1. Sir Anthony Moledy, of Roberstown, county Kildare ; 2. Redmond, of Rathwire ; and 3. Major Hugh Moledy.

MOORE. (No. 1.)

or

O'MOORE.

Lords of Leix.

Arms: Vert a lion ramp. or, in chief three mullets of the last. *Crest:* A dexter hand lying fessways, couped at the wrist, holding a sword in pale, pierced through three gory heads all ppr. *Motto :* Conlan-a-bu.

LIOSEACH LANNMOR, brother of Irial Glunmhar, who is No. 69 on the " Guinness" pedigree, was the ancestor of *O'Maoilmordha;* anglicised *O'Mulmore, O'Morra, O'Moore, Moore, Moher,* and *Mordie.*

69. Lioseach Lannmór: son of Conall Cearnach.

70. Lugha-Laoghseach: his son.

71. Lugha-Longach : his son.

72. Baccan : his son ; a quo *Rath-Baccain*.

73. Earc : his son.

74. Guaire : his son.

75. Eoghan (or Owen) : his son.

76. Lugna : his son.

77. Cuirc : his son.

78. Cormac : his son.

79. Carthann : his son.

80. Seirbealagh : his son.

81. Bearrach : his son.

82. Nadsier : his son.

83. Aongus : his son.

84. Aongus (2) : his son.

85. Beannaigh : his son.

86. Bearnach : his son.

87. Maolaighin : his son.

88. Meisgil : his son.

89. Eochagan : his son.

90. Cathal (or Charles) : his son.

91. Cionaodh : his son.

92. Gaothin Mordha : his son ; the first King of Lease (or Leix), now the "Queen's County."

93. Cinnedeach : his son.

94. Cearnach : his son.

95. Maolmordha ("mordha :" Irish, *proud*): his son; a quo *O'Maoilmordha*.

96. Cenneth : his son.

97. Cearnach (2): his son.

98. Cenneth (3): his son.

99. Faolan : his son.

100. Amergin: his son; who is considered the ancestor of *Bergin*.

101. Lioseach : his son.

102. Donall : his son.

103. Conor Cucoigcriche : his son.

104. Lioseach (2) : his son.

105. Donall (or Daniel) O'Moore : his son; King of Leix or Lease; first assumed this surname.

106. Daniel Oge : his son.

107. Lioseach (3) : his son; the last "King of Lease;" built the Monastery of Lease (called *De-Lege-Dei*), A.D. 1183.

108. Niall (or Neal): his son.

109. Lioseach (4): his son; had a brother named Daniel.

110. David : son of Lioseach.

111. Anthony : his son.

112. Melaghlin : his son; died in 1481.

113. Connall : his son; d. in 1518.

114. Roger Caoch : his son; was slain by his brother Philip; had a brother named Cedagh, who died without issue; and a younger brother named John, who was the ancestor of *Mulchay*.

115. Charles O'Moore,* of Ballinea (now Ballyna), Enfield : son of Roger Caoch; d. 1601; had an elder brother named Cedagh, who was Page to Queen Elizabeth, who granted him Ballinea.

116. Col. Roger,† son of Charles ;

---

* *Charles O'Moore :* This Charles had a younger brother named Rory Oge, who, A.D. 1587, was slain by the English.

† *Roger :* This Colonel Roger O'Moore was the "Rory O'Moore" of popular tradition in Ireland ; to whose courage and resources was, in a great measure, due the formidable Irish Insurrection of A.D. 1641. That Insurrection (see Section 12 of Paper : "New Divisions of Ireland, and the New Settlers," in the Appendix) was ostensibly the cause of the Cromwellian settlement of Ireland ; and it is remarkable that this Roger O'Moore was a descendant of one of the Chieftains of Leix, who, a century before, had been massacred by English troops at Mullaghmast. Of him Sir Charles Gavan Duffy, in his *Ballad Poetry of Ireland*, writes : "Then a private gentleman, with no resources beyond his intellect and his courage, this Rory, when Ireland was weakened by defeat and confiscation, and guarded with a jealous care constantly increasing in strictness and severity, conceived the vast design of rescuing the country from England, and even accomplished it; for, in three years, England did not retain a city in Ireland but Dublin and Drogheda ; and for eight years the land was possessed

d. 1646; had a brother named Anthony.*

117. Col. Charles: his son; Governor of Athlone; killed in the Battle of Aughrim, 12th July, 1691; his sister Anne was wife of Patrick Sarsfield of Lucan, and mother of Patrick, earl of Lucan.

118. Lewis: his son; d. 1738.

119. James O'Moore; his son;

whose daughter and sole heir, Letitia. married Richard O'Farrell, of Ballinree, county Longford.

120. Ambrose O'Farrell, of Ballyna: their son.

121. Richard Moore O'Farrell: his son; b. in 1797, d. 1880.

122. Ambrose More O'Ferrall, of Ballyna House, Enfield, co. Kildare; his son; living in 1887.

MOORE. (No. 2.)

Of Rahinduffe, Queen's County.

Arms : Same as those of " Moore " No. 1.

MURTAGH OGE MOORE, of Rahinduffe, Queen's County, gent., had :

2. John (second son), who died Nov., 1636, and was buried in St.

and the supreme authority exercised by the Confederation created by O'Moore. History contains no stricter instance of the influence of an individual mind." Before the Insurrection broke out, the people, driven to desperation by the cruelties inflicted on them by the Authorities in Ireland, had learned to know Roger O'Moore, and to expect in *him* their deliverer ; and it became a popular proverb and the burthen of national songs, that the hope of Ireland's regeneration, at that time, was in "God, the Virgin, and Rory O'Moore."

The following are a few stanzas of an Ulster ballad of that period, preserved in Duffy's "Ballad Poetry of Ireland" :

> On the green hills of Ulster the white cross waves high,
> And the beacon of war throws its flames to the sky ;
> Now the taunt and the threat let the coward endure,
> Our hope is in God and in Rory O'Moore !
>
> Do you ask why the beacon and banner of war
> On the mountains of Ulster are seen from afar ?
> 'Tis the signal our rights to regain and secure,
> Through God and our Lady and Rory O'Moore!
>
> *   *   *   *   *
>
> Oh ! lives there a traitor who'd shrink from the strife—
> Who to add to the length of a forfeited life,
> His country, his kindred, his faith would abjure ;
> No! we'll strike for our God and for Rory O'Moore.

* Anthony O'Moore joined O'Neill, earl of Tyrone ; and in a great battle defeated the English army, A.D. 1598. In the year 1600, he and Captain Tyrrell went into Munster and joined with MacCarthy there ; where, in a great engagement, the English army is defeated, and their general, the earl of Ormonde, taken prisoner. Soon after (in 1601), the Munster and Leinster confederates submit, except this O'Moore and O'Conor Faley, who are left in the lurch and slain ; and their estates and territories of Lease and Offaly (or O'Phaley) seized, confiscated, and disposed to English planters, and called by the names of the King's and Queen's Counties.—*Four Masters.*

Patrick's of Stradbally. He m. Margaret, dau. Connor Hickey, of Bulton, in the co. Kildare, gent., and had:

3. John (his eldest son), who m. Susan, dau. of James Hovendon, of the Queen's County, gent. Had a younger brother Pierce, who m. Mary, dau. of Francis Edgeworth, Clerk of ye Hanaper; and he had

five sisters :—1. Margaret, who m. Richard Jacob, co. Kildare, gent.; 2. Honora, who m. Kedagh Moor, county Tipperary, gent.; 3. Kath., who m. John Dempsey, gent.; 4. Grany, who m. Murtogh Dempsey, gent.; 5. Dorothy-Owna, who m. Oliver Grace, of Kilmanham, Queen's County, gent.

MORAN.*

Arms : Az. on a mount ppr. two lions combatant or. supporting a flag staff all ppr., therefrom a flag ar. *Crest* : Out of a mural crown a demi Saracen, head in profile all ppr. *Motto* : Fides non timet.

MOCHAN, the third son of Finghin who is No. 97 on the "Line of Ir," p. 303, was the ancestor of *O'Morain ;* anglicised *Moran,* and sometimes *Morrin.*

97. Finghin: son of Neidhe.
98. Mochan: his son.
99. Moran ("moran:" Irish, *a multitude*): his son; a quo *O'Morain.*
100. Fiachra: his son.
101. Iomchadh: his son.
102. Ferach: his son.
103. Tomhas: his son.
104. Giollaiosa (latinized Gelasius and Gillacius): his son.
105. Mulroona: his son.
106. Padraic: his son.
107. Muireadach: his son.
108. Melachlin: his son.
109. Dermod: his son.

110. Giolla (or William): his son.
111. Teige: his son.
112. Cathal: his son.
113. Rory: his son.
114. Muiredach (2): his son.
115. Lochlann: his son.
116. Muiredach (3): his son.
117. Owen: his son.
118. Donall: his son.
119. Rory (2): his son.
120. Rory Oge: his son.
121. Conor: his son; had a brother named William.
122. Tirlach O'Moran: son of Conor.

* *Moran :* Of this family was Mrs. Anne Moran, who was the mother of the late Doctor Christopher Asken, who was born in 1804, at Pimlico, in the "Liberties" of Dublin, where his father owned a cloth manufactory. He died a childless widower, in Nov. 1867, and was interred in Glasnevin Cemetery.

MULCAHY. (No. 1.)

Arms : See those of " Moore " (No. 1.) family.

JOHN, a younger brother of Roger Caoch who is No. 114 on the " Moore" (No. 1) pedigree, was the ancestor of *Mulcahy*, or (as it has also been anglicised and frequently spelled) *Mulchay.**

114. John O'Moore : son of Connall. By some this John was surnamed *Maollocha* (" loch," gen. " locha :" Irish, *a lake, the sea ;* Lat. " lac-us ;" Wels. " lhych"), meaning " The Hardy Champion," and a quo *O'Maollocha :* and by others he was surnamed *Maolcatha* (" cath ;" gen. " catha :" Irish, *battle ;* Lat. " caterva ;" Wels. "kad ;" Heb. " chath," *terror ;* Chald. " cath," *a batallion*), meaning " The Champion of the Battle," and a quo *O'Maolcatha.*

115. Cathal : his son.

116. Connall : his son.

117. Roger : his son.

118. Thomas, of Whitechurch, county Waterford : his son ; living in 1657 ; had a brother the Rev. Nicholas Mulcahy.†

119. John, of Whitechurch : his son.

120. Thomas, of Whitechurch : his son.

121. John, of Ballymakee ; his son.

122. Edmund Mun : his son ; who in 1780 married Barbara, daughter of Southwell Moore, of Ashgrove, and of his wife Elizabeth Fitzgerald, daughter of the Knight of Glyn. This Edmund had two brothers— 1. John,‡ 2. Thomas.

123. Edmund Moore Mulcahy, of Ballymakee, a J.P. for the counties of Waterford and Tipperary : his

---

* *Mulchay :* From a similarity in the pronunciation of the names, some were of opinion that *Maolcaich*, who is mentioned in the Stowe Missal, might have been the ancestor of this family. The original MS. of that Missal was written in an ancient Lombardic character which may well be deemed older than the sixth century. (The Missal is supposed to be that of St. Ruadhan, the founder of the Monastery of Lorha, in North Tipperary, who died A.D. 584.) The learned Dr. O'Connor says that portions of the MS. are written in a second and much later hand ; and, at page 71, at the end of the Canon of the Mass, the name of the second scribe is given : " *Maolcaich scripsit.*" The Rev. Dr. Todd says that the latter writing, by Maolcaich, must be referred to the eighth century ; which furnishes a strong additional evidence of the high antiquity of the original.—See the "Ecclesiastical Record," for September, 1870.

† *Rev. Nicholas Mulcahy :* This clergyman was parish priest of Ardfinnan in the co. Tipperary, at the time of the Cromwellian invasion of Ireland ; and, during the siege of Clonmel, was seized upon by a reconnoitering party of Cromwell's cavalry. Of him, Bishop Moran (in his *Historical Sketch of the Persecutions suffered by the Catholics of Ireland under the Rule of Cromwell and the Puritans.* Dublin : James Duffy, 1862), says : "Immediately on his arrest, he was bound in Irons, conducted to the camp of the besiegers and offered his pardon, should he only consent to use his influence with the inhabitants of Clonmel, and induce them to deliver up the town. These terms he rejected with scorn. He was consequently led out in sight of the besieged walls, and there beheaded whilst he knelt in prayer for his faithful people and asked forgiveness for his enemies."

‡ *John :* This John lived at Ballymakee, co. Waterford, and married Miss Quin, Loloher Castle ; no issue. His brother Thomas lived at Glasha, and married Miss Roberts : their issue were three sons—1. Frank, 2. William, 3. John ; and one daughter, Anne—all deceased, and now (1878) represented by John Roberts Mulcahy, J.P. for the county Tipperary.

son ; married Mary Cecilia Russell. This Edmund had two brothers and one sister : the brothers were—1. John Moore Mulcahy, J.P., who married Maria Bradshaw ; 2. Southwell Moore Mulcahy, who married Barbara Moore ; and the sister's name was Elizabeth, who married Edmund Power, J.P., Clashman.

The issue of this Edmund M. Mulcahy are, as follows :

124. Major Edmund Moore Mulcahy, J.P. for Waterford and Tipperary (married to Susan Purcell O'Gorman) ; Lieut.-Colonel John Russell Moore Mulcahy (married to Frances Mary Dwyre), and Cecilia Moore Mulcahy : all living in 1878.

MULCAHY. (No. 2.)

Of Ardpaddeen.

IT is believed that Thomas Mantach, who is No. 119 on this genealogy, was a brother of John, of Whitechurch, county Waterford, who is No. 119 on the foregoing "Mulcahy" (No. 1.) pedigree. Commencing with that Thomas, the following is the genealogy of *Mulcahy*, of Ardpaddeen, county Waterford :—

119. Thomas Mantach,* who fought at the Battle of the Boyne, A.D. 1690, on the side of King James the Second : son of Thomas.

120. Edmund : his son ; had a brother named John, who was the ancestor of the Mulcahys, of Killkeany, county Waterford.

121. Thomas Ban [bawn] : his son ; or "Thomas the Fair."

122. Edmund Ban : his son. The issue of this Edmund were twenty children—1. Edmund, who was born in 1773, and died 1836 ; 2. Mrs. M. Mulcahy, born in 1784, and living 1877 ; 3. Mrs. Butler, born in 1801, died 1872 ; 4. Thomas, born 1803, and living 1877 ; 5. Mrs. Catherine Norris, born 1805, living 1877 ; 6. David, born 1807, now dead; 7.

Michael, born 1809, died 1853 ; 8. Mrs. Bridget Shanahan, born 1812, died 1868 ; 9. Patrick, born 1814, died 1841 ; 10. John, born 1816, died 1868 (whose eldest son Edmund lived in Ardpaddeen, in 1877) ; 11. James, born 1818, died 1828 ; 12. Edmond, born 1821, died 1866 ; 13. Joseph, born 1823, living in 1877 ; 14. Richard, born 1825, died 1846 ; 15. David (2), who died young ; 16. Rev. David Power Mulcahy, P.P., Swords, co. Dublin, born in 1830, and living in 1881. There were four more children who died in their infancy.

123. John : son of Edmund Bann.

124. Edmund Mulcahy, of Ardpaddeen : his son ; living in 1877.

* *Mantach :* This Thomas Mulcahy owned the following townlands in the parish of Kilbrien, county Waterford : namely—Scart, Baracree, and Kilbrien ; and he afterwards got the townland of Killkeany, for his son John.

MULCAHY. (No. 3.)

Of Killkeany.

JOHN, brother of Edmund, who is No. 120 on the foregoing ("Mulcahy" of Ardpaddeen) pedigree, was the ancestor of *Mulcahy*, of Killkeany, co. Waterford.

120. John, of Killkeany, county Waterford; son of Thomas Mantach.

121. James : his son. This James had three brothers and five sisters : the brothers were—1. Patrick, 2. David, 3. John—the three of whom left no issue. The five sisters were —1. Catherine, who was married to Thomas Halloran, of Scart ; 2. Margaret, married to Denis Hacket, of Clashgannee ; 3. Johanna, married to Patrick Sheehan, of Orchardstown, county Tipperary, near Clonmel ; 4. Mary, married to Bartholomew Mulcahy, of Marlfield ; and 5. Ellen, married to James Butler, of Killnamack.

122. John Mulcahy of Killkeany : son of said James; married Margaret Power of Knockane-Brendain ; both living A.D. 1880. The surviving children of this marriage were (in 1881) the following :—1. Rev. David Bernard Mulcahy, Ballynafeigh, Belfast ; 2. John of Glashea (whose son David entered Maynooth College as an ecclesiastical student in 1880) ; 3. Nanno (deceased), m. to James Tobin, Curraghnagree ; 4. Johanna, m. to James Beresford, of Deelish, Dungarvan ; 5. James, 6. Edmond of Killkeany ; 7. Bridget, married to Michael O'Connor, Cascade Cottage, Clonmel ; 8. Rev. Patrick Mulcahy, St. Mary's, Bradford, England ; and 9. Rev. Michael Ambrose Mulcahy, St. Mary's, Bradford.

123. Edmond of Killkeany : the fourth son of the said John Mulcahy ;* m. Kate-Clare Beresford ; living in 1880, having issue.

124. John-Patrick Mulcahy : son of said Edmond ; b. in 1880.

* *Mulcahy* : The ancient fort or rath in the parish of Castleconor, co. of Sligo, known as *Rath Maoilcatha*, has suggested the idea that this family may have derived their name from the Maolcatha after whom that rath is called ; and therefore that they are descended from the royal stock from which branched the O'Connors, Kings of Connaught. That conjecture is based on the following extract from MacFirbis's Book of Genealogies, quoted by Professor O'Curry, at page 223 of his "Manuscript Materials of Ancient Irish History :" "Such is the stability of the old buildings, that there are immense royal raths (or palaces) and forts (*lios*) throughout Erinn, in which there are numerous hewn and polished stones and cellars and apartments, under ground, within their walls ; such as are in *Rath Maoilcatha*, in Castle-Conor, and in Bally O'Dowda, in Tireragh (co. Sligo), on the banks of the Moy. There are nine smooth stone cellars under the walls of this rath ; and I have been inside it, and I think it is one of the oldest raths in Erinn ; its walls are of the height of a good cow-keep still."

MULVEY.*

Arms : Same as those of " Reynolds."

DUORCAN, brother of Iomhar, who is No. 107 on the "Reynolds" pedigree, was the ancestor of *O'Mulmhiaigh* [mulvee]; anglicised *Mulvey* and *Mulvy*.

107. Duorcan : son of Maolruanaidh.

108. Dubhdara: his son.

109. Muredach : his son.

110. Mulmhiach ("mul :" Irish, *a conical heap*, and "miach," *a bag* or *measure*): his son; a quo *O'Mulmhiaigh*.

111. Gillchriosd : his son.

112. Melachlin : his son.

113. Mulmhiach (2): his son.

114. Fergall : his son.

115. Teige O'Mulvy : his son ; first assumed this sirname.

116. Anthony Buidhe Mór : his son.

117. Donall : his son ; had six brothers.

118. Anthony Buidhe (2) : his son.

119. Anthony (3) Oge: his son.

120. Tirlach : his son.

121. Maolmuire Tirlagh Oge O'Mulvy : his son.

O'CONNOR. (No. 1.)

Lords of Kerry.

Arms : Vert a lion ramp. double queued and crowned or.   *Crest* : A dexter arm embowed in mail garnished or, the hand grasping a sword erect ppr. pommel and hilt gold.   *Motto :* Nec timeo, nec sperno.

CIAR, a younger brother of Conmac, who is 65 on the " Line of Ir," p. 302, was the ancestor of *O'Ciariaidhe*, of whom *O'Connor* "Kerry" was the leading family.

65. Ciar : son of Fergus Mór, lived in the second century before Christ.

66. Mogha Taoi : his son.

67. Astaman : his son.

68. Ulacht : his son.

69. Lamhneach : his son.

70. Eunna : his son.

71. Dealbhna : his son.

72. Fionn Bhan : his son.

73. Eochaman : his son.

74. Aithrea : his son.

75. Eochoman (2) his son.

76. Orbsenmar : his son.

77. Mogha-Art : his son.

78. Saul : his son.

79. Messincon : his son.

80. Uilin : his son.

81. Iomghon : his son.

82. Hebric : his son.

83. Iomcha : his son.

* *Mulvey* : A member of this family was Doctor Farrell Mulvey, whose name is mentioned in the Second Charter granted to the College of Surgeons in Ireland, in 1828.

84. Forba : his son.

85. Rethach : his son.

86. Senach : his son.

87. Durrthacht : his son.

88. Hugh Logha : his son.

89. Multuile (" tuile :" Irish, *a flood*) : his son ; a quo *O'Maoiltuile*, anglicised *Multully, Tully,* and *Flood*.

90. Bachtbran : his son.

91. Cobthach : his son.

92. Colman : his son.

93. Flaith Fearna : his son.

94. Melachlin : his son.

95. Fionn : his son.

96. Conor : his son.

97. Dermod : his son.

98. Cu-Luachra : his son.

99. Roger : his son.

100. Teige : his son.

101. Hugh : his son.

102. Charles : his son.

103. Conchobhar (" couchobhar" : Irish, *the helping warrior*) : his son ; a quo *O'Connor (Kerry)*.

104. Maolbreath : his son.

105. Corc O'Connor : son of Maolbreath ; m. dau. of O'Keeffe, of Duhallow ; d. 1019.

106. Mahoon : his son ; chief of Kerry Luachra ; m. Joanna, dau. of Muldoon O'Moriarty of Lough Lein.

107. Dermod (2) na Sluaghach : his son ; m. Mora, dau. of Rory O'Donoghue Mór.

108. Mahoon (2) : his son ; m. Mora, dau. of Melaghlin O'Mahony, lord of Rathculler.

109 Dermod (3) : his son.

110 Connor (3) : his son.

111. Dermod (4) : his son ; m. Joanna, the dau. of the lord of Kerry.

112. Connor (4) : his son ; m. Una, dau. of MacMahon of Corcakine. This Connor was lord of Kerry Luachra, and was slain in his 58th year by the Walshes of Kerry ; had two sons—1. Dermod ; 2. Connor.

113. Connor (5) : his son ; m. Margaret, dau. of John Fitzgerald, of Callan, and was treacherously slain in 1396. This Connor's brother, Dermod, m. a dau. of O'Keeffe of Duhallow, and in 1405, his eyes were put out by Maurice Fitzgerald.

114. Connor (6), prince of Iraght and Kerry Luachra : son of Connor ; married Kathleen, dau. of John de Brunell of Kerry ; and was slain by his kinsman, Mahon O'Connor, in 1445, whilst on his way in a boat to Iniscatha (or Scattery Island), on the Shannon.

115. John : son of Connor ; was lord of Kerry Luachra and Iraghticonnor ; m. in 1451 Margaret dau. of David Nagle of Monahinny ; he founded in 1470 Lislaghtan abbey, where he was buried in 1485.

116. Connor (7) of Carrigafoyle : his son ; m. Joanna, dau. of Thomas Fitzgerald, Knight of the Valley, by whom he had issue :—1. Connor Fionn ; 2. Charles, d. s. p. ; 3. Cahir, d. s. p. : 4. Dermod, d. s. p. ; 5. Donal Maol, who m. Ellis, dau. of Thomas Fitzgerald of Billamullen, by whom he had a son, Connor.

117. Connor (8) Fionn : his son ; m. twice : first, Margaret, dau. of the lord of Kerry, by whom he had a son, Brian-*na-lana*, (or Brian of the blades), who d. in 1566 ; and, second, Slaine, dau. of O'Brien of Kilaloe, by whom he had a son, Connor. This Connor Fionn was slain in the battle of Lixnaw, in 1568.

118. Connor (9) Baccach : his son ; m. Honoria, dau. of Dermod, 2nd Earl of Thomond, by whom he had —1. John ; 2. Donal Maol ; and 3. Donoghy, who was slain in 1599, by the sons of Manus Oge McSheehy. This Connor died in 1573.

119. John-na-Cathach (or John of the Battles) O'Connor " Kerry :" his son ; m. Julia, dau. of O'Sullivan

Mór, by whom he had five children : 1. Connor who died young ; 2. Honoria, m. John Fitzgerald, Knight of Glynn ; 3. Una, m. Oliver Dela-hoyle ; 4. Julia, m. Ulick Roche ; and 5. Mary, who m. her kinsman, Connor *Cam*, and had a son John O'Connor Kerry. This John-na-Cathach, in 1600, surrendered his estates and castle of Carrigafoyle into the hands of the Earl of Thomond, President of Munster, and obtained a grant thereof from Queen Elizabeth. This chief died without male issue in 1640, where-upon the chieftaincy reverted to the descendant of Donal Maol second son of Connor Baccach, No. 118 above mentioned.

120. Connor (10): son of Donal Maol, son of Connor Baccach O'Connor "Kerry;" m. a dau. of John Fitzmaurice.

121. Connor (11) Cam : his son ; m. twice : first, Mary (d. s. p.), dau. of John-na-Cathach ; and, second,

a dau. of Murrogh O'Connor of Ballylyne, and left issue :—1. John ; 2. Donogh, who died in Flanders ; 3. Cahir ; 4. Cathal Roe, who m. Eliza, dau. of the lord of Kerry, and left issue, Mary, who d. s. p. ; and 5. Julia, who m. Charles O'Connor of Dublin.

122. John O'Connor (2) "Kerry": son of Connor Cam ; m. twice : first, Amelia, dau. of John Fitz-gerald, Knight of the Valley ; and, second, Joanna, dau. of Tadhg Mac-Carthy, of Aglish, co. Cork. In 1652, this John with Teige O'Con-nor, lord of Tarbert, suffered mar-tyrdom for their faith ; they were by stratagem seized by Cromwell's followers, brought to Tralee, and there half hanged, and next be-headed on Sheep Hill, near Kil-larney.

We are at present unable to bring down this illustrious pedigree to recent times.

According to MacFirbis, Dermod was an elder brother of Connor, No. 113, and his descendants were "the real O'Connors,"

113. Dermod* (5): son of Connor (4) O'Connor "Kerry."
114. Dermod (6) : his son.
115. Connor : his son.

116. Connor : his son.
117. John : his son.
118. Connor : his son.
119. John : his son ; living in 1666.

Of this branch was the learned Doctor Bernard O'Connor, author of a History of Poland, etc. ; and Physician to John Sobieski, King of that country. He studied in Paris, and practised in London, where he died in 1698.—See his obituary in the next genealogy, *infra*, (The "O'Connor" of Carrig-a-Foyle pedigree.)

O CONNOR. (No. 2.)

Of Carrig-a-Foyle, Dingle, West Kerry.

Arms : Vert a lion ramp. double queued and crowned or. *Crest :* A gauntleted arm, with a hand holding a dart. *Motto :* Nec timeo, nec sperno.

IN the preceding (No. 1.) genealogy we give the "O'Connor" (Kerry) pedigree from its ancestor down to No. 122 John O'Connor "Kerry" (A.D. 1652), with whom the pedigree ceases ; for at that period took place

* *Dermod :* From this Dermod is descended the family of "O'Connor (No. 2), of Carrig-a Foyle."

the Cromwellian Confiscations, when Cromwell's soldiers surprised and surrounded the O'Connor Kerry's Castle, and in the most brutal manner murdered The O'Connor himself (see No. 122 on the preceeding genealogy.) Half wild with fear and anguish, the wife of The O'Connor escaped to Bandon, then a great Protestant stronghold, taking with her their infant son ; for, she was so utterly unnerved and horrorstricken by the dreadful crimes of the Cromwellian soldiers, that she thought the only chance of safety for herself and her child from the violence of the then dominant party, was to train up the boy as a Protestant, and call him *Conner*, instead of *O'Connor*. From that boy the *Conner* family in Munster is descended.

At that period no Catholic was allowed to live in Bandon. It was on that account that Dean Swift, who deeply deplored such want of Christian charity and forbearance, wrote upon the gate of the town of Bandon the following witty lines :

> " Jew, Turk, or Atheist
> May enter here,
> But not a Papist."

The Dean's Irish servant added to his master's the equally witty lines :

> " Whoever wrote this did write it well ;
> The same is written on the gates of hell."

Among the " Forfeiting Proprietors" of the " O'Connor" Kerry family, consequent on the Irish War of 1641-1652, appear the following names : In the barony of *Iraghticonnor*—Bryan (or Bernard) O'Connor, Donnogh O'Connor, Teig O'Connor, James Connor, Morogh Connor, Thomas Connor James Connor (2) ; and in the barony of *Trughanacmy*—Bryan Connor, Dermod O'Connor, Turlagh Connor, Thomas O'Connor (" A Protestant, since August, 1654"), Redmond O'Connor, Thomas Connor (son of Turlagh), and Thomas O'Connor (son of Tirlagh).

In Vol. I., p. 514, of *The Roll of the Royal College of Physicians, of London* (Three Volumes, London : 1878 ; Edited by William Munk, M.D., F.S.A.), we read :

" Bernard O'Connor, M.D., was descended from an ancient Irish family, and was born in the county of Kerry about the year 1666. He studied at the Universities of Montpelier and Paris, but took the degree of Doctor in Medicine at Rheims, 18th Sept., 1691. In Paris he met with the two sons of the High Chancellor of Poland, then on the point of returning to their own country. They were entrusted to O'Connor's care, and he travelled with them, first into Italy. At Venice he was called to attend William Legge, Earl of Dartmouth, then seriously ill with fever, and, having recovered his patient, accompanied him to Padua. Thence he passed through Bavaria and Austria, down the Danube to Vienna, and, after some stay at the Court of the Emperor Leopold, passed through Moravia and Silicia to Cracow, and thence to Warsaw. He was well received by King John Sobieski, and, in the beginning of 1694, being then only twenty-eight years of age, was appointed physician to his Majesty. His reputation at the Polish Court was great, and it was deservedly raised by his accurate diagnosis in the case of the King's sister, the Duchess of Bedzeoil. This lady was treated by her physician for ague, but O'Connor insisted that she had an abscess of the liver, and that her case was desperate. His prediction made a great noise among the Court, more especially when it was justified by the event ; for, she died within a month, and upon examination of the body, his opinion of the malady was fully verified.

" O'Connor did not remain long at Warsaw ; but, having obtained the appointment of physician to Teresa Cunigunda, who had been espoused to the Elector of Bavaria by proxy in 1694, and was about to leave for Brussels, he accompanied the Princess on her journey. Arrived at that place, he took leave of the Princess, and, having passed through Holland, reached England in February, 1695. He stayed but a short time in London, and then went to Oxford, where he delivered a few lectures on Anatomy and Physiology. In his travels he had conversed with Malpighi, Bellini, Redi and other celebrated physicians ; and of their communications he made a proper use. In these lectures he explained the new discoveries in Anatomy, Chemistry, and Physic, in so clear a manner, that they added greatly to his reputation. This was still further increased by his publishing, during his sojourn at Oxford, *Dissertations Medico-Phgsicæ de Antris Lethiferas ; de Montis Vesuvii Incendio ; de stupendo Ossium ; de Immani Hypogastri Sarcomate.* Many very curious questions are therein discussed, and several curious facts related, which prove the author to have been a man of much thought and observation, as well as of great learning and general knowledge.

"In the Summer of 1695 he returned to London, where he read lectures as he had done at Oxford ; was elected a Fellow of the Royal Society ; and, on the 6th of April, 1696, was admitted a Licentiate of the College of Physicians of London. In 1697 he published his *Evangelium Medici, seu Medicina Mystica de Suspensis Naturæ legibus sive de Miraculis.* . . . . He subsequently published "The History of Poland," in two Volumes, containing much novel and interesting information. Doctor O'Connor died of fever, 30th October, 1698, when he was little more than 32 years of age ; and was buried at St. Giles'-in-the-Fields, London." (His Works may be consulted in the Library of the British Museum, London.)

In Cameron's *History of the Royal College of Surgeons in Ireland* (Dublin : Fanning & Co., 1886), we read that in his *Evangelium Medici,* Doctor O'Connor advanced an opinion that "generation" may be effected without actual contact of the sexes—an opinion, it is said, which has been verified by recent experimental results !

At present we are unable to trace the genealogy of this family in the *male* line for more than three generations down to the present time ; but we can trace it in the *female* line back to Mortogh Sugrue (commonly called "The Sugrue"), of Dunloe Castle, who married Sheela, daughter of the Marquis of Thomond. Commencing with that Mortogh Sugrue, the genealogy is as follows :

1. Mortogh, the Sugrue m. Sheela, dau. of O'Brien, Marquis of Thomond, and had :

2. Charles (living in 1500), who m. a dau. of MacCarthy Mór, of Pallis Castle, and had four sons and five daughters : the sons were—1. Charles, of whom presently ; 2. Mortogh, 3. Timothy, and 4. John.

3. Charles : eldest son of Charles ; m. dau. of the O'Sullivan Beare, and had :

4. Mortogh, who m. his cousin, a dau. of MacCarthy Mór, and had :

5. Charles, who m. Honoria O'Connell, and had two sons—1. Mortogh,* 2. Timothy.

6. Timothy : second son of Charles ; m. the Honble. Elizabeth Fitzmaurice, dau. of Lord Thomas Fitzmaurice, son of Fitzmaurice, Earl of Kerry, and had :

7. Denis Sugrue, who married Elizabeth, dau. of Donogh MacGillicuddy (see the "MacGillicuddy" pedigree), and had a son Charles, and two daughters :

---

* *Mortogh :* On the death of Charles Sugrue, Honoria, his widow, m. the family Tutor, who was named Mahony, a Protestant, and a native of Cork. This Mortogh was found murdered in the grounds of Dunloe Castle, and Mahony, who then seized the property, was credited with the murder. Timothy Sugrue, the younger brother of Mortogh, came to an agreement with Mahony, and kept thirty-six farms for his share, Mahony having the remainder of the estate.

I. Charles, m. Eleanor Mahony, and had two sons and two daughters :
I. James, II. Thomas.
I. Anne.
II. Elizabeth, who m. Redmond Roche, and had—1. Charles, 2. Michael, 3. James, 4. Robert, and 5. Eleanor.
I. Anne, of whom presently.
II. Winifred : the second daughter of Denis Sugrue, who married a Denis Sugrue (who did not belong to her family), and had a son Robert (who mar. Anne O'Riordan), and two daughters —1. Catherine, 2. Joanna.
8. Anne Sugrue : the elder dau. of Denis ; m. Captain Stephen Walsh,* and had a son named Stephen, and two daughters named Mary, and Elizabeth.
I. Stephen Walsh, m. Arabella Hawkins, and had two sons and four daughters ; the sons were :
I. John, who was twice mar. : first to Viana Stock ; and, secondly, to Agne Mac-Namara. By the first wife he had :
1. Stephen ; 2. Mary, who m. C. Meagher ; 3. Lizzie, 4. John (deceased), and 5. Justin.
II. Frank, who married Jane Lombard.
The four daughters of Stephen were :
I. Anne, who m. John Murphy, and had four sons and three daughters. The four sons were :
I. Stephen.
II. Edward.

III. John.
IV. James.
And the three daughters were :
I. Elizabeth, a Nun.
II. Mary, who m. T. Rearden.
III. Anne, deceased.
II. Elizabeth : second daughter of Stephen Walsh ; married T. Perry, and had three sons and four daughters. The sons were :
I. Stephen Perry, who m. M. Hegarty.
II. John, who m. —Hegarty.
III. Henry.
And Elizabeth's four daughters were :
I. Fanny, who married D. O'B. Corkery.
II. Bessy, a Nun.
III. Annie, who m. Hegarty.
IV. Mary.
III. Maria : third daughter of Stephen Walsh ; married Th. Scanlan, and had one son and five daughters :
I. Michael, deceased.
I. Elizabeth.
II. Maria, deceased.
III. Ellen.
IV. Minnie, deceased.
V. Annie.
IV. Jane : fourth daughter of Stephen Walsh ; married T. Guisani, and had three sons and three daughters :
I. Stephen.
II. John.
III. Joseph.
The three daughters of Jane were:
I. Sarah.
II. Elizabeth.
III. Jeanette.
I. Mary Walsh : the elder

---

* *Walsh :* Captain Stephen Walsh was previously married to E. Mahony, by whom he had five daughters, one of whom was Joanna, who married Charles MacCarthy, and had a son named Justin, and a daughter, Mary-Anne ; Justin married Mary Meagher ; and Mary-Anne married D. Falvey.

daughter of Anne Sugrue, of whom presently.

II. Elizabeth Walsh : the younger daughter; married John O'Sullivan, and had :

I. John, Archdeacon of Kerry.

9. Mary Walsh : elder daughter of Anne Sugrue and Captain Stephen Walsh, m. Thomas O'Connor, of Dingle (of the O'Connors of Carrig-a-Foyle, West Kerry), and had three sons.

I. Maurice, of whom presently.

II. John.

III. Thomas.

10. Maurice O'Connor : son of Thomas; m. Honoria Barrett, and had nine sons and two daughters. The sons were :

I. Arthur, deceased.

II. Patrick, who married Miss de

Pothonier, and had—1. James,*
2. Annie, 3. Fanny.

III. Thomas.

IV. Walker.

V. James, deceased.

VI. William, of whom presently.

VII. Maurice (d. 1885), who m. Anne Hawdon, and had :

I. Annie, who died 1882.

VIII. Roderick, deceased.

IX. Jordan.

The two daughters of Maurice O'Connor were :

I. Mary, who m.—— Ryan.

II. Bridget, deceased.

11. William† O'Connor (b. 1817, d. 1880) : the sixth son of Maurice ; married in 1843, Charlotte Frances O'Keeffe, (nee Day, born 1811, died 1886), and had five sons :

I. Arthur, of whom presently.

---

* *James :* This James O'Connor in 1881 married Maggie, a younger daughter of John O'Connor (of the O'Connor Connaught family, New York, who, besides other daughters named Ellie, Sarah, Fanny, &c., had a son John F. K. O'Connor, who in 1886, married Constance Hamilton, daughter of J. Hamilton Jaffrey, of Yonkers-on-Hudson, United States, America,) and had—1. John-Patrick, born 1881 ; 2. Kathleen; 3. James-Arthur-Michael, born 1886.

† *William :* Of this William O'Connor, M.D., etc., we read in the *Lancet,* of the 18th September, 1880, p. 479 (London):

" We have to record the death of Doctor William O'Connor, Senior Physician to the Royal Free Hospital (London), which took place on the 3rd instant at his residence, 30 Upper Montagu Street, Montagu Square, W. He had been in practice in this metropolis for close upon forty years, during twenty-five of which he was an active member of the institution above mentioned. He was known principally for his treatment of stomach and neuralgic affections, and for his success in the management of the diseases of children.

Doctor O'Connor was descended from an ancient Kerry family, remarkable for the great number of members whom it has afforded to our profession, including several of his brothers . . . The deceased was . . . of the same family as the celebrated Bernard O'Connor, M.D. (above mentioned), who died in 1698, historically noted for his Treatise *Evangelium Medici,* and his accurate diagnosis in the case of the Duchess of Bedzeoil, sister of the King of Poland, to whom he was Physician. Of the three surviving sons of the deceased, Arthur O'Connor, Barrister-at-Law, is M.P. for Queen's County (he is now, in 1887, M.P. for East Donegal) ; another occupies an official position ; and the third son, Bernard O'Connor, M.D., M.R.C.P. London, (late) Physician to the Westminster General Dispensary, in Gerrard Street, Soho, is in consulting practice in Brook Street, Grosvenor Square. It is a curious fact that the only possessors of the name "O'Connor" who have figured on the Roll of the Royal College of Physicians (of London) during the last three hundred years should bear the same Christian name : the one, the last named son of William ; and the other, the Physician to the Polish King already referred to."

It may be here observed that Doctor William O'Connor, referred to in this Obituary, was the first Catholic since the Reformation who was appointed to any large public Hospital or similar Institution in England.

II. William Thomas Rees, born 1845, d. 1878.

III. Ignatius (b. 1847), who in 1878, m. Mary (d. 1882), dau. of Daniel Leahy, of Rosacon, co. Cork, and had :

 I. Joseph Bernard, born 1880.

IV. Bernard,* M.D., London (b. 2nd Aug. 1849). Was twice mar.: first, in 1874, to Jane (d. 1879), another dau. of Daniel Leahy, of Rosacon, co. Cork, and by her had :

 I. Jane-Mary-Frances.

This Bernard was m., secondly, in 1883, to Mariquita Noyes (b. 1859), and has had :

 I. Bernard-Hugh-Sarsfield, born 11th May, 1884.

 II. D'Esmond-Joseph, b. 2nd August, 1885.

 III. Denis Roderick Joseph, b. 16th January, 1887.

V. Joseph, deceased.

12. Arthur O'Connor, Barrister-at-Law, of London (b. 1844, and living in 1887), M.P. for East Donegal (was late M.P. for the Ossory Division of the Queen's County): eldest son of William ; was twice married : first in 1865, to Mary Jackson (d. 1873), and by her had two sons and one daughter :

 I. Arthur-John (born 1867), of whom presently.

 II. Gerald-Bernard, b. 1871.

 I. Imelda.

Arthur was in 1875, m. to his second wife, Ellen Connolly, and by her has had issue :

 II. Ursula.

 III. Bessie.

 IV. Ellen.

13. Arthur-John O'Connor, of London : son of Arthur O'Connor, M.P. ; b. 1867, and living in 1887.

* *Bernard*: In *The Medical Directory* for 1887 (London : J. and A. Churchill), *London List*, p. 224, we read :—
"O'Connor, Bernard, 17 St. James's-place, S.W., A.B. Qu. Univ. Ireland, 1868 ; M.D. ; Master in Surgery and L.M., 1872 ; M.R.C.P. Lond. 1880 ; (studied at Queen's Coll. Cork ; Carmichael School and Whitworth, etc., Hosps. Dublin ; Univ. and Royal Infirmary, Edin. ; St. Mary's Hospital, London ; and Ecole de Médicine, Bordeaux) ; Fellow of the Royal Medical and Chirurgical Society : Member of the Pathological and Clinical Societies and British Medical Association ; Physician North London Hospital for Consumption ; Consulting Physician Convent of Refuge ; Lecturer to the National Health Society ; (late) Physician Westminster General Dispensary ; (late) Editor of *Hibernia*. Author of : "Antiseptic Treatment of Surgical Wounds, with special reference to Carbolic Acid ;" "The Medical and Allied Sciences in connection with Professional Education ;" "Sur la Liqueur Ethérée dans la Diarrhée, la Cholérine, le Mal de Mer, et quelques autres Affections," 1877 ; "A Simple View of the Essential Nature of Small-pox, and a consideration of some of the causes of Popular Objection to Compulsory Vaccination," 1883. Contributions : "Diphtheria, True and False, and the Abuse of the Term," in *Lancet*, 1878 ; "Unusual Sequel of Hœmoptysis," *ibid*., 1879 ; "Syphilitic Psoriasis," *ibid.* 1881 ; "Enuresis in Children," *ibid.* 1881 ; "Congenital Ichthyosis," *Transactions of the Clinical Society*, 1882 : "Symmetrical Gangrene," *Trans. Pathological Soc.*, 1884 ; Articles on Sanitary Science and Medical Reform and Education to the Medical Press.
The present Dr. Bernard O'Connor's first important case (1873) was an abcess of the liver in the diagnosis of which he was opposed by two other Practitioners. (So it was in 1694 in the case of Dr. O'Connor, above mentioned.) Each of the Doctors O'Connor was away on the Continent, etc., for some six years or so, from London ; and, on returning thereto, each was in *April*, admitted to the College of Physicians : the one, as a Licentiate, in 1696 ; the other, as a Member, in 1880. It is worthy of remark that Doctor O'Connor (d. 1698) was the first man to *dissect an elephant !*

O'CONNOR. (No. 3.)

Of Corcomroe, County Clare.

Arms: A man in armour shooting an arrow from a crossbow.   *Crest:* On a ducal coronet an anchor erect entwined with a cable.

CORC, the third son of Fergus Mór, who is No. 64 on the "Line of Ir," p. 301, was the ancestor of *O'Connor,* of Corcamruadh [corcomroe], in the county Clare.   The territories in Munster possessed by the descendants of this Corc* were, after him, called "*Corcamruadh*," "*Corc-Oiche*," and "*Corc Galen;*" whereof they were styled Princes or Kings until their submission to the Crown of England.

64. Fergus Mór (commonly called "Fergus MacRoy"): son of Ros.

65. Corc : his son.

66. Deadhachd : his son.

67. Ollamh (latinized "Ollavus") : his son.

68. Meadh Ruadh ("meadh:" Irish, *a scale for weighing*) : his son; a quo *Dál Meidhe* or "The tribe of Meadh."

69. Aibhilt : his son.

70. Anbheith : his son.

71. Aodh (or Hugh) Agna : his son; had a brother named Conor, who went into Scotland and there settled. This Hugh was the ancestor of the Scotch families of *Forbes* and *Urquhart.*

72. Achorb : son of Hugh Agna.

73. Neachtan : his son.

74. Mearchu : his son.

75. Oscar : his son.

76. Earc : his son.

77. Enarc : his son.

78. Earc (2) : his son.

79. Meisinsalach : his son.

80. Meisin-Dunn : his son.

81. Oscar (2) : his son.

82. Cubroc : his son; whose brother Fraoch was the ancestor of *Curtin.*

83. Broc : his son.

84. Tal : his son; a quo *Carn†MacTail.*

85. Amergin ("aimh:" Irish, a negative prefix; "eirigh," *to rise*): his son; a quo *O'Aimheirighin,* anglicised *Bergin.* (See "Bergin," under No. 100 on the "Moore" pedigree.)

86. Senach : his son.

87. Fulen : his son.

88. Dubh : his son.

89. Beocall : his son.

90. Ceallach : his son.

91. Maoldubh : his son.

92. Dubh-da-Chrioch : his son.

93. Miodhlaoch : his son.

94. Rachd-gaire (literally "a fit of laughter") : his son.

95. Dubhruadh : his son.

96. Flathartach ("flaith :" Irish, *a lord:* "beartach," gen., "beartaighe," *tricky, cunning*): his son; a quo, some say, *O'Flaithbeartaighe* (of Thomond), anglicised *O'Flaherty.*

97. Samhradhan : his son.

* *Corc:* From this Corc were also descended O'Loghlin, of Borin (now "Burren," in the county Clare); *Muintir Argha;* O'Flaherty, of Thomond ; *O'Dubhdhiorma* (or "Dermody"), lawyers and judges to O'Connor and O'Loghlin.

† *Carn:* This Irish word signifies "a pile of stones raised over the tomb of deceased heroes :" compare with the Arabic word *kern,* "a little hill."

98. Argha : his son ; a quo *Muintir Argha*.

99. Melachlin : his son.

100. Conchobhar (or " the helping warrior") : his son ; a quo *O'Concobhartha*, which has been anglicised " O'Connor" (of Corcomroe). This Conchobhar had a younger brother named Lochlann, who was the ancestor of *O'Loghlin*, of Burren, in the county Clare.

101. Flann : son of Conchobhar.

102. Conor Mear : his son.

103. Lochlann O'Connor : his son ; the first of the family who assumed this sirname ; had a brother named Cathal, who was the ancestor of *Cahill*, of the county Clare.

104. Cathal (or Charles) Mór : his son.

105. Cathal Carragh : his son.

106. Cathal Oge: his son.

107. Donall Mantagh : his son.

108. Felim an Einigh : his son.

109. Conor Shoipleith : his son.

110. Brian : his son.

111. Brian Oge : his son..

112. Murtagh Muimhneach : his son.

113. Teige : his son.

114. Rory Glas : his son.

115. Brian Caoch : his son.

116. Murtagh (2) : his son.

117. Rory (2) : his son.

118. Hugh O'Connor, of Corcomroe : his son.

O'FARRELL. (No. 1.)

Princes of Annaly.

Arms : Vert a lion ramp. or. *Crest :* On a ducal coronet a greyhound courant, with a broken chain to the collar round his neck, over that a regal crown ppr. *Motto :* Bhris me mo greim (I have broken my hold).

FEARGAL, who (see page 303) is No. 105 on the " Line of Ir," was the ancestor of this family. Had a brother named Maol-an-Eididh. This Feargal was King of Conmacne ; and was slain fighting on the side of Brian Boru, at the battle of Clontarf,* A.D. 1014 :

106. Eochaidh : son of Feargal.

107. Seanloch : his son.

108. Braon O'Farrell : his son ; first of the family that assumed this sirname.

109. Giollaiosa : his son ; had a brother named Cusleibhe, who was ancestor of *Leavy.* This name Giollaiosa has been latinized *Gillacius, Gelasius,* and anglicised *Giles.*

110. Moroch : his son.

111. Daniel, or Donal : his son.

112. Awly : his son ; living in 1268 ; his dau. Raghnalt, married Hugh O'Connor, King of Conacht, and was drowned in a bath, 1248.

113. Hugh ; his son ; ancestor of the O'Farrells of Ballinalee ; had

---

* *Clontarf :* That this Feargal was the Feargal mentioned as slain, fighting on the side of Brian Boru, at the Battle of Clontarf, A.D. 1014, is by some writers doubted, for, on searching the accounts of that Battle, and the lists of the slain, given in several accessible Annals, they can find no mention of him. But in the Annals of Ulster there is mention of a Domhnall Ua Fearghail, of the Fortuatha-Laighean, in the county Wicklow, who fell in that memorable Battle. Perhaps Feargal, who is No. 105 on the " O'Farrell " pedigree, is confounded with this Domhnall Ua Ferghail, who was a Heremonian !

two sons, Gillacius and Cuchonnacht.

114. Gillacius (2): his son; had two sons :—1. John, and 2. Moroch.

115. Moroch (2): his son.

116. Cathal (or Charles): his son; had three sons :—1. Conor, 2. Thomas, and 3. Murrogh Mór.

117. Thomas: his son; had two sons :—1. Edmund, and 2. Cathal. Edmund was father to Bryan and Geoffrey, progenitors of the *O'Farrells of Granard*.

118. Cathal (2): his son; had two sons—1. Roger, and 2. Thomas (1490). Thomas had a son Ceadach, who was father of Lisagh, ancestor of the *O'Farrells of Edgeworthstown*.

119. Roger: son of Cathal (2).

120. Brian Buidhe (pr. *bwee* or *Boy*): his son; had two sons :—1. Aodh Oge; and 2. Fachna. (1) Aodh Oge was father of Fergus (1599), who was ancestor of the *O'Farrell Buidhe;* and (2) Fachna was ancestor of the *O'Farrells of Longford*.

121. Fachna: son of Brian Buidhe; living in 1585; attended Perrott's Parliament that year in Dublin.

122. Iriol: his son.

123. James : his son.

124. Roger: his son.

125. Francis: his son.

126. Roger : his son.

127. James O'Farrell: his son; living in the 18th century.

O'FARRELL BAN. (No. 2.)

JOHN, the eldest son of Gillacius, who is No. 114 on the No. 1 " O'Farrell" Stem, was the ancestor of this family :

115. John : son of Gillacius O'Farrell ; had two sons :—1. Donal, and 2. Hugh.

116. Donal ; son of John.

117. John : his son.

118. Cormac: his son.

119. Donal (2): his son.

120. William : his son; living in 1585; attended Perrott's Parliament in Dublin in that year.

121. Ros : his son; living in 1598.

O'FARRELL. (No. 3.)

Of Rathline.

HUGH, who is No. 113 on the " O'Farrell " (No. 1) Stem, was ancestor of this family :

114. Cuchonnacht: son of Hugh O'Farrell.

115. Giollaiosa: his son.

116. Fergal : his son.

117. John: his son.

118. Cormac Ballach : his son.

O'FARRELL. (No. 4.)

Chiefs of Clanhugh.

JOHN, son of Gillacius O'Farrell, who is No. 114 on the O'Farrell " (No. 1) Stem, was the founder of this family :

115. John : son to Gillacius O'Farrell.

116. Hugh ; his son ; had two sons —1. Gillacius, and 2. Cuchonacht.

117. Gillacius : his son.

118. Murrogh : his son.

119. Cathal : his son ; had two sons—1. Murrogh, and 2. Fergal,

whose son Siacus Cam was founder of the *O'Farrells of Caltragh and Corlea.*

120. Murrogh : his son.

121. Murrogh Oge : his son.

122. Geoffrey : his son ; living in 1455.

O'FARRELL. (No. 5.)

Of Magh Treagha.

CUCHONACHT, second son of Hugh who is No. 116 on the "O'Farrell" (No. 4), of Clanhugh pedigree, was the ancestor of this family :

117. Cuchonacht: son of Hugh O'Farrell.

118. Matthew : his son.

119. Edmund : his son.

120. Hugh Mór : his son.

121. Hugh Oge : his son.

122. Gerald : his son ; living in 1497.

O'FARRELL. (No. 6.)

Of Kenagh.

CONOR, eldest son of Cathal, who is No. 116 on O'Farrell (No. 1) pedigree, was the founder of this branch of that family :

117. Conor : son of Cathal O'Farrell.

118. Ros : his son ; living in 1460.

119. Lisagh : his son ; had two sons—1. Edmund, 2. Carbry, whose

son John Ruadh was ancestor of the *O'Farrells of Killashee.*

120. Edmund : son of Carbry.

121. Fergus : his son.

O'FARRELL. (No. 7.)

Chiefs of Clanawley.

MURROGH MÓR, third son of Cathal, who is No. 116 on the "O'Farrell" (No. 1) pedigree, was the ancestor of this branch of the family:

117. Murrogh Mór: son to Cathal O'Farrell.
118. Murrogh Og: his son.
119. Brian: his son.

120. John: his son.
121. Daniel: his son; living in 1497.

O'LOGHLIN.

Chiefs of Burren, County Clare.

Arms: Gu. A man in complete armour facir g the sinister, shooting an arrow from a bow all ppr. *Crest:* An anchor entwined with a cable ppr. *Motto:* Anchora salutis.

LOCHLANN, the younger brother of Conor who is No. 100 on the "O'Connor" (Corcomroe) pedigree, was the ancestor of *O'Lochloin;* anglicised *O'Loghlin.*

100. Lochlann* ("loch:" Irish, *a sea* or *lake;* Latin "lac-us;" and Irish "lon," *powerful*): son of Melachlin; a quo *O'Lochloin*, of Burren.†
101. Melachlin: his son.
102. Amhailgadh [Awly]: his son.
103. Melachlin O'Loghlin: his son; the first of the family who assumed this sirname.
104. Amhailgadh: his son.
105. Congalach: his son.
106. Donoch: his son.
107. Annadh Cam (" cam:" Irish *crooked;* Pers. " kam;" Chald. "kam-ar;" Gr. " kam-pto," *to bend;* Lat. " cam-urus"): his son.

This Annadh (" annadh:" Irish, *delay*) was the ancestor of *O'h Annaidh,* anglicised *Hanna* and *Hanny.*
108. Melachlin Cam O'Loghlin: his son; had three brothers—1. Brian, 2. Iriall, and 3. Donoch; the generations descended from this Melachlin, and his brothers Brian and Iriall, we are at present unable to trace, but those from his brother Donoch are as follows:
109. Annadh: son of said Donoch O'Loghlin.
110. Rory: his son.
111. Melachlin: his son.
112. Anthony: his son; died A.D. 1617. This Anthony had two sons

---

* *Lochlann*: The Irish *lochlon* is the root of *lochlonnach,* which is the Irish for " a Dane:" no doubt, because the Danes were *powerful* at sea.

† *Burren*: The root of this word is the Irish *boireann,* which here means " a rocky district;" same as that at Ballyvaughan, county Clare, where stands the ancient castle of *O'Loghlin* of Burren.

—1. Uaithne (Owny or Anthony), who died before his father ; and 2. Ros.

113. Ros : son of Anthony.

114. Melachlin (or Malachi) : his son ; died, 1633.

115. Anthony (2) : his son.

116. Torlogh : his son.

117. Donogh : his son.

118. Torlogh O'Loghlin, of Burren: his son ; was living A.D. 1724.

———

Sir Colman O'Loghlin, Bart., Member of Parliament for the county Clare, who died unmarried in 1877, was the eldest son of Sir Michael O'Loghlin (the first baronet in this family), who was son of Colman, son of Hugh, son of Malachi O'Loghlin ; but we do not know the relationship which this Malachi O'Loghlin bore to Torlogh O'Loghlin, No. 118 above-mentioned (living in 1724), or to any of the names on this pedigree preceding the said Torlogh. On the death of the above-mentioned Sir Colman O'Loghlin, the second baronet, his brother Sir Bryan, of Australia, succeeded to the baronetcy ; and was elected in 1877 an M.P. for the county Clare. —*The Author.*

———

QUINN.

Lords of Muintir Gillagain, County Longford.

Arms : Vert a pegasus pass. wings elevated ar. a chief or.

GIOLLAGAN, a brother of Eimhin who is No. 101 on the "Line of Ir," p. 303, was the ancestor of *MacCuinn* and *O'Cuinn* (lords of *Muintir Gillagain* —a territory in the county Longford) ; anglicised *O'Quinn*, *MacQuinn*, *MacQueen*, *Quinn*, and *Quin.*

101. Giollagan (" giolla :" Irish, *a minister* or *page*): son of Croman ; a quo *O'Giollagain*, anglicised *Gilligan* and *O'Galligan.*

102. Sgannan : his son.

103. Gormgal : his son.

104. Conn (" conn :" Irish, *wisdom*): his son ; a quo *MacCuinn* and *O'Cuinn.*

105. Searragh : son of Conn.

106. Aodh (or Hugh) O'Quinn : his son ; first of the family who assumed this surname.

107. Donogh : his son.

108. Teige : his son.

109. Sitric : his son.

110. Amhailgadh [awley] : his son

111. Gormgal (2) : his son.

112. Dermod : his son.

113. Giolla-na-Naomh : his son.

114. Gormgal (3) : his son.

115. Cuchonacht : his son.

116. Cathal : his son.

117. Cairbre : his son.

118. Felim O'Quinn : his son.

REYNOLDS. (No. 1.)

Arms: Az. a chev. erm. betw. crosses crosslet fitchée ar.   *Crest:* An eagle close ar. ducally gorged and lined or.

EIMHIN, who is No. 101 on the "Line of Ir," p. 303, had three brothers —1. Biobhsach, who was the ancestor of *MacRadhnaill* (anglicised *Mac Rannall, MacRandall, Magrannell, Reynell, Reynolds*); 2. Gearabhan; and 3. Giollagan, who was the ancestor of *Quinn* (of Longford), as in the preceding pedigree. This Biobhsach's proportion of his father's inheritance was situate in Conmaicne Rheine, which his posterity enjoyed; and the chiefs of whom (who were called *MacRannall*) were styled "lords."

101. Biobhsach: son of Croman.

102. Eolus: his son; after whom his part of the territory of Conmaicne Rheine was called *Muintir Eoluis* ("eolus:" Irish, *knowledge*), anglicised *Wallis:* which territory is now divided into the three upper baronies of the county Leitrim, viz.: Leitrim, Mohill, and Carrigallen.

103. Maolmuire: his son; lord of Conmaicne Rheine; had two brothers—1. Brocan, who was ancestor of *Shanly*, etc.; 2. Anbeith, from whom *MacGarry* is descended.

104. Maoldun: son of Maolmuire.

105. Flann (or Florence): his son.

106. Maolruanaidh: his son.

107. Iomhar: his son; who was called the "black lord," and had a brother named Duorcan, who was the ancestor of *Mulvy*.

108. Muredach: son of Iomhar; had ten brothers.

109. Radhnal (or Randal): his son; a quo *MacRadhnaill* ("radh:" Irish, *a saying;* "anall," *over to one side from another*), first anglicised *MacRannall*.

110. Iomhar (2): his son.

111. Fergall: his son.

112. Muredach (2): his son; had a brother named Radhnall-Logg-na-Ccon.

113. Cathal Mór: his son; was the first of this sept who assumed the sirname MacRannall; had four sons, three of whom were:—1. Raghnall;

2. Conor; and 3. Iomhar (or Ivar), slain 1326.

(2). Conor, had a son Matha, who had a son Hugh, who had a son Cathal, who had seven sons—Conor, Cathal, Hugh, Brian, Manus, Owen, and Conn.

(3). Iomhar, had a son Teige, who had a son Murchadh, who had two sons—Fergal, and Anthony; Anthony had a son Cathal.

114. Raghnall, the second MacRannall: his son; had four sons—1. Iomhar; 2. Cathal; 3. William; and 4. Mahon.   Deposed 1317.

115. Iomhar (3): his son; had seven sons—1. Teige; 2. Dermod; 3. Geoffrey; 4. Fergal; 5. Edmond; 6. Melaghlin Oge; and 7. Hugh.

(5). Edmond had a son Iomhar; and 6. Melaghlin Oge had a son Dermod, died 1374.

116. Teige: his son; slain 1328, had six sons, four of whom were—1. Cathal Roe; 2. Murchadh; 3. Manus; and 4. Richard.   This Richard died on Christmas night from drinking too much whiskey.

117. Cathal (or Charles) Ruadh: his son (slain 1401); had six sons—1. Ior; 2. Conor; 3. Rory; 4. Mulroony; 5. Brian; and 6. Cathal Oge, died 1468.

(2). Conor had two sons—Edmond, lord Clan Bibacht, and Mulroony; Mulroony had two sons—Felim (d.

1503) and Herbert; Felim had a son Conor, who had a son Cathal.

(6). Cathal Oge had two sons— Teige and Conor; Teige's issue— Murrogh (lived 1468), Conor, Malachy (lived 1468), Brian; and Conor's—Teige and Hubert slain 1492.

118. Ior: his son; a quo *Slioch Ir* ("sliochd Ir:" Ir., *the progeny of Ir*: a quo *Oh-Ir*, anglicised *O'Hare*); had four sons—1. William; 2. Dermod; 3. Owen; 4. Manus. (2). Dermod had two sons—Brian and Malachy.

119. William: his son; made chieftain of Clan Malachy in 1468, and in 1492 on the death of Hubert he became chief of *Muintir Eoluis.*

120. Thomas: his son; the first of this family who omitted the prefix *Mac*, and instead of "Rannall," called himself *Reynolds.** This Thomas had two sons—1. Humphrey; and 2. Owen.

(2). Owen had a son, John, who dathree sons—Owen,† Charles, of Jamestown, and Thomas. This Charles sat at the Catholic Confederation in Kilkenny.

121. Humphrey Reynolds: his son.

122. John Reynolds of Loch Seur: his son; known as "Seaghan na g-Ceann" or *John of the Heads*, on account of a dreadful massacre he instigated of the leading chiefs of his tribe at his castle of the Island of Lough Seur which he built. This John was a captain in the Elizabethan army in Ireland, and the first of his family who conformed to the Protestant Church; he died in 1632.

123. Humphrey (2): his son.

124. William (2): his son.

125. James: his son.

126. Henry Reynolds: his son.

REYNOLDS. (No. 2.)

Of Dublin.

Arms: See those of "Reynolds" (No. 1).

121. Owen: son of Thomas, who is No. 120 on the "Reynolds" (No. 1) pedigree, had a son John.

122. John: said son of Owen; had three sons — Owen, Charles, and Thomas.

123. Thomas: said son of John. This Thomas had two sons—Ivar of Cloon, and Henry of Annaghduff.

124. Henry: second son of Thomas;

born 1610; took the National side in 1641.

125. Thomas: his son.

126. George: his son.

127. ——— MacRannall of Corduff, born 1707; had three sons:— 1. Charles, proprietor of Esker-Each and Esker-na-Coille, who left issue —Brian, Henry, and George; 2.

---

* *Reynolds*: Thomas Reynolds, pursuant to an Act of Parliament passed in Queen Elizabeth's reign, changed his name from that of *MacRannall*: "for which and for his civilizing his family and bringing his country to the obedience of the Crown of England, and introducing the English customs and fashions among them, he was called *MacRannall Gallda* (or the English MacRannall), and also *Magrannell.—Four Masters.*

† *Owen*: This Owen had a son *John Oge* who was chief of his name in Oliver Cromwell's time.

Ignatius, lived in Spain, and d. s. p.; and 3. Laurence of Clonbonny.

128. Laurence : the third son; b. 1737; had six sons:—1. Henry; 2. Mark; 3. Edmond; 4. John; 5. Patrick; and 6. Charles, whose son Henry (of the 58th Foot) died of apoplexy at Shorncliffe Camp, 1859, leaving issue.

129. Henry: son of Laurence; b.

1767, lord of *Muintir Eoluis ;* m. Margaret, dau. of Richard Bulkley, M.D., Nenagh, and left issue :

1. Thomas Reynolds, Marshal of Dublin, born January 20th, 1793.

2. John Reynolds, Alderman, J.P., M.P., ex-Lord Mayor of Dublin, born 1797 ; and

3. Henry Reynolds, born 1799.

RUDDY.

Arms : Per chev. in chief two demi lions ramp. and a mullet in base. *Crest :* A lion ramp. *Motto :* Pro rege sæpe, pro patria semper.

FICHEALLACH, brother of Neidhe, who is No. 96 on the " Line of Ir," p. 303, was the ancestor of *O'Rodoighe ;* anglicised *O'Roddy, Roddy, Reddy,* and *Ruddy.*

96. Ficheallach : son of Onchu.

97. Naradh : his son.

98. Rodoch ("rod:" Irish, *a road*) : his son; a quo *O'Rodoighe ;* had two brothers—1. Dunchean, who was the ancestor of *Duncan,* and 2. Tormach, who was the ancestor of *Tormey* of Connaught.

99. Maolin Fionn : his son.

100. Alastrum (or Alexander): his son.

101. Ardgall : his son.

102. Gillmanchan : his son.

103. Gormghall : his son.

104. Gillchriosd : his son.

105. Maoliosa : his son.

106. Feichin : his son.

107. Mulmichil: his son.

108. Giolliosa : his son.

109. Mulmuire : his son.

110. Mulmichil (2): his son.

111. Donall : his son.

112. Gillbair ("bar :"[*] Irish, *ex-*

cellence): his son; a quo *O'Giol-labair,* anglicised *Barr* and *Barre.*

113. Giolla Muire (or the " Devoted of the Blessed Virgin Mary"): his son; a quo *MacGiolla Muire,* anglicised *MacGilmary, Maryson, Marson, Marysman, Maryman, Merryman, Merriman,* and *Gilmore.* This Irish name was also anglicised *O'Morna.*

114. Eigneach : his son.

115. Giollaiosa : his son.

116. Eilia : his son.

117. Luachcas : his son.

118. John : his son.

119. Robert : his son.

120. Matthew : his son.

121. Teige : his son.

122. William : his son.

123. Bryan Buidhe : his son.

124. Teige (2): his son.

125. Teige Oge O'Roddy : his son ; who was a learned antiquarian.

---

[*] *Bar :* Compare the Irish word "bar" with the Heb. "bar," *a son ;* "bar," *corn :* "barh," *above ;* and "baar," *was famous ;* with the Syriac, Old Pers., and Chald. "bar," *high ;* the Arab, "barr," *wheat ;* and the Pers. "ber," *fruit.*

SHANLY.

Of Fernaught, County Leitrim.

Arms : Az. a lion statant or, holding out the forepaw, in chief three estoiles of the second. *Crest :* A hand from below the wrist in armour, holding a broken sword.

BROCAN, brother of Maolmuire, who is No. 103 on the "Reynolds" pedigree, was the ancestor of *O'Seanlaoich;* anglicised *MacShanly* and *Shanly.*

103. Brocan : son of Eolus.

104. Seanlaoch ("sean :" Irish, *old;* Lat. "sen-ex:" "laoch :" Irish, *a hero*) : his son : a quo *O'Seanlaoich.* This Seanlaoch had a brother named Conor, who was the ancestor of *MacCulroy* (modernized *MacElroy* and *MacIlroy*); and another brother named Giollchriosd (meaning "the devoted of Christ,") a quo *Gillchriest* and *MacGillchriest.*

105. Giollabrighid [Gillbride] : son of Seanlaoch.

106. Donoch : his son ; died in the Abbey of Boyle, A.D. 1256.

107. Dunsithe : his son.

108. Gillbaire [Gillbarry] : his son.

109. Giolla Padraic [Gillpatrick] Buidhe : his son.

110. Teige : his son.

111. Giollaiosa [Gillacius] : his son.

112. Hugh Ruadh [Roe] : his son.

113. Maothan [Mahoon] : his son. Had three brothers—1. William, 2. "The Dean," 3. Dunsithe.

114. Dermod Dubh : his son.

115. Seona : his son.

116. Cormac : his son.

117. Gothfrith [Jeffrey], of Dromod : his son ; chief of his name and clan. This Jeffrey had two sons : 1. Edmond, who had a son named Edmond Oge MacShanly ; 2. Cormac.

118. William MacShanly : son of Cormac.

119. William Shanly : his son ; lived for a time in the county Meath during the troublous times of the Commonwealth, but, upon the Restoration, returned to his old home at Dromod (or Drumod), and had grants from the Crown of certain lands in the county of Roscommon, outside of his patrimony in the county Leitrim.

120. William, of Dromod : his son ; was named in King James's Charter to Jamestown, "Sovereign" of that borough, which he represented in Parliament in 1688. This William with his three brothers were loyal adherents of King James : all four held commissions in the Army, as did also their uncle Major Michael Shanly of Cargins. The fortune of war having declared against their cause, the five were included in the list of "attainted" gentlemen in Leitrim. When peace had been restored, the aforesaid William Shanly, M.P. for Jamestown, chief of his clan, and Captain in O'Gara's Regiment, was found seized of a considerable estate, on which he fixed his residence at Fearnaught, overlooking the "stately Shannon:" here, for a century, the family was known "as Shanly of Fearnaught."

121. James Shanly, of Fearnaught : son of said William ; m. in Feb., 1709, Miss O'Farrell,* dau. of Col.

* *Miss O'Farrell:* This lady was cousin-german to Diana O'Farrell, Countess of Effingham, dau. of Major-General Francis-Fergus O'Farrell.

Roger O'Ferrall, of Mornin Castle, M.P. for Longford, by his wife, Mary, dau. of Sir Thomas Nugent.

122. William Shanly, of Fearnaught: son of James; had a brother Iriel, who d. unmarried. This William m. in May, 1734, Miss Jennings, and, with two daughters who did not marry, had four sons: 1. William ;* 2. James; 3. Tobias; 4. Michael.

123. Michael: the said fourth son of William; was an officer in the 18th Light Dragoons, and, while with his Regiment in Tipperary, m. at Nenagh a widow lady, Mrs. Constable (her name was Jane Shaw), and dying suddenly (as his brother Tobias had died) at his house in Eccles-street, Dublin, in July, 1814, left three sons—1. Robert, 2. William, 3. James.

124. Rev. Robert Shanly, Rector of Julian's-town, co. Meath: eldest son of Captain Michael Shanly; m. Miss Stewart, and had one son William, and four daughters.†

William, second son of Captain Michael Shanly, succeeded his uncle of the same name in Willyfield (1815), and, until his death (in 1824), was a grand-juror and magistrate of his county (Leitrim). He m. Charlotte, dau. of Alexander Percy of Garradise, same county,

and, with several daughters, had two sons—William, of Willyfield and Bush Hill, and James, of Riversdale. Of this family the eldest son William alone was living in 1879; he m. his cousin, Lavinia, dau. of Major John Percy of Garradise, and had one son and one daughter; his son William-John, was (in 1880) Captain in the Army.

James, the youngest of Captain Michael Shanley's three sons, Master of Arts, T.C.D., and a member of the bar, was of "The Abbey," Queen's County; Norman's-Grove, county Meath; and a magistrate of Leitrim. He m., first, Frances Elizabeth, dau. of Charles Mulvany of the City of Dublin, merchant, and, she dying in 1821, he m., secondly, Ellen, sister of his first wife; this lady d. in 1869. Mr. James Shanly emigrated to Canada in 1836, and, at his place of Thorndale, Ontario, d. 27th Oct., 1857, aged 79. Two generations of his family are now to be found in Canada, and they, with their near relatives, William Shanly, of Buttevant; William Shanly of Bush Hill, with his one son, William-John; and one other William (living somewhere abroad) son of James of Riversdale, above mentioned, are the sole representatives of their

---

* *William* : This William Shanly, of Fearnaught and Willyfield, died unmarried, He was High Sheriff of Leitrim in 1784; and, after a long life of praiseworthy record, d. at his place of Willyfield, in October, 1815, aged 80 years. His younger brother James also d. unmarried ; and the third brother Tobias, of Dromodbeg, m. Prudence, dau. of Matthew Nesbitt, of Derrycarne, and had one daughter, and a son named Tobias, who was an officer in the 16th Regiment. The said third brother Tobias, d. suddenly : An enthusiastic fisherman, it was his wont, in pursuit of his favourite pastime, to anchor his boat in some of the bays or "loughs" of the beautiful Shannon, on the banks of which he was born and had passed his life, and was so found one day, fishing-rod in hand—dead. Of this branch of the family there are no descendants in the male line.

† *Daughters* : Of the four daughters three were married : Jane, to Henry Parsons, on of the Hon. John-Clerc Parsons, brother of the Earl of Rosse; Elizabeth, to Frederick-Henry Villiers ; and Sarah, to John-Hungerford Sealy, of Barleyfield, county Cork.

house. None others of the name, wheresoever to be found, can, within any recognisable degree of consanguinity, claim kindred with the Shanlys of Fearnaught.

125. William of Buttevant Castle: son of the Rev. Robert Shanly; living in 1879; and then unmarried.

WARD.

Of Ireland.

Arms: Ar. two bars gu. each charged with as many martlets or.

EOCHA, brother of Iomchadh who is No. 85 on the "Manning" pedigree, was the ancestor of *Mac-an-Bhaird;* anglicised *Ward* and *MacWard.*

85. Eocha : son of Sodhan.
86. Nar : his son.
87. Fionnchadh : his son.
88. Reachtach : his son.
89. Nuada Dearg : his son.
90. Ughaine : his son.
91. Maighlen : his son; had a brother named Fionnagan.
92. Gilldé ("Giolla" : Irish, *a servant ;* "Dia," gen. "De," *God ;* Heb. "Yah ;" Lat. "De-us ;" Gr. "The-os," Accusat. "Dia") : his son ; a quo *O'Giolladé,* anglicised *Gildea.*
93. Eachtighearna : his son.
94. Dermod : his son.
95. Ughra : his son.
96. Murios : his son.
97. Gillde (2) : his son.
98. Melachlin : his son.
99. Ughra (2) : his son.
100. Murios (2) : his son.
101. Gillde (3) : his son.
102. Melachlin (2) : his son.
103. Ughra (3) : his son.
104. Gillcoimdhe : his son.
105. Dermod (2) : his son.
106. Maccraith : his son.
107. Conor : his son.
108. Shane (or John) : his son.
109. Owen   M a c-a n-B h a i r d* ("bhard" : Irish, *a bard ;* Heb. "baar," *was famous*), of Monycassan : his son ; a quo *MacWard,* modernized *Ward.*

* *Mac-an-Bhaird* : By some of the descendants of this Owen, this sirname was rendered *O'Bairdain,* which has been variously anglicised as follows : *Baird, Bard, Barde, Barden, Bardin, Barding, Bardon, Barten Barton, Berdan, Berdon, Burdon, Purdon, Verdon,* and *Wardin.*

THE IRIAN MONARCHS OF IRELAND.

1 & 2. Cearmna and Sobhrach : sons of Eibhric, son of Heber, son of Ir.

3. Seidnae : son of Airtri, son of Eibhric.

4. Fiacha Fionn-Sciothach : son of Seidnae.

5. Eochaidh (Ollamh Fodhla) : son of Fiacha.

6. Finachta Fionn-sneachta : son of Eochaidh.

7. Slanoll : son of Eochaidh.

8. Gead Ollghothach : son of Gead, son of Eochaidh.

9. Fiacha : son of Finachta Fionn-sneachta.

10. Bergna : son of Gead Ollghothach.

11. Olioll : son of Slanoll.

12. Fionn : son of Labhra, son of Cairbre, son of Eochaidh.

13. Siorlamhach : son of Fionn, son of Bratha, son of Labhra, son of Cairbre.

14. Argethamar : son of Siorlamhach.

15. Aodh Ruadh : son of Badhurn, son of Argethamar.

16. Diothorba : son of Diomain, son of Argethamar.

17. Cimbath : son of Fionntain, son of Argethamar.

18. Macha Mongrua (Queen) : dau. of Aodh Ruadh.

19. Ruadhri Mór : son of Sitrighe, son of Dubh, son of Fomhor, son of Argethamar.

20. Bresal Bobhiobha : son of Breasal, son of Ruadhri Mór.

21. Congall Clareineach : son of Conal, son of Ruadhri Mór.

22. Fachna Fathach : son of Ruadhri Mór.

23. Eiliomh MacConrach : son of Conrach, son of Ruadhri Mór.

24. Mal MacRochraidhe : son of Rochraidhe, son of Cathbuadh, son of Gillacha, son of Donchadha, son of Fionchadha, son of Mureadhach, son of Fiocha, son of Irial Glunmear, son of Congall Clareineach.

25. Caolbadh : son of Cruin Bradhraoi, son of Eachach, son of Lughaidh MacRosa, son of Iomchada, son of Felim, son of Cas, son of Fiacha Araidhe, son of Angusa, son of Fergus, son of Tiobhruidhe, son of Breasal, son of Mal Mac Rochraidhe.

Of the Irian race thirty-five princes became Kings of Ulster, and kept their court at Eamhain, founded by Queen Macha ; and twenty-five of them were Monarchs of Ireland, including Queen Macha.

CHAPTER IV.

THE LINE OF HEREMON.

HEREMON was the seventh son of Milesius of Spain (who is No. 36, p. 50), but the third of the three sons who left any issue. From him were descended the Kings, Nobility, and Gentry of the Kingdoms of Connaught,* Dalriada, Leinster, Meath, Orgiall, Ossory; of Scotland, since the fifth century; of Ulster, since the fourth century; and of England, from the reign of King Henry II., down to the present time.

THE STEM OF THE "LINE OF HEREMON."

OR,

THE Stem of the Irish Nation from Heremon down to (No. 81) Art Eanfhear, Monarch of Ireland in the second century, who was the ancestor of *O'h-Airt*, anglicised *O'Hart*.

" The House of Heremon,"† writes O'Callaghan, " from the number of its princes, or great families—from the multitude of its distinguished characters, as laymen or churchmen—and from the extensive territories acquired by those belonging to it, at home and abroad, or in Alba as well as in Ireland—was regarded as by far the most illustrious: so much so, according to the best native authority, that it would be as reasonable to affirm that one pound is equal in value to one hundred pounds, as it would be to compare any other line with that of Heremon."

36. Milesius of Spain.

37. Heremon : his son. He and his eldest brother Heber were, jointly, the first Milesian Monarchs of Ireland; they began to reign, A.M. 3,500, or, Before Christ, 1699. After Heber was slain, B.C. 1698, Heremon reigned singly for fourteen years; during which time a certain colony called by the Irish *Cruithneaigh*, in English " Cruthneans" or *Picts*, arrived in Ireland and requested Heremon to assign them a part of the country to settle in, which he refused; but, giving them as wives the widows of the Tuatha-

---

* *Connaught :* In other parts of this Work " Connaught" is spelled *Conacht ;* as we found it in the *MS.* or Work which we consulted.

† *Heremon :* According to the "Book of Ballymote," the river "Liffey" derived its name from the circumstance of a battle having been fought near it by the Milesians, against the Tua-de-Danans ; and the horse of the Milesian Monarch Heremon, which was named "Gabhar [gavar] Liffé" (*gabhar :* ancient Scotic and British word for the Lat. " *eq*-uus," *a horse*, which, in modern Irish, is "each" [ogh], *a steed*), having been killed there, the river was called " Liffé" or "Liffey." In Irish it was called " Amhan Liffé" (*Amhan :* Irish, *a river* ; Lat. *amn*-is), signifying the *River Liffey*, which was first anglicised " Avon Liffey," and, in modern times, changed to *Anna Liffey*—the river on which the city of Dublin is built.

de-Danans, slain in battle, he sent them with a strong party of his own forces to conquer the country then called "Alba," but now *Scotland ;* conditionally, that they and their posterity should be tributary to the Monarchs of Ireland. Heremon died, B.C. 1683, and was succeeded by three of his four sons, named Muimne,* Luigne, and Laighean, who reigned jointly for three years, and were slain by their Heberian successors.

38. Irial Faidh ("faidh" : Irish, *a prophet*): his son; was the 10th Monarch of Ireland ; d. B.C. 1670. This was a very learned King; could foretell things to come; and caused much of the country to be cleared of the ancient forests. He likewise built seven royal palaces, viz., Rath Ciombaoith, Rath Coincheada, Rath Mothuig, Rath Buirioch, Rath Luachat, Rath Croicne, and Rath Boachoill. He won four remarkable battles over his enemies:—Ard Inmath, at Teabtha, where Stirne, the son of Dubh, son of Fomhar, was slain ;

the second battle was at Teanmhuighe, against the Fomhoraice, where Eichtghe, their leader, was slain ; the third was the battle of Loch Muighe, where Lugrot, the son of Moghfeibhis, was slain ; and the fourth was the battle of Cuill Martho, where the four sons of Heber were defeated. Irial died in the second year after this battle, having reigned 10 years, and was buried at Magh Muagh.

39. Eithrial: his son ; was the 11th Monarch ; reigned 20 years ; and was slain by Conmaol, the son of Heber Fionn, at the battle of Soirrean, in Leinster, B.C. 1650.

This also was a learned King, he *wrote* with his own hand the History of the Gaels (or Gadelians) ; in his reign seven large woods were cleared and much advance made in the practice of agriculture.

40. Foll-Aich: his son ; was kept out of the Monarchy by Conmaol, the slayer of his father, who usurped his place.

41. Tigernmas† : his son; was the 13th Monarch, and reigned 77

---

* *Muimne :* This Monarch was buried at Cruachan (*cruachan:* Irish, *a little hill*) or Croaghan, situated near Elphin, in the county of Roscommon. In the early ages, Croaghan became the capital of Connaught and a residence of the ancient Kings of Ireland ; and at Croaghan the states of Connaught held conventions, to make laws and inaugurate their Kings. There, too, about a century before the Christian era, the Monarch Eochy Feidlioch (No. 72 in this stem) erected a royal residence and a great rath, called "Rath-Cruachan," after his queen, Cruachan Croidheirg (*Croidheirg :* Irish, *a rising heart*), mother of Maud, the celebrated queen of Connaught, who, wearing on her head "Aision" or *golden crown*, and seated in her gilded war-chariot surrounded by several other war-chariots, commanded in person, like the ancient queens of the Amazons, her Connaught forces, in the memorable seven years' war against the Red Branch Knights of Ulster, who were commanded by King Connor MacNessa, as mentioned in our ancient records.—CONNELLAN.

† *Tigernmas* (or Tiernmas) : This Tiernmas was the Monarch who set up the famous idol called "Crom Cruach" (literally, *the crooked heap*) on the plain of Magh Sleaght, now Fenagh, in the barony of Mohill, county of Leitrim. This idol was worshipped up to the time of St. Patrick, by whom it was destroyed. Among the idol-worship of the ancient Irish at that time was that of the sun : the sun-worship which was that of the Magi or wise men of the East, who, we are told in Scripture, were led to Bethlehem by divine inspiration to see the Infant Jesus.

This Monarch introduced certain distinctions in rank among the Irish, which were indicated by the wearing of certain colours, which, by some persons, is believed to have been the origin of the Scotch plaid. According to Keatinge, one colour was used in the dress of a slave ; two colours in that of a plebeian ; three, in that of a soldier or young

years; according to Keating, he reigned but 50 years; he fought twenty-seven battles with the followers of the family of Heber Fionn, all which he gained. In his reign gold was mined near the Liffey, and skilfully worked by *Inchadhan*. This King also made a law that each grade of society should be known by the number of colours in its wearing apparel :—the clothes of a slave should be of *one* colour; those of a soldier of *two ;* the dress of a commanding officer to be of *three* colours ; a gentleman's dress, who kept a table for the free entertainment of strangers, to be of *four* colours ; *five* colours to be allowed to the nobility (the chiefs); and the King, Queen, and Royal Family, as well as the Druids, historians, and other learned men to wear *six* colours.

This King died, B.C. 1543, on the Eve of 1st of November, with two-thirds of the people of Ireland, at Magh Sleaght (or Field of Adoration), in the county of Leitrim, as he was adoring the Sun-God, Crom Cruach (a quo *Macroom*).

Historians say this Monarch was the first who introduced image worship in Ireland.

42. Enboath : his son. It was in this prince's lifetime that the Kingdom was divided in two parts by a line drawn from Drogheda to Limerick.

43. Smiomghall : his son; in his lifetime the Picts in Scotland were forced to abide by their oath, and pay homage to the Irish Monarch ; seven large woods were also cut down.

44. Fiacha Labhrainn : his son; was the 18th Monarch ; reigned 24 years; slew Eochaidh Faobharglas, of the line of Heber, at the battle of Carman. During his reign all the inhabitants of Scotland were brought in subjection to the Irish Monarchy, and the conquest was secured by his son the 20th Monarch. Fiacha at length (B.C. 1448) fell in the battle of Bealgadain, by the hands of Eochaidh Mumho, the son of Moefeibhis, of the race of Heber Fionn.

45. Aongus Olmucach: his son; was the 20th Monarch ; in his reign the Picts again refused to pay the tribute imposed on them 250 years before, by Heremon, but this Monarch went with a strong army into Alba and in thirty pitched battles overcame them and forced them to pay the required tribute.

Aongus was at length slain by Eana, in the battle of Carman, B.C. 1409.

46. Main : his son; was kept out of the Monarchy by Eadna, of the line of Heber Fionn. In his time silver shields were given as rewards for bravery to the Irish militia.

47. Rotheachtach* : his son ; was the 22nd Monarch ; slain, B.C. 1357, by Sedne (or Seadhna), of the Line of Ir.

48. Dein : his son; was kept out of the Monarchy by his father's slayer, and his son. In his time gentlemen and noblemen first wore gold chains round their necks, as a sign of their birth ; and golden helmets were given to brave soldiers,

49. Siorna "Saoghalach" (*longævus*): his son; was the 34th Mon-

---

lord; four, in that of a brughaidh or public victualler; five, in that of a lord of a tuath or cantred ; and six colours in that of an ollamh or chief professor of any of the liberal arts, and in that of the king and queen.—BOOK OF RIGHTS.

* *Rotheachtach* : Silver shields were made, and four-horse chariots were first used, in Ireland, in the reign of this Monarch.

arch; he obtained the name "Saoghalach" on account of his extraordinary long life; slain, B.C 1030, at Aillin, by Rotheachta, of the Line of Heber Fionn, who usurped the Monarchy, thereby excluding from the throne—

50. Olioll Aolcheoin: son of Siorna Saoghalach.

51. Gialchadh: his son; was the 37th Monarch; killed by Art Imleach, of the Line of Heber Fionn, at Moighe Muadh, B.C. 1013.

52. Nuadhas Fionnfail: his son; was the 39th Monarch; slain by Breasrioghacta, his successor, B.C. 961.

53. Aedan Glas: his son. In his time the coast was infested with pirates; and there occurred a dreadful plague (*Apthach*) which swept away most of the inhabitants.

54. Simeon Breac: his son; was the 44th Monarch; he inhumanly caused his predecessor to be torn asunder; but, after a reign of six years, he met with a like death, by order of Duach Fionn, son to the murdered King, B.C. 903.

55. Muredach Bolgach: his son; was the 46th Monarch; killed by Eadhna Dearg, B.C. 892; he had two sons—Duach Teamhrach, and Fiacha.

56. Fiacha Tolgrach: son of Muredach; was the 55th Monarch. His brother Duach had two sons, Eochaidh Framhuine and Conang Beag-eaglach, who were the 51st and 53rd Monarchs of Ireland. Fiacha's life was ended by the

sword of Oilioll Fionn, of the Line of Heber Fionn, B.C. 795.

57. Duach Ladhrach: his son; was the 59th Monarch; killed by Lughaidh Laighe, son of Oilioll Fionn, B.C. 737.

58. Eochaidh Buadhach: his son; was kept out of the Monarchy by his father's slayer. In his time the kingdom was twice visited with a plague.

59. Ugaine Mór*: his son. This Ugaine (or Hugony) the Great was the 66th Monarch of Ireland. Was called *Mór* on account of his extensive dominions,—being sovereign of all the Islands of Western Europe. Was married to Cæsair, dau. to the King of France, and by her had issue—twenty-two sons and three daughters. In order to prevent these children encroaching on each other he divided the Kingdom into twenty-five portions, allotting to each his (or her) distinct inheritance. By means of this division the taxes of the country were collected during the succeeding 300 years. All the sons died without issue except two, viz:—Laeghaire Lorc, ancestor of all the Leinster Heremonians; and Cobthach Caolbhreagh, from whom the Heremonians of *Leath Cuinn*, viz., Meath, Ulster, and Conacht derive their pedigree.

Ugaine was at length, B.C. 593, slain by Badhbhchadh, who failed to secure the fruits of his murder—the Irish Throne, as he was executed by order of Laeghaire Lorc, the

* *Ugaine Mór*: In the early ages the Irish Kings made many military expeditions into foreign countries. Ugaine Mór, called by O'Flaherty, in his *Ogygia*, "Hugonius Magnus," was contemporary with Alexander the Great; and is stated to have sailed with a fleet into the Mediterranean, landed his forces in Africa, and also attacked Sicily; and having proceeded to Gaul, was married to Cæsair, daughter of the King of the Gauls. Hugonius was buried at Cruachan. The Irish sent, during the Punic wars, auxiliary troops to their Celtic Brethren, the Gauls; who in their alliance with the Carthaginians under Hannibal, fought against the Roman armies in Spain and Italy.—CONNELLAN.

murdered Monarch's son, who became the 68th Monarch.

60. Colethach Caol-bhreagh : son
of Ugaine Mór ; was the 69th Monarch ; it is said, that, to secure the
Throne, he assassinated his brother
Laeghaire ; after a long reign he
was at length slain by Maion, his
nephew, B.C. 541.

61. Melg Molbhthach : his son ;
was the 71st Monarch ; was slain by
Modhchorb, son of Cobhthach
Caomh, of the Line of Heber Fionn,
B.C. 541.

62. Iaran Gleofathach : his son ;
was the 74th Monarch ; was a King
of great justice and wisdom, ,very
well learned and possessed of many
accomplishments ; slain by Fear-
Chorb, son of Modh-Chorb, B.C.
473.

63. Conla Caomh : his son ; was
the 74th Monarch of Ireland ; died
a natural death, B.C. 442.

64. Olioll Cas-fiachlach : his son ;
was the 77th Monarch ; slain by
his successor, Adhamhar Foltchaion,
B.C. 417.

65. Eochaidh Alt-Leathan : his
son ; was the 79th Monarch ; slain
by Feargus Fortamhail, his successor, B.C. 395.

66. Aongus (or Æneas) Tuirmeach-Teamrach : his son ; was the
81st Monarch ; his son, Fiacha
Firmara (so called from being exposed in a small boat on the sea)
was ancestor of the Kings of
Dalriada and Argyle in Scotland.
This Aongus was slain at Tara
(Teamhrach), B.C. 324.

67. Enna Aigneach : the legitimate son of Aongus ; was the 84th
Monarch ; was of a very bountiful
disposition, and exceedingly muni-
ficent in his donations. This King
lost his life by the hands of Criomthan Cosgrach, B.C. 292.

68. Assaman Eamhna : his son ;

was excluded from the Throne by
his father's murderer.

69. Roighen Ruadh : his son ; in
his time most of the cattle in Ireland died of murrain.

70. Fionnlogh : his son.

71. Fionn : his son ; m. Benia,
dau. of Criomthan ; had two sons.

72. Eochaidh Feidlioch : his son ;
was the 93rd Monarch ; m. Cloth-
fionn, dau. of Eochaidh Uchtlea-
than, who was a very virtuous lady.
By him she had three children at a
birth—Breas, Nar, and Lothar (the
Fineamhas), who were slain at the
battle of Dromchriadh ; after their
death, a melancholy settled on the
Monarch, hence his name "Feidhlioch."

This Monarch caused the division
of the Kingdom by Ugaine Mór
into twenty-five parts, to cease ; and
ordered that the ancient Firvolgian
division into Provinces should be
resumed, viz., Two Munsters,
Leinster, Conacht, and Ulster.

He also divided the government
of these Provinces amongst his
favourite courtiers :—Conacht he
divided into three parts between
Fiodhach, Eochaidh Allat, and
Tinne, son of Conragh, son of
Ruadhri Mór, No 62 on the "Line
of Ir ;" Ulster (Uladh) he gave to
Feargus, the son of Leighe ; Leinster he gave to Ros, the son of
Feargus Fairge ; and the two Munsters he gave to Tighernach Teadh-
bheamach and Deagbadah.

After this division of the Kingdom, Eochaidh proceeded to erect a
Royal Palace in Conacht ; this he
built on Tinne's government in a
place called Druin-na-n Druagh, now
Craughan (from Craughan Crod-
hearg, Maedhbh's mother, to whom
she gave the palace), but previously,
Rath Eochaidh. About the same
time he bestowed his daughter the

Princess Maedhbh on Tinne, whom he constituted King of Conacht; Maedhbh being hereditary Queen of that Province.

After many years reign Tinne was slain by Maceacht (or Monaire) at Tara. After ten years' undivided reign, Queen Maedhbh married Oilioll Mór, son of Ros Ruadh, of Leinster, to whom she bore the seven Maine; Oilioll Mór was at length slain by Conall Cearnach, who was soon after killed by the people of Conacht. Maedhbh was at length slain by Ferbhuidhe, the son of Conor MacNeasa (*Neasa* was his *mother*); but in reality this Conor was the son of Fachtna Fathach, son of Cas, son of Ruadhri Mór, of the Line of Ir.

This Monarch, Eochaidh, died at Tara, B.C. 130.

73. Bress-Nar-Lothar: his son. In his time the Irish first dug graves beneath the surface to bury their dead; previously they laid the body on the surface and heaped stones over it. He had also been named Fineamhnas.

74. Lughaidh Sriabh-n Dearg: his son; was the 98th Monarch; he entered into an alliance with the King of Denmark, whose daughter, Dearborguill, he obtained as his wife; he killed himself by falling on his sword in the eighth year Before CHRIST.

75. Crimthann-Niadh-Nar*: his son; who was the 100th Monarch of Ireland, and styled "The Heroic." It was in this Monarch's reign that our Lord and Saviour JESUS CHRIST was born.

Crimthann's death was occasioned by a fall from his horse, B.C. 9. Was married to Nar-Tath-Chaoch, dau. of Laoch, son of Daire, who lived in the land of the Picts (Scotland).

76. Feredach Fionn-Feachtnach: his son; was the 102nd Monarch. The epithet "feachtnach" was applied to this Monarch because of his *truth and sincerity*. In his reign lived

---

* *Crimthann Niadh Nar:* This Monarch and Conaire Mór (or Conary the Great), the 97th Monarch of Ireland, respectively made expeditions to Britain and Gaul; and assisted the Picts and Britains in their wars with the Romans. Crimthann was married to Bainé, daughter of the King of Alba, and the mother of Feredach Fionn Feachtnach, (the next name on this Stem). O'Flaherty in the *Ogygia*, p. 181, says, "Naira, the daughter of Loich, the son of Dareletus of the northern Picts of Britain, was Crimthann's Queen, after whom, I suppose, he was called *Nia-Nair*."

This Crimthann died at his fortress, called "Dun-Crimthann" (at Bin Edar now the Hill of Howth), after his return from an expedition against the Romans in Britain, from which he brought to Ireland various spoils: amongst other things, a splendid war chariot, gilded and highly ornamented; golden-hilted swords and shields, embossed with silver; a table studded with three hundred brilliant gems; a pair of grey hounds coupled with a splendid silver chain estimated to be worth one hundred cumal ("cumal:" Irish, *a maid servant*), or three hundred cows; together with a great quantity of other precious articles. In this Crimthann's reign the oppression of the Plebeians by the Milesians came to a climax: during three years the oppressed Attacotti saved their scanty earnings to prepare a sumptuous death-feast, which, after Crimthann's death, was held at a place called "Magh Cro" (or the *Field of Blood*), supposed to be situated near Lough Conn in the county of Mayo. To this feast they invited the provincial Kings, nobility, and gentry of the Milesian race in Ireland, with a view to their extirpation; and, when the enjoyment was at its height, the Attacots treacherously murdered almost all their unsuspecting victims.

They then set up a king of their own tribe, a stranger named Cairbre (the 101st Monarch of Ireland), who was called "Cean-Cait" from the *cat-headed* shape of his head: the only king of a stranger that ruled Ireland since the Milesians first arrived there.—CONNELLAN.

Moran,* the son of Maoin, a cele-brated Brehon, or Chief Justice of the Kingdom ; it is said that he was the first who wore the wonderful collar called *Iodhain Morain ;* this collar possessed a wonderful pro-perty :—if the judge who wore it attempted to pass a false judgment it would immediately contract, so as nearly to stop his breathing ; but if he reversed such false sentence the collar would at once enlarge itself, and hang loose around his neck. This collar was also caused to be worn by those who acted as witnesses, so as to test the accuracy of their evidence. This Monarch, Feredach, died a natural death at the regal city at Tara, A.D. 36.

77. Fiacha Fionn Ola† : his son ; was the 104th Monarch ; reigned 17 years, and was (A.D. 56) slain by Eiliomh MacConrach, of the Race of Ir, who succeeded him on the throne. This Fiacha was married to Eithne, daughter of the King of Alba ; whither, being near her con-finement at the death of her hus-band, she went, and was there delivered of a son, who was named Tuathal.

78. Tuathal Teachtmar :‡ that

son ; was the 106th Monarch of Ireland. When Tuathal came of age, he got together his friends, and, with what aid his grandfather the king of Alba gave him, came into Ireland and fought and overcame his enemies in twenty-five battles in Ulster, twenty-five in Leinster, as many in Connaught, and thirty-five in Munster. And having thus restored the true royal blood and heirs to their respective provincial kingdoms, he thought fit to take, as he accordingly did with their consent, fron each of the four divi-sions or provinces of Munster, Leinster, Connaught, and Ulster, a considerable tract of ground which was the next adjoining to Uisneach (where Tuathal had a palace) : one east, another west, a third south, and a fourth on the north of it ; and appointed all four (tracts of ground so taken from the four pro-vinces) under the name of Midhe or "Meath" to belong for ever after to the Monarch's own peculiar demesne for the maintenance of his table ; on each of which several portions he built a royal palace for himself and his heirs and successors ; for every of which portions the Monarch

---

* *Moran* : See the Note "Hebrew" in page 30.

† Fiacha Fionn Ola (or *Fiacha of the White Oxen*) : According to some annalists, it was in this Monarch's reign that the Milesian nobility and gentry of Ireland were treacherously murdered by the Attacotti, as already mentioned ; but, in the "Roll of the Monarchs of Ireland" (see page 58), Cairbre, Cean-Cait, whom the Attacotti set up as a king of their own tribe, is given as the 101st, while this Fiacha is there given as the 104th Monarch of Ireland : therefore Cairbre Cean-Cait reigned before, and not after Fiacha Fionn Ola.

‡ *Tuathal Teachmar* (or Tuathal the *Legitimate*) : It is worthy of remark that Tacitus, in his "Life of Agricola," states that one of the Irish princes, who was an exile from his own country, waited on Agricola, who was then the Roman general in Britain, to solicit his support in the recovery of the kingdom of Ireland ; for that, with one of the Roman legions and a few auxiliaries, Ireland could be subdued. This Irish prince was probably Tuathal Teachtmar, who was about that time in Alba or (Cale-donia). Tuathal afterwards became Monarch of Ireland, and the Four Masters place the first year of his reign at A.D. 76 ; and as Agricola with the Roman legions carried on the war against the Caledonians about A.D. 75 to 78, the period coincides chronologi-cally with the time Tuathal Teachtmar was in exile in North Britain ; and he might naturally be expected to apply to the Romans for aid to recover his sovereignty as heir to the Irish Monarchy.—CONNELLAN.

ordained a certain chiefry or tribute to be yearly paid to the provincial Kings from whose provinces the said portions were taken, which may be seen at large in the Chronicles. It was this Monarch that imposed the great and insupportable fine (or "Eric") of 6,000 cows or beeves, as many fat muttons, (as many) hogs, 6,000 mantles, 6,000 ounces (or " Uinge") of silver, and 12,000 (others have it 6,000) cauldrons or pots of brass, to be paid every second year by the province of Leinster to the Monarchs of Ireland for ever, for the death of his only two daughters Fithir and Darina. (See Paper "Ancient Leinster Tributes,"in the Appendix). This tribute was punctually taken and exacted, sometimes by fire and sword, during the reigns of forty Monarchs of Ireland upwards of six hundred years, until at last remitted by Finachta Fleadhach, the 153rd Monarch of Ireland, and the 26th Christian Monarch, at the request and earnest solicitation of St. Moling. At the end of thirty years' reign, the Monarch Tuathal was slain by his successor Mal, A.D. 106.

This Monarch erected a Royal Palace at Tailtean ; around the grave of Queen Tailte he caused the Fairs to be resumed on *La Lughnasa* (Lewy's Day), to which were brought all of the youth of both sexes of a suitable age to be married, at which Fair the marriage articles were agreed upon, and the ceremony performed.

Tuathal married Baine, the dau. of Sgaile Balbh, King of England.

79. Fedhlimidh (Felim) Rachtmar :† his son ; was so called as being a maker of excellent wholesome laws, among which he established with all firmness that of " Retaliation;" kept to it inviolably ; and by that means preserved the people in peace, quiet, plenty, and security during his time. This Felim was the 108th Monarch ; reigned nine years ; and, after all his pomp and greatness, died of *thirst*, A.D. 119. He married Ughna, dau. of the King of Denmark.

80. Conn Ceadcathach (or Conn of the Hundred Battles*) ; his son ; This Conn was so called from *hundreds of battles* by him fought and

---

† *Felim Rachtmar* : It is singular to remark how the call to a life of virginity was felt and corresponded with first in this family in Ireland after it was Christianized. As St. Ité was descended from Fiácha, a son of this wise Monarch, so the illustrious St. Bridget was (see p. 43) descended from Eocha, another son of Felim, and brother of Conn of the Hundred Battles. St. Brigid was born at Fochard (now Faughart), near Dundalk, about A.D. 453, where her parents happened to be staying at the time ; but their usual place of residence was Kildare, where, A.D. 483, she established the famous Monastery of " Kildare," which signifies the *Church of the Oak.*—MISS CUSACK.

St. Ité or Idé is often called the Brigid of Munster ; she was born about A.D. 480, and was the first who founded a convent in Munster, in a place called Clooncrail : the name of which was afterwards changed to " Kill-Ide," now called *Killedy*, a parish in the county Limerick.—JOYCE.

* *Conn of the Hundred Fights* : This name in Irish is " Conn Cead-Cathach," a designation given to that hero of antiquity, in a Poem by O'Gnive, the bard of O'Neill, which is quoted in the " Philosophical Survey of the South of Ireland," page 423 :

" Conn of the Hundred Fights, sleep in thy grass-grown tomb, and upbraid not our defeats with thy victories."

To that ancient hero and warrior, Moore pays a graceful tribute of respect in the song—" How oft has the Benshee cried," given in the *Irish Melodies.*

According to the popular belief, the " Benshee" or guardian spirit of the House of Conn of the Hundred Fights, above mentioned, night after night, in the Castle of won : viz., sixty battles against Cahir Mór, King of Leinster and the 109th Monarch of Ireland, whom he slew and succeeded in the Monarchy; one hundred battles against the Ulsterians; and one hundred more in Munster against Owen Mór (or Mogha Nua-Dhad), their King, who, notwithstanding, forced the said Conn to an equal division of the Kingdom with him. He had two brothers—1. Eochaidh Fionn-Fohart, 2. Fiacha Suidhe,* who, to make way for themselves, murdered two of their brother's sons named Conla Ruadh and Crionna; but they were by the third son Art Eanfhear banished, first into Leinster, and then into Munster, where they lived near Cashel. They were seated at Deici Teamhrach (now the barony of *Desee* in Meath), whence they were expelled by the Monarch Cormac Ulfhada, son of Art; and, after various wanderings, they went to Munster where Oilioll Olum, who was married to Sadhbh, daughter of Conn of the Hundred Battles, gave them a large district of the present county of Waterford, a part of which is still called *Na-Deiseacha*, or the baronies of *Desies*. They were also given the country comprised in the present baronies of Clonmel, Upper-Third, and Middle-Third, in the co. Tipperary, which they held till the Anglo-Norman Invasion. From Eochaidh Fionn-Fohart decended *O'Nowlan* or *Nolan* of Fowerty (or Foharta), in Lease (or Leix), and Saint Bridget ; and from Fiacha Suidhe are *O'Dolan, O'Brick* of Dunbrick, and *O'Faelan* of Dun Faelan, near Cashel. Conn of the Hundred Battles had also three daughters : 1. Sadhbh, who m. first, MacNiadh, after whose death she m. Oilioll Olum, King of Munster. (See No. 84 on the "Line of Heber"); 2. Maoin; and 3. Sarah (or Sarad), m. to Conan MacMogha Laine.—(See No. 81 *infra*).

Conn reigned 35 years; but was at length barbarously slain by Tiobraidhe Tireach, son of Mal, son of Rochruidhe, King of Ulster. This murder was committed in Tara, A.D. 157, when Conn chanced to be alone and unattended by his guards; the assassins were fifty ruffians, disguised as women, whom the King of Ulster employed for the purpose.

81. Art Eanfhear, the 112th Monarch of Ireland, in the second century of our era, and the ancestor of *O'h-Airt*, anglicised *O'Hart.*

Dungannon, upbraided the famous Hugh O'Neill, for having accepted the Earldom of Tir-Owen, conferred on him by Queen Elizabeth, A.D. 1587. " Hence," writes O'Callaghan, " the Earl did afterwards assume the name of *O'Neill,* and therewith he was so elevated that he would often boast, that he would rather be O'Neill of Ulster than King of Spain." On his submission, however, A.D. 1603, his title and estates were confirmed to him by King James the First.—O'CALLAGHAN.

It is worthy of remark, that, while Conn of the Hundred Battles lived in the second century, we read in the *Tripartite Life of St. Patrick,* that this Pagan Monarch "prophesied" the introduction of Christianity into Ireland !

* *Fiacha Suidhe :* This Fiacha Suidhe was the father of Fiacha Riadhe, the father of Fothadh, the father of Duibhne, the father of Donn, the father of Diarmuid, usually called *Diarmuid Ua Duibhne* (or Diarmuid, the grandson of Duibhne), who married Grainné, daughter of the Monarch Cormac MacArt (or Cormac Ulfhada), and had issue by her: 1. Donchadh, 2. Eochaidh, 3. Ollann, 4. Connla. This Diarmuid O'Duibhne's mother was Corcraine, dau. of Slectaire, son of Curigh, the fourth son of the Monarch Cathair Mór (See No. 89 on the "O'Toole" pedigree). Diarmuid O'Duibhne was the founder of the Clan Campbell, known in the Highlands of Scotland as *Slioch na Diarmuid Ua Duibhne* (or "descendants of Diarmid O'Duibhne"). That Clan Campbell are now known by the name *Campbell ;* they have abandoned the old Irish sirname *O'Duibhne* or *O'Duin.*

AGNEW.

Arms: Or, an eagle displ with two heads gu. surmounted by a lymphad sa. in the dexter chief point a dexter hand couped gu. *Crest:* A raven sa. standing on a rock az.

EOIN (or John) MacDonnell, brother of Æneas Oge, lord of the Isles, who is No. 106 on the "MacDonnell" (of Antrim) pedigree, was the ancestor of *MacGniomhaighe;* anglicised *MacGnieve, O'Gnieve, Agnue,* and *Agnew.*

106. Eoin MacDonnell, surnamed *Gniomhach* ("gniomh:" Irish, *an act;* Lat. "gnav-us," *active*): son of Æneas Mór; a quo *MacGniomhaighe.*
107. Maolmuire : his son.
108. John MacGnieve, of Dunfian: his son ; first assumed this sirname.
109. Patrick: his son.
110. Mulbiadh: his son.
111. Mulbiadh Oge : his son.
112. Cormac: his son.
113. John : his son.

114. Ferdorach*: his son ; a quo *O'Ferdoraigh.*
115. Brian : his son.
116. Fearflatha O'Gnieve : his son ; was *Ollamh* (or Bard) to the O'Neill of Clanaboy, about the year 1556. His "Lament" for the unhappy state of Ireland at that period, is given in O'Connor's "Dissertations on Irish History;" of which the following few stanzas are literally translated from the Irish :

LAMENT OF O'GNIEVE.

How dimm'd is the glory that circled the Gael,
And fallen the people of green Innisfail !
The Sword of the Saxon is read with their gore,
And the mighty of nations is mighty no more.

Like a bark on the ocean long shatter'd and tost,
On the land of your fathers at length you are lost,
The hand of the spoiler is stretched on your plains,
And you're doomed from your cradles to bondage and chains.

O'Neill of the Hostages ; Conn,* whose high name
On a hundred red battles has floated to fame,
Let the long grass still sigh undisturbed o'er thy sleep ;
Arise not to shame us, awake not to weep !

O bondsmen of Egypt, no Moses appears
To light your dark steps thro' this desert of tears,
Degraded and lost ones, no Hector is nigh,
To lead you to freedom, or teach you to die !
——— DUFFY's *Ballad Poetry of Ireland.*

* *Ferdorach:* As a personal name *Ferdorach* ("ferdorcha:" Irish, *the dark featured man*) has been modernized *Frederic, Frederick,* and *Ferdinando ;* as a sirname it was *O'Ferdoraigh,* anglicised *Ferdinand.* In the "O'Neill" (of Ulster) family Ferdorach, son of Conn Baccach, who is No. 121 on that pedigree, was the ancestor of another *O'Ferdoraigh* family, of Tirowen.

† *Conn :* Meaning Conn of the Hundred Battles, the 110th Monarch of Ireland.

ALLEN.*

Arms : Or, on a chev. sa. three martlets ar. betw. as many ogresses, each charged with a talbot or, on a chief az. a demi lion ramp. betw. two dragons' heads erased of the first.

COLLA Meann, a brother of Colla da-Chrioch who is No. 85 on the "O'Hart" pedigree, was the ancestor of *MacAlain*, anglicised *Allan*, and *Allen ;* of *Clan Caroill ; Clann Benain ; Clann Criomhain ; Clann Imanaigh*, etc.

85. Colla Meann : a son of Eochaidh Dubhlen.
86. Breasal : his son; had a brother named Deadhach (or Deach) Dorn.
87. Duach : son of Breasal.
88. Fergus : his son.

89. Masin : his son.
90. Ail : his son ; had a brother named Daol.
91. Alain : his son.
92. Maoldun : his son.
93. Breasal (2) : his son.
94. Ail (2) : his son.

* *Allen* : Of this family was John Allen, Archbishop of Dublin, who had been Treasurer of St. Paul's, London, and was consecrated Archbishop, on the 14th March, 1528 ; being appointed by Cardinal Wolsey, mainly, to resist and embarrass Gerald, Earl of Kildare. During Lord Thomas' revolt in 1534, Archbishop Allen, apprehending a siege of Dublin Castle, endeavoured to escape to England. He embarked at Dame Gate, but his boat stranding at Clontarf, he took refuge in the house of a Mr. Hollywood, at Artane. Early next morning, the 28th July, 1534, Lord Thomas arrived before the house in hot pursuit of him. The Archbishop was dragged out in his shirt, and, falling on his knees, begged for mercy. "Take away the churl," exclaimed Fitzgerald to his followers. The old man was then set upon and murdered. Lord Thomas subsequently, however, insisted that he only meant that the Archbishop should be removed in custody. Archbishop Allen was the author of the *Liber Niger* of Christ's Church.

Colonel John Allen, who was an associate of Robert Emmet's in the *emeute* of 1803, and one in whom Emmet placed unlimited confidence, was also of this family. This John Allen was partner in a woollen-drapery business at 36 College Green. He was after Emmet's failure for a time concealed at Butterfield-lane, and then in Trinity College, escaping eventually as a member of the College Yeomanry Corps. On his arrival in France he entered the army, and, through his daring services, rapidly rose to the rank of Colonel. He served with distinction in the campaign of Leipsic ; he joined Napoleon on his return from Elba ; and it is stated that his surrender was demanded by the British Government, on the second occupation of Paris. At all events he was sent under guard to the frontier, to be delivered up. On the last night of the journey, one of his guard, on conducting him to his room, whispered : " Monsieur le Colonel, the room in which you are to be confined is strong, but one of the iron bars of the window is loose ; *we trust you will not escape.*" He took the hint, and regained his liberty. He spent the remainder of his life in Normandy ; the precise date of his death is not known, but he was living in 1846.

William Philip Allen, an enthusiatic Fenian, was also of this family. He was born in April, 1848, near the town of Tipperary, his father being a Protestant and his mother a Catholic. When Allen was three years old, his father moved to Bandon, where the boy was educated at a Protestant school, but he eventually became a Catholic. He was apprenticed to a carpenter; but before his apprenticeship expired, he worked in Cork, Dublin, and Chester. He incited his countrymen in Manchester to attempt the rescue of his friend Colonel Kelly. On the 18th September, 1867, with a small body of confederates he effected Kelly's release from a prison van which was strongly guarded by police. In the *melée,* a police-sergeant named Brett was killed. Allen and twenty-five others were taken and tried ; and Allen, O'Brien, Larkin,

95. Alain (2): his son; a quo *MacAlain* ("alain:" Irish, *fair*).

96. Aibhsidh : his son ; a quo *Siol Aibhsidh*.

97. Olioll: his son.

98. Artrigh : his son ; a quo *Clann Artrigh*.

99. Suibhneach: his son ; had a brother named Cathal, a quo *Clann Cathail* (or *Cahill*), of Ulster.

100. Aonan† : ("aon:" Irish, *the one*): son of Suibhneach; a quo *O'h-Aonain*, anglicised *Heenan*. This Aonan had a brother named Lagnan, a quo *O'Lagnain*, anglicised *Lannen*.

101. Solomon: son of Aonan.

102. Ostan : his son.

103. Amhailgadh : his son.

104. Gilciaran : his son.

105. Maolruanaidh MacAllen, MacAllan (or MacAlin): his son.

BAKER.

Arms: Gu. on a cross pattée or, five annulets sa.

LONGSEACH, a brother of Muireadach who is No. 98 on the "Flinn" (of Ulster) pedigree, was the ancestor of *O'Tuirtre :* anglicised *Baker.*

98. Longseach: son of Inrach-tach.

99. Aodh : his son.

100. Dubhsionach : his son.

101. Maolchobha : his son.

102. Muireachan : his son.

103. Flann : his son.

104. Muirceartach : his son.

105. Muireadach : his son.

106. Flann O'Tuirtre : his son.

BARNEWALL.*

Arms : Az. a saltire engr. betw. four crescents ar. *Crest :* An arm from the elbow vested and holding a martlet betw. two branches of laurel in orle.

BERNARD O'BEIRNE, brother of Gillcoman, who is No. 112 on the "O'Beirne" pedigree, was the ancestor of *Barnewall, Barnewell, Barne, Barnes, Bernes,* and *Berens.*

112. Bernard : son of Iomhar.

113. Edward : his son.

114. Edward Dubh : his son.

115. Edward (3) : his son.

Condon, and Maguire, were sentenced to death. Maguire was subsequently pardoned as being innocent (though sworn to by ten witnesses as an active member of the releasing party), and Condon, as an American citizen, was respited. Allen and his friends made spirited and manly speeches before sentence. It was on that occasion that the words "God save Ireland," were first uttered by one of the prisoners after conviction. Allen, O'Brien, and Larkin were executed at the old prison, Manchester, on the 23rd Nov., 1867 ; their bodies were ultimately interred in the new prison, Manchester.

* *Aonan :* This name signifies "the darling of the family."

† *Barnewall :* It is claimed for this family that their ancestors came to Ireland originally with Henry II., and received large grants of land in the county of Cork. And it is said that on the first favourable opportunity the O'Sullivan's, who had been previously in possession of those lands, rose and murdered the whole family, save one

116. Thomas: his son.
117. Richard : his son.
118. James : his son.
119. Walter : his son.
120. Edward (4) : his son.
121. George: his son.
122. Patrick: his son.
123. Edward (5): his son.

124. Sir Christopher : his son.
125. Sir Patrick : his son.
126. Sir Nicholas : his son.
127. Lord Viscount Kingsland :* his son ; the first peer in this family ; b. 1668, d. 1725.
128. Lord Viscount Kingsland : his son.

BEATTY.†

The *Arms* of "Battie" are : Sa. a chev. betw. three goats ar. each goat charged with two pellets, on a chief of the last a demi woodman with a club erect ppr. betw. two cinquefoils gu. *Crest:* A stork with a fish in the beak all ppr.

ACCORDING to Tipper's "Collection of Pedigrees," written in the Irish language, A.D. 1713, Goffrey, one of the princes from Scotland, who, siding with the Irish Monarch Brian Boru, fought at the battle of Clontarf, in 1014, was the ancestor of *Betagh,* modernized *Beattie, Beatty, Beaty, Beytagh,* and *Battie.*

1. Goffrey (or Jeffrey).
2. Comhgall : his son.
3. Maolcolum : his son ; had a

brother named Constantine, who was the ancestor of *Tobin.*
4. Alpin : son of Maolcolum.

young man who was absent studying law in England. This young man ultimately returned, and settled at Drimnagh, near Dublin. A descendant of his was John Barnewall, Lord Trimbleston, who rose to high office in Ireland, under Henry VIII., and received grants of land near Dunleer. In 1536, with Lord-Treasurer Brabazon, he made an incursion in Offaley, and drove back the O'Connor Faley, who was then ravaging the Anglo-Irish Settlements. The next year, commissioned by the Privy Council, Lord Trimbleston treated successfully with the O'Neill. He was four times married ; and died on the 25th July, 1538.

* *Kingsland:* Nicholas Barnewall, Viscount Kingsland, was born on the 15th April, 1668. The family had been ennobled by King Charles I., on the 12th September, 1645, for loyalty to his cause. Before Nicholas was of age he married a daughter of George, Count Hamilton, by his wife Frances Jennings, afterwards married to the Earl of Tyrconnell. In 1688 he entered King's James's Irish army as Captain in the Earl of Limerick's Dragoons. After the defeat of the Boyne, he was moved to Limerick ; and, being in that city at the time of its surrender, was included in the Articles and secured his estates. In the first Irish Parliament of William III., Viscount Kingsland took the oath of allegiance, but upon declining to subscribe the declaration according to the English Act, as contrary to his conscience, he was obliged to withdraw with the other Catholic lords. In February, 1703, he joined with many Irish Catholics in an unavailing petition against the infraction of the Treaty of Limerick. He died on the 14th June, 1725, and was buried at Lusk, in the county Dublin.
Evidently, John Barnewall, Lord Trimbleston and Nicholas Barnewall, Lord Viscount Kingston, mentioned in these Notes, were not of the same family !

† *Beatty:* This pedigree is here incidentally given among the families descended from Heremon ; but while *Beatty* and *Battie* are of Irish origin, the lineage of the family is not yet ascertained. The names are derived from the Irish *biadhtach* [bee-a-ta], "a public victualler"—For information in relation to the ancient *biatachs* in Ireland, see Paper "Monasteries," in the Appendix.

5. Sealbhaidh: his son.
6. Amhailgadh [awly] : his son.
7. Scanlan : his son.
8. Dolbh, of the Orkney Isles : his son.
9. Dolbh, of Loch Broin: his son.
10. Loarn : his son.
11. Constantine : his son.
12. John Mór : his son.
13. William : his son.
14. Richard: his son.

15. Garrett: his son; the first of this family who returned to live in Ireland.
16. John Betagh: his son; first assumed this sirname.
17. Henry ; his son.
18. William an Fhiona) or " William of the Wine") : his son.
19. Edward : his son.
20. John : his son.
21. Garrett Beatty : his son.

BINNEY.

Arms : Ar. a bend sa. betw. a cinquefoil in chief gu. and a sword in pale az. bladed or.   *Crest :* A horse's head bridled.   *Motto :* Virtute opere.

EACHACH BINNEACH, a brother of Muireadhach, who is No. 89 on the " O'Neill" (of Ulster) pedigree, was the ancestor of *Cinneal mBinnigh,* or *O Binnigh ;* anglicised *Binney, Binnie, Benny, Bennie,* and *Benzy.*

89. Eachach Binneach (" binn :" Irish, *melodious*): son of Eoghan ; a quo *O'Binnigh.*
90. Lairan : his son.
91. Domhnall : his son.
92. Ultan : his son.
93. Failbhe Mleme : his son.
94. Maolduin : his son.
95. Cobhrach : his son.
96. Ealghonach : his son.

97. Cugalann : his son.
98. Teidin : his son.
99. Dubhrailbhe : his son.
100. Cinneadhach : his son.
101. Ciarmhach : his son.
102. Maolduin : his son.
103. Curailge : his son.
104. Cuchairn : his son.
105. Donchadh : his son.

BIRCH.

Arms : Az. on a chev. betw. three griffins' heads ar. as many lozenges of the first. *Crest :* A griffin's head erased holding in the mouth a birch branch ppr. and charged on the shoulder with a lozenge sa.

BOIRCHE, brother of Aodh (or Hugh), who is No. 107 on the " MacSweeney" pedigree, was the ancestor of *MacBuirche ;* anglicised *Birch.*

107. Boirche (" boirche :" Irish, *a groaning*): son of Anrachan, a quo *MacBuirche.*
108. Aodh Alainn : his son.
109. Dunsleibhe : his son.
110. Fearcar : his son.
111. Giolla Colum : his son.
112. Ladhman (" ladh :" Irish,

preparation; " man," Lat. " *manus,*" *the hand*) : his son ; a quo *MacLadhmuin,* anglicised *Lamman, Lammond* and *Lavan.*
113. Giolla Colum: his son.
114. Eoin : his son.
115. Donchadh : his son.

BOLAND.

Of Ulster.

Arms : Sa. three fleurs-de-lis ar.   *Crest :* A church and spire ppr.

DUNGAL, brother of Fergal, who is No. 101 on the "Donnelly" pedigree, was the ancestor of *O'Beoilain* ("beul :" Irish, *a mouth ;* Gr. "bel-os," *a threshold*); anglicised *Beolan, Boland, Boylan,* and *Boyland.*

BOYLE.

Arms : Or, an oak tree eradicated vert.   *Crest ;* A human heart gu. betw. a cross and sword in saltire ppr.

MAOLDUN, a brother of Muriartus, who is No. 99 on the "O'Donnell" (Tyrconnell) pedigree, was the ancestor of *O'Baoghail ;* anglicised *Boghill, Boyle, O'Boyle,* and *Hill.*

99. Maoldun : son of Ceannfaola.

100. Arnel : his son.

101. Ceannfaola : his son.

102. Murtagh : his son.

103. Bradachan : his son.

104. Baoghal ("baoghal :" Irish, *peril*) : his son ; a quo *O'Baoghail.*

105. Garbhan : his son.

106. Aneisleis O'Boyle : his son ; the first who assumed this sirname.

107. Gillbrighid : his son.

108. Ceallach : his son.

109. Connor : his son.

110. Menmon : his son.

111. Aneisleis (2) : his son.

112. Aodh : his son.

113. Menmon : his son.

114. Neal Ruadh : his son.

115. Tirlogh Mór : his son.

116. Tirlogh Oge : his son.

117. Neal (2) : his son.

118. Tirlogh (3) : his son.

119. Teige : his son.

120. Teige Oge : his son.

121. Tirlogh Roe : his son ; the last chief of his name.

122. Neal Boyle : his son ; was the first of the direct line of this family that omitted the prefix *O.*

123. John Boyle, of Largey, Portgleneone, county Antrim : his son. This John was exiled to America in 1801, in consequence of his having taken part in the "Irish Rebellion" of 1798 ; he died in 1849.

124. Junius J. Boyle :* his son ; Commodore, United States Navy, America ; died in 1870. This Junius had four brothers—1. John-Franklin, 2. Eugene, 3. Cornelius,† 3. Nicholas-Bourke Boyle, and two sisters named — 1. Lavinia, 2. Catherine-Anne.

---

* *Junius J. Boyle :* Commodore Boyle died at the Naval Hospital at Norfolk, Va., in the 63rd year of his age. He was born in Maryland ; entered the United States Navy as a Midshipman in 1823 ; and deeply loved Ireland—the country of his fathers. A sailor by profession, Commodore Boyle, wishing to rest when dead under the broad ocean that had been his home while living, requested to be buried at sea ; but from some cause or other it was not thought advisable to comply with his request ; he was buried in the cemetery attached to the hospital grounds.

† *Cornelius :* This Cornelius Boyle, a physician in Washington ; was living in 1877.

125. Juan Boyle, of Washington D.C. United States, America: son of said Junius, living in 1877. This Juan had five sisters—1. Oceana-Cecilia, married to T. Stewart Sedgwick, Civil Engineer; 2. Emily-Beale, married to the Hon. Z. Potut, of Maryland; 3. Esmeralda; 4. Anna; and 5. Rebecca-Clyde.

126. Juan-Ashton Boyle; his son; born in 1876; living in 1877.

BRADY.* (No. 2.)
Of Brefny.

Arms: Sa. in the dexter chief point a sun, in the sinister vase a hand pointing thereto ppr. *Crest*: A cherub.

NEAL CAOCH O'REILLY, brother of Donal, who is No. 114 on the "O'Reilly" pedigree, was the ancestor of *MacBruide* and *O'Bruide;* anglicised respectively *MacBride*, and *O'Brady*.

114. Neal Caoch: son of Charles.
115. Maithan: his son.
116. Gilbruidhe ("bruid:" Irish, *a stupid person*): his son; a quo *MacBruidhe* and *O'Bruidhe*. This Gillbruidhe had a brother named Cathal Caoch ("caoch:" Irish, *dim-sighted*) who was the ancestor of *Clann Caoiche*, anglicised *Kee*, *Key*, *Kay*, *Kayes*, and, some say, *Cox*.

117. Tiernan O'Brady: son of Gilbruidhe; was the first of this family who assumed this sirname.
118. Giollaiosa: his son.
119. Donoch: his son.
120. Donal: his son.
121. Neal O'Brady:† his son.

* *Brady*: According to MacFirbis, Cearbhall, a brother of Dubhcron, who is No. 103 on the "O'Reilly" pedigree, was the ancestor of *MacBradaigh*, of Brefney; anglicised *Brady*.

103. Cearbhall: son of Maolmordha.
104. Bradach Mgheasdall ("*bradach :*" Irish, *roguish, love-making*); his son; a quo *MacBradaigh*.
105. Domhnall (Donall): his son.
106. Gillbruidhe: his son.

107. Tighearnan: his son.
108. Giollaiosa: his son.
109. Donchadh: his son.
110. Donall: his son.
111. Niall MacBradaigh: his son.

† *O'Brady*: Of this family was Field-Marshal Brady, who was born in the co. Cavan, in the middle of the 18th century. The son of a farmer, he gave promise of ability, and was sent to Vienna to study for the priesthood. One day the Empress Maria Theresa passed the students in review, and, observing the bearing of young Brady, remarked to Colonel Browne, an Irishman: "What a pity it is so fine a young fellow should not be in the army—what was he saying just now ?" "Your Majesty," replied Browne, "he said that your were a beautiful lady, and he only wished he had the honour to serve your Majesty." He was taken into the army and rose rapidly in the service; and as Field-Marshal and Baron distinguished himself in the defence of his adopted country against Napoleon. He married an offshoot of the Imperial family, and died without issue, at Vienna, in 1826.

BRASSIL.

BREASAL, a brother of Tuathal Cruinnbheul, who is No. 88 on the "O'Brassil" (west) pedigree, was the ancestor of *O'Breasail ;* anglicised *Brassil,* and *Brazil.*

88. Breasal (" breas :" Irish, *a prince ;* " all" *mighty*): son of Felim : a quo *O'Breasail.*
89. Fec : his son.
90. Connall : his son.
91. Olioll : his son.
92. Tuathal : his son.

93. Cronan : his son.
94. Finghin : his son.
95. Maolduin : his son.
96. Conchobar : his son.
97. Cumuscach : his son ; had a brother named Buachaill.

BREEN.

Lords of Brawney.

Arms : Or, a dexter hand couped at the wrist gu, on a chief of the last a mullet betw. two crescents ar.

CRIMTHANN, brother of Aodh (or Hugh) who is No. 91 on the "Fox" pedigree, was the ancestor of *O'Braoin ;* anglicised *Breen,* and *Brawne.**

91. Crimthan : son of Breannan.
92. Donall : his son ; had a brother named Maolfogartach, who was the ancestor of *Magawley ;* and a brother named Anmire, who was the ancestor of *Macnamee, Corgawney, Slaman,* etc.
93. Flanchaidh : son of Donall.
94. Rorc : his son.

95. Braon (" braon": Irish, *a drop*): his son ; a quo *O'Braoin,* lords of " Brawney," near Athlone.
96. Eachtighearna : his son.
97. Florence : his son.
98. Sitric : his son.
99. Eachtighearna O'Braoin (or O'Breen : his son.

* *Brawne :* Of this family the *Arms* are : Ar. three bars sa. on a canton gu. a saltire of the field.

BRENAN. (No. 1.)

Princes of Idough, or North Kilkenny.

Arms : Gu. two lions ramp. combatant supporting garb all or, in chief three swords, two in saltire, points upwards, and one fesseways, point to the dexter ar. pommels and hilt gold.　*Crest :* An arm embowed in armour grasping a sword all ppr. *Motto :* Si Deus nobiscum, quis contra nos.

BRAONAN, a younger brother of Ceallach who is No. 111 on the "Fitz-patrick" (No. 1) pedigree (and who was the 17th King of Ossory), was the ancestor of *O'Braoinan ;* anglicised *O'Brenan, Brenan, Brenon,* and *Brennan** of Idough.

111. Braonan ("braon": Irish, *a drop ;* "an," *one who*): a younger son of Cearbhall, who was King of Ossory and of the Danes of Dublin. This Braonan was created by his father the first "Prince of Idough." 112. Congalach, Prince of Idough : his son; killed in battle in his royal rath near Three Castles, co. Kil-kenny, by the King of Ossory. 113. Dunsleibhe, Prince of Idough: his son; m. dau. of O'Toole, and had Cearbhall (of whom presently), and a dau. Mairé, who m. Donal, King of Ossory. 114. Cearbhall, Prince of Idough : his son. 115. G u i d h e l g e d h, Prince of Idough; his son; m. dau. of O'Moore and had :

I. Gillacoimde, of whom pre-sently.

II. Anne, who m. Donogh, King of Ossory. III. Mairé, who m. O'Toole, Prince of Imaile. 116. Gillacoimde : son of Guid-helgedh. 117. Auliff Mór: his son; had a brother Awley. 118. Murtogh: son of Awley. 119. Auliff Oge : son of Murtogh ; m. dau. of O'Byrne. 120. Murtogh Oge : his son; had two sons:—1. Dermod Reagh, Prince of Idough, who m. dau. of Geoffrey Fitzpatrick, King of Ossory, and had Teige, his Tanist ; 2. John Ruadh, who with his bro-ther and brother's son Teige was killed† by the English in 1395. 121. Dermod Reagh: son of Mur-togh ; killed in 1395.

(For the information respecting

* *Brennan :* Of this family were Doctor John Brenan, Archbishop of Cashel, in the 17th century, and a bosom friend of the martyred Archbishop Oliver Plunket ; John Brenan, the Dramatist and Painter ; and Doctor John Brenan, the famous "Wrestling Doctor," and editor of the *Milesian Magazine.*—See the new *Dictionary of Biography* (1886.) Of this last mentioned John Brenan, WEBB, in his *Compendium of Irish Biography,* writes :—"John Brenan, M.D., born at Ballahide, county Carlow, about 1768. He was educated to the Medical Profession, and obtained a wide reputation for his successful practice in puerperal disorders. An excellent classical scholar, a man of talent and humour, whose sallies were long remembered. As editor of the *Milesian Magazine* he unhappily prostituted his talents, by ridiculing for pay the Catholic leaders of his day, and abusing the members of his own profession. He died in Dublin, on the 29th July, 1830, aged 61. In *Notes and Queries,* 3rd Series, will be found reference to a copy of the *Milesian Magazine,* in the British Museum, containing a MS. Key to Brenan's pseudonyms."

† *Killed :* In the Patent Rolls is mentioned that Dermod O'Brenan, Prince of Idough, his son Teige, and Dermod's brother John, were in 1395 killed by the English ; and it is stated that they were heads of the Irish then in rebellion.

this family, from this Dermod Reagh O'Brenan, down to the Commonwealth period, we are indebted to State Records in Ormonde Castle, Kilkenny):

1. S i r Geoffrey O'Brennan, Knighted by King Richard II.; received "Patent of English Liberty" in 1392; d. 1436.

2. S i r Gilpatrick O'Brenan, Knighted by the Earl of Ormonde, in 1440; m. dau. of Art MacMorough, Prince of Leinster; received "Patent of Liberty."

3. Sir Art O'Brenan, Knighted by Lord Ormonde (and is said to have been created a "Baron"), in 1499; m. dau. of Henry Dillon of Knockshinnagh; d. 1509; called the "Last Prince of Idough;" had two sons:—1. Gilpatrick, 2. Teige.

4. Teige, Chief of his name: son of Sir Art; living in 1520 at Castlecomer Castle; called "The Good," by the country people to this day.

5. Gilpatrick O'Brenan pardoned by Queen Elizabeth; d. 1566.

6. John O'Brenan, pardoned by Queen Elizabeth; called "Son of Gilpatrick, son of Teige;" settled at Rath Kyle Castle, near Castlecomer; m. dau. of Honble. Callogh Fitzpatrick, and had issue.

7. Gilpatrick O'Brenan of Rath Kyle Castle, the last recognized Chief of his name; Sheriff or Justice of Fassadun in 1612, and Esquire of Fassadun in 1615; m. Margaret (d. 1624), heiress and dau. of Pierce Purcell, last Baron of Ballyfoyle; d. 1628.

8. John O'Brenan of Rathkyle Castle and Ballyfoyle Castle, county Kilkenny; son of Gilpatrick; had a brother Owen, of Ardra, who had a son John Brenan, who was Archbishop of Cashel. This John (No. 8) who is, in the State Records called "John McGilpatrick O'Brenan," was a member of the Con-

federation of Kilkenny, and was dispossessed of his estates by Oliver Cromwell; m. Mary, dau. of John Grace, Baron of Courtstown; d. in poverty in 1654.

9. Gerald O'Brenan is styled "Papist and Rebel;" lived in poverty in Castlecomer.

10. John Brenan: son of Gerald; was an Officer in Hon. Colonel Edmond Butler's Infantry Regiment for James II., and was killed at the Battle of Aughrim in 1691. He m. Elizabeth, dau. of Lt. Colonel John Lalor of Tenekill, Mountrath, Queen's County, and had three sons:

I. Gerald, who settled at Knocknadoge, Castlecomer, of whom presently

II. John, of Dublin, whose son John Brenan was Dramatist and Painter, and Author of "The Painter's Breakfast."

III. Patrick (d. 1768), who settled in Kilkenny and had:—1. John, of St. Mary's parish, Kilkenny, "Gent.," who was father of Rev. Thomas Brenan, C.C., of St. Mary's, Kilkenny, and living in 1790; 2. Rev. James Brenan, P.P., of Castletown, who was b. 1734, and d. 1795.

11. Gerald: eldest son of John, settled at Knocknadoge House, Castlecomer; m. Margaret, dau. of Nicholas Lalor, of Tenekill, and had:—1. John, who, in 1776, d. unm., and in his father's lifetime; 2. Nicholas.

12. Nicholas Ruadh Brenan (d. 1799): ·younger son of Gerald, of Knocknadoge House; m. Elizabeth, dau. of James Cullinan, of Conahy House, co. Kilkenny, and had three sons and two daughters:

I. Gerald, of whom presently.

II. John, who, s. p. "died for Ireland, at the fight at Castlecomer in 1798."

2 A

III. Captain James Brenan, of Knocknadoge House, an Officer in the Kilkenny Yeomanry, d. s. p. in 1805.

The two daughters were :

I. Mary, who m. Denis Brenan of Woodview House, Woodview, co. Kilkenny, and had issue.

II. Elinor, who m. John Lalor of Dunmore Lodge, Dunmore, co. Kilkenny, and had issue.

13. Gerald (d. 1832), of Eden Hall, Ballyraggett, co. Kilkenny ; m. Elinor, dau. and heiress of Pierce Butler, lord of the Manor of Nichols-town, Queen's County (confiscated in 1554), and had two sons and one daughter.

I. John Gerald Maher Brenan, of whom presently.

II. Pierce Maher Brenan, died young.

The daughter was :

I. Mary, who m. Richard Lalor, J.P., of Cascade Place, Fresh-ford, co. Kilkenny, and had the Hon. Richard Lalor, Senator of the United States, America, Poet and Orator, who d. 1835, s. p.

14. John Gerald Maher Brenan (d. 1865), J.P., of Eden Hall, Bally-raggett, and of Nicholstown Manor :

son of Gerald ; m. dau. of Henry Loughnan, J.P. and B.A., of Crow-hill Lodge, Freshford, and had two sons and a daughter :

I. Gerald John Loughnan Brenan, J.P., of whom presently,

II. Henry Austin Diarmid Lough-nan Brenan (solicitor), of Shees-town, co. Kilkenny, and St. James's Terrace, Clonskeagh, Dublin, who m. and has issue.

I. Mary (d. 1880), who m. Joseph Maher Loughnan, late Lieu-tenant in Royal Artillery, now (1887) an Inspector of Irish National Schools, and had William Brenan Loughnan, b. 1880.

15. Gerald John Loughnan Brenan, J.P., "The O'Brenan," of Eden Hall, and Nicholstown Manor: son of John Gerald Maher Brenan ; living in 1887; b. 1840; m. Eleanor, dau. and heiress of Richard Feehan, of Carrick-on-Suir, and had :

I. John Gerald Feehan Brenan, of whom presently.

II. Richard Henry Gilpatrick Loughnan Brenan, b. 1872.

16. John Gerald Feehan Brenan : elder son of Gerald John ; b. 1869, and living in 1887.

BRENAN.* (No. 2.)

Arms : See those of " Brenan" (No. 1.)

1. Richard Brenan of Bally-brenan, county Wexford.

2. James : his second son.

3. Walter of Rosgarland, county

---

* *Brenan* : Of this family were Doctor James Brenan, of the Society of Surgeons, Ireland, who was born in 1685, and died in 1738 ; and who by his Will directed that his body should be interred in the family burial place in the Parish of New St. Michan's, in the *suburbs* of Dublin. He bequeathed his anatomical specimens to his brother, Peter Brenan, "Chirurgeon," who was born on the 30th July, 1705 (old style), and died in February, 1767. Said Peter Brenan bequeathed his surgical instruments, books, and anatomical specimens to Michael Keogh, a member of the Society of Surgeons, Dublin, and one of the first members of the College.

——; m. Margaret, dau. of James Forlong of Hoartown, co. Wexford; d. 3rd March, 1638.

4. Marck Brenan : his son ; m. Margaret, dau. of Francis Talbot of Ballinamony, county Wexford;

had one brother and two sisters: the brother was—James; and the sisters were—1. Kathleen, married to Walter Breen of Rosegarlande, 2. Anastace.

BRESLIN.

Arms: Az. two lions ramp. combatant supporting a garb or, in dexter base a crescent ar., and in the sinister, the harp of Ireland.

CONALL GREANTA, brother of Fogartach who is No. 95 on the "Fogarty" pedigree, was the ancestor of *O'Brislain;* anglicised *Breslin,* and *Brislane.*

95. Conall Greanta ("greanta:" Irish : *neat, handy*): son of Neal ; a quo *Grant.*

96. Neal : his son.

97. Fergus : his son.

98. Cearnach : his son; whose brother Muredach was the ancestor of *Spillane;* and other brother

Olioll, the ancestor of *O'Braonan,* anglicised *Brenham.*

99. Muldroman : son of Cearnach.

100. Brislann ("bris :" Irish, *to break;* Heb. "peras," *to break ;* "lann," Irish, *the blade of a sword*) : his son ; a quo *O'Brislaine.*

BRODY.

FIACHA CASAN, a brother of Rochadh, who is No. 86 on the "O'Hart" pedigree, was the ancestor of *O'Broduigh;* anglicised *Brody* and *Brodie.*

86. Fiacha Casan: son of Colla da Chrioch.

87. Fedhlim : his son.

88. Eochaidh : his son.

89. Oill : his son.

90. Amhalgadh : his son.

91. Feareadhach Culdubh: his son.

92. Maolodhar Caoch, also called brodach ("brodach :" Irish, *proud*): his son ; a quo *O'Broduigh.*

93. Sionnach : his son.

94. Dubh-da-lethe: his son.

95. Areachtach : his son.

96. Caomhan : his son.

97. Flannagan : his son.

98. Ceallach : his son.

99. Eochaidh : his son.

100. Maolmuire : his son.

101. Amhalgadh : his son.

102. Maoliosa : his son.

103. Aodh : his son.

104. Ceallach O'Broduigh: his son.

BURN.

Arms : Sa. three bezants.   *Crest :* A roundle az.

CUMASCACH, another brother of Fogartach, who is No. 95 on the " Fogarty" pedigree, was the ancestor of *O'Braoin ;* in this case anglicised *Burn, Burne, Bourns,* and *Burns.*

95. Cumascach : son of Neal ; had a brother named Conall Greanta.

96. Fogartach : son of Cumascach.

97. Cairbre : his son ; whose younger brother Fogartach was the ancestor of *MacGilcunny.*

98. Flahertach : son of Cairbre.

99. Cormac : his son.

100. Maolmordha (" mordha :" Irish, *proud :* his son ; a quo *O'Maolmordha,* anglicised *Mordie.*

101. Braon (" braon :" Irish, *a drop*): his son ; a quo *O'Braoin.*

CAHILL.

Of Connaught.

Arms : Gyronny of six ar. and vert. as many fleurs-de-lis counter changed.   *Crest :* A lion's paw holding a scimitar ppr.

AODH (or Hugh) a brother of Columhan, who is No. 94 on the " O'Shaughnessy" pedigree, was the ancestor of *MacCathail ;* anglicised *Cahill.*

94. Aodh : son of Cobhthach.

95. Bec : his son.

96. Comuscach : his son.

97. Conchobhar : his son.

98. Thorp (" torp :" Irish, *bulk*): his son ; a quo *O'Thorpa,* anglicised *Thorp, Thorpe, Torpy,* and *Tarpy.*

99. Cinaoth : his son.

100. Bracan : his son.

101. Ogan : his son.

102. Cathal (" cathal :" Irish, *valour ;* Heb. *cail,* a man's name): his son ; a quo *MacCathail.*

CAINE.

Of Manchester.

* *Arms ;* Sa. a phœnix ar.   *Crest :* A demi antelope per fesse az. and ar. collared and armed or.

THOMAS, a younger brother of Richard, who is No. 123 on the " O'Cahan" pedigree, was the ancestor of this family.

123. Thomas O'Cahan : son of Richard ; embraced the cause of King James II., and, on the over-throw of that Monarch in Ireland, at the battle of the Boyne, sought retirement in the county Leitrim.

124. Simon O'Cahan: his only child, born 1717, died 1790. Joined the standard of the "Young Pretender," in 1745; returned to Ireland, m. and had five daughters and four sons:

I. Thomas, of whom presently.

II. Dominic, had three sons and one daughter:

1. John; 2. James; 3. Myles— the three of whom died in the flower of their age and without issue: Myles the last survivor of them d. at New York in 1872.

1. Mary.

III. Myles; IV. John—both of whom died in early manhood.

I. Mary; II. Bessie; III. Sabina; IV. Bridgid; V. Honora.

125. Thomas O'Cahan: eldest son of Simon; b. 1766; d. 1844; and buried in Cloone, county Leitrim Took an active part in the Irish Insurrection* of 1798, and was present at the Battle of Ballinamuck, where he led a troop of irregular horse. He was known as the Insurgent Leader "Captain Rock," of the county Leitrim, in the latter part of the past, and early years of the present century: and in that county is still affectionately remembered, and his memory revered as the "Old Captain."

* *Insurrection*: To sustain the Irish Insurrection of 1798, French troops then landed in Ireland; and when a detachment of them had reached Cloone, on their way to the county Longford, the officer in charge was invited by a Mr. West, who lived there at that time, to share his hospitality. This hospitality the officer thankfully accepted; and, for greater security, caused the French Magazine, as advised by Mr. West (himself a Protestant gentleman), to be deposited in the Protestant church-yard of that place. Mr. West had a servant-man named Keegan, whom West induced to steal the chains of the Magazine, which Keegan did that night; so that the chains being gone, the French next morning, after having tried and broken every species of rope obtainable in the place, in their efforts to remove their guns, were reluctantly compelled to empty most of the contents of their Magazine into the Lough in the neighbourhood; and were thus rendered absolutely powerless to meet the British troops. That robbery precipitated the Battle of Ballinamuck; for, there was no intention on the part of the insurgents to engage in that vicinity: their object was to push on to Granard, where a fine body of men were awaiting the French contingent and the bold peasantry of Connaught who accompanied them.

This Thomas O'Cahan (or "Tom" O'Cahan, as he was generally called) had a friend named Terence MacGlawin, who at that Battle acted as his lieutenant, and who in the early part of the action was shot dead at the "Old Captain's" side, by a ball in the head. He had the body removed to the rear, but was at the time unable to carry it off. After the action, Captain Crofton of Lurragoe (a brother of Duke Crofton of Mohill Castle), who was going over the field, recognized the body of MacGlawin, had the ball probed for, and bought his coat from one of the human vultures who ever hang on the rear of death and destruction. The coat and ball the kind-hearted Captain Crofton gave to the unhappy mother of MacGlawin; and, two days after the Battle, gave Tom O'Cahan a "Pass," which enabled him with safety to visit the Battlefield of Ballinamuck. In presence of his royalist enemies this bold "rebel," was thus enabled to remove therefrom for interment in the family grave the body of his friend-in-arms—Lieutenant Terry MacGlawin. It was a noble idea of this Thomas O'Cahan to have back his friend's body in *death;* when the other "rebel" unfortunates who fell at that Battle were buried in ditches and all manner of holes.

Another incident of the Battle of Ballinamuck relates to a private soldier of the Longford Militia, named Magee. As the French saw there was no chance of success, they surrendered. When about doing so, this Magee rushed to one of their guns. It was loaded and ready, he applied the light, and sent the ball with unerring aim against and into a Magazine belonging to one of the English regiments. The Magazine exploded, and made death, havoc, and wide gaps in the British ranks adjacent. More fell by that one shot of Magee's than by the hand or act of any other man on that day. The British troops made for him and the gun; but the noble fellow scorned to fly: he fought to the last, and fell gun and bayonet in hand, with his face to the front! See also the Note under the "O'Dowd" pedigree.

126. Simon-Henry O'Cahan, of Manchester, England, a manufacturer, and trading as "Henry Caine and Co.:" his son; born 1805; and living in 1881. Was the first of his branch of the family that omitted the prefix *O'*, and wrote the name *Cahan*. He afterwards in 1850, assumed the name *Caine*. Surviving issue two sons and two daughters:

I. Thomas, of whom presently.

II. James-Henry, formerly of the 3rd Regiment "The Buffs;" living in 1881.

I. Helena. II. Mary.

127. Thomas Caine, of Manchester, formerly of the 3rd Regiment, "The Buffs:" son of Simon-Henry; born 1845, and living in 1881.

CAIRNS.

Arms : Gu. an anchor between three martlets or. *Crest* : A palm tree ppr. *Motto* : Virtus ad æthera tendit.

FINACHTACH (*fionn-sneachta:* Irish, "fair as snow,") who is No. 100 on the "O'Hart" pedigree, had three sons—1. Art, 2. Conmaol, and 3. Fogharthach : this Fogharthach, was the ancestor of *O'Cairn** ("carn :" Irish, *a heap;* Arab. "kern," *a little hill*), anglicised *Cairn, MacCairn, Cairnes, Cairns, Kearin, Kearins, Kearns, Kerans, Kerin, Kieran,* etc.

From the said Fogharthach are also descended the Ulster families of Carolan, Donnellan, and Flanagan.

1. Dermod O'Kerin was the first of the family who settled in Thomond.

2. Donal : his eldest son.
3. Donoch : his son.
4. Murtogh : his son.
5. Teige : his son.
6. Hubert : his son.

7. Teige (2) : his son; died in 1634 ; was buried at *Ennish* (now "Ennis"), in the county Clare.

8. Hubert O'Kerin : his son : had five brothers—1. Flann, 2. Tirlogh, 3. John, 4. Murtogh, and 5. Loghlin ; living in 1657.

CALLAN.†

Arms : Or, on a bend gu. three martlets ar. *Crest :* A demi griffin ramp. gu.

AONGUS, brother of Suibhneach, who is No. 92 on the "Colman" (of Meath) pedigree, was the ancestor of *O'Cathalain ;* anglicised *Callan.*

* *O'Cairn :* This sirname has been incorrectly written *O'Ciarain* ("ciar :" Irish, *a dark-grey colour ;* "an," *one who*).

† *Callan :* Of this family was the Very Rev. Nicholas Callan, D.D., Professor of Natural Philosophy in Maynooth College, who was born at Dromiskin, in the county Louth, in 1799. He entered college in 1817, and remained there till his death, a period of forty-seven years. Much of his leisure was devoted to the translation into English of works of piety, particularly those of St. Liguori. He died at Maynooth in 1864.

92. Aongus (or Æneas) : son of Colman Mór.
93. Maolumha : his son.
94. Fablden : his son.
95. Muiltuile : his son.
96. Congal : his son.
97. Fallain ; his son.
98. Fiachra : his son.

99. Æneas : his son.
100. Broghad (" broghad :" Irish, *opulent*) : his son.
101. Cathalan (" cathal :" Irish, *valour*), meaning " little Charles :" a quo *O'Cathalain*, in this family anglicised *Callan*.*

CANAVAN.
Of Connaught.

CAHERNACH, brother of Ficheallach, who is No. 99 on the "Fihilly" pedigree, was the ancestor of *O'Canamhain ;* anglicised *Canavan.*

99. Cahernach : son of Conbhach.
100. Flaitheimhan (" flaith :" Irish, *a chief*; "eimh," *active*; "an," *one who*) : his son ; a quo *O'Flaitheimhain*, anglicised *Fleming*, and modernized *De Fleming.*
101. Cormac : his son.
102. Maolmordha : his son.
103. Canamhan† (" can :" Irish, *to sing ;* Heb. "gan-a," *a reed* or *cane ;* Arab. "gan-i," *to sing ;* Lat.

" can-o ;" Hind. "gan-i," *to chant ;* and "amhan :" Irish, *a river*) : his son ; a quo *O'Canamhain.*
104. Aodh : his son.
105. Murtach : his son.
106. Aodh (2) : his son.
107. Moriach : his son.
108. Teige : his son.
109. John : his son.
110. Fercobhra O'Canavan : his son.

CANON. (No. 1.)

Arms : Ar. on a chev. engr. betw. three crosses patteé sa. as many martlets of the first.

AODH (or Hugh) Munderg, son of Flaithertach (latinized "Flathertius"), the 159th Monarch, and brother of Moroch, who is No. 97 on the "Mulroy" pedigree, was the ancestor of *O'Canadhnain* ; anglicised *Cananan*, and modernized *Canon, Gannon,* and *Canning.*‡

* *Callan :* See the " Carlton" pedigree which is also derived from an *O'Cathalain* family.

† *Canamhan :* This word is compounded of the Irish *can.* " to sing," and *amhan*, "a river" (Lat. *amn-is ;* Welsh, *avon ;* Corn. *avan ;* and Arm. *aun*).

‡ *Canning :* It is believed that George Canning, father of the great George Canning, was of this family. Of him WEBB says in his *Compendium of Irish*

97. Hugh Munderg.
98. Donal : his son.
99. Canadhnan (" can," " can-

adh :" Irish, *to utter, to sing ;* " an," *one who*): his son; a quo *O'Can- adhnain.*

CANON. (No. 2.)

According to MacFirbis.

Arms : Same as "Canon" (No. 1).

AODH (or Hugh) Munderg, son of Flaitheartach the 159th Monarch, and brother of Moroch, who is No. 97 on the "Mulroy" pedigree, was the ancestor of *O'Canannain ;* anglicised *Cananan, Canon, Gannon,* and *Canning.*

97. Hugh Munderg: his son.
98. Donall Cleiric: his son.
99. Longseach : his son.
100. Flaithbeartach : his son.
101. Canannan ("canadh :" Irish, *to sing*; " an," *one who*): his son ; a quo *O'Canannain.*

102. Maolfabhil : his son.
103. Cuileann : his son.
104. Longseach : his son.
105. Flaithbeartach : his son.
106. Ruadhri : his son.
107. Donall : his son.
108. Donoch : his son.

CARBERY. (No. 1.)

Of Leinster.

Arms : Ar. a lion ramp. gu. between three erm. spots.   *Crest :* A hand couped at the wrist and erect, grasping a sword all ppr.

THIS sirname is derived from Cairbre Cluitheachar, who is No. 87 on the "Dwyer" (of Leinster) pedigree, the stock from which this and the *Lee* family are descended. Faobrach, a brother of Ogan, who is No. 96 on the "Lee" pedigree, was the ancestor of *O'Cairbre* ("cairbre :" Irish, *the chief of the chariot*) ; anglicised *Carbery.*

96. Faobrach: son of Mal.
97. Gosda: his son.
98. Machair: his son.

99. Erc : his son.
100. Eiran : his son.
101. Saighir : his son.

Biography : Canning, George, an author, an Irishman, appears to have taken his degree of B.A. at the University of Dublin in 1754. His father, a gentleman of property in the north of Ireland, disinherited him for marrying, in 1768, Miss Costello, a dower-less beauty. George Canning was the author of some poems, and of a translation of *Anti-Lucretius.* He died in the Temple, London, 11th April, 1771, one year after the birth of his son, the great George Canning."

102. Fionan : his son.
103. Coman : his son.
104. Cronmhal : his son.

105. Flaithbeartach : his son.
106. Urthuile : his son.

CARBERY. (No. 2.)

Of Offaley.

Arms : Az. a lion ramp. or, betw. three pheons ar.

CAIRBRE (" corb :" Irish, *a chariot* ; "righ," *a king*), brother of Cumascach who is No. 100 on the " Colgan" pedigree, was the ancestor of this *Clann Cairbre ;* anglicised *MacCarbery*.

100. Cairbre : son of Florence ; a quo *Clann Cairbre*, of Offaley.
101. Æneas : his son.
102. Donall : his son.

103. Gorman : his son.
104. Cairbre (2) : his son.
105. Cathal MacCarbery : his son.

CARBERY. (No. 3.)

Of Orgiall.

Arms : Same as those of " Corrigan."

CAIRBRE, brother of Coraidhegan, who is No. 102 on the " Corrigan" pedigree, was the ancestor of *O'Cairbre* (of Orgiall) ; anglicised *Carbery*.

CARBERY. (No. 4.)

Of Ulster.

CAIRBRE, brother of Maoldun, who is No. 99 on the " O'Madden" (of Ulster) pedigree, was the ancestor of *Clann Cairbre* (or *Carbery*) of Ulster.

99. Cairbre : son of Dungall ; a quo this *Clann Cairbre*.
100. Cumascach : his son.
101. Eachdach : his son.
102. Artrigh : his son.

103. Eachagan : his son.
104. Muredach : his son.
105. Maoliosa : his son.
106. Patrick O'Carbery : his son ; had a brother named Randal.

CARLTON.

GARBHAN, brother of Cormac, who is No. 91 on the "O'Flanagan" (of Tuatha Ratha) pedigree, was the ancestor of *O'Cathalain;* anglicised *Cahalan, Carlton,* Carleton,†* and *Charleton.*

91. Garbhan: son of Tuathal Maolgarbh.

92. Aodh (or Hugh) : his son.

93. Suibhneach : his son.

94. Maoldun : his son.

95. Fergus Caoch : his son.

96. Conall : his son.

97. Cathal : his son.

98. Connach : his son.

99. Rathamhuil : his son.

100. Dunach : his son.

101. Cathalan ("cathal :" Irish, *valour*), meaning "little Charles :" his son ; a quo *O'Cathalain.‡*

102. Dundeadhach : his son.

103. Eighnechan : his son.

104. Mulanach :§ his son.

105. Ciardach : his son.

* *Carlton*: This name has been modernized *Gartlan*, which, in its turn has become *Garland* and *Gartland.*

† *Carleton :* Of this family was the late William Carleton, an author distinguished for his just delineation of the character of the Irish peasantry. He was born on Shrove Tuesday, 1798, at Prillisk, near Clogher, county Tyrone. He was the youngest of fourteen children. His father, who was a small farmer, was a man of considerable intelligence, endowed with a surprising memory ; his mother used to sing the old Irish songs with wonderful sweetness and pathos. "From the one," writes Webb, "he gleaned his inexhaustible store of legendary lore ; from the other, that sympathy and innerness, which have thrown a magic spell round the creations of his brilliant and fruitful fancy." Carleton attended a hedge school, travelled as "a poor scholar," and fed his literary taste by reading all the books he could lay hands on. He was destined for the Catholic priesthood ; but was prevented from entering it by his father's death, and by some conscientious difficulties that led, we are told, to his joining the late Established Church. He gained some classical knowledge at the school of Dr. Keenan, a parish priest in the diocese of Down ; and became tutor in a farmer's family in Louth. A perusal of *Gil Blas* roused within him a desire of seeing more of the world ; and throwing up his situation, he found himself in Dublin with only a few pence in his pocket. Without any definite plan, he sought everywhere for employment, even that of a bird-stuffer, of whose art he was obliged to confess complete ignorance. Driven to extremities, he contemplated enlisting, and addressed a Latin letter to the Colonel of a Regiment, who dissuaded him from his intention, and gave him assistance. Chance threw him in the way of the Rev. Cæsar Otway, who, recognizing his abilities, persuaded him to try authorship. He contributed a tale, "The Lough Derg Pilgrimage," to the *Christian Examiner.* This was favourably received ; and soon by his writings and tutorship he attained a respectable position, and married. When about thirty years of age, Carleton published a collected edition of his *Traits and Stories of the Irish Peasantry,* which was by far the most brilliant of his works. Next followed his first novel, *Fardorougha the Miser.* The facility with which he wrote was exemplified in 1845, when, on the death of Thomas Davis, who was to have supplied James Duffy with a number for his series of monthly publications, Carleton, on six days' notice, filled the gap with *Paddy-Go-Easy.* In the *Black Prophet,* which was a tale of the Famine, he has portrayed the Irish female character with matchless strength and pathos. He enjoyed a Civil List pension of £200, and latterly lived at Woodville, Sandford, near Dublin, where he died on the 30th January, 1869, aged 70 years. He was buried at Mount Jerome. In his delineations of Irish peasant life he stands perhaps unrivalled.

‡ *O'Cathalain :* See the "Callan" pedigree.

§ *Mulanach :* The root of this name is the Irish *mulan,* "a little hill," "a heap ;" and a quo *O'Mulanaigh,* anglicised *Mullany.*

106. Maolfabhal : his son.
107. Maolruanaidh : his son.

108. Uaillgarbh O'Cathalain : his son.

CARNEY.

Of Ulster.

Arms : Ar. a chev. betw. three buglehorns stringed sa.   *Crest* : A swan's head and neck erased, in the bill an annulet.

CEARNACH, brother of Coscrach, who is No. 98 on the "O'Hanlon" pedigree, was the ancestor of *O'Cearnaighe ;* anglicised *Carney, Kearney, Kerney, O'Kearney,* and *Carnagie.*

98. Cearnach (" cearnach :" Irish, *victorious*) : son of Suibhneach ; a quo *O'Cearnaige.*
99. Cumascach : his son.
100. Olioll : his son.
101. Lorcan : his son.
102. Olioll (2) : his son.
103. Cumascach (2) : his son.
104. Eocha : his son.

105. Cearnach O'Carney : his son ; the first of the family who assumed this sirname.
106. Eocha (2) : his son.
107. Ciaran : his son.
108. Cearnach (2) : his son.
109. Cumascach O'Carney : his son.

CARROLL.

Of Dundalk, County Louth.

Arms : Ar. a cross crosslet sa.   *Crest :* A bear's head sa. muzzled or, betw. two wings of the last.

THE ancestor of this family was Cearbhall (" cearbhall :" Irish *carnage*), a younger brother of Eochaidh, who is No. 90 on the " O'Hart" pedigree ; and was King of Orgiall in St. Patrick's time.   This Eochaidh, who was father of St. Donart, was an obstinate Pagan, and opposed the Apostle, who, on that account, prophesied that the sceptre would pass from Eochaidh to his brother Cearbhall (a quo *O'Carroll,* of Oriel) ; and the O'Carrolls continued Kings of Oriel (or the county Louth) down to the twelfth century, when they were dispossessed by the Anglo-Normans, under Sir John DeCourcy.   In co-operation with St. Malachy, then Archbishop of Armagh, Donoch O'Carroll, Prince of Oriel, the last celebrated Chief of this family, founded A.D. 1142, and amply endowed, the great Abbey of Mellifont in the county Louth.   At present we are unable to trace the descent from that Prince of Oriel down to—

1. James Carroll, of Drumgoolin, who was born in 1699, and d. 6th June, 1776. This James m. Anne Taaffe, and left one son :

2. Walter (b. 1727; d. January, 1804), who m. Anne Kieran, and had two sons :

I. James, of whom presently.

II. John, who m. Anne Coleman, and had two sons and four daughters; the sons were:

I. James, d. unm.

II. John, of Dublin, an M.D., who married a Miss Greene of Dublin, and had three sons: I. James. II. John. III. Frederick, living at Moone Abbey, co. Kildare, in 1884.

Of the four daughters of John, second son of Walter, one m. Peter Hoey, and had three sons, and a daughter who married R. P. Carton, Esq., Q.C., Dublin (living in 1887). Of Peter Hoey's three sons, two d. unm. ; another is the Rev. Canon Hoey, P.P., Castleblayney, living in 1887.

3. James (b. 1754; d. 1806): son of Walter; m. Anne Marmion, and had four sons and one daughter, Margaret; the sons were :

I. James, ⎫
II. John,   ⎬ the three of whom d. s. p.
III. Francis, ⎭

IV. Patrick-James, of whom presently ; born 1806.

I. Margaret, m. Edward Ferrar, and had one son:

I. Edward, living in 1884.

4. Patrick-James, who was born 1806, and d. 1879 : fourth son of James ; m. Esther Gilmore, and had three sons and six daughters, five of whom became Nuns, and one (Angela) m. as under :

I. James, of whom presently.

II. Walter, an M.D., who m. Mary O'Brien, in Sydney,and d.1883.

III. Vincent, of Dundalk, Merchant, who married Catherine McGivney, of Collan, co. Louth.

I. Angela, who married Michael Moynagh, Esq., Solicitor, Dundalk, has had issue.

5. James Carroll, of Lisnawilly, House, Dundalk, Merchant: eldest son of Patrick-James ; m. Bridget Dolan, of Dyzart, co. Louth, and has had a daughter Mary, all living in 1887.

CASEY.* (No. 3.)

Of Tirowen, Canada, and America.

Arms : Ar. a sinister hand couped at the wrist effronteé gu.

BAODAN, a brother of Donal Ilchealgach, who is No. 91 on the "O'Neill" (of Tyrone) pedigree, was the ancestor of *O'Cathasaigh*, of Tirowen ; anglicised *Cahasy*, and *Casey*.

* *Casey :* Of this family was Thomas Casey, who, about A.D. 1658, sailed from Plymouth, England, and landed in Rhode Island, U.S. America. He was married to Sarah ——, and had three sons :—1. Thomas, 2. Adam, 3. Samuel. General Silas Casey, of the late American War, was a descendant of said Adam ; and Henry-Samuel Casey (living in 1886 in Colborne, Ontario, Dominion of Canada) was a descendant of the said Samuel. In 1783, the Canada branch of this family went thither from the States, where their property was confiscated on account of their allegiance to British principles.

91. Baodan, the 137th Monarch of Ireland : third son of Muircheartach, the 131st Monarch.

92. Cudubhearg : his son.
93. Maolrubha : his son.
94. Forbhosach : his son.
95. Cathasach ("cathasach :"

Irish, *brave*) : his son; a quo *O'Cathasaigh.*

96. Maolfhuadach : his son.
97. Maolfhoghartach : his son.
98. Maolchanach : his son.
99. Colman : his son.
100. Enda: his son.

COEN.

A Branch of the "O'Dowd" Family, Princes of Hy-Fiachra.

Arms: Or, a lion ramp gu. *Crest:* A bear's head couped sa. muzzled gu.

CAOMHAN, a younger brother of Dubhda, who is No. 97 on the "O'Dowd" pedigree, was the ancestor of *O'Caomhain;* anglicised *O'Keevan, Keevan, Kevin, Kevens, Keveny, Kavanagh* (of Connaught), *Coen, Cohen, Cohan, Cowan,* and *Cuan.* This Caomhan was Chief of his Sept, A.D. 876.

The *O'Keevan* portion of the family, who were also known as *Muintir Keevan,* possessed the district of Moylena, in the county Tyrone, which was lately known as "The Closach;" and the Armorial Bearings of that branch of the *O'Caomhain* family are—

Arms: Vert a saltire or, betw. in chief and in base a lizard pass. of the last, and in fess two daggers erect ar. pommels and hilts gold. *Crest:* A dagger erect ar. pommel and hilt or, the blade impaling a lizard vert.

Tracing the pedigree to its source : Caomhan was son of Conmac, son of Duncatha,son of Cathal, son of Olioll, son of Donoch, son of Tiobrad, son of Maoldubh, son of Fiachra Ealg (or Ealgach), son of Dathi, the 127th Monarch of Ireland, son of Fiachra, brother of Niall of the Nine Hostages, whose son Eoghan (Owen) married Indorba, a princess of Britain.

The descendants of this last mentioned Fiachra were called *Hy-Fiachrach;* and gave their name to *Tir Fiachrach,* now known as the barony of "Tireragh," in the southern portion of the county Sligo. They also possessed the territories now constituting the present baronies of Carra, Erris, and Tyrawley, in the county Mayo. *Beal-atha an-fheadha (os vadi sylvæ),* now the town of "Ballina," being their chief seat.

From Caomhan, downwards, the following is the pedigree :

97. Caomhan ("caomhan :" Irish, *a noble person*) : son of Conmac; chief of the Sept, A.D. 876.

98. Cathal : his son.
99. Diarmaid : his son.
100. Giolla-na-Naomh : his son.
101. Cathal : his son.
102. Domhnall : his son.
103. Diarmaid : his son.

104. Giolla-na-Naomh : his son.
105. Tomhas : his son.
106. Domhnall : his son.
107. Tomhas : his son.
108. Diarmaid : his son.
109. Daibhidh (or David) : his son.
110. Domhnall (or Donal) : his son.
111. Giolla-na-Naomh : his son.
112. Tomhas (or Thomas) : his son.

113. David: his son.
114. Aodh (or Hugh): his son.

115. David: his son; had a brother Donal.

This list brings us down to Strafford's Viceroyalty of Ireland (*temp.* Charles I.), when the family estates were confiscated by that Viceroy.

James and Charles Coen fell as officers at the Boyne, fighting for King James II., against William III.

The late Right Rev. Thomas Coen, Roman Catholic Bishop of Clonfert, was, and the Very Rev. T. Coen, V.F., and P.P. of Aughrim (Ballinasloe), living in 1887, is, a home representative of this family. There is also settled in England a branch of this ancient Irish family, descended from the James Coen, who, as above mentioned, fell at the Battle of the Boyne. Of this branch was (1) James Coen, who died in 1860, and whose son (2) John-Joseph Coen (deceased) married Catherine, grand-daughter of James Browne (of Kilmaine, and) of Rahins, in the county of Mayo, by his wife Catherine MacNally, niece of Sir Thomas Henry Burke (of the Clanricarde family), and had one surviving son and four daughters :

I. James Coen, of whom presently.
I. Margaret, who married Francis MacKeowen.
II. Mary-Theresa, who m. John Robert Coles.
III. Nora.
IV. Katherine, both living unm. in 1887.

3. James Coen, Barrister-at-Law, of the Middle Temple, London, Ex-Captain, V.R. : son of John-Joseph ; m. Rose, dau. of Stuart Knill, Knt. of St. Gregory, J.P., Blackheath, Kent, and Alderman of London ; living in 1887.

COLEMAN. (No. 1.)

Of Meath.

Arms : Per fesse ar. and sa. a cross patonce betw. four mullets counterchanged. *Crest :* A horse's head erased ppr.

COLMAN MÓR, a brother of Aodh, who is No. 91 on the "Fogarty" pedigree, was the ancestor of *O'Columhain*, of Meath ; anglicised *Coleman*, and *Colman.*

91. Colman Mór ("columhan :" Irish, *a pillar;* mór," *great*) : son of Dermod, the 133rd Monarch of Ireland ; a quo *O'Columhain.* This Colmon Mór was the sixth Christian King of Meath.

92. Suibhneach: his son; was the Eighth King. Had a brother named Aongus or Æneas, who was ancestor of *Callan.*

93. Conall Guthbinn ("guthbinn :" Irish, *melodious voice*) : his son; the 11th King. This King is sometimes called "Conall Gulbin ;" but *Guthbinn* is the correct epithet.

94. Muireadach (by some called Armead) : his son.

95. Dermod : his son ; the 13th King.

96. Murchadh (or Moroch Midheach) : his son; the 14th King.

97. Donal : his son; the 19th King, and 161st Monarch, d. A.D. 758.

98. Donchadh (or Donoch): his son ; the 163rd Monarch.

99. Maolruanaidh : his son; the 27th King.

100. Maolseachlinn Mór (or Malachy the Great): his son : the 29th Christian King, and the 167th Monarch of Ireland. Was slain in the battle of Farrow, in the county Westmeath, A.D. 860.

101. Flann Sionnach: his son; the 32nd King, and the 169th Monarch of Ireland.

"In his time," says the Chronicler, "Cormac McCulenan, the famous King and Bishop of Munster, with a great army invaded Leinster, and did much mischief, until this Monarch came to aid Cearbhall (son of Muregan, King of Leinster), and, in a great battle fought at Magh Nalty, Cormac MacCulenan, with seven petty Kings of the south of Ireland, was slain, and their army totally routed A.D 905.

102. Maolseachlinn : son of Flann Sionnach; had a younger brother named Donchadh, who was the ancestor of O'Melaghlin.

103. Flann : son of Maolseachlinn.

104. Domhnall [Donal] : his son.

105. Murchadh O'Columhain : his son.

(In this Murchadh's time took place the invasion of Ireland by King Henry II., of England, who confiscated not only the patrimony of this family, but also the patrimonies of almost all the other Nobles of ancient Meath.)

COLEMAN. (No. 2.)

Of Orgiall.

Arms : Ar. on a chev. betw. three water bougets sa. a mullet of the first. *Crest* : A dove wings expanded ppr. in the beak a branch vert.

AIRMHEADHACH, a brother of Maolodhar Caoch, who is No. 92 on the "Brody" pedigree, was the ancestor of *Clann Columain,* of Orgiall; anglicised *Coleman, Pigeon, Pidgeon* and *Dove.*

92. Airmheadhach : son of Feareadhach Culdubh.

93. Columan (" columan :" Irish, *a little dove*): his son ; a quo *Clann Columain.*

94. Conmaol : his son.

95. Ruadhrach (" ruadh :" Irish, *lordship, valiant:* Welsh, " rhydh"): his son; a quo *O'Ruadhraigh,* anglicised *Hodges, Hodgeson, Hodgekins,* and *Hodgekinson.*

96. Ceallach : his son.

97. Ruadhacan : his son.

98. Eachachan ; his son.

99. Cumuscach : his son.

100. Oill : his son.

101. Muireadach : his son.

102. Ruaidhri (" ruaidhri :" Irish, *red king*) or *Roderick :* his son ; a quo *MacRuaidhrigh ;* anglicised *Hobkins, Hobson, Hopkins.**

103. Muireadhach O'Columain : his son.

---

* *Hopkins :* This family was quite distinct from the *O'Goibgin* (" gob :" Irish, *a beak,* Heb. " gab;" " *gin,*" *a mouth*) family, who also anglicised their name *Hopkins ;* and a branch of whom lived in Connaught in our time.

COLGAN.

Of Offaley.

Arms : Az. a lion rampant or, betw. three pheons ar

CUMASACH, brother of Æneas, who is No. 100 on the "O'Conor" (Faley) pedigree, was the ancestor of *Clan Colgain ;* anglicised "Clan Colgan," a quo *Colgan, MacColgan, and Swords.*

100. Cumascach: son of Florence.
101. Colgan ("colg:" Irish, *a sword ;* "colgan," *a swordsman*): his son; a quo *Clann Colgain.*
102. Cumascach (2): his son.
103. Conor MacColgan : his son ; first assumed this sirname.

104. Cathal : his son.
105. Fionnghon : his son.
106. Mulcoscrach : his son.
107. Donall : his son.
108. Cucogair MacColgan : his son.

COMYN.*

Arms : Az. three lozenge buckles tongues in fesse or.   *Crest*: On a chapeau gu turned up erm. a bloodhound sejant ppr.

BREANAN DALL, a brother of Cormac who is No. 95 on the "O'Kelly" (Hy-Maine) pedigree, was the ancestor of *O'Comain ;* anglicised *Coman, Comyn,* and *Comyns.*

95. Breanan Dall : son of Cairbre Crom-ris, who was also called Cairbre "MacFechine."
96. Coman ("comann:" Irish, *communion*): his son; a quo *O'Comain.*

97. Eoghan : his son.
98. Conghal : his son.
99. Seachnasach : his son.
100. Reachtghal : his son.
101. Feareadhach : his son.
102. Fogharthach ; his son.

* *Comyn :* John Comyn, Archbishop of Dublin, said to be an Englishman, but probably a member of this ancient family, was appointed to the see in 1181, but did not visit Ireland until 1184, when he was commissioned to prepare for the reception of Prince John. In 1190 he commenced and endowed St. Patrick's Cathedral, and enlarged and repaired the choir of Christ Church. He died in Dublin, 25th October, 1212, and was buried in Christ Church. One of the canons made by him, and confirmed by Pope Urban III., provides that "All archers and others who carry arms not for the defence of the people, but for plunder and sordid lucre, shall, on every Lord's-day, be excommunicated by bell, book, and candle, and at last be refused Christian burial." In consequence of a dispute with one of the Lords-Justices, he for a time laid an interdict upon his archbishopric. Ware says concerning him :—"Dempster would insinuate that he (John Comyn) was bishop of *Dunblane*, in Scotland, and not of Dublin ; but that author has up and down stuffed his catalogue of the writers of Scotland with English, Welsh, and Irish, according to his own unguided fancy, and, to confirm his assertions, has often had the impudence to forge the names of authors, works, places, and times."— WEBB.

103. Cethern; his son.
104. Cormac: his son.
105. Conall O'Comain : his son.
(At this stage in this genealogy this ancient family was dispossessed of its patrimony, as were also many other ancient families in Connaught, by the Anglo-Norman family of *De Burc*, to whom King Henry III. granted the Lordship of that Province, A.D. 1225.—See Note "Ricard Mór," under No. 18 on the "Bourke" (No. 1) pedigree.

CONAN.

Arms : Ar. a fess sa. cottised gu. betw. two fleurs-de-lis of the second.

CUININ, No. 103 on the "Donnelly" pedigree, was the ancestor of *Mac-Conein*, and *O'Conein ;* anglicised *Conan, Coonan, Cunneen, Quinan,* and *Rabbitt.*

103. Cuinin ("cuinin :" Irish, *a rabbit*): son of Dungal; a quo *Mac-Conein.*
104. Fergal : his son; had a brother named Aongus.

105. Dermod : son of Fergal.
106. Cubuidhe O'Coonan: his son.

CONCANNON.

Arms : Ar. on a mount vert, an oak tree ppr. perched thereon a falcon also ppr. belled or, betw. in base two cross crosslets fitcheé gu.   *Crest :* An elephant statant ppr. tusked or.   *Motto :* Conn gan an (meaning wisdom without guile).

DERMOD FIONN, brother of Muirgheas (or Murias) who is No. 101 on the "O'Connor" (Connaught) pedigree, was the ancestor of *MacConceannain ;* anglicised *Concannon,* and *Concanen.**

101. Dermod Fionn, the 30th Christian King of Connaught : son of Tomaltach.
102. Dathi: his son; had a brother named Connor, who was the ancestor of *Mullen.*
103. Aodh : son of Dathi.
104. Olioll : his son.

105. Murtagh : his son.
106. Teige : his son.
107. Conceannan ("con :" Irish, *of a hound ;* * cean :" *a head*): his son; a quo *MacConceannain.*†
108. Aodh (or Hugh) MacConcannon: his son; first assumed this sirname.

* *Concanen* : Matthew Concanen, a miscellaneous writer, was born in Ireland about the end of the seventeenth century.   He early went over to London, and commenced writing as an advocate of the Government, and for the Newspapers, especially for the *Speculatist.* His brilliant abilities recommended him to the Duke of Newcastle, who in 1732 procured for him the Attorney-Generalship of Jamaica, a post he held for nearly seventeen years. He published a volume of miscellaneous poems, original and translated, and was the author of a comedy, *Wexford Wells.*   Concanen died in London in 1749.   Allibone says of him :—" He is principally remembered through the celebrated letter of Warburton concerning him, and by his position in the *Dunciad*—his reward for attacking Pope."

† *MacConceannain* : By some genealogists this sirname is derived from the Irish *Conganan* ("conn :" Irish, a man's name; "gan" *without* ; "an," *a lie*), meaning " Conn the speaker of truth."

2 B

109. Muirgheas : his son.
110. Murtagh (2): his son.
111. Muirgheas (2): his son.
112. Hugh (2): his son.
113. Teige (2): his son.
114. Murtach (3): his son.
115. Malachi : his son.
116. Cathal (or Charles): his son.
117. Hugh (3): his son.
118. Teige (3) : his son.
119. Ardgall : his son.
120. Murtach (4): his son ; had a brother named Malachi, who had two sons—1. John, and 2. Muir-

ceartach. This Muirceartach (or Murtagh) was the ancestor of *Slioght Muirceartaigh ;* anglicised *Moriarty* and *Murtagh*, of Connaught.

121. Dabhach ("dabhach :" Irish, *a press or vat*): son of Murtagh ; a quo *MacDabhaighe*, anglicised *Davie.**

122. Maolseaghlainn (or Malachi) : his son; had two brothers—1. Hugh, and 2. Thomas.

123. William MacConcannon : son of Malachi.

CONNELLAN.

Arms : Per pale erm. and or, two lions ramp. combatant betw. in chief a mullet surmounted of a crescent and in base a dexter hand couped at the wrist and erect all gu.

LAEGHAIRE (latinized "Laegrius"), the 128th Monarch, son (some say the eldest) of Niall of the Nine Hostages, who is No. 87 on the "O'Neill" (Princes of Tyrone) pedigree, had three sons—1. Eanna, 2. Damin, and 3. St. Colman. This Eanna was the ancestor of *O'Condeilbhain ;* anglicised *Connellan, Cunelvan, Quinlan,*† *Quinlevan,*‡ *Conlan,* and *Conlon.*

* *Davie*: This name has been modernized *Davies* and *Davis.*

† *Quinlan* : Doctor Francis John Boxwell Quinlan, of Dublin, is of this family. He was born in Mountjoy-square, Dublin, on the 9th of May, 1834. His father was the late John Quinlan, proprietor of the *Dublin Evening Post*, a newspaper of Liberal Principles. That journal was the oldest in Ireland, having been started in 1732, and continuing up to 1871. Mr. Quinlan, however, had retired from it with a competent fortune many years before its discontinuance. He married in 1833, Wilhelmina, daughter of the late Samuel Boxwell, of Linziestown House, in the county Wexford, and grand-daughter of the late John Boxwell, J.P., of Lingstown Castle. Dr. Quinlan's primary education was conducted by the Jesuits in Belvidere College ; and subsequently in the Kingstown School, under the Rev. Dr. Stackpoole. He entered Trinity College, Dublin, in October, 1851, obtaining third place, and gained Honors in Classics and in Logics, as well as a Classical Sizarship—the only distinction of profit that was then open to Catholics. He graduated as B.A. and M.B. in 1857, and as M.D. in 1862 ; and is a Member of the Senate of the University of Dublin. On the 2nd May, 1856, he became a Licentiate of the College ; and, on the 2nd November, 1859, a Licentiate of the King and Queen's College of Physicians, of the latter of which he was elected a Fellow in 1879, and has since filled the offices of Censor and Examiner. Dr. Quinlan is a Member of the Royal Irish Academy, of the Royal Dublin Society, and of the various medical societies of Dublin. He is Senior Physician to St. Vincent's Hospital ; Professor of Materia Medica, Pharmacology, and Therapeutics in the Catholic University Medical College ; he is Examiner in the same subjects in the Royal University. He married, in 1867, Maude-Elizabeth, eldest daughter of Doctor Sir William Carroll, J.P. ; and is living in 1887.

‡ *Quinlevan* : Of this family was the late Alderman Quinlevan, of Limerick.

87. Niall of the Nine Hostages, the 126th Monarch of Ireland.

88. Laeghaire : his son, the 128th Monarch.

89. Eanna : his son.

90. Dallan : his son.

91. Libhor* [livor]: his son ; a quo *O'Libhoir*, anglicised *Livroy*, and modernized *Lefroy*.

92. Aodh (or Hugh): his son ; had a brother named Faolan, who was father of St. Cannir, virgin.

93. Flannagan : son of Hugh.

94. Maolmith : his son.

95. Maoldun Dergenech : his son

96. Fearach : his son,

97. Aongus : his son.

98. Curidh : his son.

99. Cionaodh : his son.

100. Donal : his son.

101. Mulcron : his son.

102. Condeilbhan ("con :" Irish, *of a hound ;* "deilbh," *a countenance;* "an," *one who*): his son ; a quo *O'Condeilbhain*.

CONROY.†

Arms : Gu. three beads ar. on a chief or, as many cinquefoils az.   *Crest :* A lion ramp. vert supporting a pennon gu.

ANMIRE, brother of Donall who is No. 92 on the "Breen" pedigree, was the ancestor of *MacConaire, O'Conaire,* or *O'Mulconaire ;* anglicised *MacConroi‡* (modernized *King*), *Conroy, Conry, Connery, MacConry, MacEnry, McHenry,* and *Mulconry.*

* *Libhor :* This name, analysed, is *Le-ibh-or,* which means "gold for you ;" and was first anglicised *Liver,* which became *Livroy* and, more lately, *Lefroy.* In tracing the lineage of the "House of Heber" we met another name like this.

† *Conroy :* Florence Conroy, a Catholic ecclesiastic, was born in Galway in 1560. At an early age he was sent to College in the Netherlands, and afterwards to Spain, where he entered the Franciscan Order, and distinguished himself as a student of St. Augustine's works. His defence of the doctrine of the "Immaculate Conception" enhanced his fame, and attracted the notice of Philip II. In 1588, he was appointed Provincial of the Franciscans in Ireland, and embarked in the Spanish Armada. In 1593 he published in Irish a translation of a Spanish work, *A Christian Instruction.* In 1602 he met the famous Irish Chieftain Hugh Roe O'Donnell, and acted as his chaplain during the last hours of that Chieftain, at Simancas, following his remains to their resting place in the Cathedral of Valladolid. Although he was appointed Archbishop of Tuam in 1610, the proscription of Catholicism in Ireland prevented his ever taking possession of his see. Through his exertions the Irish College at Louvain was founded, in 1616. His latter years were occupied in the publication of works on St. Augustine and his writings. He died on the 18th November, 1629, in one of the Franciscan convents at Madrid, aged about 69 years. His remains were transferred in 1654 to the Louvain College, where they repose under a marble monument.

‡ *MacConroi :* The "MacConrois" gave name to their old home of *BaileMacConroi* (anglicised "Bally MacConroy" and "Ballymaconry"), now usually · rendered "Kingston"—near Streamstown, Connemara ; and were one of the tribes who possessed West Galway, before the Joyces settled there (see the "Joyce" pedigree). The Conroi here mentioned was the first chief of the territory of Gnomore in Iar-Connaught. Of the origin of Gnomore, O'Flaherty, in his *Ogygia,* p. 387, says : "Gnomore et Gnobeg duo filii Lugaddii," etc. O'Dugan states that, in the twelfth century, *MacConroi* was chief of Gnomore, and *O'Heyny* chief of Gnobeg. The barony of Moycullen, County Galway, was created A.D. 1585 ; and was formed of the two ancient territories of Gnomore and Gnobeg. After the twelfth century the O'Flahertys seized upon this

92. Anmire: son of Crimthann.

93. Ronan: his son.

94. Foranan: his son.

95. Crunmaol: his son.

96. Maoldun: his son.

97. Fergal: his son.

98. Florence: his son.

99. Neachtan: his son; had a brother named Suibhneach, who was the ancestor of *Macnamee.*

100. Dubhdahna: son of Neachtan.

101. Brocan: his son.

102. Flaithgheal: his son; had a brother named Sealbaoth, who was the ancestor of *Slaman.*

103. Conair ("conair," gen. " conaire :" Irish, *a way*): his son; a quo *MacConaire*, etc. (as above).

104. Paul Mór: his son.

105. Maoillinn: his son.

106. Paul Oge: his son.

107. Consalach: his son.

108. Tanaidhe (Tanny or Nathaniel): his son.

109. Dunlong: his son.

110. Dunnin: his son.

111. Tanaidhe (2): his son.

112. Paidin (*Paidin :* Irish, a diminutive of "Patrick"): his son; a quo *MacPhaidin*, anglicised *MacFadden, Padden,** Patten,* and *Pattison.* This Paidin [paudeen] had a brother named Giollaiosa.

113. Conang Eolach ("eolach;" Irish, *cunning*): son of Paidin; a quo *O'Eoluighe* (of Connaught), anglicised *Gunning*; had a brother named Maurice.

114. Tanaidhe Eolach: son of Conang.

115. Conang Buidhe: his son; had a brother named Maollinn.

116. Neidhe: son of Conang Buidhe.

117. Paidin (2): his son; had a brother named Donogh.

118. Tanaidhe Mór: son of Paidin.

119. Maollinn: his son; had a brother named John Ruadh.†

120. Lochlann: his son; had a brother named Toranach (*toran* : Irish, " a great noise"), a quo *MacToranaigh*, anglicised *Torney*, and *Thunder.*

121. Paidin (2): son of Lochlann.

122. Muirgheas O'Conaire (or Mulconaire): his son.

territory, after having been themselves driven from their own ancient inheritance, on the east side of Lough Corrib, by the De Burgos (or De Burcs). Many centuries after the above-mentioned Conroi's time, some of his descendants emigrated westward towards the coast, and settled in this district of Bally MacConroy, to which they gave the name. After the introduction of the English language into Iar-Connaught, the name of the Clan *Mhic Conroi* was anglicised *MacConry*, etc., and finally, but improperly, *King*, as if the original name was *Mac-an-Righ*, which means " son of the King." The district of Bally MacConroy was also anglicised " Kingstown;" and thus the ancient name was wholly obliterated.—HARDIMAN.

* *Padden:* There was another family of *MacPaddin*, modernized *Padden*, which was descended from the Barretts of Munster; and another from Brian Oge O'Brien, of the " O'Brien" (of Thomond) family.

‡ *John Ruadh :* This John (or Shane) Ruadh had a son Donal Ruadh, who was father of Connor O'Mulconry, who was father of Maolmuire of Fullon, who was father of Maollin O'Conry (d. on 5th January, 1637), who was m. to Katherine, daughter of Teige O'Flanagan of Conneloin, county Roscommon. This Maollin had five sons—1. Thorva O'Conry, m. to Evelin, dau. of Ferdorach Branon; 2. Conry; 3. Morie; 4. Donoch; 5. Paidin.

CONWAY

Arms: Az. a lion pass. guard. paly of six ar. and or, betw. three gauntlets of the second all within a bordure engr. of the last.

CREAMTHANN, a brother of Breanan who is No. 90 on the "Fox" (of Meath) pedigree, was the ancestor of *MacConmeadha;* anglicised *Mac-Conmy, Conmy, MacConway,* and *Conway.**

90. Creamthann : son of Brian.
91. Anmireach : his son.
92. Ronan : his son.
93. Forannan : his son.
94. Cronmaol : his son.
95. Maolduin : his son.
96. Feargal : his son.
97. Flann : his son.
98. Suibhneach : his son.
99. Dubron : his son.
100. Cearnach : his son.
101. Laoghacan : his son.

102. Anbioth : his son.
103. Ruarc : his son.
104. Conn : his son.
105. Giolla Channigh : his son.
106. Cumeadh (*meadh :* Irish, metheglin) : his son; a quo *Mac-Conmeadha.*
107. Sitreach : his son.
108. Cumeadh : his son.
109. Ronan MacConmeadha : his son.

CORMACK.

Of Galway.

Arms: Az. three bezants in pale betw. two palets ar. a chief or. *Crest:* a hand couped in fesse holding a sword in pale on the point thereof a garland of laurel all ppr.

CREAMTHANN, a brother of Dalan who is No. 91 on the " O'Kelly" (of Hy-Maine) pedigree, was the ancestor of *O'Cormaic;* anglicised *Cormack.*

91. Creamthann : son of Breassal.
92. Cormac† ("*cormac :*" Irish, *a brewer*) : his son ; a quo *O'Cormaic.*
93. Secc: his son.
94. Fiontan Uallach‡ : his son.
95. Lachtnan : his son.
96. Fachtnan : his son.

97. Cucaiseal : his son.
98. Folachthach : his son.
99. Ruidhghrin : his son.
100. Maolcobhach : his son.
101. Cearbhall : his son.
102. Niall O'Cormack, of Maonmuighe : his son.

* *Conway :* In the Province of Connaught the Irish sirname *O' Connaghain* has also been anglicised *Conway.*—See the "Counaghan" pedigree.

† *Cormac :* This name originally meant "The son of the Chariot."

‡ *Uallach :* This Fiontan Uallach ("uallach :" Irish, *vain, ostentatious*), was ancestor of *O'Uallaighe;* anglicised *Howley,* and *Wallace* (of Connaught).

CORRIGAN.

Arms ; Sa. three fleurs-de-lis ar.   *Crest ;* A church and spire ppr.

CATHAL, brother of Fergal, who is No. 101 on the "Donnelly" pedigree, was the ancestor of *O'Coraidhegain* ; anglicised *Corrigan.*

101. Cathal : son of Cumascach.
102. Coraidhegan ("coraidhe :" Irish, *a hero*), meaning "the little | hero :" his son ; a quo *O'Coraidhegain ;* had a brother named Cairbre, a quo *O'Carbery,* of Orgiall.

COUNIHAN.

TIGHEARNACH, son of Muredach (or Muireadach), son of Eoghan, son of Niall of the Nine Hostages, the 126th Monarch of Ireland, and No. 87 on the "O'Neill" (of Tyrone) pedigree, was the ancestor of *O'Connaghain ;* anglicised *Counihan, Cunigham, Cunigan, Cunnigham, Cunnivane, Conyngham,* and *Conway.**

87. Niall of the Nine Hostages, the 126th Monarch of Ireland.
88. Eoghan (or Owen) : his son.
89. Muredach : his son ; had a brother named Eochaidh Binné.
90. Tighernach : son of Muireadach.
91. Daire (or Darius) : his son.
92. Cunaghan ("cu :" Irish, *the hound,* or *warrior ;* "an-agha," *of the*

battles): his son : a quo *O'Connaghain.*
93. Conall : his son.
94. Amhailgadh : his son.
95. Teige : his son.
96. Aodh : his son.
97. Owen : his son.
98. Murtagh : his son.
99. Owen (3) : his son.
100. Murtagh : his son.

.   .   .   .   .

We are unable to trace this pedigree down to the undermentioned Rodger O'Cunnivane, who was born, A.D. 1680.

1. Rodger (or Roady O'Cunnivane ; born 1680.
2. Timothy : his son.
3. Darby : his son.
4. Mihil (or Michael) : his son.
5. Thomas : his son.
6. Michael Cunningham, of Ennis, county Clare : his son.

7. John Cunningham, of Dublin : his son ; living in 1887.   Had three brothers and three sisters : the brothers were—1. Thomas (d. 1879) ; 2. Michael ; 3. Terence. The sisters are—1. Mary-Anne, m. to Patrick Dunne ; 2. Margaret ; 3. Sarah. This John was, in July, 1877, mar-

---

* *Corrigan :* Of this family was the late lamented Sir Dominic John Corrigan, Bart., M.D., of Cappagh and Inniscorrig, co. Dublin ; Vice-Chancellor of the Queen's University in Ireland, and formerly M.P. for Dublin.   Sir Dominic's Armorial Bearings were—*Arms :* Or, a chev. betw. two trefoils slipped in chief vert and a lizard in base, ppr.   *Crest :* A sword in pale point downwards, in front thereof two battle-axes in saltire, all ppr.   *Motto:* Consilio et impetu.

† *Conway:* Of this family is the Most Rev. Dr. Conway, Catholic Bishop of the diocese of Killala ; living in 1887.

ried in St. Mary's Catholic Church, Haddington Road, Dublin, to Mary-Elizabeth (d. 1st Jan., 1880), second daughter of John O'Hart, Dublin, | the Writer of this Work. Surviving issue of that marriage, one daughter named Elizabeth, living in 1887.

COWELL. (No. 1.)

Arms : Az. a lion ramp. ar. on a label of three points gu. nine bezants. *Crest :* On a chapeau gu. turned up erm. a lion pass. or, gorged with a label of three points of the first.

FEARACH, a brother of Murtogh Mór MacEarca, the 131st Monarch, and who is No. 90 on the "O'Neill (Princes of Tyrone) pedigree, was the ancestor of *MacCathmhaoill ;* anglicised *MacCawell, MacCowell, MacCaghwell, MacKevill, MacCaul, Caul, Caulfield, Caldwell, Campbell, Camphill, Colvill, Colwell, Colwill, Coghill, Coyle, Cowell, Hawell, Howell, Hemphill, Keavill, Keevill,* and *Keawell.*

90. FEARACH : third son of Muredach.

91. Fiachra : his son.

92. Fiachna : his son.

93. Suibhneach Meann ("meann:" Irish, *famous*): his son ; a quo *O'Meannaighe,* anglicised *Meanny.*

94. Edalach : his son ; had an elder brother named Cuaghan ("cuagan :" Irish, *the hinder part of the head*), who was the ancestor of *O'Cuagain,** anglicised *Coogan, Cogan,* and *Coggin.*

95. Donchar : son of Edelach.

96. Cugabhna : his son.

97. Conan : his son.

98. Donachar (2) : his son.

99. Cathmhaoïll ("cath :" Irish, *a battle ;* "maoil," *a heap*): his son ; a quo *MacCathmhaoill.*†

100. Breasal : his son.

101. Murtogh : his son.

102. Fogartach : his son.

103. Maolcolum ("colum :" Irish, *a dove*), meaning "the devoted of St. Columkill :" his son ; a quo *MacMaolcoluim,* anglicised *Malcolm,* and *Malcolmson.*

104. Suibhneach : his son.

105. Colla : his son.

106. Ranal MacCathmaoill : his son.

COWELL. (No. 2.)

Of Scotland.

IN the "Cowell" (No. 1) pedigree we see that Fearach, a brother of Muirceartach (or Mortogh) Mór MacEarca, the 131st Monarch of Ireland,

---

* *O'Cuagain :* This sirname has, by some writers, been considered the same as *MacCagadhain ;* but "MacCagadhain" and "O'Cuagain" are two distinct families.

† *MacCathmhaoill :* See at No. 99 on the "Kiernan" pedigree, for another *MacCathmhaoill* family, of the Clan Colla, and of the *Cineal Feareaduighe.*

was the ancestor of *MacCathmhaoill*. Amongst Fearach's other brothers
was Fergus Mór MacEarca, as we see in the following extract :

"In A.D. 498, Fergus Mór MacEarca (a brother of Muirceartach Mór MacEarca
above mentioned), in the twentieth year of the reign of his father, Muredach, son of
(Eugenius, or) Owen, son of Niall of the Nine Hostages . . . with a complete
Army, went into Scotland to assist his grandfather Loarn, who was King of Dalriada,
and who was much oppressed by his enemies the Picts, who were in several battles
and engagements vanquished and overcome by Fergus and his party. Whereupon, on
the king's death, which happened about the same time, the said Fergus was
unanimously elected and chosen king, as being of the Blood Royal, by his mother ;
and the said Fergus was the first absolute king of Scotland, of the Milesian Race : so
the succession continued in his blood and lineage ever since to this day.—*Four
Masters.*

As the *MacCathmhaioll* family here mentioned is descended from
Fearach, a brother of the said Fergus Mór MacEarca, it is, no doubt, the
Cowel (or *Campbel*) family mentioned in Jacob's Peerage ;* for, according
to said Peerage, we find that by letters-patent, bearing date at Kensington,
the 23rd June, 1701, Archibald, the 10th Earl of Argyle, was created
"Duke of Argyle," and amongst other titles, that of "Earl of Cambel
and Cowel." And (see No. 99 on the "Kiernan" pedigree) there was
another *MacCathmhaoill* family located in Tirowen, Ireland.

In connexion with the Scotch "Cowell" family, it is a strange fact
that the 74th Regiment, called when originally raised the "Argyll
Highlanders," wear a dark tartan, relieved by streaks of white, known as
the "Lamond." As *Fearach* was the ancestor of the family, and that the
Lamonds were called the *Clan ic Earachar*, who were afterwards known
as the "Maclamans of Lamonds," it is easy to understand that the
Lamonds were the most ancient proprietors of *Cowell*. As the traveller
passes through the Kyles of Bute he can look up Loch Striven at the
rounded tops of the "Cowall" mountains ; and, on his right, will see, at
the entrance of the Loch, Port Lomond. It is therefore not wonderful,
that a Regiment, called at its first raising the "Argyll Highlanders,"
should wear the colours of a Clan dwelling of old in *Airer Gaedhil*,†
anglicised *Argyll* and *Argyle*.

* *Peerage*: "A complete English Peerage, containing a Genealogical, Biographical,
and Historical Account of the Peers of this Realm ; together with the different
branches of each family ; including a particular relation of the most remarkable
transactions of those who have eminently distinguished themselves in the Service of
their Country, both in the Field and in the Cabinet, from the Conquest down to the
present time. To which is prefixed a succinct history of the Houses of Brunswic,
Brandenburgh, Saxe-Gotha, and Mecklenburgh. By the Rev. Alexander Jacob,
Chaplain in Ordinary to His Majesty, and Chaplain to His Grace the Duke of
Chandos. London : 1767."

† *Airer Gaedhil*: According to Dr. Joyce, the most important colony from Ireland
which settled in Scotland was that which in the fifth century was led by Fergus Mór
MacEarca and his brothers, as above mentioned ; and which was known by the name
of *Airer Gaedhil*, meaning the territory of the *Gael* or *Irish*.

COWELL. (No. 3.)

Of Logadowden, in the County of Dublin.

Arms : Erm. a hind trippant gu. *Crest :* A lion pass. guard. gu. ducally crowned and plain collared or. *Motto :* Fortis et celer.

FOR the fuller pedigree of this family see our IRISH LANDED GENTRY, pp. 616-619 (Dublin : James Duffy and Sons. First Edition, 1884, and Second Edition, 1887).

COWELL. (No. 3.)

Of Logadowden, County Dublin.

ACCORDING to the Wills (which were proved in the Prerogative Court, Dublin, in the years 1768 and 1782, respectively), of Bryan Cowell, of Logadowden, co. Dublin, and his wife Catherine, the said Bryan had six sons and three daughters. The sons were—1. Colvill, 2. Thomas, 3. George, 4. Bartholomew, 5. John, 6. Bryan ; and the daughters were— 1. Sarah, who m. George Lyddel Higgins, of the Silver Hills, co. Dublin, and left issue ; 2. Mary ; 3. Anne, who married Benjamin Helden, of Granard, county Longford, and left issue. Of the sons (1) Colvill (3) George, and (6) Bryan, we find no marriage recorded ; but the issue, so far as we can trace it, of each of the three sons (2) Thomas, (4) Bartholomew, and (5) John, is here given down to the present time. Commencing with said Thomas, the following is the issue :

2. Thomas Cowell, of Ballymore Eustace and Harristown : second son of Bryan ; was bur. at Ballymore Eustace, on the 26th June, 1782. Thomas m. on 20th Aug., 1750, Mary Kavanagh, of Kilcullenbridge, co. Kildare, and had two sons :

I. Richard, of whom presently.
II. Henry Whytehead, b. 22nd Jan., 1753 (old style); d. young.
3. Richard, of Ballymore Eustace and 30 Upper Baggot-street, Dublin : son of Thomas ; b. 20th Jan., 1752 (o.s.) Married, in 1778, as his second wife Charlotte, eldest dau. of the Rev. John Wisdom, M.A.,

Vicar of Lusk, co. Dublin, and had four sons, and three daus. :

I. John-Wisdom, who married his cousin Julia, dau. of Benjamin Helden, of Granard, co. Longford, and had three daughters, all of whom d. unm.
II. George, of whom presently.
III. Henry, who d. unm.
IV. Richard, who also d. unm.
4. George ; second son of Richard ; a Land-Surveyor ; who on the 12th Feb., 1806, m. Margaret, only dau. of Daniel Fearon, of Upper Baggot-street, Dublin, and had four sons :
I. George-Clayton (b. 1808), of whom presently.

II. Daniel Fearon, who d. young.

III. Richard-William, who d. on 25th March, 1867, s. p. legi.

IV. William-Henry, who d. young.

5. George-Clayton Cowell: eldest son of George; b. 16th May, 1808; d. 11th June, 1859, and was bur. at St. Patrick's Cathedral, Dublin, where his parents and grand-parents had also been interred. George Clayton Cowell was twice m.; first on the 20th October, 1836, to Eliza-Jane, only child of the Rev. Andrew Story Young, B.A., of Garrison House, Garrison, co. Fermanagh, by whom he had three sons and one daughter:

I. Rev. George Young Cowell, M.A.; Canon of Kildare; living in 1887.

II. Andrew-Richard. of Cullentra, co. Wexford, M.D. Retired List Bombay Army; also living in 1877.

III. William-Fearon, who d. young.

I. Mary-Anne Margaret, who d. unm.

The issue of Bartholomew, fourth son of Bryan Cowell, is as follows:

2. Bartholomew, of Harristown, who m. Jane-Davis, dau. of George Higgins, of the Silver Hills, county Dublin, and by her had (with daughters, the eldest of whom, Margaret, m. Robert Crawley) four sons:

I. George, born 1755, of whom presently.

II. Robert, a Major, —— Regt.; d. at Windsor in 1836.

III. William-Henry-Clayton, Lt.-Colonel, —— Regt., b. 26th June, 1760; m. Esther, dau. of Peter Metge, of Athlumney, co. Meath, and by her had one child:

I. John-William, b. 23rd June, 1792 (Deed registered 5th April, 1824).

IV. John-Clayton-Cowell: fourth son of Bartholomew; Lieut.-Colonel 1st Royals; A.D.C. to H.R.H. the Duke of Kent.; Governor of St. Thomas's Island; b. in 1762, and d. at Gosport, in 1819; m. in 1796, Ithamar, dau. of James Stevenson, and by her had two sons and three daughters:—1. John-Clayton, of whom presently, and 2. William, who d. young:

I. John-Clayton Cowell; Lieut. 1st Royals; born in 1800; m. in 1829, Frances Ann Hester, youngest dau. of the Rev. Richard and Lady Elizabeth-Jane Brickenden, and by her had three sons and two daughters:

I. Major-Gen. Sir John Clayton Cowell (Ret. List), R.E., K.C.B.

II. Richard-Lambart Bricken-den, Major Artillery Volunteers.

III. Hussey-Vivian-Jervis; b. in 1839, and d. in 1852.

3. George: eldest son of Bartholomew; b. 27th Feb., 1755; m. Amelia, daughter of Gilbert White, of Ardenode, co. Dublin, and had six sons:

I. George, Major 76th Regiment, who d. at Cawnpore, s. p.

II. William, Lieut.-Colonel, 42nd Regiment; C.B.; Medal with Clasp; d. s. p. legi (Will proved in the Diocese of Dublin, in 1827).

III. Henry-Clayton, born 1780, of whom presently.

IV. James-Gifford, b. 17th Aug., 1785; Captain 71st Regiment, (formerly First Royals); m. Letitia; dau. of Major Ormsby and had one child Letitia, who d. young.

V. Frederick - Luke - Gardiner, Lieut. 23rd Royal Welsh Fusiliers; m. Isabella, "dau. of Mary Johnston," of Downpatrick, and had one child:
  I. Frederica, who m. ——— de Spalier (Marriage Settlement registered on the 7th Sept., 1811).
VI. John, Lieut. 1st Royals; d. at Tobago, in 1805, s. p.
4. Henry-Clayton: third son of George; born 29th Sept., 1780; Lieut.-Colonel 1st Royals; married

Esther-Anne Parr, and had two sons and six daughters:
  I. Henry-Robert, of whom presently.
  II. James-Ormsby, who d. young.
5. Henry-Robert: son of Henry-Clayton; Lieut.-Colonel 2nd West India Regiment (formerly Captain in the Buffs); was twice married: first, to Maria Janisch, by whom he had one son and a daughter:
  I. Henry-Clayton, formerly Capt. 36th Regiment.
  I. Letitia-Louisa.

The issue of John, the fifth son of Bryan Cowell, above mentioned is as follows:

2. John, who married Sarah, sister of Benjamin Helden, of Granard, co. Longford, by whom he had two sons and four daughters:
  I. George, Captain in the Irish Artillery, who married ——— Ogilvie; no issue.
  II. John Helden, of whom presently.
3. John-Helden: second son of John; Capt. 64th Regiment; Will

proved in the Prerogative Court, Dublin, in 1799; m. Fanny Lindsay, of Hollymount, co. Mayo, and had two children:
  I. William-Helden Cowell,* who obtained his Ensigncy in the 42nd Regt. in 1815; d. unm.
  II. Matilda, who married Thomas Bayly, Capt. 1st Royals, and left two sons and one daughter.

COWELL. (No. 4.)

Of Armagh.

IN the will of Robert Cowell, of Tynan, co. Armagh, dated 4th June, 1627, the said Robert speaks of his son Henry; of his daughter Magdaline, who was then wife of Hugh Acline (see Burke's *Peerage*, for 1886, Lineage under Sir Thomas Echlin, Bart); of Matthew Lord and Robert Lord his executors: "out of my most certain lands in the co. Monaghan;" the land of the Errighe and the Grange; his son Henry was to be educated at the Dublin University; Hugh Acline (or Echlin), his son-in-law, and his daughter Magdaline, to have the reversion of his property in case of the death of his son Henry Cowell; but said Hugh and Henry were killed in action.

* *Cowell*: For fuller information respecting this "Cowell" (No. 3) family, see our *Irish Landed Gentry when Cromwell came to Ireland*.

COWELL. (No. 5.)

Of Enniscrone, County Sligo.

Arms ; A Lion passant, in dexter paw an olive branch.

JAMES COWELL m. a Miss Jones, and had three sons:

I. James, who m. a Miss Kane, and had issue.

II. John.

III. Patrick,˙ of whom presently.

2. Patrick: third son of James; married a Miss Quinn, and had six children, namely, three sons, and three daughters:

I. James, of whom presently.

II. John, who m. a Miss Carroll.

III. Peter, who m. a Miss Nolan, and had issue.

I. Bridget, who m.Bryan Kilcullen, of Enniscrone, and had issue.

II. Margaret, who m. Richard Burnett(No. 6 on the "Burnett" genealogy, *infra*) and had issue.

III. Cicily, who m. — Price, and had issue.

3. James: eldest son of Patrick;

m. Sarah (or "Sally") Kilcullen, and had three sons and three daus. :

I. Peter, of London, who m., and had a dau.; both living in 1887.

II. John, of Rose Cottage, Enniscrone, co. Sligo, living unm. in 1887.

III. Patrick, of whom presently, living in 1887.

I. Mary, who m. Patrick MacHale, of Castleconnor, and had issue.

II. Catherine, who m. Martin Gordon, and had issue.

III. Bridget, living unm. in 1887.

4. Patrick Cowell, of Enniscrone, co. Sligo: third son of James; m. and had issue, of whom were (in 1884):

I. John, of whom presently.

II. James.

III. William.

5. John Cowell: eldest son of Patrick, of Enniscrone: living in 1887.

COX.*

Of Brefny.

Arms : Sa. a chev. betw. three bucks' scalps ar.   *Crest :* On an arm ar. a bend az. the hand holding a triple branch of pinks ppr. leaved vert.

CAOCH, brother of Cathal, who is No. 113 on the "O'Reilly" pedigree, was the ancestor of *MacCoich ;* anglicised *Cox.*

113. Caoch ("caoch :" Irish, *blind*): son of Annadh.

114. Niall : his son.

115. Mathghamhan : his son.

---

* Cox: Walter, or "Watty" Cox, the son of a Westmeath blacksmith, a hanger-on of the revolutionary party in 1798, was born about 1770. He is said to have proved faithless both to his own side and to the Government. In 1797 he established the

116. Cathal: his son.
117. Aonghus : his son.

118. Mathghamhan : his son.
119. Giolla na Naomh : his son

CRAIG.

Arms: Gu. a fesse erm. betw. three crescents ar.   *Crest:* A lion's head vert, collared or.

DAVID, the youngest son of Malcolm the Third, King of Scotland, was an ancestor of *Craig*

109. Malcolm the Third, King of Scotland; died, A.D. 1094.
110. David, King of Scotland: his youngest son.
111. Prince Henry: his son.
112. David (2) : his son.
113. Isabel: his daughter; married Robert Bruce, called "The Noble," who competed with Baliol for the crown of Scotland.
114. Robert Bruce: their son; earl of Annundale, and of Carrick.
115. Robert Bruce: his son; called "King Robert the First," of Scotland.
116. Margery : his daughter; married to the *Mor Mhaor Leamhna* or "Great Steward of Lennox"— namely, Walter, the lord "steward" of Scotland, who was ancestor of *Stewart* and *Stuart*.
117. Robert Stewart : their son.
118. John: his son.
119. James: his son.
120. Ninion: his son.
121. James (2): his son.
122. Ninion (2): his son.
123. James (3): his son.

124. Christian : his son.
125. Ninion (3) : his son.
126. William: his son:
127. Mary : his daughter.
128. Mary Dickson : her daughter.
129. Matilda Bailie: her daughter.
130. Stewart Craig: her son; married Mary Graham, and had issue seven sons and three daughters. The sons were—1. Thomas-Henry ; 2. Robert-Stewart; 3. Rev. Stewart-Baillie, Vicar of St. Mark's, Hull, Yorkshire ; 4. John ; 5. William-Graham, 19, Waterloo-road, Dublin; 6. Rev. Graham, Rector of St. Catherine's, Tullamore ; 7. Hugh-Dunbar. The daughters were—1. Sarah ; 2. Mary ; 3. Maud, who died, January, 1877.
This Thomas Henry Craig (1) married Mary Charlotte Jenkins, and died October, 1872, leaving issue—1. Stewart-Charles, 102nd Regiment, who died in Naples, 1876 ; 2. Elizabeth Helen, who married Captain Marra, Italian Navy, and had issue one daughter

---

Union Star, nominally in the interests of the United Irishmen, but it was ultimately repudiated by the Directory. After a visit to America, he established his *Irish Monthly Magazine*, in which are to be found some valuable biographical details of many distinguished persons of the period. He died at 12 Clarence-street, Dublin, in poverty, on the 17th January, 1837, aged 66 years. Some years before his death he had tried to cut the head off King William's Statue in Dublin—relinquishing his task upon finding his tools unsuitable for the purpose.

named Violet. Robert-Stewart (2) married Emily Mary Noble, and had issue: 1. Edwin-Stewart, (2) Robert-Annesley. Rev. Stewart-Baillie (3) married Mary Alder, and had issue —1. John-Alder, 2. Stewart-Graham, 3. Graham. John (4) married Madelina-Louisa Boys, and had issue—1. Graham-Stewart-Lowther, 2. Dunbar, 3. John. William-Graham Craig (5) married Harriett-Ada Lawless; no issue. Rev. Graham (6) married Hellen Noble,

and had issue—1. Robert-Stewart, 2. Henry-Graham, 3. Herbert-Newcombe, 4. William-Arthur, 5. Alan.

Sarah Craig (1) married James Henry (deceased) and had issue—1. Robert, 2. Stewart : both of whom are also deceased. Mary (2) was (in 1877) unmarried.

131. Robert-Stewart Craig, of Belfast; son of Stewart Craig; living in 1877.

132. Edwin-Stewart Craig : his son ; living in 1877.

CREAN.

Of Mayo and Sligo.

Arms : Ar. a wolf ramp sa. betw. three human hearts, gu.   *Crest :* A demi wolf ramp. sa. holding betw. the paws a human heart or.   *Motto :* Cor mundum crea in me, Deus.

SCRALAGH, brother of Fionnbeartach who is No. 94 on the "Michil" pedigree, was the ancestor of *O'Creain ;* anglicised *Crean,* and *Crane.*

94. Scralach (or Tenelach): son of Endadaig (or Edalach).

95. Crean ("cre :" Irish, *earth ;* "an," an interrogative particle ; and "Crean" means *a buying*): his son ; a quo *O'Creain.*

96. Gairmliach : his son.

97. Donal : his son.

98. Crean Oge : his son.

99. Lochlann : his son.

100. Dalbach* : his son.

101. Maoldun : his son.

102. Maolmaodhog : his son.

103. Cathmaol : his son.

104. Gairmliach : his son ; a quo *O'Gairmliacha,* anglicised *Gormley,* and *Grimley,* (see the "Grimley" pedigree).

105. Maccraith : his son.

106. Meanmnach ("meanma," gen. "meanman :" Irish, *comfort*) : his son : a quo *MacMeanman,* anglicised *MacMenamin.*

107. Connor : his son. This Connor had a younger brother named Donal, who was the ancestor of *Grimley.*

108. Dermod : son of Connor.

109. Brian : his son.

110. Feral : his son.

111. Aodh (or Hugh) : his son.

112. Manus : his son.

113. Patrick : his son.

114. Donall : his son.

115. Manus (2) : his son ; had a brother named Richard.

---

* *Dalbach :* This name signifies "blind drunk :" *dall :* Irish, "blind ;" *bach,* "drunkenness." (Compare *Bac-chus,* the god of *wine*).

116. Owen : son of Manus.
117. John : his son.

118. Andrew : his son.
119. John O'Crean : his son.

CROLY.*

Arms : Gyronny of ten ar. and sa. *Crest :* A wolf pass. sa.

MAOLRUANAIDH, brother of Teige who is No. 108 on the "MacDermott" pedigree, was the ancestor of *O'Cruaidh-locha ;* anglicised *Crawley, Crolly, Croly, Crole, Crowley,*† *Campion, Hardy, Lake, Locke,* and *Poole.*

108. Maolruanaidh: son of Murtagh.
109. Teige : his son.
110. Dermod (Darby, Jeremy, or Jeremiah): his son.
111. Sioda : his son.
112. Dermod : his son ; who was called *Cruaidh-locha* (" cruaidh ;" Irish, *hard ;* Gr. "kru-os ;" Lat. " cru-dus ;" and Irish "loch," gen. "locha," *a lake, a pool,* meaning " The Hardy Champion"); a quo *O'Cruaidhlocha.*

113. Maccraith : his son.
114. Rory Mór : his son.
115. Hugh: his son.
116. Lochlann Mór : his son.
117. Lochlann Oge : his son.
118. Ranal : his son.
119. Connor : his son.
120. David : his son.
121. Donoch : his son.
122. Dermod (3) : his son.
123. Amhailgadh [awly] O'Croly: his son.

* *Croly :* Rev. George Croly, LL.D., poet, dramatic author, novelist, and divine, was born in Dublin in 1780. Having received his education in Trinity College, he went to London, and became distinguished in the world of letters. Throughout life he was a staunch Tory, in politics, and rendered material service to his party by contributions to *Blackwood* and other periodicals. He died suddenly on the 24th November, 1860, aged 80 years ; and was interred in the church of St. Stephen's, Walbrook, London, of which he had for many years been rector. His eloquence, his massive form, grave and inflexible countenance, and sonorous voice, rendered him a most attractive pulpit orator.

† *Crowley :* Peter O'Neill Crowley, a prominent Fenian, was born on the 23rd May, 1832, at Ballymacoda, county Cork, where his father was a respectable farmer. His uncle, Rev. Peter O'Neill, was flogged at Cork in 1798 for alleged complicity in the insurrection of that year. Peter inherited his farm, and cultivated it with great industry and thrift. He was a teetotaller from ten years of age ; he was studious in his habits, and was greatly beloved by relatives and friends. He early joined the Fenian movement, became one of its active propagandists, took the field in March, 1867, and formed one of a party under command of Captain M'Clure in the attack on the Knockadoon coastguard station. Afterwards he took refuge with a few comrades in Kilcloney Wood, county Cork, where, on Sunday, the 31st March, his small party was attacked and defeated by Military and Constabulary. He was mortally wounded in the fight, and died a few hours afterwards at Mitchelstown, whither he was conveyed—being treated with the greatest kindness and consideration by his captors. An immense concourse attended his funeral at Ballymacoda.

CUMMIN.

Arms : Gu. three garbs ar.

FEAREADHACH, a son of Muireadhach who is No. 89 on the " O'Neill" (of Tyrone) pedigree, was the ancestor of *Clan Cumaoin ;* anglicised *Cummin, Cuming,** and *Cumine.*

90. Feareadhach : son of Muireadhach.
91. Ferghna Fionn : his son.
92. Cumaoin ("cumaoin :" Irish, *fellowship*): his son; a quo *Clann Cumaoin.*
93. Ainmeada (or Anaileadh)¯: his son.
94. Cathmhoghtha: his son.
95. Longseach : his son.

96. Morogh : his son.
97. Murcheartach : his son.
98. Dunaleadh : his son.
99. Dalach : his son.
100. Conangan : his son.
101. Maolfabhal : his son.
102. Aodh : his son.
103. Maolmithid O'Cumaoin : his son; had three brothers—1. Cucaille, 2. Murcha, 3. Giollacolum.

DALY.

Arms : Per fesse ar. and or, a lion ramp. per fess sa. and gu. in chief two dexter hands couped at the wrist of the last.

ADHAMH [Adam], brother of Fargal the 156th Monarch of Ireland who is No. 95 on the " O'Neill" (of Tyrone) pedigree, was the ancestor of *O'Dalaighe* (of *Leath Cuinn,* or Meath, Ulster, and Connaught) ; anglicised *Daly,* and *O'Daly.*†

95. Adhamh : son of Maoldun, Prince of Ulster.
96. Corc : his son.

97. Faghnach : his son.
98. Dalach ("dall" Irish, *blind*) : his son ; a quo *O'Dalaighe.*

---

* *Cuming :* Doctor Thomas Cuming was born in Armagh on the 19th March, 1798. His father was a Presbyterian clergyman, and his mother was Eliza Black. Having spent seven years in the Royal School, Armagh, he studied medicine at Glasgow, Edinburgh, Dublin, London,and Paris. Having, in 1819, obtained an M.D. degree in Edinburgh, he came to Dublin, where he studied for three years as clinical clerk to Cheyne, at the House of Industry Hospitals. On the 21st June, 1820, he became a Licentiate ; and, on the 10th January. 1854, a Fellow of the College of Physicians. In the latter year he received, *honoris causa,* the degree of M.D. from the Dublin University. In 1829, he removed to Armagh, where he became Physician to the District Lunatic Asylum. He contributed papers, on Diseased Heart and Caverum Oris, to Vols. III. and IV. of the *Dublin Hospital Reports* ; and, on Pneumonia in Children, in Vol. V. of the " Transactions of the College of Physicians," and has published other papers and reports. Dr Cuming married, in 1826, Miss Mary Black (deceased), and had two sons and two daughters ; was in 1886, with the exception of Dr. Grattan, the Senior of the Licentiates of the College of Physicians in Ireland.

‡ *Daly :* This family is distinct from " O'Daly" of Munster

99. Gillcoimdhe: his son.

100. Teige : his son.

101. Muredach : his son.

102. Dalach (2) : his son.

103. Cuconnachta-na-Scoil O'Daly (or "Cuconnachta of the Schools):" his son; the first of this family that assumed this sirname.

104. Teige (2): his son; was "Primate of Ireland."

105. Aongus : his son.

106. Donoch Mór : his son; had two younger brothers—1. Caroll, who was the ancestor of *O'Daly*, of Brefney, Westmeath, and Connaught;* and 2. Giollaiosa.

107. Aongus (2): son of Donoch Mór.

108. Donoch Ruadh : his son.

109. Aongus Ruadh : his son.

110. Donn : his son.

111. Daire : his son.

112. Donn (2) : his son.

113. Melachlin : his son.

114. John : his son.

115. Teige (3) : his son ; had a brother named John.

116. Dermod : son of Teige.

117. Teige (4) : his son ; had four brothers—1. Dermod, 2. Donoch, 3. Ferdinando, and 4. Godfry.

118. Donoch (or Denis) : son of Teige ; had two brothers—1. Dermod, and 2. John.

119. Dermod : son of Donoch ; had two brothers—1. John, and 2. Hugh.

120. Teige (5) O'Daly : son of Dermod.

DARCY.†

Arms : Gu. three cinquefoils ar. a label az.

FIACHRA, an elder brother of Niall of the Nine Hostages, the 126th Monarch of Ireland, who is No. 87 on the "O'Neill" pedigree, was the ancestor of *O'Dorchaidhe ;* anglicised *Dorcey, Dorcy, Dorsey, Darcy, Darkey,* and *D'Arcy* (of the county Galway).

---

* *Connaught* : One of the residences of the "O'Daly" family in Connaught was *Lis-Ua-Dalaighe* (meaning the "Lis or Fort of O'Daly"), which has been anglicised *Lisadill* : now the seat of the Gore-Booth family near the town of Sligo. Of that branch of the "O'Daly" family was the famous Bard, Carroll O'Daly, the reputed composer of the exquisite Irish Melody *Eibhlén-a-Ruin*, which has been modernized *Aileen Aroon.*

Denis Daly was a member of the Irish Parliament, and the intimate friend of Henry Grattan. He represented the town of Galway in 1767, and sat for the county from 1768 until his death. A friend to Catholic rights, he opposed general parliamentary reform. He was a Privy-Councillor, and for some time Muster-Master General. Grattan considered his death an irretrievable loss to Ireland.

† *Darcy* : Patrick, Count Darcy, an engineer officer, was born at Galway, on 27th September, 1723. He was sent to an uncle in Paris in 1739. There he studied under Clairaut, and at the age of seventeen distinguished himself by the solution of some extremely difficult mathematical problems. He made two campaigns in Germany and one in Flanders—being Colonel in the Irish Brigade at Rosbach in 1757. His essay on artillery and on scientific questions display genius and solidity of judgment. He died in Paris, of cholera, on the 18th October, 1799, aged 56 years. A eulogium was pronounced upon him by Condorcet.—WEBB.

2 C

87. Fiachra : son of Eochy Moy-vane, the 124th Monarch of Ireland.

88. Dathi : his son ; the 127th Monarch.

89. Eochaidh Breac : his son.

90. Laoghaire : his son.

91. Seanach : his son.

92. Diarmaid : his son.

93. Dioma Cron : his son.

94. Dluthach : his son ; had a brother named Cuimin.

95. Dorchadh ("dorchadh:" Irish, *dark*) : his son ; a quo *O'Dorchaidhe ;* living in 1417.

The first of the " Darcy" family who settled in Galway was Bhaiter Riabhach (*baiter :* Irish, water), a quo *Atkins*, and *Atkinson*.

1. Bhaiter Riabhach.

2. Tomas : his son.

3. Padraic : his son.

4. Conchobhar : his son

5. Nioclas : his son.

6. Seamus Riabhach : his son.

7. Nioclas : his son.

8. Seamus Riabhach : his son ; had a brother named Doiminig [Dominick] : both living in 1666.

DAVIDSON.

Of the County Wexford.

Arms : Ar. a chev. sa betw. three mullets pierced gu.

MOROCH na-n Gaodhail (or " Moroch of the Gael"), brother of Dermod na-n Gaill (or "Dermod of the English," meaning Dermod MacMorough, the last King of Leinster), who is No. 114 on the " Kavanagh" pedigree, was the ancestor of *MacDaibhidh ;* anglicised *MacDavid* (meaning the *son of David*) and modernized *Davidson.*

114. Moroch na-n Gaodhail.

115. Murtogh : his son.

116. Donoch Reamhar* (" ream-har :" Irish, *wealthy, fleshy*) : his son.

117. Murtogh : his son.

118. Donoch : his son.

119. Eimhin Ruadh (" eimh :" Irish, *active ;* " ruadh," *red*), or Red Edmond : his son ; a quo *Mac-Redmond.*

120. Seanach (called Owen) : his son ; had a brother named Maurice.

121. Manus : son of Seanach.

122. David Mór : his son ; a quo *MacDaibhidh,* anglicised *Davison, Daws, Dawson, Davy,* and *Davys, MacDavy Mór, MacDamor,* and *Damer.*

123. Patrick : his son.

124. Felim : his son.

125. David (2) : his son.

126. Patrick MacDavid : his son ; known as *MacDamor,* of Gorey, co. Wexford.

* *Donoch Reamhar* [raw-wor]: This Donoch had a brother named Connor, who was father of Dermod, the father of William, the father of Maurice, the father of Murtogh, who was abbot of Ferns, in the county Wexford.

DAVIN.

Lords of Fermanagh.

Arms: A lion pass. guard. or.

CAIRBRE an-Daimh Airgid, who is No. 91 on the " O'Hart" pedigree, was ancestor of *O'Daimhin ;* anglicised *O'Davin, Davin, Davine, O'Devin, Devin,* and *Devine.*

91. Cairbre an Daimh Airgid ("airgiod :" Irish, *silver* ; Lat. " argentum ;" Gr. "arg-uros"), King of Orgiall.

92. Daimhin: his son. This Daimhin had a brother named Nadsluagh, who was the ancestor of *MacMahon,* Princes of Monaghan ; and another brother named Cormac, who was the ancestor of *Maguire,* Princes of Fermanagh.

93. Lochlann : his son ; had a brother named Tuathal Maolgharbh, and another named Clochar.

94. Fergus : his son.

95. Maoldun : his son.

96. Daimhin ("daimh :" Irish, *a poet ;* Gr. "daem-on," *a learned*

man, and "daio," *to know ;* Heb. " deah," *science*) : his son ; a quo *O'Daimhin.*

97. Foghartach ; his son.

98. E o c h a i d h L e a m h r a d h O'Daimhin ("leamhradh :" Irish, *a foolish saying*) : his son ; a quo *O'Leamhraidh,* anglicised *Lavery, Laury* and *Laurie ;* was the first of the family who assumed this sirname.

99. Dubhthire : his son.

100 Eochaidh (2) : his son.

101. Cathal : his son.

102. Muireadhach : his son.

103. Cumascach : his son.

104. Fiacha O'Daimhin :* his son ; the last lord of Fermanagh of this family.

DEMPSEY. (No. 1.)

Chiefs of Clanmaliere.†

Arms: Gu, a lion ramp. ar. armed and langued az. betw. two swords, points upwards of the second, pommels and hilts or, one in bend dexter, the other in bend sinister.

DIOMUSACH, who is No. 97 on the " Connor" Faley pedigree ; was the ancestor of *O'Diomasaighe ;* anglicised *Dempsey,* and *O'Dempsey.*

97. Diomusach : ("diomusach :" Irish, *proud, haughty, arrogant*) : son

of Congall ; a quo *O'Diomasaighe.*

98. Flann Da Congall : his son ;

---

* *O'Daimhin :* The O'Daimhin family were, in 1427, chiefs of Tirkennedy, in the county Fermanagh.

† *Clanmaliere* : This territory lay principally on both sides of the river Barrow, in the King's and Queen's counties : it contained parts of the present baronies of Geashill and Philipstown, in the King's County ; with part of Portnehinch, in the Queen's County ; and part of Offaley, in the co. Kildare, including Monasterevan and the adjoining districts ; and, according to Sir Charles Coote in his survey, the O'Dempseys had a part of the barony of Ballycowen, in the King's County.

had an elder brother named Æneas, who was ancestor of *O'Connor Faley.*

99. Cineth (by some called Tumaltach): his son; had a brother Mugron, who was the ancestor of *Hoolahan,* of " Clann Colgan."

100. Donal: his son; had a brother named Riaghan, who was the ancestor of *Dunne,* and a quo *O'Regan.* This Donal had another brother named Hugh, who was the ancestor of *O'Dempsey,* lords of Clanmaliere (as in the next following genealogy).

101. Hugh O'Dempsey: son of Donal; was the first of the family that assumed this sirname.

102. Conor : his son.

103. Maoluradh ("uradh:" Irish, *apparel, good condition*): his son; a quo *Clann Maoluraidh,* anglicised " Clanmaliere."

104. Corcran : his son.

105. Diomusach : his son.

106. Hugh O'Dempsey : his son.

107. Corcran (2) : his son.

108. Florence: his son ; was the first "lord of Clanmaliere."

109. Cubhroa : his son.

110. Dermod : his son.

111. Hugh : his son.

112. Coilen : his son.

113. Fionn : his son.

114. Melachlin : his son.

115. Dermod (2): his son.

116. Fionn (2) : his son.

117. Melachlin (2) : his son.

118. Fionn (3) : his son.

119. Dermod (3) : his son.

120. Maolmorra: his son ; lord of Clanmaliere.

121. Cahir (or Cahyr), of Ballybrittas, in the Queen's Co.: his son.

122. Hugh : his son.

123. Dermod (4) : his son.

124. Terence (or Tirloch) O'Dempsey : his son; died without issue, A.D. 1578.

DEMPSEY. (No. 2.)

Lords of Clanmaliere.

Arms. Same as those of "Dempsey" (No. 1). *Crest:* A demi lion ramp gu: langued az. supporting in the dexter paw a sword ar. pommel and hilt or. *Supporters:* Two knights in complete armour chained together by the left and right leg all ppr. *Motto:* Elatum a Deo non deprimat.

HUGH, a younger brother of Donal who is No. 100 on the foregoing "Dempsey" (No. 1) pedigree, was the ancestor of *O'Dempsey,* lords of Clanmaliere.

100. Hugh: son of Cineth; chief of his family.

101. Connor : his son.

102. Maolughra : his son.

103. Corcran : his son.

104. Diomasach : his son.

105. Corcran (2): his son.

106. Flann : his son ; in his time the family assumed the sirname *O'Dempsey.*

107. Hugh (2) : his son.

108. Conbroga : his son.

109. Dermod O'Dempsey: his son; built the Abbey of Monasterevan, A.D. 1179.

110. Hugh : his son.

111. Coilen: his son; died without issue; had a brother named Fionn.

112. Maolseachlainn: son of the said Fionn.

113. Fionn (2): his son.

114. Dermod: his son.

115. Maolmordha: his son.

116. Cahir: his son.

117. Hugh, of Loghine, Ballybrittas: his son; died in 1563.

118. Dermod Ruadh: his son; had two brothers—1. Owen, 2. Terence: both of whom died without issue.

119. Sir Terence: son of Dermod Ruadh; knighted in May, 1599, by Robert Devereux, earl of Essex, lord lieutenant of Ireland; created "baron of Philipstown" and "Viscount Clanmaliere," by patent dated 8th July, 1631, *temp.* Charles I.

120. Uaithne (Oweney, Toney, or Anthony), of Clonegauny, in the King's County: his son; died (before his father) in 1638. This Uaithne had four brothers—1. Hugh; 2. Right Rev. Edmond, Roman Catholic Bishop of Leighlin; 3. Rev. Feagh, Roman Catholic vicar-general of Kildare; 4. James.

121. Lewis: son of Uaithne; the second "lord viscount of Clanmaliere," and baron of Philipstown. This Lewis took an active part in the "Rebellion" of 1641, for which he

was outlawed and attainted; · he died intestate, and administration of his effects was granted in May, 1683. He had two brothers—1. Sir Christopher, who, when very young, was knighted by lord Falkland, lord lieutenant of Ireland, in July, 1624: this Sir Christopher died without issue; 2. James O Dempsey, of Bishop's Court, in the co. Kildare, who was a colonel in the Army of King James the Second.

122. Maximilian O'Dempsey: son of Lewis; was made lord lieutenant of the Queen's County, by King James the Second, and sat in the Parliament held by him on 7th May, 1689. This Maximilian died without issue, in 1714; his estates were, by Act of Attainder of William III., confiscated in 1691, for his adherence to the House of Stuart; he had a younger brother named Terence O'Dempsey, who, after the confiscation of the family estates in 1691, left Ireland, in his boyhood, and settled in Cheshire, England, where at an advanced age he died in 1769.

123. Thomas Dempsey, of Northchurch: son of Terence; died at Laurel House, Foxtell Park, Liverpool, England, in 1816.

124. James* Dempsey, of Liverpool: son of Thomas; d. in 1847.

DEVIN.

Of the County Clare.

Motto: Sursum corda.

THIS sirname (see the "Davin" pedigree, p. 403) is another anglicised form of *O'Daimhin*, which has been anglicised *Devin, Davine,* and *Devine.* In ancient times—down to A.D. 1427, the *O'Daimhin* family were Chiefs of

* *James:* This is the James Dempsey, Merchant, of Liverpool, mentioned in Note, p. 248 of Connellan's *Four Masters.*

Tirkennedy ; Fiacha O'Daimhin, who is No. 104 on the " Davin" pedigree, was the last lord of Fermanagh of this family. To him succeeded the Maguires, as Princes of Fermanagh. From that county, *circa* A.D. 1713, James *Devine* emigrated, and settled near Kilkee, in the county Clare. Commencing with him the pedigree is, as follows:

James Devine (I.) had, besides four daughters, four sons—1. Patrick, 2. James, 3. Martin, 4. Terence.

I. Patrick, of whom presently.

II. James: second son of James, m. and had three sons—1. Patrick, 2. Thomas, 3. Terence; and a daughter Mary, who m. Senan MacDonnell, of Kilmihill, and had two sons and two daughters. These sons were: 1. Michael, living in 1881; 2. Senan, who d. unm. ; and one of the two daughters was Mary, who m. and had a family.

I. Patrick: the eldest son of James (II.); m.——M'Grath, and had three sons and two daughters. These sons were: 1. Thomas, of Kilmihill; 2. John; 3. Patrick, of Kilmihill: I. This Thomas, of Kilmihill, married Joanna O'Shea, and had a family. II. John, living in Australia, in 1881. III. Patrick, of Kilmihill, m. and also had a family. The two daughters of Patrick were—1. Mary, m. in America, living in 1881; 2. Margaret, m. to Michael O'Connor, of Monemore, and had a family.

II. Thomas: the second son of James (II.); m. Bridget Molony, and had four sons: 1. Patrick, of Kilmihill; 2. James, of Kilmihill; 3. Michael, of Tarmon; 4. Denis, of Kilrush, co. Clare: these four sons, living in 1887.

III. Terence: the third son of James (II.); was accidentally killed when a young man.

III. Martin: the third son of James (I.) ; of him nothing is now known.

IV. Terence: the fourth son of James (I.); m. and had two sons: 1. James; and 2. Michael, of Killard.

I. This James was m. to —— Kean, and had sons and daughters, living in 1880 in Davenport, Iowa, U.S.A.

II. Michael, of Killard (living in 1881), m. Kate Talty, and had one son—John, of Killard; and three daughters—1. Mary, 2. Bridget, 3. Kate. This John of Killard, m. B. Clancy, and had a family.

2. Patrick: eldest son of James (I.); m. and had two sons and two daughters: the sons were—1. John, 2. Patrick; and the daughters were—1. Mary, 2. Norah.

I. This John, of whom presently.

II. Patrick: second son of Patrick (2); married Margaret Kean, and had four sons and one daughter: the sons were —1. Thomas, who d. in 1878; 2. Michael; 3. James; 4. John. The daughter was Bridget— all of this family living in 1887 in the United States, America.

3. John, of Corbally, Kilkee: son of Patrick (2); m. Mary MacGreen, and had three sons and four daughters. The sons were—1. Michael, who died in infancy; 2. Michael-John, of whom presently; 3. Patrick, who d. in infancy. The

daughters were—1. Kate, who d. in Iowa, United States, America, in 1861; 2. Mary; 3. Bridget; 4. Norah, unm. in 1887. This Kate was twice m.; first, to Patrick Keane, of Kilkee, co. Clare, but by him had no issue. Her second husband was John Costello, Davenport, Iowa, U.S.A., by whom she had two sons and two daughters. This Mary, the second daughter of John (3), m. Martin Hennessy, of Iowa, and had one daughter, Bridget-Fanny, living in 1887. And John's daughter, Bridget, m. Patrick Hennessy, of Davenport, Iowa, and had a son, William, and

two daughters, Bridget and Norah —all living in 1887.

4. Michael-John Devine (living in 1887), of Kilkee, co. Clare: son of John; on 29th July, 1868, m. Fanny-Mary, eldest dau. of John O'Hart, of Dublin, the Writer of this Work, and has had—1. Kathleen, who d. in infancy; 2. John Francis, who also d. in infancy; 3. Mary-Elizabeth; 4. John-Patrick; 5. Kathleen; 6. Fanny; 7. Laura; 8. Elizabeth; 9. Herbert; 10. Francis; 11. Patrick.

5. John-Patrick Devine: his son; b. 16th March, 1874, and living in 1887.

DILLON. (No. 1,)

Arms: A lion pass. betw. three crescents gu.   *Crest:* A semi lion ramp. gu. holding in the paws an estoile wavy or.

LOCHAN Dilmhain (by some called "Lochan Dilionn," from the Irish *dilé,* "a flood") was, according to the "Book of Armagh," ancestor of *Dillon,* of *Cuircneach* or "Dillon's Country," in the county Westmeath; and was, according to some of the Irish genealogists, brother of Colman Mór (king of Meath), and of Hugh Slaine, the 141st Monarch of Ireland: all three (those genealogists say), the sons of Dermod, the 133rd Monarch, who was son of Fergus Cearrbheoil, son of Connall Creamthann (the first Christian King of Meath), son of Niall of the Nine Hostages, the 126th Monarch.   And it is stated that the said Lochan killed the said Colman Mór, for refusing to let him enjoy his proportion of the Kingdom of Meath, called *Cuircneach;* and therefore fled into France, where he and his posterity remained until Robert Le Dillon, lineally descended from the said Lochan, came into Ireland (with those that Dermod Mac-Morough invited out of England to assist him in the recovery of his Kingdom of Leinster,) and laid claim to the said territory of *Cuircneach;* which having made appear, after some contest and strife, O'Melaghlin, then King of Meath, was by the interposition and mediation of O'Molloy and MacGeoghagan, then powerful men in the country, content he should enjoy; and, accordingly, he and his posterity possessed that territory from that time down to the Cromwellian confiscations of Ireland, in the seventeenth century.

That the said Lochan Dilmhain* was the ancestor of *Dillon, Delion,*

---

* *Dilmhain :* This name has been also anglicised *Dillane.*

or *Dillune*, or that he fled into France upon the murder of his brother is not gainsayed; but that he was brother of either Aodh Slaine (the 141st Monarch of Ireland), or of Colman Mór, King of Meath, is contradicted by the "Book of the Reigns of the Irish Monarchs," where giving an account of the reign of the Monarch Aodh Slaine, it is stated:

"Aodh (or Aidus) Slaine (son of Dermod, son of Fergus Cearbheoil), and Colman Rimidh, the 142nd Monarch, son of Baodan (or Boetanus), the 137th Monarch, son of Murchertus Mór MacEarca, the 131st Monarch, son of Muredach, son of Eoghan, son of Niall Mór (or Niall of the Nine Hostages), reigned jointly for six years, until Colman (rimidh) was slain by Lochan dilmhain, son of Baodan, son of Muriartus or Murchertus Mór MacEarca, son of Muredach; and Aidus Slaine was killed by Conall Guthbhinn."

According to this extract, it is evident that Lochan Dilmhain was brother of Colman Rimeach (or Rimidh), the 142nd Monarch (whom he killed), and not the brother of Colman Mór, who was King of Meath, but never Monarch of Ireland; for, Lochan Dilmhain was the fourth generation after Eoghan, son of Niall Mór, and Colman Mór was the third generation after Conall Creamthann, brother of Eoghan—both sons of the said Niall Mór (or Niall of the Nine Hostages), above mentioned.

No account can be given of the generations from the said Lochan Dilmhain to the said Robert Le Dillon, who was called "Robert the *Sacsanach*" (or Robert the *Englishman*), because he came over with the English at the time of the English invasion of Ireland; but as Roderick O'Connor, brother of Cathal Craobh-dearg, who is No. 112 on the (No. 1) "O'Connor" (Connaught) pedigree, was the Irish Monarch at the time of that invasion, we may assume that Robert Le Dillon was of the same (112th) generation as the Monarch Roderick O'Connor; and that there must have been twenty generations between Lochan Dilmhain and his descendant Robert Le Dillon.*

Down from that Robert Le Dillon, the following is the stem of the *Dillon* family:

112. Robert Le Dillon.
113. Thomas: his son.
114. William Dillon: his son; the first of the family that assumed this sirname.
115. Sir Henry: his son; built the Abbey† (or Convent) of St. Francis, in Athlone, in the reign of King John.
116. Gerald: his son.
117. Gerald Oge: his son.
118. Edmond: his son.

* *Robert Le Dillon:* Niall of the Nine Hostages is No. 87 on the "O'Neill" (Princes of Tyrone) pedigree; whose son Eoghan (or Eugenius) is therefore No. 88; whose son Muredach is No. 89; whose son Murchertus Mór MacEarca is No. 90; whose son Baodan is No. 91; whose son Lochan Dilmhain must therefore be No. 92: so that there were at least twenty generations between him and Robert Le Dillon, above mentioned.

† *Abbey:* Some persons are of opinion that "there is no such thing as a *Franciscan* Abbey;" that "the Franciscan houses are properly called *Convents*, which were never governed by Abbots;" and that, in such cases, "*Guardian* is the proper designation." In our sources of information, however, we find mention made of the "Abbey of St. Francis, in Athlone;" "Abbey of Cavan," etc., as recorded in these pages.

119. Gerald (3): his son; had three sons—1. James, 2. Gerald Oge, and 3. Richard.

120. Sir James: son of Gerald.

121. Thomas Maol: his son. This Thomas had three sons—1. Sir Theobald (or Toby), 2. Edmond, 3. Gerald.

122. Sir Theobald: son of Thomas, Maol: was the first "lord viscount Dillon," of Costello and Gallen, in the county Mayo.

123. Sir Luke: his son.

124. Robert: his son.

125. Theobald: his son; lord viscount Dillon.

126. Henry: his son; lord viscount Dillon, living in 1708.

127. Richard Dillon: his son.

DILLON. (No. 2.)

Earls of Roscommon.

Arms : Ar. a lion ramp. betw. three crescents an estoile issuant from each gu. over all a fesse az. *Crest :* On a chapeau gu. turned up erm. a falcon rising ar. belled or. *Supporters :* Dexter a griffin vert, wings expanded beaked and legged or, armed gu. ; sinister, a falcon gu. wings expanded and inverted, beaked, legged, and belled or. *Motto :* Auxilium ab alto.

As this Peerage is *dormant* since the death of Michael James Robert Dillon, the 12th Earl, the following information may assist in discovering the rightful heir to the Earldom of Roscommon.

James Dillon who was raised to the Peerage of Ireland, on the 24th January, 1619, as "Lord Dillon, Baron of Kilkenny West," was on the 5th August, 1622, created "Earl of Roscommon."

Robert Dillon, was the 2nd Earl.		
James Dillon,	„	3rd „
Wentworth Dillon,	„	4th „
Cary Dillon,	„	5th „
Robert Dillon,	„	6th „
Robert Dillon,	„	7th „
James Dillon,	„	8th „
Robert Dillon,	„	9th „
John Dillon,	„	10th „
Patrick Dillon,	„	11th „

Michael James Robert Dillon, was the 12th and last Earl.

Cary Dillon, the fifth Earl, was son of Robert Dillon, the second Earl of Roscommon.

James Dillon, the third Earl, was eldest son of Robert Dillon, the second Earl of Roscommon.

Wentworth Dillon, the fourth Earl, who d. s. p., was son of James Dillon, the third Earl of Roscommon. After Wentworth's death, the title reverted to Cary Dillon, the fifth Earl, who was brother of Robert, the second Earl of Roscommon.

Cary Dillon, the fifth Earl, was succeeded by his son Robert Dillon, who was the sixth Earl of Roscommon.

Robert, the sixth Earl, was succeeded by his eldest son Robert, who was the seventh Earl of Roscommon, who d. s. p., but was succeeded by his brother James Dillon, who was the eighth Earl of Roscommon. and who died unm.

The ninth Earl was Robert Dillon,

son of Patrick Dillon of Tuemore (who d. unmarried), and grandson of Lucas Dillon, son of James Dillon, the first Earl of Roscommon.

Robert, the ninth Earl of Roscommon, was succeeded by his brother John Dillon, the tenth Earl of Roscommon, who was twice married: by the first wife he had three daughters and no son; by the second wife he had a son Patrick, who succeeded as the eleventh Earl of Roscommon, who married and had issue an only daughter.

Michael James Robert Dillon, the twelfth and last Earl of Roscommon, was son of Michael Dillon, Esq., Captain in the County Dublin Militia, who was killed at the battle of Ross, in 1798.

(1) This Captain Michael Dillon was son of:

(2) Surgeon James Dillon, who was son of:

(3) Michael Dillon, Esq., of Rath, who was son of;

(4) Mr. Dillon, of Rath, who married Penelopé, sister of James Horan, gent., and by her had two sons, namely, said Michael (3), and Francis:

I. Michael (3) married Mary, dau. and heir of John Jennat, of Recluse and Skedan, county Dublin, and had issue—John, who died young.

II. Francis, of whom presently.

(2) Surgeon James Dillon, above mentioned, was twice married: first, to the daughter of Butler of Waterford, by whom he had no issue; secondly, to Elizabeth, dau. of Joseph Plunket, Esq., and by her had:

(1) Captain Michael Dillon, of the Dublin Militia (killed in 1798 at the battle of Ross), who m. Mary, dau. of the Rev. Richard Griffith, of Kilbritain, county Cork, and had Michael James Robert Dillon, the twelfth and last Earl of Roscommon, since whose death the Earldom has become *dormant*.

(II.) Francis Dillon, the second son of (4) Mr. Dillon, of Rath, and brother of Michael (3), m. and had:

(III.) John Dillon, who married Elizabeth Roberts and had:

(IV.) Richard Dillon, who married and had:

(V.) JOHN DILLON,* living in Montreal, Canada, in 1887, who, presumably, is the rightful heir, in the male line, to the dormant Earldom of Roscommon.

Dillon : Having found the address of this John Dillon we communicated with him to ascertain if he had any family records to sustain his claim to the Earldom of Roscommon ; and if he were the person who, some thirty or thirty-five years ago, was, to our knowledge, a claimant for the said dormant Earldom. We here subjoin his reply, as it may help to elucidate the subject :

"Address : Care of W. J. Tabb, Esq.,
"St. Antoine Hall,
"Montreal, 2nd June, 1886,

"John O'Hart, Esq.,
"Ringsend School,
"Ringsend, Dublin,
"Ireland.

"DEAR SIR,—I would have written sooner, but have been trying to find Lodge's Peerage. . . . . You asked me if I was the person who spoke to you in Kildare, and who told you he was the Heir to the Earldom of Roscommon. I may state I left Ireland when very young and did not return until January, 1880 ; and then for the purpose of looking after the Earldom . . I may also add that, when Henry Gouldburn was Home Secretary, I think about the year 1839 or 1840, the late Earl (of Ros-

DINAN.

Arms : Ar. on a mount in base vert an oak tree, the stem entwined with two serpents interwoven and erect respecting each other all ppr. *Crest :* An owl at gaze ppr.

DOIGHNAN, brother of Beice who is 98 on the "Fox" pedigree, was the ancestor of *O'Doighnain ;* anglicised *O'Dugenan, Dinan, Dinnen, Dignum,* and *Hope.*

98. Doighnan ("doigh;" Irish, *hope ;* Gr. "do-keo," *to think*): son of Tagan ; a quo *O'Doighnain.*
99. Naomhach : his son.
100. Philip : his son.
101. Paul an Fionn : his son.
102. Luke : his son.
103. Augustin : his son.
104. Malachi Ruadh : his son.
105. Magnus (or Mór): his son.

106. Dealbhbaoth : his son.
107. Magnus (2) : his son.
108. Malachi (2) : his son.
109. Magnus (3) : his son.
110. Jerome : his son.
111. John Ballach : his son.
112. Francis : his son.
113. John Ballach O'Dugenan : his son.

DOHERTY. (No. 1.)

Lords of Inishowen.

Arms : Ar. a stag springing gu. on a chief vert three mullets of the first. *Crest :* A hand couped at the wrist erect grasping a sword all ppr. *Another Crest :* A greyhound courant ar. holding in the mouth a hare ppr. *Motto :* Ar mDuthchas (For my hereditary right).

FIAMHAN, a brother of Muriartus (or Muiriartach) who is No. 99 on the (No. 1) "O'Donel" (Tirconnell) pedigree, was the ancestor of *O'Dochartaigh ;* anglicised *Docharty, Dogherty, Doherty, Dougherty,* and *O'Dogherty.*

99. Fiamhan (or Fianamhain): third son of Ceannfaola.
103. Maongal : his son.
101. Dochartach (" dochar :" Irish, *harm*): his son; a quo *O'Dochartaigh.*

102. Maongal (2) : his son.
103. Donoch : his son.
104. Maongal : his son.
105. Donal : his son.
106. Donogh Dunn : his son.
107. Donal Fionn : his son.

common) was reported as dying, my father applied for the Earldom, and, in reply, was told to send the proofs of his claim, which he did (and which were not returned), and the reply he received was that his Claim was well founded ; but the Earl, who was reported as dying, was convalescent, subsequently recovered, and outlived my father. Doctor Dillon Kelly of Mullingar is my cousin, whose mother was sister to my father, and who, I believe, has information which would prove my heirship.

"In conclusion, I beg to thank you for your kindness, and am,

"Dear Sir, your obedient servant,

"JOHN DILLON."

108. Connor : his son.
109. Dermod : his son.
110. Murtagh : his son.
111. Aongus : his son.
112. Donal Mór : his son.
113. Rory : his son.
114. Donal (4) : his son.
115. Connor : his son.
116. Aneisleis : his son.
117. Donal (5) : his son.
118. John : his son.
119. Connor-an-Einigh : his son ; was the first of the family who settled in Inishowen.
120. Donal (6) : his son.
121. Brian Dubh : his son ; had a brother Aodh ; living in 1440.
122. Connor Carrach : his son.
123. Felim : his son.
124. John Mór : his son.
125. John Oge : his son.
126. Sir Cahir O'Dogherty* : his son ; lord of Inishowen ; living in 1608 ; left no male issue. Sir Cahir had two brothers—1. Rory, who was the elder, and whose descendants live in Spain ; 2. John, who died in 1638.

127. John : son of said John ; had two brothers—1. Owen ; 2. William.
128. Cahir : son of said Owen.
129. Cahir : his son ; had a brother Owen ; d. in 1732.
130. John : son of said Owen ; d. 1762.
131. Cahir : son of John ; d. 1784.
132. Henry Dogherty, a Catholic Priest : his son ; had two brothers —1. John ; 2. Clinton Dillon. These three brothers retired to Spain with their uncle, the Rev. Henry O'Dogherty, D.D. And their pedigree, as above given, down from Sir Cahir O'Dogherty, was certified by Fortescue, Ulster King of Arms, on 4th November, 1790.— See Meehan's "*Flight of the Earls.*"

* *Sir Cahir O Dogherty* : In Connellan's "Four Masters" it is stated that, in May, 1608, Sir Cahir O'Dogherty, lord of Inishowen, a young man of great spirit and valour, then only in the twenty-first year of his age, raised an insurrection against the English in Ulster ; being unable to tolerate the insolence and tyranny of Sir George Paulett, Governor of Derry. O'Dogherty and his forces having surprised Derry, they slew Paulett and most of the garrison, and burned the town ; he also took the fort of Culmore, near Derry, from Captain Hart ; and gave the command of the fortress to a valiant chief named Felim MacDavett. O'Dogherty ravaged the settlements of the English in various parts of Derry, Donegal and Tyrone ; and defeated their forces in several engagements. Marshal Wingfield and Sir Oliver Lambert marched against him with four thousand men ; and having advanced to Culmore, MacDavett, unable to defend the place against so great a force, set fire to the fortress, and sailed off with his men towards Derry, carrying away some of the cannon, and throwing the rest into the sea. Wingfield then advanced against Burt Castle, the chief residence of O'Dogherty, near Lough Swilly. MacGeoghegan says the castle was commanded by a monk, who, not having a sufficient force to defend it, and not wishing to subject to the dangers of a siege, O'Dogherty's lady, who was Mary Preston, daughter of Lord Gormanstown, surrendered the castle on condition that the garrison should be spared ; but Wingfield put most of them to the sword, and sent O'Dogherty's wife to her brother. O'Dogherty had various encounters with the English forces, and maintained his ground for about three months in Donegal ; the lord deputy Chichester offered a reward of five hundred marks for his head ; and Sir Cahir being encamped at the Rock of Doune, near Kilmacrennan, was shot dead with a musket ball, by an English soldier, who took deliberate aim at him ; recognising the warlike chief amidst his men, from his waving plume and lofty stature. The extensive estates of O'Dogherty were confiscated, and transferred to Chichester, ancestor to the Earls of Donegal.

DOHERTY. (No. 2.)

Arms: Same as those of "Doherty" (No. 1).

ACCORDING to Dr. O'Donovan's Antiquities* of the county Donegal (at end of Vol. II.), Aodh, a brother of Brian Dubh who is No. 121 on the (foregoing) "Dogherty" pedigree, was the ancestor of this branch of that family:

121. Aodh: a younger son of Donal (6).
122. Shane Mór: his son.
123. Cormac Carrach: his son.
124. Brian Gruamach: his son.
125. Cumhaighe: his son.
126. Diarmaid: his son; living in 1608; ·was contemporary with Sir Cahir O'Doherty.
127. Niall a-Churaigh: son of Diarmaid.

128. Cahir: his son.
129. Owen: his son.
130. Cahir: his son.
131. Donogh: his son.
132. Shane: his son.
133. Donal: his son.
134. John (or Shane) O'Doherty: his son;" was a little boy in 1840."

DOLAN.†

Arms: Az. three crescents in pale or, betw. two plates a chief ar. *Crest:* A decrescent gu.

THE *Dolan* or *O'Dolan* family, of Aughawillin, Lislaughy, Lisgrudy, Lisroughty, and Lisnatullaugh, in the barony of Carrigallen, and county of Leitrim, is descended from Bryan Dolan, of Largy (or Kilargy), situate between Swanlinbar and Manorhamilton, at the north side of Cuiltagh mountain.

Bryan Dolan came with his two

---

* *Antiquities:* Preserved in the Library of the Royal Irish Academy, Dublin.

† *Dolan:* See the *Dowling* pedigree for another "Dolan" or "O'Dolan" family. We believe, however, that this family is a branch of the *O'Dolan* family, mentioned in p. 359, *ante*, as descended from Fiacha Suidhe, one of the two brothers of Conn of the Hundred Battles. That "O'Dolan" family was (see MacDermott's Map of Ancient Ireland, at the end of Connellan's *Four Masters*,) located near Croagh Patrick, in the county of Mayo. Others say that this "Dolan" family derives its name from Eochaidh *Dubhlen*, who is No. 84 on the "O'Hart" pedigree, and that, in early times, the MacGaurans were of the same stock as the O'Dolans. Be this as it may, it is worthy of remark that (See Lewes's Topographical Dictionary of Ireland), from time immemorial, these two families in the barony of Tullaghagh, county Cavan, have been proverbial for their intermarriages. In proof of this assertion we may add the following observations:—
Patrick Dolan, of Lislaughy and Lisnatullaugh, was the son of Charles Dolan and Mary McGauran. He had six sons: Jack, Tiernan, Thomas, Rodger, Felim, and Patrick. Two of these, Tiernan and Felim, were married to McGaurans; and Felim was married a second time to a McGauran. Jack and Rodger were married to two Dolans. He had three daughters: one was married to a Dolan, and the other to a Heavey, whose mother's name was McGauran. Jack Dolan, the eldest son of Patrick Dolan, had four sons and three daughters: the sons were, Thomas, Philip, Patrick,

sons Cormac and Charles to the neighbourhood of Ballymagauran, near the end of the sixteenth century. A bad time it was for priests and papists; yet, notwithstanding, Cormac and Charles rode on Sunday mornings to Killnavart, to hear Mass, a distance of some ten or twelve miles; and, having come there, they attached their horses by their bridle-reins to the branches of trees near the chapel. (Killnavart is situate between Ballymagauran and Ballyconnell, in the barony of Tullaghagh, in the county Cavan.)

Baron MacGauran was then Earl of Tullaghagh, and heard Mass at Killnavart. He observed the two strange young men at Mass, and their horses tied by their bridles to trees near the chapel; he enquired to whom the horses belonged, and where the owners were from. Having been informed on those points, the Baron invited the young men to dinner on the following Sunday; and soon afterwards proffered them a residence in the neighbourhood of Ballymagauran, and they willingly accepted the invitation. Almost immediately afterwards Cormac Dolan, the elder son, married a near relative of the Baron,—the daughter of Terence

MacGauran, who was better known as *Trealach Caoch* or "Blind Terry," in consequence of his being *squint-eyed*. But the Baron's hospitality and Dolan's marriage became a great misfortune to both parties.

In due time after the marriage a son was born to Cormac Dolan; about the same time another child was born for Baron MacGauran, who claimed that his relative Cormac Dolan's wife and daughter of Blind Terry should nurse his (the Baron's) child. Bryan Dolan took this demand as a great insult: he instructed his daughter-in-law to say that he had not come so low that she should become a "hippin-washer" to any man. This message enraged the Baron to madness; he at once rode to Dolan's house, called for the old man, whom he seized by the hair of the head and dragged him by the horse's side at full gallop, and threw him dead on the road. The sons Cormac and Charles seeing the Baron gallop furiously to their house, and immediately galloping back dragging something by his horse's side, one said to the other "the Baron is dragging something after him;" the other exclaimed with an oath "it is my father," and, snapping up a gun that

and Charles. Thomas and Patrick were married to McGaurans; Philip, to McManus; and Charles, to McGuire. Two of the daughters married McGaurans, and one an O'Rourke.

Tiernan Dolan had two surviving sons: Tiernan and Peter. Tiernan is a Catholic priest; and Peter was married to a Dolan.

Thomas Dolan had three sons: Patrick, John, and Thomas; and four or five daughters. The eldest son, Patrick, married a McGauran; and of the daughters two married McGaurans.

Rodger died without issue. Felim left two sons and one daughter, and she married a McGauran.

Patrick Dolan had three sons and two daughters: the sons and one daughter went to America; and the eldest daughter married an O'Rourke.

Abigail McGauran, the wife of Tiernan Dolan, was the daughter of Peter McGauran and Catherine McAuley. Peter McGauran had four sons: John, Eugene, James, and Edward; and three daughters: Ellen, Catherine, and Abigail. John was married to a McGuire, Eugene to a McGauran, James to a Dolan, and Edward to a McGauran. One daughter married a Dolan, one a McGauran, and the other an O'Haran.

lay near, he rushed to the road and shot the Baron dead on the spot. Old Dolan and the Baron were just buried when the relatives and retainers of the Baron came at night, broke into Dolan's dwelling, and killed the brothers Cormac and Charles. Cormac's wife exclaimed, were there none of the friends of Blind Terry there? They spared her and her child, whose name was Rodger, and reared him up as one of themselves.*

About that time society in Tullaghagh was in great confusion; but then as now occupiers were compelled to pay all exactions, rents and taxes.

It is also a tradition that young Rodger had often declared that he would revenge his father's death on McGaughran; and it is said he did so. Having been entrusted with a disagreeable office of collecting from the relatives and retainers of the Baron their several imposts, he took the opportunity on one of these occasions of searching for McGaughran, and withdrew privately from his companions to where he was informed McGaughran usually dwelt. As Rodger expected, he found him there, and at once informed him that he was come to settle an old account with him. McGaughran answered he would be ready as soon as he had finished the egg in his hand; and with haste and confidence armed himself for the encounter, in which he was worsted and lost his life.

When his friends missed Rodger, some said he was surely gone in quest of McGaughran, and some one answered " a more humble employment would suit him better." On his reappearance in a very excited state, with two *skeans* marked with blood, one of the company exclaimed : " I see you met McGaughran, I said you went in search of him; but this man said a less manly employment would suit you better." This insinuation wounded Rodger, and in his anger he said : "let him have McGaughran's *skean*, I will not dirty mine with him." And he struck the offender dead on the spot.

About this time the O'Rourkes and McGaurans were greatly reduced in the social scale. It appears that Rodger Dolan, the grandson of Blind Terry, settled with his family in Aughawillin and thereabouts. For some time there is little or nothing known about them, except their poverty and humiliation until the time of Colonel Gore, of Newtowngore, who, under the Cromwellian Settlement, became possessed of very extensive property in the neighbourhood.

Tradition reports that Colonel Gore resolved to compel Catholic tenants to become Protestants, but the Dolans of Aughawillin, Lislaughy, Liscrudy, and Lisroughty, refused to abandon the Catholic faith, and were therefore evicted from Lislaughy, etc., and their farms given to Protestants and 'verts named Whelan, who changed their name to *Heylin*, on whom their neighbours fastened the sobriquet of the *Mawleens*, or " little bags."

Patrick Dolan, who was one of the evicted, came from Lislaughry to Lisnatullaugh, where his family still remain; but a branch of the family is gone back to part of his farm of Lislaughy. It is believed that the Dolans of the counties of Meath and Louth are descended

---

* *Themselves :* It is a tradition in the locality that a man named McGaughran killed the husband of Blind Terry's daughter; and that her son grew up under the care of his mother's family, and was much esteemed by them.

from a brother of this Patrick Dolan.

1. Terence Dolan now (1887) of Lislaughy is about thirty years of age, and is son of:

2. James Dolan and Mary McGauran of Lislaughy. This James is son of:

3. Peter Dolan, late of Lisnatullaugh and Lislaughy, by his wife Mary Dolan, by whom he had—1. James, 2. Peter, 3. Thomas, who is (1887) a Catholic Priest in Howth, diocese of Dublin; 4. Michael (deceased); 5. Charles, who married Margaret O'Rourke, and has a large family; and three daughters, one of whom, the eldest, Anne, is now a Nun in the Loretto Convent, Kilkenny, the second was married to Mr. Eugene Quinn, of Kildra House, parish of Mohill, and left issue, and the third, Catherine, m. Charles Ward and has issue. This Peter (No. 3) was son of:

4. Tiernan Dolan of Lisnatullaugh, by his wife Abigail McGauran. This Tiernan was son of:

5. Patrick Dolan and his wife Catherine Routledge, of Lislaughy and Lisnatullaugh. This Patrick was son of:

6. Charles Dolan and his wife Mary McGauran, of Aughawillin, Lislaughy, Liscrudy, and Lisroughty. This Charles was son of:

7. Felim Dolan and his second wife Anne O'Rourke, of Aughawillin, Lisloughy, etc. And this Felim was son of:

8. Roger, abovementioned, who was son of:

9. Cormac Dolan, by his wife ———McGauran, the daughter of "Blind Terry." And Cormac was son of:

10. Bryan Dolan, of Killargy, by his wife, whose name we may assume was also McGauran. This is the Bryan Dolan, above mentioned, who with his two sons Cormac and Charles, settled in the neighbourhood of Ballymagauran, towards the end of the sixteenth century.

DONELAN.

Of Ballydonelan.

Arms : Ar. three ducal crowns gu.   *Crest :* A lion's paw erased, holding a sceptre in pale ppr.   *Other Arms :* An oak tree eradicated vert.   *Crest :* On a mound vert a demi lion ramp. or.

ART, a younger brother of Cathal, who is No. 103 on the "Donnellan" (of Connaught) pedigree, was the ancestor of this branch of that family :

103. Art: son of Donallan.

104. Logan (or Melaghlin): his son.

105. Cathal : his son.

106. Flann : his son.

107. Amhailgadh : his son.

108. Flann Oge : his son.

109. Lochlan : his son.

110. Cormac na g-Corn : his son. 1399.

111. Flann : his son. 1452.

112. Teige : his son. 1478.

113. Ceallach : his son. d. 1508.

114. Lochlan (2): his son.

115. Lochlan (3) : his son.

116. Lochlan (4): his son.

117. Melaghlin : his son ; died 1548.

118. Nehemias : his son ; Archbishop of Tuam.

119. John : his son. 1655.
120. Melaghlin (2) : his son. 1673.
121. John Mór : his son. 1710.
122. Melaghlin (3) : his son. 1726.
123. John, of Dublin ; died 1743. Had twenty-one children by his wife, thirteen of whom d. young.

124. Malachy : his son ; died at Ballydonelan. He had three surviving brothers and four sisters.
125. John : his son.
126. Malachy (2) : his son.
127. Arthur Donelan : his son ; living in 1843.

DON-LEVI.*

See Dunlevy, Princes of Ulidia.

THIS is the Gallic form of the Irish *Mac Dunsleibhe* family, Princes of Ulidia, in Ulster. The Hereditary Prince† of that territory, for his devotion to King James II., had in 1691 to quit Ireland and retire to France, where he died, at the Archbishopric of Treves, leaving an only son and heir—Andrew Maurice, who was born in Ireland, and d. at Coblentz on the 19th June, 1751. From him the descent was as follows :

1. Andrew Maurice Don Levi, b. in Ireland ; Lieutenant-Governor of Treves ; d. at Coblentz on 19th June, 1751, leaving four children :
  I. Christien-François, of whom presently.
  II. Wolfgang-Frederic, born at Coblentz, on 15th July, 1738, and d. at Coblentz in 1763.
  III. Wolfgang-Hartmann, b. at Coblentz, 1740 ; d. at Coblentz, 1823, leaving two children, a son and a daughter.

  I. Ferdinand, born at Coblentz, and d. in the French Army.
  I. The daughter, b. at Coblentz, and m. in Paris.
  I. Charlotte Don Levi, born at Coblentz, 14th August, 1736 ; dau. of Andrew-Maurice, and of Anna-Margueritta Flamin.
2. Christien-François : son of Andrew-Maurice Don Levi ; b. at Coblentz, 17th July, 1734 ; m. Ursule Fisher, and had two sons :
  I. Joseph-Michael, born at Leib-

---

* *Don-Levi* : Andrew Donlevy, D.D., LL.D., was born in 1694, it is thought in the county Sligo. In 1710 he repaired to Paris, and studied there in the Irish College, of which he ultimately rose to be Prefect. In 1742 he published at Paris the *Catechism of the Christian Doctrine*, a work still in extensive circulation. He died some time after 1761.

† *Prince* : This Hereditary Prince of Ulidia, on the fall of King James II., quitted Ireland for France, taking with him his only son and heir—Andrew-Maurice, then a boy ; but left behind him his wife who remained in full possession of all his property. His widow (who died in 1708) married in Ireland Count O'Donnell, by whom she left no children. It appears that, till his death (in 1751) her son, Andrew Maurice Don Levi, above mentioned, after he had attained his majority, received the rents of the landed property (situate in the counties of Down and Antrim, in Ireland), which had belonged to his father.

2 D

nertiz, in Styria (Austria), on 27th July, 1768; d. 31st May, 1811, at Vienna Leopoldstadt.

II. John.

3. John : second son of Chris-tien-François, b. at Leibernitz, in Styria, 24th Sept., 1770; m. Thecla Kormorska; d. at Berdyczou, Vol-igny, in Russian Poland, leaving four children :

I. Etienne-Stanislaus, of whom presently.

II. John, b. at Berdyczou 19th August, 1814.

I. Helene, b. at Kolodno (Vol-igny), district of the Town Dubno.

II. Mary, born at Berdyczou in 1809. Was twice married; the second marriage was to a Major in the Russian Army, named Matheu, by whom she has children ; living in Poland, 1881.

4. Etienne-Stanislaus : son and heir of John Don Levi and Thecla Komorska; b. at Berdyczou, 26th December, 1811 (old style), or 7th January, 1812 (new style); m. at Paris in 1850 Jane-Louisa Potelet, a native of Dijon, in Burgundy ; no children. Living in Paris in 1887.

DONNELLAN. (No. 1.)

Of Connaught.

Arms : Ar. a fesse betw. three stags' heads caboosed gu. *Crest* : A greyhound sejant ar.

CATHAL, brother of Inrachtach, who is No. 98 on the " O'Beirne" pedigree, was the ancestor of *O'Donallain ;* anglicised *Donnellan, Donalan, Donelan,* and *Donlan.*

98. Cathal: son of Muredach ; a quo *Clann Cathail,* anglicised *Charley* and *Charles.* This Cathal was the 18th Christian King of Connaught.

99. Ardgall : his son ; " died a saint at Hye, in Scotland, A.D. 786 ;" had a brother named Dubhionracht, who was the 22nd King of Con-naught and the ancestor of *O'Muir-eadhaigh* (" muir :" Irish, *the sea ;* "eadhach," *a protector* or *a garment*), meaning "the descendants of the man who protected the sea ;" or, " who wore garments suited to the sea ;" or, " sea-protector ;" and an-glicised *Murray.*

100. Ceneth : his son ; had a

brother named Onchu, who was the ancestor of *O'Maolmocheirghe* ("moch :" Irish, *early,* and "eirigh," *to rise ;* Lat. " erig-o"), of Con-naught, anglicised *Mulmochery, Early* and *Eardley.* (See No. 96 on the " O'Brassil West" pedigree for another *O'Maolmocheirghe* family.)

101. Moroch: son of Ceneth.

102. Donnallan (or little Donnall) his son ; a quo *O'Donallain,* lords of the territory of *Clann Cathail,* of Connaught ; had a brother named Flannagan, a quo *O'Flannagain* (" one of the twelve great lords of Cruaghan, in the county Roscom-mon"), and anglicised *Flanagan.*

103. Cathal (or Charles): son of Donallan.

104. Ardgal O'Donnellan: his son; first of the family that assumed this sirname.

105. Luaghlais ("luaghlais:" Irish, *fetters*): his son; a quo *O'Luaghlais*, anglicised *Lawless*.

106. Cathal: his son.

107. Flann Buaidh ("buaidh:" Irish, *victory;* Heb. "buagh," *to exult*): his son.

108. Amhailgadh: his son.

109. Flann (or Florence) Oge: his son.

110. Malachi: his son.

111. Cormac: his son; had a brother named Tuathal, who was the ancestor of *Donnellan*, of Rosse.

112. Florence: son of Cormac.

113. Teige: his son.

114. John: his son; had a brother named Tuathal Mór, who was the ancestor of *Donnellan*, of Bally-donnellan, Leitrim, Cloghan, etc.; and who, A.D. 1532, "built the Chapel of Kilconnell."

115. Daniel: son of John; had three brothers—1. John Oge, 2. Padraic Ruadh, 3. Amhailgadh.

116. Daniel Oge: son of Daniel.

117. Teige: his son.

118. Malachi O'Donnellan: his son.

DONNELLAN. (No. 2.)

Lords of Massarene.

Arms : Ar. a dexter arm couped betw. two swords in pale all ppr.

FINACHTACH, brother of Inrachtach who is No. 97 on the "Flin" (of North Clanaboy) pedigree, was the ancestor of *O'Donnellan*, of Orgiall.

97. Finachtach: son of Rachta-brad.

98. Longseach: his son.

99. Hugh: his son.

100. Dubhsineach ("dubh:" Irish, *black;* "sineach," *a wen*): his son.

101. Maolcraobh ("craobh:" Irish, *a bough*): his son; a quo *O'Craoibhe*, of Ulster, anglicised *Creagh,** Cre·aghe*, and *Crabbe.*

102. Donallan: his son; a quo *O'Donallain ;* had a brother named Muireigean.

103. Dubhdarach: son of Donallan.

104. Caillidh† : his son.

105. Connor O'Donnellan: his son.

---

* *Creagh :* Some genealogists are of opinion that the "Creagh," of Munster, family is a branch of the *O'Neill,* of Ulster : but that is a mistake : those Creaghs are descended from the O'Neills, of the county Clare—See p. 242.

† *Caillidh* : This name, which signifies "one who loses," is derived from the Irish, *caill,* "to lose" (Heb. *cal,* "to fail"); and seems to be the root of the Heb. *calah,* "he faileth."

DONNELLY.

Arms: Sa. three fleurs-de-lis ar.   *Crest*: A church and spire ppr.

BAODAN, the second son of Tuatan who is No. 94 on the "O'Hart" pedigree, was the ancestor of *O'Dongealaighe;* anglicised *Donnelly.*

94. Tuatan: son of Tuathal Maolgharbh.

95. Baodan : his son.

96. Failbhe : his son.

97. Faolchu (or Finchu) : his son.

98. Dubhdinna : his son ; had nine sons.

99. Lergus (or Fergus) : his son.

100. Cumascach : his son.

101. Fergal : his son. This Fergal had two brothers—1. Cathal, a quo *MacCahill* and *Cahill* of Ulster ; 2. Dungal.

102. Dungal (more properly Dongealach : "Don :" Irish, *high, noble;* "gealach," the *moon:* from "geal :" Irish, *white;* Welsh "gole," *the light*) : son of Fergal ; a quo *O'Don-*

gealaighe. This Dungal had two brothers—1. Maolfiona (*maolfiona :* Irish, "the devotee of wine"), a quo *O'Maolfhiona,** anglicised *Mulleny, O'Mulvany, O'Mulvena, Omulvena, O'Mulveny, Melveny, O'Melvena, Omelvena, O'Molina, Mulvena, Melvin, McIlvena, MacIlwane;* 2. Gabhadhan, a quo *Gavan,* etc.

103. Cuinin : his son.

104. Aongus : his son ; had a brother named Fergal.

105. Cathal : son of Aongus.

106. Cubuidhe (or "the yellow warrior") : his son ; a quo *O'Conbhuidhe,* anglicised *Convy,* etc.

107. Padraic O'Donnelly : his son.

DOWLING.

Chiefs in the County Wicklow, and Queen's County.

Arms : Ar. a holly tree eradicated ppr. on a chief engr. az. a lion pass. betw. two trefoils slipped or.   *Crest :* Out of a mural coronet a dexter arm vested, holding a sword waved.

FELIM, brother of Crimthann Cas, who is No. 95 on the "MacMorough" pedigree, was the ancestor of *O'Dublhaoidh,*† lords of Fertullagh, county Westmeath ; anglicised *Dooley, Dowley, Doolan, Dulen, Dolan,* and *Dowling.*

95. Felim : son of Eanna Cinsealach ; had a brother named

Deadhach, who was the ancestor of *O'Dea* and *Day,* of Leinster.

* *O'Maolfhiona*: One of this family, named Melaghlin O'Mulvany, who died, A.D. 1376, was poet and historian to O'Cahan, or O'Kane.—(See O'Curry's " Lectures," page 82.)

† *O'Dubhlaoidh*: Before the English invasion of Ireland, this family was driven from *Feara Tulagh (i.e. Viri Collium)*, now the barony of Fertullagh, in the county Westmeath, by the family of O'Melaghlin ; and they settled in Ely O'Carroll. The O'Dowling (or O'Dunlaing) portion of the family were chiefs in the county Wicklow and in the Queen's County.—O'DONOVAN.

96. Æneas : son of Felim.

97. Muredach (a quo *O'Muire-daigh*, of Leinster ; anglicised *Murray*) : his son ; had a brother named Uargus, who was the ancestor of *Duncan*, or *Dunkin*, of the Line of Heremon.

98. Eochaidh,* King of Leinster : son of Muredach ; fled to Scotland. He had two brothers—1. Aliol, who was the ancestor of *Maconky ;* and 2. Eoghan (Owen), who was the ancestor of *O'Harraghtan* of Leinster.

99. Brandubh : son of Eochaidh ; the tenth Christian King of Leinster ; A.D. 594.

100. Cineth : his son ; had a brother named Seicne (or Seigin), who was the ancestor of *O'Murphy* of Hy-Felimy.

101. Donal : son of Cineth.

102. Aliol : his son ; a quo "Rath Aliol."

103. Dubhlaodh (" dubh :" Irish, *black ;* " laodh," *a calf*) : his son ; a quo *O'Dublaoidh* (by some written *O'Dunlaing*, and anglicised *Dowling*).

104. Cucoille : his son.

105. Aliol (2) : his son.

106. Maolsaraan : his son.

107. Onchu : his son.

108. Flann : his son.

109. Maoluradh : his son.

110. Aliol (3) : his son.

111. Dubhlaodh (2) : his son.

112. Dubh (" dubh :" Irish, *dark-featured, great, prodigious, burned ;* Heb., " dobhe") his son ; a quo *O'Duibhe*, anglicised *O'Deevy*, and modernized *Devoy, Duff, Duffe ;* had a brother named Donough, who was the ancestor of *Connulay*.

113. Solomon : son of Dubh.

114. Padraic : his son.

115. Gillchriosd : his son.

116. Padraic (2) : his son.

117. Gillchriosd O'Dowley : his son.

DOYNE.

Of Kilkaran, Queen's County.

Arms : Az. an eagle displ. or. *Crest :* In front of a holly bush ppr. a lizard pass. or. *Motto :* Mullach abu (The summit for ever).

TERENCE DOYNE, of Kilkaran, Queen's County, had :

2. John, who d. 18th December, 1636. Was twice m. ; his first wife was Margaret, dau. of Lysah O'Dempsey, of Deskart, King's County, by whom he had three sons and three daughters :

I. Terence.

II. Anthony.

III. John.

The daughters were :

I. Elenor.

II. Sarah.

III. Elan.

John Doyne's second wife was

† *Eochaidh :* From this Eochaidh the *Keogh* of Leinster family derive their name and descent.

Helena, dau. of —— MacDonell, of Tinekill, Queen's County, Esq., by whom he had :
IV. Edmond.
V. Thomas.

IV. Margaret.
V. May.
3. Terence Doyne : eldest son of John.

DUFFE.*

Branch of the O'Connor Faley.

Arms : Vert a lion ramp. or. a crescent for diff.   *Crest* : A greyhound courant ar. collared or. a crescent for diff.

COMTHANAN, a brother of Ros Failgeach who is No. 90 on the "O'Connor" (Faley) pedigree, was the ancestor of another branch of the *O'Duibh* family; anglicised *Duffe*.

90. Comthanan: son of Cathair Mór, the 109th Monarch of Ireland.
91. Aongus : his son.
92. Eachach : his son.
93. Comthach Beag : his son.
94. Nathair : his son.
95. Nainneadh : his son.
96. Cormac : his son.
97. Cobhthach : his son.
98. Eoghan : his son.
99. Maoloctrach : his son.
100. Noinnean : his son.
101. Maoloctrach : his son.

102. Flaithreach : his son.
103. Marcan : his son.
104. Dubh ("dubh :" Irish, *dark-featured, prodigious ;* Heb. "dobhe"): his son ; a quo *O'Duibhe*.—See No. 112 on the "Dowling" pedigree.
105. Fubthag : his son.
106. Flaithman : his son.
107. Lorcan : his son.
108. Donall : his son.
109. Giolla Ciarain O'Duff : his son.

DUFFENY.

Of Tirconnell.

Arms : Ar. a sinister hand couped at the wrist affrontée gu.

BLATHMAC, brother of Niall Caille who is No. 98 on the (No. 1) "O'Neill" (of Tyrone) pedigree, was the ancestor of *O'Duibheanaigh ;* anglicised *Duffeny, Deveny,* and *Devany*.

* *Duff*: Another "Duff" family was descended from Dubh, who is No. 112 on the "Dowling" pedigree.

98. Blathmac : fourth son of Aodh Ornaighe, the 164th Monarch of Ireland.

99. Cuirc : his son.

100. Dubheanach ("dubh :" Irish, black ; "eanach," a moor) : his son ; a quo O'Duibheanaigh.

101. Gairbiadh : his son.

102. Fearmorcach : his son.

103. Giolla Conghal : his son.

104. Aongus : his son.

105. Muirceartach : his son.

DUFFY.

County Monaghan.

Arms : Vert a lion ramp. or.

FRANCIS DUFFY of Kilcrow, in the parish of Ematris, and county of Monaghan, m. a dau. of The Mac-Mahon, of Dartry, and had :

2. Patrick Mór, of Attyduffy, or Attyduff, who m. Mary, eldest dau. and co-heir of Captain John Dawson, a Cromwellian Officer, who settled at Drummany, co. Monaghan ; and by her acquired an interest in the lands of Drummany, Drumyarken, and Attyduff. By the said Mary Patrick Mór had two sons and a daughter.

I. Patrick, of whom presently.

II. Rev John, a Priest, who d. in 1744, and was buried in Ematris (otherwise called Edragoole), where his tomb still exists.

I. Mary, who m. a Mr. Colvin, of Dublin.

3. Patrick : son of Patrick ; removed from Attyduff, and settled in Monaghan. His kinsmen, the Dawsons of Drummany House (descended from Dorothea, the younger of the two daus. and co-heirs of Captain John Dawson, who m. a gentleman of her own name from Londonderry), having filed a "Bill of Discovery" against him, or adopted some such process under the Penal Laws, they "ousted" the said Patrick out of his property. He was also engaged for a long time in litigation with his brother-in-law, Mr. Colvin. This Patrick Duffy m. *circa* 1712 Elizabeth Duffy (a niece or cousin of the MacKenna of Trough), and had :

I. Philip, of whom presently.

II. Francis of Monaghan, who had :

I. John, of Monaghan, who m. Anne, dau. of Patrick Gavan, Esq., of Latnamard (by his wife Judith, dau. and co-heir of Bernard MacMahon of Rekane, who was cousin german of Ross and Bernard MacMahon, Archbishops of Armagh ; and who was grandson of Colla Dhu Mac-Mahon, titular Baron of Dartry). By Miss Gavan, John Duffy had two sons : I. Francis, who m. Miss Hope, of co. Westmeath, and left an only dau. Fanny, who m. William Maunsell, Esq. II. Charles, now (1887) the distinguished and illustrious Sir Charles Gavan Duffy, K.C.M.G.; formerly Editor and Proprietor of the Dublin *Nation*, M.P. for New Ross, and lately Prime Minister of one of our Colonies in Australia.

4. Philip: son of Patrick; m. Anne Kerr, of the co. Longford. He removed to Cootehill in 1752, and, dying in 1803, left two sons:

I. Terence, of whom presently.

II. Bernard, who, having quarrelled with his father, enlisted in the British Army. He m. Anne Jeffares of Emyvale, and

had an only child, the late:

I. General Sir John Duffy, K.C.B., who m. a dau. of General Campbell, and d.s.p.

5. Terence Duffy, of Cootehill: son of Philip; m. Anne, dau. of —— MacCabe of Lissimy, and dying, in 1831, aged 80, was buried in Ematris. He had three sons:

I. Francis.

II. Owen of Cootehill, from whose statement (in 1865) this pedigree was compiled.

III. Terence, M.D., who went out to Bolivia, or Chili, to his kinsman, General John MacKenna.

DUIGNAN.

Of Walsall, England.

THIS name was formerly *Duigenan*, one of the anglicised forms of the Irish *O'Duibhgenain** ("dubh:" Irish, *black* or *dark;* "gen," *a sword* or *wound;* "an," *one who*), an ancient celebrated family in Ireland. The O'Duigenans were located at Kilronan, in the northern division of the county Roscommon; and afterwards were landed proprietors† in the parish of Dromleas, barony of Dromaheare, county Leitrim, down to the Cromwellian Confiscations. They are especially celebrated in the Irish annals for their devotion to the history and literature of their country.

In 1339, the Church of Kilronan was begun by Ferrall Muinach O'Duigenan. It stood "over" Lough Meelagh, and has a deep national interest; as, in a vault, close to the ruins, erected for the family of MacDermott Roe, were deposited the earthly remains of the once celebrated Carolan.

At the close of the fourteenth century, Manus O'Duigenan was engaged in drawing up a considerable portion of the *Book of Ballymote.* Subsequently a Chronicle was compiled which, deriving its title from the locality of this family, was called the *Book of Kilronan*, or, sometimes the

* *O'Duibhgenain*: Other authorities give the name, in Irish, as *O'Doighnain* ("doigh:" Irish, *hope;* Gr. "do-keo," *to think*).—See the "Dinan" pedigree.

† *Proprietors*: See the Paper in the Appendix of our *Irish Landed Gentry*, headed "Books of Survey and Distribution;" under the barony of Dromaheare, and county of Leitrim.

Book of the O'Duigenans. That Book was one of the Chronicles from which the Four Masters (one of whom was Cucoigcriche or Peregrine O'Duigenan) collected their great work in 1632.

The Four Masters record, as might be expected, numerous obits of the O'Duigenan family ; each of whom is commemorated as a learned historian or philosopher.

In 1588, Duffy O'Duigenan wrote a history of the Sept of the O'Donnells.

Patrick Duigenan, LL.D.,* who was M.P. for the Borough of Old Leighlin, in the Irish Parliament of 1797, was a member of this family. That Patrick Duigenan was one of the King's Counsel, Advocate-General of the Admiralty, Judge of the Prerogative Court, Professor of Common Law in the Dublin University, Vicar-General of Dublin, a Doctor of Laws, Vicar-General of the Diocese of Meath and Leighlin and Ferns, Advocate in the Ecclesiastical Courts, etc.

In O'Clery's Genealogies the pedigree of the family is recorded down to John Ballach O'Dugenan, who was Chief of his name, when the family was dispossessed of their Kilronan patrimony; but, from his time down to the Cromwellian Confiscations, the family genealogy is not forthcoming. We have therefore been able to trace only one branch of the family ; namely, that descended from :

1. John Duigenan, of Ardagh, in county Longford, who had :

2. John, who was master of the Grammar School, at Walsall, in Staffordshire, and d. there in 1845, leaving an only surviving son, and three daughters :

   I. Henry *Duignan*, of whom presently.

   I. Mary, who m. Mr. Thomas Franklin, of Walsall.

   II. Emma, who m. Mr. William Totly, of Walsall.

   III. Ann, who m. Mr. William Holden, of Walsall.

3. Henry Duignan : son of John ; d. at Walsall, in 1873, and was buried at Rushall, leaving his only child :

4. William Henry Duignan (living in 1883) of Rushall Hall, near Walsall, who was twice m. : first, in 1850, to Mary, dau. of William Minors, Esq., of Fisherwick, in Staffordshire, and by her had three children :

   I. Florence-Mary, the wife of George Rose, M.A ; living in 1883.

   I. Ernest-Henry.

---

* Duigenan: Doctor Patrick Duigenan was twice married : his first wife was a Miss Cusack; his second, a Miss Heppenstal. This name reminds us of a Lieutenant Heppenstal, who, in 1798, acquired the sirname of the " *Walking Gallows*," from the following circumstance : " Heppenstal," writes Sir Jonah Barrington, " was a remarkably tall, robust man, and had a habit of expertly executing straggling Rebels, when he happened to meet them, by twisting his own cravat round their necks, then throwing it over his own brawny shoulder, and so trotting about at a smart pace, with the Rebel dangling at his back, and choking gradually till he was totally defunct, which generally happened before the Lieutenant was tired of bis amusement. This ingenious contrivance, and some others nearly as expert, has not been practised in any other part of the world as yet discovered ; but it was the humour of the year 1798, in Ireland, during martial law, and was not discountenanced by any military, or countermanded by any municipal authority ; nor was its legality ever investigated or called in question by any Court of Justice.—At that time Lord Clare was Chancellor."—See Vol. II. of BARRINGTON's *Historic Memoirs of Ireland.*

II. George-Stubbs.

The second wife of William-Henry Duignan was Jenny, dau. of Herr J. B. Petersen, of Stockholm, whom he there m. in 1868, and by whom he has three children (living in 1883):

III. Bernard.

IV. Carl.

V. Oscar.

5. Ernest-Henry Duignan : son of William-Henry; he and his brother George-Stubbs Duignan living in 1883.

DONEGAN.

Arms : Az. six plates, three, two, and one, on a chief or. a demi lion ramp. gu: *Crest :* An orb ar. banded and surmounted by a cross pattée or.

CORMAC, brother of Suibneach, who is No. 103 on the "Dwyer" (of Coille-na-Managh) pedigree, was the ancestor of *MacDonnagain ;* anglicised *Donegan,** and *Dungan,* Chiefs in the county Limerick.

103. Cormac : son of Dunchadh.

104. Maolmaith ("maith :" Irish, *good ;* Wel. "*mad ;*" Arm. "mat"): his son.

105. Meclachtnan : his son.

106. Donnegan (" donnegan : " Irish, *a little lord,* or *a brown lord*) : his son ; a quo *MacDonnegain.*

107. Treasach : his son.

108. Finé : his son.

109. Ruadhri : his son.

110. Tighearnan : his son.

111. Ruadhri : his son.

112. Maolseachlainn MacDonna-gain : his son.

DUNLEVY.

Princes of Ulidia.

ÆNEAS Tuirmeach-Teamrach, the 81st Monarch of Ireland, who (see p. 355) is No. 66 on the "Line of Heremon," had a son named Fiach-Fear-mara, who was ancestor of the Kings of Argyle and Dalriada, in Scotland : this Fiach (latinized "Fiachus Fearmara") was also the ancester of *Mac-Dunshleibhe* and *O'Dunsleibhe,* anglicised *Dunleavy, Dunlief, Dunlap,*† *Delap, Dunlevy, Don-Levi, Donlevy, Levingstone, Livingstone,* and *Levenston.*

---

* *Donegan :* Several branches of this family are given by MacFirbis ; the foregoing is merely the Stem.

† *Dunlap :* John Dunlap, an American Revolutionary patriot, was born at Strabane, in 1747. At the age of eight or nine years he went to live with his uncle William, a printer and publisher of Philadelphia. When but eighteen he took sole charge of his uncle's business, and in November, 1771, commenced the *Pennsylvania Packet,* and before long became one of the most successful printers and editors of the country. As printer to Congress, he first issued the "Declaration of Independence." He died in Philadelphia, on 27th November, 1812.

67. Fiach-Fearmara : son of Æneas.

68. Olioll Erann : his son.

69. Feareadach : his son.

70. Forga: his son.

71. Main Mór : his son.

72. Arndal* (" aran ;" Irish, *bread ;* Lat. " aran-s ;" Gr. " aroon," *ploughing ;* and " dal" or " dail :" Irish, *a field*) : his son.

73. Rathrean : his son.

74. Trean: his son.

75. Rosin : his son.

76. Sin : his son.

77. Eochaidh : his son ; had an elder brother named Deadhach, who was an ancester of Loarn, the last King of Dalriada, in Scotland.

78. Deithsin : son of Eochaidh.

79. Dluthagh : his son.

80. Daire : his son.

81. Fiatach Fionn : his son ; the 103rd Monarch of Ireland, a quo " *Dal Fiatach.*"

82. Ogaman : his son.

83. Fionnchada : his son.

84. Iomchaidh : his son.

85. Fergus Dubh-dheadach, the 114th Monarch : his son.

86. Æneas (or Aongus) Fionn : his son ; who is No. 34 on the Roll of the "Kings of Ulster."—See that Roll, in the Appendix.

87. Luigheach: his son ; is No. 36 on that Roll ; was the last of the "Dal Fiatach" pre-Christian Kings of Ulster.

88. Mianach : his son.

89. Dubhthach : his son.

90. Dallan : his son.

91. Forga (2) : his son.

92. Muredach Mundearg : his son; the first Christian King of Ulidia.†

93. Cairioll Coscrach : his son ; the second King.

94. Deman : his son ; the seventh King.

95. Fiachna : his son ; the twelfth King.

96. Maolcobhach (or Malcovus), the 144th Monarch, and the 15th King of Ulidia : his son.

97. Blathmac, the 150th Monarch, and 16th King of Ulidia.

98. Beag Boirche (" boirche :" Irish, *a large hind*), the 19th King ; his son.

99. Aodh (or Hugh) Roin : his son ; the 21st King.

100. Fiachna : his son ; the 23rd King ; living A.D. 743.

101. Eochaidh : his son ; the 24th King.

102. Aodh (2) : his son.

103. Eachagan : his son.

104. Aodh (3) : his son ; the 38th King.

105. Madadhan : his son.

106. Ardgal : his son ; the 44th King.

107. Eochaidh, the 46th King : his son.

108. Niall, the 48th King : his son.

109. Eochaidh (" eochaidh :" Irish, *a knight* or *horseman ;* from *each :* Irish, *a horse*), a quo *O'h-Eochaidh,* anglicised *O'Heoghy, Hoey, Howe, Haugh, Haughey,* etc. : his son; whose brother Maolruanaidh was the 47th King of Ulidia, and was slain, A.D. 1014, at the battle of Clontarf, fighting against the Danes.

110. Dunsleibhe [dunsleive] : his son ; a quo *MacDunshleibhe* and *O'Dunshleibhe.*

---

* *Arndal :* This Celtic word is the root of the sirname *Arnald,* modernized *Arnold.*

† *Ulidia :* In page 199 of first series, this Muredach is, through the author's mistake, mentioned as the son of Crimthann Liath, who was king of Orgiall (and *not* of Ulidia), at the time of the advent of St. Patrick to Ireland.

111. Connor : his son; whose brother Rory was the 54th Christian (and last) King of Ulidia.

112. Cu-Uladh [ula] MacDun-

shleibhe :* his son; living, A.D. 1177.

.   .   .   .   .   .

We are at present (1881) unable to continue the descent of this family down to the Hereditary Prince of Ulidia,† who, for his devotion to King James II., had in 1691 to quit Ireland and retire to France ; where he d. at the Archbishopric of Treves, leaving an only son and heir—Andrew-Maurice, who was b. in Ireland, and d. at Coblentz, on 19th June, 1751. From him the descent was as in the "Don-Levi" pedigree.

DUNKIN.

Arms : Sa. five eagles displ. in cross ar.

UARGUS, brother of Muredach who is No. 97 on the "Dowling" pedigree, was the ancestor of *O'Duncinn* ("dun" Irish, *a fortress ;* "ceann," gen. "cinn," *a chief ;* Chald. "knan"); anglicised *Duncan* and *Dunkin.*

97. Uargus : son of Æneas. | 98. Alioll : his son.

---

* *Dunshleibhe:* This epithet, anglicised *Dunlevy,* signifies "the fortress on the (sliabh or) mountain" (*dun :* Irish, a fortress ; Pers. *doen,* a hill ; Copt. *ton,* a mountain ; Turk. *dun,* high ; Germ. *dun,* a city ; Eng. *town*) ; but anglicised *Donlevy,* it means "the chief on the mountain" (*duine :* Irish, a man ; Hind. *dhunee,* a proprietor ; Arab., Span., and Irish, *don,* noble ; Heb., Chald., and old Persian *dan,* a chief magistrate.)

According to Dr. O'Donovan, descendants of this family, soon after the English invasion of Ireland, passed into Scotland, where they changed the name *Dunshleibhe* to *Dunlief* and *Dunlap* and even to *Livingston.* In the "*Patronimica Britanica*" it is stated that the name *Dunlop* is, in Scotland, often corrupted to *Dunlap* and *Delap ;* and that the name has been traced to A.D. 1260, when "Dom Gulielmus de Dunlop was Lord of Dunlop, in Ayrshire, an estate still in the possession of the family." It is erroneously considered by some of the name that *Delap* is derived from *De-la-Poer,* which has been modernized *Power.* (See the "Power" pedigree, p. 252, *ante.*)

The dominant family in Ulidia, when, A.D. 1177, it was invaded by John de Courcey, was that of Cu-Uladh (No. 112, above mentioned), whom Connellan styles *Cu-Uladh MacDuinshleibhe O'h-Eochadha,* and who was nephew of Rory, the 54th and last King of Ulidia. The "Cu-Uladh" portion of this name has been latinized *Canis Ultoniæ :* meaning that this chief of Ulidia (which in the twelfth century constituted the "Kingdom of Ulster") was swift-footed as a *hound.* The "Mac-Duinnshleibhe" portion of the name implies that Cu-Uladh was son or descendant of Dunsleibhe (No. 110, from whom this sirname is derived): a name which *Giraldus Cambrensis* latinized *Dunlevus :* and the "O'h-Eochadha" portion signifies that this Dunsleibhe was the son of Eochaidh, No. 109 on the foregoing pedigree.

† *Ulidia :* This Hereditary Prince of Ulidia, on the fall of King James II., quitted Ireland for France, taking with him his only son and heir, Andrew-Maurice, then a boy; but left behind him his wife who remained in full possession of all his property, and who survived him. After his death, his widow married in Ireland Count O'Donnell, by whom she left no children. This Lady O'Donnell (who died in 1708), it appears, executed a Deed by which she entrusted to the Crown the administration of her lands and property : stipulating that whenever the legitimate heir of her first husband should present himself, possession of her property should be given to him. And it also appears that, till his death in 1751, her son, Andrew-Maurice Don-Levi, above mentioned, received the rents of the landed property (situate in the counties of Down and Antrim, in Ireland), so willed by the said Lady O'Donnell to the legitimate heir of the "Donlevy" family.

DUNNE. (No. 1.)

Chiefs in the Queen's County.

Arms : Az. an eagle displ. or. *Crest :* In front of a holly bush ppr. a lizard pass. or. *Motto :* Mullach abu (The summit for ever).

RIAGHAN, brother of Donald who is No. 101 on the "Dempsey" (No. 1) pedigree, was the ancester of *O'Duin*, anglicised *Doyne, Dun, Dunn,* and *Dunne.*

101. Riaghan ("riagh:" Irish, *to gibbit*): son of Cineth; a quo *O'Riaghain*, anglicised *O'Regan*—one of "The Four Tribes of Tara."

102. Maolfiona: his son.

103. Dubhgall : his son.

104. Dun ("dun:" Irish, *a hill, or fortress*): his son; a quo *O'Duin ;* had a brother named Dubhrean, who was ancestor of *O'Regan.*

105. Ficheallach : son of Dun.

106. Amhailgadh O'Duinn: his son; the first who assumed this sirname.

107. Congalach : his son; a quo *O'Conghaile* or *O'Congalaigh*, anglicised *Congaly, O'Conolly,* and *Conolly.**

108. Cublasma : his son.

109. Caroill : his son.

110. Conbhach: his son; had a brother named Branan, a quo *Mac-Brannen.*

111. Dunsleibhe : son of Conbhach.

112. Conbhach (2) : his son.

113. Amhailgadh (or Awly) : his son.

114. Teige : his son.

115. Awly (2) : his son.

116. Awly (3) : his son.

117. Donoch : his son.

118. Roger: his son; was the first who assumed the sirname *O'Doyne.*

119. Leinach : his son.

120. Teige (Thady or Thadeus) : his son.

121. Teige (2) : his son; chief of his name; married to Margaret, daughter of Shane (an Diomuis) O'Neill.

122. Teige (3) : his son; had a brother named Brian.

123. Teige O'Doyne,† of Castlebrack, Queen's County: his son; prince of Oregon, and chief of his name; was living in 1593; had five sons, and a brother named Tirlogh, who was the ancestor of *Dunn* of Ards. (Same *Arms*.)

---

* *Conolly :* Arms : Ar. on a saltire engr. sa. five escallops of the field.

† *Teige O'Doyne :* With our present knowledge of "Land tenancy" and the "Land question," in Ireland, it may interest the reader to know the duties or "chief rents" for their lands which the Irish Chieftains exacted from their followers : The Castlebrack tenants of this Teige O'Doyne, for instance, paid one penny "heriot," per acre, on the death of each *Ceannfinne* or chief head of a family. (It may be mentioned that the word *heriot* means "a fine paid to the lord of the manor at the death of a landholder.") His tenants of Kernymore paid yearly—two beeves, twenty-four crannochs of oats, forty cakes of bread, thirteen dishes of butter, seventeen cans of malt ; eight pence, heriot, in money, on the death of each *Ceannfinne ;* one reaping hook (service) on one of every twenty acres ; custom ploughs one day in winter and one in summer.

From inhabitants of Ballykeneine Quarter: Meat and drink for twenty-four horse boys, or four shillings for their diet. From (the inhabitants of) Cappabrogan : like duties. From Garrough : like duties. These "Chief Rents" were A.D. 1613, abolished in Ireland in the reign of King James the First, by the Parliament then held in Dublin by the Lord Deputy Sir Arthur Chichester.—See Lodge MSS. Vol. I., p. 337.

DUNNE. (No. 2.)

From the De La Ponce MSS.

Arms : Same as those of "Dunne" (No. 1.)

BRIAN, a younger brother of Teige who is No. 122 on the foregoing pedigree, was the ancestor of this branch of that family.

122. Brian : son of Teige.
123. Barnaby : his son.
124. Terence : his son.
125. Edward : his son.

126. Francis : his son.
127. General Edward : his son.
128. Le Colonel Francis Dunn : his son.

DUNNE. (No. 3.)

Of Ards.

Arms: Same as those of "Dunne"(No. 1).

TIRLOGH, brother of Teige O'Doyne, who is No. 123 on the "Dunne" (No. 1) pedigree, was the ancestor of *Dunn* of Ards, in the Queen's County.

123. Tirlogh : son of Teige (3).
124. John, of Kilvavan : his son ; next in remainder to the estate of Castlebrack, in case of the extinction of the line of his elder brother Teige (Deed 21st Feb., 1616.)
125. Terence (or Tirlogh), of Kilvavan, afterwards of Ards, in the Queen's Co. : his son ; died 1680.
126. John, of Ards : his son ; died 1726'

127. Terence, of Ards : his son.
128. Lawrence : his second son ; whose elder brother Terence died without issue.
129. James, of Ards : son of Lawrence ; died in 1841 ; had two brothers—1. John, 2. Lawrence.
130. Rev. John Dunn, of Ards : son of James ; living in 1847.
131. Terence Dunn : his son.

DWYER.* (No. 1.)

Of Leinster and Munster.

Lords of Kilnamanagh, County Tipperary.

Arms: Ar. a lion ramp. gu. betw. three erm. spots. *Crest:* A hand couped at the wrist and erect, grasping a sword all ppr.

CAIRBRE CLUITHEACHAR, the youngest son of Cucorb, King of Leinster, who is No. 85 on the "O'Connor" (Faley) pedigree, was the ancestor of *O'Dwyer,* of Leinster and Munster. This Cairbre went into Munster,

* *Dwyer*: For the pedigree of this family, see also the *De la Ponce MSS.*, in the Library of the Royal Irish Academy, Dublin.

where his grandfather Conaire Mór, the 97th Monarch of Ireland, gave him the territory after him called *Dal Cairbre*, meaning "The lands of Carbery."

87. Cairbre Cluitheachar : son of Cucorb.

88. Argettmar : his son.

89. Buan ("buan:" Irish, *good, harmonious*): his son; a quo *O'Buain*, anglicised *Bowen, Bone*, and *Boon*.

90. Lughaidh : his son.

91. Ferniadh : his son.

92. Inneach : his son.

93. Ferruith : his son.

94. Finchadh : his son; whose brother Urcha was the ancestor of *MacLongachain* ("longach:" Irish, belonging to *a ship;* "an," *one who*), anglicised *Longahan, Lanigan, Lenihan*, and *Lenehan;* and of *Cooney*, etc. This Finchadh's younger brother Arbhar was the ancestor of *Trena, Cronan, Aodhan* (anglicised *Hayden*), *Brangal, Dunechy;* and *O'Corbain*, anglicised *Carbine*.

95. Macrimhe : son of Finchadh.

96. Luighneach : his son.

97. Luchair : his son ; had a brother Greallan.

98. Greallan : his son.

99. Dubhdahna : his son.

100. Donnocha : his son.

101. Suibhneach : his son ; had a brother.

102. Spellan : son of Suibhneach.

103. Dubhiir : ("dubh:" Irish, *black* or *dark;* "iir," gen. "iire," *a skirt*): his son; a quo *O'Dubhiire*, anglicised *O'Dwyer, Dwyer*, and *Diver*.

104. Caolbadh : his son.

105. Cathalan : his son.

106. Nial : his son.

107. Padraic O'Dwyer : his son ; Lord of Kilnamanagh, county Tipperary.

DWYER.* (No. 2.)

Of Kilnamanagh.

Arms : Same as those of "Dwyer" (No. 1).

GREALLAN, a brother of Luchair, who is No. 97 on the "O'Dwyer" (No. 1) pedigree, was the ancestor of *O'Dwyer*, of Coille-na-Managh, or Kilnamanagh.

97. Greallan : son of Luighneach.

98. Cruitine (or Ruadhin): his son; a quo *O'Ruadhin* ("ruadhin:" Irish, *the red little man*), anglicised *Ruane, Reddin, Rhin*, and *Rhynd*.

99. Fhuradhran : his son.

100. Conaire : his son.

---

* *Dwyer :* Of this family was Michael Dwyer, the celebrated insurgent leader in 1798, who was born in 1771. In the summer of 1798 he took refuge in the Wicklow mountains, and held out for many months against the Government—at first with Holt, and afterwards with his own band. On the evening of Emmet's *emeute* in 1803, Dwyer led nearly 500 men to his assistance at Rathfarnham, but retired to the mountains without effecting anything. Eventually he gave himself up to the Authorities, and was sent to New South Wales, where he received an appointment in the police. He is described as a handsome and intelligent man ; he died in 1815.

101. Dubh-da-Tuath : his son.
102. Dunchadh : his son.
103. Suibhneach : his son.
104. Spealan : his son.
105. Dubhodhar ("dubh : Irish, *dark;* "odhar," *pale, wan, dun*): his son; a quo *O'Duibhidhir*, or *O'Duibhir.*
106. Donchadh : his son.
107. Aodh : his son.
108. Lorcan : his son.
109. Ceallach : his son.
110. Lorcan : his son.
111. Giolla-na-Naomh : his son.
112. Lochlann : his son.

113. Giollananaomh : his son.
114. Pilip Donn : his son.
115. Tomhas : his son.
116. Lughaidh : his son.
117. Tomhas : his son.
118. Conchobhar : his son.
119. Tomhas : his son.
120. Diarmaid : his son.
121. Uaithne (Anthony): his son.
122. Pilip : his son.
123. Dermod O'Dwyer : his son; had three brothers—1. Philip, 2. Denis, 3. Edmond.
124. Philip : son of Denis : had two sisters—1. Jane, 2. Mary.

DWYER. (No. 3.)

Of Ulster.

FERACH, the eighth son of Daimhin, who is No. 92 on the " O'Hart" pedigree, was the ancestor of *O'Dubhfir ;* anglicised *Dewar* and *Dwyer,* ("dubhfear :" Irish, *the dark-featured man*). This Ferach was also the ancestor of Cumascach, King of Orgiall ; and of *O'Maoloidhe* ("oidhe :" Irish, *a guest*), anglicised *Mullody, Mulloda, Melloda,* and *Melledy.*

EARL.

Of Carbery, County Kildare.

Arms : Gu. on a chev. betw. three escallops in chief and a dolphin in base ar. as many trefoils sa. all within a double tressure engr. of the second, the outer bordure or. *Crest :* A nag's head erased sa. maned or.

THE *Errill* family, whose name has been anglicised *Earl,* was, it is believed, originally located at Errill, a village near Rathdowney, in the Queen's County, containing many ancient ruins of which Ledwich has written.

According to the MS. Vol., F. 1. 21, in the Library of Trinity College, Dublin, the Errills were in the fifteenth century located in the County Westmeath, where they remained up to the time of the Cromwellian Settlement ; after which the family was dispersed through the adjacent counties : one branch settling in Carbery, county Kildare, where *circa* A.D. 1770, we meet the name of Thomas Errill as their surviving representative, and with whom this pedigree commences :

1. Thomas Errill, of Carbury, co. Kildare, left three sons and three daughters :

I. Edward (b. 1774), who was Parish Priest of Carbury for 25 years, and died in 1846 ; he was the first of the family who wrote his name *Earl*. This good priest was possessed of considerable ability, sterling piety, and great humour; it was principally through his exertions that a stone bridge was erected over a river in Carbury. Father Earl is buried in Carbury chapel, inside of which there is a tablet to his memory, containing the following inscription:

"Sex pedes terræ me tegit,
Sex pedes solis me videt,
Sic maneo in œvum."

Respecting that epitaph Mr. W. J. Fitzpatrick, J.P., M.R.I.A. (author of the *Sham Squire*, etc.) has kindly informed us, that Father Earl left directions that the foregoing laconic inscription should be put on any monument that might be erected to commemorate him. But his bereaved parishioners hesitated to obey those directions; at the same time not wishing to disobey the dying injunctions of their *Soggarth Aroon*, they caused the modest epitaph of Father Earl's composition to be inscribed on the *back* of the monumental tablet, and had a well-merited eulogium of their own composition put on the front.

II. John, of whom presently.

III. Laurence, born in 1786, m. Catherine Maguire, and emigrated to America in 1833, accompanied by his three sisters, Mary, Alice, and Elizabeth.

2. John Errill: second son of Thomas; born 1777, d. 1837; m. another Catherine Maguire, and settled in Dublin, where he died, leaving three daughters, who died unm., and three sons:

I. George, who died unm.

II. Patrick William, of whom presently.

III. Thomas, who was educated at Erasmus Smith's School Dublin, and m. Alicia Ingram He d. in 1861, leaving issue one son and five daughters, all of whom emigrated to America about 1870.

3. Patrick William *Earl*: second son of John Errill; was born in 1823, and educated at Erasmus Smith's School, Dublin. He was the second member of his family to adopt the anglicised form of their surname; he became an eminent Analytical Chemist,* and died on

---

* *Chemist*: The following is a summary of the various biograghical notices of Patrick William Earl, which were published at the time of his decease in *The Irish Times*, *Daily Express*, *The Analyst*, *The Medical Press*, *The Farmers' Gazette*, *The Mail*, and other Irish Journals:—Mr. P. W. Earl, who died on the 4th of August last, was a member of an old Irish family named "Errill," anglicised "Earl," of Carbury, county Kildare. Mr. Earl at an early age became the pupil of the late eminent Dr Aldridge, Professor of Chemistry in the Cecilia Street School of Medicine; succeeding Professor Aldridge in the management of a large manufacturing laboratory in Dublin, in which position he spent forty years of his life, till the firm was merged into a Limited Liability Company.

Mr. Earl was well known as a talented member of his profession; though a natural diffidence which he possessed prevented his name from coming much under public notice. He took, however, an active part at one time, in an undertaking promoted by Lord George Hill, Sir James Dombrain, Professor Aldridge, and others, for the purpose of extracting and utilizing the various valuable salts found in seaweed. Amongst the chemists who graduated under Mr. Earl, and who now occupy high positions throughout the United Kingdom and the Colonies, we may mention the name of Sir Charles Cameron, M.D., Analyst to the City of Dublin, and President of the Royal College of Surgeons in Ireland.

the 4th of August, 1885. He was married to Jane, the only daughter of John Kearney, a Dublin Poplin Manufacturer. This lady was descended on her mother's side from Peter La Touche, of *Belfield, county Dublin*, who was erroneously described in her obituary announcement as of *Bellvue, co. Wicklow ;* the La Touches of Belfield being a much older branch of the family. (See BURKE'S *Landed Gentry*.)

Mrs. Jane Earl, according to the certificate of her death issued by Doctor More Madden (an eminent physician, elsewhere referred to in this volume), died of mental trouble and decline, produced by her husband's death, which event she survived only nine months; dying on the 14th of May, 1886, deeply regretted by all her friends, to whom she had endeared herself by her exceedingly gentle and amiable disposition. We were informed that the Rev. A. S. Fuller, D.D., Vicar of St. Mark's, Dublin, in preaching Mrs. Earl's funeral sermon, touchingly alluded to "the rare instance of inconsolable conjugal affection, evinced in the decease of this amiable lady, who, from a long personal acquaintance, he could testify, was truly described as—a good wife and a pious and loving mother."

The issue of Patrick William Earl and his wife, were five sons and three daughters :

I. John-Samuel, who d. young.
II. William-Samuel, who died young.

III. Frederick George Earl, born in 1852, educated at Erasmus Smith's School, Dublin, and living unmarried in 1887.
IV. John Charles Earl, born in 1855, educated at Erasmus Smith's School, Dublin, and living unm. in 1887.
V. Edward H. Earl, born in 1863, and living unmarried in 1887. He was educated at Erasmus Smith's School, Dublin, and was subsequently a pupil in Chemistry, of Sir Charles Cameron, M.D., the distinguished Irish Analyst above mentioned. Edward H. Earl was for some time the proprietor and Editor* of a Dublin Church Magazine, which received the support and patronage of the Most Rev. Lord Plunket, D.D., and other eminent Church dignitaries. He was also the author of an interesting archæological sketch of St. Dolough's Church, co. Dublin, to which church he received the honorary appointment of lay-reader from the late Archbishop Trench, in 1884, the then Rector of St. Dolough's being the talented Doctor Tisdall, Chancellor of Christ Church Cathedral, Dublin.
VI. Georgina Elizabeth Earl, living unm. in 1887.
VII. Emily Jane Earl, living unm. in 1887.
VIII. Henrietta Earl, who died young.

---

* *Editor :* The Dublin Morning and Evening *Mail*, of October 11th, 1882, in a very favourable review, thus alluded to Mr. E. H. Earl's first literary effort—the *St. Mark's Parish Magazine* . . . . "It would be unfair to close this notice without making some reference to the young gentleman, through whose energy the Magazine has struggled into existence. He is but a boy in years, and yet we believe he canvassed for the Magazine's Advertisements (of which there is a good display), supplied the news for its columns ,and wrote its introductory address—in fact, did everything for it. If but half the parishioners of St. Mark's are possessed of such devotion towards their church as this youthful editor is, a bright prospect lies before it."

O'CONOR-ECCLES.

Arms : The Armorial Bearings of "Eccles"* are—Ar. two halberts† crossed saltier-wise az. *Crest :* A broken halbert az. *Motto :* Se defendendo.

SIR HUGH O'CONOR DUN, of Ballintubber‡ Castle, county Roscommon, who is No. 124 on the "O'Conor Don" pedigree, was one of the Irish Chiefs who sat in the Irish Parliament of 1585, and signed a Deed of Composition with Queen Elizabeth, as head of his family. He was Knighted by the Lord Deputy Sir John Perrott, and was styled "Lord of Connaught;" he d. in 1632 at a very advanced age. Sir Hugh O'Conor Dun m. the daughter of Sir Brian O'Rourke, of Breffni, and by her had several sons. According to tradition the posterity of the eldest son became extinct since the reign of Charles II.

125. Hugh Oge O'Conor, of Castlerea, who d. about 1635 : second son of Sir Hugh ; m. Jane, dau. of Lord Dillon, and by her had :

126. General Daniel O'Conor, of Castlerea (who d. 1667). This Daniel O'Conor m. Anne Bermingham, dau. of Lord Athenry, and left a son :

127. Colonel Andrew§ O'Conor, who m. Honoria, dau. of Colonel Luke Dowell of Mantagh, and by her had four sons :

I. Daniel, of Clonalis, of whom presently.

II. Sir Thomas O'Conor,‖ Knight of St. Louis, and General in the French Service.

III. The Rev. Andrew O'Conor.

IV. Sir Hugh O'Conor, Knight of Calatrava ; Brigadier-General in His Catholic Majesty's

---

* *Eccles :* For the Arms of the "O'Conor" family, see those of the *O'Conor Don.*

† *Halberts :* It is worthy of remark that these Arms are identical with those of Robert Bruce, to whom the "Eccles" family of Kildonan, county Ayr, were related. The winning of these Arms by Bruce is beautifully described by Sir Walter Scott in his *Lord of the Isles.*

‡ *Ballintubber :* Sir William Wilde, in his *Fisherman of the Suck,* gives an amusing account of the siege of Ballintubber Castle. It seems that in 1786, a Will said to have been made by Hugh O'Conor, an ancestor of this line, was discovered accidentally between the leaves of a card-table which had been screwed together for a great number of years, and had lain among the effects of the late Lord Athenry. This document (from which it appeared that the castle and estate of Ballintubber, which had long before passed from the O'Conor family, had not been included in the original confiscation of their estates) passed into the hands of Alexander O'Conor, a man of very eccentric habits, who acted thereupon without further delay. He took possession of the castle, fortified it, and held high state for a short time until the matter was brought under the notice of the Irish House of Commons, which disapproved of Alexander's summary proceedings, and sent down a body of troops to dislodge him. The marks of the cannon balls fired on the occasion are yet to be seen.

§ *Andrew :* This Andrew O'Conor must have had an elder brother Roderick, who died young ; as a curious medallion or locket in possession of the family of the late Alexander O'Conor Eccles, of Roscommon, would seem to attest. The medallion is of gold, surmounted by a crown ; the front, of cut crystal covering a small painting of an allegorical figure, surrounded by a chain of fine gold. The back bears this inscription .—"Rodrik O'Connor Dun dy'd the 22nd Feby., 1722."

‖ *Thomas O'Conor :* There is in the possession of the family of the late Mr. O'Conor Eccles an old pedigree written on parchment, partly in Irish, and partly in English ; dated 6th July, 1738 ; signed and sealed by Charles Lynegar, then King-at-Arms, and

Service; and Governor of Chili.

128. Daniel O'Conor Dun, of Clonalis (d. 1769): son of Colonel Andrew O'Conor; m. Margaret Ryan, and by her had three sons and two daughters:

I. Dominic O'Conor Dun, who m. Catherine Kelly, of Lisnaneen, but by whom he had no children. He willed his property to his brothers in succession, and, failing issue by them, to his cousin* Denis O'Conor, of Belanagare, and his descendants. (From Owen, son of said Denis, the present O'Conor Don is descended.)

II. Alexander O'Conor *Don,* succeeded his brother Dominic, and d. unm. in 1820. So displeased was he at the terms of Dominic's Will, that he refused to have said Dominic interred at Kilkeevan with the rest of the family. To Alexander succeeded in the Clonalis property, Owen O'Conor, of Belanagare, according to the terms of Dominic's Will.

III. Thomas, younger brother of Alexander, d. unm.

I. Jane, of whom presently.

II. Elizabeth, who d. unm.

129. Jane O'Conor: the elder daughter of Daniel O'Conor Dun; m. William Eccles,† a scion of the Kildonan (co. Ayr) family of that name. This Jane O'Conor was educated in France, like all Catholic young ladies of her rank during the penal days in Ireland; and was returning home under the care of the Very Rev. Dr. Clifford,‡ Priest of the Sorbonne, when she seized the opportunity to elope with her lover William Eccles; knowing well that her family would never consent to her marriage with a non-Catholic. This marriage greatly displeased the O'Conor family, who had lost so heavily through their steadfast adherence to the Catholic faith; and Jane's father refused to see her again. She and her brothers, however, became reconciled; and it was understood that her only son Daniel O'Conor Eccles, was, if he survived them, to succeed his uncles, as "O'Conor Don." But Dominic, who became seized of the lands of Clonalis, under a Patent from Charles II. (the estates which he derived from Sir Hugh O'Conor having been confiscated under the Cromwellian Settlement), by his Will devised same unto his brothers successively, as above-mentioned, in strict settlement, with remainder to Denis O'Conor, of Belanagare, for life, with remainder to his eldest son Owen O'Conor, of Belanagare, and his brothers successively, in strict settlement, with remainder to

by William Walker, the Lord Mayor of Dublin at that date. That pedigree traces from the earliest times the genealogy of Thomas O'Conor, Knight of St. Louis, and General in the service of the King of France.

* *Cousin*: If Dominic O'Conor Dun thought proper to will his property to his sister Jane, in succession to his brothers Alexander and Thomas, failing issue by them, there was not, in our opinion, any English or Irish law to prevent Jane's only son Daniel O'Conor Eccles from succeeding to the property; for, we find a similar case in that of the daughter of The O'Gorman, who married a Mr. Mahon, whose son on succeeding his grandfather was known as "The O'Gorman Mahon!"

† *Eccles* : The ancestor of William Eccles came to Ireland with Edward Bruce, at the time of Bruce's Invasion of Ireland, A.D. 1315.

‡ *Clifford* : Dr. Clifford's grandnieces still (1887) live,—one at Castlerea, county Roscommon, the other at Chambéry in Savoy.

several other cousins successively; and thus, by this testament, disinherited his only nephew, the son of his sister Jane.

130. Daniel "Eccles O'Conor Don," as he continued to write his name until his death, in 1839 : only son of Jane O'Conor and her husband William Eccles. This Daniel opposed the Will of his uncle Dominic, on the ground of " undue influence," on the part of Dominic's wife; but the proofs he adduced of that alleged influence were not, in the opinion of the court, sufficient to annul the Will, which therefore, unjust as it was, held good in law. This Daniel* m. Charlotte, dau. of Benjamin Pemberton, and by her had a family of five sons and three daughters, none of whom married, save Alexander.

131. Alexander O'Conor Eccles, of

Ballinagard House, near Roscommon, who d. in March, 1877 : son of Daniel O'Conor Eccles ; married Mary, dau. of Matthew Richards, of Gorey, and by her had several children, of whom only two girls survive in 1887. (O'Brennan's *History of Ireland,* a very interesting work, refers to the descent of this Alexander O'Conor Eccles.)

132. Charlotte and Mary O'Conor Eccles: only surviving children of Alexander O'Conor Eccles ; living in 1887.

It will be seen by carefully reading this genealogy, that these two young ladies are, through their great-grandmother, Jane† Eccles (née O'Conor), the sole representatives, in the senior line, of Sir Hugh O'Conor Dun, of Clonalis, who is No. 128 on this pedigree.

* *Daniel:* Sir William Wilde, who is an excellent authority, having been born at Castlerea, where his father was family physician to the O'Conors, and whose sister moreover married Oliver Pemberton, nephew-in-law to Daniel O'Conor Eccles, adds the following interesting note to his *Memoir of Gabriel Beranger* (Gill : Dublin) :—" I am perhaps the last writer who retains a personal recollection of three of the following descendants of Cathal Crove-Dearig, one of the last Kings of Connaught. Daniel, one of the direct descendants of Sir Hugh, of Ballintubber, was The O'Conor Dun (*don* or *dubh*) or the *Dark* O'Conor, to distinguish him from O'Conor Roe (or *ruadh*), the red (O'Conor), and O'Conor Sligo and O'Conor Kerry. He lived in great state at Clonalis, near Castlerea, and died in 1769. He had three sons : Dominick, Alexander, and Thomas ; and two daughters, Jane and Elizabeth." Sir William goes on to say that Jane's marriage with a Protestant offended her family, and then adds :—" Dominick, who died in 1795, was reconciled to his sister, but made a will leaving his property to Denis O'Conor of Belinagar, failing issue by his brothers. The third son, Thomas O'Conor, lived to a great age along with his sister ' Miss Betty,' at a place called Aram, near the mill bridge at Castlerea, where my father, who was their medical attendant, used frequently to bring me to see them. Thomas O'Conor died so suddenly, that foul play was suspected, as he was supposed to have had a large sum of money in the house ; and an inquest was held on him. Both brothers and sister were very eccentric, and lived in great seclusion, but were highly esteemed by all the first families in the county. In the old house I remember seeing a beautiful Spanish picture of the Madonna, a large gold snuff-box representing on the lid the landing of Columbus in America, said to have been given by the King of Spain to one of the O'Conor family; and the silver and jewelled hilted sword of Count O'Reilly. These with the personal property of Thos. O'Conor passed into the hands of his nephew, the late Daniel Eccles, father of my esteemed friend Alexander O'Conor Eccles, of Roscommon."

† *Jane Eccles (née O'Conor):* The following inscription, copied in 1857 from a tombstone in Kilkeevan churchyard, which has been since wantonly defaced, sustains a great part of this pedigree, down to and including the name of the said Jane Eccles: " Here lies the remains of the descendants of the ancient Monarchs of Ireland. General Daniel O'Connor Don and Anne O'Connor, alias Bermingham, his wife, sister to Lord Baron Athenry ; Colonel Andrew O'Connor Don, and Honoria O'Connor, alias Dowell,

†

EDMUNDSON.

Arms: Az. a tower triple towered supported by two lions ramp. ar. as many chains descending from the battlements betw. the lions' legs or.

EDMOND KELLY, the third son of Donoch O'Kelly who is No. 113 on the "O'Kelly" (Hy-Maine) pedigree, was the ancestor of *MacEimhain*, or *MacEmuin*, ("eimh:" Irish, *brisk, active, quick*), anglicised *MacEdmond*, and modernized *Edmundson,* *Edmonds,* and *Edwards*.

114. Edmond Kelly : son of Donoch O'Kelly ; a quo *MacEimhain*.

115. Edmond Oge : his son.

116. Connor : his son.

117. William Kelly : his son ; the first who was called *MacEdmond*.

118. Edmond MacEdmond : his son.

119. Conor : his son.

120. William : his son.

121. Edmond Ruadh MacEdmond, of Gaill : his son.

EGAN. (No. 1.)

Hereditary Chief Judges of Ireland.

Arms : Az. two palets ar. over all a saltire or.   *Crest* : A cross patriarchal gu.

COSGRACH, brother of Inrachtach, who is No. 100 on the (No. 1) "O'Kelly" (Princes of Hy-Maine) pedigree, was the ancestor of *O'h-Aedhagain ;* anglicised *O'Egan, MacEgan,* and *Egan*.

The *O'Egans* or *MacEgans* were hereditary Brehons (or Chief Judges) in Connaught, in Leinster, and in Ormond. In this genealogy we are able to trace the pedigree of the Connaught (or Parent) stock of the family in regular lineal descent down to the reign of King Charles I. ; but we regret our inability to trace the regular descent down to the present time of any

his wife, daughter to Colonel Luke Dowell of Mantagh ; Daniel O'Connor Don and Margaret O'Connor, alias Ryan, his wife ; Sir Thomas O'Connor, Knight of St. Louis, and General in his Christian Majesty's service ; the Revd. Andrew O'Connor ; Sir Hugh O'Connor, Knight of Calatrava, Brigadier-General in his Catholic Majesty's service, and Governor of Chili ; Thomas O'Connor and Jane Eccles, alias O'Connor."

* *Edmundson :* William Edmundson, the father of Quakerism in Ireland, was born at Little Musgrove, Westmoreland, in 1627. He served as a trooper under Cromwell, through the campaigns in England and Scotland. In 1652 he left the army, married, joined his brother (who was also a Parliamentary trooper) in Ireland, and opened a shop at Antrim. In 1654 he and his brother, his wife and others whom he had converted, held at Lisburn the first meeting of the Quakers' Society in Ireland. In consequence of his preaching, and that of George Fox, and other expounders of the doctrine of Quakerism, the Society of Friends gained many converts in Ireland, chiefly among the English colonists of the Cromwellian Settlement. After some years' sojourn in Antrim, he removed to Rosenallis, near Mountmellick, where he died on the 31st August, 1712. It is believed that this William Edmundson was of this family.

of the Connaught and Leinster branches of this ancient noble stock. Our research enables us to trace only a few generations of two of the Ormond branches of the family, namely—the "Egan" (No. 2), and the "Egan" (No. 3), *infra*.

The following is the pedigree of the Connaught (or Parent) stock of the *O'Egan, MacEgan*, or *Egan* family :

100. Cosgrach : son of Fichollach.
101. Flaithgheal : his son.
102. Anluan : his son.
103. Flaitheamh (also called Felim) : his son.
104. Gosda : his son.
105. Aedhaghan ("aedh :" Irish, *the eye; "aghain," to kindle*) : his son ; a quo *O'h-Aedhaghain.*
106. Flann : his son.
107. Murtach : his son.
108. Donoch Mór : his son ; had a brother named Saorbhreathach, and another named Dermod.
109. Donoch Oge : son of Donoch Mór.
110. Simeon : his son ; had two sons—1. Saorbhreathach or Justin, and 2. Maoliosa.
111. Justin : son of Simeon.
112. Maoliosa : his son.
113. Flann (or Florence) : his son.
114. Finghin : his son ; who had two sons—1. Owen, and 2. Conor Ruadh.
115. Owen : son of Finghin.
116. Teige : his son.
117. Conor : his son.
118. Teige (2) : his son.
119. Melachlin Egan : his son.

· · · · · ·

At this stage in the history of this ancient Irish family the estates of Melaghlin Egan, No. 119 on this pedigree, were confiscated by the Earl of Strafford, then the Irish Viceroy, under Charles I. It appears that other members of the family held their estates down to the Commonwealth period, and others later; for (see our *Irish Landed Gentry when Cromwell came to Ireland*), among the "Forfeiting Proprietors" under the Cromwellian Confiscations in the county of Mayo, barony of Tyrawley, and parish of Leckan, we find the name of Solloman Egan of Cashelldowna and Killdavioge, in said parish, whose estate was conveyed to William Webb. Again (*ibid.*) we find among the "Connaught Certificates" of that unhappy period in Ireland the names of Carbury Egan ; Constantine Egan ; Cormac Egan ; Daniel Egan ; Eganin Egan, son of Carbury ; Feigh Egan ; Rose Egan ; Teige Egan ; and Una Egan. Next (*ibid.*) we find, among the "Names of Persons in the Grants," under the Acts of Settlement and Explanation (A.D. 1661—1665), the names of Carbery Egan ; Carbury, Dan, and Constantine Egan ; Flan Egan ; James Egan ; and Una Egan. And last (*ibid.*), among the "Forfeiting Proprietors in Ireland," under the Confiscations of William III., whose estates were sold in Dublin in 1702 and 1703, we find the name of Daniel Egan. In the Irish Parliament of 1797, we find the name of John Egan, M.P., who (a writer in *Notes and Queries*, Second Series, suggests,) was the author of a number of letters on political characters of the day that appeared during his life-time in the *Dublin Evening Post*, over the signature of "Junius Hibernicus."

(For further information respecting John Egan, M.P., see the "Egan" (No. 3) pedigree.)

EGAN. (No. 2.)

Mayor of Kilkenny.

(A Branch of the Tipperary "Egan" Family.)

The Armorial Bearings of "Egan," of Tipperary, were *temp.* Charles I.,—*Arms :* Gu. a tower ar. supported by two men in armour, their exterior hands resting on their hips, in each of the others a halbert all ppr. in chief a snake or.

THE Kilkenny branch of the *Egan* family is one of the oldest now existing of the original sept; being settled there for upwards of three centuries. Its first members migrated from Ballymac-Egan, in Tipperary, and settled in the parish of Ballycallan, county Kilkenny. During the period of the "Confederation of Kilkenny," Flan MacEgan, who at that time was one of the most eminent scholars of Munster, was in 1642 invited to proceed to Kilkenny and there superintend the printing of the Transactions of the Confederation; and from that to the present time Kilkenny has been well-known as a publishing centre.

During the Confederation period many of the Kilkenny publications were issued by Bishop Rothe, whose history may be said to be identical with that of the Confederation. It was in Kilkenny, in 1762, that Bishop de Burgo's celebrated work *Hibernia Dominicana* was published; and added to the fame which that old city had already acquired from its literary men.

In our own time, the *Transactions of the Royal Archæological Association of Ireland,* which in the main treat of the antiquities of Kilkenny, have originated there; and the works of Banim, the Novelist, as well as the historical works lately issued by the Most Rev. Dr. Moran, have well kept alive the ancient renown of the "Fairie Citie."

At the present day, Kilkenny has made a decided step in advance as a publishing centre. Mr. P. M. Egan (Patrick MacEgan), a member of the Ballycallan branch of the "Egan" family, now represents the literary fame of Kilkenny. He is descended from Daniel Egan (born in 1730), who, as it appears by the Muniments of the Kilkenny Corporation, held land in the neighbourhood of John-street, in that city, before and up to A.D. 1790. Commencing with said Daniel, the pedigree is as follows:

1. Daniel Egan, of Kilkenny, born in 1730, married and had:

2. Patrick Egan, who was educated for the Roman Catholic Priesthood, but afterwards devoted himself to trade. This Patrick (born 1770) m. and had:

3. Michael Egan (b. 1810), who m. and had:

4. P. M. Egan, Mayor of Kilkenny, in 1887.

Numerous works in connection with primary education have, from time to time, emanated from P. M. Egan's pen, all of which have been very successful in this country; while some of them have a large circulation in England and Scotland. Mr. Egan's Educational Works have, we have been informed, now reached a circulation of half a million! In illustration of the history and antiquities of Kilkenny, Mr. Egan has written an *Historical Guide* (some 400 pp.) to the County and City, which is highly popular; and he has published a large work, from the pen of Mr. John Hogan, upon *Kilkenny the Ancient City of Ossory, the Seat of its Kings, the See of its Bishops, and the Site of its Cathedral.*

Within the past twelve months Mr. Egan's first Novel, *Scullydom,* has been issued from the Kilkenny Publishing Works, and has been most favourably received by all sections of the Press, as a work of no ordinary merit; and, better still, as an omen of yet more brilliant effusions which no doubt may be expected from him. In recognition of Mr. Egan's worth as a literary man, and a citizen, the people of Kilkenny have deservedly honoured him by conferring on him the greatest favour in their gift, viz., electing him MAYOR OF KILKENNY, for the year 1887.

EGAN. (No. 3.)

Of Austria-Hungary, and Germany.

(A Branch of the "Egan" Family, of Ballymac-Egan, county Tipperary.)

The Armorial Bearings granted in 1715 to a member of the "Egan," of Bally-macEgan, family, in the County Tipperary, were:

Arms: Quarterly, 1st, gu. a tower ar. supported by two knights in complete armour, holding in their interior hands a battle axe all ppr. in chief a snake barways or; 2nd and 3rd, or, on a bend vert. three plates; 4th, gu. on a tower as in the first quarter, a swan statant ar. *Crest:* On a tower or, a knight in complete armour couped at the knees, holding in his dexter hand a battle axe all ppr. *Motto:* Fortitudo et prudentia.

JOHN EGAN,* M.P., mentioned in the last sentence of the "Egan" (No. 1) pedigree, was a younger son of Carbery Egan, who was a scion of the

---

* *John Egan, M.P.:* John Egan, Chairman of Kilmainham, co. Dublin, was born A.D. 1754, at Charleville, co. Cork, where his father was a Church of England clergyman. He entered Trinity College, Dublin, as a sizar, studied law in London, and after his return home married a widow lady of some fortune. In March, 1789, he entered Parliament as member for Ballinakill, Queen's County; and, from 1790 to the period of the Union, sat for Tullagh. He was a noted duellist, and hence was called "Bully Egan." He once fought with his intimate friend, Curran, fortunately without serious consequences. Egan, who was a corpulent man, complained of the great advantage his *size* gave to his adversary: "I'll tell you what, Mr. Egan," said Curran, "I wish to take no advantage of you whatever. Let my size be chalked out on your side, and I am quite content that every shot which hits outside that mark should go for nothing." In after life there were few of his old friends of whom Curran was accustomed to speak with greater affection than of Egan. In 1799 he was appointed Chairman of Kilmainham. His means were by that time reduced, and the post was then almost his only source of income. The office depended upon Government favour, and it was intimated that his support of the "Union" between Great Britain and Ireland would lead to further advancement. As the final debate on the question in the Irish House of Commons proceeded, it was seen that Egan was writhing under conflicting emotions; at length he rose, delivered a furious speech against the Union, and sat down exclaiming: "Ireland—Ireland for ever! and damn Kilmainham!" He died, in poverty, in May, 1810, aged 66 years.—See WEBB'S *Compendium of Irish Biography* (Dublin: Gill & Son, 1878); the *Correspondence of the Marquis Cornwallis* (London: Charles Ross 3 vols. 1859); *Curran and his Contemporaries* (Edinburgh: Charles Phillips, 1850); *Notes and Queries* (London, 1850-1878); *Public Characters of 1798* (Dublin: 1799); Walker's *Hibernian Magazine* (Dublin: 1771-1811); Brady's *Records of Cork, Cloyne, and Ross,* vol. III., p. 183.

Ballymac-Egan family, co. Tipperary, and who settled in Charleville, co Cork, as Master of the Endowed School of that place. Said Carbery afterwards entered into Holy Orders as a clergyman of the late Established Church in Ireland; and was Protestant Curate of Charleville, from A.D. 1748 to 1770. One of his sons, whose christian name we have not ascertained, also entered into Holy Orders, and afterwards became Bishop of Philadelphia, United States, America.

Considering the *date* of the grant of the Armorial Bearings which head this pedigree, and the fact that they are *identical* with those of the family of the Rev. Carbery Egan, here mentioned, who was Curate of Charleville, A.D. 1748, we are of opinion that it was to the said Carbery Egan's father those Armorial Bearings were first granted, A.D. 1715.

Commencing with the Rev. Carbery Egan, the pedigree of this family is as follows:

1. Rev. Carbery Egan, Curate of Charleville, co. Cork, from A.D. 1748 to 1770, married and had:
I. James, who m. and had:
  I. Pierce (b. 1773, d. 1849), who m. and had a son Pierce, living in 1887.
  II. John, b. 1779, d. 1862.
  III. Laurence.
This James's family settled in England.
II. Carbery, baptized 9th March, 1746.
III. Giles, bapt. 19th March, 1747
IV. Richard, baptized 1st April, 1750, d. 1751.
V. John, M.P. from 1789 to 1800, b. 1754, and of whom presently.
VI. Daniel, d. 1766.
  I. Mary, bapt. 1751.
  II. Catherine, bapt. 1758.
  III. Elizabeth,* d. 1765.

2. John Egan, M.P.; a younger son of Rev. Carbery Egan; born 1754, died 1810; entered Trinity College, Dublin, as a Sizar; studied Law in London; and after his return home married a widow lady of some fortune. In March, 1789, Mr. John Egan entered the Irish Parliament as member for Ballinakill (Queen's County); and, from 1790 to 1800, sat for Tullagh. He was "Chairman" of Kilmainham, or, as the position would now be termed, *County Court Judge of Dublin.* In Parliament he voted against the "Union" between Great Britain and Ireland; was, for so doing, deprived by the Government of his chairmanship; and, thus reduced to poverty, d. in Scotland, in May, 1810.

3. James Egan (b. 1783, d. 1834): son of John; after remaining some short time in Scotland, he went to Germany in the beginning of this century; became a Page at the Court of Zwei-Brücken, in Germany, "and a Freemason." In after years he went to reside in Austria-Hungary, mar. Theresa Price, and had four sons:
I. James, of whom presently.
II. Charles, who went to America in 1849. His son William, who is living in Mainz (or Mayençe), in Germany, has a large establishment of "sp018ditary" business, with numerous filials (or branches thereof) in Germany, Austria, and Hungary. This William has a son

named William, of minor age, in 1887.

III. Edward (d. 1880) : the third son of James (No. 3) ; was a landowner in Hungary. He had two sons and a daughter; the sons are :

I. Edward, who is (in 1887) an Inspector-General of Dairy Farming at the Hungarian Ministry of Agriculture; and whose three children—1. László, 2. Imre, and 3. Edward, are minors, in 1887.

II. Lewis : the second son of Edward, who d. in 1880 ; is Chief Engineer to the Maritime Government of Fiume and the Hungarian Croate Coast. He has one son, Béla,* a minor in 1887.

The daughter of Edward, who d. in 1880, is :

I. Irma, who is, 1887, living at her widowed mother's in "Borostyánkö-Castle."

IV. Alfred : the fourth son of James (No. 3) ; is Chief Engineer to the Hungarian States Railways. He had two sons and four daughters; the sons were:

I. Alfred, who is on the Engineer's Staff of the Hungarian States Railways.

II. Edward, who is a Clerk in the Establishment of his cousin William Egan, in Mayençe, in Germany.

The sisters of these two brothers, are : 1. Rosa, 2. Julia, both of whom are married in Budapest; 3. Josephine, 4. Louisa—both of whom are (in 1887) living at their father's in Budapest.

4. James : eldest son of James (No. 3), who was the first of the family that settled in Hungary; is (in 1887) a Professor at the University of Budapest; has one son and three daughters :

I. Lewis, of whom presently.

I. Rosa, who m. a Hungarian Nobleman and Lawyer, Dr. Victor de Hagara, member of the Hungarian Parliament, for the county of Ugocsa; and living in 1887.

II. Clara. III. Adéle, both living at their father's in 1887.

5. Lewis Egan : son of James (No. 4) ; is a Director of extensive Glass-works in Transylvania. His children are two sons and one dau. :

I. Lewis, of whom presently.

II. Victor, a minor in 1887.

I. Leona, also a minor in 1887.

6. Lewis Egan : son of Lewis (No. 5) ; living in 1887, and a minor.

FAHY.

Of Ulster.

Arms : Az. issuing from the base of the shield a dexter and sinister arm chevron-ways, vested or. hands ppr. fingers crossed.

FEAREADHACH, a brother of Muircheartach Mór Mac Earca who is No. 90 on the (No. 1) " O'Neill" (of Tyrone) pedigree, was the ancestor of *Fadhaigh*

---

* *Bela :* This name is the Hungarian for "Albert."

("fadh:" Irish, *a cut;* "ach," *a skirmish*); anglicised *Fahy, Fahie,** and *Fay.*

90. Feareadhach: third son of Muireadhach.
91. Fiachnach: his son.
92. Suibhneach Meann: his son.
93. Crunmhal: his son.
94. Maoltuile: his son.
95. Flann Fionn: his son.
96. Diochron: his son.
97. Elcan: his son.
98. Brollachan ("brollach:"

Irish, *the breast*); his son; a quo *O'Brollaghain,* anglicised *Brallaghan, Bradlaugh, Bradley, Brabacy,* and *Brabazon.*
99. Doilghean: his son.
100. Maolphadraic: his son.
101. Dubhinniseadh: his son.
102. Maolbrighid: his son.
103. Maoliosa: his son.

FALLON.

Of Clan Uadach, Co. Roscommon.

Arms: Gu. a greyhound ramp. ar. holding betw. the forepaws a tilting spear, point to the dexter or. *Crest:* A demi greyhound salient ar.

CEANNFADA, the younger brother of Ubhan who is No. 101 on the "O'Beirne" pedigree, was the ancestor of *O'Fallain;* anglicised *O'Fallon, Fallon, Fallone,* and *Falloone.*

101. Ceannfada: son of Uadach.
102. Florence: his son.
103. Fallan ("fallain:" Irish, *healthy*): his son; a quo *O'Fallain.*
104. Ferchar: his son.
105. Florence (2): his son.
106. Murtach: his son.
107. Dermod: his son.
108. Florence (3): his son.
109. Aodh (or Hugh): his son; had eight brothers.
110. Dermod (2): his son.
111. Malachi: his son.
112. Florence (4): his son.
113. Donoch: his son; had a brother named Amhailgadh [awly].
114. Hugh Mór: son of Donoch.
115. Hugh Oge: his son.
116. Teige: his son.
117. Donoch (2): his son.
118. Hugh Ballach: his son.

119. Teige Mór: his son.
120. Teige Oge: his son; had a brother named Bryan.
121. Edmond: son of Teige Oge; had five brothers—1. Daniel, 2. Teige, 3. Bryan, 4. Connor, and 5. Tirlach.
122. Hugh (5): son of Edmond.
123. Caoch Mór: his son.
124. Redmond: his son.
125. Redmond Oge: his son.
126. William: his son; had three brothers—1. Daniel, 2. Bryan, 3. Teige.
127. Edmond (2): son of William; had two brothers—1. Bryan, and 2. John.
128. Redmond (3): son of Edmond; had a brother named Teige.
129. William O'Fallon: son of Redmond.

* *Fahie:* There are several very respectable members of this family living in Dublin, in 1887.

FALVEY.

Lords of Corcaguiney, County Kerry.

ACCORDING to some authorities this family* descends from Cairbre Riada, son of the Irish Monarch Conaire II., who (see the " Genealogy of the Kings of Dalriada," in the Appendix) is No. 88 on "The Genealogy of the Kings of Dalriada;" but, according to others, the family was descended from Eocha, who was a son of Cairbre Musc, a brother of Cairbre Riada, above mentioned. From this Eocha the following is the pedigree :

88. Conaire II., the 111th Monarch of Ireland; d. A.D. 165.
89. Cairbre Musc : his son.
90. Eocha : his son.
91. Crimthann : his son.
92. Lorcan : his son.
93. Tuathal: his son.
94. Alioll : his son.
95. Dungal: his son.
96. Maolruanaidh : his son.
97. Tomaltach : his son.
98. Morogh : his son.
99. Aodh (or Hugh) : his son.
100. Duach : his son.
101. Dubhcron : his son.
102. Colga : his son.
103. Failbhe ("failbhe": Irish, *lively*) : his son; a quo *O'Failbhe ;* anglicised *O'Falvey,* and *Falvey.*
104. Lugaidh : his son.
105. Maonagh : his son.
106. Donach : his son.
107. Donall : his son.
108. Ceallach : his son.
109. Dermod : his son.
110. Connor : his son.
111. Brian : his son.
112. Conall : his son.
113. Cormac : his son.
114. Turlogh : his son.
115. Teige : his son; had two brothers, Donall and Thomas.

116. Thomas Oge : son of Teige.
117. John : his son; had a brother James.
118. Teige : son of John.
119. James : his son; had a brother named Donall.
120. Hugh : son of James.
121. Patrick : his son.
122. John : his son; living in 1641.
123. James : his son.
124. Donall : his son; living in 1718; had a brother named John.
125. Donall : son of Donall; had a brother named Dermod, who was commonly called "Jeremy," who was educated in Bandon, and was ordained a Catholic Priest in the city of Cork.
126. John : son of Donall (No. 125); b. at Drumkeen, near Inishannon, county Cork, barony of East Carbery, on 24th June, 1785 ; emigrated to New York in 1831. This John married Joanna Donovan of Bandon, who had two brothers—1. Denis, a wheelwright who died in America: 2. Jeremiah, who entered the Mexican War.
127. Thomas O'Falvey, of Taunton, Mass., United States, America : his son ; living in 1886.

* *Family :* The O'Falveys were admirals of Desmond. In ancient times they were chiefs of *Corca Duibhne* and of the territory from the Mang, westward to *Fiontraigh* (or " Ventry.") *Corca Duibhne* is now the barony of " Corcaguiney," in the county Kerry.

FEEHAN.

Arms ; Per fess sa. and erm. on a chev. or, three trefoils slipped gu. in chief three covered cups of the third.

FIACHAN, brother of Muireadach who is No. 100 on the " Lane" pedigree, was the ancestor of *O'Fiachain* ("fiach :" Irish, *a raven*): anglicised *Feehan, Fian, Fyans, Fynes*, and *Vaughan.*

FELAN.

Lords of North Decies, in Munster.

Arms : Ar. four lozenges in bend conjoined az. betw. two cotises of the last, on a chief gu. three fleurs-de-lis of the first.

FIACHA SUIDHE, a younger brother of Conn of the Hundred Battles who is No. 80 on the " O'Hart" pedigree, was the ancestor of *O'Fealain ;* anglicised *O'Faelan, O'Felan, Felan, Phelan,* Whelan, Whelen, Helan,* and *Heylin.*

80. Fiacha Suidhe : son of Felim Rachtmar.

81. Æneas : his son.

82. Artcorb : his son.

83. Eochaidh (also called Eoghan Breac) : his son.

84. Bran : his son.

85. Niadbhran : his son.

86. Earcbhran : his son.

87. Cainneach : his son.

88. Maclasre : his son.

89. Fiontann : his son.

90. Aodh (or Hugh) : his son.

91. Cumuscach ("cumus :" Irish, *power, ability ;* "cach," *all*): his

son ; a quo *O'Cumuscaigh,* anglicised *Cumisky,* and *Waters.*† This Cumuscach had two sons, one of whom was Doilbh ("doilbh :" Irish, *dark, gloomy*), a quo *O'Doilbhe,* anglicised *Doyle ;* and another Breodoilbh (a quo *Broe*), who was ancestor of *O'Bricé,* anglicised *O'Brick,* and *Brick.*

92. Doilbh : son of Cumuscach.

93. Eoghan : his son.

94. Donoch : his son.

95. Donal : his son.

96. Rorcach : his son.

97. Melaghlin : his son.

---

* *Phelan :* William Phelan, D.D., a distinguished clergyman of the late Established Church, was born at Clonmel, on the 29th of April, 1789. His parents were Catholics, and he was educated as one ; but he entered Trinity College as a Protestant in June, 1806. He soon became distinguished by his literary attainments, and was befriended by William Conyngham Plunket and Dr. Magee. In 1814 he was appointed second master in the Endowed School of Londonderry ; the same year he took Orders in the Church, and was appointed to a chaplaincy by the Bishop of Derry. In 1817 he gained a Fellowship in Trinity College, and in 1818 was elected Donnellan Lecturer ; in 1823 he resigned his Fellowship, and accepted the curacy of Keady, in the diocese of Armagh, which next year he gave up for the rectory of Killyman in the same diocese. In October, 1825, he succeeded to the college rectory of Ardtrea, and next year took the degree of D.D. He died on the 20th June, 1830.

† *Waters ;* The "isky" in the Irish sirname *Cumisky,* sounds so like the Irish "uisge" (*water, a river*), that the name "Cumisky" has been anglicised *Waters.*

98. Cormac : his son.

99. Faelan (" faelan :" Irish, *a little wolf*) : his son ; a quo *O'Faealin.*

100. Donal : his son.

101. Artcorb : his son.

102. Moroch : his son.

103. Donal O'Felan : his son ; first assumed this sirname.

104. Eochaidh : his son.

105. Faelan : his son.

106. Melachlin : his son ; living A.D. 1170.

107. Cumuscach : his son.

108. Congal : his son.

109. Donoch : his son.

110. Dungal : his son.

111. Cormac : his son.

112. Giollapadraic : his son.

113. Eoghan (or Owen) : his son ; living in 1450.

114. Teige : his son.

115. Brian : his son.

116. Donal : his son.

117. Shane : his son.

118. Edmond : his son.

119. Malachi : his son ; living in 1657.

120. James Stephenson *Whelen :* his son ; first assumed this sirname. Settled in England, and afterwards migrated to America ; m. Sarah Elizabeth Dennis, in New York, on 29th May, 1694.

121. Dennis Whelen, of Chester county, Pennsylvania : his son. Was twice married : first, to Anne Townsend, by whom we cannot find that he had any issue ; his second wife was Sarah Thompson, of Virginia, to whom he was married on the 8th Nov., 1749, and by whom he had seven children, namely—1. Ann, 2. Israel, 3. Isaac, 4. Edward,

5 and 6 Townsend and Dennis (twins).

122. Israel : son of Dennis ; m. to Mary Downing, on the 13th May, 1772, and by her had eleven children : 1. Elizabeth, m. to Joseph J. Miller ; 2. Sarah ; 3. Anne ; 4. Jane ; 5. Mary ; 6. Israel ; 7. Thomasine ; 8. Townsend ; 9. John ; 10. Susan ; 11. Maria.

123. Israel : son of Israel ; m. on 26th Nov., 1810, to Mary, dau. of Edward and Amy Siddons, of Salem, New Jersey, and by her had seven children—1. Israel, b. 10th October, 1811 ; 2. Edward Siddons Whelen, b. 22nd Aug., 1813 ; 3. Mary, b. 3rd Dec., 1815 ; 4. Henry, b. 13th Feb., 1818 ; 5. Elizabeth, b. 25th Dec., 1819 ; 6. Townsend, b. 3rd April, 1822 ; 7. Robert, b. 7th July, 1824.

124. Edward-Siddons Whelen ; son of Israel ; living in Philadelphia, in 1879. Married on 26th April, 1838, to Isabella Nevins, dau. of James and Aesah Willis, by whom he had eight children—1. Edward-Siddons Whelen, b. 23rd Dec., 1839 ; 2. Isabella-Nevins Whelen, b. 20th Dec., 1840 ; 3. Mary-Siddons Whelen, b. 17th April, 1843 ; 4. James-Nevins Whelen, b. 28th May, 1845 ; 5. William-Nevins, Whelen, b. 11th April, 1847 ; 6. Russell-Nevins Whelen, b. 21st January, 1850 ; 7. Bertha Whelen, b. 2nd April, 1851 ; 8. Emily Whelan, b. 7th July, 1853.

125. Edward-Siddons Whelen ;* of Philadelphia, United States, America : his son ; b. 23rd Dec. 1839, and living in 1879.

* *Whelen* : It may be well to observe that *O'Faelain* of North Decies, in the county Waterford, is a distinct family from the *O'Faoilain*, of Ossory ; although the roots of the two sirnames, namely "faelan," *a little wolf*, and "faoil," *wild, untameable*, are so much alike in meaning.

FERGUSON.*

Of Ulster.

Arms ; Az. a fess. betw. a star of eight rays in chief and a lion ramp. in base all or.   *Crest :* A lance in pale broken ppr. the head hanging down or, ferrule gold.

FEARGHUS, a son of Eoghan, who is No. 88 on the (No. 1) "O'Neill" (of Tyrone) pedigree, was the ancestor of *MacFearghusa ;* anglicised *Mac-Fearghus, O'Feargus, Fergus,* and *Ferguson.*

88. Eoghan: son of Niall Mór, the 126th Monarch of Ireland.
89. Fearghus: his son.
90. Aodh : his son.
91. Laoghaire : his son.
92. Forannan : his son.
93. Fioghal: his son.
94. Culena: his son.
95. Fearghus : his son.
96. Cinaodh: his son.
97. Maolcaoch : his son.
98. Branagan : his son.

99. Maolpadraic : his son.
100. Ceallach : his son.
101. Maolcamhghal: his son.
102. Colgan : his son.
103. Ceallach : his son.
104. Mathghamhan : his son.
105. Fearghus ("fear :" Irish, *a man ;* " gus," *strength*): his son ; a quo *MacFearghusa.*
106. Aodh MacFearghusa: his son.

FIHILLY.

Arms : Ar, an oak tree eradicated ppr.

MUREDACH MAOLLEATHAN, the 16th Christian King of Connaught, who is No. 97 on the "O'Connor" (Connaught) pedigree, was the ancestor of *O'Ficheallaigh ;* anglicised *Fihilly, Feely, Field, Fielden, Fielding, Tooth, O'Feeley,* and *Pickley.*

97. Muredach Mulleathan.
98. Conbhach ("conbhach:" Irish, *hydrophobia*): his son ; a quo *Clan Conbhaigh,* anglicised *Conway.*
99. Ficheallach ("fiacail:" Irish, *a tooth ;* Heb. " acal," *he eats*): his son ; a quo *O'Ficheallaigh,*

meaning "the descendants of the man who had large teeth." This Ficheallach had a brother named Cahernach, who was the ancestor of *Canavan,* of Connaught; and another brother named Dungar, who was the ancestor of *Finaghty.*

----

* *Ferguson :* Of this family was the late kind and good Sir Samuel Ferguson, Deputy Keeper of the Public Records in Ireland, and President of the Royal Irish Academy, who died in 1886.

FINAGHTY.

Arms : Ar. an oak tree eradicated ppr.

DUNGAR, a brother of Ficheallach, who is No. 99 on the "Fihilly" pedigree, was ancestor of *O'Finachtaigh* ; anglicised *Finaghty*,* *Finnerty*,† and *Snow*.

99. Dungar: son of Conbhach.

100. Fionnachtach ("fionnsneach-da:" Irish, *snow-white*): son of Dungar; a quo *O'Finachtaigh*, " one of the twelve lords of Cruaghan" (or Croaghan) in the county Roscommon.

101. Beannachdach (latinized *Benignus* and *Benedict*‡) : his son.

102. Concha : his son.

103. Cathal : his son.

104. Murtach : his son.

105. Murtach Oge : his son.

106. Teige : his son.

107. Teige Oge : his son ; the last " lord of Clannconon."

108. Charles O'Finaghty : his son; first assumed this sirname.

109. Brian : his son ; had two brothers—1. Daniel, and 2. Donoch.

110. Hugh : son of Brian.

111. Rory : his son; had two brothers—1. Hugh, and 2. Manus.

112. Donoch Granna : son of Rory.

113. Charles : his son.

114. William : his son; had two brothers—1. James, the priest, and 2. Redmond.

115. Malachy O'Finaghty : son of William.

FITZPATRICK. (No. 1.)

Princes of Ossory.

Arms : Sa. a saltire ar. on a chief ar. three fleurs-de-lis or. *Another* : Az. six lions ramp. ar. three, two, and one.

CONLA, a younger brother of Lughaidh [Luy] who is No. 78 on the " O'Connor" (Faley) pedigree, was the ancestor of *Mac Giolla Padraic*; anglicised *Mac Gillpatrick*, and *Fitzpatrick*.

---

* *Finaghty* : Of this family was James Finaghty, the Irish astrologer and exorcist, who flourished at the end of the 17th century.

† *Finnerty* : Peter Finnerty, one of the ablest reporters of his time, was born at Loughrea in 1766. In 1797 he was printer and editor of the *Press*, the organ of the United Irishmen, to which both Curran and Moore are said to have contributed. On the 22nd December, 1797, he was tried for a libel on the Government concerning the trial and execution of Orr, and, refusing to disclose the name of the author, was sentenced to stand in the pillory, pay a fine, and suffer imprisonment for two years. Arthur O'Connor, Lord Edward Fitzgerald, and others of his party, attended him at the pillory in Green-street. He died at Westminster on the 11th May, 1822.

‡ *Benedict* : From this name some derive *Bennett*.

2 F

78. Conla: son of Bressal Breac, King of Leinster.

79. Nuadad : his son.

80. Carrthach : his son.

81. Labhradh : his son.

82. Lughaidh : his son.

83. Ailill: his son.

84. Sedna: his son.

85. Iar : his son.

86. Erc : his son.

87. Crimthann Mór: his son.

88. Æneas Ossaraidhe : his son ; a quo the territory of Ossory ("ossaraidhe :" Irish, *a porter, carrier*) is so called; had a brother named Muireadach.

89. Laeghaire Bernbhradhach : son of Æneas Ossaraidhe ; had a brother named Ronan.

90. Amhailgadh [awly]: his son.

91. Eochaidh : his son.

92. Niadhcorb: his son.

93. Buan : his son ; a quo "Dal mBuain."

94. Cairbre Caomh : his son ; had two brothers—1. Dron, 2. Niadh.

95. Conall: son of Cairbre Caomh.

96. Ruamanduach : his son.

97. Lagneach Faoladh : his son ; had four brothers—1. St. Uibhne ; 2. St. Ceanfola, bishop (8th April) ; 3. St. Ceallach, a deacon (7th Oct) ; 4. St. Conall (3rd March).

98. Eochaidh (called Beagneach) Caoch : son of Lagneach; had a brother, St. Ciaran, of Saighir (3rd March).

99. Colman : son of Eochaidh.

100. Ceannfaola : his son.

101. Scanlan Mór : his son ; the 2nd King of Ossory.

102. Ronan Righfhlaith : his son.

103. Cronnmaol : his son.

104. Faelan : his son.

105. Cucaircheach : his son ; living A.D. 710.

106. Anmchadh: his son : the 9th King of Ossory.

107. Fergal : his son.

108. Dungal: his son; the 14th King of Ossory.

109. Diarmuid (or Dermod) : his son.

110. Cearbhall: his son ; the 15th King of Ossory ; had a brother Fionnan, who was the 16th King of Ossory.

111. Ceallach : son of Cearbhall ; was the 17th King of Ossory ; had a brother Dermod, who was the 19th King, and another brother Braonan ("braon :" Irish, *a drop*), a quo *O'Braonain*, anglicised *O'Brenan*, *Brenan*, and *Brenon*.

112. Donoch (or Doncha) : son of Ceallach; was the 18th King of Ossory.

113. Donal : his son.

114. Giolla - Padraig ("giolla :" Irish, *the devoted;* "Padraig," of *St. Patrick*): his son ; a quo *MacGiolla Padraig*.

115. Donoch : his son ; slain A.D. 1039 : was the 20th King of Ossory. Had a brother Teige who was the 22nd King, and who was blinded by this Donoch, A.D. 1026.

116. Donal MacGiolla Padraic : son of Donoch ; first who assumed this sirname ; died 1087.

117. Giollapadraic Ruadh : his son.

118. Scanlan : his son.

119. Donall Mór : his son ; had a brother named Connor, who settled in Thomond, and who was the ancestor of *Fitzpatrick*, of Limerick and Clare.

120. Uilliam [William] Clannach : son of Donal Mór ; was the ancestor of "Clann Donogh."

121. Geoffrey Baccach : his son : had a brother named Ostagan : ("osda :" Irish, *a host;* "gan," *without*), a quo "Clan Ostagain," anglicised *Costigan*.

122. Jeoffrey Fionn : son of Jeoffrey Baccach.

123. Donal: his son.

124. Donal Dubh: his son.

125. Flann (or Florence): his son.

126. Florence (2): his son.

127. Florence (3): his son.

128. Shane (or John): his son.

129. Brian: his son; created "Lord Baron of Upper Ossory," by Patent, dated 11th June, 1541; first of the family that assumed the sirname *Fitzpatrick*, instead of *Mac-Giolla-Padraic*, the Irish patronymic of the family; submitted to King Henry VIII., on 8th October, 1537.

130. Brian: son of Brian; a favourite to King Edward VI.; was Lord of Upper Ossory; only issue Margaret, who was wife of MacPiarras (or Bermingham). Had eight brothers—1. Florence, 3rd Baron, m. to Catherine Moore; 2. David; 3. Jeoffrey; 4. Tirlogh, who m. Ellen O'Moore, and had issue two sons—1. Donal, 2. Brian, and one dau. Kate. (This Donal m, Una Mac-Namara, and had a dau. Ellen, who m. Niall O'Neill, *alias* "Payne."—See "O'Neill" (of Tyrone) pedigree,

No. 130); 5. Dermod; 6. John; 7. Ceallach; 8. Teige.

131. Teige, 4th Baron, living 1627: son of Florence, the 3rd Baron; had a brother John, m. to Mabel St. John, and had a son Florence. This Teige had a son Barnaby, the 5th Baron (1639), who had Brian, the 6th Baron (1664), who had Brian, the 7th Baron (1731).

132. Florence: son of John and Mabel; m. to Bridget Darcy, of Platen.

133. John: their son. Married to Elizabeth Butler, and had two sons—1. Edward (1696), s. p.; 2. Richard.

134. Richard (d. 1727): second son of John; created "Lord Gowran,"* 1729. Married Anne Robinson, and had two sons—1. John; 2. Richard, m. to Anne Usher.

135. John, 2nd Lord Gowran, and 1st Viscount, 1758: son of Richard; had two sons—1. John, 2. Richard.

136. John Fitzpatrick, 2nd Viscount: son of John; m. Anne Liddell.

FITZPATRICK. (No. 2.)

Of Lissanwarny, County Clare.

Arms: Same as those of "Fitzpatrick" (No. 1).

GILLE DUFFE FITZPATRICK had:

2. Darby "Debrik," of Dounesallah, who had:

3. Florence, who had:

4. Florence (2), who had:

5. Darby, of Lissanwarny, county Clare, gent., who d. 31st Sept., 1637 He m. "Ingin Duffe," *alias* Any, dau. of Thomas MacMahon, son of Murtogh "Caume" MacMahon.

---

* *Gowran:* This Richard Fitzpatrick, Lord Gowran, was a distinguished naval commander. Entering the Naval Service, he was in May, 1687, appointed to a command, and signalized himself in several actions against the French. William III. granted him an estate in the Queen's County. On the accession of George I., he was created "Baron Gowran," and took his seat in the Irish Parliament. He died on the 9th June, 1727, leaving two sons, the eldest of whom afterwards became "Earl of Upper Ossory."

FLANAGAN.*

Of Roscommon.

Arms : Ar. out of a mount in base vert an oak tree ppr. a border of the second. *Crest :* A dexter cubit arm in armour ppr. garnished or and gu. holding a flaming sword az. pommel and hilt gold. *Motto :* Certavi et vici.

CATHAL, a brother of Inrachtach, who is No. 98 on the " O'Connor" (Connaught) pedigree, was the ancestor of *O'Flannagain* ; anglicised *Flanagan.*

98. Cathal : son of Muireadach Maolleathan.
99. Ardghal : his son.
100. Cinaoth : his son.
101. Murchadh : his son.
102. Flannagan ("flann :" Irish, *blood, red*) : his son ; a quo *O'Flannagain.*
103. Muireadach : his son.

104. Cathal : his son
105. Muireadach : his son.
106. Murchadh : his son.
107. Flaithbhearthach : his son.
108. Murchadh : his son.
109. Tadhg (Teige, or Thady) : his son.
110. Diarmaid O'Flannagain : his son.

FLINN.†

Lords of Tuirtre, or Northern Clanaboy.

Arms : Ar. a dexter arm couped betw. two swords in pale all ppr.

FIACHRA TORT, a brother of Roghan, who is No. 86 on the " Mac Uais" pedigree, was the ancestor of *O'Flainn,* of Tuirtre ; anglicised *O'Flinn, Flinn, Linn, Lyne,* etc.

86. Fiachra Tort("tort" or "toirt :" Irish, *a cake, a little loaf, bulk*) : son of Colla Uais ; a quo *O'Tuirtre ;* and a quo the territory of *Tuirtre,* more lately known as Northern Clanaboy, now the baronies of " Toome," and " Antrim."
87. Eachin (meaning " a little horse") : his son ; a quo *O'Eakin* and

Eakins ; had six brothers—1. Muireadach, 2. Cormac, 3. Main, 4. Laeghaire, 5. Aongus, 6. Nathi.
88. Fedhlim : son of Eachin ; had five brothers.
89. Daire : his son.
90. Cuanach : his son ; was King of Orgiall, as were also seven of his posterity.

---

* *Flanagan :* Among the Sligo families mentioned in the MS. Vol. 14, F. 13, (" Antiquities") by O'Donovan, and deposited in the Library of the Royal Irish Academy, Dublin, are *Coleman, Coffey* (Ui Chobhthaigh), *Roberts* (Ui Robhertaigh), etc. ; and in page 319 of that vol. is given the pedigree of another *O'Flanagan* family.

† *Flinn :* " Flinn" of Leinster is a branch of this family. In Connaught and Munster the name is spelled " Flynn," which is a distinct family from this stock. Of this family is Doctor D. Edgar Flinn, L.C.P., F.R.C.S., of Dublin ; living in 1887.

91. Bec: his son; King of Orgiall; a quo *Cineal Beice.*

92. Fuadhran: his son; King of Orgiall; ancestor of *Siol Cahesaidh* (anglicised *Casey*), and of *Siol Dubhghala.*

93. Suibhneach: his son; King of Orgiall.

94. Maolfoghartach: his son.

95. Maolchobha: his son.

96. Reachtabrad: his son.

97. Inrachtach: his son; had a brother Fionnachtach.

98. Muireadach: son of Inrachtach; had a brother Longseach, who was the ancestor of *O'Tuirtre,* strangely translated *Baker.*

99. Flann ("flann:" Irish, *blood, red*): his son; a quo *O'Flainn.*

100. Fogharthach: his son.

101. Donagan: his son.

102. Aodh: his son.

103. Maciarann ("mac:" Irish, *clear, pure, bright*; "iarann," *iron*): his son; a quo *O'Maciarainn,* anglicised *Steele.*

104. Foghlogha: his son.

105. Eachdach: his son.

106. Ruadhri an Deoraidh ("an deoraidh:" Irish, *the strong,* or *disobedient*): his son; a quo *Mac An Deoraidh,* anglicised *Dorey,* and *D'Orey.*

107. Cumidhe: his son.

108. Cu-uladh an t-Sioda ("the Silken Ulster Warrior"): his son; a quo *Cooley, Cooling, Cowley, Cully,* and *Colly.*

109. Cumidhe: his son; had a brother Murtagh.

110. Alexander: his son.

111. Muirchearthach: his son.

112. Cu-uladh: his son.

113. Domhnall: his son.

114. Ruadhri O'Floinn: his son.

FLOOD.*

Of Ireland.

Arms: Vert a chev. betw. three wolves' heads erased ar.

CORMAC, a brother of Cairbre Cluitheachar, who is No. 87 on the "O'Dwyer" (of Leinster and Munster) pedigree, was the ancestor of *O'Loimthuile,*† anglicised *Lumley,* and *Flood.*

87. Cormac: son of Cucorb.

88. Iomchadh: his son.

89. Treana: his son.

90. Labhradh: his son.

91. Lugdheach: his son.

92. Ceis: his son.

93. Treana (2): his son.

94. Lomthuile ("lom:" Irish, *bare;* "tuile," *a flood*): his son; a quo *O'Loimthuile.*†

---

* *Flood*: Henry Flood, a distinguished orator and statesman, who was born on the family estate near Kilkenny, in 1732, is believed to have been of this family; although his grandfather came to Ireland as an officer, during the war of 1641-1652. Henry Flood's father was Chief-Justice of the Queen's Bench, in Ireland. He entered Parliament in 1759 as member for Kilkenny, being the sixth of the name and family who sat in Parliament during the 18th century. He afterwards entered the British Parliament, and died at Farmley, near Kilkenny, on the 2nd December, 1791.

† *O'Loimthuile*: Meaning "the descendants of the man who was ruined by a flood."

95. Faolan : his son.
96. Furadhran : his son.
97. Ceallach : his son.

98. Nuadhad : his son.
99. Flann O'Loimthuile : his son.

FOGARTY.

Lords of Eliogarty, Tipperary.

Arms: Az. two lions ramp. combatant supporting a garb or, in dexter base a crescent ar., and in the sinister, the harp of Ireland.

CONALL CRIMTHANN, a brother of the Monarch Laeghaire, who is No. 88 on the "Connellan" pedigree, was the ancestor of *O'Fogharthaighe ;* anglicised *Fogarty.*

88. Conall Crimthann: son of Niall Mór or Niall of the Nine Hostages, the 126th Monarch of Ireland ; was the first Christian King of Meath.

89. Fergus Cearbhall : his son.

90. Diarmaid [Dermod] : his son ; the 5th Christian King, and 133rd Monarch of Ireland. Was slain at the battle of Rathbegg, by Hugh Dubh MacSweeney, King of Dal Araidhe (or Dalaradia), A.D. 558. Had an elder brother named Main, who was King of Meath next before him. It was in this Dermod's reign that the Royal Palace of Tara was deserted (see the Paper "Tara Deserted," in the Appendix).

91. Aodh (or Hugh) Slaine : son of Dermod ; the 141st Monarch. Had a brother named Colman Mór, who was the sixth Christian King of Meath.

92. Dermod Ruanach : his son. Had a brother named Congall, who was the ancestor of *O'Kelly*, of Meath—one of "The Four Tribes of Tara ;"* he had also another brother named Donoch, who was the ancestor of *Mulvey* or *Mulvy.* This Dermod Ruanach was the 149th Monarch of Ireland ; and reigned jointly with his brother Bladhmic (or Bladhmac) : both of whom died A.D. 664.

93. Cearnasotal : his son.

94. Niall: his son.

95. Fogharthach : his son ; was the 157th Monarch. He had three brothers—1. Cumascach, who was ancestor of *Burns ;* 2. Conall Greanta, ancestor of *Breslin* ; and 3. Aodh (or Hugh) Laighen, who was the ancestor of *Muldoon,* of Meath.

96. Ceallach : son of Fogharthach.

97. Tolarg ("tol :" Irish, *a church-yard :* "arg," *white* or *pale*) : his son ; a quo *O'Tolairg,* anglicised *Toler,* and *Tyler.*

98. Fogharthach (2) : his son.

99. Niull (2) : his son.

100. Fogharthach ("fogharthach :" Irish, *noisy*) : his son ; a quo *O'Fogharthaigh.*

* *Tara :* The "Four Tribes of Tara," were *O'Hart, O'Kelly* (of Meath), *O'Connolly,* and *O'Regan.*—BOOK OF RIGHTS.

FORAN.

Arms : Ar. a sinister hand couped at the wrist affrontée gu.

CONCHOBHAR, a brother of Niall Frassach who is No. 96 on the " O'Neill" (of Tyrone) pedigree, was the ancestor of *O'Furadhrain ;* anglicised *Farran, Foran,* and *Furniss.*

96. Conchobar: second son of Feargal, the 156th Monarch of Ireland.

97. Furadhran ("fuireadh:" Irish, *preparation*) : his son; a quo *O'Furadhrain.* From this Furadhran also descends the family of *O'Branagain,* of Tirowen ; anglicised *Branagan.*

98. Cumusgach: his son.

99. Sgreamdhach : his son.

100. Muireadhach : his son ; a quo *O'Muireadaigh,* of Tirowen, anglicised *Murray.*

101. Maolbrighid : his son.

102. Fachtnacht: his son.

FORBES. (No. 1.)

Of the Clann Ferbisigh.

Arms : Ar. three bears' heads couped ar. muzzled gu.

AMHAILGADH, a younger brother of Eochaidh Breac who is No. 89 on the " O'Shaughnessy" pedigree, was the ancestor of *Clann Firbisigh ;* anglicised *MacFirbis,* and *Forbes.*

89. Amhailgadh: the third son of Dathi, the 127th Monarch of Ireland.

90. Feargus : his son.

91. Muireadhach : his son.

92. Conaing : his son.

93. Enna: his son.

94. Conchobhar na Conairte (or Connor of the Pack of Hounds) : his son.

95. John : his son.

96. Lochlann, of Loch Conn, co. Mayo : his son.

97. Aongus: his son.

98. Domhnall Mór : his son.

99. Domhnall Oge : his son.

100. Fearbiseach ("fear :" Irish, *a man ;* " biseach," *prosperity,* or the *crisis of a disease ;* Heb. " bizza," *increase*) : his son; a quo *Clann Firbisigh.*

101. Giolla Phadraig: his son ; by whom St. Tighearnan,* the founder of the Abbey of Errew, in the parish of Crossmolina, near Lough Conn, was fostered.

102. Donnchadh : son of Giolla Phadraig.

---

* *St. Tighearnan :* O'Donovan, in his " Tribes and Customs of Hy-Fiachrach," states that, as a relic of antiquity, *Mias Tighearnain* ("Tiearnan's dish, or platter"), which belonged to this saint, at the Abbey of Errew, Loch Conn, is preserved by the Knox family of Rappa Castle, near Crossmolina, county of Mayo.

103. John : his son.
104. Amhlaoibh : his son.
105. Domhnall, of the School : his son.
106. Giolla na Naomh : his son.
107. Fearbiseach : his son.
108. John Carrach : his son.
109. John Oge : his son.
110. Fearbiseach : his son.
111. Donchadh Mór : his son.

112. James : his son.
113. Diarmaid Caoch : his son.
114. Dubhaltach : his son.
115. Giolla Iosa Mór : his son.
116. Dubhaltach (or Duald) Oge MacFirbis : his son; the celebrated Compiler and Writer of "Mac-Firbis's Irish Genealogies;" living A.D. 1666; had three brothers, 1. Patrick, 2. Diarmaid, 3. James.

FORBES. (No. 2.)

Earls of Granard.

Arms : Az. three bears' heads couped ar. muzzled gu. *Crest* : A bear pass. ar. gutlée de sang muzzled gu. *Supporters* : Dexter, a unicorn erminois, armed, maned, tufted, and unguled or ; sinister, a dragon, wings expanded erm. *Motto* : Fax mentis incendium gloriæ.

ACCORDING to the *Linea Antiqua*, this family derives its origin from Connor, who was a younger brother of Aodh (or Hugh), No. 71 on the "O'Connor" (Corcomroe) pedigree. But according to O'Donovan, O'Curry, and Cronnelly, it is derived from the *Clann Firbisigh*, whose pedigree is traced in the foregoing ("Forbes," No. 1) genealogy. The following is the ascertained regular descent of the family :

1. Sir Alexander de Forbes, chief of the ancient Scottish House of Forbes, created a Peer of Scotland, about 1370, by King James II., by the title of "Baron Forbes," d. 1448; m. Elizabeth Douglas, dau. of George, Earl of Angus, by the Princess Mary his wife, dau. of King Robert III.

2. James, second Lord Forbes ; m. Lady Egidia Keith, dau. of William, first Earl Marischal, by Mary his wife, dau. of James, first Lord Hamilton, and had three sons —1. William, third Lord Forbes, ancestor of the *Lords Forbes*, of Scotland ; 2. Duncan, of Corsindie, ancestor of *Forbes of Pitsligo*, etc. ;

3. Honourable Patrick Forbes, of Corss, Armour Bearer (according to the Lumsden MS.) to King James III.

3. David, of Corss, called "Traill the Axe :" son of the Hon. Patrick Forbes ; m. Elizabeth, dau. of Patrick Panter, of Newmanswaes, Old Montrose.

4. Patrick, of Corss ; m. Marjory, dau. of Robert Lumsden, of Maidler and Cushney.

5. William Forbes, Laird of Corss, county Aberdeen : eldest son of Patrick ; m. Elizabeth Strachan, dau. of the Laird of Thornton.

6. Sir Arthur Forbes, Knt. ; created, 26th Sept., 1628, a Baronet

of Nova Scotia; d. 14th April, 1632; m. Jane, dau. of Sir Robert Lauder* of the Bass, and widow of Sir Alex. Hamilton, Knt., and had two sons—1. Sir Arthur, 2. Patrick, who was killed in Poland. This Sir Arthur was Lieut.-Colonel to the Regiment of the Master of Forbes sent from Scotland to Ireland, in 1620.

7. Sir Arthur Forbes, Bart., b. 1623; elevated to the Peerage in 1673, as Baron Clanehugh and Viscount Granard; created Earl of Granard in 1684; Will dated 12th March, 1693; d. 1696; buried at Newtown Forbes, county Longford, Ireland; m. to Catherine (d. 1714), dau. of Sir Robert Newcomen, Bart., of Moss Town, co. Longford, and relict of Sir Alexander Stewart. The issue of that marriage were five sons and one daughter : the sons were—1. Arthur; 2. Robert, d. 1686, unm. ; 3. Francis, d. unm.; 4. Patrick, d. unm.; 5. Thomas, d. unm.; and the daughter was Lady Catherine Forbes (d. 1743), m. to Arthur, third Earl of Donegall.

8. Arthur Forbes, second Earl of Granard, d. 1734, and buried at Newtown Forbes ; m. Mary (d. 1724), eldest dau. of Sir George Rawdon, Bart., of Moira, co. Down. The issue of this marriage were two sons and two daughters; the sons were—1. Arthur Lord Forbes, d. unm. 1704 ; 2. George, third Earl of Granard. The daughters were— 1. Lady Jane (d. 1760), m. to Major Josias Champagné (d. 1737) ; 2. Lady Dorothy (d. unm. 1729).

9. George, third Earl of Granard, b. 1685, d. 1765, and buried at Newtown Forbes ; m. Mary (d. 1755), dau. of Sir William Stewart, first Viscount Mountjoy. The issue

of this marriage were two sons ; and one daughter, Lady Mary, m. to James Irvine of Kingcausie. The sons were—1. George, b. 1710; 2. John, Admiral of the Fleet, and General of the Marine Force, d. 1796, m. to Lady Mary Capel (d. 1782), fourth dau. of William, Earl of Essex, and had issue two daughters—1. Catherine-Elizabeth, m. to William, Earl of Mornington, 2. Mary-Eleanor, m. to John-Charles, Earl of Clarendon.

10. George Forbes, fourth Earl of Granard, b. 1710, d. 1769, and buried at Newtown Forbes ; m. Letitia (d. 1778), dau. of Colonel Arthur Davys of Hamstead, county Dublin, and had an only son.

11. George, fifth Earl of Granard, only son, b. 1740, d. 1781, and buried at Newtown Forbes ; was twice married : first, in 1759, to Dorothea (d. 1764), second dau. of Sir Nicholas Bayly, Bart., of Plas Newydd, Isle of Anglesey, and had a son George, sixth Earl of Granard ; and secondly, in 1766, to Lady Augusta Berkeley (d. 1820), eldest dau. of Augustus, Earl Berkeley, and had issue—1. Henry, 2. William, 3. Augustus, 4. Cranfield, 5. Frederick, 6. Lady Anne-Georgina, 7. Lady Augusta, 8. Lady Louisa-Georgina, 9. Lady Elizabeth.

12. George, sixth Earl of Granard, only son by the first marriage, b. 1760, created in 1806 a Peer of the United Kingdom, as "Baron Granard, of Castle Donnington," county Leicester ; d. 1837, and was buried at Newtown Forbes; m. in 1779 Lady Selina-Frances Rawdon (d. 1827), second dau. of John, first Earl of Moira, and of Elizabeth, Baroness Hastings, etc., dau. of Theophilus, Earl of Huntington, and

---

* *Lauder* : This Jane Lauder is mentioned as Jane "Lowther" in the MS. Vol. F. 418, Trin. Coll., Dublin.

had issue—1. George-John, 2. Francis-Reginald, 3. Hastings-Brudenell (d. 1815), 4. Angouleme-Moira (d. 1810), 5. Ferdinando-William (d. 1802), 6. Lady Elizabeth-Mary-Theresa (d. 1852), 7. Lady Selina-Frances (d. 1791), 8. Lady Adelaide-Dorothea (d. 1858), 9. Lady Caroline-Selina (b. 1799).

13. George-John, Viscount Forbes, eldest son, b. 1785, d. 1836, and buried in the old ruined church of Clongish, in the demesne of Castle Forbes; m. in 1832 to Frances-Mary, only dau. of William Territt, LL.D., of Chilton Hall, Suffolk, England, and had issue—1. George-Arthur - Hastings, 2. William-Francis, Colonel Leitrim Rifles, and a Resident Magistrate, b. 1836, living in 1887, m. to Phillis, dau. of John Rowe, of Ballycross House, county Wexford, and has had issue George-Francis-Reginald Forbes, b. 6th Sept., 1866.

14. George - Arthur - Hastings Forbes, seventh Earl of Granard, b.

5th August, 1833, and living in 1887, m. first, in 1858, to Jane Colclough (d. 1872), younger dau. and co-heiress of Hamilton-Knox Grogan-Morgan, M.P., of Johnstown Castle, county Wexford, and had—1. Lady Adelaide-Jane Frances, m. to Lord Maurice FitzGerald in 1880; 2. Lady Sophia Maria Elizabeth, born 1861; 3. Lady Caroline (d. an infant, 1865); and m. secondly, in 1873, to the Hon. Frances-Mary, daughter of Lord Petre, and has had issue—1. Bernard-Arthur-William-Patrick Hastings, Viscount Forbes, born 17th September, 1874; 2. the Hon. Fergus-Reginald-George, b. 20th Jan., and d. 20th Feb., 1876; 3. the Hon. Reginald-George-Benedict, and Lady Eva - Mary - Margaret (twins), b. 25th June, 1877; 4. Lady Margaret-Mary-Theresa, b. 13th Jan., 1879; 5. the Hon. Donald-Alexander, b. 3rd Sept., 1880.

FOX. (No. 1.)

Lords in Teffia, Ireland.

Arms: Az. a sceptre in bend betw. two regal crowns, and a chief or.   *Crest :* A fox sejant ppr.

MAIN, son of Niall of the Nine Hostages who is No. 87 on the " O'Neill" (of Tyrone) pedigree, was the ancestor of *MacSionnaighe;* anglicised *Sionnach, Fox, Reynard, Reynardson,* and *Seeny.*

87. Niall of the Nine Hostages, the 126th Monarch of Ireland.

88. Main : his son.

89. Brian : his son.

90. Brannan : his son.

91. Aodh (or Hugh): his son ;

had a brother named Creamthann, who was the ancestor of *Breen.*

92. Bladhmhach; son of Hugh ; had a brother named Aongus, who was the ancestor of *Loughnan* or *Loftus,* of Meath.

93. Congall : son of Bladhmach.
94. Colla : his son.
95. Giolla Brighid : his son.
96. Maolbeanachtach : his son.
97. Tagan : his son ; a quo *Muintir Tagain.**
98. Beice : his son. This Beice had three brothers—1. Deighnan, 2. Cearnachan, and 3. Gabhlach : this Cearnachan had four sons— 1. Cibleachan (" cib :" Irish, *a hand ;* " leacha," *a cheek ;* " an," *one who*), a quo *O'Cibleachain,* anglicise *Giblan ;* 2. Cathalan, who was the ancestor of a *MacQuin* family ; 3. Muireagan ; 4. Cinleachan (" ceann :" Irish, *a head ;* " leaca :" *a cheek*), a quo *O'Cinlecahain,* anglicised *Kinlehan,* and *Kinehan.*
99. Connor : son of Beice.

100. Breasal : his son.
101. Cathiarnach (" cath :" Irish, *a fight ;* Heb. " chath," *terror :* Chald. " cath," *a battalion ;* " iarann," Irish, *iron*) : his son ; a quo *O'Cathiarnaighe,* anglicised *Carney.*
102. Cathalann : his son.
103. Cathiarnach (2) : his son.
104. Rory : his son.
105. Fogartach : his son.
106. Rory (2) : his son.
107. Teige an Sionnach (" an sionnach :" Irish, *the fox*) : his son ; a quo *MacSionnaighe.*
108. Rory (3) : his son.
109. Neal : his son.
110. Malachi : his son.
111. Connor (2) : his son.
112. Rory Fox : his son.

FOX. (No. 2.)

Of Kilcoursy, King's County.

Arms : Ar. a lion ramp. and in chief two dexter hands couped at the wrist gu. *Crest :* An arm embowed in armour, holding a sword all ppr. *Motto :* Sionnach aboo (Fox for ever).

CARBRY FOX had :
2. Owen of Kilcoursy, in the King's County, who had :
3. Brassell, who had :
4. Art (or Arthur), who had :
5. Brassell, of Kilcoursy, who d. 7th April, 1639. He married Mary, daughter of Hu. MacGeoghagan, of Castletown, county Westmeath, and had one son and six daughters.
I. Hubert, of whom presently.
I. Mary, who m. Edmund Malone of Kilgarran, in the co. Westmeath.
II. Eliza, who m. Neal Molloy, of Pallis, King's County.
III. Mary.
IV. Margaret.
V. Amy.
VI. Katherine.
6. Hubert Fox, of Kilcoursy : son of Brassell ; m. Mary, dau. of Lewis Connor, of Leixlip, Esq.

---

* *Muintir Tagain :* In page 118, of first series, this people is by mistake mentioned as " Muintir Fagan."

FOY.*

Arms : Paly of eight sa. and ar. a crescent gu. *Crest :* An eel ppr.

FATHADH, a brother of Ainmireach who is No. 94 on the "Lemon" pedigree, was the ancestor of *O'Fathaidh ;* anglicised *Foy.*

94. Fathadh ("fath :" Irish, *skill ;* "adh," *a beast of the Cow Kind*) : son of Aongus ; a quo *O'Fathaidh.*
95. Furachar : his son.
96. Aongus : his son.
97. Flann : his son.
98. Colman : his son.

99. Fiochdha Salmhair : his son.
100. Colum : his son.
101. Allabhar ("*allabhar :*" Irish, *savage, wild*) : his son ; a quo *O'Allabhair,* anglicised *Oliver.*
102. Maonach : his son.
103. Cormac O'Fathaidh : his son.

FREND.

RICHARD CANE, the third son of Richard O'Cahan, of Larah Bryan, near Maynooth, co. Kildare, who is No. 123 on the "O'Cahan" Genealogy, was, maternally, an ancestor of this family :

124. Richard Cane, of Larah Bryan : third son of Richard O'Cahan. Will dated 28th December, 1754. Married Anne Cane *née* Lyons, and had three sons— 1. Richard, 2. William-Lyons, 3. John.
125. William-Lyons Cane ; second son of Richard ; m. and had three sons—1. Richard-Duke Cane, who was Major in the 5th Dragoon Guards ; 2. Hugh Cane, Captain in 22nd Regiment; and 3. Medlycott Cane.
126. Medlycott Cane : third son of William-Lyons Cane. Was in the 102nd Regiment, East Indies. This Medlycott Cane was twice married :

first to a Miss Browne (sister of Mrs. Robert Wybrants), by whom he had Major James Cane, 23rd Regiment, father of Madame de Madrid; Medlycott's second marriage was to a Mrs. Bloomfield, *née* Bayly, dau. of John Bayly, Esq., of Newtown, co. Tipperary, by whom he had—1. John-Lyons Cane, 60th Regiment; 2. Jane Cane; 3. Richard Cane, who d. 1849.
127. Richard Cane : third son of Medlycott; m. Delia-Eliza, youngest daughter of the late Rev. Meade-Swift Dennis, of Union Hill, co. Westmeath (and sister of the late Thomas Stratford Dennis, Esq., of Fort Granite, co. Wicklow), and

---

* *Foy :* Of this family is Doctor George Mahood Foy, of Dublin, who was born on the 22nd December, 1847, at Cootehill, county Cavan. His father was John Foy, a merchant, who married Jane, daughter of Michael Murphy, J.P., agent to the third Earl of Bellamont, who was noted for his violent opposition to the Union of Great Britain and Ireland. Mr. Foy is Examiner in Anatomy to the Apothecaries' Hall.

had—1. John Cane, d. s. p. ; 2. Richard-Lyons Cane, d. s. p. ; 3. James-Godfrey Cane, d. s. p. ; 4. Delia-Maria Cane, of whom presently ; 5. Elizabeth-Caroline Cane, living in 1883.

128. Delia-Maria Cane : dau. of Richard Cane ; m. in 1856, Major Frend (d. 1858), 55th Regiment, and had—1. Albert-William-John Frend, b. 1857 ; 2. Delia-Hester-Ellen-Jane Frend, living in 1883.

129. Albert-William-John Frend, B.A.: son of Major Frend and Delia-Maria Cane ; living in 1887.

GAFNEY.

Arms : Gu. a salmon naiant ppr. on a chief ar. a dexter hand apaumée of the first.

GOTHFRITH GAMHNACH, brother of Flaithbhearthach who is No. 112 on the "Maguire" pedigree, was the ancestor of *MacGamhnaigh ;* anglicised *Gafney, MacGafney,* and *Chamney.*

112. Gothfrith Gamhnach (" gamhnach :" Irish, *a cow nearly dry, a stripper*: son of Dunn Oge ; a quo *MacGamhnaigh.*

113. Gothfrith Oge : his son.

114. Niall Mór : his son.

115. Murcha : his son.

116. Diarmaid : his son.

117. Niall : his son.

118. Toirdhealbhach (or Tirloch) MacGafney : his son.

GAHAN.

Arms: Gu. three fishes haurient in a fess ar.   *Crest :* Arm embowed, holding in the hand a sword ppr.   *Motto:* Dum spiro spero.

THIS family name, as well as *Gahon, Gaghan, Gagham,* and *Getham,* is, since the reign of King Charles II., one of the anglicised forms of, and the family a branch of, *O'Cathain* or *O'Cahan,* Princes of Limavady, in the county of Londonderry.—(See the " O'Cahan" genealogy.)

In 1607, O'Cahan was implicated in the O'Neill's resistance to the English in Ireland ; he was imprisoned therefor, and his estates forfeited ; and his wife was found by the Duchess of Buckingham in great poverty. In a letter dated 1607 King James I. recommended dealing leniently with O'Cahan, and placing his son in college for the purpose of his education. That son, it is believed, was the progenitor of this family, and was the father of the Captain Daniel Gahon, who, as a soldier of the Commonwealth, was granted land in Tipperary.—(See p. 415 of our " Irish Landed Gentry when Cromwell came to Ireland." Dublin : 1884.)

According to an award of the Commissioners (which may be seen in the Public Record Office, Dublin), for the distribution of land in Ireland under the Commonwealth Rule, and which was enrolled on the 17th May, 1659, Thomas Ask became seized of the lands of Coolquill and other townlands in the county Tipperary, and devised them to his wife Susanna Ask, who afterwards became his widow and married Daniel Gahan, to whom and Susanna his wife the said lands were, under the Acts of Settlement and Explanation, granted A.D. 1666.—(See our "Irish Landed Gentry," p. 458.)

A Letter to the Duke of Ormond, dated Feby., 1663, in Letter Book 1663 to 1637, in the Signet Office, recites that Con O'Rourke of Modoragh, co. Leitrim, died without heirs, possessed of lands in 1641; his lands became the property of the Crown (not forfeited): ordered that a grant of the lands of Modoragh be made to Daniel Gagham* (rectè "Gaghan"), his heirs, etc. The grant of the estate in Tipperary was made to Daniel Gahan and his wife Susanna in 1666.

In the Irish State Papers, *temp.* Charles II., appears a Letter to the Lord Lieutenant bearing date Feby., 1663, and entered at Signet Office, directing inquiry to be made into the lands, etc., of Con O'Rourke, deceased, "of our title thereto, in the co. of Leitrim, and, being found, we make a grant thereof to Daniel Getham,* Esq."

In the Irish State Papers, 334, Charles II., appears a Letter, dated 20th Dec., 1665, from D. Gahan* to J. Williamson, Keeper of State Papers, about Con O'Rourke's Estate, county Leitrim.

Rolls Office, London: Calendar of State Papers, Domestic. Vol. 153, April 1. 16. 1666: Memo: Captain Gahan, Governor of Dublin Post Office.

21st August, 1666: Letter from Sir William Domville to Lord Arlington, Principal Secretary of State, sent by Captain Gaghan, whom he highly commends, and by whom he sends a present of a wolf dog.

Letter, 16th Nov., 1666, from Lord Lieutenant (Ormonde) recommending Mr. Gahan, who had been very diligent in the management of the Postage of this Kingdom, to be continued therein.

Daniel Gahan to Walter York, Postmaster at Barnet, in Letter of 30th Nov., 1666, recommends M. Choisin (bound for Ireland) to Postmasters on road to Chester, to furnish him with post horses.

Dec. 18th (1666): D. Gahan to Robert Leigh, at Lord Arlington's.

In 1666, Charles II. granted† to Daniel Gahan and Susanna his wife the lands of Coolquill, Killnehone, Ballynonly, and Sleveardagh, in the co. Tipperary; and by another grant‡ to Daniel Gahan himself, the lands of Modoragh, in the co. Leitrim, the estate of Con O'Rourke who, as above-

* *Gagham:* In the next entry this sirname is spelled *Getham*: an instance of the various forms which Irish sirnames assumed in their transition from the Irish to the English language. See the "O'Cahan" pedigree for other variations in English of the illustrious Irish family name *O'Cathain.*

† *Granted*: Award by the Commissioners of the Commonwealth, enrolled 17th May, 1659, may be seen in the Public Record Office, Dublin.

‡ *Grant*: Letter of Charles II. to the Duke of Ormonde, dated 10th Feb., 1663. See Irish State Papers, *temp.* Charles II.

mentioned, died without heirs. Commencing with said Daniel Gahan and his wife Susanna, the following is the pedigree :

1. Daniel Gahan m. Susanna, relict of Thomas Ask, above mentioned, and had three sons, Daniel, George, and John. He bequeathed* to his son George his estate in the co. Leitrim, and his house in Church-street, Dublin, called "Turkey Cock House :"

I. Sir Daniel, the eldest son, was Knighted for faithful services to the King; and d. intestate† and without issue. He was succeeded by his brother :

II. George, of whom presently.

III. John.

2. George Gahan : second son of Daniel ; mar. and had two sons :

I. Daniel, of whom presently.

II. George, who entered the army, settled in England, and was Governor of Scilly until his death.

George Gahan, brother of Sir Daniel, bequeathed all his real and personal estates‡ to his son Daniel.

3. Daniel : elder son of George ; m. and had (according to his Will, Prerogative, Book A-Y, 1765) three sons—Daniel, Robert, and John :

I. Daniel who m. Sarah, dau. of Joseph Smyth of Ballintubber, Queen's County. He d. without issue male surviving him. Having barred the entail of Coolquill, etc., in the co. Tipperary, the estate was inherited§ by his two daughters of his first and second marriages,

viz., Maryanne, who m. William Tighe of Woodstock ; and Penelope, who m. —— Gledstones of ——

II. Robert.

III. John, of whom presently.

4. John‖ : youngest son of Daniel; held the office of Surveyor-General; m. and had seven sons, of whom survived Beresford.

5. Beresford¶ (b. 1777) : son of John ; for some time of the 5th Dragoon Guards, 1st Royal Dragoons, and Brigade Major of the Donegal Yeomanry ; m.** Henrietta Anna Margaretta (d. 1st Feb., 1825), dau. of John Townsend of Shepperton, co. Cork, one of the Commissioners of his Majesty's Revenue in Ireland, and had nine sons :

I. John, who m. Hannah, eldest dau. of Ussher Lee, Dean of Waterford, and had three sons :

I. Beresford, who d. in infancy.

II. John, who d. leaving no male heirs.

III. Edward, supposed to be living and unmarried.

II. Beresford (2), who d. in infancy.

III. Henry, who m. Celia, dau. of —— MacDonnell, Surgeon of the 57th Regiment of Infantry, in which he held a Commission, and d. without issue. He retired from the service with the rank of Colonel.

IV. Robert, who m. Anna-Mary,

* *Bequeathed* : Prerogation, Will, Book 21, A to W, 1706-8.

† *Intestate* : Book 266. 1712 to 1716.

‡ *Estates* : Prerogative, Will, Book 33, A-W, 1731-2. Page 46.

§ *Inherited* : Prerogative, Will, Book 133, A K, 1800.

‖ *John* : Will proved, A.D. 1796.

¶ *Beresford* : Will proved, 1845.

** *Married* : Marriage Settlement dated 24th November, 1802.

eldest dau. of Richard B. Osborne of Ballycushlane, co. Kilkenny, and had two sons':

I. Beresford. II. Melmoth. This Robert d. of a wound received in the engagement of Moodkee, in India, in 1845.

V. Townsend, who d. unmarried.

VI. George, of whom presently.

VII. Alfred, who married Alicia, fourth dau. of the Rev. Henry Herbert, of Innistiogue, co. Kilkenny, and had five sons:

I. Beresford, who d. in infancy.

II. Henry:

III. Alfred, who d. in infancy.

IV. Alfred (2), who d. in boyhood.

V. Frederick.

VIII. Walter, who m. Georgina, third dau. of Charles Putland, of Brayhead, in the co. Wieklow, has no issue living.

IX. Frederick, who m. twice:— first, Henrietta, dau. of Edward Byrne of Carlow, who d. s. p.; and secondly, Katharine-Jane, eldest dau. of Edward Hume Townsend of Cuilnaconara, near Clonakilty, co. Cork, and had seven sons:

I. Frederick, who d. in infancy.

II. Edward, who d. in boyhood.

III. Townsend.

IV. Beresford.

V. Stirling.

VI. Reginald.

VII. Walter.

6. George: the sixth son of Beresford; is unm. and in America.

Of the nine sons of Beresford Gahan, three survive (1887), viz., George, Walter, and Frederick.

GALLAGHER.

ANMIRE (latinized Anmireus), who was the 138th Monarch of Ireland, and the brother of Fergus, who is No. 91 on the "O'Donnell" (of Tirconnell) pedigree, was the ancestor of *O'Gallchobhair;* anglicised *Galchor,* and *Gallagher.*

91. Anmire: son of Seadneach; slain A.D. 566.

92. Aodh (or Hugh): his son; the 140th Monarch.

93. Maolchobhach (latinized Malcovus): his son, who was the 144th Monarch; had a brother named Donal, who was the 146th Monarch, and the ancestor of *Mulroy.*

94. Ceallach: son of Maolchobhach.

95. Donal: his son.

96. Donoch: his son.

97. Rory: his son.

98. Rorcan: his son.

99. Gallchobhair," ("gall:" Irish, *a foreigner;* "chobhair," *help):* his son; a quo *O'Gallchobhair;* A.D. 950.

100. Manus: his son.

101. Donoch (2): his son.

102. Amhailgadh [awly]: his son.

103. Donal (2): his son.
104. Dermod: his son.
105. Hugh (2): his son.
106. Maolruanaidh: his son.
107. Nichol: his son.
108. Donoch (3): his son.
109. Fergall: his son.
110. Hugh (3): his son.
111. Gillcoimdhe: his son.

112. Nichol (2): his son.
113. Eoin (or John): his son.
114. Hugh (4): his son.
115. Rory (2): his son.
116. John (2): his son.
117. Cormac Buidhe: his son.
118. John (3): his son.
119. Owen O'Galchor: his son.

GALWEY.*

Arms: Or, on a cross gu. five mullets of the field.

1. JEOFFREY GALWAY (modern-ized *Galwey*), of Kinsale, co. Cork, had:

2 John, of Limerick: his son.

3. James, of Limerick, Ald.: his son.

4. Jeoffrey, of Limerick, Knt. and Bart.: died at Kinsale. This Jeoffrey was thrice married: first to Anne, dau. of Nicholas Comyn, Ald., Limerick; secondly, to Mary, dau. of Maurice MacSheehy, of Ballenan, co. Limerick, gent., by whom he had four daughters, Martha, Margaret, Grace, and Clara; and thirdly, to More, dau.

of Morough O'Brien, of Twogh, co. Limerick, by whom he had a daughter Eleanor. The children of the first marriage were—1. John; 2. Gabriel; 3. Patrick; 4. Jenet, *m.* to William Galwey of Kinsale; 5. Mary, *m.* to Nicholas Stritch, of Limerick; 6. Anne, *m.* to John Stritch, of Limerick, 7. Kathleen, *m.* to Maurice Caha O'Brien, of Twogh, co. Limerick; 8. Christian.

5. John: son of Geoffrey; *m.* Eliza, dau. of—— Betts, of Norfolk, England.

6. Sir Jeoffrey Galwey, Bart., his son.

GARVALY.

Arms: Same as those of "O'Hart.'

BRIAN, a brother of Daimhin who is No. 92 on the "O'Hart" pedigree, was the ancestor of *O'Garbhgeille;* anglicised *Garuly*, and *Garvaly*.

92. Brian: son of Cairbre an-Daimh-Airgid, King of Orgiall.

93. Fergus Garbhgeill ("garbh:"

Irish, *rough;* "geill," *to yield*): his son: a quo *O'Garbhgeill*.

94. Hugh: his son.

* *Galwey*: This sirname is derived from a branch of the "Bourke" family, in the county Galway, which settled in Cork in the 14th century; and hence have been distinguished by the territorial name of *Galway, Galwey*, and *Gallwey*.

2 G

95. Faolan : his son.
96. Mactigh : his son.
97. Cuborin : his son.
98. Cumagan : his son.
99. Maolagan ("maolagan:" Irish,

the bald little man) : his son ; a quo
O'Maolagain, anglicised *Mulligan*,
and *Molyneux*.
100. Muireadach O'Garvaly : his
son.

GARVEY. (No. 1.)

Of Orgiall.

Arms : Erm. two chevronels betw. three crosses pattée gu.

FIACHRA CEANNFIONNAN, brother of Niallan who is 89 on the "O'Hanlon"
pedigree, was the ancestor of *O'Gairbhidh*, of Orgiall ; anglicised *Garvey*.

89. Fiachra Ceannfionnan
("ceannfionnan:" Irish, *the fair-
haired*) : son of Feig ; a quo *O'Ceann-
fionnain ;* anglicised by some *Cannon.*
90. Luachmhar : his son.
91. Failbhe : his son ; had a
brother named Cumann ("cu-
mann :" Irish, *acquaintance*), a quo
O'Cumuinn (of Moyne), anglicised
Cummins, and *Commins.*
92. Fohach : his son.

93. Crunmaol : his son.
94. Dubthirr : his son ; a quo
O'Dubthire, anglicised *Duffry*, and
Dooher.
95. Failbhe (2) : his son.
96. Fionnan : his son.
97. Fearach : his son.
98. Maoleadach : his son.
99. Gairbiadh ("gairbiadh :"
Irish, *shouting for food*) : his son ; a
quo *O'Gairbhidh*, of Orgiall.

GARVEY. (No. 2.)

Of Tirowen.

EOCHAIDH BINNE, brother of Muireadach [muredach], who is No. 89 on
the "*Cuonaghan*" pedigree, was the ancestor of *O'Garvey* of Tyrone.—
See the derivation of this sirname in the foregoing pedigree.

89. Eochaidh Binne ("binn :"
Irish, *melodious*) : son of Eoghan ; a
quo *Cineal Binne* in Scotland, a
Binney in Ireland.
90. Claireadanach* ("claireadanach:" Irish, *broadfaced*) : his son.
91. Donal : his son.

92. Ultach ("ultach :" Irish, *an
Ulsterman ;* his son ; a quo *MacAn-
Ultaigh*, anglicised *MacNulty*, *Nulty*,
and *Nalty.*
93. Failbhe : his son.
94. Maoldun : his son.
95. Conrach : his son.

* *Claireadanach* : Some of this man's descendants call themselves *Clarendon.*

96. Elgenan : his son.
97. Cucolann : his son.
98. Danaille : his son.
99. Mulfabhal : his son.
100. Toiceach ("toiceach :" Irish, *wealthy*) : his son.

101. Gairbiadh: his son ; a quo *O'Gairbidh* (of Tirowen), anglicised *Garvey.*

GAVAN.

Arms : Erm. on a saltire engr. az. five fleurs-de-lis.

GABHADHAN ("gabhadh :" Irish, *danger ;* "an," *one who*), brother of Dungal, who is No. 102 on the "Donnelly" pedigree, was the ancestor of *O'Gabhadhain ;* anglicised *Gavan,* and *Gavahan.*

GAWLEY.

Arms : Ar. on a chev. gu. betw. three ancient galleys with three masts, sails furled, flags flying sa. a lion ramp. or, armed and langued az.

LUIGHACH, who is No. 90 on the "Quirk" pedigree, was ancestor of *O'Gabhlaighe* ("gabhlach :" Irish, *forked or longlegged*) ; anglicised *Gavala, Gawley, Gowley,* and *Gooley.*

90. Luighach : son of Labhrach ; had six brothers, but there is no account of their issue.
91. Brollach : his son.
92. Connla : his son.
93. Iomchadh : his son.
94. Dulach : his son.
95. Croch : his son.
96. Maith ("maith :" Irish, *a*

chief, a nobleman, a leader) : his son; a quo *O'Maith,* anglicised *May** and *Maye ;* had two brothers—1. Iomchadh, 2. Earc.
97. Ceannfionnan : son of Maith.
98. Iomchadh (2) : his son.
99. Sionamhuil   O'Gabhlaighe : his son.

* *May :* See the "May" (Lords of Orgiall) pedigree, for another family of this name, but of a different stock from this family, and differently derived.

GERAGHTY.

Arms : Ar. a saltire and a border gu.

CATHAL (or Charles), brother of Teige Mór who is No. 102 on the "O'Connor" (Connaught) pedigree, was the ancestor of *MacOrcachta ;* anglicised *MacOiraghty, MacGeraghty, Geraghty, Gerty, Garrett, Garratt,* and *Gerrotte.*

102. Cathal : son of Muirgheas.

103. Aodh (or Hugh): his son.

104. Morogh: his son.

105. Duncath : his son.

106. Orcacht (" orc :" Irish, *a small warrior ;* " acht," gen. achta," *an act*): his son ; a quo *MacOrcachta.*

107. Duncath Mór : his son ; had two brothers—1. Morogh, 2. Orcacht.

108. Duncath Oge : son of Duncath Mór.

109. Duncath (4): his son.

110. Hugh : his son.

111. Malachi : his son.

112. Tumaltach (or Timothy) : his son.

113. Morogh : his son.

114. Donall ; his son.

115. Connor : his son.

116. Timothy (2): his son.

117. Malachi (2): his son.

118. Manus : his son.

119. Manus MacOiraghty : his son.

GILLON.

Arms : Or, three fleurs-de-lis gu.   *Crest ;* A dexter hand holding up a bomb, fired ppr.

GIOLLAFINNEAN, who is No. 105 on the "Mulroy" pedigree, was the ancestor of *MacGiolla-Finnein ;* anglicised *MacGillfinen, Gillfinan, Gillfinan, Gillion, Gillon, Gillinan, Glennon, Leonard,* etc.

105. Giollafinnean ("finnen :" Irish, *a shield*): son of Maolruanaidh ; a quo *MacGiolla-Finnein.*

106. Maccraith MacGiolla Finnein : his son ; first assumed this sirname.

107. Giollapadraic : his son.

108. Concobhar : his son.

109. Donall : his son.

110. Giolla Midhe (or Giolla of Meath): his son.

111. Ranall : his son.

112. Henry Crosach : his son.

113. Tirlogh: his son.

114. Donoch : his son.

115. Lochlann : his son.

116. Lochlann Oge : his son.

117. Brian : his son.

118. Shane MacGiolla-Finnein : his son.

GILMARTIN.

Arms : Ar. a sinister hand couped at the wrist affrontée gu.

FEARCAR, brother of Aodh Ornaighe who is No. 97 on the "O'Neill" (of Tyrone) pedigree, was the ancestor of *MacGiolla Marthain ;* anglicised *Gilmartin, Kilmartin,* and *Martin.*

97. Fearcar : son of Niall Frassach, the 162nd Monarch of Ireland.
98. Bearach : his son.
99. Maolgarbh : his son.
100. Cearnach : his son.
101. Donchadh : his son.

102. Dubhfionn : his son.
103. Giolla Marthain : his son : meaning "the devotee of St. Martin" ("marthain :" Irish, *life*); a quo *MacGiolla Marthain.*

GRIFFIN.

Of Leinster.

Arms : Gu. three griffins' heads, two in chief couped ar. and one in base erased or.

CRIOMHTHANN, a brother of Ros Failge who is No. 91 on the "O'Connor" (Faley) pedigree, was the ancestor of *O'Criomhthainn ;* anglicised *Griffin,* * *Cramton,* and *Crampton.*

91. Criomhthan : son of Cathair Mór, the 109th Monarch of Ireland.
92. Aongus : his son.
93. Eochaidh : his son.
94. Criomhthan Beag ("criomhthan :" Irish, *a fox*): his son ; a quo *O'Criomhthain.*
95. Naneadh : his son.
96. Cormac : his son.
97. Cobthach : his son.
98. Eoghan : his son.
99. (   ): his son.
100. Dubhdacrioch : his son.

101. Congal : his son.
102. Dungal : his son.
103. Ceannfaola : his son.
104. Murchadh : his son.
105. Dubhfhel : his son.
106. Uchbhisi : his son.
107. Uchbhisi (2) : his son.
108. Urchail : his son.
109. Uchbhisi (3); his son.
110. Dubh : his son.
111. Giolla Muire : his son.
112. Maolmordha : his son.
113. Giolla-na-Naomh : his son.

* *Griffin :* There was another family of this name descended from Crimthann Liath, who is No. 89 on the "O'Hart" pedigree. The *Arms* of that "Griffin" family were : Gu. a lion ramp. or, within a bordure innecked ar.

GRIMLEY.

Arms : Ar. a wolf ramp. sa. betw. three human hearts gu.

DONAL, brother of Connor who is No. 107 on the " Crean" pedigree, was the ancestor of *O'Gairmliacha* ("gairm:" Irish, infmt. of "goir" *to call ;* and "liach," gen. " liacha," *a spoon*); anglicised *Gormley,* and *Grimley.*

107. Donal: son of Meanmnach.
108. Connor: his son.
109. Dalbach : his son.
110. Donal (2) : his son.
111. Niall : his son.

112. Connor (2) : his son.
113. Sithric : his son.
114. Melachlin O'Gormley : his son.

GUTHRIE.

Of Brefney.

Arms : Vert two lions ramp. combatant or, supporting a dexter hand couped at the wrist erect and apaumée bloody ppr.

FEARGAL, a brother of Cathal (orCharles) who is No. 111 on the "O'Reilly" pedigree, was the ancestor of *MacGothfrith ;* anglicised *Guthrie,* and *Mac-Guthrie.*

111. Feargal: son of Gothfrith.
112. Cathal Dubh : his son.
113. Gothfrith (" goth :" Irish, *straight;* " frith," *small*) : his son ; a quo *MacGothfrith.*

114. Muirchearthach : his son.
115. Feargal : his son.
116. Donchadh : his son.
117. Niall MacGuthrie : his son.

GWARE.

Arms : A tower triple-towered ar.

GUAIRE AIDHNE, who is No. 95 on the "O'Shaughnessy" pedigree, was the ancestor of *Gware, Gerry,* and *Gurry.*

Guaire Aidhne: son of Columhan.

. . . . .

1. John Gware of Courtstown, county Kilkenny, Kt.

2. Oliver : his son.
3. John : his son.
4. Robert : his son.
5. Oliver, of Courtstown, gt. :

his son; married to Joan, dau. and heiress of Sir Ciprian Horsfall, of Inisharag, county Kilkenny, Knt.; *d.* 6th July, 1637.

6. John Gware : son of Oliver.

This John had three brothers and two sisters : the brothers were—1. Redmond, 2. Ciprian, 3. Robert; the sisters, 1. Mary, 2. Ellen.

HANLY.

Chiefs of Doohy-Hanly, in the County Roscommon.

Arms : Vert a boar pass. ar. armed, hoofed, and bristled or, betw. two arrows barways of the second, headed of the third, that in chief pointing to the dexter, and that in base to the sinister. *Crest* : Three arrows sa. flighted ar. pointed or, one in pale, the other two barways, the upper one pointing to the dexter, the lower to the sinister. *Motto* : Saigheadoir collach abu (The strong archer for ever).

ARCA-DEARG, brother of Conall Orison who is No. 88 on the "O'Malley" pedigree, was ancestor of *O'h-Anleagha ;* anglicised *Hanly* and *Henly.*

88. Arca-Dearg : son of Brian.
89. Æneas : his son.
90. Dubhthach : his son; had a brother named Onach, who was the ancestor of *MacBrannan* family.
91. Uan ("uan," gen. "uain :" Irish, *a lamb*): his son; a quo *O'Uain,* anglicised *Lamb* and *Lambe.*
92. Cluthmhar : his son.
93. Maoldun : his son.
94. Murtuile : his son.
95. Anliaigh (" an :" Irish, *the ;* "liaigh," gen. "leagha," *a physician*) : his son; a quo *O'h-Anleagha,* meaning "the descendants of the Physician."
96. Murtagh : his son.
97. Teige : his son.
98. Donal : his son.
99. Murtagh (2) : his son.
100. Ranald Catha Brian : his son; meaning Randal who was slain at the battle of Clontarf, A.D. 1014, fighting on the side of the Irish Monarch Brian Boroimhe.
101. Muireadach : his son.

102. Idir (or Odhar) : his son.
103. Anliaigh (2) : his son.
104. Donal O'Hanly : his son; the first who assumed this sirname.
105. Iomhar : his son.
106. Donal (3) : his son.
107. Connor : his son.
108. Aodh (or Hugh) : his son.
109. Gilbert : his son.
110. Rory Buidhe : his son.
111. Donal (4) : his son.
112. Teige (2) : his son.
113. Gilbert (2) : his son.
114. Neamhach (or Nehemiah) : his son.
115. Hugh (2) : his son.
116. Tireach : his son.
117. Hugh (3) : his son.
118. Gilbert (3) : his son.
119. Teige (3) : his son.
120. Edmund Dubh : his son.
121. William : his son.
122. Teige : his son.
123. Teige Oge : his son.
124. Connor O'Hanly : his son.

HANRAGHAN.

Arms: Gu. a lizard pass. in fess or, in chief a trefoil slipped between two holly leaves ar. in base a garb of the second. *Crest*: An arm erect, couped below the elbow, vested vert, cuffed ar. holding in the hand ppr. a holly leaf vert. *Motto*: An uachtar.

NOCHAN, brother of Seagal who is No. 101 on the "O'Murphy" (No. 1) pedigree, was the ancestor of *O'h-Anracain*, of Leinster; anglicised *Hanraghan*, and *Rakes*.

101. Nochan ("nocha:" Irish, *ninety;* "an," *one who*): son of Seicin.

102. Fiach: his son.

103. Maolleathan: his son.

104. Snidhgobhan: his son.

105. Tiomainach ("t i o m a i n:" Irish, *to fall on*): his son; a quo *O'Tiomainaighe* (of Leinster), anglicised *Timony*.

106. Sliabhan ("sliabh:" Irish, *a mountain*): his son; a quo *O'Sliabhain*, anglicised *Slevin*.

107. Anracan ("racan:" Irish, *mischief;* "raca," *a rake*): his son; a quo *O'h-Anracain*.

HARDIMAN.

Arms: Ar. three chev. gu. a canton sa. *Crest*: On a serpent nowed a hawk perched all ppr.

EOGHAN (or Owen), brother of Alioll who is No. 98 on the "Maconky" pedigree, was the ancestor of an *O'Airachdain* family; anglicised *Harraghtan, Harrington, Hargadan,* and *Hardiman.**

98. Eoghan (or Owen): son of Muireadach.

99. Owen (2): his son.

100. Beice: his son.

101. Lagnen: his son.

102. Mochtighearna: his son.

103. Forgalach: his son.

104. Owen (3): his son.

105. Cronmaol: his son.

106. Coscrach: his son.

107. Snagaidhil: his son.

108. Melachlin: his son.

109. A i r a c h d a n ("airachda:" Irish, *of great stature*): his son; a quo *O'h-Airachdain*.

110. Owen (4): his son.

111. Beice O'Harraghtan: his son.

---

* *Hardiman*: James Hardiman, a distinguished Irish writer, and lawyer, said to be a native of Galway, was born about the end of the 18th century. His important work, *The History of Galway*, appeared in Dublin, in 1820; his *Irish Minstrelsy*, 2 vols. 8vo, in London, in 1831; *Statute of Kilkenny*, in 1843; and in 1846 he edited O'Flaherty's *West or Iar Connaught* for the Irish Archæological Society. He was a prominent member of the Royal Irish Academy, and was for some time sub-commissioner on the Public Records. He spent the latter part of his life in Galway as librarian to the Queen's College, and died in 1855.

HART. (No. 1.)

Of America.

THERE are several families of this name in America since the beginning of the 17th century : some of them claiming to be of Irish ; some, of English; and some, of Scotch descent. The prevailing way of spelling the name, which, however, has obtained in the New World, is: " Hart," " Harte," " Hartt," " Heart," and " Hearte."

Some of those families are descended from Stephen Hart* (or Harte), a Puritan, who, about 1632, emigrated from (it is supposed) Braintree, in Essexshire, England, to Massachusetts, United States of America; and from whom " Hart's Ford" (more lately rendered "Hartford") on the Connecticut river, took its name. That Stephen Hart was a farmer and large landholder ; he and the company with whom he went to America settled in Braintree, Mass., and afterwards removed to Newtown (since called " Cambridge"), Mass., and there constituted themselves a church, of which the said Stephen was elected " deacon :" hence has he been called " Deacon Stephen Hart." He was in Cambridge (Mass.) in 1632, and admitted a freeman there, on 14th May, 1634. He went to Hartford in 1635 ; was there a proprietor in 1639 ; and became one of the eighty-four proprietors of Farmington, in Connecticut, in 1672. At his death, in March, 1682-3, he was 77 years of age, and then lived at the village of Farmington, on a tract of land (bordering the present town of Avon) which is still known by the name of " Hart's Farm." His children were : 1. Sarah, who on the 20th November, 1644, m. Thomas Porter ; 2. Mary, who was twice married—first, to John Lee, and, secondly, on the 5th Jan., 1672, to Jedediah Strong; 3. John, who m. Sarah ——; 4. Stephen, the name of whose wife is not known ; 5. Mahitabel, who m. John Cole; 6. Thomas, b. 1643, who m. Ruth Hawkins. From those six children of Deacon Stephen Hart, have descended many of the families of distinction, now (1883) living in the Great Western Republic.

The sirname of said Stephen appears as *Hart*, in the list of Winthrop's New England, among those who took the freeman's oath on the 14th of May, 1634 ; while his brother Edmund's name appears in the same list as *Harte*, where the *e* final is added. The history of Dorchester, Massachusetts, makes that Edmund one of the first settlers of that town, and there he had his house-lot in 1632; but he subsequently removed to Weymouth. His children were, according to Savage, all daughters. It is worthy of remark that Stephen Harte, of Westmill, in Hertfordshire, England, was the first of the name recorded as living in that country. And (see the " Harte" pedigree) it was in the 12th century that a junior branch of the " O'Hart" family anglicised their name *Harte*, from the Irish *O'h-Airt*, and first employed the *e* final in the name.

Another distinguished branch of the " Hart" family in America is that descended from John Hart, who was born at Witney, in Oxfordshire,

* *Stephen Hart*: See the " Genealogical History of Deacon Stephen Hart and his descendants, 1632-1875." By Alfred Andrews, New Britain, Conn. (Hartford : Lockwood, Brainard, and Co. 1875.)

England, on the 16th of November, 1651, and who went to America with William Penn. He was a Quaker preacher of note, and settled near Philadelphia. He was elected a member of the Assembly for the county of Philadelphia, and took his seat therein on the 12th March, 1683. He died at his residence in Warminster, in Sept., 1714, in the 63rd year of his age. From that John Hart is descended General W. W. Hart-Davis, of Doylestown, Pennsylvania, living in 1883. All things considered, we are of opinion that the above mentioned Stephen Hart, the Deacon; Stephen Harte, of Westmill, in Hertfordshire, England; and John Hart, the celebrated Quaker preacher, were all of the same stock and of *Irish* origin.

Another eminent branch of the "Hart" family in America is that descended from Edward Hart, of Hopewell township, formerly in Hunterdon county, New Jersey, who fought under Wolfe on the Heights of Abraham (Quebec). His son John Hart (see Note,† "Independence," p. 76, *ante*) was one of the Signatories who, on the 4th of July, 1776, signed the famous "Declaration of American Independence;" and is still remembered in America as:

"Honest John Hart."

This John was born at Hopewell, N J., in 1715; and, in 1774, was first elected to the General Congress, at Philadelphia. New Jersey was soon invaded by the British Army, who devastated Mr. Hart's estate, and made special exertions to take him prisoner. He, however, frustrated their designs, by wandering through the woods from cottage to cottage, and from cave to cave, constantly hunted by the English soldiery; so that he never ventured to sleep in the same place twice in succession. The capture of the Hessians by General Washington put an end to that state of things: Mr. Hart was enabled to return to his estate, on which he passed the remainder of his life. He had two sons in the War of the Revolution: Edward, and Daniel; and three of his sons (supposed to be Jesse, Nathaniel, and John) acted as General Washington's guides while he was campaigning in New Jersey.

The said John Hart married Deborah Scudder (who died on the 26th October, 1776), and, according to entries in his writing in the Family Bible, the following were their children:

1. Sarah,	born 16 Oct. (year not legible.)		8. Abigail,	born 10 Feb., 1754
2. Jesse,	„	19 Nov., 1742	9. Edward	„	20 Dec., 1755
3. Martha,	„	10 Apl., 1746	10. Scudder,	„	20 Dec., 1759
4. Nathaniel,	„	29 Oct., 1747	11. (A daughter)	„	16 Mar., 1761
5. John,	„	29 Oct., 1748	12. Daniel,	„	13 Aug., 1762
6. Susannah,	„	2 Aug., 1750	13. Deborah,	„	11 Aug., 1765
7. Mary,	„	7 Apl., 1752			

Sarah married a Mr. Wyckoff; and her grandson, Samuel S. Wyckoff, was in 1882 a prominent merchant in Murray Street, New York City. Susannah m. Major Polhemus, an Officer of the Revolution, and was the mother of Mrs. Kurts. Deborah m. Joseph Ott. Daniel went to Virginia.

Joseph Hart, a grandson of the said John Hart, was in 1874 living on the top of Rich Mountain, in West Virginia; and H. S. Hart, of

Circleville, 'Kansas, living in 1874, was a great-grandson of John, the Signer of the Declaration.   The said John's personal appearance was, it is recorded, very prepossessing : he was tall and straight, with black hair and dark complexion.   The time of his death has been variously stated by different writers : Sanderson, in his "Lives of the Signers," puts it in the year 1780 ; others make the time 1778 ; but we believe we are correct in saying the true time is the 11th of May, 1779.

There is a Monument erected to his memory at Hopewell, New Jersey, on the *Front* of which are the words : "John Hart, a Signer of American Independence, July 4, 1776 ;" on its *Right side*, the words : "Erected . . . by the State of New Jersey, by Act Approved, April 5, 1865 ;" on its *Left side*, the words : "First Speaker of Assembly, August 27, 1776," and "Member of the Committee of Safety, 1775-1776;" on the *Rear*, the words : "Honor the Patriot's Grave."   Around the Monument are the graves of those who were his companions and associates.

Patrick Hart, of Youngstown, Ohio, living in 1877, and Thomas Hart, living in 1880, near Courtland, Decalb county, Illinois, are (see the "O'Hart" pedigree) members of our own family.

There is yet another branch of the "Hart" family located in Pittston, Pennsylvania, which we cannot connect with any of the foregoing families, but which, judging by its coat of arms, is, in our opinion, a branch of our own family.   We can trace the descent of that branch only from Jeremiah* Hart, who when a young man lived in Duchess County, State of New York ; removed to Saratoga County in said State, there married, owned a large farm, and lived and died.   He had two elder brothers—1. John, 2. Richard : that John had a son John, both of whom held commissions in the English Army during the American Revolution, after which the younger John came to reside in England ; Jeremiah remained faithful to the American cause ; but we have learned nothing of Richard and his descendants.   Commencing with Jeremiah the following is the descent from him:

1. Jeremiah Hart, of Saratoga County, State of New York, b. *circa* 1750 ; m. Abigail Purcell (née Macomber), and had five sons and three daughters — 1. John, 2. Stephen, 3. Reuben, 4. Philip, 5. Jeremiah, 1 Hannah, 2. Sarah, 3. Phebe.   He died at Stillwater, Saratago county, N.Y,, about 1825.

2. Philip : the fourth son of Jeremiah ; b. about 1775 ; m. Anna, dau. of Joseph Seeley and —— Millard, and had five sons and four daughters — 1. Philip, 2. Theodorus, 3. Henry, 4. Lorenzo D., 5. Rebuen B., 1. Maria, 2. Abby, 3. Amy, 4. Sarah-Anne.   He d. at Pine Island, in Minesota, about 1860.

3. Theodorus : his second son ; b. 5 Aug., 1809; m. Eliza, dau. of Sylvester Ruland and Rebecca Lobdell, on the 30 Mar., 1821, and had four children—1. Alonzo, 2. Theodorus, 3. Adelia, 4. Marion - Ellen — all living in 1883.

4. Theodorus Hart, Jun., of Pittston, Pennsylvania, U.S.A. : second son of Theodorus ; born 10 Sept., 1847 ; and living in 1883 ;

* *Jeremiah* : This is another name for the Irish *Dermod.*

m. Rebecca (b. 11 June, 1849), dau. of William Dymond and Malvina (Slocum) Eyet, and had in 1883

one child—Mary-Lawson-Dymond, b. 13 July, 1875.

HART. (No. 2.)

Of America.

JOSEPH HART, born near Kells, in the county Meath, migrated thence in 1798 or 1799, to Slieve Baugh, county Fermanagh. He married the sister of Bishop Carlin, in the county Meath, and had four daughters and three sons, viz.—1. Patrick, 2. Philip, 3. James.

I. Patrick, m. a Miss McPhilip, of Ahabog, co. Fermanagh, and had four sons and three daus.; the sons were:—1. Patrick, 2. Henry, 3. James, 4. Hugh. Patrick, James, and Hugh were ordained priests in the Catholic Church; and it is thought that Henry had no issue.

II. Philip, the second son of Joseph, m. but had no issue.

III. James, the third son of Joseph Hart, married a Miss MacGowan, of Dartry, county Letrim, and had two sons and one dau., namely—1. Joseph, 2. Patrick, and 3. Rose. This Joseph died at St. Louis, Mo., without issue; and Patrick, his younger brother, married a Miss O'Connell, of the O'Connell family, of Mallow, county Cork, and had one son and three daughters (all living in 1881): namely—1. Joseph, 2. Catherine, 3. Jane, 4. Rose.

When (in 1845) Texas was annexed to the United States, this

Patrick Hart, the second son of James, enlisted in the U. S. Army, and served through the Mexican War, in Colonel James Duncan's Light Battery A., 2nd U.S. Artillery; and in 1850 reached home as first Sergeant of that Battery. He was transferred to the Ordnance Department in 1858, as first Sergeant; joined the Paraguay Expedition; and, on the breaking out of the late American War, he was promoted to the rank of Captain commanding Battery B, Irish Brigade, which took a prominent part in the Battle of Gettysburg, Pa., in 1864. Captain Patrick Hart was promoted on the battlefield of the Yellow-Tavern, on the Weldon Railroad, to the rank of Brevet-Major.

It is worthy of remark, in connexion with this brave soldier Major Patrick Hart, that he had fought in sixty-eight battles. He was living in Port Hudson, La., in August, 1881.

HARTE. (No. 1.)

Ireland.

Arms : Same as those of " O'Hart."

ART, who is No. 101 on the " O'Hart" pedigree, had a brother named Congeal (a quo *Teallach Congeal* or " The territory of Congeal"), and two sons—1. Donall, Prince of Tara, and ancestor of *O'Hart ;* 2. Lochlann : The descendants of this Lochlann were the first that employed the *e* final in the anglicised form of their sirname—as *Harte,* lately *Hart.*

101. ART ; a quo *MacArt ;* and according to MacFirbis, *O'Hart.*

1	2
102. Donall, Ancestor of *O'Hart.*	102. Lochlann.
	103. Teige : son of Lochlann.
	104. Fearmara : his son.
	105. Teige (2) : his son.

1	2
106. Fearleighinn.*	106. Flannagan.

At this stage in this family pedigree, King Henry the Second of England invaded Ireland, A.D. 1172 ; and by his Charter to Hugh DeLacey, granting to him the Kingdom of Meath, dispossessed the *O'Harts* of their patrimony, as Princes of Tara, in that kingdom. Thus dispossessed, the family was scattered : some of them settled in England, some in Scotland, some in France, some in Germany, etc., and some of them remained in Ireland. Branches of them who settled in Leinster called themselves *Hart, Hort,* and *Hartey ;* in England, *Harte,* and more lately, *Hart ;* in Scotland, *Hart ;* France, *Hart, LeHart, Harts, Hardies, Hardis ;* in Germany, *Hart, Harte, Hartt, Hartz, Hardts, Herdts,* etc. In parts of Ireland some of the family anglicised the name *Harte, Hairt, Hairtt, Hairtte, Hartte ;* and, in Scotland, according to MacPherson, *Artho,* or *Arthur.*

HARTE. (No. 2.)

Of England.

STEPHEN HARTE, of Westmill, Hertfordshire, England, is the first of the name recorded as living in that Country ; where, possibly, his father or grandfather settled after the English invasion of Ireland by King Henry

---

* *Fearleighinn* [farlane] : This word means "a lecturer ;" while *MacLeighinn,* means "a scholar," "a student." The name is derived from the Irish *fear* "a man," and *leighionn,* "a lesson," "instruction," "erudition ;" and implies that the man who was so called was a person of superior education. Some consider that this *Fearleighinn* was the ancestor of *MacFarlane.*

the Second A.D. 1172. From the said Stephen down to the present time the *Harte* (of England) pedigree, is as follows :—

1. Stephen Harte,* of Westmill, Hertfordshire.

2. Havekin, of Westmill: his son.

3, William, of Westmill: his son; afterwards of Abbotsbury and Papworth, in Cambridgeshire.

4. William, of Papworth: his son; returned to Hertfordshire. This William was twice married :—first, to Mary, daughter of John Humphreys, by whom he had a son and heir named John; secondly, to Alice ——, by whom he had a son named William.

5. John: eldest son of the said William Harte, of Papworth; living A.D. 1430; married to Joane, dau. of William Dayly, of Lincolnshire.

6. William, of St. Dunstan's, in the west of London, and of Ware, in Hertfordshire: son of John; was married to Alice, dau. of Robert Sutton, of London; living in 1480; had a sister named Alice, who was wife of William Callow, of Sholford, Kent, one of the English Judges.

7. John Harte, of the Middle Temple, London, Barrister-at-Law: son of William; married to Elizabeth, daughter of Sir William Peche, Knight, and sister and heir of Sir John Peche, Knight and "Banneret;" died 16th July, 1543; and was buried in St. Mary Cray Church, London.

8. Sir Percival Harte, of Lull-

ington (now "Lullingstone") in Kent, knight: son of John; married Frideswide, daughter of Edward, Lord Bray, and sister and heir of John, Lord Bray; had a sister who was wife of Sir James Stanley; died 21st May, 1580, aged 84 years; was buried at Lullington. *Harte* (now *Hart*) of Donegal is, we believe, descended from this Sir Percival; but, as yet, we are unable to trace the descent.

9. Henry Harte: son of Sir Percival; married to Cecily, daughter of Sir Martin Bowes, Knight; died without issue. This Henry had two younger brothers—1. Sir George Harte, of Lullington, also a "Knight of the body to the King," who was married to Elizabeth, daughter of John Bowes, and sister of Sir Hieron and Sir John Bowes, Knights, and who died on the 16th July, 1587, and was buried at Lullington; 2. Francis Harte, of Halwell, Devonshire, who was the ancestor of *Harte* of the counties of Clare, Limerick, and Kerry, in Ireland.

10. Sir Percival Harte, of Lullington, Knight: son of the aforesaid Sir George. Sir Percival was twice married: 1st, to Anne, daughter of Sir Roger Manwood, Knight; by whom he had a son named William, who was married to Eliza-

* *Stephen Harte*: Considering that John Harte, No. 5 on this Stem, was living, A.D. 1430, and that between A.D. 1172 (when King Henry II. invaded Ireland) and 1430 there elapsed a period of 258 years, the ancestor of this Stephen Harte, who first settled in England, could have been his father, or at most his grandfather; for, taking 36 years as the average age of each generation of the family, 258 divided by 36 would give seven generations. But the said John was the fifth in descent down from Stephen; then counting back to the said Stephen's grandfather would make at most seven generations. As, therefore, it was at that period (see the foregoing "Harte" pedigree) that the *e* final was first added to the anglicised form of the Irish name *O'h-Airt*, there is reason to believe that the said Stephen Harte, of Westmill, Hertfordshire, England, was of Irish origin; and was descended from the O'Hart family. —See the "O'Hart" pedigree.

beth, daughter of Sir Anthony Weldon, of Swanscombe, Kent, this William died without issue in 1671, and was buried at Lullington. Sir Percival's second wife was Jane, daughter of Sir Edward Stanhope, of Grimstone, knight: the issue of this marriage were—1. Percival Harte, who died without issue; 2. Jerome Harte, *obiit, s. p.;* 3. Sir Harry Harte, of Lullington, knight, K.B., died (before his father) in 1636; 4. Edward; 5. George. This Sir Percival had three brothers—1. Robert Harte, *ob. s. p.;* 2. George Harte, 3. Sir Peter Manwode Harte.

11. Sir Percival Harte, of Lullington, knight: son and heir of the aforesaid Sir Harry Harte, who died in 1636; Will proved in 1642; had a brother named George Harte.

12. Percival Harte, of Lullington; son of Sir Percival; married to Sarah, daughter of Edward Dixon, of Hilden; left an only daughter and heir named Anne Harte; died in 1738.

13. Anne Harte; their daughter. This Anne was twice married: first, to John Blunt, of Holcombe Regis, Devonshire, who died without issue, A.D. 1728; secondly, to Sir Thomas Dyke of Horeham, Sussex, baronet, who died in 1756, leaving three sons and one daughter, namely—1. Thomas Hart-Dyke, who died without issue: 2. Sir John Dixon Dyke, of Horeham, baronet; 3. Percival Dyke, who died without issue; and the daughter (whose name was Philadelphia) was married to William Lee, and left four children—1. William Lee, 2. Philadelphia Lee, 3. Harriet Lee, 4. Louisa Lee. From this marriage of Anne Harte and Sir Thomas Dyke is derived the sirname *Hart-Dyke.*

14. Sir John Dixon Dyke, of Horeham, baronet: son of Anne Harte and Sir Thomas Dyke; married to Philadelphia, daughter of George Horne, of East Grinstead.

15. Sir Thomas Dyke, of Horeham, baronet; their son; *ob., s. p.;* had one brother—Sir Percival Hart-Dyke, baronet; and two daughters—1. Philadelphia, 2. Anne. This Sir Percival was married to Anne, eldest daughter of Robert Jenner of Wenvoe Castle, Glamorganshire.

16. Sir Percyvall Hart-Dyke, of Lullingstone Castle, Dartford: their son; d. 1875. This Sir Percyvall, who was born in June, 1799, married Elizabeth, daughter of John Wells, of Bickley, Kent.; and had five brothers and four sisters. The brothers were—1. John Dixon, 2. Francis Hart, 3. Peche Hart, 4. Augustus Hart, 5. Decimus Townshend; and the sisters—1. Harriett-Jenner, 2. Georgiana-Frances, 3. Laura, 4. Philadelphia.

17. Sir William Hart-Dyke, M.P. for Mid-Kent: eldest son of Sir Percyvall; born in August, 1837, and living in 1887; had two brothers and six sisters. The brothers were—1. George Augustus Hart, 2. Reginald-Charles Hart; the sisters were—1. Frances-Julia, 2. Eleanor-Laura, 3. Catherine-Sybella, 4 Sybella-Catherine, 5. Emily-Anne 6. Gertrude. This Sir William Hart-Dyke was married to Lady Emily Caroline Montagu, eldest daughter of the Earl of Sandwich; had a son named Percyvall, born in October, 1871, and a daughter named Lina Mary.

18. Percyvall: son of Sir William Hart-Dyke; living in 1887.

HARTE. (No. 3.)

Of Clare, Limerick, and Kerry.

FRANCIS HARTE, of Halwell, Devonshire, youngest brother of Henry, who is No. 9 on the foregoing genealogy, was the ancestor of *Harte*, of the counties of Clare, Limerick, and Kerry.

9. Francis Harte, of Halwell: third son of Sir Percival Harte of Lullington, Kent.

10. Rev. Richard Harte: his son. Was Vicar of Rochestown, *alias* Ballywilliam, in the diocese of Emly; of Adare, in Limerick; and of Stradmore, in Killaloe, A.D. 1615. This Richard married a daughter of John Southwell, of Barham, in Suffolk, and Sister of Sir Richard Southwell, of Singleland, in the county Limerick, knight, and by her had three sons—1. Richard Harte, 2. Percival Harte, 3. Henry Harte, of Carrigdiram in the county Clare, who died intestate in March, 1665.

11. Richard Harte: son of the Rev. Richard; had a grant of the lands of Cloghnamanagh, Ballyboure, and Carriglapon, in the co. Limerick (part of the possessions of the Monastery of Nenagh, in Tipperary), by Patent dated 11th Feb., 1638; Will dated 24th Jan., 1661. This Richard was twice married—by the first wife he left an only son—Richard, of Grangebridge, county Limerick; and by the second, three sons—1. Francis, 2. John, 3. Percival.

12. Richard Harte, of Grangebridge: eldest son of the aforesaid Richard; in 1667 married Elizabeth, dau. of Thomas Amory, of Galy, in Kerry; left three sons—1. Richard, 2. John, 3. Edmond.

13. Richard Harte, of Grange, and of Lisofin, county Clare: eldest son of Richard. Was a Colonel in

the Army of King William the Third; was twice married: by the first wife he left an only son named Percival; and by the second wife (who was living a widow A.D. 1697) he had two sons—1. Henry Harte, of Coolrus, whose Will was dated 16th April, 1737, and proved 26th June, 1742; and 2. John Harte, whose only daughter and heir was married to — Hayes, of Cahirguillamore, in the co. Limerick, who was the father of Jeremiah Hayes, the father of Honora Hayes, who was marrried to Standish O'Grady, the father of Darby (or Dermod) O'Grady, Cahirguillamore.

14. Percival Harte, of Lissofin, in Clare, and of Grange, in Limerick: son of Richard; left two sons —1. Richard, 2. Percival; and a daughter named Anne, who was wife of William Johnson, of Flemingstown, co. Cork. This Percival had a brother named Henry, of Coolruss.

15. Richard Harte, of Grange: son of Percival. This Richard left two daughters—1. Margery, wife of Thomas Franks, of Carrig, in the county Cork, who inherited Grange: 2. Margaret, wife of Robert Bradshaw, of the co. Tipperary—married A.D. 1758, but had no issue. Richard, having left no male issue, was succeeded by his younger brother, Percival Harte, of Lissofin.

16. Sir Richard Harte, of Lissofin and Coolruss: son of said Percival, was knighted by the Duke of Richmond, in 1807; died in 1824. This

Sir Richard was twice married: first to Anne, daughter and heir of William Johnson, of Flemingstown, county Cork, by whom he had three sons—1. William Johnson Harte; 2. Percival Harte, who settled in the West Indies; 3. Kilpatrick Harte, who died at School. Sir Richard's second wife was Margaret, daughter of Richard Meredyth, and relict of James Mahony, of Batterfield, in the county Kerry.

17. William Johnson Harte, of Coolruss, Croom, co. Limerick: son of Sir Richard; married in 1796 to Marion, daughter and heir of James Mahony, of Batterfield, in Kerry;

died 1814. This William left three sons and six daughters: the sons were—1. Richard, 2. James Mahony Harte, of Batterfield, county Kerry, 3. Rev. William Harte.

18. Richard Harte, of Coolruss: eldest son of William; married Anne, daughter of Andrew Vance,* of Rutland-square, Dublin (who d. in 1849), and sister of John Vance, M.P., who died in 1875. This Richard died in 1842.

19. Richard Harte, of Coolruss, Croom, county Limerick: his son; living in 1877; had a sister named Mary Harte, who died in 1859.

HARTE. (No. 4.)

Of Castleconnell.

HENRY HARTE of Coolruss, brother of Percival, of Lisofin, in Clare, who is No. 14 on the foregoing genealogy, was the ancestor of *Harte* and *Hart*, of Castleconnell.

14. Henry: son of Richard Harte; Will proved 26th June, 1742.

15. Richard of Coolrus: his son; had a brother named William.

16. Percival of Coolruss: son of Richard; Will proved in 1791; left his estates to William Johnstone Harte, who died in March,

1791, *s.p.;* had a brother named Richard Harte, of Tonagh.

17. Richard, of Castleconnell: son of Richard Harte, of Tonagh.

18. Richard Harte, of Gurteen, in the county Limerick: his son; living in 1877; had a brother, the Rev. Henry Harte, Fellow of Trinity College, Dublin.

HARTE. (No. 5.)

Of the Queen's County.

DERMOD MACMURROUH, the 58th Christian King of Leinster, who is No. 113 on the " MacMorough" pedigree, and who died A.D. 1175, married

---

* *Andrew Vance*: See the " Vance" Genealogy.

Mór, daughter of Muirceartach, King of the *Ui-Muirceartaigh* (who d. 1164), and had :

114. Eva, who m. Richard de Clare, surnamed "Strongbow," and had :

115. Lady Isabel *de Clare* (d. 1220), who m. William le Marechal, third Earl of Pembroke, and had :

116. Lady Isabel *Marshall*, who m. Gilbert, fifth Earl of Hereford and Gloucester, and had :

117. Richard, Earl of Gloucester and Hereford, who m. and had :

118. Gilbert de Clare, Earl of Gloucester and Hereford (d. 1295), married (at St. John's Monastery, Clerkenwell, 30th April, 1290), the Princess Joan (b. 1273), dau. of Edward I., King of England and of Eleanor of Castile; and had :

119. Elizabeth de Clare, who m. David de la Roche (living, 1315), son of Alexander de la Roche, and had :

120. Sir David de la Roche, Knt. (17 Edward III.), who m. Anna Fleming, and had :

121. John de la Roche, Lord Fermoy (*temp.* 1382), who m. the dau. and heiress of the Tanist of one of the MacCarthy Mórs, and had :

122. Morris (or Maurice) Lord Roche and Fermoy (d. 1439), who m. Anne, dau. of Maurice, Earl of Desmond (by Beatrice, his wife, dau. of the Earl of Stafford), and had a daughter, who m. the Earl of Kildare, and a son David.

123. Said David Lord Roche and Viscount Fermoy (d. 1492), surnamed "Moore," m. Jane, dau. of Walter Bourke MacWilliam *Iachtar*, and had five sons, and a dau. Ellena who m. James de Courcy, 13th Lord Kinsale. Of the five sons were :

I. Thomas, whose direct descendant, the late Rev. George Tierney, Vicar of Stradbally, would have been "Lord Fermoy," had not the title been attainted. The present title of "Lord Fermoy" is a new creation.

II. Edmund Roche, the third son (d. 1540).

124. Edmund Roche (d. 1540), the said third son, m. and had :

125. Joan Roche, who, in 1508 m. David de Courcy, 15th Baron Kinsale (son of Nicholas, the 12th Baron, who m. Nora, dau. of O'Mahony, Chief of his Sept and name), and had :

126. Edmund de Courcy, second son (who was 26th in lineal male descent from Charlemagne, King of France), who m. Juliana, dau. of William Barry, Viscount Buttevant, and had :

127. Edmund (the eldest son), who m. Juliana, dau. of Dermod Mac Teige O'Hurley, Lord of Knocklong, and Chief of his name, and had :

128. John de Courcy (d. 1625), the 18th Baron of Kinsale, who was twice m. : first, to Catherine, dau. of William Cogan, by whom he had no issue ; secondly, to Mary, dau. of Cornelius O'Cruly (or O'Crowly), and by her had :

129. Patrick, the 20th Baron of Kinsale, who m. Mary, dau. of John FitzGerald, of Dromanagh, Lord of Decies, and had :

130. Myles de Courcy, the third son, who m. Elizabeth, dau. of Anthony Sadleir, of Arley Hall. co. Warwick, and had :

131. Gerald de Courcy (d. 1759), the 24th Baron Kinsale, who m. Margaretta, dau. and heiress of John Essington of Ashlyns, county Herts, and Grossington Hall, co. Gloucester, and had :

132. Elizabeth Geraldine de Courcy (second dau. and co-heiress), who in 1751 m. Daniel MacCarthy, of

Carrignavar, who (see p. 135) is No. 128 on the "MacCarthy" (No. 13) pedigree, and had:

133. Elizabeth Geraldine de Courcy MacCarthy (only daughter), who m. Maurice Uniacke* Atkin, of Leadinton, co. Cork, who was Lieut.-Col. in the North Cork Militia, and son of Walter Atkin, of Leadinton, High Sheriff of the co. Cork in 1766, who m. Barbara Uniacke, only child of Maurice Uniacke, of Ballymacody, co. Cork (who m. Catherine, dau. and heiress of James Uniacke, of Cappa, co. Tipperary, and Cappamushree, co. Cork, by Barbara, his wife, dau. of John Power of Clashmore, co. Waterford), third son of Thomas Uniacke of Woodhouse and Stradbally, co. Waterford, M.P. for Youghal, who m. Helena, dau. of Christian Borr of Borrmount, co. Wexford.

Elizabeth Geraldine de Courcy MacCarthy had:

134. Barbara Atkin (d. 3rd Feb., 1835), second dau., who on the 16th May, 1825, m. Rev. Charles *Harte*, M.A., T.C.D. (b. 5th Sept., 1794), son of Edward Harte, M.D., son of Edward *Hart* of Durrow and Raheenshira, Queen's County, by Arabella Bathorn his wife. Rev. Charles Harte was Rector of Whitechurch, Carrick-on-Suir; and m. secondly, Frances, only surviving child of Captain John Dawson (62nd Grenadiers, and son of J. Dawson, Comptroller of the Customs, in Jamaica, and a scion of a branch of the co. Monaghan family of Dawson, now represented by Lord Viscount Cremorne and Earl of Dartry), who married Frances, only daughter of Robert Fuller, Esq., Barrister-at-Law, of Cork, who assumed the name of *Harnett* (see the co. Kerry "Fuller" family, in Foster's *Royal Descents*). The Rev. Charles Harte had:

135. Captain Edward Harte, late 3rd Batt. Prince Albert's Light Infantry, who was in 1826 born at Durrow, Queen's County; and who m. Eliza Susannah, dau. of Edward Parfitt, of Wells, Somerset (eldest son of Rev. Peter Lewis Parfitt, Vicar of the Cathedral Church of St. Andrew, in Wells, and Vicar of Westbury Sub-Mendip, Somerset), Deputy Register of the Diocese of Bath and Wells, by his wife Mary Susannah, only dau. of James Roche, and sister of James John Roche, lord of the manor of Glastonbury, co. Somerset, who was a descendant of John Rocke, M.P. for the city of Wells, *temp.* Henry VI Captain Edward Harte had:

136. Edward Charles Harte of Wells, Somerset, England; b. 1859, and living in 1887.

HENNESSY.

Of Clan Colgan, King's County.

Arms: Vert a stag trippant ar. betw. six arrows, two, two, and two, saltireways or.   *Crest*: Betw. the attires of a stag affixed to the scalp or, an arrow, point downwards gu. headed and flighted ar.

AONGUS, brother of Fogharthach who is No. 103 on the "Hoolahan" (of

---

* *Uniacke*: This family of "Uniacke" is descended from a Geraldine branch of the House of Desmond.

Clan-Colgan) pedigree, was the ancestor of *MacAongusa;* anglicised *Mac-Hennessy, Hennessy,* and *Harrington.*

102. Aongus ("aon:" Irish, *excellent;* "gus," *strength*) : son of Cumascach ; a quo *MacAongusa.*
103. Donall : his son.
104. Teige : his son.

105. Uallachan : his son.
106. Teige : his son.
107. Uallachan : his son.
108. Aodh (or Hugh): his son.
109. Donall MacAongusa : his son.

HENRY.*

Arms : Az. a fess betw. three pelicans ar. vulned ppr. *Crest :* A pelican's head erased vulning itself ppr. *Motto :* Fideliter.

HENRY, brother of Aibhneach who is No. 114 on the "O'Cahan" pedigree, was the ancestor of *Clan Henry,* modernized *Henry, MacHenry* and *Fitzhenry.*

114. Henry† O'Cahan or O'Kane : son of Dermod; a quo "Clan Henry."

115. Dermod Henry: his son ; first assumed this sirname.
116. Conor: his son.

* *Henry :* Of this family was James Henry, M.D., scholar and author, born in Dublin in 1799. Having been bequeathed a large legacy, he abandoned the medical profession, and devoted himself to literary pursuits. About the year 1848, he began to travel through Europe with his wife and only child, and to make researches on his favourite author, Virgil. After the death of his wife in the Tyrol (where he succeeded in cremating her and carrying off her ashes, which he preserved ever after), he continued to travel with his daughter, who, brought up after his own heart, emulated him in all his tastes and opinions, and who learned to assist him thoroughly and ably in his Virgilian studies. It was the habit of this curious pair to wander on foot, without luggage, through all parts of Europe, generally hunting for some ill-collated MS. of Virgil's *Æneid,* or for some rare edition or commentator. Having examined every MS. of the *Æneid* of any value, he returned to Dublin, when declining years disposed him to rest, and where the Library of Trinity College afforded him a rich supply of early printed books on his subject. In 1873 appeared his *Æneidea : or Critical, Exegetical, and Æsthetical Remarks on the Æneid,* with the following dedication : "To my beloved daughter, Katherine Olivia Henry, etc., I give, dedicate, and consecrate all that part of this work which is not her own." His daughter's death, shortly after the appearance of that book, was a terrible blow to him. He himself passed away, on the 14th July, 1876. A full list of his publications will be found in the *Academy,* of the 12th August, 1876, in the ample notice, by his friend Dr. Mahaffy, from which this sketch is taken.— WEBB.

† *Henry :* The name "Henry" is derived from the Irish *An Righ* [an ree], "the king." This Henry O'Kane is considered to have been so called after one of the Henrys, kings of England. As *MacHenry* and *FitzHenry* signify "the sons or descendants of Henry," and that *Harry* is the common name for "Henry," some are of opinion that "MacHenry" is another name for *Harrison,* which would mean "the son of Harry ;" and that *Harris* and *Fitzharris* are branches of the "Clan Henry."

117. Giolla-Padraic : his son.
118. James : his son.
119. Giolla-Padraic (2) : his son.
120. Geoffrey Henry: his son;
living in 1691.
(This family is (in 1887) represen-

ted by Mitchell Henry, Esq., of
Kylemore Castle, county Galway,
and of Stratheden House, Hyde
Park, S.W., London ; but in this
edition we are unable to trace the
descent.)

HIGGINS.*

Of Westmeath, and Galway.

The ancient *Arms* were : Vert three cranes' heads erased ar.

UIGIN, brother of Eochaidh who is No. 89 on the "Molloy" pedigree, was
the ancestor of *O'h-Uigin ;* anglicised *Higgin, Higgins, MacHiggin* (which
has been modernized *Higginson*), and *Huggins*

89. Uigin (" uige :" Irish, *knowledge*) son of Fiacha.
90. Cormac : his son.
91. Flaithbeartach : his son.
92. Tumaltach ; his son.
93. Flannagan : his son.
94. Ibhear : his son.
95. Conchobhar (or Conor): his
son.
96. Uigin (2) : his son; a quo
O'h-Uigin.
97. Robeartach (or Robert): his
son.
98. Goffrey O'Higgin; his son;
first assumed this sirname.
99. Aneisleis : his son.
100. Lochlann : his son.
101. Cormac : his son.
102. Ranall : his son.
103. Cathall : his son.

104. Morogh : his son.
105. Niall : his son.
106. Teige Mór : his son.
107. Giollacolum (by some called
" Giolla na-Naomh") : his son.
108. Teige (2) : his son; had an
elder brother named Giolla Chriosd.
109. Fergal Ruadh : his son.
110. Teige Oge : his son ; had a
brother named Brian.
111. Giollananaomh : his son.
112. Manus : his son.
113. Aodh (or Hugh) : his son.
114. Donall Cam : his son.
115. Brian : his son.
116. Brian Oge : his son.
117. Maolmuire : his son.
118. Teige Oge : his son; living
in 1657; had three brothers—1.

* *Higgins* : WEBB, in his *Compendium of Irish Biography*, mentions the names of
five distinguished men of this family in Ireland—namely : 1. Bryan Higgins, born in
the county Sligo, about 1737, who was a distinguished physician and chemist. 2.
William Higgins, also a distinguished chemist, who was a nephew of the preceding, and
was born in the county Sligo. 3. Francis Higgins, who was a High Church clergyman,
and Archdeacon of Cashel ; he was born in Limerick about 1670, died in August, 1728,
and was buried in St. Michael's Church, Dublin. 4. Francis Higgins, the "Sham
Squire" (born 1750, died in January, 1802), was a Dublin celebrity in his day. 5.
Matthew James Higgins, better known as "Jacob Omnium," was born about 1810,
and died on 14th August, 1868.

Maithan, 2. Giolla-Colum, and 3. Giolla-Iosa.

119. William Higgin* : son of Teige Oge : omitted the prefix "O ;" first of the family who, in 1677, owned Carropadden, county Galway ; died in 1693.

120. Thomas, of Addergoole, co. Galway : his son ; died 1717 ; willed the lands of Carropadden to his son Nicholas.

121. Nicholas *Higgins* : his son ; first of the family who settled in Carropadden.

122. Thomas (2): his son ; died 1770.

123. Nicholas (2) : his son ; died 1812.

124. Thomas (3): his son ; died 1846.

125. Thomas Higgins, of Carrowpadden, solicitor, Tuam, living in 1877 ; his son ; married to Kate MacHale,† daughter of Mr. Patrick MacHale, of Tubbernavine (in Irish, *Tobar na Feiné* or "The Well of the Fenians"), county Mayo, and sister of His Grace the Most Rev. John MacHale, Archbishop of Tuam ; no children. This Thomas had a brother named James, married to —— Hanly, by whom he had a son named Thomas-William.

126. Thomas - William Higgins : son of said James ; living in 1877.

HOLAHAN. (No. 1.)

Of Kilkenny.

WE have traced the *Holahans* (or *Hoolahans*) of Kilkenny back to James Holahan, who was born in 1694, and died in 1759 ; from that James the following is the descent :

1. James Holahan, born A.D. 1694; died in 1759. This James had two sisters ; and an elder brother John, who was born at Skoghathorash, in 1687, and died at Royal Oak, county Carlow, in May, 1779.

2. Richard : son of James ; died in 1810; had three sisters—1. Mary, 2. Sarah, 3. Margaret.

3. James (2): his son ; died (in 1805) before his father. This James had one sister and two brothers : the brothers were—1. Rev. Walter,

who died in 1823, and 2. Patrick ; the sister's name was Judith.

4. Richard (2): son of James. This Richard had three brothers— 1. Rev. John, 2. Walter, 3. Michael ; and three sisters—1. Mary, 2. Eleanor, 3. Judith.

5. John Holahan: son of Richard. This John (living in 1877), had a brother, the Rev. James Holahan, C.C., of Ballycallan, diocese of Ossory, living in 1877 ; and a sister named Bridget.

---

* *William Higgin* : In consideration of the family estates in Westmeath confiscated by Cromwell, this William Higgin was, in 1677, granted twenty-six townlands, some in the co. Galway and some in the county Roscommon, forfeited in 1641 by the Bermingham family ; of these lands, Carropadden, Beagh, and Keeloge—situate in the county Galway, were (in 1877) in possession of Thomas Higgins, Tuam, No. 125 on this ("Higgins") pedigree.

† *Kate MacHale* : See the "MacHale" genealogy.

HOOLAHAN. (No. 2.)

Of Clan Colgan, King's County.

Arms . Gu. a lion ramp. ar. armed and langued az. betw. two swords points upwards of the second, pommels and hilts or., one in bend dexter, the other in bend sinister.

MUGRON, a brother of Cineth who is No. 99 on the "Dempsey" pedigree, was the ancestor of *O'h-Uallachain*, of Clan Colgan; anglicised *Holahan*, and *Hoolahan.*

99. Mugron: son of Flann Da Conghal.
100. Colgan: his son.
101. Cumascach : his son.
102. Fogarthach: his son; had a brother Aongus.
103. Uallachan (" uallachan : " Irish, *a coxcomb, a fop*): his son; a quo *O'h-Uallachain*, of Clan Colgan.

104. MacTire : his son; first of this family who assumed this sirname.
105. Connor: his son.
106. Cuileann : his son.
107. MacTire O'h-Uallachain : his son.

HOOLAHAN. (No. 3.)

Chiefs of Siol Anmchada in Hy-Maine.

Arms: Az. a tower or, supported by two lions ramp. ar. in base two crescents of the last, on a chief of the third three annulets gu.

Of OULAHAN (a Branch of this family) the *Arms* are : Az. two lions argent, supporting a Castle of four turrets of the second, or, in the centre chief point a cross gu. in base two crescents* argent, and in chief three annulets gules. *Crest* :† A demi-savage, handcuffed.

FLANCHADH [Flancha], brother of Cobthach who is No. 100 on the "O'Madden" (of Connaught) pedigree, was the ancestor of *O'h-Uallachain ;*‡ anglicised *O'Hoolahan, Hoolahan, Oulahan,* etc.

* *Crescents* : The "crescent" is the distinctive mark of the *second* branch of a family. In this case "O'Madden" (a branch of "O'Kelly" of Hy-Maine, Ireland,) is the head family.

† *Crest* : See "Fairbairn's Crests," Plate 10. O'Dugan, in his Topography, says : "A rough fettering lord of distinguished valour is *O'h-Uallachain.*" "O'Kelly" of Hy-Maine has this crest; and so have "O'Kelly," "Hollyland," and "Holyland" in England : a fact which would go to prove that "Hollyland" and "Holyland" are *Houlahan* disguised ; and that "O'Kelly," of England, is a branch of "O'Kelly" of Hy-Maine. For another crest of "O'Kelly" of Hy-Maine, see Burke's "General Armory."

‡ *O'h-Uallachain :* After this family was dispossessed of their territory in Hy-Maine, in Connaught, branches of them settled in Dublin, Galway, Kildare, Kilkenny, King's County, Mayo, Meath, and Westmeath ; and assumed one or other of the following sirnames : Colaghan, Coolacan, Coolaghan, Halahan, Halegan, Halligan, Holahan,

100. Flanchadh : son of Maoldun (or Maoldubhan).

101. Flann : his son.

102. Uallachan ("uallach :" Irish, *proud, haughty, merry, supple, vain*): his son : a quo *O'h-Uallachain.*

103. Iomrosan : his son.

104. Cartmil : his son.

105. Laidir Ara : his son.

106. Duilleabhar : his son.

107. Luchd : his son.

108. Logach : his son.

109. Lughach Leathdearg : his son.

110. Bromansutal Fionn : his son.

111. Bruithe : his son.

112. Brandabhach Beuldearg : his son.

113. Iodnaoidhe : his son.

114. Fearmuin : his son.

115. Columan : his son.

116. Umhan : his son.

117. Fionnachtach : his son.

118. Brangaile : his son.

119. Ros : his son.

120. Fliuchgaile : his son.

121. Corcrann : his son.

122. Dubhdhar : his son.

123. William O'Huolaghane : his son. He was the first of the family who settled at Killea (Rahilla or Red Hills), county Kildare. He built a residence, and outhouses on a farm there, between A.D. 1657 and 1660. There is a tomb over his remains in Lacka grave-yard, west of the town of Kildare.

124. William Houlaghan, of Killea : his son. There is a headstone to his memory in Carna grave-yard, south of the Curragh.

125. Simon* Houlahan, of Killea (Rahilla or Red Hills), county Kildare, who was son of William, d. 12th May, 1790, aged sixty years, He m. a farmer's dau., of Rathbride, county Kildare, named Margaret Moore† (d. 16th March, 1808, aged eighty years), and had :

I. William.

II. Pierce, of Lacka, who m. a Miss Doorley, sister of the Gallant Captain Doorley, one of the Kildare "Rebels" of 1798.

III. John, of whom presently.

IV. Christopher.‡

This Simon (No. 125) had a

Holhane, Holbgane, Holighan, Holland, Holligan, Hoolaghan, Hoolaghane, Hoolahan, Houlaghan, Houlaghane, Houlahan, Howlegan, Howlan, Hulegan, Huolaghane, Olehan, Oulahan, Oullaghan, Oullahan, Woolahan, and Merrie, Merry, FitzMerry, Mac-Merry, Nolan (of Mayo), Noland (in England), Proud, Proude, Soople, Suple, Supple, Vain, Vane, Whelton, and Wilton.

* *Simon* : On the tombstone (or headstone) over the remains of this Simon, in the graveyard of Carna, near Suncroft, Curragh Camp, Kildare, are the following words : "Erected by Pierce Houlahan in memory of his father Simon Houlahan, who departed this life May the 12th, 1790, aged 60 years.

"Also his mother 'Margret' Houlahan, *alias* Moore, who departed this life March 16th, 1808, aged 80 years. Also his sister Honor Houlahan who departed August 26th, 1805, aged 35 years. May they rest in peace. Amen."

† *Moore* : This Margaret Moore was the aunt of a saintly invalid priest, Father Moore of Rathbride, on north edge of the Curragh, who blessed a well on his widowed mother's farm which (well) became locally famous : and "Father Moore's Blessed Well" is still the resort of the afflicted, for miles around : "thousands having been cured of various diseases by its healing waters."

‡ *Christopher* : This Christopher *Oulahan* had six children : 1. Simon, 2. William, 3. Honora, 4. Mary, 5. Pierce, 6. Christopher. And this Pierce (5) had also six children : 1. Christopher, b. in 1854 ; 2. Mary, b. in 1856 ; 3. Simon, b. in 1858 ; 4. John, b. in 1860 ; 5. Elizabeth, b. in 1862 ; 6. Marcella, b. in 1864.

brother William,* who was father
of John *Oulahan*, known as "Little
John," who was the father of John,
who was the father of two children
living in 1877 in the old homestead
of Killea, co. Kildare.

126. John Houlahan, of Killea:
son of Simon ; b. at Killea in 1750,
and d. at his farm at Tully (south
of the town of Kildare) in 1834.
He was one of the leaders of the
Kildare *United Irishmen*, in 1798.
He m. a Miss MacCabe, dau. of a

farmer, near the Hill of Allen, co.
Kildare (who was the first person
buried in Allen graveyard),and had:
I. Simon, who was killed at the
   battle of Monastereven, on the
   24th May, of that year, under
   the command of Roger Garry.
II. John.
III. Patrick.†
And two daughters :
I. Anne, who m. a Mr. Higgins.
II. Mary, who m. Peter Mac-
   Daniel.

* *William* : In our opinion this William was the ancestor of the Dublin branch of
this family ; from him the descent was as follows :
125. William *Oullahan*, a merchant in Dublin. Will dated 6th Dec., 1781; proved
20th April, 1782.
126. Henry: his son ; had five brothers: 1. William, 2. Daniel, 3. Robert, 4.
Thomas, 5. Joseph ; and a sister named Anne.
127. Robert: son of Henry ; had six brothers : 1. John, 2. Henry, 3. William
(whose son John was, in 1877, living in Baltimore, Maryland, United States America),
4. Lawrence, 5. Richard, 6. James.
128. Denis J. Oullahan, of the Firm of "Oullahan and Co.," Miners, City of
Stocton, California : son of Robert ; had three children living in 1877 ; a sister named
Kate, who then was a Nun in Canada ; and a brother named Richard.

† *Patrick* : This Patrick Oulahan married Anastatia Farrell, by whom he had a
daughter named Bridget, who married P. Ryan of Frenchfurze : both living at North
Aams, Mass., in 1881 ; had twenty-one children—seventeen of whom are now living :
viz.—1. Mary, 2. Anne (Kane), 3. John, 4. Patrick, 5. Kate (Madden), 6. Lawrence,
7. Bridget, 8. Joseph, 9. Frank, 10. Agnes (m. to a Ryan), 11. Teresa, 12. Thomas,
13. Jane, 14. Peter, 15. Charles, 16. Anastatia, 17. Gertrude.
According to the Patent Rolls, 15° Jac. I., p. 1, Thomas Nolan (in Irish, *Tomhas
O'h-Uallachain*), of Ballinrobe, co. Mayo, gent., obtained a grant by patent, of the
four quarters of land in Ballinrobe, for ever, which belonged to the "Fryers' House,
of Ballinrobe." Before the date of that Grant the said Thomas Nolan resided at
"The Crevaghe" (now called Creagh), in the barony of Kilmain and county of Mayo.
In the Indenture of Composition for that county, A.D. 1585, it was provided that he
should have the Castle of the Creavaghe and three quarters of land thereto adjoining,
free from the Composition rent, "in respecte of his sufficiencie to act as a *Clerke* in the
said countrey." It may be here added, as a matter merely coincident, that the next
grantee of those very lands in the succeeding century, under the Act of Settlement,
was Mr. James Cuffe, ancestor of the late Baron Tyrawley, and of the late (if not the
present) proprietor of the Crevaghe, whose first appearance here was in the capacity
of *clerk* or secretary to Cromwell's Commissioners of Transplantation to Connaught
(see Hardiman's "West Connaught," p. 251).
The above Thomas Nolan was one of the first "English Tavern" Keepers in
Connaught. When the old Irish *Biatachs* (see Stat. Kilkenny, p. 4) and "Houses of
Hospitality" ceased, they were succeeded by "English Inns" or Taverns. On 21st
December, A.D. 1616, a licence was granted to John Coman of Athlone, merchant,
and Thomas Nolan, of Ballinrobe, Esq., to keep taverns, and sell wines and spirituous
liquors : to the former in almost every town in the county Galway, and in some towns
of the counties of Mayo, Roscommon, Sligo and Westmeath ; and "to Thomas Nolan,
in the town of Callow, and in the whole barony of Kilconnell, and in the town and
barony of Kilmaine, in Mayo county, during their own lives and those of Barnaby
Coman, brother of John ; of John Nolan, son of Thomas ; of Peter Nolan, son of
Richard Nolan, late of Athlone, merchant, deceased ; and of Jane or Jennet Coman,
daughter of the said John Coman." *Rot. Pat.* 15 *Jac.* I., p. 2. *d.* No. 58.

127. John *Oulahan :* son of John; b. at Friarstown, near Red Hills, in 1790, and d. in Dublin, 29th May, 1825. He m. Alice, dau. of Richard Byrne, of Donoughmore Mills, co. Meath (a farmer and miller, who d. in Dublin in 1856), and had two surviving sons and a daughter:

I. John, who d. unm. in Dublin, in 1856.

II. Richard, of whom presently.

I. Mary-Anne.

128. Major Richard Oulahan, of Washington, D.C., United States of America: son of John; bapt. 24th Feb., 1822, and living in 1887. In 1849, this Richard emigrated from Dublin to New York, United States; served as first Lieutenant in the 164th New York Volunteers (Irish Legion) in the late American Civil War; and in 1864, after muster out of the Military Service, he received from President Andrew

Johnson, a commission of Brevet-Major of United States Volunteers, and an appointment in the Treasury Department, Washington, D.C., which he still (1887) holds. This Richard* had three sons and two daughters;

I. John-Kenyon, of whom presently.

II. Joseph, b. in 1857, and living in 1887.

III. Richard Oge, b. in 1867, living in 1887.

The two daughters:

I. Alice, m. to John W. Sanderson, of Washington, by whom she had — I. Marie-Louise, born 1876; II. Alice-Irene; and III. Charlie; all living in 1887.

II. Mary, living in 1887.

129. John-Kenyon Oulahan, of Washington, D.C.: son of Major Richard Oulahan; b. in 1851, and living in 1887.

HUGHES.†

Arms : Ar. a chev. betw. three fleurs-de-lis gu.   *Crest :* A lion ramp. or, holding a thistle slipped ppr.

EANNA Ceannsalach, King of Leinster, who is No. 94 on the "Mac Morough" pedigree, had seven sons: Deadhach, the seventh of these sons, was the ancester of *O'h Aodha ;* anglicised *Hay, Hayes, Haiz, Hughes, Hewes, O'Hay, O'Hugh, O'Hea.*

95. Deadhach . son of Eanna Ceannsalach.

96. Æneas: his son; had a bro-

ther named Eoghan, who was the ancestor of St. Moling, whose feast is on the 17th June.

---

* *Richard :* See the 164th Regiment (Irish Legion), of the "Irish American Brigades," in the Appendix.

† *Hughes :* The late Judge Hughes, and his brother, Dr. James Stannus Hughes, Professor of Surgery, 1863-1884, were of this family. They were sons of James Hughes, solicitor, by his wife Margaret, daughter of Trevor Morton, solicitor, of Golden-lane. Doctor Hughes married Margaret, daughter of Walter Blake, of Meelick, co. Galway, but he had no children. The Doctor was born at 100 Capel-street, Dublin, on the 20th July, 1812, died at 1 Merrion-square, on the 1st of June, 1884, and was interred in Glasnevin Cemetery.

97. Aodh : son of Æneas.
98. Conmaol: his son.
99. Dubh-dacrioch: his son.
100. Eanachan : his son.
101. Deimhin : his son.
102. Aodh ("aodh:" Irish, *fire*, the Vesta of the Pagan Irish) : his son ; a quo *O'h-Aodha*.
103. Moroch : his son.

104. Donal O'Hugh : his son; first assumed this sirname.
105. Giolla (or William): his son.
106. Eachtighearna : his son.
107. Cinaodh (or Cineth) : his son.
108. Dunlong : his son.
109. Gillmoling: his son.
110. Dunsliabh: his son.
111. Hugh O'Hughes: his son.

HYNES.

Arms: Ar. a chev. gu. betw. three demi lizards couped vert.

AIDHNE, brother of Braon who is No. 107 on the "O'Clery" pedigree, was the ancestor of *O'h-Eidhin ;* anglicised *O'Heyne, Heyne, Hine, Hinds, Hynds,* and *Hynes.*

107. Aidhne ("aidhne:" Irish, *an advocate, a pleader*) : son of Congalach; a quo *O'h-Eidhin.*
108. Giolla-na-Naomh : his son.
109. Flann : his son.
110. Connor : his son.
111. Aodh (or Hugh): his son.
112. Giollaceallach : his son.

113. Goilla-na-Naomh : his son.
114. Owen : his son.
115. Shane (or John): his son.
116. Hugh : his son.
117. Donoch; his son.
118. Muirceartach (or Muriartach) O'Heyne: his son; had a brother named Owen.

For several branches of this family, see " Tribes and Customs of Hy-Fiachrach;" which may be seen in the library of the Royal Irish Academy, Dublin.

KANE.

Of Drumreaske, County Monaghan.

Arms : Gu. three fishes haurient ar. in the centre chief point an estoile or. *Crest*: A naked arm embowed ppr. charged with an estoile gu. and holding in the hand a sword also ppr.

AODH (or Hugh) a younger brother of Sir Donal Ballach who is No. 119 on the (No. 1) "O'Cahan" pedigree, was the ancestor of *Kane,* of Drumreaske, county Monaghan.

119. Hugh : second son of Rory Ruadh; m. Mary, dau. of O'Connor Faile.

120. Richard : their son; was twice m. : first, to Julian O'Dempsey, by whom he had two sons—1. John,

2. Mathew (or Ferdorach); and, secondly, to Mary O'Dunn, of Brittas, county Dublin, by whom he had Hugh, who m. Anne Mac-Coghlan, and had an only child Sarah O'Cahan.

121. John (or Shane): the eldest son of Richard; married Catherine O'Mulloy.

122. Mathew (or Ferdorach), who d. 1699 : eldest son of John ; m. the said Sarah O'Cahan, his first cousin, and had Joseph ; Nathaniel ; and other children who died young. This Joseph who was Lord Mayor of Dublin, 1725, d. without male issue.

123. Nathaniel, Lord Mayor of Dublin, 1734 : second son of Mathew ; founded the Bank of "Kane and Latouche." Married Martha Thwaites (who d. 1741) and had—1. Nathaniel, who d. s.p. and unm. 1750 ; 2. Joseph ; 3. Elizabeth, m. to Mathew Weld, and had a dau. m. to the Right Rev. John Brinkley, Astronomer Royal of Ireland, and Lord Bishop of Cloyne ; 4. Martha, d. unm. 1778 ; 5. Mary, m. to John Walker, of Dublin ; 6. Esther, died 1752.

124. Joseph (d. 1801): second son of Nathaniel ; m. Mrs. Mary Maxwell, née Church, and by her had— 1. Nathaniel ; 2. Joseph-Thomas (d. 1837), who was twice married, and left issue ; 3. John-Daniel, Col. 4th Regiment, who was thrice m., and left issue.

125. Nathaniel (d. 1826), Col. 4th Foot : eldest son of Joseph. Married Elizabeth Nisbett (d. 1858), and had—1. Joseph ; 2. Nathaniel (d. 1844) ; 3. Rev. Francis, Rector of Fenagh, county Leitrim, m. in 1864 to Anne Shea ; 4. John, of the Castle of Mohill, D.L., b. 1810, m. twice : first, in 1839, his cousin Matilda Nisbett, and by her had issue ; and, secondly, in 1859, m. Anne Hyde, and by her had one son Arthur Hyde Kane, b. 1860, died 24th May, 1880 ; 5. William, a Medical Doctor ; 6. Mathew, an A.M., and M.D.

126. Joseph : eldest son of Nathaniel ; m. Eliza-Jane, Madlle. de Vismes, and had—1. William-Francis-de Vismes Kane, 2. Eliza-Jane-Margaret (d. 1861).

127. William-Francis de Vismes Kane, of Drumreaske, county Monaghan, J.P. : son of Joseph ; b. 1840, and living in 1887 ; m. 2nd Sept., 1862, Amelia-Maria-Jane, only dau. of the Rev. Charles-James Hamilton, Incumbent of Kimberworth, county of York, England, and has had issue—1. Joseph-George-Auriol Kane (b. 29th June, 1865), 2. Emmeline-Rosa-Margaret—both living in 1887.

KAVANAGH. (No. 1.)

Lords of Leinster.

Arms : Ar. a lion pass. gu. in base two crescents of the last.

DERMOD na-Ghall, who is No. 113 on the "MacMorough" pedigree, had a son named Donal Caomhanach, who was the ancestor of *O'Caomhanaighe ;* anglicised *Kavanagh,* and *Cavanagh ;* and a quo *Cavaignac,* in France.

114. Dermod na-nGhall: son of Donoch MacMorough; died 1171; was the 58th Christian King of Leinster.

115. Donal Caomhanach ("caomh:" Irish, *gentle ;* Lat. " com-is ;" Arab. " kom," *noble*): son of Dermod na-nGhall (or " Dermod of the strangers," meaning that he sided with the English); a quo *O'Caomhanaighe.* This Donal Kavanagh who was slain in 1175, was fostered at Kilcavan; had two sons—1. Connor, who was slain at Athlone in 1170, and 2. Donal Oge. He had a brother Eanna Ceannsalach, a quo *Kinsela.*

116. Donal Oge: son of Donal; was Prince of Leinster; had two sons—1. Art, who was beheaded in 1281, and 2. Muirceartach.

117. Muirceartach: younger son of Donal Oge; was Prince of Leinster.

118. Muiris (or Maurice): his son; living in 1314; had two sons—1. Muirceartach, 2. Art (or Arthur).

119. Muirceartach : elder son of Muiris; Prince of Leinster; slain in 1307.

120. Art Mór Kavanagh: his son; Prince of Leinster; living in 1361; had two sons—1. Donal Mór ; and 2. Art Oge.

121. Art Oge: second son of Art Mór; living in 1417; Prince of Leinster; had two sons—1. Gerald; and 2. Diarmuid *Lamhdearg.*

122. Diarmuid *Lamhdearg (i.e. " Red Hand")*: younger son of Art Oge: Lord of Leinster; d. 1417.

123. Diarmuid (2), of St. Malins : his son.

124. Art Buidhe, of St. Malins, and Poulmonty, co. Carlow: his son; Lord of Leinster.

125. Cahir MacArt : his son ; Lord of Leinster; was created for life " Baron Ballyanne," 1554.

126. Brian : his son ; Lord of Leinster; d. 1572.

126. Morgan : his son; Lord of Leinster; d. 1636.

127. Brian (2): his son; Lord of Leinster; d. 1662.

128. Morgan (2): his son ; Lord of Leinster; died 1700.

129. Morgan (3): his son; died 1720; had issue.

130. Brian (3): son of Morgan; d. 1741.

131. Thomas: his son; d. 1789.

132. Thomas (2): his son ; d. 1837.

133. Arthur MacMurrough Kavanagh, of Borris: his son; Chief of his name, born 25th March, 1831, and living in 1887.

KAVANAGH. (No. 2.)

Of Clonmellon, County Carlow.

Arms: Ar. a lion pass. gu. in base two crescents of the last.

122. GERALD : elder son of Art Oge, who is No. 121 on the "Kavanagh" (No. 1) pedigree.

123. Donal Reac: his son; had two sons—1. Arthur Buidhe, and 2. Maurice.

124. Arthur Buidhe : son of Donal Reac.

125. Murtagh, of Clonmellon, co. Carlow: son of Arthur Buidhe; d. 1547.

126. Cathaoir (Cahyr) Carrach: his son.

127. Donoch, of Clonmellon: his son.

128. Donal-*an-Spaineach* (or "Donal the Spaniard"), of Clonmellon: his son; died 1631. From this Donal some derive the sirname *Spaine*.

129. Sir Moroch Kavanagh*: his son.

This branch of the "Kavanagh" family emigrated to France after A.D. 1690.

KAVANAGH. (No. 3.)

Arms: Same as those of "Kavanagh" (No. 1).

130. HARVEY KAVANAGH: second son of Morgan, who is No. 129 on the "Kavanagh" (No. 1) pedigree; d. 1740.

131. Morgan (4): his son; died 1817.

132. Walter: his son; d. 1853.

133. Morgan (5): his son; died 1848.

134. Morgan Butler Kavanagh: his son; Barrister-at-Law; living in 1874.

KAVANAGH. (No. 4.)

Of Garryhill,† County Carlow.

Arms: Same as those of "Kavanagh" (No. 1).

ARTHUR MÓR, who is No. 120 on the "Kavanagh" (No. 1) genealogy had two sons—1. Donall Mór, 2. Arthur Oge. From the Donal Mór here mentioned this branch of the "Kavanagh" family was descended.

---

   * *Sir Morogh Cavanagh:* Colonel Charles Kavanagh was second son of Sir Morogh Cavanagh, of Clonmullen; and is designated in the Attainders of the time as of "Carrickduff, co. Carlow." His regiment formed part of the besieging force at Derry. He married Mary Kavanagh, of the Borris family, and had two sons—1. Ignatius, 2. James. Colonel Charles raised his regiment himself, and appointed his son Ignatius Captain of the Grenadier Company. This Captain served with his regiment through the Irish war; and with his father and brother James was attainted by the Williamites. On the termination of hostilities, he retired with the army to France, where he entered the Irish Brigade, and again rose to the rank of Captain. He married Catherine, daughter of Andrew Browne, of Galway, of the Castle McGarrett family, and left three sons—Nicholas, Andrew, and Charles, who were living in France in 1776.

   † *Garryhill:* The descendants of this branch of the "Kavanagh" family, having been deprived of their Estates by the Cromwellian Settlement, emigrated to France in 1691, after the violation of the Treaty of Limerick.

121. Donal Mór : eldest son of Arthur Mór.
122. Murtagh : his son.

123. Murtagh (or Morough) : his son.
124. Morough Ballach : his son.

KAVANAGH. (No. 5.)

Of Kilballyowen, County Wicklow.

THOMAS KAVANAGH, of Kilballyowen, m. Mary, only dau. and heiress of Charles Dumble, an Englishman, who, under the Act of Settlement, became possessed of that property.

2. Matthew, of Kilballyowen : son of said Thomas ; m. and had
1. Darby, of whom presently :
2. Winefrid.*
3. Darby, of Kilballyowen : son of Matthew ; m. and had :
I. The Rev. James Kavanagh : D.D., and P.P., of Kildare ; died 1887.

II. Mathew, who m. Anne Loghlin, and (in 1883) had two daughters—1. Mary, 2. Jane.
III. Thomas.
4. Thomas Kavanagh, of Kilballyowen ; third son of Darby ; married —— Byrne, and, in 1887, had a family of sons and daughters.

KEANE. (No. 1.)

Of Cappoquin, County Waterford.

Arms : Gu. three salmon naiant in pale ar. *Crest :* A cat sejant ppr. supporting in the dexter paw a flag-staff, thereon a union jack ppr. *Motto :* Felis demulcta mitis.

DANIEL (or Donall), brother of Donoch an-Einigh, who is No. 116 on the (No. 1) "O'Cahan" pedigree, was the ancestor of *Keane,* of Cappoquin, county Waterford.

116. Daniel : son of John.
117. Richard : his son. This

Richard married Elizabeth, daughter of Alexander MacDonnell, of An-

---

+ *Winefrid :* This Winefrid m. Darby Whelan, of Ballymanus, and had one son and three daughters. The son William (d. *circa* 1876), m. a dau. of Lawrence Byrne of Redna, county Wicklow, and had three sons and four daughters, all living in 1883, save one daughter, who died in that year ; the sons were—1. William, 2. Darby, 3. Lawrence. And the three daughters of the said Darby Whelan were : 1. Margaret, who m. John Redmond, and had issue ; 2. Julia (died 1886) who m. —— Kavanagh, and had issue ; 3. Catherine (d. 1886), who m. William Byrne (d. 1881) of Ringsend, Dublin, but formerly of Redna, as above, and had : 1. Mary, who married Nicholas Warren, of Ringsend, Dublin, —— both living in 1887, and having issue ; 2. Patrick, born 1871, and living in Ringsend in 1887.

trlm, by whom he had six sons— 1. Conbhach Ballach; 2. John, ancestor of the Barons Kingston; 3. Daniel, ancestor of *Keane*, of the county Clare; 4. Roger, ancestor of *Keane*, of Cappoquin; 5. Magnus, ancestor of *O'Cahan*, of the south of the county Derry; 6. Richard, who died without issue; 7. Thomas.

118. Roger: the fourth son of Richard.

119. Magnus: his son.

120. Hugh: his son.

121. Thomas: his son.

122. Daniel (2): his son.

123. John: his son.

124. George: his son; alive in 1716.

125. John (2): his son; got a lease of the Cappoquin estate, from Richard, Earl of Cork and Burlington, dated July, 1738; died in 1756.

126. Richard: his son; died before his father.

127. Sir John Keane: his son; created a "baronet" in 1801; died 1829.

128. Sir Richard, the second baronet: his son; died 1855.

129. Sir John Henry Keane, the third baronet: his son; born in 1816, died 1881: had a brother named Leopold George-Frederick, who had a son named Frederick, living in 1877.

130. Sir Richard Francis Keane: son of Sir John; born in 1845; and living in 1887; married to Adelaide-Sidney, daughter of the late John Vance,* M.P. for Armagh, and formerly M.P. for Dublin.

131. John Keane: son of Richard; born in 1874, and living in 1887; had a younger brother named George Michael Keane.

KEANE. (No. 2.)

Of the County Clare.

Arms: Gu. three salmon naiant in pale ar.

DANIEL, the third son of Richard O'Cahan, who is No. 117 on the "Keane" (of Cappoquin) pedigree, was the ancestor of *Keane* of the county Clare.

118. Daniel O'Cahan: son of Richard; settled in the co. Clare, where he married a daughter of the Chief, Teige MacMahon, of Carrigaholt, who gave the said Daniel fourteen ploughlands in the western part of that county, as a marriage portion with his wife, the said daughter.

119. Hugh: son of Daniel; had a

brother James, living in 1543, who resided on Scattery Island, and from whom, it is believed, the "Keane" family of Beech Park (*Keane* No. 3) is descended.

120. Bryan: son of Hugh.

121. Owen: his son.

122. Charles: his son.

123. Robert: his son; married a MacNamara; had a brother

* *Vance*: See the "Vance" genealogy.

Owen (or Eugene), who died unmarried, of wounds received by him from one of Cromwell's staff officers, whom he killed.

124. Bryan: his son; married Mary, daughter of Daniel MacDonnell, whose grand-nephew was M.P. for the county of Clare. The issue of that marriage were fourteen sons and seven daughters. The eldest of these sons, Eugene, raised a company of 100 men at his own expense, at the time of the formation of the Clare Regiment, of which he was afterwards Captain; and was killed at the battle of Marsaglier, in Piedmont. Three other brothers of this Eugene, namely,—1. Charles, 2. Nicholas, and 3. Andrew (who died in 1755) went to, and also served as officers of distinction in, the Army of France, where some of their descendants still reside. One of the daughters of this Bryan was the mother of Lord Clare.

125. Robert, commonly known as "Robert of Ross" (Ross near Kilkee): son of Bryan; married to Anne Creagh. This Robert conformed to the Protestant Religion, and thus retained the estate in the county Clare; he was the first of this branch of the "O'Cahan" family who assumed the name *Keane*.

126. Charles of Kildimo: son of "Robert of Ross;" married Mary, daughter of Dean Freeman, of Castlecur, county Cork. This Charles had three brothers and two sisters: The brothers were—1. Thomas, who married Elizabeth, daughter of Captain Christopher O'Brien, of Ennistymon, widow of Charles MacDonnell, and mother of Charles MacDonnell of Kilkee, who was M.P. for the co. of Clare, in 1765, and for the borough of Ennis, in 1768, above alluded to; 2. Eugene, who was Captain in the Clare Regiment, was married to the sister of Francis Haller of the county of Kent, in England, and died without issue, in the service of France: 3. Richard, who became a barrister, and died young and unmarried. The sisters were— 1. Anne (Anne Ruadh), who was richly married to Robert Keane* of Ballyvoe, Kilmaley, near Ennis; and 2. Margaret, who was married to Edmund Fitzgerald,† of Abbeyfeale, county Limerick.

127. John Buidhe, of Raha: son of Charles of Kildimo; had three sisters.

128. Charles, of Raha: his son. Had four brothers—1. John; 2. Robert; 3. Thomas; and 4. Owen, who was reputed one of the

---

* *Robert Kean*: This Robert Kean and Anne Keane were the parents of—1. Robert, who had a son named "Tom;" 2. Charles of Ballyvoe, and 3. Patrick. This Charles Kean, second son of Robert, was the first of this family who added *e* final to the name; he married a Miss Harding, and by her had two sons—1. Robert Fada, of Beech Park, near Ennis, county Clare, and 2. Charles, who was a Major in the Artillery, and died unm. This Robert Fada m. a Miss Delahunty, by whom he had eleven sons (three of whom d. in infancy), and five daughters: The sons who survived were—1. Charles, 2. Francis, 3. Thomas, 4. Giles, 5. Robert, 6. Marcus, 7. Rev. William, 8. Henry.

Marcus Keane, of Beechpark, Ennis (living in 1881), the sixth surviving son of Robert Fada, m. a Miss Westby, by whom he had a family.

† *Edmund Fitzgerald*: This Edmund Fitzgerald and Margaret Keane were the parents of Robert Fitzgerald, who died in 1806, aged 63 years. And this Robert was the father of Captain Charles (known as "Governor") Fitzgerald, R.N., C.B., of Kilkee, county Clare, living in 1887. To the courtesy of this Captain Fitzgerald we are largely indebted for much information (oral and MS.) in relation to this branch of the O'Cahan family.

strongest men in Munster; and one sister who was married to —— MacMahon, of Kilcradare, Carrigaholt, who by the said sister was father of Lucy MacMahon (living in 1880), the widow of Michael Collins of Kilkee.

129. Charles, of Ballard, near Kilkee: only son of Charles of Raha.

130. Patrick, of Ballard : son of Charles; had three younger brothers—1. Charles, 2. Lawrence, 3. Thomas—all living in 1880.

131. Thomas Keane: eldest son of Patrick; b. Dec., 1859; had four brothers and three sisters : the brothers were—1. Peter, 2. Charles, 3. Patrick, 4. John—all living in 1880.

KEANE.* (No. 3.)

Of Beech Park, Ennis, County Clare.

Arms : Quarterly : Gu. and or, in the 1st and 4th quarters a salmon naiant ar. ; in the 2nd and 3rd quarters, a tree vert. *Crest :* A wild cat ramp. guard. ppr. gorged with an antique Irish crown or, and charged on the shoulder with a trefoil vert. *Motto :* Felis demulcta mitis.

ACCORDING to Dwyer, the O'Cahans, of whom the "Keane" family of Beech Park is a branch, had in the county Clare two castles in the reign of Queen Elizabeth ; one on *Inis Catha* (or Scattery Island), at Kilrush, occupied by a Charles O'Cahan (living in 1584), who was called a "corboe," and who filled some official position, *temp.* King Henry VIII. ; and another at Ballykett, occupied by a James Cahane. That Charles (who, in Parrot's Registry of Irish Castles of that date, is described under the name of "Colloo," and who was slain by a follower of O'Donnell, Chief of Tirconnell, in his raid to the county Clare, A.D. 1599,) was the son of James O'Cahan, who also resided on Scattery Island in 1543; and from whom this family is descended.

A golden bell which belonged to the Abbey on Scattery Island, and which until lately was in the possession of Captain Fitzgerald, R.N., C.B., Kilkee, was transferred by that gentleman to, and was in 1881 in the

---

* *Keane :* There were also in the county Clare members of an ancient Irish family named *O'Cain* ("cain :" Irish, *chaste*), pronounced "O'Koin," and variously anglicised *Cain, Kain, Kean, Keane,* and *Coyne ;* but that family was quite distinct from the "O'Cahan" family, Princes of Limavady, in the county Derry. Some of the "O'Cahan" family also settled in the counties of Westmeath and Mayo ; but in Clare they were, as distinguished from the "O'Cahan" family, known as *O'Cain Tón le Gaoth.*

Of the *O'Cain* family was Joseph Stirling Coyne, born at Birr in 1805. He was son of an officer, and received his education at Dungannon School. He was intended for the Bar, but ultimately devoted himself entirely to literature, chiefly dramatic. His first piece, *The Phrenologist,* was produced at the Theatre Royal, Dublin, in 1835. . . . He contributed to several London papers, and, with Mark Lemon and Henry Mayhew, was one of the projectors and original contributors to *Punch.* Coyne was the author of *The Scenery and Antiquity of Ireland,* and some works of fiction. He died on the 18th July, 1868.

possession of, the late Mr. Marcus Keane, of Beeck Park, by whom it was up to his death carefully preserved.

Commencing with James, brother of Hugh O'Cahan who is No. 119 on the "Keane" (No. 2) pedigree, the following is the genealogy, as far as we can trace it:

119. James O'Cahan, of Scattery Island, Kilrush, county Clare: son of Daniel; living in 1543.

(We are unable to trace the descent down to Owen O'Cahan,* who, about the middle of the 17th century, settled at Ballyvoe, near Ennis, and married Judith, dau. of Sir Robert Shaw, of Galway, and had issue. — See Burke's *Landed Gentry*.)

KEARY.

Of Fore, County Westmeath.

Arms: Az. a lion pass. guard. or.   *Crest:* An arm in armour embowed, holding a spear, point downwards, shaft couped all ppr.

THIS family is believed to be a branch of the "Cahill" family of Connaught, which derived its name from Cathal, who is No. 102 on the "Cahill" of Connaught pedigree; and was in Irish known as *O'Ciardha* ("ciar:" Irish, *a dark-grey colour*), anglicised *O'Cearry, O'Carry, O'Carrie, Carry, Carey,* and *Keary.*

Thomas O'Ciardha, brother of Dermod O'Ciardha of Offaley, called Thomas *Baintreabhachd* (or Thomas "the Widower"), was the ancestor of "Keary," of Fore, county Meath. This Thomas lived on the Hill commanding a view of the famous Abbey founded at Fore by St. Fechin; and was killed at the burning of the Abbey by the Cromwellians, A.D. 1654. Commencing with said Thomas, the following is the pedigree of this family:

1. Thomas had three sons, Thomas, Patrick, and James, the three of whom sought refuge, and found it, with Hugh O'Byrne, of Dublin, one of the Confederate Catholics; Patrick and James d. unm., but the eldest son:

2. Thomas m. Mary O'Byrne, niece of the above-named Hugh, and had three sons:

I. Thomas;

II. Patrick; III. Hugh, both of whom went to Spain, where the latter died in 1700. Patrick entered the Spanish service.

3. Hugh m. Margaret, dau. of Dermot O'Brien, of Naas, and had issue: Dermot, Thomas, Patrick, John, and Mary.

4. John m. in 1745, Mary, dau.

---

* *Owen O'Cahan:* Some are of opinion that the Keanes of Beech Park are connected only in the Female line with the O Cahans of Scattery Island; and that this Owen who settled at Ballyvoe, about the middle of the 17th century, went there from the North of Ireland, at the time of the Plantation of Ulster.

of Owen M'Kewen of Clontarf and Swords, and had one son, Thomas (b. 1747), and a daughter, Ellen (b. 1749), who m. in 1780 Hugh O'Moore, of the O'Moores of Longford.

5. Thomas m. Julia, dau. of Roderick Murphy of Castledermot, and had issue : Thomas, John, Patrick, and Michael.

6. Thomas m. in 1815, Mary, dau. of John Keogh of Castlepollard; he was the first of the family to omit the prefix *O'* from the family name then *O'Cary*, and assumed the name, *Keary*.* This Thomas d. in Dublin in 1836, and was interred in the church-yard of Artane, where his tomb can be seen; leaving issue :

I. Patrick, of whom presently.
II. John;
III. Michael, who d. in Liverpool in 1870.
I. Bridget;
II. Mary.

7. Patrick Keary : son of Thomas; m. Anne, youngest dau. of James Butler of Fairview, Ballybough, Dublin, and d. in 1884, leaving issue :

I. Thomas.
II. Francis.
III. Michael.
IV. James.
V. John.
VI. Peter.
VII. Joseph.
VIII. Matthew.
IX. Patrick, of whom presently.
I. Mary-Anne.

8. Patrick J. Keary (Cahill): son of Patrick (7); of 22 Colville Terrace, Ballybough Road, and of Wellington Quay, Dublin; m. in 1875, Elizabeth, only daughter of Patrick Cahill, and has living in 1887 :

I. William-Laurence Cahill Keary, b. 1877.
II. John-Francis, b. 1887.
I. Mary-E.
II. Christina.

KEENAN.

Chiefs in Fermanagh.

Arms: Gu. a lion pass. guard. or, in base a human heart ar.

MURTAGH, the fourth son of Ceallach who is No. 97 on the "O'Hart" pedigree, was the ancestor of *O'Caoinain* ("caoin :" Irish, *mild,* "an" *one who;* Heb. "chen," *favour*); anglicised *O'Keenan, Keenan, Kennan, Kinane, Kinnane,* and *Keon.*

From the said Murtagh are also descended the Ulster families of *Dongan, Donegan, Rogan,* etc.

A worthy representative of the *O'Keenan* family is The Right Hon. Sir Patrick Joseph Keenan, P.C., C.B., K.C.M.G., M.R.I.A., of Delville, Glasnevin, Dublin; b. 1826, and living in 1887; son of John Keenan, of

---

* *Keary:* Daniel O'Ciardha (or O'Cary), a nephew of this Thomas, having conformed to the Protestant religion, Thomas (m. 1815), above mentioned, called together the remnant of his family; and, in order to distinguish themselves from the said Daniel, they solemnly pledged to assume thereafter the name *Keary,* and to abandon the prefix *O',* and the "Carey" form of spelling the name.

Phibsborough, Dublin; m. in 1860, Elizabeth-Agnes, daughter of the late Michael Quinn, J.P., of Waterville, co. Limerick, and has had issue. Sir Patrick Joseph Keenan is a *Resident Commissioner of National Education in Ireland ;* a Governor of the Royal Hibernian Military School, and J.P. co. Dublin ; was employed in 1869 in the West Indies as Commissioner to inquire into the state of education in Trinidad ; and in 1878 in Malta as Commissioner to inquire into the University, Lyceums, and Primary Schools of that colony. For his Educational services in Trinidad and Malta he was created a K.C.M.G. in 1881.

KELLY. (No. 1.)

Of Tuam, County Galway.

Arms ; See those of "O'Kelly." (No. 1.)

1. Anthony Kelly of Turrick, Castle Park, near Mount Talbot, co. Galway, m. Margaret (b. 4th October, 1736, died 1822), dau. of Jasper Ouseley,* of Prospect, Dunmore.

2. Jasper Kelly of Loughrea: their only son; married Frances, daughter of Edward Davis,† of Fahy, Loughrea, county Galway.

3. Richard Kelly: their eldest son; born 1810, at Loughrea ; now (1880) of Bayview-avenue, Dublin, but formerly of Tuam, where, in 1837, he founded the "Tuam Herald" Newspaper; m. Margaret,

daughter of Dominick Tully, of Dunmore, by whom he had issue —1. Jasper, 2. Susan, 3. Fannie, 4. Lizzie, 5. Richard, 6. Robert.

4. Jasper: eldest son of Richard; for many years Proprietor of the "Tuam Herald ;" married Delia, third eldest daughter of John Daly of Tuam and Westport, by whom he had issue—1. Richard-John, 2. Margaret, 3. Mary, 4. Susan; died October, 1866.

5. Richard-John Kelly: son of Jasper; born 1856; living at Tuam in 1887, as the Proprietor of the "Tuam Herald" Newspaper.

* *Ouseley :* Jasper Ouseley was the son of Jasper, who, in 1772, m. Julia Bodkin (d. 1790), of Kilclooney. Said last-mentioned Jasper was son of Richard Ouseley (b. 1697, d. 1761), who was son of Jasper Ouseley, of Ballycogley, co, Wexford (b. 1630), who was the eldest son of Richard Ouseley of Courteen Hall, Northampton, England, (b. 1570).

† *Davis :* John Davis, of Fahy, Loughrea, was son of Robert Davis (b. 1737, d. 1813), who was the son of Geoffrey Davis (d. 1757), who was the son of William Davis, of Aughrim (d. 1721).

KELLY. (No. 2.)

Chiefs of Hy-Maile, County Wicklow.

Arms : Ar. on a mount in base vert an oak tree acorned ppr.

CEATHRAMHADH, a brother of Cormac who is No. 87 on the "O'Connor" (Faley) pedigree, was, according to the *Linea Antiqua*, the ancestor of *O'Ceallaigh*, of Cualan ;* anglicised *O'Kelly*, and *Kelly*.

87. Ceathramhadh : son of Niadh Corb.
88. Ceallach Cualan ("ceallach :" Irish, *strife*): his son ; a quo *O'Ceallaigh*, of Cualan.
89. Edirsceal : his son.
90. Ceallach : his son.
91. Cathal : his son.
92 Mothudan: his son.

93. Dubhdatuagh: his son.
94. Flann : his son.
95. Raghilleach : his son.
96. Madudhan : his son.
97. Clochar : his son.
98. Tuathal : his son.
99. Amhailgadh : his son.
100. Cathal O'Ceallaigh : his son.

KELLY. (No. 3.)

Chiefs of Hy-Maile, County Wicklow.

Arms : Ar. on a mount in base vert an oak tree acorned ppr.

ACCORDING to MacFirbis, Main Mal, a younger brother of Cathair Mór, Monarch of Ireland in the second century, and who is No. 89 on the "O'Connor" (Faley) pedigree, was the ancestor of *O'Ceallaigh*, of Cualan; anglicised *O'Kelly* and *Kelly*.

89. Main Mal: son of Felim Fiorurglas ; a quo *Hy-Maile* of the Glen of "Imaile," in the county Wicklow.
90. Tuathal Tigheach : his eldest son.
91. Fergus Forcraidh : his son.
92. Aengus Ailce : his son.
93. Etersceol: his son.
94. Carthann Muadh : his son.

95. Seanach Diodhach : his son.
96. Aodh Dubhcean : his son.
97. Ronan Cruaic : his son; by some authorities reckoned as King of Leinster.
98. Diocolla Dana : his son.
99. Gertighe : his son; living A.D. 702.
100. Ceallach Cualain ("ceallach" : Irish, *strife*) : his son ; a quo

---

* *Cualan:* This ancient territory originally comprised the present county Wicklow with parts of the counties of Dublin and Kilkenny ; and the O'Kellys here mentioned were chiefs of *Hy-Maile*, now the barony of "Imaile," in the county Wicklow.

O'Ceallaigh, of Cualan. Had a brother named Fiannamhail, who was Abbot of Clonard.

101. Etersceol: son of Ceallach Cualan; slain, 721. Had seven brothers and two sisters: the brothers were—1. Crimthan (slain, 721), King of Leinster, who had Tuathal, who had Fiacra; 2. Comgan of Turrieff, North Britain (October 13th); 3. Cobthach (d. 730); 4. Coincean (d. 739); 5. Aedh (slain, 717); 6. Fiacra, and 7. Fiannamhail—both slain A.D. 707, at Selgge, in Ferthuath Laighen. The sisters were—1. Muirean, who was wife of Irgalach, son of Conaing, and had Ceneth, the 158th Monarch of Ireland ; 2. Cainteghern, who was wife of Feredach (of the Dal Fiatach of Ulster), and had Faelan (January 9th) of Cluan Mescna, and Strathfellan, N.B. (see *Acta Sanct-*

orum, pp. 49-50, and MacFirbis, p. 221).

102. Ceallach: son of Etersceol. Had two sons—1. Oilill, slain, 739; 2. Cathal, also slain, 739.

103. Cathal: younger son of Ceallach.

104. Madudhan: his son.

105. Dubhdatuagh: his son.

106. Flann: his son.

107. Riaghallach: his son.

108. Madudhan: his son.

109. Clochar: his son; died, A.D. 915.

110. Tuathal: his son. Had two sons—1. Amhailgadh, 2. Aedh.

111. Amhailgadh: eldest son of Tuathal.

112. Cathal O'Ceallaigh, Prince of Ui-Cualain : his son ; slain with his wife, A.D. 1034. This Cathal had a younger brother Giollacaemgin, who was slain A.D. 1057.

KENNEDY.*

Of Tirowen.

Arms : Ar. on a fesse az. three mullets of the field.

DIARMAID, brother of Flaithbheartach who is No. 97 on the "Morley" pedigree, was the ancestor O'Cineadhaigh, of Tirowen ; anglicised *Kennedy*.

97. Diarmaid: son of Conchobhar.

98. Baoghal: his son; had a brother named Maolpadraic.

99. Cineadhach ("cineadh :" Irish, *decreeing ; "* ach," *a skirmish)*: son of Baoghal; a quo *O'Cineadhaigh*.

---

* *Kennedy* : The name of Cornet Thomas Kennedy does not appear in Mr. Dalton's "King James's Army List ;" but the omission of the name must have been a mistake. It is believed that the Cornet's family was a branch of the O'Kennedys of Ormond, which, in the 16th century, settled in Dublin, where they became wealthy merchants, and after whom "Kennedy's Land" has been named. This officer commenced his military career as Cornet in Tyrconnell's own Regiment of Horse, who appointed him one of his *Aides-de-Camp*, and presented him with his own miniature ; a relic still in the Kennedy family. At the capitulation of Limerick, he retired to France, where he rose to the rank of Colonel ; and in 1706 married the daughter of a Dutch Noble, after which he resided in Brussels. He was in 1718 accidentally killed by the Duchess of

KEOGH.* (No. 1.)

Of Connaught.†

Arms : Ar. a lion ramp. gu. in dexter chief a dexter hand couped at the wrist, and in the sinister a crescent both of the second. *Crest :* A boar pass. az.

DERMOD KELLY, the fifth son of Daniel O'Kelly who is No. 111 on the (No. 1) "O'Kelly" (Hy-Maine) pedigree, and whose patrimony was "The

Oldenberg, who, driving in his carriage to a hunt, saw a wild boar cross the road, and in firing at it the barrel of her fowling piece burst, and mortally wounded the colonel. He had three children by his wife, two of whom are considered to have died young ; because, when his widow came to Ireland in 1720 she is said to have been accompanied by *her son.* 1. Cornet Thomas Kennedy married Elizabeth Von Vryberge, and had :

2. Marinus James, who lived in France, and was active in the service of Prince Charles Edward Stuart, the "Pretender ;" returned to Ireland, and in 1763 was strangled in Clondalkin Castle, county Dublin, for sake of some gold he was known to keep in his house. He m. Henrietta Creagh, niece to Duke of Ormond, and had :
I. Thomas, of whom presently.
II. Walter, a poet of some talent. Taking advantage of the "Gavel Act," he divided the family in 1776, and died in 1790, leaving :
    I. Marinus-James, who served in the German and Spanish Armies. On the admission of Roman Catholics to the English Army, he was appointed to the 18th Royal Irish Regiment, and killed in 1811 in Java. It does not appear that he left any issue.
3. Thomas : elder son of Marinus-James (No. 2) ; was apprenticed to a merchant in Amsterdam ; lived some time in Cadiz ;

returned to Dublin ; was a great musician. He m. in 1764 Frances-Arabella, dau. of Doctor Fergus, an eminent Roman Catholic Physician, and representative of the Irish Sept called *Clan Fergus.* (See the "Ferguson" pedigree, *ante,* p. 448). He d. 1791, leaving two sons :
I. Marinus, a distinguished Trinity College man, who d. in 1852 or 1853, s.p.
II. Macarius.
4. Macarius : son of Thomas ; was a solicitor ; m. and had :
I. Thomas, a barister, and member of the original "Comet Club ;" he d. in 1840, s. p.
II. Marinus.
III. Macarius, of whom presently.
IV. Philip.
5. Macarius : third son of Macarius (No. 4) ; served in the Portuguese Army in 1832-3 & 4 ; m. and had :
6. James Marinus Kennedy, of Clondalkin, co. Dublin ; d. at 15 Lower Mount Street, Dublin, on 29th July, 1876.

* *Keogh :* Of this family was, it is thought, John Keogh of Mount Jerome, a Dublin merchant, and prominent Catholic leader of his time, who was born in 1740. In his own words, he "devoted near thirty years of his life for the purpose of breaking the chains of his countrymen." Of him, Henry Grattan, junior, says : "He was the ablest man of the Catholic body . . . . . At the outset of life Keogh had been in business, and began as an humble tradesman. He contrived to get into the Catholic Committee, and instantly formed a plan to destroy the aristocratic part, and introduce the democratic. The Act of 33 George III., c. 21, was passed mainly through his instrumentality." He died in Dublin on the 13th November, 1817, and was buried in St. Kevin's churchyard, under a stone he had erected to his father and mother.

† *Connaught :* This branch of the "O'Kelly" (No. 1) family were Chiefs of Onagh, in the parish of Taghmaconnell, barony of Athlone, county of Roscommon ; in which county many respectable people of the "Keogh" family still reside. *Cambrensis Eversus* in Note, p. 256, says that, "subsequently the territory of Breadach, county Roscommon, containing forty quarters of land, and comprising the whole parish of Taghmaconnell, in the barony of Athlone, fell into possession of the O'Kellys, who took the name Mac-Eochaidh, now Keogh, of whom the father of the late Mr. Justice Keogh was the Chief Representative."

forty quarters of Moyfin," near Elphin in the county Roscommon, was the ancestor of *MacEochaidh*, or, more properly, *MacEachaigh ;* anglicised *MacKeogh*, and modernized *Kehoe*, and *Keogh*.

112. Dermod Kelly : son of Daniel O'Kelly.

113. Eochaidh (" each" or " eoch :" Irish, *a steed ;* Gr. " ikkos ;" Lat. " equus"), meaning a horseman or knight :" his son ; a quo *Mac-Eochaidh*.

114. Thomas Kelly : his son ; ancestor of *Kelly*, of Moyfin, etc.

115. Nicholas : his son ; was Prior of Athenry ; had a brother named Simeon, who was dean of Clonfert.

116. Nicholas Oge : son of Nicholas ; divided his estates amongst his four sons ; first who assumed the sirname *MacKeogh*.

117. Donoch : his son ; had three

brothers—1. Thomas, 2. Daniel, 3. William.

118. Hugh : his son.

119. Connor : his son.

120. Teige : his son.

121. Melaghlin an - Bearla (or Melaghlin who spoke English) : his son.

122. William Keogh : his son ; the first of the family who omitted the prefix " Mac ;" had a brother named Colla.

123. Melaghlin (2) : his son ; had two brothers—1. named John, 2. Daniel.

124. Edmond Keogh : his son.

KEOGH. (No. 2.)

Of Leinster.

Arms : Ar. a lion rampant gu. betw. a dexter hand apaumée in the dexter, and a crescent in the sinister chief point, both of the second.   *Crest :* A boar passant ppr. *Motto :* Resistite usque ad sanguinem ; and, by some of the family, Malo mori quam fœdari.

EOCHAIDH, who (see p. 421, *ante*,) is No. 98 on the " Dowling" pedigree, was the ancestor of *MacEochaidh* (" eachach :" Irish, *a horseman* or *abounding in horses*) of Leinster. That Eochaidh was (see p. 391 of the Book of Leinster,) son of Muredach, son of Aongus, son of Felim (a quo *Hy-Felimy*), son of Eanna Ceannsalach, King of Leinster, in St. Patrick's time in Ireland.

But Eochaidh, brother of Feach, who is No. 108 on the " O'Meagher" pedigree, was the ancestor of MacEochaidh,* Chiefs of Uaithne Tire, a

* *MacEochaidh :* Of this family was John Keogh, D.D., a learned divine, born at Clooncleagh, near Limerick, in the middle of the 17th century. His family lost their property in the Cromwellian Wars. He entered Trinity College in 1669, was a scholar in 1674, and M.A. in 1678. Entering into Holy Orders, he was by his relative John Hudson, Bishop of Elphin, given a living in that diocese, and was collated and installed Prebendary of Termonbarry, in 1678. There he continued for forty-seven years, until his death, devoting himself to literary pursuits. His biographer in *Walker's Magazine* (in 1778) writes of him : " Although the Doctor had a very numerous issue, not less than twenty-one children, males and females, yet he never would take tythe from a poor man."

territory situated in ancient Owney,* which comprised the present baronies of " Owney" and " Arra," in Tipperary ; and " Owneybeg," in the county Limerick. In each case the family name in Irish has been anglicised, as in the case of " Keogh" (No. 1), *MacKeogh*, *Kehoe*, and *Keogh*.

In pp. 259 (Note) of *Cambrensis Eversus*, we read : " This (Leinster) branch of the Kehoes or Keoghs occupied the plains of Maghlaighlan and Magh Liffé, about the northern half of the present county Kildare." Their possessions comprised the present baronies of Clane and Salt, and the greater part of Oughteranny, the town of Naas, and the churches of Clane, Laraghbrien (near Maynooth), Donaghmore, Cloncurry, and Feighcullen. (See O'Donovan's *Book of Rights*.) The Clan Kehoe or Keogh were driven from this fertile territory, about A.D. 1202, by Meyler Fitz-Henry and his followers, when the Kehoes had to retire into Wicklow.

In Connellan's Annals of the Four Masters, p. 223 (Note), it is recorded that MacKehoe of Wicklow, together with O'Doran, chief Brehon of Leinster, and O'Nolan, the King's marshal, attended at Cnoc-an-Bhoga, when the MacMurroughs (now " Kavanaghs") were inaugurated as Kings of Leinster, during the reign of Queen Elizabeth.

In the *Transactions of the Iberno-Celtic Society* for 1820, Vol. I., Part I., pp. 143-145, we find mention of Donald McKehoe writing a poem on the Journey of O'Byrne, 1584.

Among the attainted in 1642 were Thomas MacMaolmuire MacKehoe,† and William MacShane MacFarrel MacKehoe of Knockandarragh, county Wicklow. But the Laws against using the distinctive Irish prefixes *O'* and *Mac* in Irish sirnames were so rigidly enforced in the counties of Carlow, Wicklow, and Wexford, that the *Mac* was abandoned in this family name after that period. The family estates were confiscated by Cromwell ; but portions of them were restored by Charles II., who, according to the Down Survey, gave Rathgarvan (now known as Clifden) to Arthur, Earl of Anglesea.

In the List of the " Persons Transplanted in Ireland" under the Cromwellian Confiscations we find (see our " Irish Landed Gentry when Cromwell came to Ireland") the name of Mahon Keogh, gent., of Cloncleafe, co. Limerick, and other members of the family from the same county ; and (*ibid.*) the names of others of the family appear among the " Connaught Certificates" of the Commonwealth period, in Ireland.

Among the Irishmen who served in the Spanish Netherlands, in 1660, we find the name of Don Theodoro Keogh.

In 1693, Thomas Kehoe (grandson of Thomas MacMaolmuire Mac-Kehoe of Knockandarragh, co. Wicklow), who had served as a Captain in the Army of King James II. (see Dalton's Army List, Vol. II., p. 404), and fought at the Boyne and Aughrim, settled in the co. Carlow. The family subsequently intermarried with those of Coughlan, Doyle, Brewster, and Blanchfield—a family resident in the co. Kilkenny since the time of

---

* *Owney* : Among the ancient families of Irish descent in Munster, Lynch in his *Cambrensis Eversus*, names O'Loingsigh, as lord of Uaithne-Tire, now the barony of Owney, in Tipperary.

† *MacKehoe* : This name means : "Thomas, son of Maolmuire MacKehoe ;" and the next : " William, son of Shane, son of Farrel MacKehoe."

the Tudors.   Sir Edward Blanchfield married Elizabeth Butler, daughter of the second Earl of Ormond.*

We also find that in 1703 the Blanchfield properties were again confiscated by William III.; in which alone 2,903 acres were forfeited, and a portion of them sold by the Crown to W. Edward Worth, of Rathfarnham.

The lands of Rathgarvan (or Clifden) continued to be leased by the Blanchfields until the death (in 1874) of Miss Mary Blanchfield, when they came into possession of her nephew the late Myles W. Keogh, a Lieutenant-Colonel of the 7th Regiment, United States Cavalry, of whom hereafter.   Colonel Myles W. Keogh gave his right and title of Clifden to his sister Margaret Keogh, the present occupant.

1. Captain Thomas Kehoe† (b. 1660, d. 1720), who, as above mentioned, fought in King James' Army at the Boyne and Aughrim, and afterwards settled in the county Carlow, married and had:

2. Patrick‡ (b. 1697, d. 1760), of Ballywilliamroe, co. Carlow, who m. Bridget Doyle, and had:

3. James (b. 1723, d. 1779), of Orchard and Ballywilliamroe, who m. Julia Coughlin (d. 1812), and had four sons and three daughters:

I. James Kehoe, of Oldtown.

II. Patrick *Keogh*, who, according to Cox's Magazine, was on the 9th of June, 1798, hanged at the town of Carlow (on the same morning as Sir E. Crosbie), because of his connection with the United Irishmen of that period.

III. Thomas, who d. unm.

IV. John Keogh, of whom presently.

I. Joanna, who m. J. Ennis.

II. Bridget, who m. W. Cummins.

III. Margaret, who m. J. Donohoe.

4. John Keogh, of Orchard, co. Carlow: fourth son of James; m. Margaret Blanchfield of Rathgarvan§ (or Clifden), and had five sons and seven daughters:

I. James, who d. unm.

II. Patrick *Kehoe*, Coroner of the co. Carlow, of whom presently.

III. Thomas *Keogh*, of Park, Carlow, who in 1870 m. Alice, daughter of Richard Kehoe, of Bagenalstown, and had issue:

IV. John, who d. unm.

V. Myles|| Walter Keogh, Lieutenant-Colonel, United States Army, who also d. unm.

The daughters were:

---

* *Ormond:* See Graves' and Prim's *History of St. Canice's;* also Tomb in N. W. Aisle of the Kilkenny Cathedral.

† *Captain Thomas Kehoe:* The present representatives of this branch of the "Kehoe" family are—Patrick Kehoe, of Orchard, Leighlin Bridge; the Kehoes of Bagenalstown—two families; Surgeon-Major Keogh, J.P., Castleroe, co. Kildare; James Kehoe, of Milford; James Kehoe, of Blanchfield Park, co. Kilkenny; Thomas Keogh, of Park, Carlow; and Richard J. Kehoe, of Chicago, United States, America.

‡ *Patrick:* This Patrick had other brothers, from whom descended the Kehoes of Bagenalstown; P. Kehoe, M.D., Cork (family extinct); Anthony Kehoe, Kilcommany and Teninscourt (family extinct); and others.

§ *Rathgarvan:* Rathgarvan (or Clifden) was the property of James Blanchfield, who, with Garret, Edmond, and Sir Edward, "Irish Papists," lost their estates by the Confiscations in 1656.—See the Down Survey, in the Royal Irish Academy.

|| *Myles:* Colonel Keogh was serving with the Papal Army when the American War (of 1861-1865) broke out.   After the capture of Ancona, in Italy, in 1860, Mr.

I. Julia, who d. unm.

II. Mary, who m. John Sullivan, of the co. Tipperary.

III. Joanna, who m. J. A. Kehoe, of the county Kildare.

IV. Bridget, who married James Kehoe, of Milford.

V. Ellen, who m. M. Donohoe, of Clocristie.

VI. Margaret, the present occu-pant of Clifden (or Rath-garvan).

VII. Fanny, who m. John Delany, M.D., of Freshford, county Kilkenny.

5. Patrick *Kehoe*, Coroner of the co. Carlow: eldest surviving son of John Keogh, of Orchard, m. Marion, dau. of L. Nolan, of Tennaclash; and has issue; living in 1886.

KETT.

CEAT MIC MAGHACH, one of the sons of the Irish Monarch Cahir Mór, is said to have been the ancestor of *O'Ceat;* ("ceat:" Irish, *a pillar, a prop*), anglicised *Kett*, and *Keats*.

1. Connor Kett was the first of the family who went from Burren, near Ballyvaughan, county Clare, and settled in Kilbaha, in the west of that county; living in 1690. This Connor had a brother, who was a Medical Doctor in the Spanish Fleet.

2. John: son of Connor; had a brother Joseph; and two sisters— 1. Honor, 2. Margaret.

3. Darby*: son of John. Had

Keogh, then a Sub-Lieutenant, offered his services to President Lincoln, from whom Mr. Keogh received a Lieutenant's Commission. He was afterwards appointed *Aide-de-Camp* to General Shields, who was then operating in Shenandoah Valley; received honourable mention for his services in the battle of Port Republic; and was trans-ferred to General McClellan's Staff, with whom he served in the battle of Antietam, receiving a letter of thanks for his gallant conduct. A splendid horseman, Colonel Keogh was appointed to the Cavalry Command of General Buford, on whose personal Staff, Mr. Keogh served at the battles of Madison, Cedar Mountain, Kelly's Ford, and was especially mentioned for gallantry and good conduct. In 1863, Colonel Keogh still served with General Buford in the brilliant cavalry actions in which his division took part at Beverly, Boomboro', William Port, Culpepper, Rappahannock, etc., and, on the death of General Buford, was transferred to the Staff of General Stoneman, with whom he served through the Atlanta campaign; receiving at Reseca the personal thanks of General Sherman, and a Brevet Majority for gallant and meritorious services at the battle of Gettysburg. Colonel Keogh continued on active service until the termination of the War, receiving his Commission of Lieu-tenant-Colonel by Brevet for "gallant and meritorious services at the battle of Dallas." Some months after the fall of Richmond, and the surrender of the Southern Armies, Colonel Keogh was ordered with his Regiment (the 7th Cavalry) on frontier duty, where he was killed, together with General Custer, fifteen officers, and three hundred men, in the unfortunate skirmish with Sioux Indians, near the Yellowstone River; thus closing a brilliant military career at the early age of six-and-thirty. In recogni-tion of Colonel Keogh's services the American Army have named in his memory an important post in Montana—"FORT KEOGH."—*Record on File, War Department, Washington.*

* *Darby*: This Darby had two sons, and two daughters: the sons were— 1. Martin, the eldest son, who lately died in America; 2. Joseph, who died unmarried. Three of this Martin's sons were—1. Mathias; 2. Darby; and 3. Thomas, who emigrated with him to America.

two brothers—1. Michael; 2. Joseph;
and no sisters.

4. Thomas Kett, of Farrahy, near
Kilkee; son of said Michael; born
1826, living in 1886. Had three brothers—1. John (deceased), 2. Darby
(who emigrated to America), 3.

Joseph; and two sisters—1. Catherine, 2. Mary.

5. Michael Kett: son of Thomas.
Has had three brothers—1. Jeremiah
(or Darby), 2. Joseph, 3. Connor;
and two sisters—1. Ellen, 2. Mary:
all living at Farrahy in 1886.

KIERNAN.

Arms: See those of the " O'Hart" family.

CAIRBRE an-Daimh-Airgid, who is No. 91 on the " O'Hart" pedigree, was
the ancestor of *O'Ciarnain,* and *MacCiarnain;* anglicised *Kiernan,* and
*MacKiernan.**

91. Cairbre and Daimh Airgid,
King of Orgiall.
92. Aodh (or Hugh): his son;
whose eldest brother Daimhin was
an ancestor of *O'Hart;* had two
younger brothers—1. Cormac, who
was the ancestor of *Maguire;* 2.
Naidsluagh [nadslo], the ancestor
of *MacMahon,* of Monaghan.
93. Fergus : his son.
94. Cormac : his son.
95. Eanachan : his son.
96. Iorghuileach : his son.
97. Lughan : his son.
98. Cearnach : his son.
99. Feareadhach (" feareadhach :"
gen. " feareaduighe :" Irish, *a dressy
man*): his son; a quo *Cineal Feareaduighe* or *O'Feareaduighe,* anglicised *Faraday.* The family of *Mac-
Cathmhaoill,* anglicised *Campbell* and
MacCampbell (of Tyrone), are of
this *Cineal Feareaduighe.* (See Note
under the " Cowell " No. 1 pedigree.)
100. Maoldun : son of Fearedach.
101. Maolruanaidh [mulroona] :
his son.

102. Tighearna   (" tighearna :"
Irish, *a lord, an owner;* Lat. " tyr-
ann-us ;" Gr. " turann-os"): his son;
a quo *O'Tighearnaighe,* anglicised
Tierney.
103. Ciarnain (" ciar :" Irish, *dark-
grey,* and " ciar," *a comb;* " an,"
one who): his son; a quo *O'Ciarnain* and *MacCiarnain.*
104. Cearnach (2) : his son.
105. Lochlann : his son.
106. Donoch : his son.
107. Lochlann (2) : his son.
108. Feargal : his son.
109. Torloch : his son.
110. Flaitheartach : his son.
111. Tighearnan : his son.
112. Michiall [Michael] : his son.
113. Eocha : his son.
114. Aongus : his son.
115. Murtagh : his son.
116. Teige : his son.
117. Giollachriosd : his son.
118. Concobhar [connor] : his son.
119. Hugh (2): his son; had a
brother named Connor.
120. Melaghlin : his son.

* *MacKiernan :* There is a " McKiernan" family in the county Leitrim and in
America, which we are as yet unable to connect with the foregoing Stem. For the
present we give that genealogy in its alphabetical order.

121. Teige : his son.
122. Hugh MacKiernan : his son ; living A.D. 1709 ; first of the family who, after the battle of the Boyne, settled in the county Leitrim ; had a brother named Michael.

KILBRIDE.

Arms : Or, an oak tree eradicated vert.

BRADACHAN, who is No. 103 on the "Boyle" pedigree, had a younger son named Giolla-Brighid, who was the ancestor of *MacGiollabrighid ;* anglicised *Gilbride,* and *Kilbride.*

103. Bradachan: son of Murtagh.
104. Giollabrighid (meaning " the devoted of St. Bridget") : his son ; a quo *MacGiollabrighid.*
105. Murtagh : his son.
106. Dermod : his son.
107. Ranall : his son.
108. Fionngal : his son.

109. Teige : his son.
110. Rory : his son.
111. Giollabrighid (2) : his son.
112. Fionn : his son.
113. Aongus : his son.
114. Giollabrighid MacGilbride : his son.

KILKELLY. (No. 1.)

Arms : Vert two lions ramp. combatant, supporting a tower triple-towered or, all between three crescents ar.

FERGAL, brother of Hugh, who is No. 97 on the "O'Shaughnessy" pedigree, was ancestor of *O'Giollaceallaighe ;* anglicised *Gillic, Gilly, Gilkelly, Killikelly, Kilkelly,* and *Cox.**

97. Fergal ; son of Artgal.
98. Tiobrad : his son.
99. Camogach : his son.
100. Cumascrach : his son.
101. Edalach : his son.
102. Cleireach : his son ; a quo *O'Clery.*
103. Eidhean : his son.
104. Flann : his son.
105. Maolfabhal (" fabhal :" Irish, *a report, a fable;* Lat. " fabul-a") :

his son ; a quo *O'Maolfabhail,* anglicised *Mulfavill,* and *Mulhall.*
106. Cugeal : his son.
107. Giollabeartach (or Gilbert) : his son.
108. Aodh (or Hugh) : his son.
109. Giolla Ceallach (" ceallach :" Irish, *war, strife*) : his son ; a quo *O'Giollaceallaighe.*
110. Moroch : his son.
111. Giollapadraic : his son.

---

* *Cox :* Of this family is the respected Dr. Cox, of 45 Stephen's Green, Dublin, Physician to St. Vincent's Hospital ; living in 1887.

112. Gillruaidhe ("ruaidhe :" Irish, *erysipelas*) : his son.
113. Morogh (2) : his son.

114. Florence MacGillkelly : his son.

KILKELLY. (No. 2.)

Of the O'Clery Stock.

Arms : Or, three nettle leaves vert.

GIOLLA-NA-NAOMH, a brother of Braon who is No. 107 on the " O'Clery" pedigree, was the ancestor of *O'Giolla Ceallaigh ;* anglicised *Kilkelly.*

107. Giolla na Naomh : son of Congalach O'Clery.
108. Flann : his son.
109. Conchobhar : his son.

110. Aodh : his son.
111. Giolla Ceallaigh : his son ; a quo *O'Giolla Ceallaigh.*
112. Giolla na Naomh : his son.

KINSELLA.

Chiefs of Hy-Cinselagh, in the County Wexford.

Arms : Ar. a fess gu. betw. in chief two garbs of the last, and in base a lion pass. sa.

EANNA CEANNSALACH, younger brother of Donal Caomhanach who is No. 115 on the "Kavanagh" pedigree, was the ancestor of *O'Ceannsalaighe* (ceann :" Irish, *the head ;* " salach :" *unclean*) ; anglicised *Kinselagh, Kinsela, Kingsley, Kinsley,* and *Tinsley.*

115. Eanna Ceannsalach : son of Dermod-na-nGall, King of Leinster ; first assumed the sirname *Kinselagh.*
116. Tirlach (" tor," gen. " tuir :" Irish, *a tower* or *bulwark ;* Lat. " tur-ris ;" and " leac :" Irish, *a stone*) : his son ; a quo *MacTorleice,* anglicised *MacTirloch, MacTerence, MacTerry,* and *Terrie.*
117. Moroch : his son.
118. Thomas Fionn : his son.
119. Dermod : his son ; had an elder brother named Art, who was slain by MacMorough, in 1383, and from whom descended *Slioght Thomas Fionn.*
120. Art : his son.
121. Donoch : his son.
122. Arthur : his son.
123. Donoch (2) : his son.
124. Edmund Kinselagh : his son.
125. Dermod Dubh : his son ; Chief of the sept in 1580.

KIRWAN. (No. 1.)

Of Galway.

Arms : Ar. a chev. sa. betw. three Cornish choughs ppr.

ANDREW KIROVANE, of Galway, gent., had :

2. Peter (or Patrick) who had :

3. Robert (his fourth son), of Galway, gent., who died 23rd December, 1636. He m. Maria, dau. of Nicholas Martin,* of Galway, gent., and had four sons and three daughters :

I. Nicholas.
II. John.
III. Richard.
IV. Robuck.
I. Joan.
II. Agnes.
III. Margaret.
4. Nicholas Kirwan :   son of Robert.

KIRWAN. (No. 2.)

Of Galway.

Arms : Same as those of " Kirwan" (No. 1).

THOMAS KEOGH (or Caoch) KIR-WAN, of Galway, had:

2. Thomas Oge, Alderman, who had :

3. Andrew, Alderman, who had :

4. Patrick, Alderman, who had :

5. Andrew, of Galway, Alderman, who d. 11th January, 1639. He m. Margaret, dau. of Edmund French,

of Galway, Alderman, and had three sons and three daughters :

I. Patrick.†
II. Martin.
III. William.
I. Giles.
II. Mary.
III. Katherine.

* *Martin* : The study of the origin of *Family Arms* has often interested us. Richard Martin (of Ballinahinch, in Connemara), M.P. for the county of Galway, the author of the Act of Parliament for Prevention of Cruelty to Animals, popularly known as " Martin's Act ;" and his son Thomas Martin, M.P. for said county, used to state that the *origin* of the Arms borne by their family, was as follows :

In days when the various Irish septs, if they had no common enemy to oppose, were engaged in fighting among themselves, the Martins and the O'Flaherties were thus amusing themselves. The O'Flaherties advanced against the Martins in such force, that the utter extirpation of the latter family must have necessarily followed upon their defeat. The fateful encounter of the opposing parties took place on a Good Friday, and, after a fearful struggle, the Martins proved victorious, and were enabled to return home safely for the celebration of Easter. In grateful commemoration of this signal deliverance from " ye bloodie O'Flaherties," they (the Martins) adopted thenceforward for the family Arms a *Calvary Cross*, etc. ; with the Motto : *Auxilium meum a Domino.*

† *Patrick* : Patrick Kirwan was (in 1646) a member of the " Supreme Council of the Catholic Confederation," whose son Martin married into the Bodkin family, and was the father of Captain Patrick Kirwan, of Lord Bofin's Infantry, in the service of King James II. Captain Kirwan married in 1703 Mary, daughter of Richard Martin, of Dangan, and on the death of his father in 1705, succeeded to the Cregg estates.

LAFFAN.

Arms : Or, on a chief indented az. three plates

1. JAMES LAFFAN of Garristown, co. Tipperary.
2. Thomas: his son.
3. James of Garristown : his son.
4. Thomas of Lurgoe, county Tipperary : his son ; m. Ellen, dau. of Thomas Den, of Grenane, county Kilkenny, by whom he had Henry, No. 5 on this stem. This Thomas, who d. 6th December, 1638, was secondly married to Joan, dau. of Edmund Tobyn of Kilnegogonah, county Tipperary, and by her had issue—1. James, who m. Elin, dau. of David Bourke ; 2. Edmund, m. to Mary, dau. of William Dillon of Roscommon ; 3. Edward ; 4. Richard ; 5. Patrick.

5. Henry: eldest son of Thomas ; m. first, Mary, dau. of Edmund Mandeville ; and, secondly, Ellen, dau. of John Butler, uncle of Richard (Lord Mountgarrett), and of Edward Butler ; d. s. p.

LANE.

Of Ulster.

Arms : Gu. a lion pass. guard. betw. three saltires couped or.

FEARACH, one of the eight sons of Daimhin, who is No. 92 on the "O'Hart" pedigree, was the ancestor of *O'Lainne* ("lann :" Irish, *the blade of a sword ;* Lat. "lan-io," *to cut*); anglicised *Lane*, and *Laney*. By some the Irish name is spelled *O'Lainidh*.

93. Fearach : son of Daimhin.
94. Maoldun : his son.
95. Fogharthach : his son.
96. Eochaidh : his son.
97. Dur ("dur :" Irish, *dull ;* Lat. "dur-us"): his son ; a quo *Clan Duire* (lords of Fermanagh), anglicised *Dwyer*.
98. Eochaidh (2) : his son.

99. Cathal : his son.
100. Muireadach : his son. This Muireadach had six brothers, one of whom, named Congmhail, was ancestor of *Larkin ;* another named Eochaidh was ancestor of *Malone ;* and another named Fiachan was the ancestor of *Feehan, Vaughan,* etc.

He had two sons by that lady :—1. Martin, who succeeded him, and 2. Richard (died 1779), who was an officer in Dillon's regiment of the Irish Brigade. Martin, married Mary, daughter of Hyacinth French of Cloughballymore, co. Galway, and had four sons :—1. Patrick, who was killed in a duel, s. p. ; 2. Richard, LL.D., the celebrated Chemist and Geologist (mentioned in p. 227 of Webb's *Compendium of Irish Biography*), and President of the Royal Irish Academy, he died in Dublin, on the 22nd of June, 1812 ; 3. Andrew ; 4. Hyacinth.

2 K

LARKIN.

Arms : Chequy gu. and ar. a cross az.

CONGMHAIL, brother of Muireadach, who is No. 100 on the "Lane" pedigree, was the ancestor of *O'Lorcain*, ("lor :" Irish, *enough*, and "can," *to sing ;* Hind. "gan-i," *to chant*), anglicised *Larkin*, and *Larcom*.

LAVAN.

Of Clan Colla.

Arms : Or, six lozenges gu.

ORGIALL, who is No. 101 on the "Maguire" pedigree, had a brother named Dallach, who was the ancestor of *O'Lamhain* ("lamh :" Irish, *a hand ;* Gr. "lab-o," *I take*), meaning "the descendants of the man with the small or withered hand ;" anglicised *Lavan*.

LAWLOR.

Of Monaghan.

Arms : Or, a lion ramp. guard. gu.

DONACHAN, brother of Paul who is No. 99 on the "MacMahon" (of Ulster) pedigree, was the ancestor of *O'Leathlabhair ;* anglicised *Lalor*, and *Lawlor*.

99. Donachan : son of Foghartach.

100. Fogharthach : his son.

101. Lagnan : his son.

102. Muireadach : his son.

103. Fogharthach : his son.

104. Leathlabhair : his son ; a quo *O'Leathalabhair*. This name is derived from the Irish, "leath" [lah], *a half ;* "labhair" *to speak* (old Irish "labh ;" Lat. "labium," *a lip*), and "leabhar" (Lat. "Liber," Fr. "livre"), *a book*. *O'Leathlabhair* means "the descendants of the man who stammered ;" as *O'Labhairmor* (anglicised *Larmour*) means those descended from "the man who was a great speaker."

LEE.

Arms : Ar. a cross betw. four fleurs-de-lis sa.

ARMHORACH, a brother of Finchadh who is No. 94 on the " O'Dwyer" (of Leinster) pedigree, was the ancestor of *O'Macliaigh ;* anglicised *MacLea,* and *Lee.*

94. Armhorach : son of Fearruith.
95. Mal : his son.
96. Ogan : his son.
97. Olchon : his son.
98. Macliagh ("mac :" Irish, *bright ;* "liagh, *a physician*) : his son ; a quo *O'Macliaigh.*

99. Caolbha : his son.
100. Dioma : his son.
101. Sinil : his son.
102. Maoldobhron : his son.
103. Eathac : his son.
104. Caolbha : his son.
105. Duneccneach : his son.

LEMON.

Arms : Az. a fess betw. three dolphins hauriant ar.

LOMAN, a brother of Lughach who is No. 92 on the (No. 1) " O'Kelly" (of Hy-Maine) pedigree, was the ancestor of *O'Lomain ;* anglicised *Lemon,* and *Lowman.*

92. Loman ("loman :" Irish, *an ensign*) : a son of Dallan ; a quo *O'Lomain.*
93. Aongus : his son.
94. Ainmireach : his son.
95. Eathach ; his son.
96. Maolandadh : his son.
97. Maolduin : his son.
98. Reachtaghan ("reachtgha :" Irish, *a law imposed by force of arms*) :

his son : a quo *O'Reachtaghain,* anglicised *Rhattgian.*
99. Coibdealg : his son.
100. Fomosach : his son.
101. Condmuigh : his son.
102. Eathach : his son.
103. Droigheann : his son.
104. Conliogan : his son.
105. Ruadhri O'Lomain : his son.

LEONARD.

Arms : Or, on a fesse az. three fleurs-de-lis ar.   *Crest* : Out of a ducal coronet or, a tiger's head ar.

GIOLLAFINNEAN, who is No. 105 on the " Mulroy" pedigree, was the ancestor of *MacGiollafinneain ;* anglicised *MacGillfinen, Gillfinan, Gill-*

finnon, Gillinan, Gillion, Gillon, Glennon, Lennard, Leonard, and *Linden.* (See the "Gillon" pedigree.)

105. Giollafinnean : son of Maol-ruanaidh Mór.

106. Rath : his son.

107. Aongus, Feargal, Uillimed, Donall, Conchobar Dhall, and Giolla Phadraic : his sons.

LOFTUS.

Arms : Vert a dexter hand couped apaumée, and in chief an arrow fessways ar.

AONGUS, brother of Bladhmhach, who is No. 92 on the "Fox" pedigree, was the ancestor of *O'Lachtnain ;* anglicised *Loughnan,* and *Loftus.*

92. Aongus: son of Hugh.

93. Bladhmhach : his son.

94. Congmhail : his son.

95. Beice: his son.

96. Congmhail (2) : his son.

97. Conang : his son.

98. Maolciaran : his son.

99. Lachtnan (*lachtna :* Irish, " a coarse grey dress," *an,* " one who") ; a quo *O'Lachtnain.*

LOGAN.*

Arms : Or, three passion nails in point piercing a man's heart gu.

LOCHAN, a son of Daimhin who is No. 92 on the "O'Hart" pedigree, was the ancestor of *O'Lochain* ("lochan :" Irish, *chaff, a pool*) ; anglicised *Logan, Logue,* and *Pool.*

* *Logan :* James Logan, a statesman, and secretary to William Penn, was born at Lurgan, on the 20th October, 1674. His parents were members of the Society of Friends. He became Chief Justice of the State of Pennsylvania, Provincial Secretary, and Commissioner of Property, and for nearly two years governed the Province as President of the Council. He visited England in 1710, where he successfully vindicated himself from charges brought against him by a faction in the Assembly. He did not retire from public life until about 1747. Thenceforward, living in dignified leisure at Stenton, near Germantown, he devoted himself to literature, translated Cicero, and penned those scientific papers which will be found appended to his *Memoirs.* Some of his works were printed by his friend Benjamin Franklin. He died at Stenton, 31st October, 1751, and was interred in the Friends' burial ground, Arch-street, Philadelphia.

LONGAN.

Arms : Vert three lions ramp. or.

BREASAL, brother of Beice, king of Orgiall who is No. 98 on the "Magellan" pedigree, was the ancestor of *O'Longain ;* anglicised *Long, Longan, Langan,* and *Langhan.*

98. Breasal: son of Cumascach.
99. Fiachnach : his son.
100. Longan ("long :" Irish, *a ship ;* "an," *one who*) : his son ; a quo *O'Longain.*

101. Eiteach : his son.
102. Eachagan : his son.
103. Eatach : his son.
104. Giollachriosd O'Longan: his son.

LYNCH.

Of Tirowen.

Arms : Ar. a cross sa. betw. four lions ramp. gu. armed and langued az.

LONGSEACH, a brother of Diarmaid who is No. 97 on the "Kennedy" (of Tirowen) pedigree, was the ancestor of *O'Loingsigh,* of Tirowen; anglicised *Linch, Lynch,* and *Lynskey.*

97. Longseach ("longseach :" Irish, *a mariner*): son of Conchobhar ; a quo *O'Loingsigh.*
98. Conchobhar : his son.
99. Branan : his son.
100. Cinaoth : his son.

101. Maoldoradh: his son.
102. Cathalan : his son.
103. Giollagrinde : his son ; had two brothers—1. Giolla-Tighearnach, 2. Cearnach.

MacANASPIE.

Arms : Per fess or and erm. a fess az. betw. in chief a bishop's hat vert, and in base two gem rings of the first, gemmed of the third.   *Crest :* Out of a ducal coronet or, a rock ppr.

THIS sirname is derived from Giolla-Easbuig ("giolla :" Irish, *the devoted of ;* "easbog," gen. "easbuig," *a bishop ;* Lat. "episcop-us"), who is No. 102 on the "O'Hagan" (Lords of Tullaghoge) genealogy ; as are also the sirnames : *McGillanespick, McAnespick, McAnespie, McAnaspie, McAnaspog, Gillaspy, Gillaspie, Gillespy, Gillespie, Gillesbie,* etc. We are, however, unable to give the pedigree of the family.

MACAULAY.

Arms : Ar. a lion ramp. gu. armed and langued az. in chief two dexter hands couped at the wrist of the second. *Crest :* A demi lion ramp. gu.

MAOLFOGHARTHACH, brother of Donall, who is No. 92 on the "Breen" pedigree, was the ancestor of *MacAmhailgaidh;* anglicised *Macaulay, MacAuley, MacAwley, MacGawly, Magauly, MacGawley, McGauly,* and *Wythe.* (Some genealogists would derive these families from Ithe, the Uncle of Milesius of Spain.)

92. Maolfogharthach : son of Creamthann.

93. Conn : his son.

94. Aodh (or Hugh) : his son.

95. Cathasach : his son.

96. Conn (2) : his son.

97. Donall : his son.

98. Suibhneach : his son.

99. Foranan ("foran :" Irish, *anger, a short verse*) : his son ; a quo *O'Foranain,* anglicised *Foran.*

100. Cucroidhe (" croidhe :" Irish, *a heart;* Gr. "kardia") : his son.

101. Feargal : his son.

102. Amhailgadh ("amhail:" Irish, *like ;* " gad," *a withe, a willow twig*) : his son ; a quo *MacAmhailgaidh.*

103. Hugh MacGawly : his son ; first assumed this sirname.

104. Florence : his son.

105. Donall : his son.

106. Murtogh : his son.

107. Mór (or Magnus) : his son.

108. Hugh (3) : his son.

109. Murtogh (2) : his son.

110. Amhailgadh [awly] : his son.

111. Awly Oge : his son.

112. Awly (4) : his son.

113. Brian : his son.

114. Awly Mór : his son.

115. Awly Maol : his son.

116. Feargal (or Farrell) Carrach : his son.

117. Farrell Oge : his son.

118. Awly (5) : his son.

119. William, of Williamstown, in Westmeath : his son.

120. Murtogh, of Williamstown : his son ; married to Eliza, dau. of Hugh Coffey of Ro...... , co. Westmeath ; died on 24th Feb., 1632.

121. Awly Magawly : his son. This Awly, who m. Elleanor, dau. of James FitzGerald, of Laragh, co. Westmeath, had five brothers—1. Owen, 2. Robert, 3. Richard, 4. Felim, 5. Gerald ; he had also two sisters—1. Elizabeth, wife of Thomas Dillon of Lissenack, co. Westmeath ; and 2. Beamone, wife of Donoch O'Daly, son of Æneas O'Daly of Clonerillick, in the co. Westmeath.

MacBRADY.*

From the De La Ponce MSS.

Barons of Loughtee, County Cavan.

Arms : Sa. in the sinister base a dexter hand couped at the wrist ppr. pointing with the index finger to the sun in splendour in the dexter chief or.

1. Denis MacBrady, married Susan McKernan.

2. Charles : his son ; married

Elizabeth O'Donnell, daughter of Prince of Tirconnell.

* *MacBrady :* This "MacBrady" family of Calry had the *alias* "O'Carroll."

3. Charles: his son; married Jeanne MacMahon.

4. Gillaume: his son; married Therise O'Rourke.

5. Daniel: his son; married Honoria MacBrady.

6. Martin, lord of Loughtee: his son; married Anna O'Dooley. Had a brother Jean, who had Patrice, who had Bernard, who had Jacques-Bernard.

7. Gillaume: son of Martin.

8. Alexis-Joseph Augustin: his son: had three sons—1. Eugene, d. 1767, s. p.; 2. Felix, d. 1770, s. p.; 3. Francois-Joseph, d. 1820.

9. Francois - Joseph: son of Alexis.

10. Benoit Jh. Constant Mac-Brady: his son.

MacBRANNEN.

Arms : Sa. an eagle displ. or, and a border compony az. and gu.

BRANAN, a brother of Combhach, who is No. 110 on the "Dunne" pedigree, was the ancestor of *MacBranain*, anglicised *MacBrannen*, and *Brannen*.

110. Branan ("bran :" Irish, *a raven**: son of Caroill; a quo *Mac-Branain*.

111. Congalach: his son.

112. Cusliabh: his son.

113. Caroill: his son.

114. Giollacumhdach: his son.

115. Amhailgadh [awly] : his son.

116. Melachlin: his son.

117. Awly (2) : his son.

118. Murtagh : his son.

119. Awly (3) : his son.

120. Awly Oge MacBrannen: his son.

MacCAWELL.

THIS family name in Irish (see the "Cowell" No. 1 pedigree, p. 391) is *Mac Cathmhaoil*. From O'Donovan's Annals of the Four Masters we learn the following information respecting this ancient family:

A.D. 1185. Gilchreest MacCawell, Chief of Kinel-Farry,† and of the

---

* *Raven* : This Branan must have had hair as dark as a raven ; or, in battle, have been as impetuous as a mountain torrent: for *bran*, which also means "chaff," has those meanings. It may be here observed that *bran* is the root of the sirnames *Brain, Brian, Brien, Bryan, Bryant, Byrne, Byron, O'Brien, O'Byrne,* and of the Latin *Bren-us.* And it may be added that "Brannen" and "Brennan" are distinct sirnames.

† *Kinel-Farry* : Of this Clan, Dr. O'Donovan, in Note *m* in the Annals, under the year 1185, says : "Kinel-Farry (in Irish, *Cinel Feareaduighe*) and the Clans. The territory of Kinel-Farry, the patrimonial inheritance of the MacCawells (the descendants of Fergal, son of Muireadhach, son of Eoghan, son of Niall of the Nine Hostages), was nearly co extensive with the barony of Clogher, in the county of Tyrone ; in which barony all the clans here mentioned were located, except the Hy-Kennoda and the

Clans, viz., Clann Aengus, Clann Duibhinreacht, Clann Fogarty, Hy-
Kennoda, and Clann Colla in Fermanagh, and who was chief adviser of all
the north of Ireland, was slain by O'Hegny and Muintir-Keevan, who
carried away his head, which, however, was recovered from them in a
month afterwards.

A.D. 1215. Murrough MacCawell, Chief of Kinel-Farry, died.

A.D. 1238. Flaherty MacCawell, Chief of Kinel-Farry, and Clann-
Congail, and of Hy-Kennoda in Fermanagh, the most illustrious in Tyrone
for feats of arms and hospitality, was treacherously slain by Donough
MacCawell, his own kinsman.

A.D. 1215. Donough MacCawell, Chief of Kinel-Farry, was slain by the
men of Oriel.

A.D. 1252. Conor MacCawell, Chief of Kinel-Farry and many other
territories, and peace-maker of Tirconnell, Tyrone, and Oriel, was slain by
the people of Brian O'Neill, while defending his protegés against them, he
himself being under the protection* of O'Gormley and O'Kane.

The name *MacCawell* also occurs in O'Donovan's Annals of the Four
Masters, under the following years: A.D. 1261—1262—1346—1358—
1365 — 1366—1368—1370—1379—1403—1404—1432—1434 — 1444—
1461—1467 — 1474—1480—1481—1492—1493—1498—1508 — 1515—
1518—1519.

Dr. O'Donovan also mentions the Kinel-Farry, or *Cinel Fereadaigh*,
under the following years : A.D. 626—632—1082—1120—1129—1166—
1507—1511—1516—1531.

In the Index to Wills, Diocese of Derry District Registry of Londonderry, the following names occur: Robert MacCawell, of Drumragh, A.D.
1734. Owen MacCawell of Drumragh, 1718. Thomas MacCawell of
Drumragh, 1723. Hugh MacCawell, 1737, to be buried in the churchyard
of Clogher.

In the Index to Wills, Clogher District, Registry Armagh, appear the
names: Patrick MacCawell, Bolies, county Tyrone, A.D. 1790. Owen
MacCawell, Cavan, co. Tyrone, 1806. Bernard MacCawell, Scotstown, co.
Monaghan, 1809. Rev. Fergus MacCawell, of Cornamuck, 1758. And
Hugh MacCawell, of Aughanameena, co. Monaghan, 1802.

In the *Fate and Fortunes of Hugh O'Neill, Earl of Tyrone, and Rory
O'Donel, Earl of Tyrconnel*, by the Rev. C. P. Meehan, M.R.I.A., we read that

---

Clan-Colla, who were seated in Fermanagh. The Hy-Kennoda gave name to the
barony of *Tir-Kennedy*, which is situated in the east of Fermanagh, adjoining the
barony of Clogher, in Tyrone.—See it mentioned in the Annals at the years 1427, 1468,
and 1518 ; and in the "Davin" pedigree, *infra*.
　　The family of *MacCathmhaoil* (a name generally anglicised *MacCawell*, and
latinized *Cavellus*), who supplied several bishops to the see of Clogher, are still
numerous in this their ancient territory, and the name is also found in other counties,
variously anglicised *Camphill*, *Cambell*, *Caulfield*, etc., and even *Howell;* but the
natives, when speaking the Irish language, always pronounce the name *MacCathmhaoil*.

　　* *Under the protection* : This passage is not in the Dublin copy of the Annals of
Ulster, but, in the old translation preserved in the British Museum, it is given in
English, as follows : "A.D. 1252. Conner MacCathmoyle, kingly chief of Kindred
Feragh and many other places, also the upholder of liberality and fortitude of the
North of Ireland ; the peace-maker of the Connells and Owens, and Airgialls also,
killed by the Rutes (*cohortes*) of Brien O'Neal, defending his comrick from them, being
upon O'Garmely and O'Cahan's word himself."

Rev. Father Hugh Cawell or MacCawell was afterwards Archbishop of Armagh, in 1626 ; and in the same volume we meet the name of Hugh Cawell or MacCaughwell.—See pp. 249, 322, 324, and 327 of that great work.

And in the Registry of Deeds Office, Dublin, we find in Book 79, p. 244, Memorial 55,639, the name of Bryan McCowell of Bishop's Court, county Kildare, gent., as a witness to a Deed made respecting Robert Colvill of Newtown, co. Down, son and heir of Hugh Colvill of same ; and registered on the 17th April, 1735. It is possible that this Bryan McCowell, of Bishop's Court, in 1735, was the Bryan Cowell, of Logadowden, in the county Dublin, mentioned in the "Cowell" (No. 3) pedigree, whose Will was proved in 1768 in the Prerogative Court, Dublin.

MacDERMOT. (No. 1.)

Princes of Moylurg, County Roscommon.

Arms : Ar. on a chev. gu. betw. three boars' heads erased az. tusked and bristled ar, as many cross crosslets ar.   *Crest :* A demi lion ramp. az. holding in the dexter paw a sceptre crowned or.

MAOLRUANAIDH [MULROONA] MÓR, a younger brother of Conchobhar (or Connor) who is No. 106 on the "O'Connor" (Kings of Connaught) pedigree, was the ancestor of "Clan Mulroona ;" the leading family of which was *MacDiarmuid*, anglicised *MacDermott*. Among the other families of "Clan Mulroona" were—1. *Mulrooney*, modernized *Rooney*, *Roney*, and *Rowney* ; 2. *MacDonough*, *O'Crolly*, etc.

106. Mulroona Mór : son of Teige, married the dau. of Flann Abraid O'Malley.

107. Murtogh : his son ; Prince of Moylurg ; m. the dau. of O'Dowd, Lord of Tyrawley.

108. Teige : his son ; had a brother Mulroona, who was the ancestor of *O'Crolly*.

109. Mulroona : second son of Teige.

110. Teige Mór : his son.

111. Diarmaid ("diarmaid :" Irish, *the god of arms*) : his son ; a quo *MacDiarmuid*. Had two brothers —1. Donoch, the ancestor of *O'Morris ;* 2. Teige Oge, ancestor of *MacLaughlan*, of Connaught.

112. Conchobhar (or Connor) : his son ; was the first of this family who assumed this sirname.

113. Tomaltach (or Timothy) na Carriga ("cairig :" Irish, *a rock*) : his son.

114. Cormac, Lord of Moylurg : his son ; had a brother Donoch.

115. Conchobhar, Lord of Moylurg : son of Cormac ; living A.D. 1251.

116. Giollachriosd : his son ; had a brother Diarmaid Dall, who was the ancestor of MacDermott Roe (Ruadh).

117. Mulroona : son of Giollachriosd.

118. Timothy : his son.

119. Conor : his son.

120. Hugh : his son.

121. Rory Caoch*: his son.

122. Rory Oge : his son.

123. Teige : his son.

124. Rory : his son.

125. Brian : his son.

126. Brian Oge : his son ; d. 1636.

127. Tirlogh (or Terence) : his son ; died unmarried in 1640. Had a brother named Charles, who died in 1693 ; and another brother named Teige na n-Gadhar.

128. Hugh : son of said Charles ; died 1707. Was an officer under James II., and a prisoner at the Battle of Aughrim ; had a brother Timothy, who had Andrew, who had John† and other children.

129. Charles (2) : his son ; d. 1758 ; got Coolavin ; had a brother Terence, an M.P. in King James's Parliament, and attainted.

130. Myles : his son ; d. 1777 ; had a brother Terence, and another Hugh. This Hugh had Charles, who m. Arabella O'Rourke, and had several children.

131. Hugh (2) : his son ; d. 1824.

132. Charles : his son ; d. 1873.

133. Hugh MacDermott, of Coolavin, Q.C., J.P., living in 1887 : his son ; Chief of the Clan, and known as the "Hereditary Prince of Coolavin."

MacDERMOT ROE. (No. 2.)

Of Kilronan.

Arms : Same as those of " MacDermott" (No. 1).

DIARMAID Dall, a brother of Giollachriosd who is No. 116 on the (No. 1) "MacDermott" pedigree, was the ancestor of *MacDermott Ruadh* (or MacDermott Roe.")

116. Diarmaid Dall : son of Conchobhar (or Connor), Lord of Moylurg, who was living in 1251.

117. Cormac : his son.

118. Diarmuid Ruadh ("ruadh :" Irish, *red*) : his son ; a quo *MacDermott Roe* ; living in 1320.

119. Cormac Oge : his son.

120. Melaghlin : his son.

121. Teige : his son.

122. Eoghan : his son.

123. Diarmaid : his son ; had a brother Owen.‡

124. Maghnus : his son.

---

* *Caoch :* This Rory Caoch is the first name on the (No. 3) "MacDermot" pedigree, *infra*, which is taken from the MS. Volume, F. 3. 27, in the Library of Trinity College, Dublin.

† *John :* This John had three sons : 1. Edward, whose only son suffered death in 1798 ; 2. John ; and 3. another son who was a General in the American Service, and settled there. This last mentioned John had John Wynne MacDermott, who had four sons :—1. John-Wynne, 2. James, 3. Phibbs, 4. William. This branch may be looked on as the third line of the sept.

‡ *Owen :* This Owen had Teige : who had Connor (Patentee of 1608) ; who had Charles Dubh : who had Henry of Kilronan (who, in 1667, had confirmation of his estates on a Decree of Innocence) : who had two sons—1. Henry (d. s. p.) ; 2. John, B.L., who had four sons—1. Charles (d. s. p.) ; 2. Thomas (died 1823), of whom presently ; 3. A son, who was a Roman Catholic Bishop of Ardagh : 4. Matthew, an M.D., who had Charles, an M.D. ; 5. Charles. This Thomas (who died 1823) had two sons—1. French ; 2. Molloy ; and French had—1. Thomas MacDermot Roe, and 2. William-French MacDermot Roe, of the 49th Regiment.

125. Maghnus : his son.
126. Cathal (or Charles) : his son.
127. Conchobhar : his son ; living in 1657.

128. Dubhaltach (or Dudley) Mac-Dermott Roe : his son.

MacDERMOT. (No. 3.)

Of Carrig, County Roscommon.

Arms : Ar. three boars pass. az. armed and bristled or.   *Crest :* A boar's head erased az.

RORY KEOGH (*recté "Caoch"*) MAC-DERMOT* had :

2. Rory, who had :
3. Teige, who had :
4. Rory, who had :
5. Bryan, who had :
6. Bryan,† of Carig, co. Roscommon, Esq., who d. 8 Jan., 1636. He m. Margaret, dau. of Richard Bourke, of Derrymaclaghny, co. Galway, Esq., and had :
  I. Tirlogh, of whom presently.
  II. Connor, s.p.

III. Brian.
IV. Teige.
7. Tirlogh : the eldest son of Bryan ; m. twice : his first wife was Margaret, dau. of Feagh Burke MacDavy. His second wife was Ellenor, dau. of William Molloy, of Croghan, co. Roscommon, Esq. But in F. 3. 27 it does not appear that by either marriage there was any issue.—See No. 127 on the "MacDermot" (No. 1) pedigree.

MacDONAGH.

Of the County Galway.

Arms : Ar. a lion pass. gu. betw. in chief a mullet sa.   *Crest :* A dexter arm erect, couped at the elbow, vested az. cuffed ar.

TERENCE MACDONOGH, of Creevagh, M.P. for Sligo, in 1689, and who d. in 1718, was the only Catholic Counsel who was admitted to the Bar in Ireland, up to his death, after the violation of the Treaty of Limerick,

---

* *MacDermot :* This is the Rory Caoch MacDermot who is No. 121 on the "Mac-Dermot" (No. 1) pedigree.

† *Bryan :* In Ulster's Office the Fun. Entry of this Brian MacDermot is dated 1637.

in 1691. From that Terence the descent, so far as we have yet ascertained, is as follows:

1. Terence MacDonogh, M.P. for Sligo in 1689, m. and had five sons:
I. John.
II. Redmond, of whom presently.
III. Daniel.
IV. Nicholas.
V. John, who went to America.

2. Redmond: second son of Terence; m. and had two sons:
I. Daniel, of whom presently.
II. Redmond, who m. and had a daughter Mary, and three sons.
I. Patrick, who had two daus. and three sons:
I. Admiral William Mac-Donagh, who fought under General Washington; and after whom "MacDonagh County" in G e o r g i a, U.S.A., is so called. Some of this Patrick's descendants are now (1887) living in Rhode Island, and one of them is Recorder there.
II. John, ancestor of Joseph MacDonagh, of San Francisco.
III. Henry.
Patrick's two daughters were:
I. Mary, who m. Geraghty of Knockerasser; with him emigrated to America; and whose family now (1887) resides in Lockport, State of New York.
II. Jude, who m. one of the Joyces, of Joyces' Country, West Galway.

3. Daniel: eldest son of Redmond; m. Miss O'Sullivan, and had two sons.

4. Daniel, the second son of Daniel, settled in Joyces' Country; m. Miss O'Grady, and subsequently removed to Craughwell, county

Galway, where he possessed a large farm and died. This Daniel had four sons and three daughters. The sons were:
I. Richard, who (in 1887) resides in California; is m. and has issue:
I. Daniel, m., and living in 1887.
II. Patrick: second son of Daniel, of whom presently.
III. John, m. in California, and has a numerous issue.
IV. Michael, living in California in 1887; no issue.
The three daughters of Daniel were:
I. Mary, who m. T. Ryne, and had:
I. William Ryne of Chicago;
II. Maria Ryne, who m. M. Ashe, of Galway.
II. Norah, who m. J. Conroy, and had two daughters:
I. Ellen, who m. J. Finnegan of Boston, U.S.A.
II. Honor, who m. T. Healy.
III. Bridget, residing (1887) in New York, unm.

4. Patrick, who died in 1881: second son of Daniel; was twice m.: first, to Miss MacGeoghegan, by whom he had one daughter named Ellen, who is m. in India; and, secondly, to Miss Cahill, by whom he had two sons and two daughters. The sons are:
I. Daniel, of whom presently; and
II. Henry-James, living in 1887.
The daughters of Patrick are:
I. Mary-Anne, who married John Gaffy, merchant in Troy, New York.
II. Matilda-Jane, living in 1887 in New York.

5. Daniel MacDonagh: eldest son of Patrick; living in 1887.

MacDONALD.

Of Wicklow, and of San Francisco.

BRIAN, a younger brother of Fearach who is No. 119 on the "MacDonnell" (of Leinster) pedigree, was the ancestor of MacDonnell, MacDonald, and McDonald, of the county Wicklow.

119. Brian MacDonnell: son of Hugh Buidhe [boy.]

120. Alexander: his son; m. a daughter of Thomas Archbold, of Wicklow.

121. Brian, who assumed the name MacDonald : * his son ; m. Mary, dau. of John Doyle, of Arklow, in the co. Wicklow. Was there engaged in the Tanning trade, which is still carried on in that county. Served in an Irish Volunteer Regiment, in the cause of King James II.; and, in 1691, after that cause was lost, this Brian MacDonald emigrated to America, with his wife and five children:—1. John, 2. William, 3. James, 4. Brian, 5. Mary. He settled near New Castle, Delaware, U.S.A., and had two more children—6. Richard, 7. Anabel; and d. 1707.

122. Brian: his fourth son; m. Catherine . . . , and had five sons and four daughters. The sons were—1. Richard, b. 1716 ; 2. James, b. 1718; 3. Edward, born 1720 ; 4. Joseph, b. 1722 ; 5. Bryan, b. 1732; the daughters were—1. Rebecca, b. 1724 ; 2. Catherine, b. 1727 ; 3. Mary, b. 1730; 4. Priscilla, b. 1734. Moved, about 1754, to Botetourt, county, Virginia where some of his descendants still live; d. 1757.

123. Joseph; his fourth son; m. Elizabeth Ogle and had nine sons and one daughter. The sons were —1. Bryan, b. 1753; 2. John, b. 1756 ; 3. Joseph, born 1758; 4. Edward, b. 1761 ; 5. Richard and 6. Alex. (twins), b. 1763 ; 7. William, b. 1766; 8. Jonas,† b. 1771 ; 9. James, b. 1774. The daughter

* Brian MacDonald : According to the MS. Vols. F. 2. 4, and F. 2. 6, in the Library of Trinity College, Dublin, the possessions of this family stretched along the foot of the mountain range, upon the marshes of the Pale, and bore the name of "The Clandonnell's Countrie," as late, at least, as 1641. Dr. O'Donovan in his edition of the Four Masters, Vol. V., p. 1641-2, writes: "In Col. Francis Toole's regiment of foot, in the service of King James II., was Lieut. Brian MacDonnell, fourth in descent from whom is Alexander MacDonnell, Esq., J.P., of Bonabrougha, in the county of Wicklow, who married Marcella, heiress of Charles O'Hanlon, Esq,, of Ballynorran, in the same county." Whether the Brian MacDonnell here mentioned by O'Donovan, were the Brian, who is No. 121, on this pedigree, we are unable to say. If they were not identical, they must have been both members of the Wicklow branch of the Mac-Donnell family.

† Jonas : This Jonas, who lived where many of the descendants now (1881) live, near Blackburg, Montgomery county, Va., and who d. 1856, m. Elizabeth Foster, and had ten children—1. Charles, b. 1798 ; m. Dioney Dickinson ; and d. 1864. 2. William, b. 1800 ; m. Lucinda Patton ; living near Blackburg, Va., in 1876. 3. Joseph, b. 1802 ; m. Lorena Ross ; d. 1855. 4. Nancy, b. 1806 ; married William McDonald ; living in 1876. 5. Elizabeth, b. 1808 ; m. Bryan McDonald, d. unm. 1871. 6. Mary, b. 1810 ; m. James N. Pierce; d. 1872. 7. Exceoney, b. 1812 ; d. unm., 1832. 8. James-Lewis, b. 1814 ; living unm. near Blackburg, Va., 1879. 9. John Alexander, b. 1816 ; m. Harriet McDonald ; living near Blackburg, Va., 1881. 10. Floyd-Fectig,

was Elizabeth, b. 1768. This Joseph and his family removed about 1768 to near Blackburg, Montgomery county, Virginia, were he died 1809.

124. Major Richard : fifth son of Joseph ; married Mrs. John Martin (née Mary Long), and had three sons and three daughters, all born near Mackville, Washington county, Kentucky. The sons were —1. James, b. 1797 ; 2. Joseph, b. 1799 ; 3. Griffin, b. 1801. The daughters were—1. Elizabeth, b. 1804 ; 2. Mary, b. 1804 ; 3. Ursula, b. 1808.

125. Colonel James : his son ; b. 1797 ; married near Macksville, Washington county, Kentucky, on 28th September, 1819, Martha Shepard Peter (living in San Francisco, California, in 1881 ; dau. of Jesse Peter and Milly Sweeney), and had twelve children. He was a Colonel in the State Militia, and was elected to the Kentucky Legislature in 1828, 1829, and 1832 ; and to the Kentucky Senate, from 1832—1837. He also held various other public offices. He went to Missouri in 1851, and to California in 1859, where he died 1865. Their

children were—1. Richard Hayes, born 1820 (who is No. 126 *infra*). 2. Milly-Ann, born 1822 ; married Dr. M. F. Wakefield ; died 1858. 3. Martin Pierce, born 1824 ; died 1824. 4. James-Monroe,* b. 1825 ; living unmarried in San Francisco, California, 1881. 5. Dewitt-Livingston, born 1828 ; married Martha Ellenor Hunter ; living in San Francisco, 1881. 6. Marion Jasper, born 1831 ; married Alice Booth ; living in San Francisco, 1881. 7. Marcus-Linsey, b. 1833 ; m. Ralphine North ; living in San Francisco, 1881. 8. Joseph William, born 1835 ; died unmarried, 1855. 9. Josephine Bonaparte, born 1837 ; married Robert W. Elliott ; living in San Francisco, 1881. 10. Maria-Louisa, b. 1840 ; married Alvin W. Whitney, died 1870. 11. Alice Fisk, born 1842 ; d. unm. 1867. 12. Martha Harriet, born 1848 ; married Frank Swift, died 1874.

126. Dr. Richard - Hayes Mc-Donald † of San Francisco, California: son of Colonel James ; b. near Macksville, Ky., 1820 ; m. 5th Aug. 1851, in Sacramento, Cal., Mrs. Sarah Maria Steinagel (née

b. July, 1819: m. Jane Black; living at Blackburg, Va., 1881. This Floyd has been for years one of the most intelligent and zealous labourers in the researches of this family.

* *James Monroe* : This James was (in 1881) one of the prominent men of the Pacific coast. He was State Senator in California Legislature in 1859 and 1860, and he has held a number of public offices. He and his brother Marion Jasper are both most successful capitalists.

† *McDonald :* Dr. R. H. McDonald was one of the California Pioneers, and has been a citizen of that State since 1849. His life has been eventful and historically interesting, and a biography of it is in preparation. He has been prominently connected with the whole development of the State ; and was (in 1881) President of the Pacific Bank in San Francisco, Cal., of which his brother Captain James and himself have been almost two of the founders. It was *solely* through Dr. R. H. McDonald's love of family, and his liberality in expressing it, that the large sum of nearly £2,000 which has been needed to collect the data in the genealogies of the several branches of this family, was secured. He also bore the entire expense of printing those data in three handsome and neatly compiled volumes ; with copies of which we have been favoured. To those volumes we would refer those anxious for more details ; they are compiled by Frank V. McDonald, Esq., Law Student, Harvard University, Cambridge, Mass., U.S.A., who is No. 127 on this pedigree.

Whipple), who d. 21st Oct., 1866. They had three children, all born in Sacramento, Cal.—1. Frank-Virgil, b. 20th April, 1852 (who is No. 127 *infra*). 2. Richard-Hayes, Junior, b. 28th Aug. 1854 ; is unm. ; studied abroad, and is (in 1881) graduating at Yale College, New Haven, Connecticut. 3. Martha Shepard, b. 7th April, 1859; studied abroad, and for three years at Vassar College, Poughkeepsie, New York : m. 17th Feb., 1879, John C. Spencer, Junior, both living in New York City, 1881.

127. Frank V. McDonald : son of Dr. Richard Hayes McDonald ; b. 20th April, 1852 ; unm. in 1881 ; was a student for some years in Germany, France, and England ; was graduated A.B., at Yale College, New Haven, in 1878, and at Harvard College, Cambridge, Massachusetts, in 1879—where in 1881 he was a Student-at-Law.

MacDONNELL. (No. 1.)

*Of Antrim.**

Arms ; Or, a lion ramp. gu.

COLLA UAIS [oose], a younger brother of Colla da Chrioch who is No. 85 on the "O'Hart" pedigree, was the ancestor of *MacDomhnaill*, of Antrim,

---

* *MacDonnell of Antrim :* There is a pedigree of this ancient family contained in the *De La Ponce MSS.*, deposited in the Library of the Royal Irish Academy, Dublin, which would well repay perusal.

In Connellan's *Four Masters* it is said :—Some of the ancestors of the tribe "Clan Colla" having gone from Ulster in remote times, settled in Scotland, chiefly in Argyle, and the Hebrides, and according to Lodge's Peerage on the MacDonnells, earls of Antrim, they became the most numerous and powerful clan in the Highlands of Scotland, where they were generally called MacDonalds. In the reign of Malcolm the Fourth, king of Scotland, in the 12th centuary, Samhairle (Somerled, or Sorley) Mac-Donnell was Thane of Argyle, and his descendants were styled lords of the Isles or Hebrides, and lords of Cantyre ; and were allied by intermarriages with the Norwegian earls of the Orkneys, Hebrides, and Isle of Man. The MacDonnells continued for many centuries to make a conspicuous figure in the history of Scotland, as one of the most valiant and powerful clans in that country. Some chiefs of these MacDonnells came to Ireland in the beginning of the thirteenth century ; the first of them mentioned in the *Annals of the Four Masters* being the sons of Randal, son of Sorley MacDonnell, the Thane or Baron of Argyle above mentioned ; and they, accompanied by Thomas MacUchtry (MacGuthrie or MacGuttry), a chief from Galloway, came, A.D. 1211, with seventy-six ships and powerful forces to Derry ; they plundered several parts of Derry and Donegal, and fresh forces of these Scots having arrived at various periods, they made some settlements in Antrim, and continued their piratical expeditions along the coasts of Ulster. The MacDonnells settled chiefly in those districts called the Routes and Glynnes, in the territory of ancient Dalriada, in Antrim ; and they had their chief fortress at Dunluce. They became very powerful, and formed alliances by marriage with the Irish princes and chiefs of Ulster ; as the O'Neills of Tyrone and Clanaboy, the O'Donnells of Donegal, the O'Kane of Derry, the MacMahons of Monaghan, etc. The MacDonnells carried on long and fierce contests with the Mac-Quillans, powerful chiefs in Antrim, whom they at length totally vanquished in the 16th century ; and seized on their lands and their chief fortress of Dunseverick, near the Giant's Causeway. The MacDonnells were celebrated commanders of galloglasses in Ulster and Connaught, and make a remarkable figure in Irish history, in the and of the lords of the Isles and chiefs of Glencoe; anglicised *MacDonnell*, in Ireland, and *MacDonald* and *Donaldson* in Scotland.

85. Colla Uais, the 121st Monarch of Ireland: son of Eochaidh Dubhlen.

86. Eochaidh: his son. Had two brothers—1. Roghain (" roghain :" Irish, *a choice*), who was ancestor of *O'Fiachry*, *MacUais*, etc., and a quo *O'Roghhain*, anglicised *Rowan ;* 2. Fiachra Tort, ancestor of *O'Flinn*, of Tuirtre (now the baronies of Toome and Antrim), of *O'Geuranaigh* (anglicised *Gurney*, and *Gernon*), of *O'Dubhdera*, *O'Bassil*, *O'Casey*, etc.

87. Earc (or Eachach): his son.

88. Carthann (" carthann :" Irish, *charity*, *friendship*, *kindness*): his son; a quo *MacCarthainn*, anglicised *MacCartan*, and *Cartan*, of Lough Foyle. Had one daughter and six sons—1. Earc; 2. St. Teresa, virgin, whose Feast is commemorated on the 8th July; 3. Muireadhach; 4. Forgo; 5. Olioll; 6. Laoghaire; 7. Tren — "from the last five of whom many saints are descended."

89. Earc: son of Carthann.

90. Fergus: his son.

91. Gothfrith: his son.

92. Main: his son.

93. Niallgus: his son.

94. Suibhneach: his son.

95. Meargach (Ineargach): his son.

96. Solamh (or Solomon): his son.

97. Giolla Adhamnan): his son.

98. Giolla Brighid: his son.

99. Samhairle (Savarly, Sorley, Somerled, or Samuel) was, A.D. 1140, the eighth and greatest Thane of Argyle; lord of Cantyre; lord of the Hebrides; founder of the " Kingdom of the Isles ;" m. Sabina, dau. of Olad the Red, King of the Isle of Man (the " Insula *Mevania*" of the ancients), by whom he possessed the Isles and Man (See Paper "Isle of Man," in the Appendix); had a brother Dubhgall, who was ancestor of *MacDowell ;* d. 1164.

100. Randal :* son of Sorley ; lord of Oergeal and Cantyre; founder of the Cistercian Monastery, and benefactor of the Abbey of Paisley.

101. Aongus (or Æneas), of the Isles: his son; living in 1211 (See the Four Masters under that year.)

102. Domhnall: his son.

103. Alexander: his son.

various wars and battles, from the thirteenth to the seventeenth century, and particularly in the reign of Elizabeth ; they were sometimes called "Clan Donnells," and by some of the English writers "MacConnells." The MacAlustrums or Mac-Allisters of Scotland and Ireland were a branch of the MacDonnells, and took their name from one of their chiefs named Alastrum or Alexander; and as the name " Sandy" or " Saunders" is a contraction of "Alexander" some of MacAllisters have anglicised their names " Saunderson." The MacSheehys, according to Lodge, were also a branch of the MacDonnells, who came from Scotland to Ireland ; and they also were celebrated commanders of galloglasses, particularly in Munster, under the FitzGeralds, earls of Desmond, Sir Randal MacDonnell, son of Sorley Buighe (*Buighe :* Irish, *yellow*), son of Alexander, was created earl of Antrim, by King James the first.

* *Randal :* This Randal, whose daughter was married to Hugh O'Connor, had a brother Alexander, who had Randal, who had Alexander, who had John, who had Alan, who had Donald, who had Alan, who had John, who had Alan, who had John, who had Alexander, who had Randal *MacDonald*, who had five sons—1. Donald, 2. John, 3. Æneas (or Ence), 4. Randal, 5. Alan.

104. Domhnall ("domhan :" Irish, *the world*; "all," *mighty*): son of Randal ; a quo *MacDomhnaill*, lords of the Hebrides, and of Cantyre, etc., in Scotland, and chiefs of Glencoe. This sirname has also been anglicised *Danielson,* and *Donaldson.* Had a brother Alexander, who was ancestor of the Sept called "MacDonnell of Ulster ;" and a brother Rory, who was ancestor of *MacRory,* modernized *Rogers,* and *Rodgers.*

105. Aongus (or Æneas) Mór Mac-Donnell : son of Domhnall ; lord of the Isles ; m. —— Campbell ; had a brother Alustrum (or Alexander), who was ancestor of *Alexander, MacAllister, MacSheehy, Saunders, Saunderson,* and *Sheehy,* etc. ; assumed this sirname.

106. Æneas Oge MacDonnell : son of Æneas Mór ; lord of the Isles ; fought at the Battle of Bannock-burn, A.D. 1314, on the side of Robert Bruce, King of Scotland. Had an elder brother Alexander, who was ancestor of the MacDon-nells, "Galloglasses of Ulster," and slain in 1296 ; and another brother Eoin, who was sirnamed "The Gnieve."

107. Randal (or Reginald) : son of Æneas Oge.

108. Shane : his son.

109. Eoin Mór, who d. in 1378 : his son ; lord of the Isles ; m. twice : by his first marriage he was ancestor of the chieftains of *Clann Raghnail* or Clanronald, and of Glengarry ; he was secondly married to Margaret, dau. of Robert the Second, King of Scotland, and by her had a dau. Margaret, who was wife of Nicholas, earl of Sunderland,

and another dau. Elizabeth, who was wife of Lachlan MacLean of Dowart ; and he had three sons—1. Donal na Heile ("eile :" Irish, *prayer, adoration*), a quo *Hale,* whose descendants were lords of the Isles, and who, in 1411, at the head of ten thousand vassals, convulsed the Kingdom of Scotland, and fought the famous battle of Harlaw, in defence of his right to the earldom of Ross, the heiress of which he had married ; 2. Eoin Oge ; 3. Alexander, who was ancestor of MacDonnell of Kappagh. This Eoin Mór had a brother named Marcach (slain 1397), and another named Donal.

110. Eoin Oge : the second son of Eoin Mór : m. Margery, dau. of Lord Bissett, of the Glinns of Antrim.

111. Donal Ballach : son of Eoin Oge ; m. Joan, dau. of O'Donnell, lord of Tirconnell. Had a brother Marcach (or Marcus*) who m. a dau. of O'Cahan.

112. Eoin : son of Donal Ballach ; m. Sarah, dau. of Phelim O'Neill, lord of the Clanaboys.

113. Eoin Cathanach : son of Eoin ; hanged, A.D. 1499 ; so surnamed because he was fostered in northern Ulster, in the family of *O'Cathain* or O'Cahan ; m. to Cecilia, dau. of Robert Savage, of Ards.

114. Alexander : his son ; lord of the Route and Glens, in Ireland ; m. to Catherine, dau. of Murcha MacCahalan of Derry. Had a brother Æneas MacDonnell, who was called "MacParson" (Scotticised *MacPherson*), and anglicised *Parsons.*†

This Alexander had eight sons—

---

* *Marcus :* In p. 1641 of O'Donovan's Four Masters this Marcus is mentioned as the son of "Aengus Oge," the hero of Sir Walter Scott's *Lord of the Isles.*

† *Parsons :* The final *s* in this sirname is a contraction for *son,* and represents the *Mac* in "MacParson ;" as the final *s* in the English sirname "Jennings" is a contraction for the *Mac,* in the Irish sirname *MacEoinin.*—See "Jennings."

1. Giolla Espuig Daoinech, 2. Donal Ballach, 3. James, whose son Æneas d. in 1545, 4. Aengus the Proud, 5. Alasdar Oge, 6. Colla, 7. Sorley Buidhe, 8. Donal Gorm.

115. Sorley Buidhe [boy], of Dunluce Castle, county Antrim, who d. 1590: seventh son of Alexander; m. Mary, dau. of Conn Baccach O'Neill, who was created "Earl of Tyrone," in 1542. This Sorley Buidhe had six sons—1. Donal (who had Colla, and Visduin or Euston), 2. Alasdran, 3. Sir James, of Dunluce Castle, 4. Raghnall of Arran, 5. Aengus of Ulster, 6. Ludar.

116. Sir James, of Dunluce, who d. in 1601: third son of Sorley Buidhe; knighted in 1597 by King James the Fourth of Scotland; left his youngest son Alasdar Carragh, a ward with his younger brother Raghnall or Randal, who was the first "Earl of Antrim." Sir James had six sons—1. Gilla Espuig, 2. Aengus, 3. Raghnall, 4. Colla, 5. Donal Gorm, 6. Alasdar Carragh or Sir Alexander, who d. in 1634.

117. Gilla Espuig: eldest son of Sir James.

118. Coll-Kittagh,* who died in 1647: son of Gilla Espuig; had— 1. Sir Alexander (or Alaster) who in the Cromwellian war was exe-

cuted on the 13th Nov., 1647, 2. Angus, 3. Gilla Espuig (or Archibald).

119. Sir Alexander: eldest son† of Coll-Kittagh; had three sons:

I. Colla of Kilmore, Glenariff, co. Antrim, of whom presently.

II. John of Tanaughconny.

III. Gillaspick (or Captain Archibald Mór) who d. in 1720. This Archibald m. Anne (d. 1714), dau. of Capt. Stewart of Redbay, and had a son Colla, and a dau. Catherine, who m. a MacDonnell, who had property in the Route. The son Colla (d. 1737), m. Anne McDonnell of Nappan, and had:

I. Alexander of Cushindall (d. 1782), who m. Anne Black (d. 1835), and had one son and two daughters; the son was Alexander, who d. young, in 1791; and the daughters were Rachel (d. 1805), and Anne (d. 1825), who m. Archibald McElheran, Esq., of Cushindall.

120. Colla of Kilmore, m. Anne Magee, and had:

121. Alexander of Kilmore, who was twice m.: first to Miss McDonnell of Nappan, by whom he had:

---

* *Kittagh*: This word (properly *ciotach*) signifies left-handed ; but as here applied it means that Coll or Colla, son of Gilla Espuig, could when occasion required wield his sword with the *left hand* equally as well as with the right.

† *Eldest son*: This Alexander (or Alaster) MacDonnell, Major-General, was created Knight of the Field by Montrose, after the battle of Kilsyth in 1645. He was a Scottish chieftain. In the summer of 1639, having refused to accept the Covenant, he, with 300 other persons, took refuge in Ulster. There he was hospitably received by his kinsfolk, and his Highlanders became an effective aid to the northern Irishi n the War of 1641—1652. Early in the war he overthrew an Anglo-Irish force of about 900 men near Ballymoney. Afterwards, in June, 1642, he was, with Sir Felim O'Neill, defeated at Glenmaquin, in Raphoe. Next year he was appointed by the Earl of Antrim to command the force sent into Scotland to assist Montrose, and took a prominent part in the war in that country. In 1647 he returned to Ireland, and was, by the Supreme Council of the Catholic Confederation appointed Lieutenant-General of Munster, under Lord Taaffe. He was killed in an engagement with Lord Inchiquin, at Knocknaness, between Mallow and Kanturk, on the 13th November, 1647, and was buried in the tomb of the O'Callaghans, in Clonmeen churchyard, Kanturk. He is described as of gigantic stature and powerful frame.—WEBB.

I. Michael Ruadh [Roe], of whom presently.

The second wife of Alexander of Kilmore was Miss McVeagh, by whom he had a son:

II. John, who succeeded to the Kilmore property, and who m. Rose, dau. of George Savage, Esq., and had:

I. Randal, of Kilmore, who m. Mary, dau. of Archibald McElheran, Esq., of Cloney, and had two sons and three daughters. The sons were:

I. Alexander of Kilmore and Dublin (who d. 1862), and who, in 1851, m. Margaret, daughter of Alexander McMullin, Esq., of Cabra House, co. Down, and had Rachel-Mary-Josephine.

II. Lieut.-Col. John McDon- nell, J.P., of Kilmore (living in 1885), who, in 1870, m. the Honble. Madeline (deceased), dau. of the lamented Lord O'Hagan, late Lord Chancellor of Ireland.

122. Michael Ruadh: the elder son of Alexander of Kilmore, had:

123. James McDonnell, of Belfast, (d. 1845), who had two sons:

I. Sir Alexander* McDonnell Bart. (d. s. p.), late Resident Commissioner of National Education in Ireland; d. 1875.

II. John McDonnell, M.D., late Poor-Law Commissioner for Ireland, who had:

124. Robert McDonnell, Esq., M.D., of 89 Merrion Square, Dublin; and living in 1887.

MACDONNELL. (No. 2.)

Earls of Antrim.

Arms: For the ancient Arms of the family see "MacDonnell" (No. 1) pedigree.

SIR RANDAL MACDONNELL, a younger brother of Sir James, of Dunluce, county Antrim, who is No. 116 on the (foregoing) "MacDonnell" (No. 1) pedigree, was the ancestor of *MacDonnell*, earls of Antrim.

---

* *Alexander*: Sir Alexander MacDonnell, Bart., was born in Belfast in 1794. He was educated at Westminster and Oxford, where he displayed the most brilliant abilities, and was called to the English Bar at the age of thirty. In 1839 he was appointed Resident Commissioner of National Education, of which he became the presiding and animating genius. A zealous Protestant, he uniformly sustained the principle that the faith of the children of his poorer fellow-countrymen should be protected in the spirit as well as in the letter. He was made a Privy-Councillor in 1846; he resigned the Commissionership in 1871, at the age of 77, and was created a baronet early in the following year. Of him the *Spectator* said : . . . "He was in his daily life and amongst his friends an example of how high a creature the Celt may become under the fairest influences of culture; for, he was a Celt of the Celts, if an ancestry of a thousand years could make him so." He died on the 21st January, 1875, aged 80 years, and was interred at Kilsharvan, near Drogheda. A beautiful statue has been erected by his friends and admirers to his memory, on the grounds at the Education Office (Tyrone House), Marlborough-street, Dublin.

116. Sir Randal* : a younger son of Sorley MacDonnell; created in 1618 "Viscount Dunluce," and advanced to the "earldom of Antrim" in 1620 ; died in 1636.

117. Randal : his son ; created "marquis† of Antrim;" died in 1682 ; was succeeded by his brother Alexander, the third earl of Antrim, who died in 1699.

118. Randal: son of said Alexander ; was the fourth earl of Antrim ; died in 1721.

119. Alexander: his son ; the fifth earl ; d. 1775.

120. Randal-William : his son ; the sixth earl; had no issue but two daughters—1. Anne-Catherine, 2.

Charlotte, to whom in 1785 new Patent with remainder was granted ; with this Randal-William the old earldom of Antrim became extinct ; he died in 1791.

121. Anne-Catherine MacDonnell: his daughter ; countess of Antrim in her own right; died in 1834. Her sister Charlotte succeded her as countess of Antrim, and married lord M. R. Kerr ; she died in 1835.

122. Hugh-Seymour, earl of Antrim : their son ; died in 1855 ; had a brother named Mark who succeeded him, and was earl of Antrim.

123. William-Randall MacDonnell, third earl of Antrim, under new Patent : son of the said Mark.

* *Randal :* Sir Randal MacDonnell, first Earl of Antrim, succeeded to the family estates on the death of his brother James, in 1601. He was known as *Arranach,* from having been fostered in the island of Aran. In the autumn of 1602 he abandoned the cause of Hugh O'Neill, and joined Sir A. Chichester, offering to serve against his former ally with 500 foot and 40 horse, maintained at his own expense. He was subsequently knighted by Mountjoy. In 1603, James I. granted him 333,907 acres between Larne and Coleraine. About 1604 he married Alice, daughter of O'Neill. His position after the flight of O'Neill and O'Donnell was very perilous ; but, by devoting himself entirely to the consolidation and improvement of his estates, his movements, as O'Neill's son-in-law, ceased to excite the suspicion of the authorities ; and when he had occasion to visit London in 1608, he was cordially received at Court. In 1618 he was created "Viscount Dunluce," a member of the Privy Council, and Lieutenant of the county Antrim ; and two years afterwards the title of "Earl of Antrim" was conferred on him. Besides estates in Ulster, he owned lands on the Scottish coast, the sustainment of his rights in which gave him at times no little trouble. The Earl died at Dunluce on the 10th December, 1636, and was buried at Bonamargy.

* *Marquis :* This Randal, Marquis, and second Earl, of Antrim, was bred in the Highland way ; "he wore neither hat, cap, nor shoe, nor stocking, till seven or eight years old." In 1635 he married the widow of the Duke of Buckingham, who thereupon returned to Catholicism, which she had renounced on her first marriage. On the breaking out of the war in Scotland he was appointed by Charles I. one of his lieutenants and commissioners in the Highlands and Islands. In June, 1640, he took his seat in the Irish House of Lords, and continued to reside in Dublin until the War 1641-'52 broke out. On the 26th January, 1644, he received a Marquisate. The Cromwellian Settlement deprived him of his estates for a time ; but in July, 1666, he was restored to the possession of 87,086 acres in Dunluce and Glenarm. He died at Ballymagarry on the 3rd Feb., 1682, and was buried in state in the family vault at Bonamargy.

MacDONNELL. (No. 3.)

Of the County Clare.

Arms : The ancient Arms same as "MacDonnell" (No. 1).

SIR ALEXANDER (or ALASDAR CARRAGH) MACDONNELL, younger brother of Gilla Espuig, who is No. 117 on the (No. 2) " MacDonnell" (of Antrim) pedigree, was the ancestor of *MacDonnell*, of the county Clare.

117. Sir Alexander MacDonnell, of Kilconway and Moye, who died 1634 : youngest son of Sir James of Dunluce ; was created a baronet in 1627.

118. Sir James of Eanagh and Ballybannagh* : son of Sir Alexander ; died after 1688 ; was second baronet. This Sir James MacDonnell m. Mary O'Brien, by whom he had six sons : 1. Sir Alexander (commonly called "Alastrum Mór"), who m. Lady E. Howard, and by her had a son Randal, who d. *s. p. ;* 2. Sir Randal, who succeeded, and and m. Hannah Roche, by whom he had James, Randal, Sir John, and Richard ; 3. Darby ; 4. Daniel, who was ancestor of MacDonnell of Clare, and who died *v. p. ;* 5. Alneas, who d. unm. ; 6. Sorley. According to Lodge, Alneas and Sorley died young.

119. Daniel : fourth son of Sir James ; deprived of his patrimony in Antrim, settled at Kilkee, county of Clare, where he obtained leases of several lands from his kinsman Lord Clare : died about 1675.

120. James, of Kilkee : his son ;

Captain† in Lord Clare's Dragoons ; acquired extensive estates in Clare, Limerick, and Longford ; died 1714. Had a brother John MacDonnell, of Moyne.

121. Charles (1), of Kilkee : his son (succeeded his elder brother Randal, who died unmarried in 1726) : died 1743.

122. Charles (2), of Kilkee, M.P. for the county of Clare, in 1765, and for the borough of Ennis in 1768 : his son ; died 1773.

123. Charles (3), of New Hall and Kilkee, M.P. : his son ; died 1803.

124. Bridget : his only daughter, and in her issue heiress ; married William Henry Armstrong, M.P., of Mount Heaton, King's Co. ; she died 1860.

125. William Edward, of New Hall and Kilkee, Colonel of the Clare Militia : her son ; succeeded his uncle the late John MacDonnell in 1850, and assumed by Royal Licence the sirname and Arms of MacDonnell ; died 1881.

126. Charles Randal MacDonnell : his son ; born 1862 ; living 1887.

* *Ballybannagh :* His eldest son, Colonel Sir Alexander, as well as his cousin Sir Alexander ("MacCollkittagh") were both killed in the battle of Knocknaness, 13th November, 1647. The second son, Sir Randal, succeeded as third baronet, but was attainted, forfeited his estates, 10th July, 1691, and entered with Lord Clare into the service of the King of France.

† *Captain :* This Captain James MacDonnell (or "MacDaniel," as he is called in Dalton's *King James's Army List*), married Penelope, sister of Honora, second Viscountess of Clare, and became a purchaser of a part of the forfeited estates of Daniel, Viscount Clare.—See " Poems on the MacDonnell family," in Lenihan's *History of Limerick*, p. 613.

MacDONNELL. (No. 4.)

Of Fairy Hill, County Clare.

Arms: Quarterly: 1st or, a lion ramp. gu.; 2nd, or, a hand issuing from a cloud at the sinister fess point ppr. holding a cross croslet fitchée az.; 3rd, ar. a ship with its sails furled up, sa.; 4th, parti per fess az. and vert, the latter wavy, a dolphin naiant ppr. Quartering Bourke: or, a cross gu., and in the dexter canton a lion ramp. of the last. *Crest:* A dexter arm, couped at the shoulder, attired gold, turned down ar. holding a cross crosslet fitchée as in the arms. *Motto:* Tout jours prest.

JOHN MacDONNELL of Moyne (living in 1700), eldest son of Daniel, who is No. 119 on the "MacDonnell" (No. 3) pedigree, was the ancestor of this branch of that family.

120. John : son of Daniel; living in 1700.

121. Charles, of Moyne: his son.

122. Timothy: his son; married Catherine Rochford.

123. Michael, of Kilrush, county Clare: their son; m. Honoria, dau. of P. Buggy, of Doonass, co. Clare.

124. John (b. 1805) of Fairy Hill, co. Clare: their son; living in 1886; J.P. for Clare and Limerick, and was High Sheriff for Limerick, m. Catherine-Sarah, dau. of Stephen Chester Bourke, Esq., of Limerick.

125. Robert* : their son; living in 1886; J.P. for Limerick; was High Sheriff in 1874, and Mayor of Limerick City in 1871; m. Minnie, dau. of Matthew Hare de Courcy of Shannon Ville, Limerick.

126. John MacDonnell : their son; b. 1869, and living in 1886.

MacDONNELL. (No. 5.)

Of Leinster.

Arms: The ancient Arms same as those of "MacDonnell" (No. 1)·

MARCUS ("marcach:" Irish, *a horseman;* Lat. "marcus") or Mark MacDonnell, brother of Donal Ballach, who is No. 111 on the (No. 1) "MacDonnell" (of Antrim) pedigree, was the ancestor of *MacDonnell* of Leinster.

111. Marcus : son of Eoin.

112. Tirlogh Mór: his son; died 1435.

113. Tirlogh Oge : his son; first of the family who settled in Leinter.†

114. Donoch : his son.

115. Eoin Carrach : his son.

---

* *Robert:* This Robert had two sisters :—1. Norah, who married Thomas Greene, Esq., J.P., of Greenlawn, Ennis; and 2. Kathleen, who married Matthew J. de Courcy, Esq., of Allington, Corbally, Limerick.

† *Leinster:* The MacDonnells of Leinster formed three septs, of whom two were seated in the Queen's County, and the third in the present barony of Talbotstown, in county of Wicklow.

116. Tirlogh (3) : his son.

117. Charles, also called Calbhach ("calbh:" Irish, *bald;* Heb. "chalak"): his son; living in 1569.

118. Hugh Buidhe* [boy], of Tenekille, Queen's County: his son; m. Mary Moore; died 1618. Had a brother Alexander, who was slain in 1577.

119. Fearach : son of Hugh Buidhe. Had two younger brothers—1. Brian ; 2. Fergus, who died 1637. And a sister Helen married to John Doyne.

120. James : son of Fearach: b. 1617; died in London, A.D. 1661. Was a Colonel of the Confederate Catholics. On the 8th February, 1641, the Lords Justices proclaimed a reward of four hundred pounds (£400), and a free pardon, for his head.

121. Hugh (2) : his son.

122. Dermod : his son.

123. Dermod Oge : his son.

124. William : his son; died in 1810.

125. John, of Saggart, in the co. Dublin: his son ; had two sons.

126. Joseph : his son.

127. John-Daniel MacDonnell, of Pembroke-road, Dublin : his son ; had a brother named Joseph, and two sisters—all living in 1886.

MacDONNELL.† (No. 6.)

Of the County Mayo.

Arms : The ancient Arms of this family same as those of "MacDonnell" (No. 1).

DONAL, brother of Eoin (or John) Mór who is No. 109 on the " Mac-Donnell" (of Antrim) pedigree, was the ancestor of *MacDonnell*, of Tyrawley, in the county Mayo.

109. Donal : son of Eoin.

110. Randal : his son.

111. Shane (or Eoin) : his son.

112. Aongus : his son.

113. Marcach (or Marcus) : his son.

114. Tirlogh : his son.

115. Feareadach Mór, of Tyrawly : his son.

116. Duine-eadach : his son : a quo *Slioght Duineaduigh* (" sliochd :" Irish, *seed, offspring ;* " duine-ea-

---

* *Hugh Buidhe*: This Hugh was Chief of one of "the three septs of galloglasses of the Clandonnells," in Leinster in his time ; another of the Chiefs was Maolmuire, of Rahin, both Hugh and Maolmuire living in the Queen's County ; and the third Chieftain was Tirlogh Oge MacDonnell, of the county Wicklow, whose indenture of composition with the Lord Deputy Sidney (dated 7th May, 1578) is enrolled on the record branch of the Office of Paymaster of Civil Services, Dublin. That Tirlogh Oge was "son of Alexander, son of Tirlogh, son of Maolmuire MacDonnell of Balliranan, Generosus" ("generosus :" Latin, *noble,* of *noble birth*), who possibly was a son of Donoch, No. 114 on this pedigree.

† *MacDonnell:* Major Francis MacDonnell, a distinguished officer in the Austrian Service, was born in Connaught in 1656. At the surprise of Cremona (1st February, 1702) he particularly signalized himself. On that occasion he took Marshal Villeroy prisoner, and refused brilliant offers of rank and money to connive at his escape. On the other hand, he did not scruple to endeavour by bribes to bring over the Irish regiments serving with the enemy. He fell at the battle of Luzzara, in August, 1702.

dach," *a dressy person*). This Duine-eadach had two brothers—1. Brian Buidhe; and 2. Cathal, a quo *MacCathail*, anglicised *MacCail*, modernized *MacHale*, etc.

117. Rory: son of Duine-eadach.

118. Feareadach (2): his son.
119. Feardorcha: his son.
120. James MacDonnell, of Tyrawley: his son; had a brother named Aongus; living in 1691.

MacDONNELL. (No. 7.)

Lords of Clan Kelly, County Fermanagh.

Arms: Gu. a lion pass. guard. or.

LOCHLAN, a brother of Donall who is No. 102 on the "O'Hart" pedigree, was the ancestor of *MacDomhnaill*, of Clankelly, County Fermanagh, anglicised *MacDaniel, Daniel, MacDonnell*, and *O'Donnell*.

102. Lachlan: son of Art.
103. Teige MacDonnell, his son; first of this family that assumed this sirname.
104. Fearmarcach ("marcach:" Irish, a *horseman*): his son; a quo

O'Marcaigh, anglicised *Markey, Horseman, Knight, MacKnight, Rider, Ryder, Riding, Ryding*, etc.
105. Teighe: his son.
106. Flanagan: his son.

MacDONOUGH. (No. 1.)

Lords in the County Sligo.

Arms: Per chev. invected or and vert. in chief two lions pass. guard. gu. in base a boar pass. ar

DONOCH,* a brother of Cormac who is No. 114 on the "MacDermott" pedigree, was the ancestor of *Clann Domhnaigh* also called *Clann Donchada* (of Connaught), anglicised *MacDonough,† Macdonogh, Macdona*, and *Donoghue*.

114. Donoch ("domnach:" Irish, *Sunday*): son of Tomaltach.

115. Muirgheas: his son.
116. Tomaltach (2): his son.

* *Donoch :* This name is anglicised "Dennis" and "Denny;" and thus "Mac-Donough" has been modernized *Dennison, Denny*, and *Dennis*. The latinized form of "Donoch" (or Doncha) is *Dionysius*.

† *MacDonough :* This family was distinct from MacDonough, Lords of Duhallow, in Munster.

117. Teige: his son. This Teige had a brother named Cormac na-Beag-feada (or Cormac of "the little whistle,") who was the ancestor of "MacDonough" of *Tir-Olliolla* (now the barony of "Tirerill)," in the County Sligo.

118. Brian: his son.

119. Teige: his son.

120. Cormac: his son.

121. Cairbre: his son.

122. Maolseaghlainn (or Melaghlin) Oge: his son.

123. Connor: his son.

124. John Oge MacDonough, of *Baile-an-Duin:* his son.

MacDONOUGH. (No. 2.)

Lords of Corran and Tirerill, County Sligo.

Arms : Same as those of "MacDonough" (No. 1).

CORMAC na-Beag-feada, brother of Teige who is No. 117 on the foregoing ("MacDonough") pedigree, was the ancestor of *MacDonough*, of Tirerill, County Sligo.

117. Cormac na-Beag-feada: son of Tomaltach.

118. Morogh: his son.

119. Donoch: his son.

120. Owen: his son.

121. Cathal (or Charles) Mac-Donough, of *Tirolliolla:* his son.

MacDONOUGH. (No. 3.)

Of Wilmont House, Parish of Portumna, Co. Galway.

Arms : The ancient Arms of this family same as those of "MacDonough" (No. 1).

THIS is a Catholic branch of the ancient family of "MacDonough,"[*] Lords of Corran and Tirerill, in the county Sligo. Of that family was Terence MacDonogh, of Creevagh, who was M.P. for Sligo in 1689 ; and who d. in 1718 ; he was the only Catholic Counsel who was admitted to the Bar in Ireland, up to his death, after the violation of the Treaty of Limerick in 1691. Since that period we find a branch of this family settled as country gentlemen and Justices of the Peace in the co. Galway ; holding lands of their own, and others in lease under their ancient kinsmen, the Clan Mac William, now Marquises of Clanrickard.

* *MacDonough :* By reference to "MacDonough" (No. 1) pedigree, it will be seen that "MacDonough," Lords of Corran and Tirerill, were a younger branch of the great house of McDermott, Princes of Moylurg, who were a younger branch of the O'Connors, Kings of Connaught ; details of whose wealth and territories, of their wars and alliances, are given in the Annals of the Four Masters.

1. Francis MacDonogh, held lands at Gort, and at Wilmont, in the parish of Portumna, and county of Galway, in the middle of the 18th century. To him succeeded :

2. Matthew MacDonogh, who held both those places, and who d. *circa* 1779. He had :

I. Allen, who succeeded him, and of whom presently.

II. James.

3. Allen MacDonogh, of Wilmont, J.P. for the co. Galway, who d. in July, 1825 ; son of Matthew ; m. Mary, dau. of —— Doolan, of Derry, in the King's County, and had issue, four sons and four daughters :

I. Matthew, of whom presently.

II. William, who d. s.p.

III. Thomas, b. 1st Sept., 1805, d. s.p.

IV. Allen MacDonogh, now (1884) of Athgarven Lodge, the Curragh, co. Kildare, who m. Charlotte Elizabeth, only dau. and eventual sole heiress of the late George Houghton, Esq., of Leicester (by Chailoth-Elizabeth, daughter and co-heiress of —— Cheatle, Esq.), and had issue an only daughter :

I. Charlotte - Murray - Houghton, who in 1871 married John Pym Yeatman, Esq., of Springfield House, Sheffield, in the co. of York, England, (a Barrister of Lincoln's Inn, and of the family of *Yeatman*, in the county of Dorset), and has three sons and four daughters :

I. John - Francis - Joseph - Pym Yeatman, b. 25th November, 1873.

II. William-Goel-de Percival, born 25th February, 1877.

III. Patrick - Allen - Irvine, b. 25th Oct., 1878.

I. Ethel - Charlotte - Murray-Houghton.

II. Maud-Mary-Theophila-Farr.

III. Sybil-Mary-Josephine.

IV. Olive-Mary.

The four daughters of Allen MacDonogh, of Wilmont, were :

I. Eleanor.

II. Hanna.

III. Frances-Elizabeth.

IV. Margaret.

4. Matthew MacDonogh, J.P. for the county of Galway, who died 25th Dec., 1877 : eldest son of Allen ; was Captain in the 10th Hussars. He married Jemima, daughter of James Lynch, M.D., of Lough, county Galway, and had an only son :

5. Frank MacDonogh of Wilmont House, in the co. Galway, b. 18th June, 1844, and living in 1884 ; m. on the 19th Mar., 1865, Kate-Mary, dau. of Thomas Bodkin, M.D., of Tuam, and had issue six sons and two daughters :

I. Matthew-Joseph, b. 26th Jan., 1867.

II. Thomas - Aloysius, b. 19th June, 1870.

III. Joseph-Patrick, b. 19th Feb., 1875.

IV. Francis-James, b. 5th Jan., 1877.

V. Allen, b. in 1879.

VI. Charles, b. in 1882.

I. Mary-Esmina, b. 1868, d. 17th March, 1873.

II. Esmina-Mary.

6. Matthew-Joseph MacDonogh, of Wilmont House : son and heir of Frank ; b. in 1867, and living in 1884.

MacDOWALL.*

Arms : See the Arms of "MacDonnell" (No. 1) pedigree.

DUBHGHALL, brother of Samhairle (or Sorley) who is No. 100 on the "MacDonnell" (of Antrim) pedigree, was the ancestor of *MacDubhghaill ;* anglicised *MacDougall, MacDougald, MacDowell,* and *MacDowall.*

100. Dubhghall ("dubhghall:") Irish, *a black foreigner*): son of Giollabrighid [gillbride]: a quo *MacDubhghaill ;* was King of the Isles; living A.D. 1144.

101. Donoch : his son ; had a brother named John, who was the ancestor of *MacDowell,* of Larne, county Antrim.

102. Lochlann : his son.

103. Duhhghall (2) : his son.

104. Iomhar ("iom-ar :" Irish, *much slaughter*): his son; a quo *MacIomhair.†*

105. Giollacolum : his son.

106. Iomar MacDubhghaill : his son. This Iomhar had two brothers—1. Lochlann ; and 2. Fercar ("fear :" Irish, *a man,* "caor," a *fire-brand ;* Heb. "charah," *it blazed forth ;* Chald. "charei," *lighted up*), a quo *Ferrar.* By some genealogists "Ferrar" is derived from the Irish *fear-ard* (Lat. "ard-uus)," meaning "the tall or high man." And "Farrell" has been also anglicised *Ferrar,* by some members of that family.

MacFETRIDGE.

Arms : The Arms of this family were the same as those of "MacUais."

CATHACH, brother of Criochan who is No. 95 on the "MacUais" pedigree, was the ancestor of *O'Fiachraidh* and *MacFiacraidh* ; anglicised *Fiachry,* and *MacFetridge.*

95. Cathach : son of Maolfogha.

96. Aodh (or Hugh) : his son.

97. Maolbreasal : his son.

98. Maolcuairt ("cuairt :" Irish, *a visit ;* Eng. "court ;") a quo *MacCuarta,* anglicised *MacCourt.*

---

* *MacDowall* : Patrick MacDowell, R.A., was born in Belfast, on the 12th Aug., 1799. His father dying early, the family moved to London, and although Patrick showed a decided taste for art, and desired to follow it, he was apprenticed to a coach-maker. When he had served about four years, his master became bankrupt, and the lad, then sixteen years of age, was thrown on his own resources. Accident brought him to lodge in the house of a French sculptor, M. Chenu. He indulged once more in his old tastes, copied from his landlord's models, and soon delighted him with a "Venus," for which he obtained eight guineas. Mr. MacDowell thenceforth became eminent as an artist ; he died in London, on the 9th December, 1870, aged 71 years.

† *MacIomhair* : This sirname has been anglicised Emer, Emerson, Iver, Ivir, Ivor, Howard, MacIvir, MacIvor, McIvor, and McKeever. It was the Author's mistake, in Note 111, page 396 of the first series (published 1876), to derive some of these sirnames from *MacIdhir.*

99. Maolruainaidh : his son.
100. Maolmuire : his son.
101. Hugh (or Cinaodh): his son.
102. Maolpadraic: his son.
103. Maolruanaidh (2): his son.

104. Fogharthach : his son.
105. Neal O'Fiachry, of *Ardstratha* (or Ardstraw), in the co. Tyrone : his son.

MacGEOGHAGAN.

Lords of Moycassell and Fertullagh, in Westmeath.

Arms : Ar. a lion ramp. betw. three dexter hands couped at the wrist gu. *Crest*: A greyhound statant ar. *Motto* : Semper patriæ servire presto.

FIACH, a brother of Main who is No. 88 on the " Fox " pedigree, was the ancestor of *MacEachagain ;* anglicised *MacGeoghagan, Geoghagan, Macgeoghagan, Geagan, Gegan, Gaghan, Gahagan, Gahan,* and *MacGahan.*

88. Fiach : son of Niall of the Nine Hostages, the 126th Monarch of Ireland.
89. Tuathal : his son; whose brother Eochaidh was ancestor of *Molloy,* and other brother Uigin, the ancestor of *Higgins.*
90. Amhailgadh [awly] : son of Tuathal.
91. Coscrach : his son.
92. Eachagan ("each :" Irish, *a horse;* Lat. " eq-uus ;" Gr. " ikk-os"), meaning a little horse :" his son; a quo *MacEachagain.*
93. Rory : his son.
94. Awly (2) : his son.
95. Giollacolum : his son.
96. Creamthann : his son.
97. Eochaidh : his son.
98. Florence : his son.
99. Awly (3) : his son.
100. Donoch : his son.
101. Congal : his son.
102. Anluan : his son.
103. Coscrach (2) : his son ; a quo *Cnoc Ui Coscraigh.*
104. Malachi : his son.
105. Murtach : his son.
106. Congal (2): his son.
107. Cucogar : his son.
108. Cucalma (" calma :" Irish,

brave; Heb. "chalam," *he prevailed*) : his son ; a quo *MacCalma,* anglicised *MacCalmont,* and *Culm.*
109. Murtach (2) : his son.
110. Congal (3) : his son.
111. Congal (4) : his son.
112. Donoch (2) : his son.
113. Congal (5) : his son.
114. Murtach Mór : his son.
115. Donoch (3) : his son.
116. Dermod : his son.
117. Hugh Buidhe : his son.
118. Conla : his son; had one brother.
119. Leineach Cairach : his son.
120. Conchobhar [connor] : his son.
121. Conla (2): his son.
122. Ros : his son.
123. Neal : his son ; had three brothers.
124. Conall : his son ; had an elder brother named Ros, whose only son named Richard died without issue.
125. Conla (2): son of Conall.
126 Charles : his son; had two brothers.
127. Connor MacGeoghagan of Moycassell : his son; living in 1690. Had three brothers — 1. Conla, 2. Antoine, 3. ——

MacGILLCUNNY.

FOGHARTACH, brother of Cairbre who is No. 97 on the "Burns" pedigree, was the ancestor of *MacGiollamocunaidh;* anglicised *MacGilcunny.*

97. Foghartach : son of Foghartach.
98. Congall : his son.
99. Ciarnach : his son.
100. Foghartach (2) : his son.

101. Giollamocunadh ("mo :" old Irish, *a man;* Lat. "ho-*mo*" and "ne-*mo*;" "cunadh:" Irish, *a wood*) : his son ; a quo *MacGiolla-mocunaidh.*

MacGILLFINEN.

Arms : Same as those of "Leonard."

GIOLLAFINNEAN ("finne :" Irish, *whiteness*), No. 105 on the "Mulroy" pedigree, was the ancestor of *MacGiollafinneain;* anglicised *MacGillfinen.* (See the "Leonard" pedigree).

MacHALE.

Of Tubbernavine, Parish of Addergoole, County of Mayo.

Arms : Same as those of "MacDonnell" (No. 1).

DUINE-EADACH, who is No. 116 on the "MacDonnell" (of Mayo) pedigree, had two brothers—1. Brian Buidhe ; 2. Cathal : this Cathal ("cath :" Irish, *a battle,* "all," *great*) was the ancestor of *MacCathail;* anglicised *MacCail, MacCael, MacCale, MacKeal,* and *MacHale.**

* *MacHale*: John, the late Catholic Archbishop of Tuam, was the first of the family who wrote the name—"MacHale." At p. 22 of *The Life and Times of the Most Rev. John MacHale, Archbishop of Tuam* (Dublin : Gill and Son, 1882), the Very Rev. Canon Ulick J. Bourke, the worthy author of that Volume, expresses the opinion that the sirname *MacHale,* as borne by Archbishop MacHale's family, is derived from *Clan-heil,* which is of Welsh origin, and a quo the sirnames *Hoel, Howell,* etc. It is worthy of remark, however, that some of the Archbishop's ancestors spelled their name *Mac-Cail,* while his father and grandfather spelled it *MacKeal;* and that in the "Book of Survey and Distribution," for the barony of Tyrawley and county of Mayo, the *Clan Keale* are entered as proprietors, in 1641, of Cuming and Ballymacramagh, in the parish of Adergoole, where the Archbishop's immediate ancestors resided. The *Cail* and *Keal* portion of the name so closely resembling in sound the *Keale* in *Clan Keale,* is also worthy of notice ; as is the fact that it was from MATHEW HALE, an eminent Englishman in his day, and in no way related to the Archbishop's family, that His Grace, the Most Rev. Doctor MacHale, assumed the *Hale* portion of his name, and ceased to write it *MacKeal!*

117. Seamus (or James) *MacCail*, living A.D. 1641, had:

118. Searun, who had:

119. Ricard, who had:

120. James, who m. Mary *MucCale*, and had:

121. Maolmuire (or Myler) *Mac-Keal*, who d. in 1790. He married Anne Moffett (d. 1795), and had:

122. Patrick *MacKeal*, of Tubber-navine (or *Tobar na Feiné*, meaning the "Well of the Fenians"), in the parish of Adergoole, barony of Tyrawley, and county of Mayo, who d. in 1837. He was twice m.: first, to Mary Mulkieran (who d. in 1806), by whom he had six sons and three daughters; his second wife was Catherine MacCale, by whom he had three danghters and two sons. Of the daughters by the second marriage, Catherine was m. to Thomas Higgins, of Carropadden, Solicitor, Tuam, living in 1881. (See the "Higgins" Genealogy). Patrick MacKeal had a sister named Margaret* (who died in 1816), who was m. to Patrick Sheridan, joiner and farmer, from Lagan.

123. Thomas: eldest son of the said Patrick MacKeal. Had six brothers and three sisters,—the issue of his father's first marriage: 1. Martin; 2. Myler; 3. Patrick; 4. His Grace, the Most Rev. John MacHale, Archbishop of Tuam, living in 1881; 5. Rev. James; 6. Edmund. The sisters were: 1. Anne, 2. Mary, 3. another Catherine, who d. young.

MacHUGH.

Of Ulster.

Arms: Vert a white horse fully caparisoned, thereon a knight in complete armour, on his helmet a plume of ostrich feathers, and his right hand brandishing a sword all ppr.

AMHAILGADH, brother of Flaitheartach who is No. 112 on the "Maguire" pedigree, was the ancestor of *MacAodh;*† anglicised *MacHugh, Hughson, Hewson,‡ McCoy, McCue, McCuy, MacKay, MacKey, McKay, Mackey, McKee,* and *Magee.*

112. Amhailgadh [awly]: second son of Dun Oge Maguire.

113. Philip: his son; had four brothers.

114. Aodh: his son; a quo *Mac-Aodh.*

115. Patrick MacHugh: his son.

116. Giolladubh: his son; a quo

---

* *Margaret*: Of the daughters of Margaret and Patrick Sheridan, Cecilia was married to Ulick Bourke, who is No. 34 on the "Bourkes of Lough Conn and Ballina" pedigree.

† *MacAodh:* For the derivation of this sirname see the "Hughes" pedigree. In the transition of the Irish sirnames from the Irish to the English language, the name *Aodh* was by the English sometimes pronounce "Od:" hence *MacAodh* was angli-cised *Odson*, and in the course of time, *Hodson* and *Hudson;* each meaning the *sons* or *descendants* of *Aodh.*

‡ *Hewson:* This name has been rendered *Hewston* and *Houston.*

MacGiolladuibh ; anglicised *Mac-Gilladuff, Gillduff* and *Killduff.*
117. Neal: his son.

118. Edmond: his son.
119. Cormac: his son.
120. John MacHugh: his son.

MacKENNA.* (No. 1.)

Lords of Cruagh (or Truagh), in the County Monaghan.

Arms: Vert. a fess ar. betw. three lions' heads affrontée or.   *Crest*: A salmon naiant ppr.

THIS family was in Irish called *MacIonaigh* (" ionach :" Irish, *a dirk*), and was descended from Colla-da-Crioch who is No. 85 on the "O'Hart" pedigree.

O'Donovan says:

"It is remarkable that there is no pedigree of this (" MacKenna") family either in MacFirbis or in the Book of Leacan."

In Shirley's *History*† of the County Monaghan, we read (Part II., p. 136):

"Neal MacKenna of Portinaghy, in the parish of Donagh, was seized in fee of

---

* *The MacKenna*: The following is a Translation of an Address presented by the Lord of Truagh to Hugh Roe (or Red Hugh) O'Donnell, then in his 15th year of age, on the occasion of his escape from Dublin Castle (see the Four Masters, under A.D. 1587, 1590, and 1592), when the said Red Hugh was making his way home to Tirconnell :

The Truagh Welcome.

"Shall a son of O'Donnell be cheerless and cold
　　While MacKenna's wide hearth has a faggot to spare ?
　　While O'Donnell is poor, shall MacKenna have gold ?
　　Or be clothed, while a limb of O'Donnell is bare ?

While sickness and hunger thy sinews assail,
　　Shall MacKenna, unmoved, quaff his madder of mead ?
On the haunch of a deer shall MacKenna regale,
　　While a Chief of Tirconnell is fainting for food ?

No ; enter my dwelling, my feast thou shalt share ;
　　On my pillow of rushes thy head shall recline ;
And bold is the heart and the hand that will dare
　　To harm but one hair of a ringlet of thine.

Then come to my home, 'tis the home of a friend,
　　In the green woods of Truagh thou art safe from thy foes:
Six sons of Mackenna thy steps shall attend,
　　And their six sheathless skeans shall protect thy repose."

† *History:* The *History of the County Monaghan* (London : Basil Montagu Pickering, 196 Piccadilly, 1877 and 1878), by Evelyn Philip Shirley, Esq., M.A., F.S.A., M.R.I.A., of Lough Fea, is published in Three Parts : Parts I. and II. in 1877, and Part III. in 1878.   Price, each Part, 12s.   May be seen at the Royal Irish Academy, Dublin.

thirty-two townlands. He was in rebellion in 1641. It is added that he transported himself into Spain in November, 1653 ; the lands being then in possession of one Walter Crimble. (Carew MSS. 1603-24, Calendar, p. 223.) Portinaghy being one of the townlands granted by Queen Elizabeth to Patrick MacKenna, Chief of his name in 1591, I conclude that Neal was his descendant, and was probably his grandson and the representative of the family. He it is, I suppose, who is alluded to in the deposition, after the Rebellion in 1641, of Mrs. Elizabeth Petre, as ' —— M'Kenna of the Trough (Truagh), Esq., the principal man of that sept.' " It would appear by the Inquisitions that Patrick MacKenna, of the Lower Trough, died before the 10th June, 1625.

A John or Shane MacKenna, living in 1626, sold five townlands to Thomas Blaney and his heirs.

A Neale M'Kenna of Portinaghy, in the Parish of Donagh (above mentioned), was High Sheriff for the City.

In 1640 there were sixteen landed proprietors in the Barony of Trough, of the tribe of the MacKennas. Their estates, however, were small, seldom exceeding a townland or two in extent ; and of this number three were Protestants.

(In page 137 *ibid.*) The last of the principal line of this family I suppose to have been Shane or John, who was killed ' in open and actual rebellion at Glaslough, on the 13th of March, 1689.'

In 1659, there were no less than ninety-one heads of families of this Clan, and but one hundred and twelve of the MacMahons in the whole county."

In p. 140, Part II.* of Shirley's *County Monaghan*, is a pedigree of MacKenna of Lower Trough, from the Inquisitions, P.M. :

Patrick MacKenna of Lower Trough, to whom the three Ballybetaghs of Ballydavough, Ballymeny, and Ballylattin, and twelve (es)tates besides were granted by Queen Elizabeth, on the 10th September, 1591 ; died 1625. He left four sons : 1. Owen (supposed to have been the father or grandfather of Neale MacKenna, of Portinaghy, Esq., above mentioned, who rebelled in 1641, and withdrew into Spain, in 1653); 2. Shane or John of Lower Trough, who sold his land to Thomas Blaney before 1626, and was in rebellion in 1641 ; 3. Dunslieve (d. 10th January, 1600), who had Patrick, aged seven years in 1608; 4. Tool MacKenna, of Lower Trough, who sold his land to B. Brett, of Drogheda, merchant, before 1626, and who had two sons: 1. James, in rebellion in 1641, and 2. Shane.

* *Part II.* In Part II. also may be seen the pedigrees of the following families— commencing at page 152 of that volume : Leslie ; Anketill, of Grove ; Maxwell; Johnston, of Fort Johnston ; Singleton, of Fort Singleton ; Dawson, of Dawson Grove, Earl of Dartry ; Ker, of Newbliss ; Corry, of Glen ; Madden, of Hilton ; MacMahon, of Monaghan ; Westenra, lord of Rosmore ; Cairnes, of Monaghan ; Lucas, of Castleshane ; Fleming, of Derry ; Foster, of Tullaghan ; Richardson, of Poplar Vale ; Owen, of Monaghanduffe ; Cole, of Brandrum ; Wright (now " Wood-Wright") of Golagh ; Evatt, of Mount Louise; Montgomery, of Ballyleck, County Louth ; Mitchell, formerly of Drumreaske ; Hamilton, of Cornacassa ; Blayney, lord of Blayney ; Blayney, of Gregynogge Hall, Wales ; Leslie, of Ballybay ; Tennison, of Lough Bawn ; Rothwell (now Fitzherbert), of Shantonagh ; Devereux, Earl of Essex ; Shirley, Earl Ferrers.

MacKENNA. (No. 2.)

Of Dundalk.

Arms : Same as those of " MacKenna" (No. 1).

UP to going to press with this Work, we have not met with the genealogy of this family down to the Chief of Truagh, who, with five young sons, was murdered by Cromwell's soldiers, after sacking the place and setting it on fire. One of the Chief's sons, who was then a child at fosterage up in the mountains, escaped the massacre, and was afterwards THE MACKENNA (commonly called the " Major"), who in March, 1689, was killed defending the Fort of Drumbanagher, near Glaslough, for King James II.; and who was buried in the family grave in Donogh, parish of Donogh, county of Monaghan, and diocese of Clogher. A grandson of that " Major" was Francis MacKenna, of Mulmurry, whose brother Charles was ordained a Catholic Priest on the Continent, was Chaplain to the Irish Brigade at Fontenoy, said Mass on that Battlefield, on the day of that memorable battle, afterwards settled in Ireland and became Parish Priest of Donogh, in the diocese of Clogher. Commencing with said Francis the pedigree is as follows :

1. Francis MacKenna of Mulmurry : a grandson of The Mac-Kenna who, in March, 1689, was killed while defending the Fort of Drumbanagher, for King James II. Was twice married : first to Letitia Adams ; and secondly to a Miss Gernon. The children of the first marriage were—1. William* or " Big Billy ;" 2. James, who settled in Philadelphia early in life ; 3. Felim or Felix ; 4. Margaret, m. to a Mr. Brennan. The said Francis MacKenna went to Dundalk, and as above mentioned married secondly a Miss Gernon of the county Louth, and became the owner of an estate near Castlebellingham in that co.

2. John MacKenna of Dundalk : youngest son of Francis ; d. 1820.

3. William-Alexander McKenna of Dundalk, solicitor : his son ; m. in 1839, Ellen McKenna, his cousin, who d. 1849.

4. Philip McKenna of Londonderry : his son ; living in 1882.

---

* *William :* This William (or "Big Billy") MacKenna of Wilville near the town of Monaghan, who d. 1816, and was buried in Donogh ; married Ellen O'Reilly of Bally-maurin, co. Longford, and by her had twenty-two children, some of whom were—1. John McKenna, a general in the Spanish Service, d. 1814. (This John being an officer in the Spanish Service inclines us to believe that the pedigree of this family could be found among the public records at Madrid, or Cadiz) ; 2. Philip, of Tobago, d. unm. in Bristol, about 1832 ; 3. Captain William, d. unm. in Chelsea, about 1843 ; 4. Francis, a merchant in Drogheda, who m. Mary Markey ; 5. James, who d. 1843 ; 6. Christopher, who d. young ; and 7. a daughter Ellen, b. 1819. The aforesaid William was buried in a grave under a stone which has the following inscription :—" Here lyeth the Body of Phelemy MaKenna deceased the 15th April, 1666." It is the belief of some educated persons in that neighbourhood, that The MacKenna who was (as above-mentioned) killed at Drumbanagher in 1689, was buried in the same grave.

MacKENNA. (No. 3.)

Of Ardo House, Ardmore, County Waterford.

Arms : Same as those of "MacKenna" (No. 1).

1. Owen MacKenna had:
2. Michael who lived a long time in Philadelphia, United States, America, and who had:
3. Michael, of Dublin (d. 1854), who had:
  I. Sir Joseph Neale McKenna, of whom presently.
  II. William Columban, living in 1882.
4. Sir Joseph Neale McKenna,

M.P. : son of Michael ; b. 1819, and living in 1887. Was twice m. : first, in 1842, to Esther Louisa (d. 1871), dau. of the late Edmond Howe, Esq., of Dublin ; secondly, in 1880, to Amelia, dau. of G. K. Brooks, Esq., and widow of R. W. Hole, Esq. Residence in Ireland : Ardo House, Ardmore, co. Waterford.

MacKENNA. (No. 4.)

Of Tirowen.

Arms : Ar. a sinister hand couped at the wrist affrontée gu.

CINAOTH, a brother of Furadhran who is No. 97 on the "Foran" pedigree, was the ancestor of *Clann Cionaotha ;* anglicised *MacKenna,** and *Kenny.*

97. Cinaoth : son of Conchobar.
98. Maolbreasal : his son.
99. Maonan : his son.
100. Maolciaran : his son.
101. Diarmaid : his son.
102. Maolmoicherge : his son.
103. Faghartach : his son.

104. Diarmaid : his son.
105. Cinaoth ("cin" or "gan :" Irish, *without ;* "aoth," *servile work*): his son ; a quo *Clann Cionaotha ;* had three brothers—1. Deaghadh, 2. Egneach, 3. Donn.

* *MacKenna* : There were other families of this name in Ireland, but not derived from the same epithet, nor descended from the same stock. For instance : *MacKenna,* lords of Cruagh or Truagh, in the co. Monaghan, were in Irish called *MacIonaigh* ("ionach ;" Irish, *a dirk*), and were descended from Colla-da-Crioch, who is No. 85 on the "O'Hart" pedigree.

MacKEOGH. (No. 1.)

Of Connaught.

Arms : Ar. a lion ramp. gu. in dexter chief a dexter hand couped at the wrist, and in the sinister a crescent, both of the second.   *Crest :* A boar pass. az.

MELAGHLIN, the second son of Donoch who is No. 113 on the (No. 1) "O'Kelly" (of Hy-Maine) pedigree, was the ancestor of *Clann-Eochaidh*, of Connaught; anglicised *MacEocha*, *MacKeogh*, *Kehoe*, and *Keough*.

114. Melaghlin: son of Donoch O'Kelly.

115. Eochaidh Kelly: his son; a quo *Clann Eochaidh* (" each" [ogh]: Irish, *a horse*), meaning " the clan of the knight or horseman."

116. Cairbre Ruadh: his son.

117. Daniel MacEochaidh: his son; first assumed this sirname; had two brothers—1. Dermod Reagh, 2. Teige.

118. Edmond: son of Daniel.

119. Donoch: his son.

120. Col (" col :" Irish, *impediment*): his son.

121. Donoch: his son.

122. Edmund (2): his son; had a brother named Daniel Ruadh.

123. Eochaidh: son of Edmund.

124. Francis MacEochy (or MacKeogh): his son.

MacKEOGH. (No. 2.)

Of Derrylea.

Arms : Same as those of "MacKeogh" (No. 1).

DERMOD REAGH, brother of Daniel who is No. 117 on the foregoing ("MacKeogh") pedigree, was the ancestor of *MacEochaidh*, of Derrylea; anglicised *MacKeogh*.

117. Dermod Reagh MacEocha: son of Cairbre Ruadh.

118. Daniel: his son.

119. Eochaidh: his son.

120. Eochaidh Mór: his son.

121. Giolladubh: his son.

122. Eochaidh (3): his son.

123. John MacEochy (or John MacKeogh), of Derrylea: his son.

MacLAUGHLAN.

Arms : Ar. a sinister hand couped at the wrist affrontée gu.

DONAL, King of Aileach (a territory in the county Donegal), and a younger brother of the Monarch Niall Glundubh who is No. 100 on the

(No. 1) " O'Neill" (of Tyrone) pedigree, was the ancestor of *MacLochlainn ;* anglicised *MacLaughlan, MacLoughlan,** and *Macklin.*

100. Donal: son of the Monarch Aodh Fionnliath.

101. Murtagh: his son; had six brothers, one of whom named Fergus was King of Aileach.

102. Donal, King of Aileach: his son.

103. Donal Oge, King of Aileach: his son.

104. Muireadach, King of Aileach: his son.

105. Lochlonn ("lochlonn :" Irish, *strong at sea*), King of Aileach: his son ; a quo *MacLochloinn.*

106. Ardghal, King of Aileach: his son; first of this family that assumed this sirname.

107. Donal: his son; King of Aileach; and the 179th Monarch of Ireland. This Donal, as Monarch, reigned jointly with Murchertach O'Brien, King of Munster; and alone for thirty-five years, both before and after Murchertach. Most of that time was spent in bloody wars and devastations between these two competitors for the Monarchy, until at length they agreed to the old division of "Leath Mogha" and "Leath Cuinn," between them ; and both ended their days very penitently: Murchertach, in the Monastery of Lismore, A.D. 1119; and Donal, in the Monastery of Columbkille at Derry (now Londonderry), A.D. 1121. In 1088 he destroyed the Monarch Brian Boru's palace of Kincora, in the county Clare, the ancient royal seat of the Kings of Thomond.

108. Neil: his son ; who was King of Aileach ; had a brother named Connor.

109. Murchertach MacLoghlin: his son. This Murchertach was King of Aileach, and the 182nd (and last save one) Monarch of Ireland of the Milesian Irish Race. He was a warlike, victorious, and fortunate Prince ; brought all the provinces of Ireland under his subjection ; forced hostages from them ; and after ten years' absolute reign, was, by Donoch O'Carroll, King of Oriel (that part of the kingdom of *Orgiall*, now the county Louth), slain in battle A.D. 1166.

110. Muirceartach (2): his son; lord of *Cineal Eoghain* (or "Tirowen"); heir presumptive to the throne of Ireland; called "The Demolisher of the Castles of the English ;" was slain by Donoch O'Cahan, A.D. 1196.

111. Donal: his son; known as " Donal of the Battle of Caimirge," fought in 1241. This Donal invaded Tirconnell with the English, in 1232 ; slew Donal, son of Hugh O'Neill, in 1234, and was elected "lord of *Cineal Eoghain*," in his stead. In 1238, Fitzmaurice, Lord Justice of Ireland, together with the Earl of Ulster, marched into *Cineal Connaill* (or Tirconnell); deposed this Donal, and made Brian O'Neill, chief. In 1241, this Brian fought the battle of Caimirge (or Caim Eirge) with Donal, whom he slew, along with nine of his chief kinsmen ; after which the O'Neills were chiefs of *Cineal Eoghain.*

112. Morogh MacLoghlin: son of Donal.

113. Eoghan (or Owen) Mór: his son.

114. Niall : his son.

† *MacLoughlan* : For the derivation of *MacLoughlan*, see the "O'Loghlin" pedigree, p. 342, *ante.*

115. Owen (2): his son.
116. Niall (2): his son.
117. Aibhneach (also called Forbneach): his son; living in 1441.
118. Hugh: his son.
119. Dermod: his son.
120. Dubhaltach: his son; living in 1551: had two brothers—1. Manus Muire, and 2. Hugh Carragh.
121. John MacLaughlan: son of Dubhaltach; had four brothers—1. Dermod, 2. Hugh Buidhe, 3. Giolla Glas, 4. Edmond Gruama.

MacLEIGH.

A Branch of the "MacNamee" family.

Arms of McLeay : Ar. on a chev. gu. betw. three bucks' heads of the last, armed or, a hawk's head erased of the last betw. two salmon erect ppr. on a chief az. an anchor betw. two garbs or. *Crest ;* A buck's head erased ppr. *Motto :* Spes anchora vitæ.

THIS sirname is derived from the Irish "leigh," *a physician,* and means "the son of the physician." The name has been modernized *McLeigh, McLea,* McLeay, McAlea,* etc.

The name is found in the counties Down, Tyrone, and also in Derry. In Lanigan we find *MacLiag* (King Brian Boru's Poet), anglicised *McLigh.* At the Norman Invasion of Ireland we had an Archbishop of Armagh named Gilla *McLiagh,* whose name is latinized Gelasius. Of this family is the Rev. Thomas *McLeigh,* of St. Martin's, Brown County, Ohio, United States, America.

MacMAHON.† (No. 1.)

Lords of Farney, County Monaghan.

Arms : Ar. an ostrich sa. holding in the beak a horseshoe or. *Crest :* A naked arm embowed holding a sword all ppr. the point pierced through a fleur-de-lis sa. *Motto :* So dorn don a dhubhfuiltibh (meaning "here is a fist for the dark-blooded"). *Another :* Manus hæc inimica tyrannis.

CAIRBRE AN DAIMH AIRGID, who is No. 91 on the "O'Hart" pedigree, had a younger son Nadsluagh, who was the ancestor of *MacMaghghamhna,*

---

* *McLea :* This name is believed to be a modern form of *McLear,* and of *McAler.* In the graveyard of Lower Langfield, near Drumquin, county Tyrone, are tombstones with the following inscriptions : On one of them—"Here lyeth the body of Edmund McLear who departed this life February 16 ano Dom 1721, aged 68." And on the other tombstone : " Here lyeth the body of Neckel McAler who died the 11 of April ano Dom 1708, aged 22 years."

† *MacMahon :* Of this family was Con MacMahon who was wounded at the Boyne. Dr. O'Brennan in his *Ancient Ireland,* says that this officer commanded a body of cavalry at the Boyne, where he was wounded ; that he afterwards assisted Sarsfield in his famous interception of the Williamite artillery. His wife was Ellen, of Clonina, a niece of the illustrious Sarsfield.

Lords and Princes of Monaghan; anglicised *MacMahon*, *Mahon*, *Mathew*, *Mathews*, and *Mathewson*.

91. Cairbre an Daimh Airgid: son of Eochaidh.

92. Nadsluagh: his son.

93. Fergus: his son.

94. Ronan: his son.

95. Maolduin (also called Maol-Temin): his son; had a brother named Fogharthach.

96. Fogharthach: son of Maol-duin.

97. Ruadhreach: his son; had a brother Athachtach.

98. Fogharthach: his son; had a brother named Cearbhall.

99. Poil: his son. Had two brothers—1. Flannagan, 2. Dunnagan, who was the ancestor of *Lawlor*, of Monaghan.

100. Cearbhall: son of Poil.

101. Lagnan: his son.

102. Maghghamhuin ("maghghamhuin:" Irish, *a bear*); his son; a quo *MacMaghghamhna*.

103. Donal: his son; first in this family that assumed this sirname; had a younger brother named Cana.

104. Cu-Casil: his son.

105. Donoch: his son; had a brother named Murtagh.

106. Niall: his son.

107. Aodh (or Hugh): his son.

108. Maghghamhuin: his son.

109. Manus: his son.

110. Niall: his son.

111. Maghghamhuin: his son.

112. Eochaidh: his son.

113. Rodolph: his son.

114. Eochaidh: his son.

115. Brian Mór: his son.

116. Ardghul: his son.

117. Ruadhri (or Roger): his son; had eight brothers.

118. Eoghan [owen]: his son; Lord of Dartry, county Monaghan; had two brothers.*

119. Owen: his son.

120. Hugh: his son.

121. Shane (or John) Buidhe: his son.

122. Hugh: his son.

123. Hugh Oge: his son.

124. Sir Bryan, Lord of Dartry: his son; d. 10th Oct., 1620. Married the Lady Mary, widow of his kinsman Sir Ross MacMahon, and dau. of Hugh O'Neill, the great Earl of Tyrone, whose "flight," A.D. 1607 (see "The Flight of the Earls," in the Appendix), afforded such facilities for the "Plantation of Ulster." By this Lady Sir Bryan MacMahon left at his death two sons—1. Art, 2. Brian Oge; and daughters.†

125. Art MacMahon, Lord of Dartry: his son; married Evaline, dau. of Ever MacMahon, of Lissanisky, in the county Monaghan; died at Ballinure in 1634, leaving issue an only son.

126. Patrick: only son of Art; died at Dublin, in 1635, leaving three sons—1. Colla Dubh [dhu], 2. Constantine, who died *s. p.*, 3.

* *Brothers:* One of those brothers was Edmund, who was father of Cormac, who was father of Collo, who was father of Patrick MacMahon, of Drumgiston, county Monaghan, who died A.D. 1637.

† *Daughters:* Una (or Agnes), one of the daughters of this Sir Bryan MacMahon, Lord of Dartry, married—first, Gerald Byrne, Esq., of Roscrea, and secondly, Charles, son of Morgan (son of Bryan) Kavanagh, of Polomonty, in the county of Carlow, and Katherine was married Captain Hugh Reilly, Liscannow, county Cavan.

Writing in 1608 of this Sir Bryan MacMahon, Sir Henry Dillon says: "That he is the best followed of any man in the country, and it were well he were not discontented."

the Rev. Arthur Augustine,* Provost of St. Peter's, at Casselle, in Flanders.

127. Colla Dhu MacMahon, titular Lord of Dartry: son of Patrick. This Colla married Aileen, daughter of The O'Reilly (who was styled "Earl of Cavan"), and niece of the illustrious Owen Roe O'Neill, by whom he had issue—1. Bernard, who married a daughter of Art Oge, son of Art Roe MacMahon, of Slack's Grove; 2. Hugh, who was administrator of Kilmore, was consecrated bishop of Clogher in 1708, became primate of Armagh in 1709, and who died in August, 1737; 3. Con; 4. Patrick; and two other sons whose names have not been recorded, but who are stated to have fought at Derry, etc.

128. Patrick of Corravilla: the fourth son of Colla Dhu; married a lady named MacMahon, by whom he had four sons—1. Cullagh, 2. Bernard,† who died 27th May, 1747, aged 69 years, 3. Ross (who died October 29th, 1748, aged 49), 4. Roger.

129. Cullagh MacMahon, of Rockfield, county Monaghan: son of Patrick; nominated to the Family Bourses, until he "conformed,"

when the privilege appears to have passed to the co-heiresses of Mr. Peter MacMahon of Rekane,‡ under a clause in the Will of the Rev. Arthur Augustine MacMahon, above mentioned.

130. Hugh, of Rockfield: son of Cullagh; married Miss Griffith of Laurel Hill, county Monaghan.

131. Charles of Carrickmacross: their son; married in 1821 Rose, daughter of ——— Coleman, Esq., county Louth, by whom he had two sons—1. Charles, 2. Patrick (who, in 1853, died, *s. p.*); and one daughter, Eliza.

132. Charles MacMahon, of Brookfield, Dundalk: son of Charles; living in 1881; Clerk of the Crown and Peace, for the county Louth; was, when only twelve years of age, called upon to nominate to the Family-Bourses. He married Alice, daughter of James Gartlan, Esq., of Carrickmacross, by whom he had issue one son, Charles, and two daughters—1. Alice, married to W. Russell, Esq., of Downpatrick; 2. Rose, married to William Mulholland, Liverpool, Barrister-at-Law.

133. Charles MacMahon, A.B.: his son; living in 1887.

* *Augustine* : This Rev. Arthur Augustine MacMahon, by his Will, dated 1710, founded many Bourses for the education of young men for the priesthood : "The preference being given to members of the families of MacMahon, Maguire, O'Reilly, and O'Neill, ... and amongst the four families aforesaid shall be preferred those of the name and parentage of the Founder."

† *Bernard* : This Bernard MacMahon was consecrated Bishop of Clogher in 1709 (in succession to his uncle Hugh, the second son of Colla Dhu, above mentioned), and was translated to the primatial chair of Armagh, in 1738 ; and his brother Ross was, in succession to him, consecrated Bishop of Clogher, in 1739, and was translated to Armagh, in 1747. In the churchyard of Edragoole (or Ematriss), county Monaghan, Roger MacMahon, the younger brother of these two primates, erected A.D. 1750, a monument to their memory, on which the following is the inscription :

"Hic jacent Rochus (vel Rossius) et Bernardus MacMahon, fratres germani : uterque successivé archiepiscopus Armacanus, totius Hiberniæ primates, quorum nobilissimi generis memor pietas, atque æmula doctrina, vitaque titulos non impar morientem patriam decoravere. Bernardus obiit 27 Maii 1747, ætat. 69. Rochus, die 29 Oct., 1748, ætat. 49. Ambo pares virtute, pares et honoribus ambo."

‡ *Rekane:* See Note under under No. 11 of the "Fay" pedigree.

MacMAHON.* (No. 2.)

Of Drumgiston, County Monaghan.

Arms : Same as those of "MacMahon" (No. 1).

ARDELL MACMAHON had :
2. Rory, who had :
3. Edmund, who had :
4. Cormac, who had :

5. Collo, who had :
6. Patrick MacMahon, of Dromgiston, co. Monaghan, Esq., who d. in 1637.

---

* *MacMahon :* Heber MacMahon, Bishop of Clogher, and General of the Ulster Irish, was a Catholic prelate who took a prominent part in the War 1641—1652, in the interest of Charles I. Clarendon speaks of him as " much superior in parts to any man of that party." He was created Bishop of Clogher in June, 1643. On the death of Owen Roe O'Neill, in November, 1649, he was appointed at Belturbet, Commander of the Ulster Irish, and received his commission from the Earl of Ormond. He immediately put himself at the head of 5,000 foot and 600 horse, and marched to Charlemont, where he issued a manifesto inviting the Scots serving under Coote and Venables to make common cause with the Irish ; but only a small number of them joined his standard. On the 21st of June, 1650, he attacked at Scarriffhollis, two miles from Letterkenny, the united forces of Coote and Venables ; in the early part of the engagement his troops carried all before them, but they were afterwards defeated and almost annihilated. Major-General O'Cahan, many officers, and 1,500 soldiers were killed on the spot ; and Carte says that Colonels Henry Roe O'Neill and Felim O'Neill, Hugh Maguire, Hugh MacMahon, and many more were slain after quarter was given. The Bishop quitted the field with a small party of horse. His fate is related by Clarendon, as follows :—"Next day, in his flight, he had the misfortune, near Enniskilling, to meet with the governor of that town, at the head of a party too strong for him, against which, however, the Bishop defended himself with notable courage ; and, after he had received many wounds, he was forced to become a prisoner, upon promise, first, that he should have fair quarter ; contrary to which, Sir Charles Coote, as soon as he knew that he (the Bishop) was a prisoner, caused him to be hanged, with all the circumstances of contumely, reproach, and cruelty which he could devise." Cox, in his *History of Ireland*, says :—"Nor is it amiss to observe the variety and vicissitude of the Irish affairs ; for, this very Bishop (MacMahon), and those officers whose heads were now placed on the walls of Derry, were within less than a year before confederate with Sir Charles Coote, raised the siege of that city, and were jovially merry at his table, in the quality of friends."

MacMANUS.*

Of Fermanagh.

Arms : Vert a griffin segreant or, in chief three crescents ar.   *Crest :* A hand and arm couped below the elbow erect, holding a long cross ppr.

MANUS,† brother of Giollaiosa who is No. 109 on the "Maguire" pedigree, was the ancestor of *MacManus.*

109. Manus: son of Dun Mór Maguire ; a quo *MacManus.*
110. Rory : his son.
111. Manus (2) : his son.
112. Patrick : his son; had two brothers.

113. Matthew : his son.
114. Patrick (2) : his son.
115. Connor MacManus : his son.

MacMOROUGH.

Kings of Leinster ; and Chiefs of " Clan Moroghoe."

Arms : Sa. three garbs or. (*Another* : Gu. a lion ramp. ar.)   *Crest :* Out of clouds a hand erect holding a crown betw. two swords in bend and bend sinister, points upwards all ppr.

LABHRADH, a brother of Eanna Niadh who is No. 92 on the "O'Toole" pedigree, was the ancestor of *MacMuircha ;* anglicised *MacMorough,‡ Mac-Morrow,* and *Morrow.*

92. Labhradh: son of Breasal Bealach, the second Christian King of Leinster ; had two sons:

I. Eanna Ceannsalach.
II. Deagh, a quo *Ui Deagha Mór ;* in Hy-Cinnselach.

---

* *MacManus* : Terence Bellew MacManus, a distinguished "Young Irelander," was born about 1823. At the time of the Young Ireland agitation in 1848 he was in business as a shipping agent in Liverpool. In the summer of that year he threw up everything, managed to give the detectives the slip in Dublin, joined Smith O'Brien at Killenaule, and shared the fortunes of the small band of insurgents until their dispersion at Ballingarry. When all hope was over, he was for a time concealed by the peasantry, and then managed to make his way to Cork, and was on board a vessel in the harbour about to sail, when he was arrested. On the 9th October, 1848, he was brought to trial for high treason, at Clonmel, found guilty, and condemned to death. His sentence was subsequently commuted to transportation for life. He was sent to Tasmania, whence he escaped to California, on the 5th June, 1851. He died in California nine years after-wards ; but his remains were conveyed to Ireland, and buried in Glasnevin, on the 10th November, 1861.

† *Manus* : Some derive this name from the Irish *mainis,* "a lance or spear" (*main* : Irish, "the hand :" Lat. *man-us*) ; in which case *MacManus* would mean "the son of the man who could wield a spear."

‡ *MacMorough* : The ancient kings of Leinster had fortresses or royal residences at Dinnrigh, near the river Barrow, between Carlow and Leighlin ; at Naas, in Kildare ;

93. Eanna Ceannsalach : elder son of Labhradh ; mar. Conang ; was called Ceann-Salach (unclean head) by Cednathech the Druid, whom he slew at Cruachan Cleanta (Croghan Hill, in the King's County), where Eanna defeated Eochaidh Muigh Meadhoin (Eochy Moyvone), the Monarch, A.D. 365. Had issue:

I. Feidhlimidh (or Felim).

II. Eochu (or Eochaidh) Ceann-salach, who was exiled to Scotland by the Irish Monarch Niall of the Nine Hostages, whom said Eochu assassinated near Boulogne, on the river Leor (now the Lianne).

III. Crimthann Cass, of whom presently.

IV. Earc.

V. Aongus.

VI. Conal.

VII. Trian.

VIII. Cairpre.

94. Crimthann Cass : third son of Eanna Ceannsalach ; was King of Leinster for 40 years ; baptized by St. Patrick at Rathvilly, *circa* 448 ; slain in 484 by his grandson Eochaidh Guinech of the Hy-Bairche. Married Mell, dau. of Erebran of the Desies in Munster (son of Eoghan Bric, son of Art Cuirb, son of Fiacha Suighde, son of Felim Rachtmar), and had issue:

I. Ingen, wife of Daire Mac-Ercadh of the Hy-Bairche.

II. Nathach (or Dathi).

III. Fiacra.

IV. Eithne Uathach, wife of Aongus MacNadfraech, King of Munster.

V. Fergus, who defeated Diarmuid MacCearbhaill at Drum Laeghaire, by the side of Cais in Hy-Faelain, defending the *Boromha.*

VI. Aongus.

VII. Etchen.

VIII. Cobthach.

95. Nathach : son of Crimthan Cass ; was King of Leinster for 10 years ; bapt. in his infancy by St. Patrick. Had issue:

I. Owen Caoch, of whom presently.

II. Cormac.

III. Faelan, who had a son named Fergus.

IV. Olioll.

96. Eoghan (or Owen) Caoch : eldest son of Nathach; had two sons:

I. Siollan, of whom presently.

II. Fergus, ancestor of *O'Ryan.*

97. Siollan (" siollan :" Irish, *a skinny, meagre person*): son of Eoghan Caoch ; a quo *O'Siollain,* anglicised *Sloan.*

98. Faelan : his son ; was King of Leinster for 9 years.

99. Faolchu : his son ; had three sons:

I. Elodach, King of Leinster for 7 years.

II. Onchu, of whom presently.

III. Aongus, slain A.D. 721 at Maisden, Mullaghmast.

100. Onchu : son of Faolchu.

and in after-times at the city of Ferns in Wexford, which was their capital ; and also at Old Ross in Wexford; and at Ballymoon in Carlow. The MacMoroughs were inaugurated as kings of Leinster at a place called *Cnoc-an-Bhogha*, attended by O'Nolan, who was the King's Marshal, and Chief of Forth in Carlow ; by O'Doran, Chief Brehon of Leinster ; and by MacKeogh, his Chief Bard ; and the MacMoroughs maintained their independence, and held the title of " Kings of Leinster," with large possessions in Wexford and Carlow down to the reign of Queen Elizabeth. The Hy-Cavanagh or O'Cavanaghs were chiefs of the ancient territory which now comprises the barony of Idrone East, in the county Carlow ; and in modern times became the representatives of the MacMoroughs, Kings of Leinster.

* *Boromha* : For the explanation of this tribute, see the Paper " Ancient Leinster Tributes," in the Appendix.

101. Rudgal: his son; had two
sons:

    I. Aodh (or Hugh), of whom pre-
sently.

    II. Flann, slain at Allen, in the
co. Kildare, A.D. 722.

102. Aodh: son of Rudgal; had
two sons:

    I. Diarmuid, of whom presently.

    II. Bruadar, slain in 853.

103. Diarmuid: son of Aodh; had
two sons:

    I. Cairbre, of whom presently.

    II. Tadhg, slain in 865.

104. Cairbre: son of Diarmuid;
slain in 876.

105. Ceneth: his son; slain by
the Danes of Loch Carmen; was
King of Leinster for 13 years. Had
two sons:

    I. Echtighern, King of Leinster
for 9 years; slain in 951 by the
sons of Ceallach, his brother.
He had issue:—1. Cairpre,
abbot of Clonmore, who d. in
974; 2. Aodh, who slew Donal
Cloen, in 983; and 3. Bruadar
(Bran?) who d. 982, and was
King of Leinster for 4 years.

    II. Ceallach, slain in 945.

106. Ceallach: second son of
Ceneth; was slain by the Ossorians
in 945, at Athcliath (or Dublin).
He had two sons:

    I. Doncadh, King of Leinster for
6 years.

    II. Donal.

107. Donal: second son of Ceallach; was King of Leinster for 9
years; slain by the Ossorians in 974.
Had issue:

    I. Aodh.

    II. Doncadh, slain by Donal
Cloen in 983.

    III. Diarmuid, of whom pre-
sently.

    IV. Maolruanaidh, who was King
of Leinster for 13 years.

108. Diarmuid: third son of

Donal; was King of Leinster for
13 years; d. in 997.

109. Donoch Maol-na-mBo: his
son; was King of Leinster for 9
years. Had two sons:

    I. Donal Reamhar, slain in 1041
at Killmolappog, co. Carlow,
had three sons:—1. Donchadh,
slain in 1089 by O'Connor
Failghe (Faley); 2. Donal,
who was a hostage of Tirlogh
O'Brien; and 3. Ruadh, who
gave Clonkeen (now known as
the "Kill-o'-the Grange"), near
Kingstown, to Christ Church
in Dublin.

    II. Diarmuid, slain in 1072.

110. Diarmuid: second son of
Donoch Maol-na-mBo; was the 47th
Christian King of Leinster, and the
177th Milesian Monarch of Ireland;
was slain on the 23rd Feb., 1072, at
Odhba, near Navan; m. Darbhforgal
(d. 1080), grand-daughter of the
Monarch Brian Boromha, and had
issue:

    I. Murcha, of whom presently.

    II. Glunairn, who in 1071, was
slain by the Meath men at
Donlah, and buried at Duleek.

    III. Enna, who had a son Diar-
muid, slain in 1098.

111. Murcha ("muirchu:" Irish, *a
sea hound*, meaning *a sea warrior*,
also called Morogh or Morough), a
quo *MacMuirchu* or *MacMorough*:
eldest son of Diarmuid. From this
Murcha, also (and not from his son
Murcha), the *ClanMorochoe* is
so called; which has been anglicised *O'Moroghoe*, and modernized
O'Murphy, Murrough, and *Murphy*.
This Murcha was the eldest son of
Diarmuid; was the 50th Christian
King of Leinster; invaded the Isle
of Man in 1070; d. in Dublin on
the 8th December, 1090. Had
issue:

    I. Donal, who was King of Dublin, d. after three days' illness in 1075.

II. Gormlath, who was Abbess of Kildare, d. 1112.

III. Donoch, of whom presently.

IV. Enna, who had a son Diarmuid, d. 1113, at Dublin.

V. Glunairn, whose daughter Sadhbh (d. 1171) was Abbess of Kildare.

VI. Murcha (or Moragh).

112. Donoch *MacMorough :* the third son of Murcha, No. 111 ; was King of Dublin, and the 56th Christian King of Leinster ; slain in 1115 by Donal O'Brien and the Danes at Dublin. He had two sons :

I. Diarmuid-na-nGhall, of whom presently.

II. Murcha* (or Moroch)-na n Gaodhail, from whom descended *Davidson* or *MacDavy Mór.* This Murcha was in 1166 elected successor to his brother as King of Leinster, when Diarmuid-na-nGhall was deposed.

113. Diarmuid - na - nGall ("na-nGall :" Irish, *of the foreigners*) : the elder son of Donoch MacMorough ; was the 58th Christian King of Leinster ; is known as "Dermod MacMorough ;"† became King of Leinster in 1135 ; was in 1166 deposed by the Monarch Roderick O'Connor, aided by Tiernan O'Ruarc, Prince of West Brefni ; d. in Ferns in January, 1171. Dermod MacMorough had :

I. Aifé (or Eva), who was m. to Richard de Clare, known as "Strongbow ;" she d. in 1177.

II. Art, slain in 1170 at Athlone, by the Monarch Roderick O'Connor, to whom said Art was given as a hostage.

III. Donal Caomhanach, a quo *O'Kavanagh.* (See the "Kavanagh" pedigree.)

IV. Eanna Ceannsalach, a quo *O'Kinsela.* (See the "Kinsela" pedigree.)

V. Orlacan, who m. Donal Mór, No. 110 on the "O'Brien" (No. 1) pedigree.

---

* *Murcha :* We have seen it stated in a Genealogical Chart in one of the Kilkenny Arch. Journals, that the *Clan-Morochoe* descended, and derived their name, from this Murcha ; but MacFirbis distinctly states that the *Clan-Morochoe* is descended and takes its name from Murcha, who is No. 111 on this pedigree.

† *MacMorough :* In 1153 Dermod MacMorough carried off Dearvolga, daughter of O'Melaghlin, the last King of Meath, and the wife of O'Ruark, Prince of Brefney. On this subject Webb writes :—"The transaction cannot have had much of the romance usually associated with the idea of an elopement. She was forty-four years of age, and did not leave her lord without carrying off her cattle and furniture. This was fifteen years before Dermot sought Anglo-Norman assistance ; so that the invasion (of Ireland) can scarcely be attributable to the elopement. . . . Dearvorgal spent much of her later life in religious exercises, and part of her substance in endowing churches. She survived until 1193, when she died at Mellifont Abbey, county of Meath, which she had enriched with many presents. Although Dermot's Kingdom nominally passed into Earl Strongbow's family after his decease, much of it appears to have been soon again occupied by the MacMurroughs, by whom it was held in almost undisputed sway for several centuries."

MacNAMEE.

Arms : Gu. three bends ar. on a chief or, as many cinquefoils az.

SUIBHNEACH, brother of Neachtan who is No. 99 on the "Conroy" pedigree, was the ancestor of *Macnamidhe ;* anglicised *Macnamee*, and *Mee.*

99. Suibhneach : son of Florence.
100. Dubhron ("dubhron :" Irish, *sorrow*) : his son ; a quo *O'Dubhroin*, anglicised *Doran.**
101. Cearnach : his son.
102. Lochan : his son.
103. Anbeith : his son.
104. Rorc : his son.

105. Conn : his son.
106. Giolla Cumidhe [cumee] : his son.
107. Cumidhe ("cu :" Irish, *a warrior ;* "midhe," *Meath*), meaning "the warrior of Meath :" his son ; a quo *Macnamidhe.*

MACONKY.

Arms (of "Maconochie") : Az. three dexter hands couped fesseways in chief, each holding a bunch of arrows ppr. and in base a royal crown gold, all within a bordure gyronny of eight or and sa.

ALIOLL, brother of Eochaidh who is No. 98 on the "Dowling" pedigree, was the ancestor of *MacOnchuin ;* anglicised *MacOnchon*, *Maconchy*, *Maconky*, and *Maconochie.*

98. Alioll : son of Muireadach : had two brothers—1. Eochaidh, 2. Eoghan.
99. Creamhthann : son of Alioll.
100. Caomhan : his son.
101. Failbhe : his son.
102. Dicneadh ("dicneadh :" Irish, *without a wound*) : his son ; a quo *O'Dicneidhe*, anglicised *Dickney*, which has been modernized *Dickens.*
103. Onnchu ("onnchu :" Irish, *a leopard*) : his son ; a quo *MacOnchuin.*

104. Cu-cuan ("cuan :" Irish, *a little warrior*) : his son ; a quo *O'Cuain ;* anglicised *Quain*,† *Quane*, and *Quan.*
105. Irgus : his son.
106. Forabuidh : his son.
107. Maoldun : his son.
108. Cronmaol : his son.
109. Irgus (2) : his son.
110. Seachnasach : his son.
111. Guaire MacOnchon : his son.

---

* *Doran* : There was another "Doran" or *Ui Dheorain* family descended from the "O'Sullivan Mór" Stock.

† *Quain* : For another "Quain" family, see the "Quin" pedigree, p. 256, *ante.*

MacSHEEHY.

Arms : Quarterly, 1st, az. a lion pass. guard. ar. ; 2nd, ar. three lizards vert ; 3rd, az. three pole-axes in fess or ; 4th, ar. a ship with three masts sa.

ALASTRUM (or Alexander), brother of Æneas (or Aongus) Mór who is No. 105 on the "MacDonnell" (of Antrim) pedigree, was the ancestor of *O'Sithaigh,* and *MacSithaigh ;* anglicised *MacSheehy,* and *Sheehy.*

105. Alastrum ("ala :" Irish, *a swan ;* "astraim," *to carry*), or Alexander : son of Donall ; a quo *Alexander, Lester, MacAllister, Macalister, Saunders,* and *Saunderson.*

106. Eachdun : his son.

107. Si th a ch an D o r n a d o i r ("sioth :" Irish, *an atonement ;* "ach," *one who*), meaning " Sithach the Boxer :" his son : a quo *O'Sithaigh ;* living in 1380.

108. William Fionn : his son.

109. Dunsithach MacSheehy : his son ; first assumed this sirname.

110. William (2) : his son.

111. Dermod Baccach : his son.

112. William (3) : his son.

113. Dermod (2) : his son.

114. John : his son.

115. Dermod MacSheehy : his son.

MacSWEENY. (No. 1.)

Of Fanad.

Arms :[*] Or, on a fess vert betw. three boars pass. sa. a lizard ar. *Crest:* An arm in armour embowed, holding a battle-axe all ppr.

AODH ANRACHAN, a younger brother of Donal an Togdhamh who is No. 106 on the (No. 1) "O'Neill" (Princes of Tyrone) pedigree, was the ancestor of *MacSuibhaneaighe ;* anglicised *MacSweeney, MacSwiney, MacSwiggan, Sweeney, Sweeny, Swiggan, Swiney, Swyney, Swayne, Swain,* and *Sweney.*

106. Aodh (or Hugh) Anrachan : second son of Aodh Athlamh, Prince of Tyrone.

107. Aodh Alainn (or Hugh the Beautiful) : his son.

108. Dunsleibhe : his son ; had a brother named Giollachriosd, who was the ancestor of *MacLaghlan, MacLachlan, MacLaughlan,* and other families, in Scotland.

109. Suibhneach ("suibh :" Irish,

a strawberry plant, Welsh, " syfi ;" or " subha," *mirth ;* and "neach," *some one, any one, a spirit* or *apparition*) : son of Dunsleibhe ; a quo *MacSuibhaneaighe.* This Suibhneach had a brother named Fearchar, who had a son named Giollacoluim, who was father of Ladhman, a quo *O'Laidmain,* anglicised *Layman.*

110. Maolmuire ; son of Suibhneach ; first assumed this sirname.

---

* *Arms :* The *Arms* of MacSweeney, according to De la Ponce, were : "D'argent á deux Sangliers affrontés de gueules, accompagnés en chef de deux haches de combat d' ázur placés en sautoir."

111. Moroch Mór: his son; living A.D. 1267.

112. Maolmuire: his son.

113. Moroch Mir ("mir:" *a part* or *portion*): his son. Had two sons —1. Moroch, ancestor of *MacSweeney* of Fanad; 2. Maolmuire, who was the ancestor of *MacSweeney na Doe* (or MacSweeney *na Tuaidh*). Some annalists derive *tuaidh* from "tuagh:" Irish, *an axe;* or from "tuagh catha:" Irish, *a battle axe;* Gr. "tuo;" Fr. "tuer;" and some, from "tuaith:" Irish, *a territory.**

114. Moroch: elder son of Moroch Mir.

115. Maolmuire: his son.

116. Tirloch Mór Caoch: his son.

117. Tirloch Ruadh [roe]: his son.

118. Maolmuire: his son.

119. Ruadhri: his son.

120. Tirloch: his son.

121. Donal: his son.

122. Donal Gorm: his son.

123. Donal Oge: his son.

124. Donal Gorm (2): his son.

125. Hugh MacSweeney, of Fanad: his son; had a brother named Donal.

MacSWEENEY. (No. 2.)

Na-Tuaighe, or "Na Doe."

Arms : Az. two boars ramp. combatant or, in chief two battle axes in saltire of the last. *Crest :* A demi griffin ramp. or, holding in the claws a lizard ppr.

Maolmuire, the second son of Moroch Mir who is No. 113 on the (No. 1) "MacSweeney" pedigree, was the ancestor of *MacSuibhaneaighe na Tuaighe.*

113. Moroch Mir: son of Maolmuire.

114. Maolmuire (or Myler): his younger son; had a brother named Moroch, who was the ancestor of *MacSweeney*, of Fanad.

115. Donoch (also called Daniel: his son; had two brothers—1. Dubhghall, 2. Tirloch.

116. Tirloch: son of Donoch; had a brother named Geoffrey.

117. Neal na Tuaighe: son of Tirloch; had a brother named Maolmuire MacSweeney, of Desmond.†

118. Daniel: son of Neal.

119. Donoch: his son.

120. Hugh Buidhe: his son.

† *Territory*: The territories of MacSweeney na Tuaighe (or, as some have it, "na d-Tuath," or *na Doe*) comprised the parishes of Menagh, Clondahorky, Raymunter, Doney, and Raytullaghobigly. And the names of the three Tuaths (or territories) contained in "MacSweeney's Country," in the County of Donegal, are yet retained among the old inhabitants; namely—Ross-Guill (or Rossgul), Tuath-Tory, and Cloghaneely.

* *Desmond :* Branches of the "MacSweeney" family settled in Connaught, in Clanrickard, in Thomond, in Ormond, in Desmond, and other parts of Munster.
—*Four Masters.*

121. Maolmuire : his son.

122. Owen Mór ; his son.

123. Owen Oge :* his son ; living in 1587.

124. Neal Bearnach : his son.

125. Morogh (2): his son.

126. Sir Maolmuire [or Mulmurry] : his son.

127. Donoch Mór : his son ; had a brother Moroch.†

128. Maolmuire : son of Donoch Mór.

129. Tirloch : his son ; living in 1768.

130. Hugh : his son ; married to Eleanor Scott. Had a brother Maolmordha (or Myles) ; and a sister Mary, m. to James Dunlevy‡ of Ballygawley ; d. aged 103 years, and buried in Sligo Abbey.

131. Hugh (or "Hugo Smoke :") son of Hugh ; m. in 1790 Ellen Dunlevy. Had four brothers and four sisters : the brothers were—1. Doyle, m. to Elizabeth Stuart, and had issue§ four daughters and two sons ; 2. Morgan, whose son George m. Mary Gordon, no issue ;

---

* *Owen Oge*: It was with this Owen Oge MacSweeney, the lord of Rathmullan Castle, county Donegal, that Hugh Roe O'Donnell (see the Four Masters, under A. D. 1587, 1590, and 1592), then in his 15th year, with other nobles of the country, were enjoying the far-famed hospitality of the said Owen Oge MacSweeney, and looking out on the beautiful bay before them. A ship was observed coming up the bay, with a deceptive ensign, under the pretext of being a Spanish vessel freighted with the choicest wines. The news of its arrival being immediately spread abroad, the young chieftain with some others incautiously went on board, where they were most graciously received by the captain, who invited them down to the saloon, where he gave them the most delicious wines. Whilst, however, they were enjoying his hospitality, the hatches were secured, and O'Donnell was carried off to Dublin Castle ; where he remained a prisoner for three years and three months, when he contrived to escape, first in 1590. This Owen Oge MacSweeney was foster-father to that Hugh O'Donnell, and he proffered other hostages and sureties in lieu of him, but it was of no avail ; for there was not a hostage in the province of Ulster the English would take in his stead:

—— The generous Prince Red Hugh,
Unguarded, quits the fortress walls and stands amidst the crew.
Down with the hatches, set the sails, we've won the wished-for prize,
Above the Rebel's prison cell to-morrow's sun shall rise.
Untasted foams the Spanish wine, the board is spread in vain,
The hand that waved a welcome forth is shackled by a chain.
Yet faster, faster, through the deep the vessel glideth on,
Tirconnell's towers, like phantoms fade, the last faint trace is gone.

† *Moroch :* From this Moroch the descent was as follows :

127. Moroch : son of Sir Mulmurry.

128. Donoch Oge : his son.

129. Tirlogh : his son.

130. Emon : his son.

131. Donoch : his son.

132. Tirlogh MacSweeney : his son : living in September, 1835, in Dunfanaghy, county Donegal, when (see O'Donovan's

MSS. Antiquities deposited in the Library of the Royal Irish Academy, Dublin,) John O'Donovan, LL.D., then engaged on the Ordnance Survey in that district met the said Tirlogh, and his two sons, then "stalwart young men."

133. (These two sons).

‡ *James Dunlevy :* The issue of that marriage were six children—1. Mary, *s.p.* ; 2. Alicia, *s.p.* ; 3. Ellen, m. in 1790, to Hugo Smoke MacSweeny, No. 131, *supra ;* 4. Morgan, m. Margaret Sweeny, by whom he had five children ; 5. Denis, m. to Countess de Perigny, no issue ; 6. Owen, m. to ——, and had Rev. James Dunlevy, Dean in Roman Catholic Church, Sligo, *s.p.* The five children of Morgan were—1. James, who d. *s.p.*, an Officier d'Artillerie à Auxome, France ; 2. Denis, d. *s.p.* U.S.; 3. Owen, m. to Clara King, had three daughters ; 4. Nial-Morgan, *s.p.* in U.S. ; 5. Mary, *s.p.* in U.S.

§ *Issue :* 1. Elizabeth-Stuart, d. *s.p.* ; 2. Elinor, m. Edwin Myers, had a dau.

3. John, m. to Susan Fromberger, issue, three daughters; 4. Nial. The sisters were—1. Rose, m. John Gaelrick; 2. Honora, m. to John Ormsby, grandfather of John Ormsby of Ballina, county Mayo, living in 1878; 3. Nelly, m. to — Fitzgerald, no issue; 4. Margaret, married to Morgan Dunlevy. This "Hugo Smoke" MacSweeney had three sons and two daughters: the sons were—1. Hugh MacSweeney, who d. *s.p.* in 1845, was the last of this family that retained the prefix *Mac ;* 2. Frederick-Morgan Sweeny (No. 132 on this pedigree); 3. Charles (d. in India), m. — Shooks, and had a son Charles. Hugo's daughters were—1. Mary Sweeny, m. to Bartholomew Brennan, issue two sons and one daughter;* 2. Alicia, m. to — Christy, issue two daus.—Mary-Ellen, and Alicia (*s.p.*)

132. Frederick-Morgan Sweeny: second son of "Hugo Smoke;" b. in Sligo 1795, died 1845. Married to Rachel (b. in Philadelphia, Penn-sylvania, and d. 1841), daughter of Geo. Ormsby, of Sligo, son of John Ormsby by his wife Ellinor Morgan. This last mentioned John was the son of John Ormsby by his wife Lady Anne Gore, all of the county of Sligo. This Frederick had four children—1. Emmet, d. in infancy, in Philadelphia; 2. Robert Ormsby-Sweeny, No. 133 on this pedigree; 3. Mary Alicia, married to William Lowber Banning, issue seven children;† 4. Catherine, m. to Jacob-Henry Stewart, M.D., issue three children—Ursula, Jacob-Henry, and Robert.

133. Robert Ormsby Sweeny, of St. Paul, Minnesota, United States, America: son of Frederick Morgan Sweeney; born in Philadelphia, in 1831, and living in 1886; married Helen Benezet, and had issue.

134. Robert Ormsby Sweeny, of St. Paul, Minn.: their son; born 1869, and living in 1886. Had a sister Helen Benezet Sweeny, who died in infancy.

MacSWEENEY. (No. 3.)

Of Banagh.

Arms : Same Arms and Crest as "MacSweeney" (No. 2).

Dubhghall, of Dun Usnaigh, brother of Donoch who is No. 115 on the (No. 2) "MacSweeney" na Tuaighe (or Na Doe) pedigree, was the ancestor of MacSweeney, of *Tir Boghaine,* now the barony of "Banagh," in the county Donegal.

Frances-Cecilia; 3. Doyle-Edward Sweeny, Captain U.S. Army, d. 1847, married Catherine Hanlon, had one son and two daughters; 4. Nial Sweeny, d. *s.p. ;* 5. Rose-Anna, m. T. H. Walsh, and had issue three sons and two daughters; 6. Fanny, *s.p.*

* *Daughter:* The two sons were—1. Michael Brennan, m. to Dorinda Leslie, issue three children, namely—Ellen, *s.p.*, Robert, *s.p.*, and Dorinda, *s.p. ;* 2. Hugh Brennan, d. in Hong-Kong, China. The daughter, Ellen-Mary Brennan, living in Sligo in 1880.

† *Children :* The children were—1. William-Lowber Banning, *s.p. ;* 2. Ellen-Barrows; 3. Evans, *s.p.*; 4. Mary-Alice ; 5. Frederick-Dunlevy Banning ; 6. Kate-Stewart; 7. William.

2 N

115. Dubhgall : son of Maolmuire.

116. Owen Conachtach ("conachtach :" Irish, *an inhabitant of Connaught*): his son; a quo *O'Conachtaigh* (anglicised *Conaty*), of Cabra, in the barony of Tireragh, county Sligo.

117. Owen na Lathaighe (or Owen of the Mire) : his son; slain 1351 ; a quo *O'Lathaighe*, anglicised *Lahy*, and *Myers.*

118. Maolmuire : his son.

119. Eoghan : his son.

120. Niall (or Neal) Mór:* his son ; died 1524.

121. Maolmuire (2): his son; slain by his brother Niall in 1535 ; had a brother Eoin Modardha (or John the Stern), who died 1543.

122. Maolmuire Meirgeach (" meirgeach):" Irish, *rusty ;* his son.

123. Donogh : his son ; living in 1588.

124. Neal Meirgeach MacSweeney: his son; had four brothers — 1. Maolmuire, 2. Oliver, 3. Henry, 4. Alexander.

MacSWEENEY. (No. 4.)

Of Castlemore, Moviddy, County Cork.

Arms : The *Armorial Bearings* of MacSweeney-na-Doe family, according to Cæsar Otway who wrote in 1839, were a salmon, a lion pass. and a bloody hand.

TIRLOCH, a younger brother of Donoch who is No. 115 on the (No. 2) "MacSweeney" Na Tuaighe (or Na Doe) genealogy, was the ancestor of this branch of that family :

115. Tirloch : son of Maolmuire.

116. Dubhdara: his son.

117. Eoghan : his son.

118. Donall : his son.

119. Eoghan an Locha : his son.

120. Brian : his son.

121. Eoghan : his son.

122. Maolmuire : his son.

123. Murcadh : his son ; had :

    I. Maolmuire.

    II. Eoghan.

    III. Eileen.

    IV. Murcadh.

124. Maolmuire : son of Murcadh ; m. Kathleen O'Mahony, of Kilmurry, and had :

    I. Murcadh Beag.

    II. Tirlogh.

125. Murcadh Beag : son of Maolmuire ; born in Castlemore, Moviddy, and removed thence to Macroom ; m. Mary, dau. of Bryan O'Sullivan, of Castleisland, county Kerry, and had :

    I. Murcadh.

    II. Maolmuire.

* *Niall Mor*: Of this Niall, the Four Masters record, under the year 1524 :

" MacSweeney of Tir Boghaine, i.e., Niall Mór, the son of Eoghan, the most renowned constable of his own noble tribe for action and heroism, for determination of mind and counsel, for arraying and attacking, for hospitality and generosity, for great troops and active warriors, by whom most dangerous passes were forced, died, after extreme unction and repentance, in his own castle at Rathaine (Rahan, St. John's Point), on the 14th of December."

III. Kathleen.
IV. Eoghan.
V. Eileen.
VI. Shane.
VII. Mary.
126. Murcadh (Patrick Morgan):
son of Murcadh Beag ; m. Margaret,
dau. of Michael O'Donovan (whose
son, Very Rev. Jeremiah O'Donovan, D.D., was the author of *Rome
Ancient and Modern*, and the Translator of the Catechism of the Council
of Trent, &c.), and had surviving
issue : I. Diarmaid, II. Grania ;
living in 1886.
127. Diarmaid (Jeremiah) of Dublin : son of Murcadh ; living in 1887 ;
m. Maria, eldest dau. of Joseph
O'Longan, of the Royal Irish Academy, and has had :
I. Murcadh.
II. Diarmaid (Jeremiah Myles).
III. Eoghan (Eugene).
IV. Michael.
V. Mary.
VI. Margaret.
VII. Grania (Grace).
VIII. Eugene-Joseph.
128. Murcadh (or Patrick Morgan) MacSweeney : son of Diarmaid
(or Jeremiah), of Dublin ; living in
1887.

MacSWEENEY. (No. 5.)

Arms : Same *Arms* and *Crest* as " MacSweeney" (No. 1).

ACCORDING to p. 118 of the Vol. F. 4. 18, in the MS. Lib. of Trin. Coll.
Dublin, Maolmuire who is No. 112 on the " MacSweeney" (No. 1) pedigree,
had a brother Moroch Oge, from whom the descent was as follows :

112. Moroch Oge : son of Moroch
Mór.
113. Maolmuire : his son.
114. Tirloch Clogh : his son.
115. Tirloch Ruadh : his son.
116. Maolmuire : his son.
117. Rory : his son.
118. Tirloch : his son.
119. Donal : his son.
120. Donal Gorm : his son ;
121. Donal : his son.
122. Donal Gem, " Dux Militum
de Rynedevocharigy, Co. Donegall,
Arm., ob. ib. 17th Feb., 1636, Sepul-
tus in Clondawydoge :" son of
Donal ; m. Honora, dau. of Owen
MacSweeny na Tuaighe, " de Castle-
naduagh, Co. Donegall, Arm.," and
had six sons and four daughters.
The daughters were—1. Mary ; 2.
Grana ; 3. Honora ; 4. Alice ; and
the sons were—1. Hugh, *s.p.* ; 2.
Daniel ; 3. Walter, m. to Mary,
dau. of Walter, son of Lochlan
MacSweeney of Ray, co. Donegal,
arm. ; 4. Mal ; 5. Hugh Buidhe ;
6. Moroch.
123. Daniel : second son of Donal
Gem ; m. Ellen, dau. of Fachnach,
O'Ferrall " de Moat, co. Longford,
arm.," and had two sons and two
daughters. The sons were—1.
Richard ; 2. John, who was a priest
(sacerdos) ; and one of the daughters was the wife of a Mr. Kirwan
(uxor Ciravan).
124. Richard MacSweeney : the
son of Daniel ; m. " Honestas, filia
Christr. Neterville, de Fethard, co.
Tip. ;" *s.p.*

MacSWEENEY. (No. 6.)

Of Desmond.

Arms : The same *Armorial Bearings* as "MacSweeney" (No. 2).

MAOLMUIRE, a brother of Neal na Tuaighe who is No. 117 on the (No. 2) "MacSweeney" (na Tuaighe) pedigree, was the ancestor of *MacSweeney,* of *Desmond.*

117. Maolmuire : son of Toirdheal- bhach [Tirloch].
117. Donchadh : his son.
119. Maolmuire : his son.

120. Tiordhealbhach : his son.
121. Murchadh na Mart (or Mur- cha of the Beeves); his son;* living in 1588.

MacTIERNAN. (No. 1.)

Of Brefney.

Arms : Erm. two lions pass. gu.   *Crest :* A griffin statant gu. wings erect vert.

BRUNAN, a younger brother of Hugh Fionn who is No. 93 on the "O'Rourke" pedigree, was the ancestor of *MacTighearnain,*† of Brefney ; anglicised *MacTiernan, MacTernan, McKiernan, McTernan, MacMaster, McMaster, Masterson, Lord,* and *Tiernan.*

93. Brunan : son of Feargna.
94. Baothan : his son.
95. Maonach : his son.
96. Doncha : his son ; a quo *Siol Donchadha ;* a quo *O'Donoghue,* of Connaught.
97. Gormgal : his son.
98. Connor : his son.
99. Gothfridh : his son.
100. Teige : his son.
101. Aongus : his son.
102. Rory : his son.
103. Giolla-na Naomh : his son.
104. Maonach : his son.

105. Tighearnan   (" tighearna :" Irish, *a lord,* or *master*) : his son ; a quo *MacTighearnain.*
106. Amhailgadh : his son.
107. Giollachriosd : his son.
108. Iomhar : his son.
109. Tighearnan : his son.
110. Duarcan : his son.
111. Sitreach : his son.
112. Giollaiosa : his son.
113. Tomas : his son.
114. Cuconnacht MacTighearnain : his son.

---

* *Son :* The Four Masters make this Murrogh-na-Mart, the son, and not the *grandson,* of Maolmuire, as rendered by MacFirbis. Among the present representa- tives of this branch of the "MacSweeney" family we find (in 1881) the worthy Commendatore, Peter Paul MacSwiney, J.P., 23 Lower Sackville-street ; and Jeremiah J. MacSweeney, Esq., Secretary of the Society for the Preservation of the Irish Lan- guage, 9 Kildare-street, Dublin.

† *MacTighearnain :* Another family of this name was descended from Donal, a younger brother of Tiernan, who is No. 112 on the "O'Rourke" pedigree. But the genealogy of that family is, we fear, lost.

MacTIERNAN. (No. 2.)

Of Clan Colla.

Arms : Same *Arms* as those of " Maguire"(No. 1).

FEARGAL, brother of Odhar who is No. 100 on the "Maguire" pedigree, was the ancestor of *MacTighearnain,* of Clan Colla ; anglicised *MacTiernan,* etc., (as in the foregoing pedigree).

100. Feargal : son of Cearnach.
101. Maolduin : his son.
102. Tighearnan : his son ; a quo *MacTighearnain.*
103. Cearnach : his son.

104. Lochlann : his son.
105. Feargal : his son.
106. Torloch : his son.
107. Flaithbheartach MacTighearnain : his son.

MacUAIS.

Arms : Az. a wolf pass. ar. in chief three bezants. *Crest :* A hand couped at the wrist erect, grasping a snake all ppr.

COLLA UAIS, the 121st Monarch of Ireland, who is No. 85 on the "MacDonnell" (of Antrim) pedigree, was the ancestor of *MacUais ;* anglicised *MacEvoy, MacVeagh, MacVeigh, Noble,* and *Vey.*

85. Colla Uais ("uais :" Irish, *noble*) : son of Eochaidh Dubhlen [Dublin] : a quo *MacUais.*
86. Roghain : his son ; had two brothers—1. Eochaidh, 2. Fiachra Toirt.
87. Earc : his son.
88. Carthann : his son ; had a younger brother named Fiachra.
89. Dochartach : his son.
90. Cormac : his son.
91. Anmire : his son ; had a younger brother named Fergus.
92. Foranan : his son.
93. Guaire : his son.

94. Maolfogha : his son.
95. Criochan (" criochan :" Irish, *striving*) : his son ; a quo *O'Criochain,* anglicised *Creehan* and *Crehan ;* had an elder brother named Cathach, who was the ancestor of *MacFetridge.*
96. Aodh (or Hugh) : son of Criochan.
97. Brandubh : his son.
98. Caornan : his son.
99. Coibhdheanach : his son.
100. Robeartach (" ro :" Irish, *very,* " beartach," *tricky*) : his son ; a quo *MacRobeartaighe,** sometimes written *MacRoiberd,* and anglicised

---

* *MacRobeartaighe :* There was an *Ui Robeartaigh* family in the county Sligo, but quite distinct from this *MacRobeartaighe.*

According to Smibert and to Douglas's Baronage, the *MacRobeartaigh,* or Robertsons are descended from the Lords of the Isles, who (see the "MacDonnell," of Antrim, pedigree) were, like this family, descended from Colla Uais, the 121st Monarch of Ireland. The name by which the Roberstons are called in Scotland is, *Clann Donnachaidh,* meaning the descendants of King Duncan, the eldest son of King Malcolm III., of Scotland.—See the "Robertson" pedigree.

Roberts, Robins, Robinson, and *Robertson.*

101. Maolbrighid : his son.
102. Feardacrioch : his son.
103. Flaitheartach : his son.
104. Hugh (2) : his son.
105. Muireadach : lfis son.
106. Brian : his son.
107. Muran ("mur :" Irish, *a fortification ;* Lat. "murus") : his son ; a quo *O'Murain,* anglicised *Murrin.*
108. Donoch : his son.
109. Curaioach (also called Dubhros) : his son.
110. Padraic :* his son.
111. Dubhgall : his son.
112. Donoch (2) : his son.
113. Moroch : his son.
114. Niall : his son.
115. Rory : his son.
116. Tirloch : his son.

117. Cairbre : his son.
118. Eoghan : his son.
119. Padraic (or Patrick) : his son ; living in 1691.
120. Brian : his son.
121. Donoch (3) : his son.
122. James : his son ; living in 1760.
123. John† : his son ; died in 1815. This John was twice married.
124. Patrick‡ : his youngest son : born in 1802 ; died in 1871.
125. James :§ his son ; living in 1878 ; had four brothers, of whom Henry, who died in 1873, was created by Queen Isabella, of Spain, a "Knight of the Golden Fleece."
126. James D. McVeigh : son of said James ; born in 1848 ; living in 1878.

---

* *Padraic :* At this stage in this family genealogy, the *O'h-Aongusa* (or "O'Hennessy") dispossessed the *Mac-Uais* family of their territory, called *Hy-mac-Uais,* now the barony of "Moygoish," in Westmeath ; and the "MacUais" family then branched into *MacEvoy* (still a highly respectable family in the county Meath), *MacVeagh, MacVeigh,* etc., as above.

† *John :* This John MacVeigh, who was born A.D. 1765, and died in 1815, entered the English Army, and was engaged in the American War, under Generals Sir Henry Clinton and Lord Cornwallis ; he afterwards served under the Duke of York, in Flanders and Holland, and retired from the Army in 1794. Having acquired large landed property in the United States, he married a Miss Stuart, by whom he had five sons and one daughter : descendants of those five sons were (in 1877) prominent citizens in America. Becoming a widower he married Margaret, daughter of H. Burns, Esq., by whom he had only child—a son named Patrick.

‡ *Patrick :* This Patrick MacVeigh, only child of John, by his second marriage, married in 1823 Helen, daughter of H. O'Hare, Esq., of an old Irish family ; and by her had five sons and three daughters. In 1849 he finally left Scotland ; settled on his property in Kentucky, United States, America ; and died in 1871, his wife having died in 1868. Of the five sons by that marriage, Henry MacVeigh, of Madrid, married in 1851, Jacoba, daughter of Duke Fernandez y-Nunez, grandee of Spain, by whom he had three sons—1. Henry, 2. Alfred, 3. James : this Henry was created by Queen Isabella of Spain a "Knight of the Golden Fleece ;" and died in 1873.

§ *James :* Of this James, under the heading "MacVeigh James, Esq., of Wallacetown and Castlebank, Drumfriesshire," Walford, in his *County Families* (1877), says : "Third surviving son of the late Patrick MacVeigh, Esq., Planter of Kentucky, U.S., America, by Helen, daughter of John O'Hehir, Esq., of Ballyna, county Down ; b. 1829, m. 1847 Mary, second daughter of Captain James Dalgiel, of the Glenæ and Carnwath family ; and has issue James D., b. 1848 (m. 1874, Mina, daughter of J. Parsons, Esq., Brighton), and a daughter, Caroline Cassendra."

"Mr. MacVeigh is a merchant in London, and purchased the Wallacetown property from the old family of Fergusons ; and Castlebank from the last of the Watson family. Residences—Wallacetown, Dumfriesshire ; Castlebank House, near Dumfries ; and 10 Maxwell Road, S.W. (London)."

MacVADDOCK.

Arms: Sa. three garbs or.

MOROCH-NA-NGAODHAIL, brother of Diarmaid-na-nGhall who is No. 114 on the "MacMorough" pedigree, was the ancestor of this branch of that family.

114. Moroch-na-nGaodhail : son of Donoch, King of Leinster.

115. Morogh : his son ; slain, A.D. 1193.

116. Donoch Reamhar : his son.

117. Murtagh : his son.

118. Donoch :* his son.

119. Redmond : son of Donoch. Had a younger brother Dermot who was the father of Maurice, father of Donoch† Dubh [dhu].

120. Sheanach : son of Redmond ; had a brother Maurice.

121. Manus : son of Sheanach.

122. Daibhidh Mór : his son ; a quo *MacDaibhidh Mór*, anglicised *MacDavid-Mór*, *MacDamore*, *David-son*, *Davis*, *Davison*, *Daws*, *Dawson*, *Davy*, and *Davys*. Had a brother Richard. The descent from this Daibhidh (or David) Mór MacMorough is carried down four generations more on the "Davidson" genealogy, namely down to Patrick MacDavid‡ Mór.

123. Bhadhach ("badhach :" Irish, *loving, famous*) MacMorough : son of Richard ; a quo *MacVaddock*, in Irish *MacBhadhaigh*. In English this Bhadach's name was written "Bhaday." The patrimony of this family was about Gorey, county Wexford.

Of this Sept was Teige Mac Vaddock, who was living *temp.* King Henry VIII.; and whose son Donal McVaddock and Teige obtained a pardon on 20th Nov. 6 Edward VI., A.D. 1552. Thomas MacVaddock, who was Chief of the Sept, A.D. 1641, married Grany, dau. of Dowling Kavanagh of the county Carlow. The name "MacVaddock" has been latterly corrupted into *Wadeck*.

* *Donoch* : This Donoch (No. 118) had a brother named Connor, who was father of Dermod, father of William, father of Maurice, father of Murtogh, who was Abbot of Ferns, co. Wexford.

† *Donoch Dubh* : Some members of the "O'Murphy" (of Wexford) family are of opinion that this Donoch Dubh MacMorough was their ancestor ; but (see the "Murphy" No. 1 genealogy, we must go much farther back than Donoch Dubh MacMorough, for the ancestor of the "O'Murphy" (of Hy-Felimy) family.

‡ *MacDavid* : The patrimony of the "MacDavid Mór" family lay about Glascarrig, co. Wexford, and is now known as the *Macnamores*. Redmond MacDavid Mór was the chief of this sept. A.D. 1611.

MADDEN. (No. 1.)

Of Hy-Maine, Connaught.

Arms : Sa. a falcon volant seizing a mallard ar.   *Motto* : Fide et fortitudine.

OWEN BUAC, brother of Owen Fionn who is No. 96 on the (No. 1) "O'Kelly" (Hy-Maine) pedigree, was the ancestor of *O'Madadhain*, of Connaught; anglicised *O'Madden*, and *Madden*.

96. Owen Buac (" buacach;" Irish, *beauish*) : son of Cormac.

97. Moroch : his son; had a brother named Anmchadh, a quo *Siol-Anmchadha*.

98. Dungealach (or Dungal): son of Moroch.

99. Maoldun : his son.

100. Cobthach : his son. This Cobthach had two brothers—1. Flanchadh, who was ancestor of *Clancy* and *Glancy* (of Hy-Maine), and of *Hoolahan* ; 2. Dungal.

101. Longseach: son of Cobthach ; had a brother named Droighnean, who was father of Treasach ("treas :" Irish, *a battle*, or *skirmish*), a quo *O'Treasaigh*, of Connaught ; anglicised *Tracey*, *Treacy*, and *Treassy*. (See " Trasey," page 134).

102. Donoch : son of Longseach.

103. Garadh : his son; had a brother named Cineadh [Kinnee], a quo *Kenny*, of Connaught.

104. Donoch (2) : his son.

105. Olioll : his son.

106. Aodh (or Hugh): his son.

107. Dermod : his son.

108. Dunoagh : his son.

109. Garadh (2) : his son.

110. Madadhan (" madadh :" Irish, *a dog, a warrior*): his son ; a quo *O'Madadhain ;* slain, 1008.

111. Dermod (2) : his son.

112. Madadhan Mór: his son.

113. Cathal (or Charles): his son.

114. Moroch : his son.

115. Owen: his son ; died 1347.

116. Moroch (2): his son. Had two brothers—1. Donoch-na-Heireceach ; 2. Dermod Caoch. Died 1371.

117. Owen (2): his son; died 1411.

118. Morogh (3) : his son.

119. Morogh (4) O'Madden : his son ; had three brothers—1. Owen, 2. John, 3. Cathal.

120. John O'Madden : second son of Morogh.

121. Bresal : son of John; had two sons—1. John, 2. Melaghlin.

122. John : son of Bresal ; became chief of Siol Anmchadha in 1554, and slain in 1556 by Bresal Dubh O'Madden ; after which two chiefs were elected, namely the said Bresal Dubh and Melaghlin Modardha, son of Melaghlin the brother of John.

123. Domhnall (or Donall): son of John. Of him Dr. O'Donovan says :

" He was the last chief who ruled the territory of Anmchada according to the old Irish system, and was perhaps the most powerful and celebrated chieftain of that territory since the time of Eoghan, who died in 1347."

In 1567 Queen Elizabeth appointed him Captain of his nation ; in 1585 he attended a Parliament convened in Dublin, to which the Irish chiefs who were obedient to the Queen were summoned ; and in 1595 we find him, according to the Four Masters, "in open rebellion." In 1602, "he came in," and dying shortly afterwards, was succeeded by his son :

124. Anmchadh (or Ambrose)

O'Madden, chief of his name : son of Donall ; d. in 1637.

125. John *Madden* (living in 1677): son of Ambrose O'Madden ; first of this family who omitted the prefix *O*'; had two sons—1. Daniel, 2. Patrick.

126. Daniel Madden, chief of his name : son of John ; is the last of his race given in the *Linea Antiqua*, by O'Farrell.

127. Brasil Madden: son of Daniel: Will dated 1745, in which he mentions his three sons :

I. Ambrose (living in 1791), who married Margery, a daughter of Malachy Fallon, Esq., of Bally-vahen, in the county of Roscommon, and had Brasil, who m. Juliet, daughter of Francis Lynch, Esq., of Omey, and had Ambrose of Streamstown, in the north-west of the co. Galway, living in 1843. A sister of this Brasil (son of Ambrose) m. —— Madden, Esq., of Fahy, whose son Laurence Madden, of Fahy, was, not many years ago, in possession of 300 acres of the original territory of the O'Maddens.

II. Daniel.

III. John, of whom presently.

128. John Madden, of Kilternan, near Enniskerry, county Wicklow : third son of Brasil ; b. *circa* 1708, and d. *circa* 1765. This John had a brother (his Christian name unknown), whose son William Madden, of Merchant's Quay, Dublin, d. in old age in 1817.

129. Edward Madden : son of John ; born 1739, died 1829, in his 91st year ; was an eminent merchant in Dublin before the Union ; was a Catholic Delegate in 1782 ; had a sister Jane, b. in 1734. This Edward was married to Elizabeth Forde, of Corry, county Leitrim ; had twenty-one children : of whom

his youngest daughter, m. Brian Cogan, and had one son, the Right Hon. William Forde Cogan, D.L., Tinode ; and the youngest son was Richard-Robert (No. 130 on this pedigree), who left issue.

130. Richd-Robert Madden, M.D., F.R.C.S. London : the twenty-first and youngest child of Edward; b. in 1798 in Dublin ; married Harriet Elmstil, who by a singular coincidence was, like her husband, the twenty-first and youngest child of her father, the late John Elmstil of Berners-street, London, and of Surge Island Estate, Jamaica. This lady, who has survived her husband, being of high intellectual attainments, shared largely in his literary labours ; and when in Cuba, where Doctor R. R. Madden was then engaged in the abolition of the Slave Trade, embraced her husband's religion,—becoming, like him, a fervent Roman Catholic. By this marriage were :

I. William Forde Madden, who, just after passing through a very distinguished course in the Polytechnic College of Engineering at Paris, perished in his 19th year by drowning in the Shannon, whilst engaged on Public Works for relief of distress, then (March 1849) prevailing in. Ireland.

II. Thomas-More Madden, who is No. 131 on this pedigree.

In 1824, Doctor R. R. Madden, in company with the late Sir Moses Montifiore, visited the Turkish Empire, where he remained for about four years, and of which he published an account in his *Travels in the East*. Subsequently Doctor Madden practised as a physician ; at first at Naples, and afterwards in London, and at St. Leonard's near London. In 1833, however, being deeply interested in the *anti*-slavery movement then in progress, he relinquished his practice and entered the public service as special Magistrate for the abolition of slavery in Jamaica; and subsequently was appointed British Representative and Acting Judge Advocate in the International Commission in the Havana, for that purpose. In 1841 he was selected by Lord John Russell as Commissioner of Inquiry on the Western Coast of Africa; in 1847 he was appointed to the Colonial Secretaryship of Western Australia; and soon after his return home from Australia he was appointed Secretary of the Loan Fund Board in Dublin, which he continued to hold for nearly thirty years, when he retired from it in 1880. Notwithstanding the absorbing nature of his public duties, Dr. Madden found time to cultivate his literary tastes, and acquire distinction as an author. He has written largely and excellently in the departments of politics, sociology, history, travels, and *belles lettres.* His works are so varied and numerous— amounting to no less than forty-seven published volumes, besides a vast number of contributions in prose and verse to magazines and reviews, as well as to the newspaper press with which he was connected at home and abroad during a considerable portion of his earlier years— that we cannot refer to them in detail, but must content ourselves with briefly indicating some of the most important. Of these perhaps the best known is his *History of the United Irishmen,* which make up a series of seven volumes, the publication of which commenced in 1842, and terminated in 1866, and has been since more than once republished in England and America. Doctor R. R. Madden, fortified up to his last moment by the sacra-

ments of the Catholic Church, died at 3 Vernon-terrace, Booterstown, co. Dublin, in his 88th year, on the 5th of February, 1886; and was interred with his father in the old churchyard of Donnybrook, near Dublin. R.I.P.

131. Thomas More Madden (living in 1887), M.D., F.R.C.S. Ed., of 55 Merrion-square, Dublin: son of Dr. R. R. Madden; born at Havana, in Cuba; Ex-President of Obstetric Section, Academy of Medicine in Ireland; now (1887) Obstetric Physician, Mater Misericordiæ Hospital; Physician, St. Joseph's Children Hospital. Has published many works— amongst them :— "*The Health Resorts of Europe and Africa;*" "*Child Culture, Moral and Physical;*" "*Spas of Germany, France, and Italy;*" "*Chronic Diseases of Women;*" "*Medical Knowledge of the Ancient Irish;*" etc. Married to Mary-Josephine Caffrey, eldest dau. of the late Thomas McDonnell Caffrey, of Crosthwaite Park, Kingstown, and has had :

I. Richard-Robert, of whom presently.

II. Thomas MacDonnell Madden; b. 1870; educated at Downside Catholic College, near Bath.

III. William-Joseph H. Forde Madden; born 10th January, 1871, died at 5 Cavendish Row, Dublin, 14th Sept., 1871.

I. Mary-Josephine; born 1868; educated at New Hall Convent Essex, and at Jette St. Pierre, near Brussels.

II. Bridget - Gertrude - Harriet ("BEDA"), a child of rare endowments and great promise, who was early called to God; b. 17th July, 1875, and died at 55 Merrion-square, on the Feast of the Sacred Heart, 16th June, 1882.

132. Richard - Robert   Madden : in 1869, and living in 1887; edu-
eldest son of Dr. More Madden ; b. cated at Downside Catholic College.

MADDEN. (No. 2.)

Of Longford, County Galway.

Arms : Same as "Madden" (No. 1).

CAHALL O'MADDEN, of Longford, *alias* Derrylewny, in the co. Galway, Prince of his Tribe, had :
2. Donogh, who had :
3. Farragh, who had :
4. Brazill, who had :
5. Daniel, who had :
6. John, of Longford, co. Galway, gent. ; who d. 5th Feb., 1639, and was bur. in Kilnemoholg. He m. Fenola, dau. of Connor O'Horan, of Faha, co. Galway, Prince of his Tribe, and had two sons and one daughter.
  I. Daniel.
  II. Melaghlin.
  I. Anabella, who married Daniel O'Madden, of Boluske, Galway, gent.
7. Daniel O'Madden : son of John ; m. Evelyn, dau. of Kyras Tully, of Gorbally, co. Galway, Esq.

O'MADDEN. (No. 3).

Of Balbriggan, County Dublin.

Arms : Same as "Madden" (No. 1).

THIS, according to Dr. O'Donovan, is a branch of the "Madden" (of Hy-Maine) family :

1. Hugh Madden, of Bloxham, Beauchamp, gent., had :
2. Thomas, of Bloxham, who had :
3. John, of Bloxham, who had :
4. Thomas, of Baggotsrath, and who died 1640. Had a brother, Robert,* and a son :
5. John, of Maddentown, who d. 1661. He had :
6. John, of Dublin, M.D., who d. 1703, and who had :

---

* *Robert :* This Robert Madden, of Donore, co. Dublin, who d. 1635, was father of Jane Madden, the mother of Robert Goldsmith, father of Rev. Charles Goldsmith, the father of Oliver Goldsmith, M.D., who was born at Auburn, in the co. Westmeath (as proved by an entry on the fly-leaf of his father's Bible, dated the 29th of November, 1728), and d. in London, on the 4th of April, 1774. This was the celebrated Oliver Goldsmith whose statue is in front of Trinity College, Dublin.

7. Very Rev. John* Madden, Dean of Kilmore, D.D., who died 1751, and who had:

8. Rev. John Madden, of Londonderry, D.D., b. 1725. Had a brother Samuel,† and a son:

9. John Eles Madden, Dublin, who d. 1817, and who had:

10. John Madden, of Inch House, Balbriggan, co. Dublin, who died 1833, and who had:

11. John Travers Madden, of Inch House, Balbriggan; living in 1843.

MADDEN.‡ (No. 4.)

Of Ulster.

Arms : Gu. a lion pass. guard. or.

BREASAL,§ brother of Tuathal Cruinnbheul who is No. 88 on the "O'Brassil West" pedigree, was the ancestor of *O'Madden*, of Ulster.

88. Breasal: son of Felim; a quo *O'Brassil* East; had a brother named Feig.

89. Feig: son of Breasal.

90. Conall: his son.

91. Olioll: his son.

92. Tuathal: his son.

93. Ronan: his son.

94. Finghin: his son.

95. Maoldun: his son.

96. Connor Cairach ("cairach :" Irish, *scabby ;* Heb. "karach"): his son; a quo *O'Cairaighe*, anglicised *Corry* and *Carey* (which has been

---

* *John :* This Very Rev. John Madden had an elder brother, Rev. Samuel Madden, commonly called "*Premium Madden,*" who d. in 1765, and who was the father of John Madden (d. 1791), the father of Samuel Madden (d. 1814), the father of Colonel John Madden, of Hilton, who was living in the year 1843, and was then the Head of this branch of the "Madden" family.

† *Samuel :* This Rev. Samuel Madden, who d. in 1800, had a son, Major Charles Madden, who was the father of the Rev. Samuel Madden, Prebendary of Blackrath, co. Kilkenny, and living in 1843.

‡ *Madden :* Samuel Madden, D.D., *Premium Madden,* as he was called, was a distinguished writer, and one of the founders of the Royal Dublin Society ; he was born in Dublin on the 23rd December, 1686. He took the degree of B.A. at Trinity College in 1705, and was collated to Drummully, near Newtownbutler, in 1721. In 1723 he took the degree of D.D. He wrote several works ; and promoted a system of quarterly premiums at Trinity College, which obtained for him the appellation of "Premium Madden." Having spent a life of exemplary piety and charity, and devoted his talents and liberal fortune to the improvement of the condition of his fellow-creatures, he died at Manor Waterhouse, in the county of Fermanagh, on the 31st December, 1765, aged 79 years. It is believed that he was of the "Madden" of Ulster family. His son, Samuel Molyneux Madden, who died in 1798, bequeathed his estate in the Corporation of Belturbet, together with the residue of his personal estate, for the founding of a prize to be given to the best of the disappointed candidates at the Fellowship examinations at Trinity College, Dublin.

§ *Breasal :* This Breasal was also the ancestor of *O'Brassil* Macha, and *O'Brassil* Ruadh.

modernized *Carew* and *Carewe*); had a brother named Aodh (or Hugh).

97. Buachall (" buachaill :" Irish, *the boy;* Arab. " bukawal;" Gr. " boukol-os"): son of Conor Cairach; a quo *O'Buachaill.** Had a brother named Cumascach.

98. Dungall : son of Buachall.

99. Maoldubhan (*maoldubhan :* Irish, "the devotion of St. Dubhan :" *Dubhan* here meaning " a dark-complexioned man"): son of Dungal; a quo *O'Maoldubhain*, of Ulster, anglicised *Muldoon*. This Maoldubhan (or Maoldun) had a brother named Cairbre, a quo *Clann Cairbre* or *Carbery*, of Ulster.

100. Aodh (or Hugh) : son of Maoldun.

101. Gairbiadh (" gair :" Irish, *a shout;* " biadh," *food*) : his son : a quo *O'Gairbidh*, anglicised *Garvey*.†

102. Ceallachan : his son.

103. Treinfear (" treine :" Irish, *strength*, and " fear," *a man ;* Heb. "fear," and " fir ;" Lat. " vir") : his son; a quo *O'Treinfir*, anglicised *Train* and *Traynor*.

104. Hugh : his son.

105. Madadhgan (" m a d a d h :" Irish, *a warrior;* " gann," *small*), meaning " the little warrior :" his son; a quo *O'Madadhgain* and *Mac-Madadhgain*, anglicised *Madagan*, *Madden*, and *Maddison ;* had a brother named Arca O'Brassil, a quo *O'Brasil* East.

106. Padraic : son of Madadhgan.

107. Lorcan O'Madagan : his son.

MAGAURAN.

Arms: Ar. out of a mount vert an oak tree ppr. on a chief az. a crescent betw. two mullets ar. *Crest*: An oak tree ppr.

BREANNAN, brother of Hugh Fionn who is No. 93 on the " O'Rourke" pedigree, was the ancestor of *MacSamhradhain ;* anglicised *MacGauran*, *MacGovern*, *Magauran*, *Magovern*, *McGowran*, *Saurin*,‡ *Somers, and Summers.*

* *O'Buachaill:* This sirname has been anglicised *Boy*. Some genealogists are of opinion that *Ball, Boal,* and *Bole,* are also anglicised forms of this old Irish sirname.

† *Garvey :* This sirname signifies " the descendants of the man who used to shout for food ;" and is akin to *O'h-Arbhidh* (" ar :" Irish, *a ploughing*; Lat. " ar-o," *to plough;* " biadh," gen. " bidh :" Irish, *food*), which means " the descendants of the man who ploughed the land, to produce food," and which is anglicised *Harvey*, modernized *Hervey*.

‡ *Saurin :* There was a Huguenot refugee in Ireland named Saurin, whose grandson was William Saurin, an eminent lawyer, who was born in the North of Ireland in 1757. This William's father was a Presbyterian Minister. William was educated at the University of Dublin, and was called to the Bar in 1780. With indignant ardour he threw himself into the agitation against the proposal for the Union between Great Britain and Ireland. He was elected a member of the House of Commons for Blessington. For at least twenty-three years after the passing of the Act of Union he never set foot upon English soil. In 1807 he was appointed Attorney-General, and he may be said to have governed Ireland for fifteen years. He instituted proceedings against the Catholic Board; popular excitement was the result : from being one of the most popular men in Ireland, he grew to be an object of aversion. In 1822, on some official changes then being made, he was offered, and in a fit of vexation refused, the

93. Breannan: son of Fergnath [fergna].
94. Baothin: his son.
95. Maoinach: his son.
96. Eochaidh: his son; a quo *Teallach Eochdhaidh*.
97. Dungaile: his son.
98. Coscrach: his son.
99. Iomhar: his son.
100. Ruarc: his son.
101. Teige: his son.
102. Connor: his son.
103. Samhradhan ("samhradh:" Irish, *summer*); a quo *MacSamhra-dhain*.

104. Muireadhach: his son.
105. Giollananaomh: his son.
106. Giollaiosa: his son.
107. Giollananaomh (2): his son.
108. Donoch: his son.
109. Brian Breug ("b r e u g:" Irish, *a lie*): his son.
110. Thomas: his son.
111. Fergal: his son.
112. Brian MacSamhradhain: his son; had four brothers—1. Thomas na-Feasoige, 2. Donoch Ballach, 3. Maolseaghlainn, 4. Cormac.

MAGELLAN.

Arms: Same as those of "Madden" of Ulster.

BEICE (King of Orgiall), son of Cumasach, brother of Buachall, who is No. 97 on the "Madden" (of Ulster) pedigree, was the ancestor of *MacGealain;* anglicised *Magellan, Magillan,* and *Gealan*.

97. Cumascach: son of Connor Cairach.
98. Beice Gealan ("gealan:" Irish, *lighting*): his son; a quo *Mac-Gealain*. This Beice had two brothers—1. Breasal, who was the ancestor of *O'Longan;* and 2. Maoldum.
99. Cearnach: his son.
100. Breasal: his son.

101. Eochaidh: his son.
102. Cearnach (2): his son.
103. Tuathal: his son.
104. Cathal: his son.
105. Tighearnach: his son.
106. Tuathal Magealan: his son; had a brother named Giollachriosd MacGealain, who was called *Mac-Gillan*.

MAGOFREY.

Arms: Vert a white horse fully caparisoned, thereon a knight in complete armour, on his helmet a plume of ostrich feathers, and his right hand brandishing a sword all ppr.

GUTHRIGH (anglicised Goffrey, Geoffrey, Jeoffrey, and Godfrey), brother of

place of Chief Justice of the King's Bench, whereupon he returned to his old position at the Bar. Mr. Saurin married a sister of the Marquis of Thomond. He died at his residence, Stephen's Green, Dublin, on the 11th of February, 1839, aged 82 years.

Dun Oge who is No. 111 on the "Maguire" pedigree, was the ancestor of *MacGuthrigh;* anglicised *Magofrey, Maguthrie,* and *Guthrie,* of Orgiall.

111. Guthrigh ("guth" [guff]: Irish, *a voice;* "righ: *of a king*): son of Donal; a quo *MacGuthrigh.*

112. Rory : his son.

113. Guthrigh Bearnach ("bearnàch" Irish, *gapped*): his son; a quo *MacBearnaighe,* of Fermanagh, anglicised *MacBirney.*

114. Niall Mór : his son.

115. Dermod : his son.

116. Moroch : his son.

117. Niall (2) : his son.

118. Tirlach Magofrey : his son.

MAGRATH.*

Of Ulster.

Arms : Ar. three lions pass. gu.

DUBHCULIN, brother of Gairbiadh who is No. 98 on the "O'Brassil West" pedigree, was the ancestor of *MacCraith,* of Ulster ; anglicised *MacCraith, Maccrae, Magrath, MacGrath, McGrath,* and *Creeth.*

98. Dubhculin : son of Cearnach.

99. Giollachriosd : his son.

100. Dallgan ("dall:" Irish, *blind ;* "gan," *little*): his son; a quo *O'Dallgain,* anglicised *Dalgan, Dallan,* and *Dolan.*

101. Maolbrighid : his son.

102. Macraith ("craith :" Irish, *to weave*) : his son ; a quo *MacCraith.*

* *Magrath :* Miler Magrath, Archbishop of Cashel and Bishop of Emly, was born in the county of Fermanagh about the year 1522. Originally a Franciscan Friar, he became a Protestant, and was consecrated Bishop of Clogher, and in 1570-'71 advanced to the Archbishopric of Cashel and Bishopric of Emly. He also held the Bishoprics of Waterford and Lismore *in commendam* from 1582 to 1589, and from 1592 to 1607, when he resigned them, and was placed in charge of Killala and Achonry. He had four sons and four daughters ; some of the sons, although being Catholics, contrived to possess themselves of several church livings. After occupying the Archbishopric for fifty-two years, he died at Cashel in December, 1622, aged 100 years, and was buried in the Cathedral under a monument previously erected by himself, which may still be seen. There is a tradition that he returned to Catholicity before his death, and directed his body to be secretly buried elsewhere.

MAGUIRE.* (No. 1.)

Princes of Fermanagh.

Arms : Same as those of " Magofrey," *ante. Another* : Gu. a salmon naiant in fess ar. in chief a dexter hand apaumée of the last. *Another* : Gu. a salmon naiant ppr. on a chief ar. a dexter hand apaumée of the first.

CORMAC, a younger brother of Daimhin who is No. 92 on the "O'Hart" pedigree, was the ancestor of *MacUidhir ;* anglicised *MacGwyre,* and *Maguire.*

92. Cormac: son of Cairbre an Daimh Airgid.

93. Aodh : his son.

94. Fergus : his son.

95. Cormac (2) : his son.

96. Egneach (or Fechin) : his son.

97. Iargallach : his son.

98. Luan (" luan :" Irish, *a hero, a woman's breast, the moon,* etc.) : his son.

99. Cearnach : his son.

100. Odhar: his son; had a brother named Feargal.

101. Orgiall: his son ; had a brother named Dalach, who was the ancestor of *O'Lavan* and *Lavan,* of Fermanagh.

102. Searrach : son of Orgiall.

103. Odhar (" odhar," gen. " uidhir :" Irish, *pale* or *palefaced*): his son ; a quo *MacUidhir.*

104. Orgiall (2): his son.

105. Searrach (2) : his son.

106. Odhar Oge: his son.

107. Randal : his son.

108. Donn Mór : his son ; Lord of Fermanagh.

109. Giolla Iosa : his son ; had a younger brother named Manus.

110. Donall: son of Giollaiosa.

111. Donn Oge (also called Donn Carrach), the first Prince of Fermanagh : his son ; d. 1315. Had a younger brother named Guthrigh Gamhnach, who was the ancestor of *Guthrie* and *MacGuthrie* of Oirgiall.

112. Flaithearthach : his son. Had two younger brothers—1. Amhail gadh [Awly], who was the ancestor of *MacHugh ;* 2. Mahoun.

113. Hugh Ruadh, the fourth Prince of Fermanagh : son of Flaithearthach ; d. 1360.

114. Philip : his son; the fifth Prince of Fermanagh : d. 1375.

115. Thomas Mór (also called Giolladubh), the sixth Prince of Fermanagh : his son ; d. 1430.

116. Thomas Oge, the seventh

---

* *Maguire* : The Maguires supplied Chiefs or Princes to Fermanagh, from about A.D. 1264, when they supplanted the former Chieftains (O'Daimhin, or Devin), and continued in power till the reign of King James II., of England. (See the Paper in the Appendix, headed : " Princes of the ' Maguire' family.")

The Maguires were inaugurated as Princes of Fermanagh on the summit of Cuilcagh, a magnificent mountain near Swanlinbar, on the borders of Cavan and Fermanagh ; and sometimes also at a place called *Sciath Gabhra* or *Lisnasciath,* now Lisnaskea. They possessed the entire of Fermanagh : hence called " Maguire's Country ;" and maintained their independence as Lords of Fermanagh down to the reign of James the First, when their country was confiscated like other parts of Ulster ; but Connor Roe Maguire obtained re-grants of twelve thousand acres of the forefeited lands of his ancestors, and was created Baron of Enniskillen—a title which was also borne by several of his successors. Cathal or Charles Maguire, archdeacon of Clogher in the fifteenth century, who assisted to compile the celebrated " Annals of Ulster," was of this family. For an interesting account of the Maguires, in the reign of King James the First, see the works of Sir John Davies.—CONNELLAN's *Four Masters.*

Prince : his son ; d. 1480 ; had a brother named Philip.

117. Philip: son of Thomas Oge. Had two brothers—1. Connor Mór, the tenth Prince, d. 1518; 2. Edmond, who was the eighth Prince of Fermanagh, and who d. 1488.

118. Brian : son of Philip.

119. Cu-Chonacht : his son.

120. Cuchonacht (2), the eleventh Prince : his son ; d. 1538.

121. Cuchonacht (3), the fourteenth Prince : his son ; d. 1589.

122. Hugh,* the fifteenth Prince : his son ; slain at Kinsale, 1602.

123. Brian : his son.

124. Cuchonacht :† his son.

125. Brian Maguire : his son.

† *Hugh* : This Hugh Maguire, Prince of Fermanagh, took a prominent part in the war during Elizabeth's reign. He was a cousin of Hugh O'Neill. His mother was Nuala, daughter of Manus O'Donnell. On the death of his father he became possessed of the estates held by his ancestors since 1302. He soon took up a defiant attitude towards the Government, replying, when told by the Deputy FitzWilliam that he must allow the Queen's writs to run in Fermanagh : " Your sheriff shall be welcome, but let me know his *eric*, that if my people should cut off his head I may levy it upon the country." He succoured Hugh Roe O'Donnell in his escape from Dublin Castle. In 1593 he besieged the sheriff and his party in a church, and would have starved them out, but for the intervention of Hugh O'Neill, then an ally of the Anglo-Irish. On the 3rd July of the same year Maguire carried off a large prey of cattle from Tulsk from under the eyes of Sir Richard Bingham, Governor of Connaught. Under that year the Four Masters give a spirited account of the engagement : Sir William Clifford and a few horsemen were slain on Bingham's side, while Maguire lost, amongst several of his party, Edmond MacGauran (Archbishop of Armagh) and Cathal Maguire. Some months later he unsuccessfully endeavoured to prevent Marshal Bagnall and Hugh O'Neill crossing the Erne at Athcullin. We are told that his forces, a great number of whom were slain, consisted of Irish, armed with battleaxes, and some Scotch allies, armed with bows. In the contest Hugh O'Neill was severely wounded in the thigh. . . He threw himself heart and soul into O'Neill's war, and took part in the victory of Clontibret and Kilclooney, and was in command of the cavalry at Mullabbrack in 1596, where the Anglo-Irish were defeated with heavy loss. The same year he was, with O'Neill and O'Donnell, formally outlawed, and a price was set upon his head. In 1598 he held a command at the defeat of Marshal Bagnall at the Yellow Ford. Next year Maguire joined O'Donnell in a marauding expedition into Thomond, and took Inchiquin Castle. In March, 1600, he commanded the cavalry in Hugh O'Neill's expedition into Leinster and Munster. Accompanied by a small party, he reconnoitred the country towards Cork, but was intercepted by Sir Warham St. Leger and Sir Henry Power, with a superior force. Nothing daunted, he struck spurs into his horse, and dashed into the midst of the Deputy's band, where St. Leger inflicted on him a deadly wound with his pistol. Maguire, summoning his remaining strength, cleft his adversary's head through his helmet, and then fell exhausted and almost immediately expired. Hugh Maguire's name will probably live longest in the ode addressed to him by his bard, O'Hussey, which has been so forcibly rendered into English by Mangan.—WEBB.

† Colonel Cuchonacht Maguire was sheriff of the county Fermanagh in 1687, and, on the breaking out of the Revolution of 1688, he mortgaged the greater part of his estates to raise and arm a regiment for the service of his King, James II. He was shot at the Battle of Aughrim, where his regiment was cut to pieces, after nearly destroying the 2nd regiment of British Horse. When he was killed, and the fate of the day decided, an officer of his regiment, named Durnien, cut off the brave Maguire's head, which he put in a bag, and, starting from the fatal field, slept neither night nor day until he reached the family burying ground in the Island of Devenish, where he interred his commander's head with the remains of his ancestors. Colonel Maguire was married to Mary, daughter of Ever Maguire, and left three sons.—From *Memoirs of* BRIAN MAGUIRE.

MAGUIRE. (No. 2.)

Of France.

(From the De La Ponce MSS.)

Arms : Same as " Maguire" (No. 1).

ZACHAIRE, believed to have been a brother of Cuconnacht who is No. 120 on the " Maguire" pedigree, was the ancestor of *Maguire,* of France.

120. Zachaire : son of Cuconnacht ; m. Eliza O'Neill, of Tyrone.

121. Francis : their son ; m. —— du Poncet ; had a brother Zachaire.

122. Nicholas : son of Francis ; m. —— Philippe.

123. Etienne : his son ; m. in 1649 Margaret Morel.

124. Pierre : his son ; m. in 1697, Henriette de ....

125. Rene-Etienne-Nicholas : his son ; m. in 1725 Elizabeth Daniell.

126. Jean - Baptiste - Daniel : his son ; m. Genevieve Jeane Viol.

127. George-Corry Maguire : his son.

MAHON.

Of Connaught.

Arms : Or, a lion ramp. az.   *Crest* : A demihusbandman holding over the dexter shoulder an ox-yoke ppr.

SIR BRYAN MACMAHON, who is No. 122 on the "MacMahon" (of Monaghan) pedigree, had a son named Sir Bryan, who was the ancestor of *Mahon,* of Connaught.

122. Sir Bryan MacMahon, lord of Darty : son of Hugh Oge ; died A.D. 1620.

123. Sir Bryan : his son ; had a brother named Art, who died in 1634, and who was ancestor of *Mac-Mahon,* of Dartry. This Sir Bryan was the first of the family who, in the reign of Queen Elizabeth, settled in Connaught.

124. James : his son ; acquired by purchase the estate of Lisduff, in the county Galway.

125 Bryan : his son ; married Magdalin, daughter of Poer (or Power) of Loughrea ; died in 1695.

126. Bryan *Mahon* : his son ; first of the family that omitted the prefix *Mac ;* married in 1693 Ellinor, daughter of Ross Gaynor of Westmeath ; had an elder brother named James, who was the head of the "Mahon" family of Beechill.

127. Ross Mahon : his son ; m. in 1721 Jane Usher ; had three sons— 1. Ross, 2. John, 3. Peter : both John and Peter died unmarried. This Ross had two brothers—1.

James, 2. Peter—both of whom also died unmarried.

128. Ross Mahon : son of Ross; married in 1762 the Hon. Lady Anne Brown (daughter of John, then lord Monteagle, but afterwards earl of Altamont), by whom he had seven sons—1. Ross, who, in 1818, became the first baronet ; 2. John, who married Lady Charlotte Brown, daughter of Peter, the second earl of Altamont, and died leaving no male issue ; 3. George, who d. young and unmarried; 4. Henry*; 5. James†; 6. Charles, who d. unm.; 7. George, who married Sophia Ker, and died leaving one son Charles, who died leaving no male issue.

129. Sir Ross Mahon, eldest son of Ross ; married in 1786 Lady Elizabeth Browne, daughter of Peter, second earl of Altamont, and by her had no male issue. In 1805 he married, secondly, Diana, daughter of —— Baber, Esq., of Park-street, Grosvenor-square, London, and by her (who died in 1807) he had one son, Ross, who died an infant. He

married, thirdly, Maria, daughter of the Right Hon. James Fitzgerald, and by her had five sons—1. Ross, 2. James, 3. William, 4. John, 5. Henry; was created a baronet in 1818 ; and died 1837.

130. Rev. Sir William Ross Mahon, the fourth baronet ; rector of Rawmarsh, Rotherham, Yorkshire, England, third son (by the third marriage) of Sir Ross Mahon, the first baronet : living in 1877. His eldest brother, Sir Ross Mahon, the second baronet died unmarried, and was succeeded in the baronetcy by his next brother Sir James, who was the third baronet, and who also died unmarried. This Sir William (Vesey) Ross Mahon had two surviving brothers—1. John Ross Mahon (J.P., county Roscommon), of Castlegar, Ahascragh, county Galway ; 2. Henry.

131. William-Henry : son of Sir William Ross Mahon; born 1856, and living in 1877 ; had then four surviving brothers—1. John, 2. James-Vesey, 3. Edward, 4. Gilbert.

MALONE.‡

Of Ulster.

Arms : Vert a lion ramp. or, between three mullets ar.

EOCHAIDH, brother of Muireadach [muredach] who is No. 100 on the "Lane" pedigree, was the ancestor of *Malone*, of Ulster. (There was

---

* *Henry*: This Henry Mahon married Anne, daughter of Rev. Abraham Symes, D.D., and died in 1838, leaving three sons—1. Ross, 2. Henry, 3. George : this Ross Mahon (of Belgrave-square, Monkstown, county Dublin, living in 1877), married, first, Jane, daughter of Sir Hugh Crofton, Bart, and by her had no issue ; the said Ross married, secondly, Hariet, daughter of Rev. Henry King, of Ballylin, in King's County, and by her had four sons—1. Henry, 2. Ross, 3. George, 4 Arthur, the four of whom living in 1877.

† *James* : This James Mahon married Frances Kerr, and by her had one son John, who married Frances Dillon, by whom he had two sons (living in 1877)—1. James, 2. George.

‡ *Malone*: Along with Anthony Malone, a distinguished politican, who was born

another *Malone* family in Connaught: see No. 112 on the No. 1 " O'Connor," Kings of Connaught pedigree.)

MANTUA AND MONTFERRAT.

SCARRON, who was Court Poet, *temp.* Louis XIV., described the *Armorial Bearings* of this family, in a parody written with reference to Regnier, Duc d'Anjou, King of Sicily. That description was, at the request of Duke Archibald of Mantua, translated by Thomas Moore, as follows :

> " Six mighty realms, beneath the helmet crowned,
> Shine on the shield of Charlie the renowned :
> Byzantium, Baleares and Bar, Arragon, France, and Mantua,
> Are blazoned all in chief ; and underneath the shield fair Navarre.
> Thus is our courteous Knight, and none such known,
> A king of kings, a noble generous son.
> The war-cry " Olympus Fides" doth he choose
> In battle-field or Tournay's shock to use ;
> And, with his emblems, birds of plumage rare,
> That his brave shield may be their constant care.
> With that (his loving Worship) may be seen
> The Paternoster crosses of a Queen."

As in pp. 59-63 of "The Pedigree of Her Royal and Most Serene Highness, the Duchess of Mantua, Montferrat, and Ferrara" (London, 1885), this family pedigree is elaborately traced in regular lineage, in the " Table of Descent from the Irish Kings," from Heremon, son of Milesius of Spain, down to the Duchess and her son Charles, Prince of Mantua (living in London, in 1887), we are content with here inserting the following extract from pp. v., vi., and vii. of that carefully compiled volume ; containing the opinion of Sir John Holker, Her Majesty's Attorney-General, on the claims and Titles of the Duchess of Mantua and Montferrat, and her son :

" I am of opinion on the following grounds," says Sir John Holker, " that Anne Napier, widow of Charles Edward Groom, Esquire, Prince of Gaeta, is entitled to the appellation Duchess of Mantua and Montferrat, she having proved her claim thereto. I have read over and critically examined all the certificates and other documents which prove Duchess Ann to be the lineal descendant and heir of Ferdinand, Duke of Mantua and Montferrat, by his wife Camilla. I have read the documentary evidence which

---

in Ireland on the 5th December, 1700, we may mention his nephew Edmond Malone, Shaksperian commentator and author, who was born in Dublin on the 4th October, 1741. Lord Sunderlin, who was Edmond's brother, buried him near the family mansion at Baronstown in Westmeath. Rev. William Malone, best known for his challenge to Protestant writers and Archbishop Ussher's reply, was born in Dublin about 1586. At an early age he was sent to Portugal, and then to Rome, where in his twentieth year he entered the Order of Jesuits. After a sojourn in Ireland, he was sent for to Rome and appointed Rector of St. Isidore's College. He returned to Ireland as Superior of the Jesuit Mission. He excited the suspicion of the Government and was arrested ; but contrived to make his escape to Spain, where he died Rector of the Irish College at Seville, in 1659.

proves the claim of the aforesaid Duchess Ann to the title and states of the Duchy of Ferrara, of the Duchy of Este, Duchy of Modena, of the Duchy of Guastalla, of the Duchy of Bozzola, of the Duchy of Sabioneta, of the Principality of Castiglione, of the Counties of Canossa and Novellara, and to be the heiress of the line of Medici, Dukes of Florence and Grand Dukes of Tuscany. I am likewise of opinion, having considered all the acts and settlements of Louis XIV., Louis XV., Louis XVI., and of Napoleon I., Kings and Emperor of France, that the Duchess is entitled to style herself Duchess of Nevers, Réthel, and Alençon in France and Cleves in Flanders. I am likewise of opinion that the aforesaid Duchess Ann is the heiress of the line of Paleologi or last Emperors of Costantinople, and one of the heirs general of Charlemagne, Emperor of Germany and King of France ; to be heiress also of the old Emperors and Kings of Italy ; and to be heiress of the Kings of Jerusalem and of the Kings of Cyprus ; the Balearic Isles and Candia ; and of the King of Thessaly ; and I am likewise of opinion that the aforesaid Duchess Ann is heiress of the Royal House of Stewart, as the chief of the line of descent of the Earls of Menteth. I am likewise of opinion that the Duchess Ann has made out her claim to be heiress of the line of Duncan, Earl of Lennox, both on account of her being the representative and lineal descendant of Lady Margaret, who is proved to be the second daughter of Duncan, who married Sir Robert Menteth, of Rusky, by whom Lady Margaret had one son, who died unmarried, and two daughters. Agnes, the eldest, became the wife of Sir John Haldane, of Gleneagles. I have read the certificate of the baptism of Agnes, which describes her as the eldest daughter of Lady Margaret, and Sir Robert Menteth, his wife. The second daughter of Lady Margaret, Elizabeth, married John Napier, of Merchiston, and the certificate of her baptism now before me describes her as the second daughter of the Lady Margaret and her husband, Sir Robert Menteth, and the certificate showing that Agnes was two years older than Elizabeth. And I am further of opinion that the Duchess has proved her line of descent as heiress of the Haldanes, of Gleneagles, and to be chief of their family, as well as to claim priority over the other claimants to the Earldom of Lennox. I have examined the certificates of the marriage of Mungo Haldane, Esq., M.P. for Stirlingshire, with Mary Scott, of Edinburgh. He was erroneously reported to have died unmarried. Also the marriage certificate of his daughter, Mary Jane Haldane, with the Rev. Archibald Napier, the claimant to the Earldom of Lennox as heir general of Elizabeth Menteth, the wife of John Napier of Merchiston. I am likewise of opinion that the two lines of descent from the sisters Agnes and Elizabeth are now represented by the Duchess of Mantua and Montferrat. I am likewise of opinion that she has proved her claim to be the representative of the line of the Napiers of Merchiston, Tobago, and of the line of the Napiers of Kilmahew. I am also of opinion that the Duchess has brought proof that her grandfather, the Rev. Archibald Napier, and her father, Archibald, were acknowledged by King George II., and King George III., as Earls of Lennox, Fife and Menteth ; the Attorney General in King George II.'s time, having reported in favour of the Rev. Archibald Napier's claim.

" I am likewise of opinion that the Duchess of Mantua and Montferrat has proved her pedigree as a descendant of the ancient Kings of Ireland, and the Princes of Wales, and as such entitled to be a representative family as regards pedigree in both these countries. And I am likewise of opinion that the Duchess is Sovereign of the Order of Knight Templars, founded 1119, by Baldwin II. ; Sovereign of the Order of Siardino del Palestina, instituted 1197, by Baldwin, King of Jerusalem ; Sovereign of the Most Ancient Order of the Sword in Cyprus ; the Most Sacred Order of the Redemption ; and the Most Ancient Order of the Annunciad, or St. Michael, in Mantua ; of the Noble Order of the Swan, of Cleveland ; of the Illustrious Order of the White Eagle, of Este ; dignities which are associated with the representation of the families which constituted them, and are personal and not geographical, as I have proved by reference to the statutes of each.

" I am likewise of opinion that the Duchess can claim to exercise all the powers which her ancestors exercised over these Orders, and I am further of opinion that the Duchess has inherited all the powers of creation which were vested in her ancestors, of which she is the lineal representative. And I am likewise of opinion that she has proved her claim to be the hereditary Sheriff of the Counties of Lennox and Dumbarton, in Scotland. And I am likewise of opinion that the Duchess Ann has proved her claim to the old Barony of Lennox, the representative of the ancient Thanes of Lennox ; and to the titles of Countess and Baroness de Lennox, in France ; and to the titles of

Baroness de Tabago and Merchiston, in Tobago. And I am likewise of opinion that the Duchess is entitled to the appellation of Royal and Most Serene Highness.

"And I am likewise of opinion that to her son, His Royal and Most Serene Highness Charles, belong the titles of Prince of Mantua and Montferrat ; Prince of Ferrara, Prince of Este, Prince of Guastalla, Prince of Bozzola, Prince of Castiglione, Prince of Modena, and Marquis of Viadona, and Count de Canossa, in Italy ; Prince of Nevers, Réthel and Alençon, in France ; Prince of Cleves, in Flanders ; Prince of the House of David, King of Israel ; Master of Lennox, Fife and Menteth, and Master of Kilmahew, in Scotland ; Baron de Tabago, in the West Indies ; Grand Master of the Order of the Knights Templars ; Grand Master of the Order of Siardino del Palestina ; Grand Master of the Most Ancient Order of the Sword, of Cyprus ; Grand Master of the Most Sacred Order of the Redemption, of Mantua ; Grand Master of the Ancient Order of the Annunciade of St. Michael, of Mantua ; Grand Master of the Illustrious Order of the White Eagle, of Este ; Grand Master of the Noble Order of the Swan of Cleveland.

"I have, with the aid of Sir George Jessel, Master of the Rolls, examined five ancient Pentateuchs, which contain the Genealogical line of descent from David, the ancient King of Israel ; and a Genealogical Table contained in a manuscript, written by Moses Maimonides, which is a Commentary upon the Old Testament. I have likewise examined Genealogical Tables and Charters of the line of Paleologus, and Genealogical Tables made at different times by order of the House of Gonzaga, Captains, Marquises, and Dukes of Mantua, and I am able to trace and see clearly proved a connection between the two lines of descent from David, King of Israel, and the Houses of Paleologus and Gonzaga, their representatives. And I am likewise of opinion that the Prince of Mantua and Montferrat is descended in lineal descent from Zerrubabel, he having shown a continuous descent therefrom, and as such, is entitled to the appellation of Prince of the House of David.

"JOHN HOLKER, A.G."

Having been asked my opinion as to the correctness of three lines of descent from the House of David, as now represented by the Duchess of Mantua and Montferrat, or her son, the Prince of Mantua and Montferrat, I, having examined all the documents on which this claim is founded, more especially five ancient Pentateuchs, containing at the end Genealogical lines of descent from King David, and a manuscript commentary by Moses Maimonides on the Old Testament, and sundry Genealogical Tables relating to the families of Paleologus, Gonzaga, and Groom, am strongly of opinion that the Duchess and Prince of Mantua and Montferrat are entitled to the appellation of Princess and Prince of the House of David.

J. Montgomery.   (Signed)   "GEORGE JESSEL,* M.R."

On the 5th November, 1878, the Comte de Chambord (de jure Henri V., King of France and Navarre,) issued Letters Patent to the Duchess Ann and her son Charles, confirming the Acts of Louis XIV., Louis XV., Louis XVI., and Louis XVII., Kings of France, acknowledging them (the Duchess and her son) to be " Their Royal and Most Serene Highnesses, the Duchess and Prince of Mantua, Montferrat, and Ferrara, Nevers, Réthel, Alençon, and Cleve, and Prince of Charleville, etc. ; Baron and Baroness de Tobago ; and that they should have precedence in France next to the House of Orleans, when it pleases God to give me my Rights." They were to discontinue the names of *Groom* and *Napier*, and assume the sirnames of *Bourbon, D'Este, Paleologus, Gonzaga;* and the Arms of those families, with the Quarterings for Gonzaga, Paleologus, Nevers, Réthel, Alençon, Cleve, and Navarre : being the Arms borne by Duke Charles IV. of Mantua, and

* *George Jessel :* For the Genealogical Tables and Letters Patent above referred to by Sir John Holker, Attorney General, and Sir George Jessell, Master of the Rolls, see "The Pedigree of H.R. and M.S.H. the Duchess of Mantua, Montferrat, and Ferrara; with the Roll of the Mantuan Medallists ; compiled by John Riddell, the Comte de Chambord, etc. New Edition, with Portraits, 4to (London : Dulan and Co., 1865) ;" a work which shows the origin of these families from a very remote period.

assumed by their ancestor James *Dalrymple*.   In accordance with these Letters Patent, the Prince of Mantua and Montferrat succeeded to the property entailed by Duke Charles IV., and with his mother assumed the surnames of *de Bourbon, d'Este, Paleologus, Gonzaga*, which act was enrolled in the High Court of Justice (London), Chancery Division, on the 11th of October, 1884.

Letters Patent were in 1885 issued by Her Majesty Queen VICTORIA, reciting their Titles; and similar Letters Patent have been issued by the French Republic, the Italian and other principal Powers of Europe, and by the United States.

MAYE.*

Lords of Orgiall.

Arms : Ar. a chev. sa. betw. three roses or, a chief of the last.   *Crest :* A leopard's head ppr.

IOMCHADH, a brother of Rochadh who is No. 86 on the " O'Hart" pedigree was the ancestor of *O'Mheith ;* anglicised *May*, and *Maye.*

86. Iomchadh : son of Colla da Chrioch.

87. Muireadach Meith (" meith :" Irish, *corpulent*) : his son ; a quo *O'Mheith.*

88. Brian: his son.
89. Eoghan : his son.
90. Fiachra : his son.
91. Aodh : his son.
92. Fingin : his son.
93. Sgannlan : his son.
94. Maoliomlan : his son.
95. Muireadach : his son.

96. Inreachtach : his son.
97. Tadhg [Teige]: his son.
98. Dubhinreachtach : his son.
99. Maolpol: his son ; meaning " the devoted of St. Paul."
100. Anbith : his son.
101. Gairbith: his son.
102. Inreachtach : his son.
103. Sgannlan : his son.
104. Dubhdarach : his son.
105. Muirceartach : his son.
106. Iomhar O'Mheith : his son.

MAYNE.

Arms : Ar. three chevronels sa. each charged with an escallop of the first, on a chief of the second three mullets of the field.

MAON, a brother of Muircheartach Mór MacEarca, the 131st Monarch of Ireland, who is No. 90 on the " O'Neill" (No. 1) pedigree, was the ancestor of *O'Maoin ;* anglicised *Main, Mayn*, and *Mayne.*

* *May :* In the Vol. F. 4. 18, in Trin. Coll. Dub., it is recorded that James **May**, Merchant, Dublin, m. Frances (d. 5th May, 1635, and buried in St. Audoen's, Dublin), dau. of Sir Thade Duffe, of Dublin, Knt., by his wife —— Burnett ; and had issue— 1. Bartholomew May, 2. James May.

90. Maon (" maon :" Irish, *a hero*): son of Muireadach; a quo *O'Maoin*.

91. Colman : his son.

92..Faolan : his son.

93. Endalach : his son.

94. Teandalach : his son ; a quo *Clann Teandalaigh*.

95. Gairmleadach : his son.

96. Dalbhach : his son.

97. Maolmithidh : his son.

98. Cathmhaol : his son.

99. Gairleadach : his son.

100. Macrath : his son.

101. Meanman : his son.

102. Domhnall : his son.

103. Conchobhar : his son.

104. Endalach : his son ; had a brother Domhnall.

105. Niall : son of Endalach.

106. Conchobhar : his son.

107. Sithreach : his son.

108. Maol ( ) : his son.

109. Conchobhar O'Maoin : his son.

McCANN.

Lords of Clanbrassil, County Armagh.

Arms : Az. fretty or, on a fess ar. a boar pass. gu. *Crest* : A salmon naiant ppr. *Motto* : Crescit sub pondere virtus.

CANA, a younger brother of Donal who is No. 103 on the " MacMahon" (of Ulster) pedigree, was the ancestor of *MacCana* (anglicised *McCann*), Lords of Clanbrassil, county Armagh.

103. Cana ("can :" Irish, *to utter ;* Lat. " can-o :" Heb. " gan-a, *a cane ;* Hind. " gani," *to chant*): son of Maithgamhuin ; a quo *MacCana*.

104. Cana Mór McCan : his son ; first assumed this sirname.

105. Cana Oge : his son.

106. Cathal (or Charles) McCann : his son.

107. Charles (2): his son.

108. Hugh the Valiant : his son.

109. Terence, the wine drinker : his son.

110. Donal (or Daniel) : his son ; lord of Clanbrassil.

111. Hugh (2) : his son.

112. Cairbre Oge : his son.

113. Neal : his son.

114. Neal Oge : his son.

115. Cairbre Mór · his son.

116. Hugh Mòr : his son.

117. Hugh Mór : his son.

118. Terence, of Upper Clanbrassil, in Armagh : his son.

119. Cairbre : his son.

120. Brian Buidhe : his son ; lord of Upper Clanbrassil.

121. Lochlann : his son ; lord of Clanbrassil.

122. Cormac, lord of Clanbrassil : his son.

123. Brian Ruadh : his son.

124. Glaisneach McCann : his son ; had a daughter named Elizabeth, who was married to John Hamilton, by whom she had six sons : one of whom was killed at the battle of Aughrim, on the 12th of July, A.D. 1691.

McKIERNAN.

Arms : Same as those of "MacTiernan" (No. 1).

THIS family derives from Michael Oge McKiernan, of Arderry, parish of Drumrielly, barony of Carrigallen, and county of Leitrim, Ireland; who was born about 1680, and died 1750.

1. Michael Oge McKiernan. This Michael was twice married: by the first wife he had eighteen children; by the second, six. Of the twenty-four children we have ascertained the names of five; of the other nineteen, fourteen were sons and five were daughters. The five whose names we have ascertained were—
1. Michael, of Fenagh, co. Leitrim, born in 1716, and died in 1800.
2. Farrell, of Keenheen, co. Leitrim, b. 1720, m. Jane Webb, of county Longford, died in 1820, aged 100 years.
3. Lawrence, of Arderry, co. Leitrim, b. 1722, married in Ireland, emigrated to Maryland in 1773, d. 1805, was ancestor of *Gale* of Maryland.
4. Susan, b. 1729, married a Mr. Plunkett of Mullingar, county Westmeath.
5. Brian Ruadh [roe], of Aughalough, county Leitrim, b. 1733, was twice married—first, to Mary Johnston, and secondly, to Jane Portis, d. 1800.

2. Michael, of Fenagh, county Leitrim : son of Michael Oge; b. 1716; married to Frances Connellan, of county Mayo; emigrated to Maryland in 1773; died 1800. This Michael had ten children : 1. Peter, born at Fenagh, 1747, emigrated to Maryland in 1773, and d. unmarried in Virginia, in 1812. 2. Patrick, who died in infancy, in Ireland. 3. Susan, who also died in infancy, in Ireland. 4. Charles, born at Fenagh, in 1753; married Mary Duigenan of Keshcarrigan (who died in 1788); emigrated to Maryland in 1790, and married Jane MacDonnell, of

Virginia, in 1795; died in 1797. 5. Michael, born at Fenagh in 1755; emigrated to Maryland in 1775; and d. unmarried in Virginia, in 1801. 6. Catherine, born at Fenagh in 1757 (d. 1832); first married Patrick O'Ferrall—her second husband was Andrew Goulding—both of Maryland; from her is descended the Rev. Robt. W. Brady, S.J. 7. Margaret, b. at Fenagh in 1759; m. Patrick Tiernan of Virginia; she died in 1814: from her are descended the *Tiernans* of Pittsburgh, Pennsylvania. 8. Susannah, born at Feenagh, in 1761: was thrice married : 1. to Florence Mahony of Virginia; 2. to a Mr. Quinn of Pennsylvania; and 3. to a Mr. Lewis of Louisiana: she died in 1827. 9. Lawrence, b. at Feenagh, in 1763; emigrated to Maryland in 1775; married Elizabeth Butler of Virginia; died in 1846; he was ancestor of the *McKiernans* of Illinois. 10. Frances, born at Feenagh, in 1765; married Ignatius O'Ferrall of Virginia; from her are descended the *O'Ferralls* of Virginia (Berkeley Springs); she died in 1843.

3. Charles : the third son of Michael; b. 1753; d. 1797. ' This Charles had seven children—1. Frances, b. 1773; d. 1859: was twice married—first to Timothy Monohan; and secondly to a Mr. Melton, both of Maryland; from her is descended John MacKiernan Monohan, of Louisville, Kentucky, living in 1877. 2. Michael, b. 1776, d. 1837; married Mary Protzman,

of Pennsylvania; resided at Hancock in Maryland, and had two children —1. Alice (who died young), 2. John. 3. Ella, b. 1778, d. 1845; was twice married—first, to George Sharkey; and secondly to John O'Ferrall, both of Maryland; from her are descended the *O'Ferralls* of Lewis county, Missouri. 4. John, b. 1780; d. 1824, unmarried, in Tennessee. 5. Peter, b. 1782, d 1837; married Mary Stonebraker, of Maryland; resided at Frederick, in Maryland; left no issue. 6. Francis, born 1784, died 1828; married Catherine Smith of Maryland; resided at Frederick, Md.; left a son named George S. McKiernan, who was born in Frederick, in

Maryland, in 1818, and was married in 1852 to Mary Hull who died in 1875: this George S. McKiernan was living in 1877, in New Albany, Indiana. 7. Bernard, b. 1786, d. 1858; was married to Marianne Waters of Maryland; resided in Alabama, and was the ancestor of the *MacKiernans* of North Alabama.

4. Michael: the second son of Charles; born 1776, died 1837.

5. John: his son; born in Hancock, in Maryland; removed to Ohio; died in Louisiana, in 1840

6. Warren: his son; born in Ohio in 1831; residing in Indianopolis, Indiana, in 1877.

7. John: son of Warren; born 1858, and living in 1877.

MICHEL.

Arms (of Mulvihill): Per fess ar. and gu. in chief a salmon naiant ppr. betw. two lions ramp. combatant az. supporting a dexter hand of the second, in base a harp or, betw. two battle-axes in pale, the blade turned outwards ppr.

MAOIN, a brother of Muirceartach (latinized "Muriartus") Mór MacEarca, the 131st Monarch of Ireland, and who is No. 90 on "The (No. 1) O'Neill" (of Tyrone) pedigree, was the ancestor of *O'Maolmicheille;* anglicised *Michil,** *Michel, Mitchell, Mulvichill, Mulvihill, Melvill,* and *Mulville.*

90. Maoin: son of Muireadach.

91. Columan ("columan:" Irish, *a little dove*); his son; a quo *O'Culumain* (of Tirowen), anglicised *Colman.*

92. Faelan: his son.

93. Endadaidh: his son.

94. Fionnbeartach: his son.

95. Tuathal: his son.

96. Dungal: his son.

97. Maolmichiall ("michiall:"

Irish, *folly*): his son; a quo *O'Maolmicheille* and *O'Maolmichil.*

98. Uiruiman ("uiruim:" Irish, *obedience*): his son.

99. Ardait: his son.

100. Eachteoragan: his son.

101. Giollachriosd: his son.

102. Murcha: his son.

103. Duinesidhe ("duine:" Irish, *a man;* "sidh," gen. "sidhe," *of a fairy hill*): his son; a quo *O'Duin-*

* *Michil*: Another family of this name, whose pedigree we did not yet meet, is descended from Giollamichiall, a descendant of Colla-da-Crioch, who is No. 85 on the "O'Hart" pedigree; but, while *Maolmichiall*, No. 97 on the foregoing stem, literally means "bald Michael," the name *Giollamichiall* means "the devoted of St. Michael."

esidhe, anglicised *Dennesy*, and *Dennehy*.

104. Breannan : his son.
105. Eachmarcach : his son.
106. Coma : his son.
107. Giollachriosd (2) : his son.

108. Muireadach : his son.
109. Niall : his son.
110. Giolla* Blein O'Maolmichil, "of the Battle Axes" ("blein:" Irish, *the groin*); his son; a quo *MacBleinne*.†

At this stage in this genealogy the family was expelled by the O'Connors, of Connaught, from *Corca Eachlinn ;* when they settled in the county Clare, at *Doon Maolmichiall*, which they possessed up to the time of the Cromwellian confiscations in Ireland. In 1554 the castle of Doon Maolmichiall was besieged by the O'Briens ; and Owen O'Maolmichil, of Doon Maolmichiall and Killowen, was the last of the family who possessed that estate—of which he was deprived by Oliver Cromwell. From this Owen descended Daniel O'Mulvihill, of Knockanira, county Clare, who died in 1820. This Daniel had five sons—1. Charles ; 2. Daniel, of Kilglassy, county Clare ; 3. George ; 4. William ; 5. Henry—the three last of whom were Medical Doctors. This Doctor William (fourth son of Daniel of Knockanira), of Gort, co. Galway, had a son—the Rev. Urquhart S. Mulville, A.B., living in 1881, in Strand-street, Tramore, co. Waterford. The fifth son, Henry Mulville, was a Medical Doctor in Dublin : this Henry had a son named Urquhart. Daniel O'Mulvihill, Kilglassy, had three sons, the eldest of whom was Captain Charles Blood Mulville, late of the 3rd Dragoon Guards, who, in 1881, was head of the family ; whose dau. m. Captain French. This Daniel's (of Kilglassy) second son Neptune Blood Mulville was in 1881 living, and a wealthy merchant in the city of Sacramento, California.

Maolmichiall, No. 97 on the foregoing pedigree, did, in his advanced age, shave his head, and become a monk, very eminent for his sanctity : hence his name, which signifies "bald Michael;" on account of the monks *shaving* their heads in the tonsure. He had been a chief or prince of *Tuatha Corca Eachlinn* (or " the north swampy plain"), on the banks of the river Arigna (a tributary of the river Shannon), in the county Roscommon. In the "*Monasticon*" is mentioned, as an eminent ecclesiastic of this name, a dean of Cluan Dochrach, and professor of Divinity of Cluan MacNorisk.

The "Annals of the Four Masters," O'Dugan's "Topography," Lynch, in his *Cambrensis Aversus*, and the Books of Leacan and Ballymote all mention this family as lords of Corca Eachlinn, which they continued to hold down to about A.D. 1416. The Four Masters state, under the year 1189, that on the trial, for treason, of the son of Roger (Roderick) O'Connor, king of Connaught, by the chiefs and nobles of Connaught, O'Maolmichiall (or O'Maolmichil) was the fourth on the list. Under the year 1210, the Four Masters also state that the O'Connors of Connaught

---

* *Giolla* : This Giolla Blein O'Maolmichil, "of the Battle Axes," possessed the *Tuatha* (or North *Corca Eachlinn*), in the county Roscommon, near the river Arigna, a branch of the Shannon.

† *MacBleinne* : It is considered that *Blean, Blain, Blane, Blaney, MacBlane*, and *MacBlain*, are anglicised forms of this Irish sirname.

invaded Corca Eachlinn, but were beaten out of it with loss by
O'Maolmichil ; and, in 1232, a similar event took place, in which O'Connor's son, MacDermott, and O'Kelly were all slain by O'Maolmichil, "of
the Battle Axes :" which raised the hero's fame so high, that it became
an adage to say—" Maolmichil of the Battle Axes could not accomplish
it." The O'Connors, however, eventually expelled the O'Maolmichil
family from Corca Eachlinn ; when they settled in the county Clare, at
Doon Maolmichil, which they lost by confiscation in Cromwell's time.

MEEHAN.*

Of Ballaghmeighan, County Leitrim.

Arms : Gu. on a chev. ar. three bucks' heads erased of the field, attired or, in base
a demi lion ramp. of the second.   *Crest* : A griffin's head erased, wings endorsed or.

THIS is a county Leitrim family ; and is the anglicised form of *O'Maoithain*
("maoth :" Irish, *tender*) and of *O'Miadhachain* (" miadhach :" Irish, *noble,
honourable*), two ancient families of that county, but of different descent.
The latter family was anglicised *O'Mehegan*, as welll as *O'Meehan ;* but the
pedigree of either family is not forthcoming.

MILMO.

Arms : Gu. a lion ramp. ar.

SOME Genealogists derive this family from Maol-na-mBo ("maol :" Irish,
the devotee ; " na-mBo," *of the cows or cattle*), who is No. 110 on the
" MacMorough" genealogy ; and a quo *O'Maoilmbo*. Of this Irish sirname
Mildmay is considered another anglicised form.
    The *Milmo* family, after the English invasion of Ireland, settled in
Connaught, and intermarried with (among others) the ancient families of
" O'Dowd," and " Crean," in the co. Sligo.
    The Venerable Archdeacon O'Rorke, in his " Ballisadare and Kilvarnet,
county Sligo," mentions that the " Milmo" family is one of the oldest and
most respectable families in the parish of Ballisadare. Of this family is

---

* *Meehan* : The Sept of *O'Meehan* or *O'Meighan* possessed Beallach, now the parish
of Ballymeehan, in the county Leitrim. The Four Masters record the death, A.D.
1173, of Edru O'Miadhachain (or Edru Meehan), bishop of Clonard. In Burke's
Armory we read : " A curious relic, consisting of a metal box, which contained the
gospel of St. Molaise, of Devenish, a celebrated saint of the sixth century, is still in
possession of the family, the Sept having preserved it for more than 1200 years."
Christopher *O'Meighan*, an officer in the army of James II., fell at the battle of the
Boyne.

Don Patricio Milmo, of Mexico, who was born in Collooney, in the county Sligo; and who in his youth, went to Mexico to a rich unmarried uncle, who helped his nephew to lay the foundation of his present colossal fortune.

One of Don Patricio Milmo's brothers was a Prize man of the Catholic University, Dublin, in 1856; and another brother, Daniel Milmo, was in 1883 head of the "Milmo National Bank," in Laredo, Texas.

Don Patricio m. the dau. of the celebrated Mexican statesman General Vidaurri, who, taking sides with Maximilian, shared that Emperor's unhappy fate. As an instance of warm attachment to Faith and Fatherland, for which his fathers suffered so much, it is mentioned that this good Irishman Don Patricio (or Patrick) Milmo had his eldest son educated in Dublin under a Catholic professor; and has also taken from the Irish capital a Catholic governess for his daughters; while, during the late famine in Ireland, the said Patrick Milmo sent a handsome donation to the Priests of his native county, for distribution among the distressed.

It is to the realms of fiction that one must look for counterparts to the careers of some of our scattered Irish exiles; for, the lives of not a few of them have even eclipsed in romantic and adventurous elements any of the "forms" that imagination has ever bodied forth. Scarcely a year passes without our meeting some record of a wonderful achievement by one or other of poor Ireland's "Wild Geese," in some distant land. The life of the honoured subject of this paper is such a one; for Mr. Patrick Milmo, of Mexico, is eminently one of our countrymen who, in exile, have shed lustre on their Nation and their Race.

MOGHAN.

Arms : Vert a tower triple-towered ar. from each tower a pennant flotant gu. supported by two lions ramp. combatant or.

CONN BEARNEACH, brother of Conall who is No. 91 on the "O'Shaughnessy" pedigree, was the ancestor of *O'Mochain ;* anglicised *Moghan* and *Mohan.*

91. Conn Bearnach : son of Owen.
92. Cathal : his son.
93. Flann : his son.
94. Connor : his son.
95. Algan ("alga:" Irish, *noble,* "an," *one who ;* Gr. "agla-os") : his son.
96. Teige: his son.
97. Tighearnach: his son.
98. Tioith : his son.
99. Æneas (Aongus) : his son.
100. Mochan ("moch:" Irish, *early,*

"an," *one who*) : his son; a quo *O'Mochain.*
101. Morogh : his son.
102. Morogh Oge : his son.
103. Athasach : his son.
104. Minmoin : his son.
105. Fionn : his son.
106. Muireadach : his son.
107. Murtagh : his son.
108. Donoch : his son.
109. Donal : his son.
110. Nicholas : his son.

111. Simeon : his son.
112. Gregory : his son.
113. John : his son ; had two sons, named—1. Mór, 2. Dermod.

114. Mór (or Mangus) O'Moghan : his son.

MOLLOY.* (No. 1.)

Lords of Fircall, King's County.

Arms : Ar. a lion ramp. sa. betw. three trefoils slipped gu. *Crest :* In front of an oak tree growing out of a maint all ppr. a greyhound springing sa. collared or.

EOCHAIDH, brother of Tuathal who is No. 89 on the "MacGeoghagan" pedigree, was the ancestor of *O'Maoluaidh ;* anglicised *O'Molloy,* and *Molloy.*

89. Eochaidh : son of Fiacha. Had a brother named Tuathal, who was the ancestor of *MacGeoghagan,* and another brother Uigin, who was ancestor of *Higgins.*
90. Duncatha : son of Eochaidh.
91. Bran : his son.
92. Duineocar ("duine :" Irish, *a person ;* "ocar," gen. "ocair," *usury*) : his son ; a quo *O'Duinocair,* anglicised *Donacar, Donagher,* and *Dooner.*
93. Anmchadh : his son.
94. Donnceann : his son.
95. Maoluadh : his son.
96. Donoch : his son.
97. Lorcan : his son.
98. Bogach : his son.
99. Maoluadh ("luadh :" Irish, *motion*) : his son ; a quo *O'Maoluaidh,* lords of the territory of Fircal, in the King's County.
100. Duach : his son.
101. Dubh : his son.
102. Donoch (2) : his son.
103. Donal O'Molloy : his son ; first assumed this sirname.

104. Teige : his son.
105. Cathal : his son.
106. Florence : his son.
107. Fiongan ("fionn :" Irish, *wine ;* Heb. "yain ;" Lat. "vin-um ;" Gr. "oin-os" or "fion-os ;" and "gan :" Irish, *without*), meaning "without wine :" his son ; a quo *O'Fionagain,* anglicised *Finnegan.*
108. Fergal : his son.
109. Murtach : his son.
110. Hugh Mór : his son.
111. Hugh Oge : his son.
112. Rory : his son ; had a brother named Cuileann, who was ancestor of *Molloy,* of Connaught.
113. Neal : son of Rory.
114. Hugh (3) : his son.
115. Conn (also called Constantine, and Cosnamh) : his son.
116. Cathair (or Cahyr) : his son.
117. Conall : his son.
118. Caolach : his son.
119. Cahyr (2) : his son.
120. Calloideach : his son ; had a brother named Art (or Arthur). This Art had a son named Conall

* *Molloy :* O'Donovan is of opinion that the *Clann Taidhg* or *Molloys* of Oakport, county Roscommon, were a distinct family from *O'Molloy,* of Fircall, King's County ; but we are of opinion that the *Molloys* of Oakport are descended from Cuileann, brother of Rory, who is No. 112 on this pedigree.—(See "Molloy" (No. 2), next after this genealogy.)

O'Molloy, lord of Fircall, who, in 1590, surrendered his lands to Queen Elizabeth, and got a re-grant thereof.

121. Arthur O'Molloy : son of Calloideach ; and lord of Fircall.

MOLLOY. (No. 2.)

Of Aghadonoher, King's County.

Arms : Same as "Molloy" (No. 1).

"COCOGHERY" O'MOLLOY, of Kilmanahan, had :

2. Rory, who had :

3. John, who had :

4. Donogh, of Aghadonoher (now "Aghadonagh"), in the barony of Ballycowan, King's County, who d. 16th Nov., 1637. He m. Ellenor, dau. of Andrew Briscoe, of Strahyker, King's County, gent., and had three sons and two daughters :

I. Dominick.
II. Cosnyagh.
III. Rory.
The daughters were :
I. Margaret, who married Hobart Farrell, of Aghadonoher gent.
II. Sheela.
5. Dominick O'Molloy : son of Donogh.

MOLLOY. (No. 3.)

Of Harperstown and Oakport, County Roscommon.

Arms ; Same as those of "Molloy." (No. 1.)

CUILEANN, brother of Rory who is No. 112 on the "Molloy" (No. 1) pedigree, was the ancestor of this family.

1. William Mór, known as " The Great William O'Molloy," had four sons :

I. Connor, of whom presently.
II. Edward.
III. Arthur ; and
IV. Terence.
This Edward m. Mary O'Connor Don, and had :
    Greene O'Molloy, who was a

Capt. in O'Gara's regiment, in the Army of King James
II. Greene had William (also an officer in O'Gara's regiment), who was attainted on the 2nd November, 1696, and who had two sons : 1. Theobald, a Capt. of Horse in Portugal ; and 2. Ignatius.
2. Connor : eldest son of William

Mór ; was the founder of the Harperstown and Oakport " O'Molloy" families. He had two sons :

I. Theobald, of whom presently.

II. William.

3. Theobald : son of Connor ; was a Captain in the Army of William III. ; had :

4. Charles, who was pressed into the Jacobite army. He had :

I. John, who d. s.p.

II. Coote.

5. Coote *Molloy :* second son of Charles ; had four sons :

I. Tobias, of whom presently.

II. James.

III. Coote.

IV. William.

6. Tobias, B.L. : eldest son of Coote ; d. 1825. He had two sons :

I. Coote, of whom presently,

II. Charles, who had three sons.

7. Coote Molloy : son of Tobias ; had three sons :

I. Rev. Coote, of whom presently.

II. Charles.

III. William-James, who had William-Soyes.

8. Rev. Coote Molloy : eldest son of Coote ; and had three sons.

I. Coote, of whom presently.

II. Robert.

III. William.

9. Coote Molloy : son of Rev. Coote Molloy.

MOODY.*

Arms ; Az. a chev. erm. betw. three pheons ar.

DONOCH, brother of Dermod Ruanach who is No. 92 on the "Fogarty" pedigree, was the ancestor of *O'Maolmodha ;* anglicised *Mulmuog, Mulmody, Moody,* and *Mulmy.*

92. Donoch: son of Aidus (or Aodh) Slaine, the 141st Monarch of Ireland.

93. Finachtach Fleadhach : his son who was the 153rd Monarch.

94. Cathal : his son.

95. Tomaltach : his son.

96. Cumascach : his son.

97. Cearnach : his son.

98. Maolmodh ("modh," gen. " modha :" Irish, *a mode* or *manner;* Lat. "mod-us"): his son ; a quo *O'Maolmodha.*

* *Moody :* John Moody, a well-known actor, was born in 1727. In a notice that throws some doubt on his Irish birth, the *Gentleman's Magazine* calls him the "father of the English stage." But of him the poet Churchill wrote :

" Long from a nation ever hardly used,
At random censured, wantonly abused,
Have Britons drawn their sport with partial view,
Formed general notions from the rascal few."
• • • • • •

These lines would show that Moody was an *Irishman.* In 1796 he retired from the stage, after fifty years' service, and died in London on the 26th December, 1812.

MOONEY. (No. 1.)

Of Ulster.

Arms : Gu. a lion pass. guard. or.

MAIGNAN, brother of Aongus who is No. 90 on the "O'Brassil West" pedigree, was the ancestor of *O'Maoinaigh* of Ulster, anglicised *O'Mooney*, *Mooney*, and *Moynagh*.

90. Maignan: son of Colcan.

91. Cumann: his son; had a brother named St. Furanan. (See Calendar, 25th June.)

92. Maoinan: son of Cumann.

93. Cumann (2): his son.

94. Osbiseach ("biseach: Irish, *increase ;* Heb. "bizza") : his son.

95. Maoinach: his son; a quo *O'Maoinaigh.*

96. Fear-coir ("coir:" Irish, *virtuous ;* Heb. "chor," *noble*) : his son; a quo *O'Fearcora*, anglicised *Faraher*, and modernized *Corr.*

97. Flann: his son.

98. Cearnach: his son.

99. Felim O'Mooney: his son.

MOONEY. (No. 2.)

Of Ballaghmooney, King's County.

Arms : Ar. a holly tree eradicated vert, thereon a lizard pass. or, a border compony counter-compony of the first and second.

EOGHAN (or Owen), brother of Berchan who is No. 93 on the "O'Gorman" pedigree, was the ancestor of *O'Maoinaigh ;* anglicised *O'Mooney*, *Mooney*, and *Money.*

93. Owen: son of Feig.

94. Alioll Mór: his son.

95. Maoinach ("maoin," gen. "maoine," Irish, *wealth ;* Engl. "money"): his son; a quo *O'Maoinaigh*, and the territory of *Feara Maoinaigh* (anglicised "Fermanagh,") which was given to him by his uncle, the then Irish Monarch.

96. Corcran: son of Maoinach; had two brothers — 1. Fiachra, ancestor of *Mooney*, of Lochern,

and 2. Iardun, ancestor of *Clann Rorc.*

97. Conall: son of Corcran.

98. Ionglan: his son.

99. Gilearan ("gile:" Irish, *whiteness*, and "aran," *bread*) : his son; a quo *O'Gilearain*, anglicised *Gilleran*, and *Gillard.*

100. Maoltoghadh: his son.

101. Conadhgan: his son.

102. Gallan: his son.

103. Dallgan: his son.

2 P

104. Canamhuin (see *canmen*, old Lat. form of "carmen :") his son.
105. Coscrach : his son.

106. Giollabrighid : his son.
107. Cearnach : his son.
108. Ranall O'Mooney : his son.

MOONEY. (No. 3.)

Of Ringstown, County Meath.

Arms : Same as those of "Mooney" (No. 2).

WILLIAM MOONEY, had :
2. Daniel, who had :
3. James, who had :
4. William, of Ringstown, co. Meath, who had :

5. Thomas Mooney, of Garishe, co. Meath, who d. unm. 30th May, 1638.

MORGAN.

Arms : Gu. three towers ar.

MUIREGAN, brother of Donelan who is No. 102 on the "Donnellan" (of Ulster) pedigree, was the ancestor of *O'Muiregain ;* anglicised *Murigan*, and *Morgan.*

102. M u i r e g a n ("muiregan :" Irish, *a mariner*) : son of Maol-craoibhe ; a quo *O'Muiregain.*
103. Flann : his son.

104. Murtagh : his son.
105. Muireadach : his son.
106. Flann O'Murigan : his son.

MORIARTY.

Of Connaught.

Arms : Ar. three lions pass. guard. gu.

MUIRCEARTACH (or Murtagh), the second son of Malachi, the brother of Murtogh who is No. 120 on the "Concannon" pedigree, was the ancestor of *MacMuirceartaigh ;* anglicised *Moriarty*, and *Murtagh.*

120. Malachi: son of Ardgall.

121. Muirceartach ("muir:" Irish, *the sea;* "ceart," *just* or *upright*), meaning "a protector at sea," or, "an admiral"): his son; a quo *MacMuirceartaigh.*

122. Edmond: his son; had a brother named John.

123. Hugh: son of Edmond.

124. Elmond (2): his son

125. Hugh O'Moriarty: his son.

MORLEY.

Arms: Per pale gu. and az. a leopard's face jessant-de-lis or.   *Crest*: Out of a mural coronet a griffin's head betw. two wings.

FLAITHBHEARTACH, brother of Furadhran who is No. 97 on the "Foran" pedigree, was the ancestor of *MacMhearlaoigh;** anglicised *Morley, Marlay, Marley, Mahrlé, Mehrlé, Merlé, Merley, Murley,* and *Varley.*

97. Flaithbheartach: son of Conchobhar.

98. Cathal: his son.

99. Baoghal: his son.

100. Conchobhar: his son; had a brother Cineadhach, a quo *O'Cineadhaigh,* of Scotland, anglicised *Kennedy.*

101. Flaithbheartach: his son.

102. Bruadaran ("bruadair:" Irish, *a dream*): his son; a quo *Mac-Bruadarain,* anglicised *MacBroderick,* and *Broderick,* of Ulster.

103. Tadchaidh: his son.

104. Duncathach: his son.

105. Cucaille: his son.

106. Giolla Dhabheog: his son.

107. Dubhleacan: his son.

108. Mearlaoch ("mear:" Irish, *quick,* Heb. "maher," *to hasten;* "laoch," *a hero*): his son; a quo *MacMearlaoigh.*

MORRIS.

Arms: Same as those of "MacDermot" (No. 1).

DONOGH, brother of Diarmod who is No. 111 on the "MacDermott" pedigree, was the ancestor of *MacMuirios,* or *O'Muirfeasa;* anglicised *Morishy, Morris, Morrisey,* and *MacMorris*—modernised *Morrison.*†

* *MacMearlaoigh*: This name has been also rendered *O Mearlaoigh.*

† *Morrison:* Like other Scotch families of the present day, a member of the *Mac-Muirios* or *O'Muirios* family settled in Scotland in early times; who was the ancestor of *Morrison.* Sir Richard Morrison, President of the Institute of Architects, was born in Cork, in 1767. He was at first employed in the Government service in the Ordnance Department; but afterwards devoted himself to private engagements, and erected many important public buildings in Ireland—as Sir Patrick Dun's Hospital, Dublin, and the County Court Houses at Carlow, Clonmel, Dundalk, Galway, Maryborough, Naas, Roscommon, and Wexford. He was knighted in 1841, and died on the 31st of October, 1849.

111. Donoch : son of Teige Mór.

112. Teige : his son.

113. Muirios ("muir," Irish, *the sea;* "fios" or "feas," gen. "feasa," *knowledge;* Lat. "vis-us"), meaning "intelligence from the sea :" his son ; a quo *MacMuirios*, etc.

114. Tomaltach (or Timothy) : his son; first assumed this sirname.

115. Murtach : his son.

116. Donal : his son.

117. Malachi : his son.

118. Ceallach : his son.

119. Murtach : his son.

120. Manus : his son.

121. Maolruanaidh (or Mulroona) : his son.

122. Malachi (2) : his son.

123. Manus (2) : his son.

124. Duald (or Dudley) : his son.

125. Ferdinand O'Muirios,* or *MacMuirios.*

MULDOON. (No. 1.)

Of Meath.

Arms : Vert a dexter hand couped ar. between three crescents or, issuant therefrom as many estoiles of the second. *Crest :* A dexter hand ppr. surmounted by a crescent or, therefrom issuant an estoile ar. *Motto :* Pro fide et patria.

AODH (or Hugh) Laighen, brother of Fogharthach who is No. 95 on the "Fogarty" pedigree, was the ancestor of *O'Maoldubhain*, of Meath, anglicised *Muldoon*, and *Meldon.*

95. Aodh Laighen : son of Neal (or Niall).

96. Donal : his son.

97. Maoldun : his son.

98. Adhnachan : his son.

99. Assachan : his son.

100. Maoldun ("Maol-Dubhan" : Irish, the *devoted of St. Dubhan*) : his son ; a quo *O'Maoldubhain.*

* *O'Muirios :* Another "Morris" family was descended from Tiomain Muirios, the younger brother of Tiobrad, who is No. 91 on the "O'Dowd" pedigree ; as follows :

91. Tiomain Muirios : son of Maoldubh, who was son of Fiachra Ealgach (or Ealleach), who was son of Dathi, the 127th Monarch of Ireland.

92. Aodh (or Hugh) ; his son.

93. Murtagh : his son.

94. Murtagh Oge : his son.

95. Teige O'Murios : his son.

MULDOON. (No. 2.)

Of Tirowen.

Arms ; Ar. a sinister hand couped at the wrist affrontée gu.

MAOLDUIN, a brother of Niall Caille who is No. 98 on the "O'Neill" (No. 1) pedigree, was the ancestor of *Siol Maoilduin;* anglicised *O'Muldoon.*

98. Maolduin ("maol:" Irish, *the devotee ; "* duin," *of the fortress*): second son of Aodh Ornaighe, the 164th Monarch of Ireland; a quo *Siol Maoilduin.*
99. Niall : his son

100. Donnagan : his son.
101. Maolduin : his son.
102. Clercen ("clerc:" Irish, *a curl; "* en," *one*): his son; a quo *O'Cleircin,* anglicised *Curley,* and *Curling.*

MULFINNY.

Arms : Same as those of "Donnelly," of Ulster.

MAOLFION ("fionn:" Irish, *wine*), brother of Dungal who is No. 102 on the "Donnelly" (of Ulster) pedigree, was the ancestor of *O'Maolfhiona ;* anglicised *Mulfinny, Feeny,* etc.—See the "Donnelly" pedigree for other anglicised forms for the Irish sirnames *O'Maolfhiona.*

MULHEERAN.

Of Offaley.

Arms : Ar. on a mount in base vert an oak tree acorned ppr.

CEALLACH, a brother of Æneas who is No. 100 on the "O'Connor" Faley pedigree, was the ancestor of *O'Maolciarain,* of Offaley, anglicised *Mulkeeran, Mulheeran,* and *Mulhern.*

100. Ceallach : son of Florence.
101. Dungal : his son.
102. Ceallachan : his son.

103. Maolciaran ("ciaran:" Irish, *one who is dark grey*): his son; a quo *O'Maolciurian.*

MULLALLY.

Of Moenmoy, County Galway.

Arms : Ar. three eagles displ. gu. two and one, each holding in the beak a sprig of laurel ppr. betw. as many crescents, one and two az.   *Crest* : An eagle, as in the Arms.

O'DUGAN in his Topographical Poems says :

> " The Kings of Maonmagh of chiefs,
> To whom the rich plain is hereditary,—
> Two who have strengthened that side,—
> O'Naghten* and O'Mullally ;
> Their fight is heavy in the battles ;
> They possess the land as far as *Hy-Fiachrach*."

Of the O'Mullallys, Doctor John O'Donovan writes : " This family was afterwards removed from Maonmagh to the parish of Tuam (in the county Galway), where they resided in the Castle of Tollendal, four miles to the north of the town of Tuam."   .   .   .   The Lallys and O'Naghtens were chiefs in turn of Maonmagh (Moenmoy), according to the power of each ; but about the period of the English Invasion of Ireland they were driven out of Moenmoy, and obliged to settle at Tulach-na-dala (Tollendal), *i.e.* " hill of the meeting," in the territory of Conmaicne Duna Moir, where they became tenants to the Lord Bermingham. It appears from an Inquisition taken at Athenry, on the 16th of September, 1617, that Isaac Laly, then the head of this family, who was seated at Tullaghnadaly (or Tulach-na-dala, as it is above written) ; William Laly, of Ballynabanaby ; and Daniel Laly, of Lisbally, were all tributary to the Lord Bermingham.

Moenmoy is the rich plain lying round Loughrea, and comprising Moyode, Finnure, and other places mentioned in old Irish documents. It was bounded on the east by the (O'Madden) territory of Siol Anmchada (now the barony of Longford), on the south by the celebrated mountain of Sliabh Echtghe (now known as " Slieve Aughtee"), and on the west by the diocese of Kilmacduagh ; its northern boundary is uncertain ; but we know that it extended so far to the north as to comprise the townland of Moyode.

After the defeat of the Irish, at the Battle of Aughrim, the head of the O'Mullally family removed to France, and was the ancestor of the celebrated statesman and orator Count Lally Tolendal, who was created Marquis by Napoleon I. " The French and Tuam branches of this family," says O'Donovan, " are now extinct, but there are many of the name still in the original territory of Moenmoy, who retain the original form of the name, except that in writing it in English they reject the prefix *O'*, which has become a general practice among the Irish peasantry."

From an ancient pedigree drawn up about 1709 for the French branch of this family, from old Irish MSS., much curious information is given by O'Donovan (in his " Tribes and Customs of Hy-Many," p. 178).   The

---

* *O'Naghten :* While in the Third and present Edition of this work we give the pedigree of this family, we were, until lately, unable to trace the pedigree of the " O'Mullally" family.

document is entitled "Extracts from the Genealogy of the most ancient and illustrious House of *O'Maollala*, afterwards *Mullally*, or *O'Lally*, of the Kingdom of Ireland, collected from the old Irish MSS. Books of Pedigrees, as well as from the Records preserved in the Exchequer, Auditor-General and Rolls Offices in the said Kingdom. By WILLIAM HAWKINS, ESQ., Ulster King of Arms, and principal Herald of all Ireland, under the Seal of his office, &c."

From that document we can give ten generations of the " O'Mullally" family commencing with—

1. Melaghlin *O'Maollala.*·

2. John : son of Melaghlin ; was sirnamed *Giallaoch*, or the " warlike hostage," because in the siege of Boulogne, in 1544, he distinguished himself very much with his galloglasses, etc. He m. Shely (or Judith), daughter to Hugh O'Madden, chief of his name, and lord of the territory of Siol Anmchada, county Galway, by whom he had Dermod. His brothers were William O'Lally, Archbishop of Tuam, who d. 1595 ; and John O'Mullally, who, dissatisfied with the submission of his father to the crown of England, and with the supremacy of Henry VIII., went to Rome with his red eagles painted in black on his escutcheon, offered his services with many companions to the Pope, and warred for Octava Farnesse.

3. Dermod : son of John ; chief of his Sept ; d. 1596.

4. Isaac *O'Mullally*, of Tolendal : his son ; d. 1621.

5. James O'Mullally, of Tolendal : son of Isaac ; forfeited in 1652 part of his estate, consequent on the Cromwellian Confiscations ; he d. 1676. His brothers Donal and William *Lally* espoused the cause of King Charles II. ; were outlawed and all their estates forfeited. William m. and had Edmund Lally, who m. Elizabeth Brabazon.

6. Thomas O'Mullally, chief of Tully Mullally or Tolendal : son of James ; m. a sister of Lord Dillon (the seventh Viscount), father of Arthur Count Dillon, Lieutenant-General in the French Service.

7. Colonel James *Lally :* their eldest son ; was "sovereign" of the Corporation of Tuam, for King James II., in 1687 ; a member of James's last Parliament in 1689 ; was outlawed the same year, fled to France, entered the French army, a Colonel in that Service, Commandant of the Lally's battalion in Dillon's regiment in 1690, and killed in 1691 during the blockade of Mount Mellan (or Melian). Colonel James Lally had four brothers :—1. Sir Gerard,* who became highly distinguished in the French Service, and d. a Brigadier-General and designed Marèchal de Camp in 1737 ; he m. Madlle. de Bressac, by whom he had Thomas-Arthur, of whom presently. 2. William, who was a Captain in Dillon's regiment,

---

* *Gerard :* On the death of his brother Colonel James Lally, this Sir Gerard succeeded to the Chiefship ; he appears to have passed through the Irish war, and, after the capitulation of Limerick, to have accompanied the army to France. His son, Thomas-Arthur, bravely upheld the French flag in India ; he was beheaded in 1766, but his cruel and undeserved fate stamped indelible disgrace on the Bourbons of France. Thomas-Arthur, General Count Lally of Tolendal, left a son Trophime Gerard, Count and Marquis de Lally, who laboured for many years to remove the stain from his father's name, in which he at length succeeded. He was made a Peer of France, on the second restoration of the Bourbons, and died in 1830, leaving an only daughter who brought the peerage of Lally Tollendal into the family of her husband, the Count D'Aux.

and killed in 1697. 3. Michael, who m. a Miss O'Carroll, by whom he had a son Michael, who was a Brigadier-General, and who d. at Rouen in 1773.

8. Thomas-Arthur, General, Count Lally of Tolendal: son of Sir Gerard Lally ; was Colonel of an Irish regiment in the French Service, of his name ; beheaded in 1766.

9. Trophime Gerard Compte et Marquis de Lally Tolendal, Peer of France, Minister of State, etc.; son of Thomas Arthur ; m. Charlotte Wedderburne Halkett (having a common grandfather with Alexander Wedderburne, Lord Loughborough, who was Lord Chancellor of England,) by whom he had an only child (a daughter), who m. the Count D'Aux, to whom in 1817 the peerage of his father-in-law was to descend, as the genealogical notice appended to the Pedigree by Hawkins states.

"Authenticated by signature, dated 29th October, 1817.

"LALLY TOLLENDAL,

" Peer of France and Minister of State."

The last survivor of the senior branch of the male line in Ireland of this very ancient family, who was named Thomas Lally, died without issue, in September, 1838. The calamitous history of some members of the family in France is very singular.

MULLEN.*

Arms : Ar. on a mount vert an oak tree ppr. perched thereon a falcon also ppr. belled or, betw. in base two cross crosslets fitchée gu.

CONNOR, brother of Dathi who is No. 102 on the " Concannon" pedigree, was the ancestor of *O'Maolain ;* anglicised *Malin, Mallin, Mollan, Mollon, Mollin, Moline, Moylan,*† *Moleyns, De Moleyns, MacMullen, Mullen,* and *Milne.*

102. Connor: son of Dermod Fionn, the 30th Christian King of Connaught.

103. Donall : his son.

104. Maolan ("maolan:" Irish, *a bald-pated man*): his son ; a quo *O'Maolain ;* had a brother named Fionn ("fionn:" Irish, *fair, handsome*), a quo *O'Finne,* anglicised *Finn.*

---

* *Mullen :* Allen Mullen, or Moline, M.D., an eminent anatomist of his time, was born in the north of Ireland, in the middle of the 17th century. He took his medical degree in the University of Dublin in 1684, removed to London in 1686, and was elected a member of the Royal Society. Harris's *Ware* gives a list of six surgical treatises from the pen of Allen Mullen, published between 1682 and 1689 ; he died in 1690.

† *Moylan :* Stephen Moylan, Brigadier-General in the United States revolutionary army, was born in Ireland in 1734. He was one of the first to answer the call to arms against the British at Cambridge, Massachusetts ; and who distinguished himself in many of the operations of the war. A man of education and gentlemanly address, he for a short time acted as *aide-de-camp* to Washington. He was made Brigadier-General by Brevet, in November, 1783, and after the peace occupied some civil posts in Pennsylvania. He died on the 11th April, 1811. His brother was Catholic Bishop of Cork .

MULRENNAN.

Arms: Ar. an oak tree eradicated ppr.

MUIREADACH Maoilleathan, the 16th Christian King of Connaught who is No. 97 on the (No. 1) "O'Connor" (Connaught) pedigree, was the ancestor of *O'Maolbrennain ;* anglicised *O'Mulrennan*, and *Mulrennan*.

97. Muireadach Maoilleathan ("maoilleathan :" Irish, *broad-faced*); a quo *O'Maoilleathan*, anglicised *Molohan*, and *Mullehan*.

98. Cathal: his son; the 18th Christian King; was the ancestor of *Finnerty* and *Finaghty*.

99. Dubhinrachtach : his son.

100. Oireachtach : his son.

101. Aongus Maoldun : his son.

102. Breanan (*an :* Irish, one who ;" *brean*, "an offensive smell") : his son ; a quo *O'Maoilbreannain*.

103. Ruarc : his son.

104. Culuachrach : his son ; first assumed this sirname.

105. Tomaltach : his son.

106. Murtogh : his son.

107. Dermod : his son.

108. Giollachriosd ("giollachri-

osd :" Irish, *a devotee of Christ*) : his son ; a quo *MacGiollachriosd*, and (in Scotland) *MacCriosdora*, anglicised *Gillchriest*, *Christian*,[*] *Kit*, *Kits*, and *Kitson*.

109. Dermod (2) : his son.

110. Aodh (or Hugh) : his son.

111. Giollachriosd (2) : his son.

112. Maithan : his son ; had a brother named Aodh.

113. Hubert : his son.

114. Hubert Oge : his son.

115. Hugh (2) : his son.

116. Rory Granna ("granna :" Irish, *not handsome*) : his son ; a quo *MacGranna*, anglicised *Mac-Grane* and *Magrane*.

117. Edmund Mulbrennan : his son.

---

[*] *Christian:* We have traced this family back to Gilbert Christian, a native of Scotland, who settled in the North of Ireland, A.D. 1702, and there married Margaret Richardson, by whom he had children : that Gilbert was, we find, the great-great-grandfather of J. R. Christian, living in 1877, in Holly Springs, Mississippi, United States, America ; subject to whose correction we write this notice of his family. And, we find, that Duncan Campbell, of Inverary, Scotland, whose wife was Mary McCoy, and who settled in Ireland at the time of the "Plantation of Ulster," by King James II., of England, was one of Mr. Christian's maternal ancestors. This Duncan lived near Londonderry, where his son Patrick Campbell purchased some land. Patrick's youngest son, John, when far advanced in life, migrated to America, A.D. 1726 : from him and his numerous children and other kindred have descended a large progeny, spread over the Southern States of the American Union.

In 1722, the above-mentioned Gilbert Christian, accompanied by a large number of his countrymen, migrated to America ; and, having some time remained in Pennsylvania, he ultimately settled in Virginia, whither many of his name and family had preceded him from Ireland. Israel Christian, a Scot, once a merchant in Dublin, followed him ; and among those who then also went to America from various counties in Ulster were members of the following families : Allen, Brakenridge, Campbell, Christian, Cunningham, Given, Henry, Lewis, Lockhart, McClanahan, McCue, [Mac-Hugh], McDonald, McDowell, McGavock, Montgomery, Rerton (or Rereton), Russell, Trimble, Wilson, etc. The descendants of those families, in America, have there so multiplied during a residence of a century and three quarters in the country, and have become so connected by marriage, as to constitute a relationship between a large proportion of the population of the Southern United States ; disclosing the important fact that the people of that vast region in America are almost entirely *Celtic*.

MULROY.

Arms : Same as " O'Donnell" (No. 1).

ANMIRE, the 138th Monarch, brother of Fergus who is No. 91 on the " O'Donnell" (Tirconnell) pedigree, was the ancestor of *O'Maoldaraighe*, ancient Princes of Tirconnell; anglicised *Dary*, *Muldory*, *Malory*, and *Mulroy*.

91. Anmire (" mire :" Irish, *frolic*): son of Seadneach ; ancestor of *O'Gallagher*.

92. Aodh : his son.

93. Donall : his son.

94. Aongus : his son.

95. Longseach : his son ; was the 154th Monarch.

96. Flaithertach : his son ; the 159th Monarch.

97. Maolbreasal : his son.

98. Morogh : his son ; had a brother named Aodh Munderg, who was the ancestor of *Canning*, of Tirconnell.

99. Aongus : his son.

100. Maoldarach (" darach :" Irish, *an oak*): his son ; a quo *O'Maoldaraighe*.

101. Maolbreasal : his son.

102. Aongus : his son.

103. Murtogh : his son.

104. Maolruanaidh O'Maoldaraighe : his son ; first assumed this sirname. Had a brother Criochan, who was the father of Giollacoluim, father of Niall, father of Flaithbeartach.

105. Giollafinnean : his son ; a quo *MacGillfinen*. This Giollafinean was the last Prince of Tirconnell, of the *Muldory* (or *Mulroy*) family. After him the O'Donnells, who were of the same illustrious stock, became by conquest Princes of Tirconnell ; and remained so down to the beginning of the 17th century. —See the " Flight of the Earls," in the Appendix."

MURRAY.*

Of Leitrim.

Arms : Same as those of " O'Beirne."

MUIREADHACH, a brother of Beirin who is No. 103 on the " O'Beirne" pedigree, was the ancestor of *O'Muireadhaigh*, na-Haidhnighe (" aidhnidhe :" Irish, *an Advocate*) ; anglicised *Murray*, *Meredith*, and *Meredyth*.

* *Murray*: Nicholas Murray, D.D., a distinguished divine and author, was born at Ballinasloe, on the 25th December, 1802. He went to the United States in 1818, and was appointed to the printing house of Harper Brothers. Subsequently he studied theology and became pastor of a Presbyterian Church in Pennsylvania. In 1849 he was Moderator of the Presbyterian General Assembly. He was the author of numerous works on archæology and social statistics, travels, and sermons. He died at Elizabethtown, New Jersey, on the 4th of February, 1861.

103. Muireadhach("muireadhach:"
Irish, *a lord*) : son of Cineadh ; a
quo *O'Muireadhaigh*, na-Haidnighe.
104. Muircheartach : his son.
105. Dubhslatach : his son.
106. Britriabhach : his son.

107. Conghalach : his son.
108. Giolla Calma : his son.
109. Conghalach : his son.
110. Giolla Calma : his son.
111. Conghalach : his son.
112. Giollachriosd : his son.

NAGHTEN.*

Chiefs of Maonmagh, Hy-Maine.

Arms : Quarterly, 1st and 4th, gu. three falcons close ppr. ; 2nd and 3rd, vert three
swords ar. pommels and hilts or, one in pale, point downwards, the others in saltire,
points upwards. *Crest :* A falcon close ppr.

FIACHRA FIONN, brother of Lughach who is No. 92 on the (No. 1) "O'Kelly"
(Hy-Maine) pedigree, was the ancestor of *O'Neachtain* and *MacNeachtain ;*
anglicised *Naghten, Natten, Naughton, MacNaughtan,*† and *Norton.*

92. Fiachra Fionn : son of
Dallan.
93. Amhailgadh [awly] : his son.
94. Congal : his son.
95. Inleigh : his son.
96. Tuathal : his son.
97. Olioll : his son.
98. Æneas : his son ; had a brother named Maoleala (" eala :" Irish,
a swan), a quo *O'Maoleala,* anglicised
Swan, Lally, and *Mullally.*
99. Maolceir : his son.
100. Neachtan (" neach :" Irish,
a spirit ; " teann," *bold, daring*) :
his son ; a quo *O'Neachtain.*
101. Aodh (or Hugh) : his son.
102. Fiontain (" fion :" Irish, *wine ;*
" teann," *daring*) : his son ; a quo
O'Fiontain, anglicised *Finton.*

103. Fearballach (" ballach :" Irish,
speckled), meaning the " freckled
man :" his son ; a quo *O'Fear-
ballaighe,* anglicised *Farrelly, Farley,*
and *Freely.*
104. Fergus Fionn : his son.
105. Connor Catha Brian (or Connor who fought on the side of the
Monarch Brian Boroimhe [Boru], at
the battle of Clontarf, A.D. 1014) : his
son. This Connor was the first
that assumed the sirname *O'Neachtain.*
106. Amhailgadh [awly] : his son.
107. Awly Oge : his son.
108. Melachlin : his son.
109. Teige, of Loughrea : his son.
110. Hugh (2) : his son.
111. Connor (2) : his son.

---

* *Naghten :* As showing the wealth and piety in early times of this ancient
family, we subjoin a copy of an inscription on a tomb in Drum Church, Athlone :
"ONaghten Nobilissimus Satrapes ex Stirpe Hugonii Magni Totius Hiberniæ
Monarchæ Hoc Templum Edificavit Sanctæque Mariæ Dedicavit Anno Domini 550.
Sub hoc Tumulo Sepelitur Tandemque Illustrissima Antiquissimaque Ejus prosapia
Requiescant in Pace Amen."

† *MacNaughtan :* Some MacNaughtens were of opinion that they were of *Pictish*
origin ; and that the family was one of the three clans descended from the old
Maormors of Moray—sovereigns of that ancient Pictish race, which, from the earliest
times, occupied the district of Moray, in Scotland.

112. Melachlin (2): his son.
113. Awly (4): his son.
114. Donall: his son.
115. Creachmhoill: his son.
116. Cathal: his son.
117. Awly (5): his son.
118. Giollachriosd: his son.
119. Roger: his son.
120. Giolla (or William): his son.

121. Hugh (3): his son.
122. Donogh: his son.
123. Edward: his son.
124. Thomas Naghten, of Crofton House, Hants, England: his son.
125. Arthur R. Naghten, of Bligh mont, Southampton, M.P. for Winchester: his son; living in 1878.

NEALAN.

Arms: Sa. two unicorns pass. in pale ar. horned and hoofed or. *Crest*: A dexter hand erect, couped at the wrist, grasping a dagger all ppr.

COLLA-DA-CRIOCH, who is No. 85 on the "O'Hart" pedigree, had a son named Fiachra Casan, who was the ancestor of *O'Niallain ;* anglicised *Nallin, Nealan, Neiland, Neylan, Neillan, Neyland, Newland, Niland, Nally,* and *MacNally.*

85. Colla-da-Crioch, the first king of Orgiall.
86. Fiachra Casan: his son.
87. Felim: his son.
88. Feich: his son.
89. Niallan ("niall:" Irish, *a champion*): his son; a quo *O'Niallian.*
90. Eoghan ("ogan:" Irish, *a youth*): his son; a quo *MacEoghain,* of Ulster; anglicised *MacOwen, McEwen, Ewing, McCune, McKeowen, MacKeown, MacKeon, Keon, McGeown, Keown, Owens, Owenson,* and *Johnson.*
91. Muireadach: his son.
92. Baothain ("Baoth:" Irish, *simple ;* Heh. "baha," *was vain*): his son; a quo *O'Baothin,* anglicised *Boytan, Boyton,* and *Batten.*
93. Ronan ("ron:" Irish, *hair*), meaning "the man with a profusion of hair:" his son; a quo *O'Ronain,* anglicised *Ronan,* and *Ronayne.*
94. Subhaneach: his son.
95. Colga: his son.
96. Eiginneach: his son.

97. Subhaneach (2): his son.
98. Cosgrach: his son.
99. Dermod: his son.
100. Anluaneach: his son.
101. Flann Line: his son.
102. Aodh: his son.
103. Dermod: his son.
104. Flaithertach: his son.
105. Dermod O'Niallain: his son; first assumed this sirname. Had a brother named Hugh, who was the ancestor of *Neylan,* of England: the first of whom, named Edmund O'Neylan, went there A.D. 1120.
106. Teige: son of Dermod.
107. Cathal Caomh: his son.
108. Thomas: his son.
109. Dermod (3): his son.
110. Donoch: his son.
111. Teige (2): his son.
112. David: his son; a quo *Slioght Daibhidh* ("sliochd:" Irish, *posterity*), meaning the posterity of Davy: his son; a quo *O'Daibhidh,* of Orgiall, anglicised *Davy, Davies,* and *Davis.*

113. Connor : his son.
114. Thomas (2): his son.
115. David (2) : his son.
116. William : his son.

117. John : his son.
118. Denis O'Neylan, of Slioght
David : his son.

NIGHT.

Arms (of MacNight) : Sa. three lions' heads erased or.

FEARGAL, a brother of Charles who is No. 111 on the "O'Reilly" (Princes of East Brefney) pedigree, was the ancestor of *Mac-na-Hoidhche* [macna-heeha] ; anglicised *MacNight, Night*, and *McNeight*.

111. Feargal : son of Gothfrith.
112. Cathal Dubh : his son.
113. Gothfrith (" goth :" Irish, *straight ;* "frith," *small*): his son; a quo *MacGothfrith* (meaning "the son of the small straight man"), of Brefney, and anglicised *MacGuthrie, Maguthrie, Guthrie*, and *Godfrey*.

114. Muirceartach : his son.
115. Feargal : his son.
116. Donchadh : his son.
117. Niall MacNight (who was also called Niall Guthrie): his son.

NOWLAN.*

Princes of the Foharta, now the Barony of Forth, County Carlow.

Arms : Ar. on a cross gu. a lion pass. betw. four martlets of the first, in each quarter a sword erect of the second. *Crest :* A martlet ar.

EOCHAIDH FIONN FOHART, a younger brother of the Monarch Conn of the Hundred Battles, who (see p. 358) is No. 80 on the "Stem of the Line of Heremon," was the ancestor of *O'Nuallain ;* anglicised *O'Nowlan,* and *Nolan.* Foharta, or, more properly, Foghmhartach ("foghmhar :" Irish, *harvest*), gen. Foghmhartaigh, being the name by which the descendants of this Eochaidh were called; and the two principal districts inhabited by them still retain the name, viz.—the baronies of "Forth," in the counties of Wexford and Carlow.

* *Nowlan :* Of this family is John Nolan, who in 1887 resided in Dundas-street, Edinburgh, Scotland, whose ancestors were for the last century chiefly located in Ballinamona, near Ballycanew, county Wexford. On his mother's side he comes from two very old and respectable families, viz., the Gilberts and Dickensons, the representatives of whom still reside in the vicinity of Inch, near Gorey. Mr. John Nolan married in 1874 Jane, eldest daughter of John Hughes, of Killygordon, and had issue : 1. Mary-Jane, 2. John-Gilbert, 3. Thomas-Oakes, 4. Heremon-Hughes—all living in 1887.

80. Eocha Fionn Fohart : son of the Monarch Felim Reachtmhar.

81. Æneas : his son.

82. Cormac : his son.

83. Cairbre : his son.

84. Art-Corb : his son.

85. Mughna : his son.

86. Cuibhe : his son.

87. Iar : his son.

88. Feach (or Fiacha) : his son.

89. Ninneadh : his son.

90. Baithin : his son.

91. Eocha : his son.

92. Ronan : his son.

93. Fionnan : his son.

94. Maonach : his son.

95. Fergus : his son.

96. Congal : his son.

97. Dungus : his son.

98. Dunan : his son.

99. Faelan : his son.

100. Nuallan (" nuall :" Irish, *a howl, famous;* " an," *one who*) : his son ; a quo *O'Nuallain.*

101. Moroch : his son.

102. Dungus (2) : his son.

103. Cuinee : his son.

104. Eile : his son.

105. Dunlong : his son.

106. Eocha (3) Fionn : his son.

107. Eocha (4) Oge : his son.

108. Eocha (5) : his son.

109. Melaghlin : his son.

110. Ughare : his son.

111. Awly : his son.

112. Donogh : his son.

113. Teige : his son.

114. John (or Shane) : his son.

115. Donal (or Daniel) : his son.

116. John O'Nowlan : his son; was called " John the Poet." Had two daughters—co-heiresses : one of them was married to —— Beaumont of Hydepark, county Wexford ; the name of the other was Anne.

117. Anne O'Nowlan : dau. of said John ; m. Brian O'Brien, of Ballinvalley, county Carlow.

118. John O'Brien : their son.

119. William : his son ; had a brother named Brian, who emigrated.

120. John : his son ; had a brother named Brian. This John O'Brien also emigrated.

O'BEIRNE.*

Arms : Ar. an oak tree eradicated and fructed ppr. in base a lizard vert in the dexter base point a saltire couped gu. on a chief az. the sun in his splendour or, and a crescent of the first.

AODH (or Hugh) Balbh, brother of Murgal who is No. 99 on the (No. 1)

* *O'Beirne :* Thomas Lewis O'Beirne, Bishop of Meath, was born in the county of Longford in 1747. He was intended for the Catholic priesthood, and was sent with his brother to St. Omer's ; but eventually he joined the late Established Church. He was appointed chaplain in the British fleet under Lord Howe ; and whilst in this service he published a pamphlet in defence of his patron, the Admiral. In 1782 he accompanied the Duke of Portland, Lord Lieutenant, to Ireland as his private secretary. He was in 1791 collated to the rectory of Templemichael and vicarage of Mohill, county Leitrim, in the diocese of Ardagh, where his brother was at the same time a Parish Priest. In 1795 he became chaplain to Lord Fitzwilliam, who obtained for him the bishopric of Ossory, whence, in 1798, he was translated to Meath. In his place in the Irish House of Lords he objected to the recall of Lord Fitzwilliam, then Irish Viceroy, and was one of those peers who voted against the Union, and signed the Lords' Protest. He died at Ardbraccan, on the 17th of February, 1823, and was there buried.

" O'Connor" (Connaught) pedigree, was the ancestor of *O'Beirin ;* anglicised *O'Beirne, Beirnes, Barne, Barnes, Barnewall,* and *Barnewell.*

99. Aodh Balbh* (" balbh :" Irish
stammering, dumb ; Lat. " balb-us") :
son of Inreactha, the 23rd Christian
King of Connaught. Some say
that this Aodh Balbh was the 26th
King, instead of Flaithrigh (2).

100. Uadhach : son of Aodh Balbh ;
a quo *Clann Uadhaigh.*†

101. Ubhan (" ubh :" Irish, *the
point of a thing*) : his son ; a quo
O'h-Ubhain, anglicised *Hoban.* Had
a brother named Ceannfada, who
was the ancestor of *Fallon.*

102. Cineadh : son of Ubhan.

103. Beirin (" beir-in :" Irish, *fit
to bear or carry ;* Lat. " fer-o :" Gr.
" pher-o ;" Pers. " bar") : his son ;
a quo *O Beirin.*

104. Murtach Mantach : his son.

105. Dermod : his son.

106. Murtach (2) : his son.

107. Cuconnacht : his son.

108. Giollachriosd : his son.

109. Donall : his son.

110. Giollaiosa : his son.

111. Iomhar : his son.

112. Giollacoman : his son ; had a
brother named Bernard, who was
the ancestor of *Barnewall,* etc.

113. Maithan : son of Giollacoman.

114. Giollachriosd : his son.

115. Iomhar (2) : his son.

116. Giollachriosd (2) : his son.

117. Donall (2) : his son.

118. Donoch : his son.

119. Cormac : his son ; had five
brothers.

120. Cairbre : his son ; had six
brothers.

121. Teige : his son.

122. Teige Oge : his son.

123. Donoch : his son.

124. Brian : his son.

125. Donoch (2) : his son.

126. Teige (3) : his son.

127. Henry : his son.

128. Hugh : his son ; was a J.P.
for the county Roscommon ; died
in 1813.

129. Francis : his son ; was a J.P.
and D.L. for the county Leitrim ;
died in 1854.

130. Hugh O'Beirne, D.L., Jamestown House, Drumsna, co. Leitrim :
his son. Has a younger brother,
Colonel Francis O'Beirne, late an
M.P. for the county Leitrim ; both
living in 1887.

131. Francis O'Beirne, b. in 1864 :
son of the said Hugh. This Francis
had three brothers—1. Hugh-James,
b. in 1866 ; 2. Joseph, b. in 1874 ;
and 3. George-John, b. in Dec.,
1877.

* *Balbh* : This word is the root of the sirname *Balfe.*

† *Clann Uadhaigh* : The sirnames *Wood* and *Woods* are considered anglicised
forms of this Clan-name ; which literally means " except from him" (*uadh* : Irish,
" from him ;" *ach,* "save or except"). But *Wood* and *Woods* are anglicised forms of
the Irish sirname *O'Coillte* (" coill :" Irish, *a wood*).—See No. 103 on the " O'Mealla"
pedigree.

O'BRANNAN.

Of Ulster.

Arms : Ar. a lion ramp. az. in chief two dexter hands couped at the wrist apaumée gu.

OLIOLL, a brother of Cearnach who is No. 98 on the " Breslin" pedigree, was the ancestor of *O'Brannain*, of Ulster ; anglicised *O'Brannan*, and *Brannan.*

98. Olioll : son of Fergus.
99. Connor : his son.
100. Brannan ("bran :" Irish, *a*

mountain torrent) : his son ; a quo *O'Brannain,*

O'BRASSIL.

Arms : Gu. a lion pass. guard. or.

FIACHRACH CASAN, younger brother of Rocadh, who is No. 86 on the " O'Hart" pedigree, was the ancestor of *Clann Brassil ;* a quo *O'Brassil,* in the county Armagh, and, some say, the name of the Empire of " Brazil," in South America.

86. Fiachra Casan (" cas :" Irish, *means* or *income*, and " an," *one who ;* or " casan" means a *pathway)* : son of Colla-da-Crioch ; a quo *O'Casain,* anglicised *Cashin.*

87. Felim : his son.

88. Tuathal Cruinnbheul ("cruinn- beul :" Irish, *a gathered mouth)* : his son ; a quo *O'Beil.** Had a brother named Breasal, and another named Feig : This Feig was the ancestor of *O'Hanlon.*

89. Colcan : son of Tuathal Cruinnbheul ; had a brother named Sacan (" sacan :" Irish, *a short corpulent man*), literally " a little sack."

90. Aongus : son of Colcan ; had six brothers—1. St. Baodan (5th February). 2. Saraan, whose three sons were, St. Ronan Fionn, St.

Beican (17th August), and St. Cear- nach (16th May). 2. Hugh, from whom were descended St. Cobh- thach, St. Libren (11th March), St. Tuoa (virgin), St. Maimon, bishop (18th Dec.), a quo " Kilmainham," near Dublin. 4. Maignan ("maignan :" Irish, *one with a proud gait*), a quo *O'Maignan*, anglicised *Magnan* and *Mangan* : this Maignan was ancestor of *O'Mooney*, of Ulster. 5. Lamhan. 6. Firbis, who was the ancestor of *O'Connor* of Ulster.

91. Diceilidh : son of Aongus.

92. Ultan : his son.

93. Cuanach (" cuan :" Irish, *a coast*) : his son ; a quo *O'Cuanaigh*, anglicised *Cooney* (of Clanbrassil), and *Quiney.*

94. Inreactha : his son.

95. Donoch : his son.

* *O'Beil :* The sirnames *Bale* and *Bell* are considered anglicised forms of this sir- name.

96. Dalgan: his son; had a brother named Maolmocheirigh ("moch:" Irish, *early;* "eirigh," *to rise*), a quo *O'Maolmochheirghe,* of Orgiall.—See No. 100 on the "Donnellan" of Connaught pedigree, for the derivation and present anglicised forms of this Irish sirname.

97. Cearnach : son of Dalgan.
98. Gairbiadh: his son; had a brother named Dubhculin, who was the ancestor of *McGrath,* of Ulster.
99. Longseach : son of Gairbiadh.
100. Conamhail : his son.
101. Aodh : his son.
102. Breasal : his son ; a quo *O'Brassil* West.

O'BRICK.

Lords of South Decies, in Munster.

Arms : Same as those of "Felan."

BREODOILBH, a younger brother of Doilbh who is No. 92 on the "Felan" pedigree, was the ancestor of *O'Bricé;* anglicised *O'Brick,* and *Brick.*

92. Breodhoilbh : son of Cumuscach.
93. Donoch : his son.
94. Donal : his son.
95. Cormac : his son.
96. Rorchach : his son.

97. Melaghlin : his son.
98. Faelagh : his son.
99. Artcorb : his son.
100. Breac ("breac:" Irish, *speckled;* Chald. "brakka;" Arab. "abrek") : his son ; a quo *O'Brice.*

After O'Brick's issue failed, the whole of Decies (North and South) went to O'Felan.

O'BRIEN. (No. 11.)

Of Fermanagh.

Arms : Gu. a lion pass. guard. or.

BRIAN, a brother of Daimhin who is No. 92 on the "O'Hart" pedigree, was the ancestor of *O'Briain,* of Fermanagh; anglicised *O'Brien,* and *Brien.*

92. Brian ("brian:" Irish, *great strength*): son of Cairbre an Daimh Airgid ; a quo *O'Briain.*
93. Baodan : his son.

94. Beacan ("beacan:" Irish, *a mushroom*): his son; a quo *O'Beacain,* anglicised *Bacon.*

2 Q

95. Oisin : his son.
96. Allbhreun ; his son.
97. Drobhellach : his son.
98. Dunghal : his son.
99. Cathasach : his son.

100. Cuileann Ban : his son.
101. Fuagartha : his son.
102. Oisin : his son.
103. Conghallach : his son.
104. Eochaidh : his son.

O'BRIEN. (No. 12.)

Of Donegal.

Arms : Ar. a sinister hand couped at the wrist affrontée gu.

BRAON DIA, brother of Aodh Fionnliath who is No. 99 on the (No. 1) " O'Neill" (of Tyrone) pedigree, was the ancestor of *Clann Braoin,* of Magh Ithe, in the county Donegal ; anglicised *O'Brien.*

99. Braon Dia (" braon :" Irish, *a drop ;* "dia," *abundance*): son of Niall Caille, the 166th Monarch of Ireland ; a quo *Clann Braoin,* of Magh Ithe.
100. Cathal : his son.
101. Ruarcan : his son.

102. Maolduin : his son.
103. Gairbiadh : his son.
104. Feargal : his son.
105. Niall : his son.
106. Flaithearthach : his son.
107. Donchadh O'Brien : his son.

O'BYRNE.* (No. 1.)

Lords of Ranelagh, County Wicklow.

Arms : Gu. a chev. betw. three dexter hands couped at the wrist ar. *Crest :* A mermaid with comb and mirror all ppr. *Motto :* Certavi et vici.

EVEN in the annals of Ireland it would be hard indeed to find a nobler record than that of the O'Byrnes of Wicklow. Through a long line of warriors and chieftains they were eminently distinguished for devotion to

* *O'Byrne :* Feagh O'Byrne, who is No. 130 on this pedigree, and who is commonly known as " Feagh MacHugh O'Byrne" (which means *Feagh, son of Hugh O'Byrne*), resided at Ballinacor, in Glenmalure ; and was chief of that sept of the O'Byrnes called *Gabhail Raighnaill* (pr. " Gaval Rannall"). His father, Hugh, who died in 1579, was far more powerful than The O'Byrne, and possessed a large tract of territory in the county Wicklow. Upon the death of The O'Byrne, in 1580, Feagh MacHugh O'Byrne became the leader of his clan, and one of the most formidable of the Irish Chieftains. In 1580 he joined his forces to those of Lord Baltinglass, and defeated Lord Grey. After holding out in the rocky fastnesses of his principality for several years, he was, in 1595, driven up Glenmalure, and his residence at Ballinacor was

the sacred cause of Faith and Country.   High-souled in their patriotism, fearless and fierce in defence of their Nation's rights, proud of their race, and intensely attached to the mountain crags and exquisitely picturesque glens of their ancient patrimony, they, during centuries of wrong, persecution, plunder and perfidy, held their ground invincibly, and fought against their ruthless oppressors with courage indomitable and fortitude heroic.   Their motto *Certavi et Vici* was truly appropriate.   The love of freedom, "bequeathed from bleeding sire to son," burned so fiercely in their hearts, that it can scarcely be considered an exaggeration to say, they contended for four hundred years unconquered.   It was almost as natural to them to fight as it was to breathe, and, in a sense, as necessary; because they were perpetually assailed, and every element of force and every base subterfuge, that fiendish minds could conceive, were made available to ruin and annihilate them.   By nature dauntless and combative, yet merciful and humane; and by the treachery of perfidious enemies obliged to be ever watchful, it may be believed, that they almost slept with their battle-axes grasped, at all times ready to spring at the foe, repel aggression, aid their kinsmen, and jealously guard their stronghold, wooded hills and crystal watered valleys of the beauteous region which they ruled and loved.   Not only do they figure prominently in the pages of Irish history, but their deeds and exploits have furnished touching themes for song and story.   No persecution, however malignant, could deter them, no allurement could seduce them.   Threat and overture they spurned with equal contempt; and to their eternal honour it is stated, that there was never "a king's or a queen's O'Byrne," and that they were the very last of the Irish clans to yield to the Saxon.   Some writers seem to think, that they did not always receive that prompt aid from other septs which their common cause demanded; but it is not our purpose to draw contrasts, and most assuredly it is not our desire to pass, perhaps, unmerited censure.   All created beings have their faults and follies, and

occupied by an Anglo-Irish garrison.   He then made terms, but seized the first opportunity of driving out the garrison, and razing the fort.   He was killed in a skirmish with the forces of the Lord Deputy, in May, 1597, and his head was impaled on Dublin Castle.   The family estates were confirmed to his son Felim (or Phelim), by patent of Queen Elizabeth, but he was ultimately deprived of them by the perjury and juggling of adventurers under James I.; and although in 1628 acquitted of all the charges brought against him, he was turned out upon the world a beggar.—WEBB'S *Compendium of Irish Biography.*

Of this family also is Doctor John Augustus Byrne, of Dublin, living in 1887; who was born in 22 Wellington-quay, Dublin, on the 9th of April, 1827.   Having received his preliminary education at Mr. Walsh's school in Bolton-street, Mr. O'Grady's in D'Olier-street, and from private tutors, Dr. Byrne entered Trinity College, and graduated B.A. and M.B. in 1848.   In 1858 he became Assistant Master to the Rotunda Lying-in-Hospital, under the Mastership of Dr. McClintock; taking, in 1864, the diploma of the College of Physicians.   Doctor Byrne is Professor of Midwifery in the Catholic University Medical School, and Gynæcological Surgeon to St. Vincent's Hospital.   He is a past President of the Dublin Obstetrical Society, Physician to the Grand Canal-street Dispensary, and Honorary Fellow of the San Francisco Obstetrical Society.   He has contributed a large number of papers to the *Dublin Journal of Medical Science* and to the *Medical Press.*   Doctor Byrne's mother was Anne, daughter of W. Griffith, an extensive leather merchant, in his time, in Dublin.   He is married to Kate, daughter of the late John Quinn, of Aubrey House, Shangannagh, and has one son and three daughters.

exemption from the sins and frailties of human nature cannot be claimed for the O'Byrnes; but it can be pleaded in extenuation of their errors, that their virtues were many and their sufferings great.   Numbers of the O'Byrnes, in different generations, consecrated themselves to the service of the Church, at the altar, and in the cloister; some of them founded abbeys and generously maintained them.   Their Faith was as warm in them as the burning rays of the noonday sun, and as immovable as the base of "The Golden Spears" which tower high in their beloved Wicklow; and proudly it can be proclaimed, that the mother of the great Saint Laurence O'Toole was an O'Byrne.   At the present day, the descendants of the O'Byrne clan are, perhaps, more numerous than those of any other.   At all events, they appear to be more concentrated, and to cling more tenaciously to the historic county of their ancestors.   The saying that: "You will find a Byrne in every bush in Wicklow," can be easily understood; but it is strange and sad to think, that few of them have retained the distinctive prefix *O'*. No clan has a more rigid right to it.   One historian alludes to the name of the O'Byrnes as "heroic;" surely, those who bear it should be proud of it, and all the O'Byrnes—those who can trace their pedigree connectedly, and those who cannot, should keep before their vision the noble example of their martyred forefathers.   The old spirit of clanship should bind them firmly together in love for kith and kin and country.   The past glories of our land should urge them to labour incessantly for her future greatness.   Thank God, she is not now as she was in generations gone by, still she is sadly placed in many respects, and her children are bound by ties the tenderest, and obligations the most sacred, to make every effort that the precepts of religion, the principles of justice, the dictates of honour, and the chastened sympathies of exalted minds can sanction for her elevation amidst the proudest nations of the earth. Ireland is a country of beauty, fruitfulness, and holiness.   The O'Byrnes of the past loved her with all the intensity of their impassioned souls.   In proof of their faithfulness to God and their country, they hesitated not to pour out their blood in crimson streams.   The same sacrifices are not now required from their descendants, but the latter should be guided and governed by the characteristic instincts of their great race, which would infallibly teach them, that their first and highest aspiration should be to live and die for God and Ireland.

MOROGH (or Murcha), who is No. 102 on the "O'Toole" pedigree, had a younger son Faolan, who was the ancestor of *O'Brain ;* anglicised *O'Byrne, Byrne, Byron, Brain*, etc.

103. Faolan, the 18th Christian King of Leinster : son of Morogh.

104. Rory: his son; the 23rd King whose brother Bran was the 28th King.

105. Diarmaid: his son; had a brother Roderick who was the 29th King.

106. Muregan (or Morogh): his son, the 35th King; whose son Donal was the 37th King; and son Cearbhall, the 38th King.

107. Maolmordha: his son; m. Joan, dau. of O'Neill, Prince of Ulster.

108. Bran Fionn ("bran:" Irish, *impetuous as a mountain torrent ;* "fionn," *fair-haired*): his son; the

42nd King; a quo *O'Brain ;* m. the dau. of O'Sullivan Beara.

109. Morogh, the 45th King: his son; m. the dau. of O'Mahony of Carbery.

110. M a o l m o r d h a : his son; the 51st King; had a brother Faolan.

111. Bran, the 54th King; son of Maolmordha; taken prisoner in battle by the Danes of Dublin, who put out his eyes, and afterwards put him to death.

112. Donoch na Soigheadh ("soighead" or "saighead:" Irish, *a dart, an arrow ;* Lat. "sagit-ta"): his son ; was the first of the family who assumed this sirname.

113. Donoch Mór : his son.

114. Donal na Scath ("scath :" Irish, *a shadow*): his son.

115. D u n l a n g Dubhchlarana ("dubhchlarana :" Irish, *a small, dark person*) : his son.

116. Olioll an Fiobhbha ("fiobh-bha :" Irish, *a wood* : his son ; had a brother named Angar.

117. Moroch Mór : his son.

118. Donoch : his son. Had two brothers—1. Melachlin ; 2. Dalbh, a quo *Gabhail Dailbh.*

119. Ranal : son of Donoch ; a quo *Gabhail Raighnaill ;* had a brother named Lorcan.

120. Philip : son of Ranal.

121. Lorcan : his son.

122. Ranal : his son.

123. Connor : his son.

124. Donal Glas : his son.

125. Hugh : his son.

126. Shane (or John): his son.

127. Redmond : his son.

128. John : his son.

129. Hugh : his son; d. 1579.

130. Fiacha (or Feagh) : his son.

Defeated Lord Grey de Wilton, at Glendalough, in 1580 ; and in 1597 was killed by the English soldiers, under Sir W. Russell. Had a brother John, who commanded a military contingent from Wicklow, in aid of the O'Neill, Prince of Tyrone, against the English army in Ireland, *temp.* Queen Elizabeth ; two other brothers—1. Connell, 2. Charles, both of whom were slain in battle ; and a sister Esibel. Was twice married: first wife was a Miss O'Byrne ; second wife, Rose, dau. of Luke O'Toole of Fercoulen and Castle-pevir. Had three sons and two daughters : the sons were — 1. Phelim ; 2. Raymond, a J.P. for Wicklow ; living in 1625 ; buried at Killevany Castle, shown on the Ordnance Map as "Raymond's Castle." 3. Tirloch, who, attempting to betray* his father, was by him delivered to the English, and executed in Dublin. One of the daughters was married to Rory Oge O'Moore ; the other to Walter Reagh Fitzgerald.

131. Phelim : eldest son of Fiacha. Submitted to Queen Elizabeth, in 1600, who granted him lands in the co. Wicklow. Will is in the Probate Office, Dublin ; it is dated from Clonmore, 1632. He was M.P. for Wicklow in 1613 ; in prison in Dublin, 1628 ; and d. at Clonmore, in 1632. Married Winifred M. Toole, and had nine sons and one daughter : the sons were—1. Brian, who was committed to Dublin Castle, 1625; was at Meeting of the Confederate Catholics in Kilkenny in 1641; and is mentioned in Cromwell's Denunciation, 1652.

---

* *Betray :* By some members of this family this assertion has been strenuously denied.

2. William, ancestor of *Brain*,* in England. 3. Hugh, a Colonel of the Confederate Catholics, 1641; proclaimed a "Rebel," same year; living in 1652. 4. Gerald (or Garrett), living in 1604. 5. James, living in 1603. 6. Tirloch, living in 1628, had three sons and one daughter: the sons were—Henry, Gregory, and Hugh; the daughter was Mary, m. (according to the De La Ponce MSS.) to Owen O'Rourke. 7. Feagh, *alias* Luke. 8. Cahir (slain at Aughrim, co. Wicklow, 1657), who had Hugh,† who had Charles, who was living about 1697, and is mentioned in the *Leabhar Brannagh*. 9. Colla. The daughter m. John Wolverton, and d. in Connaught.

132. Brian: eldest son of Phelim. Had two sons—1. John, who was a Colonel of the Confederate Catholics, in 1641; 2. Hugh.

133. Hugh: second son of Brian.

134. William: his son.

135. John: his son.

136. Lawrence: his son; migrated to America, in 1818.

137. Brian (2): his son.

138. Lawrence Byrne, of Pikeville, near Baltimore, Maryland, United States, America: his son; living in 1877.

139. Richard MacSherry Byrne: his son. Had two brothers—1. Charles, 2. Bernard; and two sisters —1. Anna, 2. Eliza: all living in 1877.

O'BYRNE. (No. 2.)

Of Cabinteely, County Dublin.

Arms : Gu. a chev. between three dexter hands couped at the wrists, or.   *Crest* : A mermaid, in the dexter hand a mirror, in the sinister a comb, all ppr.   *Motto* : Certavi et Vici.

DUMHLAN DUBHCLUASACH, a younger brother of Donal na Scath, who is No. 114 on the (No. 1) "O'Byrne" (Lords of Ranelagh) genealogy, was the ancestor of this branch of that family.

114. Dumhlan Dubhcluasach ("dubh :" Irish, *prodigious ;* "cluas," *the ear*): son of Donoch Mór O'Byrne; m. dau. of MacMurrough Kavanagh, and had :

115. Ughdar, who married the daughter of Magenis, and had :

116. Feagh na Fhiagh, who m. dau. of O'Brennan, and had six sons, all of whom had issue.

---

* *Brain :* This sirname appears to be derived, by metathesis from "Brian." Unhappily, at that period and long afterwards, an Irishman might not, under his Irish patronymic, expect favour or affection from the authorities in England or Ireland. Hence the changes, at the time, of many Irish sirnames; and hence some members of the "O'Byrne" family, for instance, anglicised their names *Byron, Brain,* etc.

† *Hugh :* This Hugh had, besides Charles, two other sons—1. James; 2. Edmond, who was buried in Clonmore Church-yard, co. Carlow, in 1777, and who left three children—namely, Murtogh, John, and Anne who married a Ryan, in the co. Carlow. This James of Clonmore, but then of Ballyspellin, co. Kilkenny, son of Hugh, had four sons : 1. Pierre, 2. Edmond, 3. James, 4. Phelim. This Pierre had Margaret, who m. —— Meagher, and had Maryanne, who m. John Cosgrave, of Castlewood-avenue, Rathmines, co. Dublin.

117. Dumhlan : the eldest son of Feagh na Fhiagh ; m. dau. of O'Dunn, and had :

118. Donoch, who m. dau. of O'Connor Faley, and had :

119. Gerald, who m. dau. of O'Brien, of Ara, and had :

120. Moroch, who m. Ann, dau. of O'Brennan, of Iveagh, and had :

121. Philip, who m. Joanne, dau. of O'Dempsy, and had :

122. Brian Ruadh, who m. dau. of Morgan Kavanagh, and had :

123. Donoch, who m. dau. of O'Toole, and had :

124. Bryan, who married dau. of O'Moore, and had :

125. Teige Mór, who m. Mary Kavanagh, and had :

126. Garrett, who married dau. of O'Byrne, of Killiman, and had :

127. Teige Oge, who m. dau. of O'Byrne, of Ballinakill, and had two sons : 1. Brian, 2 Donoch (or Denis).

128. Brian O'Byrne : the son of Teige Oge ; m. Catherine, dau. of Kavanagh, of Gorahill, and had three sons and a daughter :

   I. Teige (or Thady), of whom presently.

   II. Brian, who m. Margaret, dau. of O'Byrne, of Rodran, and had a daughter Margery, who died unm.

   III. Morough, who was killed in battle.

   I. The dau. m. a son of O'Byrne, of Rodran.

129. Thady : eldest son of Brian ; m. Mary, dau. of Dermod O'Byrne, of Dunganstown, and had two sons and a daughter :

   I. Charles, of whom presently.

   II. Thady, from whom descended the O'Byrnes, of Killboy.

   I. Honor, who d. unm.

130. Charles : the son of Thady ; whose estates were confiscated under the Cromwellian Settlement; m. Grizel, dau. of O'Byrne, of Bal-

linacarbeg, and had three sons and a dau.

   I. Hugh, who removed to Dublin, and afterwards returned to the co. Wicklow, where he purchased landed property, and resided in Ballinacarbeg up to his death. This Hugh was twice married : his first wife was Catherine, great granddaughter of Richard Archbold, Constable of Dublin Castle, *temp.* Henry VII., by whom he had two sons and four daus. :

   I. George (d. 27th Dec., 1697), who m. Amey, dau. of James Bell, Esq., Surgeon-General of Ireland, and had two sons and two daughters : 1. Gregory, who m. Mary, dau. of Richard Butler, brewer of Dublin, by whom he left no surviving issue ; 2. William, who d. s. p.; and 3. Elizabeth, who was heiress to her brother, and who d. unm. in 1732.

   II. Charles : the second son of Hugh ; had (besides a dau. who m. Bartholomew Hadsor), an only son Emanuel, who, being educated in France, became a Friar of the Order of St. Francis, and had in " Confirmation " taken the name of "Francis." " Father Francis," generally known as "Father Huson," d. at Cornel's Court, Cabinteely, on the 30th August, 1743 ; having bequeathed to his cousin all his rights, title and interest in the Ballinacarbeg estate.

Hugh's four daus. were :

   I. Catherine.

   II. Ann.

   III. Marian.

   IV. Margaret.

II. John, of Ballinclough, in the co. Wicklow : second son of Charles ; m. Cecilia, dau. of Garrett O'Byrne, of Cualanarle, and left three daughters :
I. Mary, who m. John Byrne, a brewer, of Dublin.
II. Elinor, who m. Dudley Keoghe, of Ballinclough.
III. Catherine, who m. James Byrne.
III. Daniel, of whom presently.
I. Sarah, the daughter of Charles, m. Turlogh Byrne.

131. Daniel *Byrne* : third son of Charles ; m. Anne, dau. of Richard Taylor, Esq., of the family· of Swords, and had four sons and two daus. :
I. Gregory,* who inherited the Lordships of Sheen and Timogue, and in 1671 was created a Baronet.
II. John, of whom presently.
III. Walter, a Captain in the Army of King James II. ; died at St. Germain's ; m. Dorcas Crosby, and had a son who went to sea, and a dau.
IV. Joseph, a Merchant in Dublin, who was also a Captain in the Army of King James II., and was killed at the battle of Aughrim. This Joseph left two daus. : the elder m. to a Mr. Gibson, of London ; and the younger, Elinor, m. twice, but d. without issue.

The two daus. of Daniel Byrne were :
I. Mary, whose first husband was John Walsh, Esq., of Old Connaught, by whom she had two sons :
I. Edward.
II. John.
Her second husband was Sir Luke Dowdall, Bart., by whom she had three sons and two daus. :
III. Sir Daniel Dowdall, second

---

* *Gregory :* Sir Gregory Byrne, Bart., of Timogue, was twice married: his first wife was Penelope, daughter of Colonel Calwall, of Yorkshire, in England, by whom he had (with younger children) :
I. Daniel (d. v. p.), who married Miss Warren, daughter of —— Warren, Esq., of Chorley, in Lancashire, and left a son :
I. John, who thus became heir to his grandfather, the said Sir Gregory ; and of whom presently.
Sir Gregory's second wife was Alice Fleming, dau. of Randal, Lord Slane, and by her had (with other children) a son :
I. Henry, of Oporto, who married Catherine, daughter of James Eustace, of Yeomanstown, in the co. Kildare, and left an only child :
I. Catherine Xaveria Byrne (died July, 1779), who married George Bryan, Esq., and left a son :
I. George Bryan, Esq., of Jenkinstown, in the co. Kilkenny, who was the father of the late George Bryan, of Jenkinstown, M.P. for said county.
Sir John Byrne, of Timogue (the son of Daniel, son of Sir Gregory Byrne), became the second Baronet ; he married Meriel, widow of Fleetwood Leigh, Esq., of Bank, and only daughter and heiress of Sir Francis Leicester, of Tabley, and had :
Sir Peter Byrne, of Timogue (died 1770), the third Baronet, who, under the Will of his maternal grandfather, assumed in 1774, the sirname and Arms of *Leicester.* He married Catherine, daughter and co-heir of Sir William Fleming, Bart., of Rydale, in Westmorelandshire, England, and (with several other children) had a son and heir :
Sir John Fleming Leicester (died 1827), the fourth Baronet, who, on the 16th July, 1826, was raised to the Peerage, as "Baron de Tabley," of Tabley House, in Chestershire, England. He married in 1810, Georgiana-Maria, daughter of Colonel Cottin, and had :
Sir George Leicester, Baron de Tabley, of Tabley House ; and a Baronet of Ireland ; born 28th October, 1811, and living in 1883 ; as second Baron de Tabley, Sir George succeeded his father, on the 18th June, 1827 ; and in 1832, assumed by "Sign Manual," instead of his own patronymic, the sirname *Warren* only.

Bart., who took Orders in the Church of Rome.

IV. James Dowdall, who d. unm.

V. ———— Dowdall, who m. Margaret Allen, of St. Wolstans, near Celbridge.

One of the daughters of Sir Luke Dowdall, m. Amon Clark, Esq., the other dau. m. Ulick Wall, Esq., of Colland House.

    II. Margaret : second daughter of Daniel Byrne ; m. Terence Dunn, Esq., of Brittas, in the Queen's County, and had three sons :

        I. Daniel Dunn, who m. a dau. of Colonel Nugent, brother of Thomas, then Earl of Westmeath, and had surviving issue, two daus. : 1. Alice, who m. Richard Plunket, Esq., of Dunshaughlin ; 2. Mary, who m. James Hussey, Esq., of Westown, in the county of Kildare.

        II. Barnaby Dunn, who m. Miss Molloy, of the King's County, and left two surviving daus.

        III. Edward Dunn, who m. the sister of Thomas Wyse, Esq., of Waterford.

132. John, of Cabinteely : second son of Daniel ; inherited from his father the town and lands of Kilboy, Ballard, and other estates in the co. Wicklow, and was High Sheriff for that county. Studied in England and was called to the Irish Bar ; m., in 1678, Mary, dau. of Walter Chevers, Esq., of Monkstown, and had two sons and a dau. :

    I. Walter, who inherited from his father, m. Clara, dau. of Christopher Mapas, Esq., of Roachestown, but left no issue :

    II. John, of whom presently.

    I. Alice, who died young.

133. John, Barrister - at - Law :

second son of John ; succeeded his brother Walter in the family estates ; died suddenly in 1681, and left two sons :

    I. Walter (died January, 1731), of Cabinteely, who m. Clara, dau. of Christopher Mapas, Esq., of Roachestown ; but dying without issue was succeeded by his brother John.

    II. John.

134. John, who died in 1741 : the second son of John, a Merchant of Dublin ; succeeded his elder brother Walter ; m. Marianna, younger daughter of Col. Dudley Colclough, of Mohory, in the county Wexford, and had eight sons and five daughters :

    I. George, of whom presently.

    II. Dudley, who married Elizabeth, daughter of James Dillon, Esq.

    III. John, who was a Wine Merchant in Bordeaux, where he was the proprietor of extensive vineyards at La Hourangue et Macon. This John O'Byrne had Letters of Nobility granted to him by Louis the XVI., King of France, in 1770 ; and was always styled in France, and in Ireland, "The Chevalier O'Byrne of Macon La Hourange, Bordeaux." He was twice m : his first wife being Mary, dau. of Richard Gernon, Esq., of Gernonstown, in the co. Louth, by whom he had a son and successor :

        I. Richard O'Byrne (d. 1803), who m. Elizabeth, dau. of Richard William Stack, Esq., M.D., of Bath, England, and had two sons and three daus. : I. Robert O'Byrne, who m. Martha Trougher, dau. of Joseph Clark, Esq., and had two sons : 1. William R. O'Byrne (living in 1887), late of Cabinteely, and late M.P. for the co. Wicklow; 2. Robert O'Byrne, Barrister-at-Law, London, and living in 1883. II. John O'Byrne, who m. Elizabeth, dau. of Thomas O'Brien, Esq., of Stephen's Green, Dublin, and had: 1. Mary-Louisa O'Byrne (living in 1887), the talented Authoress of "The Pale and the Septs" (Dublin: Gill & Son, 1876); "Leixlip Castle" (Dublin: Gill & Son, 1883); and other National Works, all worthy of perusal. 2. Richard-Gregory. 3. John-Jeremiah. 4. William. 5. Aileen, who d. young. 6. Elizabeth, who also died young. 7. Walter. 8. Francis. 9. Clare, living in 1883. Of these children Richard, in his boyhood went to America, and was there engaged in the late Civil War, on the side of the Confederates; John and Francis went to Australia; and William went to New Orleans.

Richard O'Byrne's three daus. were:

I. Marianne, who m. and had Mr. P. Stack, Registrar of the Board of Works, Dublin, and living in 1883.

II. Harriet, who m. Thomas, son of the above-mentioned Thomas O'Brien, Esq., of Stephen's Green, Dublin.

III. Eliza, who m. William Henry Coppinger, of the Barryscourt family, in the county Cork, and nephew of the Right Rev. William Coppinger, Bishop of Cloyne.

The Chevalier O'Byrne's second wife was Miss Laffan, dau. of —— Laffan, Esq., of the co. Kilkenny, by whom he had four sons:

II. Thomas, who d. unm.

III. Dudley, who d. unm.

IV. Michael, who m. Miss Cahill, and d. s. p.

V. James, who m. dau. of Francis Kindillon, Esq., of the City of Dublin, and had two sons:

I. John, who m. Miss Beleasis, allied to the family of the Duke of Norfolk and others of the Catholic Nobility.

II. Francis, who m. the dau. of George Gillow, Esq., of Clifton Hill, Lancashire, and had four children: I. James O'Byrne, of Sandridge House, Birkdale, Southport. II. Robert, who d. in Melbourne. I. Anne-Maria: II. Mary-Agnes: both now dead.

IV. Francis: the fourth son of John, No. 134; d. unm.

V. Walter, who d. unm.

VI. Gregory,* who was a Lieutenant in the Duke of Berwick's Regiment.

VII. Daniel.

VIII. Joseph, who entered the German Service.

The five daughters of John O'Byrne, No. 134, were:

I. Mary, who married Walter Blackney, Esq., of Ballycormack, in the co. Carlow.

II. Frances, who m. Edward Masterson, Esq., of Castletown, in the co. Wexford.

III. Harriet, who m. Anthony

---

* *Gregory*: This Gregory O'Byrne was attached to the Court of Louis the XVI., and was one of the 500 Royalists (many of whom were Officers of the Irish Brigade in which the said Gregory and his Uncle Colonel O'Byrne had served), who enrolled themselves as a guard of honour to, and protected the flight of, the Duchess d'Angoulême, daughter of Louis XVI., upon the occasion of her rash enterprise in appealing in person to the National Assembly.

Lynch, Esq., a Merchant in Dublin.

IV. Marianne, who m. Adam Colclough, Esq.

V. Ann, who d. young.

135. George O'Byrne, of Cabinteely : eldest son of John ; m. Clare, second dau. of Captain Michael Nugent* of Carlanstown, in the co. Westmeath, aud had three sons and one daughter :

I. Michael, of Cabinteely, who d. unm. ; and at whose death his brother John succeeded to the family estates.

II. Gregory, who d. unm.

III. Robert, of whom presently.

The dau. was Mary, who married William Skerret, Esq., of Finvara, co. of Clare.

136. Robert O'Byrne (d. in 1798), of Cabinteely : third son of George ;

m. Mary, dau. of Robert Devereux, Esq., of Carrignenan, in the county Wexford, and left three daus.

I. Mary-Clare, who succeeded to her father's estates ; of whom presently.

II. Clarinda-Mary.

III. Georgina-Mary.

137. Miss Mary-Clare O'Byrne : eldest dau. of Robert ; succeeded to her father's estate ; but, dying unm. in 1810, she was succeeded by her next sister Miss Clarinda-Mary, living in 1843 ; and this Miss O'Byrne was, after her death, succeeded by her sister Miss Georgiana O'Byrne. This Lady also d. unm., when her cousin Mr. William R. O'Byrne (living in 1887), late M.P. for the co. Wicklow, succeeded to the Cabinteely, and the other estates of the family.

O'BYRNE. (No. 3.)

Of Ballymanus, County Wicklow.

Arms : Same *Armorial Bearings* as "O'Byrne" (No. 1).

RAYMOND, second son of the renowned Feagh (M'Hugh) O'Byrne, who is No. 130 on the O'Byrne (No. 1) pedigree, who was called by the English " *The Firebrand of the Mountains,*" and described by historians as " one of the noblest spirits of his race and age," was ancestor of this branch of the " O'Byrne" family.

131. Raymond : second son of Fiacha ; living in 1625. Had three | sons—1. Phelim, of Killevany (see Borlace, p. 86) ; 2. Feagh, of Kil-

* *Nugent* : This Michael was the father of Robert Nugent, Esq., of Gossfield, in Essex, who, on the 20th December, 1776, was, in the Peerage of Ireland, created "Baron Nugent and Viscount Clare," and in the same Peerage he subsequently became "Earl Nugent." This Robert had an only dau. and heir, the Lady Mary Elizabeth Nugent (d. 16th March, 1813), who on the 16th April, 1775, married George Grenville (born 17th June, 1753), the second Earl Temple, who, by Royal permission, assumed, on the 2nd December, 1779, the sirnames of *Nugent* and *Temple* before that of Grenville." This George Nugent-Temple-Grenville (d. 1813), was on the 4th Dec. 1784, created "Marquis of Buckingham ;" and was in 1782 and 1787 Lord Lieutenant of Ireland.

cloran, proclaimed a "Rebel," 8th Feb., 1641; 3. John, of Kiltiomon, obtained a grant of lands from King Charles I., dated 24th May, 1628.

132. John, of Kiltiomon : third son of Raymond. Had three sons—1. Raymond, who had Hugh of Ballinacar, living in 1710; 2. Charles, of whom presently; 3. Patrick, for whom, tradition says, the Pope's Legate in 1641 stood in baptism; and is considered to be identical with Patrick Byrne of Ballygannon, who was buried at Kilcoole, 1707.

133. Charles : second son of John. Forfeited Kiltiomon (or Kiltimon) to Sir John Borlace; according to book in Landed Estates Record Office, in which he is mentioned as "Charles Byrne, J.P. (Irish Papist)."

134. Hugh : his son. M.P. in 1689. Had two sons—1. Garrett; 2. Hugh, living in 1713.

135. Garrett Byrne, of Ballymanus : son of Hugh. Obtained from Sir Lawrence Esmond of Clonegal, Catherlough (Carlow), a grant dated 13th Jan., 1700, of the lands of Ballymanus, Mycredin, Clogheenagh, etc. Will dated 1713-14, is in Probate Office. Buried at Rosehane. Had two sons—1. Garrett; 2. Thomas, who is mentioned in his father's Will.

136. Garrett (2), of Ballymanus : son of Garrett; m. to Miss Colclough of Tintern. Will dated 1767. Had three sons—1. Garrett; 2. John of Wicklow, who m. Miss Byrne of Wicklow, and from whom Colclough Byrne of Ballysepple

claims descent; 3. Colclough of Drumquin, who m. Miss Galway of Cork, great grand-niece of James, first Duke of Ormond, and who died in London. This Colclough had two sons—1. Garrett* of Drumquin, 2. William-Michael.

137. Garret Byrne (3) of Ballymanus : son of Garrett; married Miss Hynes. He lived at Ballymanus until his son Garrett's marriage, when he removed to Arklow, where, in 1793, he made his Will, and died in 1794. He was buried at Rosehane. He had five sons and two daughters : the sons were—1. Garrett, who m. Miss Sparling of Hacketstown (died in Dublin in 1834), commanded the "Rebels" at the Battle of Hacketstown, co. Carlow, in 1798; 2. John, d. unm.; 3. Colclough, d. unm. at Harold's Cross, in 1807; 4. Edward, who d. in 1824, married twice: first to a Miss O'Byrne; secondly, in 1802, to Mary Kavanagh, who d. in 1847; 5. William (or Billy), who fought as a "Rebel" at the Battle of Hacketstown, and was hanged at Wicklow in 1799. The two daughters were Nelly and Fanny, both of whom died in Dublin, in 1831.

138. Edward : fourth son of Garrett (3); died in 1824. Had five sons and two daughters. The sons were—1. John-Edward, married Miss Byrne of Mullinahack, and died s.p. in Dublin in 1830; 2. William died s.p. in India; 3. Colclough, who d. young, and was buried at Rosehane; 4. Edward, of whom presently; 5. Francis, who

---

* *Garrett* : This Garrett Byrne of Drumquin, m. Miss Lyons of Kilkenny; d. at Inch Cottage, county Carlow, in 1838, and was buried at Dunleckney. His wife d. in Gardiner-street, Dublin, in 1850. Their daughter d. unmarried at Newcomen-terrace, North Strand, Dublin, in 1849.

Garrett's brother, William-Michael, m. Miss Hoey of Dublin; in 1798, at Green-street, Dublin, he was executed as a "Rebel." His daughter, Mary, who m. a Mr. Moore, solicitor, had several children, and d. in 1867.

emigrated to America. The daughters were—1. Fanny;* and 2. Christina, who died unmarried.

139. Edward: fourth son of Edward; married Joanna Kennedy; d. July, 1864. Had two sons and four daughters. The sons were—1. Joseph Edward, born 1843, died 1845; 2. Edward-Colclough, of whom presently; 3. Mary, who m. T. Delany, and had Edward Delany; 4. Fanny, born Nov., 1848, died 1874; 5. M. Angela, d. 1867; 6. Joanna, died at Rathmines, 1867.

140. Edward-Colclough Byrne (or O'Byrne), of Hollyville, Rathmines, Dublin, who died June, 1870.

O'BYRNE. (No. 4.)

Of Ballycapple.

Arms : Same as those of "O'Byrne" (No. 1)

137. JOHN O'BYRNE: second son of Garrett, who is No. 136 on the (No. 3) "O'Byrne" of Ballymanus genealogy; settled in Dunganstown, and m. Miss Byrne of Wicklow. He had two sons:
I. William, who m. Miss Bury and had two sons :
  I. William.
  II. James, who m. Miss Newsome, and had one daughter, who is (in 1887) wife of Robert Caldwell, of Wicklow.
II. Garrett-Michael, of whom presently.

138. Garrett-Michael: second son of John, succeeded to part of his father's lands in Ballycapple. His wife was descended from the O'Byrnes of Kiltimon. He had one son, William Colclough, and four daughters :

I. William-Colclough, of whom presently.
I. Margaret, who m. John Redmond.
II. Mary-Anne, who m. Joseph Byrne, who was descended from another chief branch of the "O'Byrne" race. She had eight sons and four daughters —1. James, 2. John, 3. Garrett Michael, 4. Patrick, 5. Joseph, 6. William-Colclough, 7. John-Kennedy, 8. William-Andrew. The four daughters are—1. Sarah, 2. Anne, 3. Bride-Anna, 4. Julia-Mary-Ellen. Of these children :
I. James, of Carlow, Contractor.
II. John, who died young.
III. Garrett-Michael, the third son of said Mary-Anne, was M.P. for the co. of Wexford

---

* *Fanny* : This Fanny Byrne m. James Power of Dublin, and had—1. John Power, living in Dublin in 1867; 2. William Power, Lieutenant of Inniskilling Dragoons; 3. James Power, d. in Australia; 4. Mary Power, who m. F. R. Cruise (living in 1887), M.D., of Merrion-square, Dublin, and had Francis Cruise, James Cruise (deceased), Ellen Cruise, John Cruise, Robert Cruise, Mary Cruise, William Cruise, Joseph Cruise, Edward Cruise, Thomas Cruise, Augusta Cruise—all these children, except James, living in 1881.

more than three years. He resigned in 1883, and at present (in 1887) has the honour of representing West Wicklow—"the cradle of his race," in Parliament.

IV. Patrick, of Wicklow, who died in 1867.

V. Joseph, who died young.

VI. William-Colclough, who d. young.

VII. John-Kennedy O'Byrne, the seventh son, who wrote "The O'Byrnes, Chieftains of Wicklow,"and contributed many sketches and articles to the press; m. Monica-Cecilia, dau. of P. Kennedy, author of several works of Irish Literature. This John assumed his wife's name before his own, and resumed the prefix *O'*, as the rigid right of his family.

VIII. William-Andrew, of Massachusetts, America.

IX. Sarah (in Religion "Mother Mary - Chrysostom"), Rectress of the Sisters of Charity Convent, Kilkenny.

X. Anne, who m. Joseph Anderson, of Dublin.

XI. Bride-Anna.

XII. Julia-Mary-Ellen, married to James J. Fowler, of London.

III. Catherine : third daughter of Garrett-Michael O'Byrne, of Ballycapple, married James Kinsella; their daughter "Mother Mary - Stanislaus," was Abbess of St. Clare's Convent, Harold's Cross, Dublin.

IV. Julia, m. Abraham Manifold.

139. William-Colclough O'Byrne : son of Garrett-Michael; had four sons and two daughters, of whom three sons and one daughter are (in 1887) living :

I. Garrett-Michael, of whom presently.

II. John-Joseph, of Dublin.

III. William-Colclough, who still retains Ballycapple.

I. Anna-Frances, m. to J. J. Byrne, of The Rathmore family.

140. Garrett - Michael O'Byrne, Merchant, of Wicklow : son of William-Colclough O'Byrne ; living in 1887.

O'CAHAN. (No. 1.)

Princes of Limavady, County Londonderry.

Arms : Az. on a fess per pale gu. and ar. betw. in chief out of the horns of a crescent, a dexter hand couped at the wrist and apaumée, surmounted by an estoile, betw. on the dexter a horse counter-saliant, and on the sinister a lion ramp. each also surmounted by an estoile, and in base a salmon naiant all ar. on the dexter side three lizards pass. bend sinisterways gu. and on the dexter an oak tree eradicated vert, over all an escutcheon ar. charged with a cross calvary on three grieces ppr. *Crest ;* A cat-a-mountain ramp. ppr. *Motto :* Felis demulcta mitis.

CONCHOBHAR [connor], Prince of *Leim-an-Madaidh* [" Limavady"], and a younger brother of Niall Frasach, the 162nd Monarch of Ireland, who is

No. 96 on the (No. 1) " O'Neill (of Tyrone) pedigree, was the ancestor of *O'Cathain;* anglicised *O'Cahaine, O'Cahane, O'Cahan, O'Cane, O'Kane, O'Keane, O'Caen, O'Chane, Cahan, Caine, Cane, Gahan, Gethan, Kane, Kean, Keane, Keen,* and *Kyan.*

96. Connor : second son of Fargal, the 156th Monarch of Ireland ; a quo *O'Connor,* of Moy Ith, county Donegal ; had a brother named Hugh.

97. Gruagan (" gruag :" Irish, *the hair*), meaning " the hairy man :" his son ; a quo *O'Gruagain,* anglicised *Grogan* and *Gregan;* had a brother named Dermod, who was ancestor of *O'Connor,* of Moy Ith.

98. Dungan : son of Gruagan.

99. Cathan (" cath :" Irish, *a battle,* and " an," *one who;* Heb. " chath," *terror*) : his son ; a quo *O'Cathain.*

100. Cathusach : his son.

101. Dermod : his son ; had a brother named Flaitheartach.

102. Conn Cionntach* O'Cahan : son of Dermod ; first assumed this sirname ; had a brother named Annselan, who was the ancestor of *O'Bocainain* (" bocain :" Irish, *fairies;* " an," *one who*), anglicised *Buchanan.* This Annselan was the first of the family who settled in Scotland.

103. Giollachriosd : his son.

104. Iomhar : his son.

105. Ranall : his son.

106. Eachmarcach : his son.

107. Donall : his son.

108. Rory : his son.

109. Manus Catha an Duin : his son ; Prince of Limavady ; killed by the English in the " battle of Down," A.D. 1260': hence the epithet *Catha an Duin.*

110. Cumagh-na-nGall† (or " Cumagh of the English") : his son.

111. Dermod (2) : his son.

112. Cumagh (2) : his son ; living, A.D. 1350.

113. Dermod (3) : his son.

114. Aibhneach : his son ; had a brother named Henry, a quo the " Clan Henry," or *Henry.*

115. John (or Shane) : son of Aibhneach ; d. 1498.

116. Donoch-an-Einigh (or " Donoch the Affable") : his son ; a quo *Macaneinigh,* anglicised *MacAneny;* ‡ d. 1523. Had a brother named Donall or Daniel,§ who was ances-

* *Cionntach* : From this name (" cionntach :" Irish, *guilty*) some derive *Mac-Cionntaigh,* anglicised *Maginty* and *Ginty.*

† *Cumagh-na-nGall* : On the tomb of this Cumagh O'Cahan, in the church of Dungiven, the Arms of this Prince of Limavady display the *salmon,* as do the Arms of the O'Neill, from whom the " O'Cahan" family are an offshoot.

‡ *MacAneny* : This name in Irish is more properly written *Mac-an-Eineaigh,* and is derived from the Irish " eineach," *affability.* Some genealogists confound this family with *Mac-an-Eanaigh.* (See the Note " MacNeny," under the families of Ulster descended from Colla-da-Chrioch, who is No. 85 on the " O'Hart" pedigree, *infra.*)

§ *Donall* : From this Donall (or Daniel), the fourth son of John O'Cahan, No. 115 on this Genealogy, also descended General Sir Richard O'Cahan, of the 18th Foot, who was Governor of Minorca, etc. This Sir Richard was b. on 20th December, 1666, and d. 19th December, 1736. According to the subjoined epitaph, he first entered on his military career at the Siege of Derry. The descent was as follows :—

116. Daniel, of Coolbryan, son of John, had
117. Richard, of Coolbryan and Dungiven, who had
118. Thomas, m. to Catherine O'Skullen, and had

tor of *Keane*, of Cappoquin, and *Keane*, of the county Clare, etc.

117. Manus: son of Donoch an Einigh ; slain 1548.

118. Rory Ruadh [roe]: his son ; d. 1598.

119. Donall Ballach :* his son ; lord of the Route, and of Limavady, in the county Derry. This Donall, in 1602, surrendered to the English the Castle of Oinough (or Eanagh), and all the lands between the river

119. Thomas O'Cahan, of Carrickfergus (d. 1665), who m. Margaret, dau. of James Dobbin of Duneane, county Antrim, and had

120. General Sir Richard O'Cahan, of the 18th Foot, Governor of Minorca, etc. ; assumed the name *Kane*. Excuses himself for having been obliged, on account of his profession of arms in the British Service, etc., to abandon the Irish patronymic " O'Cahan."

The following is a copy of the Latin epitaph on the handsome Cenotaph, erected in Westminster Abbey to his memory; which Cenotaph was, in 1880, restored by Captain Maurice-Hugh Cane, of 60 Dawson-street, Dublin, the fourth son of Richard, who is No. 126 on this pedigree :—

M. S.
RICARDI KANE.

Ad arcem Balearicæ Insulæ Minoris. A. S. Philipps dictam, depositi Qui, an Xti MDCLXVI Decemb. 20 Dumanii in agro Antrimensi natus in memorabili Derriæ obsidione tyrocinium miles fecit.   Unde, sub Gulielmo Tertis felicis memoriæ, Domi ad subjugatam, usque totam Hibernicam foris in Belgio cum magno vitæ discrimine Namurre præsertim gravissime vulneratus perpetuo militarit.

Anno MDCCII.

Recrudescente sub Annæ auspiciis bello ad Canadanam usque cui intersint Expedi-tionem in Belgio iterum castra posuit.

Anno MDCCXII.

Sub inclyto Argatheliæ et Grenovici duce mox sub Barone Carpenter Balearicam Minorem Legatus Administravit.   Ubi ad omne negotium tam civile quam militare instructus et copiis maritimis atque terrestribus profectus.   Qui quid Insulæ in pace et bello, terra marine conservandæ necessarium utile quit commodium foret dignorit constituit stabilirit.

Anno MDCCXX.

A Georgio I. evocatus e Balearica in Calpen trajecit, Hispanisque arcem ex improviso occupandam meditantibus irrita reddidit consilia.

Anno MDCCXXV.

Per octodecem menses in cadem sudarit arena hostesque peninsulam gravi obsidione prementes omni spe potiumdæ exuit.

Post tot autem tantasque res legati nomini strenue gestas, anno MDCCXXXIII, Georgio Secundo jubente ad istum ut ad alios uberios honores nec ipse ambrens necdum sciens evectus Balearicæ summo cum imperio præfuit.   At, At, humana omnia incerta, qui quatuor sub Regibus, summa cum prudentia fortitudine et dignitate militaverat, qui nullis erga Deum officiis defuerat nec Christiani minas quam militis boni partes sustinuerat fide pura moribus antiquis, amicis carus, sociis jocundus, civilibus mitis et comis omnibus beneficus et munificus et per omnia utilitati publicæ magis quam suæ confidens triste sui desiderium insulanis, tam Hispanis quam Brittannis reliquit, sex-tumque supra sepituagesimum annum agens Decemb. 19 anno MDCCXXXVI. diem obiit supremum.

* *Ballach*: In the First and Second Editions of this Work, No. 119 on this family genealogy is incorrectly given as " Donoch Ballach" (*ballach* : Irish, *freckled*) ; but, thanks to Mr. W. F. de Vismes Kane (No. 127 on the " Kane" of Drumreaske Pedigree) and to the Four Masters, we find that " Donoch Ballach" should have been written "Donall Ballach," and that Nos. 119 and 120 in those Editions were only *one* person—Sir Donall Ballach O'Cahan, the son of Rory Ruadh.

Foghan and Lough Foyle, as far as the Bann ; and obtained a grant of escheated lands in the co. Waterford; was Knighted at Drogheda, in 1607, by Sir Arthur Chichester, lord deputy of Ireland. Sir Donall O'Cahan had four younger brothers —1. Hugh, who was the ancestor of *Kane,* of Drumreaske, co. Monaghan ; 2. Manus ; 3. Rory ; 4. Shane (or John) Carrach* (" carrach :" Irish, *scabbed, bald ;* Heb. " karrach," *stony, rocky).*

120. Rory†: a younger son of Sir Donall Ballach; had an elder brother, Donall Gobhlach.

121. Eanagh: son of Rory. This Eanagh O'Cahan m. Jana (or Jane) Ware.‡

122. Richard : the second son of Eanagh. Had five brothers—1. John (who was the eldest), 2. Roger, 3. Henry, 4. Eanagh, 5. Patrick ; and five sisters—1. Elizabeth (who was married to a Roger O'Cahan of the Route), 2. Maria (m. to Lysah Ferall, of Newton, co. Longford), 3. Jana, 4. Margaret, 5. Norah.

123. Richard O'Cahan, of Laragh Bryan, near Maynooth, co. Kildare : son of Richard ; had a younger brother, Thomas O'Cahan, who, after the Battle of the Boyne, settled in the county Leitrim, and was the ancestor of *Caine,* of Manchester, England. Richard, after the same memorable Battle, settled in the county Kildare, assumed the name *Keane,* more lately *Kean,* and lastly *Cane.* In 1695 he occupied (according to Leases in the Duke of Leinster's Rent Office) a farm at Donaghstown, near Maynooth; and, in 1698, became seized of a large farm at Laragh Bryan. Since that period the Church-yard of Laragh Bryan has been the burial-place of his branch of this family. This Richard had three sons—1. William, of Dowdstown (or Dowstown), near Maynooth, who is No. 124, *infra,* on this Genealogy. 2. Joseph, who d. 1756. 3. Richard, of Laragh Bryan (Will dated 28th December, 1754), who m. Anne Cane,§ and by her had three sons and two daus. : the sons were—1. Richard, 2. William-Lyons, 3. John ; the daughters were—1. Jane, 2. Alice.

124. William Cane, of Dowdstown (d. at Dowdstown, 1st Sept., 1739) : eldest son of Richard (No. 123), of Laragh Bryan ; m. 7th Oct.,

* *Carrach* : The epithet applied by others to this John is the Irish "carach," which means *friendly,* or *faithful* ; as well as *deceitful* and *tricky.* According to Shaw, the Irish word " carach" also means *terrible* and *meandering.*

† *Rory* : In page 292 of the MS. Vol. F. 3. 23, in the Library of Trinity College, Dublin, this Rory is styled lord " of the Rout in county Derry." But, in his time, that " Lordship" must have been only *titular ;* for, to make room for the " Ulster Plantation," Rory's family patrimony was then confiscated.—See the " Flight of the Earls," in the Appendix.

‡ *Ware* : According to the Vol. F. 3. 23, in the MSS. Library of Trinity College, Dublin, this Jane Ware (whose brother James, and sister Martha, d. s.p.) was a daughter of John, son of James Ware, Gen. Mil., by his wife Elizabeth Piers (who was secondly m. to William, son of Edmond Fitzgerald, of Gorteen, in Ophaly or Offaley, and by whom also she had issue). And this Elizabeth Piers was the fourth daughter of Henry Piers, Arm., of Tristernah, county Westmeath (who d. 16th Dec., 1623), by his wife Jana Jones, a daughter of Thomas Jones, who, at his death, on the 10th April, 1619, was Protestant Archbishop of Dublin. And this Thomas Jones was the third son of Henry Jones, whose parentage we cannot trace.

§ *Cane* : For the pedigree of a " Cane" family, of English origin in Ireland, quite distinct from the Canes of St. Wolstan's, Celbridge, see p. 83 of the MS. Vol. F. 4. 18, in the Library of Trinity College, Dublin.¶

2 R

1712, Alice Stowell, by whom he had eight sons and five daughters:

I. Richard, b. 1713; d. young.

II. Rev. John, b. 1714, m. Grace Proby, of Hannington, co. of Wilts, and living at Leixlip, co. Kildare, in 1739. Their only child, Grace-Alice, m. Thomas Atkinson, Esq., of the Royal Horse Artillery.

III. James, b. 1715, lived at Inchicore, Dublin, and left two sons—1. William, 2. James, of Ratoath, and two daughters; living in 1739. The son William was a Lawyer, born in Dublin, 8th July, 1742; m. a Miss Johnston; retired to France before 1786; died at Tours, on 30th April, 1818, leaving issue one son: William, Lieut. 17th Foot, b. in London, 4th March, 1772; d. at Martinique, 10th July, 1794, leaving issue two sons: 1. William, born at Tours, 1st September, 1795, d. at Tours, 5th Feb., 1815. 2. James, of 39 Rue Royale, Tours; b. at Tours, 7th Dec., 1798; died unm. April, 1868. 2. James, of Ratoath, co. Meath, second son of James, of Inchicore; Captain 12th Dragoons; m. Jane, third dau. of William Roe,* Esq., of Roe's-Green, co. Tipperary, and had issue one son, William. 1. Jane, the eldest dau. of James Cane, of Inchicore, married Andrew

Walsh, of Oatlands, co. Meath, and had three sons and a dau. The sons were: 1. William Jeremy Walsh, who left no issue. 2. James Walsh, m. and had three sons and three daus. The sons were: 1. William-Henry Walsh, living unm. in 1879. 2. John Walsh, living unm. in 1879. 3. Henry Walsh, living in 1879; had one son and three daus. The son is: 1. James Walsh, of Clifton, England, living in 1879. 3. Henry - Thomas Walsh, the third son of Jane and Andrew Walsh, of Oatlands, co. Meath, left no issue. 2. Mary the second dau. of James Cane, of Inchicore.

IV. Hugh Cane, of Dowdstown, co. Kildare, Lt.-Col. 5th Dragoons, the fourth son of William and Alice Cane; b. 1716, died 19th January, 1793; was M.P. for Tallaght, co. Dublin. This Hugh was twice married: first to Louisa,† dau. of Edward Riggs, Esq., county Cork; and secondly, to Annabella, Lady Blakiston, relict of Sir Mathew Blakiston, who was Lord Mayor of London when King George III. was crowned. Of this second marriage there was no issue. The issue of the first marriage were two daughters— 1. Anne,‡ m. to Sir Edward Leslie, Bart., of Tarbert, co.

* *William Roe*: This William Roe m. Jane, fifth and youngest daughter and co-heir of Major Samuel Green of Killaghy, county Tipperary, M.P. for Cashel, by Jane, his wife, daughter of Oliver Latham, Esq., of Ballyshehane, county Tipperary. The other daughters of this William Roe were—1. Frances, m. to William Despard, of Killaghy Castle; 2. Anne-G., m. to Sir Charles Levinge, Bart.; 3. G. m. to Stephen Moore, Esq., of Killworth; 4. Dorothea-G., m. to the Hon. Richard Allen, M.P.

† *Louisa*: The Settlement between this Louisa and her husband Lt.-Col. Hugh Cane, was executed on the 13th July, 1741. And, as he had no issue by his second marriage, this Hugh Cane's property went to his two daughters by the first marriage, namely—Anne and Louisa.

‡ *Anne*: The Settlement between this Anne and her husband, Sir Edward

Kerry, by whom she had a dau. Louisa, who m. Lord Douglas Hallyburton, son of Charles, fourth Earl of Aboyne; 2. Louisa, m. to Col. Austey.

V. Charles, the fifth son of William and Alice, d. young.

VI. Maurice, Lt.-Col. 5th Foot, m. and had one son and two daughters: 1. Rev. William Augustus, Chaplain to the Duke of Northumberland, m. a Miss Ogle, but left no issue. He d. at 39 Hans-place, London, in 1839. 1. A daughter, married a Col. Scott; 2. Another dau., m. a Mr. Reynolds.

VII. William, the seventh son of William and Alice, b. in Fishamble - street, on 1st Sept., 1730, and, according to the Baptismal Register of St. John's Episcopalian Church, Dublin, was baptised on 22nd Sept., 1730: "Sept. 22, 1730. William, son of William and Alice Cane, gent.;" d. young.

VIII. Edward, Major 43rd Foot, the eighth son of William and Alice Cane, b. at Inchicore; of whom see No. 125, infra.

The five daughters of William and Alice were:

I. Mary, b. 1718, d. young.

II. Elizabeth, b. 1719, d. young.

III. Emilia, b. 1721, d. young.

IV. Alice, m., 13th May, 1752, Stephen Wybrants, of Rutland-square, Dublin (senior descendant of Joseph Wybrantz, of Antwerp, whose son and heir, Peter, settled in Ireland, temp. Car. I.), and left issue (with two daughters who died unm.) Peter and Robert, whose lines are extinct, and Gustavus (Rev.), whose only son Stephen, d. unm., and whose eldest daughter, Mary-Anne, m. Col. Wm.-Middleton, and left issue; the eldest of which, Isabella-Henrietta-Letitia, is a co-heiress, by devise, to her cousin Robert Wybrants, of Rutland-square, who d. s.p. 28th Aug., 1875, and wife of Wm. Geale-Wybrants, J.P., who, together with Captain Phipson, who m. her sister Georgina, assumed the name and arms of Wybrants by Royal License, dated 16th of March, 1877. The twelve children of Stephen and Alice Wybrants were seriatim: 1. Peter Wybrants, a Barrister, b. 1754; was Chairman of the co. Westmeath; m. and had two daus., d. 12th June, 1802. 2.

Leslie, Bart., was executed on the 29th July, 1773, after the death of her grand-father Edward Riggs, Esq., and was signed by the Rev. Archdeacon Leslie; the Rev. Richard Cane; Duke Tyrrell, of Claremount, in the county Westmeath; Christopher Kirwan Lyster, of the city of Dublin; and by Hugh Cane, Anne Cane, Louisa Cane (the 2nd daughter), Edward Leslie.

The Rev. Richard Cane, here mentioned as one of the signatories to the marriage Settlement between Anne Cane and Sir Edward Leslie, Bart. (and who is believed to have been an O'Cahan), was Rector of Maynooth, co. Kildare, and was buried at Laragh Bryan. By his Will, dated 13th December, 1798 (to be seen in the Public Record Office, Four Courts, Dublin), this Rev. Richard Cane left legacies of fifty guineas each to his nieces Caroline and Louisa Cane, and left all else to his nephew Richard Duke Cane, whom he made sole executor.

In his Will, that clergyman requests the following lines to be engraved on his Tombstone:

"Here lies the Rev. —— ——, vain and misplaced claim;
Can the cast slough of sin deserve that name?
Shall falsehood dare profane the sacred stone?
And pride exalt what Providence pulls down?"

Robert, b. 1755; m. 1st Sept., 1786, his first cousin, Christian Browne, by whom he had five children; died 1826, and was buried at Laragh Bryan. This Robert's children were: 1. Stephen, b. 27th June, 1787; d. 22nd December, 1787. 2. Robert, of 47 Rutland-square, Dublin; born 20th May, 1788. This Robert, m., first a Miss Trevelian; and, secondly, on 18th June, 1839, Maria Mac-Gregor Skinner; but left no issue by either marriage. He d. at Bray Head House, 28th August, 1875, and was buried in Mount Jerome, Dublin. 3, 4, and 5, d. in early infancy. 3. William, the third son of Stephen and Alice Wybrants, b. 1756, d. 3rd Nov., 1793. 4. Stephen, b. 1757, died 1758. 5. The Rev. Gustavus, b. 1758. 6. A second Stephen, Captain 67th Regiment, b. June, 1757, d. April, 1797. 7. John, born July, 1760, d. April, 1763. 8. A boy, b. 1761. 9. Hugh, b. 1762, died 30th March, 1763. 10. Deane, born 1764, died 5th September, 1788. 11. Alice, b. 1765, d. 19th Feb., 1840. 12. Margaretta, b. 1766, died December, 1833.

V. Maria, the fifth daughter of William and Alice Cane, m. —— Browne, Esq., and had three daus., of whom were: 1. Christina, who m. her first cousin, Robert Wybrants, 47 Rutland-square, Dublin. 2. Another daughter, married Medlycott Cane, of Multifarn-

ham, co. Westmeath, and of the 102nd Reg., East Indies. The issue of this marriage was James Cane, Major 23rd Regt.; He lived at Cheltenham and Tours, in France. This Major James Cane m. Miss Mortimer of Cheltenham, and had a dau., Madame de Madrid. Medlycott Cane married, secondly, Mrs. Bloomfield, née Bayly, dau. of John Bayly, Esq., of Newtown, co. Tipperary; and his granddaughter, Mrs. Frend (widow since 1858), née Delia Maria Cane, was living in 1883, —See the "Frend" pedigree, infra.

125. Edward Cane, of Donnybrook, county Dublin, Major 43rd Regiment of Foot; the eighth son of William and Alice; b. at Inchicore, 9th Sept., 1732, and d. 28th July, 1810. This Edward m. in the parish of St. Margaret, next Rochester, on the 24th Nov., 1765, Mary, only dau. of Admiral Robert Erskine, of Dun (who was Port Admiral at Chatham, and there buried on 13th Nov., 1766). The issue of this marriage were six sons and three daughters:

I. William, Capt. 61st Regt., b. at Chatham, 1768; d. 1792.

II. Rev. Robert* Erskine Cane, Rector of Creagh, co. Cork, as well as of Skibbereen, d. 1806. This Robert m. Dorothea, dau. of Hewett Poole, of Mayfield, co. Cork.

III. Edward, Army Agent, 60 Dawson-street, Dublin, born at Chatham, 1771; died, unm., in 1802.

* Robert : The Indenture by and between the Rev. Robt. Erskine Cane, of Creagh, in the county Cork, and his wife Dorothea, second daughter of Hewett Poole, as above, was made on the 19th June, 1801. The Trustees on the occasion were—Samuel McCall, of Glentown, in the county Cork; and Thomas Kemmis, of the city of Dublin, Attorney-at-Law. The Settlement was signed by Robert Erskine Cane; Dorothea Poole; and Samuel McCall.

IV. Maurice, Major 83rd Reg.,
" Comissr. Acct. Ireland," died
at Foster-place, Dublin, 4th
September, 1830 ; buried in
St. Paul's parish, Dublin.

V. Henry, Capt. 40th Regt., d.
at Minorca.

VI. Richard, Army Agent, of 60
Dawson-street, Dublin, and of
St. Wolstan's, Celbridge, co.
Kildare : who is No. 126 on
this Genealogy.

The three daughters of Edward
and Mary Cane were :

I. Alice-Rebecca, b. at Chatham,
1767 ; died unm., at Boulogne,
April, 1826, and is there interred.

II. Elizabeth, born at Chatham,
Dec., 1774 ; m. 11th March,
1808, the Honble. John Jones ;
died 1811.

III. Annabella, m. 26th Feb.,
1808, Frederick - Nathaniel
Walker, of the Manor House,
Bushey, co. Herts, England,
K.C.H., a General in the Army,
R.A. (and a younger brother of
Sir George Townshend Walker,
who d. 3rd Feb., 1857). This
Annabella d. at Calais, in May,
1827, and is buried in the
cemetery at Boulogne. The
issue of that marriage, as far
as we have ascertained, were
as follows : 1. Sir Edward-
Walter-Forestier W a l k e r,
K.C.B., of Manor House,
Bushey, Herts ; General in the
Army ; Colonel 50th Foot ; b.
18th February, 1812 ; m., first,
20th July, 1843, Jane, only
dau. of Francis Grant, sixth
earl of Seafield, and by her
(who d. 16th Sept., 1861) has
had : 1. Frederick - William-
Edward - Forestier, Lieut. Col.
Scots' Guards, born 16th April,
1844 ; m. 15th Feb., 1887, at
St. George's, Hanover-square,

London, to Mabel Louise, dau.
of Colonel Ross (Northumberland Fusileers), of county Fermanagh. 2. Francis - Lewis-
George Forestier, b. 2nd Jan.,
1847 ; d. February, 1854. 3.
Douglas-Henry-Walter -Fores-
tier, born May, 1849 ; died an
infant. 4. Montague-Charles-
Brudenel-Forestier, 60th Rifles,
born 7th August, 1853.

Sir Edward W. F. Walker, m.,
secondly, 15th Oct., 1862, the Lady
Juliana-Caroline-Frances, dau. of
Thomas, second Earl of Ranfurley,
and by her had a daughter, Mary-
Juliana-Forestier, who d. an infant
in 1863. 2. Frederick-Brudenell
Walker, second son of Frederick-
Nathaniel and Annabella Walker,
d. April, 1822 ; and their daughters
were : 1. Henrietta-Maria Walker,
d. Oct., 1824. 2. Augusta-Eliza, d.
1876. 3. Isabella-Louisa, m. 19th
May, 1858, to Colonel James-John
Graham. 4. Georgiana-Adelaide, m.,
first, 31st Aug., 1854, to William
Stuart, of Aldenham Abbey, Herts ;
and, secondly, 15th Dec., 1875, to
the Hon. James Grant, brother of
the Earl of Seafield. 5. Amelia-
Forestier, d. unm. 11th Jan., 1845
6. Caroline-Albinia, m. to the Rev.
Percy Monro, Incumbent of Colden
Common, Hants, England.

126. Richard Cane, Army Agent,
60 Dawson-street, Dublin, and of
St. Wolstan's, near Celbridge, co.
Kildare ; the sixth son of Edward ;
died at 60 Dawson-street, on 9th
February, 1853, and was buried at
Laragh Bryan, near Maynooth.
This Richard Cane, m., 9th May,
1812, Isabella, youngest child of
Arthur Dawson, Esq., of Castle
Dawson, county Derry, and grand-
daughter of George-Paul Monck,
Esq., and the Lady Araminta
Monck, née Beresford. This Isabella
died 22nd Feb., 1845, and is buried

at Laragh Bryan. The issue of this marriage were four sons and three daughters; the sons were :

I. Edward Cane, of St. Wolstan's, Celbridge, born Feb., 1813 ; died 22nd Sept., 1877, at 60 Dawson-street, Dublin ; was buried at Laragh Bryan.

II. Arthur-Beresford Cane, Lieut. 10th Foot, and afterwards Receiver for the Constabulary in Ireland ; of whom presently.

III. Richard Cane, of St. Wolstan's, Celbridge ; living in 1886 ; m. at Florence, 4th April, 1854, Louisa-Mary, only daughter of the Hon. William Dawson-Damer. She d. at Biarritz, 6th May, 1855, and is buried in the cemetery there.

IV. Maurice-Hugh Cane, Army Agent, 60 Dawson - street, Dublin, and of Allen's Grove, Celbridge, living in 1887 ; late Captain XXth Regiment ; and late Governor of the Bank of Ireland.

The three daughters of Richard and Isabella Cane were:

I. Catherine-Harriet, who d. at St. Wolstan's, 6th July, 1828, and is buried at Laragh Bryan.

II. Louisa, living in 1887.

III. Caroline-Frances, living in 1887.

127. Arthur Beresford Cane, Lieut. 10th Foot, and afterwards Receiver for the Constabulary in Ireland : the second son of Richard and Isabella Cane ; died at Marseilles 13th May, 1864, and was there buried. This Arthur Beresford Cane was twice m. : first at St. George's, Hanover-square, London, on 5th July, 1849, to Selina, youngest daughter of John Trant,* Esq., of Dovea, county Tipperary. She d. 5th Nov., 1859, and is buried in Mount Jerome, Dublin. Their issue were two children :

I. Edith-Caroline-Isabella, who d. 9th Dec., 1884, and is buried at Laragh Bryan.

I. Richard-Claude, who is No. 128 on this genealogy.

Arthur Beresford Cane's second marriage was, on the 23rd Feb., 1864, to Eliza, eldest dau. of Rev. Joseph Stevenson, Rector of Clonfeacle, county Armagh, and granddaughter of Sir John Stevenson, Mus. Doc. ; and had issue :

II. Arthur Beresford Cane; born 2nd Dec., 1864, and living in 1887.

128. Richard Claude Cane, of St. Wolstan's, Celbridge, late Captain Royal Artillery : elder son of Arthur Beresford Cane, born 29th October, 1859, and living in 1887 ; m. on 1st March, 1882, Eva, second daughter of W. H. Mackintosh, Esq., M.D., of St. Julian's, Malta, and has issue :

I. Maurice, of whom presently.

I. Evadne, b. 4th Sept., 1884.

129. Maurice : son of Richard Claude Cane ; born 22nd December, 1882, and living in 1887.

---

* *Trant :* Caroline, eldest daughter of this John Trant, married James Hamilton, of Abbotstown, M.P. for county Dublin, whose second son, Ion Trant Hamilton, D.L., of Abbotstown House, Castleknock, late one of the M.P.'s for the county Dublin, m. Victoria, dau. of Lord Charles Wellesley, and sister of the present Duke of Wellington.

O'CAHAN. (No. 2.)

Arms : Same as " O'Cahan" (No. 1).

JOSEPH, a younger brother of William, who is No. 124 on the (foregoing) " O'Cahan" (No. 1) pedigree, was the ancestor of this branch of that family.

124. Joseph : second son of Richard ; died 1756.

125. Rev. Richard O'Cahan : his son. Had three younger brothers— 1. William,* who settled in the co. Cork ; 2. Lewis, who settled in the co. Mayo ; 3. John, who assumed the name *Kean*, settled in Mullingar† in 1751, and afterwards resided in the city of Dublin. This John Kean had five sons—1. William ; 2. John ; 3. Robert ; 4.

Patrick ; 5. Richard, who died in 1795.

126. John Kean, of Dublin: second son of John ; became connected with the "United Irishmen," on account of which he had to fly the country, in 1798. When those troublous times in Ireland had passed away, he returned to Dublin ; assumed the name *Kane;* and died in 1832.

* *William* : This William and Lewis assumed the name *O'Keane.*

† *Mullingar* : Following up our research with reference to this John Kean, we visited Mullingar, in November, 1879, and there learned (see Note, under the " Keane," of the county Clare, pedigree) that an *O'Cain* family lived in the county Westmeath, in the early part of the eighteenth century. In the *Liber Baptisatorum* of the Catholic Church at Mullingar occurs the following entry :—"1742. July 19th. Bap. Margaret *Cain*, daughter to William and Margaret Darcy." In that Baptismal Register also occur, since 1742, the names of *Coyne, Kain, Kane,* and *Kean* ; all of them anglicised forms of the Irish *O'Cain*. The oldest branch of the " Cain" family that settled in the county Westmeath, lived in Killpatrick, near Rathconrath. Descendants of that family have been :

1. Patrick Kean of Templepatrick, Moyvore, near Ballymahon, and his five brothers, John, Matthew, James, William, and Christopher, all living in 1879 : the sons of

2. James Keane of Rathcolman, who had three brothers—1. Rev. Patrick ; 2. John, who died unmarried ; and 3. ———— : sons of

1. Patrick Kean, who had an elder brother Hugh, and three younger brothers— 1. a Doctor, 2. a Priest, 3. Richard. The Hugh here mentioned had five sons and four daughters : one of those daughters was Mrs. Marcella Canton, of Greville-street, Mullingar, living in 1879. The sons were : 1. James, 2. Nicholas, 3. Christopher, 4. Hugh, and 5. William. The first four of these five sons of Hugh died unm. ; but the youngest son William, who died on the 17th of March, 1878, was married, and left two children—1. Bridget, 13 years old ; and 2. Hugh, 8 years old : both living in 1879, Patrick Keane (No. 3) and his brothers were the sons of

4. James (or Shemus), who was sirnamed " Brooteen Kean," and who "had an uncle a Priest."

O'CAHAN. (No. 3.)

Of Ballymaclosty (or Ballymaclosky), County Londonderry.

Arms: Gu. three salmon haurient, two and two or.   *Crest:* A mountain cat salient ppr.   *Motto:* Inclytus virtute.

SHANE O'CAHAN, Chief of his Name, who d. 1498, and who is No. 115 on the (No. 1) "O'Cahan" (Princes of Limavady) genealogy, had:

2. Donell (or Daniel), of Colryan (? Coolbryan), who had:

3. Richard, who had:

4. "Quoy" (or Conbhach) Ballach O'Cahane, of Ballymaclosty, county Londonderry, who died 10th July, 1637. He m. Una, dau. of Dermot O'Cahan, of Lekyn, and had two sons:

I. Manus, who m. Evelin, dau. of Cormack O'Neill.

II. Richard.

5. Richard: second son of "Quoy" Ballach; m. Margaret, dau. of Sir Donogh O'Cahan, of Limavady, Knt., and had:

I. Donogh.

II. Richard.

6. Donoch O'Cahan: son of Richard.

O'CLERY.

Arms: Or, three nettle leaves vert.

FEARGALL, brother of Artgall who is No. 96 on the "O'Shaughnessy" pedigree, was the ancestor of *O'Cleirigh,* and *MacCleirigh;* anglicised *O'Clery, Cleary, Clark, Clarke,* and *Clarkson.*

96. Fergall: son of Guaire Aidhneach [aidhne].

97. Toirbheartach: his son.

98. Cathmogh: his son.

99. Cumascach: his son.

100. Ceadach: his son.

101. Cleireach ("cleireach:" Irish, *a clerk;* Lat. "cleric-us"): his son; a quo *O'Cleirigh.*

102. Maolfabhal: his son; died A.D. 887.

103. Maolceardachd (called Flann): his son.

104. Comhailltan (" comhaill:" Irish, *to perform a duty*): his son; a quo *O'Comhailltain,* anglicised *Coulton;* died A.D. 976.

105. Giollaceallach: his son; a quo *Gilkelly,* and *Kilkelly.*

106. Congalach O'Clery: his son;

first assumed this sirname; died 1025.

107. Braoin: his son; had a brother named Aidhne, who was the ancestor of *Hynes;* and another brother Giolla na Naomh, who was the ancestor of *Kilkelly;* d. 1033.

108. Eoghan (or Owen): his son.

109. Donall: his son.

110. Giollananaomh: his son.

111. Tighearnach: his son.

112. Muireadach: his son.

113. Teige: his son.

114. Giollaiosa: his son.

115. Donall (2): his son.

116. Shane Sgiamhach (or John the Elegant): his son. This John had three brothers—1. Donall, 2. Thomas, 3. Cormac: from Shane Sgiamhach are descended the

O'Clerys of Tirconnell; from Donall, the O'Clerys of Tyrawley, in Mayo; from Thomas, the O'Clerys of Brefney-O'Rielly; and from Cormack, the O'Clerys of the county Kilkenny.

117. Dermod: eldest son of Shane Sgiamhach [skeevagh].

118. Cormac: his son; the first of the family who settled in Tirconnell.

119. Giollabrighid: his son.

120. Giolla Riabhach: his son.

121. Dermod na-Ttri-sgol (or "Dermod of the Three Schoals," namely,

one school for Reading, another for History and Genealogy, and another for Poetry): his son.

122. Teige Cam: his son.

123. Dermod (3): his son.

124. Cucoigcrioch [cucocry]: his son.

125. Maccon: his son.

126. Lughach O'Clery:* his son; had four brothers—1. Giollabrighid, 2. Maccon Meirgeach ("meirge:" Irish, *an ensign;* meaning "Maccon, the standard bearer"), 3. Cucoigcrioch or Peregrine, and 4. Dubhceann.

O'CONNOR. (No. 1.)

Kings of Connaught.

Arms: Ar. an oak tree eradicated ppr.

BRIAN, the eldest brother of Niall Mór, who is No. 87 on the "O'Neill" (Princes of Tyrone) pedigree, was the first King of Connaught, of the Hy-Niall Sept, and ancestor of *O'Conchobhair*, of Connaught; anglicised *O'Connor, O'Conor, Connor, Conor,* and *Conyers.*

87. Brian: eldest son of Eochaidh Muigh-Meadhoin [Moyvane], the 124th Monarch of Ireland.

88. Duach Galach: his youngest son; the first Christian King of Connaught. His brothers, who left any issue, were Conall Orison, Arca-Dearg, and Aongus, etc.

* *O'Clery*: The princely residence of the O'Clerys was the Castle of Kilbarron, within a short distance of Ballyshannon, in the county Donegal. In describing that Castle, the late Dr. Petrie says: "This lonely insulated fortress was erected as . . a safe and quite retreat in troubled times for the laborious investigators and preservers of the history, poetry, and antiquities of their country. This castle was the residence of the *Ollamhs,* bards, and antiquarians of the people of Tirconnell, the illustrious family of the O'Clerys."

The following stanza is from *Kilbarron's Last Bard to his Harp*:

Wake, let the despot's knell
Peal from thy wires,
Hope hath a tale to tell,
Harp of my sires;
Tyranny's rayless night,
Erin's degrading blight
Sinks, that thy strains may light
Liberty's fires.

89. Eoghan Sreibh : son of Duach; the fifth Christian King of that province.

90. Muireadach : his son.

91. Fergus : his son.

92. Eochaidh Tiormach : his son. Had two younger brothers—1. Feargna, who was the ancestor of *O'Rourke*, etc.; 2. Duach-Teang-Umh, who was the ancestor of *O'Flaherty*, and *MacHugh* (of Connaught), etc.

93. Aodh (or Hugh) Abrad : son of Eochaidh ; was the eighth Christian King.

94. Uadach : his son; the ninth King. Had a brother named Cuornan.

95. Raghallach : son of Uadach; was the 11th King.

96. Fergus : his son.

97. Muireadach Maolleathan : his son; the 16th King.

98. Inreachtach : his son; was the 17th King. Had two brothers —1. Cathal, 2. Conbhach.

99. Murgal : son of Inreachtach. Had a younger brother named Aodh Balbh.

100. Tomhailtach (or Timothy) : his son.

101. Muirgheas (or Murias) : his son; d. A.D. 815. Had a brother Diarmaid Fionn, who was the ancestor of *Concannon, Fahy* (of Connaught), etc.

102. Teige Mór: son of Murias; had a brother named Cathal.

103. Conchobhar: his son.

104. Cathal : his son. Had a younger brother Maolclothach, who was the ancestor of *O'Tomhailtaigh* ("tomhailt:" Irish, *wasting, consuming*), anglicised *Tomalty*, and *Talty ;* and of *MacMorrissy*.*

105. Teige: his son; d. 956. He married Creassa, dau. of Arca, lord of West Connaught. (Arca's other dau. Beavionn was the mother of Brian Boru, the famous Monarch of Ireland.)

106. Conchobhar ("concobhar: Irish, *the helping warrior*): son of Teige; a quo *O'Conchobhair*. Had a brother named Maolruanaidh [Mulroona] Mór; and another brother Teige, who was the ancestor of *O'Taidhg* (anglicised *Tighe*), who were collectors to the King of Connaught. This Conchobhar [connor] was the 40th Christian King; he d. 973.

107. Cathal: his son; the 42nd Christian King.

108. Teige an Each [ogh] Ghal (or Teige of the White Steed): his son; the 43rd Christian King.

109. Aodh an Gath Bearnaigh : his son ; the 44th King.

110. Ruadhri [Rory] an Saight heach Buidhe : his son ; the 46th King.

111. Tirloch Mór : his son ; the 48th King of Connaught, and the 181st Monarch of Ireland ; d. 19th May, 1156, at Dunmore, co. Galway, aged 68 years ; bur. at Clonmacnoise. Married three times : 1st, to Talteina, dau. of Murtogh O'Melaghlin, King of Meath; 2ndly, to Dervorgilla, dau. of Donal O'Melaghlin, Prince of Meath ; 3rdly, to Dubhcola, dau. of Mulroona MacDermott, Prince of Moy lurg.

112. Cathal Craobh-Dearg : his son by Dubhcola; the 51st King; d. 1224. This Cathal (or Charles) had seventeen younger brothers—1. Roderick O'Connor, the 183rd Monarch of Ireland, who d. 1198; 2. Brian, who was the ancestor of *O'Connor* (Sligo); 3. Donal Mór; 4. Hugh Dall, ("dall:" Irish, *blind*

---

* *MacMorrissy* : See the "Morris" pedigree, for another *MacMorrissy* Genealogy.

or *near-sighted*), a quo *O'Doille*, anglicised *Doyle ;** 5. Muirceartach,† a quo *MacMuirceartaih*, anglicised *MacMorrisy*, and *MacMoriarty*; 6. Maoliosa, Bishop of Roscommon, who had a son named Maol Eoin (meaning a devotee of St. John), a quo *O'Maoil Eoin*, anglicised *Malone ;* 7. Manus, a quo *MacManus* of Tir Tuathail ; 8. Connor, who was King of Meath, and the ancestor of *Cuniffe*. According to O'Dugan this Connor was the ancestor of *Nugent*, Earls of Westmeath ; 9. Teige ; 10. Brian Oge ; 11. Donoch ; 12. Malachi ; 13. Teige Oge ; 14. Cathal Oge ; 15. Dermod ; 16. Donal Oge ; 17. Murios.

113. Aodh (or Hugh) : son of Cathal Craobh-Dearg ; King of Connaught ; d. 1228 ; had a brother Felim.

114. Roderick : son of Aodh ; Lord of Connaught. Had five brothers ; and a sister Una, who m. Robert de Gernon.

115. Eoghan [Owen] : his son ; lord of Connaught ; killed 1274 ; had one brother.

116. Hugh : his son ; lord of Connaught, 1293—1306 ; had two brothers.

117. Felim : his son ; lord of Connaught. Had two brothers—1. Tirloch, who was the ancestor of *O'Connor Don ;* 2. Cathal.

118. Hugh : son of Felim.

119. Tirloch Ruadh ("ruadh :" Irish, *red*) : his son ; a quo the *O'Connor Roe* is *so* called.

120. Teige O'Connor Roe : his son.

121. Charles O'Connor Roe : his son.

122. Teige Buidhe O'Connor Roe : his son.

123. Tirlogh Ruadh O'Connor Roe : his son. Had three sons—1. Hugh ; 2. Teige ;‡ 3. Cairbre.

121. Hugh O'Connor Roe : eldest son of Tirlogh.

125. Charles Oge O'Connor Roe : his son.

126. Teige O'Connor Roe : his son.

127. Hugh O'Connor Roe : his son.

128. Charles O'Connor Roe : his son ; died without issue.

---

* *Doyle* : This family of *O'Doille* is distinct from *O'Doilbhe* (or "Doyle") of North Decies.—See No. 91 on the "Felan" pedigree, *ante*.

† *Muirceartach* : See the "Moriarty" (of Connaught) Genealogy, for another family of this name, of the Line of Heremon.

‡ *Teige* : This Teige, the second son of Tirlogh Ruadh, was the father of Diarmaid and Teige Caoch : said Diarmaid was the father of Brian, who was father of another Diarmaid ; and said Teige Caoch was the father of another Diarmaid. And Teige's youngest brother, Cairbre, was the father of Felim, who was father of Tirlogh, who was father of Tirlogh Oge ; and said Felim was also the father of Hugh, who was father of Brian Ballach, who was father of Dermod, who was father of Cairbre.

O'CONNOR ROE. (No. 2.)

Of Lanesborough.

Arms : Erm. an oak tree eradicated and acorned ppr.   *Another* : Ar. an oak tree eradicated and acorned ppr. over all on a fess wavy az. a unicorn's head erased between two salmon naiant of the first.

SHANE O'CONNOR Ruadh (pr. " Roe") had :

2. Teige* (or Thaddeus), who lived at Cloonfree, was styled the "O'Connor Roe," m. daughter of O'Brannan, and had :

3. Denis O'Connor Roe, who m. daughter of O'Hanly of Sheehane, and had :

4. Thadeus, who m. a Miss Foster of Esker, county Dublin, and had :

5. Denis, of Lanesborough, b. 1765, who m. dau. of Plunket, of Ardkeenagh, and had :

6. John, who m. daughter of Costello of Gurteen, near Coolavin, and had :

7. John O'Connor Roe.

O'CONOR DON.† (No. 3.)

Arms: Ar. an oak tree vert surmounted by a crown.

TIRLOCH, a brother of Felim who is No. 117 on the (No. 1) "O'Connor" (Kings of Connaught) Genealogy, was the ancestor of *O'Conchobhair Duinn ;* anglicised *O'Connor Dun,* and, more lately, *O'Conor Don.*

117. Tirloch : son of Hugh "lord of Connaught ;" d. 1345.

118. Hugh : his son ; lord of Connaught ; had a brother named Rory ; d. 1356.

119. Tirloch Dun ("dun :" Irish, here means *a darkish brown colour,* as distinguished from the O'Connor Ruadh [Roe] : son of Hugh ; d. 1406.

120. Felim Geancach : his son ; "lord O'Conor Dun ;" who attended a Parliament held in his time ; d. 1474.

121. Owen Caoch : his son ; lord O'Conor Dun ; d. 1485.

122. Cairbre : his son ; lord O'Conor Dun ; d. 1546.

123. Dermod : his son ; lord O'Conor Dun ; had a brother named Tuathal ; d. 1585.

124. Sir Hugh : his son ; lord O'Conor Dun ; knighted by Sir John Perrott, lord deputy of Ireland ; d. 1632, at a very advanced age.

125. Cathal (or Charles) : his third son ; d. 1634. Had a younger

----

* *Teige* : It is claimed that this is the Teige O'Connor, who was a Colonel in the French army, A.D. 1700.

† *O' Conor Don* : The pedigree of the "O'Connor (Connaught)" family, contained in a Book by Roderick O'Conor, of Tulsk, would well repay perusal.

brother, Brian, who was the ancestor of the O'Conors of Dundermott and Milton, co. Roscommon.

126. Cathal Oge: his son; d. 1696.

127. Donogh (or Denis): his son; d. 1750.

128. Charles: his son; an eminent Antiquary; d. 1791.

129. Denis: his son; d. 1804. Had a younger brother Charles, of Mount Allen, co. Roscommon, b. 1736, d. 1808. This Charles m. a dau. of John Dillon of Dublin, and by her had three children—1. Thomas, who settled in New York; 2. Denis, and 3. Catherine—both of whom d. in America. This Thomas (d. 1855) was father of Charles O'Conor, Barrister-at-Law, (b. 1804), of New York, U.S.A., and who d. May, 1884, leaving no children.

130. Owen: son of Denis; the first Catholic Member of Parliament for the co. Roscommon, since the Reformation. This Owen became The O'Conor Don, on the death, in 1820, of Alexander O'Conor Don (See No. 128 on the "O'Conor-Eccles" pedigree), the last male representative of the elder sons of Sir Hugh (No. 124); had a brother named Mathew, who was the ancestor of O'Conor, of Mount Druid, co. Roscommon.

131. Denis: son of Owen; M.P. for Roscommon; d. 1847.

132. Charles-Owen O'Conor, known as "The O'Conor Don:" his son; was M.P. for the county Roscommon; had a younger brother named Denis (deceased), who was M.P. for the county Sligo; living in 1887. According to Burke's "Landed Gentry, 1879," this Charles-Owen m. 21st April, 1868, Georgina-Mary (who d. Aug. 1872), dau. of T. A. Perry, of Bitham House, co. Warwick, England, and by her had four children—1. Denis-Charles, b. 1869; 2. Owen-Felim, b. 1870; 3. Charles-Hugh, b. 1872; 4. Roderick, b. 1872, d. 1878. (For later particulars, see "Walford's County Families, 1879.")

133. Denis-Charles O'Conor Don: eldest son of Charles-Owen O'Conor Don, of Belanagare and Clonalis, co. Roscommon; living in 1887.

O'CONNOR SLIGO. (No. 4.)

Arms : Per pale vert and ar. in the dexter a lion ramp. to the sinister, in the sinister on a mount in base, vert an oak tree ppr.

BRIAN, brother of Cathal Craobh Dearg, the 51st Christian King of Connaught who is no 112 on the (No. 1) "O'Connor" (Connaught) pedigree, was the ancestor of *O'Connor Sligo.*

112. Brian: son of Tirlogh Mór, the 48th Christian King of Connaught, and 181st Monarch of Ireland.

113. Andreas: his son; was the first that assumed the sirname *O'Connor Sligo.*

114. Brian (2): his son.

115. Teige: his son.

116. Donal (or Daniel): his son.

117. Murtach: his son; had a brother named Cathal (or Charles); died 1327.

118. Daniel: his son; had five brothers—1. Malachi, 2. Manus, 3. Murtach, 4. Donoch, 5. Malachi Oge.

119. Owen: son of Daniel; had five brothers—1. Felim, 2. Tirloch Fionn, 3. Brian, 4. Tirloch Cairach, 5. Murtach Baccach.

120. Daniel (2): son of Owen.

121. Charles Mór: his son.

122. Teige (2): his son.

123. Charles Oge :* his son.

124. Teige (3): his son.

125. Martin: his son; had four brothers—1. Teige, 2. Charles, 3. Brian, 4. Hugh.

126. Owen: son of Martin.

127. Daniel: his son.

128. Dermod: his son.

129. Charles: his son.

130. Denis (2): his son; died in 1750.

131. Connell: his son, died 1782.

132. Denis (3): his son; died 1835.

133. Peter O'Connor, J.P., Cairnsfort, Sligo: his son; born in 1803, living in 1887; had no son. This Peter had three brothers—1. Connell; 2. Patrick, who died in 1832; 3. John: Connell (who died in 1866), had three sons; Patrick (who died in 1832) had three sons and four daughters; John (who d. in 1852) had one son named Patrick. This Peter O'Connor had also one sister named Ellen, who was married to Simon Cullen: the issue of that marriage were two sons and two daughters.

134. Peter O'Connor: son of Patrick, who, as above mentioned, died in 1832; born 28th June, 1832, living in 1887.

O'CONNOR. (No. 5.)

Of Annagh, County Roscommon.

Arms: Same as (No. 1) "O'Connor," Connaught.

TIRLOGH O'CONNOR, of Annagh, had:

2. Carbery, who had:

3. Phelimy Buoy, who had:

4. Tirlogh, who had:

5. Tirlogh of Annagh, who died June, 1638. This Tirlogh married Benmy, dau. of Dualtach Mac-Connor of Tulsk, co. Roscommon, gent., and had one son and one daughter:

I. John.

I. Una, who m. Daniel Albanah.

6. John O'Connor: son of Tirlogh; m. Mór, dau. of William Flanagan.

---

* *Charles* (or *Cathal*) *Oge:* According to Wood-Martin's *History of Sligo*, this Charles had a son Donal, whose son was Sir Charles O'Connor Sligo; and that Teige, living in 1536, was the first who assumed the title of "*O'Connor Sligo*,"—the previous title of the family having been:

"*MacDonail MacMuircheartaigh.*"

which was derived from a lord of Sligo, bearing that name, and who died A.D. 1395.

O'Donovan says that the last chief of this family died at Brussels, on the 7th February, 1756, a Lieut.-General in the Austrian Army; which would go to show that Teige, No. 124, was a younger son of Charles Oge, No. 123.

O'CONNOR. (No. 6.)

Of Moy Ith, County Donegal.

Arms : Same as " O'Cahan" (No. 1.)

DERMOD, brother of Gruagan who is No. 97 on the " O'Cahan" pedigree, was the ancestor* of *O'Connor*, of Moy Ith, in the barony of Raphoe, and county Donegal.

97. Dermod : son of Connor.

98. Baoghal O'Connor : his son ; first of the family who assumed this sirname.

99. Carlan (" an :" Irish, *one who ;* " carla," *a wool-comb*) : his son ; a quo *O'Carlain*, anglicised *Carlin*, *Carolan*, and *Kerlin*.

100. Maoldun : his son.

101. Aongus : his son.

102. Rory : his son.

103. Aodh (or Hugh) : his son.

104. Maolruanaidh [mulroona] : his son.

105. Aodh (2) : his son.

106. Maolruanaidh O'Connor, of Magh [Moy] Ith : his son.

O'CONNOR. (No. 7.)

Of Orgiall, in Ulster.

Arms ; Gu. a lion pass. guard. or.

FIRBIS, brother of Aongus (or Æneas) who is No. 90 on the " O'Brassil West" pedigree, was the ancestor of *O'Connor* of Orgiall, or of Clann Colla.

90. Firbis : son of Colcan.

91. Tuathal : his son.

92. Sercan : his son.

93. Maonachan (" maoin :" Irish, *esteem, wealth*) : his son ; a quo *O'Maoinachain*, of Ulster, or Orgiall, anglicised *Monahan*, and *Monaghan*. From this Maonachan the territory of " Monaghan" was first so called.

94. Rimhiadh : his son.

95. Concobhar (" con :" Irish, *of a warrior*, and " cobhar," *help*) : his son ; a quo *O'Conchobhair*, anglicised *O'Connor*.

96. Maolmichil (meaning the devoted of St. Michael) : his son ; a quo *Michil*, and *Mitchell*, of Clan Colla.]

*Ancestor : Other genealogists state that the ancestor of this family was Moroch, son of Longseach, son of Flaitheartach, who was brother of Dermod O'Cahan, No. 101 on the " O'Cahan" (No. 1) pedigree.

97. Dubhdara: his son.

98. Seanghain (*Seanghain :* Irish, "a child near its time of being born"): his son; a quo *O'Sheanghain,** anglicised *Shannon,* and *Hyde.*

99. Giolla Dun O'Connor: his son.

O'CONNOR FALEY. (No. 8.)

Lords of Offaley.

Arms : Ar. on a mount in base vert an oak tree acorned ppr.

LAEGHAIRE LORC, an elder brother of Cobthach Caol-bhreagh who is No. 60 on the "Line of Heremon," was the ancestor of *O'Connor Faley.*

60. Laeghaire Lorc, the 68th Monarch of Ireland: son of Ugaine Mór; began to reign, B.C. 593.

61. Olioll Aine: his son.

62. Labhradh Longseach: his son.

63. Olioll Bracan: his son.

64. Æneas Ollamh: his son; the 73rd Monarch.

65. Breassal: his son.

66. Fergus Fortamhail, the 80th Monarch: his son; slain B.C. 384.

67. Felim Fortuin: his son.

68. Crimthann Coscrach: his son; the 85th Monarch.

69. Mogh-Art: his son.

70. Art: his son.

71. Allod (by some called Olioll): his son.

72. Nuadh Falaid: his son.

73. Fearach Foghlas: his son.

74. Olioll Glas: his son.

75. Fiacha Fobrug: his son.

76. Breassal Breac: his son. Had two sons—1. Lughaidh, 2. Conla, between whom he divided his country, viz.—to his eldest son

Lughaidh [Luy], who was ancestor of the Kings, nobility, and gentry of Leinster, he gave all the territories on the north side of the river *Bearbha* (now the "Barrow"), from Wicklow to Drogheda; and to his son Conla, who was ancestor of the Kings, nobility, and gentry of Ossory, he gave the south part, from the said river to the sea.

77. Luy: son of Breassal Breac.

78. Sedna: his son; built the royal city of *Rath Alinne.*

79. Nuadhas Neacht: his son; the 96th Monarch.

80. Fergus Fairgé: his son; had a brother named Baoisgne, who was the father of Cubhall [Coole], who was the father of Fionn, commonly called "Finn MacCoole," the illustrious general in the third century of the ancient Irish Militia known as the *Fiana Eirionn,* or "Fenians of Ireland."

81. Ros: son of Fergus Fairgé.

82. Fionn Filé ("filé:" Irish, *a poet*): his son.

* *O'Sleanghain :* This sirname is quite distinct from *O'Sheanchain* ("seancha :" Irish, *an antiquary* or *genealogist ;* "an," *one who*), anglicised *Shanahan,* and modernized *Shannon.*

83. Conchobhar Abhraoidhruaidh: his son ; the 99th Monarch of Ireland.

84. Mogh Corb : his son.

85. Cu-Corb* : his son ; King of Leinster.

86. Niadh [nia] Corb : his son.

87. Cormac Gealtach : his son. Had a brother named Ceathramhadh.†

88. Felim Fiorurglas : his son.

89. Cathair [cahir] Mór‡ : his son ; the 109th Monarch of Ireland. Had a younger brother named Main Mal, who was the ancestor of O'Kelly, of Cualan (of Wicklow, etc.) ; and another, Eithne.

90. Ros Failgeach : son of Cahir Mór ; a quo Hy-Failgeagh ("failgeach :" Irish, abounding with rings), meaning the descendants of this Failgeach, and afterwards the name of the territory itself which they possessed, which has been anglicised Offaley, and which is the origin of the epithet applied to the O'Connors of this territory — namely, the O'Connors "Faley," signifying the O'Connors of Offaley. Ros Failgeach had a brother named Dairé, who' was the ancestor of O'Gorman ; and a brother Comthanan, who was the ancestor of Duff, of Leinster.

91. Nathi : son of Ros Failgeach.

92. Eoghan : his son.

93. Cathal (or Cathair) : his son.

94. Maolumha : his son.

95. Foranan : his son.

96. Congal : his son.

97. Diomusach (" diomusach :" Irish, proud, haughty, arrogant) · his son ; a quo O'Diomusaigh, anglicised O'Dempsey, and Dempsey.

98. Flann (or Florence) Da Conghal : his son.

---

* Cu-Corb : This Cu-Corb had four sons—1. Niadh Corb. 2. Messincorb, a quo Dal Messincorb. 3. Cormac, a quo Dal Cormaic, and who was the ancestor of Quirk. 4. Cairbre Cluitheachar, who was the ancestor of Donegan (lords of Dal Aracht) ; of O'Dwyer (lords of Killnamanagh) ; of O'Urcha (which has been anglicised Archer) ; of O'Cooney, O'Kearnan, O'Conalty, O'Hartley ; O'Arrachtan (modernized Harrington) ; O'Skellan (modernized Skilling) ; O'Congal, Clan Brian, O'Dubhcron, MacLongachan, O'Trena, O'Aodhan, O'Brangal, O'Corban, O'Dunedy, etc.

86. Messincorb : second son of Cucorb.

87. Eochaidh Lamh-dearg : his son.

88. Fothach : his son.

89. Garchu : his son ; ancestor of O'Concuan, O'Tuatan, O'Cosney, O'Cearda, O'Conatta, O'Rappan, O'Hechinn, O'Broin (of Deilgne,or Delgany), O'Ceallagh, O'Dubhan, O'Gobham (O'Gowan), O'Marcan (Marks), etc. This Garchu had two brothers—1. Naspre, who was ancestor of O'Fallan, O'Dinachar, O'Conag, O'Dubhcron, O'Donnan, O'Saran, O'Briony, Clan Ciaran, O'Teachtar, O'Convoy, O'Monay, etc. ; and 2. Nar, who was ancestor of O'Birinn, O'Deman, etc. ; all of these being Leinster families ; but many of whom are now extinct.

† Ceathramhadh : According to some authorities Cormac Gealtach had a brother named Crimthan Culbuidh, who, in succession to his grand-nephew Cathair Mór, was by the Monarch Conn Ceadcathach made King of Leinster. This Cormac Gealtach is supposed to be the "Galgacus" of Tacitus, who led an army to Alba, to aid the Scots and Picts against the Romans, and was defeated by Agricola at the Grampion Hills. —See O'Halloran's History of Ireland, p. 217.

‡ Cahir Mór : This Monarch was King of Leinster in the beginning of the second century. He divided his great possessions amongst his thirty sons, in a Will called " The will of Cahir More," contained in the "Book of Leacan" and in the "Book of Ballymote." His posterity formed the principal families in Leinster : namely, the O'Connor "Faley," Princes of Offaley ; O'Dempsey, O'Dunn, O'Regan, MacColgan, O'Harty, MacMurrough, Kings of Leinster ; Cavenagh, O'Byrne, O'Toole, O'Murphy, O'Mulrian, or O'Ryan, O'Kinsellagh, O'Duffy, O'Dowling, O'Cormac, O'Muldoon, O'Gorman, O'Mullen, O'Mooney, and O'Brenan, chiefs in Kilkenny, etc.—CONNELLAN.

2 S

99. Æneas: his son; one of whose brothers, Cairbre, was the ancestor of *MacCarbery;* and another brother, Ceallach, was the ancestor of *Mulkeeran.*

100. Mugron: son of Æneas.
101. Ceneth : his son.
102. Flannegan (or Flanchadha): his son.
103. Conchobhar ("conchobhar:" Irish, *the helping warrior*): his son; a quo *O'Conchobhair Failge;* anglicised *O'Connor Faley.*
104. Maolmordha : his son.
105. Fionn : his son.
106. Congallach : his son.
107. Conchobhar: his son.
108. Braorban : his son.
109. Dunsleibhe : his son.
110. Congallach : his son.
111. Murtagh : his son.
112. Conaibhneach : his son.

113. Donoch : his son.
114. Murtagh : his son.
115. Maolmordha : his son.
116. Murtagh (of Kilkenny) : his son. Had five brothers—1. Flaitheartach ; 2. Tumaltach ; 3. Inreachtach ; 4. Irgalach ; 5. Cathasach.
117. Murtagh (of Dublin): his son.
118. Murtagh (of Carrig) : his son.
119. Murtagh Oge: his son.
120. Moroch : his son.
121. Calaoch : his son.
122. Conn: his son ; had a brother named Dermod.
123. Cahir: son of Conn; had a brother named Tirloch.
124. Patrick: son of Cahir; had two brothers—1. Cahir, 2. Brian.
125. Teige : son of Patrick.
126. Patrick O'Connor Faley: his son ; living in 1691.

O'CONNOR FALEY. (No. 9.)

Of America.

Arms: Same as " O'Connor Faley" (No. 8).

127. BRIAN : son of Patrick O'Connor Faley, who was living in 1691, and who is No. 126 on the (No. 8) "O'Connor Faley" pedigree.
128. John : his son; had a brother named Christopher. This John had two sons, namely:—1. Christopher; 2. Nicholas, of whom presently.

This Christopher was born *circa* 1759; went to India in 1783; returned to Ireland, and emigrated to America; he was living in Philadelphia in 1798; was twice married : first to . . . . . ; secondly to Ann Maria, daughter of Archibald, and sister of the late Judge Randall. Christopher died

27th April, 1820; most of his descendants returned to France ; his male line became extinct by the death of his son Arthur Emmett O'Connor, s. p., in 1880.
129. Nicholas: the second son of John ; born 1785; was educated in France; emigrated to America and was living in Philadelphia, where, in 1809, he married Sarah, granddaughter of General Ross; he d. 28th Jan., 1822.
130. John-Christopher, of New York City : son of Nicholas; b. 9th March, 1811 ; m. 24th Dec., 1838, Elizabeth, dau. of Captain Richard and Harriet (Miles) Hepburn; living in 1883.

131 John-Christopher O'Connor, of New York City, Alderman, living in 1886: eldest son of John-Christopher; b. 20th Aug., 1847; m. 15th Nov.,1881, Maria-Jephson,* dau. of Colonel Henry A. V. Post, of New York City, by his wife Maria Farquhar Taylor, dau. of George Elliott Taylor, of the Taylors of Pennington, England.

O'DONEL. (No. 1.)

Princes† of Tirconnell.

Arms : Or, issuing from the sinister side of the shield an arm fessways vested az. cuffed ar. holding in the hand ppr. a cross crosslet fitchée gu. *Motto :* In hoc signo vinces.

CONALL GULBAN, a brother of Eoghan who is No. 88 on the (No. 1) " O'Neill" (of Tyrone) pedigree, was the ancestor of *O'Domhnaill*, of Tirconnell; anglicised *O'Donel, O'Donell, O'Donnell,* etc.

88. Conall Gulbhan: son of Niall Mór, the 126th Monarch of Ireland.

89. Fergus Ceanfada: his son.

90. Sedna (seadnach): his son (" sead :" Irish, *a jewel*).

91. Fergus (2): his son; had a younger brother named Ainmireach.

92. Lughach: his son.

93. Ronan: his son.

94. Garbh [garv]: his son.

95. Ceannfola: his son.

96. Maolduin: his son.

97. Arnall: his son.

98. Ceannfola (2): his son.

99. Muirceartach: his son. Had a brother named Maolduin, and another Fiaman.

100. Dalach: his son; a quo *Siol n-Dalaigh*.

101. Eignechan: his son.

102. Domhnall (" domhan :" Irish, the *world*, " all," *mighty*): his son ; a quo *O'Domhnaill*, and *Muintir‡ Domhnaill* of the county Clare.

103. Cathbharr: his son.

104. Giollachriosd: his son.

105. Cathbharr (2): his son.

106. Conn: his son.

107. Teige: his son.

108. Aodh (or Hugh): his son.

109. Domhnall [Donal]: his son.

110. Donoch (or Doncha): his son.

111. Eignechan: his son.

112. Donal Mór: his son.

113. Donal Oge: his son.

114. Hugh: his son.

115. Neal Garbh: his son; died 1380.

116. Tirloch an Fiona (" anfiona :" Irish, *of the Wine*): his son ; Chief of Tirconnell): died 1422. Had eighteen sons.

* *Jephson :* For the lineage of this family, see Burke's Peerage, title "Norreys ;" and for the lineage of the *Taylors* of Pennington, England, see Burke's Landed Gentry, and History of the Commoners.

† *Princes :* The O'Donnells, were inaugurated as Princes of Tirconnell, on the rock of Doune, at Kilmacrenan ; and had their chief castle at Donegal. —CONNELLAN.

‡ *Muintir Domhnaill :* See Note " Niall Garbh," in pp. 644-645.

117. Niall Garbh* (2), C.T. (or Chief of Tirconnell) : his son ; died in captivity, in the Isle of Man, in 1439.

118. Hugh Ruadh, C.T. : his son ; d. 1497.

119. Hugh Dubh, C.T. : his son ; d. 1537.

* *Niall Garbh :* In O'Ferrall's *Linea Antiqua*, compiled about A.D. 1709, it is stated that this Niall " had an elder brother named Shane-a-Loirg (or Shane of Lurg), who was banished by his father from Tirconnell, and who settled in Tipperary ; and that from this Shane the O'Donnells of Tipperary, Clare, and Limerick, are descended." But O'Ferrall cites no authority for those assertions, namely :—1. That Shane was the eldest son ; 2. that he was banished ; 3. that he settled in Tipperary ; 4. that the O'Donnells in Tipperary, Clare, and Limerick are his descendants.

In Betham's *Antiquarian Researches,* published in 1826, it is said : " Tirloch an-Fhiona had eighteen sons—Shane, the eldest, having given offence to his father, was banished, and settled in the county Tipperary, where his descendants still exist." This statement was taken by Betham from the *Linea Antiqua.*

The evidence of the Records and of the Genealogies is, we find, opposed to that statement ; for they show that Shane of Lurg was not only *not* the eldest son, but they render it doubtful that he was even legitimate. According to the loose notions of the period, all sons, whose mothers had been married, even though a previous wife was living, were considered as Heirs or *Roydamnas*, i.e. were eligible to be Tanists and Chiefs. Thus, O'Clery, in his Book of Pedigrees, p. 20, deposited in the Royal Irish Academy, Dublin, recognises these distinctions in recording, at length, the family of Tirlogh :—

" The eighteen sons of Tirlogh an-Fhiona were—By the daughter of Niall Mór O'Niall, Niall and Naghtan, who succeeded as Kings of Cinell Conail, and Donel, who was a *Roydamna*. Manus, who was the son of a daughter of O'Doherty ; he was also a *Roydamna*. Egneghan, son of the daughter of Conor (the Hospitable) O'Doherty ; he was also a *Roydamna*. Conor. son of the daughter of John Mór O'Connor ; he was a *Roydamna*, also. (Here the Roydamnas or Heirs cease.) Hugh and Neil Beg were the two sons of the daughter of McMailin. Donogh of the Wood was the son of the daughter of Teige Oge O'Durneen Shane of Lurg was the son of the daughter of the son of Fergus O'Boyle." . . . . And so on to the end of the eighteen sons of Tirloch an-Fhiona.

Duald MacFirbis, in p. 153 of his "Book of Genealogies" (deposited in the Royal Irish Academy, Dublin), gives a brief outline of the sons of Tirlogh-an-Fhiona, naming seven of them, of whom Shane of Lurg is placed last :

" Nial Garv, the son of Tirlogh ; whose brothers were—Naghten and Donel, Hugh. Egneghan, Donogh, Conor, and Shane of Lurg."

Whenever sons, who were Roydamnas, grew up to man's estate, they always took a prominent part in leading their Clans in battle. and thus the sons, Niall and Naghtan and Donel are frequently mentioned in the Annals of the Four Masters, as in the years 1398, 1420, 1421, 1422 ; but nowhere is there mention of Shane of Lurg, his name never appears even once in the Annals. We cannot see how that fact can be accounted for, if Shane of Lurg were the eldest son ; unless on the supposition that he was banished in his youth, before he could take a prominent part in the events of his day. But this supposition is destroyed by the fact that he lived in Donegal, to leave a long family after him, namely—" Art and John, the two eldest, Godfrey, Dermod, and Niall." (See O'Clery's *Irish Pedigrees*, p. 20, where Shane's descendants are given for three generations.)

Again, supposing that he was banished, we may ask how comes it that Shane's sons never asserted their prior claims, if he were the eldest son, nor struggled for the Chieftainship, which they would be sure to do, as the history of those times proves by abundant instances.

In the eleventh and twelfth centuries, when family sirnames came be to adopted in Ireland, the name *O'Donnell* came, we would say, into use in West Munster and South Leinster, as well as in Donegal, without any affinity of common origin ; just as a southern family took the name of " O'Connor," which was totally distinct from the O'Connors of Connaught, or the O'Connors of Offaley, etc. In the Annals we read that the O'Donnell, of Leinster, was slain, A.D. 1161, in an attack on the foreigners of Wexford. In 1158, O'Donnell, lord of Corca Bhaiscin, was slain. In 1090, Mael-

120. Manus :* his son ; d. 1555.

121. Calbhach : his son ; C.T., from 1555 to 1556. Had a younger brother named Sir Hugh, who was chief of Tirconnell, and who d. in 1592. This Sir Hugh had two sons —1. Hugh Ruadh (roe], who was Chief of Tirconnell from 1592 to 1602, and who was, according to Froude, poisoned on the 9th of October, 1602, at the castle of Simancas, in Spain, by James Blake, who, at the instigation of the President of the English in Munster, sailed from Cork for that purpose ; and 2. Rory, Earl of Tirconnell, in 1603, who died in Rome, in 1608. This Rory had a son named Hugh, who was Page to the Infanta of Flanders, 1618 ; and was known as "Earl of Tirconnell."

122. Conn : son of Calbhach, unsuccessfully contested the chieftainship of Tirconnell with his uncle Sir Hugh, above mentioned. This Conn, who died in 1583, had three sons—1. Sir Nial Garbh [garv], who was ancestor of *O'Donnell*, of Newport-Mayo ; 2. Hugh Buidhe, ancestor of *O'Donnell*, of Larkfield, county Leitrim ; and 3. Conn Oge, ancestor

of *O'Donel* of Oldcastle and Castlebar, in the county Mayo, and of *O'Donnell*, of Spain and of Austria.

123. Sir Nial Garbh : eldest son of Conn ; contested the chieftainship with Hugh Ruadh ;† who, as above stated, died in Spain, in 1602 : in which year Sir Nial Garbh was inaugurated "chief of Tirconnell." He was afterwards, in 1608, imprisoned in the Tower of London, where he died in 1626.

124. Manus : his son ; a Colonel in the army of Owen Ruadh O'Neill ; was killed at the battle of Benburb, in 1646.

125. Rory (or Roger), of Lifford, in the county of Donegal: his son ; was transplanted to the county Mayo by Oliver Cromwell.

126. Col. Manus O'Donnell, of Newport-Mayo : his son ; admitted to benefit of Limerick Treaty, in 1698 ; died in 1737. This Manus had two sons—1. Charles (called Calbhach Ruadh), and 2. Hugh, of Newport-Mayo : This Charles, who died in 1770, had three sons—1. Manus, a Major-General in the Austrian service, who died in 1793, was buried at Strade, in Mayo,

mordha, son of O'Donnell, King of Ui-Cinnsealigh, was slain ; and so on with similar entries, showing that, for centuries before Shane of Lurg existed, there were O'Donnells in the South of Ireland—doubtless the progenitors of the families of that name now existing there.

* *Manus* : This is the Manus O'Donnell, Chief or Prince of Tirconnell, who made with Teige O'Connor (Sligo) the stipulations mentioned in the Paper in the Appendix headed—"Wardership of Sligo ;" which was written in the Abbey of Donegal, on the 23rd day of June, 1539.

† *Hugh Ruadh* : Dalton, in his *King James's Army List*, speaking of Captain (or Colonel) Manus O'Donnell, of the Earl of Antrim's regiment, says that a Daniel O'Donnell was, in December, 1688, appointed a Captain in the Royal Service, and in 1689 authorised to rank as Colonel. That Captain Daniel O'Donnell was son of Turlogh, son of Caffer, son of Hugh Ruadh or Red Hugh O'Donnell, who was called "The Achilles of the Irish Race." In Doctor O'Donovan's Memoirs of the family he has noticed the gallant services on the Continent in the French Army, of the said Captain O'Donnell, till 1719, when he was made a Brigadier-General. He afterwards retired to St. Germain en Laye, where he died without issue on the 7th July, 1735, aged 70 years. This officer is remarkable as having been the possessor of the celebrated O'Donnell *relique*, called the *cathach of St. Columbkille* ; for an account of which see Sir William Bethan's *Antiquarian Researches,* and O'Callaghan's *Irish Brigades.*

obiit s. p. m.; 2. Conn; and 3. Lewis, of Rosslands, who died in 1822—aged 108 years. This Lewis had a son named Lewis, who died in 1841; and this last mentioned Lewis had a son named Charles, who died in 1853, *s.p.* Thus the line of Charles (called Calbhach Ruadh) became extinct.

127. Hugh O'Donnell, of Newport-Mayo: second son of the aforesaid Col. Manus O'Donnell.

128. Sir Neal ODonnell, of Newport-Mayo: his son; created a "baronet," in 1780; died 1811.

129. Sir Neal O'Donnell, the second baronet: his son. This Sir Neal had two sons—1. Sir Hugh, who was the third baronet, and who died in 1828, *s. p. m.*; 2. Sir Richard.

130. Sir Richard O'Donnell, of Newport-Mayo, the fourth baronet: second son of Sir Neal; died 1878. This Richard had two sons—1. George; 2. Richard, who died *s. p. m.*

131. Sir Geogre O'Donell, of Newport-Mayo, fifth baronet: the elder son of Sir Richard; born in 1832, and living. in 1887. (The *Arms* of this branch of the family are: Gu. issuing from the sinister side a cubit sinister arm vested az. cuffed or, the hand ppr. grasping a cross fitchée of the third.)

O'DONEL. (No. 2)

Of Oldcastle and Castlebar.

Arms: Per saltire or and gu. issuing from the dexter side in fess an arm sleeved of the first, with the hand ppr. in the centre, holding in pale a passion cross of the second.

CONN OGE O'DONNELL, another younger brother of Sir Nial Garbh who is No. 123 on the "O'Donnell" (of Newport-Mayo) pedigree, was the ancestor of *O'Donel*, of Oldcastle and Castlebar, in the county Mayo; and of *O'Donell*, of Austria and Spain.

123. Conn Oge: son of Conn; killed at the siege of Donegal Castle, in 1601.

124. Manus: his son; a Colonel under Owen Roe O'Neill.

125. Calbhach Ruadh: his son; a Colonel in the Royalist Army Wars of King Charles the Second; settled in the county Mayo.

126. Hugh, of Oldcastle, in the county of Mayo: his son.

127. Charles (called Calbhach Dubh), of Oldcastle: his son. This Charles had three sons—1. Manus, of Wilford Lodge, born in 1720; 2. Joseph, who was a Lieutenant-General in the Spanish service; 3. Henry, who was a Major-General in the Austrian service.

128. Manus, of Wilford Lodge: son of Charles. This Manus had two sons—1. Joseph; 2. Charles, who was a General of Cavalry in the Austrian service, and who died of wounds in 1805, *s.p.*

129. Joseph: son of said Manus; a Captain in the Spanish service; died in Santa Cruz.

130. Joseph (2), of Castlebar, in the county Mayo: his son; born

in 1780, died in 1834. This Joseph had three sons—1. Manus, who died in 1857, *s. p.* ; 2. Charles ; 3. Lewis, who died in 1862. This Lewis had two sons—1. Manus, born in 1858 ; 2. Charles, born in 1860—both living in 1887.

131. Charles Joseph O'Donel, of 47 Leeson-street, Dublin, Barrister, Chief Magistrate Dublin Metropolitan Police: second son of Joseph ; born in 1818, and living in 1887.

132. Manus O'Donel : his son ; born in 1871, and living in 1887.

O'DONELL. (No. 3.)

Of Leitrim and Greyfield.

Arms : Same as "O'Donell" of Newport.

HUGH BUIDHE [boy], brother of Sir Nial Garbh [garv] who is No. 123 on the "O'Donnell" (Princes of Tirconnell) genealogy, was the ancestor of this branch of that family.

123. Hugh Buidhe : second son of Con ; d. 1649.

124. John : his son ; died 1665. Had two sons :

  I. Hugh, who was called *Balldearg O'Domhnaill* ("balldearg:" Irish, *red spot*), was living in 1690 ; was Chief of his name in 1701 ; and left no issue.

  II. Connell.

125. Connell: second son of John ; appointed Lieutenant of the county Donegal, by King James the Second, in 1689.

126. Hugh, of Larkfield, county Leitrim : his son ; d. 1754. This Hugh had three sons :

  I. Conal Count O'Donel, Knight Grand Cross of the Order of Maria Theresa ; Governor-General of Transylvania ; and a Field Marshal in the Austrian Service. He d. unm. in 1771.

  II. John, Count O'Donel, a General in the same service, who had :

    I. Hugh, a Major in the Austrian Service, who was killed at Nervinden.

  III. Con, of Larkfield.

127. Con, of Larkfield : third son of Hugh. This Con had two sons :

  I. Hugh, of Greyfield, of whom presently.

  II. Con, of Larkfield.

128. Hugh, of Greyfield, county Roscommon : the elder son of Con ; d. in 1848, aged 84 years. This Hugh had three sons :

  I. Con, of whom presently.

  II. Hugh.

  III. Robert.

129. Con: eldest son of Hugh of Greyfield ; d. in 1825. This Con had an only child :

130. The Rev. Constantine O'Donel, A.B., formerly Vicar of St. Peter's, Allenheads, but lately (1883) Rector of Thockrington, and Minister of Kirkheaton, Northumberland, England. This Rev. Constantine had two sons and two daughters :

  I. Constantine-Richard-Annesley, of whom presently.

II. Hugh Roe, b. in 1861.
I. Mary.
II. Rose.
The three children living in 1883.

131. Constantine-Richard-Anthony O'Donel: elder son of the Rev. Constantine O'Donel; b. in 1851.

O'DONEL. (No. 4.)

Of Larkfield, county Leitrim ; and Greyfield, county Roscommon.

Arms : Same as " O'Donel" (No. 3.)

CON, a younger son of Con who is No. 127 on the foregoing (No. 3) "O'Donel" (of Leitrim and Greyfield) pedigree, was the ancestor of this branch of that family.

128. Con, of Larkfield : second son of Con ; d. *circa*, 1835.
129. John, of Larkfield : his son : d. 1874.

130. Hugh O'Donel, of Larkfield : his son ; b. 1844. Had a younger brother named John, born in 1862 : both living in 1877.

O'DONELL. (No. 5.)

Of Spain.

JOSEPH, the second son of Charles, of Oldcastle, in the county Mayo, who is No. 127 on the (" O'Donel") pedigree (No. 2), was the ancestor of *O'Donell*, of Spain.

127. Charles, of Oldcastle, near Swineford, county Mayo.
128. Joseph : his second son ; a Lieutenant-General in the Spanish Service ; b. in 1722. This Joseph had four sons—1. José, who was a General in the Spanish Service, a Captain-General of Castile, a K.G.C. St. Ferdinand, and died in 1836, *s.p.m. ;* 2. Carlos, who was a Lieutenant-General, a K.G.C. St. Ferdinand, and died in 1830 ; 3. Alejandro, who was a Colonel in the Spanish Service, and died in 1837 ; 4. Henrique, Conde de Abisbal, a Lieutenant-General in the Spanish Service ; Regent in 1812 ; died in 1833. This Henrique's only son Leopoldo, was a Captain in the Spanish Royal Guards, and was shot in 1833, *s. p. ;* and the Alejandro here mentioned, who died in 1837, left a son named José, who was born in 1806, and died in 1882. This José had two sons—1. José (born in 1846), a Captain of Infantry ; 2. Leopoldo (born in 1853), also a Captain of Infantry— both sons living in 1887.
129. Carlos : second son of Joseph ;

died in 1820; had two sons—1. Carlos, and 2. Leopoldo, who was Duke of Tetuan, and a field-marshal in the Spanish Service. This Leopoldo died in 1867, *s. p.*

130. Carlos (2): eldest son of Carlos; was a General of Cavalry; killed in 1835, aged 33 years.

131. Carlos (3) : his son; second Duke of Tetuan; late Spanish Minister at Vienna; born in 1834, and living in 1887. This Carlos had then three sons—1. Carlos; 2. Juan, b. 1864; 3. Leopoldo, b. in 1874—all three living in 1887.

132. Carlos O'Donell, of Spain : son of Carlos, Duke of Tetuan, born 1863, and living in 1887.

O'DONELL. (No. 6.)

Of Austria.

HENRY, the third son of Charles (of Oldcastle in the county Mayo) who is No. 127 on the " O'Donel" of Oldcastle and Castlebar pedigree, was the ancestor of *O'Donell*, of Austria.

128. Henry: son of Charles; a Major-General in the Austrian Service.

129. Joseph Count O'Donell: his son; was Minister of Finance to the Emperor Francis the Second.

130. Maurice, Count O'Donell: his son; Field-Marshal-Lieutenant; died in 1843. This Maurice had two sons—1. Maximilian, Count O'Donnell, who saved the life of the Emperor, in 1853; and 2. Maurice, born in 1815, and living in 1887. This last named Maurice had then two sons—1. Henry, born 1845; and 2. Hugo, born in 1858; both living in 1887, together with Henry's son, who is named Rory, and was born in 1871.

131. Maximilian, Count O'Donell: a Major-General: elder son of Maurice; was born in 1812, and living in 1887.

O'DONNELL. (No. 7.)

Lords of Clankelly.

Arms : Same as " O'Hart" (No. 1).

DONALL, who is No. 99 on the " O'Hart" pedigree, was the ancestor of *O'Domhnaill*, of Clankelly, in the county Fermanagh; also anglicised *MacDonnell*, *MacDonald*, *Daniel*, and *MacDaniel*.

99. Donall ("domhan :" Irish, *the world ;* and "all," *mighty*) : son of Colga : a quo *O'Domhnaill.*

100. Art : his son.

101. Fionnachtach : his son.

102. Lachnan ("lachna :" Irish, *yellow*) : his son ; a quo *O'Lachnain* of Fermanagh, anglicised *Loughnan.*

103. Teige : his son.

104. Fearmorradh [farmor-ra], literarally "the great speaking man :" his son.

105. Teige (2) : his son.

106. Flannagan O'Donnell, of Clankelly : his son.

O'DOWD.*

Princes of Hy-Fiachra, in Connaught.

Arms : Vert a saltire or, in chief two swords in saltire, points upwards, the dexter surmounted of the sinister ar. pommels and hilts gold.

FIACHRA Ealg, brother of Eocha Breac who is No. 89 on the "O'Shaughnessy" pedigree, was the ancestor of *O'Dubhda ;* anglicised *Doody, Dowd, Dowde, O'Dowd,* and *O'Dowda.*

89. Fiachra Ealg : son of Dathi, the 127th Monarch of Ireland.

90. Maoldubh : his son.

91. Tiobrad : his son ; had a younger brother named Tiomain Murios.

92. Donoch : son of Tiobrad.

93. Olioll : his son.

94. Cathal : his son.

95. Duncatha : his son.

96. Conmac : his son. This Conmac had two sons—1. Dubhda ; 2.

---

* *O'Dowd* : Of this ancient family is (in 1887) the Rev. Patrick Dowd, the venerable pastor of St. Patrick's, Montreal, Canada ; whose Golden Jubilee was on the Feast of the Ascension, in May last, celebrated by the Irish Catholics of Montreal.

The Reverend Patrick Dowd was born in 1813, of respectable and well-to-do parents, at the inland village of Dunleer, county Louth, Ireland, and is consequently seventy-four years of age. From his earliest childhood he was remarkable for his piety, and his heart continually burned with an ardent desire to give his life up in the service of God. His good parents were not slow in noticing this, and immediately sent him to pursue his classical studies at Newry college, after which the young ecclesiastic was sent to study theology in the Irish college at Paris. In 1837 he saw his fondest hopes realized, and was ordained priest by the Archbishop of Paris, Monseigneur Quelen.

The young priest returned to his native land soon after his ordination, and pursued his priestly functions for ten years in different sections of the country. In 1847 he joined the illustrious order of St. Sulpice, of which he is to-day one of the most esteemed members, and in 1848 he bade an affectionate farewell to the green hills of his beloved Ireland, and set sail for distant Canada. After a long passage Father Dowd landed in Montreal, a very small town at that remote date, and immediately after entered upon his ministerial duties in connection with St. Patrick's Church. For nearly forty years this distinguished clergyman has been working assiduously for the spiritual and temporal welfare of the people of St. Patrick's parish, as well as for the Irish citizens in general throughout Montreal, who have known him so long and so well.

The year after his arrival in this country Father Dowd founded the St. Patrick's

Caomhan ("caomh:" Irish, *gentle;* Arab. "kom," *noble;* Lat. "com-is,") who was the ancestor of *O'Caomhain.* (See the "Coen" pedigree).

97. Dubhda ("dubhda:" Irish, *dark-complexioned*): son of Conmac; a quo *O'Dubhda.*

98. Ceallach: his son.

99. Aodh (or Hugh): his son.

100. Maolruanaidh [mulroona]: his son.

101. Malachi: his son; had a brother named Donall.

102. Niall (or Neal): his son.

103. Talach: his son.

104. Hugh (2): his son.

105. Murtagh: his son.

106. Hugh (3): his son.

107. Talach (2): his son.

108. Hugh (4): his son.

109. Donoch: his son.

110. Mulroona: his son.

111. Talach (3): his son.

112. Brian: his son.

113. Donall: his son.

114. Roger O'Dowd: his son. This Roger had two brothers—1. Teige Ruadh [roe]; 2. Malachi.

Orphan Asylum, which is to-day a splendid monument to the untiring devotion and charitable instincts of the aged priest. St. Bridget's Home and the Night Refuge were established through his energy in 1865, and the present commodious Home and Refuge on Lagauchetiere-street, built in 1866-67, and the handsome building known as the St. Patrick's School. Such are the buildings which owe their inception to the man whom his admiring countrymen have more than once designated Montreal's Irish Bishop.

Father Dowd has been repeatedly offered the highest dignities of the Church, but has always declined them, preferring to remain with his St. Patrick's congregation rather than wear the mitre—the Sees of Kingston and Toronto having been offered to him.

In 1877 he organized the great Irish pilgrimage to Lourdes and Rome, and everyone can recollect the painful anxiety that was felt when the vessel carrying the pilgrims and their beloved pastor was not heard of for several agonizing weeks. Prayers were offered in all churches without distinction of creed, a pleasing proof of the high appreciation in which the esteemed pastor is held by even those disbelieving in Catholicism. Father Dowd has more than once earned for himself the gratitude of his fellow-citizens by the loyal stand he has taken when the law of the land was menaced or when constituted authority was set at defiance, and the grandeur of his jubilee celebration to-day will be a fitting testimonial of the esteem in which he is held.

In the Note "Insurrection" (of 1798) under Thomas O'Cahan, No. 125 on the "Caine" pedigree, p. 373, *ante,* we mention about the Battle of Ballinamuck, and the chains of the French Magazine having been stolen by Keegan. A circumstance that occurred after that Battle was the hanging of a Mayo gentleman named Captain O'Dowd, a member of this family. When on the cart (for a cart was the scaffold employed on the occasion), Duke Crofton, of Mohill Castle, a royalist, addressing O'Dowd, said : "You have brought yourself to a nice pitch. I believe you're a gentleman, and that your father keeps a pack" (of hounds). O'Dowd replied : "Yes he keeps three packs, and his whippers-in are better gentlemen than you." Continuing, he said : "As I have to die, I shan't die like a trooper." His hands and arms were tied, yet he succeeded in removing his boots—one foot assisting the other. "Now," he said, "I am ready !"

David, the eldest son of David, THE O'DOWD, was an officer in the Irish Army of King James II., and was slain at the Battle of the Boyne. In stature he was more than seven feet. (All the O'Dowds, including the females, even to the present day are extra tall.)

James, next son of the THE O'DOWD, fought at the Boyne, Athlone, and Aughrim, where he was killed. When found among the dead, his hand was so swollen, that the guard of his sword had to be filed, before the hand could be extricated therefrom.

O'FLAHERTY.*

Princes of Iar (or West) Connaught.

Arms : Ar. two lions ramp. combatant, supporting a dexter hand couped at the wrist all gu. in base a boat with eight oars sa.

DUACH TEANG UMH ("teang-umh:" Irish, *brazen-tongue*), brother of Eochaidh Tiormach who is No. 92 on the "O'Connor" (Kings of Connaught) pedigree, was the ancestor of *O'Flaithbhearthaigh*, of West (or Iar) Connaught; anglicised *O'Flaherty, O'Fflahertie,* and *Flaherty.*

92. Duach Teangumh : son of Fergus.

93. Aodh (or Hugh) : his son.

94. Colga : his son.

95. Ceannfaola : his son.

96. Amhailgadh [awly] : his son.

97. Flann (or Florence) Robhadh : his son.

98. Fianngall : his son.

99. Flathnia : his son.

100. Moroch (also called Maonach): his son ; died A.D. 892.

101. Urban : his son.

102. Moriach : his son.

103. Maonach : his son.

104. Moriach (2) : his son.

105. Eimhin : his son.

106. Flaithbheartach ("flaith:"

Irish, *a lord ;* "beartach," *rich, wealthy*) : his son ; a quo *O'Flaithbhearthaigh,* of West Connaught; living, A.D. 970.

107. Maolculair : his son.

108. Moriach Mór : his son; first of this family that assumed this sirname.

109. Ruadhri (or Roger) : his son.

110. Hugh : his son.

111. Muireadach : his son.

112. Hugh : his son.

113. Roger : his son.

114. Murtagh : his son.

115. Donal : his son. Had two sons—1. Hugh Mór; 2. Brian : the stem of the family descended from each of these sons is, as follows :

116. Hugh (4) Mór : his son.

117. Donal (2) : his son.

118. Owen : his son.

119. Owen (2) Oge : his son.

120. Morogh : his son.

121. Gillduffe : his son.

122. Donal : his son.

123. Morogh : his son.

124. Sir Morogh : his son.

125. Morogh O'Flaherty : his son.

116. Brian : son of Donal.

117. Morogh : his son.

118. Donal : his son.

119. Roger (3) : his son.

120. Roger (4) : his son.

121. Morogh : his son.

122. Roger : his son.

123. Teige : his son.

124. Donal : his son.

125. Sir Morogh : his son.

126. Teige : his son.

127. Bryan : his son.

128. Col-Morogh : his son; who died, A.D. 1652.

129. Bryan O'Flaherty : his son.

At page 362, in O'Flaherty's *West Connaught,* by Hardiman, this family genealogy is more fully given.

* *O'Flaherty :* The Breitheamh or Judge to O'Flaherty of Iar Connaught, was

O'FLANAGAN. (No. 1.)

Of Fermanagh.

Arms : Ar. a sinister hand couped at the wrist affrontée gu.

CAIRBRE, son of Niall of the Nine Hostages, the 126th Monarch of Ireland and who is No. 87 on the (No. 1) " O'Neill" (of Tyrone) pedigree, was the ancestor of *O'Flanagan*, of Tuatha Ratha (now the barony of " Magheraboy"), in the county Fermanagh.

88. Cairbre : son of Niall of the Nine Hostages.

89. Cormac Caoch : his son.

90. Tuathal Maolgarbh : his son. Some annalists make this Tuathal the 132nd Monarch of Ireland.

91. Cormac (2): his son ; had a brother named Garbhan, who was the ancestor of *Carleton*.

92. Donall Dunn ("d u n n :" Irish, *a doctor*) : his son.

93. Flann : his son.

94. Maolruanaidh : his son.

95. Malachi : his son.

96. Lochlann : his son.

97. Ardgal : his son.

98. Longseach : his son.

99. Flannagan (" flann :" Irish, *blood*), meaning the "red faced little

man :" his son ; a quo *O'Flannagain*, of Ulster, anglicised *O'Flanagan*.

100. Padraic : his son.

101. Brian : his son.

102. Donall an-Fhiona (or Donall of the Wine): his son.

103. Hugh : his son.

104. Dermod : his son.

105. Cormac an-Neach (or Cormac the Apparition) : his son.

106. Aodh (or Hugh) : his son.

107. Dermod Balbh : his son.

108. Brian (2) : his son.

109. Cormac (4) : his son ; had a brother named Hugh.

110. Murtogh : son of Cormac.

111. Giollaiosa Ruadh : his son.

112. Cormac (5) : his son.

113. Giollabrighid : his son.

114. Manus : his son.

O'Maoilampail written by Duald MacFirbis *O'Maoilfabhuill*, pronounced " O'Mullawill," and anglicised *Lavelle.*

Roderic O'Flaherty, historian and antiquary, was born at Moycullen Castle, Galway, in 1629. His father, Hugh, who was last chief of the race, died when Roderic was an infant. He was educated by Dr. Lynch, author of *Cambrensis Eversus,* and was intimate with Duald MacFirbis, of Lecan. Roderic devoted his life to the study of the history and antiquities of Ireland. He had scarcely arrived at manhood when, in 1652, without having taken any part in politics, he was included in the general Cromwellian proscription. On appeal to the Parliamentary Commissioners sitting at Athlone, he was allowed a portion of his estates in West Connaught, but it was so burdened with taxes and dues, that he was reduced to great destitution. He was disappointed in an alleviation of his circumstances at the Restoration, and wrote : " I live a banished man within the bounds of my native soil ; a spectator of others enriched by my birth-right ; an object of condoling to my relatives and friends, and a condoler of their miseries." His first important work was a reply to Doctor Borlace's *History of the Rebellion.* He also wrote *A Description of West Connaught,* which was first published by the Irish Archæological Society, in 1846. His great work, the *Ogygia,* "remains a lasting monument of our author's learning and genius." His *Ogygia Vindicated,* which followed, remained in manuscript until published by Charles O'Connor, in 1775. O'Flaherty was of a commanding presence, and was proud of his blood and ancestry. He died in 1718, aged about 89 years, leaving an only son, Michael, to whom, in 1736, a portion of the family estates was restored.

115. Padraic : his son.
116. Hugh (3) : his son.
117. Murtogh (2) : his son.

118. Giolla (or William) O'Flanagan, of Tuatha Ratha : his son.

O'FLANAGAN. (No. 2.)

Of Orgiall.

Arms: Ar. a fess betw. three stags' heads cabossed gu.

FLANNAGAN, brother of Donallan who is No. 102 on the "Donnellan" pedigree, was the ancestor of *O'Flannagain*, of Clann Colla ; anglicised *O'Flanagan.*

102. Flannagan : son of Moroch ; a quo *O'Flannagain.**
103. Moreach : his son.
104. Cathal : his son.
105. Cugranna : his son.
106. Moreach (2) : his son.
107. Murtogh : his son.
108. Donall : his son.
109. Moreach (3) : his son.
110. Murtogh (2) : his son.
111. Flaitheartach : his son.
112. Murtogh (3) : his son.
113. Teige : his son.
114. Dermod : his son.

115. Jeoffry : his son. This Jeoffry had two brothers—1. Shane, a quo *Clann Shane* ;† 2. Connor.
116. Connor : son of Jeoffry.
117. Dermod : his son.
118. William : his son.
119. William Oge : his son ; had a brother named Malachi.
120. Edmond : son of William Oge ; had a brother named Teige.
121. Brian : son of Edmond.
122. Brian Oge O'Flanagan : his son.

O'FLYNN.

Of Connaught.

Arms: Ar. a dexter arm couped betw. two swords in pale all ppr.

CUORNAN (" corn : Irish, *a horn ;* Arab. " kurn," *a horn ;* Lat. " corn-u"), brother of Uadach, the 9th Christian King of Connaught who is No. 94

---

* *O'Flannagain* : For the derivation of this sirname see No. 99 on the foregoing genealogy.

† *Clan Shane* : The sirnames *Jacks* and *Johns* are considered to be derived from this " Clann Shane."

on the "O'Connor" (Connaught) pedigree, was the ancestor of *O'Flainn;* anglicised *O'Flynn, Flynn, Lynn,* and *Blood* (of Connaught).

94. C u o r n a n : son of A o d h Abraidh [abrad], the 8th Christian King of Connaught.

95. Maolruanaidh: his son; a quo *Siol Maolruana.*

96. Annadh : his son.

97. Eocha : his son.

98. Donoch : his son.

99. Moroch : his son.

100. Muireadach : his son.

101. Beolan ("beol:" Irish, *the mouth*) : his son; a quo *O'Beolain,* of Connaught, anglicised *Beolan* and *Boland.*

102. Donall : his son.

103. Flann ("flann :" Irish, *blood*), meaning "the man with the red complexion:" h i s s o n; a quo *O'Flainn,* and the name of the mountain called *Sliabh-ui-Fhloinn.*

104. Fothach : his son.

105. Feach O'Flynn : his son;

the first of the family that assumed this sirname.

106. Eocha (2) : his son.

107. Eachtighearnach : his son.

108. Flann (or Florence): his son.

109. Fiachrach : his son.

110. Giallbeartach (" giall :" Irish, *a hostage;* "beartach," *tricky*) : his son; a quo the sirname *O'Giallbeartaigh,* anglicised *Gilbert.*

111. David : his son.

112. Fiachrach (2) : his son.

113. Brian : his son; had a brother named Florence or Flann.

114. David (2) : his son.

115. Fiachrach (3) : his son.

116. Florence (2) : his son.

117. Fiachrach (4) : his son.

118. Melaghlin : his son.

119. Colla : his son.

120. Edmond O'Flynn : his son.

O'GORMAN. (No. 1.)

Chiefs of Ibrickan, County Clare.

Arms: Az. a lion pass. betw. three swords erect ar.   *Crest*: An arm embowed in armour, grasping in the hand a sword blade wavy, all ppr.

DAIRE, a younger brother of Ros Failgeach,* who is No. 90 on the No. 1 "O'Connor" (Faley) pedigree, was the ancestor of *MacGormain;* anglicised *MacGorman,*† *Gorman,* and *O'Gorman.*

90. Daire: second son of Cathair [Cahir] Mór, King of Leinster and the 109th Monarch of Ireland.

91. Feigh : his son; had a brother Breacan (*breacan:* Irish, " a party-coloured or striped stuff, an-

---

* *Failgeach :* This word is the root of the terms *Faley* (as in the name " O'Connor Faley,") *Phaley* and *Offaly ;* and *Ros Failgeach* (*Rosa:* Irish, " a rose ;" Lat. *rosa ; failge :* Irish, " an ouche," " a ring," " a jewel," " a wreath,") means " Ros of the Rings," etc.

† *MacGorman :* The MacGormans were originally located in Leinster. After their expulsion from Leinster, shortly after the English invasion, they were granted by O'Brien, Prince of Thomond, a territory in the barony of Ibrickan, co. Clare, where they settled.

ciently used by different people as their trowse* and cloaks" †), who was the ancestor of *Mulvy;* and a quo *O'Breacain,* anglicised *Bracken.*

92. Berchan : son of Feig ; had a brother Owen (Eoghan), who was the ancestor of *Mooney,* of Fermanagh.

93. Earc : son of Berchan ; had a brother St. Fiagh (12th October).

94. Æneas : son of Earc ; had a brother Dallan.

95. Eocha : son of Æneas.

96. Dermod : his son.

97. Cormac : his son.

98. Gorman : ‡ his son ; had a brother Cormac.

99. Donal : son of Gorman.

100. Suibhneach : his son.

101. Maoilmuire : his son.

102. Gobhgan : his son.

103. Eocha : his son.

104. Gorman ("gorm :" Irish, *illustrious*) : his son ; a quo *MacGormain.* A member of this family built *Caislean MacGormain,* in the co. Meath ;§ from which " Gormanstown" takes its name.

105. Dunagan : his son.

106. Gasan : his son.

107. Duach Dubh : his son.

108. Treasach : his son.

109. Aodh (or Hugh) : his son.

110. Donoch : his son.

111. Murtach : his son ; the first of the family that settled in Munster.

112. Gorman (3) : his son.

113. Scannall : his son.

114. Eachtighearnach : his son ; had a brother Maccraith.

115. Moroch (a corruption of the Irish *muirchu,* which signifies " a sea hound or warrior") : his son. This name has also been written "Murcha," and " Morogh."

116. C u m e i d ("m e a d," gen. " meid :" Irish, *bulk* or *bigness*) : his son ; a quo *O'Meid,* anglicised *Mead* and *Meade.*

117. Concobhar : his son.

118. Donal (2) : his son.

119. Cumeid (2) : his son.

120. Conbhach : his son.

121. David : his son.

122. Dathi : his son.

123. John : his son.

124. Dermod : his son ; had a brother Conbhach.

125. Donal : son of Dermod ; had a brother Melaghlin.

---

* *Trowse :* A *trouse* or *trowse* was a tight-fitting article of dress that comprised in one piece " britches, stockings, and socks or sandals." We read that Sir John Perrot, lord deputy of Ireland, would not admit members habited in the Irish mantle (or cloak) and trowse, to attend the Parliament he had convoked, A.D. 1586 ; and to induce those members summoned to that assembly to appear in English attire, he bestowed both " gownes and cloakes of velvet and satten on some of them :" a full dress, whatever it might be now, not being an inappropriate gift for a gentleman, at a time when a rich robe was often a most acceptable present to the Queen.—See *Ware.*

† *Cloaks :* From the Irish word *breac,* which means "speckled or of various colours," some of the Gauls were called *Galli Braccati,* and their country *Gallia Braccata.* Diodorus Siculus (*Lib.* 6,) mentions that the garments of those Gauls were rough and party-coloured ; and calls them *Braccœ.* Dr. O'Brien, in his Irish Dictionary, observes at the word " breacan," that the Irish Scots preserved this kind of garment up to his time (A.D. 1768). *Breac,* " a trout," is so called from the various colours of its skin.

‡ *Gorman :* This Gorman (No. 98) was, by Geoffry, of Monmouth, called " King Gurmandus," who invaded and devastated a large part of Britain, *circa* A.D. 593.

§ *Meath :* The migration of members of this family to Meath took place in the ninth century, where their descendants remained until the 15th century, when Gormanstown passed into the possession of the English family of Preston. It is very probable that the celebrated martyrologist, Marian or Maelmuiré O'Gorman, Abbot of Knock (Cnoc-na-napstol), near Louth, was of this branch of the family. In 1171 this Marian

126. Conbhach (2) : son of Donal.
127. Donal (3) : his son.
128. Maolseaghlainn (or Melaghlin) : his son.
129. Dermod (3) : his son.
130. Donal (4) : his son ; had a

brother named Cu-na-mBochd, who settled in the county Westmeath.
131. Melaghlin : his son.
132. Dermod (4) : his son.
133. Nicholas O'Gorman :* his son ; living in 1691.

O'Gorman composed a calendar generally known as the *Calendar of Marianus.* Though their property was lost to them, the Meath O'Gormans did not forsake their ancient district ; at the present time they are numerous in Monknewtown and Slane, but some of them in reduced circumstances. Slane had been their burial-place, and in that church-yard numerous tombstones belonging to them still exist. At the period of the Revolution the family had a respectable standing ; for, we find a member of it, a James O'Gorman, holding the position of a lieutenant in Lord Slane's Infantry regiment, in the service of King James II. From that James O'Gorman the descent to the present day is as follows :

1. James O'Gorman, Lieut. in Lord Slane's regiment. After the war he entered into trade as a timber-merchant, in Oxmantown—now Queen-st., Dublin.

2. Patrick *Gorman,* of Queen-street : his son ; dropped the prefix *O',* and m. Cecily Christie. Will dated 3rd Nov., 1744 ; directs his body to be buried in Slane, county Meath.

3. Thomas Gorman, of Queen-street : his son ; m. Mary ——, and d. intestate in January, 1785 ; was buried in Slane. He had an only son :

4. Thomas Gorman, of Queen-street, who m. Alice, daughter of —— Carberry, of Ballyleas, co. Dublin (descended from an "Innocent Papist" of the days of Charles II.) ; died July, 1836, and was buried in the new cemetery at Golden Bridge, near Dublin. His eldest son was :

5. Thomas Gorman, who m. Catherine Aungier, niece of the celebrated John

Keogh, of Mount Jerome, co. Dublin—the "Magog" of Wolfe Tone's *Memoirs.* (See Note * in p. 504 *ante.*) This Thomas Gorman's eldest son was :

6. Thomas *O'Gorman,* who resumed his Celtic prefix *O',* and m. Annabella, eldest daughter of Edmond Hanley, of Lakeview, co. Roscommon, (who, there is reason to believe was the head of the grand old family of Kinel Doffa, the patron saint of which was Saint Bearagh, whose Pastoral Staff known for ages in the co. Roscommon as the *Bachal Gear* (or short staff) was in said Hanley's possession until 1862 or 1863, when it passed into the collection of the Royal Irish Academy, Dublin, where it is now preserved.) This Thomas O'Gorman, of RathGorman, Sandymount, Dublin, has two sons and one daughter surviving in 1887, namely, 1. Victor, 2. Chamberlayne, and 1. Josephine.

* *Nicholas O'Gorman* : There was a Nicholas Purcell O'Gorman, who, in 1829, was Secretary of "The Catholic Association," of Ireland, who died in 1857, and whose genealogy down from "Mallacklin (or Melaghlin) McGorman," living in 1544, is as follows :

1. Mallacklin McGorman, who on the 31st day of December, 1544, obtained from King Henry VIII., a grant of the "Countrie of *Hy-Brecane*," now known as "Ibrickane."

2. Donal : his son ; obtained from Queen Elizabeth a grant of the advowsons of Kilmichil and Kilmurry, in the county Clare, bearing date the 25th day of Aug., 1570 ; was Sheriff of Thomond in 1572.

3. Donn : his son ; was Sheriff of Thomond in 1614 ; d. 1626.

4. Mahon : his son ; d. 1665.

5. Melaghlin : his son ; Sheriff of the co. Clare, in 1689 ; d. 1707.

6. Thomas : his son ; d. 1717.

7. Mahon (2) : his son ; d. 1741.

8. James : his son ; d. 1787.

9. Nicholas Purcell O'Gorman : his son ; d. 1857.

10. Nicholas Smith O'Gorman, of Bellevue, Kilrush, county Clare, J.P.: his son ; was sheriff in 1878. This Nicholas had a younger brother, Major Purcell O'Gorman ; and a sister, Susan, married to Major Edmund Moore Mulcahy, No. 124 on the "Mulcahy" pedigree : all living in 1881.

11. Nicholas : son of Nicholas ; a Capt. in the 10th Regiment, living in 1881.

2 T

O'GORMAN. (No. 2.)

Of Monamore, County Clare.

Arms : Same as " O'Gorman" (No. 1).

CONBHACH, a younger brother of Dermod who is No. 124 on the (No. 1) " O'Gorman" (Chiefs of Ibrickan) pedigree, was the ancestor of this family.

124. Conbhach: son of John. Had three sons—1. Melaghlin, 2. Dermod, 3. Donal; from whom, respectively, sprung the three houses of Cahir Morogher, Drumelie, and Tullychrin—all in the county Clare.

125. Melaghlin: his eldest son; m. a daughter of Roger O'Dea, of Tullydea (brother of Cornelius O'Dea, 15th Bishop of Limerick).

126. Donal: his son.

127. Melaghlin: his son; married Anne, dau. of Maccon MacNamara of Clancuillen.

128. Melaghlin: his son ; m. dau. of Terence MacMahon, lord of Corca Baiscind.

129. Donal: his son; m. dau. of MacMahon of Moyarta and Clonderla, in county Clare; built the castle of Morroghee.

130. Donus (or Daniel): his son ; m. daughter of Richard Gallery of Cregbrien, sirnamed "The Hospitable.'

131. Mathew: his son; m. dau. of MacMahon, of Doonbeg, near Kilkee. His brother Bonaventure was Abbot of Quin, in county Clare. Another brother Denis was Captain in the Confederate Armies against Cromwell; and (see Brodinus, p. 712) suffered martyrdom for his faith, in 1652.

132. Melaghlin: his son; married Jane, dau. of Richard Harold, of Ennis; distinguished himself in the Battles of the Boyne and Aughrim (1689). His son Loghlin Oge went to England with his kinsman Sir Donough O'Brien: this Loghlan held a commission in the Irish Army and also distinguished himself in the Battle of Aughrim. Thomas O'Gorman, of Inchiquin, brother of Melaghlin, left Ireland at this time and settled in France, at Tonnerre, in Burgundy; his grandson, the Chevalier O'Gorman, m. Marguerite d'Eon de Beaumont.

133. Donus (or Daniel): son of Melaghlin; m. Mary, daughter of Stephen Roche.

134. James: his son; born 1688, in the castle of Bunratty, co. Clare, and d. 1736; went in 1724 to live at Limerick. He married Christina (d. 1764), third dau. of Thomas Harold and Alicia Enright, and had four children, who were protected by their maternal uncle Lawrence Harold. The four children were—1. John, d. 1750; 2. Thomas ; 3. Michael, m. Rebecca Stackpoole, but died 1818 *s.p. ;* 4. Christina, m. William Wall and had two children—Thomas, and Christina, who m. a Mr. Stirling and had one daughter Christina.

135. Thomas: second son of James; b. 1724; went to England in 1747, and in 1764 m. Alicia, eldest dau. of Edmond Sexton and Alicia Nihell, and by her had fourteen children : I. Edmond-Sexton, born 1810.

I. Edmond-Sexton O'Gorman, b. 1810 ; Married Dorothy Munkhouse of Winton Hall, Kirby Stephen, Westmoreland, and at his marriage added the name *Munkhouse* to his own (*O'Gorman Munkhouse*). He lived in Switzerland, in the Chateau de Müncingen, and had five children : 1. Dorothy, died. 2. Thomas, died. 3. Jane. 4. Anna, m. to Amédée de Watteville, and (up to 1880) had six children (she, at her marriage, added her maiden name to her husband's ; her children are *de Watteville O'Gorman*). 5. Edmund Munkhouse ; two children.

II. Thomas-Harold, died 1880.

III. James, died.

IV. Michael-Arthur, who is No. 136 *infra*.

V. William, died unm. 26th Dec., 1857 ; buried at Chelsea.

VI. and VII. Twins : Sylvester, died 1777 ; Charles, 1778.

VIII. James-Denis, died at Limerick, 1797.

IX. Charles-Thaddeus, born 27th May, 1785, and died 23rd Sept. 1853. Was appointed consul-general of Mexico in 1826 ; m. Anita Noriego y Vicario (sister of the Marchioness di Vivanco, and General Moran), and had seven children : 1. John, born 1827 ; married his cousin Anita Santiago Moreno. 2. Eustace-Harrold. 3. Miguel. 4. Francis. 5. Anita. 6. Teresa. 7. Maria, died 1869.

X. George, m. Elizabeth Barry, and had one son—George, who died without issue.

XI. Catherine, died 1771.

XII. Alicia, died unmarried 3rd August, 1846.

XIII. Maria-Christina, m. James Tobin of Cumsinagh, Chevalier de St. Louis, commandant du Chateau de Nantes, and had served for many years in the Irish Brigade in his cousin Victe. Walsh de Serrant's Regiment. She had five children : 1. Alicia, died 1874. 2. Maria. 3. Edmond, died. 4. James, married Irmenilde, dau. of Colonel d'Almaida-Allen, and had a son in the "Garde Imperiale"—James. 5. Emily, died at Nantes, 1871.

XIV. Margaret, d. in a convent at Liege.

136. Michael-Arthur : fourth son of Thomas ; m. in 1810, Miss Chare, and by her (who died 1821) had six children :

I. Michael-Harold, b. 12th Jan., 1817, died 1840, serving in the French Army against the Arabs in Algeria.

II. Edmond-Anthony, No. 137 on this pedigree.

III. Maria Christina, born 11th December, 1811.

IV. Catherine-Lutetia, born 30th March, 1814.

V. Mary-Emily, born 1818 ; m. William Garrett Roope, and had one son William, ordained priest in 1871.

VI. Louisa, died an infant, 1816.

137. Edmond-Anthony O'Gorman, of Monamore, county Clare : second son of Michael-Arthur ; b. 6th Oct., 1820, and living in 1881. He m. in Jan., 1856, Sophia Pereira (who died October, 1863), and by her had five children :

I. Joseph-Vincent, born 21st May, 1857 ; made his vows in the Society of Jesus, in London, July, 1877.

II. Francis-Edmond, born 17th November, 1859.

III. Ignatius-Thomas, born 31st July, 1860 ; in the Society of Jesus, 7th September, 1880.

IV. Mary-Alicia, d. an infant 1871.

V. Mary, born 11th Oct., 1863.

In 1865 he m. Ellen, daughter of Capt. Edward Whyte, R.N.,

of Loughbrickland, and by her (who died in Nov., 1867) had one son:

VI. Edmond-John Whyte.

In 1871 he m. Margaret Barclay, eldest daughter of Mervyn Archdall Nott Crawford (see the "Crawford" pedigree), of Millwood, county Fer-

managh, and by her had three children:

VII. Mervyn Archdall, born 19th December, 1871.

VIII. Cecil Carleton Crawford, born 6th April, 1873.

IX. Bernardine Beauchamp-Col-clough, born 1st Nov., 1874.

O'HAGAN.

Lords of Tullaghoge, County Tyrone.

Arms : Quarterly : ar. and az. in 1st quarter a shoe ppr. on a canton per chev. gu. and erm three covered cups or ; in 2nd quarter a flag of the first charged with a dexter hand of the fourth ; in third quarter a lion ramp. of the sixth ; and in the fourth a fish naiant ppr.

FERGUS, a son of Niall of the Nine Hostages, the 126th Monarch of Ireland, who is No. 87 on the (No. 1) "O'Neill" (Princes of Tyrone) pedigree, was the ancestor of *O'h-Again ;* anglicised *O'Hagan.*

88. Fergus: son of Niall of the Nine Hostages.

89. Caolbath : his son.

90. Cairbre : his son.

91. Felim : his son.

92. Dermod : his son.

93. Conall Bracaidh : his son.

94. Cuanach : his son.

95. Dongaile : his son.

96. Cumuscach : his son.

97. Oilioll : his son.

98. Maolgarbh : his son.

99. Cionaoth : his son.

100. Ogau (also called Agan): his son ; a quo *O'h-Ogain*, of Ulster, and *O'h-Again* ("ogan:" Irish, *a youth*), anglicised respectively *O'Hogan* and *O'Hagan.**

101. Eoghan (or Owen) : his son.

102. Giolla Easbuig ("giolla :" Irish, *the devoted of ;* "easbog," gen. "easbuig," *a bishop*—Lat. "episcop-us") : his son ; a quo *O'Giollaeasbuig*, anglicised *Gillaspy*, *Gillespy*, *Gillesby*, and *MacAnaspie.*

103. Flann O'Hagan: his son ; the first that assumed this sirname.

104. Aodh (or Hugh): his son.

105. Ranall : his son.

106. Owen (2): his son.

107. Maolruanaidh : his son.

108. Maolseachlainn (or Melaghlin): his son.

109. Amhailgadh [awly) : his son.

110. Teige: his son.

111. Owen (3): his son.

112. Hugh (2) : his son.

113. Giollachriosd : his son.

† *O'Hagan :* One of the O'Hagans, of Tirowen acquired territorial hold and standing in Meath by marrying into the family of "O'Melaghlin," of that ancient kingdom. Walter DeLacy having by charter secured to the said O'Hagan all his acquired territorial rights, titles, and interests in Meath, O'Hagan changed his name to *Fagan ;* and thereafter was a devoted follower of the standard and fortunes of his Anglo-Norman friend and protector. Thus we see that "Fagan" is of Irish, and *not* of English, descent.

114. Teige (2) : his son.

115. Roger: his son.

116. Donall : his son.

117. Tirlogh : his son.

118. Teige (3) : his son.

119. Niall : his son.

120. Brian : his son.

121. Tirlogh (2) : his son; living 1601.*

122. Giollachriosd (2) : his son.

123. Shane† (or John): his son.

124. Hugh (3): his son; died in 1708.

125. Shane Ban [bawn]: his son; first of the family who, after the Revolution, settled in the county Derry.

126. Frank : his son.

127. Charles : his son.

128. Edward : his son.

129. Thomas, Lord O'Hagan (deceased): his son ; created a "Baron" of the United Kingdom in 1870. This Thomas was born 29th May, 1812 ; m. first in 1836, Mary (d. 1868), dau. of Charles Hamilton Teeling, of Belfast, and had one son and five daughters.

I. Charles, b. 1838; d. young.

I. Mary-Ellen, d. unm.

II. Anne-Catherine, d. unm.

III. Caroline, d. unm.

IV. Madeleine (d. 1875), m. Colonel John MacDonnell, of Kilmore, co. Antrim. (See the "Mac-Donnell of Antrim" pedigree.)

V. Frances, m. 1866 to John O'Hagan, Q.C., and living in 1887.

Secondly, Lord O'Hagan m. 2nd August, 1871, Alice-Mary, youngest dau. and co-heir of the late Colonel Towneley, of Towneley, co. Lancaster, England, and by her had :

VI. Kathleen-Mary, b. 13th May, 1876.

II. Thomas Towneley, born 5th Dec., 1878.

VII. A. daughter, b. and d. 5th Nov., 1877.

VIII. Clare-Elizabeth-Mary, died 23rd Dec., 1880.

---

* 1601 : The O'Hagans, whose principal seat was at Tullaghoge, were the Law-givers to the O'Neills, Princes of Tyrone.   In the year 1602, the lord-deputy Mount-joy remained at Tullaghoge, for five days, and "broke down the chair whereon the O'Neills were wont to be created ; it being of stone planted in the open field."—See Fyne's Moryson's *Rebellion of Hugh* (*O'Neill*), *Earl of Tyrone*, Book iii., c. i.

Sir Nicholas Malby in a report on the state of Ireland, which he made to Queen Elizabeth, in 1579, describes the O'Hagan of Tullaghoge, barony of Dungannon, and county of Tyrone, as one of the principal men of note in that part of the country.

† *Shane* : In "King James's Army List (1689)," preserved in the MS. Vol. F. 1. 14, in the Lib. of Trin. Coll., Dublin, and published by Dalton in 1855, are the names of "Art O'Hegan," and "John O'Hegan ;" and of "Art O'Hagan, Cormuck O'Hagan, and Daniel O'Hagan." The John there mentioned could have been a son of the Shane (or John) who is No. 123 on this pedigree, and who fought against the Cromwellian Army, at the Battle of Ticroghan, in June, 1650.

O'HALLORAN.

Lords of Clan Fergail, County Galway.

Arms: Gu. a horse pass. ar. saddled and bridled ppr. on a chief of the second three mullets az. *Crest*: A lizard or. *Motto*: Clan Fergail abu.

AONGUS (or Æneas), a brother of Duach Galach who is No. 88 on the (No. 1) " O'Connor" (Kings of Connaught) pedigree, was the ancestor of *O'h-Allmhurain*; anglicised *O'Halloran.**

88. Aongus: son of Brian.

89. Mortogh: his son.

90. Allmhuran (" allmhuire:" Irish, *importation*; "an," *one who*): his son; a quo *O'h-Allmhurain*.

91. Fergallach: his son.

92. Cucolle: his son.

93. Aodh (or Hugh): his son.

94. Dermod: his son.

95. Connor Chatha-Luireach: his son.

96. Donall: his son.

97. Teige, the Strong: his son.

98. Fergal: his son; a quo *Clan Fergail*.

99. Hugh: his son.

100. Connor: his son.

101. Giolla-Sdefain, of the Plunder: his son.

102. Mulroona: his son.

103. Donall: his son.

104. David: his son.

105. Awley: his son.

106. Teige: his son.

107. Giolla-Chriost: his son.

108. Donall: his son.

109. Seonac: his son.

110. Dabhaic: his son.

* *O'Halloran*: This family were, as the name implies, "importers" of Wine; and were lords of *Clan Fergail*, a district in which Galway town is situate; and had their castle at Barna, close to the sea-side, about three miles west of Galway. The MS. Vol. H. 2. 17, in the Library of Trinity College, Dublin, states that " O'Halloran is the chief of the twenty-four townlands of Clan Fergail; and of these are the O'Antuiles and O'Fergus of Roscam." That statement refers to the twelfth century. These twenty-four townlands of Clan Fergail lay east of the river *Gallimh* (or " Galway.") The name "Clan Fergail" is now obsolete; but " Roscam," on which are the remains of a round-tower, is still well known. It lies about three miles S. E. of Galway. In the 13th century the O'Hallorans were dispossessed of their ancient inheritance of Clan Fergail, by the De Burgos; and were obliged to emigrate, with the O'Flahertys, to Iar (or West) Connaught, where they built the castle of O'Hery in Gnomore; and also, according to tradition, the castle of Rinvile in Northern Connemara. O'Flaherty, in his *Ogygia*, claims for the House of Clan Fergail the celebrated Saint Finbar of Cork. According to the Chronicles of the Wars of Thomond, at A.D. 1309, there was another family of the O'Hallorans in Thomond, descended from the stock of the O'Briens and other Dalcassians in Munster.—See HARDIMAN'S *West Connaught*.

O'HANLON.

Lords of Orior, in the County Armagh.

Arms : Vert on a mount in base ppr. a boar pass erm. Crest ; A lizard displ vert.
Another Coat : Ar. on a mount vert a boar pass. ppr. armed or.

FEIG, brother of Breasal who is No. 88 on the "Madden" (of Ulster)
pedigree, was the ancestor of Oh-Anluain; anglicised Hanlon, Henlon,
and O'Hanlon.

88. Feig: son of Felim; had a
brother named Eachach, who was
the ancestor of Rogan.

89. Niallan: son of Feig. This
Niallan had a brother named
Fiachra Ceannfinan,* who was
ancestor of Duffry and Garvey; and
another brother Oronn, who was
ancestor of Mooney, of Orgiall.

90. Eoghan (or Owen): son of
Niallan; had a brother named
Muireadhach, who was the ancestor
of St. Colman, of Kill.

91. Muireadach: son of Owen.

92. Baodan : his son.

93. Ronan : his son.

94. Suibhneach : his son; had a
brother named Crunmoal.

95. Colgan : his son.

96. Eagnach : his son.

97. Suibneach (2): his son.

98. Cosgrach: his son; had a
brother named Cearnach (" cearnach:" Irish, victorious), a quo
another O'Cearnaighe family, anglicised Carney, and Carnagie, of Clan
Colla.

99. Dermod : son of Cosgrach.

100. Anluan (" an-luan :" Irish,
the champion) : his son ; a quo
O'h-Anluain.

101. Flann : his son.

102 Aodh (or Hugh): his son.

103. Dermod : his son.

104. Flaitheartach : his son.

105. Cumascach : his son.

106. Maccraith : his son.

107. Flann (2) : his son.

108. Moroch : his son; had a brother named Giollapadraic.

109. Ardgal: son of Moroch.

110. Moroch Ruadh : his son.

111. Edmond : his son.

112. Eocha: his son.

113. John O'Hanlon: his son;
first assumed this sirname; had a
brother named Patrick.

114. Eocha (2) : son of John.

115. Shane Oge: his son.

116. Eocha (3) : his son.

117. Shane (2) : his son.

118. Giollapadraic Mór: his son.

119. Eocha (4) : his son.

120. Shane (3) : his son.

121. Shane (4) Oge: his son. This
Shane had five sons—1. Eocha
(called "Oghy"). 2. Patrick, 3.
Melaghlin, 4. Shane Oge, 5. Felim.

122. Sir Oghy O'Hanlon, of Ton-
regee (now Tanragee), knight ; son
of Shane Oge ; Chief of his name;
lord of Upper and Lower Orior; in
Armagh ; attainted, but pardoned
on the 12th February, 1605.

123. Owen Oghy Oge: his son;
lord of Orior ; had two brothers—
1. Tirlogh (who was the eldest son),
and 2. Edward, who was the
youngest.

124. Patrick Mór: son of Owen
Oghy Oge.

125. Edmond: his son; an officer
in the service of King James the
Second.

126. Felix, of Killeavy, in the co.
Armagh : his son.

---

* Ceannfinan, or, more properly, ceannfionnan, means "white headed."

127. Edmond Ruadh, of Killeavy: his son.

128. Hugh, of Newry: his son; d. in April, 1807, aged 86 years.

129. Patrick, of Newry: his son; had an elder brother named Hugh, who, in 1828, died without issue. This Patrick became a Barrister-at-Law, and was living in Calcutta in 1830.

130. Hugh O'Hanlon: his son; was Law Adviser to the Irish Office in London, in 1831; his brother, Pringle O'Hanlon, was Captain in the First Bengal Cavalry; and his other brother, Edward, was killed at Rangoon, in the East Indies.

O'HART. (No. 1.)

Princes of Tara, and Chiefs in Sligo.

Arms : Gu. a lion passant guardant or, in base a human heart argent. *Crest* : A dexter cubit arm holding a flaming sword all ppr. *Motto* : Fortiter et fideliter.

ART EANFHEAR, who (see p. 359) is No. 81 on the "Line of Heremon," and son of the Monarch Conn of the Hundred Battles, was the ancestor of this family:

81. Art* Eanfhear ("art:" Irish, *a bear, a stone ; noble, great, generous ; hardness, cruelty.* "Ean:" Irish, *one ;* "fhear," " ar," *the man ;* Gr. "Ar," *The Man, or God of War*): son of Conn of the Hundred Fights; a quo *O'h-Airt*, anglicised *O'Hart.*†

This Art, who was the 112th Monarch of Ireland, had three sisters—one of whom Sarad was the wife of Conaire Mac Mogha Laine, the 111th Monarch, by whom she had three sons called the "Three Cairbres," viz.—1. Cairbre (*alias* Eoch-

---

* *Art* ; In Old High-German, the word "hart" (which is evidently derived from the Celtic *art*) means *inexorable.*

According to Keating's History of Ireland, the epithet *Eanfhear* applied to this Art means "The Solitary ;" because he was the *only one* of his father's sons that survived : his two brothers Conla Ruadh and Crionna, having been slain by their uncles, as above mentioned. His grief on account of that fact was so intense, that, in old writings, he is often called "Art, the Melancholy."

This Art's descendants gave Kings to Connaught, Meath, and Orgiall ; Kings or Princes to Clanaboy, Tirconnell, and Tirowen ; and with only two or three exceptions, Monarchs to Ireland, up to the Anglo-Norman Invasion. From this Art also descended the Kings of Scotland, from Fergus Mór Mac Earca, in the fifth century, down to the Stuarts : See No. 81 on "The Lineal Descent of the Royal Family of England," *ante.*

† *O'Hart* : As an illustration of the transitions which many of the ancient Irish sirnames underwent, it may be observed that, in the early ages, the "O'Hart" family was called *Cin-Airt* and *Muintir-Airt*, meaning respectively, the "kindred," and the "people, of the Monarch Art Ean Fhear" (or Art Enaar); the ancestor of the family ; but after the introduction of sirnames in Ireland, the family name was at one time *Ua-Airt*, next *Ua-'Airt* (using the aspirate before the name "Airt"), next *Ua-Hairt*, and lastly *O'h-Airt*, anglicised *O'Hairt, O'Harthiee*, etc.—(See the "Harte" pedigree, for other changes in the anglicised forms of this family name.)

aidh) Riada—a quo "Dalriada," in Ireland, and in Scotland ; 2. Cairbre Bascaon ; 3. Cairbre Musc, who was the ancestor of *O'Falvey*, lords of Corcaguiney, etc. Sabina (or Sadhbh), another sister, was the wife of Mac-Niadh [nia], half King of Munster (of the Sept of Lughaidh, son of Ithe), by whom she had a son named Maccon ; and by her second husband Olioll Olum she had nine sons, seven whereof were slain by their half brother Maccon, in the famous battle of Magh Mucroimhe* [muc-crove], in the county of Galway, where also the Monarch Art himself fell, siding with his brother-in-law Olioll Olum against the said Maccon, after a reign of thirty years, A.D. 195. This Art was married to Maedhbh, Leathdearg, the dau. of Conann Cualann ; from this Queen, Rath Maedhbhe, near Tara, obtained its name.

82. Cormac Ulfhada :† son of Art Eanfhear ; m. Eithne, dau. of Dunlang, King of Leinster ; had three elder brothers — 1. Artghen, 2.

Boindia, 3. Bonnrigh. He had also six sons—1. Cairbre Lifeachar, 2. Muireadach, 3. Moghruith, 4. Ceallach, 5. Daire, 6. Aongus Fionn : Nos. 4 and 5 left no issue. King Cormac Mac Art was the 115th Monarch of Ireland ; and was called " Ulfhada," because of his *long beard.* He was the wisest, most learned, and best of any of the Milesian race before him, that ruled the Kingdom. He ordained several good laws ; wrote several learned treatises, among which his treatise on " Kingly Government," directed to his son Carbry Liffechar, is extant and extraordinary. He was very magnificent in his house-keeping and attendants, having always one thousand one hundred and fifty persons in his daily retinue constantly attending at his Great Hall at Tara ;* which was three hundred feet long, thirty cubits high, and fifty cubits broad, with fourteen doors to it. His daily service of plate, flagons, drinking cups of gold, silver, and

---

* *Magh Mucroimhe* : See Note " Art Eanfhear," in page 59.

† *Cormac Ulfhada* : This Monarch was commonly known as " Cormac Mac Art ;" he died at Cleitach, on the Boyne. Before his death he gave directions that, instead of at Brugh, a famous burial place of the Irish pre-Christian kings, he should be buried in Ross-na-Ri [Rosnaree] near Slane—both in the county of Meath ; and that his face should be towards the *East*—through respect for the Saviour of the World, whom he knew to have been there born and crucified.

‡ *Great Hall of Tara* : In the ancient work called "The Book of Ballymote," stanzas, in Irish, occur, of which the following is a translation :

> " Temor (Tara), the most beautiful of hills,
>   Under which Erin is warlike ;
> The chief city of Cormac, the son of Art,
>   Son of valiant Conn of the Hundred Battles.

> " Cormac is worth excelled ;
>   Was a warrior, poet, and sage ;
> A true Brehon ; of the Fenian men
>   He was a good friend and companion.

> " Cormac conquered in fifty battles,
>   And compiled the ' *Psalter of Tara.*'
> In that Psalter is contained
>   The full substance of history.

precious stone, at his table, ordinarily consisted of one hundred and fifty pieces, besides dishes, etc., which were all pure silver or gold. He ordained that ten choice persons should constantly attend him and his successors—Monarchs of Ireland, and never to be absent from him, viz.—1. A nobleman to be his companion; 2. A judge to deliver and explain the laws of the country in the King's presence upon all occasions; 3. An antiquary or historiographer to declare and preserve the genealogies, acts, and occurrences of the nobility and gentry from time to time as occasion required; 4. A Druid or Magician to offer sacrifice, and presage good or bad omens, as his learning, skill, or knowledge would enable him; 5. A poet to praise or dispraise every one according to his good or bad actions; 6. A physician to administer physic to the king and queen, and to the rest of the (royal) family; 7. A musician to compose music, and sing pleasant sonnets in the King's presence when thereunto disposed; and 8, 9, and 10, three Stewards to govern the King's House in all things appertaining thereunto. This custom was observed by all the succeeding Monarchs down to Brian Boromha [Boru], the 175th Monarch of Ireland, and the 60th down from

" His great house of a thousand heroes,
    With tribes it was delightful ;
A fair bright fortress of fine men ;
    Three hundred feet was its measure.

" Its circuit was well arranged ;
    Nor was it narrow by a faulty construction ;
Nor too small for separate apartments ;
    Six times five cubits was its height.

" Grand was the host which attended there,
    And their weapons were glittering with gold ;
There were three times fifty splendid apartments ;
    And each apartment held fifty persons.

" Three hundred cup bearers handed around
    Three times fifty splendid goblets
To each of the numerous parties there :
    Which cups were of gold or silver—all

" Ornamented with pure and precious stones ;
    Thirty hundred were entertained
By the son of Art on each day.

        .   .   .   .   .   .

" The household of the hosts let us enumerate ;
    Who were in the house of Temor of the tribes ;
This is the exact enumeration—
    Fifty above a thousand warriors.

" When Cormac resided at Temor,
    His fame was heard by all the exalted ;
And a king like the son of Art-Ean-Fhear,
    There came not of the men of the world.

        .   .   .   .   .   .

                                —CONNELLAN.

Cormac, without any alteration only that since they received the Christian Faith they changed the Druid or Magician for a Prelate of the Church.

What is besides delivered from antiquity of this great Monarch is, that (which among the truly wise is more valuable than any worldly magnificence or secular glory whatsoever) he was to all mankind very just, and so upright in his actions, judgments, and laws, that God revealed unto him the light of His Faith seven years before his death; and from thenceforward he refused his Druids to worship their idol-gods,* and openly professed he would no more worship any but the true God of the Universe, the Immortal and Invisible King of Ages. Whereupon the Druids sought his destruction, which they soon after effected (God permitting it) by their adjurations and ministry of damned spirits choking him as he sat at dinner eating of salmon, some say by a bone of the fish sticking in his throat, A.D. 266, after he had reigned forty years. Of the six sons of Cormac Mac Art, no issue is recorded from any [of them], but from Cairbre-Lifeachar;† he had also ten daughters, but there is no account of any of them only two— namely, Grace (or Grania),‡ and Ailbh [alve], who were both successively the wives of the great champion and general of the Irish Militia, Fionn, the son of Cubhall [Coole]. The mother of Cormac MacArt was Eachtach, the dau. of Ulcheatagh.

Cormac was married to Eithne Ollamhdha, dau. of Dunlang, son of Eana Niadh; she was fostered by Buiciodh Brughach, in Leinster.

83. Cairbre-Lifeachar, the 117th Monarch of Ireland: son of King Cormac Mac Art; was so called

---

* *Idol-Gods :* A vivid tradition relating the circumstance of the burial of King Cormac Mac Art has been very beautifully versified by the late lamented Sir Samuel Ferguson, in his poem—"The Burial of King Cormac."

> "Crom Cruach and his sub-gods twelve,"
> Said Cormac, "are but craven treene ;
> The axe that made them, haft or helve,
> Had worthier of our worship been ;

> "But He who made the tree to grow,
> And hid in earth the iron stone,
> And made the man with mind to know
> The axe's use, is God alone."

. . . . . .

> "The Druids hear of this fearful speech, and are horrified !

> "They loosed their curse against the King.
> They cursed him in his flesh and bones,
> And daily in their mystic ring
> They turned the maledictive stones."

For the full poem of "The Burial of King Cormac," see *The Story of Ireland* (Dublin : A. M. Sullivan).

† *Cairbre-Lifeachar* : This Cairbre is the Monarch referred to in Note, page 9, as having composed the poem in relation to the Gaelic language—a stanza translated from which is there given.

‡ *Grania* : Grania m., first : Diarmuid (Fionn's Lieutenant), son of Donn, son of Duibhne, son of Fothadh, son of Fiacha Riadhe, son of Fiacha, son of Feidhlimidh ; and had by him four sons—Donnchadh, Tollann, Ruchladh, and Ioruadh.

from his having been nursed by the side of the Liffey, the river on which Dublin is built. His mother was Eithne, daughter of Dunlong, King of Leinster. He had three sons—1. Eochaidh Dubhlen; 2. Eocho; and 3. Fiacha Srabhteine, who was the 120th Monarch of Ireland, and the ancestor of *O'Neill*, Princes of Tyrone. Fiacha Srabhteine was so called, from his having been fostered at Dunsrabhteine, in Connaught; of which province he was King, before his elevation to the Monarchy.* After seventeen years' reign, the Monarch Cairbre Lifeachar was slain at the battle of Gabhra [Gaura], A.D. 284, by Simeon, the son of Ceirb, who came from the south of Leinster to this battle, fought by the Militia of Ireland, who were called the *Fiana Erionn* (or Fenians), and arising from a quarrel which happened be-

tween them; in which the Monarch, taking part with one side against the other, lost his life.

84. Eochaidh Dubhlen: the eldest son of Cairbre Lifeachar; was so called from his having been nursed in Dublin ("Dubhlen:"† Irish, *black stream*, referring to the *dark* colour, in the city of Dublin, of the water of the river Liffey, which flows through that city). Eochaidh Dubhlen was married to Alechia, daughter of Updar, King of Alba, and by her had three sons, who were known as "The Three Collas,"‡ namely—1. Muireadach, or Colla da Chrioch (or Facrioch), meaning "Colla of the Two Countries" (Ireland and Alba); 2. Carioll, or Colla Uais (meaning "Colla the Noble"), who was the 121st Monarch of Ireland; 3. Colla Meann, or "Colla the Famous." From the Three Collas descended many noble

---

* *Monarchy*: Under the laws of "Tanistry," the Crown in Ireland and Scotland was hereditary in the *Family*, but not exclusively in Primogeniture.—(See the Paper "Election of Kings, Princes, and Chiefs," in the Appendix). On this subject Sir Water Scott, in his *History of Scotland*, observes:—

"The blood of the original founder of the family was held to flow in the veins of his successive representatives, and to perpetuate in each chief the right of supreme authority over the descendants of his own line; who formed his children and subjects, as he became by right of birth their sovereign, ruler, and lawgiver. With the family and blood of this chief of chiefs most of the inferior chieftains claimed a connection more or less remote. This supreme chiefdom or right of sovereignty, was hereditary, in so far as the person possessing it was chosen from the blood royal of the King deceased; but it was so far elective that any of his kinsmen might be chosen by the nation to succeed him; and, as the office of sovereign could not be exercised by a child, the choice generally fell upon a full-grown man, the brother or nephew of the deceased, instead of his son or grandson. This uncertainty of succession which prevailed in respect to the crown itself, proved a constant source of rebellion and bloodshed: the postponed heir, when he arose in years, was frequently desirous to attain his father's power; and many a murder was committed for the purpose of rendering straight an oblique line of succession, which such preference of an adult had thrown out of a direct course."

† *Dubhlen*: According to Connellan, the name "Dubhlen," is the root of *Dubhlana*, which has been corrupted *Eblana*—the name of the city of *Dublin*, as marked on Ptolemy's Map of Ireland. Another ancient name for the city of Dublin was *Dromcollchoille*, which signifies "the back of the hazel wood."

‡ *The Three Collas*: The descendants of the Three Collas were called "The Clan Colla." The word "*Clan*," writes the Rev. Dr. Todd, F.T.C.D., "signifies *children* or *descendants*. The tribe being descended from some common ancestor, the Chieftain, as the representative of that ancestor, was regarded as the common *father* of the Clan, and they as his *children*.

families: Among those descended
from Colla Uais are—Agnew, Alexander, Donelan, Flinn, Healy, Howard (of England), MacAllister,
MacClean, MacDonald, lords of the
Isles, and chiefs of Glencoe;* MacDonnell, of Antrim; MacDougald,
MacDowell, MacEvoy, MacHale,
MacRory, MacVeagh (the ancient
MacUais), MacVeigh, MacSheehy,
O'Brassil, Ouseley, Rogers, Saunders, Saunderson, Sheehy, Wesley,
etc.

"The barony of Cremorne in Monaghan," writes Dr. Joyce, "preserves the
name of the ancient district of *Crioch-Mughdhorn* or Cree-Mourne, *i.e.*, the
country (crioch) of the people called
Mughdorna, who were descended and
named from Mughdhorn (or Mourne), the
son of Colla Meann."

And among others descended
from Colla Meann was Luighne
[Lugny], who was the ancestor of
Spears; and who, by his wife Basaire
of the Sept of the Decies of Munster, had a son called Fearbreach
[farbra] ("farbreach:" Irish, *the
fine-looking man*), who was bishop of
Yovar, and who (according to the
Four Masters) was fifteen feet in
height !

The following are among the
families of Ulster and Hy-Maine
descended from Colla da Chrioch:
Boylan, Carbery, Cassidy, Corrigan,
Corry, Cosgrave, Davin, Davine,
Devin, Devine, Devers, Divers,
Donegan, Donnelly, Eagan, Enright, Fogarty (of Ulster), Garvey,
Gilchreest, Goff, Gough, Hart,
Harte, Hartt, Hartte, Higgins,
Holland, Holligan, Hoolahan, Hort,
Keenan, Kelly, Kennedy, Keogh,
Lally, Lannin, Larkin, Laury,
Lavan, Lalor, Lawlor, Leahy,
Loftus, Loingsy (Lynch), Looney,
MacArdle, MacBrock, MacCabe,
MacCann, MacCoskar, MacCusker,
MacDaniel, MacDonnell (of Clan-Kelly), MacEgan, MacGeough, MacGough, MacHugh, MacKenna (of
Truagh, co. Monaghan), MacMahon

---

* *Glencoe* : For a poem on the "Massacre of Glencoe," see the Paper No. 89 in the
Appendix.

The orders to the officers engaged in that Massacre of the MacDonalds of Glencoe,
A.D. 1692, are still preserved; they are, according to the Inverness *Highlander*, as
follows :—

" To Captain Robert Campbell.

"Thou art hereby commanded to seize the rebels, the Clan M'Donald of Glencoe,
and slay every soul of them under three score years and ten. Thou shalt take special
care that the Old Fox and sons do not make their escape. Begin thy work sharp at
five o'clock to-morrow morning. I will endeavour to be forward with a strong force at
that hour. If I am not there, delay not a moment, but begin at the hour specified.
The foregoing is the King's special command. See that thou yield implicit obedience.
If not, thou art considered unfaithful to thy trust, and unworthy of holding a commission in his service.—I am, ROBERT DUNCANSON.—Ballachaolish, 2nd mo., 1692."

The following is the letter of Colonel Hamilton to Major Duncanson :—

"Thou, and those of the Earl of Argyll's Regiment under thy command, must
execute the Glencoe order. Be thou therefore prepared. See that every pass be made
secure. Begin thy work at five o'clock to-morrow morning. I will endeavour, with
my men, to be in position at that very hour. Thou shalt make secure every pass on the
south side of the Glen, and have the ferry well guarded, lest the Old Fox or one of his
whelps make their escape. Under the age of three score years and ten leave not a soul
of them alive, nor give the nation trouble nor expense by making prisoners.—I am,
JAMES HAMILTON.—Ballachaolish, 2nd mo., 1692."

(of Ulster), MacManus, MacNeny,[*] MacTague (anglicised Montague), MacTernan, MacTully, Madden, Magrath, Maguire, Malone, Mac-Ivir, MacIvor, Meldon, Mitchell, Mooney, Muldoon, Mullally, Muregan, Naghten, Nawn, Neillan, Norton, O'Brassil, O'Callaghan (of Orgiall), O'Carroll of Oriel (or Louth), O'Connor of Orgiall, O'Duffy, O'Dwyer, O'Flanagan, O'Hanlon, O'Hanratty, O'Hart, O'Kelly, O'Loghan, O'Loghnan, O'Neny, Oulahan, Rogan, Ronan, Ronayne, Slevine, Tully, etc.

85. Colla da Chrioch: son of Eochaidh Dubhlen; had three sons —1. Rochadh; 2. Imchadh; 3. Fiachra Casan, a quo *Oirthearaigh*. This Fiachra was the ancestor of *O'Mooney* of Ulster; *O'Brassil;* St. Maineon (18th December), bishop, a quo "Kilmainham," near Dublin; *O'Connor*, etc. Colla da Chrioch was the founder of the Kingdom of Orgiall. The Clan Colla ruled over that Kingdom, and were styled "Kings of Orgiall," down to the twelfth century.

86. Rochadh: son of Colla da Chrioch.

87. Deach Dorn: his son.

88. Fiach (or Feig): his son; had a brother Labhradh, a quo *Laury;*

and a brother Brian, a quo *O'Brien*, of Arcaill.

89. Criomhthan Liath[†] (" criomhthan :" Irish, *a fox*): son of Fiach; a quo *O'Criomhthainne*, of Ulster, anglicised *Griffin;* was King of Orgiall, and, as the epithet *Liath* implies ("liath:" Irish, *gray-haired*), was an old man when St. Patrick came to Christianize Ireland. He had five sons—1. Eochaidh; 2. Fergus Ceannfada (" ceannfada :" Irish, *long-headed*, meaning *learned*), who is mentioned by some writers as "Fergus Cean," and a quo *O'Ceannatta*, anglicised *Kennedy* and *Kinitty;* 3. Luighaidh, a quo *Leithrinn-Lughaidh ;* 4. Muireadach, who was the ancestor of *MacBrock*, now *Brock;* 5. Aodh (who was also called Eochaidh), the ancestor of *Slevin*. The Fergus Ceannfada here mentioned was one of the three antiquaries who assisted the Monarch Laeghaire; Corc, King of Munster; Daire, a Prince of Ulster; St. Patrick, St. Benignus, St. Carioch, etc., "to review, examine, and reduce into order all the monuments of antiquity, genealogies, chronicles, and records of the Kingdom."

90. Eochaidh [Eochy],[‡] King of Origall: the son of Criomhthan

---

[*] *MacNeny*: This family name in Irish is *Mac-an-Eanaigh* ("ean :" Irish, *a bird*; " eanach," *a moor* or *marsh*), and has been variously anglicised *MacNeny, O'Nena, O'Neny, Bird, Bourd, Byrd, Byrde, Naun*, and *Nawn*. And the *Mac-an-Eanaigh* family is quite distinct from the *Mac-an-Eineaigh* (" eineach :" Irish: *affability*), which has been anglicised *MacAneny*.—See Note "MacAneny," under No. 116 on the "O'Cahan" pedigree.

[†] *Criomhthan Liath* : This Crimthann Liath's descendants were very celebrated; some of them settled in Slane in the county of Meath. Of them Colgan says in his *Trias Thaumaturga* : " Est regiuncula Australis Orgielliæ, nunc ad Baroniam *Slanensem* spectans, vulgo Crimthainne dicta."

[‡] *Eochy* : " Soon after St. Patrick's arrival in Ireland," writes Dr. Joyce, " one of his principal converts was St. Donart, Bishop, son of Eochy, king of Ulster."

The Saint's name—a very significant one—was " Domhan-Gabh-Art" (*domhan* : Irish, *the world*, and *gabh*, *I take*), which means *I take Art from the world* (to serve his Heavenly Master). By contraction the name became " Domhang'hart," and ultimately " Domhanghart"—Anglicised " Donart."

St. Donart founded two churches—one at Maghera, on the northern side of the

Liath. Had a brother Cearbhall (" cearbhall :" Irish, *carnage*), who was the ancestor of and a quo *O'Carroll*, Kings of Oriel (or county Louth), down to the twelfth century.

91. Cairbre an Daimh Airgid (" an :" Irish, *the def. article ;* "daimh" [dav], *a learned man* or *poet ;* and " airgid," *wealth, money ;* Lat. "argentum ;" Gr. "arg-uros"), King of Orgiall : his son ; d. 513 ; " was so called from the many presents and gifts of silver and gold he usually bestowed and gave away to all sorts of people." He had many sons, viz. :—1. Daimhin, a quo *Siol Daimhin ;* 2. Cormac, a quo the territory *Ua Cormaic,* and who was the ancestor of *Maguire ;* 3. Nadsluagh, a quo *Clann Nadsluaigh,* and who was the ancestor of MacMahon, of Ulster ; 4. Fearach ; 5. Fiacha ; 6. Longseach ; 7. Brian ; 8. Dobhron, etc.

92. Daimhin,* King of Orgiall : son of Cairbre an Daimh Airgid ; d. A.D. 566. Had many sons. From Fearach his eighth son are descended *Devers, Divers, Dwyer, Feehan, O'Leathain* (" leathain :" Irish, *broad*), anglicised *Lahin, Lehane, Lane,* and *Broad ; Larkin,*

Malone, Orr, etc. ; and Cumuscach, who was King of Uriel.

93. Tuathal Maolgharbh : son of Daimhin. Had two brothers—1. Lochlann, ancestor of *O'Davin* ; 2. Clochar, from whom the present town of *Clogher,* in the county of Tyrone, takes its name. This Clochar (" clochar :" Irish, *a college*), was, himself, so called because of the *college* which he founded in that ancient town.

94. Tuatan : son of Tuathal Maolgharbh. Had two sons—1. Maolduin ; 2. Baodan : from this Baodan the following families descended— *Coscry, Cusker, MacCusker,* and *Cosgrave, Conan, Coonan, MacCoonan; Boylan, Cahil, Carbery, Corrigan, Donnelly, Gavan,* etc.

95. Maolduin : son of Tuatan.

96. Tuathal : his son.

97. Ceallach : his son ; a quo *Clan Kelly,* in the county Fermanagh, and from whom descended *Kelly,* of Ulster. Had five sons, from the fourth of whom, Murtagh, the following families descended—*Dongan, Donnegan, Dunegan, Keenan, Morgan, Murrin, Rogan,* etc.

98. Colga : son of Ceallach ; a quo *Colgan,* of Ulster.

99. Donall : his son ; a quo

mountain called Slieve *Donard,* in Ulster ; and the other, according to Colgan, A. SS. page 743, on the very summit of the mountain itself, far from all human habitation. The ruins of this little church existed down to a recent period on Slieve Donard, which takes its name from St. *Donart ;* and the name of the mountain stands as a perpetual memorial of the saint, who is still held in extraordinary veneration by the people among the Mourne mountains.—Joyce.

* *Daimhin :* From this Damhin " Devinish Island," in Lough Erne, near Enniskillen, in the county of Fermanagh, takes its name ; and St. Damhin, a descendant of that prince of Fermanagh, was the founder of the Abbey of Devinish, which is situated on Devinish Island.   In Irish it was called " Damhin-Inis," contracted to " Damhinis," and anglicised " Devinish," which means *Damhin's* (or Devin's) *Island.* Devinish Island was incorrectly anglicised the " *Island of the Ox,*" on account of the Irish word " damh" [dov], *an ox,* being, in sound, so like the word " daimh" [dav], *a learned man* : hence the observation by Colgan, in reference to the name of that island, namely— " quod Latine *sonat* Bovis Insula." Some of the abbots of Devinish were also styled bishops, until, in the twelfth century, it was annexed to the see of Clogher.

The Clan " Damhin" were long represented by the *Davins* or *Devins,* and so late as the fourteenth century, by the family of Diver or Dwyer, as lords of Fermanagh. The Maguires, also of the same stock, next became princes of Fermanagh, which, after them was called " Maguire's Country."—Four Masters.

MacDomhnaill, of Clan Kelly. (See No. 102, *infra*).

100. Fionnachtach : his son. Had three sons—1. Art; 2. Congall; 3. Foghartach, from whom descended *Cairn, Cairns, Flanagan, Donnellan, Kearns*, etc.,—all of Ulster.

101. Art: the son of Fionnachtach : a quo, according to MacFirbis, *O'h-Airt* (see No. 81, *supra*); but a quo only *MacArt*, according to O'Ferrall's *Linea Antiqua.*

102. Donall: the son of Art ; had a brother Lochlann, who was the ancestor of *MacDomhnaill*, of Clan Kelly, anglicised *MacDonnell, MacDaniel, Daniel*, and *O'Donnell*, of Fermanagh. (See No. 99 *supra*.)

103. Felim O'Hart: son of Donall ; the first of the family who assumed this sirname. From the second century down to this period (the eleventh century), when sirnames were first introduced into Ireland, this family was known as *Cin Airt*, and *Muintir Airt* : signifying, respectively, *the kindred* and *people of Art*, who is No. 81 on this pedigree.

104. Maolruanaidh [Mulrooney] : son of Felim ; some of whose descendants were called *O'Maoilruanaidh* (anglicised *Mulrooney, Rooney, Rowney*), and were lords of Fermanagh.

105. Tomhas (or Thomas) : his son.

106. Shane : his son ; living A.D.

1172 ; was the last prince of Tara. At that period took place the English invasion of Ireland ; when, as the name of Melaghlin, King of Meath, was *not* amongst the few signatures sent to Rome (Chartis subsignatis, oraditis, ad Romam transmissis), notifying Pope Adrian IV. of their assent to his transfer of their respective sovereignties to King Henry II., of England, that Monarch, by virtue of Adrian's Grant of Ireland to England, dispossessed Melaghlin of his Kingdom, and all his nobles of their patrimonies ; and conferred on Hugh De Lacy the Kingdom of Meath :

> No more to chiefs and ladies bright
>   The harp of Tara swells ;
> The chord alone that breaks at night
>   Its tale of ruin tells.
> Thus Freedom now so seldom wakes,
>   The only throb she gives
> Is when some heart indignant breaks,
>   To show that still she lives.
> —MOORE.

It was then that, deprived of his patrimony* in that Kingdom, by King Henry II., this Shane first settled in Connaught, in the barony of Carbury (county Sligo), which then belonged to the Principality of Tirconnell, and which O'Malory (or O'Mulroy), the then Prince of Tirconnell, granted to the said Shane, as an inheritance for him-

---

* *Patrimony* : In the "Topography" of O'Dugan (who died, A.D. 1372), the O'Harts, as Princes of Tara, rank next to Murcha, Meath's last King ; and, according to Connellan's "Four Masters," the Princes of Tara were also styled "Princes of Magh Breagh ;" *Magh Breagh* (latinized *Bregia*) signifying the "Magnificent Plain :" that vast plain extending between the rivers Liffey and the Boyne, from the city of Dublin to the town of Drogheda, thence to Kells in the county Meath, and containing the districts about Tara, Trim, Navan, Athboy, Dunboyne, Maynooth, Clane, Celbridge, Lucan, Leixlip, and all that part of the county Dublin north of the river Liffey. The "Magnificent Plain" here mentioned contains about half a million of acres of the finest land in Ireland ; and, up to the English invasion, formed a portion of "O'Hart's Country," in the Kingdom of Meath. The other portion of the family patrimony in that Kingdom was in *Teabhtha* (latinized *Teffia*), now known as the county Westmeath ; where some of the family remained.

self and his people. Some of Shane's descendants afterwards acquired landed property in the barony of Leyney, etc., in the co. Sligo, which they held down to the period of the Cromwellian Settlement of Ireland. (See Part IX. c. iv. ; and sect. 12 of the paper No. 94, in the Appendix.) Thus dispossessed, by King Henry II., of their territories in Bregia (or East Meath) the O'Hart family settled — some of them in Leinster, some in Ulster, some in England, some in Scotland, some in France, some in Germany ; and this the senior branch of the family, settled, as above stated, in that part of Connaught, now known as the county Sligo. At the time of the English Invasion of Ireland, the town of Kells, in the Principality of Tara, was called *Ceanannas* ("ceann :" Irish, *a head ; "* ceannas :" *authority, power*); where, according to Dr. O'Brien, " a national council of the clergy of Ireland was held about the year 1152, in which Cardinal Papyron gave the first Pallia to the four Archbishops of Armagh, Cashel, Dublin, and Tuam."

107. Art: son of Shane ; chief of his name.

108. Conchobhar : his son ; chief of his name.

109. Tirloch : his son; chief of his name.

110. Giollachriosd : his son; chief of his name.

111. Brian : his son ; chief of his name.

112. Teige : his son ; chief of his name.

113. Amhailgadh [awly] : his son ; chief of his name.

114. Teige : his son: chief of his name.

115. Melaghlin (or Malachi): his son ; chief of his name.

116. Giollachriosd Caoch : his son ; chief of his name ; who, according to the " Betham Collection," in the office of Ulster King-of-Arms, had five sons—1. Aodh (or Hugh)* Mór ; 2. Brian ; 3. Teige ; 4. William ; 5. Rory. By MacFirbis only three of those sons are mentioned, namely—1. Aodh Mór, who built the Castle of " mBotuinn ;" 2. Brian, who built the Castle of Ardtarmon ;† 3. Teige Brughaid Coilte agus an Botuinn, who built

---

* *Hugh* : According to the " Betham Collection," this Hugh's Brother, Brian, was the father of Donal, who was the father of Teige Ruadh [roe], the father of another Donal Glas ; Teige was the father of Teige Caoch, who was the father of Connor, the father of Hugh ; William was the father of Connor, who was the father of Brian ; and Rory was the father of Neale, living in 1635.

† *Ardtarmon* : As showing the social status of this family in the county Sligo, before the unhappy advent of Cromwell to Ireland, one of them, Pheolyme [Phelim] O'Hart, of Ardtarmon, ranks next to the O'Connor Sligo, amongst the Signatories (in 1585) of the Indenture between Sir John Perrott and the Chieftains of Sligo, *temp.* Queen Elizabeth. According to O'Flaherty's *West Connaught*, by Hardiman, p. 341, the following persons were the parties to that Indenture :—" Right Honorable Sir John Perrott, Knight, Lord Deputy-General of Ireland for and on the behaulfe of the Queen's most excellent Majesty, of the one partye ; and the reverend fathers in God John Bishop of Elphine—Owyn Bishop of Aconry—Owine electe Bishop of Killalae— Sir Donyll O'Connor of Sligo, Knight—Pheolyme O'Hart of Ardtarmon otherwise called O'Hart, chief of his name—Owen O'Connor of the Grawndge, gen.—Edmond O'Dowey (O'Dowda) of Killglasse, otherwise called O'Dowey, chief of his name— Hubert Albanaghe of Rathly, gen.—Breen McSwyne of Ardneglasse, gen.—Davy Dowdy of Castle-Connor, gen.—Cormocke O'Harey, (O'Hara of Cowlany, otherwise called O'Harey buy, chief of his name—Ferrall O'Harry of Ballinefennock otherwise

the Castle of Grainsioch Tuaidh (or North Grange). These were the latest built castles of the family; for, in Magherow (commonly called "O'Hart's Country"), at Ardtarmon (more properly "Art-tarmon:" *Art* being the name a quo the sirname *O'Hart*, and *tarmon* being the Irish for "sanctuary" or "protection," and sometimes meaning "church lands"), and at Ballinfull, near Lisadill,* the beautiful seat of Sir Henry-William-Gore Booth, Bart., are to be seen the remains of the O'Hart older castles in the county Sligo. But it was in the beginning of the 17th century, that Aodh Mór O'Hart built, in the Tudor style, on the shore of Lough Gill, the Castle of *mBotuin* (corruptly anglicised "Newtown"), in the parish of Dromleas, barony of Dromoheare (now "Dromahair"†), and co. of Leitrim; that his brother Brian O'Hart built in the same Tudor style the castle at Ardtarmon; and that the younger brother Teige built the castle at North Grange. The remains of these once splendid castles at Ardtarmon and Newtown are in tolerable preservation; but it may here be remarked that the stone which was embedded in the front wall immediately over the entrance to the Newtown Castle has mysteriously been removed therefrom. On that stone perhaps were engraved the name and Arms of the person who built it, and the date of its erection: if so, it would help to explain *why* the said stone has been removed therefrom, and is said to have been buried in Mr. Wynne's garden, at Hazelwood, Sligo, and thence to Lisadill by the Gore Booth family, who were in the female line the lineal descendants of the Captain Robert Parke, who, according to the Civil Survey, was the recognized owner of Newtown in 1641, and who, it is conjectured by McParlan, was a probable (?) founder of that castle. But why the said stone was removed from its place over the Newtown Castle entrance, or by whose orders it was taken away, remains a *mystery!*

Our curiosity being thus aroused on the subject, on the occasion of our visit to the locality in August, 1886, we wrote to Mr. Roger Parke, J.P., of Dunally, Sligo, the present

---

called O'Harry reoghe, chief of his name—Breene O'Harry of Tulwy, gen.—Owene O'Harey of Cowlany, gen.—Ferrdorraghe McDonoghe of Cowleae, otherwise called McDonoughe Tyrreryll, chief of his name—Mellaghlyne McDonoghe of Ballyndowne, gen.—Melaghlyne McDonogh of Cowlwony, gen.—Morryshe McDonoghe of Clonemahyne, gen.—Cene McHughe of Bryckleawe, gen.—John Croftone of Ballymote, gen.—George Goodman of Taghtample, gen.—Manus Reoghe of Rathmollyne, gen.—Manus McTeig bwy of Lysconnowe, gen.—Alexander McSwine of Loughtnevynaghe, gen.—Urryell Garry of Moye, otherwise called O'Garry, chief of his name—Rory O'Garry of Kearowercoghe, gen.—and Manus M. Byrne Reogh of Levally, gen.—of the other partie."

* *Lisadill :* The Gore-Booth mansion at Lisadill was, we were informed, built principally with the stones taken from the Ballinfull and Ardtarmon old castles.

† *Dromahair :* Standing at the ruins of O'Rourke's Castle at Drumahair, and looking towards the town of Sligo, Lough Gill, with its charmingly wooded islands, presents to the eye of the spectator that enchanting view which inspired the immortal Moore when, in his *Song of O'Ruarc, Prince of Brefni,* he well describes it as—

"The valley lay *smiling* before me."

courteous and respected owner of Newtown Castle, requesting some information respecting that stone, etc. Mr. Parke replied as follows :

"Dunally, Sligo,
"15th November, 1886.

"*Stemmata quid faciunt.**

"John O'Hart, Esq.

"SIR,—Yours of the 7th November, '86, to hand. In reference to *Newtown*, there are two castles there, as also a chapel in the which, as per tombstone therein, are deposited the remains of Robert and Maggy, children of Captain Robert Parke, and it is dated at 1677. McParlan says either Durroch O'Rorke or the Parke family were the founders. Perhaps O'Rorke built the older one, which is on a kind of peninsula in the lake (Lough Gill), and Robert Parke the other one. I have no MSS. or work bearing on these Castles' histories, but a small pamphlet published by Hardiman in Mullany's R.C. Magazine, being the diary of Sir Frederick Hamilton, of date 1642.

"Though a namesake and collaterly related to said Robert Parke, I am not his lineal descendant; the Gore Booths are. I purchased Newtown Castle and the townland called Culmore, otherwise Kelmore, otherwise Newtown, in 1871, Culmore, probably the proper name (the big way), as the formation of the lake on which the Newtown estates† stand would indicate.

"There is some mystery as to the removed stone that was over the newer Castle gate : some say it went to Hazelwood and was (buried) in the garden there ; others reckon it was thence removed to Lisadill. I enquired from the deceased, Right Hon. John Wynne, whether he knew anything about it, but he told me he had never heard of such a stone. My deceased old Newtown herd, Francis Cunningham, said he heard there was on it "609" (probably "1609"), at which period I would infer said castle was built, from its Tudor architecture. As to the claim of the O'Harts building said castle, I never heard of it till you mentioned it, but possibly you may be right. They built, I believe, a castle near Lisadill, and people say they were once owners of this place, Dunally and its castle, the latter now no longer in being. It is certain, however, from the Annals of the Four Masters, that Kaffer O'Donnell owned Dunally Castle at one time, I believe in the reign of Henry the Seventh. I found in the Quit Rent Office in Dublin, that in 1636 Roger Parke (from whom I am descended) owned half the castle of Dunally. He and our family were probably connected with the Cavalier party, and the whole family probably followers of the great Earl of Strafford, to whose represen tative I now pay a Chiefry for the lands of Dunally. . . .

"I am well aware the O'Hart family were once a very powerful Clan here, and the name much disseminated through the county. Of course it is only a conjecture of mine, as I am not well up in Irish, MacFirbis might have meant *Moteen*‡ (a little moat), which would correspond with the older castle, which is nearly surrounded by water in Lough Gill. Newtown (in Irish "Ballynew") would correspond with the kind of settlement Parke made there. . . . . Without wishing to offend you I repeat again : "*Stemmata quid faciunt;*" and most particularly in these democratic times.

"Yours faithfully,
"ROGER PARKE.'

---

* *Faciunt* : In its entirety the passage, which is taken from JUVENAL, runs thus : *Stemmata quid faciunt, quid prodest, Pontice longo sanguine censeri.*

Translated : Of what avail are pedigrees, or to derive one's blood from a long train of lofty ancestors?

† *Estates* : Of the nineteen forfeited townlands returned in the Civil Survey as having been in Captain Robert Parke's possession in 1641, there is no *Culmore* mentioned ; but No. 6 of those townlands was named *Shraghmore*, or "the big strand," which is adjacent to the castle of *mBotuin*, or Newtown. Strange to say that, while in 1641 Captain Parke is in the Civil Survey described as of "Newtown," Donoch O'Hart held that castle against the Cromwellian forces until June, 1652.—See No. 120, next on this genealogy.

‡ *Moteen* : The name of the castle which Aodh Mór O'Hart in the beginning of the 17th century built on the shore of Lough Gill, near Dromahair, was called *not*

117. Aodh (or Hugh) Mór: eldest son of Giollachriosd; had two sons —1. Aodh Oge, and 2. William. This William was the father of Ir, who was father of Brian, the father of Giolladubh, the father of Rory, the father of Giolladubh and Connor, who where living in the latter part of the 18th century.

118. Aodh Oge: the son of Aodh Mór; living in 1616.

119. Felim: his son; had two sons—1. Donoch Gruama, 2. John. This John (who is mentioned by MacFirbis, but not in the *Linea Antiqua*), was the father of William Granna, whose family were called "Muintir-Brughaid-coilte." In this (Felim's) time some of the family estates in the barony of Carbery, co. Sligo, were held by Brian O'Hairt and Owen O'Hairtt, and some more of the family estates in the barony of "Leny," same county, were held by

Katherine Hairtt—all "Papist Proprietors," whose estates* were confiscated under the Cromwellian Settlement. This Felim O'Hart was, as a Catholic Proprietor, dispossessed of his estates by the Earl of Strafford, the Viceroy of Ireland, *temp.* Charles I. The only inheritance that remained to him (Felim) was his poor but proud *birthright* as "Hereditary Prince of Tara;" but, so intense at that time was the hatred which political and religious differences had created between the English and the Irish peoples, and so great the antipathy then existing in England towards everything *Irish*, it is not to be wondered at that his "birth-right" did not serve him; for, unhappily, those were sad times in Ireland.

120. Donoch Gruama† ("gruama:" Irish, *sullen, morose*), of Newtown Castle,‡ above mentioned: son of

"Moteen," which means "a little moat," but *mBotuin*, which, as the name implies, means "The Castle of the Prey of Cattle" (*botuin* or *botain*: Irish, "a prey of cattle"), and which has, as above mentioned, been corruptly anglicised "Newtown," although there has been in that locality no such place as *Ballynew*, which would be the Irish for "Newtown."

* *Estates*: In his description of Connaught, A.D. 1614, Sir Oliver St. John states that "The O'Dowds, the MacDonoghs, the O'Hares, and the O'Harts retained the residue of the county Sligo, besides that which O'Connor Sligo held." For further information in connection with the Harts and O'Harts of the county Sligo, see O Flaherty's "West Connaught," by Hardiman; Prendergast's "Cromwellian Settlement;" and Archdeacon O'Rorke's "Ballysadare and Kilvarnet, county Sligo."

† *Gruama*: In the Betham Genealogical Collections, the epithet applied to this Donoch is incorrectly written *granna*. But the epithet which is properly applied to him in other State Records is *gruama*, which in his case is a very significant one; for, he naturally became *sullen* in manner, when he found that his patrimonial estates were unjustly and hopelessly confiscated. Crushed by the Cromwellian Settlement in Ireland, this Donoch had not left him, of his own, whereon to lay his head.

‡ *Newtown Castle*: The following Extract is taken from p. 332, Part VI. of Gilbert's *History of Affairs in Ireland*, respecting Donoch O'Hart, of Newtown Castle, on the shore of Lough Gill:

DONOGH O'HART.

"Articles of Agreement made and concluded by and between Donogh O'Hart, of the one parte, and Major Robert Ormesby, on the other parte, in behalfe of Sir Charles Coote, Knight and Baronett, Lord President of Connaght, for and concerning the surrender of the Castle or Holt of Newtowne, in the barony of Drumaheare (and county of Leitrim), unto the said Lord President or whome hee shall apoynt for the Parliament of the Commonwealth of England, June 3d., 1652:

1. "The said Donnogh O'Hart doth conclude and agree to deliver up the said Holt of Newtowne with all the armes, ammunicion and necessaries of warr not here-

Phelim O'Hart; was dispossessed under the Cromwellian Settlement of Ireland, on the 3rd June, 1652. Up to that date, the said Donoch was the possessor of the Castle of Newtown, in the parish of Dromleas, barony of Dromaheare, and county of Leitrim; while the Civil Survey and in the Book of Survey and Distribution for the County of Leitrim, the name of Capt. Parke* is entered as the Proprietor of said Newtown, in 1641. Among the Troopers† who claimed as Soldiers under the Act of Settlement, appears the name "Parke;" and, according to the Genealogical MSS. in the Library of Trinity College,

after excepted, unto the said Lord President or whome hee shall apoynt, at or by twelve of the clocke to-morrow without prejudice or embezilment. In consideracion whereof the said Major Ormesby doth conclude and agree that the said Donnogh O'Hart and those souldiers in that Holt shall have quarters for their lives, and shall have liberty to march away with their bagg and baggage, without impeachment, except arms and ammunition."

2. "The said Donnogh O'Hart (if hee desire the same) shall have a protection graunted to him and his men, to live in the State's Quarters, with his and their families, as to other protected persons.

3. "That the said Donnogh O'Hart shall have the full benefitt of the little corne that hee and those souldiers in pay in the said Holt sowed themselves, without rent, or contribucion for this yeare, and a howse assured them to keep their corne in, safe from any under the Parliament's comand.

4. "The said Donnogh O'Hart (if hee submit to protection) shall haue for this yeare the grazeing of twenty cowes free from contribucion.

5. "The said Donnogh O'Hart is to haue the small boat and cotts which hee hath on Newtowne Lough without any impeachement. Lastly: the said Donnogh O'Hart is to haue six musquiteers and six pikes allowed him and his men out of their armes, which they are to deliver up, with his owne sword (in case hee submitt to protection), for his necessary defence against Tories, which hee is to give security shall not bee employed against the State."

It may be here mentioned that the "Tories" of that period, who were more lately known as *Rapparees*, were bands of men, who, headed by some of the dispossessed gentlemen, retired to the wilds and mountains, and incessantly attacked the Cromwellian planters. The Calvagh O'Hart, who, as one of those Tories, joined the celebrated Rapparee Redmond O'Hanlon, is believed to have been a son of the aforesaid Donoch Gruama O'Hart.

* *Parke :* The letters "C.S." prefixed to Captain Parke's name, in the Book of Survey and Distribution, indicate that the said entry was taken from the *Civil Survey*, or that the said Parke was a *Cromwellian Soldier ;* but, in either case the entry is misleading, for the Cromwellian soldiers were not disbanded, at soonest, before September, 1653, and up to that time they certainly had received no grants of Land in Ireland. Among the names of those who (see the Paper in the Appendix of our *Irish Landed Gentry,* headed "Soldiers of the Commonwealth, in Ireland") claimed as Soldiers, or in right of Soldiers, who served in Ireland in the Commonwealth period, is that of Captain Parke, who is there entered as claiming "in right of pre-emption;" but it is not mentioned from whom he "purchased" the townlands above stated to have been in his possession in 1641. Before the Books of Distribution were compiled (in 1666), Captain Parke could have *purchased* from the Cromwellian soldiers the townlands respectively assigned to them ; and thus Parke's name could, in the List of Claims above mentioned, appear as claiming "in right of pre-emption."

† *Troopers :* According to Wood-Martin, the following are among the names of the Cromwellian Troopers who were disbanded in the county Sligo : Allan, Armstrong, Barber, Barclay, Benson, Black, Brown, Carter, Charlton, Cole, Davis, Dennison, Duke, Fleming, Gilbert, Gilmore, Glass, Grey, Hall, Henry, Hughes, Hunter, Irwin, Johnston, Lang, Little, McKim, Macklin, McIlroy, Morrison, Nichols, Noble, *Parke,* Porter, Reynolds, Rogers, Smith, Trimbel, Wallis, White, Williams, Wilson, Winne. It will be seen that some of these names are of Irish origin.

Dublin, there was *no Parke* family in Ireland before the Viceroyalty of Stafford in Ireland.

Under date A.D. 1636, we first meet with the name "Parke" in Ireland: the name "Roger Parke" appears as tenant, under the Earl of Strafford, of half the Castle of Dunally; after Strafford had ruthlessly dispossessed almost all the Catholic Proprietors of Connaught, but especially those of the *old Irish race* in his time in Ireland. The Parke family, therefore, who were followers of Strafford, could not have been the founders of the Newtown Castle, which, according to the mysterious stone above mentioned, was built A.D. 1609, in the reign of James I.: just sixteen years before the reign of Charles I., under whom the Earl of Strafford was Viceroy of Ireland! And the O'Rorkes had no castle south of Dromahair. It is worthy of remark that, on the accession of King Charles II. (who, himself, had drunk deeply of the bitter cup of adversity, during the "Protectorate" of Cromwell), not even a portion of their estates was restored to any member of the O'Hart family.

121. Teige: son of Donoch Gruama O'Hart: had a younger brother named Calvagh.

122. Shane (2): his son; the last recognized chief of his name; married Mary, daughter of Manus Mór O'Laydon. To hide his poverty, this Shane migrated* from Magherow, in the county Sligo, to the neighbouring county Mayo; and there, in comparative retirement, far from home and kindred, settled near his wife's friends on a farm at Doonbreeda, which they procured for him on the Bourke (of Carrowkeel) property, in Glen Nephin. He was buried in the O'Laydon burial-ground in *Cill Muire* (Kill Mary), now called "Kilmurray," in the parish of Crossmolina, barony of Tyrawley, and said county of Mayo; which cemetery since then became the burial-place of the members of this family resident about Crossmolina.

123. Shane (3), of Doonbreeda: only son of Shane (2); m. Mary, dau. of Michael Martin and his wife Catherine Berry, of Glenavne, near Doonbreeda; was buried in *Cill-Muire*. The issue of this marriage were two sons and one daughter:

I. Shane (or John) O'Hart, of Crossmolina, of whom presently.

II. Martin, of Glenhest, who was twice married: first to Catherine Moran, by whom he had four children:

1. John, m. to Mary, daughter of Thomas Regan, of Moygownagh; d. 12th Nov., 1886, leaving issue.

2. Mary, m. to James Kearney.

3. Michael, twice married but left no issue.

4. Anthony, m. to Judith MacGreevy, by whom he left five children—1. John, 2. Brian, 3. Michael, 4. Thomas, 5. Martin.

Martin, of Glenhest, was secondly m. to Bridget Boggin, by whom he had five children—1. Bridget; 2. Martin; 3. Nancy (m. to Martin McHale, by whom she had three children—1. Mary; 2. Bridget; 3. Thomas); 4. Patrick, of Youngstown, Ohio, living in 1877 (emigrated to America in 1858); and

---

* *Migrated:* After the Cromwellian Confiscations in Ireland some of this family migrated to America; and (see No. 15 in Note "Independence," page 76) JOHN HART, one of their descendants, was one of the Signatories to the "Declaration of American Independence," on the 4th July, 1776.

5. Thomas Hart, who emigrated to America in 1855, and living in 1880, near Courtland, Decalb county, Illinois, United States.

I. Mary Hart, m. to Thomas Cormack, by whom she had five children—Bridget, Martin, Mary, Catherine, and Rose.

1. Bridget, who was twice married: first, to Luke Forristal, by whom she had two children—Mary; and Bridget, m. to Frank Cormack. By her second marriage she had a son Brian MacGreevy.

2. Martin, m., and had six children—1. Thomas; 2. Mary, m. to Michael Coyne; 3. James; 4. Bridget; 5. Catherine; 6. Martin.

3. Mary, m. to Patrick Mac-Manamnin, and had six children—1. Mary, m. to John Gannon; 2. Martin; 3. Felim; 4. Margaret, m. to John Commins; 5. Bridget; 6. Patrick.

4. Catherine, m. to — Cormack, had four children—1. Daniel; 2. Mary, m. to Luke Forristal; 3. Anne; 4. Rose.

5. And Rose Cormack, who was twice married: by her first marriage she had three children—1. John Moran; 2. Catherine Moran, m. in America to Bryan Mulroy; 3. Mary Moran, m. to Peter Cawley, of Curraghmore. The said Rose was secondly m. to Edward Mulroy, by whom she had two children—1. Celia, 2. Bridget.

124. Shane (or John), of Crossmolina: son of Shane (3); m. in 1800 Nora (who died in 1844), eldest dau. of Peter Kilroy and his wife Mary Geraghty, of Keenagh, in the old parish of Glenhest, but now attached to the parish of Crossmolina; d. in 1841; he and his wife were buried in the family grave in *Cill Muire*, above mentioned. The issue of this marriage were six sons and four daughters:

I. Michael; II. another Michael —both of whom died in infancy.
III. The Rev. Anthony, a Catholic Priest of the Diocese of Killala; d. 7th March, 1830.
IV. Patrick, m. in 1844, Bridget (d. in 1847), daughter of John Mannion, of Castlehill, near Crossmolina, by whom he had two children, who died in infancy. This Patrick died in 1849, in Carbondale, United States, America.
V. John, the writer of this Work, of whom presently, at No. 125 *infra*, on this Genealogy.
VI. Martin, who died in infancy.
I. Mary, who d. unm. in 1831.
II. Anne, who d. in 1840, m. to James Fox, of Crossmolina, by whom she had three children—1. Mary Fox, living in 1878, and m. to J. Sexton, of Rockford, Illinois, United States, America, and had issue; 2. Catherine, who d. young, and unm.; 3. Anthony, who d. in infancy.
III. Bridget, living in 1879, m. John Keane, of Cloonglasna, near Ballina (Tyrawley), by whom she had three sons and two daughters: 1. James; 2. Mary, d. unm.; 3. Francis; 4. Bridget; 5. Patrick—all four of whom were living in 1879 near Scranton, Pennsylvania, United States, America.
IV. Catherine, who d. in Liverpool in 1852, was m. to John Diver, of Crossmolina, by who she had two sons—1. Patrick, 2. John.

125. John O'Hart, of The School, Ringsend, Dublin: only surviving son of John, No. 124; b. in Dec., 1824, and living in 1887.

Of this John, *The Dublin Journal* of the 16th May, 1887, writes:

"John O'Hart, F.R.H.A.A.I., M.H.S.,

was born at Crossmolina, county of Mayo, in December, 1824. He received his early English education at the school conducted in his native town by Mr. Alexander M'Hugh ; and at the age of ten years he was placed in the classical school presided over by Mr. John Corley—also situated in Crossmolina. The death of his brother (who was a priest of the diocese of Killala), and other domestic disappointments so affected the means of his parents that while yet a boy in years he was withdrawn from his classical studies and reduced to the alternative of entering the Constabulary Force. He was place in the Depôt of Ballinrobe, then under the superintendence of Major Priestly, Provincial Inspector of Connaught. That officer apparently did not consider young O'Hart physically fitted for the rougher duties of his position ; for, one day on parade he jocosely told the future genealogist that he "might hide behind a fishing rod," at the same time expressing his belief that he would be more congenially situated in a County Inspector's office. Accordingly, O'Hart was allocated to West Galway, and placed as an assistant clerk in the office of the County Inspector at Oughterard ; and when his officer was removed to another county some months afterwards, O'Hart accompanied him. His youth, his efficiency, and a knowledge of the untoward destiny that had so rudely compelled him to abandon his studies, secured him the respect and sympathy of all his officers save one. After a year or two O'Hart retired from the force; and in 1845 entered the service of the Commissioners of National Education in Ireland. In the autumn of that year he was admitted to the Board's Training Department, Marlborough-street. Here he attracted the favourable notice of Sir Alex. M'Donnell, then Resident Commissioner of National Education ; the late Robert Sullivan, LL.D., then one of the Board's Professors ; and Sir Patrick J. Keenan, P.C., K.C.M.G., C.B., &c., the present Resident Commissioner. In 1856 he was appointed to the Ringsend School as a Stepping-stone to promotion, under the patronage of the late Lord Herbert of Lea ; for the appointments to Inspectorships were then made by patronage. When, however, in 1859, the National Education Department was, for examination purposes, placed in connection with the Civil Service Commissioners, and that, thereafter, Inspectorships could only be obtained by nomination and examination,

the *age* clause frustrated Mr. O'Hart's eligibility for a nomination. From that time to the present he has devoted himself ardently to antiquarian and genealogical research. His greatest work is, "*Irish Pedigrees ; or, the Origin and Stem of the Irish Nation.*" The first volume of this laborious and exhaustive work was published in 1875 ; the second in 1878 ; and the third (or latest edition) in 1881. He has also written "*The Last Princes of Tara,*" "*Irish Landed Gentry when Cromwell came,*" and was a contributor to *Hibernia,* a monthly magazine lately published in London. A fourth and enlarged edition of the "Irish Pedigrees" is, we have been informed, now passing through the press ; and we need scarcely say that we wish it every success. . . . It is clearly the duty of Irishmen to support and encourage native literature. Here is a countryman of ours who has attained a high rank among contemporary archæologists by perseverance in face of circumstances often adverse ; and it were surely a disgrace and a stigma on cultured Irishmen if his works should fail to receive their well-won meed of recognition and reward."

He m. on the 25th May, 1845, in the Catholic Church of Crossmolina, above mentioned, Elizabeth (living in 1887), dau. of Patrick Burnett and his wife Margaret Bourke, of Enniscrone, co. Sligo. The issue of that marriage were three sons and seven daughters :

I. Patrick Andrew O'Hart, who is No. 126 on this pedigree.

II. John-Anthony, b. 3rd June, 1859 ; d. 4th Oct., 1861.

III. Francis-Joseph, born 11th March, 1865 ; d. 16th Aug., 1866.

I. Fanny-Mary, m. Michael John Devine, of Kilkee, co. Clare, and has a family—(See the "Devin" pedigree, p. 405, *ante*.)

II. Mary-Elizabeth (d. 1st Jan., 1880), m. John Cunningham, of Dublin (see the "Cunningham" pedigree), and left one child, Bessie.

III. Margaret, who m. John Bourke, of Ringsend, Dublin,

and has—1. John, 2. Bessie, both living in 1887.

IV. Eliza.

V. Annie.

VI. Louisa, m. in 1887, to Thomas Joseph Maguire.

VII. Hannah.

126. Patrick - Andrew O'Hart, Public Auditor and Accountant, 45 Dame-street, Dublin : son of John O'Hart,* the writer of this Work ; b. 27th February, 1849, and living, unm., in 1887, when this Edition was published.

O'HART. (No. 2.)

Of Ardtarmon, County Sligo.

Arms ; The *Armorial Bearings* same as those of " O'Hart" (No. 1).

BRIAN, a younger brother of Aodh Mór who is No. 117 on the (No. 1) " O'Hart" (Princes of Tara) pedigree, was the ancestor of *O'Hart,* of Ardtarmon, county Sligo.

117. Brian: son of Giollachriosd Caoch.

118. Donal Glas : his son ; had a younger brother Felim,† who was father of William, the father of Felim, father of the four brothers— 1. Rory Ballach, 2. William, 3.

John, 4. Owen, who were called *Muintir Ardtarman.*

119. Giolladubh : son of Donal Glas ; had a brother Teige Ruadh. This Teige Ruadh had two sons— 1. Donal Glas, 2. Teige Oge : Donal Glas was the father of the four

---

* *O'Hart :* The following are living representatives of the " O'Hart" family in the county Cork, in 1887 :

Harte, Mrs. Mary, Scott's-square Hotel, Queenstown.
Hart, William, Harbour-row, Queenstown.
Hart, Henry, Aghabullogue, Cork.
Harte, W., South Main-street, Bandon.
Harte, John, Strand-road, Clonakilty.
Harte, Cornelius, Ballynacole, Dungourney, Midleton.
O'Hart, Jermiah, Farranalough, Newceston, Enniskean.
O'Hart, Stephen,   do.,   do.
O'Hart, James, Derrygarbh, Bandon.
O'Hart, Stephen,   do.,   do.
Hart, James, Ballinvriskig, Riverstown.
Hart, Thomas, Transtown,   do.
Hart, Patrick, Kilruane, Rosscarbery.
Harte, Henry, Mountrivers, Rylane, Cork.
Harte, Daniel, Ballinvriskig, White Church.
Harte, Patrick,   do.,   do.
Hart, Hannah, 7 Coburg-street, Cork.
Hart, J. S., 73 George's-street, Cork.
Harte, John, 9 Buxton-hill, Cork.
Harte, Mrs., 14 Patrick-street, Cork.

† *Felim :* This Felim was the " Pheolyme O'Harte of Ardtarmon, otherwise called O'Hart, chief of his name," who (See Note, page 000) was one of the Signatories of the Indenture (in 1585) between Sir John Perrott and the chieftains of Sligo, *temp.* Queen Elizabeth.

brothers, Muircheartach, Teige Oge, Brian, and Ferdorach—who were known as *Muintir Duin Fhuar ;* and Donal Glas's brother Teige Oge and his family were known as *Muintir Duin Fuil.**

120. Cormac : son of Giolladubh. Had three brothers—1. Owen Lochtach; 2. Rory; 3. Scabhar. Owen

Lochtach appears to have left no issue ; Rory left two sons namely —Giolladubh, and Connor ; and Scabhar was the father of Giollapadraic, the father of Owen.

121. John Caoch O'Hart : son of Cormac ; had two brothers—1. Giollapadraic, 2. Rory Garbh.

O'HART. (No. 3.)

Of North Grange, or Drumcliffe, County Sligo.

Arms : Same as those of "O'Hart" (No. 1).

TEIGE, another younger brother of Aodh Mór who is No. 117 on the "O'Hart" pedigree, was the ancestor of *O'Hart*, of the Grange, county Sligo ; or "Muintir Grainsighe," as they were called.

117. Teige : son of Giollachriosd Caoch.

181. Teige Caoch : his son ; had a brother named Rory Dubh.

119. Cormac-na-Cuideachta : son of Teige. Had three brothers—1. Connor ; 2. Melaghlin ; and 3. another Cormac : this Connor was the father of Hugh : Melaghlin was the father of Teige, the father of Niall, father of the three brothers

Cormac, Frederick and Felim ; and of Cormac's descendants, see the "O'Hart" (No. 5) pedigree.

120. Hugh : son of Cormac-na-Cuideachta ; had a brother named Owen, who was father of Rory, the father of Niall.

121. Teige : son of Hugh.
122. Owen : his son.
123. Niall O'Hart : his son.

O'HART. (No. 4.)

Of the Grange, or Drumcliffe, County Sligo.

Arms : Same as "O'Hart" (No. 1).

RORY DUBH, a brother of Teige Caoch who is No. 118 on the foregoing pedigree, was the ancestor of other branches of this family.

118. Rory Dubh : son of Teige.
119. Hugh : his son. Had two sons—1. Giollapadraic ; 2. Maolruan : this Maolruan was father of Rory Dubh, and of Niall ; and this Niall was father of Brian.

120. Giollapadraic : son of Hugh.
121. Hugh : his son.
122. Connor Dubh O'Hart : his son.

* *Duin Fuil* : This name has been modernized *Ballinfull,* above mentioned, near Lisadil.

O'HART.* (No. 5.)

Another Branch of the Grange Family.

Arms: Same as "O'Hart" (No. 1).

CORMAC, a brother of Cormac-na-Cuideachta who is No. 119 on the "O'Hart" (of Drumcliffe) pedigree, was the ancestor of other branches of this family.

119. Cormac: son of Teige Caoch; had three sons—1. Owen, 2. Teige, 3. Hugh: this Teige was the father of Donoch, the father of the three brothers, Giollachriosd Caoch, Maolruan, and Owen; and Hugh was the father of Teige, Hugh Oge, and Melachlin: this last-mentioned Teige was the father of the seven brothers—Owen, Hugh Oge, Brian, Cormac, William Granna, Giollachriosd Caoch, and Teige.

120. Owen: son of Cormac.

121. Rory: his son.

122. Niall: his son; had two brothers—1. Felim, 2. Teige Caoch.

123. James: son of Niall (or Neil); lived in Ballygilgan (one of the seven cartons of Lisadil), married Mary Kilbride, and had:

124. Thady (or Teige), of Ballygilgan, who m. Catherine Mannion, and had four sons and three daughters; the sons were:

I. James, of whom presently.

II. Patrick.

III. Michael.

IV. Thady.

The daughters were: 1. Else, 2. Mary, 3. Bridget. In 1833, the family with others was evicted by Sir Robert Gore Booth, of Lisadil, Bart., and the three brothers and three sisters of James emigrated to America; and the townland has since been turned into grazing farms.

125. James† O'Hart, of North Grange, co. Sligo, living in 1886: son of Thady; purchased a holding

---

* *O'Hart*: In the "Records of Ireland; Patent Rolls; James I.," pp. 20 and 21, many of the "O'Harts," and "O'Hartes," are mentioned as having obtained Pardons.

† *James*: Having visited North Grange, on the 29th of July, 1886, we had the pleasure of there meeting Mr. James O'Hart, who was then 85 years of age, and who naturally feels a laudable pride in the ancient lineage of our family. "My sons," said he, "write their name *Harte*, but the correct name is *O'Hart*." "Can you, sir," I said, "show me even one stone of the old Castle of Grange, which I came all the way from Dublin to see?" "Yes," he replied; "see (pointing to a stone embedded in the front wall of one of his houses) where I have preserved a stone of the arch that was over the front entrance to the castle of my ancestors." And there sure enough, has Mr. James O'Hart preserved that to him precious relic, as a *souvenir* of his family castle, which had once towered in North Grange, but was lately razed, to supply the stones with which the spacious Catholic church which now stands on the site of said castle, the presbytery, and the walls around the church, have been built.

We may observe that we, too, wrote our name *Harte*, up to 1873, and omitted the prefix *O'*; because, on account of our parents' reduced circumstances, that prefix was omitted by my brother, to whom, as a Catholic clergyman, the family naturally looked for the mode of spelling the name in its transition from the Irish to the English language, and who from his boyhood (as we find his autograph in some of his books,) variously wrote his name *Hairtt*, *Hairtte*, *Hartte*, and *Harte*. The last mentioned form was the orthography adopted by the members of the family who, in the 12th century, first in Drumcliffe, after the family was evicted from Ballygilgan ; married Ellen, daughter of Michael Cryan, of Drumcliffe, and lived there for some fourteen years. He subsequently purchased (for £100) from Mr. Gethen, of Ballymote, in the year 1848, another farm in North Grange, on which stood the ruins of the castle built in the beginning of the 17th century by Teige O'Hart, brother of Aodh (or Hugh) Mór, who (see p. 000) is No. 117 on the (No. 1) "O'Hart" pedigree. The children of this James O'Hart were six sons; and one daughter, Catherine :

I. Patrick, of whom presently.

II. Timothy, living at Garrison, co. Fermanagh ; married Mary Ellen Clancy, dau. of Andrew Clancy, of Stracomer, county Leitrim, and has had issue.

III. Michael, living in America, and there married.

IV. James, living at Caldragh, near Bundoran, married Ellen, daughter of Joseph Barker, of Muninane, co. Sligo, and has had issue.

V. John, living at Grange, has there a Drapery Establishment; married to Anne, dau. of James McGarraghy, of Grange, and has had two in family :—1. James, 2. Mary-Kate.

VI. Bernard, unm. in 1886; living in North Grange, and there keeps a Bakery and a Vintner's Establishment.

I. Catherine, m. James McSharry, of Mount Temple, near Grange, and had six children (living in 1886): 1. Bridget, 2. Mary, 3. Kate, 4. Ellie, 5. Annie, 6. Michael.

126. Patrick *Harte*, of North Grange, county Sligo : son of James O'Hart ; unmarried in 1886.

O'KELLY. (No. 1.)

Princes of Hy-Maine.

Arms : Az. a tower triple-towered supported by two lions ramp. ar. as many chains descending from the battlements betw. the lions' legs or. *Crest :* On a ducal coronet or, an enfield vert. *Motto :* Turris fortis mihi Deus.

IOMCHADH, the second son of Colla-da-Chrioch, who is No. 85 on the (No. 1) "O'Hart" (Princes of Tara) pedigree, was the ancestor of *O'Ceallaigh*, Princes of Hy-Maine (in the counties of Galway and Roscommon); anglicised *O'Kelly, Kalloch, Kellogg,* and *Kelly.* In the *Macariæ*

settled in England, and descendants of whom came back therefrom and settled in Ireland, *temp.* Elizabeth ; and, possibly, because (until lately) that was the *English* mode of spelling the name, our dear brother thought it *fashionable* to adopt that form of orthography ; or, because, from the same motive, Furlong, in his English translation of Carolan's song in honour of Bishop O'Hart (of the diocese of Achonry) wrote the name *Harte,* with an e final, and without the prefix *O' ;* while Dr. W. Maziere Brady, in his *Episcopal Succession in England, Scotland, and Ireland,* Vol. ii., p. 191, writes the name *O'Harte,* thus restoring the prefix *O';* but, in the Irish orthography of the sirname (*O'h-Airt*) there is no final e.

*Exidium** (or "The Destruction of Cyprus"), published in 1850, by the Irish Archæological Society of Ireland, in small quarto, of about 520 pages, this family is traced down to our times.

86. Iomchadh : son of Colla-da-Chrioch.

87. Domhnall : his son.

88. Eochaidh : his son.

89. Main Mór ("mor :" Irish, *great, large*; "main," *riches.* "Main" also means *the hand.* Lat. "manus") : his son ; a quo the territory of *Hy-Maine.*

"The descendants of Main Mór," says O'Clery, "had many privileges and immunities from the Kings of Connaught and their successors; viz.—they were hereditary marshals or generals of the Connaught armies; they possessed and enjoyed the third part of all the strongholds, and sea-port towns in the province; also a third part of all prizes and wrecks of the sea, and of all hidden treasures found under ground, and of all silver and gold mines and other metals, belonged to them, together with a. third part of all *Eric* or Reprisals gained and recovered by the Kings of Connaught from other provinces for wrongs received; with many other the like enumerated in the ancient Chronicles."

90. Breasal : son of Main Mór.

91. Dallan : his son.

92. Lughach : his son ; had a brother Fiachra.

93. Fearach : son of Lughach.

94. Cairbre Crom Ris : his son.

95. Cormac : his son.

96. Eoghan Fionn : his son. Had a younger brother named Eoghan [Owen] Buac, who was ancestor of

Madden, Clancy, Tracey, Hannan, Kenny, Hoolahan, etc.

97. Dithchiollach : son of Eoghan Fionn.

98. Dluitheach : his son.

99. Fiacalach : his son.

100. Inreachtach : his son ; had a brother Coscrach.

101. Olioll : his son.

102. Fionnachtach : his son.

103. Ceallach ("ceallach :" Irish, *war, strife*) : his son ; a quo *O'Cealliagh,* of Hy-Maine, A.D. 874.

104. Aodh (or Hugh) : his son.

105. Moroch : his son.

106. Teige : his son ; the first of the family that assumed this sirname. This Teige, as King of Hy-Maine, was slain at the Battle of Clontarf, A.D. 1014, fighting on the side of the Irish Monarch, Brian Boroimhe [boru], and is called " Teige Catha Briuin," meaning *Teige who fell in Brian's Battle* (of Clontarf). This Teige O'Kelly, Brian Boru, and Brian Boru's son Moroch—all three slain at the Battle of Clontarf—were buried at Kilmainham, near Dublin.

107. Conchobhar (or Connor) : his son ; whose brother Taidhg was ancestor of *MacTague*—modernized *Montague.*

108. Dermod : son of Connor.

109. Connor : his son. This Con-

* *Exidium* : The *Macariæ Exidium* is a secret history of the Revolution in Ireland, by Col. Charles O'Kelly, of Skryne or Aughrane, in the county Galway ; and was edited from four English copies, and a Latin Manuscript preserved in the Royal Irish Academy, Dublin, with Notes and Illustrations, and a Memoir of the Author (of that work), and his descendants, by John Cornelius O'Callaghan, the esteemed Author of " The Irish Brigades, in the Service of France," etc.

Captain Denis O'Kelly, of Galmoy's Regiment, was the eldest son and heir of the aforesaid Col. Charles O'Kelly, author of the *Macariæ Exidium* ; he had a horse shot under him at Aughrim. He mar. Lady Mary Bellew, daughter of. second Lord Bellew, but d.s.p., and left his estates to his cousin John Kelly of Clonlyon, by whom the line had been carried on to the present day.

nor O'Kelly "built twelves churches in Monvoy" (now 'Monivea'), in the county Galway; and bought 365 chalices of gold and silver, and as many copes and other necessaries for the Altar, of the richest stuffs that could be had, and distributed them among the clergy, to pray for his soul." He was King of Hy-Maine, and the seventh "O'Kelly."

110. Teige, of Talten: his son; the last King of Hy-Maine. In his time took place the English Invasion of Ireland.

111. Donal: his son. Had five sons, from the fifth of whom, who was named Dermod, is descended *Keogh*. This Donal's younger dau. who was named Amy or Mary, was the mother of Richard (or Rickard) de Burgo, the younger, a quo (see No. 18 on the "Bourke Genealogy) *Clanrickard*.

112. Connor: son of Donal.

113. Donoch: his son; was the thirteenth "O'Kelly." Was twice married: by his first wife he had three sons—1. Main, from whom descended the eldest branch of the O'Kelly family, of Hy-Maine; 2. Melaghlin; 3. Edmond. By his second wife he had one son, named William Buidhe [boy], who (al-

though the youngest son) held, himself and his posterity, the power, chief rule, and government from the three elder brothers and their issue.

114. Main: eldest son of Donoch.

115. Philip: his son.

116. Murtagh: his son. After this Murtagh O'Kelly became a widower, he entered into Holy Orders; and was, by Pope Boniface IX., made Archbishop of Tuam.

117. Melaghlin: his son. Had a brother named Donal, who was father of Thomas, the father of William, the father of Edmond, the father of William, the father of Ferdorach, the father of Hugh, the father of William Kelly.

118. Donoch: son of Melaghlin.

119. Connor: his son.

120. William: his son.

121. William (2): his son.

122. Edmond: his son. Had a brother named Donoch Granna, who was father of Ferdorach, the father of Conor Kelly.

123. William (3): son of William.

124. William Oge: his son. Had a brother named Edmond, who was the father of Edmond Oge Kelly.

125. Edmond O'Kelly, of Coilla-voy (or Coillaboggy): son of William Oge.

O'KELLY. (No. 2.)

Of Tiaquin, County Galway.

Arms: Same *Armorial Bearings* as " O'Kelly" (No. 1).

WILLIAM BUIDHE [boy] O'KELLY, the youngest son of Donoch who is No. 113 on the (foregoing) " O'Kelly" (Princes of Hy-Maine) pedigree, was the ancestor of *O'Kelly*, of Tiaquin.

114. William Buidhe: son of Donoch; built the Abbey of Kil-connel.

115. Melaghlin: his son; lord of Hy-Maine, and the 22nd " O'Kelly."

116. Donoch O'Kelly, of Tiaquin: his son; the 24th " O'Kelly."

117. Teige: his son; the 26th " O'Kelly;" had a brother named Breasal, who was the 27th "O'Kelly."

118. Melachlin: son of Teige; was the 28th " O'Kelly."

119. Teige Dubh, of Gallach : his son.

120. Hugh O'Kelly, lord abbot of Knockmoy: his son.

O'KELLY. (No. 3.)

Of Gallagh* (now " Castle Blakeney"), County Galway.

Arms: Same as " O'Kelly" (No. 1).

DONOGH O'KELLY, of Gallagh, co. Galway, Esq., had:

2. William, who had:

3. Melaghlin, who had.

4. William, of Callagh, Esq., who had:

5. Teige, of Clonbreak, who had:

6. Connor, of Clonbreak, who had:

7. Donal, of Down, co. Galway, who had:

8. Donal Reagh, who had:

9. Donogh, of Down, gent., who d. 1639. He m. Mary, dau. of Richard Bourke of Ballynacreagh, gent., co. Galway, and had:

10. Melaghlin, whose first wife was Una, daughter "Doo Dala" O'Kelly, of Fohananin, co. Galway, gent. ; and whose second wife was Katherine, dau. of Enehan O'Kelly.

11. Donogh O'Kelly : son of said Melaghlin.

O'KELLY. (No. 4.)

Of Aughrim, County Galway.

Arms: Same as " O'Kelly" (No. 1).

KELLAH O'KELLY, of Aughrim, co. Galway, Chief of his Name, had :

2. Ferdoragh, who had:

3. Melaghlin, of Aughrim, who d. Dec., 1637. He was twice m. :

first to Onora, daughter of William Bourke, of Cloghchrok, co. Galway, Esq., by whom he had two sons :

I. Teige.

II. Hugh, s.p.

---

* *Gallagh* : The O'Kellys were expelled from Gallagh by an English military officer named Blakeney ; so that the site of Gallagh is the present Castle Blakeney— situated between Mount Bellew and Ballinasloe. The modern Gallagh near Tuam was so called in honour of the ancient seat of that name.

The second wife of Melaghlin was Rose, dau. of Arthur, Viscount Iveagh (and the widow of Maelmorra O'Reilly), by whom he had a son :

III. John.

And Melaghlin's third wife was Gyles, dau. of Sir Hugh O'Conor Don, by whom he had three sons :

IV. Brian.

V. Ferdoragh.

VI. Kellagh.

4. Teige O'Kelly ; eldest son of Melaghlin.

O'KELLY. (No. 5.)

Of Meath.

Arms : Same as those of " Fogarty."

CONGALL, brother of Dermod Ruanach who is No. 92 on the "Fogarty" pedigree, was the ancestor of *O'Ceallaigh* (chiefs of *Tuath Leigh*, parts of the present baronies of "West Narragh" and "Kilkea," in the county Kildare) ; anglicised *O'Kelly.**

92. Congall: son of Aodh (or Aidus) slane, the 141st Monarch.

93. Conang Curra: his son.

94. Congall (2): his son.

95. Amhailgadh [awly]: his son.

96. Conang (2): his son.

97. Congall (3): his son.

98. Ceallach (" ceallach :" Irish, *war, strife*): his son ; a quo *O'Ceallaigh*, of Meath.

99. Flannagan : his son.

100. Maolmaoth : his son.

101. Congall (4): his son ; was the 172nd Monarch.

102. Donal : his son.

103. Donoch : his son.

104. Ceallach O'Kelly : his son.

O'MALLEY.†

Chiefs of the Baronies of Murrisk and Burrishoole, County Mayo.

Arms : Or, a boar pass gu.   *Crest :* A ship with three masts, sails set, all ppr.

BRIAN, the first King of Connaught of the Hy-Niall Sept, who is No. 87 on the (No. 1) " O'Connor" (Connaught) pedigree, and who was the eldest

---

* *O'Kelly* : These O'Kellys, who were one of the " Four Tribes of Tara," possessed the district about Naas, and had their chief residence and castle at Rathascul (or the Moat of Ascul) near Athy. The territory comprising these districts was known as " O'Kellys' Country."

+ *O'Malley*: Of this family were the celebrated Connaught-Princess Grace O'Malley, who flourished in the 16th century (see " Meeting of Grace O'Malley and Queen Elizabeth" in the Appendix) ; and the Rev. Thadeus O'Malley, " The Father of Federalism in Ireland," as he called himself, who died in Dublin on the 2nd January, 1877.

of the five sons of Eochaidh Muighmeadhoin, the 124th Monarch of Ireland, had twenty-four sons, whereof three only left issue, namely—1. Duach Galach (the first Christian King of Connaught), who was the youngest son and the ancestor of "O'Connor" (Connaught); 2. Conall Orison; 3. Arca (or Archu) Dearg: this Conall Orison was the ancestor of O'Maille; anglicised O'Mally, and O'Malley, and modernized Manly, Mallet, and De Mallet.

87. Brian: eldest brother of the Monarch Niall of the Nine Hostages.

88. Conall Orison: his son.

89. Armeadh: his son.

90. Tuathal: his son.

91. Eochaidh [Eocha] Sinne: his son.

92. Æneas: his son.

93. Cumuscrach: his son.

94. Mortach: his son.

95. Maill ("maill:" Irish, delay): his son; a quo O'Maille.

96. Seachnasach: his son.

97. Flann Abhraidh [abrad]: his son.

98. Dubhdara: his son.

99. Mortach (2): his son.

100. Dubhdara (2): his son.

101. Mortach (3): his son.

102. Donal Fionn O'Mally: his son; first assumed this sirname.

103. Mortach (4): his son.

104. Brian: his son.

105. Donal: his son.

106. Dermod: his son.

107. Owen: his son.

108. Dermod (2): his son.

109. Dermod (3): his son. This Dermod had seven sons—1. Teige; 2. Dubhdara; 3. Owen; 4. Dermod; 5. Hugh; 6. Brian, and 7. John.

110. Teige O'Mally: son of Dermod (3).

O'MEALLA.

Arms: Same as those of "MacMorough."

GUAIRE, brother of Siolan who is No. 98 on the "MacMorough" pedigree, was the ancestor of O'Meala; anglicised Mealla, O'Mealla, and Mill.

98. Guaire: son of Eoghan (or Owen).

99. Maolodhar: his son.

100. Foranan: his son.

101. Maolfothach: his son.

102. Cumeala ("mil," gen. "meala:" Irish, honey; Gr. "mel-i;" Lat. "mel"): his son; a quo O'Meala.

103. Cu geilt* (geilt: Irish, "a person who inhabits woods): his son; a quo O'Coillte; anglicised Kielty, Quilty, Galt, Wood, and Woods.

104. Dungall: his son.

105. Dunlong: his son.

106. Cathal: his son.

107. Cairbre O'Mealla: his son.

---

* *Geilt*: This word, according to O'Brien's Dictionary, originally meant "a wild man or woman," one that inhabits woods or deserts (coill and coillte: Irish, "woods" Welsh, guylht, "a wild man," and gelhtydh, "wood"). Compare the Irish words geilt and coillte, and the Latin Celtæ, with the Hebrew word celat, "refuge;" for the Celtæ frequented woods and groves, either for their places of refuge and residence, or to perform their religious rites and other ceremonies.—See TACITUS, De Morib. Germ., and CÆSAR Commentar.

O'MELAGHLIN.

Kings of Meath.]

Arms: Per fess, the chief two coats, 1st, ar. three dexter hands couped at the wrist gu. ; 2nd ar. a lion ramp. gu. armed and langued az., the base wavy az. and ar. a salmon naiant ppr.

DONCHADH, a younger brother of Maolseachlinn who is No. 102 on the "Coleman" (of Meath) pedigree, was the ancestor of *O'Maoilseachlainn ;* anglicised *O'Melaghlin, MacLaughlin,* and *McLaughlin.*

102. Donchadh: son of Flann Sionnach; the 35th Christian King of Meath, and the 171st Monarch of Ireland.

103. Donal: his son; the 40th King of Meath.

104. Maolseachlann ("maol :" Irish, *the devoted of ;* "Seachnal," *St. Seachnal,** or St. Secundinus): son of Donchadh; a quo *O'Maollseachlainn.* Was the 45th Christian King of Meath, and the 174th Monarch of Ireland ; and known as King Malachi II. He resumed the throne after the Monarch Brian Boroimhe [boru] was slain at the Battle of Clontarf, A.D. 1014; killed and destroyed such of the Danes as fled from that memorable Battle, and settled the Kingdom; building, re-edifying, and repairing many churches, monasteries, and colleges, formerly burnt and destroyed by the Danes; built St. Mary's Abbey, in Dublin, and settled sufficient maintenance as well upon that and other monasteries and Abbeys, as upon colleges and public schools, for the encouragement of learning and learned men ; maintained three hundred scholars out of his own private revenue; and having spent nine years of his second reign as Monarch in the well-ruling and governing his country, in these pious

and charitable employments, he retired into the little island of *Cro-Inis,* on Lough Annin, in the co. Westmeath, where he ended his days penitently and holily, A.D. 1023 ; others say, in 1034.

105. Donal: son of Malachi II., was the 47th King of Meath. Had three brothers—1. Connor, 2. Murtagh, 3. Flann. This Flann had one son named Murcha or Moroch, who was the last King of Meath, and the father of Dearvorgill, the wife of Tiernan O'Ruarc, the last Prince of Brefney.

106. Connor, the 48th King of Meath: son of Donal; was murdered by his brother, A.D. 1073.

107. Donal: his son.

108. Moroch: his son.

109. Malachi: his son.

110. Arthur: his son.

111. Cormac : his son.

112. Art (or Arthur): his son.

113. Niall (or Neill): his son.

114. Cormac (2): his son.

115. Cormac Oge : his son.

116. Conn Mór : his son.

117. Felim : his son.

118. Felim Oge : his son.

119. Charles: his son:

120. Moroch : his son.

121. Charles (2): his son.

122. Cormac (4) : his son.

123. Arthur O'Melaghlin, of Bal-

---

* *St. Seachnal* : After this saint, the town of "Dunshaughlin," in the county Meath, is so called.

lindony: his son. [It is stated
by O'Connellan that this family,
since the reign of Queen Anne, | have changed their sirname to *Mac-*
Laughlin, or *McLaughlin.*]

O'MURPHY.* (No. 1.)

Lords of Hy-Felimy, County Wexford.

Arms :† Quarterly, ar. and gu., four lions ramp. counterchanged ; on a fesse sa.
three garbs or.   *Crest :* A lion ramp. gu. supporting a garb or.   *Motto :* Fortis et
hospitalis.

SEICNE (or Seigin), brother of Cineth who is No. 100 on the "Dowling"
pedigree, was the ancestor of *O'Muircatha* (sometimes written *MacMurchada,*

* *O'Murphy :* According to Dr. O'Donovan, this family was originally seated at
Castle Ellis and Ouleartleagh (*abhalghortliath :* Irish, "grey orchard ;" and from which
"Oulart" is derived), in the barony of Ballaghkeen (*bealach caoin :* Irish, "the
smooth or pleasant roadway"), in the east of the county Wexford. The country of
the O'Murphys is still called the "Murroes."
    The Sept of O'Morchoe of Hy-Felimy possessed the territory extending from the
bounds of Hy-Kinsellagh at the river Ounavara to the bounds of "Sinnott's Land" in
the barony of Shelmalier, which comprised almost the whole of the present baronies of
Ballaghkeen North and South, county Wexford.   The Sept kept their ancient customs
and retained their gallowglasses (or armed soldiers), known as *O'Morchoes Police,* down
to the 16th century, and were allowed to hold their lands by descent, according to the
English custom, and not by Tanistry, which was the Irish custom. (See State Papers
of Ireland.)
    In 1611, the advowson of the Rectory and Vicarage of Kiltennel was granted by
the Crown to Sir Edward Fisher, Knt., his heirs and assigns. Same time there was
granted to him 1,500 acres Irish measure, of the towns, lands and hamlets, situated in
the territory called *Mac-de-mores,* the territory of the Sept of O'Morchoe, together with
the river Ounevara, and the mountain of Torchill (Tara hill), the whole of which was
by letters patent erected into the manor of Fisherstown or Fisher's Prospect. This
Sir Edward Fisher was one of the Commissioners appointed for the settlement of this
county. By the records of the Royal Visitation (1622) it is shown that the rectory of
Kiltennel had been an appropriation of the Monastery of Glascarrig, and that the
vicarage was in the gift of the Crown.
    In 1628 Adam Colclough was created a Baronet. He died in 1634, leaving but one
son, Sir Cæsar, who dying without male issue, the Baronetcy became extinct.
    In 1608 the borough and Castle of Wexford were granted to the Corporation of that
town at a yearly rent.
    February 4th, 1619.—It appearing that considerable disputes were occurring
between the *Morowes* (or O'Morchoes) and Sinnotts about their boundaries, King James
issued orders for an Inquisition to be held to settle the matter in dispute between them.
The Commissioners accordingly met in the Town of Wexford, and the following is
their award :—"The true meares (boundaries) between the territory of the Morowes
and Synotts land were in manner following—that is to say, from Loughnepeast to
Askenebea, from Askenebea to Clashnekern, from thence to Dowlogh, and from thence
along the suike or valley leading to the heigh way, where the valley called Glane
Ballehtein, leaving Kilmoghoor, Coroghtloe, Tailorstowne, and Rawen, with all the
lands and other members to them and every of them belonging, to be within Synotts
land, and no part of the said territory of the *Morowes,* were within the precincts
thereof, as appeareth by the said meares."

† *Arms :* On Plate XXXIX, Vol. IV., Part 1, of the *Fac Similes of Ancient MSS.
of Ireland,* we see that the Arms of " O'Murrogh" (or O'Murphy) in A.D. 1617, were :
    A lion ramp. gu. on a white (argent) shield.
    This simple device was evidently the *basis* of the present Bearings ; but we know
not when the "O'Murphy" Arms were "quartered."

MacMurchadain, O'Muirchu, O'Moroghu, O'Morchoe, and *O'Murchada*); angli-
cised *Murchoe, Murrough, Murphy, Murphie, Murpy, Morphie, Morphy,
Morpie, Morpy, O'Murphy,* and *Morrin.* The tribe name of the family was
Hy-Felimy.

100. Seicne : son of Brandubh.

101. Seagal* (" seagal :" Irish, *rye,*
Fr. " seigle ;" Lat. " secal-e") : his
son ; had a brother Nochan, who was
ancestor of *Hanrahan,* of Leinster.

102. Mochtighearna : his son.

103. Dungalach : his son.

104. Aodh Fionn : his son.

105. Alioll : his son.

106. Murcha : his son.

107. Aongus : his son.

108. M u i r - c a t h (Muirchu or
Morogh) : his son ; a quo *Mac
Muircatha* (" muircatha :" Irish, *a
sea battle*), and *O'Muirchu* (" muir-
cu :" Irish, *a sea warrior*), etc.

109. Dunsliabh : his son.

110. Donoch : his son.

111. Donal Ruadh : his son. In
the *Book of Leinster,* page 391, the
" O'Murphy" (of Leinster, or Hy-
Felimy) pedigree is traced down to
this Donal Ruadh, thus : Donal
Ruadh, son of Donchadh (or Donogh),
son of Dunslebhe, son of Murchadh,
son of Aongus, son of Murcha, son
of Oilill, son of Aodh Fionn, son of
Dungalach, son of Mochtighearna,
son of Siadhal, son of Seigin, son of
Brandubh, son of Eochaidh (a quo
Keogh, of Leinster), son of Muredach,
son of Aongus, son of Felim (a quo

Hy-Felimy), son of Eanna Ceannsalach—King of Leinster.

112. Donal Ban [bawn] : his son.

113. Dermod : his son.

114. Donoch : his son.

115. Donoch Oge : his son.

116. Cathal : his son.

117. Murtagh : his son.

118. Phelim : his son.

119. Donal : his son. This Donal,
"Chief of *Hy-Felimy,* was in 1381
slain by the Hy-Kinselagh."—See
O'Donovan's *Four Masters,* Vol. IV.,
p. 685.

120. Eimin : son of Donal.

121. Murtagh O'Morchoe,† of
Tobberlimnich (now rendered
" Toberlumny"), Chief of his Sept.
Had, A.D. 1461, a charter‡ to entitle
him to use *English law* over his
Sept and his country ; according to
a Petition still preserved among
the State Papers in England. This
Murtagh, together with Kavanagh,
Kinselagh, and MacDavy Mór held
their lands by *descent* or primogeniture, according to the English Law,
and not by Tanistry—which was
the Irish Custom.§

122. Teige : his son.

123. Art : his son ; had a younger
brother named Mahon, who, accord-

---

* *Seagal* : In page 391 of the " Book of Leinster," this name is " Siadhal" (siad-
hail : Irish, *sloth,* or *sluggishness*), a quo *OSiadhail,* anglicised *O'Shiel* and *Shiel.*

† *O'Morchoe* : This sirname is now rendered *Murphy.*

‡ *Charter* ; In the Third Edition of this Work we gave by mistake A.D. 1460 ;
and in our " Irish Landed Gentry when Cromwell came to Ireland," also 1460 as the
date of this Charter ; but in Calendar of Patent and Close Rolls of Chancery, Ireland,
page 268, we find that said Charter was granted to said Murtagh O'Morchoe or O'Murrough in the first year of the reign of Edward IV., which was 1461.　See also Haverty's
History of Ireland, p. 328 (Dublin : 1865) ; and Connellan's *Four Masters,* p. 267, and
Note on p. 273.

§ *Custom* : This Sept, however, cared but little for " English Law," as they still
continued to follow their ancient laws and customs ; retaining power and jurisdiction,
as well as territory for a considerable period subsequent to that date—their chiefs

ing to the Annals of the *Four Masters*, Vol. IV., page 1159, was in 1488, treacherously slain by Donogh, son of the lord of Hy-Kinselagh.

124. Donal Mór: son of Art; Chief of his Sept. Was possessed of the "Wilde Orcharde" *alias* "Owllarde Lyah" (more recently rendered *Ouleartleagh*), and was "aggressed to pay yearly as Kildaris Duties for the defence of 'O'Moroghe Country,' at Michaelmas XX Kyne or X Milkine, A.D. 1537." Had a brother Teige. This Donal, Chief of his Sept, was the O'Morchoe, *temp.* Henry VIII., and Edward VI. In the latter reign, after long resistance, he was overthrown, attainted, and his estates and the territory of the Sept were confiscated to the Crown.* A considerable portion of this confiscated property was granted, in the reigns of Elizabeth and James I. to the Synnotts, as rewards for their "fidelity and noble service in suppressing common enemies."† The overthrow of Donal Mór and the subjugation of his followers (*temp.* Edward VI.) broke the power of the Sept "O'Murphy," from which, as an independent Sept, they never rallied. Many of them dispersed and settled in Carlow, Kilkenny, and the neighbouring counties, where they afterwards became numerous.‡ Some went to Spain where they distinguished themselves in arms.§ Later on, in the Cromwellian period, and after the capitulation of Limerick, numbers followed Sarsfield to France, many took refuge in Spain and other countries, where they also distinguished themselves in arms and diplomacy.‖ In the Patent and Close Rolls in Chancery, 5th Edward VI., Donal Mór is styled "*Lord O'Morgho*" (O'Murphy), which establishes the position of the Sept, and its Chief at that time, as an independent family.¶

125. Art, of Tobberlimnich: son of Donal Mór; Chief of his Sept.

126. Donal, of Tobberlimnich: his son; Chief of his Sept; had two sons:—1. Conall; 2. Brian, whose son Art, of Ouleartleagh, escaped the Cromwellian confiscations.

127. Conall O'Morchoe, of Tobberlimnich:** son of Donal: Chief of his

keeping gallowglasses (or armed soldiers) for offensive and defensive purposes, and for levying dues from their subjects. In the middle of the sixteenth century "The O'Morchoe" (Donal Mór, No. 124 on this pedigree) enforced "cain" (*cain*, Irish, rent, tribute, fine) due to him as Tighearna or Chief of the Sept.

* *Crown*: See Patent and Close Rolls in Chancery, 27th Queen Elizabeth, A.D. 1584; and also Dalton's "*King James's Army List*," p. 161, First Edition.

† *Enemies*: See *Proceedings of the Kilkenny Arch-Society*, for 1861, p. 81.

‡ *Numerous*: See Connellan's *Four Masters*, Note 7, on page 224.

§ *Arms*: See O'Connor's *Military Memoirs of the Irish Nation*, p. 73.

‖ *Diplomacy*: See in the Appendix the "Irish Brigades in the Service of France, Spain, the Spanish Netherlands, Austria, America, etc."

¶ *Family*: See Patent and Close Rolls in Chancery, 5th Edward VI. (A.D. 1551), p. 241, Vol. I., Dublin, 1861.

** *Tobberlimnich*: This place is now called *Toberlumny* ("tobar:" Irish, *a well,* "luim," *milk*), and is situated in the parish of Meelnagh, in the barony of Ballaghkeen. Quoting from Dr. O'Donovan in his "Antiquities," preserved in the Royal Irish Academy, Dublin, "The last head of the family resided at Oulartleagh, in the barony of Ballaghkeen" (who, according to the Book of Rights, p. 208, retained their property, till very recently).—See "O'Murphy" (No. 2) pedigree, p. 696.

Arthur Murphy, the translator of Sallust and Tacitus, was of this Wexford family; so was Edward Murphy, the editor of Lucian; but their pedigrees are not on record.

Sept; died October, 1634, and was buried at Castle Ellis.* This Conall married Joan, daughter of Donal an Spaineacht† Kavanagh, of Clonmullen, county Carlow, and had five sons and seven daughters: The sons were—1. Teige, of whom presently; 2. Phelim, who d. unm. in 1634; 3. Pierce, living in 1634; 4. David (or Daniel), living in 1634; 5. Gerald, living in 1634; the daus.

were: 1. Joan, who married James, son of Donoch O'Morchoe, of Ruanmore, gent.; 2. Ellen or Elinor, who mar. Edmond O'Morchoe, of Ballymacdonaghfyn, gent.; 3. Mary, who married Thomas Synnot, of Clone. 4. Ellenor, living in 1634; 5. Elizabeth, living in 1634; 6. Honor or Onora, living in 1634; 7. Margaret, who married John Rowe, of Ballybrennan.

Of this Wexford family was also Lieutenant-Colonel Murphy, who served in the French Army with great distinction under General Lally in India, and was present at all the principal engagements in that country, until taken prisoner at the battle of Wandewash in 1759.—O'Callaghan in his *History of the Irish Brigade in the Service of France*, after noticing the fact of Colonel Murphy being taken prisoner, introduces the following note :—"The Sept of O'Murchudha, pronounced O'Murraghoo, at first anglicised O'Murchoe, and finally Murphy, were likewise designated Hy-Felimy, or descendants of Felim ; from their progenitor, a son of the celebrated Enna Kinsellagh, King of Leinster, contemporary of St. Patrick, in the 5th century. The territory of the Sept consisted of the Murroes or Macdamores, in the county Wexford ; the seat of the Chieftain being at Castle Ellis, where, in 1634, Conal O'Murchudha, the head of the race, died, and was interred ; and, till within the present century, a respectable branch of the family still possessed a considerable estate at Oulartleigh. (See the " O'Murphy" No. 2 pedigree, *infra*.) To be a Murphy is to be proverbially associated, at home and abroad, with old Irish or Milesian extraction, even without the prefix of O'; 'Don Patricio O'Murphy, the steward of the Duke of Wellington's estates in Spain, being,' writes Dr. O'Donovan, in 1861, 'the only man living, who retains the O' in this name.' During the war of the Revolution in Ireland, the Murphys were represented in the Jacobite army among Hamilton's, Kenmare's, Tyrone's, Bellew's, Kilmallock's, and Hunsdon's infantry, by several officers, from the rank of Major to that of Lieutenant; and seven of the name, in Wexford alone, besides many more in other counties, are to be seen in the attainders of the Jacobites. From the sailing of the Irish forces for France, after the Treaty of Limerick, in 1691, to the reign of Louis XVI., there were various Murphys also, from the rank of Major to that of Lieutenant, in the Irish regiments of Charlemont, Clancarty, Limerick, Fitzgerald, Galmoy, Dillon, and Clare. besides those in the French regiments ; the Lieutenant-Colonel of the regiment of Lally having been, so far, the highest in rank of his name." Some years previous to the death of Conal Murchudha, or Murphy, alluded to above, 66,800 acres of the district, between the river Slaney and the Sea, were cleared of the old Irish inhabitants. Of 447 Irish (mostly Murphys) claiming freeholds, only 21 families were allowed to retain their ancient house and habitations, 36 others were to be elsewhere provided for, and all the rest of the freeholders, 390 in number, together with the other inhabitants, estimated to be 14,500 men, women, and children, were removable at the will of the new planters.—On the 7th day of May, 1613, the Sheriff of Wexford proceeded to put the latter in possession of the several portions of the lands specified in their patents, broke open the doors of such of the ancient proprietors as resisted, and turned them out. They probably felt all this the more, as they had been previously informed that nothing was intended unto them by that plantation but their good ; and that the civilizing of the country was the chief thing aimed at. They all offered, but in vain, to pay such rents, and to perform such buildings, as the new undertakers were to perform. (*Vide* Prendergast's Cromwellian Settlement.) Previous to this clearing, the name of Murphy was scarcely known in Forth or Bargie.

* *Castle Ellis* : According to "Molyneux's Visitation of the County Wexford," preserved in the Office of Ulster King-of-Arms, Dublin Castle, this Conall O'Morchoe died in 1634, and was buried at Castle Ellis.

† *Spaineach* : See No. 128 on the "Kavanagh" (No. 2) pedigree, p. 494, *ante*.

128. Teige : eldest son of Conall. Succeeded his father in 1634, being then of full age; married Anne, daughter of David Redmond, of Rahin-Callengallen (or Rahinedrum-gullion), gent., and had Brian of whom presently. This Teige

"was seized in fee on 23rd October, 1641, of Tobberlimnich and Tourknick : 170 acres ; Garrybranagh, 182 acres ; Monganbo, 111 acres ; Crymure and Kilmaloney, 109 acres : Total, 572. Barony of Ballaghkeene, county Wexford. Being so seized, he was in actual rebellion, and commanded a company of 500 Rebels, with whom he marched towards the City of Dublin, where he was slain in Battle : when his lands were forfeited."—*Inquisition taken at Wexford, 7th May, 1663, Anno 15 Charles II.*

129. Brian : son of Teige.

130. Art (or Arthur), of Ballyellen, county Carlow ; son of Brian ; living in 1690; d. s. p. Had two younger brothers—1. Teige, who d. unm. 2. Edmund, born 1693, died 16th May, 1763, and was buried in Old Leighlin churchyard, county Carlow. This Edmund had four sons.

I. David, b. 1723 ; d. 3rd Sept., 1777.

II. James, born 1730; died 12th October, 1754.

III. Daniel, b. 1740; died 27th December, 1777.

IV. Andrew (of whom presently), b. 1741 ; d. 28th Sept., 1793. (As far as we can find, David, James, and Daniel, here mentioned, d. unm.)

131. Andrew, of Ballyellen : fourth son of Edmund, who was the third son of Teige; b. 1741, d. 1793, and was buried also in Old Leighlin churchyard, co. Carlow ; mar. Margaret Dunn, and had five sons and one daughter :

I. Edmund, b. 1779 ; died unm. 17th December, 1837.

II. James, born 1782 : died unm. 26th December, 1857.

III. Daniel (of whom presently), b. 1785 ; died 17th November, 1846.

IV. David, b. 1789 ; d. 8th May, 1829 ; m., and left two daus.

V. Michael, born 1790 ; d. unm. 30th November, 1862.

I. The daughter d. young.

132. Daniel Murphy, of Ballyellen, co. Carlow, Ireland, and afterwards of Montreal, Canada: third son of Andrew ; born 1785 ; removed to Canada in 1824, where he resided till his death, in 1846. He mar. in 1817, Mary, dau. of Peter Byrne, of Knockullard, gent., and his wife, Diana Rudkin, of Corris, co. Carlow, and had five sons and two daus. :

I. Edward, b. in 1818 in parish of Dunleckney, co. Carlow (see No. 133 *infra* on this Genealogy).

II. Peter-Sarsfield, b. in Corris, county Carlow ; m. in 1851, to Jane-Amelia, dau. of Allen Perry ; issue (in 1883) one son, Edward-Albert, b. 1864 ; and three daughters.

III. Bernard-Rudkin, b. in Corris, co. Carlow ; dead.

IV Daniel, born in Montreal, Canada, 1824; dead.

V. Patrick-Alexander, born in Montreal ; unm. in 1883.

The two daughters were:

I. Margaret - Diana, born in Montreal; married in 1865, A. A. Meilleur, son of J. B. Meilleur, M.D., and LL.D., of Montreal.

II. Eliza-Anne, b. in Montreal; dead.

133. Edward Murphy, of Montreal, Canada, J.P., Knight of the Order of the Holy Sepulchre: eldest son of Daniel ; b. 1818, and living in 1887. Married, first, in Jan., 1848, to Elizabeth, dau. of Thomas M'Bride,

of the co. Donegal, Ireland, gent., and by her had two sons and three daughters:—I. Edward-Byrne Murphy, died; II. Patrick - Sarsfield Murphy, d. ; I. Mary, m. in 1871, to Edward C. Monk, son of the Hon. Samuel Cornwallis Monk, one of Her Majesty's Justices of Appeal for the Province of Quebec ; II. Elizabeth-Diana, a nun, in religion "Sister Mary Edward," died; III. Emily-Hester, living in 1883. Secondly, in February, 1863, this

Edward Murphy married Maria-Georgiana, dau. of the Hon. William Power, Judge of the Superior Court of Quebec, Canada, and by her had one son and three daughters: III. William-Sarsfield Murphy, who is No. 134 *infra ;* IV. Grace-Maria, living in 1887 ; V. Amy-Susan, living in 1887 : VI. Alice-Lily, d.

134. William - Sarsfield Murphy, born 1865 : eldest surviving son of Edward, of Montreal, living in 1887.

O'MURPHY. (No. 2.)

Of Ouleartleagh, County Wexford.

Arms : Ar. an apple tree eradicated fructed ppr. on a chief vert a lion ramp. also gu. holding betw. the paws a garb or. *Crest :* On a chapeau gu. turned up erm. a lion ramp. also gu. holding betw. the paws a garb or. *Motto* : Fortis et hospitalis, over the motto—Vincere vel mori.

TEIGE, a brother of Donal Mór who is No. 124 on the "O'Murphy" (No. 1) pedigree, was the ancestor of this branch of that family :

124. Teige O'Morchoe, of Ouleartleagh, or "Fracht Lea," as it was sometimes called : son of Art.

125. Art Ruadh: his son ; obtained a pardon A.D. 1551—5 Edward VI.

126. Hugh Ballach, of Ouleartleagh and Cooleknockmore: son of Art Ruadh.

127. Brian O'Morchoe, of Ouleartleigh : his son; named in all the patents of his lands as "Brian MacHugh Ballagh" or Brian, son of "Freckled Hugh." Had a grant by patent, Anno 15 James I., of the lands of Ouleartleigh More, Tenneberney, and Ballymabodagh, Cooleknockmore, Coolenaboy next Tomlean, and Kian, in the barony of Ballaghkeene, in the territory of the

"Murrows," in co. Wexford. Made a deed of entail of these lands, in 1634.

He forfeited, after the rebellion of 1641, Oulartleigh and his other lands which were granted *in trust* for his son, to Richard Kenny, except Oulartleigh-beg which was granted to Richard Franklin under the Act of Settlement.

128. Art O'Morchoe of Ouleartleigh : son of Brian ; escaped the Cromwellian confiscations.

129. Daniel Morchoe of Ouleartleigh ; son of Art ; named in chancery bill of 14th December, filed by his son Arthur Murphy, as "Daniel Murphy *alias* Morchoe ;" succeeded to Ouleartleigh, Tenneberney, and Ballynamodagh, under

his grandfather's entail of 1634, as tenant for life. Will dated 26th May, 1679; died same year. Will proved in Ferns, 5th June, 1680; desired to be buried at Kilmallock: "Mr. John Dalton and well-beloved cousin Edward Kavangh of Borris (co. Carlow), to be his Executors and overseers."

The following are a few extracts from this Daniel's Will (of the 26th May, 1679):

"6thly. I leave fourtie pounds if any other children come to perfection of mine.

"9thly. I leave thirtie shillings to the Clercie (clergy) for my Soule, that is to say fifteen shillings to the Parish Priest, and the other fifteen shillings to the rest of the Clercie, as my overseers will order."

"I do leave a lease of 100 years upon Balliebudagh, Oullerleagh, and Tigebornin, to the within-named my daughter Bridget *Murphie*, for five pence an acre per annum, in raisance of the within-named my son Arte (or Arthur) *Murphie* should die without lawful issue, and if the said Ellinor should die without issue lawfully, I leave to my sonne John *Murphie* the afforesaid lease of the above-named townes and to his heirs lawfully begotten, and if the said John should die without lawful issue, I leave to my cousin James Keoghoe and to his heirs lawfully begotten. As witness my hand and seale, the 26th May, 1679.

"DAN. MORCHOE."

"Witness being present:
"GEO. KEOGHOE.
"EDMOND KEOGHOE."

This Daniel Morchoe had, also, a son George;* and another daughter Ellinor, to whom by his will he bequeathed £50.

130. Arthur Morchoe *alias* Murphy of Oulartleagh and of Ballycomin, co. Kilkenny: eldest son of Daniel; married, 1st, to Elizabeth, dau. of Thomas Knox of Taguanon, county Wexford, by whom he had one child, a daughter Dorcas, from whom Baron Halsbury, Lord High Chancellor of England, is descended; 2nd, on the 17th April, 1704, to Elizabeth, dau. of William Turner, by whom he had eight sons and four daughters:

I. Daniel (of whom presently).
II. William, who succeeded to Oulartleigh.
III. Arthur.
IV. Thomas.
V. James.
VI. Francis.
VII. Henry.
VIII. Kenny.

Daughters:
I. Jane.
II. Elinor.
III. Lucy.
IV. Elizabeth.

Will dated 28th March, 1761; will proved in Ferns, by his son Thomas, 21st April, 1761; desired to be buried at Kilmallock, county Wexford.

131. Daniel Murphy of Oulartleigh: eldest son of Arthur; joined his father in levying a fine, but neglected to suffer a recovery; died in his father's lifetime in 1758, leaving an only child, a son James, who was an idiot from his birth, and who was born in 1740, and died, May, 1759, aged 19, when his uncle William, became his heir and successor to his estates.

132. William Murphy, brother of Daniel, succeeded said James, under the entail referred to in the Chancery Bill of 14th December, 1692; married Elizabeth, dau. of John Hawkins, Ulster King of Arms (marriage licence, 26th June, 1727), by whom he had two sons:

I. Arthur, who was his successor.

---

* *George*: Unless this George had died s.p. before his father's Will was made; or, that he died young, it appears strange that by the said Will the Estate should be leased to Bridget, in case her brother Arthur died without issue.

II. Carey, who had a fortune of £1,000 with his wife.

133. Arthur Murphy of Oulartleigh, born 1732: eldest son of William; Party to deeds of 13th and 14th June, 1758; Defendant in Chancery Bill of 23rd May, 1760; named in his grandfather's will; succeeded to Oulartleigh, Ballynamodagh, and Tinneberney, as heir of entail, under the deed of entail 1634. Will dated 19th August, 1789; proved 10th April, 1793; married Esther, dau. of John Pounden, Esq., of Enniscorthy (marriage licence 29th January, 1766), by whom he had two sons and three daughters:

I. Arthur, his successor.
II. William of Bloomfield.
I. Margaret.
II. Eleanor.
III. Charlotte.

134. Arthur Murphy of Oulartleigh : eldest son of Arthur ; succeeded to Oulartleigh, Ballynamodagh and Tinneberney ; named in his father's will; made a mortgage of his estate, 9th November, 1795; will dated 5th September, 1805 ; buried at Kilmallock, county Wexford ; married Margaret, dau. of Rev. Shapland Swiney, Rector of Templeshambo, county Wexford (marriage licence, 18th March, 1791), by whom he had one son and two daughters:

I. Arthur, his successor.
I. Katherine, wife of Robert Shaw.
II. Hester, wife of Henry Grattan Douglas, Esq., M.D., Surgeon to Louis Phillipe, King of the French.

135. Arthur Murphy, of Oulartleigh : only son of Arthur, inherited Oulartleigh, Ballynamodagh and Tinneberney; made a further mortgage of his estate 15th March, 1830; mortgages foreclosed in a suit of "Jane Cooke v. Arthur Murphy;" and by decree of the Court of Chancery, dated 26th November, 1839, and order of 7th December, 1840, estates sold 13th November, 1841. Died at Gorey, county Wexford, 21st August, 1867; buried at Monamolin, county Wexford ; he married, 1st, Elizabeth, dau. of John Millet, Esq., of Lisinarta, county Tipperary, who died without issue ; 2nd, Rebecca, dau. of Rev. John Bagwell Creagh, Rector of Rincurran, and Vicar of Carrig, county Cork (named in the "Royal descents," as 15th in descent from King Edward III.); marriage settlements, 20th February, 1834. By his second wife this Arthur had an only child, a son, Arthur-MacMurrogh.

136. Arthur MacMurrogh Murphy of Monamolin, co. Wexford, and Ailesbury Road, Dublin, and formerly of Oulartleigh, co. Wexford; born 4th January, 1835; and living in 1887 ; married Susan-Elizabeth, dau. of Thomas Bradley, Esq., M.D., of Kellysgrange, county Kilkenny (married at Kells, November, 1863), by whom he has had three sons and four daughters:

I. Thomas-Arthur-MacMurrogh Murphy, born 22nd March, 1865 ; B.A., T.C.D.
II. Arthur-MacMurrogh Murphy, born 22nd September, 1866.
III. William - MacMurrogh Murphy, born 12th July, 1868.
I. Sophia-Rebecca MacMurrogh Murphy.
II. Gertrude-Susan MacMurrogh Murphy ; d. 29th June, 1882; bur. at Mount Jerome, Dublin.
III. Edith MacMurrogh Murphy.
IV. Mary-Augusta MacMurrogh Murphy.

137. Thomas-Arthur MacMurrogh Murphy : eldest son of Arthur; a B.A. of T.C.D.; born, 1865, and living in 1887.

O'MURPHY. (No. 3.)

Of the County Carlow.

Arms: See those of " Murphy" (No. 1).

At the Great Rebellion of 1641, Mathew Murphy held considerable estates in Wexford, chiefly in the districts of Palace and Clonroche. With the larger portion of Ireland, Wexford also rose in Rebellion, and, under the leadership of Sir Morgan Kavanagh, marched to join the insurgent forces. Among these, with his kinsmen and tenants, was Mathew Murphy, who was made a Captain on the 15th April, 1642. The disastrous battle of Blackheath was fought between the Irish forces under Lord Mountgarret and the Kings troops under the Duke of Ormonde, in which the former were worsted. After the battle, the head of Colonel Kavanagh was brought to Lord Ormonde. Captain Murphy, with a company formed from the wreck of the Irish forces, followed the fortunes of the Confederate Army, until a wound received in the battle of Lynch's Cross incapacitated him for further service. He then returned home, and, fearing attainder of the family estates, settled in a district of the county Carlow, some few miles from Borris, in the shadow of the Blackstairs, called after him " *Ballymurphy*." Here he married a sister of Daniel Oge Kavanagh, and cousin of the slain chief. To him were born—1. Laurence; 2. Mathew; 3. Jane; and 4. Richard. Cromwell on his march to Ross passed along these mountains, and burned the castle which Captain Matthew Murphy had erected, and all were obliged to take refuge in the mountains, in the cave universally known in that district as " Cahir's Den." Of these children Laurence died young. In the Williamite wars the three others joined the troops of Lord Galway, and were present at the battle of the Boyne. James was badly wounded, and returned home; but the two other brothers continued with the army until the Siege of Limerick was raised, when they sailed with Sarsfield and the "Wildgeese" for France. Matthew was killed in action at the battle of Neerwinden or Lauden, when Marshal Duke of Luxemburg and William III. contended for mastery. Richard served in the regiment of Lord Clancarty, as captain. He married and had two sons, one of whom, Mathew, exchanged into the Spanish service, and his descendants hold civil and military offices there to the present day. The other, Richard, attached himself to Count Lally Tollendal's regiment, where, by successive acts of bravery, he rose to the position of Lieutenant-Colonel. As captain, he sailed with the regiment to Scotland, to the aid of Prince Charles, and was taken prisoner with the remnant of the regiment, at Inverness, the day after the battle of Culloden. Being exchanged he went to India with Count Lally, was present at the battle of Wandewash, in Jan., 1760, and was one of the officers taken prisoner after the complete overthrow of the French.

James returned from the Boyne to Ballymurphy, and married a sister of Bryan Oge Kavanagh, of Ballyleagh—this latter also marrying a sister of his. Bryan Oge was an officer in Dillon's regiment, and was famous as a swordsman. He had previously served in Spain. Many stories of him are current to this day in the Barony of Idrone. It is told of him that, in one of the conflicts attendant on the passage of the Boyne, being engaged with an officer of Schomberg's force, so powerful was his arm and so keen his sword, that, getting a clear sweep at his enemy, his blade clove swiftly through his neck without disturbing the head! It was only when the officer moved, that his head fell off, exclaiming as it touched the ground: " Bloody Wars!"

In the ancient abbey of Saint Moling, beside the flowing waters of the Barrow, the following moss-covered tablet is to be seen:—" Here lieth the body of Bryan Kavanagh of Drumin, of the family of Ballyleagh. A man remarkably known to the nobility and gentry of Ireland by the name of Bryan Na-Sthroka, from his noble actions and valour, in King James's troop, in the battles of the Boyne and Aughrim. He died February 8th, 1735, aged 74 years. Also Mary Murphy his wife with four of their children.—R.I.P."

Of James Murphy there were born Richard and Mathew. Of the former there was born Martin, of whom Richard, and of whom Laurence, Mathew, and James. The two latter were killed among the insurgent forces at the battle of Ross. Laurence had children: Richard, Andrew, James, and Matthew. The two first went to America; one of whom, Andrew, rose to great opulence in Columbus, Ohio, leaving several children. Mathew settled in Glynn, county Carlow, and had five sons, one of whom died in action in the passage of "Island No. 10," by Admiral Farragut at New Orleans in the War of Secession. James, the youngest son, is author of the "Forge of Clohogue," "Convict No. 25," and several other Irish national novels. He has several sons: Mathew, Michael, Thomas, Martin; and daughters Lizzie, Margaret, Mary—all living in Dublin, in 1887.

O'MURPHY. (No. 4.)

Of the "Clan Moroghoe" Sept.

Arms : See those of "MacMorough," *ante.*

MURCHA (or Morogh) MacMorough, son of Murcha who (see p. 553, *ante*) is No. 111 on the "MacMorough" pedigree, was the ancestor of this branch of that family :

112. Morogh MacMorough (a quo *Clan Moroghoe*): son of Murcha. From this Clan is derived the name *O'Moroghoe*, which has been anglicised *O'Murphy*, *Murrough*, and *Murphy*.

113. Morogh: son of Morogh; had a brother Donogh, who had a son named Morogh.

114. Morogh-na-Maoir (of the Stewards): son of Morogh (No. 113); living A.D. 1193.

115. Donogh Reamhar : his son ; a quo *O'Murphy Reamhar.* (See the "O'Murphy" No. 10 pedigree.)

116. Morogh : his son.

117. Donogh na-Coille :* his son.

118. Diarmuid :† his son.

119. Maurice : his son.

120. Donogh Dubh MacMorough

O'Murphy : his son.   From this Donogh it is said that *Clan Donagh* was so called; and from the territory of *Clan Donagh*, the present barony of "Clandonagh," in the Queen's County, on the border of the co. Kilkenny, derives its name.

O'MURPHY. (No. 5.)

Of Cork : Of the "Clan Moroghoe" Sept.

Arms : Quarterly, ar. and gu., four lions ramp. counterchanged, on a fess sa. three garbs or.   *Crest :* A lion ramp. gu., holding in fore paws a garb or.   *Motto :* Fortis et hospitalis.

THIS family is a branch of the *Clan Moroghoe* Sept, whose genealogy is traced in the "O'Murphy" (No. 4) pedigree; and is a branch of the "O'Murphy" family of Muskerry, in the county Cork; which ancient clan went from Leinster about the thirteenth century; and, as may be seen by ancient Maps, possessed the territory between Cork and Macroom, on the northern side of the River Lee.

At the commencement of the eighteenth century, in the year 1709, just after the enactment of the Penal Laws‡ of the reign of Queen Anne, *Nicholas Murrough* or *Murphy,* a descendant of the once powerful *Clan Moroghoe,* of Leinster, migrated from the land then held by the Sept to

---

* *Coille :* Donagh-na-Coille had a brother named Dermod *Muimneach* (or Dermod the "Munsterman"), who was father of Donogh, the father of Donal, the father of Dermod, the father of Donogh, who was living in the 15th century.   Dermod Muimneach O'Moroghoe was the first of the family that, in the 13th century, settled in Munster.

† *Diarmuid :* This Diarmuid (or Dermod) MacMorough O'Murphy had two brothers—1. Reman, who was the father of Seonach, the father of Manus, the father of David ; and 2. Luke, who had a son named Donogh.

‡ *Penal Laws :*

> In that dark time of cruel wrong, when on our country's breast,
> A dreary load, a ruthless code, with wasting terrors press'd—
> Our gentry stripp'd of land and clan, sent exiles o'er the main,
> To turn the scales on foreign fields for foreign monarchs' gain ;
> Our people trod like vermin down, all fenceless flung to sate
> Extortion, lust, and brutal whim, and rancorous bigot hate—
> Our priesthood tracked from cave to hut, like felons chased and lashed,
> And from their ministering hands the lifted chalice dashed—
> In that black time of law-wrought crime, of stifling woe and thrall,
> There stood supreme one foul device, one engine worse than all :
> Him whom they wished to keep a slave, they sought to make a brute—
> They banned the light of heaven—they bade *instruction's* voice be mute.

which he belonged in the barony of "Clandonagh," Queen's County, and settled at Cloghroe, in Muskerry, county Cork.

In the year 1756, one of the last "Bills of Discovery," in that part of the country, was filed against his son *Jeremiah Murphy*, of Cloghroe, as a "Papist," by one Samuel Windus, of Grafton-street, Dublin, an informer. Jeremiah Murphy refusing to conform to Protestantism, and preferring the loss of his property to that of the Faith of our Fathers, was thereupon dispossessed of his lands. By his marriage with Mary-Anne Kedmond of the county Tipperary (a descendant of an adherent of King William III., who came with him to Ireland in one of his Danish regiments), Jeremiah Murphy, whose wife embraced the Catholic religion, had two children, both being sons : 1. Daniel, 2. Jeremiah. The altered circumstances of the family consequent on this confiscation, obliged the second son Jeremiah to engage in trade and commerce in the city of Cork, in which both he and his descendants have, since then, been singularly successful ; thus verifying in a remarkable manner the words of a great Catholic Writer :

"God never permits himself to be outdone in generosity."

Jeremiah Murphy married Mary O'Hallinan, and had issue :
I. James, of Ringmahon, Cork, born in 1769.
II. John, who was Catholic Bishop of Cork, b. 1772.
III. Jeremiah, of Hyde Park, Cork, b. 1779.
IV. Daniel, of Belleville, Cork, b. 1780.
V. Nicholas, of Clifton, Cork, b. 1783.
And Mary-Anne, who married Mr. John Murphy, of the Fermoy Sept, and was the mother of the late Jeremiah-John Murphy, Master in Chancery ; and of Michael Murphy, late Official Assignee to the Court of Bankruptcy, Dublin.

There are numerous descendants of the above named children of Jeremiah Murphy resident in the county and city of Cork ; in other parts of Great Britain and Ireland ; in the United States of America ; in Canada ; Australia, etc. ; and in the Church, Army, and Navy.

There are no descendants of Daniel, the elder brother of Jeremiah Murphy, that can be traced in Ireland, at present ; but a grandson and two granddaughters of his are (1887) still living in the Colony of Victoria, Australia.

This ancient Irish family would be perfectly within their rights in, at any time, re-assuming their original patronymic "MACMOROUGH-MURPHY ;" for it is their *birthright*.

O'MURPHY. (No. 6.)

Of Muscry, County Cork.

Arms: See those of "MacMorough," *ante*.

THE following are some of the different Septs of this family in Muscry, in 1887 :

1. Murphy Dubh ("dubh:" Irish, *dark featured*) reside at Deshure, Kilmichael.

2. Murphy Bog ("bog:" Irish, *soft*), at Canovee.

3. Murphy Stuac ("stuac:" Irish, *summit, top, declivity of a hill*), at Kilmichael and Kilmurry.

4. Murphy Bán ("ban:" Irish, *white, fair*), at Currabeh and Pullerick, in Kilmurry.

5. Murphy Leib ("ledhb:" Irish, *a piece of untanned leather, a fragment*), in and about Cork City.

6. Murphy Buidhe ("buidhe:" Irish, *yellow*), at Templemartin, Moneens, Kilbarry, Dunbollog, and Kilbrittain.

7. Murphy Reamhar or Roghmhar ("reamhar:" Irish, *fat, bulky, wealthy*), at Inchirahill, Moviddy, Templemartin, and Tasmania (the

Most Rev. D. Murphy, D.D., Catholic Bishop of Tasmania, is of this family).

8. Murphy Derbh ("deirbh:" Irish, *a churn*), at Cork, Kilmurry, Corrach, and Murragh.

9. Murphy Géire ("geire:" Irish, *sharp, sharpness, bitterness*), at Mount Music, Kilmichael, Currabeh, Lisarda.

10. Murphy Caol ("caol:" Irish, *slender*), in the parish of Kilbonane, and at Kilcrea.

11. Murphy Pound, at Ahabullog.

12. Murphy Crón ("cron:" Irish, here means *brown, swarthy*), living at Kilmichael.

13. Murphy Taranige, of Murragh.

14. Murphy Purtinee, Fuide, Cullanee, etc., variously located.

In the "O'Murphy" (No. 4) pedigree we see that Dermod Muimneach O'Moroghoe was the first of the family that, in the 13th century, settled in Munster. He and his people settled in Muscry, where they obtained various grants of land from the MacCarthys and O'Mahonys. We learn that there were some thirty-five families of them, all sprung from the original Leinster Sept, who can trace their descent from Felim (or Felimidh), son of Enna Cean Salach, King of Leinster, *temp*. St. Patrick, in Ireland.

The original location in the county Cork, of the family, was, and is still, named "Bally-Murphy," a townland north of Innishannon, near Upton. Before A.D. 1641, the senior branch of the family lived there, and was distinguished by the name *Buidhe*, which they still bear. At that time they were deprived of their possessions ; and the eldest living member of the family, who was then about 14 years of age, removed to the north of Cork, took service under the Blarney MacCarthys, and assisted in the defence of Dunbolg Castle, near Carrignavar.

O'MURPHY. (No. 7.)

O'Murphy Buidhe, County Cork.

1. JOHN MURPHY, of Ballmurphy: son of Philip ; removed at the age of 14 years to Dunbolg, assisted in the defence of that castle against the English ; married there and had issue :

2. Philip (2) : his son.
3. Philip (3) : his son.
4. Philip (4) : his son.
5. John (2) : his son ; had three sons :
  I. Martin, of whom see the "O'Murphy" (No. 8) pedigree.
  II. Patrick, of whom presently.
  III. Denis.
6. Patrick : second son of John.
7. John (3) : his son ; had three sons :
  I. Rev. William Murphy, Parish Priest of Murragh, Temple-martin, and Kinneigh, co. Cork,

who died at Mountpleasant in 1862, and was buried at the Catholic Church of Temple-martin.
  II. John, of whom see "O'Murphy" (No. 9).
  III. Patrick, of whom presently.
8. Patrick : son of John (No. 7) ; m. a Miss Carney and had issue :
  I. Rev. William, of whom presently.
  II. Another son, d. s. p.
  III. Mary, living unm. at Kilbrittain, in 1887.
  IV. Margaret, d. young.
  V. Hannah, m. Timothy Murphy Reamhar. (See No. 7 on the "O'Murphy," No. 10 pedigree).
9. Rev. William Murphy : son of Patrick ; Parish Priest of Kilbrittain ; living in 1887.

O'MURPHY. (No. 8.)

O'Murphy Buidhe—continued.

6. MARTIN MURPHY : eldest son of John, who is No. 5 on the "O'Murphy" (No. 7) pedigree ; remained at Dunbolg ; m. there and had issue.
7. Michael : his son.
8. Martin (2) : his son.

9. James : his son ; living at Ballynabortagh, Dunbolg, in 1887 ; m. and has had issue.
10. Martin Murphy : his son ; a Deacon in Maynooth College, in 1887.

O'MURPHY. (No. 9.)

O'Murphy Buidhe—continued.

8. JOHN MURPHY: second son of John, who is No. 7 on the O'Murphy" (No. 7) pedigree; removed to Kinalmeaky, and there married Elizabeth, dau. of Timothy Murray, of Kilbarry (Kinalmeaky), by his wife Ellen O'Farrell, and had issue:

I. Rev. John Murphy, C.C., who died at Kilbrittain, 30th Nov., 1874, and was buried at the Templemartin Catholic Church.
II. William, who died 1881; m. but left no issue.
III. Timothy, of whom presently.
IV. Patrick, emigrated to America, m. and has issue.
V. Ellen, living unm. at Kilbarry, in 1887.
VI. Martin, d. an infant.
VII. Martin (2), living in London, m. and has issue.
VIII. Bartholomew, m. by the Rev. J. Cummins, P.P., in the Catholic Church of Templemartin, to Ellen, dau. of the late Patrick O'Casey of Ballyvolane, by his wife Mary O'Driscoll (Dooleen), on the 18th June,

1881; living at Moss Grove Cottage, near Bandon, and has issue :—1. John, b. 5th April, 1882; 2. William, born 15th November, 1883; 3. Patrick, born 6th Feb., 1885; and 4. Timothy, b. 15th Feb., 1886.
IX. Eliza, who m. in 1886, Teige (or Timothy) O'Long of Ballinadee, near Bandon, has issue a dau. Mary, in 1887.
X. Daniel, m. in America to Mary, dau. of Daniel O'Donovan, by his wife Mary O'Crowley; living in 1887 at 237 Commercial Street, Dorchester, Boston, Mass., U.S.A., and has a daughter Elizabeth.

9. Timothy Murphy (Buidhe): son of John; m. by the Rev. Father Lucy to Hannah, dau. of John O'Donovan of Barryroe, by his wife Ellen Cunningham; has issue:
I. William, b. 28th Dec., 1882.
II. John, b. 22nd June, 1886.
This Timothy represents this branch of the family in Kinalmeaky, in 1887.

O'MURPHY. (No. 10.)

O'Murphy Reamhar, of Muscry and Kinalmeaky.

THE chief seat of this branch of the " O'Murphy" family in the county Cork, was Rereamhar (pronounced " rerour"), a townland in the parish of Kilbonane, and barony of Muscry.

1. Michael, living at Rerour (or Rereamhar), circa 1632.
2. Conn Reamhar: his son; living at Rerour in 1656; had two sons:
I. Michael.

II. John, of whom see " O'Murphy" (No. 11) pedigree.
3. Michael: son of Conn Reamhar.
4. Conn: his son; left Rerour

2 Y

and settled in the parish of Murragh, in Carbery.

5. Michael, of Farranalough: son
of Conn; m. Mary O'Mahony and
had issue by her:

I. Conn, of whom presently.

II. Denis, who m. a Miss Cooney,
and had:—1. Michael, who
d. s. p.; 2. Mary (living in 1887),
who m. Patrick Cahill of Far-
nanes, county Cork, and has
had issue; 3. Ellen, who became a Sister of Mercy in
Kinsale; and other children
who d. young.

III. Daniel, who m., and had:
1. Michael who m. twice: first,
to Mary Wall (see the "Wall"
pedigree), and by her had—
Mary, Kate, and Daniel; mar.,
secondly, to Mary Regan, and
by her also had issue:—William, who emigrated; Mary, m.
in Kinsale, and had issue.

IV. Michael of Insirahill (Crookstown), who m. Mary Mac-
Swiney of Clodagh, and by her
had: 1. Michael, who d. s. p.
2. Conn, twice mar.—first to
Miss Ahern, by whom he had:
Michael, who went with his
parents to America; Denis,
Daniel, and Mary, who d. s. p.
in Ireland; Anne, Kate, and
Ellen, who also went to America.
This Conn, married, secondly,
in America, and by his second
wife had: Denis, Daniel, James,
Peter, and Bridget. 3. Denis,
the third son of Michael (IV),
of Insirahill, was Parish Priest
in Kinsale. 4. Daniel, who is
now (1887) Lord Bishop of
Tasmania; he first became a
Priest on the Indian Mission;
was, in 1846, consecrated
Bishop of Hydrabad; and in
1866 translated from that See
to Tasmania. 5. Mary, who m.
Robert Beechinor of Clonakilty,

and has had: Daniel, who is a
Parish Priest in Tasmania;
Michael, who is also a P.P. in
Tasmania; Denis, and Jeremiah
who (in 1887) are farmers at
Killeh, near Midleton; Mary,
who was a Nun, died in San
Francisco; Ellen (in religion
"Sister Francis Xavier"), a Nun
in Tasmania, living in 1887;
Anne, d. s. p.; Margaret, who
m. John MacSwiney, C.E.,
county Mayo, and has issue:
Margaret - Mary, Mary - Ellen,
Honoria (a Nun, deceased), and
Kate. 6. Anne (in religion,
" Sister Mary Joseph"), a Nun
in the Presentation Convent,
Bandon, which she entered in
1838, living in 1887. 7. Ellen
(in religion "Sister Mary
Xavier"), a Nun, dead.

V. Anne: the fifth child of
Michael (No. 5); married a Mr.
Donegan of Carrigaline, near
Cork, and has had issue.

VI. Ellen, married a Mr. Murphy
(Caol) of Kilcrea, and has had
issue.

VII. Mary, who m. Thomas Wall
of Gurranamuddach (see the
"Wall" pedigree), and had
issue.

6. Conn: second son of Michael,
married twice: 1st, to Miss O'Crowley, by whom he had:

I. Michael, who d. s. p.

II. Mary, who married Jeremiah
MacCarthy of Inshirahill, and
had:—1. Jeremiah, who emigrated; 2. Margaret, living in
1887; 3. William, who m. a
Miss Lordan, and has issue.

This Conn m., secondly, Anne
O'Daly, and by her had:

III: Denis, of whom presently.

IV. Daniel, who d. a student in
Maynooth College.

V. Conn, a Parish Priest in Ballin-
hassig.

7. Denis: son of Conn (No. 6); married a Miss O'Healy, and has had —1. Conn, 2. Anne, 3. Ellen.

8. Conn: son of Denis; living at Inshirahill, unm. in 1887.

O'MURPHY. (No. 11.)

O'Murphy Reamhar, of Muscry—continued.

3. JOHN: second son of Conn, who is No. 2 on the "O'Murphy" (No. 10) pedigree; m. and had :—
4. Denis, of Rerour : his son ; had many children who settled in various parts of the county Cork.
5. Timothy: his eldest son ; settled at Thoames, near Macroom ; mar. Joanna Murphy (Stuac), and had :
I. Denis, who d. s. p.
II. John, of whom presently.
III. Timothy, who m. Margaret Kenealy, and had : 1. Timothy, who emigrated; 2. Rev. Edward, C.C., Kinsale, dead ; 3. Joanna, who m. Richard Bourke, of Coachford ; 4. and 5. Mary and Ellen, who both emigrated to Australia; 6. Jane, who m. Michael Murphy, of Annahalla; 7. and 8. Hannah, and Lizzie reside in the Victoria Hotel, Macroom.
6. John: second son of Timothy ; m. Margaret Hallihin, and had :
I. Denis, who married Catherine Kenealy of Mishanaglas, and d. s.p.
II. Joanna, who m. John Foley, of Maulnadrough, Murragh, and has had : 1. Patrick: 2. John J., of Macroom, a solicitor; 3. Margaret, died ; 4. Julia, 5. Mary-Anne, 6. Ellen, 7. Hanora.
III. Timothy, of whom presently.
IV. Jeremiah, who m. Mary,

O'Downey, of East Thoames, and d. s. p.
V. Margaret, who m. William Murphy (Bán) of Currabeh, Kilmurry, and has issue: 1. William, 2. Hanora, 3. John, and 4. Margaret.
VI. Ellen, who married Jeremiah Murphy of Finnis (Brinny), and has issue : 1. Timothy, 2. Margaret, 3. Ellen, 4. Hanora, 5. Mary, 6. John.
VII. Mary, who married Patrick Buckley of Capeen, and has issue.
7. Timothy: son of John; m. Hannah (d. 9th Jan., 1880), dau. of Patrick Murphy (Buidhe) of Dunbolog, by his wife, who was a Miss Carney, and has issue :
I. John-Patrick, of whom presently.
II. Margaret-Genevive.
III. Maryanne-Symphorosa.
IV. Patrick-John, b. 12th Nov., 1871.
V. Elena-Dymphna.
VI. Hannah-Theresa.
This Timothy removed from Thoames to Curravordy, in 1863.
8. John-Patrick Murphy (Reamhar) : eldest son of Timothy : born 8th May, 1864 ; of the St. Finbar's seminary, Cork, and residing at 3 Great George's-street, in that City, in 1887.

O'NAUGHTEN.

Of Lislea, County Roscommon.

Arms: Same as those of "Naghten."

MURTOGH BUOY O'NAUGHTEN had :
2. Donogh, who had :
3. Rory Duffe, who had :
4. Dermod Reagh of Lislea, co. Roscommon, who d. 1st Jan., 1637. He m. Unah, dau. and co-heir of

MacHugh Buoy O'Kelly, and had :
I. Murtogh, of whom presently.
II. Dermod.
5. Murtogh O'Naughten : son of Dermod Reagh ; m. Katherine,dau. of Donal O'Brien, of Westmeath.

O'NEILL.* (No. 1.)

Monarchs of Ireland, Kings of Ulster, and Princes of Tyrone.

Arms ; Ar. a sinister red hand couped at the wrist affrontée gu.

FIACHA SRABHTEINE,† third son of Cairbre-Lifeachar, the 117th Monarch of Ireland (see p. 667) who is No. 83 on the " O'Hart" pedigree, was ancestor of this branch of that family.

84. Fiacha Srabhteine, King of Conacht, and the 120th Monarch of Ireland: son of Cairbre-Liffechar ; married Aoife, dau. of the King of Gall Gaodhal. This Fiacha, after 37 years' reign, was, in the battle

* *O'Neill :* There were four distinct families of Hy-Niall or *O'Neill*, in Ireland ; namely—1. O'Neill, of Ulster ; 2. O'Neill, of the county Clare, from whom the Creaghs of Munster are descended ; 3. O'Neill, in the barony of Shillelagh, in the county Wicklow, which (see Annals of the Four Masters, at A.D. 1088) is sometimes called *Farron O'Neale ;* 4. O'Neill, of the Ui Eoghain Finn tribe, in Northern Deisi, in the present county Tipperary.

† *Fiacha Srabhteine :* The three Collas being very valiant, warlike, and ambitious princes, combined against their uncle King Fiacha, and aspired to the Monarchy ; they collected powerful forces, and being joined by seven *catha* (or legions) of the Firbolg tribe of Connaught, they fought A.D. 322, a fierce battle against the army of the Monarch Fiacha, at Criogh Rois, in Bregia, in which the royal army was defeated, and many thousands on both sides, together with King Fiacha himself, were slain. This was called the battle of Dubhcomar, from "Dubhcomar," the chief Druid of King Fiacha, who was slain there ; and the place where the battle was fought was near Teltown, between Kells and Navan, near the river Blackwater in Meath. After gaining the battle, Colla Uais became Monarch and regined nearly four years ; when he was deposed by Fiacha's son, Muiredach Tireach, who then, A.D. 326, became Monarch of Ireland. The three Collas and their principal chiefs, to the number of three hundred, were expelled from Ireland (hence the name "Colla :" Irish, *prohibition ;* Gr. "*koluo,*" *I hinder*), and forced to take refuge among their relatives in Alba ; but, through the friendly influence of their grandfather, the king of Alba, and the mediation of the Druids, they were afterwards pardoned by their cousin, then the Irish Monarch, who cordially invited them to return to Ireland.—CONNELLAN.

of Dubhcomar, A.D. 322, slain by his nephews, the Three Collas, to make room for Colla Uais, who seized on, and kept, the Monarchy for four years. From those three Collas the "Clan Colla" were so called.

85. Muireadach Tireach : son of Fiacha Srabhteine ; m. Muirion, dau. of Fiachadh, King of Ulster ; and having, in A.D. 326, fought and defeated Colla Uais, and banished him and his two brothers into Scotland, regained his father's Throne, which he kept as the 122nd Monarch for 30 years.

86. Eochaidh Muigh-Meadhoin* [Moyvone]: his son; was the 124th Monarch ; and in the 8th year of his reign died a natural death at Tara, A.D. 365 ; leaving issue four sons, viz., by his first wife Mong Fionn : —I. Brian ; II. Fiachra; III. Olioll ; IV. Fergus. And, by his second wife, Carthan Cais Dubh (or Carinna), daughter of the Celtic King of Britain,—V. Niall Mór, commonly called "Niall of the Nine Hostages." Mong Fionn was dau. of Fiodhach, and sister of Crimthann, King of Munster, of the Heberian Sept, and successor of Eochaidh in the Monarchy. This Crimthann was poisoned by his sister Mong-Fionn, in hopes that Brian, her eldest son by Eochaidh, would succeed in the Monarchy. To avoid suspicion she herself drank of the same poisoned cup which she presented to her brother ; but, notwithstanding that she lost her life by so doing, yet her expectations were not realised, for the said Brian and her other three sons by the said Eochaidh were laid aside (whether out of horror of the mother's inhumanity in poisoning her brother, or otherwise, is not known), and the youngest son of Eochaidh, by Carthan Cais Dubh, was preferred to the Monarchy.   I. Brian, from him were descended the Kings, nobility and gentry of Conacht—Tirloch Mór O'Connor, the 121st, and Roderic O'Connor, the 183rd Monarch of Ireland.   II. Fiachra's descendants gave their name to Tir-Fiachra ("Tireragh"), co. Sligo, and possessed also parts of co. Mayo.   III. Olioll's descendants settled in Sligo—in Tir Oliolla (or Tirerill). This Fiachra had five sons :—1. Earc Cuilbhuide ; 2. Breasal ; 3. Conaire ; 4. Feredach (or Dathi) ; and 5. Amhalgaidh.

87. Niall Mór† : his son ; a quo

---

* *Muigh-Meadhoin :* From the Irish "Magh," a *plain ;* and "Meadhoin," a *cultivator.*

† *Niall Mór :* This Niall of the Nine Hostages was, as above mentioned, son of Carinna, daughter of the king of Britain ; and his son Eoghan (*og-an :* Irish, *a young man*) or Owen, was also married to another princess of Britain, named Indorba ; a proof of the intimacy which existed in the fourth and fifth centuries between Britain and Ireland. From A.D. 378 to 405—the period of the "Decline and Fall" of Druidism in Ireland—Niall of the "Nine Hostages" was Monarch ; and he was so called in reference to the principal hostile powers overcome by him and compelled to render *so many pledges* of their submission. He was chiefly renowned for his transmarine expeditions against the Roman empire in Britain, as well as in Gaul. In one of those expeditions Niall Mór, A.D. 388, carried home from Gaul some youths as captives ; amongst whom was Succat (meaning "brave in the battle"), then sixteen years of age, with his sisters Dererea and Lupida. That Succat afterwards, as St. Patrick ("Patrick :" from the Irish *Padraic ;* Latin, *pater ;* Ital., *padre,* a father,—here meant in a religious sense), became the Apostle of Ireland. (See St. Patrick's pedigree, p. 43.) And when, many years later, that illustrious liberated captive, entering, in a maturity of manhood and experience, upon his holy mission, was summoned before the supreme assembly at Tara, to show *why* he presumed to interfere with the

the "Hy-Niall" * of Ulster, Meath, and Conacht. He was twice married:—his first Queen was Inne, the dau. of Luighdheach, who was the relict of Fiachadh; his second Queen was Roigneach, by whom he had Nos. I., II., III., IV., V., VI., and VII., as given below. This Niall Mór succeeded his Uncle Crimthann; and was the 126th Monarch of Ireland. He was a stout, wise, and warlike prince, and fortunate in all his conquests and achievements, and therefore called "Great." He was also called *Niall Naoi-Ghiallach* or "Niall of the Nine Hostages," from the royal hostages taken from *nine* several countries by him subdued and made tributary: viz.,—1. Munster, 2. Leinster, 3.

Conacht, 4. Ulster, 5. Britain, 6. the Picts, 7. the Dalriads, 8. the Saxons, and 9. the Morini—a people of France, towards Calais and Piccardy; whence he marched with his victorious army of Irish, Scots, Picts, and Britons, further into France, in order to aid the Celtic natives in expelling the Roman Eagles, and thus to conquer that portion of the Roman Empire; and, encamping on the river Leor (now called Lianne), was, as he sat by the river side, treacherously assassinated by Eocha, son of Enna Cinsalach, king of Leinster, in revenge of a former "wrong" by him received from the said Niall.† The spot on the Leor (*not* "Loire") where this Monarch was murdered is still called the "*Ford of Niall,*" near

old religion of the country, by endeavouring to introduce a new creed, it was Laeghaire [Leary], the son of his former captor Niall, who presided as sovereign there.—O'CALLAGHAN.

Happy captivity, which led to Ireland's Christianity!

* *Hy-Niall:* A branch of the Hy-Niall (or Ui-Niall) settled in Gaul, at an early period, and are mentioned by Cæsar, as the *Unelli*, which is the latinized form of *Ui-Neill*, but here meaning descendants of this Niall Mór, the 126th Monarch of Ireland. Cæsar also mentions the *Eberdovices* or *Eberdocii*, meaning descendants of *Eber*, or *Heber*, the eldest son of Milesius, of Spain.

Some of the *Unelli* of France settled in England before the English invasion of Ireland, and assumed the following names: O'Ni'el, Neylle, Nihil, Noel, Nevell, Newell, Nevil, Nevill, Nevylle, etc. One of the family, Sir Geoffrey Neylle, was, A.D. 1205, a subscribing witness to the Charter of Waterford. In 1408, Thomas Neoylle was made Dean of Ferns; and, in 1480, Dr. Lawrence Neoylle was made bishop of Ferns, by Pope Sixtus IV. David Nevell, Baron of Nevill, was attainted in the reign of King Henry VIII., and suffered the loss of extensive landed property in the county Wexford. See the "Needham" pedigree for another *Neville* family, but which was of the Ithian race.

† *Niall :* The cause of the difference between the Monarch Niall, and Eocha, Prince of Leinster, arose out of two distinct causes :—On the death of Niall's uncle, Crimthann, this Eocha, being ambitious, attempted to take possession of the Royal Palace at Tara, by sleeping there *nine* nights in succession, so as to qualify himself for the Monarchy of Ireland. For doing this he was severely censured by the Arch-Druid, as no person who had not the order of Knighthood dare sleep in the Royal Palace. Then Eocha withdrew from Tara, and in shame and vexation, relinquished his pretensions to the Crown.

On Eocha's journey from Tara to his own province, he arrived at the house of Laidhgon, the son of Bairceadha, the Arch-Druid; whilst staying there he took offence from some expressions made use of to him, and, in a rage, he slew the Druid's son. Immediately, Niall was applied to for justice; he then invaded Leinster, and, after some skirmishing, to avoid bloodshed, the people delivered up the murdering prince into the Monarch's hands. The Druid chained Eocha to a rock where criminals were wont to be executed; but when he saw the executioners coming to despatch him, he, by a nearly superhuman effort, wrenched asunder the chain, and effected his escape to Scotland. On arriving in Scotland, Eocha requested and obtained the protection of

Boulogne-sur-mer. It was in the ninth year of his reign that St. Patrick was first brought into Ireland, at the age of 16 years, among two hundred children brought by the Irish Army out of Little Brittany (called also Armorica), in France. Niall Mór was the first that gave the name of *Scotia Minor* to "Scotland," and ordained it to be ever after so called ; until then it went by the name of "Alba."

Niall had twelve sons:—I. Eoghan; II. Laeghaire (or Leary), the 128th Monarch, in the 4th year of whose reign St. Patrick, the second time, came into Ireland to plant the Christian Faith, A.D. 432 ; III. Conall Crimthann, ancestor of *O'Melaghlin*, Kings of Meath; IV. Conall Gulban, ancestor of *O'Donnell* (princes, lords, and earls of the territory of Tirconnell), and of *O'Boyle, O'Dogherty, O'Gallagher*, etc.; V. Fiacha, from whom the territory

from Birr to the Hill of Uisneach in *Media Hiberniæ* (or Meath) is called "Cineal Fiacha," and from him *MacGeoghagan*, lords of that territory, *O'Molloy*, *O'Donechar*, *Donaher* (or *Dooner*), etc., derive their pedigree ; VI. Main, whose patrimony was all the tract of land from Lochree to Loch Annin, near Mullingar, and from whom are descended *Fox* (lords of the Muintir Tagan territory), *MacGawley*, *O'Dugan*, *O'Mulchonry* (the princes antiquaries of Ireland), *O'Henergy*, etc. ; VII. Cairbre, ancestor of *OFlanagan*, of Tua Ratha, "Muintir Cathalan" (or *Cahill*) etc. ; VIII. Fergus (a quo "Cineal Fergusa" or *Ferguson*), ancestor of *O'Hagan*, etc. ; IX. Enna ; X. Aongus or Æneas ; XI. Ualdhearg ; and XII. Fergus Altleathan. Of these last four sons we find no issue.

88. Eoghan (Eugene,[*] or Owen) : son of Niall Mór ; from whom the

---

Gabhran, the son of Domhangairt, the General of the Dalriada, with whom he went into France so as to get near Niall, and murder him. The Irish Monarch, on being informed of Eocha being in the allied army, would not allow him into his presence ; but he one day secreted himself in a grove near a ford of the Leor, and, whilst Niall was in the act of crossing, the assassin shot him through the body with an arrow.

[*] *Eugene :* Before the arrival of St. Patrick in Ireland, this son of Niall the Great acquired the territory of Aileach, which in many centuries afterwards was called after him—"Tir-Owen" or *Owen's Country.* At Aileach he resided, A.D. 442, when he was converted to Christianity by St. Patrick. "The man of God," says the old biographer of the Apostle, "accompanied Prince Eugene to his court, which he then held in the most ancient and celebrated seat of kings, called Aileach, and which the holy bishop consecrated by his blessing." The MacLoghlins being descended from the same family stem as the O'Neills, a MacLoghlin, or an O'Loghlin, as well as an O'Neill, was sometimes Prince of Aileach, until A.D. 1241, when Donell O'Loghlin, with ten of his family, and all the chiefs of his party, were cut off by his rival, Brian O'Neill, in the battle of "Caim-Eirge of Red Spears ;" and the supreme power of the principality of Aileach thenceforth remained with the O'Neills.—O'CALLAGHAN.

In the thirteenth century the "Kingdom of Aileach" ceased to be so called, and the designation "Kingdom of Tir-Owen," in its stead, was first applied to that territory. Sixteen of the Ard Righs or Monarchs of Ireland were princes or kings of Aileach—descended from this Eugene or Owen.

The O'Neills had their chief seat at Dungannon, and were inaugurated as princes of Tyrone, at Tullaghoge, a place between Grange and Donaghenry, in the parish of Desertcreight, in the barony of Dungannon ; where a rude seat of large stones, called Leach-na-Ree or the Flag stone of the kings, served them as a coronation chair. —CONNELLAN.

We learn that, about A.D. 442, St. Patrick visited Ulster ; at which time he took his route through that romantic pass called *Bearnas-mór* of *Tir-Aodha ;* thence he emerged into Magh Ith, an extensive plain in the present barony of Raphoe, where

territory of " Tir-Eoghan" (now
Tirowen or Tyrone), in Ulster is so
called.   From this Owen came

(a m o n g o t h e r s) the following
families : O'Cahan, or O'Cane, O'Daly
of "Leath Cuinn" (or the kingdoms

he founded the church of Donaghmore, near the town of Castlefinn.   The Prince
Owen kept his private residence at Fidh-mór, now called Veagh, between the church of
Donaghmore and the palace of Aileach. St. Patrick went into the Aileach, and before
entering he said to his people, "Take care that you meet not with the lion, Eoghan,
the son of Niall."   So as to honour St. Patrick, Owen sent a guard to meet him, under
the command of Muireadhach, his son, who, being in front, was accosted first by
Seachnall in these words :—"You shall have a reward from me, if you could persuade
your father to believe."   "What reward ?" asked he.   "The sovereignty of thy tribe
should for ever belong to thy heirs," said Seachnall.   Muiredhach agreed to this
arrangement.   The Saint first saw Eoghan at Fidh-mór, preached to him there, when
he embraced the Faith, a large leac (or stone) being set up there to commemorate the
event.   St. Patrick promised this prince :—" If you would receive the salutary doctrine
of Christ in your country, the hostages of the Gaedhil should come to you ;" meaning
that in his posterity the Regal Race should be—a promise verified by time.
    Eoghan held the Castle of Aileach forty-seven years prior to St. Patrick's visit.
This fort the Apostle blessed, left the old coronation stone there, and prophesied that
Kingship and pre-eminence should be over Erinn from Aileach : "When you leave
your fort out of your bed to the flag, and your successors after you," said St. Patrick,
"the men of Erinn shall tremble before you."   He blessed the Island of Inis-Eoghan
(Inishowen was an island then), and after this gave a blessing of valour to Eoghan :

    " My blessing on the tuatha [territories]
      I give from Belach-ratha,
      On you the descendants of Eoghan
      Until the Day of Judgment.

    " Whilst plains are under crops,
      The palm of battle shall be on their men,
      The armies of Fail [Ireland] shall not be over your plains ;
      You shall attack every tetach [tribe].

    " The race of Eoghan, son of Niall,
      Bless, O fair Brigid !
      Provided they do good,
      Government shall be from them for ever.

    " The blessing of us both
      Upon Eoghan MacNeill ;
      On all who may be born from him,
      Provided they are obedient."
        (i.e., as long as they keep the Faith.)

    These blessings were pronounced from Belachratha, now known as Ballagh, barony
of Inishowen East, parish of Clonca, near Malin Head, where are the ruins of a church
founded by St. Patrick.
    Eochaidh, son of Fiachra, son of Eoghan, was baptised with Eoghan : during the
ceremony the Apostle's Staff is said to have accidentally pierced the naked foot of the
prince.
    The old Fortress of the Irish Monarchs, and Princes of Ulster, was an ancient
Tuatha da Danaan Sith or Lios, and called Grianan Aileach, which here signifies "a
stone house in a beautiful or sunny situation."   Formerly there was a great wood
around it, to Whitefort and along the east banks of the Foyle.   This fort stands on an
elevation of 802 feet, and lies in the parish of Burt, barony of Inishowen.   The
outermost enclosure on the circular apex of the hill contains 5½ acres ; within the
second are 4 acres ; within the third about one acre ; while within the Cashel there is
about ½ acre of surface.
    The Cashel has been restored, since 1874, with great labour and expense, by Dr.
Walter Bernard, of Derry.   A square headed doorway enters the Cashel, and three

of Meath, Ulster, and Conacht), *O'Crean, Grogan, O'Carolan*, etc.

This Eoghan, Prince of Ulster, was baptized by St. Patrick at the Royal Palace of Aileach ; and our Ulster Annalists state that it was *his* foot which was pierced by the Bacchal Iosa during the ceremony. (See the "Line of Heber Stem," No. 91.)

89. Muireadach (III.): son of Eoghan ; was married to Earca, dau. of Loarn, King of Dalriada in Scotland, and by her had many sons and daus., two of them are especially mentioned : — Muirceartach Mór, and Fergus Mór, both called "Mac Earca." From this Fergus Mór descended the Kings of Scotland, and thence, through Queen Matilda, the Kings of England, including the Royal Houses of Plantagenet, Stuart, and D'Este.

This Muireadach who had a brother named Eachagh Binneach, had twelve sons :—I. and II. above mentioned ; III. Fearach (or Fearadach), a n c e s t o r of Mac Cathmhaoil (or *Cowell, Campbell*, etc.) ; IV. Tigernach, ancestor of *O'Cunigan*, and *O'h-Easa* (anglicised *Hosey, Hussey*, and *O'Swell*) ; V. Mongan, ancestor of *O'Croidhen* (*Creedon* or *Croydon*), *O'Donnelly*, etc. ; VI. Dalach : VII. Maon, ancestor of *O'Gormley, OMaolmichil, O'Doraigen*, ("dor:" Ir. *a confine ;* "aigein," *the ocean*), anglicised *Dorrine, Dorien*, and modernized *Dorrian ;* VIII.

Fergus ; IX. and X. named Loarn ; XI. and XII. called Aongus.

In the 20th year of the reign of the Monarch Lughaidh, the son of Laeghaire, with a complete army, Fergus Mór Mac Earca,* (with his five brothers, VIII., IX., X., XI., and XII., above mentioned went into Scotland to assist his grandfather King Loarn, who was much oppressed by his enemies the Picts; who were vanquished by Fergus and his party, who prosecuted the war so vigorously, followed the enemy to their own homes, and reduced them to such extremity, that they were glad to accept peace upon the conqueror's own conditions; whereupon, on the King's death, which happened about the same time, the said Fergus Mór Mac Earca was unanimously elected and chosen king as being of the blood royal by his mother. And the said Fergus, for a good and lucky omen, sent to his brother, who was then Monarch of Ireland, for the Marble Seat called "*Saxum Fatale*" (in Irish, *Liath Fail*, and *Cloch-na-Cinneamhna*, implying in English the *Stone of Destiny* or *Fortune*), to be crowned thereon ; which happened accordingly; for, as he was the first absolute King of all Scotland of the Milesian Race, so the succession continued in his blood and lineage ever since to this day.

90. Muirceartach (or Muriartach)

---

distinct platforms ascend by means of side stone steps within the circle, which reaches interiorly 77 feet 6 inches from wall to wall. In the highest part the wall is about 17 feet 3 inches on an average. The width of this circular wall, at the base, is about 13 feet. Several old roads from this Cashel can still be traced on the hill-sides.

Here is still seen a stone called after St. Columbcille, and believed to be the old coronation stone of the Tuatha da Danaan, and the Hy-Niall races, blessed by St. Patrick as stated above. (See the *Tripartite Life of St. Patrick*.)

---

* *Fergus Mór Mac Earca :* According to the *Linea Antiqua*, Muireadach had only two sons by his wife Earca. But some writers confound this Fergus Mór Mac Earca, the grandson of Loarn (the last King of Dalriada, in Scotland), with Ferghus Mór, the son of Earc, who is No. 96 on the "Genealogy of the Kings of Dalriada," and who was therefore a brother of Loarn, the last King of Dalriada.

Mór Mac Earca : his son. This Muriartach, the eldest son of Muireadach (3), was the 131st Monarch of Ireland ; reigned 24 years ; and died naturally in his bed, which was rare among the Irish Monarchs in those days ; but others say he was burned in a house after being "drowned in wine" (meaning that he was under the influence of *drink*) on All-Halontide (or All-Hallow) Eve, A.D. 527. Married Duinseach, dau. of Duach Teangabha, King of Conacht. He had issue—I. Donal Ilchealgach ; II. Fergus, who became the 135th Monarch ; III. Baodan (or Boetanus), who was the 137th Monarch of Ireland, and was the father of Lochan Dilmhain, a quo *Dillon*, according to some genealogists ; IV. Colman Rimidh, the 142nd Monarch ; V. Neiline ; and VI. Scanlan.

91. Donal Ilchealgach (*Ilchealgach :* Irish, deceitful) : eldest son of Muirceartach ; was the 134th Monarch ; reigned jointly with his brother Fergus for three years : these princes were obliged to make war on the people of Leinster ; fought the memorable battle of Gabhrah-Liffé, where four hundred of the nobility and gentry of that province were slain, together with the greater part of the army.

In this reign Dioman Mac Muireadhach, who governed Ulster ten years, was killed by Bachlachuibh. Donal and Fergus both died of "the plague," in one day, A.D. 561.

92. Aodh (or Hugh) : Donal's son; Prince of Ulster. This Aodh Uariodhnach was the 143rd Monarch ; he had frequent wars, but at length defeated his enemies in the battle of Odhbha, in which Conall Laoghbreag, son of Aodh Slaine, was killed. Soon after this battle, the Monarch Aodh was killed in the battle of Da Fearta, A.D. 607.

93. Maolfreach : his son ; Prince of Ulster; had at least two sons :—1. Maoldoon ; and II. Maoltuile, a quo *Multully*, *Tully*, and *Flood* of Ulster.

94. Maoldoon : his son ; Prince of Ulster ; had two sons : I. Fargal ; and II. Adam, who was ancestor to *O'Daly* of "Leath Cuin." His wife was Cacht, daughter of Maolchabha, King of Cineall Connill.

95. Fargal : son of Maoldoon, was the 156th Monarch of Ireland ; was slain, in A.D. 718, by Moroch, King of Leinster. Married Aithiochta, dau. of Cein O'Connor, King of Conacht. This Fargal had four sons : I. Niall Frassach ; II. Connor (or Conchobhar), who was ancestor of *O'Cahan ;* III. Hugh Allan (or Aodh Olann), the 160th Monarch, and ancestor of *O'Brain*, of Ulster ; and IV. Colca, a quo *Culkin.*

96. Niall Frassach : son of Fargal ; married Bridget, dau. of Orca, son of Carrthone ; was called "frassach" from certain miraculous *showers* that fell in his time (a shower of honey, a shower of money, and a shower of blood) ; was the 162nd Monarch of Ireland ; and, after seven years' reign, retired to St. Columb's Monastery at Hye, in Scotland, A.D. 765, where he died in A.D. 773 ; issue : Aodh Fearcar, and Aodh Ordnigh.

97. Aodh Ordnigh : son of Niall Frassach ; was the 164th Monarch ; and, after 25 years' reign, was slain in the battle of Fearta, A.D. 817. Was married to Meadhbh, dau of Ionrachtach, King of Durlus. In his reign prodigious thunder and lightning occurred, which killed many men, women, and children all over the Kingdom, particularly in a nook of the country between Corcavaskin and the sea in Munster, by which one thousand and ten persons were destroyed. In his reign occurred many prodigies—the forerunner of the Danish Invasion,

which soon after followed. This Monarch had four sons: I. Niall Caille; II. Maoldoon, a quo "Siol Muldoon;" III. Fogartach, ancestor of Muintir Cionaodh or *Kenny;* and IV. Blathmac.

98. Niall Caille: son of Aodh Ordnigh; was the 166th Monarch of Ireland; and was so called after his death from the river "Caillen," where he was drowned, A.D. 844, after 13 years' reign. He fought many battles with the Danes and Norwegians, in most of which although the Danes were worsted, yet the continual supplies pouring unto them made them very formidable; (so much so) that in this reign they took and fortified Dublin and other strong places upon the sea-coasts. Married Gormfhliath, dau. of Donogh, son of Donal. This Monarch had five sons: I. Aodh Finnliath; II. Dubhionracht, a quo *O'Dubhionrachta;* III. Aongus; IV. Flahertach, ancestor of *O'Hualairg* or *Mac Ualairg,* anglicised *Mac Golderick, Goderick, Golding, Goulding, Waller,* etc.; V. Braon, a quo *Clan Braoin* of Mogh Ithe (Moy Ith).

99. Aodh Finnliath, i.e. *Hoary:* son of Niall Caille; was the 168th Monarch of Ireland; reigned for

sixteen years, during which time he fought and defeated the Danes in several battles and was worsted in others; he died at Drom-Enesclann, A.D. 876. This Aodh married Maolmare or Mary, dau. of Keneth, the son of Alpin—both Kings of Scotland. He had two sons: I. Niall Glundubh; and II. Donal, who was King of Aileach, and ancestor of the family of *MacLaughlin* (or *O'Laughlin*), some of whom were Monarchs of Ireland; and of *O'Donnelly,* whose chief was, A.D. 1177, slain at Down by Sir John de Courcey, first "Earl of Ulster."

100. Niall ("niall," gen. "neill:" Irish, *a champion*) Glundubh [gloonduv]: son of Aodh Finnliath, was the 170th Monarch of Ireland; and reigned for three years. He had many conflicts with the Danes, in which, generally, he was victorious. At length, making up a great army, in order to besiege Dublin, a great battle was fought between them, wherein the Monarch lost his life, and after great slaughter on both sides, his army was routed, A.D. 919. He revived the great Fair at Tailtean.

From this Monarch the sirname *O'Neill** or "Clan-na-Neil," *Neilson,*

---

* *O'Neill:* Niall Glundubh attained to the Monarchy, A.D. 914, after the death of Flan Siona, King of Meath ; and was slain in a battle with the Danes, at Rathfarnham, near Dublin. The following passage from one of the many "Lamentations," written at the time by the Irish bards on his death, shows the affection entertained for him by his people :—

" Sorrowful this day is sacred Ireland,
Without a valiant chief of 'hostage' reign ;
It is to see the heavens without a sun,
To view Magh Neill without Niall."

" Magh Neill," here mentioned, signifies *the plain of Niall :* meaning, no doubt, the " O'Neill-land" forming the two baronies of that name in Armagh, which constituted the ancient patrimony of the Hy-Niallain, or the descendants of Niallan, who was collaterally descended in the fifth degree from Colla-da-Chrioch, who, writes O'Callaghan, " overthrew the dominion of the old Irian Kings of Uladh," whose heraldic emblem was the " Red Hand of Ulster." That emblem The O'Neill in after ages assumed, together with the Battle Cry of " Lamh Dearg Abu" [lauv darig aboo], which means—*The Red Hand for Ever.*
In the humble but honourable position of a Teacher of a National School (see No.

Nelson and *Nilson* are derived.
Niall Glundubh left issue : I. Muriartach na-Cochall, Prince of Ulster,
who left no issue ; and II. Murchertach.

101. Murchertach : that second son
(called "The Hector of Western
Europe") and Roydamna ; was married and left issue. This Prince was
slain by Blacaire, lord of the Danes,
26th March, A.D. 941.

102. Donal of Armagh :* his son ;

was the 173rd Monarch ; died at
Armagh, after 24 years' reign, A.D.
978. During his long reign we find
but little progress by him (made)
against the encroaching Danes ; he
wholly bent his arms against his
subjects ; preying, burning, and
slaughtering the people of Conacht,
whether deservedly or otherwise we
know not, but we know it was no
reasonable time for them to fall
foul upon one another, while their

134 on the "O'Neill" (No. 2) pedigree), the lineal representative of the Monarch Niall
Glundubh now (1887) resides in a secluded part of the co. Cork, under a name which
some of his forefathers assumed, in order to preserve a portion of their estates, which,
however, have since passed away from the family. But, modest though be his position,
the gentleman to whom we allude is, perhaps, more happy—he is certainly far more free
from care—than were the latest of his illustrious ancestors on the throne of Tirowen,
the Principality of the ever-famed O'Neill ; of whom the following lines convey but a
faint idea :

> " His Brehons around him—the blue heavens o'er him,
> His true clan behind, and his broad lands before him,
> While group'd far below him, on moor, and on heather,
> His Tanists and chiefs are assembled together ;
> They give him a sword, and he swears to protect them ;
> A slender white wand, and he vows to direct them ;
> And then, in God's sunshine, "O'NEILL" they all hail him :
> Through life, unto death, ne'er to flinch from, or fail him ;
> And earth hath no spell that can shatter or sever
> That bond from *their* true hearts—*The Red Hand for Ever !*
>
> Proud lords of Tir-Owen ! high chiefs of Lough Neagh !
> How broad-stretch'd the lands that were rul'd by your sway !
> What eagle would venture to wing them right through,
> But would droop on his pinion, o'er half ere he flew !
> From the Hills of MacCartan, and waters that ran
> Like steeds down Glen Swilly, to soft-flowing Bann—
> From Clannaboy's heather to Carrick's sea-shore
> And Armagh of the Saints to the wild Innismore—
> From the cave of the hunter on Tir-Connell's hills
> To the dells of Glenarm, all gushing with rills—
> From Antrim's bleak rocks to the woods of Rostrevor—
> All echo'd *your* war-shout—' *The Red Hand for Ever !* ' "
>
> —O'CALLAGHAN.

* *Donal of Armagh :* This Donal was succeeded in the Monarchy by the famous
Malachi the Second, King of Meath ; and is by some writers called Donal *O'Neill ;*
but it is to be observed, that it was not until some time after the death of Malachi
the Second (who died A.D. 1023), and, who, as Monarch, succeeded this Donal of
Armagh, A.D. 978, that Moriartus-na-Midhe was the first of the family that ever
assumed the sirname "O'Neill." Donal of Armagh ascended the throne, A.D. 954,
and died A.D. 978. He was son of Muircheartach (Murkertagh or Murtagh), the
northern chieftain who was the "Roydamna" or *heir apparent* to the throne, as being
the son of Niall Glundubh, above mentioned. Donoch the Third of Meath succeeded
Niall Glundubh in the Monarchy, A.D. 917 ; and, with the exception of a victory over
the Danes, at Bregia (a part of the ancient kingdom of Meath), passed his reign in
comparative obscurity. Murkertagh (*muir :* Irish, *the sea ;* Lat. *mare :* Arab. *mara :*
and *ceart ;* Irish, *righteous ;* Lat. *certus*) had conducted a fleet to the Hebrides, whence

common enemy was victoriously triumphing over them both.

103. Moriartach na-Midhe* : his son ; was the first that assumed the sirname and title of "THE GREAT O'NEILL, *Prince of Tyrone*, and of Ulster.

104. Flathartach An Frostain : his son; Prince of Ulster.

105. Aodh Athlamh : his son; Prince of Tyrone; had two sons :— I. Donall an Togdhamh ; and II. Aodh Anrachan, who was ancestor of *MacSweeney.*

106. Donall an Togdhamh: his son; Prince of Ulster, had a dau. Joan.

107. Flahertach Locha Hadha : his son ; was Prince of Tyrone.

108. Connor na-Fiodhbha : his son; Prince of Ulster and Tyrone; was murdered, A.D. 1170.

109. Teige Glinne : his son ; Prince of Tyrone.

110. Mortogh Muighe Line : his son ; Prince of Ulster.

111. Aodh (or Hugh) an Macaomh Toinleasg : his son ; slain A.D. 1177, by Malachlan and Ardgal O'Loughlin (his kinsmen), but the latter fell by the hand of O'Neill in the conflict. This Aodh was styled "Lord of Tirowen," "King of the Cineal Owen," "King of Aileach," "King of North Erin," etc. He had two sons—1. Niall Ruadh ; and 2. Aodh (or Hugh) Dubh, who, some say, was the elder son. But as the *Linea Antiqua,* in the Office of Arms, Dublin Castle, continues the line of "O'Neill," Princes of Tyrone, from Niall Ruadh, we give the descent from him in the "O'Neill" (No. 2) pedigree, next *infra.* And from his brother, Aodh (or Hugh) Dubh, we give, in the "O'Neill" (No. 3) genealogy, the pedigree of *O'Neill,* Princes of Clanaboy.

he returned flushed with victory. He assembled a body of troops of special valour, and, at the head of a thousand heroes, commenced his "circuit of Ireland :" the Danish chief, Sitric, was first seized as a hostage ; next Lorcan, King of Leinster ; next the Munster King, Callaghan of Cashel (who then had leagued with the Danes, and in conjunction with them invaded Meath and Ossory, A.D. 937), "and a fetter was put on him by Murkertagh." He afterwards proceeded to Connaught, where Connor, son of Teige, came to meet him, "but no gyve or lock was put upon him." He then returned to Aileach, carrying these Kings with him as hostages ; where, for five months, he feasted them with knightly courtesy, and then sent them to the Monarch Donoch, in Meath. Murkertagh's valour and prowess procured for him the title of—"The Hector of the west of Europe ;" in two years after his justly famous exploit he was, however, slain by "Blacaire, son of Godfrey, lord of the foreigners," on the 26th March, A.D. 941 ; and "Ardmacha (Armagh) was plundered by the same foreigners, on the day after the killing of Murkertagh."—MISS CUSACK.

* *Moriartach na-Midhe :* This name, analysed, means "Mor-Neart na Midhe" (*moir-neart :* Irish, *mighty power ; na Midhe, of Meath*) ; and, as the word "neart" means *great strength,* implies, that this prince was powerfully strong—in person or in the forces at his command.

O'NEILL. (No. 2.)

Princes of Tyrone.

Arms: Ar. two lions ramp. combatant gu. armed and langued az. supporting a sinister red hand couped at the wrist erect, palm outward. *Crest*: A right arm couped below the elbow cased grasping a naked sword. *Motto*: Lamh dearg Abú (The Red Hand for ever).

112. Niall Ruadh ("ruadh:" Irish, *red*): son of Aodh (or Hugh) an Macaomh Toinleasg, who is No. 111 on the "O'Neill" (No. 1) pedigree, next *ante;* a quo *O'Ruaidh*, anglicised *Roe* and *Rowe:* a family honourably represented (in 1887) by Henry Roe, Esq., of Thomasstreet, Dublin.

This Niall Ruadh was Prince of Ulster, and was m. to Nuala (died 1226), dau. of Roderic O'Connor, the 183rd Monarch of Ireland.

113. Brian Catha Duin: his son; may be reckoned as the 184th Monarch of Ireland. Had three sons :—I. Donal; II. Niall, d. 1314; III. Murrogh, d. 1356.

Under A.D. 1258, the Four Masters say of this Brian :—

"Hugh, the son of Felim O'Connor and Teige O'Brien, marched with a great force to Caol Uisge (near Newry), to hold a conference with Brian O'Neill, to whom the foregoing chiefs granted the sovereignty over the Irish; and they agreed that the hostages of Hugh O'Connor should be given to him as sureties for the fulfilment of this compact, and that the hostages of O'Reilly's people, and also those of Hy-Briuin, from Kells to Drumcliff, should be likewise given to Hugh, the son of Felim O'Connor."

After this Brian's death on the battlefield of Drom Deirg, at Dunda-

leathglas (Downpatrick), commanding the Irish forces against the English, in defence of his Crown and kingdom, he was succeeded in the Principality of Ulster by the famous Hugh Buidhe, son of Donal Oge, son of Hugh Dubh, the ancestor of *O'Neill* of Clanaboy.

114. Donal (VI):* his son; King of Ulster, and heir to the Monarchy of Ireland, became *The O'Neill*, on the death of Aodh Buidhe (or Yellow Hugh), in 1283. After the battle of Bannockburn, in Scotland, A.D. 1314, Edward, brother to the illustrious Robert Bruce, was invited to accept the Sovereignty of Ireland. In his favour this Donal sought to resign his title, which, owing to the Irish Constitution (the Brehon Law), he could not do. (See Paper in the Appendix, headed: "Invasion of Ireland by Bruce.")

Donal had five sons :—I. Hugh; II. Roderic, slain, 1365; III. Shane, slain, 1318; IV. Brian, slain, 1319; and V. Cu Uladh, killed, 1325.

115. Hugh: his son; Prince of Ulster, etc.; "the best Irishman of his time:" d. 1364. Issue: I. Neil Mór; II. Brian (d. 1369); and four daughters.

116. Neil Mór:† his son; was

---

* *Donal:* In the MS. Vol. E. 3. 22, in the Library of Trinity College, Dublin, this Donal (or Donald) O'Neill is styled—

"Rex Ultoniæ, et omnium Regulorum Hiberniæ." . . . .

† *Neil Mór:* In the last page of the MS. Vol. E. 3. 10, in the Library of Trin. Coll. Dublin, there is a copy of a letter, written by this Neil Mór, as "Princeps Hibernicorum Ultoniæ," to King Richard II., of England :

" . . . Litteræ missæ ad Regem Richardum II., per Nellanum O'Nell, Principem Hibernicorum Ultoniæ, Anno 18° ejusdem Regis."

"Prince of the Irish in Ulster," when Richard II., King of England, visited Ireland (at Dundalk), in 1394. He was styled "*Le Grand O'Neill*" by the Anglo-Normans; and by the Irish he was called "the defender of Ireland," "the champion of dignity, and pre-eminence of the principality," "the unyielding tower against tyranny," etc. He had issue:—I. Neil Oge. II. Henry (d. 1392), who had issue—1. Donal; 2. Hugh (who escaped from the prison in Dublin, in 1412, having been confined ten years there by the English); 3. Niall (d. 1430); 4. Brian (d. 1401). III. Graine (d. 1429), m. Turlogh O'Donnell "of the Wine." IV. Cu Uladh Ruadh (d. 1399).

This Neil Mór was married to Gormley (d. 1397), dau. of John O'Donnell.

117. Neil Oge: his son; Prince of Tyrone, etc.; m. to Una (d. 1417), daughter of Donal O'Neill. Issue :

I. Owen; II. Brian (d. of small-pox, 1402); six other sons; and a dau., Una, m. to Rory O'Sullivan, Prince of Dunkerron. This Neil Oge died in 1402, and was succeeded in the Principality by Donal, son of Henry, son of Neil Mór. (See above.) This Donal (called "Donal Bocc") was, in 1432, slain in O'Cahan's Country, by Donal Aibhne O'Cahan.

118. Owen: son of Neil Oge; was, in 1432, on the death of Donal Bocc, inaugurated* *The O'Neill*; m. Catherine (d. 1427), dau. of Ardgal MacMahon. Issue :—I. Henry; II. Hugh, of the Fews, d. 1475; III. Felim, d. 1461; IV. Murtagh; V. Art, died 1458; VI. Connor; VII. Niall; VIII. Brian Mór; IX. Conla; X. Donal Claragh, killed 1493. This Owen died in 1456, and was succeeded by :

119. Henry: his son; Prince of Ulster, etc.; m. Gormley Cavenagh (d. 1465), dau. of MacMurrogh,

* *Inaugurated :* After the destruction of the ancient Palace of Aileach, A.D. 1101, the princes of the O'Neill fixed their residence in the south of the present county of Tyrone, at Ennis Enaigh, now Inchenny, in the parish of Urney; and the stone chair upon which each of these princes was proclaimed, was at Tullahoge (or the hill of the youths), now Tullyhawk, in the parish of Desertcreagh, and barony of Dungannon ; where was seated down to Cromwell's time the family of O'Hagan, the lawgiver of Tullahoge, whence the present Baron O'Hagan (see the "O'Hagan" pedigree) takes his title ; and where, on the stone chair above mentioned—the Leac-na-Righ (or Flagstone of the Kings), the princes or kings of Tir-Owen were inaugurated by O'Hagan, "and called O'Neill after the lawful manner." That *Leac-na-Righ* was A.D. 1602, demolished by the lord-deputy Mountjoy.

"According to the tradition in the country," writes John O'Donovan, LL.D., "O'Hagan inaugurated O'Neill, by putting on his golden slipper or sandal ; and hence the *sandal* always appears in the armorial bearings of the O'Hagans." With reference to the observance in Ireland, of a superior prince or chief, when inaugurated, having his shoe, slipper, or sandal put on by an inferior potentate, but still one of consideration, we find that at the inauguration of the O'Connor in Connaught, the same office was performed for him by MacDermott, the powerful chief of Moylurg (the old barony of Boyle, county Roscommon), as that performed by O'Hagan for the O'Neill in Ulster. There is a resemblance between this custom at the inauguration of the old princes of Ireland, and that connected with the ceremonial of the later Roman emperors or those of Constantinople, on their creation as such. Under the head of "Honours and Titles of the Imperial Family," Gibbon notes that "the Emperor alone could assume the purple or red buskins." And subsequently relating how the celebrated John Catacuzene assumed A.D. 1341, the imperial dignity, he mentions John being "invested with the purple buskins;" adding "that his right leg was clothed by his noble kinsman, the left by the Latin chiefs, on whom he conferred the honour of knighthood;" this office of putting on the buskins being one of honour in the *east*, like that of putting on the shoe or sandal in the *west.*—O'CALLAGHAN.

King of Leinster. This Henry "was inaugurated *The O'Neill*, in 1455, by the coarb of St. Patric, together with Maguire, MacMahon, O'Cahan, and all the O'Neills, at Tullaghoge, according to the usual customs." Issue: I. Conn; II. Roderic Baccach, killed by the sons of Art O'Neill, 1470; III. Tuathal, killed by the Anglo-Normans, who intruded on the Plain of O'Neill, 1476; IV. Donal, died Aug., 1509; V. Henry Oge, d. 1498; VI. Slaine, married to Turlogh Donn O'Brien; VII. Art, killed in 1502, by Art, son of Conn, son of Henry (see No. 118). This Henry died in 1489, and was succeeded by:

120. Conn: his son, as Prince of Ulster, of Tyrone, etc.; m., in 1483, Elinora (d. 1497), dau. of Thomas (the 7th Earl), the son of John Cam, the 6th Earl of Kildare; and had by her issue: I. Conn Baccach; II. Art Oge (d. 1519) had a son, Neal Connelagh, who had a son Turlogh Luinagh, whose son was called Sir Arthur O'Neill; III. Niall, d. 1497; IV. Turlough killed by MacMahon, 1501, left no issue; V. John of Kinard, had a son, whose son was Sir Henry O'Neill, whose son was Sir Henry O'Neill, who had a son Sir Phelim, murdered by the English, 1650; VI. Deila; VII. Judith, married to Manus O'Donnell, she d. Aug., 1535, aged 42 years, and was interred in the Franciscan Convent, Donegal; VIII. Eliza, m. to Zachaire Maguire.

In 1493, this Conn, "the bountiful bestower of valuable presents and property, was (say the Four Masters) treacherously slain by his his own brother, Henry Oge;" and was succeeded in the Principality by his uncle Donal, who was opposed by Henry Oge; which opposition was not lawful, as Donal was the senior. They quarrelled till 1497,

when Henry Oge gave great presents to Donal, in horses and armour, for resigning the title. In 1498, "Henry Oge was (according to the Four Masters) slain in the house of Art, son of Hugh, son of Owen (No. 118), in Tuath Eachach (Iveagh, county Down), by the two sons of Conn, son of Henry, son of Owen, namely Turlogh and Conn Bacchach, in revenge of their father Conn, who had been previously killed by Henry, in the year 1493." Donal thus became undisputed Prince of Tyrone; he died unlamented, on the 6th of Aug., 1509. Art, son of Hugh, son of Owen (No. 118), was chosen his successor. This Art d. in 1514, when Art Oge, son of Conn (No. 120), son of Henry (No. 119), was made *The O'Neill*. In 1519 Art Oge died and was succeeded by his brother:

121. Conn Bacchach: son of Conn, as Prince of Ulster. Hugh, the son of his uncle Donal, gave him no little trouble, as he too aspired to the Principality, until in the year 1524, in a bloody engagement between them, the said Hugh lost his life; and being thus rid of all competitors, Conn began to follow the example of his ancestors, who, upon all occasions and prospects of success, were up in arms in opposition to the English invaders, endeavouring to drive them from the country; and recover their liberties and their right to the Irish Crown, worn by their ancestors for many ages, successively, as above shown; but all in vain. And this Conn Bacchach trying his fortunes in the same manner, and finding his endeavours to be to as little purpose as were those of his forefathers, did for a time submit; and, going into England, was, upon his openly renouncing his ancient title of *O'Neill* and *Prince of Tyrone*, favour-

ably received by King Henry VIII., in Greenwich, in 1542.

Conn thus seemingly renounced a title " in comparison of which," says Camden, "the very title of Cæsar is contemptible in Ireland ; and taking upon him the barbarian Anglo-Saxon title of *Iarl*, or Earl of Tyrone ; and doing homage to Henry as King of Ireland and Head of the Church ; who on his side adorned him with a golden chain, saluted him 'beloved cousin,' and so returned him richly plated." At the same time the title of " baron of Dungannon" was conferred on his illegitimate son, who is called "Mathew" by Sir James Ware in his *Annals of Ireland*, but in the *Pedigree* is entered "Ferdorach." These foreign titles, with Conn's conduct, were so deeply resented by SHANE AN DIOMUIS (by Ware called "Shane Dowlenach" or O'Dongaileach, from being fostered by O'Dongaileach or O'Donnelly, Chief of Ballydonnelly, or Charlemont, in Tyrone), the eldest of Conn's legitimate sons, that he, with O'Donnell, MacGuire, and the other Ulster chieftains broke out in rebellion against him. This act of Conn's, in submitting to a foreign prince, has met with universal astonishment, inasmuch as he on a former occasion solemnly *cursed* his offspring if he should ever speak the Saxon tongue, sow corn, or build houses in imitation of the English ; and who led

his troops to the south, burned Atherdee and Navan to the ground, and from the Hill of Tara—the palace of his ancestors—warned off the servile nobles of the Pale from the frontiers of Ulster. But this one act alienated his subjects, and Shane was made *The O'Neill* in his place.

Ferdorach was executed in 1558. Conn Bacchach m. Alice, dau. of Gerald Fitzgerald, 8th Earl of Kildare, and had by her issue : I. Shane ; II. Tirlogh ; III. Felim Caoch, who had a son Turlogh, who was father of Phelim ; IV. Mary, who d. in 1582, and who m. Sorley Buidhe MacDonnell ; with three other daughters. This Conn was born 1484, died 1559, and was succeeded by his son :

122. Shane* an Diomuis (*i.e.* John the Proud or Haughty) : eldest legitimate son of Conn Bacchach ; set no value on his father's " earldom," refused such badge of servitude, was duly inaugurated *The ONeill*, and " King of Ulster" about A.D. 1550. Not receiving due submission from O'Donnell, he, in 1556, went to war with him, and, in 1559, Calvach O'Donnell, Prince of Tirconnell, was subdued and taken prisoner. In 1560, Shane was undisputed Ruler of Ulster, from " Drogheda to the Erne." In 1563, he visited Queen Elizabeth, as an independent sovereign prince, when she recognized him as *The O'Neill*, "with all the

* *Shane :* In 1565, Shane O'Neill assumed the title of "Monarch of Ireland," and led the Irish Army of Ulster against the English Government. He maintained, at his own cost, a standing army of 4,000 foot, and 1,000 horse, and always took care to have his Chiefs and their dependents well instructed in the art of war. Queen Elizabeth in vain attempted to reduce him, either by force, or by kindness. She offered to him the titles of "Earl of Tyrone," and "Baron of Dungannon." Shane received these proposals with a haughtiness expressive of his contempt for any such titles, which he looked upon as beneath his dignity as the O'NEILL. The commissioners who were intrusted with the negociations, received from him this reply : "If Elizabeth, your mistress, be Qeen of England, I am O'Neill, King of Ulster ; I never made peace with her without having been previously solicited to it by her. I am not

2 z

authority and pre-eminence of his ancestors." After a time the English recommenced to encroach on his territories, planted soldiers on his frontiers, his subjects were incited to rebel against him by the English Government; till at length, in 1567, he is betrayed by the Scots (the MacDonnells), instigated by an English officer named Piers; and slaughtered, with most of his followers, in North Clan-atha-buidhe (or North Clanaboy), near Cushendun, in the county of Antrim. After he had been buried four days, William Piers exhumed the body, cut off his head, and carried it " pickled in a pipkin," to Dublin, to Sir Henry Sydney, who ordered it to be placed on a pole on the top of Dublin Castle ! Piers got one thousand marks for thus so effectually carrying out the instructions of his government. Shane's headless trunk was re-interred where he was murdered, about three miles from Cushendun, where the tourist can still be shown the " Grave of Shane O'Neill."

This Shane was m. to Mary (d. 1561), dau. of Calvach O'Donnell (by his first wife), Prince of Tir-Connell; and had issue :—I. John Oge, killed 1581, s. p.; II. Conn; III. Thomas; IV. Elana; V. Henry;

VI. Art, died from exposure in the Wicklow mountains, in 1592; VII. Margaret, m. to Teige O'Doyne; with two others. He had, besides, illegitimate children, one of whom was named Hugh Geimhleach (*i.e.* " of the Fetters"), and was also incorrectly called " Conn MacShane," by a few modern writers. This Hugh, was, in 1590, for betraying to the English Aodh O'Neill's dealings with the Spaniards, seized by orders of his lawful Prince, and tried for various robberies and murders which he had committed within The O'Neill's jurisdiction; for which he was sentenced to death, and in January, 1590, said Hugh Geimhleach was hanged by Loughlin Mac-Murtogh and his brother—both natives of Fermanagh.

In A.D. 1569, the English passed an Act of Attainder against the "late John O'Neill;" and all his extensive estates, nearly all the Tribe Lands of the Sept, together with the greater part of Tyr-Owen, were seized by the English Crown, and various parts thereof planted with English and Scotch settlers.

Immediately after the murder of Shane, the Prince of Ulster, Tirlogh Luineach* (or Turlogh Luinagh —see No. 120) was, at the instigation of the English Government,

ambitious of the abject title of ' earl ;' both my family and birth raise me above it ; I will not yield precedence to any one: my ancestors have been Kings of Ulster ; I have gained that kingdom by my sword, and by the sword I will preserve it." (Cox, *Hist. Irel.*, p, 321.)

On Shane's visit to Queen Elizabeth, when reference was made to the natural son of Conn (Ferdoroch, Baron of Dungannon) as likely to succeed his father in Tir-Owen, Shane said that Ferdoroch (" Mathew") was the son of the wife of a blacksmith of Dundalk, by Conn, his father, subsequent to the marriage of the said Conn O'Neill and Alice, of whom he, Shane, was the eldest legitimate son, and that consequently he alone had a right to succeed to his father's inheritance. He added that the surrender which had been made by his father, of the Principality of Tir-Owen, to King Henry VIII., and the restitution his father had received from that King by letters patent, were null; since his father's right to that principality was confined to his own life, whilst he (Shane) had been acknowledged THE O'NEILL, by a popular election according to custom.

* *Luineach* : This Tirloch Luineach left a son, Sir Art O'Neill.

made *The O'Neill*, in preference to Shane's two brothers—Tirloch and Felim Caoch ("caoch:" Irish, *dim-sighted*), or to Shane's son Conn. Tirloch Luineach d. at Strabane in 1595, and was buried at Ardstraw (Irish, *Ardstratha*) in Tyrone.

Feardorach (or Mathew), son of Conn Bacchach, and half brother of Shane, was, by the English, made "Baron of Dungannon;" he married Judith, daughter of Cuchonnacht Magennis, and had by her : I. Brian, the second "Baron of Dungannon," who was slain, s. p. in 1561; II. Aodh (or Hugh), virtual *Ard Righ*, of whom again ; and two illegitimate sons; III. Sir Cormac, who had a son, Conn, whose sons were Hugh Oge, and Brian, both died s. p.; IV. Sir Art. This Sir Art m. and had three sons :—1. Art Oge, who was father of Hugh Dubh,* the renowned defender of Limerick and Governor of Clonmel, in 1650; 2. the famous *Owen Roe O'Neill,*† who

---

* *Hugh Dubh* was born in the Spanish Netherlands. He is mentioned as one of "the brave warriors and prime captains who, out of the martial theatre of Flanders, enlisted under the banner of Owen Roe O'Neill, and came to Ireland in 1642." He was taken prisoner at the battle of Clones, in 1642, and did not regain his liberty till released by exchange after the battle of Benburb in 1646. In that year he was appointed Major-General of the Ulster Army. During the illness of his uncle, Owen Roe, he commanded the Ulster Army, and was with Ferrall despatched in October, 1649, to the Marquis of Ormond with a body of two thousand men. After Owen Roe's death he was anxious to succeed him as commander of the Ulster Army. His qualifications were strongly urged by Daniel O'Neill (*a*), as being a "man who knew the ways Owen Roe O'Neill took to manage the people, and one not unacceptable to the Scots, and one who would do nothing contrary to Ormond's commands."

After defending Clonmel he retired, and was by Ormond appointed military governor of Limerick. In a reply to the demand of Sir Hardress Waller to surrender the city, in September, 1650, he declared "he was determined to maintain it for the use of his majesty, Charles II., even to the effusion of the last drop of his blood."

Finding that his name was not included in the treaty on the surrender of Limerick he rode up to Deputy Ireton and offered him the pommel of his sword. Ireton received him most kindly, and commanded his own guard under pain of death to attend and bring him to a place of safety. A few days after the taking of Limerick, Ireton died ; but before his death he commanded Edmund Ludlow to behave well to O'Neill, send him to England, and bestow on him three horses, one for himself, and two for two servants, and means to defray his charges.

O'Neill arrived in London, on the 10th January, 1652, and was committed to the Tower, for being in arms against the Parliament. Twenty shillings a week were allowed for his support. Don Alonzo Cardenas, the Spanish Ambassador, proposed to the Council of State in July, 1652, to give permission to the Irish troops to pass into Spain, especially to Don Hugo O'Neill, since he was born in Flanders, and consequently a Spanish subject; having, besides, borne no part in the first insurrection in Ireland, nor in the excesses which took place there. He seems to have gone to Spain, for there is a letter of his to Charles II., dated Madrid, October 27th, 1660, in which he solicits the restoration of his family to that king's favour. He there assumed the title of "Earl of Tyrone."

† *Owen Roe O'Neill:*

EPITAPH OF OWEN ROE O'NEILL.

EUGENII O'NEILLI, COPIARUM ULTONIENSIUM PRÆFECTI GENERALIS, EPITAPHIUM.

Hic jacet ille ingens patriæ defensor O'Nellus,
 Nobilis ingenio, sanguine Marte, fide.
Qui genus et magni mensuram stammatis implens,
 Per sua Catholicos arma probavit avos,
Quem neque vis dubii potuit perfringere belli,
 Nec mutare boni spesve timorve mali.

was Commander-in-Chief of the Irish Confederate Forces in Ulster, in the war subsequent to 1641, and who was poisoned, he died at Clough Oughter Castle, on the 6th of Nov., 1649. Owen Roe m. and left four sons:—1. Henry (slain in 1649), who left a son Hugh; 2. Brian, whose son was Owen, the last Earl of Tyrone, in Spain; 3. Conn, who had two sons:—Owen, a Colonel in the French Service; and Luaghadh (or Lewis) an officer in the French Service; and 4. John, who became a monk. The third son of Sir Art was Conn, who had two sons:—1. Daniel,* and 2. Brian, whose son Conn died in Spain.

On the "Plantation of Ulster" Sir Art (MacBaron) in his old age was removed from his own territory of O'Neilan, and got in exchange an estate of 2,000 acres during the lives of himself and his wife.

(II.) Aodh O'Neill, the second son of Feardorach, above mentioned, was, during the lifetime of Tirlogh, designated his successor, in 1587; Queen Elizabeth solemnly made him "Earl of Tyrone:" in order, says Connellan, " to suppress the name and authority of O'Neill;" and in May, 1588, with Tirlogh's consent, he was duly and solemnly inaugurated The O'Neill, in the Rath of Tullaghoge. On the Stone of Royalty,

Quem tria conjuncto pertierunt agmine regna,
    In caput unius tot coiere manus.
Celsus in immota mentis sed constitit arce,
    Et cœptum infracto pectore duxit iter.
Spem contra humanam, cœlum tamen adfuit ausis,
    Cumque suo Christus milite miles erat.
Impia Catholicorum seu strinxit in agmina ferrum,
    Discolor hæretica cæde madebat humus.
Sive fugam simulat, simulando comprimit hostem,
    Nec minus arma viri quam metunda fuga.
Hoc tamen, hoc urgens et inexpugnabile Marti,
    Pectus humi positum spicula mortis habent.
Æmula nam crebris Parca invidiosa triumphis,
    Vincendi et vitæ sit tibi finis, ait.
Fata sed Eugenium nequeunt ita sternere servent
    Postuma Romanam quominus arma fidem.
Hanc lapis et cineres, sed et ipsa cadavera spirant,
    Et Petrum litui, tela tubæque sonant.
Magni viri merces, tot palmas astras coronant,
    Sic præstant meritum terra polusque decus.

* (a) *Daniel O'Neill*, like Hugh Dubh, was a nephew of Owen Roe. His father and grandfather were owners of Upper Claneboy and Great Ardes, and had served the English in the war against their own kindred. His father was induced to transfer these lands, amounting to 66,000 acres, to Sir Hugh Montgomery and James Hamilton for the sum of £60, and a yearly rent of £160. He spent the early part of his life in Holland, in the army of the Prince of Orange; later, he entered the English service. At the beginning of the Irish "Rebellion," he was accused of high treason, and imprisoned in the Tower. He escaped in disguise, after a confinement of six months. Soon after he was a Lieutenant-General of Prince Rupert's Horse. Ormond gave him a command in the Irish Army : he was sent by Ormond to make proposals to Owen Roe, and it was mainly owing to his exertions that the treaty was brought about between them. Ormond was anxious that this Daniel should succeed Owen Roe in command of the Ulster Army, but his religion stood in the way,—he was a Protestant. He left Ireland for Spain in 1650, with 5,000 men for service in Holland. After the Restoration of Charles II., Daniel was made Postmaster-General. He died in 1664. On the occasion of his death Charles II. wrote to the Duchess of Orleans, "This morning poor O'Neill died of an ulcer in his guts. He was as honest a man as ever lived. I am sure I have lost a good servant by it."

amidst the circling warriors, the Bards and Ollamhs of Uladh, he took the oath "to preserve all the ancient former customs of the country inviolable," etc.; and on the death of Tirlogh, he became the Prince of Ulster. He was four times married: first, to Judith, daughter of Sir Hugh O'Donnell, and sister to the celebrated Red Hugh, she d. early in 1591; he m., secondly, in July, 1591, Mabel Bagnal, who d. 1596; thirdly, to Catherine, dau. of Magennis of Down; and, fourthly, to —— ; he had issue by Catherine: 1. Hugh (d. 1609), called "Baron of Dungannon;" 2. Henry (d. s.p.), a Colonel in the Spanish Service; 3. John, Conde de Tyrone, a General in the Spanish Service; 4. Bryan (a page to the Archduke), who was strangled in his bedroom at Brussels, in 1617, by an English assassin; and 5. Conn, a natural son, a prisoner in the Tower, who had a son—Fear-dorach, of whose descendants we, at present, know nothing.

From his great military genius, this Aodh has been called "The Irish Hannibal." In the reign of Queen Elizabeth this Aodh (or Hugh*) exercised the authority of *Ard-Righ* or Monarch, in electing both native and Anglo-Norman chieftains, etc. He died at Rome, blind and worn out, in 1616.

123. Conn: son of Shane an Diomuis; hereditary Prince of Ulster; was elected "The O'Neill" in 1590, as successor to Aodh; but his patrimony being now wrested from him, his people disorganized, and strangers in his strongholds, he was forced to lead an inactive life. He resided usually at Strabane; was m. to Nuala O'Donnell, and by her had issue: I. Art Oge; II. Cu-Uladh, who retired to Scotland, where he m. and had issue; III. Mór, became a Nun; IV. Eoghan, married and had issue; V. Brian, who was killed by an Englishman named Tempest; VI. Flann, d. unm. at Strabane. This Conn d. in 1598, at an advanced age.

124. Art Oge: his son; hereditary Prince of Ulster. Owing to the seizure of his country by James I., of England, and the consequent "Ulster Plantation," this Art's inheritance was overrun by Scotch and English settlers, many of whom generously held for him part of his estates in trust. He was born in 1565; resided partly in Strabane and Dungannon; married Sinead Ni Airt (or Joanna O'Hart), by whom he had four children: I. Conn Ruadh, who d. s.p.; II. Shane; III. Rose; IV. Aodh Dubh, who was a Major-General in the Austrian Army, m. in 1641, Mary Sibylla, dau. of a German Prince, and had issue; died 1650. (See "O'Neill-Bridge" Stem, *infra*.)

---

* *Hugh*: Hugh O'Neill had served some years in the English army, when a young man; acquired a great knowledge of military affairs, and was a favourite at the Court of Elizabeth. On his return to Ireland, he continued some time in the service of the queen; but, having revolted, he became the chief leader of the Northern Irish, and was (perhaps with the exception of his relative, Owen Roe O'Neill) the ablest general that ever contended against the English in Ireland. He, however, became reconciled to the state in the reign of James the First, who, A.D. 1603, confirmed to him his title and estates; but, for alleged political reasons, Hugh O'Neill and Rory O'Donnell, Earl of Tirconnell, were, A.D. 1607, forced to fly from Ireland: they retired to Rome, where Hugh died, A.D. 1616; and Rory or Roderick O'Donnell, A.D. 1617. (See the "Flight of the Earls," in the Appendix.)

For further information in connection with this Hugh O'Neill, see "The Life and Times of Aodh O'Neill, Prince of Ulster; called by the English, Hugh, Earl of Tyrone. With some Account of his Predecessors, Conn, Shane, and Tirlogh." (Dublin: James Duffy. 1845.)

Art Oge O'Neill died in 1622, in Strabane, and was buried at Ardstraw.

125. Shane : his second son ; hereditary Prince of Ulster ; lived, like his father, in Strabane and Dungannon ; b. 1599 ; m. when only 19 years of age, Kathleen O'Donnell of Tirconnell, by whom he had issue : I. Thomas ; II. Art, d. s.p. ; III. Conn, who married and removed to Munster ; IV. Eoghan, who m. and emigrated to North America ; V. Robert, who m. and had issue—extinct in 1866 ; VI. Meadhbh, who m. a French officer.

Shane died in 1643, at Strabane, and was buried with his fathers at Ardstraw.

126. Thomas : his son ; hereditary Prince of Ulster ; b. 1619 ; married Angelina, the dau. of Aodh Dubh O'Neill, by whom he had issue : I. Teige ; II. Shane, who entered the Spanish Army ; III. Mór, who m. a Scotch " laird ;" and IV. Kate.

This Thomas resided at Inishowen, and, in 1670, was found dead on the western shore of Lough Foyle, a dagger being stuck to the hilt in his back : a deed performed, it was believed, by two English spies. He was buried in Derry-Colum-cill (now Londonderry).

127. Teige : his son ; hereditary Prince of Ulster ; b. in 1641 ; resided at Dungannon ; married Mary O'Donnell, by whom he had issue : I. Henry ; II. Brian ; III. John. (These two brothers—Brian and John—went as "soldiers of fortune" to France, thence to Portugal ; they m. two cousins of Maguire, of Fermanagh, before leaving Ireland ; eight of their descendants, in 1807, on the invasion of Portugal by the French, went with the House of Braganza to Brazil, where some of their descendants now (1887) reside.) IV. Robert, married a Miss Stuart, of Argyle, and had issue ; V. Rose, m. a gentleman named MacCallum, of Scotland.

This Teige died in 1690, and was buried at Ardstraw.

(IV.) Robert with his family emigrated to the United States of North America, where he changed his name to *Paine*, so as to preserve his life from assassins. It was one of his descendants who, under the name of " Robert Francis Paine," signed the *Declaration of American Independence*, on the 4th of July, 1776 ; and whose portrait is still to be seen in the old Congress Hall at Philadelphia. Descendants of this Robert are now holders of large estates in many of the States of the great American Republic, and many others of them are engaged in mechanical and mercantile pursuits in that rising nation.

128. Henry : eldest son of Teige ; hereditary Prince of Ulster ; b. in Dungannon, 1665 ; m. Fionualla O'Gormley, by whom he had issue : I. Art ; II. Judith, and III. Kate (twins) ; IV. Aodh ; V. Shane (d. s.p.) ; VI. Roderic, and VII. Nora (twins) ; VIII. Cu-Uladh, who entered the English Army under a feigned name, and was strangled in London ; IX. Delia, married George MacCarthy, had issue ; X. Cormac, born three months after his father's death, m. and removed to co. Cork, where his descendants yet are to be found amongst the peasantry.

Kate died in infancy, Judith went to her cousins in Portugal, with Roderic and Nora, all m. and had issue. Aodh m. Matilda O'Connor, had issue, location now (1887) unknown.

This Henry O'Neill was cousin to Colonel Sir Neill, who was, in 1690, killed at the Boyne. He (Henry) changed his name to *Paine* (modernized *Payne*), so as to preserve both his life and a portion of his Ulster estates. He entered the Army of William III., and obtained the "head rents" of large tracts of land in the county of Cork, and other parts of Ireland, in addition to a small portion of the Sept lands he still held in Ulster. He resided for a short time in North Clanaboy; afterwards at Dungannon, whence he removed to the shelter of his kinsman Neal O'Neal of Cloon, co. Leitrim, where, notwithstanding all his precautions, he fell a victim to his hereditary enemies, being assassinated in 1698, at Foxford, co. Mayo.

129. Art O'Neill, *alias* "Payne:" son of Henry; hereditary Prince of Ulster; b. 1687; made The O'Neill on May Eve, 1709, at Aileach; m. Kate O'Toole, daughter of Garret O'Toole, of Power's Court, county Wicklow (see "O'Toole" Stem, No. 128), and had by her: I. Nial. II. Thomas, who emigrated to America; III. Francis, who m. a Miss Bellsang, and had issue; IV. Lawrence, who m. a Miss Collins, and had two sons and one daughter; V. Nuala, died in infancy; VI. Rose, who m. James Talbot, went with him to England, and had issue; VII. Ada, who m. also a Talbot, and went to England; VIII. Mór, who m. Henry O'Cahan, of Derry; IX. Joan, who m. Felim MacCarthy, d. s.p.

This Art lived a roving life, partly in Tyrone, Wicklow, and Cork, and kept large deer-hounds; died in co. Cork,1732, and was bur. in St. Helen's, Moviddy, whence his remains were taken to Ardstraw, by his son:

130. Nial: hereditary Prince of Ulster; b. 1711; m. Ellen, dau. of Donal Fitzpatrick (of Ossory), by his wife, Una Mac Namara, and by her had issue: I. Richard (or Roderic); II. William, who married Ellen Toler, and by her had a dau. named Nora, who m. Cormac Mac

Carthy, the hereditary Earl of Clan Carthy; and a son, Henry (d. 1843), who m. Lina Seton, of Bucks, and by her had two sons and one dau.; this Henry, on the death of his uncle Roderic (or Richard), was duly elected "The O'Neill," by representatives of the old clans. His two sons were Conn and Aodh; the daughter was Delia, who m. Henry Seton, and is now (1887) in some part of France, and has issue; the son, Conn, d. an infant; and Aodh, on the eve of 1st of Nov., 1847, was made Prince of Ulster, he d. unm., in 1859. Soon after some of the Irish in Paris and New York proceeded to elect his successor; and we learn that Mac Carthy Mór and James Talbot took Richard, who is No. 134 on this Stem, to London, where he was acknowledged as the future Representative of his Race; and we learn that on May Eve, 1862, in the ruined fort of Aileach, the white wand was put into his hand by Daniel O'Connor, of Manch, and the old Pagan ceremonies were performed, as they were some hundreds of years before, when the chieftains elected "O'Neill." (See No. 134 below.) The other children of this Niall were: III. Kate, d. unm; IV. Mary, who m. Phelim O'Neill, and had a dau., Ada, who m. a Mac Loughlin, whose dau. Eva, married Donogh Mac Carthy of Cork; V. Rose, who m. Dermod, hereditary lord of Muscry, and Earl of Clancarthy. (See Stem of Mac Carthy, Lords of Muscry Family, Nos. 129, 130, 131).

This Nial lived in the western part of the county, and in the City of Cork; lived an extravagant life; took a leading part, under various disguises, in political events; sold out to his trustees the remains of the tribe lands in Ulster. The penal laws being in force, his possessions in the South of Ireland were held in trust for him by Protestant friends, many of whom eventually ignored his right, and, taking advantage of the *Law*, excluded him and his heirs from the head rents. Then he engaged in manufacturing pursuits, by means of the remnant of his property, which proved abortive ; finally, he died in 1772, and was buried in Moviddy. In 1780, his remains were removed by his son to Ulster.

131. Richard (or Roderick) : his son; hereditary Prince of Ulster ; b. in Kilmichael, co. Cork, in 1743; m. Margaret, dau. of Donal Mac Carthy Reagh, by his wife Kate O'Driscoll (see No. 125 on the "Mac Carthy Reagh" Stem), and had issue : I. Robert ; II. Rachel, who married John O'Sullivan Mór (Prince of Dunkerron), a native of Berehaven, and by him had issue : Richard, Donogh, and Nora (see the "O'Sullivan Mór" pedigree) ; III. Mary, m. to Philip Ryder, has (in 1887) no issue ; IV. Alice, m. Richard Good, and had issue : 1. Anne (d. s. p.) ; 2. Mary, m. John

Forde, of Bandon, and has one dau. Jane ; 3. Jane, m. Simon Long, issue : James, Daniel, and Elizabeth ; 4. Richard, who m. Anne Good, both d. s.p. ; and V. Bessy, d. s.p.

This Richard was duly elected "The O'Neill," on May Eve, 1766, and was inaugurated in the old Rath of Tullaghoge, west of Lough Neagh, in Tyrone, by the O'Hagan, who was then reduced to indigence. This Richard (or Roderic) lost the remainder of the "head rents" of those lands in co. Cork, which were granted to Henry (No. 128) ; he removed to East Carbery, where he died, in 1817, and was buried in Moviddy. He was, during the most part of his life, unostentatiously the rallying point of all the Celtic princes and chieftains of Erinn, as his elected position indicated.

132. Robert : his son ; m. Eleanor or Nelly, eldest daughter of Corlis O'Baldwin, of Lios-na-Cait, near Bandon, county Cork. [This Corlis was eldest son of William,* son of Robert, son of John, Mayor of Cork, 1737, and descended from William

---

* *William :* This William had three sons and two daughters : the sons were—I. Corlis, m. to a Miss Jenkins ; 2. James, m. to a Miss Banfield—family extinct ; 3. Henry, d. unm. The eldest daughter m. Edward Herrick, of Belmount, gent. ; the youngest, m. Walter MacCarthy, solicitor, a scion of the Blarney MacCarthys.
The second daughter of Corlis m. Mr. McCrate, and d. s.p. McCrate m. secondly to former wife's cousin—a daughter of James. From the following inscription on an obelisk-like monument in the old church-yard of Templemartin, diocese of Cork, we learn that the *Baldwin* family no longer reside or hold possession in Ireland :

✠

"Sacred to the Memory of Barbara Baldwin and her husband Robert Baldwin, of Summer Hill, near Carrigaline, co. Cork, and afterwards of Annarva, Baldwin's Creek, co. Durham, Upper Canada. She died at Summer Hill, 21st Jan., 1791, 42 years of age, and lies buried here among the ancestors of her husband. He died at City of Toronto (then the town of York), Upper Canada, 24th Nov., 1816, aged 75 years ; and lies buried in the grave-yard of St. James's Church in that city. He was the second son of John Baldwin, of Lios-na-Cait, Alderman of Cork. After his wife's death he emigrated with the greater number of their children to Upper Canada, in the years 1798-99. This stone, under the superintendence of his eldest son, Robert Baldwin, is erected to the memory of his much-loved parents by William Warren Baldwin, of Spadina, in the county of York, in Upper Canada, their eldest surviving son, and the present head of the eldest male branch of their descendants, who are all now through the merciful goodness of the Almighty successful and happily settled in that Province —1836."

of Lisarda, son of Henry, who is No. 7 on the "Baldwin" pedigree.] Issue: I. Richard, who m. Mary O'Nolan, and had by her—Robert, Henry, Eleana, Richard, and Una : Henry died in Ireland ; the others with their parents, emigrated to North America, from 1847 to 1854, and all of whom are now (1887) dead. II. Robert, whose lineage is here traced. III. William. IV. John. V. Thomas: — these last three also emigrated to New Jersey, and thence to Kentucky, where they resided, unm., in 1880. VI. Francis, an officer in the United States Army, killed many years ago by American Indians. VII. Margaret, d. unm. in Ireland. VIII. Mary, m. to — Linzey, an officer in the Anglo-Indian Army, d. some years ago, s.p.

This Robert, in 1847, died at Mount Pleasant, and was buried at St. Helen's, Moviddy, co. Cork.

133. Robert: second son of Robert ; born 1816 ; m. Jane Anne, dau. of Richard Wall, of Ardnaclog (Bellmount), parish of Moviddy, county Cork, by his wife Jane "Welply," or more correctly, Jane Mac Carthy, dau. of William Mac Carthy Mór, *alias* "Welply," of Clodagh Castle. (See Mac Carthy Mór pedigree, No. 129.) Issue : three sons and two daughters : I. William, who died in infancy. II. Richard-Walter. III. Marmaduke, an officer in the English Army—the "Connaught Rangers," Renmore Barracks, Galway (living in 1887), born at Lios-na-Cait, 4th June, 1845 ; married, and has issue two sons, and four daughters. IV. Jane Anne, b. at Lios-na-Cait, 13th June, 1848, m. William Farrow, son of William Farrow by his wife Jane Mitchel, both natives of Ipswich, in

Suffolk, England ; this Jane Anne with her husband reside at 2 Albert Villas, King-street, New Brompton, Kent, England, and has no issue. V. Elizabeth-Lavinia, born at Ardna-clog (Bellmount), Muscry, 6th September, 1852, and resides (1887) at the Connecticut Training School, State Hospital, New Haven, Connecticut, U. S. America ; unm.

This Robert died in New Jersey about 1851.

134. Richard W. O'Neill (*alias* "Payne"[*]) : his son ; born at Lios-na-Cait, 13th Sept., 1842 ; living at St. Martin's, Farranavane, Bandon, county Cork, in 1887 ; and acts as Principal Teacher of Mount Pleasant National School. (See Note, "The O'Neill," under Niall Glundubh, No. 100, on the "O'Neill" (No. 1) pedigree.)

This Richard, known over most part of Ireland as "The O'Neill," (see No. 130 on this pedigree) was m., in June, 1864, to Mary, only dau. of John Harris, of Moss Grove, by his wife Eliza O'Connor, in the Catholic Church of Murrogh, by the Reverend John Lyons, C.C. (now P.P. of Kilmichael, co. Cork) and has had issue :

I. John Canice, b. at Moss Grove, 12th January, 1867.
II. Luaghaidh (Lewy)-Thomas, b. 7th June, 1870.
III. Jane-Anna-Maria, born 2nd February, 1873.
IV. Aodh ⎱ twins, born 9th
V. Caroline ⎰ Aug., 1876.
Aodh d. at the age of ten months.
VI. Rose-Adelaide, b. 28th Aug., 1880.

135. John: son of Richard (2) ; living in St. Martin's, Farranavane, Bandon, in 1887.

---

[*] *Payne :* This family is not even remotely connected with any other, bearing a like name in Great Britain, or Ireland.

O'NEILL. (No. 3.)

*Princes of Clanaboy.**

Arms :† Per fesse wavy the chief ar. the base representing waves of the sea, in chief a dexter hand couped at the wrist gu. in base a salmon naiant ppr.   *Crest* : An arm in armour embowed the hand grasping a sword all ppr.   *Motto :* Lamh dearg Eirin.

Of the present Hereditary Princes of Clanaboy the *Arms* are : In chief ar. a dexter hand couped and erect, supported by two lions ramp. surmounted by three mullets, the whole gu., the base waves of the sea ppr. whereon a salmon naiant ppr.   The shield is surmounted by a mediæval princely crown‡ of three strawberry leaves. *Crest :* A dexter arm in armour embowed ppr. garnished or, holding in the hand a dagger also ppr., pommel and hilt gold.   *Motto :* Cœlo, solo, salo, Potentes.   *War Cry :* Lamh dearg Eirin Abú.

In the old graveyard of Lower Langfield, near Drumquin, county Tyrone, there are two tombstones of the O'Neills with the following inscriptions —" Here lieth the body of Fardoragh O'Neill, who departed this life March 20, 1738, aged 99 years." The second—" Here lieth the body of Charles O'Neill, who dyed Desember the 8, 1739, aged 23 years."   On the first stone the arms of O'Neill are cut in relief, and agree with the above, except that on the stone the arm embowed has behind it cross bones. (*No Arms on the second stone*).

The ruins of an old castle of the O'Neills are to be seen in the townland of Kerlish, near the graveyard.

AODH (OR HUGH) DUBH ONEILL, brother of Niall Ruadh, who is No. 112 on the " O'Neill" (No. 2) pedigree, Princes of Tyrone, was the founder of this House.

---

* *Clanaboy :* In modern times some representatives of this family assumed the title-name of *Castlereagh.*

† *Arms :* In the earlier part of the history of the " O'Neill" (of Ulster) family the Arms were (as in " O'Neill" No. 1), the *Red Right Hand*, which a writer in Queen Elizabeth's time, designated as " that terrible cognizance ;" and from which is derived the war-cry : *Lamh dearg Eirin Abú*, or " The Red Hand of Eirin for ever."   In fact this warlike symbol is Ireland's heraldic emblem, *par excellence :* and is for her what the *Roses* are for England, and the *Fleur-de-lis* for France.   The " O'Neill" Arms in this simple form appear in the ancient heraldic records ; and we have it in the beautiful silver signet belonging to Hugh O'Neill (d. 1364), and described in p. 64 of Vol. I. of Ulster Journal of Archæology.   At a later period the Coat of Arms displays a greater number of figures, and we successively meet with the *salmon* (attributed to the O'Neill dominion over Lough Neagh), and more lately the *mullets* ; and it is in the latter complete form that we find it used by Hugh O'Neill, Earl of Tyrone, who had it represented in mosaic in natural colours on the tombstone of his son, at St. Pietro in Montorio, Rome ; and also by Sir Daniel O'Neill, and the celebrated Owen Roe O'Neill, whose signet seal was discovered by the Rev. James Graves in the "evidence chamber" of Kilkenny Castle.   It is this more elaborate display that the branches of the House of " O'Neill" of Clanaboy who emigrated to the Continent have adopted, and with it the *parlant* Motto of " Cœlo, Solo, Salo, Potentes."   We are told that in the archives of Shane's Castle, Antrim, an old MS. refers to this Motto : truly a fit one to revive the proud traditions of a family which, for the number of its Saints, of its Kings, and of its Heroes, can be said to be qualified as great in Heaven and on Earth.   We cannot trace any origin for the mullets in the Arms of this family, we can only say that they are met with in the Arms of several other Irish families.   As to the *salmon* it seems to be of a remote origin : it is on the tombstone of Cumagh-na-nGall O'Cahan (see No. 110 on the " O'Cahan" pedigree), who was Sovereign Prince of Limavady, in the latter end of the thirteenth century, and who was buried in the church of Dungiven ; for, the " O'Cahan" family is an off-shoot of the " O'Neill," which explains the identity of this heraldic figure in their Arms !

‡ *Crown :* This Crown is no heraldic one.   Crowns are believed to have been unknown to native Irish heraldry ; but the House of O'Neill having maintained its

112. Hugh (6) Dubh O'Neill* (d. 1230): son of Hugh an Macaomh Teinleasg; surnamed "dubh," because he was *dark-featured;* was 12th in descent from Niall Glundubh, the 170th Monarch of Ireland; was Sovereign Prince of Tyrone, and King of Ulster, A.D. 1186. He defeated the English at Dungannon, in 1199; and in 1210 visited King John at Carrickfergus, but made no submission to him. Hugh Dubh m. and was succeeded by his son:

113. Donal (4) surnamed Oge (or the young); slain A.D. 1234.

114. Hugh (7), surnamed "Buidhe"† (or yellow), in Irish "Aodh Buidhe:" son of Donal Oge; was Prince of Tirowen from A.D. 1260 to 1283, when he died. From him is derived the name "Clanaboy" which in Irish was *Clan Aodh Buidhe,* meaning the "Clan of Yellow Hugh;" by which designation the territories which said Hugh then brought under his dominion have been known to this day. The House of Clanaboy maintained its sovereign rights down to the time of James I., of England; and such was

sovereign honours down to the 17th century, a mediæval princely crown was logically adopted by its more modern representatives, and is the one we meet with in the family signets of the last century. Although crowns and coronets were not adopted as an heraldic emblem in the display of the coat of Arms of the ancient Irish, they were in use as regal ornament, but their shape was apparently not subordinate to any heraldic rules. One of these crowns, found in 1692 under ground in Barnanely, is of pure gold, and is described by Dr. Petrie in the Dublin *Penny Journal.* On the tomb of Felim O'Connor, in Roscommon, and on that of Connor O'Brien (both reigning Princes), another form of Crown appears, which was in use in England and on the Continent by Sovereign Princes, till the 15th century.

* *Hugh* (6) *Dubh O'Neill:* Some authorities assume that Hugh Dubh O'Neill was the elder and not the younger brother of Niall Ruadh; that therefore, the Clanaboy branch of the "O'Neill" would be the senior; and, as such, the representative of Kinelowen.—See No. 111 on the "O'Neill" (No. 1) pedigree.

† *Buidhe:* In A.D. 1275, the English Municipality of Carrickfergus mention Aodh Buidhe O'Neill to King Edward I. of England, as: "Ad. O'Neill regem de Kinelowen." (See O'Callaghan's *Irish Brigades in the Service of France.*) Among the splendid collections of Lord Braye, there exists a beautiful silver seal, with the O'Neill badge carved thereon, and the legend: "Sigillum Adonis O'Neill, Regis Hiberniæ coram Ultoniæ," attributed to Hugh O'Neill.

The Clan of this Aodh (or Hugh) Buidhe passed the river Ban into Eastern Ulster or Antrim and Down; and wrested from the mixed population of old natives and the descendants of the English settlers, the territory hence designated "Clanaboy" or the *Clan of Yellow Hugh.*

The "Clanaboy" territory was divided into north and south; the former situated between the rivers Ravel and Lagan, embracing the modern baronies of the two Antrims, two Toomes, two Belfasts, Lower Massarene, and county of the town of Carrickfergus; the latter, south of the river Lagan, including the present baronies of Upper and Lower Castlereagh. Upon the hill of Castlereagh, about two miles from Belfast, was the stone chair on which the Rulers of the Clanaboy principality (of which Conn O'Neill, in the reign of James the First, was the last chief) were inaugurated. From the chieftain-line of this second "Hy-Niall," sprang the last lineal representative of the Clanaboy branch of the O'Neill in Ireland: namely, The Right Honourable John Bruce, Richard O'Neill, third Viscount and Baron O'Neill, of Shane's Castle, County Antrim; a Representative Peer of Ireland; General in the Army; Vice-Admiral of the Coast of Ulster; and Constable of Dublin Castle: b. at Shane's Castle, Dec., 1780; and deceased, February, 1855, in his 75th year. His estates devolved to the Rev. William Chichester, Prebendary of St. Michael's, Dublin, who hence took the name of "O'Neill;" and was, A.D. 1868, in the Peerage of Great Britain and Ireland, created "Baron O'Neill," of Shane's Castle, County of Antrim.—O'CALLAGHAN. (See the "O'Neill" (No. 4) pedigree, p. 736, *infra.*)

its power in the time of Henry VIII., that (according to Cox, quoted by MacGeoghagan,) its representatives recovered from the English not only the territories called the "Clanaboys" and the "Ards," but also a tributary tax from "the British authorities of the Pale."

The *Annals of the Four Masters* record this Prince's death in the following terms:

"Hugh O'Neill, the fair Prince of Tyrone, the head of the generosity and valour of the Irish, the most distinguished man in the North for gifts and for wealth, the most dreaded and victorious of his House, and a worthy Heir to the Throne* of Ireland, was killed by Bernard Mac-Mahon." . . .

Hugh (6) Buidhe O'Neill was succeeded by his eldest son:

115. Brian (1), or Bernard, Sovereign Prince of Tyrone and of Clanaboy, A.D. 1291, who was slain in 1295, and was succeeded by his son:

116. Henry (1), Sovereign Prince of Clanaboy, who was succeeded by his son:

117. Muriertach or Murtagh (7), anglicé Maurice, who was surnamed *Ceannfada* (meaning "long-headed" or "prudent"). He was Sovereign Prince of Clanaboy; lord of the baronies of Castlereagh, and Lower Ards, in the county Down; of the baronies of Tuam (now "Toome"),

Antrim, Belfast, and Massarene; of the towns of Carrickfergus, Belfast, and Lisnegarry; and of the barony of Loghlinslin,† in the county Derry. He died A.D. 1395, and was succeeded by his son:

118. Brian (2), surnamed *Ballach* (or "freckled"). He was Sovereign of Clanaboy, and lord of the lordships over which his father had held sway. Having obtained several victories over the English and the O'Neill of Tyrone, this Brian was slain in 1425, under which date his death is recorded by the Four Masters, thus:

"Brian Ballach, the most distinguished man of his time for hospitality, goodness, and learning, and the knowledge of many sciences, was killed by the people of Carrick."

It was this Brian who imposed an *eric* on the English of Carrickfergus, Carlingford, etc., called "Brian Balla's eric," which was paid until it was by Act of Parliament discontinued in the reign of Henry VIII., and by Proclamation in the reign of Queen Elizabeth. He was succeeded by his son:

119. Hugh (8) Buidhe, Sovereign Prince of Clanaboy, whose name is honourably mentioned by the Four Masters. Had three brothers—1. Murtagh Ruadh, 2. Henry Caoch,‡ 3. Niall Galdha. This Hugh occu-

---

* *Heir to the Throne:* According to the Laws of Tanistry, all the members of the House of O'Neill were eligible to the Monarchy, as well as to the Chieftainship of any of the Principalities belonging to the family. They had therefore a right to be styled Heirs to the Throne of Ireland, and of Ulster; Hereditary Princes of Tyrone, of Clanaboy, etc.

† *Loghlinslin:* A very interesting relic of the regal power of the Princes of Clanaboy was to be seen some years ago in the house of a gentlemen of elegant tastes, namely, Mr. R. C. Walker, of Granby Row, Dublin. It was, according to Dr. Petrie, the coronation chair of their sovereigns.

† *Henry Caoch:* According to the Rev. Dr. Reeves, this Henry was a brother and not a son of Brian Ballach; but, according to Burke's "Vicissitudes of Families," Henry Caoch was *son* of Brian Ballach, No. 118. A lineal descendant of said Henry was Sir Francis O'Neill, who was married to a Miss Fleming, and who, being a Roman Catholic, "was robbed of his property in the course of law." Sir Francis then took a

pied an important position in the wars of his time; and was slain in 1444. He was m. to Finola, dau. of Charles O'Connor, lord of Offaley; she died a Nun in the Convent of Killeigh, in 1493. He was succeeded by his eldest son:

120. Conn (1) or Constantine, of Edendubh-carrig, Sovereign Prince of Clanaboy. *Edendubhcarrig* means "the brow of the dark rock," and was the name of the castle and domains where this Prince usually resided on the borders of Lough Neagh. In more modern times, as will be seen hereafter, this name was changed for that of *Shane's Castle*, when the estates passed under British influence to a junior branch of the family. This Conn is styled by the Four Masters:

"Worthy heir to the throne of Ulster," and his death is by them recorded under A.D. 1482.

121. Niall (5), surnamed Mór (or the Great): son of Conn; married Innedubh, dau. of O'Donel Roe.* This Niall was celebrated for his valour and religion; the Annals of the Four Masters affirm that in 1497 the Convent of Carrickfergus was founded by him, by permission of the Holy See, for the benefit of the monks *De Minor. de Observantia.* The same Annals also mention him as the proprietor of the Castle of Edendubhcarrig, as well as the Castle of Carrickfergus. He died on the 11th of April, 1512, and, according to the Four Masters, "was a pious and learned Prince, able in the sciences of history, poetry, and music." He had four sons whose names appear in history in the following order: 1. Hugh,† whose descent is extinct, and who died Sovereign Prince of Clanaboy in 1524; 2. Brian Ballagh, of whom

farm, but having a large family of fourteen children, he became encumbered with debt and was again ejected. His eldest son Henry went to Spain and served in his relative's regiment; last heard of in 1798. Another son John m. Catherine Murtagh, and had Francis, who, in 1859, was a working mill-wright in Drogheda. Another of the sons was James, who was a working baker in Dublin, and who d. in 1800. And Bryan, the youngest son, served as a soldier for many years in the Peninsula, etc.; was chief officer of the Newgate guard in 1830, and on its break up he took the house No. 95, Cook-street, where he resided in 1859, and where his eldest son carried on the business of a coffin-maker. (That son's name was Francis, who, in 1868, was the keeper of the Cork Model School, and who then had several children.)

* *O'Donel Roe*: The O'Neills and O'Donels often intermarried. They were worthy of each other for their pedigrees. On the Continent these two families always met with due consideration. In Austria, an O'Donnell married in 1754 a cousin of the Empress Maria Theresa, with the latter's consent; such was the esteem his pedigree was held in. As an illustration of the high consideration entertained for the Irish pedigrees on the Continent, we may quote the opinion of a learned French writer, M. Julés Paulet, du Parais, who, in his *Manuel Complet du Blason*, says: "L' aristocracie Anglaise in elle est la plus forte et la plus vivace de toute, est aussi de toute la plus nouvelle. Ses plus hautes pretentions ne remontent guére qu'aux Plantagenets, et l'on considére comme tres anciennes les races dont l'Illustration date des guerres des deux Roses. Comparez a ces généalogies celles des familles patriciennes de Venise des grandesses Espagnoles, de ritters Allemands, celles de la noblesse Celtique d'Irlande, des O'Neills, des O'Brien, des O'Connor, voise celles des grands barons Français contemporains de Charlemagne, et vous n'aurez qu'une médiocre estime pour les origines de la noblesse Britannique. Le sang des Howards lui-même ne nous semblera pas aussi précieux."

† *Hugh*: This Hugh had Niall, who had Niall Oge of Killelagh, county Antrim; (his patent, A.D. 1606: Calendar Patent Rolls, Jac. I., p. 94; and Erck, p. 285), and Hugh, who was joined by his brother in the patent of 1606, and who (or his son) was the Hugh Mergach of the Inquisition, *temp.* King Charles I. (See Montgomery MSS., p. 137.)

presently ; 3. Niall Oge,* who died Sovereign Prince in 1537, and whose posterity ended with the late Miss O'Neill of Banville; 4. Phelim Baccagh, who never became Sovereign Prince of Clanaboy, but whose son Brian (known as Brian Mac-Phelim O'Neill) was renowned as such. This Phelim Baccagh, fourth son of Niall Mór, was the ancestor of the Lords O'Neill, of Shane's Castle, to whose branch of the family the estates of Edendubhcarrig devolved under British influence. (See Ware, quoted by O'Donovan in the Four Masters under the year 1555.) Brian MacPhelim's son, Shane, changed the name of Eden-dubhcarrig to " Shane's Castle," after his own name, and was chosen by the English Government for " Captain of Clanaboy," on the grounds that *" he was a modest man that speaketh English ;"* which shows that it was no particular right on Shane's part, but merely his friendly disposition towards the English, that was the cause of their preference in his favour. (See State Papers, Vol. CIV., 28, August 23rd, 1583). Shane's son Henry conformed to the Protestant religion ; was knighted, and got a patent from King James I., of the estates of "Shane's Castle;" and thus the old family domains of Edendubh-carrig passed to the posterity of the

fourth son of Niall Mór, to the prejudice of the senior branch of the family who clung to the Catholic Faith.

122. Brian (3) Ballagh : second son of Niall Mór ; was, according to the Four Masters, slain in 1529, by MacQuillan, " who went out of Carrickfergus in company and friendship with him." According to a letter from Captain Piers, serving in Ireland, to Secretary Walshingham, and dated 12th June, 1580, in the Second Volume of State Papers for Ireland (*apud*, A.D. 1580), this Prince for some time enjoyed the sovereignty of Clanaboy. That letter contains the following paragraph :

" O'Neill (Tyrone) was encamped before the town of Carrickfergus and the colour (or pretext) of his coming was to demand certain buying for one Brian Ballagh O'Neill, sometime Lord of Clanaboy, a kinsman of his, who was killed by the townsmen of Carrickfergus about sixty years past ; and the buying forgiven by Sir Bryan McPhelim, in his life-time, and now, as it seemeth, newly revived by O'Neill."

That extract from the letter of Captain Piers shows that Brian MacPhelim O'Neill, representative of the junior branch of the Clanaboy family, courted British protection, and hastened to ignore the buying, and throw into oblivion the

---

* *Niall Oge* : This Niall was the ancestor of Sir Daniel O'Neill (died 1669), who was Chamberlain to King Charles I., and Page of Honour to Charles II. The descent was as follows:

122. Niall Oge : son of Niall Mór. Had three sons—1. Aodh, of Belfast, slain 1555 ; 2. Conn ; 3. Brian Ferlagh.
123. Brian Ferlagh (or Faghartach) : son of Niall Oge ; slain, 1548.
124. Niall : his son ; 1577.
125. Conn, of Castlereagh : son of Niall ; made a grant of Land in 1606 ; m. Ellice O'Neill. Had two sons—1. Hugh Buidhe [boy], 2. Conn Oge.
126. Conn Oge : his son ; killed in 1643

at the Battle of Clones, after quarters had been granted.
127. Sir Daniel O'Neill : his son. Chamberlain to Charles I., and Page of Honour to Charles II. Married Lady Catherine Stanhope, widow of Henry Stanhope, son of Philip, first Earl of Chesterfield— According to the Rev. Dr. Reeves, this Sir Daniel was son of Conn Oge ; but, according to the Montgomery MSS., p. 321, Sir Daniel was Conn Oge's brother.

traditions of his senior kinsman.* Brian (3) Ballagh O'Neill† m., first, dau. of O'Neill, Prince of Tyrone; and, secondly, Sibile, dau. of Maguire of Fermanagh. His son by the first marriage was his successor:

123. Murtagh (8), Hereditary Prince of Clanaboy. A Memoir on the State of Ireland by Lord Chancellor Cusack, in 1552, states of this Murtagh: "In Clanaboy is one Murtagh Dulenach, one of the O'Neills, who hath the name as Captain of Clanaboy, but he is not able to maintain the same; he hath eight tall gentlemen to his sons and (yet) they cannot make past twenty-four horsemen. There is another sept in that country of Felim Baccagh's sons, tall men, which taketh part with Hugh McNeill Oge, till now of late." This again shows that, despite his efforts, Murtagh's power was fast declining, under the unceasing persecution of his junior kinsmen, the sons of Niall Oge and of Felim Baccagh, who, as we have already shown, enjoyed British preference and support. Murtagh, like his father, was a strenuous Roman Catholic, and, evidently, this circumstance did not contribute to make them favourites of the English. He married, Margaret, dau. of O'Byrne, of Wicklow, and had:

124. Daniel (5), who had:

125. Constantine (2), whose son and successor was:

126. Felix (1), who married a dau. of O'Neill of Kilultagh. He distinguished himself as Colonel under the celebrated Owen Roe O'Neill, in 1649; and was succeeded by his son:

127. Ever (1), who joined the National movements of the time; and married Catherine, daughter of Ever O'Neill, of Killitragh, ancestor of O'Neill, of Austria, Counts of the Holy Roman Empire, etc. He had a son:

128. Felix (2), who was an officer in Lord Galmoy's regiment for James II. He was deprived of the remnant of his family estates, under the persecution generally suffered by Roman Catholics in those Penal days in Ireland; and, after the surrender of Limerick, he followed King James II. to the Continent, and died on the field of battle of Malplaquet, on the 13th September, 1709, as an officer of the Irish Brigade. He was twice married: first, to Catherine Keating; and, secondly, to a dau. of O'Dempsey, Viscount Clanmaliere; he left only one son by his first marriage, namely Constantine]

129. Constantine (3), the said son of Felix (2); was a Citizen of Dublin, who married Cecilia, dau. of Felix O'Hanlon, a Capt. of Infantry in the Army of James II., who was the son of Colonel Edmond O'Hanlon, who is No. 125 on the "O'Hanlon" (Lords of Orior) pedi-

---

* *Kinsman*: These family dissensions have long since passed away; and we are aware that the late Lord John Bruce Richard Viscount O'Neill, of Shane's Castle, who died in 1855, maintained a very friendly intercourse with his Portugese kinsmen.

† *O'Neill*: Brian Ballagh's descent is traced as follows, in a Pedigree written in Latin upon parchment in 1756, and preserved by the present representatives of the family, as one of the most precious relics of their tradition. This document is authenticated by the then Archbishop of Armagh; the Bishop of Dromore, who vouches "for the constant and not yet interrupted tradition," and his own "certain knowledge of its facts;" and other high Ecclesiastical authorities. All the signatures are legalised, and the whole is certified by the Prothonotary Apostolic, who bears witness in public faith to its truthfulness. In this Pedigree also Brian (3) Ballagh is declared to be, by hereditary right (*hereditario jure*), Sovereign of the Upper and Lower Clanaboy.

gree. Constantine had three sons and seven daughters ; the eldest son was :

130. John, who settled in Portugal, and purchased an estate on the left bank of the river Tagus, near Almada, in front of Lisbon. He is mentioned by the Italian traveller G. Barretti, in his *Letterre Famigliari*. In 1750 he m. Valentina, dau. of José Ferreira, a landed proprietor in the environs of Lisbon, from whose family descended maternally the families of *Palyart, Clamanse*, and of the French general *De Negrier*. This John had several sons and daughters ; amongst the latter— Cecilia and Anna who both took the veil, and became successively Prioresses of the Convent of Irish Sisters of Bone Successo, near Lisbon, where they died and lie buried. Two of the sons d. without issue ; and he was succeeded in the seniority of the name by his youngest son :

131. Charles, who was educated at the College of St. Omer, in France. He married in 1784 Anna-John, daughter of Jacob Torlade (Consul of the Hanseatic Cities at St. Ubes), son of Henry Torlade, a Judge and Banker in Hamburg in 1713, whose Coat of Arms is described under that date in the City Registers. Charles O'Neill possessed extensive landed property at St. Ubes and Lisbon ; and received at his house at St. Ubes the visit of the King of Portugal, John VI. and his daus. the Infantas.* He was a Knight of the Order of Christ. He left three sons—1. José-Maria, 2. Joaquin, and 3. Henry ; and several daus., all of whom left issue ; the eldest son being also represented in the male line by the now (1887) existing members of the family.

O'NEILL. (No. 4.)

Of Shane's Castle, County Antrim.

The ancient *Arms* were : Per fess wavy the chief ar. the base representing waves of the sea, in chief a dexter hand couped at the wrist gu. in base a salmon naiant ppr. *Crest:* An arm in armour embowed the hand grasping a sword all ppr. *Motto :* Lamh dearg Eirin (The Red hand of Erin).

PHELIM BACCACH, a younger brother of Brian Ballach who is No. 122 on the "O'Neill" (Princes of Clanaboy) pedigree, was the ancestor of this branch of that family.

122. Phelim Baccach : son of Niall Mór ; d. 1533 ; some of whose male descendants are the O'Neills of Ballymoney. Had two sons — 1. Hugh,* 2. Brian.

† *Infantas* : This family has since received the visits of other members of the Portguese Royal Family at their houses at St. Ubes, namely : Queen Donna Maria II. ; King Don Ferdinand ; King Don Peter V. ; and his brothers Don John ; and Don Luis, the present King.

*₁*Hugh* : This Hugh MacFelim O'Neill, lord of Kilultagh, mar. and had : 1. Hugh Oge ; 2. Niall, of whom presently ; and three other sons, who owned the territory of Kilultagh, in Clanaboy.

123. Brian*: his second son; died 1574.

124. John: his son; had a brother named Conn; was twice married—the only issue by the first marriage was Sir Henry O'Neill; this John died 23rd April, 1617.

125. Sir Henry†: his son; had a daughter named Rose, who was his only heir, and who married Randal MacDonnell, Earl of Antrim (a quo "Randalstown"), but left no issue. This Sir Henry O'Neill, whose Will is dated the 13th September, 1637, had four brothers—1. Arthur, of Shane's Castle, who was the heir of his brother Henry, in the event of his daughter Rose (Marchioness of Antrim) having no issue; 2. Phelim; 3. Shane Oge, who died without issue, A.D. 1620; and 4. Hugh, who also died, sine prob. Arthur O'Neill, of Shane's Castle, here mentioned, had two sons — 1. Charles (no issue recorded); 2. Captain John O'Neill. This Captain John O'Neill had two sons— 1. Arthur, who died unmarried, in Flanders, in 1702; and 2. Colonel Charles O'Neill, of Shane's Castle, who died without issue. After this Col. Charles O'Neill's death, Henry O'Neill administered on 10th Sept., 1716, but died s.p. The estates then reverted to "Shane an Franca" (or "French John"), son of Brian,

2. Niall: son of Hugh MacFelim Baccach; had great disputes with the sons of Sir Brian MacFelim O'Neill respecting territory. (See Antrim Survey.) This Niall m. and had: 1. Niall Oge of Killilagh, and 2. Hugh.

3. Niall Oge of Killilagh (b. 1606): son of Niall; m. and had:

4. Sir Henry (b. 1625), who was knighted in 1666, and who m. and had:

    I. Sir Neill, of whom presently.

    II. Sir Daniel, who succeeded on the death of his brother, left one daughter who mar. Hugh O'Reilly, of Ballinlough, to whom William III. gave a fortune of £20,000.

    I. Rose, who m. Captain Con O'Neill, of the Fews.

5. Sir Neill O'Neill: elder son of Sir Henry; was Colonel of Dragoons in the service of King James II. Sir Neill mar., in 1677, Lady Frances, dau. of the third Viscount Molyneux. He raised and equipped his regiment, and fought with the utmost gallantry at its head, at the Battle of the Boyne, in 1690, when thrice he charged through the river and beat back Schomberg's choicest troops. Here he was wounded in the thigh (according to O'Callaghan), and was carried to Dublin, and thence to Waterford where, by the negligence of his surgeons, he died of his wounds. His tomb is still extant in the ruined church of the Franciscan Abbey in the city of Waterford; it is a limestone flag or slab on the ground inside the church walls; the Arms and Crest of the departed are on it, and, from the inscription, it appears he died on the 8th July, 1690, aged 32 years and 6 months. He left no male heir, but was succeeded in his title by his only brother, Sir Daniel O'Neill. Sir Neill had five daughters, who with their mother retired to their grandmother's relatives—the Talbots of Cartown, county Kildare: 1. Rosa, became wife of Nicholas Wogan, of Rathcoffey, whose daughter and co-heir, Frances, married John Talbot, of Malahide; 2. Anne, married to John Segrave, of Cabra; 3. Mary; 4. Elizabeth. We know not the fifth daughter's name.

* Brian : Primogeniture, though not universal, was yet coming into use among the Irish about this time; for, see Notification, in Bagenal's Description of Ulster, of Sir Brian MacFelim having been able to get himself elected Prince of the two Clanaboys, because his elder brother Hugh was held in prison by the English.

† Sir Henry : At p. 82 of the MS. Vol. F. 3. 27, in the Lib. of Trin. Coll., Dublin, occurs the following entry: " Martha, dau. of Sir Francis Stafford, governor of Ulster, born ibid. 1599, Oct. 8, was wife to Sir Henry O'Neill of ye Lower Claneboyes, and had issue, Rosey, wife to Sir Randal (MacDonnell), Earl of Antrim. The said Martha d. 19th April, bur. 4th June, 1678, in Carigfergus."

son of Phelim, the second brother of Sir Henry O'Neill, No. 125 on this pedigree.

126. Brian : son of the said Phelim, the second brother of the said Sir Henry O'Neill ; had a brother named Arthur.

127. Shane* an Franca (or "French John") : son of Brian ; Will proved 1739 ; had two brothers—1. Henry, and 2. Hugh.

128. Henry O'Neill : the eldest son of Shane an Franca ; had a dau. Mary, who was his only heir. This Henry had two brothers--1. Charles, who, after Henry's death, took possession of Shane's Castle ; 2. Clotworthy, who left no issue. The said Charles died in August, 1769, leaving two sons—1. The Right Hon. John O'Neill, who, on the 25th October, 1793, was created "Baron," and in 1795, "Viscount,

O'Neill ;" 2. St. John O'Neill. This John Viscount O'Neill left two sons —1. Charles Henry St. John, Viscount (in August, 1800, created "Earl") O'Neill, and 2. John Bruce Richard, Viscount O'Neill†—each of whom died without issue. St. John O'Neill, the younger brother of the Right Hon. John, the first "Viscount O'Neill," here mentioned, died in March, 1790, leaving an only child, Mary O'Neill, of whom no issue is recorded.

129. Mary : daughter and only heir of Henry O'Neill (No. 128 on this stem), the eldest son of Shane an Franca ; m. to the Rev. Arthur Chichester.

130. Rev. Wm. Chichester, known as "Doctor Chichester:" their son. This William had two sons—1. Sir Arthur Chichester, to whom the Clanaboy Estates were willed, and

---

* *Shane :* This was the Shane O'Neill who built the Clanaboy Tomb at Shane's Castle, of the inscription on which the following is a copy : "This Vault was built by Shane, MacBrien, MacPhelim, MacShane, MacBrien, MacPhelim O'Neill, Esq., in the year 1722, for a Burial Place to himself and family of Clanneboy."

† *John Bruce Richard O'Neill :* In connexion with the Seal of John Bruce Richard, Viscount O'Neill (born at Shane's Castle, in December, 1780, and died in February, 1855 : see Note " Aodh Buidhe," p. 731, *ante*), we read from a paper by the Right Rev. Doctor Reeves, in pp. 256-258, Vol. I., of the *Ulster Journal of Archæology,* that said Seal was a shield with the right hand extended, supported by two nondescript animals, with the legend : " S Odonis (an attempt to latinize *Aodh*) O'Neill Regis Hybernicorum Vltonie . . ." The death of this Aodh (or Hugh) O'Neill is recorded in the Annals, under the year A.D. 1364. (See No. 115 on the "O'Neill," Princes of Tyrone, pedigree.) Of that Seal Doctor Reeves says : "This beautiful specimen of the Sphragistic art is the finest work of the kind connected with Ireland which remains, and far exceeds in elegance the other seals of the O'Neill family . . . It is to be observed, too, that the hand, as in other early seals of the family, is a *Dexter* one— the same as that which now (in 1853) appears on the Arms of the present lord. *Argent a hand gules* was the heraldic characteristic of Baronetcy when created in 1611 and 1619, *in consideration of O'Neill's extermination ;* and it was remarkable to find Sir Bryan O'Neill, of Bakerstown, in 1642, and Sir Henry O'Neill, of Killilagh, in 1666— the one in the English, and the other in the Irish, Baronetage—adopting an achievement which they were supposed to *win from themselves.* . . . All that is known of its History is, that it came into the hands of Horace Walpole, in the course of the last century, from the neighbourhood of Belfast. This appears from his own description of Strawberry Hill, printed there in 1784."

In p. 64 of said *Ulster Journal of Archæology* we read : "A SILVER seal, extremely ancient, of Hugh O'Neill (d. 1364), King of Ulster, brought out of Ireland by Mr. William Bristow."

The Seal of Brian O'Neill, King of Tyrone, from A.D. 1241 to 1260, who was killed at the Battle of Down, in 1260, consists of (apparently), a mounted king with a drawn sword, and the legend :

" S Brien Regis de Kinel Eogain."

who died unm. ; 2. Rev. Edward Chichester.

131. Rev. Edward : second son of the Rev. William Chichester. This Edward had four sons—1. Rev. William ; 2. Rev. Robert, who died in June, 1878 ; 3. Arthur, who died young, in 1830 ; 4. Rev. George Vaughan Chichester.

132. Rev. William Chichester, of Shane's Castle : eldest son of the Rev. Edward Chichester; created "Baron *O'Neill*" (United Kingdom, 1868) ; d. 18th April, 1883. This Rev. William, Lord O'Neill, had three sons — 1. Edward Baron O'Neill ; 2. The Hon. Arthur O'Neill, who died unm., in 1870 ; 3. The Hon. Robert Torrens O'Neill, M.P. for Mid Antrim ; and one daughter, The Hon. Anne O'Neill.

133. Edward Baron O'Neill; eldest son of the Rev. William Baron O'Neill ; living in 1887. Has had three sons and three daughters, viz.,

I. The Hon. William T. Cochrane, who died in 1882.

II. The Hon. Arthur - Edward Bruce O'Neill.

III. The Hon. Robert-William-Hugh O'Neill.

I. Louisa-Henrietta-Valdevia.

II. Rose-Anne-Mary.

III. Alice-Esmeralda.

O'NEILL. (No. 5.)

Baron of Dungannon, and Earl of Tyrone.

Arms : Ar. two lions ramp. combatant gu. armed and langued az. supporting a sinister hand couped at the wrist gu. in chief three etoiles of the same and in base a salmon naiant ppr. *War-cry :* Lamh dearg Eirinn. *Motto :* Cœlo, solo, salo, potentes.

ACCORDING to documents in possession of the present representative of this family, the Count de Tyrone, of Paris, is descended from one of the sons of the celebrated Hugh O'Neill, Prince of Tyrone. In the reign of Queen Elizabeth this Hugh (see Note " Hugh," p. 725, *ante*) exercised the authority of *Ard-Righ* or Monarch of Ireland, in electing both native and Anglo-Irish chieftains, etc. Commencing with this Hugh, the pedigree is as follows :

122. Hugh, Baron of Dungannon, and Prince and Earl of Tyrone, who, in May, 1588, was inaugurated THE O'NEILL.

123. John : son of Hugh.

124. Patrick: his son; m. Catherine O'Dogherty, and had :

125. James : his son ; godson of D o m i n i c k O'Donnell, and of Honoria de Burgh. This James, after the accession of James II., of England, settled in the Island of Martinique.

126. Henry : son of James : was born in 1688, in Ireland, and was brought by his father to Martinique, where he died on the 9th October, 1756. He was married on the 25th Sept., 1724, to Rose Plissonnean.

127. James-Henry: son of Henry; m. Mary-Anne Teyssier, and had :

128. Paul-Francis, who m. Anne Louisa Hurlot, and had :

129. James, who married Anne Modeste Hugonnenc, and had :

130. Francis-Henry (second son)

O'Neill (living in 1887), Count de Tyrone, who mar. Hermine de la Ponce, and who is, with his younger brother Julien, and his cousin Charles Count O'Neill de Tyrone (unm.) a worthy representative of the branches * of the O'Neills, descended from Hugh, the famous Earl of Tyrone. The Count de Tyrone had:

I. Mary-Auguste-Eugenia-Valentine, mar. to Hermann Baron de Bodman ("Grand Duché de Baden").
II. Mary-Anne Margaret.
III. Mary-Anne-Thérése, d. unm., 1877.

O'NEILL. (No. 6.)

Of Mayo and Leitrim.

Arms ; Per fess wavy the chief ar. and the base representing waves of the sea, in chief a dexter hand couped at the wrist gu. in base a salmon naiant ppr. *Crest :* A naked arm embowed, brandishing a sword all ppr. *Motto :* Hæc manus pro patriæ pugnando vulnera passa.

HUGH O'NEILL, of the Fews, a brother of Henry who is No. 119 on the (No. 2) "O'Neill" (Princes of Tyrone) pedigree, was the ancestor of *O'Neill*, of Mayo and Leitrim.

119. Hugh O'Neill; second son of Owen, Prince of Ulster.

120. Art: his son; died 1514.

121. Felim Ruadh, of the Fews: his son; in "rebellion," *tempore* King Edward the Sixth.

122. Henry, of the Fews: his son.

123. Sir Tirlogh, of the Fews: his son; married Sarah dau. of Sir Tirloch Lynagh O'Neill; died 23rd Feb., 1639.

124. Henry: his son; mar. Mary, dau. of Sir John O'Reilly, of the co. Cavan, Knt. Had a brother Art, m. to Kathleen, dau. of Sir Henry O'Neill, of Kinnaird, co. Tyrone; and three sisters: 1. Kathleen, married to Robert Hovedon of Ballynametah,

county Armagh; 2. Jane, married to Colla (MacBrian) MacMahon of Loghgoise, county Monaghan; 3. Rose, married to Felim O'Reilly, of Rathkenny, county Cavan.

125. Tirlogh† : his son; transplanted from the Fews to Newcastle, in the county Mayo; died 1676; had a brother named Shane‡ (or John) O'Neill, of Dungannon, in the county Tyrone. This Shane's son, Thomas, first assumed the sirname *MacEoin, MacSeoin, Mac-Seaain,* or *MacShane ;* anglicised *Johnson,* which has been modernized *Johnston, Johnstone, Jackson, Jenkins, Jenkinson,* and *Fitzjohn.*

126. Conn O'Neill, of the Fews:

* *Branches :* Another branch of this family was worthily represented by Don Juan O'Neill, of Spain, "Le Marquis de la Granja, en Espagne."

† *Tirlogh :* Some of the descendants of this Tirlogh O'Neill have changed their sirname to *Neale.*

‡ *Shane :* The proper Irish word for "Shane" is *Sheaghan* ("seah :" Irish, *esteem ;* "an," *one who*) ; so that the sirname *MacShane* or *Johnson* literally means "the son of the man who was esteemed."

son of the said Tirlogh ; was also transplanted to Newcastle, county Mayo.

127. Henry O'Neill, of Foxford, co. Mayo : his son ; was a Captain in the Army of King James the Second, A.D. 1689.

128. Neal O'Neill, of Cloon, co. Leitrim : son of Henry ; living in 1717.

129. Henry of Carrowrony, co.

Mayo : his son ; went to France, there studied Law.

130. Neal (also called Nicholas) : his son ; born in 1734 ; went to Spain, and there died a Lieutenant-Colonel. This Neal had a brother named Arthur, born in 1736, who also went to Spain, where he was Lieutenant-General.

131. Neal O'Neill : son of Neal ; left one daughter named Elinor.

O'NEYLON.

Protestant Bishop of Kildare.

Arms : Ar. a dragon pass. wings elevated ppr. *Crest :* A hand couped at the wrist holding a sword erect, the point pierced through a boar's head couped fessways all ppr.

DANIEL O'NEYLON, Bishop of Kildare ; living in 1583.

2. William, of Turlagh, county Clare : his son.

3. Daniel, of Turlagh ; his son ; d. 2nd March, 1639. He m. Mary, dau. of Tirlogh MacMahon, of Clondrallagh, co. Clare, and had four sons :

I. William.

II. Daniel.

III. Michael.

IV. John.

4. William O'Neylon : son of Daniel.

ORD.

Arms : For the Armorial Bearings of this family, see Burke's "General Armory."

THIS sirname, it may be said, is of English origin, and should not therefore be inserted among Irish genealogies. But, according to some, it is derived from the Irish *oradh,* " excellency ;" and to others from *ord,* " order." At present, however, we can only trace the lineage of the following branch of this ancient family. Edward the First, King of England, who (see p. 38) is No. 115 on the "The Lineal Descent of the Royal Family," was twice married, first to Eleanor, sister of Alphonso XI., King of Castile, in Spain ; and, second, to Margaret, daughter of Philip III., King of France. Of this second marriage was born Thomas Plantagenet, from whom this family is descended.

115. Edward the First, King of England ; died 1307.

116. Thomas Plantagenet : his son.

117. Lady Margaret: his daughter.

118. Elizabeth: her daughter; who married John, lord Mowbray.

119. Catherine: their daughter.

120. Sir Thomas Grey: her son; who married Alice, daughter of Ralph Neville, the great Earl of Westmoreland.

121. Elizabeth: their daughter; who married Philip, lord Darcy and Mennell.

122. John, lord Darcy: their son; who married Margaret, daughter of Henry, lord Grey and Wilton.

123. John, lord Darcy, their son: who married Iran, daughter of John, lord Greystock.

124. Richard: their son; who married Eleanor, daughter of John, lord Scroop of Upsal.

125. William, lord Darcy: their son; who married Euphemia, dau. of Sir John Langton.

126. Jane: their daughter; who married Sir Roger Grey, of Horton.

127. (————): their daughter (whose name we do not know); who married Edward Muschamp, of Barmore.

128. (————): their daughter (whose name we do not know); who married Gawin Ord, of Fenwick.

129. Oliver: their son.

130. Lionel, of Fishburn: his son.

131. Ralph: his son.

132. Lionel, of Sedgefield: his son.

133. Thomas: his son.

134. George (commonly called the "Patriarch of the Ords of Newton-Ketton"): his son.

135. John, of Newton-Ketton: his son.

136. Thomas, of Newton-Ketton: his son.

137. John, of Newton-Ketton: his son.

138. John Robert Ord, of Houghton Hall, Darlington, England: his son; living in 1880.

O'REGAN.

Arms: Az. an eagle disp. ar.

DUBHREAN, a younger brother of Dun who is No. 104 on the "O'Dunn" pedigree, was the ancestor of *O'Riaghain* (one of the "Four Tribes of Tara"); anglicised *O'Regan.*

104. Dubhrean: son of Dubhghall.

105. Dubhda: his son.

106. Maolcroine: his son.

107. Giollamuire Caoch O'Riag-hain ("riagh:" Irish, *to gibbet*): his son; Chief of *Hy-Riaghain*—now the barony of "Tinehinch," in the Queen's County.

O'REILLY.* (No. 1.)

Princes of East Brefney.

Arms : Vert two lions ramp. combatant or, supporting a dexter hand couped at the wrist erect and apaumée bloody ppr.

MAOLMORDHA, a younger brother of Aodh or Hugh who is No. 102 on the "O'Rourke" pedigree, was the ancestor of *O'Ragheallaigh*, or *O'Radheollaigh ;* anglicised *O'Rahilly, O'Reilly, O'Rielly, Rahilly, Raleigh, Reyley, Rielly, Riley, Radley, Ridley, Ryley,* and *Reillé.*

102. Maolmordha or Myles: son of Cobthach.

103. Dubhcron : his son.

104. Cathalan : his son.

105. Ragheallacht† ("ragh :" Irish, *a race;* "eallach," *gregarious*): his son; slain at the Battle of Clontarf, 1014; a quo *O'Ragheallaigh.*

106. Artan : his son.

107. Artgal : his son.

108. Connachtach: his son; d.1089.

109. Macnahoidhche (" oidhche :" Irish, *the night*): his son ; a quo *Mac-na-Hoidhche,* anglicised *Mac-Night, Night,* and *McNeight ;* killed 1127.

110. Gothfrith [godfrey]: his son ; killed, 1161.

111. Charles : his son ; died 1196. Had a younger brother named Feargal.

112. Annadh [annay]: his son ;

---

* *O'Reilly :* Of this family were (see the "O'Reilly," No. 3 pedigree) Count Alexander O'Reilly, a Spanish General, who was born at Baltrasna, in 1722 ; Count Andrew O'Reilly, an Austrian Field-Marshal, who was born in Ireland in 1740; the Most Rev. Edward O'Reilly, Archbishop of Armagh, who was born in Dublin in 1606 ; Edward O'Reilly, author of an *Irish-English Dictionary,* of *A Chronological Account of nearly Four Hundred Irish Writers* (Dublin, 1820), and other works relating to Ireland ; Hugh O'Reilly, a Barrister born in the county of Cavan, who was Master in Chancery, and Clerk of the Council under James II. in Ireland, and who about 1693 published *Ireland's Case Briefly Stated : or, a Summary Account of the most Remarkable Transactions of the Kingdom since the Reformation.*

And of this family was the celebrated Myles "the Slasher" O'Reilly, of A.D. 1641 fame, whose son Colonel John *Reilly* was, according to O'Donovan, the first of the family who dropped the Irish distinctive prefix *O'* in connection with his name ; it was, however, soon afterwards, resumed by his desendants. Colonel John Reilly resided at Clonlyn and Garryrocock, in the county Cavan, from which he was returned as Member to the Parliament held in Dublin by King James II. On the breaking out of hostilities, this John Reilly raised, at his own expense, a regiment of Dragoons, called "REILLY'S DRAGOONS," for the service of his sovereign ; at the head of which, he fought at Derry, Belturbet, the Boyne, Aughrim, and Limerick. He was included in the Articles of Limerick, and so saved his property from confiscation. His regiment does not appear in Dalton's *King James's Army List ;* but there can be no doubt of its existence, and of its having been in active service from the Siege of Derry, in 1689, till the surrender of Limerick. The only officers of that regiment, of whom we have yet read, were members of the Colonel's own family. From him descended O'Reilly, of Heath House, Queen's County ; and O'Reilly, of Knock Abbey Castle, county Louth.

† *Ragheallach :* Some writers consider *Radheolach* ("radh :" Irish, *a saying ;* "eolach," *learned, skilful*) as the correct spelling of this name. In this case *O'Radheollaigh* would be the correct Irish form of the name.

was the last King* of East Brefney;
d. 1220. Had two sons—1. Charles;
2. Fergus (also called Feargal).

113. Charles, lord of Lower Brefney: son of Annadh; was killed at
the battle of Moysleaghta, A.D.1256;
had a brother named Farrell
Reilly, who was the ancestor of
"Clann Goffrey."

114. Donal: son of Charles: also
killed at the said battle of Moysleaghta, in 1256; had a brother
named Neal Caoch, who was the
ancestor of *Brady.*

115. Giollaiosa: his son; lord of
Lower Brefney; built the Abbey
of Cavan; had two brothers; died
in 1330.

116. Philip, lord of Lower Brefney:
his son; died in 1384.

117. John, lord of Lower Brefney:
his son; died in 1402.

118. Owen na Feasog, lord of
Lower Brefney: his son; d. 1449.
According to some genealogists this
Owen na Feasog ("feasog," gen.
"feasoige:" Irish, *a beard*) was the
ancestor of *Vesey* and *Vosey.*

119. Charles, lord of Lower Brefney: his son; d. 1467.

120. John, lord of Lower Brefney:
his son; d. 1510.

121. Myles, lord of Lower Brefney:
his son; d. 1565.

122. Hugh Conallach, lord of
Lower Brefney: his son; d. 1583.

123. John Ruadh [roe]: his son.
According to some records this
John, in June, in 1596, resigned the
chieftaincy to his brother Philip,
who died in 1601; but, according
to others that brother's name was
Edmond, of Kilnacrott, the last
"O'Reilly" of the county Cavan,
who was elected chief in 1585, and
who was wounded in the wars
against Queen Elizabeth; of which
wounds he died in May, 1601, and
was buried in the Monastery of the
Franciscan Friars at Cavan. John
Ruadh had a brother Mulmore (or
Myles), whose Funeral Entry in
Ulster's Office is dated A.D. 1636.

124. Hugh, lord of Lower Brefney:
son of John Ruadh.

125. Myles: his son.

126. Colonel Edmond Buidhe
[boy]: his son; resumed the title
"O'Reilly;" d. in France in 1693;
had a brother named Hugh, who
was a Captain in France, in 1711.

127. Connell O'Reilly: his son;
had a brother named Owen, who
was Chief of his name; both living
in France in 1711.

* *Last King:* The O'Reillys were inaugurated on the Hill of Seantoman or Shan-
toman, a large hill between Cavan and Ballyhaise, on the summit of which may still
be seen the remains of a Druidical temple consisting of several huge stones standing
upright. In after times the O'Reillys were inaugurated on the Hill of Tullymongan,
above the town of Cavan; and took the tribe name of Muintir Maolmordha or the
People of Maolmordha, one of their celebrated chiefs. This name Maolmordha or
Mulmora was Latinized "Milesius" and anglicised "Miles" or "Myles,"—a favourite
Christian name with the O'Reillys.

O'REILLY. (No. 2.)

Of Scarva, County Down.

Arms : Quarterly, 1st and 4th, same Arms as "O'Reilly" (No. 1); 2nd and 3rd, ar. on a mount an oak tree a snake descending the trunk all ppr. supported by two lions ramp. gu. *Crest :* 1st.—An oak tree with a snake entwined descendant ppr. issuing out of a ducal coronet or ; 2nd—An arm mailed in armour, couped at the elbow the gauntlet grasping a dagger all ppr. *Motto :* Fortitudine et prudentia.

EDMOND, brother of John Ruadh who is No. 123 on the foregoing (No. 1) "O'Reilly" pedigree, was the ancestor of *O'Reilly*, of Scarva, county Down.

123. Edmond, the last "O'Reilly ;" lived at Kilnacrott, where he built a large castle ; was twice married : first to Mary Plunket, daughter of Lord Dunsany, and secondly to Elizabeth Nugent, dau. of Thomas Lord Delvin. By the first marriage this Edmond had three sons—1. Cahir, 2. John, 3. Terence ; by the second marriage, three sons—1. Myles, surnamed "The Slasher ;" 2. Farrell, 3. Charles. This Edmond d. in 1601 ; was attainted after his death by an Act of Parliament, in the eleventh year of the reign of King James I.; and his estates forfeited to the Crown.

124. Terence : third son of Edmond, by the first marriage ; had two sons—1. Brian, 2. John.

125. Brian : elder son of Terence ; had two sons—1. John, of Belfast, 2. Miles, who was a Captain.

126. John, of Belfast: son of Brian.

127. Miles of Lurgan: his son. This Miles had five sons—1. John, 2. James, 3. Charles, 4. Marlow, 5. another John.

128. John : the fifth son of Miles ; married in 1738, Lucy Savage, by whom he had two sons—1. Daniel, who died young, and 2. John.

129. John, M.P. for Blessington : second son of John ; married Jane Lushington, by whom he had three sons—1. John-Lushington, 2. William-Edmond, 3. James-Myles.

130. John-Lushington Reilly, son of John ; married Louisa Temple, by whom he had five sons, whose names—except the eldest—we have not yet ascertained.

131. John Temple Reilly, D.L., Scarva-House, Scarva, co. Down : son of John-Lushington Reilly ; living in 1878.

"O'REILLY." (No. 3.)

Of Heath House, Queen's County.

Arms : Same as "O'Reilly" (No. 2).

MYLES, surnamed "*The Slasher*," a younger brother of Terence (or Tirlogh), who is No. 124 on the "O'Reilly" (No. 2) pedigree, was the ancestor of this branch of that family.

124. Myles O'Reilly, "The Slasher:" son of Edmond, of Kilnacrott, who was the last " Prince of Brefney."

125. Colonel John *Reilly* : son of Myles : omitted the prefix *O'* ; raised at his own expense for the service of King James II., a regiment called "Reilly's Dragoons," at the head of which he fought at Derry, Belturbet, the Boyne, Aughrim, and Limerick, but saved his property from confiscation by being included in the Articles of the Treaty of Limerick. He married Margaret, dau. of Owen O'Reilly, Esq., by whom he had five sons and two daus., some of whom d. without issue. He died on the 17th Feb., 1717, and was buried in the old churchyard of Kill, parish of Cross-arlough, county Cavan, where, in 1836, his tomb was in good preservation. His surviving children were :

I. Connor, who was a Captain in his father's regiment, d. s. p.

II. Myles, who was a linen-draper in Dublin, had three sons who all d. s. p.

III. Bryan, also a Captain in his father's regiment, and of whom presently.

IV. Thomas, who was a Lieut. in his father's regiment, mar. and had four sons and an only daughter :* 1. Patrick, d. s. p. ; 2. Philip, a Priest ; 3. James ;† 4. Count Alexander O'Reilly,

of Spain,‡ born 1722 (see Note " O'Reilly," under *O'Reilly*, No. 1 pedigree, p. 743).

126. Bryan O'Reilly : third son of Colonel John Reilly ; had six sons, all of whom except the eldest d. s. p.

127. Myles : the eldest son of Bryan ; had three sons :

I. Dowell, of whom presently.

II. John Alexander O'Reilly, a Colonel in the Spanish Service, d. s. p.

III. Matthew, who had seven sons:

1. Matthew, who d. s. p.

2. John, who d. s. p.

3. Myles, who d. s. p.

4. William, who was father of the late William Patrick O'Reilly, Major in the Pope's Brigade, and Assistant Commissioner of the Board of Intermediate Education in Ireland.

5. Walter, who d. s. p.

6. Dowell, of Jamaica.

7. Richard.

128. Dowell O'Reilly : eldest son of Myles ; was the first of the family that conformed to the late Established Church in Ireland.

129. Myles John O'Reilly, of Heath House, Queen's County : son of Dowell.

130. Myles George O'Reilly : son of Myles John ; representative of Colonel John Reilly ; living in 1861.

* *Daughter :* This only daughter of Thomas O'Reilly, the fourth son of Colonel John Reilly, married a Captain Adams, who assumed the name *O'Reilly* ; from that marriage the " O'Reillys" of Belmont are descended.

† *James :* This James O'Reilly had two sons : 1. Thomas, and 2. Anthony, who d. s. p. This Thomas had six sons : I. James, of whom presently ; II. Robert ; III. Thomas ; IV. Anthony ; V. Stephen ; VI. John. And this (1) James had : 1. James, who d. s. p.; 2. Thomas, who d. s.p. ; 4. Anthony, who had James W. Fortescue O'Reilly, the representative of the line of Thomas O'Reilly, the fourth son of Colonel John Reilly, son of Myles O'Reilly, "The Slasher."

‡ *Spain :* For the descent of this Count Alexander O'Reilly of Spain, see Burke's *Landed Gentry.*

O'REILLY. (No. 4.)

Of Ballynahern, County Wexford.

Arms : Same as " O'Reilly" (No. 1.)

OWEN O'REILLY had:
2. Arthur, who had:
3. Hugh, who had:
4. Cahir, who had:
5. Morogh (his second son), of Ballynahern, co. Wexford, gent., who d. 5th Dec., 1638. He married

Joan, dau. of John MacDonough, of Ballanakilly, in the co. Wexford, and had:
I. Cahir.
II. Brian.
6. Cahir O'Reilly : son of Morogh.

O'REILLY. (No. 5.)

Of Timothan, County Dublin.

Arms : Same as " O'Reilly" (No. 1.)

PHELIM O'REILLY had :
2. Hugh, of Lismyne, co. Cavan, who had :
3. Glasney, of Parton, co. Meath.
4. Barnaby, of Timothan, in the co. Dublin : the fifth son of Glasney ; d. 29th June, 1638. He married

Rose, dau. of Richard Arthur, of Culmullen, co. Meath, and had two sons : 1. Bartholomew ; 2. Gerot.
5. Bartholomew : son of Barnaby ; m. Amy, dau. of Robert Usher, of Cromlin.

O'ROURKE. (No. 1.)

Princes of West Brefney.

Arms : Or, two lions pass. in pale sa. *Crest*: Out of an ancient Irish crown or, an arm in armour erect, grasping a sword ppr. pommel and hilt gold. *Motto* : Buagh (meaning "Victory") ; *Another* : Serviendo guberno.

FEARGNA, a younger brother of Eochaidh who is No. 92 on the " O'Connor" (Kings of Connaught) pedigree, was the ancestor of *O'Roairc ;* anglicised *O'Rourke, O'Rorke, O'Ruarc, Rourke, Rooke,* and *Rorke.*

92. Feargna : son of Fergus. Had two sons—1. Hugh Fionn ; 2.

Brunan, by some incorrectly written " Brennan."

93. Hugh Fionn : son of Feargna.
94. Scanlan : his son.
95. Crimhthann : his son.
96. Felim : his son.
97. Blamhach: his son.
98. Baothan : his son.
99. Donchadh : his son.
100. Dubhdara : his son.
101. Cobthach (by some called Carnachan) : his son.
102. Aodh (or Hugh): his son. Had a younger brother named Maolmordha (or Myles), who was the ancestor of *O'Reilly*, lords and princes of East Brefney, now the county Cavan.
103. Tighearnan (or Tiernan): son of Hugh. Was prince or lord of West Brefney; which contained the three lower baronies of the county of Leitrim. Had twelve sons.
104. Roarc ("ro:" Irish, *very;* "arc," *swift, small*): his twelfth and youngest son; a quo *O'Roairc,* by some written *O'Ruairc;* died A.D. 893.
105. Art (or Arthur): his son.
106. Feargal Sean ("sean;" Irish, *old*): his son; the 39th Christian King of Connaught; died 954.
107. Hugh: his son. Had a brother named Art Coileach (" coileach:" Irish, *a cock*), a quo *O'Coileaigh,* anglicised *Colly.*
108. Arthur the Righteous, King of Connaught: son of Hugh; slain 1046.
109. Hugh: his son; slain 1077.
110. Niall (or Neil): his son.
111. Uailarg: his son. Had two sons—1. Tiernan; 2. Donal, who was the ancestor of another *Mac Tighearnain* family, of Brefney.
112. Tiernan: eldest son of Uail-

arg ("uail:" Irish, *a wailing,* Lat. "ulu-latio," and "arg," Irish, *milk.*) This Tiernan married Dearvorgal*; daughter of Murcha, the last king of Meath: that Dearvorgal, whose abduction by Dermod MacMurrogh, King of Leinster, was the ostensible occasion of the invasion of Ireland by King Henry the Second of England.
113. Donal: his son; was the last Prince† of West Brefney.
114. Feargal: his son; lord of West Brefney.
115. Donal (2): his son; lord of West Brefney; had five brothers, the fifth of whom, Congal, was the ancestor of *MacNeill* and *McNeill,* modernized *Neilson,* and *Nelson.*
116. Arthur: son of Donal; had two brothers—1. Hugh; 2. Lochlann.
117. Amhailgadh [awly], lord of West Brefney: son of Arthur.
118. Donal (3): his son; had three brothers—1. Tiernan; 2. Connor; 3. Rory.
119. Uailarg Mór: son of Donal; had five brothers.
120. Tiernan Mór: his son.
121. Teige na Goir ("g o i r:" Irish, *to call;* Lat. "gar-uo," *to prate* or *prattle;* Syriac, "kar-o," *to name;* Gr. "ger-uo," and "gar-uo," *to prate*): his son; lord of West Brefney: a quo *MacGoir* ‡; had eight brothers, one of whom was Tiernan, from whom descended the O'Rourkes of Dromahaire, county Leitrim.
122. Tiernan Oge, lord of West Brefney: his son; had two younger brothers.
123. Donogh: his son.

124. Owen, lord of West Brefney : his son.

125. Brian Ballach : his son ; lord of West Brefney : died in 1562.

126. Brian-na-Mota: h i s s o n ; warred with Queen Elizabeth, and was beheaded in England ; Indenture between him and Sir H. Sidney, in 1578 ; and between him and Sir John Perrott, in 1585 ; had a younger brother named Owen.

127. Teige an-Fhiona: his son; had a brother named Brian Oge.

128. Brian (3): son of Teige an-Fhiona.

129. Brian (4) : his son.

130. John : his son.

131. Thomas : his son.

132. Edmond Roche O'Rourke : his son ; living in Nancy, in France, A.D. 1777.

O'ROURKE.* (No. 2.)

Chiefs of Carrha, County Leitrim.

Arms: Same as "O'Rourke" (No. 1).

ARTHUR, one of the two younger brothers of Tiernan Oge who is No. 122 on the " O'Rourke" (Princes of West Brefney) pedigree, was the ancestor of this branch of that family.

122. Arthur: a younger son of Teige na Goir.

123. Loghlan : his son.

124. Shane : his son.

125. Shane Oge : his son.

126. Owen: his son ; married to Margaret Nugent, of the family of the Earls of Westmeath.

127. Shane Oge : his son.

128. Brian: his son : married to Bridget O'Rourke, dau. of Owen Oge, who was son of Owen Mór, who was son of Tiernan, who was a brother of Brian na Mota, who is No. 126 on the foregoing (O'Rourke) pedigree.

129. Owen : son of Brian.

130. Count John O'Rourke, living in 1782 : his son; had two brothers—1. Brian ; 2. Con. This Con, who was a colonel of horse, was m. to a niece of Count Lacy, who was a field marshal in the service of Austria.

This John O'Rourke was born at a village near the ancient castle of Woodfort, in the county Leitrim, which was the residence of his ancestors. In his 25th year of age he went to London, where he remained for five years, experiencing many disappointments, but ulti-

---

* O'Rourke : In the Fiants Elizabeth, A.D. 1585, July 6th, is the following :

"4732. Commission to Sir Richard Bingham, Knight, Chief Commissioner of the Province of Connaught and Thomond ; Ullic, Earl of Clanrickard ; John, Bishop of Elfyn ; Lyseus, Bishop of Ardagh ; Edmd., Baron of Athenry ; Sir Thomas Le Strange, Knt., one of the Privy Council ; Thomas Dillon, Chief Justice of the Province ; Charles Calthorp, Attorney-General ; Sir Brien O'Rowirk (and) Sir Donell O'Conor, Sligo, Knights ; Owen O'Harte, and others, to be Commissioners under the Statute of 11° Elizabeth in the Province of Connaught and Thomond, to survey all the 'countries' in that Province that are not now their ground, and to divide them into counties, baronies or hundreds, or add them to any counties or baronies now being."— See Appendix to 15th Report of the Deputy Keeper of the Public Record Office, Dublin.

mately fixed on the military profession as the best suited to his genius and disposition. In the first troop of Horse Guards he received the rudiments of arms; but, being a Roman Catholic, he was forced to resign. He then went to France, and presented to the King, at Versailles, a petition, specifying his princely origin, and praying for a regiment. In consequence of which he was, in the year 1758, made a Captain of the "Royal Scotch" in that service. As a few instances of irregular promotions had been made in the brigade, the lieutenants were hurt at his appointment, and resolved to contest the matter with him. Accordingly this John O'Rourke, in the space of a few days, fought four duels, in which he gained great reputation—not more by his gallantry in the field, than by his honourably confessing that he thought it an injury to the national regiment, that he as a foreigner should be thrust upon them. He therefore gave up his commission, informing the French monarch that it was a dear purchase to fight for

it every day. With strong recommendations from France to the Court of St. Petersburgh, John O'Rourke went to Russia, which being then engaged in a war with Prussia, was a scene for adventure and fame. He was appointed first major of horse cuirassiers in the regiment of body guards; and, in the course of the war, he greatly distinguished himself, in particular, by storming the City of Berlin, which he laid under contribution. At the end of that war he returned to France with certificates of his gallant conduct from Peter the Third, Prince-General Wolkousky, and General de Sonverow; and was appointed by King Stanislaus one of his chamberlains in the year 1764. In 1770 he was appointed by the French king a colonel of horse, was enrolled among the nobility of France, was granted a pension from the French civil list, and in 1774 was honoured with the order of St. Louis.

For interesting incidents in the life of Count John O'Rourke, the reader is referred to the *Hibernian Magazine* for March, 1782.

O'ROURKE. (No. 3.)

Of Innismagrath, County Leitrim.

Arms, Crest, and *Motto,* same as "O'Rourke" (No. 1). *Another* Coat of Arms of this family was; *Arms:* Or, a lion ramp. on the left, and a spotted cat, ramp. on the right. *Crest:* A hand and dagger. *Motto:* Buagh; and Serviendo guberno.

THE following lines (author unknown), which refer to the *Arms* and *Crest* of "O'Rourke," may interest the reader:

The rampant Lion and spotted Cat,
The Hand and Dagger come next to that
Those Royal emblems may well divine
The O'Rourkes belong to a royal line.

OWEN, a younger brother of Brian-na-Mota, who is No. 126 on the (No. 1)

"O'Rourke" (Princes of West Brefney) pedigree, was the ancestor of this branch of that family :

125. Brian Ballach, last lord of Brefney, died A.D. 1562. This is the man to whom Sir Henry Sydney alludes in the following passage, which has been quoted by Dr. O'Donovan: "I found him (O'Rourke) the proudest man that ever I dealt with in Ireland." This Brian built Leitrim Castle,* in A.D. 1540—that famous castle in which his grandson, the chivalrous Brian Oge O'Rourke,† son of Brian-na-Mota, who was beheaded, A.D. 1592, received the brave Donal O'Sullivan Beare after his retreat from Dunboy, A.D. 1602—a retreat described by Davis as "the most romantic and gallant achievement of the age." Besides Leitrim Castle which, most probably, was built for military purposes, this Brian possessed two other castles in Brefney : Castle Carr, evidently a military stronghold, having been built on a *Crannoge* (or artificial island) in a small lake in the romantic and picturesque valley of Glencarr ("The valley lay smiling before me," of the immortal Moore), between Manorhamilton and Sligo ; and the Castle of Dromahaire or

"Ballyrourk" as it was then called, where, on the left bank of the "Bonet" (*Buaniad* or lasting river), near its entrance into Lough Gill, the parents of this Brian, namely, Owen O'Rourke and Margaret O'Brien, daughter of Conor O'Brien, King of Thomond, founded in A.D. 1508 the Franciscan Abbey of Crevelea, now a ruin, on the spot known to be *Leac Phadric*‡ or "Carrick Patrick." Here the said Margaret O'Brien, who founded it, was buried, A.D. 1512; and "The Abbey" continued long afterwards to be the *Natale Solum* of the O'Rourkes, and doubtless still does, for the branches of that ancient sept who live in its vicinity. In his "*Records relating to the Diocese of Ardagh and Clonmacnoise*," p. 379, the Very Rev. John Canon Monaghan, D.D., P.P., V.G., Cloghan, King's County, says of this Abbey : "The walls of this abbey are still entire, and the altar is nearly so. There are several curious figures inserted in the walls and over some graves of the Murroghs, the Cornins—a very ancient family, the O'Ruarks, etc., etc. ; The Great O'Ruark lies

* *Leitrim Castle ;* To the rear of the Constabulary Barrack in the village of Leitrim, four miles north of Carrick-on-Shannon, an ivied wall about nine feet high may be seen —the ruin of this once powerful stronghold. The appearance of it to the "mangled and bleeding fugitives" of Donal O'Sullivan Beare is thus described by A. M. Sullivan, in his *Story of Ireland*, p. 322 : "When they saw through the trees in the distance the towers of Leitrim Castle, they sank upon the earth, and for the first time since they quitted Beara, gave way to passionate weeping, overpowered by strange paroxysms of joy, grief, suffering, and exultation."

† *Brian Oge :* Of this Brian Oge O'Rourke, the son of Brian-na-Mota, the Ven. Archdeacon O'Rorke, P.P., in his *History of Ballysadare and Kilvarnet*, p. 345, says : "A father and son that bore as persevering hostility to the English as Hamilcar and Hannibal did to the Romans." The reply of Brian-na-Mota to the apostate Archbishop Miler Magrath, who had been sent to afford him spiritual consolation on the scaffold, is characteristic of his fidelity to his creed and country : "No; but do you remember the dignity from which you have fallen ? Return to the bosom of the ancient Church, and learn from my fortitude that lesson which you ought to have been the last man on earth to disavow."

‡ *Leac Phadric :* So called from having been sanctified by the presence of our National Apostle, *St. Patrick*, in his Missionary tour through Connaught.

at full length on a tomb over the burial ground of his family."

It is only simple justice to the memory of the dead to state here, that, of the few people in Leitrim who take any interest in such matters, most of them believe that Centy (H y a c i n t h) O'Rourke, a gentleman who lived at a place called Carrigeenboy, county Sligo, on the border of Roscommon, and who died in the early part of the present century, was the lineal descendant of Brian Oge O'Rourke. This Centy had a brother, Hugh Buidhe (his father also was Hugh), who died in the middle of the present century, leaving one son (Hugh), who died in 1886, in the Colony of Victoria, Australia.

Centy O'Rourke was nephew to another man of the same name (Centy), who fell in a duel, about the year 1770, with one of the Percevals, of Templehouse, county Sligo. It was believed by many of his numerous friends and admirers in Leitrim, that he was *murdered:* that he fought with a pistol handed to him by his second, and charged with powder only. Up to the middle of the present century, when the people declined in their use of the Irish language, the valour of this popular favourite, handed down in "song and story," was a favourite topic at all social gatherings.

126. Owen : son of Brian Ballach.

127. Tiernan Bán: his son. By referring to the Annals of the Four Masters, A.D. 1590, it will be seen that this man was in alliance with his kinsman Brian Oge O'Rourke, in resisting the encroachments of Sir Richard Bingham, then the Queen's Governor of Connaught. Doubtless, he was among "wild Breffny's warlike band,* who, led "by gallant Brian Oge, turned the scale of victory"† against Sir Conyers Clifford, at "Curlieu's Pass," near Boyle, on that memorable Feast of the Assumption, A.D. 1600.

128. Owen : son of Tiernan Bán; fought against Sir Frederick Hamilton. Had two sons : 1. Hugh ; 2. Owen.‡ This Owen had two brothers—1. Brian, 2. Con : the former slain during the events of 1641-9, and the latter executed during the same unhappy period. Tradition tells that this execution took place in the presence, or within view, of his brother Owen, and in front of, or convenient to their father's house.

This is the "Owen O'Rourke, who lived on the banks of Lough Allen, in Leitrim," for whom, according to Hardiman, Carolan, the last of the Irish bards, composed his "Dirge on the death of Owen O'Rourke," and for whose wife, Mary McDermott, he composed the song *Mhaire-an-Chulfhin,* or "Fair-

---

* "With nodding plumes of emerald green before his fearless clan,
   O'Donnell stands with dauntless mien and marshals Erin's van ;
   While Brave O'Ruairc commands the rear (wild Breffny's warlike band),
   Bold mountaineers, with swords and spears, embattled for the land.

'Twas then O'Ruairc, with Breffny's Clan, came thundering to the front,
   Unheeding blade or bullet they faced the battle's brunt ;
   Against the Saxon column they rushed with might and main,
   And hurled them back with slaughter, upon the open plain."
   —*Irish World* (America), 11th April, 1874.

† O'Brennan's *History of Ireland,* Vol. II., p. 304.

‡ *Owen :* It is believed that this Owen's issue is extinct. A *souvenir* of him preserved with jealous care in the family, and made of cast iron, having thereon the armorial bearings of the O'Rourkes, and dated A.D. 1688, is now (1887) in possession of Denis O'Rourke, who is No. 134 on this pedigree.

haired Mary." The spot, "on the banks of Lough Allen in Leitrim," where Owen O'Rourke lived is about two hundred yards from the water's edge.—See *Hardiman's Memoir of Carolan*, Vol. I., pp. liii. and lxii.

129. Hugh: the elder son of Owen; living A.D. 1688. Before the events of 1641, these brothers Hugh and Owen lived in the parish of Drumlease, but possessed several quarters (townlands) of land in the parish of Innismagrath, all of which were confiscated.* Hugh's portion having been "conveyed" to a man named Richard Barry; and Owen's to a man named Hugh Campbell. The brothers, Hugh and Owen, were soldiers, and took part in the campaign of 1688-91, ending their military career fighting under that brave man, Sir Teige O'Regan, author of an expression which has become historic, an expression which is characteristic of the man's valour. "Let us change commanders, and we will fight the battle over again."

After these events the brothers Hugh and Owen lived in Innismamagrath.†

130. Con: only son of Hugh. The place where he lived is still called in Irish *Alla Cuinn*, which means "Con's Hall," but in English it is called by the name of "Grouse Lodge." He left three children: one son, and two daughters. One of the daughters, Ellen O'Rourke, lived down to about the year 1820.

She died unmarried at a very advanced age; she died in poverty and obscurity in that parish, a *portion* of which was wrested from her grandfather in 1641, and the *whole* of which was ruled by her ancestors long before the Norman Barons assembled at Runnymede.

131. Donoch (or Denis): his only son; had four sons: 1. John 2. Frank (d. 2nd Feb., 1854), 3. Teige, 4. Michael, all of whom left families.

132. John: eldest son of Denis; d. 11th Nov. 1845, aged 80 years, leaving three sons: 1. Hugh, 2. Con, 3. Michael. Hugh d. 1866; his family have all left the country. Con. d. 1846, s.p.

133. Michael: youngest son of John; d. 13th April, 1859, leaving five sons: 1. Denis, 2. John, born 1838, and living in the parish of Innismagrath, county Leitrim; 3. Michael, born 1848, and living in Knoxville, Tenn., U. S. A.; 4. Francis, born 1851, and living in Sydney, New South Wales; 5. James, born 1856, and teacher of Tarmon National School, Drumkeerin, co. Leitrim—all living in 1887.

134. Denis: eldest son of Michael; b. 22nd Sept., 1836, and living in 1887, at Mount Allen, county Roscommon, as Teacher of the National School of that place; married, 30th June, 1860, Julia, dau. of Thomas Clarke, of Geevagh, co. Sligo, and has had issue thirteen children (seven sons and six daughters), of whom six sons and three daughters

---

* See *Book of Survey and Distribution for " Leitrim, Sligo, and Tyrawley,"* deposited in Public Record Office, Dublin.

† *Innismagrath*: This parish is called in Irish *Muintir Ceann Aodh*, or, as it is mentioned in some works on Irish history, "*Muintir Kenny.*" The popular account of the origin of this name is that it was called so after (No. 129) Hugh O'Rourke, or from people of Hugh's name *Muintir Ceann Aodh*, "Hugh the chief's people." If it were called after a man of that name it is not probable that it was this Hugh; but that it was called after some Hugh who had lived previously, as the term *Muintir* was scarcely applied for the first time, so late as 1641, or 1688.

died; the surviving children are:
1. Kate, Teacher of Corderay
National School, Drumshambo, co.
Leitrim, who mar., 6th Feb., 1884,
Joseph Nangle, Teacher of the Male
Department of the same School,
and has had issue (Fannie); 2. Julia-
Bridget; 3. Teresa-Mary: 4. Francis-
Joseph, all living in 1887.

135. Francis-Joseph O'Rourke:
only son of Denis; born 17th Sept.,
1880, baptised in the Catholic
Church, Keadue, co. Roscommon,
on the 18th Sept., 1880, and living
at Mount Allen, in 1887.

O'SHAUGHNESSY.

Chiefs of Cineal Aodha [Kinelee], County Galway.

Arms; Vert a triple-towered ar. from each tower a pennant flotant gu. supported
by two lions ramp. combatant or. *Crest:* An arm in chain armour embowed, the hand
grasping a spear-shaft broken, all ppr.

FIACHRA Folt-leathan, brother of Brian who is No. 87 on the (No. 1)
"O'Connor" (Connaught) pedigree, was the ancestor of *O'Seachnasaigh;*
anglicised *O'Shaghnasy, O'Shannessy,* and *O'Shaughnessy.*

87. Fiachra Folt-leathan ("folt:"
Irish, *vein;* "leathan," *broad*):
the second son of Eochaidh Muigh-
Meadhoin, the 124th Monarch of
Ireland; a quo were called the territories in Connaught known as *Tir
Fiachra,* or "Fiachra's Country,"
and a quo *O'Fuillleathan,* anglicised
Fulton. This Fiachra had two sons
—1. Amhailgadh, and 2. Dathi:
the former was the second Christian
King of Connaught, who died without issue; it was after him that
the territory of *Tir Amhailgaidh,*
now the barony of "Tyrawley," in
the county Mayo, was so called.

88. Dathi: second son of Fiachra
Folt-leathan; was the 127th Monarch. This Dathi (in imitation of
the heroic actions of his uncle, the
Monarch Niall of the Nine Hostages, and in prosecution of the conquest of France undertaken by the
said uncle, but prevented by his
death,) went with a great army
into France; and, marching over
the Alps, was there killed by a
thunderbolt, which put an end to his
conquest and life together, A.D. 428.

89. Eocha Breac: his son. This
Eocha had three brothers—1. Olioll
Molt, the 129th Monarch of Ireland, who, leaving no issue, was slain
in the battle of Ocha, A.D. 478;
and 2. Fiachra Ealg, who was the
ancestor of *O'Dowd;* 3. Amhailgadh,
who was the ancestor of *Forbes* and
MacFirbis.

90. Eoghan (or Owen): son of
Eocha Breac. This Owen had a
daughter named St. Faoileann,
whose feast is on the 13th Sept.

91. Conall: his son; had a brother named Conn Berneach, who
was the ancestor of *Moghan.*

92. Gobhneann: his son.

93. Cobthach: his son.

94. Columhan ("columhan:"
Irish, *a prop;* Lat. "columna;"
Welsh, "colovn; "Span. "coluna:"
Gr. "kolona"): his son; was the
10th Christian King of Connaught,
and the ancestor of *Colman,* of that
province. Had a brother Aodh
who was the ancestor of *Cahill,* of
Connaught.

95. Guaire Aidhne: his son; the
12th Christian king; a quo *O'Guaire,*

("guaire :" Irish, *rough hair*); anglicised *Gware* and *Gurry ;* had a
brother named Hugh.

96. Artgall : his son.

97. Aodh (or Hugh): his son.
This Hugh had two younger brothers—1. Dermod Ruadh [roe],
who was the ancestor of *Ruane*,
modernized *Rowan ;* 2. Fergall,
who was the ancestor of *O'Clery*, etc.

98. Morogh: his son.

99. Brian Leath-dearg: his son.

100. Breannan :* his son.

101. Duach : his son; had a brother named Tuadan, who was the
ancestor of *Scanlan.*

102. Gabhran : son of Duach.

103. Agna ("agna :" Irish, *wisdom ;* Gr. "agneia," *chastity*—
"chastity" being the surest sign of
a wise man) : his son.

104. Nochbuaidh : his son.

105. Sidhmach : his son.

106. Maolguala : his son.

107. Cas : his son.

108. Maolciaran : his son.

109. Feargal : his son.

110. Cu-maighe : his son.

111. Donoch : his son.

112. Seachnasach ("seachnaim :"
Irish, *to escape*): his son; a quo
O'Seachnasaigh ; A.D. 1100.

113. Giall - Buidhe ("buidhe :"
Irish, *yellow ;* "giall," *a hostage*)
O'Shaghnasy: his son; a quo *O'Giall-
Buidhe,* anglicised *O'Gilby, Ogilby,
Galvey, Galwey, Gilbey,* and *Gilboy.*

114. Randal : his son.

115. Giall-Beartach : his son.

116. Roger : his son.

117. Gilbert (2): his son.

118. Owen : his son.

119. John : his son.

120. William : his son.

121. Dermod : his son.

122. Giall-Dubh : his son.

123. Dermod Reach : his son.

124. Sir Roger (2): his son;
knighted in 1567.

125. Dermod (2) : his son.

126. Captain Roger (3) O'Shaugh-
nasy† : his son ; Chief of his name ;

---

* *Breannan :* Acccording to some genealogists, the following is the pedigree of
O'Shaughnessy, down from this Breannan—

100. Breannan : son of Brian Leath-dearg.
101. Tiobrad : his son.
102. Gabhran : his son.
103. Agna : his son.
104. Nochbuaidh : his son.
105. Siodhmhuine : his son.
106. Maoltuile : his son.
107. Maolciaran : his son.
108. Feargal : his son,
109. Cumagh : his son.
110. Donoch : his son.
111. S e a c h n a s a c h : his son ; a quo
O'Seachnasaigh.
112. Giall Buidhe O'Shaghnasy ("geall"
or "giall :" *a hostage ;* "buidhe," *yellow*):
his son ; first assumed this sirname.

113. Radhnall (or Randall) . his son.
114. Giolla-na-niomh [neev]: his son.
115. Gilbeartach (or Gilbert): his son.
116. Owen : his son.
117. John Buidhe (or Yellow John) :
his son.
118. William : his son.
119. Dermod : his son.
120. Gialldubh : his son ; d. 1569.
121. Dermod (2) : his son ; d. 1607.
122. Gialldubh, *i.e.* Rory : his son ; died
1655.
123. Dermod (3) : his son.
124. Rory : his son.
125. William O'Seachnasy : his son.

† *Captain Roger O'Shaughnasy :* This Roger m. Helen O'Brien, dau. of Connor,
second Lord Clare, who was son of Sir Donal O'Brien, first Lord Clare, who married
Catherine, dau. of Gerald, the 16th Earl of Desmond. (See the "O'Brien," Lord Clare,
pedigree, *ante.*) For further information in relation to this ancient family, see Blake-
Foster's excellent work, " *The Irish Chieftains ; or, A Struggle for the Crown*" (Dublin :
M. H. Gill & Son, 1872) ; Hardiman's " *West Connaught,*" p. 57 ; and the *Tribes and
Customs of Hy-Fiachra.*

In 1843, a barber in Galway was supposed to represent this once noble family.

living in 1690; had an only son named William, a Major-General, who died unm., in France, on the 2nd January, 1744; and an only brother named Charles, of Ardmilevan, who, on the death of his nephew, the said William,* would have become chief of his name, but that he had died in 1721, leaving three sons:

I. Joseph (d. 1732, s. p. m.), who went to law to recover the family property, in which action he was sustained by the Butlers of Cregg, county Galway. Of those Butlers was the late Major Toby Butler of Cregg, whose aunt was an O'Shaughnasy.

II. Colman (s.p.), who was in Holy Orders, and was Bishop of Ossory, became Chief of his name, on the death of his first cousin Major-General William, in France, in 1744.

III. Robuck, of whom presently.

127. Robuck (d. 1754): third son of Charles, who was brother of Captain Roger; on the death of his brother, Colman succeeded to the Chieftaincy, and d. in 1754; went into law also, striving to recover the family property, but was unsuccessful.

128. Joseph O'Shaughnasy: son of Robuck; conformed to the late Established Church in Ireland; went to law to recover his family property, but did not succeed.

O'SHEA.

Of Limerick.

Arms : Same as " O'Shee."

JOHN, the fifth son of Sir Richard, who is No. 6 on the " O'Shee" Genealogy, next, *infra*, was the ancestor of this branch of that family.

7. John: son of Sir Richard, had:
8. Lucas, who had:
9. Nicholas, who had:
10. Richard, who had:
11. William, who had:
12. Martin, who had two sons:
  I. William, of whom presently.
  II. Henry, who had four children:
    I. William, Duke de Santucar, created a Grandee of Spain, who m. Christina, daughter of the Duke of Villamar.
    II. Henry, who mar. Marie, daughter of the Count de Montebello.
    III. Christine, who m. Col. Fane, of Fulbeck, in Lincolnshire, England.
    IV. Mary, who m. Honble. George Vaughan.

13. William O'Shea,† living A.D. 1798, who went to Spain: son of

---

* *William* : This William had a sister Helen, who married Theobald Butler, and had : Francis Butler (living in 1784), who had : Walter Butler, who had two sons—1. Francis, of Cregg ; 2. Theobald, who mar. Nicola St. George, and had : Nicola Butler, living in 1867.

† *William O'Shea* : This Pedigree is authenticated by the Lord Bishop of Limerick, Ardfert and Aghadoe, under the Consistorial Seal, dated 1st June, 1818; also by the Mayor and Sheriff of the Citizens of Limerick.

Martin. This William married
Margaret, dau. of John Howley, of
I. Henry, of whom presently.
Rich Hill, Limerick, and had three
sons :

  II. John, who m. Senora Dona
    Ysabel Hurtado de Corcuera,
    of Madrid.
  III. Thaddeus, who m. Margaret,
    daughter of Edward Craneach
    Quinlan, of Rosanna, co. Tip-
    perary.
This branch of the family is
  therefore partly Spanish and
  partly Limerick.
14. Henry O'Shea: son of Wil-

liam ; m. Catherine (a Countess of
Rome), daughter of Edward C.
Quinlan, above mentioned, and had
a son and a daughter :

  I. William-Henry, of whom pre-
    sently.
  I. Countess Marie O'Shea, Cha-
    noinesse, and Lady of the
    Royal Order of Theresa of
    Bavaria; d. unm., Dec., 1884.
15. William-Henry O'Shea: son
of Henry; late M.P. for Galway;
J.P. for the county of Clare; late
Captain 18th Hussars; living in
1887; is an Hereditary Count of
the Holy Roman Empire.

O'SHEE.

Chiefs of Iveragh, County Kerry.

Arms : Per bend indented az. and or, two fleurs-de-lis counterchanged. *Crest* : A
swan rousant sa. beaked and legged gu.

THE *O'Seaghdha** ("seaghdha :" Irish, *stately, majestic, learned*) were lords
of Corcaguiney and Iveragh, in Desmond ; of the line of Heremon ; and
descended from Corc, a son of Cairbre Musc, who was a son of Conaire
II., the 111th Monarch of Ireland, who (see the Appendix in Vol. II.)
is No. 88 on ' The Genealogy of the Kings of Dalriada." While
some members (and the great majority) of the Sept write the name
O'Shea, this branch of the family write it *O'Shee.* *O'Seaghdha* was pronounced in Irish "O'Shay-ah" or "O'Shé-a," and hence it has been
variously anglicised *O'Shea, O'Shee, Shea,* and *Shee.* This branch of the
family, in anglicising the name, omitted the final letter of " O'Shé-a,"
and doubled the then final *e* in "O'Shé," as in *O'Shee.* In England *temp.*
Queen Elizabeth, and later, the name *Shee* would be pronounced "Shay."
  So early as A.D. 1095, we find mention made of Mathgamhain
O'Seaghdha, lord of Corcaguiny, who died in that year; and in the
following year another chief of the same name, and same territory, died.
  Oda (or Odanus) Chief of the Sept, settled in the county Tipperary
early in the twelfth century. Odoneus, tenth in descent from him,

---

* *O'Seaghdha* : According to Cronnelly's "Irish Family History," there was also
in Desmond a family named *O'Seagha* ("seagha :" Irish, *ingenious, crafty, cunning*),
of the line of Heber, who took their name from Seagha, a descendant of Eoghan Mór,
son of Olioll Olum, who is No. 84 on the "Line of Heber," *ante.* The two sirnames
O'Seaghdha and *OSeagha* would be pronounced alike ; but, it may be observed that
the Four Masters do not mention the latter name.

obtained (15th Richard II.) letters of English "denizenship" at Clonmel, 6th Nov., 1381. In the pedigree and patent of arms, attested in 1582, by Clarencieux Roy d'Armes, the sirname is written *O'Shee.*

Robert O'Shee, fifth in descent from Odoneus, settled in the county Kilkenny in 1489, and had Richard.

[As we had not time before going to press with this Genealogy, to compile the names on the pedigree in their entirety, we here commence with that Robert, as No. 1; from whom the following are the names in regular succession, down to 1887.]

1. Robert O'Shee. 1489.
2. Richard : his son.
3. Robert: his son.
4. Richard : his son.
5. Robert :* his son ; m. Margaret Rothe, and had—1. Sir Richard Shee, of whom presently; and 2. Elias† Shee, of Cranmore, from whom descended Sir George Shee, of Dunmore, county Galway, and also, Sir M. A. Shee, President R. Academy.
6. Sir Richard Shee, Knt., of Upper Court, and Bonnetstown or "Bonnestown:" eldest son of Robert. Omitted the prefix *O'.* Was twice m. : first to Margaret Sherlocke ; and, secondly, to Margaret Fagan,‡ by whom he had no issue. There were nine children by the first marriage, namely— 1. Robert, who d. unm. in the lifetime of his father. 2. Lucas, of Upper Court, his heir, who was m. to the Hon. Ellen Butler,§ sister of Lord Mountgarrett ; and who was the ancestor of *Shee,* of Cloran, family. To this Lucas, Sir Richard Shee left the whole of his Tipperary,

and most of his Kilkenny, estates, which were forfeited after 1641. This branch of the family went to France, and entered the French service. Seventh in direct descent from the said Lucas was Colonel William O'Shea (Cloran), of Pontoise, Seine-et-Oise, France, who had no male issue. 3. Thomas of Freinstown, m. Ellen, dau. of Ald. Nicholas Dobbyn of Waterford, and by her left no issue. 4. Marcus (of whom presently) who m. Ellen, daughter of Oliver Grace, Baron of Courtstown, and had five sons— 1. Richard, 2. John, 3. Lucas, 4. James, 5. Thomas. 5. John, the fifth son, who was the ancestor of *O'Shea,* of Limerick, and of *O'Shea,* Duke de Sanlucar, in Spain. 6. Lettice, m. to John Grace of Courtstown, and had issue. 7. Catherine, who was twice married : first, to Edmund Cantwell of Moycarkey Castle, in the county Tipperary ; and, secondly, to Richard Fforstal, of Fforstaltown and Ologan Castles. 8. Margaret, m. to James Walshe, Esq. And 9. Elizabeth, married to

---

* *Robert*: According to the Kilkenny Journal, 1864, p. 54, this Robert and his son Sir Richard acquired, by purchase, property in the counties of Kilkenny, Tipperary, and Wexford.

† *Elias :* According to Holingshed, Elias Shee of Cranmore was "a scholar of Oxford, of a passing wit, a pleasant conceited companion full of mirth without gall. He wrote in English divers sonnets."

‡ *Fagan:* In the Kilkenny Journal, for 1850, p. 179, and for 1853, p. 212, see Prim's description of two Wayside Crosses erected to Sir Richard Shee, Knt., by his second wife Dame Margaret Fagan.

§ *Butler :* At Freshford a Wayside Cross was erected to the memory of Lucas Shee and his wife Ellen Butler, the site of which is called *Bun na Croisé.*

David Rothe, Esq., of Tullaghmain, in the county of Kilkenny. Sir Richard* Shee (who died at his Castle of Bonnetstown, on the 10th August, 1608) founded (see the Kilkenny Journal, 1861, p. 320) the *Hospital of Jesus*, at Kilkenny, which was called after him *"Shee's Alms House."* To that Alms House a charter was granted on the 4th November, in the sixth year of the reign of King James I. (1609).

7. Marcus Shee, of Sheestown : fourth son of Sir Richard, who left the said Marcus the rest of his (Sir Richard's Kilkenny property, which was also subsequently forfeited in the rebellion of 1641, but in part restored.

8. Richard : eldest son of Marcus, m. Rose, dau. and heir of Peter Rothe, Esq.

9. Marcus, of Sheestown (Will dated 1684): son of Richard; m. Mary, dau. of Nicholas Plunkett, Esq., of Dunsoghly, and had—1. Richard, 2. Marcus, 3. Nicholas,

4. John, ancestor of *Shee*, of Bally-reddan.

10. Richard (who died 10th Dec., 1748): son of Marcus; mar. the Hon. Dymna Barnewall, daughter of Robert, the twelfth Lord Trimblestown.

11. Marcus: son of Richard ; m. Thomasina, daughter of Thomas Masterson, Esq., of Castletown, and had: 1. John, 2. (   ) who was a General in the French Service, 3. Philip, 4. Mary.

12. John : son of Marcus; m. Elizabeth, dau. and heir of Richard Power, Esq., of Garden Morres, in the co. Waterford (by Anne, dau. and heir of —— Morres, Esq., of Bally-naven, in said county), by whom he acquired Garden Morres (more lately Garran Morres and Garran Mór), and had—1. Richard, 2. Arnold, 3. John (who was a Col-onel in the Austrian Service), and died unm. at Sheestown, in 1809.

13. Richard Power O'Shee, of Garden Morres and Sheestown, who

---

* *Sir Richard* : In the "Description of Ireland, Anno 1598," edited by Rev. Father Hogan, S.J., the name of Sir Richard Shee appears amongst "men of accompt," living in the co. Kilkenny in 1598. Father Hogan, in a note, states that Sir Richard Shee hailed from Upper Court, in the county Kilkenny, and Cloran in Tipperary ; that he was the son of Robert Shee and Margaret Rothe ; a member of Gray's Inn ; Seneschal of Irishtown in 1568 ; Deputy Treasurer to the Earl of Ormonde (Lord Treasurer of Ireland), in 1576 ; Knighted in 1589 ; and that he died at his Castle of Bonnetstown in 1608. By his Will he left an injunction on his son Lucas to build an Alms House, and he left his curse on any of his descendants who should ever attempt to alienate the property provided for its maintenance, which consisted chiefly of impropriate tithes.

Henry Shee, a first-cousin of Sir Richard Shee, was Mayor of Kilkenny, A.D. 1610-11. Robert, son of said Henry, died 27th Sept., 1615 ; and his son Henry Shee, junior, was m. to Dorothy, dau. of Lucas Shee and his wife the Honble. Ellen Butler, above-mentioned. For a letter from Sir Richard Shee to Sir George Carew, President of Munster, dated 19th April, 1600, see the Kilkenny Journal, for 1861, p. 406 ; and, for further information respecting this family, see the same Journal for 1864, and for 1861, pp. 320 and 406.

According to Shearman's *Loca Patriciana*, p. 363, William Shee, burgess of Kil-kenny, who d. 18th April, 1584, and whose tomb is still extant behind the chancel of St. Mary's Church, was ancestor of the Shees of Sheepstown, represented by the late Baron Richard de Shee, of Paris ; by the late Judge Shee, who was a native of Thomastown, co. Kilkenny, where he had property ; and of the Shees, of Rosencany, now (1881) represented by James-John Shee, J.P., of Abbeyview, Clonmel. Judge Shee was succeeded by George Shee, of the Mall House, Thomastown ; and by Henry Shee, of the English Bar—both living in 1881.

died in 1827 : son of John ; married Margaret, dau. of Nicholas Power, of Snowhill, in the co. Kilkenny, and had two sons—1. John Power O'Shea; 2. Nicholas R. Power O'Shea, who succeded his brother John.

14. Nicholas R. Power O'Shee, D.L., of Garran Mór, Kill, county Waterford, and of Sheestown, co. Kilkenny; born 1821, and living in 1887.

O'TOOLE.* (No. 1.)

Anciently Chiefs of Hy-Muireadaigh, County Kildare; afterwards Kings of Leinster and Princes of Imaile.

The Armorial Bearings† are—*Arms*: Gu. a lion pass. ar.   *Crest*: A boar pass. ppr.   *Motto:* Virtute et fidelitate.

COMMENCING with Cathair Mór, King of Leinster, who was the 109th Monarch of Ireland, and who is No. 89 on the (No. 1) "O'Connor" (Faley) pedigree, the following is the genealogy of this family :

89. Cathair Mór, Monarch of Ireland: son of Felim Fiorurglas. Had amongst other children : 1. Ros Failgeach, from whom descended the *O'Connor* (Faley); 2. Daire, ancestor of *O'Gorman;* 3. Comthanan, ancestor of *Duff,* of Leinster; 4. Curigh, who was slain by Fionn MacCumhal (Finn Mac-Coole); 5. a daughter, Landabaria, who, according to the *Ogygia,* p. 315, was the third wife of the (110th) Irish Monarch Conn Ceadcathach (or Conn of the Hundred Battles), who succeeded Cathair Mór in the Monarchy; 6. Fiacha Baicheda.

Curigh, No. 4 here mentioned, who was slain by Fionn MacCumhal, had a son named Slectaire;

* *O'Toole* or *Ui Tuathail* : The O'Tooles were Kings of Leinster and Princes of Imaile (now the counties of Wicklow and Kildare), Chieftains of Hy-Murray, Castle Kevin, Glendalough, and Powerscourt; and Omey in West Connaught. We are indebted to the Rev. Patrick Laurence O'Toole, O.C.C., Whitefriar-street Church, Dublin, for permission to inspect an elaborate genealogy of this family in that gentleman's possession ; from which we here trace the genealogy more fully than we gave it in our Third Edition of "IRISH PEDIGREES."

† *Armorial Bearings* : According to other authorities the Armorial Bearings of the O'Tooles are :
Arms—A white lion on red grounds (signifying a course without relaxation);
Crest—Two palms, a Cross surmounted by a laurel branch over a princely crown ;
Supporters—The shield accompanied by two battle axes and two Irish pikes ; under the shield, two branches of shamrock—the national symbol of Ireland ;
Motto—" Virtute et Fidelitate." One Branch of the Family has " Spero ;" another: " Semper et Ubique Fideles."
The *War Cry* was : " Fianæ Abu," and sometimes "Ui Tuathail Abu :" the former meaning " Victory to the Fenians ;" and the latter, "Victory to the O'Tooles."

and a daughter named Uchdelbh (or Uchdamhuil), who was wife of Fionn Fothart, a son of Conn of the Hundred Battles. This Slectaire, son of Curigh, had a daughter Corcraine, who was the mother of Diarmid Ua Duibhne,* and of Oscar, son of Oissin.

90. Fiacha Baicheda: youngest son of Cathair Mór; d. 220.

91. Breasal Bealach ("bealach:" Irish, *large-lipped*): his son; a quo *O'Bealaigh*, anglicised *Bailey, Bailie, Baily, Bayly*, and *Bewley*. Was the second Christian King of Leinster.

92. Enna Niadh: his son. Had a brother Labhradh.

93. Dunlong: son of Enna Niadh. This Dunlong slew the Royal maidens at the Claenfert of Tara: in revenge of which twelve Leinster Princes were slain, and the *Boromha* tribute exacted. He had eight sons; and a brother named Brian† Leth-dearg a quo Ui Briuin Cualan (or *O'Brien* of Cualan). Some of the children of this Dunlong were:—1. Olioll (or Ailall); 2. Maonach, a quo *O'Mooney* of Cualan; 3. Dubhtach; 4. Fergus, from whom descended Justus, the Deacon, and his brother Daire.

94. Muireadach: son of Dunlong.

95. Alioll (or Olioll), the fifth Christian King of Leinster: his son. Baptized at Naas by St. Patrick, A.D. 460; was at the battle of

Ocha, where Olioll Molt, the 129th Monarch, was slain; d. 526. Had: 1. Cairbre; 2. Cormac; 3. Felim, who was baptized by St. Patrick at Naas; 4. Mugan.

96. Cormac: second son of Olioll. Was King of Leinster for nine years; abdicated A.D. 515, and d. a monk at Bangor, 567. Had: 1. Cairbre Dubh, King of Leinster, who d. in 546; 2. Felim, from whom descended Cormac, of Tullac; 3. Iolladon, priest of Desert Iolladoin (now "Castledillon"), who had St. Criotan (11th May), of Magh Credan and Acadfinnech (on the river Dodder), and of Crevagh Cruagh, co. Dublin.

97. Cairbre Dubh: eldest son of Cormac. Had: 1. Mainchin, a quo Ui Mainchin (between Cineal Nucha and the river Liffey); 2. Cillen Mór, a quo Ui Nemri; 3. Cillen Beg, a quo Siol Aedha; 4. Colman, King of Leinster for thirty years, who d. 576; 5. St. Coman, bishop (8th March); 6. St. Sedealbh (10th Nov.); and 7. St. Cumaine (8th March); these last two were called "daughters of ardent charity" (29th March) at Domnach-Inghen Baithe (now "Donabate"), in the county Dublin.

98. Colman (or Columan): the fourth son of Cairbre Dubh. Had: 1. Faolan; 2. Cobhthach, a quo "Rathcoffey" in the county Kildare; 3. Felim, 13th Christian King of Leinster; 4. Ronan,‡ the

---

* *Diarmid Ua-Duibhne:* See Note "Fiacha Suidhe," in p. 359, *ante*.

† *Brian:* This Brian Leth-dearg had a son Feidhlimidh (or Felim), who had three sons: Conal, a quo Ui Elgenaigh; 2. Fiachra Caech, who had Ronan, who had Foranan; and 3. Cobhthach, a quo Ui Ernine.

‡ *Ronan:* This Ronan had: 1. Maelfoghartach, slain by his father's orders; 2. Maeltuile, a quo Ui Maeltuile; 3. Maelochtrach, who had Maelcaech (who had Maelgarbh of Naas) and Ailechda. This Ailechda had Monach, who had Fianamhail (d. 694), who had Ceanfela, who had Ceallach, Abbot of Kildare, living in 720. This Maeltuile, the second son of Ronan above mentioned, had two sons—1. Maelfoghartach, anker. at Inisbofin, slain in 732; and 2. Fianamhail, King of Leinster, who was baptised by St. Moling, and mortally wounded by Foisechan, one of his own people.

11th King of Leinster; on the resignation of Aedh Dubh;* 5. Aedh Dubh, King of Leinster, who in 591 retired to Kildare, where he d. a bishop, in 638; 6. Aedh Fionn, from whom descended Aengus (or Æneas), abbot of Kildare; 7. Crimthan Cualan, 12th Christian King of Leinster, from whom descended Dalthach of St. Kevin's, slain at Ath Goan (now "Kilgowan"), in Iachtir Liffé, A.D. 628; 8. Molumba, who had Maelandfidh, who had Aedhroin, who had Dunmaduind, who had Berchan. Colman d. 676.

99. Faolan: eldest son of Columan; was King of Leinster; educated by St. Kevin at Glendalough; d. 663.

100. Conall: son of Faolan.

101. Bran Muit ("muit:" Irish, *dumb*): his son; 14th Christian King of Leinster; d. 689. Had four sons: 1. Moroch (or Murchadh) Mór; 2. Congal, who defeated the men of Cualan at Inisbreoghan, in 727; 3. Faolan, d. 733; 4. Iomcadh.

102. Moroch Mór: eldest son of Bran Muit; was the 16th King of Leinster. Had three sons:—1. Muireadach; 2. Doncha, the 17th King of Leinster, slain A.D. 727, and a quo Ui Donchada or *O'Donoghue* of Cualan; 3. Faolan, the 18th King of Leinster, who d. 734, and a quo Ui Faolain or *O'Felan* of Cualan.

103. Muireadach: son of Moroch

Mór; d. 755; and a quo Ui Muireadaigh or *O'Murry* of Cualan.

104. Bran Ardcean: his son; m. Eithne, dau. of Domhnal Mideach; she and her husband were slain, A.D. 780, by Finachda Catherdere, son of Ceallach, at Cill Cuile-duna (now "Kilcoole"), near Newtown Mount Kennedy, in the co. Wicklow.

105. Muireadach: son of Bran Ardcean; d. 818, according to the "Chronicon Scotorum." Had four sons—1. Bran, Tanist of Leinster, who was defeated at Dunbolg, by Cearbhall, King of Ossory, in 808; 2. Dunlong; 3. Arthur, who d. in 845, and from whom descended Garbith, Tanist of Leinster, who d. 881; 4. Maelbrighid, father of Tuathal, the 31st King of Leinster.

106. Dunlong, the 32nd King of Leinster: second son of Muireadach; d. a Monk in Kildare, 867. Had: 1. Ailill; 2. Cairbre,† the 34th King of Leinster, who was a hostage to Cearbhall, King of Ossory, and who died 881; 3. Donal, Tanist of Leinster, d. 862.

107. Ailill: eldest son of Dunlong; slain by the Danes in 809. Had: 1. Ugaire; 2. Ceallach, who was abbot of Kildare and Hy, 854-865; d. in "Pictland" (Scotland).

108. Ugaire (or Angaire), King of Leinster: son of Ailill; slain, 915. Had: 1. Tuathal; 2. Art (or Arthur), d. 934.

---

* *Aedh Dubh*: This Aedh Dubh had two sons: Crimthan Cael, and Erc (who had Nessan). This Nessan had: 1. Braon, Bishop (8th August) of Fidhcullin ("Feighcullen," in the county Kildare); 2. Cairrell (13th June), Bishop of Tir Rois; 3. Flann (4th Jany.); 4. Muireadach (15th May); 5. Dichuil, abbot of Cluain Mór Dicholla; 6. Munissa, who had Nadsluadh (15th March), of Inis Mac Nessain, now known as "Ireland's Eye," Howth, co. Dublin.

† *Cairbre*: This Cairbre had: 1. Donal (d. 864), Tanist of Leinster, who had Muireadach, Tanist of Leinster (slain, 906); 2. Dunlong, who also d. in 906.

‡ *Tuathal*: Some derive this name from the Irish "tuatha," *territories*: meaning one possessed of large landed property.

109. Tuathal‡ ("tuathal:" Irish, a man's name; left-handed), King of Liffé: son of Ugaire; a quo O'Tuathail, anglioised O'Toole, Toole, Tootal, Tuohill, Tuthill, etc.; d. 956. Had: 1. Dunlong; 2. Donal; 3. Doncadh, Tanist of Leinster, who died 964; 4. Angaire;* Tanist of Leinster, who was slain by the Danes at Bithlin ("Belin," in the co. Kildare).

110. Dunlong: eldest son of Tuathal; fought at the battle of Clontarf, 1014, and was slain there. Had: 1. Donal; 2. Murcadh, who in 1042 was slain by the King of Ossory; 3. Gillacamghin, who in 1019 was slain by the men of Leix; 4. Duncuan; 5. Angaire, who defeated Sithric the Dane at Delgany in 1021; 6. Doncadh, who in 1037 was blinded at Castledermott by Dunchadh MacGillapatrick, King of Ossory; 7. Muirceartach, who was slain by the Ossorians in 1026; 8. Dunlong; 9. Eachdun, Tanist of Leinster, slain, 1042; 10. Boclan, slain at Clontarf, in 1014; and 11. Longseach, who was also slain at Clontarf in 1014.

111. Duncuan, "the Simpleton:" fourth son of Dunlong. Was made King of Leinster by Malachy II., Monarch of Ireland, and slain by the King of Ossory in 1018.

112. Gillacomghall: son of Duncuan. Was, in 1041, by violence taken by his uncle Murcadh from the Church of Kildare; and "the successor of Bridget was violated;" died 1041; first that assumed this family sirname.

113. Gillacaemghin: son of Gillacomghall. Was in 1056 slain by Murcha, who is No. 112 on the "MacMorough" genealogy, who was the 50th Christian King of Leinster.

114. Duncuan Baccach: son of Gillacaemghin; who in 1075 slew Doncadh and Gillacaemghin, sons of Angaire Ua Lorcain, of the Ui Doncadh. In 1076 his people were slain by the Ui Lorcain, and sixty-three of their heads were carried to a hill south of Castledermot.

115. Gillacomghall Baccach: his son; lord of Ui Muireadaigh: slain in 1119. Had: 1. Gillacaemghin; 2. Ugaire, slain in 1131 by the Ossorians; 3. Gillacomghall, abbot of Glendalough, who in 1127 was slain by the Foghmhartaigh (Fohartat†), of the barony of Forth, in the county Carlow; 4. Murcadh, who in 1141 was blinded by Diarmaid na-nGall, King of Leinster, who is No. 113 on the "MacMorough" pedigree; 5. Muirceartach,‡ King of the Ui Muirceartaigh, who in 1154 slew the King of Ui Enachglais, and d. "after penance" in 1164.

116. Gillacaemghin Faitche: eldest son of Gillacomghall Baccach; died 1160.

---

* Angaire: This Angaire had Tuathal, who A.D. 1014, was wounded at the battle of Clontarf; died same year at Glendalough, and is there buried. And Tuathal had Aedh, living in 1034.

† Foharta: See the "Nowlan" genealogy, in pp. 605-606 ante, for the meaning of this term.

‡ Muirceartach: This Muirceartach had: 1. Gillacomghall, lord of Ui Muireadaigh; 2. Tuathal; 3. Ruadh; 4. Aodh; 5. Conchobhar; 6. Mór, wife of Diarmaid MacMorough (or Diarmaid na-nGall), the last King of Leinster; and 7. Lorcan (Saint LAURENCE O'TOOLE), Archbishop of Dublin, who, on 14th Nov., 1180, died at Eu, in France, where his relics are still preserved and revered. It was at the instance of St. Laurence O'Toole that Earl Strongbow added a steeple and two chapels to Christ Church Cathedral, Dublin. With five other Irish prelates, St. Laurence O'Toole attended a Council at Rome in 1179, a promise having been first exacted from him by

117. Bhaltair (Walters or Walter): his son; slain 1200.

118. Gillacaemghin na Ficheall ("ficheall:" Irish, *a buckler*); his son; a quo *MacFicheaill*, anglicised *Buckley*. Had: 1. Felim (by some called "Faolan"); 2. Bathair, whose son Adam Dubh O'Toole was in Easter week, A.D. 1326, burnt in "Hoggin Green" (now College Green), Dublin; 3. Dunlong,* who settled in the Island of Omey, in Iar Connaught, and was the ancestor of *O'Toole* of Connemara.

119. Felim (or Faolan): son of Gillacaemghin na Ficheall.

120. David: his son; taken in 1327 by John Wellesley, and in 1328 was hanged at Dublin. Had: 1. Aedh (or Hugh); 2. Donal; 3. David, slain in 1368; 4. John, killed by a clown in 1328.

121. Aedh, Prince of Imaile: son of David; slain by the English, in 1376. Had 1. Dermod; 2. Felim, died 1404; 3. Aed, who died of the plague, 1404; 4. Shane (or John)

Ruadh, who had: Ruadh, lord of Imaile, who was the ancestor of O'Toole, of Toole's Castle (now called "Talbotstown"), of O'Toole of Coillsi, of O'Toole of Balleyedan, of O'Toole of Knight's Castle (or Castleruddery, in Imaile), O'Toole of Ballyhubbock, of Newtown, and of Rathdangan. Shane Ruadh, the fourth son of Aedh, had:

I. Edmond.

II. Shane, who was slain by Gerald, Earl of Kildare. This Shane had:

III. Shane (died 1571), who in 1526 m. a dau. of Sir James Fitzgerald of Leixlip, Knight of Rhodes, and had:

IV. Tirlogh, who was slain in rebellion, and forfeited his estates in Imaile to the Crown: these estates were given to Lord Chichester (see the State Papers for the year 1608). Tirlogh had:

V. Felim (slain in battle), who had:

VI. Cahir, of Castleruddery, who had:

King Henry II., that he would there urge nothing detrimental to the King's interests in Ireland; because, after the Anglo-Norman invasion, he (St. Laurence O'Toole) exerted all his influence to urge his countrymen to united resistance to the English invaders, and, in the enemy's assault on Dublin, braved every danger—encouraging the defenders of the city, and administering spiritual consolations to the wounded. When all hope of successful resistance was over, he gave in his adhesion to the Anglo-Normans, and in 1172 attended Henry II.'s Synod of Cashel, where many new canons were enacted for the government of the Irish Church. In 1180, Archbishop O'Toole was entrusted with the delivery of the son of the Monarch Roderick O'Connor, to Henry II., as a hostage. He followed the King to Normandy; but taking ill almost immediately after his arrival there, died at Eu, as above mentioned.

* *Dunlong*: This (119) Dunlong of Omey in *Iar Connaght* had: (120) Tuathal, who had: (121) Doncuan, who had: (122) Diarmid Sugach, who had: (123) Diarmid Oge, who had: (124) Amhailgadh, who had: (125) Aedh, who had: (126) Tuathal, who had: (127) Tuathal Oge, who had: (128) Felim, who had: (129) Tiboid (or Theobald), of Omey, who was hanged in 1586 by Sir Richard Bingham, and whose Estates were confiscated to the Crown. This Tiboid had: (130) Edmond, who had: (131) Fergnan, who had: (132) Cornelius or Connor O'Toole, who fought for King James II. at the Battle of the Boyne, and then settled at Kilcogny, in the co. Cavan. This Cornelius had: (133) Connor, who had four children, namely—1. Mathew, 2. Richard, 3. Margaret, 4. Mary. This (134) Mathew had four children, namely—1. Cornelius, 2. Richard, 3. Catherine, 4. Margaret (died 1876). This (135) Cornelius O'Toole, a merchant in Dublin, and living in 1883, has had: (136) Cornelius O'Toole; Joseph O'Toole; Rev. Mathew B. O'Toole, O.C.C., Carmelite College, Terenure, co. Dublin: Eliza; Rosanna; Josephine (dead); and Mary, wife of Mr. Farrelly, merchant, living in 1883.

VII. Dermot, who d. in 1622.—
See his will, which is one of
the oldest in the Record Office.
Dermot had:

VIII. Cahir (or Charles) of Ballyhubbock, in Imaile, who forfeited his lands to Cromwell.
Hoping to regain his estates
he joined the Standard of
King James II., and fought
at the battle of the Boyne,
where he shot the Duke of
Schomberg, while crossing the
river; d. 1702. Charles had:

IX. Patrick, of Newtown and
Oldmill, in Imaile, who died
1770, and had:

X. Patrick, of same place, who
d. 1830, and had—1. Michael,
of whom presently; 2. John;
3. Laurence; 4. Thomas; 5.
Christopher.

XI. Michael, of Newtown, the
eldest son of Patrick, d. 1846,
and had: 1. Patrick, of Holly-
park, Rathfarnham, co. Dublin;
2. Mary; 3. James; 4. Bridget;
5. John of Raheen, in Imaile.

XII. Patrick, the eldest son of
Michael, m. Sarah Grehan, of
Donard, and had:

XIII. 1. Thomas (a student in
Terenure College); 2 Patrick;
3. Jane; 4. Mary; all living in
1883.

Castlekevin Branch.

122. Dermod: eldest son of Aedh;
slain in 1445, at the age of eighty
years.

123. Theobald: his son; d. 1460.

124. Edmond: his son; slain in
1488 by the sons of Teige
O'Byrne.

125. Art: son of Edmond; died
1499. Had: 1. Art Oge, of Castlekevin; 2. Felim; 3. Tirlogh, slain
in 1542. This Art Oge,'of Castlekevin, was slain in 1517. He had:

I. Aedh (or Hugh), who in 1523
was slain by the O'Byrnes;
and Luke (died 1578) who m.
Rice Basnett, and had:—1.
Felim; 2. Donoch; 3. Hugh;
4. Alexander; 5. Barnaby, who
died 17th January, 1597.

II. Barnaby, the fifth son of Luke,
who m. Honor O'Moore and
had:—1. Luke (died 1652); 2.
Arthur; 3. Cahir; 4. Margery.

III. Luke, the eldest son of
Barnaby, who, at the age of 75,
d. in 1652 in prison in Dublin
Castle. Had: 1. Barnaby (d.
1691), of Harold's Grange;
2. Donogh, who was a Lieut.-
Col. in the Irish Confederate
Army of 1642; 3. Christopher,
a Major in the same Confederate Army, and slain in the
Wars of the Revolution;
4. Tirlogh, who was also a
member of the Irish Catholic
Confederation of that period,
and from whom the present
O'Tooles of Castlekevin and
Glendalough are descended.

IV. Barnaby (d. 1691), of Harold's
Grange: son of Luke. Had:
1. Luke, of Fairfield, county
Wexford; 2. Arthur; 3. Francis, M.P. for Wicklow in 1688,
and who d. 1720.

V. Luke O'Toole, of Fairfield:
the eldest son of Barnaby, who
d. 1750. Had:

VI. Laurence (d. 1794), who had:

VII. Laurence (d. 1782), who had:

VIII. Laurence (d. 1820), who
had;

IX. Joseph Laurent (living in
1883); President de la Chambre
du Commerce de l'Ile de la
Reunion France. Had:

X. Thomas O'Toole, living in
1883.

Powerscourt Branch.

126. Tirlogh O'Toole, of Powers-

court: third son of Art; slain in 1542 by Shane O'Toole of Imaile. Had: 1. Luke; 2. Tirlogh, slain *ante* 1542; 3. Brian an Cedach ("cedach:" Irish, *a mantle*), who in 1547 defeated the Fitzgeralds at Three Castles, near Blessington; 4. Felim (slain, 1599), lord of Powerscourt, in the co. Wicklow, who in 1590 forfeited his lands, which in 1603 were granted to Sir Richard Wingfield, an ancestor of the present Lord Powerscourt, of Enniskerry; 5. Dermod, who had:

I. Donoch O'Toole, who had:
II. Garret O'Toole, of Powers-court, who had:
III. Kate, who was m. to Art O'Neill, *alias* Payne, who is No. 129 on the (No. 2) "O'Neill" (Princes of Tyrone) genealogy.
127. Felim O'Toole: the fourth son of Tirlogh; slain in 1599.

128. Garrett: his son; slain in 1582.
129. Tirlogh*: his son; m. Miss Kavanagh; slain at Dublin Castle in 1625. Had a sister, Winefrid, who was married to a son of Feagh (MacHugh) O Byrne, a celebrated Chieftain in the county Wicklow, who is No. 130 on the "O'Byrne" (Lords of Ranelagh) pedigree.
130. Donoch, of O'Toole's Castle, near Kiltegan, son of Tirlogh; slain in battle, 1690.
131. Tirlogh (or Terence): his son; who, refusing to conform to the Protestant religion, forfeited his estate, and migrated to Drum-quin, near Kiltegan, in Imaile: d. 1725.
132. Patrick (d. 1790), of Bally-toole and Ballymooney, in Imaile: his son; m. Mary Donohoe. Had:
I. Terence, of Ballymooney and Donard, of whom presently.

* *Tirlogh* : Deprived of almost all his family patrimony this Tirlogh lingered amongst his friends and kinsfolk on the western side of the mountains near Kiltegan, county Wicklow; expecting to be able to muster a sufficient number of his clansmen and friends to retake his family Castle and Estates of Powerscourt; as may be seen by reference to the State Papers of A.D. 1608. Writing to the Earl of Salisbury, the then Lord Chancellor of Ireland says:

" . . . Has received advertisement of stirs to be raised in Leinster during the absence of the Lord Deputy, by some of the O'Tooles, Kavanaghs, and others. Has been careful to discover their purposes. And first, for the O'Tooles: Has heard that that base uncle plotted with a nephew named Tyrlagh O'Toole, to surprise the Castle of Powerscourt, within eight miles of Dublin, possessed by Mr. Marshall, to kill his ward there, to gather forces, and to enter into action of rebellion. The said Tyrlagh has also used his credit to gather lately some companies of the O'Moores out of the Queen's County (which Sept will prove a dangerous one, ready to be entertained for mischief upon all occasions), and to allow some confederates of the Kavanaghes, and other loose persons of these mountains near Dublin to take his part; who have all given him promise of assistance. As yet, however, he sees no fear of danger. Tyrlagh lurks secretly amongst his friends; the want of arms and munitions and powder is some stay to him and the rest, but the principal thing that stayed them is their expectation of foreign forces, the return of Tyrone, and the uncertainty of severe chastisement in the return of the Lord Deputy.

St. Sepulcre's, near Dublin,
    7th August, 1608."

This Tirlogh O'Toole and his descendants never recovered Powerscourt; on the contrary, they forfeited to the Crown whatever remained of his estates in Imaile; and, as above shown, he was slain at Dublin Castle in 1625. His descendants were reduced to the position of farmers, compelled to labour, and till those lands their fathers once held in fee:

"Alas! that might could conquer right."

II. Denis (d. 1850), who removed to Slieveroe, near Blessington, co. Wicklow, and m. Miss Finn, by whom he had:
I. John (died 1879), of whom presently.
II. Mary.
III. Terence.
IV. Patrick.
V. Denis.
VI. Sarah.
VII. Edward.
VIII. James.
IX. Timothy.
X. Catherine.

John, the eldest son of John, son of Denis, had: I. John, II. Patrick, III. Henry, IV. Thomas, V. Kate, VI. Jane, VII. Eliza, VIII. Sarah.

III. John (d. 1812), the third son of Patrick, had:
I. Patrick (living in 1883), who had:
II. John, also living in 1883.
IV. Mary, who d. 1815.
V. Sarah, who d. 1812.

133. Terence (or Tirlogh), of Ballymooney and Donard: eldest son of Patrick, who died 1790; m. Mary Headon; d. 1817. Had: 1. Terence, who d. s.p.; 2. Mary, wife of William Mooney; 3. Anne, died 1826; 4. Denis, of whom presently; 5. Patrick, d. 1832; 6. Sarah.

134. Denis: fourth son of Terence; married Anne Byrne, died 1849. Had: 1. Terence; 2. Mary, who d. 1863; 3. Anne, who died 1862; 4. Anthony, who died 1834; 5. Rev. Patrick Laurence O'Toole, O.C.C., living (in Dublin) in 1883; 6. Anthony, of Mountpleasant Square, co. Dublin, living in 1883 (who married Alice O'Donohoe, and had: I. Kevin, II. Alice, III. Anne, IV. Lawrence, V. Eva (died young), VI. Cathleen, VII. Arthur—all, except Eva, living in 1883): 7. Denis, who d. 1879; 8. Sarah, wife of James Meythen, Merchant, 35 South King Street, Dublin (living in 1883); 8. Lawrence, d. young.

135. Terence: eldest son of Denis; d. in 1872 in St. Louis, United States, America. Was married to Margaret Barry, of Buttevant, county Cork, and had:—1. Denis, 2. Anthony, 3. Mary, 4. Sarah, 5. Margaret—all of whom living in St. Louis, in 1883.

136. Denis O'Toole, of St. Louis, United States, America: eldest son of Terence; b. 1862; and living in 1883.

O'TOOLE. (No. 2.)

Of Connemara.

Arms : Same as those of "O'Toole" (No. 1).

DUNLONG, a brother of Faolan who is No. 118 on the (foregoing) "O'Toole" (Princes of Imaile) pedigree, was the ancestor of *O'Toole*, of Connemara.*

---

* Connemara : About the time of King Henry VIII., a branch of the O'Tooles of Leinster migrated to the West of Ireland, and settled in the island of Omey, in *Iar* (or West) *Connaught*, where their descendants still remain. Under A.D. 1586, Tiboid (or Theobald), who is No. 127 on the foregoing pedigree, is, in the Annals of the Four

119. Tuathal : son of Dunlong.
120. Duncuan : his son.
121. Dermod Sugach : his son.
122. Dermod Oge : his son.
123. Awley : his son.
124. Hugh : his son.

125. Tuathal : his son.
126. Felim : his son.
127. Tiboid (or Theobald) : his son ; living in 1586.
128. Edmond O'Toole : his son.

QUIRK.

Arms : Ar. on a mount in base vert an oak tree acorned ppr.

CORMAC, the third son of Cu-corb, King of Leinster, who is No. 85 on the "O'Connor" (Faley) pedigree, was the ancestor of ' *O'Cuirc* ("cuirc :" Irish, *a head, a whittle, a swathe*); anglicised *Cuirk, Quirk, Quirke, Head,* and *Whittle.*

86. Cormac : son of Cucorb.
87. Iomcdadh : his son.
88. Labhradh : his son.

89. Lugaidh [luy] : his son ; had six brothers. This Luy was the ancestor of *Gawley.*

REILY.

Of Redland Grove, Clifton, County of Somerset, England.

*Arms :** Ar. on a mound an oak tree entwined by a serpent descending the trunk all ppr., and supported by two lions ramp. gu. *Crest :* A mailed arm grasping a dagger, couped at the elbow, all ppr. *Motto ;* Fortitudine et prudentia.

A BRANCH of the "O'Reilly" (No. 2) family, after their property had been confiscated under the Cromwellian Settlement, settled in the county Cork about the middle of the seventeenth century :

1. John Reily (armig.), of Scarva House, had :

I. John, who went abroad in 1818.

Masters, described as " a supporter of the poor, and keeper of a house of hospitality" (i.e. *a Biatach*) ; and was hanged by a party of English soldiers under Sir Richard Bingham, who were sent on a predatory excursion to *Iar-Connaught.* "The present O'Tooles of Connemara," says Dr. John O'Donovan, " are reduced to poverty ; and are utterly ignorant of their origin."

* *Arms :* According to Warren's *Guide to the Study of Book Plates*, P. II., p. 20. " The book plate of John Reilly, Esq., of the Middle Temple, 1679, is on a mound an oak tree, a snake descending the trunk, supported by two lions rampant. *Crest :* Out of a ducal coronet an arm mailed in armour couped at the elbow, and grasping a dagger. *Motto :* Fortitudine et prudentia."

II. Joseph, of whom presently.
III. Isaac, went to India.
IV. Jacob, also went to India.
V. George, who d. unm.
VI. James, also d. unm.
VII. Jane, who m. John Hazle, Esq., of Rock Castle, co. Cork, and had: 1. John Hazle, who married a daughter of George Shaw, of Cork (sister of John George Shaw, Esq., who was twice Mayor of Bristol, England), but had no issue; 2. William, who m. Eliza Jane Hamilton; 3. Henry, who died unm. at Paris in 1830; 4. Eliza-Jane, who m. Fitzmaurice, of Dunmanway, and had one son (a lawyer), and one daughter.
VIII. Elizabeth, who m. Don Bibra de Bilboa.
IX. Mary.
X. Isabella.
2. Joseph Reilly, of "Kingsaile" (now "Kinsale"): second son of John; born 29th March, 1773, died 21st March, 1834; married Ellen, sister of Major James Sweeny, of Her Majesty's 62nd Regiment of Foot (Deputy Governor-General of Canada under Lord Dalhousie), and had issue:
I. Joseph, eldest son, born 1806, died 1859.

II. Jane, b. 3rd Jan., 1800, died 3rd Jan., 1862; m. Christopher Cleburne, of Rock Cottage, Esq.
III. Ellen, b. 1808, d. unm. 30th Mar., 1859.
IV. William Henry, b. 1809, d. 1st March, 1839.
V. Bridget, born 1810, died 23rd Oct., 1845.
VI. Bessie, born 1812, d. 1847; married Mr. Coffey.
VII. James, b. 1811, died 29th July, 1851; m. Isabella Torey, and had issue James, b. 1844, and Isabella.
VIII. John, b. 1814, died 22nd May, 1848.
IX. Sampson, of whom presently.
X. George, born 1819, died 24th Aug., 1847.
XI. Roger, b. 1818, d. 7th March, 1845; married Matilda Hillier, in 1843, and had Matilda, b. 1844, who m. Mr. Collins (a lawyer) of London.
XII. Ann-Isabella, b. 1823, died 17th July, 1837.
XIII. Mary.
3. Sampson Reily, of Leinster-Villa, Redland Grove: son of Joseph; b. 14th May, 1815.

ROBERTSON.

Chiefs of Clann Donachaidh.

Arms : Gu. three wolves' heads erased ar.   *Crest* : A dexter hand erect, holding an imperial crown all ppr.   *Motto* : Virtutis gloria merces.

ACCORDING to Skene (the author of "Celtic Scotland"), King Duncan, the eldest son of Malcolm III., was the ancestor of *Robertson;* and the Robertsons are called *Clann Donnachaidh*, which means "the descendants of Duncan." (See, in p. 565, Note under "MacUais" pedigree.) As

3 c

Malcolm III. of Scotland is (see p. 38) No. 109 on "The Lineal Descent of the Royal Family of England," his son Duncan must be No. 110.

110. Duncan : eldest son of Malcolm III. of Scotland.

111. Robert : son of Duncan.

112. Duncan (2): his son.

113. Duncan (3): his son.

114. Robert: his son.

115. John : the son of Robert. Assumed the sirname *Robertson;* living in 1448.

116. Laurence: his son ; had a brother named William. John Robertson, son of Laurence, having died without issue, was succeeded by his uncle William.

117. John, son of William ; second son of John No. 115; was a man of great strength and courage, and was therefore called " Stalwart John." He married, first, a dau. of Hugh Rose, of Kilravock, by whom he had an heir and successor. He married, secondly, a dau. of Fearn, of Pitcullen, by whom he had three sons and one daughter.

118. William : one of those three sons, by the second marriage; became first of the Robertsons of Kindeace. He married Elspeth, dau. of the Rev. Thomas Howison, minister of Inverness, by whom he had six sons and three daughters. The first two, William and George, d. unmarried, before their father.

119. Gilbert, of Kindeace : third and eldest surviving son of William, No. 118. He mar. Margaret, eldest dau. of Colin Mackenzie of Redcastle, by whom he had two sons

and several daughters. The eldest son William, died before his father, unmarried.

120. Colin, of Kindeace, the second son of Gilbert; married a daughter of Sir Robert Munro, Bart., of Fowlis, by whom he had two sons, William and George.

121. William, of Kindeace : eldest son of Colin. He was twice married—first, to Catherine, daughter of Robertson of Shipland, by whom he had two sons and several daughters; secondly, to Anne, daughter of Sir John Munro, Bart., of Fowlis, by whom he had no issue.

122. George: second son of William, of Kindeace; was Sheriff-Depute and Commissary of Ross. He married Agnes, daughter of John Balfour, of Aldourie, by whom he had four sons.

123. Andrew Robertson: eldest son of George; was Provost and Sheriff-Substitute of Dingwall. He married Anne, daughter of Colin Mackenzie, a Bailie of Dingwall, by whom he had, among others, a daughter Anne who married, as his second wife, the late Sir John Gladstone, Baronet, of Fasque, Kincardineshire, by whom she had issue, amongst other children, the Right Hon. William Ewart Gladstone,* of Hawarden, in Flintshire, M.P., and First Lord of the Treasury in 1884.

* *William Ewart Gladstone :* This venerable gentleman (living in 1887) is descended on the mother's side from the ancient Mackenzies of Kintail, through whom is introduced the blood of The Bruce, of the ancient Kings of Man, and of the Lords of the Isles, and Earls of Ross ; also from the Munros of Fowlis, and the Robertsons of Strowan and Athole. His descent on the father's side is from the ancient Scottish family of *Gledstaine* ("gleadh :" Irish, *tricks, humour;* "stain," tin or *latten*). Mr. Gladstone is thus eminently *Celtic* in origin and descent both on the father's, and mother's side.

ROE.

NEIL RUADH (*ruadh :* Irish, "red ;" Wel. *rhydh ;* Lat. *ru-fus ;* Fr. *rou-ge ;* Gr. *eruth-ros*), who is No. 112 on the " O'Neill" (Princes of Tyrone) pedigree, was the ancestor of *O'Ruaidhe ;* anglicised *Roe*, and *Rowe*.

ROGAN.

Arms : Vert on a mount in base ppr. a boar pass er.

EACHACH, brother of Feig who is No. 88 on the "O'Hanlon" pedigree, was the ancestor of *O'Ruagain ;* anglicised *Rogan*.

88. Eachach ("eachach :" Irish, "having many horses"): son of Felim ; a quo *Ua Eachaigh*, and *MacEachaigh*, anglicised *Mageough*, *Magough*, *Magoff*, *Goff*, *Gough*, and *Magahy*.

89. Olioll : his son ; lord of the territory of *Eachach Mór ;* had a brother, named Cathfoighid, who was lord of *Eachach Beag*.

90. Amhailgadh [awly] : son of Olioll ; a quo *Cineal Amhailgadh*, now "Clanawley," in the co. Down.

91. Fearach : his son ; had two brothers—1. Rory, 2. Fraochran.

92. Giall-Dubh : son of Ferach.

93. Armeadh : his son ; a quo *Clann Armeidh ;* had a brother named Sineach, a quo *Clann Sineaigh*.

94. Conmaol : son of Armeadh ; had a brother named Cineadh ("cineadh," gen. " cinuidh :" Irish, *a nation, a kind ;* Lat. "gen-us ;" Gr. " gen-os"); a quo *O'Cinnidh*, anglicised *Kenny* (of Ulster).

95. Ruarach : son of Clonmaol.

96. Ceallach : his son ; had a brother named Allen.

97. Ruagan ("ruaig :" Irish, *to pursue ;* "an," *one who*): son of Ceallach ; a quo *O'Ruagain*.

98. Eochagan : his son.

99. Cumascach : his son.

100. Olioll : his son.

101. Muireadach : his son.

102. Rory : his son.

103. Morogh Fionn O'Ruagain : his son.

ROGERSON.

Arms : Az. a fess betw. a fleur-de-lis in chief and a mullet in base all or.

RORY, brother of Donal who is No. 104 on the "MacDonnell" (of Antrim) pedigree, was the ancestor of *MacRuadhri* and *O'Ruadhri*, of *Ardstratha* (or

"Ardstraw"), in the county Tyrone; anglicised *MacRory* and *Rory*, and modernized *Rodgers, Rogers, Roger,* and *Rogerson.*

104. Ruadhrigh ("ruadh": Irish, *red haired;* Lat. "ru-fus;" and 'righ:" Irish, *a king*): son of Alexander; a quo *MacRuadhri,* etc.

105. Allan: his son.

106. Rory MacRory: his son; first of the family that assumed this sirname.

107. Randal MacRory,* of Ardstraw: his son.

ROYAL FAMILY

Of England.

Arms :† The ancient *Arms* were : Gu. three lions pass. or.

THE following names carefully trace the Stem of the Royal Family, from King Malcolm III. (or Malcolm Ceann Mór) down to Walter, lord steward of Scotland, the *Mór Mhaor Leamhna* (or "Great Steward of Lennox") of the Irish annalists; a quo (see the "Stewart" pedigree) the sirname *Stewart.* As Malcom III. (see p. 38) is No. 109 on the "Lineal Descent of the Royal Family of England," we commence this genealogy with that number :

109. Malcolm the Third, king of Scotland, ascended the throne, A.D. 1057, and d. A.D. 1094. Malcolm's father, King Duncan, was murdered by Macbeth, A.D. 1041, upon which occasion this Malcolm and his brother Donald Bane who d. 1098 (*ban*: Irish, *white; bahin*: Heb. *bright*), to avoid the same fate from Macbeth, fled into Ireland, where, and in England, they spent the most part of their time during the life of the usurper. Malcolm's eldest son was also Duncan II., King of Scotland, who d. 1095.

110. David : Malcolm's youngest son; King of Scotland; d. 1153; m. Maud of Northumberland.

111. Henry, prince of Scotland : his only son; who d. in his father's life-time, leaving issue three sons, viz.: King Malcolm the Fourth, who

---

* *Randal MacRory :* At present we are unable to supply the links in this genea logical chain down to Thomas MacRory (or MacRogers), who A.D. 1689, was living in "The Three County March," parish of Ardstraw, in the co. Tyrone. This Thomas was twice married : his son Daniel, by the first marriage, had six sons, five of whom settled in America, and one died without issue. A lineal descendant of that Thomas MacRory, by the first marriage, was Philip Rogers, builder, living (in 1877) in or near Limerick ; son of Philip, who lived in the county Fermanagh, who was son of the said Daniel. By the second marriage, the said Thomas had fifteen sons ; some of whose descendants to this day live in and about Ardstraw, and some in America.

† *Arms* : Of the Kings of England, of the Norman Race, it was Henry II. who, in the Royal Banner, first assumed three lions : " *Gu. Three Lions Passant gardant, or.*" As Henry, through his mother Maude, claimed to be of *Irish lineal descent*, and that Milesius of Spain, the ancestor of the *Milesian* Irish Nation, bore *three lions* in his shield, the fact of *three* lions on the escutcheon of King Henry II. is very significant.

died without issue, A.D. 1163; William, surnamed "the Lion," who died A.D. 1214; and, after this William, his son and grandson, both named Alexander, reigned successively, and their issue became extinct.

112. David : the third son of Henry. The issue of this David were three daughters, of whom Margaret (the wife, first of Alan Fitz-Roland, and next, of Mal, king of Galloway) was mother of Dorna-

gill, who was wife of John Baliol, king of Scotland for a time in *her right*, by the award of Edward the First, king of England.*

113. Isabel : the second daughter of David. This Isabel m. Robert Bruce, called "The Noble;" who competed with Baliol for the crown of Scotland.

114. Robert Bruce (2): son of the said Robert and Isabel ; was earl of Annundale (Annandale) and of Carrick, in right of his wife Martha,

* *King of England*: When, A.D. 1296, Edward the First conquered Scotland, he carried away from Scone to London, the crown and sceptre surrendered by Baliol; and the "stone of destiny" on which the Scottish monarchs were placed when they received their royal inauguration.   That stone or seat Fergus Mór Mac Earca had, for the purpose of his inauguration, sent to him, it is said, from Ireland to Scotland, by his brother Murchertus MacEarca, the 131st monarch ; and that stone-seat, the "stone of destiny" or *Lia Fail* of the ancient Irish, it is by some persons believed, is now preserved in Westminster Abbey, under the Coronation Chair.

This "Lia Fail" was, before Christ 1897, brought to Ireland by the Tua-de-Danans ; and on it they crowned their kings.   It is believed to be the stone on which Jacob reposed : hence the veneration with which it was regarded, and which for ages secured its preservation in Ireland and Scotland.

Of that "Stone of Destiny" Sir Walter Scott observes :

" Its virtues are preserved in the celebrated leonine verse—

"Ni fallat fatum, Scoti, quocunque locatum
Invenient lapidem, regnare tenentur ibidem.

" Which may be rendered thus :

" Unless the fates are faithless found,
And prophet's voice be vain,
Where'er this monument is found
The Scottish race shall reign."

" There were Scots who hailed the accomplishment of this prophecy at the accession of James the Sixth to the crown of England ; and exulted, that, in removing this palladium, the policy of Edward resembled that of the people who brought the Trojan horse in triumph within their walls, and which occasioned the destruction of the royal family.   The stone is still preserved, and forms the support of King Edward the Confessor's chair, which the sovereign occupies at his coronation ; and, independent of the divination so long in being accomplished, is in itself a very curious remnant of extreme antiquity."

Without attaching any superstition whatever to the *Saxum Fatale* or "stone of destiny," which it is alleged, thus forms the support of King Edward the Confessor's chair in Westminster Abbey, one cannot help thinking that, after all, there is some force in the "divination" respecting it, contained in these lines—

——"Scoti, quocunque locatum
Invenient *lapidem*, regnare tenentur ibidem ;"

for, in the person of our gracious Sovereign, the *Scottish Race* now reigns (as it did in the person of the monarch who, in Scott's time, swayed the sceptre of the British empire) where the Irish *Lia Fail* is said to be so carefully preserved ! But some antiquarians assert that the *Lia Fail* is still at Tara.

who was daughter and heiress of the earl of Carrick.

115. Robert Bruce (3): his son. After much trouble and many wars between this Robert and his competitor Baliol, Bruce recovered his right to the kingdom, and was crowned the 57th king of Scotland; which he maintained for twenty-four years against Baliol, and against Edward the First and Edward the Second of England.

This Robert Bruce* had one son named David, who was king of Scotland, and died without issue, A.D. 1370; and one daughter named Margery, upon whose issue by her husband the "Mór Mhaor Leamhna" or *Great Steward of Lennox,* namely: Walter, the lord steward of Scotland, the crown was entailed in case of the failure of her brother's issue. This Walter, lord "steward," was ancestor of *Stewart,* and of the *Stuarts* who were kings of Scotland and England.

Queen Matilda was the only dau. of Malcolm the Third, king of Scotland; was the wife of king Henry the First of England, who was the youngest son of William the Conqueror: she was crowned at Westminster on the 11th Nov., A.D.

1100. Queen Matilda's marriage to Henry the First united the Irish or Scottish, Saxon, and Norman Dynasties; in her and her daughter, Princess Maude, continues the *lineal descent* of the present Royal Family of Great Britain and Ireland.

The Princess Maud was, as alrealy mentioned, daughter of King Henry the First of England and of Queen Matilda; Queen Matilda was dau. of Malcolm the Third of Scotland and of Princess Margaret; Princess Margaret was the eldest daughter of Prince Edward and of Agatha; and Agatha was the dau. of Henry the Third, Emperor of Germany. Prince Edward was son of Edmund Ironside and of Algitha; and, after his father's death, was banished from England to Hungary, by Canute, the Danish king. Canute died A.D. 1036; and Prince Edward afterwards returned to England, and died in London A.D. 1057.

In Cox's *Hibernia Anglicana* the following passage is quoted from a speech delivered by King James the First, at the Council Table in Whitehall, on the 21st of April, 1613:—

"There is a double cause why I should

* *Robert Bruce*: Notwithstanding that King Edward the First of England conquered Scotland, carried Baliol a prisoner to London, and destroyed all records of antiquity (which came within his reach) that inspired the Scots with a spirit of national pride:—

"Still are the Scots determined to oppose
And treat intruding Edward's friends as foes;
Till the revengeful king, in proud array,
Swears to make Scotland bend beneath his sway."
—MacDonald.

Bruce made several fruitless attempts to recover the independence of his country, which, since Baliol resigned it, King Edward the First considered as his own; who, with his last breath, enjoined his son and successor, Edward the Second of England, to prosecute the war with Scotland, "till that obstinate nation was finally conquered." It was not, however, until the "Battle of Bannockburn," A.D. 1314, that the Scots, under this Robert Bruce—afterwards called "King Robert the First"—established their independence.

be careful of the welfare of that (the Irish) people : first, as King of England, by reason of the long possession the Crown of England hath had of that land ; and, also, as King of Scotland, for the ancient Kings of Scotland were descended from the Kings of Ireland."

After the death of Queen Anne, George the First, Elector of Hanover, son of Ernest Augustus and of the Princess Sophia, ascended the throne of England A.D. 1714, pursuant to the "Act of Succession." Ernest Augustus, himself, formed a double line of the pedigree, for he, as well as his wife, was descended from Henry the Second. That pedigree is thus traced : Ernest Augustus was son of George, son of William, son of Ernestus, son of Henry, son of Otho the Second, son of Frederick, son of Bernard, son of Magnus, son of Albert the Second, son of Albert the First, son of Otho the First, Duke of Bruns-wick and Lunenburg ; son of Henry, Duke of Saxony, who was the husband of Princess Maud, the eldest daughter of King Henry the Second of England, who was son of *the* Princess Maude, daughter of Queen Matilda ; who was daughter of King Malcolm the Third of Scotland, as above.

According to the learned Hardiman, George the Fourth,* when passing in view of the Hill of Tara, during his visit to Ireland A.D. 1821,

"Declared himself proud of his descent from the ancient monarchs of the land."

And Forman says:

" The greatest antiquity which the august House of Hanover can boast, is deduced from the Royal Stem of Ireland."

In this Work (see pp. 37-41) that " Royal Stem" is carefully compiled.

RYAN† (No. 1.)

Lords of Idrone, County Carlow.

Arms : Gu. three griffins' heads erased ar.   *Crest* : A griffin segreant gu. holding in the sinister claw a dagger ppr.

CORMAC, brother of Eoghan (or Owen) who is No. 97 on the " Mac-Morough" pedigree, was the ancestor of *O'Righin;* anglicised *Mulrian, O'Ryan, Ryan,* and *Ryne.*

---

* *George the Fourth* : According to Gaskin, the visit in 1821 by His Majesty George the Fourth was the first instance in Irish history of an English Monarch visiting Ireland as a friend ; for, before him, when other Monarchs came over, it was not a visit, but a *visitation* : blood heralded their approach; blood marked their progress; blood tracked their return. Even their Viceroys, till the accession of the Brunswick Dynasty, but too truly justified the bitter witticism of the late Sir Hercules Langrish :
" In what history," said a modern Viceroy (Earl Fitzwilliam), " in what history, Sir Hercules, shall I find an account of all the Irish Lords Lieutenant ?"
"Indeed I do not know, my lord," replied Langrishe, " unless it be in a continuation of *rapine* (Rapin)."—Gaskin's *Irish Varieties.*

† *Ryan* : According to O'Donovan's " Antiquities," deposited in the Royal Irish Academy, Dublin, the O'Ryans of Idrone, county Wexford, are a distinct family from

97 Cormac: son of Nathi.

98 Colman (also called Colum): his son; a quo *Siol Coluim*, now *Colum*.

99. Ronan : his son.

100. St. Crohnmaol (22nd June): his son.

101. Aodh (or Hugh) Roin : his son.

102. Colman (2): his son.

103. Laignen : his son.

104. Cairbre : his son.

105. Hugh: his son.

106. Bruadar ("bruadar:" Irish, *a reverie*) : his son ; a quo *O'Bruadair*, anglicised *Broder*, *Broderick*, and *Bradner*.

107. Dubhghall : his son.

108. Righin ("righin :" Irish, *sluggish*, *dilatory*): his son ; a quo *O'Righin*.

109. Cairbre (2): his son.

110. Teige : his son.

111. Donoch : his son.

112. Melachlin : his son.

113. Lucas : his son.

114. Daithi (or David): his son.

115. Neimheach : his son.

116. Jeoffrey : his son.

117. Henry : his son.

118. Henry Mulrian : his son.

RYAN. (No. 2.)

From the Vol. F. 4. 18, in the MSS. Library of Trin. College, Dublin,

Arms : Same as "Ryan" (No. 1.)

1. Darby O'Ryan.

2. Mahowne : his son.

3. Daniel : his son.

4. Darby : his son.

5. Daniel : his son.

6. William O'Mulryan, of Salloghade Mór: his son; d. 14th Aug., 1637; m. Margaret, dau. of John

Cantwell of Mokarhy, co. Tipperary, and had five sons—1. Darby ; 2. Donoch (or Denis); 3. Henry; 4. James ; 5. John.

7. Darby O'Mulryan : eldest son of William ; m. Kathleen, dau. of Thomas Fitzmorice, of Cahiressa, co. Limerick.

SCANLAN.

Arms : Vert a tower triple-towered ar.

TUADAN, brother of Duach, who is No. 101 on the "O'Shaughnessy" pedigree, was the ancestor of *O'Scannla ;* anglicised *Scanlan*.

the O'Ryans of the counties of Tipperary and Waterford. Others, however, say that all these families are of the same stock.

Richard Ryan was born in 1796; his father was a London bookseller. He wrote a *Dictionary of the Worthies of Ireland* (Two Vols., 1821) ; *Ballads on the Fictions of the Ancient Irish* (1822) ; and *Poetry and Poets* (Three Vols., 1826). He died in 1849.

101. Tuadan : son of Breannan.
102. Garbhan : his son.
103. Nathseanach : his son.
104. Conla : his son.
105. Nobilleud : his son.
106. Tiomail : his son.
107. Maoltuile : his son.
108. Maolguala : his son.
109. Casadhmanach : his son.
110. Maolciaran : his son.
111. Feargal : his son.
112. Scannail ("scannail :" Irish, *scandal*: Lat. "scandal-um;" Gr. "skandal-on"): his son ; a quo *O'Scannla.*

113. Aodh (or Hugh): his son.
114. Gileneach: his son.
115. Concobhar (or Connor): his son.
116. Hugh (2) : his son.
117. Tirlach : his son.
118. Hugh (3) : his son.
119. Teige : his son.
120. Murios : his son.
121. Connor (2) : his son.
122. Murios (2) : his son.
123. Brian : his son.
124. Art : his son.
125. Owen O'Scanlan : his son.

SHEANE.

Arms: Gu. a lion pass. guard. or.

SEAGHAN (Shane or John), brother of Colcan, who is No. 89 on the "O'Brassil" (West) pedigree, was the ancestor of *O'Seaghain;* anglicised *Shean,* and *Segan.*

89. Seaghan ("seagh :" Irish, *esteem*): son of Tuathal Cruinn-bheul (or "Tual of the gathered mouth").
90. Glasceann : his son.
91. Muirios [murrish] : his son.
92. Aongus : his son.

93. Cubreathan : his son.
94. Dunbo : his son.
95. Dungal : his son.
96. Tighearnach : his son.
97. Cananan : his son.
98. Anbuidh O'Seaghain ("ana-buidh :" Irish, *immature*) : his son.

SPILLANE.

Arms: Sa. a fess erm. a bend pean.

MUIREADACH [muredach], brother of Cearnach, who is No. 98 on the "Breslin" pedigree, was the ancestor of *O'Speilain;* anglicised *Spellan, Spelman, Spilman, Spillane, Spollen,* and *Spillers.*

98. Muiredach : son of Fergus.
99. Foghartach : his son.
100. Speilan ("speil :" Irish, *a*

herd, particularly *of swine;* "an," one *who*) : his son ; a quo *O'Speilain.*

SWEENY. (No. 1.)

Of Connaught.

Arms : Az. two boars ramp. combatant or, in chief two battle axes in saltire of the last. *Crest* : A demi griffin ramp. or, holding in the claws a lizard ppr.

DOMHNALL AN MADHMANN, brother of Maolmuire who is No. 118 on the "MacSweeney" (of Banagh) pedigree, was the ancestor of *Sweeny*, of Connaught.

118. Domhnall an Madhmann: son of Eoin (or Eoghan) na Lathaighe.
119. Donoch: his son.
120. Aodh: his son.

121. Maolmuire: his son.
122. Ruadhri: his son.
123. Maolmuire: his son.
124. Brian MacSweeny: his son; living in 1690.

SWEENY, (No. 2.)

Of Clanrickard.

Arms: Same as "Sweeny" (No. 1).

MUIRCHEARTHACH, a brother of Donoch who is No. 119 on the "Sweeny" (of Connaught) pedigree, was the ancestor of *Sweeny*, of Clanrickard.

119. Muirchearthach: son of Donall an Madhmann.
120. Ruadhri: his son.
121. Murchadh: his son.

122. Donall: his son.
123. Donall Sweeny, of Clanrickard: his son; living in 1666.

SWEENY. (No. 3.)

Of Thomond.

Arms: Same as those of "Sweeny" (No. 1).

CONCHOBHAR, a brother of Aodh who is No. 120 on the "Sweeny" (of Connaught) pedigree, was the ancestor of *Sweeny*, of Thomond.

120. Conchobhar: son of Donoch.
121. Giolladubh: his son.
122. Colla: his son.

123. Eoghan Sweeny: his son; living in 1666.

SWENEY. (No. 4.)

Of Redwing, Minnesota, United States, America.

Arms : Az. two boars ramp. combatant or, in chief two battle axes in saltire of the last. *Crest* : A demi griffin ramp. or, holding in the claws a lizard ppr.

MYLES (or Maolmordha), a younger brother of Hugh, who is No. 130 on the (No. 2) "MacSweeney" (Na Tuaighe, or Na Doe) genealogy, was the ancestor of this branch of that family :

130. Myles MacSweeney, of Letterkenny, county Donegal; son of Tirloch; lived to a very old age.

131. Daniel *McSwine:* his son; m. Jane, dau. of John Burns.

132. Nicholas Major *Sweney:* his son; m. Fanny Bell Barclay.

133. Alexander M o n t g o m e r y Sweney: his son; born 1783; m.

Mary M. Kehr. Had an elder brother, George, who left no male issue.

134. Doctor William Wilson Sweney of Red Wing, Minnesota, United States of America: son of Alexander; b. 18th December, 1818, in Northumberland County, Pennsylvannia; and living in 1881.

SWEENY (OR SWYNY). (No. 5.)

Of Kinsale, and West Bandon, County Cork.

Arms : The ancient Armorial Bearings of this family were : An orle of eight az. and or. *Motto* : Baillailah aboo. More lately the *Arms* were: Ar. on a fess vert betw. three boars pass. sa. a lizard gu. *Motto* : Buailtir cabair a buaigh.

THIS branch of the "MacSweeney" of Ulster family settled in the county Cork *circa* 1630; and many of its members distinguished themselves in the service of England and France.

1. John Sweeny, gent., m. Jane Lyon (niece of Rear Admiral Lyon, Royal Navy), and had issue :

I. James, of whom presently.

II. Sampson, d. unm.

III. Roger, who was twice mar.: first, to a noble Sicilian by whom he had a son Roger Swiny, who went to Sicily; secondly, to Amelia, daughter of Major Bent of the British army, by whom he had one son James (who died young) and

a dau. Amelia, married to Mr. Gerrard of London (a lawyer), by whom she had several children.

IV. Ellen, born 29th Sept., 1779, d. 10th Jan., 1864; married to Joseph Reily, Esq., and had issue (see "Reily").

V. Mary, m. to George Willison, gent., and had, with several other children, Eliza-Ann, who m. Colonel Singleton of the Army, by whom she had one son, Sydenham, who d. young, and a daughter, Lucy, unm.

VI. Bridget, married to Abraham Ellis, and had : 1. Ellen (a spinster), 2. Bessy, who m. Captain Edward Ellis, and had one son James (who went to Africa), and three daus., the eldest of whom Isabel, married a son of the Rev. Joseph Kingsmith, of Brighton, and has issue.

2. James Sweeny, a Major in Her Majesty's 62nd Regiment; *aide-de-camp* to General Riall, at Grenada, West Indies (*see British Army List*): was appointed Deputy Governor-General of Canada to Lord Dalhousie, 1817 ; m. Elizabeth, dau. of O'Brien Bellingham, Esq., of Castle Bellingham,* co. Louth (brother of Sir William Bellingham, Private Secretary to Pitt), and died without issue.

TATLY.

Arms (of " Tatlock") : Az. a bend cotized or, in chief a dolphin naiant ar. *Crest* : Out of a mural coronet az. a dexter arm brandishing a sword wavy ppr.

AODH, a brother of Taithleach who is No. 103 on the "O'Dowd" pedigree, was the ancestor of *MacTaithleigh ;* anglicised *Tatly, Tatlock,* and *Tatlow.*

103. Aodh ; son of Niall.
104. Brian Dearg : his son.
105. Maolseachlainn : his son.
106. Aodh Alain : his son.
107. Taithleach   (" taithleach :" Irish, *quiet, pleasant, handsome*) : his son : a quo *MacTaithleigh.*
108. Muirchearthach-na-Fuineaoige

(" Fuinneog :" Irish, *a window*) : his son.
109. Taithleach Oge : his son,
110. Conchobar : his son.
111. Ruadhri : his son.
112. Corc : his son ; had two brothers—1. Taithleach, 2. Seaan (or Shane).

TIERNEY.
Of Ulster.

Arms : Ar. a chev. sa. a chief gu. *Crest* : An oak tree ppr.

TIGHEARNACH, a son of Muireadach who is No. 89 on the (No. 1) " O'Neill" (of Tyrone) pedigree, was the ancestor of *Cineal Tighearnaigh ;* anglicised *Tierney.*

---

* *Castle Bellingham*: "The neighbourhood is embellished with several handsome country seats, of which those of Lady Bellingham, Miss Bellingham, Major Sweeney, and Mrs. Filgate are the chief." (See Lewis's *Topograph. Dict. of Ireland.*) The extensive Brewery and Malt-houses at this place were greatly enlarged by Major Sweeney, and Major Wolsley, father of the present Sir Garnet Lord Wolsley, the hero of Magdala.

90. Tighearnach ("tighearna :" Irish, *a lord*): son of Muireadhach; a quo *Cineal Tighearnaigh*.
  91. Dathgil : his son.
  92. Ruadan (or Ruarcan): his son.
  93. Feardalach (or Columan): his son.

94. Fanred; his son.
95. Cirdeag (or Firdheodh): his son.
96. Cronghiolla : his son.
97. Aodh: his son.
98. Cel : his son.
99. Rath : his son.
100. Tighearna : his son.

TIGHE.*

Of Woodstock, County Kilkenny ; and Rosanna, County Wicklow.

Arms : Per chev. embattled ar. and sa. nine crosses crosslet, five in saltire in chief, and four in cross in base counterchanged. *Crest :* A wolf's head erased ppr. gorged with a plain collar az. thereon a cross crosslet or, between two bezants. *Motto :* Summum nec metuam diem nec optem.

MAIN MAL, one of the youngest brothers of Cathair Mór, the 109th Monarch of Ireland, and who is No. 89 on the "O'Connor" (Faley) genealogy, was the ancestor of *O'Taidhg ;* anglicised *Tighe.*

89. Main Mal : son of Felim Fiorurglas; a quo *Hy-Maile*, and the territory in the county Wicklow called *Imaile.*
90. Amhailgadh : his son. Had three elder brothers—1. Tuathal Tigheach, 2. Berach, 3. Sedna Cromdana. This Sedna had a son named Aedh, who had twelve sons.
  91. Fergus : son of Amhailgadh.
  92. Feargna : his son.
  93. Dioma : his son.

94. Diacolla: his son. Had an elder brother, Aedh Acrach, who was the father of Cobthach, the father of Fiachra Fionn ; and a younger brother, Berchan, who was the father of Dubhtire, the father of Leathola, father of Flann, father of Rudgail, father of Dungealach, father of Aedhgus, father of Cinneth, father of Mithighan, father of Ceallach, father of Cionneth, father of Cairbre, lord of Imaile, who died

* *Tighe :* Of this family was Alderman Richard Tighe, Mayor of Dublin in 1651 ; High Sheriff of the county Dublin in 1655, and of the county Kildare in 1662 ; to whom the above Armorial Bearings were, according to Burke's *General Armory,* granted by St. George, Ulster King-of-Arms, in 1665 ; and who, *temp.* Charles I. and Charles II., acquired estates in the counties of Carlow, Dublin, and Westmeath ; he died, A.D. 1673. His grandson, the Right Hon. Richard Tighe, M.P. *temp.* George I., married Barbara, dau. and co-heir of Christian Borr, Esq., of Drinagh and Borrmount, county Wexford, and was grandfather of William Tighe, Esq., of Rosanna, county Wicklow, M.P., who married Sarah, only child of the Right Hon. Sir William Fownes, Bart., of Woodstock, county Kilkenny. Their son and heir, William Tighe, of Woodstock, M.P., married, in 1793, Marianne, dau. and co-heir of Daniel Gahan, of Coolquil, county Tipperary (see the "Gahan" pedigree), and eventually co-heir of her maternal uncle, Matthew Bunbury, of Kilfeacle, in the same county, and was father of the Right Hon. William Frederick Fownes Tighe, of Woodstock, P.C., Lord Lieutenant and Custos Rotulorum, of the county Kilkenny.

A.D. 847. This Cairbre had a brother Dungealach (see Mac-Firbis's Genealogies, p. 211).

95. (   )
96. Siolan : son of No. 95.
97. Faeleb : his son.

98. Faolbran : his son.
99. Dungal : his son.
100. Tadhg ("tadhg:" Irish, *a poet, philosopher*) : his son ; a quo *O'Taidhg*.

TULLY.

Of Ulster.

Arms : Vert a chev. betw. three wolves' heads erased ar.   *Crest* : A wolf's head couped ar.

MAOLTUILE, a younger brother of Maoldoon, who is No. 94 on the (No. 1) "O'Neill" (of Tyrone) genealogy, was the ancestor of *O'h-Maoltuile ;* angli cised *Multully, Tully,* and *Flood* (of Ulster).

94. Maoltuile ("tuile:" Irish, *a flood*) : son of Maolfireach ; and a quo this family name.
95. Hugh : his son.
96. Cormack : his son.
97. Cairbre : his son.
98. Owen : his son.
99. Teige : his son.
100. Connor : his son.
101. Donal : his son.
102. Murrogh : his son.
103. Muirceartach : his son.
104. Conla : his son.
105. Aongus : his son.
106. Maoltuile : his son.
107. Giollabreac : his son.
108. Congal : his son.
109. Conang : his son.
110. Griorrha : his son.
111. Muriartach : his son.
112. Cathal : his son.
113. Connor : his son.
114. Cormac : his son.

115. William *Tully* : his son.
116. Iollan : his son.
117. Kyras Tully : his son. Was Dean of Clonfert, co. Galway ; died 31st Dec., 1637. This Kyras was twice m. : by his first wife Sheela, a dau. of Thomas O'Kelly, Esq., he had five sons :
I. Mathew.
II. Mark.
III. Luke.
IV. John.
V. Connor.
The second wife of Kyras Tully was Katherine, a dau. of John na Moy O'Kelly, of Criagh, by whom he had three sons :
VI. Edward.
VII. Conla.
VIII. Nicholas.
118. Mathew Tully : eldest son of Kyras.

THE foregoing are the pedigrees of those of the Irish Gaels, or *Milesian* Irish families, which, as yet, we have been able to collect; and we need not say the collection and compilation of those genealogies were to us a "labour of love." In respect to any inaccuracies or blemishes which may still be found in the Work, we trust that the magnitude of our labour will plead our excuse. Any inaccuracies, however, which shall be pointed out to us, shall be corrected in future editions; and the blemishes, if any, expunged.

It will be observed that some of the genealogies are traced down to the time of the English invasion of Ireland; some, to the reign of Queen Elizabeth; some, to the Plantation of Ulster; some, to the Cromwellian, and others to the Williamite, confiscations; and some down to this year of our Lord, 1887. But we are satisfied that, so far as our sources of information enabled us to do so, each generation of each pedigree is herein faithfully recorded.

It will be also seen that, of those families whose pedigrees are continued down to 1887, some contain more generations than others; but this is easily accounted for by the fact, that many families were more long-lived than others; that many of the names recorded in the Irish Genealogies were *Chiefs* of Clans, and that the Chiefs of *dominant* Irish families in the past were often slain in early manhood: because, in war, the Chief headed his Clan, and, thus in *front* of the battle, was always exposed to the onslaught of his foe. Hence the average age of the generations is low in the Pedigrees of those families which longest continued to be *dominant;* thus accounting for the greater number of generations.

To render IRISH PEDIGREES as interesting as possible to future generations of those Irish, Irish-American, Norman-Irish, Anglo-Irish, Danish, Scottish, Welsh, Huguenot, and Palatine families, whose genealogies are recorded in the Work, we would receive reliable information from the representatives of those families, at home, or abroad, who can, from where we leave off in any genealogy, continue their pedigrees down to themsleves; with the view of having such information when verified, inserted in future editions of this Work. And, as the Work caters to the prejudices of no sect or party, there is no valid reason for withholding such information; on the contrary, the man who can assist in rescuing his family genealogy from oblivion, and will not do so, incurs, in our opinion, the reproach so justly applied by Sir Walter Scott, in the following lines, to him, if such there be, whose soul is dead to " Love of Country:"

> High though his titles, proud his name,
> Boundless his wealth as wish can claim ;
> Despite those titles, power and pelf,
> The wretch, concentred all in self,
> Living, shall forfeit fair renown,
> And, doubly dying, shall go down
> To the vile dust, from which he sprung
> Unwept, unhonoured, and unsung.

IRISH MONARCHS OF THE LINE OF HEREMON.

1. Heremon : son of Milesius of Spain.
2. Muimne ⎫
3. Luighne ⎬ : sons of Heremon.
4. Laighne ⎭
5. Irial, The Prophet : son of Heremon.
6. Eithrial : son of Irial.
7. Tighearnmas : son of Follain, son of Eithrial.
8. Fiacha Lamhraein : son of Smiorgioill, son of Eanbothadh, son of Tighearnmas.
9. Aongus Ollmucach : son of Fiacha Lamhraein.
10. Rotheacta : son of Maoin, son of Aongus Ollmucach.
11. Siorghnath Saoghalach : son of Dein, son of Rotheacta.
12. Giallcadh : son of Olioll Olchaoin, son of Siorghnath.
13. Nuadhas Fionnfail : son of Giallcadh.
14. Simeon Breac : son of Nuadhas Fionnfail.
15. Muireadach Bolgach : son of Simeon Breac.
16. Eochaidh : son of Duach Teamhrach, son of Muireadach Bolgach.
17. Conang Beag-Eaglach : son of Duach Teamhrach, son of Muireadach Bolgach.
18. Fiacha Tolgrach : son of Muireadach Bolgach.
19. Duach Ladhrach : son of Fiacha Tolgrach.
20. Ugaine Mór : son of Eochaidh Buaidhaig, son of Duach Ladhrach.
21. Bancadh : son of Eochaidh Buaidhaig.
22. Laeghaire Lorc : son of Ugaine Mór.
23. Cobthach Caoil-bhreagh : son of Ugaine Mór.
24. Labhra Longseach : son of Oilioll Aine, son of Laeghaire Lorc.
25. Melg Molbhthach : son of Cobhthach, son of Cobthach Caoil-bhreah.
26. Aongus Ollamh : son of Oilioll, son of Labhra Longseach.
27. Iarn Gleofathach : son of Melg Molbhthach.
28. Conla Caomh : son of Iarn Gleofathach.
29. Olioll Casfiacalach : son of Conla Caomh.
30. Eochaidh Altleathan : son of Olioll Casfiacalach.
31. Fergus Fortamhail : son of Breasal Breac, son of Aongus Gailine, son of Olioll Brachain, son of Labhra Longseach.
32. Aongus Turmeach-Teamreach : son of Eochaidh Altleathan.
33. Conall Collaimrach : son of Eidirsgeoil, son of Eochaidh Altleathan.
34. Eanna Aigneach : son of Aongus Turmeach-Teamreach.
35. Crimthann Cosgrach : son of Feidhlim Fortruin, son of Fergus Fortamhail.
36. Eochaidh Feidlioch : son of Finn, son of Finlogha, son of Roignein Ruadh, son of Easamhuin Eamhna, son of Eanna Aigneach.

37. Eochaidh Aireamh : son of Finn, son of Finloga, son of Roignein Ruadh, son of Easamhuin Eamhna, son of Eanna Aigneach.

38. Edersceal : son of Eoghan, son of Oilioll, son of Iar, son of Deagha, son of Luin, son of Roisin, son of Trein, son of Rotherein, son of Airindil, son of Maide, son of Forga, son of Fearadhach, son of Oiliolla Euron, son of Fiacha Fearmara, son of Aongus Turmeach-Teamreach.

39. Nuadhas Neacht : son of Seadna Siothbach, son of Lughaidh Fiorbric, son of Lughaidh Loitfin, son of Breasal Breac, son of Fiachadh Fiorbric, son of Oiliolla Glas, son of Fearadhach Foglas, son of Nuaghat Follamhain, son of Alloid, son of Art, son of Criomthan Cosgrach.

40. Conaire Mór : son of Edersceal (No. 38).

41. Lughaidh Sriabh-n Dearg : son of Bress-Nar-Lothar, son of Eochaidh Feidlioch (No. 36).

42. Conchobhar : son of Feargus Fairge, son of Nuadhas Neacht (No. 39).

43. Crimthann Niadh-Nar : son of Lughaidh Sriabh-n Dearg (No. 41).

44. Feareadach Fionnfeachtnach : son of Crimthann Niadh-Nar.

45. Fiatach Fionn : son of Daire, son of Dluthig, son of Deitsin, son of Eochaidh, son of Suin, son of Rosin, son of Trein, etc. (see No. 53).

46. Fiacha Fionn-Ola : son of Feareadach Fionnfeachtnach (No. 44).

47. Tuathal Teachtmar : son of Fiacha Fionn-Ola.

48. Felim Rachtmar : son of Tuathal Teachtmar.

49. Cathair Mór : son of Feidhlimhidh Fionirglais, son of Cormac Gealta Gaoth, son of Niadh Corb, son of Concorb, son of Modha Corb, son of Conchobhar (No. 42).

50. Conn Ceadcatha : son of Tuathal Teachtmar (No. 47).

51. Conaire MacMogha Laine : son of Modha Cromcinn, son of Luigheach Allathach, son of Cairbre Cromcinn, son of Daire Dornmór, son of Cairbre Fionnmór, son of Conaire Mór (No. 40).

52. Art Eanfhear : son of Conn Ceadcatha (No. 50).

53. Fergus Dubh-Dheadach : son of Fionchada, son of Eogamhuin, son of Fiathach, son of Finn, son of Daire, son of Dluthig, son of Deitsin, son of Eochaidh, son of Suin, son of Rosin, son of Trein, son of Rothrein, son of Airiondil, son of Main, son of Forga, son of Feareadhach, son of Oiliollaran, son of Fiacha Fearmara, son of Aongus (No. 32).

54. Cormac MacAirt ("Ulfada") : son of Art Eanfhear.

55. Eochaidh Gunta : son of Feig, son of Iomachaidh, son of Breasal, son of Fionchadha, son of Fiachadh Fionn, son of Dluthig, son of Deitsin, etc. (See No. 53).

56. Cairbre Liffechar : son of Cormac MacAirt.

57. Fiacha Srabhteine : son of Cairbre Liffechar.

58. Colla Uais (Carioll) : son of Eochaidh Dubhlen, son of Cairbre Liffechar.

59. Muireadach Tireach : son of Fiacha Srabhteine.

60. Eochaidh Muigh Meadhoin : son of Muireadach Tireach.

61. Niall Mór (of "The Nine Hostages") : son of Eochaidh Muigh Meadhoin.

62. Fereadach (Dathi) : son of Fiachradh, son of Eochaidh (No. 60).

63. Laeghaire : son of Niall Mór.

64. Lughaidh : son of Laeghaire.

65. Muirceartach Mór Mac Earca : son of Muireadach, son of Eoghan, son of Niall Mór.

66. Tuathal Maolgharbh : son of Cormac Caoch, son of Cairbre, son of Niall Mór.

67. Diarmid : son of Feargus Ceirbheoil, son of Conal Creamthann, son of Niall Mór.

68. Donal ⎫
69. Fergus ⎭ : sons of Muirceartach Mór Mac Earca (No. 65).

70. Eochaidh : son of Donal, son of Muirceartach Mór Mac Earca.

71. Boitean : son of Nineadhadh, son of Feargus Ceannfada, son of Conall Gulban, son of Niall Mór.

72. Anmire: son of Seadhna, son of Feargus Ceannfada, etc. (See No. 71).

73. Boitean.

74. Aodh : son of Anmire (No. 72).

75. Aodh Slaine: son of Diarmuid, son of Feargus Ceirbheol, son of Conal Crimthann, son of Niall Mór (No. 61).

76. Colman Rimidh (reigned jointly with Aodh Slaine) ; son of Muirceartach (No. 65).

77. Aodh Uar-iodhnach : son of Donal (No. 68).

78. Mallcobh : son of Aodh (No. 74).

79. Suimneach Meann : son of Fiachra, son of Feareadhach, son of Murtough, son of Muireadach, son of Eoghan, son of Niall Mór.

80. Donall : son of Aodh (No. 74).

81. Ceallach ⎫
82. Congall ⎭ : sons of Maolchobha, son of Aodh (No. 74).

83. Diarmid Ruadhnigh ⎫
84. Bladhmhac ⎭ : sons of Aodh Slaine (No. 75).

85. Leachnasach ⎫
86. Ceanfail ⎭ : sons of Bladhmhac.

87. Finachta Fleadhach : son of Dunchada, son of Aodh Slaine.

88. Longseach : son of Donal (No. 80).

89. Congall Cionnmaghair : son of Feargus Fanuid, son of Conall Gulban, son of Niall Mór.

90. Feargall : son of Maoldun, son of Maolfireach, son of Aodh (No. 74).

91. Foghartach : son of Neill, son of Cearmuigh Sotuill, son of Diarmuid, son of Aodh Slaine (No. 75).

92. Ceneth : son of Iargallach, son of Conuing Charraig, son of Congall (No. 82).

93. Flaithertach : son of Loingseach, son of Aongus, son of Donal (No. 80).

94. Aodh Olann (or Allan) : son of Feargall (No. 90).

95. Donall : son of Murough, son of Diarmuid, son of Anmire Caoch, son of Conall Guthbhin, son of Srubhne, son of Colman Mór, son of Feargus Ceirbheoil, son of Conall Creamthann, son of Niall Mór.

96. Niall Frassach : son of Feargall (No. 90).

97. Doncha : son of Donall (No. 95).

98. Aodh Ornigh : son of Niall Frassach.

99. Conchobhar : son of Doncha (No. 97).

100. Niall Caille : son of Aodh Ornigh.

101. Malachi: son of Maolruanaidh, son of Doncha (No. 97); his mother was Arog.

102. Aodh Fionnliath : son of Niall Caille (No. 100).

103. Flann Sionnach : son of Malachi (No. 101).

104. Niall Glundubh : son of Aodh Fionnliath.

105. Doncha : son of Flann Sionnach.

106. Congall : son of Maolmithig, son of Flanaghan, son of Ceallach, son of Conuing, son of Congalla, son of Aodh Slaine.

107. Donall : son of Muirchertach, son of Niall Glundubh.

108. Malachi : son of Flann Sionnach (No. 103).

109. Diarmid, King of Leinster (d. 1072) : son of Donoch Mael-na-mbho, son of Diarmid, son of Donall, son of Cellach, son of Cineath, son of Cairbre, son of Diarmid, son of Aodh, son of Rugalach, son of Oneu, son of Faelcu, son of Faelan, son of Sillan, son of Eoghan Caech, son of Dathi, son of Crimthann, son of Enna Cinnselach, son of Labraidh, son of Bresal Beolach, son of Fiach Baicheda, son of Cathair Mór.

110. Donall Mac Loghlin : son of Ardgal, son of Lochlonn, son of Muireadach, son of Donal Oge, son of Donal, son of Murtagh, son of Donal, son of Aodh Fionnliath (No. 102).

111. Tirloch Mór O'Connor : son of Ruadhri, son of Aodh, son of Teige, etc., son of Brian, son of Eochaidh Muigh Meadhoin (No. 60).

112. Muirceartach Mac Loghlin : son of Neil, son of Donall (No. 110).

113. Roderic O'Connor : son of Tirloch Mór (No. 111).

(114.) Brian O'Neill : son of Neill Ruadh, son of Aodh, son of Mortogh, son of Teige Glinne, son of etc.,—Donal (No. 107).

—(See " O'Neill," Princes of Tyrone.)

(115.) Edward de Bruce : son of Robert, son of Isabel, dau. of David, son of Henry, son of David, son of Malcolm, son of Duncan, etc.

—(See "Stem of Royal Family of England.)

(116.) Shane O'Neill : son of Conn Bacchach, son of etc., etc.

—(See O'Neill Stem), son of Brian O'Neill (123).

(117.) Aodh O'Neill : son of Ferdoroch, son of Shane.

(118.) Art Oge O'Neill : son of Conn, son of Shane ; was Monarch *Elect*, but never exercised regal powers.

(Nos. 114, 115, 116, 117, and 118 were acknowledged Kings of Ireland by the Irish people, but not by the English.)

PART IV.

ADDENDA.

COLLINS.

INSTEAD of the third paragraph in p. 183, *ante*, commencing with "William Collins," read:

William Collins, "the finest English poet which England has produced," was, though a native of England, of *Irish* extraction; he was the son of a hatter in Chichester, being born there on the 25th December, 1720; his uncle was a Colonel in a Foot regiment; he died a lunatic in his sister's house, in Chichester, in 1756.

For the fourth paragraph in same page, read:

"Of the Cork family was the late Stephen Collins, Esq., Q.C., whose son, John T. Collins, Esq., Barrister-at-law, is (in 1887) the chief representative."

And at the end of the "O'Collins" paper, same page, we should have added the following:

There are a few families of the name of *Collins*, settled in Ireland, which are considered of English extraction. About 1651, a Cadet of a Cornish "Collins" family (which was probably founded there by an offshoot of the family of the Lords of Lower Connello, who migrated from Ireland in the 13th or 14th century), acquired property and settled in the county Galway. His descendants intermarried from time to time with members of the Blake, French, Daly, and Kelly families; and his representative at the beginning of this century was John Collins, Esq. (born 1775, died 1826), who married Ellen, daughter of Rev. Joseph Tenison,* Rector of Wicklow, and left issue:

I. William Tenison Collins, M.D.; m. and left issue, who d. s.p.

II. Joseph Tenison Collins, now (1887) Manager of the National Bank, Ballinasloe, who m. as second wife Sarah MacCarthy (for whose descent see "MacCarthy Reagh," No. 4, page 126, *ante*, and foot note), and had issue by her:

I. Charles MacCarthy Collins, born 1850; a member of the Irish, English, and Queensland Bars; a J.P. for Queensland; M.R.I.A.; Fellow of the Institute of Bankers (Lond.);

---

* *Tenison*: Rev. Joseph Tenison was great-grandson of the Rt. Rev. Dr. Edward Tenison, Bishop of Ossory, who was nephew of Most Rev. Dr. Thomas Tenison, Archbishop of Canterbury, and great-grandson of Very Rev. Philip Tenison, Archdeacon of Norwich (1586-1660).—[Burke's *Landed Gentry*: "Tenison of Portnelligan."]

author of *History, Law, and Practice of Banking,* and other works; m. in 1879 Elizabeth-Isabel, dau. of Wm. Crompton-Ashlin, Esq., of Cloughton, Birkenhead, and has issue, a son and daughter.

II. Alfred Tenison Collins, now (1887) Secy. of Hibernian Bank, Dublin; married and has issue.

III. Mary MacCarthy Collins, unm.

III. Philip Tenison Collins, M.D. of Wednesbury, died 1882, leaving issue:

Edwd. Tenison Collins, M.D., of Wednesbury, married.

EARL.

THE following is the epitaph inscribed by Father Earl's parishoners on his monumental tablet in Carbury Chapel, county Kildare, referred to in the " Earl" pedigree, p. 433, *ante :*

" Underneath lie the remains of the Rev. Edward Earl, late Parish Priest of Carbury and Dunforth, which he governed for 25 years with great piety and enlightened zeal. He died on the 29th Sept., 1846, in the 72nd year of his age, sincerely regretted and beloved by all his people.

Beati Mortui qui in Domino Moriuntur. Requiescat in pace. Amen."

MACCARTHY.

IN Note at foot of page 126, *ante*, read as follows :

128. Charles : son of Charles ; born 1778, d. *circa* 1846 ; married Miss Turner, of Rosanna, Tipperary ; was a Lieutenant in Tipperary Militia, and a Civil Engineer ; had issue : 1. Charles Ffennell ; 2. Solomon (lost at sea, unm.) ; 1. Sarah (see below), and several other daughters.

129. Rev. Charles-Ffennell Mac-Carthy, his son, D.D. : Rector of St. Werburgh's, Dublin ; born 1818 ; m. Miss Sophia Reardon, and had issue : 1. Charles ; 2. William ; and four daughters ; he died 1877, and was buried in the crypt of Werburgh's church.

130. Charles : his son ; an M.D. ; resident at Hong-Kong : married and has issue.

Sarah, daughter of Charles (No. 128 *supra*), married in 1848 Joseph Tenison-Collins (eldest surviving son of John Collins, Esq., of Dominick-street, Dublin, by Ellen, daughter of Rev. Joseph Tenison, of Wicklow, great-grandson of Right Rev. Dr. Edward Tenison, Bishop of Ossory, who was son of William, elder brother of His Grace Dr. Thomas Tenison, Archbishop of Canterbury (1636-1715), and great-grandson of Rev. Philip Tenison, Archdeacon of Norwich (1586-1660); she d. 1854, leaving issue two sons and one daughter :

I. Charles MacCarthy Collins, b. 1850 ; called to the Irish Bar, 1879 ; to the English Bar

(Middle Temple) 1884; to the
Queensland Bar, 1883; a
Member of the Royal Irish
Academy; a Fellow of the
Institute of Bankers; J.P. for
the Colony of Queensland;
author of "*History, Law, and
Practice of Banking*," "*Celtic
Irish Songs and Song Writers*,"
and other works. He married
in 1879 Elizabeth-Isabel, dau.

of Wm. Crompton-Ashlin, Esq.,
of Cloughton, Birkenhead, and
has issue: 1. Julian Tenison, b.
1885; 1. Eva-Mabel, b. 1880.
Resident in Brisbane, Queensland; living in 1887.

II. Alfred Tenison Collins, born
1852; Secretary of Hibernian
Bank, Dublin (1887); married
and has issue:

I. Mary MacCarthy Collins, unm.

MAGAURAN.

OF this family is (see p. 573, *ante*) "McGowran," which is one of the
anglicised forms of the Irish sirname *MacSamhradhain*.

The ancient Armorial Bearings of "McGowran" were: *Arms*—Gu. two lions ppr.
and one lion pass. surmounted with a crown in centre. *Crest:* A demi ramp. lion gu.
Motto: Vincit veritas.

The McGoverns or McGowrans, etc., are of the Hy-Briuin race, and
are descended from Brian, the first King of Connaught of the Hy-Niall
Sept, and the eldest brother of the Monarch Niall of the Nine Hostages,
who is No. 87 on the "O'Neill" (No. 1), of Tyrone, pedigree. They were
the Lords and Chieftains of the ancient barony of Tullaghaw, co. Cavan,
generally known (see the "Dolan" pedigree, *ante*,) as the Kingdom of
Glan or Glangavlin or the Country of the MacGaurans. (See Lewis's
Topographical Dictionary of Ireland, 1837.) "MacGauran's Country" is
about sixteen miles in length by seven in breadth. In Queen Elizabeth's
reign Commissioners were in 1584 sent there, and by them the whole
territory of the County Cavan was partitioned into seven baronies, one of
those baronies (Tullaghaw) being assigned to the Sept MacGauran. On
the confiscation of six counties in Ulster, during the Ulster Plantation, in
the reign of James I., the County Cavan was planted with British colonies,
and, according to Connellan, the MacGaurans received 1,000 acres.

A complete list of the chiefs, from A.D. 1220 to 1532, is given in
O'Donovan's translation of the "Four Masters." The Sept prides itself
on having had a Catholic Archbishop, viz., Edmond MacGauran, Primate
of Armagh, and two bishops.

A Mr. Bartholomew Joseph McGovern went to Liverpool about the
year 1846, and there attained a high social position. R.I.P. He left
two sons, viz., the Rev. John Bernard McGovern, and Mr. Joseph Henry
McGovern, architect, who are the authors of a History of the Clan,
together with a number of other works. Both living in 1887.

CORRIGENDA.

MacDONNELL. (No. 1.)

ACCORDING to some genealogists, Gilla Espuig, who (see p. 530, *ante*) is No. 117 on the " MacDonnell" (No. 1) pedigree, was son, *not* of Sir James of Dunluce, but of Colla, the elder brother of Sorley Buidhe, who is No. 115 on that page. That Colla, who mar. a MacQuillan, was known as Coll-dhu-na-Gappal (or " dark-featured Colla, of the Horses"), and died in May, 1558.

Commencing with No. 124 on p. 531, the pedigree should read as follows :—

124. James McDonnell, Barrister-at-Law (living in 1887), who mar. Rosanna Cairns (sister of Earl Cairns), and has two daughters, but no male issue. This James has a brother Robert, M.D., of 89 Merrion-square, Dublin (also living in 1887), who mar. Susan, dau. of Sir Richard McCausland, and has one son John.

125. John McDonnell: son of said Robert; living in 1887.

MADDEN. (No. 1.)

COMMENCING with No. 130, on this family pedigree, p. 569, the first sentence should read :—

130. Richd.-Robert Madden, M.D., F.R.C.S., London: the twenty-first and youngest child of Edward; b. in 1798 in Dublin; mar. Harriet Elmslie, who by a singular coincidence was, like her husband, the twenty-first and youngest child of her father, the late John Elmslie of Berners-street, London, and of Surge Island Estate, Jamaica.

O'BYRNE. (No. 3.)

COMMENCING with No. 136, p. 620, *ante*, read :—

136. Garrett (2), of Ballymanus: son of Garrett; mar. to Miss Colclough of Tintern. Will dated 1767. Had three sons : 1. Garrett; 2. John of Dunganstown, who mar. Miss Byrne of Wicklow, and from whom William Colclough O'Byrne of Ballycapple was descended; 3. Colclough, etc. (same as is recorded in the remainder of the paragraph.)

And, commencing with Anna-Frances, who (see p. 622) is the daughter of William-Colclough O'Byrne, No. 139 on the same pedigree, read :—

I. Anna-Frances, mar. to Garrett Byrne of Ballyvaltron.
140. Garrett - Michael O'Byrne, Merchant of Wicklow: son of William Colclough O'Byrne; living in 1887.

I.—ENGLISH INVASION OF IRELAND.

IN the middle ages the Popes claimed and exercised great temporal power, which, in the main, they exercised for the general good. The Merovingian dynasty was changed on the decision of Pope Zachary. If Frederick the First did not renounce all pretensions to ecclesiastical property in Lombardy, he was threatened by Pope Adrian with the forfeiture of the Crown received from him and through his Unction.

In 1211, Pope Innocent the Third pronounced sentence of Deposition against King John of England, and conferred that kingdom on Philip Augustus, who instantly prepared to assert his claim; although he had no manner of title, except the Papal Grant. And, in 1493, Pope Alexander the Sixth gave the whole continent of America to Ferdinand and Isabella of Spain; ostensibly because the nations which then inhabited that continent were *infidels*.

King Henry II., of England, ascended the throne, A.D. 1154, and was contemporary with Pope Adrian the Fourth, who was, himself, an Englishman, and whose name originally was Nicholas Brakespeare; to whom Henry sent John of Salisbury, the Secretary of Thomas-à-Becket, archbishop of Canterbury, to make certain representations and stipulations respecting the Kingdom of Ireland, which Henry had long coveted.

In the exercise of his temporal power, Pope Adrian IV. did, regardless of every right, transfer the sovereignty of Ireland to the Crown of England; not because the Irish people of that period were "infidels"* (which they certainly were not), but because Adrian IV., in his love of country, naturally wished to aggrandize England !

Among the volumes in the MS. Library of Trinity College, Dublin, is the *Collectanea Hiberniæ*, marked E. 3. 10, which includes the "Invasion and first Invaders of Ireland under Henry II.;" together with some interesting Annals relating to Ireland, commencing with A.D. 322, and ending A.D. 1590. Of those Annals the first is a strange one; for, it asserts that for thirteen years—namely, from 322 to 335, a certain Lady of the Pictish race had been engaged in the conversion of the Irish people to Christianity :

"Prin. Fid. Anno Dom. 322. Fuit conversio ad Christum Hibernorum, 335.

Mulier quædam genere Picta, Anno 322, reginæ infirmata Christi nomen illi inwisite prædicedit . . . effecit, regina regem docuit populum."—*Hector Boethus, Lib.* 6. *Historiæ Scotiæ.*

---

* *Infidels :* To the great piety and zeal of the Irish people for the glory of God, not only at the time of the English invasion, but since Christianity was first introduced into Ireland, the many remains of Abbeys, Churches and other Christian Monuments throughout the land even at the present day, bear ample testimony :

"Who sees these ruins, but will demand
What barbarous invader sacked the land :
And when he hears no Goth nor Turk did bring
The desolation, but a Christian King ;
While nothing but the name of Zeal appears
'Twixt our best actions and the worst of theirs,
What must he think, our sacrilege would spare,
When such the effects of our devotion are."

And the next entry asserts that in 432 Saint Patrick came from Rome to Ireland:

"A.D. 432. S. Patricius venit ad Hiberniam a Roma."

Later on in those Annals it is stated that, in 1142, the Abbey of Mellifont, in the county Louth, then known as the Kingdom of Uriel, was founded:

"A.D. 1142. Mellifons fundatur."

In page 48 of E. 3. 10, the following passage occurs:

"Apud Johannem Rossum Warricensem, De Terris Coronæ Anglicæ Annexis, extat Declaratio quomodo Dominum Hiberniæ ad Coronam Anglicæ devotutum, P. Adrianus (inquit.) Anno Dom. 1150 (1155, legend. ex. Mart°. Paris, et Rob°. de Monte) . . . concessit Regi Anglicæ Henrico Secundo Conquisitionem Hiberniæ . . . . Cujus . . . potestatem, causam et modum in Bulla sua ad Regem directa exprimit in his verbis: Adrianus, Servus Servorum Dei, Legibur Papale hoc Diploma, apud Girald. Cambr. De Expng. Hiberniæ, Lib. 2. Cap. 6. (pag.787, Edit. Camden) . . . et a Vernaculis Annalib. Johannis Stowe, ubi ex MS°. quo ille usus, ut Girald. Cambrensis exemplari . . . . Diplomati huic subjiciuntur, Orabo Dominica et Symbolum Apostolicum Anglicana lingua descripta, et Adrianus (ut videtur) populares suos transmissa."

And we have it on the authority of Mathew Parker, Archbishop of Canterbury, that Cardinal Pole, in a speech delivered by him in the Parliament of Westminster, announced that Pope Adrian, "led by his love of country," granted the Sovereignty (Imperium) of Ireland to Henry II., King of England:

"Hinc Cardinalis Polus in Oratione quam in patria lingua Westmonsterii in Parliamento habuit, dixit: Hadrianum Quartum Papam fuisse Angln. qui Noriegiam primus Christiana fide imbuit, amore que patriæ ductus, Imperium Hiberniæ, quæ Pontificiæ ditionis fuerat, Henrico Secundo Anglorum Rege concessit." (*Ut est apud Mat. Parker, in Cant. Archiep. Histor., pag.* 415. *Lib.* 33.)

Acting, however, under the advice of his Mother, the Princess Maude, Henry II. did not for many years advance any pretensions to the sovereignty of Ireland, under the Papal grant. But, A.D. 1167, occurred a plausible opportunity for realizing the dream of his life—the *Annexation* of Ireland to England; when, unhappily, Celt was pitted against Celt, on account of the abduction* of the unfortunate Dearvorgal ("dear :" Irish, *a daughter*; "forgil," *purely fair*), the wife of Tiernan O'Rourke (No. 112 on the

---

* *Abduction*: The Dearvorgal here mentioned was daughter of Murcha, the last King of Meath. In his *Irish Melodies*, in "The Song of O'Ruarc," Thomas Moore commemorates that event of melancholy importance to Ireland; of that song the following is a stanza:

> " There *was* a time, falsest of women !
>   When Breffni's good sword would have sought
> That man, through a million of foemen,
>   Who dared but to doubt thee *in thought !*
> While now——O degenerate daughter
>   Of Erin, how fallen is thy fame !
> And through ages of bondage and slaughter,
>   Our country shall bleed for thy shame."

" O'Rourke" pedigree, Prince of West Brefney, by Dermod MacMorough King of Leinster, which led in that year to the invasion of Dermod's Kingdom by the Irish Monarch, Roderick O'Connor, King of Connaught, who espoused the cause of O'Rourke. Defeated by the Irish Monarch King Dermod fled to England, to invoke the aid of Henry II.; offering to become his liegeman if Henry would assist him :

"A.D. 1167. Diarmicius, Rex Laginiæ (Leinster), transfretavit in Anglia ad adducendos Anglicos."

On receiving Dermod's Oath of Allegiance, Henry II. granted a general licence to all his English subjects to aid King Dermod in the recovery of his Kingdom. Dermod then engaged in his cause Richard de Clare, commonly known as " Strongbow,"† through whose influence an army was raised, headed by Robert Fitzstephen, Myler Fitzhenry, Harvey de Monte Marisco, Maurice Prendergast, Maurice Fitzgerald, and others; who in May, 1168, landed in Ireland, in Bannow, in the county Wexford (a portion of Dermod's Kingdom) :

"A.D. 1168. Circa Kal. Maii applimerunt Anglici primo apud Bannam."

When, to relieve Fitzstephen, Strongbow was marching to the town of Wexford, through the barony of Idrone, he was confronted and briskly assaulted by O'Rian, Chief of that territory; but O'Rian being slain by an arrow, shot at him by Nichol the Monk, O'Rian's troops were scattered and many of them slain. It was there that Strongbow's only son, a youth about seventeen years old, frighted with the numbers, ululations, and prowess of the Irish troops, ran away from the battle and made towards Dublin; but, being informed of his father's victory, the son came back to congratulate him. Strongbow, however, having first reproached his son with cowardice, caused him to be immediately executed, by cutting him off in the middle with a sword. The epitaph on Strongbow and his son in Christ Church Dublin, is as follows :

"Nate ingrate mihi pugnanti terga dedisti; Non mihi sed genti Regno quoque terga dedisti."

St. Thomas a-Beckett, Archbishop of Canterbury, was, in 1170, assassinated; at the instance, it was said, of King Henry II., who, to divert public attention in England from that crime, then prepared to advance his claim to Ireland, under the Papal grant :

" A.D. 1170. "Martyr. est B. Thomas, Cant. Archiep."

Accordingly, King Henry lost no time in conveying through his friends to the Irish people the knowledge of the Papal grant with respect to Ireland, conferred on him by Adrian IV.; for, Henry by that time knew how hopeless it was for him to expect the conquest of Ireland by *force of arms;* and he well knew that, in their deep veneration for the Pope, the Irish would consider it a grievous crime to combat Papal Authority, on the subject, even though that authority had unjustly deprived them of their country and their liberty. However, Henry, in 1171, sent over Strongbow with two thousand soldiers and other warriors; to assist, so far as the

† *Strongbow* : See Paper, headed " Strongbow," in the Appendix to Vol. II.

display of a military force could do so, in the promulgation in Ireland of Pope Adrian's Bull:

"A.D. 1171. Richardus Strongbow Comes Pembrochiæ intravit Hiberniam in 2,000 militib. et aliis bellatoribus."

And afterwards, in the same year, King Henry II., himself, with great pomp and ceremony, came into Ireland :

"A.D. 1171. Henricus Rex Angliæ in Hiberniam venit."

The promulgation in Ireland of Pope Adrian's Bull acted as a *Spell* on the Irish people; for, says Prendergast*—

" The English coming in the name of the Pope, with the aid of the bishops . . . were accepted by the Irish. Neither King Henry the Second nor King John ever fought a battle in Ireland."

In obedience to the Bull† of Pope Adrian IV. (and believing the promises of King Henry II., that he only desired the *annexation* of Ireland to England, but in no instance to disturb or dispossess any of the Irish Kings, Chiefs, or people), the States (Ordines) of Ireland ; Roderick O'Connor, Monarch of Ireland: Dermod MacCarthy, King of Cork ; Donal O'Brien, King of Limerick ; O'Carroll, King of Uriel ; MacShaghlin, King of Offaley; O'Rourke, King of West Brefney ; O'Neill,‡ King of Ulster, and all their Nobles, did, in 1172, under their Signs Manual, transfer to King Henry the Second of England all their Authority (Imperium) and Power:

"Recitato P. Adriani Diplomate, subdit Johannes Rossus : Rex ergo Henricus circa Festum S. Michaelis, Winton Parliamento de conquirenda Hibernia cum suis optimatibus tractavit . . . Sed ex consilio Matris ejus Matildis Imperatricis res in aliud tempus dilata . . . Anno postea 1172°. omne imperium suum et potestatem in Henricum Secundum transtulerunt Hiberniæ Ordines ; Rothericus O'Conor Dun, Hiberniæ Monarcha; Dermot Mac Cartye, Rex Corcagii ; Donald O'Bren, Rex Limerici ; O'Carol, Rex Urielæ ; MacShaghlin, Rex Ophaliæ ; O'Rork, Rex Brefniæ ; O'Neal, Rex Ultoniæ ; proceres que reliqui et populus ipsorum, Chartis subsignatis, oraditis, ad Romam transmissis." (*Camden pag.* 731, *ex Girald. Camb. et MS.° pere Baronem Houth.*)

"Johannes Hardingus in Chronicis suis, Cap. 132°, hac de re in hunc modum scribit :"

> " The King Henry then conquered all Ireland
> By Papal dome, there of his royaltee
> The Profytes and revenues of the lande
> The Dominacion and the Soveрayntee
> For ewour which against the spirituallee
> They held full long, and would not be connecte
> With heresyes, with which they were infacte."

---

* *Prendergast :* See Prendergast's " Cromwellian Settlement of Ireland" (Dublin : McGlashan and Gill, 1875).

† *Bull :* That such a Bull ever existed is sometimes disputed ; but, unfortunately, it is but too true that Adrian IV., in the exercise of his temporal power as Pope, did issue a Bull annexing the Kingdom of Ireland to the Crown of England. (See the Paper headed " The Invasion of Ireland by Bruce," in the Appendix to Vol. II.)

‡ *O'Neill :* It is right to mention that this statement relating to O'Neill, King of Ulster, is disputed. We, however, give the statement as we found it in the MS. Volume *Collectanea Hiberniæ,* marked E. 3.10 in the Library of T.C.D., Dublin.

Et Cap. 241°. Rego Edwardi jus ad dominia sua breviter explicans :

"To Ireland also, by King Henry le Fytz of Maude, daughter of firste King Henry that conquered it, for theyr great heresye."

Harding, in the two foregoing Extracts, says that (1) Henry "conquered all Ireland by Papal dome ;" and (2) that he "conquered it, for theyr great heresye." But, in Ireland, there was no "heresye" (in the religious sense of the term) then known ; unless indeed that the *refusal* of some of the Irish Kings and Princes to acknowledge the right of Pope Adrian IV. to transfer their sovereignty to King Henry II., may have been considered a "heresy !" In the military sense of the term, there never was a *conquest* of Ireland by King Henry the Second of England.

It will be seen that the name of Murcha O'Melaghlin, the last King of Meath, was not amongst the signatures above mentioned as sent to Rome (Chartis subsignatis, oraditis, ad Romam transmissis), notifying Pope Adrian IV. of their assent to his transfer of their respective sovereignties to King Henry II. ; for, while second to none in their veneration for the Pontiff, and their zeal for the advancement of the Christian religion, Murcha* and his Nobility could not recognize in Pope Adrian IV. any authority to transfer to King Henry II., or to any other foreign potentate, the sovereignty of their kingdom, and, with their sovereignty, the power of dispossessing themselves and their people of their ancient patrimonies.

But Henry II. had his revenge ; for one of his first public acts in Ireland was to depose King Murcha, confiscate his and most of his nobles' patrimonies, and confer on Hugh de Lacy the Kingdom of Meath : as a nucleus for an English Plantation of Ireland. That kingdom afterwards formed the principal portion of the English Pale.† In 1172, King Henry II. landed at Waterford with five hundred horsemen, to enter into possession of the Kingdom of Ireland, under the Papal grant ; and, in that year also, Murcha (called in State Papers Murchard), the last King of Meath, died of a broken heart :‡

"A.D. 1172. Henricus Rex cum 500 equitibus Waterfordia. Fraiectis tota Middia Hugoni De Lacii donavit. Et (ut aiunt) hoc anno Murchardus obit."

---

* *Murcha :* Giraldus Cambrensis and other English writers, of his *anti*-Irish stamp have grossly libelled the Irish people ; to justify their subjugation by King Henry II., of England. Yet, among the many other Irish Kings and Princes who founded and endowed the Abbeys of Ireland before its annexation to England, it was this Irish King, who, in his great piety, founded and endowed the Abbey of Bective, in the county Meath.

† *English Pale :* This was the portion of Ireland which was subject to the regular jurisdiction of the King of England and his laws ; while that portion of Ireland which was outside the English Pale was called the "Irish Country." In 1603, however, the distinction between the "English Pale" and "Irish Country" terminated, by the submission of Hugh O'Neill, Earl of Tirowen : for it was in that year, and by that submission, that the English conquest of Ireland was first effected.

‡ *Broken Heart :* This Murcha, as already mentioned, was the father of the unfortunate Dearvorgil, who was the ostensible cause of the invasion of Ireland by Henry II. Unhappily, Murcha insisted that she should marry O'Rourke, Prince of Brefney, in preference to Dermod MacMorough, King of Leinster, with whom she afterwards eloped ; for Dearvorgil loved MacMorough "not wisely but too well."

The Irish Monarch, Roderick O'Connor, finding that King Henry II. had thus so soon violated his solemn promise, that he would not dispossess any of the Irish people of their ancient patrimonies, sincerely regretted having given his assent to the Papal grant of Ireland by Adrian IV. to Henry II.; for O'Connor saw that Henry would act towards the Kings and Princes of other parts of Ireland as he had done to the King and Nobles of the Kingdom of Meath.   Accordingly the Irish Monarch assembled an Army to resist Hugh de Lacy's possession of that Kingdom.

We read in page 16 of the MS. Vol. F. 3. 16, in the Lib. of Trin. Coll., Dub., that:

"Hugh de Lacy had built a strong castle at Tryme [Trim], surrounded with a deep and large ditch; which being furnished and competently garnished, he departed for England, leaving the same in the custody of Hugh Tirrell. The king of Connaught, to destroy it, assembled all the forces he could make; the principal of his Armie who were Commanders and Chieftains were—O'fflahertie, M'Dermond, M'Ghorathie; O'Kelly, King of O'Many; O'Harthiee, O'Himathie, O'Carbry, O'fflanogan, O'Manethan, O'Dude; O'Shaghnes of Poltiloban; the King O'Malachlin, the King O'Rory (alias O'Rourke); O'Noil of Kinell; O'Malory; M'Donleve, King of Ulster; the King O'Carvill; M'Tarvene, M'Skilling, M'Cartan, M'Garraga, M'Kelan; O'Neale, King of Kinelogmh, and manie others whose names are omitted that put themselves into O'Connor's Armie, with purpose to destroye ye castle of Trym."*

"Hugh Tirrell being advertised of their comeinge dispatched messengers unto the Earle, beseeching him to come to his aid.   The Earle presently assembled his forces and marched towarde Trim; but Hugh Tirrell seeing the Enemie at hand, and findinge himselfe too weak to make resistance against their multitude, abandoned the castle and burned it.   The Irish Kings perceiving that done to their hande which they intended to have done by force, returned towards their own countries.   The Earle upon his way meeting with intelligence that Trim was burned, marched on, and when he came thither he neyther found castle nor house to lodge in, wherefore he made noe staie but pursued the Enemie and fell upon the reare, of whom 150 were slain; which done he returned to Dublin, and Hugh Tirrell to the ruined castle of Trim, to reedifie the same before Hugh de Lacy his return out of England."

King Henry's emissaries throughout Ireland continued unceasing in proclaiming to the Irish people the Bull of Pope Adrian IV. conferring on Henry II. the sovereignty of Ireland.   In their simplicity the people believed that the said Bull was Heaven-inspired, and that it would be blasphemy or worse to gainsay it.   They therefore relaxed (and most of them ceased) their resistance to King Henry's pretensions to the sovereignty of Ireland, under the Papal grant; but some of the Irish Chiefs,† while bowing in matters spiritual to the authority of the Pope, maintained their national independence, down to A.D. 1603.

---

* *Trym* : The present anglicised forms of the names of the Commanders and Chieftains in the Irish Monarch's Army on that occasion were—O'Flaherty, MacDermott, MacGeraghty, O'Kelly, O'Hart, O'Hughes, O'Carbery, O'Flanagan, O'Monaghan, O'Dowde, O'Shaughnessy; Murcha O'Melaghlin, the King of Meath; O'Neill, O'Mulroy, MacDonleavy; O'Carroll, king of Uriel; . . . . MacGarry, MacKilleen, O'Neill, etc.

† *Irish Chiefs:*—

" Oh! to have lived like an IRISH CHIEF when hearts were fresh and true,
   And a manly thought, like a pealing Bell, would quicken them through and through;

Thus, by virtue of the Papal grant, King Henry II. obtained possession of the Kingdom of Ireland ; and Hugh de Lacy and his barons obtained and held possession of the Province of Meath.

In the Charter granting the Kingdom of Meath* to Hugh de Lacy, and dated at Wexford, A.D. 1172, King Henry II. says :

"Henry, by the grace of God, king of England, duke of Normandy and Aquitain, and earl of Anjou, to the archbishops, bishops, abbots, earls, barons, justices, and to all his ministers, and faithful subjects, French, English, and Irish, of all his dominions, greeting : Know ye that I have given and granted, and, by this my Charter, confirmed unto Hugh de Lacy, in consideration of his services, the land of Meath, with the appurtenances ; to have and to hold of me and my heirs, to him and his heirs, by the service of fifty knights, in as full and ample manner as Murchard Hu-Melaghlin held it, or any other person before him or after him ; and, as an addition, I give to him all fees which he owes or shall owe to me about Duvelin [Dublin], while he is my bailiff, to do me service in my city of Duvelin. Wherefore I will and strictly command, that the said Hugh and his heirs shall enjoy the said land, and shall hold all the liberties and free customs which I have or may have therein, by the aforesaid service, from me and my heirs, well and peaceably, freely, quietly and honourably, in wood and plain, in meadows and pastures, in water and mills, in warren and ponds, in fishings and huntings, in ways and paths, in sea-ports and all other places appertaining to the said land, with all liberties which I have therein, or can grant or confirm to him by this my Charter.

"Witness, earl Richard (Strongbow), son of Gilbert ; William de Brosa (and many others), at Weisford (Wexford)."—WARE.

At the Synod of the bishops and clergy, held at Waterford, A.D. 1175, William Fitzadelm de Burgo (who succeeded Strongbow as chief governor of Ireland) published the Bull of Pope Alexander III., confirming the Papal grant of Ireland by Adrian IV., to King Henry II. of England.

According to Rymer's *Fœdera*, Vol. i., p. 31 (Folio. London : 1816), King Henry II., in 1175, at Windsor, after the publication, at the Synod of Waterford, of the Bull of Pope Alexander III., entered into a Treaty with the Irish Monarch, which was signed on O'Connor's behalf, as King of Connaught and Chief King of Ireland, by two of the Pope's new Archbishops of Ireland. By that treaty Roderick O'Connor is made to become the King's liegeman, and to be King of Connaught, and Chief King of Ireland under Henry the Second. The Irish Monarch undertakes :

"That the Irish shall yield to the King of England annually one merchantable hide for every ten cows in Ireland, which Roderick O'Connor is to collect for him

---

And the seed of a generous hope right soon to a fiery action grew,
And Men would have scorned to talk and talk, and never a deed to do.

Oh ! the iron grasp
And the kindly clasp
And the laugh so fond and gay ;
And the roaring board,
And the ready sword,
Were the types of that vanished day."

CHARLES GAVAN DUFFY.

* *Meath :* The Kingdom of Meath consisted of two great divisions, namely, *Magh Breagh* (or Bregia), and *Teabhtha* (or Teffia). Bregia, which was that magnificent plain situated in the eastern part of the kingdom, comprised five *triocha-cheds* or baronies, and included Fingal, a territory lying along the coast between Dublin and Drogheda ; and Teffia comprised the present County Westmeath, with parts of Longford and the King's County. Some of the chiefs of that kingdom, particularly those of Teffia, held their estates down to the Cromwellian confiscations.

through every part of Ireland, except that which is already in the possession of King Henry II. and his barons—namely, Dublin, Meath, and Leinster, with Waterford as far as Dungarvan. The rest of the Kings and people of Ireland are to enjoy all their lands and liberties as long as they shall continue faithful to the King of England, and pay this tribute through the hands of the King of Connaught."—See Prendergast's *Cromwellian Settlement*, p. 14.

According to that treaty it appears that King Henry II. never effected the *military* conquest of Ireland, and that his authority in that country was acquired solely through the influence on the Irish people, of Pope Adrian's Bull in Henry's favour ; for, says Prendergast—

"Two systems were thus established side by side in Ireland, the Feudal and the Brehon systems ; for the Irish, as Sir John Davis remarks, merely became tributaries to the King of England, preserving their ancient Brehon law, and electing their chiefs and tanists, making war and peace with one another, and ruling all things between themselves by this law, until the reign of Queen Elizabeth ; and this, as Spenser remarks, not merely in districts entirely inhabited by Irish, but in the English parts."—*Ibid.* p. 15.

As Ireland had long acknowledged the jurisdiction of the Holy See (*Pontificiæ ditionis fuerat*), it grieves us to find that Adrian IV., as a Pontiff of the Church to which we belong, was so swayed by his love of country (*amore patriæ*), as to issue the now famous Bull annexing Ireland to England ; for, that Bull, it may be said, was the *fons et origo* of all the wrongs since inflicted on Ireland by England. But :

"Could the chain for an instant be riven
Which tyranny flung round us then,
Oh ! 'tis not in man nor in Heaven
To let tyranny bind it again."

—Moore.

II.—CROMWELLIAN DEVASTATION OF IRELAND.

As one of the ancient Irish families which have drunk to the dregs of the bitter cup of adversity, consequent on the Cromwellian confiscations in Ireland, we have ventured to introduce this Paper by a few observations on our own family :

At the time of the English invasion of Ireland the O'Harts were located in the Kingdom of Meath ; and, as Princes of Tara, ranked next to Murcha, Meath's last King. For a short history of that invasion, its causes, and some of its unhappy consequences to Ireland, the reader is referred to the " English Invasion of Ireland," next, *ante ;* and, for the patrimony of our family, see Note (*), p. 672.

Dispossessed of that patrimony by King Henry II., Shane O'Hart, No. 106, p. 672, who was the last Prince of Tara, settled in the territory now known as the barony of Carbury, in co. Sligo,* which O'Mulroy, the Prince of

---

* *Sligo :* " Carbury," in the county Sligo, where the last Prince of Tara settled after he was dispossessed of his patrimony in the kingdom of Meath, then belonged to the principality of Tirconnell.

Tirconnell, of that period, granted to him.   The Prince of Tara's descendants acquired and held other landed property in the barony of Leyney,
in the said county ; down to the middle of the seventeenth century, when,
as they were "Papist Proprietors" (see No. 120, p. 676), their estates
were, A.D. 1652, confiscated, under the Cromwellian settlement of Ireland.

At the Restoration, some of the Irish gentry, who had good interest
at court, got back their estates, which had been confiscated under the
"Protectorate" of Cromwell; others obtained decrees of the Court of
Claims, to be restored to their ancient inheritances ; but as the Cromwellian
adventurers,* officers, and soldiers in possession were not to be removed
without being first reprised (that is, provided with other lands of equal
value, which were not to be had, so large was the number of Cromwellian
claimants for whom provision had to be made in Ireland), the dispossessed
owners, especially the ancient Irish, were not restored.

> "The master's bawn, the master's land, a surly *bodagh*† fills ;
> The master's son, and outlaw'd man, is riding on the hills."

Driven from their homes and lands, these dispossessed Irish owners
wandered, many of them, about their ancient inheritances, living upon the
bounty of their former tenants, or joined some band of Tories :‡

"The poor Irish peasantry," writes Prendergast, "with a generosity characteristic of their race and country, never refused hospitality to the dispossessed owners,
but maintained them as gentlemen ; allowing them to 'cosher' upon them as the Irish
called the giving their lord a certain number of days' board and lodging."

Archbishop King (see King's "State of the Protestants of Ireland
under the Government of King James the Second."   Dublin : 1730.) and
the Cromwellian possessors of the lands of these dispossessed Irish gentlemen complained much of their pride and idleness in not becoming
labourers to them (the new possessors) !

"Their sons or nephews," writes King, "brought up in poverty, and matched
with peasant girls, will become the tenants of the English officers and soldiers ; and,

---

* *Adventurers :* In sect. 12, of the Paper in the Appendix to Vol. II., headed "The
New Divisions of Ireland, and the New Settlers," see the names of the Adventurers for
Land in Ireland, at the time of the Cromwellian Settlement of that unhappy country.

† *Bodagh :* The correct Irish word is *bodach*, which means "a churlish, surly
fellow."

‡ *Tories :* The "Tories" of that period, who were more lately known as *Rapparees,*
were bands of men who retired to the wilds or mountains rather than transplant themselves from any of the other provinces wherein their confiscated estates were situated ;
and, headed by some of the dispossessed gentlemen, incessantly attacked the Cromwellian planters.   In those troublous times in Ireland, the *Priest* and the *Tory* were
classed with the *wolf*, as the three burdensome "beasts" on whose heads were set
rewards ; for, according to "Burton's Parliamentary Diary," of the 10th June, 1657,
Major Morgan, Member for the county Wicklow, in the first United Parliament of the
Three Kingdoms, at Westminster, A.D. 1657, deprecated the taxation proposed for
Ireland, by showing that the country was then in ruins, and said : "We have three
beasts to destroy, that lay burdens upon us.   The first is the wolf, on whom we lay
five pounds a head if a dog, and ten pounds if a bitch.   The second beast is a priest,
on whose head we lay ten pounds ; if he be eminent, more.   The third beast is a Tory,
on whose head if he be a public Tory we lay twenty pounds ; and forty shillings on a
private Tory.   Your army cannot catch them ; the Irish bring them in ; brothers and
cousins cut one another's throats."

thence reduced to labourers, will be found the turf-cutters and potato-diggers of the next generation."

The dispossessed Irish proprietors, or their sons, who remained in Ireland, were the gentlemen, who, in 1707, were described in the (Irish) Act, 6 Anne, c. 2, "For the more effectual suppression of Tories;" and who were, on presentment of any Grand Jury of the counties which they frequented, to be seized and sent on board the Queen's fleet, or as slaves to Barbadoes, or to some of the English Plantations in America :

"One of the first steps towards the Cromwellian Settlement of Ireland," writes the learned Prendergast, "was to get rid of the disbanded *Irish* soldiery. Foreign nations were apprised by the Articles of Kilkenny, that the Irish were to be allowed to engage in the service of any state in amity with the Commonwealth. The valour of the Irish soldier was well known abroad. From the time of the Munster Plantation by Queen Elizabeth, numerous Irish exiles had taken service in the Spanish Army. There were Irish regiments serving in the Low Countries . . . Agents from the King of Spain, the King of Poland, and the Prince de Condé, were contending for the services of Irish troops . . . The thirteen years' war,* from 1641 to 1654, followed by the departure from Ireland to Spain of 40,000 Irish soldiers, most with the chief nobility and gentry, had left behind a mass of widows and deserted wives with destitute families. There were plenty of other persons too, who, as their ancient properties had been confiscated, had 'no visible means of livelihood. Just as the King of Spain sent over his agents to treat with the Government for the Irish swordsmen, the merchants of Bristol had agents treating with it for men, women, boys, and girls, to be sent to the sugar plantations in the West Indies. The Commissioners for Ireland gave to those agents orders upon the governors of garrisons, to deliver to them prisoners of war ; upon the keepers of gaols, for offenders in custody ; upon masters of workhouses, for the destitute in their care ' who were of an age to labour, or, if women, were marriageable and not past breeding;' and gave directions to all in authority to seize those who had no visible means of livelihood, and to deliver them to the agents of the Bristol sugar merchants; in the execution of which direction Ireland must have exhibited scenes in every part like the slave hunts in Africa. How many girls† of gentle birth must have been caught and hurried to the private prisons of these men-catchers none can tell . . . Ireland, in the language of Scripture, now lay void as a wilderness. Five-sixths of her people had perished. Women and children were found daily perishing in ditches, starved. The bodies of many wandering orphans, whose fathers had embarked for Spain, and whose mothers had died of famine, were preyed upon by wolves. In the years 1652 and 1653, the plague and famine had swept away whole countries, that a man might travel twenty or thirty miles and not see a living creature. Man, beast, and bird, were all dead, or had quit those desolate places."

At that gloomy period in Irish history, the Irish people, it may be said, had realized the fate foretold (Leviticus xxvi. 31, 32,) for the Jews ; for, like that nation, the ancient Irish Proprietors and their children, who survived the Cromwellian devastation in Ireland, were, alas! scattered among all people, from one end of the earth unto the other.

By industry and education, however, many of the descendants of those

---

* *War*: See Note (†) under No. 116, p. 324.

† *Girls*: Morison, in his *Threnodia Hiberno Catholica* (Innsbruck : 1659), relates that, in his presence, Daniel Connery, a gentleman in the county Clare, was, in 1657, sentenced to banishment by Colonel Henry Ingoldsby, for harbouring a priest. Mr. Connery had a wife and twelve children. His wife fell sick and died in poverty. "Three of his daughters, beautiful girls, were transported to the West Indies, to an island called the Barbadoes ; and there, if still alive," he says, "they are miserable slaves."

3 E

Irish exiles, and of others who more lately were driven to seek homes in foreign lands, have, in those lands, attained to positions of social eminence; and, in England, Scotland, Canada, Australia, the great Western Republic, etc., possess considerable political influence. It is calculated that, in the United States of America, alone, the Irish race now constitutes an "Irish Nation," in population at least twice that at present in Ireland:

> "Long, long be my heart with such memories fill'd.
> Like the vase, in which roses have once been distill'd—
> You may break, you may shatter the vase if you will,
> But the scent of the roses will hang round it still."
> —MOORE.

APPENDIX.

I.—THE CHIEF IRISH* FAMILIES OF MUNSTER.

The following is a brief summary of the Irish families in Munster, beginning with the three branches of the race of Heber : namely, the Dalcassians, the Eugenians, and the Clan Cian.

I. *The Dalcassians :* According to Connellan, the chief families of this sept were—Lysacht, MacArthur, MacBruodin, MacClancy, MacConry, MacCurtin, MacDonnell, MacEniry, MacGrath, MacMahon, MacNamara, O'Ahern, O'Brien, O'Brody, O'Casey, O'Cashin, O'Considine, O'Davoran, O'Dea, O'Duhig, O'Grady, O'Hanraghan, O'Hartigan, O'Hea, O'Healy (modernized Haley and Hayley), O'Heap, O'Heffernan, O'Hehir, O'Hickey, O'Hogan, O'Hurly (modernized Harley), O'Kearney, O'Kennedy, O'Liddy, O'Lonergan, O'Meara, O'Molony, O'Noonan (or O'Nunan), O'Quinn, O'Shanahan (or O'Shannon), O'Sheehan, O'Slattery, O'Spillane, O'Twomey, etc.

The following were also of the Dalcassian race : the families of MacCoghlan, chiefs in the King's County ; O'Finnelan (or O'Fenelon), and O'Skully, chiefs in Teffia, or Westmeath.

II. *The Eugenians :* Of these the chief families were—MacAuliffe, MacCarthy, MacDonagh, MacElligot, MacFinneen, MacGillicuddy, O'Callaghan, O'Cullen, O'Donohoe, O'Finnegan, O'Flannery, O'Fogarty, O'Keeffe, O'Kerwick (anglicised "Berwick" and "Kirby"), O'Lechan (or Lyons), O'Mahony, O'Meehan, O'Moriarty, O'Sullivan, O'Treacy, etc.

III. *The Clan Cian* were, as already stated, located in Ormond or the present county of Tipperary ; and the heads of the Clan were O'Carroll, princes of Ely. The other families were—MacKeogh (or Kehoe), O'Corcoran, O'Dulbunty (anglicised O'Delahunty), O'Meagher. O'Connor, chiefs of Cianaght (now Keenaght) in the county Londonderry ; and O'Gara and O'Hara, lords of Lieny and Coolavin in the county Sligo, were also branches of the Clan Cian of Munster.

IV. The Ithians, who were also called Darinians, were descended from Ithe, or Ithius, uncle of Milesius.

V. The Clan-na-Deagha were also called Degadians and Ernans, from two of their distinguished ancestors ; they were celebrated chiefs in Munster, but were originally descended, as already shown, from the Heremonians of Ulster. Of this Clan the

---

* *Irish :* According to Connellan, many penal Acts of Parliament were in the reigns of the Henrys and Edwards, Kings of England, passed, compelling the ancient Irish to adopt English "surnames," and the English language, dress, manners, and customs ; and, no doubt, many of the Milesian Irish did take English surnames in those times, to protect their lives and properties, as, otherwise, they forfeited their goods and were liable to be punished as Irish enemies. Hence, many of the ancient Irish families did so twist and anglicise their names, that it is often difficult to determine whether those families are of Irish or English extraction ; and hence, many of them of Irish origin are considered of English or French descent. In modern times, too, many of the Irish families omitted the *O'* and *Mac* in their surnames ; but such names lose much of their euphonious sound by the omission, and, besides, are neither English nor Irish.

Some of the Danish families who settled in Ireland were those of Dowdall, Dromgoole, Sweetman and Palmer, in Dublin, Meath, and Louth ; Gould, Coppinger, Skiddy, and Trant, in Cork ; and Haroid (modernized *Harold*), of Limerick and Clare. Of those Danish families, some took Irish sirnames, and more of them prefixed "Mac" to their names, as did many of the Anglo-Norman and English families in early times. The following families adopted Irish surnames :—De Burgo, of Connaught, took the name of MacWilliam, and some of them that of MacPhilip ; De Angulo or Nangle, of Meath and Mayo, changed the name to MacCostello ; De Exeter of Mayo, to MacJordan ; Barrett, of Mayo, to MacWattin ; De Staunton of Mayo, to MacAveely (*mileadh :* Irish, *a hero*), signifying "The son of a hero ;" De Bermingham of Connaught and other places, to MacFeorais or MacPeoruis (signifying "The son of Pearse" or Percy, and a quo Pearse, Pearce, Peirs, Piers, Pearson, Pierson, Peterson), from one of their chiefs ; Fitzsimon of the King's County, to MacRuddery (*ridire :* Irish, *a knight*), signifying "The son of the knight ;" Le Poer (anglicised "Power") of Kilkenny and Waterford, to MacShere ; Butler, to MacPierce ; Fitzgerald to MacThomas and MacMaurice ; De Courcy of Cork, to MacPatrick ; Barry of Cork, to MacAdam, etc. But it does not appear that any of those families adopted the prefix "O," which, according to the Four Masters, was confined chiefly to the Milesian families of the highest rank.—CONNELLAN.

principal families in Munster were—O'Falvey, hereditary admirals of Desmond; O'Connell, of Kerry, Limerick, and Clare; O'Donegan, O'Fihilly, O'Flynn, O'Shee or O'Shea, O'Baisan or O'Basken, and O'Donnell of the county Clare, etc.

VI. The Irians (or "Clan-na-Rory") of Ulster also settled several families of note in Munster, as early as the first and second centuries; of whom were the following: O'Connor, lords or princes of Kerry; O'Connor, lords of Corcomroe in Clare; and O'Loghlin, lords of Burren, also in Clare. Of this race were also O'Farrell, lords or princes of Annaly; MacRannal (anglicised "Reynolds"), lords of Muintir Eoluis, in the county Leitrim, etc.

VII. Of the Leinster Milesians of the race of Heremon, were some chiefs and clans of note in Munster, as O'Felan, princes of Desies in Waterford; and O'Bric, chiefs in Waterford; O'Dwyer and O'Ryan, chiefs in Tipperary; and O'Gorman, chiefs in Clare.

King Henry the Second, A.D. 1180, granted part of the kingdom of Thomond to Herbert Fitzherbert; but he having resigned his claims, it was granted by King John to William and Philip de Braosa. In the thirteenth century, King Henry the Third gave to Thomas de Clare, son of the earl of Gloucester, a grant of the whole kingdom of Thomond or "O'Brien's Country," as it was called; but the O'Briens and other chiefs in Thomond maintained for centuries fierce contests with the Anglo-Norman and English settlers, in defence of their national independence.

II.—THE TERRITORIES OF THE ANCIENT IRISH FAMILIES.
I.—IN LIMERICK AND CLARE.
The Ancient Thomond.
(a) THE IRISH CHIEFS AND CLANS.

THE following were the Irish chiefs and clans of ancient Thomond, or the counties of Limerick and Clare: 1. **O'Dea**, chief of Dysart-O'Dea, now the parish of Dysart, barony of Inchiquin, county Clare. 2. **O'Quinn**, chief of Muintir Ifernain, a territory about Corofin in the county Clare. The **O'Heffernans** were the tribe who possessed this territory; over whom **O'Quinn** was chief. These **O'Quinns** had also possessions in Limerick, where they became earls of Dunraven. 3. **O'Flattery**, and **O'Cahil**, chiefs of Fianchora. 4. **O'Mulmea** (or **Mulmy**), chief of Breintire, now Brentry, near Callan hill, in the county Clare. 5. **O'Haichir** (or **O'Hehir**), chief of Hy-Flancha and Hy-Cormac, districts in the barony of Islands; and (according to O'Halloran) of Callan, in the county Clare. 6. **O'Duibhgin, O'Dugan,** (or **O'Deegan**), chief of Muintir Con-lochta, a district in the parish of Tomgraney, in the barony of Tullagh, county Clare. 7. **O'Grady**, chief of Cineal Dongally, a large territory comprising the present barony of Lower Tullagh, county Clare. The O'Gradys had also large possessions in the county Limerick; and, in modern times, the Right Hon. Standish O'Grady, Chief Baron of the Exchequer in Ireland, was A.D. 1831, created Viscount Guillamore. 8. **MacConmara** or **MacNamara** (literally *a warrior of the sea*) was chief of the territory of Clan Caisin, now the barony of Tullagh, in the county Clare. The Macnamaras were also sometimes styled chiefs of Clan Cuilean, which was the tribe name of the family; derived from Cuilean, one of their chiefs in the eighth century. This ancient family held the high and honourable office of hereditary marshals of Thomond. 9. **O'Connor**, chief of the territory of Fear Arda and of Corcomroe, at present a barony in the county Clare. 10. **O'Loughlin**, chief of Burren, now the barony of Burren, county Clare, which was sometimes called Eastern Corcomroe. The O'Loghlins and O'Connors here mentioned were of the same descent: namely, a branch of the Clan na Rory, descended from the ancient kings of Ulster of the race of Ir. 11. **O'Connell**, chief of Hy-Cuilean, a territory south-east of Abbeyfeale, in the barony of Upper Connello, on the verge of the county Limerick, towards the river Feale, and the borders of Cork and Kerry. According to O'Halloran, the O'Connells had their chief residence in Castle Connell, in the county Limerick. In the twelfth century the O'Connells settled in Kerry, where they had a large territory on the borders of their ancient possessions. According to O'Halloran, the O'Falvies, admirals of Desmond; the O'Connells, of Kerry; O'Sheas, chiefs of Muskerry, in Cork; and several other chiefs, were descended from the Clan na Deaga, celebrated chiefs of Munster, originally a branch of the Here-monians of Ulster. Of the Clan na Deaga, was Conaire the Second, Monarch of Ireland, who was married to Sarad (daughter of his predecessor, Conn of the Hundred Battles, Monarch of Ireland in the second century), by whom he had a son, named Cairbre Riada, from whom were descended the Dalriedians of Ulster, and of Scotland. A son of Cairbre Riada got large possessions in South Munster, in the present counties of Cork and Kerry. 12. **MacEneiry**, chiefs of Corca Muiceadha, also called Conaill Uachtarach, now the barony of Upper Conello, in the county Limerick. The Mac-Eneirys were descended from Mahoun, king of Munster, and brother of Brian Boru; and had their chief residence at Castletown MacEneiry. 13. **O'Billry**, a chief of Hy Conall Guara, now the baronies of Upper and Lower Conello, in the county Limerick. 14. **O'Cullen, O'Kenealy**, and **O'Sheehan**, were chiefs in the baronies of Conello, county Limerick. 15. **O'Macassa (Macassey**, and **Maxey)**, chief of Corca Oiche: and **O'Bergin**, chief of Hy-Rossa, districts in the county Limerick. 16. **O'Mulcallen**, a chief of Conriada, now the barony of Kenry, county Limerick. 17. **O'Clerkin** and **O'Flannery**, chiefs of Dal Cairbre Eva, in the barony of Kenry, county Limerick. 18. **O'Donovan**, chief of Cairbre Eva, now the barony of Kenry, which was the ancient territory of O'Donovan, O'Cleircin, and O'Flannery. The O'Donovans had their chief castle at Bruree, county Limerick. 19. **O'Ciarmhaie** (or **O'Kerwick**), chief of Eoganacht Aine, now the parish of Knockaney, in the barony of Small County, county Limerick. 20 **O'Muldoon**, also a chief of Eoganacht Aine, same as O'Kerwick. 21. **O'Kenealy**, chief of Eoganacht Grian Guara, a district comprising parts of the baronies of Coshma and Small County in Limerick. 22. **O'Gunning**, chief of Crioch Saingil and Aosgreine: Crioch Saingil, according to O'Halloran, is now "Single Land," and is situated near Limerick; and both the territories here mentioned are, according to O'Brien, com-prised in the barony of Small County, in Limerick. 23. **O'Caolidh** or **O'Keely**, and **O'Malley** are given as chiefs of Tua Luimnidh or "the district about Limerick." 24. **O'Keeffe**, chief of Triocha-Cead-an-Chaliadh, called Cala Luimne, that is the "port or ferry of Limerick." 25. **O'Hea**, chief of Muscry Luachra, a territory lying between Kilmallock and Ardpatrick, in the barony of Coshlea, in the county Limerick. 26. **MacDonnell** and **O'Baskin**, chiefs of the territories of Corca Baisgin or Baiscind, now the barony of Moyarta, in the county Clare. O'Mulcorcra was chief of Hy-Bracain, now the barony of Ibracken; and O'Keely—probably the O'Keely above named—was another chief of the same place. One of the Corca Baiscinds here mentioned was the present barony of Clonderlaw. 27. **MacMahon**. The MacMahons succeeded the above chiefs, as lords of Corca Baisgin; and possessed the greater part of the baronies of Moyarta and Clonderlaw, in the county Clare. In O'Brien's Dictionary these Mac-Mahons and MacDonnells are given as branches of the O'Briens, the posterity of Brian Boru; and, therefore, of quite a different descent from the MacMahons, princes and lords of Monaghan, and the MacDonnells, earls of Antrim, and the MacDonnells of Kilkee, county Clare, who were of the race of Clan Colla. 28. **O'Gorman**, chief of Tullichrin, a territory comprising parts of the baronies of Moyarta and Ibrackan, in the county Clare. 29. **O'Diocholla** and **O'Mullethy** or **Multhy**, were chiefs in Corcomroe. 30. **O'Drennan**, chief of Slieve Eise, Finn, and of Cinel-Seudna, a district on the borders of Clare and Galway. 31. **O'Neill**, chief of Clan Dalvy and of Tradree, a district in the barony of Inchiquinn, county Clare. A branch of this family went in the tenth century to Limerick, to assist in the expulsion of the Danes, over whom they gained several victories; and on one occasion, having worn green boughs in their helmets and on their horses' heads, they, from this circumstance, got the epithet *craebhach* (*i.e.* Ramifer), signifying *of the branches*: a name which has been anglicised "Creagh." Of these *Mac Gilla Craeibhe* or "Creagh" family there are still many respectable families in the counties of Clare, Cork, and Tipperary. Some of those O'Neills, who were of the *Ui-Bloid*, of the race of Heber, changed their name to Nihel, and some to Newell; but they were all of the same stock as the O'Briens of Thomond. 32. **O'Davoran**, chief of Muintir Lidheagha (or O'Liddy), the tribe name of this clan; whose territory was situated in the barony of Corcomroe, and at Ballynalaken, near Lisdoonvarna, county Clare. 33. **O'Moloney**, were chiefs of Cuiltenan, now the parish of Kiltonanlea, in the barony of Tulla, county Clare. 34. **O'Kearney**, as chiefs of Avon-Ui-Cearney or O'Kearney's River, a district about Six-Mile-Bridge, in the baronies of Tulla and Bunratty, county Clare. 35. **O'Casey**, chiefs of Rathconan, in the barony of Pubblebrien, county Limerick. 36. **O'Dinan** or **Downing**, chiefs of Uaithne, now the barony of Owneybeg, in Limerick. 37. **O'Hallinan** and **MacSheehy,** chiefs of Ballyhallinan, in the barony of Pubblebrien, county Limerick. O'Halloran, chiefs of Fay Ui-Hallurain, a district between Tulla and Clare, in the county Clare. 38. **Lysaght**, placed in a district about Ennistymon ; **MacConsidine**, in the barony of Ibrackan ; **O'Daly** of Leath Mogha or Munster, in the barony of Burren ; **MacGillereagh** (MacGilroy, MacGilrea, Gilroy, Kilroy) in the barony of Clonderlaw ; **MacClancy**, in the barony of Tulla ; and **MacBruodin**, in the barony of Inchiquin : all in the county Clare. **MacArthur** and **O'Scanlan**, in the barony of Pubblebrien ; and **O'Morny**, in the barony of Lower Conello: all in the county Limerick ; etc.

(b) The New Settlers in Limerick and Clare,
Or Thomond

THE following were the chief families of early settlers, in the counties of Limerick and Clare : De Burgo, Fitzgerald, Fitzgibbon—a branch of the Fitzgeralds, De Clare, De Lacey, Brown Barrett, Roche, Russell, Sarsfield, Stritch, Purcell, Hussey, Harold, Tracey, Trant, Comyn, White, Walsh, Wolfe, Dongan, Rice, Aylmer, Nash, Monsell, Massy, etc. The Fitzgeralds, earls of Desmond, had vast possessions in Limerick ; and of the estates of Gerald, the sixteenth earl of Desmond, in the reign of Elizabeth, about one hundred thousand acres were confiscated in the county Limerick, and divided amongst the following families :—Annesley, Barkley, Billingsley, Bouchier, Carter, Courtenay, Fitton, Mannering, Stroude, Trenchard, Thornton, and Uthered.

Limerick was formed into a county as early as the reign of King John, A.D. 1210 ; and Clare, in the reign of Elizabeth, A.D. 1565, by the Lord Deputy Sir Henry Sidney.

(c) The Modern Nobility of Limerick and Claré,
Or Thomond

QUOTING from Connellan, the following have been the noble families in Limerick and Clare, since the reign of Henry the Eighth :—O'Brien, earls and marquises of Thomond, earls of Inchiquin, barons of Ibrackan, and barons of Burren, also viscounts of Clare, and barons of Moyarta ; Bourke, barons of Castleconnell ; Roche, barons of Tarbert ; and Fitzgerald, knights of Glin, in the county of Limerick ; Sarsfield, viscounts of Kilmallock, in the county of Limerick ; Dongan, earls of Limerick ; Hamilton, viscounts of Limerick ; Fane, viscounts Fane and barons of Loughguire, in Limerick ; Southwell, barons Southwell of Castlematross in Limerick ; Fitzgibbon, earls of Clare ; Perry, earls of Limerick ; Quinn, earls of Dunraven and barons of Adare, in Limerick ; O'Grady, viscounts Guillamore in Limerick ; the lords Fitzgerald, and Vesey or Vesci, in the county of Clare ; Massey, barons of Clarina in Limerick ; Monsell, barons of Emly.

2.—CORK AND KERRY.
The Ancient Desmond.
(a) The Irish Chiefs and Clans.

CORK (in Latin "Corcagia," and also "Coracium") got its name from Corc (No. 89, p. 69), a prince of the Eugenian race, who was King of Munster, in the fifth century ; Kerry (in Latin "Kerrigia") got its name from Ciar, son of Fergus Mac Roy, by Meava or Maud, the celebrated Queen of Connaught, a short time before the Christian era. This Ciar, in the first century, got a large territory in Munster, called from him Ciar Rioghact, signifying *Ciar's Kingdom*: hence, the word "Ciaraidhe," anglicised "Kerry."

The Eugenians, we saw, ruled as kings over Desmond or South Munster, which comprised the whole of the present county Cork, and the greater part of Kerry, together with a portion of Waterford, and a small part of the south of Tipperary, bordering on Cork; while the Dalcassian kings ruled over Thomond. From each race was alternately elected a king of all Munster; and, in that kingdom, this mode of government continued from the third to the tenth century, when Brian Boru, of the Dalcassian race, became king of Munster. After that period the O'Briens alone were kings of Munster and kings of Thomond; and the MacCarthys, who were the head of the Eugenian race, were kings and princes of Desmond.

When, on the English invasion, King Henry the Second landed at Waterford, in October A.D. 1171, Dermot MacCarthy, king of Desmond, waited on him the day after his arrival, delivered to him the keys of the city of Cork, and did him homage.[*]   A.D. 1177, Henry II. granted to Robert Fitzstephen and Milo de Cogan, for the service of sixty knights to himself and his son John and their heirs, the whole kingdom of Desmond, with the exception of the city of Cork and the adjoining cantreds, which belonged to the Ostmen or Danes of that city, and which Henry reserved to hold in his own hands. The MacCarthys maintained long contests for their independence, with the Fitzgeralds, earls of Desmond, the Butlers, earls of Ormond, and other Anglo-Norman and English settlers; and held their titles, as princes of Desmond, with considerable possessions, down to the reign of Elizabeth. They were divided into two great branches, the head of which was MacCarthy Mór: of whom Donal MacCarthy was, A.D. 1565, created earl of Glencare or Clancare, by Queen Elizabeth; the other branch, called MacCarthy Reagh, were styled princes of Carbery. Besides the earls of Clancare, the MacCarthys were also created at various periods barons of Valentia, earls of Clancarty, earls of Muskerry, and earls of Mount Cashel; and, had several strong castles in various parts of Cork and Kerry.

There are still in the counties of Cork and Kerry many highly respectable families of the MacCarthys; and several of the name have been distinguished commanders in the Irish Brigades in the service of France and Spain.

COUNTY CORK.

The Irish Chiefs and Clans.

In Cork, the following have been the Irish chiefs and clans:—1. **O'Sullivan** had the ancient territory of Beara, now the baronies of Beare and Bantry in the county Cork; and were called O'Sullivan Beara, and styled princes of Beara. Another branch of the family, called O'Sullivan Mór, were lords of Dunkerron, and possessed the barony of Dunkerron, in the county Kerry; and their chief seat was the castle of Dunkerron, near the river Kenmare. A third branch of the O'Sullivans were chiefs of Knockraffan, in Tipperary. The O'Sullivans are of the Eugenian race, of the same descent as the MacCarthys, princes of Desmond; and took their name from Suileabhan, one of their chiefs in the tenth century. In the reign of James the First, their extensive possessions were confiscated, in consequence of their adherence to the earls of Desmond and Tyrone in the Elizabethan wars; and the heads of the family retired to Spain, where many of them were distinguished officers in the Spanish service, and had the title of Counts of Bearhaven. 2. **O'Driscoll**, head of the Ithian race, chief or prince of Corcaluighe, called Cairbreacha, comprising the ancient extensive territory of Carbery, in the south-west of Cork. The O'Driscolls were lords of Beara, before the O'Sullivans in after times became possessors of that territory. 3. **O'Keeffe**, chief of Glen Avon and of Urluachra. Glen Avon is now called Glanworth, a place in the barony of Fermoy, county Cork. This family had afterwards a large territory in the barony of Duhallow, known as "Pobal O'Keeffe." In ancient times the O'Keeffes, the O'Dugans, and O'Cosgraves, were chiefs in Fearmuighe Feiné, now the barony of Fermoy; which was afterwards possessed by the family of Roche, viscounts of Fermoy, and called "Roche's Country." The O'Keeffes at one time were marshals and military leaders in Desmond, and were styled princes of Fermoy. 4. **MacDonogh**, chief of Duhalla, now the barony of Duhallow, in the county Cork. The MacDonoghs of Munster were a branch of the MacCarthys, and were styled princes of Duhallow;

---

[*] *Homage:* See "The Clan of MacCaura," by Denis Florence MacCarthy, in p. 107, *ante.*

their chief residence was the magnificent castle of Kanturk. 5. **O'Mahony**, chief of Ivaugh, and Kinalmeaky. The O'Mahonys also possessed the territory of Cinal Aodha (now the barony of "Kinalea"), and a territory in Muskerry, south of the river Lee : both in the county Cork ; and another territory called Tiobrad, in the county Kerry. They were sometimes styled princes ; and possessed several castles, as those of Rosbrin, Ardintenant, Blackcastle, Ballydesmond, Dunbeacan, Dunmanus, Ringmahon, etc.— all along the sea-coast. 6. **O'Callaghan**, chief of Beara, and of Kinalea, in the county Cork. The chief of this family was transplanted into Clare by Cromwell, who gave him at Killarney considerable property, in lieu of his ancient estates. A branch of this family (who are of the Eugenian race) are now viscounts of Lismore. 7. **O'Lehan (Lyne, or Lyons)** was lord of Hy-Lehan and Hy-Namcha, afterwards called the barony of Barrymore, from the family of the Barrys, who became its possessors. Castle Lehan, now Castlelyons, was the chief seat of this family. 8. **O'Flynn**, chief of Arda (a territory in the barony of Carbery), and Hy-Baghamna, now the barony of "Ibane" and Barryroe, adjoining Carbery. The castle of Macroom was built by the O'Flynns. 9. **MacAuliffe**, chief of Glean Omra, in the barony of Duhallow, and a branch of the MacCarthys. Their chief seat was Castle MacAuliffe, near Newmarket. O'Tedgamna was another ancient chief of this territory. 10. **O'Donnegan (or Dongan)**, chief of "Muscry of the three Plains," now the half barony of Orrery, in the county Cork. O'Cullenan was chief on the same territory, and was hereditary physician of Munster. 11. **O'Hinmanen**, chief of Tua-Saxon. 12. **O'Mulbhehan**, chief of Muscry Trehirne. 13. **O'Breoghan** (this name "Breoghan" is considered the root of *Brown*), O'Glaisin (Glashan, or Gleeson), O'Mictyre* and O'Keely were chiefs of Hy-Mac-Caille, now the barony of "Imokilly," in the county Cork. 14. **O'Curry**, chief of Ciarraidhe Cuire, now the barony of "Kerrycurrehy," in the county Cork. 15. **O'Cowhey or O'Coffey**, of Fuin Cleena, chief of Triocha Meona, now the barony of West Barryroe, in the county Cork. These once powerful chiefs had seven castles along the coast, in the barony of Ibawne and Barryroe. 16. **O'Fihilly** were also chiefs in West Barryroe. 17. **O'Baire**, anglicised O'Barry, chief of Muintir Baire, part of ancient Carbery in the county Cork ; and also chief of Aron. This family was of the Ithian or Lugadian race. 18. **O'Leary**, chief of Hy-Laoghaire or "Iveleary," and Iveleary, or "O'Leary's Country," lay in Muskerry, in the county Cork, between Macroom and Inchageela. 19. **O'Hea and O'Dea** are mentioned among the families of Thomond ; they were also chiefs of Carbery, county Cork. 20. **O'Donovan**, also mentioned in Thomond, settled in Cork, and were chiefs of Clan Cathail, in West Carbery. 21. **O'Beice or Beeky**, chief of Beanthraidhe, now the barony of Bantry. 22. **O'Casey**, chief of a territory near Mitchelstown, in the county Cork. 23. **O'Healy or Hely**, chief of Domhnach-Mór-O'Healy or Pobal O'Healy, a parish in the barony of Muskerry, county Cork. 24. **O'Herlihy or Hurley** is mentioned in the families of Ormond ; they were also chiefs in the barony of Muskerry. 25. **O'Nunan or Noonan**, chief of Tullaleis and Castlelissen, now the parish of Tullilease, in the barony of Duhallow, county Cork. 26. **O'Daly**, bard to MacCarthy, O'Mahony, Carews, and other great families. The O'Dalys were eminent poets in Munster. 27. **O'h-Aedhagan** (anglicised "Mac Egan") was hereditary Brehon or judge in the counties of Cork and Kerry, under the MacCarthys, kings of Desmond. The MacEgans were also hereditary Brehons of Ormond. 28. **MacSweeney**, military commanders under the MacCarthys, who, in the thirteenth century, brought a body of them from Tirconnell or Donegal, where they were celebrated as chiefs under the O'Donnells ; and hence the head of the clan was styled MacSuibhne-na-dTuadh or MacSweeney of the Battle Axes. In Munster, the MacSweeneys had the parish of Kilmurry, in the barony of Muskerry, and had their chief castle at Clodagh, near Macroom, and had also Castlemore in the parish of Movidy. 29. **Mac-Sheehy** : This family was a warlike clan, brought from Connaught in the fifteenth century by the Fitzgeralds, Earls of Desmond, who appointed them their body-guards. Some of them changed the name to "Joy ; " and of this family was the Irish judge, Baron Joy. They are considered to be originally the same as the Joyces of Connemara —a race of men of tall and manly stature. The MacSheehys and O'Hallinans were chiefs of Ballyhallinan, in the parish of Poblebrien, county Limerick ; and the O'Hallorans were chiefs of Faith-Ui-Hallurain, a district between Tulla and Clare, in the county Clare. 30. **O'Kearney** were chiefs of Hy-Floinn, near Kinsale, in the county Cork. 31. **O'Riordan**, a clan of note in Muskerry ; and distinguished military chiefs in

---

* *O'Mictyre:* This sirname ("mactire :" Irish, *a wolf*) has been anglicised *Wolfe*.

ancient times. 32. **O'Crowley**, chiefs of Kilshallow, west of Bandon, and originally a clan from Connaught. 33. **O'Murphy** (originally from Wexford), a clan in Muskerry. 34. **O'Ahern, ORonanye**, and **OHeyne** (or Hynes), were old and respectable families in the county Cork.

COUNTY KERRY.

In Kerry, the following have been the Irish chiefs and clans: 1. **O'Connor**, king or prince of Kerry, was descended from Ciar, of the Irian race already mentioned; and took the name from Con, one of their chiefs, in the eleventh century, and from Ciar, their great ancestor; thus making the word "Conciar" "Conior," or Conchobhar, anglicised "Connor" (See No. 103, page 331). From a portion of the ancient inheritance of this family the present barony of Iraghticonnor takes its name. 2. **O'Donoghoe** was of the Eugenian race, and chief of Lough Lein; a branch of this family was the O'Donoghoe Mór, lord of Glenfesk or O'Donoghoe of the Glen. 3. **O'Donnell** (of the same race as O'Donoghoe), chief of Clan Shalvey (a quo Shelly); comprising the district called Iveleary, and a great portion of Muskerry. 4. **O'Carroll**, prince of Lough Lein. 5. **O'Falvey**, chief of Corca Duibhne (now the barony of "Corcaguiney"), and lord of Iveragh: both in the county Kerry. The O'Falveys were hereditary admirals of Desmond. 6. **O'Shea**, chief of Iveragh. 7. **O'Connell**, chief or Magh O g-Coinchinn, now the barony of "Magonihy," in Kerry. These O'Connells were a branch of the O'Connells of Thomond; descended from Conaire the Second, the 111th Monarch of Ireland. O'Leyne or Lane, chief of Hy-Fearba; and O'Duividin, chief of Hy; Flannain: districts in the county Kerry. 9. **O'Neide**, chief of Clar Ciarraidhe or the Plain of Kerry. 10. **O'Dunady**, chief of Slieve Luachra, now Slievlogher, on the borders of Limerick and Kerry. 11. **O'Muircheartaigh** (Moriarty, or Murtagh), and O'Hinnesvan (or Hinson), chief of Aos Aisde of Orlar Eltaigh, a district which comprised the parish of Templenoe, in the barony of Dunkerron. 12. **The MacGillicuddys** (a branch of the O'Sullivans) were chiefs of a territory in the barony of Dunkerron: from this family the Mac Gillicuddy's Reeks in Kerry got their name: and some of this family anglicised the name "Archdeacon." 13. **MacElligot** (or **Elligot**), an ancient family in Kerry, from whom the parish of Ballymacelligott, in the barony of Troughenackmy, got its name. From MacElligott the name of "MacLeod" was said to be derived; but "MacLeod" is of *Scotch* origin. 14. **MacFinneen**, MacCrehan, O'Scanlan, and O'Harney (or Harnet), were also clans of note in Kerry.

(*b*) THE NEW SETTLERS IN CORK AND KERRY,

Or Desmond.

As already stated, King Henry the Second gave a grant of the kingdom of Desmond to Robert Fitzstephen and Milo de Cogan. With that Robert Fitzstephen came Maurice Fitzgerald and other Anglo-Norman chiefs, A.D. 1169, who assisted Strongbow in the invasion of Ireland. In 1173, Maurice Fitzgerald was appointed by Henry the Second chief governor of Ireland; and he and his descendants got large grants of land in Leinster and Munster, chiefly in the counties of Kildare, Wicklow, Wexford, Cork, and Kerry. He died, A.D. 1177, and was buried in the abbey of the Grey Friars at Wexford. A branch of the Fitzgeralds were, down to the reign of Elizabeth, earls of Desmond; and had immense possessions in the counties of Cork and Kerry. Another branch of them became barons of Offaly,* earls of Kildare, and dukes of Leinster. The Fitzgeralds trace their descent from the dukes of Tuscany: some of the family from Florence, settled in Normandy, and thence came to England with William the Conqueror. The Geraldines, having frequently joined the Irish against the English, were charged by English writers as having become Irish in language and manners: hence, the origin of the expression—"Ipsis Hibernis Hiberniores" or *More Irish than the Irish themselves.* The Fizgeralds, who were created earls of Desmond, became one of the

* *Offaly:* The ancient territory of Offaly comprised a great part of the King's County, with part of the Queen's County and Kildare.

most powerful families in Munster; and several of them were lords deputies of Ireland in the fourteenth and fifteenth centuries. Gerald Fitzgerald, sixteenth earl of Desmond, was one of the greatest subjects in Europe; he held the rank of a "Prince Palatine," with all the authority of a provincial king. Having resisted the Reformation in the reign of Elizabeth, and waged war againt the English government, the earl of Desmond's forces after long contests were defeated, and he himself was slain in a glen near Castle Island, in the county Kerry, on the 11th of November, A.D. 1583; his head was cut off and sent to England, by Thomas Butler, Earl of Ormond, as a present to Queen Elizabeth, who caused it to be fixed on London Bridge. James Fitzgerald (nephew of Gerald, Earl of Desmond) attempting to recover the estates and honours of his ancestors, took up arms and joined the standard of Hugh O'Neill, Earl of Tyrone. This James Fitzgerald was styled Earl of Desmond; but his title not being recognized, he was designated the *sugan earl*, which signifies the "earl of straw." His forces being at length defeated and himself taken prisoner, he was sent to England along with Florence MacCarthy, and imprisoned in the Tower of London, where he died, A.D. 1608; and thus terminated the once illustrious House of Desmond.

The vast estates of Gerald, Earl of Desmond, were confiscated in the reign of Elizabeth, and granted to various English settlers (called planters or undertakers), on conditions that no planter should convey any part of the lands to any of the "mere Irish:" and the English settlers were also prohibited to intermarry with the Irish, and none of the Irish were to be maintained in any family! The following are the names of the new settlers in Ireland who obtained grants of the Desmond estates in Cork and Waterford, thus confiscated: Sir Walter Raleigh,* Arthur Robins, Fane Beecher, Hugh Worth, Arthur Hyde, Sir Warham St. Leger, Hugh Cuffe (in Irish "Durneen"), Sir Thomas Norris, Sir Arthur Hyde, Thomas Say, Sir Richard Beacon (in Irish "Beagan") and (the poet) Edmond Spencer. In the county Kerry, the following persons got grants of the Desmond estates: Sir William Herbert, Charles Herbert, Sir Valentine Brown (ancestor of the earls of Kenmare), Sir Edward Denny, and some grants to the families of Conway, Holly, and others. Of the families who got the Desmond estates in Limerick, an account has been given in the names of the new settlers in "Thomond."

The other principal families of the county Cork, were Cogan, Carew (or Carey), Condon (or Canton), De Courcy, Barry, Barnwall, Barrett, Roche, MacGibbon and Fitzgibbon (a branch of the Fitzgeralds); Fleming, Sarsfield, Nagle, Martell, Percival, Russel, Pigott, Prendergast, Lombard, Lavallan, Morgan, Cottor, Meagh (or May), Murrogh, Supple, Stackpole, White, Warren, Hodnet, Harding, Field, Beecher, Hyde, Jephson, Garrett, Kent, Delahide (or Delahoyd), De Spencer, Deane, Daunt, Vincent, Gardiner, Beamish, Courtenay, Cuffe, Gore, Hore, Newenham (or Newman), etc.

Coppinger, Gould, Galway, Skiddy, and Terry were, in former times, very numerous and powerful families in Cork.

Some of the family "De Courcy" took the Irish name MacPatrick; some of the "De Barrys," that of MacDavid; the "De la Rupe," that of Roche, who became viscounts of Fermoy; some of the family of "Hodnet" took the name MacSherry, etc.

In Kerry, the following have been the chief Anglo-Norman and English families:— Fitzmaurice, earls of Kerry, descended from Raymond le Gros, a celebrated warrior who came over with Strongbow. Raymond having formed an alliance with Dermot MacCarthy, King of Desmond, got large grants of land in Kerry, in the territory called Lixnaw. The other principal families were those of Herbert, Brown, Stack, Blennerhasset, Crosbie, Denny, Gunn, Godfrey, Morris, Rice, Spring, etc.

---

* *Sir Walter Raleigh:* To Sir Walter Raleigh we are are indebted for the introduction into Great Britain and Ireland (consequent upon his voyage in A.D. 1585 to colonize Virginia, in North America) of the potato plant, and the use of tobacco; the former of which has since become an almost universal article of diet, and the latter a most productive source of revenue. Sir Walter Raleigh it was who first planted potatoes in Ireland, in a field near Youghal, about A.D. 1610. In his time, too, the publication of newspapers in England is said to have originated. Copies of the "English Mercurie," relating to the threatened descent of the Spanish Armada, are still preserved in the British Museum.

(c) The Modern Nobility of Cork and Kerry,
Or Desmond.

In the county Cork the following have been the noble families, since the reign of King John : De Courcy, barons of Kinsale and Ringrone ; Fitzgerald, earls of Desmond, barons of Decies, and seneschals of Imokilly ; Fielding, earls of Denbigh in England, has the title of earls of Desmond. Of the Royal Family, the dukes of Clarence were earls of Munster. The Carews were marquises of Cork ; MacCarthy, earls of Clancare, earls of Clancarthy, earls of Muskerry, and earls of Mountcashel ; Barry, barons of Olethann, viscounts of Buttevant, and earls of Barrymore ; Roche, barons of Castlelough, and viscounts of Fermoy ; Boyle, barons of Youghal, Bandon, Broghill, and Castlemartyr, viscounts of Dungarvan and Kinnalmeaky, earls of Cork, Orrery, and Shannon, and earls of Burlington in England ; Percival, barons of Duhallow, Kanturk and Ardee, and earls of Egmont ; St. Leger, viscounts of Doneraile ; Touchet, earls of Castlehaven ; Bernard, earls of Bandon ; White, viscounts of Berehaven, and earls of Bantry ; Berkley and Chetwynd, viscounts of Berehaven ; Broderick, viscounts Midleton ; Moore, earls of Charleville ; and Moore, earls of Mountcashel ; King, earls of Kingston ; O'Callaghan, viscounts of Lismore in Waterford, are originally from Cork ; Evans, barons of Carbery ; Deane, barons of Muskerry ; Tonson, barons of Riversdale ; and the family of Cavendish, barons of Waterpark.

In the county Kerry the following have been the noble families since the reign of King John :—Fitzmaurice, barons of Lixnaw ; and O'Dorney, viscounts of Clanmaurice, and earls of Kerry ; Petty, or Fitzmaurice-Petty, barons of Dunkerron, viscounts Clanmaurice, earls of Kerry, earls of Shelbourne, and marquises of Lansdowne in England ; Fitzgerald, knights of Kerry ; Brown, earls of Kenmare, and viscounts of Castlerosse ; Herbert, barons of Castleisland ; Child, viscounts of Castlemaine, and earls of Tilney in England ; Monson and Palmer, viscounts of Castlemaine ; Power, viscounts of Valencia ; Crosbie, viscounts of Brandon, and earls of Glandore ; Wynn, barons Hedley ; De Moleyns, barons of Ventry ; Hare, barons of Ennismore, and earls of Listowell ; and Spring-Rice, barons Monteagle of Brandon.

Down to the last century, the mountains of Cork and Kerry were covered with ancient forests of oak, ash, pine, alder, birch, hazel, and yews of immense size ; and afforded retreats to wolves and numerous herds of red deer. It is needless to speak of the majestic mountains and magnificent lakes of Kerry, celebrated as they are for their surpassing beauty and sublime scenery.

3.—ANCIENT ORMOND AND DESIES,
Or Tipperary and Waterford.

The territories which formed ancient Ormond and Desies have been already mentioned. As this territory is closely associated with the Anglo-Norman invasion of Ireland, the following observations may not here be out of place :

Waterford is celebrated as the chief landing-place of the Anglo-Norman invaders, under Strongbow and his followers ; and is also remarkable as the chief place where several kings of England landed on their expedition to Ireland. In May, A.D. 1169, Robert Fitzstephen, Maurice Fitzgerald, David Barry, Hervey de Monte Marisco, Myler Fitzhenry, Maurice Prendergast, and other chiefs from Wales (being the first of the Anglo-Normans who invaded Ireland) landed at the bay of Bag-an-bun or Bannow, in the county Wexford, near the bay of Waterford ; where they were joined by their ally Dermod MacMurrough, King of Leinster. In May, 1170, Raymond le Gros and other Anglo-Norman chiefs landed near the rock of Dundonnel, about four miles from Waterford, near the river Suir. In August, 1170, Strongbow landed near Waterford, and was there married to Eva, daughter of Dermod MacMurrough, who then conferred on his son-in-law the title of "heir presumptive" to the kingdom of Leinster.

A.D. 1171, King Henry the Second embarked at Milford Haven, landed at Croch, now Crook, near Waterford, on the 18th of October ; and was attended by Strongbow,

William FitzAdelm, Hugh de Lacy, Humphrey de Bohun, and other lords and barons. The day after Henry's arrival, Dermot MacCarthy, king of Desmond, waited on him at Waterford; delivered to him the keys of the city of Cork; and did him homage. Henry, at the head of his army, marched to Lismore, and thence to Cashel; near which, on the banks of the Suir, Donal O'Brien, King of Thomond, came to meet him, delivered to him the keys of the city of Limerick, and did him homage as Dermot MacCarthy had done. MacGillpatrick, Prince of Ossory; O'Felan, Prince of Desies; and other chiefs, submitted soon after. From Cashel, Henry returned through Tipperary to Waterford, and shortly afterwards proceeded to Dublin; where he remained during the winter, and in a style of great magnificence entertained the Irish kings and princes who had submitted to him. In February, 1172, Henry returned to Waterford, and held a council or parliament at Lismore; and also convened a synod of bishops and clergy at Cashel. After remaining in Ireland about six months, King Henry embarked at Wexford, on Easter Monday, the 17th of April, 1172; set sail for England, and arrived the same day at Port Finnain in Wales. A.D. 1174, Raymond le Gros landed at Waterford, with a large force from Wales, to relieve Strongbow, then besieged by the Irish in that city; and succeeded in rescuing him. A.D. 1175, according to Lanigan, King Henry sent Nicholas, abbot of Malmesbury, and William FitzAdelm to Ireland, with the Bull of Pope Adrian IV., and the brief of Pope Alexander III., conferring on King Henry the Second the kingdom of Ireland; when a meeting of bishops was convened at Waterford, where these documents were publicly read; it being the first time they were ever published. A.D. 1185, Prince John, Earl of Morton, son of King Henry the Second, landed at Waterford, accompanied by Ralph Glunville, Chief Justice of England, and by Giraldus Cambrensis, his secretary and tutor. A.D. 1210, King John landed at Waterford, and soon after proceeded to Dublin, and from thence through various parts of Meath and Ulster.

Waterford is also celebrated as the place of landing and embarkation of other kings of England: namely, of Richard the Second, in the years 1394 and 1399. On the 2nd of September, A.D. 1689, King William the Third embarked at Waterford for England; and, being again in Ireland, at the siege of Limerick, A.D. 1690, he came to Waterford and embarked for England on the 5th of September. On the 2nd of July, 1690, King James the Second, after the battle of the Boyne, arrived at Waterford, whence he set sail for France.

Amongst the ancient notices of Waterford, it may be mentioned that, A.D. 1497, in consequence of the loyalty of the citizens of Waterford, against the mock princes and pretenders to the crown of England—namely, Lambert, Simnel, and Perkins Warbeck, King Henry the Seventh granted, with other honours, to the city the motto—

Intacta Manet Waterfordia :

hence, it is designated the "Urbs Intacta." In 1536, Henry the Eighth sent by Sir William Wyse to the citizens of Waterford a gilt sword, to be always borne before the Mayors, in remembrance of their renowned fidelity.

(a) THE IRISH CHIEFS AND CLANS OF TIPPERARY AND WATERFORD,
Or Ormond and Desies.

In Desies or Waterford, the following were the chiefs and clans :—1. **O'Felan,** whose territory was, after the Anglo-Norman invasion, transferred to the Le Poers, and other settlers; but there are still very respectable families of the O'Felans (some of whom have changed the name to Phelan and Whelan) in the counties of Waterford, Tipperary, Kilkenny, and Queen's County. The O'Felans were princes of Desies, and held an extensive territory comprising the greater part of the present county of Waterford, with part of Tipperary, as already explained; and were descended from the Desians of Meath, who were of the race of Heremon. Some of the family in America spell the name "Whelen." 2. **O'Bric,** of the same descent as O'Felan. 3. **O'Brien,** a branch of the O'Briens of Thomond. 4. **O'Crotty,** also a branch of the O'Briens of Thomond. 5. The **McGraths** were old and respectable families of Waterford; as were also those of O'Shee, O'Ronayne, O'Hely, O'Callaghan, O'Coghlan, O'Meara, etc.

In Ormond or the county Tipperary, the following have been the chiefs and clans of note :—1. **O'Donoghoe** (or **O'Donohoe**), of the Eugenian race, and of the same descent as the MacCarthys, kings of Desmond. One of the O'Donoghoes is mentioned by the Four Masters, at the year A.D. 1038, as "king presumptive" of Cashel. The ancient kings of Munster, of the Eugenian race, were inaugurated on the rock of Cashel; and those of the Dalcassian race, or the O'Briens, kings of Thomond, had their place of inauguration at Magh Adair, situated in the townland of Toonagh, parish of Cloney, barony of Upper Tulla, in the county Clare. 2. O'Carroll, Prince of Ely, ruled, according to O'Heerin, over eight subordinate chiefs; and had their castle at Birr, now Parsonstown, in the King's County. O'Carroll was the head of the Clan Cian race, as the MacCarthys were of the Eugenians: and the O'Briens, of the Dalcassians. The territory of "Ely" got its name from Eile, one of its princes, in the fifth century; and from being possessed by the O'Carrolls, was called "Ely O'Carroll;" which comprised the present barony of Lower Ormond, in the county Tipperary, with the barony of Clonlisk and part of Ballybrit, in the King's County; extending to Slieve Bloom Mountains, on the borders of the Queen's County. The part of Ely in the King's County belonged to the ancient province of Munster. 3. O'Kennedy, chief of Gleann Omra; several of them are mentioned by the Four Masters as lords of Ormond. The O'Kennedys (of Munster) were of the Dalcassian race; and possessed the barony of Upper Ormond, in the county Tipperary. 4. O'Hurley: a branch of this family (who were also of the Dalcassian race) settled in Limerick, in the barony of Owneybeg, and in the parish of Knocklong, in the barony of Coshlea, county Limerick, where the ruins of their chief castle still remain. Other branches of the O'Hurleys were settled in Galway, and had large possessions in the baronies of Kilconnell, Killian, and Ballymore; of which family were Sir William and Sir John Hurley, baronets. 5. O'Hern (Hearne, Heron, Ahearne, Ahern), chiefs of Hy-Cearnaidh. 6. O'Shanahan (or O'Shannon), descended from Lorcan, a king of Munster, who was grandfather of Brian Boru: hence, the O'Shanahans or Shannons are a branch of the Dalcassians, who were also designated Clan Tail. The O'Shannons were chiefs of a territory called Feadha Hy-Rongaile or the Woods of Hy-Rongaile— comprising the country about Eibhline; and, as Slieve Eibhline is stated in the old writers to be near Cashel, this territory appears to have been situated either in the barony of Middlethird or of Eliogarty. 7. O'Duffy. 8. O'Dwyer, chief of Hy-Aimrit, was a branch of the Heremonians; and possessed extensive territory in the present baronies of Kilnamanach, county Tipperary. Some of the O'Dwyers were com manders in the Irish Brigade in the Service of France. MacGeoghagan mentions General O'Dwyer as governor of Belgrade; and there was an Admiral O'Dwyer in the Russian service. 9. O'Dea, and O'Hoillolla (or O'Hulla), are given by O'Heerin as chiefs of Sliabh Ardach, now the barony of "Slieveardagh," in Tipperary. 10. O'Carthy, chief of Muiscridh Iarthar Feimin—a territory which, according to O'Halloran, was situated near Emly, in Tipperary. 11. O'Meara,* chief of Hy-Fathaidh, Hy-Niall, and Hy-Eochaidh-Finn. The O'Mearas had an entensive territory in the barony of Upper Ormond, county Tipperary; and the name of their chief residences Tuaim-ui-Meara, is still retained in the town of "Toomavara," in that district. The Hy-Nialls here mentioned were of the race of Eugenius of Munster. 12. O'Meagher or Maher, chief of Crioch-ui-Cairin, or the land of Hy-Kerrin, now the barony of "Ikerin," in the county Tipperary. 13. O'Flanagan, chiefs of Uachtar Tire and of Cinel Agra. The district of Uachtar Tire (or the Upper Country) was situated in the barony of Iffa and Offa, on the borders of Tipperary and Water-ford; and that of Cinel Agra, in Ely O'Carroll, in the King's County. 14. O'Breslin, chief of Hy-Athy of Ely, which appears to have been a part of Ely O'Carroll, situated near the Shannon; and these O'Breslins were probably a branch of the O'Breslins of Donegal, who were Brehons or judges to the O'Donnells, princes of Tirconnell, and to the MacGuires, princes of Fermanagh. 15. O'Keane, chief of Hy-Fodhladha, a district supposed to be on the borders of Tipperary and Waterford. 16. O'Donegan (or O'Dongan) prince of Aradh, was of the race of Heremon. The O'Donegans were styled princes of Muiscrith Tire, now Lower Ormond, in Tipperary; and possessed Aradh Cliach, now the barony of Owney and Arra, also in Tipperary. 17. O'Donnelly or O'Dongally, and O'Fuirig (or O'Furey), also chiefs of Muiscrith Tire. 18. O'Sullivan,

---

* *O'Meara:* Of this family we find the following, in p. 36 of the Vol. F. 3. 27, in the MSS. Library of Trinity College, Dublin: 1. Donell O'Meara. 2. William of Lismiskey, co. Tipperary: his son and heir. 3. Teige of Lismisky: his son; m. Honora, dau. of Robert Grace of Corktown, co. Kilkenny. 4. Daniel O'Meara: his son: had two brothers and two sisters: the brothers were—1. William, 2. Patrick, the sisters were—1. Ellin, 2. Elan.

chief of Eoganacht Mór of Knock Raffan, already mentioned. **19. O'Fogarty,** chiefs of South Ely, now the barony of Eliogarty, in Tipperary, had their chief seats about Thurles ; it was called South Ely, to distinguish it from North Ely or Ely O'Carroll. **20. O'Cullen,** chief of Eoganacht of Arra ; and O'Keely, chief of Aolmoy : these two districts appear to have been in the barony of Owney and Arra, in Tipperary. **21. O'Duinechair** and **O'Dinan,** chiefs of Eoganacht Uaithne Ageamar [Owney Agamar]. This territory comprised part of the counties of Tipperary and Limerick, now the baronies of Owney and Owneybeg. **22.** The **O'Ryans** or **O'Mulrians** of Tipperary, afterwards possessed Owney in Tipperary, and Owneybeg in Limerick. A branch of the O'Ryans were princes of Hy-Drone, in Carlow. **23. O'Mearns,** chief of Eoganacht Ross Airgid. **24. MacKeogh** or **Kehoe,** chief of Uaithne Tire, a territory situated in ancient Owney, which comprised the present baronies of Owney and Arra, in Tipperary ; and Owneybeg, in Limerick. In that territory also dwelt the O'Linskeys or Lynches, who are described as "men of lands," dwelling in the neighbourhood of the Danes, who possessed Limerick. **25. O'Heffernan** and **O'Callanan** were chiefs of Owney Cliach,* a territory situated in the barony of Owney and Arra, county Tipperary ; these O'Heffernans were a branch of the O'Heffernans of Clare, whose name is mentioned under "Thomond." **26. MacLenehan** (Irish MacLongachain), chief of Crota Cliach, and Hy-Coonagh. This territory was situated partly in the barony of Owney and Arra, in Tipperary, and partly in the barony of Coonagh, county Limerick. The O'Dwyers, already mentioned as chiefs of Kilnamanagh, in Tipperary, were also located in this territory. **27. O'Lonergan,** ancient chiefs and proprietors of Cahir, and the adjoining districts in Tipperary, till the fourteenth century, when they were dispossessed by the Butlers, earls of Ormond. **28. Mac-I-Brien** or **MacBrien,** a branch of the O'Briens of Thomond, had large possessions in the barony of Owney and Arra, in Tipperary, and in the barony of Coonagh, county Limerick ; and were styled lords of Arra and Coonagh. **29. MacCorcoran,** chief of Clan Rooney, "of the flowery avenues." **30. O'Hogan,** chief of Crioch Cian, about Lower Ormond, in Tipperary. **31. MacGillfoyle** or **Gilfoyle,** chief of Clan Quinlevan. The MacGillfoyles appear to have been located on the borders of Tipperary and King's County ; and some of the O'Quinlevans have changed the name to "Quinlan." **32. O'Bannan** or **Bannin,** chief of Hy-Dechi, a territory situated in the north of Tipperary. **33. O'Ailche,** chief of Tuatha Faralt. **34. O'Cahil,** chief of Corca Tine, situated on the borders of Tipperary and Kilkenny. **35. O'Dinnerty** and **O'Amry,** clans located on the borders of Tipperary and Kilkenny. **36. O'Spillane,** chief of Hy-Luighdeach, situated on the borders of Tipperary and Kilkenny. **37. MacEgan,** in the barony of Arra, were hereditary Brehons ; and O'Cullenan or MacCullinan, hereditary physicians in Ormond. **38. O'Scully,** O'Hanrahan, O'Lanigan, and MacGrath, were also clans of note in Tipperary ; and O'Honeen, who changed their name to "Green," and "Hoyne," were numerous in Tipperary and Clare.

Ormond and Desies were formed into the counties of Tipperary and Waterford, A.D. 1210, in the reign of King John. Waterford was called by the ancient Irish Cuanna-Grian, signifying the "Harbour of the Sun," and afterwards, Glean-na-nGleodh or the "Valley of Lamentations," from a great battle fought there between the Irish and the Danes in the tenth century. By the Danes it was called *Vader Fiord* ("vader :" Danish, *to wade ;* "fiord," a *ford* or *haven*), signifying the *fordable* part of the *haven :* hence, "Waterford" is so called. Tipperary is, in Irish, *Tobardarainn,* signifying the "Well of Arainn ;" and so called from the adjoining territory of Arainn. In Tipperary are valuable coal and iron mines, and extensive slate quarries. Affane in Waterford was famous for cherries ; first planted there by Sir Walter Raleigh, who brought them from the Canary Islands.

(*b*) The New Settlers in Tipperary and Waterford,

Or Ormond and Desies.

A.D. 1177, Henry the Second gave a grant of Desies, or the entire county of Waterford, together with the city, to Robert Le Poer, who was his marshal. The Le Poers were

---

* *Cliach :* Some authorities say that the present barony of "Owneybeg," in the county Limerick, was the territory of (*Uaithne Cliach* or) Owney Cliach, of which O'Heffernan and O'Hallinan were chiefs.

at various periods from the thirteenth to the seventeenth century, created barons of Donisle, and of Curraghmore, viscounts of Desies, and earls of Tyrone ; and many of them changed the name to " Power." The Fitzgeralds, earls of Desmond, had extensive possessions and numerous castles in the county Waterford, in the baronies of Coshmore and Coshbride ; and had also the title of barons of Desies. In the reign of Henry the Sixth, A.D. 1447, Sir John Talbot, Earl of Shrewsbury, Lord Lieutenant of Ireland, got grants in Waterford, together with the castle and land of Dungarvan, and the title of Earl of Waterford, and Viscount of Dungarvan. The family of Villiers, earls of Jersey in England, got, in the seventeenth and eighteenth centuries, large possessions in Waterford, by intermarriage with the Fitzgeralds of Dromana, a branch of the earls of Desmond ; and were created earls of Grandison. The chief families who settled in Waterford were the following :—Aylward, Anthony, Allan, Alcock, Butler, Brown, Barker, Bolton, Bird, Barron, Burke, Bagg, Boat, Boyd, Creagh, Carr, Corr, Comerford, Croker, Cook, Christmas, D'Alton, Dobbyn, Disney, Drew, Ducket, Everard, Fitzgerald Green, Gamble, Gough, Grant, Hale, Jackson, King, Key, Lombard, Lea or Lee, Leonard, Mandeville, Morgan, Morris, Madan or Madden, and Mulgan or Mulligan, Newport, Nugent, Osborne, Odell, Power, Prendergast, Rochfort, Roche, Rice, Sherlock, Strong, Tobin, Usher, Wall, Walsh, Wadding, Wyse, Woodlock, White, etc. The early English families principally possessed the territoy called from them *Gal-tir* (" gal:" Irish, *a foreigner;* " tir," a *country*), now the barony of " Gaultiere,"and signifying " the country of the foreigners." The Walshes (called, by the Irish, Brannaghs or Breathnachs, signifying Britons or Welshmen, as they originally came from Wales) are still very numerous in Ireland ; and there are many respectable families of them in the counties of Waterford and Kilkenny.

Otho de Grandison, an Anglo-Norman lord, got a grant of Ormond ; but the family of Butler became the chief possessors of Tipperary. The ancestors of the Butlers came from Normandy to England with William the Conqueror. Their original name was Fitz-Walter, from Walter one of their ancestors; and Theobald Fitz-Walter came to Ireland with Henry the Second, and had the office of Chief Butler of Ireland conferred on him : the duty attached to which was, to attend at the coronation of the kings of England, and present them with thefirst cup of wine. From the office of Butlership of Ireland, they took the name of " Butler." In the reign of Edward the Third, Tipperary was formed into the " County Palatinate of Ormond,"* under the Butlers; who thus became so powerful, that different branches of them furnished many of the most distinguished families in Ireland.

(c) The Modern Nobility of Tipperary and Waterford,
Or Ormond and Desies.

The following have been the noble families in Tipperary and Waterford, from the reign of King John to the present time :

In Waterford, Le Poer, barons of Donile and of Curraghmore, viscounts of Desies, and earls of Tyrone. Beresford, by intermarriage with the Le Poers, became earls of Tyrone, marquises of Waterford, and barons of Desies. Fitzgerald, barons of Desies and earls of Desmond ; Talbot, earls of Shrewsbury, in England, and earls of Waterford and Wexford, in Ireland ; the family of Villiers, earls of Jersey in England, and earls of Grandison in Ireland ; the Scottish family of Maule, earls of Panmure, have the titles of barons Maule and earls of Panmure in Waterford and Wexford ; the family of Lumley, earls of Scarborough in England, are viscounts of Waterford ; Boyle, earls of Cork, and viscounts of Dungarvan ; O'Brien, earls of Clare, in the reign of James the Second, had also the title of viscounts of Lismore : O'Callaghan, viscounts of Lismore, but resident in Tipperary ; St. Leger, barons of Kilmeden ; Villier and Stuart, barons of Desies ; and Keane, barons Keane of Cappoquin.

In Tipperary : The Dukes of Cambridge, in the Royal Family, have the title of earls of Tipperary. The Butlers were earls, marquises and dukes of Ormond, and also had the following titles in Tipperary :—Earls of Carrick, earls of Glengall, viscounts of

---

* *County Palatinate of Ormond :* A "palatinate" was the province of a palatine ; and a " palatine" was one possessed of such royal privileges, as to rule in his palatinate almost as a king.

Thurles, viscounts of Ikerrin, and barons of Cahir. The MacCarthys were earls of
Mountcashel ; afterwards the Davises, and, in modern times, the Moores, are earls of
Mountcashel ; the Buckleys, viscounts of Cashel; the Scotts, earls of Clonmel; the
Hely-Hutchinsons, earls of Donoghmore ; the Kings, earls of Kingston ; the Yelvertons,
viscounts of Avonmore ; the Maudes, viscounts Hawarden ; the family of Fairfax,
viscounts of Emly (that of Monsell is now baron of Emly); the Carletons, barons
Carleton ; the Pritties, barons of Dunally ; the Bloomfields, barons Bloomfield ; and
the Mathews, earls of Landaff.

III.—THE PRINCIPAL FAMILIES OF ULSTER.

1.—THE COUNTY LOUTH OR ANCIENT ORIEL.

(a) THE IRISH CHIEFS AND CLANS.

IN the Appendix to Vol. II., under the heading "The Clan Colla," a sketch of the history
of ancient Oriel is given ; and it is there mentioned that the O'Carrolls were princes of
Oriel down to the Anglo-Norman invasion. Amongst the other chief clans who
possessed Louth were those of MacCann, MacCartan, O'Kelly, O'Moore, O'Callaghan,
O'Carragher, MacColman, MacCampbell, MacArdle, MacKenny, or MacKenna,
O'Devin, O'Markey, O'Branagan, MacScanlan, and others.

In the reign of King John, A.D. 1210, Louth was formed into a county ; and
acquired its name from the town of Louth, in Irish *Lugh Mhagh*, which signifies the
"Plain of Lugh or Lugaid"—and which probably was so called after some ancient
chief.

(b) THE ANGLO-NORMAN FAMILIES,

AND

(c) THE MODERN NOBILITY,

In Louth.

ACCORDING to Connellan, the chief Anglo-Norman or British families settled in Louth
were—De Lacy, De Verdon, De Gernon, De Pepard ; De Flemming, barons of Slane ;
Bellew, of Barmeath, who had formerly the title of barons of Duleek ; De Bermingham,
earls of Louth, a title afterwards possessed by the Plunkets ; Taaffe, earls of Carlingford
(in the peerage of the United Kingdom, Mr. Chichester Fortescue, late M.P. for the
county Louth, was A.D. 1874, created "baron Carlingford") ; Ball, Brabazon, Darcy,
Dowdal, and Clinton, etc. ; Fortescue, now earls of Claremont ; and, in more modern
times, the family of Gorge, barons of Dundalk; and Foster, viscounts Ferard, and
barons of Oriel.

2.—MONAGHAN.

(a) THAT part of the kingdom of Orgiall called Monaghan was overrun by the forces of
John de Courcy, in the reign of King John, but the MacMahons maintained their
national independence to the reign of Elizabeth ; when Monaghan was formed into a
county, and so called from its chief town *Muineachan*, which signifies the "Town of
the Monks."

(c) THE MODERN NOBILITY IN MONAGHAN.

The noble families in Monaghan have been those of Dawson, barons of Cremorne ;
Westenra, lords Rossmore ; and Blayney, lords Blayney. The other chief landed
proprietors are the families of Shirley, Leslie, Coote, Corry, and Hamilton, etc.

3.—ARMAGH.

(a) THAT part of Orgiall, afterwards forming the county Armagh, was possessed partly by the families of O'Hanlon and MacCann, and partly by those of O'Neill, O'Larkin, O'Duvany or O'Devany ; and O'Garvy, of the Clan-na-Rory, who, according to O'Brien, possessed the Craobh Ruadh [Creeveroe] or the territory of the famous Red Branch Knights of Ulster ; O'Hanratty or Enright, of Hy-Meith-Macha ;* and O'Donegan, of Breasal Macha.† Ancient Orgiall included the territory embraced in the present counties of Tyrone and Derry ; but of that territory the Clan Colla were gradually dispossessed by the race of Owen (son of Niall of the Nine Hostages), from whom it derived the name Tir-Owen.

The native chiefs held their independence down to the reign of Elizabeth, when Armagh was formed into a county, A.D. 1586, by the Lord Deputy, Sir John Perrott.

(b) THE NEW SETTLERS IN ARMAGH.

In the Armagh portion of ancient Orgiall, the following were the chief English families :—Acheson, Brownlow, Powell, St. John, Hamilton, Cope, Rowlston (or Rolestone), etc.

(c) THE MODERN NOBILITY IN ARMAGH.

The modern noble families in Armagh have been—Acheson, earls of Gosford ; Caulfield, earls of Charlemont ; and Brownlow, barons of Lurgan. The Hamiltons in former times had the title of earls of Clanbrassil.

4.—FERMANAGH.‡

(a) THE IRISH CHIEFS AND CLANS.

THE following were the Chiefs and Clans of Fermanagh, and the territories they possessed in the twelfth century :—1. **MacUidhir** (anglicised MacGuire and Maguire)

---

* *Hy-Meith-Macha* : The descendants of Muireadach Meith, son of Iomchadh [Imcha], who was a son of Colla-da-Chrioch, were called Hy-Meith or Ui-Meith. There were two territories of this name in the Kingdom of Orgiall : one called sometimes Ui Meith-Tire (from its inland situation), and sometimes Ui-Meith-Macha, from its contiguity to Armagh ; and the other Ui-Meith Mara, from its contiguity to the sea. The latter was more anciently called " Cuailghne ;" and its name and position are preserved in the anglicised name of " O'Meath," a district in the county Louth, comprising ten townlands, situate between Carlingford and Newry. The " Hy-Meith Macha" or " Hy Meith Tire" is a territory in the present county Monaghan, comprising the parishes of Tullycorbet, Kilmore, and Tehallan, in the barony of Monaghan. Of this territory the O'Hanrattys were the ancient chiefs, before they were dispossessed by the sept of the Mac Mathghamhna (or MacMahons) ; and Saint Maeldoid, the patron saint of Muckno, at Castleblayney, was of the same stock as the O'Hanrattys. That Saint Maeldoid, according to Colgan, was a lineal descendant of Colla-da-Crioch : " S. Maldodius de Mucknam, filius Fingini, filii Aidi, filii Fiachri, filii Fiachæ, filii Eugenii, filii Briani, filii Muredachi, filii Colla-fochrioch (or Colla-da-Chrioch)." The Muintir Birn (some of whose descendants have anglicised their name *Bruen*), a district in the south of the barony of Dungannon, adjoining the territory of Trough in the county Monaghan, and Toaghie, now the barony of Armagh, were descended from the same progenitor as the Ui-Meith, namely, Muredach Meith, as above.

† *Breasal Macha* : This was the territory of the Ui-Breasal, or, as they were called, the Ui Breasal Macha ; descended from Breasal, son of Felim, son of Fiachra Casan, son of Colla-da-Chrioch. In later ages this territory was more usually called *Clann Breasal*, anglicised "Clanbrazil" or "Clanbrassill." The tribe of O'Garvey were the ancient chiefs of this territory ; but in more modern times it belonged to the MacCanns, who were descended from Rochadh,†the son of Colla-da-Chrioch. This territory was on the south of Lough Neagh, where the Upper Bann enters that lake, and was co-extensive with the present barony of O'Neilland East, in the county of Armagh ; and according to a map of Ulster made in the reign of Queen Elizabeth, or James the First, it would appear that, in the formation of the baronies, more than one territory was placed in that of O'Neilland. The fact is, that all the eastern part of the Kingdom of Orgiall, called " Oirthear," was occupied by septs of the race of Niallan : that district including the present baronies of East and West O'Neilland and also those of East and West Orior ; for, the sept of O'h-Anluain (or the O'Hanlons), who possessed the two latter baronies, were descended from the aforesaid Niallan, another descendant of Colla-da-Chrioch.—*Book of Rights.*

‡ *Fermanagh* : In the early ages, according to our old annalists, the lake called Lough Erne suddenly burst forth and overflowed a great tract of land which was called *Magh Geannain* or the " Plain

3 F

was chief of *Feara Monach* (or "Fermanagh"). 2. **O'Muldoon**, chief of Muintir Maolduin and Feara Luirg, now known as the barony of "Lurg." 3. **Muintir Taithligh**, Tilly or Tully, chiefs of Hy-Laoghaire, of Lough Lir, a district which lay in the barony of Lurg, near Lough Erne, towards Tyrone. 4. **MacDuilgen** or **Mac-Dwilgan**, not mentioned in O'Dugan, is A.D. 924, in the Annals of the Four Masters, given as Fergus MacDuilgen, lord of Lurg. 5. **O'Flanagan**, chief of Tuath Ratha (a name retained by the mountain "Tura") or the District of the Fortress, a territory which extended from Belmore to Belleek, and from Lough Melvin to Lough Erne, comprising the present barony of Magheraboy. 6. **Gilfinan**, chief of Muintir Peodachain of the Port, on the borders of Fermanagh and Donegal; and still traceable in the name of "Pettigo." (By metathesis we might derive "Pakenham" from this Irish clan: Peodachain, Pachain, Pachena, Pakenha—Pakenham). 7. **Mac Giolla Michil** or **Gilmichael** (anglicised "Michil" and "Michael") was chief of Clan Congail. In the Annals of the Four Masters, at A.D. 1238, it is stated that Clan Congail and O'Ceanfada [O'Kennedy] lay in Tir Managh or Fermanagh: this Clan or Tir O'Ceanfhada is probably the present barony of "Tirkennedy." 8. **O'Mulrooney** and **O'Heany**, who were chiefs of Muintir Maolruanaidh (as the descendants of Maolruanaidh, No. 104, page 672, were called), and of Maoith Leirg Monach. 9. **MacDonnell**, chief of Clan Celleagh, now the barony of "Clankelly."

The following clans, not given in O'Dugan, are collected in Connellan's Four Masters from other sources:—10. **MacManus**, a numerous clan (chiefly in Tirkennedy), who had the control of the shipping on Lough Erne, and held the office of hereditary chief managers of the fisheries under Maguire. 11. **MacCassidy**, who were hereditary physicians to the Maguires. Roderick MacCassidy, archdeacon of Clogher, who partly compiled the "Annals of Ulster," was a distinguished member of this important family. 12. **O'Criochain** (who were descended from Colla-da-Chrioch), anglicised O'Creighan, O'Greighan, Cregan, Crehan, Creighton, Creehan, Grehan, and Graham,* were a numerous clan in Fermanagh. 13. **MacGrath**, who held possession at Termon M'Grath, where they had a castle in the parish of Templecarne.

"Maguire's Country" was, in the reign of Queen Elizabeth, A.D. 1569, formed into the county Fermanagh, by the lord deputy Sir Henry Sidney.

(b) THE NEW SETTLERS IN FERMANAGH.

On the "Plantation of Ulster," in the reign of King James the First of England, the following English and Scotch families obtained extensive grants of the confiscated lands in Fermanagh, as given in Pinnar's Survey, A.D. 1619, quoted in Harris's *Hibernia*:—Sir James Belford, Mr. Adwick, Sir Stephen Butler, ancestor of the earls of Lanesborough; John Sedborrow, Thomas Flowerdew, Edward Hatton, Sir Hugh Wirrall, Sir John Davies, who was Attorney-General to King James the First, and a celebrated writer; Sir Gerrard Lowther, John Archdall, Edward Sibthorp, Henry Flower, Thomas Blennerhasset, Sir Edward Blennerhasset, Francis Blennerhasset; Sir William Cole, ancestor of the earls of Enniskillen; Sir Henry Folliot (now Ffolliot), Captain Paul Gore, Captain Roger Atkinson, Malcolm Hamilton, George Humes, Sir

---

of Geannan," so called from Geannan, one of the Firbolg kings. This lake was anciently called Lough Saimer; and, according to Walsh, in quoting *Cambrensis Eversus*, derived the name "Erne" from Erna, the favourite waiting-maid of Maud or Meav (the famous queen of Connaught) who was drowned there. In the tenth, eleventh, and twelfth centuries, the head chief of this territory was O'Duibhdhara or O'Dwyer, whom O'Dugan mentions as chief of the race of Daimhin (No. 92 on the "O'Hart" pedigree) and several of the names are mentioned in the Annals of the Four Masters, at A.D. 1086, and in Mac Firbis's genealogical work, page 304; amongst others, Giolla Chriosd O Duibhdara, prince of Fermanagh, who A.D. 1076, was killed at Daimhinis or Devenish Island, in Lough Erne.

* *Graham or Grahame*: The author of that excellent American work, "Irish Family Names," lately published, says:—"The Montrose family, the most eminent of the modern representatives of this grand old Celtic stock, trace their pedigree back to the first half of the fifth century of our era, and to Græme, the distinguished general, who administered the affairs of Scotland in the interest and during the minority of Eugene II., grandson of Fergus II. (A.D. 411-429), of the Dalriadic line of Kings of what we now know as Scotland. Many of the Grahams of Ulster trace their descent from this illustrious stock, originally of the oldest of the 'old Irish' element. The Graham tartan suggestively enough gives prominence, in its make-up, to the '*Emerald green*.'"

John Humes, and John Dunbar. Two or three of the natives obtained grants, namely—Connor (Mac Shane) O'Neill, 1,500 acres; Bryan Maguire, 2,000 acres; and Connor Roe Maguire, who obtained large grants, and was created baron of Enniskillen.

(c) The Modern Nobility in Fermanagh

The following have been the noble families in Fermanagh since the reign of King James the First: Cole, earls of Enniskillen; Creighton, earls of Erne; Corry, earls of Belmore; Verney, viscounts of Fermanagh; and Butler, barons of Newtown-Butler, and earls of Lanesborough. The family of Loftus, marquises of Ely, have a seat in Fermanagh.

5.—ULIDIA,* OR DOWN AND PART OF ANTRIM

(a) The Irish Chiefs and Clans.

The Chiefs and Clans of Ulidia, and the territories they possessed in the twelfth century, as collected from O'Dugan's Topography, are as follows:—

The Craobh Ruadh [Creeveroe] or the portion of the Red Branch Knights of Ulster, a large territory which comprised the central parts of the present county Down, with some adjoining parts of Armagh, is given by O'Dugan as the head territory of Ulidia. The principal chiefs of the Creeveroe were—1. O'Duinnshleibhe or MacDunnshleibhe, kings or princes of the territory (of this family was Rory, the last king of Ulidia. This name has been anglicised "Donlevy," "Dunlevy" and "MacDunlevy"); O'Heochadha (anglicised "O'Heoghy," "Hoey," "Howe," etc.) a branch of the O'Dunlevys; O'Haidith (Heady or Head), O'Eochagain (or O'Geoghagan), O'Lavary, O'Lowry, O'Luingsigh (anglicised Longsy, Linskey, Linch, and Lynch), O'Moran, and O'Mathghamhna (O'Mahon, MacMahon). O'Garvey and O'Hanvey, were chiefs of Hy-Eachach Coba, now the barony of "Iveagh." 2. MacAongusa, chief of Clan Aodha or Clan Hugh, the tribe name of the family. (The MacAongusa, or Guinness, MacGuinness, and Magenis, had the baronies of Iveagh, and Lecale, and part of Mourne; and were lords of Iveagh, Newry, and Mourne. They were the head of the Clan-na-Rory in Ulster). 3. MacArtan, chief of Cinel Fogartaigh, now the baronies of "Kinelarty," and Dufferin. 4. O'Duibheanaigh (Devany, Duffeny, Dooney, Downey), chief of Cinel Amhalgaidh, now "Clanawley," in the county Down. 5. MacDuileachain or O'Duibhleachain (Doolecan or Doolan), chief of Clan Breasail MacDuileachain, near Kinelarty, in the barony of Castlereagh. 6. O'Coltarain, (Coleton, Coulter), chief of Dal Coirb, in the barony of Castlereagh. 7. O'Flinn, and O'Domhnallain or O'Donnellan, chiefs of Hy-Tuirtre: a people seated on the east side of the river Bann and Lough Neagh in Antrim; and descended from Fiachra Tort, grandson of King Colla Uais. Hy-Tuirtre comprised the baronies of Toome and Antrim, and was afterwards known as northern Clanaboy. 8. O'Heirc (Eric, Earc, Hirk), chief of Hy-Fiachra Finn, in the barony of Massarene. 9. O'Criodain (Credan, Creden, and

---

* *Ulidia*: The name "Uladh" was applied to the province of Ulster, but in after times was confined, as mentioned in the chapter on Orgiall, to a large territory on the east of Ulster, called Ulidia. This territory was also called Dalaradia (*dal*: Irish, a part or portion, and *Araidhe*, a man's name), signifying the descendants of Araidhe, a king of Ulster in the third century; and comprised the present county Down, with a great portion of Antrim, extending from Iubhar or Newry, Carlingford Bay, and the Mourne mountains, to Slieve Mis mountain in the barony of Antrim; thus containing, in the south and south-east parts of Antrim, the districts along the shores of Lough Neagh and Belfast Lough, Carrickfergus, and the peninsula of Island Magee to Larne; and thence in a line westward to the river Bann. The remaining portion of the county Antrim obtained the name of Dalriada. Ulidia is remarkable as the scene of St. Patrick's early captivity (it being there that he was sold as a slave to a chieftain named Milcho, whose flocks he tended near Mis mountain), and is celebrated as the place where he made the first converts to Christianity; and finally, as the place of his death and burial. He died at Sabhal, afterwards the parish of "Saul;" and was buried in the cathedral at Dune, which, in consequence, was called *Dunepatrick* or "Downpatrick."—CONNELLAN.

Creed), chief of Machaire Maedhaidh, now the parish of "Magheramisk," in the barony of Massarene. 10. O'Haodha, O'Hugh or Hughes, chief of Fearnmhoighe or Fernmoy, a district in the county Down, on the borders of Antrim, in the barony of Lower Iveagh. 11. O'Caomhain* or Kevin, chief of Magh Lini, now Moylinny, a district in the barony of Antrim. 12. O'Machoiden, chief of Mughdhorn or Mourne. 13. O'Lachnain or O'Loughnin, chief of Modharn Beag or Little Mourne. In addition to those clans given by O'Dugan, the following clans in Ulidia are given from other authorities :—14. MacGee or Magee, of Island Magee. 15. MacGiolla-Muire (Mac-Gillmore or Gilmore), who possessed the districts of the great Ards. 16. MacRory or Rogers, chiefs of Killwarlin. 17. O'Kelly of Clanbrasil Mac Coolechan, in the county Down. 18. Ward or Mac Ward. 19. Gowan (*gobha :* Irish, *a blacksmith*) and Mac-Gowan (modernized "Smith," "Smeeth," and "Smythe") were of the Irian race and of the Clan-na-Rory, and were mostly expelled by the English into Donegal, whence large numbers of them emigrated to the county Leitrim, and more lately to the county Cavan. Dal Buinne, a district in Ulidia, was not given by O'Dugan ; but it was situated on the borders of Down and Antrim, and contained the parish of Drumbo, in Down, with those of Lisburn, Magheragall, Magheramask, Glenavy, Aghalee, and Aghagallen, in Antrim. The Dal Buinne were of the Irian race.

In the fourteenth century, Hugh Buidhe O'Neill, prince of Tyrone, with his forces, crossed the Bann and took possession of the northern part of Ulidia, which, from its being possessed by his posterity, who were called *Clan Aodh Buidhe*, was anglicised "Clanaboy," or "Clandeboy." This territory was divided into North Clanaboy and South Clanaboy. A part of North Clanaboy also obtained the name of "Brian Carragh's Country," from its having been taken from the O'Neills by a chief of the MacDonnells, who was called Brian Carragh. South Clanaboy comprised the baronies of Ards, Castlereagh, Kinelarty, and Lecale ; and extended, according to Mac-Geoghegan, from the Bay of Dundrum to the Bay of Carrickfergus on Belfast Lough.

(b) THE NEW SETTLERS IN DOWN AND ANTRIM,

Or Ulidia.

John De Courcy with his forces overran a great part of Orgiall and Ulidia ; and for a period of twenty years carried on an incessant warfare with the native chiefs. As already mentioned, he fixed his head-quarters at Downpatrick. After De Courcy had been driven out of Ireland by his great rivals, the De Lacys, lords of Meath, the latter obtained possession of Ulidia, and were created earls of Ulster. The De Burgos next became possessors of Ulidia, and earls of Ulster ; which title and possessions afterwards passed to the Mortimers, earls of March, in England. The chief settlers in Ulidia, under De Courcy and his successors, were those of Audley, Bisset, Copeland, Fitzsimon, Chamberlain, Bagnall, Martell, Jordan, Mandeville, Riddle, Russell, Smith, Staunton, Logan, Savage, Walsh, and White. In the reign of Queen Mary, the Fitzgeralds, earls of Kildare, obtained *Leath Chathail* or "Lecale," a well-known barony in the county Down, anciently called Magh Inis or the Insular Plain.

(c) THE MODERN NOBILITY IN DOWN AND ANTRIM,

Or Ulidia.

The following noble families in more modern times settled in the county Down :— Hamilton, barons of Clanaboy and earls of Clanbrassil. Montgomery, earls of Mount Alexander, in the barony of Ards. Cromwell, viscounts of Ardglass—a title after-wards possessed by the Barringtons. Hill, barons of Kilwarlin, viscounts of Hills-borough, and now marquises of Downshire. Annesley, barons of Glenawley, and viscounts Annesley of Castlewellan. Rawdon, Hastings, earls of Moira. Jocelyn, barons of Clanbrassil, and earls of Roden. Stewart, viscounts Castlereagh, now mar-quises of Londonderry. Dawney, viscounts of Down. Ward, barons of Bangor.

---

* *O'Caomhain:* See the "Coen" pedigree for another family of this name, in Ireland.

Needham, earls of Kilmorey, and viscounts of Newry and Mourne. Smyth, viscounts of Strangford. Blackwood, barons of Dufferin, etc.

Down, in Irish "Dun" (signifying *a fortress*), was in ancient times called Dundaleathglas, and afterwards DunPadraic or Downpatrick, from St. Patrick having been buried there. Down comprised the greater part of ancient Ulidia or Dalaradia; and was, in the reign of Edward the Second, formed into two counties, namely, Down, and the Ards (or Newtown); but in the reign of Queen Ellzabeth, both were formed into the present county Down, which got its name from the chief town Dune or Downpatrick, and is Latinized "Dunum."

6.—DALRIADA,* OR PART OF ANTRIM AND DERRY.

(a) The Irish Chiefs and Clans.

The chief clans in Dalriada were as follows:—The O'Cahans, and MacUidhilin or MacQuillan, who held the territory of the Routes, and had their chief seat at Dunluce. The MacDonnells of the Hebrides invaded, A.D. 1211, the territories of Antrim and Derry, where they afterwards made settlements. In the reign of Elizabeth, Somhairle Buidhe MacDonnell or "Sorley Boy," as he was called by English writers,—a chief from the Hebrides, descended from the ancient Irish of the race of Clan Colla, came with his forces and took possession of the Glynns. After many long and fierce battles with the MacQuillans, the MacDonnells made themselves masters of the country, and dispossessed the MacQuillans. Dubourdieu, in his *Survey of Antrim*, says:—"A lineal descendant of the chief MacQuillan lives on the road between Belfast and Carrickfergus, near the Silver Stream, and probably enjoys more happiness as a respectable farmer, than his ancestor did as a prince in those turbulent times." The MacDonnells were created earls of Antrim. The O'Haras, a branch of the great family of O'Hara in the county Sligo, also settled in Antrim; and several families of the O'Neills. The other clans in this territory were the O'Siadhails or Shiels; the O'Quinns, O'Furries, MacAllisters, MacGees or Magees, etc.

(c) The Modern Nobility in Dalriada.

The following have been the noble families in Antrim, in modern times:—The viscounts O'Neill; Chichester, earls of Belfast, and marquises of Donegal; earl MacCartney, baron of Lisanoure; Clotworthy, and Skeffington, earls of Massareene; and Vaughan, barons of Lisburn.

Antrim was formed into a county in the reign of King Edward the Second: and took its name from the chief town, in Irish *Aendruim*, which is said to signify the "Handsome Hill:" from "Aen" or "Aon," *excellent*, and "druim," *a hill*. It is Latinized "Aendromia" and "Antrumnia."

---

* *Dalriada:* This ancient territory comprised the remaining portion of the county Antrim, not mentioned under Ulidia in the last chapter, together with a small part of the present county Derry: as Dunboe, now the parish of Dunboe, in the barony of Coleraine, county Derry, was (according to the Four Masters) in ancient Dalriada. As elsewhere mentioned, this territory was named after Cairbre Riada, son of Conaire (or Conary) the Second, Monarch of Ireland, in the second century. Dalriada is connected with some of the earliest events in Irish history. In this district, according to our old Annalists, the battle of Murbolg was fought between the Nemedians and Fomorians, two of the earliest colonies who came to Ireland; and here Sobairce, Monarch of Ireland, of the race of Ir, long before the Christian era, erected a fortress in which he resided; which, after him, was called *Dunsobairce* or the *Fortress of Sobairce*, now "Dunseverick," which is situated on a bold rock projecting into the sea near the Giants' Causeway: And it is mentioned by the Four Masters that at this fortress of Dunseverick, Roitheachtach, No. 47, page 353, was killed by lightning. In after times, the chief O'Cathain had his castle at Dunseverick, the ruins of which still remain. Dalriada was divided into two large districts: 1st, "The Glynns" (so called from its consisting of several *large glens*), which extended from Olderfleet or Larne to the vicinity of Ballycastle, along the sea-shore; and contained the barony of Glenarm, and part of Carey; 2nd. "The Routes," called Reuta or Ruta, which comprehended the baronies of Dunluce and Kilconway.—Connellan.

7.—TIROWEN.*

(a) THE IRISH CHIEFS AND CLANS.

THE chiefs and clans of Tir-Owen, and the territories they possessed in the twelfth century, as given by O'Dugan, are as follows :—1. **O'Neill** and **MacLoghlin** ,as princes. 2. **O'Cahan,** of the race of Owen, and who was chief of Cianacht of Glean Geibhin (or Keenaght of Glengiven). The O'Cahans were also chiefs of the Creeve, now the barony of Coleraine ; and in after times, possessed the greater part of the county Derry, which was called "O'Cahan's Country ;" they also, at an early period, possessed part of Antrim, and had their seat at the castle of Dunseverick. 3. The **O'Connors,** who were chiefs of Cianacta before the O'Cahans, and were descendants of Cian, son of Olioll Olum, King of Munster : hence their territory obtained the name of Cianachta, a name still preserved in the barony of "Keenaught," county Derry. 4. **O'Duibhdiorma** or **O'Dwyorma,** sometimes anglicised O'Dermot or O'Dermody, but a distinct clan from MacDermot, prince of Moylurg, in Connaught. The O'Dwyorma were chiefs of Breadach which comprised the parishes of Upper and Lower Moville, in the barony of Innishowen. The name of this district is still preserved in the small river "Bredagh," which falls into Lough Foyle. **O'Gormley** or **Grimly,** chief of Cineal Moain, now the barony of Raphoe, county Donegal. 6. **Moy Ith** and **Cineal Enda,** partly in the barony of Raphoe, and partly in the barony of Tirkeran in Derry. O'Flaherty places Moy Ith in Cinachta or Keenaught. According to O'Dugan, the following were the chiefs of Moy Ith :— O'Boyle, O'Mulbraisil, O'Quinn, and O'Kenny. 7. **O'Broder, O'Mulhall** and **O'Hogan,** chiefs of Carruic Bachuighe, still traceable by the name "Carrickbrack," in the barony of Inishowen. 8. **O'Hagan,** chief of Tullaghoge in the parish of Desertcreight, barony of Dungannon, and county Tyrone. 9. **O'Donegan** or **Dongan, MacMurchadh** or **MacMorough,** O'Farrell or **Freel,** and **MacRory** or **Mac-Rogers,** chiefs of Tealach Ainbith and of Muintir Birn, districts in the baronies of Dungannon and Strabane. 10. **O'Kelly,** chief of Cineal Eachaidh or Corca Eachaidh, probably "Corcaghee," in the barony of Dungannon. 11. **O'Tierney,** and **O'Kieran** chiefs of Fearnmuigh. 12. **O'Duvany,** Oh-Aghmaill or **O'Hamil,** and **O'Heitigen** or **Magettigan,** chief of three districts called Teallach Cathalain, Tealach Duibhrailbe, and Tealach Braenain. 13. **O'Mulfoharty,** and **O'Heodhasa** or **O'Hosey,** chiefs of Cineal Tighearnaigh. 14. **O'Cooney,** and **O'Bailey** (Bayly, or Bailie), chiefs of Clan Fergus. 15. **O'Murchada, O'Murphy,** and **O'Mellon,** chiefs of Soil Aodha-Eanaigh. 16. **MacFet ridge,** chief of Cineal Feraidaigh, in the north of Tyrone. In the Annals of the Four Masters, under A.D. 1185, mention is made of Gillchreest MacCathmhaoil (MacCampbell or MacCowell), head chieftain of the Cineal Fereadaidh, who was slain by O'Negnaidh

---

* *Tirowen:* After the conquest of Ulster by the three Collas, this territory was comprised within the Kingdom of Orgiall ; but Niall of the Nine Hostages, the 126th Monarch of Ireland, conquered that part of it called the "Kingdom of Aileach," of part of which (Tirowen) his son Eoghan or Owen, and of the other part (Tirconnell), his other son, Conall Gulban, were the first princes of the Hy-Niall sept. In after ages the territory of Tirowen expanded by conquest, so as to comprise the present counties of Tyrone and Derry, the peninsula of Inishowen (situate between Lough Foyle and Lough Swilly), and the greater part of the barony of Raphoe, in the county Donegal. This ancient territory is connected with some of the earliest events in Irish history. The lake now called Lough Foyle, according to Keating and O'Flaherty, suddenly burst forth in the reign of the Monarch Tiernmas, No. 41, page 354, and overflowed the adjoining plain, which was called Magh Fuinsidhe. This lake, mentioned in the Annals of the Four Masters as Loch Feabhail Mic Lodain, obtained its name from Feabhail (or Foyle), son of Lodan, one of the Tua-de-Danan chiefs, who was drowned in its waves. In this territory, on a high hill or mountain called Grianan. on the eastern shore of Lough Swilly, south of Inch Island, was situated the celebrated fortress called the Grianan of Aileach (from "Grianan," *a palace* or *royal residence,* and "Aileach" or "Oileach," which signifies *a stone fortress*), This fortress was also called "Aileach Neid" or "Oileach Neid," from Neid, one of the Tua-de-Danan princes ; and was for many ages the seat of the ancient Kings of Ulster. It was built in a circular form of great stones without cement, of immense strength, in that style called "Cyclopean" architecture ; and some of its extensive ruins remain to this day. It was demolished, A.D. 1101, by Murtogh O'Brien, King of Munster and the 180th Monarch of Ireland. This palace of Aileach is supposed to have been the "Regia" of Ptolemy, the celebrated Greek geographer, in the second century ; and the river marked "Argita" on his map of Ireland, is considered to have been the *Finn,* which is the chief branch of the Foyle river. The territory surrounding the fortress of Aileach obtained the name of Moy Aileach or the Plain of Ely. Tirowen was peopled by the race of Owen or the Clan Owen, some of whom, on the introduction of sirnames, took the name of "O'Neill," from their ancestor Niall Glundubh, the 170th Monarch of Ireland ; and some of them, the name MacLoghlin, from Lochlan, one of the Kings of Aileach. Some of the MacLoghlins, during the eleventh and twelfth centuries, were princes of Tirowen, and some of them were Monarchs of Ireland. Altogether, according to O'Flaherty, sixteen of the Clan Owen were Monarchs of Ireland.

or O'Neney, aided by Muintir Chaonain or the O'Keenans. That Gillchreest Mac-Cathmhaoil, was also head chieftain of clan Aongus, clan Dubhinreacht, clan Fogarty O'Ceanufhoda, and clan Colla of Fermanagh—"the chief of the councils of the north of Ireland." These Cathmhaoils were a powerful clan in Tyrone, and many of them in Monaghan, Louth and Armagh. 18. The clans of **Maolgeimridh** (Mulgemery, or Montgomery) and of **Maolpadraig** or **Kilpatrick**, who possessed the two districts of Cineal Fereadaidh (or Faraday), in the east of Tyrone. 19. **Muintir Taithligh** of Hy-Laoghaire of Lough Lir, a name anglicised MacTully or Tully. 20. **O'Hanter** or **Hunter**, chiefs of Hy-Seaain.

The following chiefs and clans, not given by O'Dugan, are collected in Connellan's Four Masters, from various other sources : 1. **O'Criochain** or **O'Crehan** (mentioned in the Annals of the Four Masters, under A.D. 1200), chief of Hy-Fiachra, a territory which comprised the parish of Ardstraw, and some adjoining districts in Tyrone. 2. **O'Quinn**, chief of Moy Lugad and of Siol Cathusaigh (a quo Casey), as given by the Four Masters, under A.D. 1218. Moy Lugad, according to the Books of Lecan and Ballymote, lay in Keenaght of Glengiven, county Derry. 3. The **O'Cearbhallins** (O'Carolans, or **Kerlins**), a name sometimes anglicised "Carleton," were chiefs of clan Diarmaida, now the parish of Clandermod or Glendermod, in Derry. 4. The **O'Brolachans**, by some changed to Bradley, etc., were a branch of the Cineal Owen. 5. **MacBlosgaidh** or **MacClosky**, a branch of the O'Cahans, was a numerous clan in the parish of Dungiven and the adjoining localities. 6. **O'Devlins**, chief of Muintir Dubhlin, near Lough Neagh, on the borders of Derry and Tyrone. 7. The **O'Looneys**, chiefs of Muintir Loney, a district known as the Monter Loney Mountains in Tyrone. 8. **O'Connellan**, chief of Crioch Tullach in Tyrone. 9. **O'Donnelly**, chiefs in Tyrone, at Ballydonnelly and other parts. 10. **O'Nena** (*ean :* Irish, *a bird*), **O'Neny** or **MacNeny** were chiefs of Cineal Naena, in Tyrone, bordering on Monaghan ; of this family was Count O'Neny of Brussels, in the Austrian service, under the Empress Maria Theresa. 11. **O'Flaherty**, lord of Cineal Owen, but a branch of the great family of O'Flaherty in Connaught. 12. **O'Murray**, a clan in Derry. 13. **MacShane** (a name anglicised "Johnson"), a clan in Tyrone. 14. **O'Mulligan**, anglicised "Molineux," were also a clan in Tyrone. 15. **O'Gnive** or **O'Gneeve** (anglicised "Agnew") were hereditary bards to the O'Neills.

The O'Neills maintained their independence down to the end of the sixteenth century, as princes of Tyrone ; and in the reigns of Henry the Eighth and Elizabeth, bore the titles of Earls of Tyrone and barons of Dungannon. The last celebrated chiefs of the name were Hugh O'Neill, the great Earl of Tyrone, famous as the commander of the northern Irish in their wars with Elizabeth ; and Owen Roe O'Neill, the general of the Irish of Ulster in the Cromwellian wars, A.D. 1641. Several of the O'Neills have been distinguished in the military service of Spain, France, and Austria. In consequence of the adherence of the Ulster chiefs to Hugh O'Neill, in the wars with Elizabeth, six counties in Ulster were confiscated, namely: Tyrone, Derry, Donegal, Fermanagh, Cavan, Armagh—all in the reign of King James the First. A project was then formed of peopling these counties with British colonies ; and this project was called the "Plantation of Ulster."

(c) The Modern Nobility in Tir-Owen.

In the survey of Ulster by Captain Pynnar, A.D. 1619, as stated in Harris's *Hibernica*, the following English and Scotch families are given as those who settled in Tyrone : Hamilton—the earl of Abercorn (more lately the title was "marquis," and now, in 1881, his grace the *Duke* of Abercorn is the representative of that ancient family), Sir George Hamilton, Sir Claude Hamilton, Sir Robert Newcomen, Sir John Drummond, the Earl of Castlehaven, Sir William Stewart, Sir John Davis, the Lord Ridgeway, George Ridgeway, Sir Gerrard Lowther, the Lord Burley, Sir Francis Willoughby, Sir William Cope, John Leigh, William Parsons, Sir Robert Heyborne ; Stewart, Lord of Uchiltree; Captain Saunderson, Robert Lindsay, Alexander Richardson, Andrew Stewart, David Kennedy, the Lord Chichester, Sir Toby Caulfield, Sir Francis Roe, Sir Francis Annesley, and the Lord Wingfield.

Since the reign of James the First the following noble families have settled in Tyrone :—the Le Poers were earls of Tyrone, a title which afterwards passed by intermarriage to the Beresfords. Blount, viscounts Mountjoy, a title which afterwards passed to the families of Stewart and Gardiner. Trevor, viscounts Dungannon. Stewart, viscounts Castlestewart. Knox, earls of Ranfurley. And Alexander, barons of Caledon.

Derry : In the reign of Elizabeth, "O'Cahan's Country" was formed by Sir John Perrott into a county, which was called from its chief town, the "County of Colerain ;" and in the reign of James the First, on the plantation of Ulster, a company of under-takers, consisting of merchants and traders from London, got grants of the "County of Colerain," and town of Derry : hence the city and county got the name of "London-derry."

Derry, in Irish, "Doire," signifies an *Oak Wood ;* and the town was anciently called "Doire-Calgach," signifying the *Oak Wood of Calgach,* from a chief of that name ; and afterwards "Derry-Columbkille," from the abbey founded there by that saint. The territory which now forms the county Derry was part of Tir-Eoghain or Tirowen ; and O'Cahan being the head chief it was called "O'Cahan's Country."

Derry is Latinized "Derria."

The following noble families derive their titles from this county :—The family of Pitt, formerly marquises of Londonderry, a title now possessed by the Stewarts. Hamilton, earls (now Dukes) of Abercorn, and barons of Strabane. The families of Hare and Hanger, barons of Coleraine.

Part of ancient Tyrone was, about A.D. 1585, formed into the county Tyrone by the lord deputy Sir John Perrott. The ancient "Tir-Eogain" has been Latinized "Tironia," and sometimes "Eugenia." Tirowen in later times was called "O'Neill's Country."

8.—TIRCONNELL.*

(a) THE IRISH CHIEFS AND CLANS.

THE following clans and chiefs, in Tir Conaill in the twelfth century, are given by O'Dugan under the head of Cineal Conaill :—1. **O'Maoldoraigh** or **Muldory, O'Canannain,** and **Clan Dalaigh,** were the principal chiefs. In the tenth century some of the head chiefs of the Clan Connell took the tribe name Clan-na-Dalaigh, from Dalagh, one of their chiefs, whose death is recorded by the Four Masters, at A.D. 868 ; but they afterwards took the name O'Dombnaill, or O'Donnell, from Domhnall or Donal, grandson of Dalagh. 2. **O'Boyle** were chiefs of Clan Chindfaoladh of Tir Ainmireach, and of Tir Boghaine—territories which comprised the present baronies of Boylagh and Banagh : Crioch Baoighilleach or the country of the O'Boyles gave name to the barony of "Boylagh ;" Tir Boghaine was the barony of "Banagh." 3. **O'Mulvany,** chief of Magh Seireadh or Massarey. 4. **O'Hugh,** chief of Easruadh [Esroe] or Ballyshannon, in the barony of Tir Hugh. 5. **O'Tairceirt** or **Tarkert,** chief of Clan Neachtain and of Clan Snedgaile or Snell. 6. **Mac Dubhaine** or **Mac Duane,** chiefs of Cineal Nenna or Cineal Enda, a district which lay in Inishowen. 7. **MacLoingseachain,** chiefs of Glean Binne ;

---

* *Tir-Connell :* This territory comprised the remaining portion of Donegal not contained in Tir-Owen, the boundary between both being Lough Swilly ; but in the twelfth century the O'Muldorys and O'Donnells, princes of Tir-Connell, became masters of the entire of Donegal : thus making Lough Foyle and the rivers Foyle and Finn the boundaries between Tir-Connell and Tir-Owen. This territory got its name from Conall Gulban, who took possession of it after its conquest by Niall of the Nine Hostages. He was brother to Owen, who possessed Tir-Owen ; from him the territory obtained the name of Tir-Connaill or "Connell's Country ;" and his posterity were designated Cineal Conaill or the race of Connell, a name which was also applied to the territory.

Some of the earliest events in Irish history are connected with this territory, amongst which the following may be noticed :—Inis Saimer was the residence of Bartholinus or Partholan, who first planted a colony in Ireland ; and this island gave the name Saimer to the river now called the Erne, and Lough Erne, which in ancient times was called Lough Saimer. The waterfall at Ballyshannon is connected with another early event, the death of Aodh Ruadh, an ancient king of Ireland who was drowned there ; hence it was called Eas-Aodha Ruaidh or the Cataract of Red Hugh ; and hence "Eas-Ruadh" [Ashroe] was the ancient name of Ballyshannon.

In the tenth century a branch of the Cineal (or Clan) Connell took the name of O'Canannain, many of whom were celebrated chiefs ; and another branch of them took the name of O'Maoldoraidh (angli-cised O'Muldory and Mulroy). and became princes of Tir-Connell. The O'Donnells, in the twelfth century, became princes of Tir-Connell. Rory O'Donnell, the last chief of the race was created earl of Tir-Connell, but died in exile on the Continent ; and his estates were confiscated in the reign of James the First.

and O'Breislen or Breslein, chief of Fanaid or Fanad, on the western shore of Lough Swilly. 8. **O'Dogherty**, chief of Ard Miodhair. In the Annals of the Four Masters, at A.D. 1197, Eachmarcach [Oghmarkagh] O'Doherty is mentioned as chief of all Tirconnell. The O'Doghertys maintained their rank as chiefs of Inishowen down to the reign of James the First. 9. **MacGilleseamhais** (anglicised Gilljames, James, and Fitzjames), chief of Ros-Guill, now "Rosgul," in the barony of Kilmakrenan. 10. **O'Kernaghan**, and **O'Dallan**, chiefs of the Tuath Bladhaidh. 11. **O'Mulligan**, chief of Tir Mac Caerthain. 12. **O'Donegan**, and **MacGaiblin** or **MacGiblin**, chiefs of Tir Breasail; and O'Maolgaoithe, chief of Muintir Maolgaoithe (*gaoth*: Irish, the *wind*; pronounced "ghee"). Some of this clan anglicised their name "Magee;" and others, "Wynne"—another form of "wind," the English for the word "gaoth," as above. 13. **MacTernan**, chief of Clan Fearghoile or Fargal. The following chiefs and clans not given by O'Dugan are collected from the Four Masters and other sources :—14. **MacSweeney** (strangely anglicised MacSwiggan), a branch of the O'Neills, which settled in Donegal, and formed three great families, namely, MacSweeney of Fanaid, who had an extensive territory west of Lough Swilly, and whose castle was at Rathmullin; MacSweeney Boghainach or of Tir Boghaine, now the barony of Banagh, who had his castle at Rathain, and in which territory was situated Reachrain Muintir Birn, now Rathlin O'Beirne Islands; and MacSweeney Na d-Tuath, signifying *MacSweeney of the Territories*. His districts were also called "Tuatha Toraighe" or the districts of *Tory Island*. This MacSweeney's possessions lay in the barony of Kilmacrenan. According to O'Brien, he was called "MacSweeney Na d-Tuath," signifying *MacSweeney of the Battle-axes*—a title said to be derived from their being chiefs of gallowglasses, and from their being standard bearers and marshals to the O'Donnells. A branch of these MacSweeneys, who were distinguished military leaders, settled in Munster in the county Cork, in the thirteenth century; and became commanders under the Mac-Carthys, princes of Desmond. 15. **O'Gallagher**, descended from a warrior named "Gallchobhar," were located in the baronies of Raphoe and Tir Hugh, and had a castle at Ballyshannon, and also possessed the castle of Lifford; they were commanders of O'Donnell's cavalry. Sir John O'Gallagher is mentioned in the wars of Elizabeth. 16. **O'Furanain** (or Foran), chief of Fion Ruis, probably the "Rosses," in the barony of Boylagh. 17. **O'Donnely**, chief of Fear Droma, a district in Inishowen, is mentioned in the Annals of the Four Masters, at A.D. 1177. 18. **O'Laney or Lane**, chief of Cineal Maoin, a district in the barony of Raphoe. 19. **O'Clery or Clarke**, hereditary historians to the O'Donnells; and the learned authors of the Annals of the Four Masters, and other valuable works on Irish history and antiquities. They had large possessions in the barony of Tir Hugh, and resided in their castle at Kilbarron;[*] the ruins of which still remain on a rock on the shores of the Atlantic near Ballyshannon. 20. **MacWard**, a clan in Donegal, were bards to the O'Donnells, and were very learned men.

Tir Connell was formed into the county Donegal by the lord deputy Sir John Perrott, in the reign of Queen Elizabeth.

(b) The New Settlers in Tirconnell,

Or Donegal.

On the confiscation of Tirconnell, and the settlement of British colonies called the "Plantation of Ulster," in the reign of King James the First, the following families are, in *Pynnar's Survey*, A.D. 1619, given as the possessors of Donegal :—John Murray got all Boylagh and Banagh. The following had various districts :—Captain Thomas Dutton, Alexander Cunningham (or Conyngham), John Cunningham, James Cunningham, Cuthbert Cunningham, Sir James Cunningham, James MacCullagh; William Stewart, the Laird of Dunduff; Alexander MacAwley, *alias* Stewart; the Laird of Lusse, Sir John Stewart, Peter Benson, William Wilson, Thomas Davis, Captain Mansfield, Sir John Kingsmill, Sir Ralph Bingley, Sir Thomas Coach, Sir George Marburie, Sir William Stewart, Sir Basil Brooke, Sir Thomas Chichester, Sir John Vaughan, John Wray, Arthur Terrie, Captain Henry Hart, Captain Paul Gore, Nathaniel Rowley, William Lynn, and Captain Sandford.

---

[*] *Kilbarron:* See Note, p. 633.

(c) The Modern Nobility in Tirconnell.

The following have been the noble families in Donegal since the reign of James the
First :—1. Fitzwilliam, earls of Tirconnell. 2. Richard Talbot, Lord Lieutenant of
Ireland, in the reign of James the Second, was created Duke of Tirconnell. 3. The
families of Brownlow and Carpenter have been subsequently earls of Tirconnell. 4.
Chichester, earls of Donegal. 5. Conyngham, earls of Mountcharles. 6. Cockayne,
barons of Cullen. 7. Hewitt, barons of Lifford. Etc.

Tirconnell was, about A.D. 1585, formed into a county by the lord deputy Perrot ;
and called Donegal, from its chief town. The names Donegal and Tirconnell are
Latinized " Dungallia" and "Tir-Connellia," and sometimes " Conallia."

Donegal, in Irish " Dun-na-nGall," signifying the *Fortress of the Foreigners*, got its
name, it is said, from a fortress erected there by the Danes. This ancient territory
was called Tir-Conaill or the Country of Conall, from Conall Gulbin, brother of Owen,
and son of Niall of the Nine Hostages, as already mentioned. In modern times the
head chiefs of this territory were the O'Donnells : hence it was called " O'Donnell's
Country."

9.—BREFNEY.*

(a) The Irish Chiefs and Clans.

The chiefs and clans of Brefney and the territories they possessed in the twelfth century,
are, according to O'Dugan, as follows :—1. O'Ruairc or O'Rourke ; 2. O'Raghallaigh
or O'Reilly : these were the princes of the territory of Brefney. 3. MacTighearnain (*tighearna :* Irish, a *lord* or *master*), anglicised MacTernan, McKiernan, and
Masterson, were chiefs of Teallach Dunchada (signifying the tribe or territory of
Donogh), now the barony of "Tullyhunco," in the county Cavan. 4. The MacSamhradhain (anglicised MacGauran, Magauran, and Magovern) were chiefs of Teallach

* *Brefney :* In Irish this word is " Breifne" or " Brefne," which signifies the *Hilly Country* ; it was
called by the English "The Brenny," and has been Latinized "Brefnia" and "Brefinnia." This
ancient territory comprised the present counties of Cavan and Leitrim, with a portion of Meath, and a
part of the barony of Carbury in Sligo ; O'Rourke being prince of West Brefney or Leitrim ; and
O'Rielly, or O'Reilly, of East Brefney or Cavan. Brefney extended from Kells in Meath to Drumcliff in
the county Sligo ; and was part of the Kingdom of Connaught, down to the reign of Queen Elizabeth,
when it was formed into the Counties of Cavan and Leitrim, and Cavan was added to the province of
Ulster. In this territory Tiernmas, the 18th Monarch of Ireland, was the first who introduced Idol
worship into Ireland ; and set up at Moy Slaght (now Fenagh, in the barony of Mohill, county Leitrim)
the famous idol, Crom Cruach, the chief deity of the Irish Druids, which St. Patrick destroyed. Brefney
was inhabited in the early ages by the Firvolgians (who are by some writers called Belgæ and Firbolgs),
who went by the name of "Ernaidhe," "Erneans," and "Ernaechs;" which names are stated to have
been given them from their inhabiting the territories about Lough Erne. These Erneans possessed the
entire of Brefnc٫. The name "Brefney" is, according to "Seward's Topography," derived from "Bre,"
a *hill*, and therefore signifies the country of hills or the hilly country : a derivation which may not
appear inappropriate as descriptive of the topographical features of the country, as innumerable hills
are scattered over the counties of Cavan and Leitrim. On a vast number of these hills over Cavan and
Leitrim are found those circular earthen ramparts called forts or raths, and some of them very large ;
which circumstance shows that those hills were inhabited from the earliest ages. As several thousands of
these raths exist even to this day, and many more have been levelled, it is evident that there was a very
large population in ancient Brefney. The erection of these raths has been absurdly attributed to the
Danes, for it is evident that they must have formed the chief habitations and fortresses of the ancient
Irish, ages before the Danes set foot in Ireland ; since they abound chiefly in the interior and remote
parts of the country, where the Danes never had any permanent settlement. Ancient Brefney bore
the name of Hy Briuin Breifne, from its being possessed by the race of Brian, King of Connaught, in
the fourth century, brother of Niall of the Nine Hostages, and son of Eochy Moyvane, Monarch of
Ireland from A.D. 357 to 365, and of the race of Heremon. That Brian had twenty-four sons, whose
posterity possessed the greater part of Connaught, and were called the "Hy-Briuin race." Of this race
were the O'Connors, kings of Connaught ; O'Rourke, O'Rielly, MacDermott, MacDonogh, O'Flaherty,
O'Malley, MacOiraghty (MacGeraghty, or Geraghty), O'Fallon, O'Flynn (of Connaught), MacGauran,
MacTiernan, MacBrady or Brady, etc. In the tenth century Brefney was divided into two principalities,
viz., Brefney O'Rourke or West Brefney, and Brefney O'Rielly or East Brefney. Brefney O'Rourke
comprised the present county Leitrim, with the barony of Tullaghagh and part of Tullaghoncho in the
county Cavan ; and Brefney O'Rielly, the rest of the present county Cavan : the river at Ballyconnell
being the boundary between Brefney O'Rourke and Brefney O'Rielly ; the O'Rourkes being the principal
chiefs. "O'Rourke's Country" was called Brefney O'Rourke ; and "O'Rielly's Country" Brefney
O'Rielly. The O'Rourkes, and O'Riellys maintained their independence down to the reign of James the
First, and had considerable possessions even until the Cromwellian wars; after which their estates were
confiscated.—CONNELLAN.

Eachach (which signifies the tribe or territory of Ecchy), now the barony of "Tullaghagh," county Cavan. This sirname is by some rendered "Somers," and "Summers," from the Irish word "Samhradh" [sovru], which signifies *summer*. 5. **MacConsnamha** (snamh : Irish, *to swim;* anglicised "Ford" or "Forde"), chief of Clan Cionnaith or Clan Kenny, now known as the Muintir Kenny mountains and adjoining districts near Lough Allen, in the parish of Innismagrath, county Leitrim. 6. **MacCagadhain** or **MacCogan**, chief of Clan Fearmaighe, a district south of Dartry, and in the present barony of Dromahaire, county Leitrim. O'Brien states that the Mac-Egans were chiefs of Clan Fearamuighe in Brefney : hence MacCagadhain and Mac-Egan may, probably, have been the same clan. 7. **MacDarchaidh** or **MacDarcy,** chief of Cineal Luachain, a district in the barony of Mohill, county Leitrim, from which the townland of Laheen may be derived. 8. **MacFlannchadha** (rendered Mac-Clancy), chief of Dartraidhe or Dartry, an ancient territory co-extensive with the present barony of Ross-Clogher in Leitrim. 9. **O'Finn** and **O'Carroll,*** chiefs of Calraighe or Calry, a district adjoining Dartry in the present barony of Dromahaire, and comprehending, as the name implies, an adjoining portion of Sligo, the parish of "Calry" in that county. 10. **MacMaoilliosa** or **Malliscn,** chief of Magh Breacraighe, a district on the borders of Leitrim and Longford. 11. **MacFionnbhair** or **Finvar,** chief of Muintir Gearadhain (O'Gearon or O'Gredan), a district in the southern part of Leitrim. 12. **MacRaghnaill** or **MacRannall** (anglicised Reynolds), who were chiefs of Muintir Eoluis, a territory which comprised almost the whole of the present baronies of Leitrim, Mohill, and Carrygallen, in the county Leitrim, with a portion of the north of Longford. This family, like the O'Farrells, princes of Annaly or Longford, were of the race of Ir or Clan-na-Rory ; and one of their descendants, the celebrated wit and poet, George Nugent Reynolds, Esq., of Letterfian, in Leitrim, is stated to have been the author of the beautiful song called "The Exile of Erin," though its composition was claimed by Thomas Campbell, author of "The Pleasures of Hope." 13. **O'Maoilmiadhaigh** or **Mulvey,** chief of Magh Neise or Nisi, a district which lay along the Shannon in the west of Leitrim, near Carrick-on-Shannon. The following clans in the counties of Cavan and Leitrim, not given by O'Dugan, are collected from other sources : 14. **MacBradaigh** or **MacBrady,** was a very ancient and important family in Cavan ; they were, according to MacGeoghagan, a branch of the O'Carrolls, chiefs of Calry. 15. **MacGobhain, MacGowan,** or **O'Gowan** (*gobha* : Irish, *a smith*), a name which has been anglicised "Smith," etc., were of the race of Ir ; and were remarkable for their great strength and bravery. Thus Smith, Smyth, Smeeth, and Smythe, may claim their descent from the Milesian MacGowan, originally a powerful clan in Ulidia. 16. **MacGiolladuibh, MacGilduff,** or **Gilduff,** chiefs of Teallach Gairbheith, now the barony of "Tullygarvey," in the county Cavan. 17. **MacTaichligh** or **MacTilly,** chief of a district in the parish of Drung, in the barony of Tullygarvey. 18. **MacCaba** or **MacCabe,** a powerful clan originally from Monaghan, but for many centuries settled in Cavan. 19. **O'Sheridan,** an ancient clan in the county Cavan. Richard Brinsley Sheridan, one of the most eminent men of his age, as an orator, dramatist, and poet, was of this clan. 20. **O'Corry** was a clan located about Cootehill. 21. **O'Clery** or **Clarke** was a branch of the O'Clerys of Connaught and Donegal, and of the same stock as the authors of the Annals of the Four Masters. 22. **O'Daly** and **O'Mulligan,** were hereditary bards to the O'Riellys. 23. **Fitzpatrick,** a clan originally of the Fitzpatricks of Ossory. 24. **Fitzsimon,** a clan long located in the county Cavan, are of Anglo-Norman descent, who came originally from the English Pale. 25. **O'Farrelly,** a numerous clan in the county Cavan. 26. Several other clans in various parts of Cavan, as O'Murray, MacDonnell, O'Conaghy or Conaty, O'Connell or Connell, MacManus, O'Lynch, MacGilligan, O'Fay, MacGafney, Mac-Hugh, O'Dolan, O'Drom, etc. 27. And several clans in the county Leitrim, not mentioned by O'Dugan, as MacGloin of Rossinver ; MacFergus, who were hereditary *erenachs* of the churches of Rossinver, and whose name has been anglicised "Ferguson ;" O'Cuirnin or Curran, celebrated bards and historians ; MacKenny or Keaney, MacCartan, O'Meehan, etc.

---

* *O'Carroll :* According to the *De La Ponce MSS.,* "O'Carroll" of Calry, has been modernized *MacBrady.*

(c) The Modern Nobility of Brefney.

Leitrim : The following were the chief settlers to whom large grants of land were given in the reigns of Elizabeth and James the First :—Hamilton, who erected a castle at Manorhamilton ; and the family of Villiers, dukes of Buckingham. Skerrard, in after times barons of Leitrim, and the family of Clements are at present earls of Leitrim.

Cavan : The following have been the noble families in the county Cavan, since the reign of James the First :—Lambert, earls of Cavan : Maxwell, earls of Farnham ; Coote, earls of Bellamont ; Pope, earls of Belturbet ; Verney, barons of Belturbet. Amongst the great landed proprietors, but not resident in the county, were the marquises of Headford, the earls of Annesley, and the earls of Gosford. And among the landed proprietors resident in the county have been—the earls of Farnham, the families of Burrowes, Clements, Coote, Humphreys, Nesbitt, Pratt, Saunderson, Vernon, etc.

Cavan is derived from the Irish "Cabhan" (pronounced " Cawan"), which signifies *a hollow place ;* and corresponds with the situation of the town of Cavan, which is located in a remarkable hollow.

In the reign of Queen Elizabeth, Brefney O'Rourke was, by the lord deputy, Sir Henry Sidney, formed A.D. 1565, into the county Leitrim, and so called from the town of Leitrim ; and in the same reign, A.D. 1584, Brefney O'Reilly was, by the lord deputy, Sir John Perrott, formed into a county, and called Cavan, from its chief town. Cavan was added to Ulster, and Leitrim was left in Connaught.

The name " Leitrim," in Irish *Liath-Druim*, signifies the *Grey Hill :* and from the town, the county was called Leitrim. as the county Cavan was called from the town of Cavan. Leitrim is Latinized " Leitrimnia ;" and Cavan, " Cavania."

IV.—ANCIENT MEATH. THE PRINCIPAL FAMILIES IN THE KINGDOM OF MEATH..

I.—IN THE COUNTY MEATH.

(a) The Irish Chiefs and Clans.

O'Dugan in his Topography says :

" Let us travel around Fodhla (Ireland),
    Let men proceed to proclaim these tidings ;
From the lands where we now are,
    The five provinces we shall investigate.

" We give the pre-eminence to Tara,
    Before all the melodious mirthful Gael,
To all its chieftains and its tribes,
    And to its just and rightful laws.

" The princes of Tara I here record :
    The Royal O'Hart, and likewise O'Regan ;
The host who purchased the harbours
    Were the O'Kellys and O'Connollys."

The " harbours" here mentioned were those of the river Shannon, bordering on the ancient Kingdom of Meath.

The Kingdom of Meath included Bregia and Teffia. The chiefs and clans of the Kingdom of Meath, and the territories they possessed, are as follows.: 1. O'Melaghlin, kings of Meath. Of this family Murcha was the king of Meath at the time of the Anglo-Norman invasion ; whose Kingdom was granted by King Henry the Second to Hugh de Lacey. 2. O'h-Airt or O'Hart were princes of Tara ; and when, on the Anglo-Norman invasion of Ireland, they were dispossessed of their territories in Bregia or the eastern portion of the Kingdom of Meath, they were lords in Teffia* or the western portion of that ancient Kingdom. Connellan styles O'Regan, O'Kelly, and O'Connolly, princes of Tara; and O'Donovan states that they were of the four families who, by pre-eminence, were known as the "Four Tribes of Tara."† The princes of Tara were also styled princes of Bregia,‡ a territory which extended between the Liffey and Boyne, from Dublin to Drogheda, thence to Kells; and contained the districts about Tara, Trim, Navan, Athboy, Dunboyne, Maynooth, Lucan, etc.; the territory comprising these districts and that part of the present county Dublin, north of the river Liffey, was known as "O'Hart's Country." O'Kelly of Bregia were chiefs of Tuath Leighe, parts of the baronies of West Narragh and Kilkea, in the county Kildare; they had also the district about Naas, and had their chief residence and castle at Rathascul or the Moat of Ascul, near Athy: the territory comprising these districts was known as "O'Kelly's Country." These O'Kellys are distinct from the O'Kellys of Clan Colla, who were princes of Hy-Maine, a territory in Galway and Roscommon. O'Regan were chiefs of Hy-Riagain, now the barony of Tinnehinch in the Queen's County. 3. O'Connolly, respectable families in Meath, Dublin, and Kildare; were chiefs in the county Kildare. 4. O'Ruadhri or O'Rory, now Rogers, lord of Fionn Fochla in Bregia. 5. O'Fallamhain or Fallon, lord of Crioch-na-gCeadach: so called from Olioll Cedach, son of Cahir Mór, King of Leinster, and the 109th Monarch of Ireland. The "Country of the O'Fallons" was near Athlone in the county Westmeath, but they were afterwards driven across the Shannon into Roscommon. 6. O'Coindeal-bhain (O'Kendellan, or O'Connellan), princes of Ibh-Laoghaire or "Ive-Leary," an extensive territory in the present counties of Meath and Westmeath, which was possessed by the descendants of Leary, Monarch of Ireland, at the time of St. Patrick. The parish of Castletown Kendellan in Westmeath shows one part of this ancient territory, and the townland of Kendellanstown, near Navan, shows another part of it. 7. O'Braoin or O'Breen, chief of Luighne, now the parish of "Leney," in the barony of Corcaree, Westmeath. 8. O'h-Aongusa or O'Hennessy, chief of Hy-Mac-Uais, now the barony of "Moygoish," in Westmeath. The Clan-Mac-Uais or MacEvoy, sometimes called MacVeagh and MacVeigh, of the race of Clan Colla, were the original chiefs of this territory. 9. O'h-Aodha (anglicised O'Hughes and O'Hayes), chief of Odhbha (probably "Odra" or "Oddor," in the barony of Skrine, near Tara). 10. O'Dubhain or Duane, chief of Cnodhbha, probably "Knowth," near Slane. 11. O'h-Ainbeath or O'Hanvey, chief of Fearbhile, now the barony of "Farbill," in Westmeath. 12. O'Cathasaigh or O'Casey, chief of Saithne, now "Sonagh," in Westmeath, where one of the castles of De Lacy stood, who conferred that property on the Tuite family. 13. O'Lochain or O'Loughan, chief of Gailenga, now the parish of "Gallen" in the barony of Garrycastle, King's County. 14. O'Donchadha or O'Donoghoe, chief of Teallach Modharain, probably now "Tullamore, in the King's County. 15. O'Hionradhain, chief of Corcaraidhe, now the barony of "Corcaree" in Westmeath. 16. O'Maolmuaidh or O'Mulloy, Prince of Ferceall, comprising the present baronies of Ballycowen, Ballyboy, and Eglish or "Fercall," in the King's County. 17. O'Dubhlaidhe or O'Dooley, chief of Fertullach, the present barony of "Fertullagh," in Westmeath. 18. O'Fionnallain or O'Fenelan (of the race of Heber, and tribe of the

---

* *Teffia:* Another great division of ancient Meath was called Teabhtha Latinized "Teffia," which comprised the present county Westmeath, with parts of Longford and the King's County; and was the territory of Main, son of Niall of the Nine Hostages. It was divided into North and South Teffia. North Teffia or Cairbre Gabhra (or Gaura) was that portion of Annaly or the county Longford, about Granard; and South Teffia comprised the remaining portions of Annaly and Westmeath.

† *The Four Tribes of Tara:* "The Four Tribes of Tara, according to the Battle of 'Magh-Rath' [Moria], page 9, where those tribes are mentioned, were the families of O'h-Airt [O'Hart]; O'Ceallaigh [O'Kelly], of Breagh or Bregia; O'Conghaile (considered to be O'Connolly); and O'Riagain [O'Regan]." —*Book of Rights.*

‡ *Bregia:* The great plain of Meath, which included the greater part of the present counties of Meath and Dublin, was known by the name Magh Breagh (*magh breagh:* Irish, the *magnificent plain*) signifying the Plain of Magnificence. It was Latinized "Bregia" and by O'Connor called *Campus Brigantium* or the "Plain of the Brigantes," from its being possessed by the Brigantes or Clan-na-Breoghan, as the descendants of Breoghan (No. 34, page 50), were called. That plain, situated in the eastern part of the ancient kingdom of Meath, comprised five triocha-cheds or baronies, and included Fingal, a territory lying along the coast between Dublin and Drogheda. This territory was so called because of a colony of Norwegians, who settled there in the tenth century, and who were called by the Irish *Fionn Ghaill,* or "Fair-haired Foreigners": hence the term "Fingal," which was applied to the Norwegians; while *Dubh Ghaill* or "Black Foreigners" was the term applied to the Danes.

According to Connellan's Four Masters, Bregia, which was a portion of the territory possessed by the princes of Tara, presents vast plains of unbounded fertility: containing about half a million of acres of the finest lands in Ireland.

Dalcassians), lord of Delbhna Mór, now the barony of "Delvin," in Westmeath.
19. **O'Maollugach**, chief of Brogha, part of the now baronies of Delvin and Farbill.
20. **MacCochlain** or **MacCoghlan** (of the Dalcassians), lord of Dealbhna-Eathra, now the
barony of Garrycastle in the King's County. 21. **O'Tolairg** or **O'Toler** and **O'Tyler**,
chief of Cuircne (*cuircne*: Irish, *the progeny of Cuirc*, anglicised "Quirk"), now the
barony of Kilkenny West, in Westmeath. 22. **MacEoghagain** or **MacGeoghagan**, Prince
of Cineal Fiacha, now the barony of Moycashel, with parts of Rathconrath and
Fertullagh. The MacGeoghagans were one of the principal branches of the Clan
Colman, and were called Cineal Fiacha, from one of the sons of Niall of the Nine Hostages. 23. **MacRuairc** or **MacRourke**, chief of Aicme-Enda, descended from Enna
Finn, another son of Niall of the Nine Hostages. This clan was located in the district
in which is situated the Hill of Uisneach, in the barony of Rathconrath, in Westmeath.
24. **O'Cairbre** or **O'Carbery**, chief of Tuath Binn. 25. **O'Heochadha** (O'Heoghey, O'Hoey,
O'Howe, etc.), chief of Cineal Aengusa. 26. **O'Maelcolain** or **O'Mellon**, chief of Delvin
Beg or Little Delvin adjoining the barony of Delvin.

O'Dugan, in the continuation of his Topography of Meath, enumerates the different
chiefs and their territories in Teffia; among whom were the following:
1. **O'Catharnaigh** or **O'Kearney.** 2. **O'Cuinn** or **O'Quinn.** 3. **O'Confiacala** or
O'Convally. 4. **O'Lachtnain** or **O'Loughnan**, anglicised Loftus. 5. **O'Mureagain**,
(Murrin or Murrigan). The O'Quinns were chiefs of Muintir Giolgain, and had their
chief castle at Rathcline, in Longford. The other chiefs were:—1. **O'Flannagain** or
O'Flanagan, chief of Comar, which O'Dugan places beside "O'Braoin's Country."
2. **O'Braoin** or **O'Breen** of Breaghmhuine, now the barony of "Brawney" in Westmeath.
3. **MacConmeadha** or **Conmy**, of Muintir Laodagain. 4. **MacAodha** or **MacHugh**, of
Muintir Tlamain. 5. **MacTaidhg** or **MacTague**, of Muintir Siorthachain. By some of
the family the name has been anglicised "Montague." 6. **MacAmhailgadh** (anglicised
respectively, MacAwley, Macaulay, Magauley, and MacGawley), chief of Calraidhe or
Calrigia, a territory on the borders of Westmeath and the King's County; comprising
(according to MacGeoghegan) the barony of Kilcourcy, in the King's County. 7. **Mac-
Garghamna** (anglicised MacGorgan), of Muintir Maoilsionna. 8. **O'Dalaigh** or **O'Daley**,
of Corca Adhaimh or Corcadium, a territory in or contiguous to the barony of Clonlonan, in Westmeath. 9. **O'Scolaidhe** or **O'Scully**, of Dealbhna Iarthar or West Delvin.
10. **O'Comhraidhe** (anglicised O'Corry), of Hy-Mac-Uais or Moygoish in Westmeath.
11. **O'Haodha** or **O'Hea**, of Tir Teabtha Shoir or East Teffia. 12. **O'Cearbhaill** or **O'Carroll**, of Tara. 13. O'Duin, O'Doyne, or **O'Dunne**, of the districts of Tara. 14. **MacGiolla
Seachlan** or **O'Shaughlin**, of Deisceart Breagh, now the parish of "Dysart" in Westmeath. 15. **O'Ronain** or **O'Ronayne**, of Cairbre Gaura or northern Teffia. 16. **O'h-
Aongusa** or **O'Hennessy**, of Galinga Beg,* now the parish of "Gallen" in the King's
County.

The following chiefs and clans in Meath and Westmeath have not been given by
O'Dugan:—
1. **O'Sionnagh** (anglicised Fox), of the southern Hy-Niall, lords of Muintir Tadhgain
in Teffia, containing parts of the baronies of Rathconrath and Clonlonan in Westmeath,
with part of the barony of Kilcourcy, in the King's County. The head of this family
was distinguished by the title of "The Fox," and obtained large grants of land from
Queen Elizabeth, with the title of Lord of Kilcourcy. 2. **O'Malone**, a branch of the
O'Connors, Kings of Connaught, who had large possessions in the barony of Brawney,
in Westmeath. In former times, these chiefs had the title of "Barons of Clan-Malone,"
and afterwards obtained that of "Barons Sunderlin," of Lake Sunderlin, in Westmeath.
3. **O'Fagan**, a numerous clan in Meath and Westmeath, of which there were many respectable families, the head of which had the title of "Baron of Feltrim," in Fingal. The
following were also clans of note in Westmeath, namely, 4. **O'Cobthaidh** or **O'Coffey.**
5. **O'Higgin.** And in Meath, O'Loingseach or O'Lynch. 6. **O'Murphy.** 7. **O'Murray.**
8. **O'Brogan**, etc. The chiefs and clans of ancient Meath were, with few exceptions, of
the same race as the southern Hy-Niall; in our days, there are but few families of note,
descendants of the ancient chiefs and princes of Meath.

* *Galinga Beg*: According to O'Donovan, "Galinga Beg" included Glasnevin, near Dublin, north
of the river Liffey; but this Galinga Beg could not be the same as the Galinga Beg, in the King's
County.

(b) The New Settlers in Meath.

King Henry the Second having granted to Hugh de Lacy,* for the service of fifty Knights, the Kingdom of Meath, De Lacy divided that ancient Kingdom amongst his various chiefs, who were commonly denominated De Lacy's barons: 1. **Hugh Tyrrell** obtained Castleknock, and his descendants were for a long period barons of Castleknock. 2. **Gilbert de Angulo** (or Nangle) obtained Magherigallen, now the barony of "Morgallion," in Meath. 3. **Jocelin**, son of Gilbert Nangle, obtained Navan and Ardbraccan. The Nangles were afterwards barons of Navan; and many of them took the Irish name of "MacCostello," and from them the barony of *Costello* in Mayo derived its name. 4. **William de Missett** obtained Luin; and his descendants were barons of Lune, near Trim. 5. **Adam Feipo** or **Phepoe** obtained Skrine or Skryne, Santreff or Santry, and Clontorth (which means either Clonturk or Clontarf). This family had the title of barons of Skrine, which title afterwards passed to the family of Marward. 6. **Gilbert FitzThomas** obtained the territories about Kenlis; and his descendants were barons of "Kells." 7. **Hugh de Hose** obtained Dees or the barony of "Deece," in Meath. 8. **Hussey**, barons of Galtrim. 9. **Richard** and **Thomas Fleming** obtained Crandon and other districts. The Flemings became barons of Slane; and a branch of the family, viscounts of Longford. 10. **Adam Dullard** or **Dollard** obtained Dullenevarty. 11. **Gilbert de Nugent** obtained Delvin; and his descendants were barons of Delvin, and earls of Westmeath. 12. **Richard Tuite** obtained large grants in Westmeath and Longford; his descendants received the title of barons of Moyashell, in Westmeath. 13. **Robert de Lacy** received Rathwire in Westmeath, of which his descendants were barons. 14. **Jeoffrey de Constantine** received Kilbixey, in Westmeath, of which his descendants were barons. 14. **William Petit** received Castlebreck and Magheritherinan, now the barony of "Magheradernon" in Westmeath. The Petits became barons of Mullingar. 15. **Myler Fitzhenry** obtained Magherneran, Rathkenjn, and Athinorker, now "Ardnorcher." 16. **Richard de Lachapelle**, brother of Gilbert Nugent, obtained "much land."

(c) The Modern Nobility in Meath.

The following families settled in Meath in early times :—1. **De Geneville** succeeded the De Lacys as lords of Meath: and afterwards the great family of Mortimer, earls of March in England. 2. **Plunket** became earls of Fingal; and branches of them barons of Dunsaney, and earls of Louth. 3. **Preston**, viscounts Gormanstown; and another branch of them viscounts of Tara. 4. **Barnwall**, barons of Trimblestown, and viscounts Kingsland. 5. **Neterville**, barons of Dowth. 6. **Bellew**, barons of Duleek.† 7. **Darcy**, of Platten, some of whom were barons of Navan. The family of Jones were afterwards

* *Hugh de Lacy:* The De Lacys (see the "Lacy" pedigree) came from Normandy with William the Conqueror, and were earls of Lincoln in England. Hugh de Lacy came to Ireland with King Henry the Second, A.D. 1171, and obtained from that monarch a grant of the whole kingdom of Meath, as already mentioned. He was lord palatine of Meath, and many years chief governor of Ireland. He erected numerous castles, particularly in Meath and Westmeath, as those of Trim, Kells, Ardnorcher, Durrow, etc., and endowed some monasteries. He is thus described in Holingshed :—"His eyes were dark and deep-set, his neck short, his stature small, his body hairy, not fleshy, but sinewy, strong and compact; a very good soldier, but rather harsh and hasty." It appears from Hanmer and others, that he was an able and politic man in state affairs, but very ambitious and covetous of wealth and great possessions; he is also represented as a famous horseman. De Lacy's second wife was a daughter of King Roderick O'Connor; and his descendants, the De Lacys, were lords of Meath, and earls of Ulster, and founded many powerful families in Meath, Westmeath, and Louth, and also in Limerick, some of whom were distinguished marshals in the service of Austria and Russia. The castle of Dearmagh or "Durrow," in the King's County, was erected by De Lacy on the site of a famous monastery of St. Columkille, which he had thrown down; and his death was attributed by the uneducated Irish to that circumstance as a judgment from Heaven. The man who killed De Lacy fled to his accomplices in the wood of Clair or "Clara ;" but it appears from MacGeoghegan and others, that the Irish attacked and put to the sword the English retinue at the castle of Durrow, and that having got De Lacy's body into their possession, they concealed it nearly ten years, when, A.D. 1195, it was interred with great pomp in the abbey of Bective, in Meath; Mathew O'Heney, Archbishop of Cashel, and John Comyn, Archbishop of Dublin, attending at the ceremony.—CONNELLAN.

† *Duleek:* This word is in Irish "Doimhliag," signifying a *house* made of *stone.* This village was formerly a parliamentary borough; and in early times was the seat of a small dioces afterwards united to the see of Meath

barons of Navan. 8. **Cusack**, barons of Clonmullen. 9. **FitzEustace** (see the "Eustace" pedigree), barons of Portlester 10. **De Bathe** of Athcarn. 11. **Dowdall**, of Athlumney. 12. **Fleming**, of Stalhomock. 13. **Betagh** (or Beatty), of Moynalty. 14. **Cruise**, of Cruisetown and Cruise-Rath, etc. 15. **Drake**, of Drake-Rath. 16. **Corbally.** 17. **Everard.** 18. **Cheever**, some of whom had the title of barons of Mount Leinster. 19. **Dardis.** 20. **Delahoyd.** 21. **Balffe.** 22. **Berford** or **Bedford.** 23. **Caddell.** 24. **Scurlock** or **Sherlock.** 25. **Dillon.** In modern times the following families :—26. **Brabazon**, earls of Meath. 27. **Butler**, barons of Dunboyne. 28. **Wharton**, Baron of Trim. 29. **Schomberg**, Viscount Tara. 30. **Cholmondeley** (modernized "Chomley"), Viscount Kells. 31. **Hamilton**, Viscount Boyne. 32. **Colley Welsley** or **Wellesley**, of Dangan, Earl of Mornington, afterwards Marquis Wellesley, and Duke of Wellington. 33. **Taylor**, earls of Bective, and marquises of Headfort. 34. **Bligh**, earls of Darnley. 35. **The Marquis Conyngham**, at Slane. 36. **Langford Rowley**, Baron of Summerhill. 37. **Gerard, Garnet, Barnes, Lambert, Nappier** of Loughcrew, Waller, Tisdall or Tiesdale, Winter, Coddington, Nicholson, and Thomson, respectable families in modern times in Meath.

2.—WESTMEATH.

(c) The Modern Nobility.

In Westmeath the following families were located, together with those already enumerated :—1. **The Dillons** were originally of Irish descent, and of the race of Heremon. Their ancestor (see the "Dillon" pedigree) was descended from a branch of the southern Hy-Niall, in Meath ; went to France, in the seventh century ; and, being a famous warrior, became Duke of Aquitaine. One of his descendants came to Ireland with King John, and got large grants of land in Westmeath and Annaly ; his descendants were lords of Drumrany, in the barony of Kilkenny West ; and having founded many great families in Meath and Connaught, became earls of Roscommon, viscounts Dillon in Mayo, barons of Clonbrock, and barons of Kilkenny West ; and several of them were counts and generals in the French and Austrian Service. 2. **Dalton**, and **Delamere** obtained large possessions in Westmeath and Annaly. The chief seat of the Daltons was at Mount Dalton, in the barony of Rathconrath, of which they were lords ; and some of them were distinguished in the service of foreign states. 4. **Dease**, in Meath, and Westmeath. In more modern times the following families had titles in Westmeath : 5. **Rochford**, earls of Belvidere. 6. **De Ginkell**, earls of Athlone.

In Meath, up to very recently, the following baronets were located :—Sir William Somerville, Sir Henry Meredith, Sir Francis Hopkins, Sir Charles Dillon ; and in Westmeath the following : Sir Percy Nugent, and Count Nugent, Sir Richard Nagle, Sir John Bennet Piers, Sir Richard Levinge, and Sir John O'Rielly or O'Reilly.

Ancient Meath constituted the chief part of the English Pale,* and was divided into the counties of East Meath and Westmeath, in the reign of Henry the Eighth ; but its extent was diminished, as East Meath in early times contained parts of Dublin and Kildare, and Westmeath contained parts of Longford and King's County.

3.—ANNALY, OR LONGFORD.

Anghaile or "Annaly," which was formed out of the ancient territory of Teffia, comprised the whole of the county Longford, and was the principality of O'Farrell. His chief residence was the town of "Longford," anciently called Longphort-Ui-Fhearghail or the *Fortress of O'Farrell.* This territory was divided into Upper and Lower Annaly : the former comprising that part of Longford south of Granard, and a part of the county Westmeath, was possessed by O'Farrell O'Buidhe (or O'Farrell the *Yellow*) ; the latter, or that portion north of Granard, was possessed by O'Farrell Ban

* *English Pale:* The "English Pale" meant that part of Ireland occupied by the English settlers. In A.D. 1603, the distinction between the "Pale" and the "Irish Country" terminated, by the submission of Hugh O'Neill, Earl of Tyrone.

(or O'Farrell the *Fair*). The O'Farrells were dispossessed of the eastern portion of this territory by the Tuites and the Delameres, who came over with Hugh de Lacy in the twelfth century.

(a) THE IRISH CHIEFS AND CLANS OF LONGFORD.

Besides the O'Farrells, princes of Annaly, the following were among the ancient clans in the county Longford : 2. **O'Cuinn** or **O'Quinn**, who had his castle at Rathcline. There was also a powerful family of the O'Quinns in the county Clare (see "Thomond"), distinct from this family in Annaly. 3. **MacGilligan.** 4. **Muintir** (or people of) Megiollgain (Magillan or Magellan) were located in the territory of Muintir Eoluis, in the northern portion of the county Longford ; and their chief was O'Quinn. 5. **O'Mulfinny** or **Mul Feeney,** whose district was called Corcard. 6. **MacCormack.** 7. **MacCorgabhan.** 8. **O'Daly.** 9. **O'Slaman** or **O'Slevin.** 10. **O'Skolly** or **O'Skelly.** The O'Farrells maintained their sovereignty till the reign of Elizabeth ; when Annaly was formed into the county Longford, by the lord deputy Sir Henry Sidney.

(c) THE MODERN NOBILITY OF LONGFORD.

In modern times the following families have formed the nobility of Annaly:— 1. **Aungier,** earls of Longford ; afterwards Fleming ; and next Pakenham. 2. **Lane,** earls of Lanesborough, and next Butler. 3. **Gore** were earls of Annaly. 4. The family of **Forbes** are now earls of Granard.

4.—DUBLIN,* KILDARE,† AND KING'S COUNTIES.

(a) THE IRISH CHIEFS AND CLANS.

THE following accounts of the ancient chiefs of the territories now forming the counties of Dublin and Kildare, together with some of the princes and chiefs of Meath (of whom a full account has not been given in the Chapter on "Meath") have been collected from the Topographies of O'Dugan, O'Heerin, the Annals of the Four Masters, O'Brien, O'Halloran, MacGeoghegan, Ware, O'Flaherty, Charles O'Connor, Seward, and various other sources. As already mentioned, O'Connor, princes of Offaley ; O'Moore, princes of Leix ; O'Dempsey, lords of Clanmaliere, all possessed parts of Kildare. The O'Tooles, princes of Imaile, in Wicklow, also possessed some of the southern parts of Kildare ; and the O'Tooles, together with the O'Byrnes, extended their power over the southern parts of Dublin, comprising the districts in the Dublin mountains—1. **MacFogarty,** lords of South Bregia, are mentioned by the Four Masters in the tenth century. 2. **O'Ciardha** or **O'Carey,** chiefs of Cairbre O'Ciardha, now the barony of "Carbery" in the county

* *Dublin:* The grant of the Kingdom of Meath by King Henry the Second to Hugh de Lacy, A.D 1172, included that part of Bregia, containing those parts of the present county Dublin, north of the river Liffey. This grant, King John confirmed to Walter de Lacy, lord of Meath, the son of Hugh ; and gave him, besides, his fees in Fingal, to hold to him and his heirs for ever.
Parts of the territories of Moy Liffey and Bregia, with a portion of Cualan (or Wicklow), were formed into the county Dublin, A.D. 1210, in the reign of King John. In the sixteenth century, according to D'Alton's "History of Dublin," the county Dublin extended from Balrothery to Arklow —thus comprising a great part of the present county Wicklow.

† *Kildare:* In the reign of King John, parts of the territories of Moy Liffey, Offaley, Leix, and Cualan, were formed into the county Kildare ; but it was only a "liberty" dependent on the jurisdiction of the Sheriffs of Dublin, until A.D. 1296, in the reign of Edward the First, when Kildare was constituted a distinct county. It was called *Coill-Dara,* or the "Wood of Oaks," as oak forests abounded there in ancient times ; or, according to others, *Cill-Dara* or the "Church of the Oaks," as it is said that the first church founded at the present town of Kildare was built amidst oak trees.

3 G

Kildare. 3. **O'Murcain** or **O'Murcan**. 4. **O'Bracain** or **O'Bracken**, chiefs of Moy Liffey. The O'Murcans and O'Brackens appear to have possessed the districts along the Liffey, near Dublin. 5. **O'Gealbhroin**, chiefs of Clar Liffé, or the Plain of the Liffey, a territory on the borders of Dublin and Kildare. 6. **O'Fiachra**, chiefs of Hy-Ineachruis at Almhuin [Allen]; and O'Haodha or O'Hea, chiefs of Hy-Deadhaidh: territories comprised in the county Kildare, 7. **O'Muirthe** or **O'Murtha**, chiefs of Cineal Flaitheamhuin (or Clan Fleming); and O'Fintighearan, chiefs of Hy-Mealla : territories also situated in the county Kildare, it would appear in the baronies of East and West Ophaley or Offaley. 8. **O'Cullin** or **O'Cullen**, chiefs of Coille Culluin (or the Woods of Cullen), now the barony of "Kilcullen" in the county Kildare. 9. **O'Colgan**, MacDonnell, O'Dempsey, and O'Dunn, were all chiefs of note in Kildare. 10. **O'Dubthaigh** or **O'Duffy**, one of the Leinster clans of the race of the Monarch Cahir Mór ; and of the same descent as MacMorough, kings of Leinster, and O'Toole and O'Byrne, chiefs of Wicklow. Originally located in Kildare and Carlow, and afterwards in Dublin and Meath, the O'Duffys migrated in modern times to Louth, Monaghan, Cavan, Galway, and Roscommon. 11. **O'Fagan** or **MacFagan** are considered by some to be of English descent. D'Alton, in his "History of the County Dublin," mentions some of this family who, in the thirteenth, fourteenth, and fifteenth centuries, were high sheriffs, in Meath and Dublin. In former times the Fagans of Feltrim, near Dublin, and other parts of that county, were highly respectable, and held extensive possessions. 12. **O'Murphy**, chiefs in Wexford, were also numerous in the counties of Dublin and Meath. 13. **O'Mullen**, numerous in Meath, Dublin, and Kildare. 14. **MacGiollamocholmog** or **Gilcolm**, and O'Dunchada or O'Donoghoe, are mentioned by O'Dugan as lords of Fingal, near Dublin ; and, as mentioned in the chapter on "Hy-Kinsellagh," there was another MacGiollamocholmog, lord of a territory on the borders of Wicklow. 15. **O'Muircheartaigh**, or O'Moriarty, or O'Murtagh, chiefs of the tribe of O'Maine ; and O'Modarn, chiefs of Cineal Eochain, are mentioned by O'Dugan as chiefs of the Britons or Welsh ; and appear to have been located near Dublin. 16. **MacMuireagain**, lords of East Liffey, in the tenth century.

(*b*) THE NEW SETTLERS IN DUBLIN AND KILDARE.

As explained in the account of the grant of the Kingdom of Meath to Hugh de Lacy by King Henry the Second, De Lacy and his barons became possessed of the greater portion of the present county Dublin ; Hugh Tyrrell got the territory about Castleknock, which was long held by his descendants, as barons of Castleknock ; the Phepoes got Santry and Clontarf, and, according to MacGeoghegan, Vivian de Cursun got the district of Raheny, near Dublin, which belonged to Giollamocholmog.

In Dublin:—In the county and city of Dublin, the following have been the principal families, from the twelfth to the eighteenth century, but some of whom, it will be seen, are of Irish descent:—Talbot, Tyrrell, Plunket, Preston, Barnwall, St. Lawrence, Taylor, Cruise, Cusack, Cogan, White, Walsh, Wall, Warren, Wogan, Woodlock, Darcy, Netterville, Marward, Phepo, Fitzwilliam, Fleming, Fitzsimons, Archbold, Archer, Allen, Aylmer, Ball, Bagot, De Bathe, Butler, Barry, Barret, Bermingham, Brett, Bellew, Blake, Brabazon, Finglas, Sweetman, Hollywood, Howth, Hussey, Burnell, Dowdall, Dillon, Segrave, Sarsfield, Stanihurst, Lawless, Cadell, Evans, Drake, Grace, Palmer, Eustace, Fyan or Fynes, Foster, Gough, Berrill, Bennet, Brown, Duff, Nangle, Woder, Tuite, Tew, Trant, Peppard, Luttrell, Rawson, Vernon, Delahoyde, Usher, Garnet, Hamilton, Domville, Coghill, Cobb, Grattan, Molesworth, Latouche, Putland, Beresford, Shaw, Smith, etc. For accounts of all those families and others, see D'Alton's Histories of Dublin and Drogheda.

In Kildare:—In the county Kildare, the following have been the chief families of Anglo-Norman and English descent :—Earl Strongbow (a quo, probably the names "Strong" and "Stronge") having become heir to the kingdom of Leinster, as son-in-law of Dermod MacMurrough, king of that province, as already mentioned, gave grants of various parts of Leinster to his followers. Amongst other grants, Strongbow gave in Kildare to Maurice Fitzgerald, Naas and Offelan, which had been part of "O'Kelly's Country ;" to Myler Fitzhenry he gave Carbery ; to Robert de Bermingham, Offaley, part of "O'Connor's Country ;" to Adam and Richard de Hereford, a large territory about Leixlip, and the district called *De Saltu Salmonis* or the Salmon Leap (on the banks of the river Liffey, between Leixlip and Celbridge), from which the baronies of North and South "Salt" derive their name; and to Robert FitzRichard he gave the barony of Narragh. The family of De Riddlesford, in the reign of King John, got the district of Castledermot, which was part of the territory of O'Toole, prince of Imaile, in Wicklow; and Richard de St. Michael got from King John the district of Rheban, near Athy, part of "O'Moore's Country;" and from the St. Michaels, lords of Rheban, the manors of Rheban and Woodstock in Kildare, with Dunamase in the Queen's County, passed to the Fitzgeralds, barons of Offaley, A.D. 1424, by the marriage of Thomas Fitzgerald with Dorothea, daughter of Anthony O'Moore, prince of Leix. As already mentioned, the county Kildare, in the thirteenth century, became the inheritance of Sibilla, one of the daughters of William Marshall, Earl of Pembroke, by Isabella, daughter of Strongbow, and grand-daughter of Dermod MacMurrough, King of Leinster; and Sibilla having married William Ferrars, Earl of Derby, he became in right of his wife lord of Kildare; which title passed (by intermarriage of his daughter Agnes) to William de Vesey, a nobleman of the De Veseys, barons of Knapton in Yorkshire; and this William de Vesey was appointed by King Edward the First lord justice of Ireland, and was lord of Kildare and Rathangan. But having some contests with John FitzThomas Fitzgerald, baron of Offaley, who charged him with high treason, it was awarded to decide their disputes by single combat. De Vesey, having declined the combat and fled to France, was attainted, and his possessions and titles were conferred on Fitzgerald, who, A.D. 1316, was, by King Edward the Second, created earl of Kildare; and his descendants were, in modern times, created dukes of Leinster (see the "FitzGerald" pedigree). The other chief families in Kildare have been those of Aylmer, Archbold, Bagot, Burgh or Bourke, Butler, Brereton, Burrough, Boyce, Dungan or Dongan, Keating, Eustace or FitzEustace, Preston, Lawless, Wogan, Warren, White, Woulfe, Ponsonby, Nangle, Hort, etc. Some of the Aylmers of Kildare became barons of Balrath in Meath; and Arthur Woulfe, chief justice of the Queen's Bench, who was created "Viscount Kilwarden," was of the Wolfes or Woulfes of Kildare.

(c) The Modern Nobility of Dublin and Kildare.

The following have been the noble families in the counties of Dublin and Kildare since the reign of King John:—

In Dublin:—As already explained, the De Lacys were lords of Meath and of a great part of Dublin. In the year 1384, Robert de Vere, Earl of Oxford, and Lord Lieutenant of Ireland, was created Marquis of Dublin and Duke of Ireland; and, in the present Royal Family of Great Britain and Ireland, some of the dukes of Cumberland were earls of Dublin. Talbot, a branch of the Talbots, earls of Shrewsbury, Waterford, and Wexford, have been celebrated families in Dublin and Meath, chiefly at Malahide and Belgard in the county Dublin; and were created barons of Malahide, and barons of Furnival: of these was Richard Talbot, the celebrated duke of Tyrconnell, Lord Lieutenant of Ireland, under King James the Second. The Plunkets, great families in Dublin, Meath, and Louth, were created barons of Killeen and earls of Fingal; and branches of them, barons of Dunsany in Meath, and barons of Louth; William Conyngham Plunket, formerly Lord Chancellor of Ireland, was created "Baron Plunket." Preston, viscounts Gormanstown, and some of them viscounts of Tara. St. Lawrence, earls of Howth. Barnwall, viscounts of Kingsland, and barons of Turvey; and also barons of Trimblestown in Meath. De Courcey, barons of Kilbarrock. Fitzwilliam, viscounts of Merrion. Rawson, viscounts of Clontarf. Beaumont, viscounts of Swords; the Molesworths, viscounts of Swords. Temple, viscounts Palmerstown or Palmerston. Treacy, viscounts of Rathcoole. Patrick Sarsfield, the celebrated commander of the Irish forces under King James the Second, was created "Earl of Lucan;" and the Binghams are now earls of Lucan. The Marquis of Wharton, Lord Lieutenant of Ireland, was created earl of Rathfarnham; and the family of Loftus, viscounts of Ely, were also earls of Rathfarnham. Luttrell, earls of Carhampton. Leeson, earls of Miltown. Harman, viscounts of Oxmantown (the name of an ancient district in the vicinity of Dublin); and the family of Parsons, earls of Rosse, in the King's County, are barons of Oxmantown. Wenman, barons of Kilmainham. Barry, barons of Santry. Caulfield, earls of Charlemont, resided until lately at Marino, Clontarf. Brabazon, earls of Meath, have extensive possessions in Wicklow and Dublin. And Thomas O'Hagan, of Dublin, Lord Chancellor of Ireland under the Gladstone Administration, was A.D. 1870, in the peerage of the United Kingdom, created "Baron O'Hagan."—See the "O'Hagan" pedigree.

In Kildare the following have been the noble families since the Anglo-Norman invasion : Fitzgerald, barons of Offaley, earls and marquises of Kildare, and dukes of Leinster. The title of "Earl of Leinster" was, A.D. 1659, borne by the family of Cholmondely; and the title of "Duke of Leinster" was, A.D. 1719, held by a descendant of Duke Schomberg. De Vesey or De Vesci, lords of Kildare and Rathangan. De Lounder, barons of Naas; Preston, also barons of Naas. St. Michael, barons of Rheban. FitzEustace, barons of Kilcullen in Kildare, of Portlester in Meath, and viscounts of Baltinglass in Wicklow. Bourke, barons of Naas, and earls of Mayo. Bermingham, barons of Carbery. Wellesley, barons of Narragh. Allen, viscounts of Allen in Kildare, and barons of Stillorgan in Dublin. Burgh, barons Down. Pomeroy, barons Harberton, and viscounts of Carbery. Agar, barons of Somerton, and earls of Normanton. Lawless, barons of Cloncurry. The barons De Roebeck. Moore, earls and marquises of Drogheda, and barons of Mellifont in Louth, reside at Monasterevan in Kildare. Scott, earls of Clonmel ; and the family of Clements, earls of Leitrim, have seats in Kildare.

V.—THE ANCIENT KINGDOM OF LEINSTER.*

1.—HY-KINSELLAGH AND CUALAN ; OR WEXFORD, WICKLOW, CARLOW, AND PART OF DUBLIN.

UNDER this head will be given the history and topography of the ancient territories comprised in the present counties of Wexford, Wicklow, and Carlow, with their chiefs and clans, and the possessions of each in ancient and modern times. The territory of "Hy-Cinsealach" [Hy-Kinsela] derived its name from Enna Cinsealach, King of Leinster in the time of St. Patrick ; and comprised at one time the present counties of Wexford and Carlow, with some adjoining parts of Wicklow, Kilkenny, and Queen's County.

---

* *Leinster :* The ancient kingdom of Leinster comprised the present counties of Wexford, Wicklow, Carlow, and Queen's County, the greater part of Kildare, of King's County, Kilkenny, and that part of Dublin south of the river Liffey. Parts of Kilkenny bordering on Tipperary, and the southern parts of the King's County, belonged to ancient Munster ; and some of the northern part of the King's County belonged to the province of Meath. The above named territories continued to be the limits of Leinster down to the reign of Queen Elizabeth ; but in after times the old kingdom of Meath was added to Leinster, and also the county Louth, which was a part of the ancient kingdom of Ulster.

Leinster in early times was called Gaillian or Coigeadh Gaillian, from its being possessed by the tribe of Firvolgians called Fir-Gaillian, signifying spear-men ; but it afterwards got the name of Laighean [Laen] from the following circumstance : A few centuries before the Christian era, an Irish prince, named Labhra Loingseach or Laura of the Ships (Latinized Lauradius Navalis), having been banished to Gaul, became commander of the forces to the king of that country : and afterwards led an army of Gauls to Ireland for the recovery of the crown. He landed at a place more lately called Lough Garman (now Wexford Bay), and proceeded 'to Dinnrigh, an ancient fortress of the kings of Leinster, which was situated near the river Barrow, between Carlow and Leighlin, and there put to death the Monarch Cobthach Caolbhreagh (No. 60, page 355), son of the Monarch Hugony the Great ; and became himself the Ardrigh of Ireland. The name "Garman" was afterwards applied to the whole of the territory now forming the county Wexford; and the people called "Garmans," because this Gaulish colony who settled there came from those parts of *Germany* adjoining Gaul. The Gaulish troops brought over by Laura were armed with green broad-headed spears, called Laighin, which were introduced amongst all the forces of the province: hence it got the name of *Coigeadh* [*coogu*] *Laighean* or the "province of the spears ;" and from Laighean or Laen came the name *Laen-Tir*, which has been anglicised "Leinster" or the Territory of the Spears.

When the Firvolgians invaded Ireland, some of them landed in large force in Connaught, at Erris, in Mayo ; and were called Firdomnians or Damnonians. Another body of them landed under one of their commanders named Slainge, the son of Dela, at a place called after him *Inbhear Slainge* [Inver Slaney], now the Bay of Wexford, from which the river "Slaney" takes its name. These Firvolgians were called Fir-Gaillian or spear-men as already mentioned ; and possessed the counties of Wexford, Wicklow, and Carlow, under the name of "Galenii" or "Galenians." This territory was in after ages

O'Dugan, the learned historian of the O'Kellys, princes of Hy-Maine, gives a full account of all the chiefs and clans of *Leath Cuin* (i.e. Conn of the Hundred Battles' half of Ireland or the kingdoms of Meath, Ulster, and Connaught—see No. 83, page 67), and collected part of the topography of Leinster ; but O'Heerin, another learned historian, who died A.D. 1420, wrote a continuation of O'Dugan's Topography, commencing thus : *Tuilleadh Feasa air Eirinn Oigh*, or " An Addition of Knowledge on Sacred Erin ;" in which he gives an account of all the chiefs and clans of Leath Mogha (i.e. Mogha's half of Ireland or the kingdoms of Leinster and Munster), and the territories they possessed in the twelfth century.

(a) THE IRISH CHIEFS AND CLANS OF HY-KINSELAGH AND CUALAN.

The following accounts of the chiefs and clans of Wexford, Wicklow, and Carlow, and the territories possessed by each, have been collected from the Topographies of O'Heerin, O'Dugan, O'Brien, O'Halloran, and other sources. It appears that O'Dugan collected part of the topography of Leinster ; but it was chiefly compiled by O'Heerin, who says :

> " Leath Mogha, the portion of Heber the Fair,
> The two southern territories of Erin !
> Thus the plain of Leinster is mine ;
> And each brave man to the Bay of Limerick."

1. **O'Tuathail** or **O'Toole**, chiefs of Hy-Murray, an extensive territory comprising the greater part of the baronies of Talbotstown and Shilelagh in the county Wicklow, and extending as far as Almain, now the Hill of Allen, in the county Kildare ; thus containing a great portion of the baronies of Naas, Kilcullen, Kilkea and Moone, and Connell, in that county. The O'Tooles were princes of Imaile ; of the same race as the MacMurroughs ; and like them eligible to be kings of the province of Leinster. The celebrated St. Lawrence O'Toole was of this family. 2. **O'Brain, O'Broin**, or **O'Byrne**, were chiefs of Hy-Briuin Cualan (which comprised the greater part of the barony of Ballinacor, called " O'Byrne's Country"), and also the Ranelagh : hence the O'Byrnes were styled lords of Ranelagh. 3. **O'Ceallaigh** or **O'Kelly**, and **O'Taidhg**, chiefs of Hy-Maile [Imaile] and of Hy-Teigh. This ancient family of O'Teigh have anglicised the name " Tighe ;" and the O'Kellys here mentioned were of the same race as the MacMurroghs, O'Tooles, O'Byrnes, etc. The territory of Hy-Teigh was also called Crioch Cualan or " Cualan's Country," which comprised the baronies of Rathdown, Newcastle, and Arklow. 4. **MacGiollamocholmog**, chiefs of Cualan. 5. **O'Cosgraidh** or **O'Cosgrave**, and **O'Fiachraidh**, other chiefs in Cualan. 6. **O'Gaithin**, and **O'Dunlaing** or **Dowling** (some of this family have anglicised the name " Laing"), chiefs of Siol Elaigh and the Lagan ; this territory of Siol Elaigh is now the barony

called Hy-Cinsealach, which derived its name from Enna Cinsealach, King of Leinster at the advent of St. Patrick to Ireland ; and comprised the present counties of Wexford and Carlow, with some adjoining parts of Wicklow, Kilkenny, and Queen's County.
The territories now forming the counties of Dublin and Kildare are connected with some of the earliest events in Irish history : Partholan or Bartholinus, the Scythian, who planted the first colony in Ireland, had his residence at Binn Eadair, now the Hill of Howth. At this place Bartholinus was cut off by a plague, together with his entire colony ; all of whom were buried, according to some authors, at Moy-nEalta or the Plain of Birds, afterwards called Clontarf ; but according to O'Brien these people were buried at a place called Tamlachta Muintir Partholain (signifying the burial cairns of the people of Bartholinus), which is now the Hill of *Tallaght*, near Dublin. Crimthann Niadh-Nar, Monarch of Ireland when Christ was born (see No. 75, page 356), had his chief residence and fortress, called Dun Crimthann or Crimthann's Fort, on the Hill of Howth ; and so had Conary the Great, the 97th Monarch of Ireland. Crimthann Niadh-Nar was a famous warrior, celebrated for his military expeditions to Gaul and Britain ; and brought to Ireland from foreign countries many valuable spoils, amongst other things a gilded war-chariot, two hounds coupled together with a silver chain, and valued at three hundred cows ; according to the Glossary of King Cormac MacCullenan of Cashel, this was the first introduction of greyhounds into Ireland. The ancient Irish kings and chieftains (like their Celtic or Scythian ancestors), as well as those of Gaul and Britain, fought in war-chariots, in the same manner as did Maud (elsewhere mentioned), the famous heroine and Queen of Connaught ; and as did the British Queen Boadicea, etc. Numerous memorials of the most remote ages still exist in the counties of Dublin and Kildare, as in all other parts of Ireland ; of which full accounts may be found in D'Alton's History of the County, and of the Archbishops of Dublin ; Ware's and Grose's Antiquities ; Vallancey's Collectanea, etc.—CONNELLAN.

of "Shilelagh," in the south of the county Wicklow. 7. **O'Murchada** or **O'Murphy**, chiefs of Crioch O'Felme or Hy-Feidhlime [Hy-Felimy], and of the same race as the MacMurroughs, kings of Leinster. Hy-Felimy extended along the sea coast, and was commonly called the "Murrowes;" and comprised the barony of Ballagheen in the county Wexford. 8. **O'Gairbidh** or **O'Garvey**, other chiefs in Hy-Felimy. 9. **O'Cosgraidh** or **O'Cosgrave**, chiefs of Beantraidhe, now the barony of "Bantry," county Wexford. 10. **O'Duibhgin**, probably **O'Dugan**, chiefs in Shelbourne, a barony in Wexford. 11. **O'Lorcain** or **O'Larkin**, chiefs of Fothart, the territory of the Foharta, now the barony of "Forth," in the county Wexford; the O'Larkins had their fortress at Carn, now the headland called Carnsore Point. 12. **O'h-Airtghoile** (*O'h-Airtghaol*: Irish, *the kindred of O'Hart*), anglicised "Hartly" and "Hartilly," chiefs of Crioch-na-gCenel (the country of the clans) or Criochnageneal, a territory near "O'Larkin's Country," above mentioned. 13. **O'Riaghain** or **O'Ryan**, lord of Hy-Drona, a territory which comprised the present baronies of "Idrone," in the county Carlow. The O'Ryans were styled princes of Hy-Drona, and were the stock of the O'Ryans who had extensive possessions in Tipperary. 14. **O'Nuallain**, **O'Nolan**, or **O'Nowlan**, chiefs of Fotharta Feadha, now the barony of "Forth," in the county Carlow. 15. **O'Kinsellagh**, **O'Cahill**, **O'Doyle**, **O'Bulger**, and **MacCoskley**, were powerful clans and had large possessions in the counties of Wexford and Carlow. O'Brien or MacBrien, and O'Moore, were also respectable families in Wexford. O'Doran held the high office of hereditary Brehons of Leinster; and, being the judges of that province, had extensive possessions under its ancient kings. Donald Caomhanach [Cavanagh], a son of King Dermod Mac-Murrough, succeeded partly to the inheritance of the kingdom of Leinster; and from him some of his descendants took the name of *Kavanagh* or *Cavanagh*, or MacMur-rough-Kavanagh.

(b) NOTICE ON HY-KINSELAGH.

The counties of Waterford and Wexford were intimately connected with the Anglo-Norman invasion under Strongbow and his followers: Dermod MacMurrough, King of Leinster, after giving his daughter Eva in marriage to Richard de Clare, Earl of Pembroke (commonly called Strongbow), at Waterford, A.D. 1171, also conferred on him the title of "Heir Presumptive to the Kingdom of Leinster." After Dermod's death Strongbow succeeded to the sovereignty of Leinster, in right of his wife Eva, by whom he had an only daughter Isabel, who became heiress of Leinster; and was married to William Marshall, earl of Pembroke; who, in right of his wife, enjoyed the sovereignty of Leinster. Marshall, Earl of Pembroke, had by his marriage with Isabel five sons and five daughters; all the sons, namely, William, Richard, Gilbert, Walter, and Anselm, became in succession earls of Pembroke, and lords or princes of Leinster; but all having died without issue, the male line became extinct; the five daughters were all intermarried into noble families in England, and the different counties of Leinster were divided amongst them and their posterity (see "Hanmer's Chronicle;" and Baron Finglas's "Breviate of Ireland," in Harris's *Hibernica*).

(c) THE NEW SETTLERS IN HY-KINSELAGH.

The New Settlers who joined Strongbow in Ireland, and got large grants of lands, were:

In Wexford—Maurice Fitzgerald, ancestor of the earls of Kildare and Desmond; Harvey de Monte Morisco, and Robert Fitzstephen. The other families who settled in Wexford were those of Carew, Talbot, Devereux* Stafford, Sinnott, Sutton, Keating, Power, Walshe, Fitzharris, Fitzhenry, Derenzy, Masterson, Butler, Brown, Rositer,

---

* *Devereux:* This is the gallicised form of the Irish sirname *Leimhearois* ("leimhe:" Irish, *simplicity, folly, silliness;* "aros," *a dwelling, a house,* or *habitation*. Compare with it the French *Vereux*, "worm-eaten" "rotten," etc.); of which family Tcmhas Leimhearois (or Thomas Devereux) was an Irish Catholic Bishop, *temp.* Queen Elizabeth.

Redmond, Esmond, Hore, Harvey, Hay, Hughes, Codd, Comerford, Colclough, Lambert, Boyce, Morgan, Tottenham, Ram, Furlong, etc. In the first volume of the *Desiderata Curiosa Hiberniæ*, an account is given of various patentees and undertakers who, in the reigns of Elizabeth and King James the First, got extensive grants of forfeited lands which were confiscated in the county of Wexford. The following persons obtained lots of those lands :—Sir Richard Cooke, Sir Laurence Esmond, Sir Edward Fisher, Francis Blundell, Nicholas Kenny, William Parsons, Sir Roger Jones, Sir James Carroll, Sir Richard Wingfield, Marshal of the Army ; Sir Adam Loftus, Sir Robert Jacob, Captain Trevellian, Captain Fortescue ; and Conway Brady, Queen Elizabeth's footman. Several families of the Old proprietors in Wexford are enumerated, with the lands they possessed, and the re-grants of part of those lands which they obtained ; as those of Masterson, MacMurrough, MacBrien, MacDowling, MacDermott, Malone, Cavanagh, Moore, O'Bulger, O'Doran, Sinnot, Walsh, Codd, etc.

In Carlow the following have been the chief old English families :—De Bigod, earls of Norfolk, by intermarriage with the daughter of William Marshall, Earl of Pembroke, became lords of Carlow in the thirteenth century ; and, A.D. 1346, the county of Carlow was granted to Thomas Plantagenet or De Brotherton, Earl of Norfolk and Marshal of England : whose successors, the Mowbrays, and Howards, dukes of Norfolk, possessed the county of Carlow down to the reign of King Henry the Eighth, when they were deprived of it in consequence of the law against absentees being enforced ; and after that time the Butlers, earls of Ormond, became possessed of a great part of Carlow. It may be here observed, that in the fourteenth century the Courts of Exchequer and Common Pleas were for a long period held at Carlow. The other chief families who settled in Carlow were the following :—Butler, Brown, Burton, Bagnal, Carew, Cooke, Eustace, Rochfort, Cheever, Ponsonby, Astle or Astly, Bunbury, Blackney or Blackeney, Doyne, Bruen, etc.

In Wicklow, Maurice Fitzgerald and his descendants, in the reigns of Henry the Second and King John, got extensive grants of land about Arklow ; and Walter de Riddlesford, who had the title of "Baron of Brey," got from King John a grant of the lands of Imaile in Wicklow, and of Castledermot in Kildare ; both of which belonged to the ancient principality of O'Toole. The other chief families of Wicklow were Butler, Talbot, Eustace, and Howard.

––––––

(d) THE MODERN NOBILITY OF HY-KINSELAGH.

The following have been the noble families in Wexford, Wicklow, and Carlow, since the reign of King John :—

In Wexford, in the thirteenth century, the noble English families of De Mountchensey, and De Valence, got large possessions, with the title of lords of Wexford, by intermarriage with a daughter of Marshall, Earl of Pembroke, above mentioned ; and by intermarriage with De Valence, Talbot, earls of Shrewsbury, became lords of Wexford, in Ireland ; the family of Petty, marquises of Lansdowne, in England, and earls of Shelbourne, in Wexford ; Butler, viscounts Mountgarret ; Keating, barons of Kilmananan ; Esmond, barons of Limerick ; Stopford, earls of Courtown ; the family of Loftus, earls and marquises of Ely ; the family of Phipps, barons Mulgrave, barons of New Ross in Wexford, earls of Mulgrave, and marquises of Normandy in England ; Ponsonby, viscounts of Duncannon ; Annesley, viscounts Mountmorris ; Carew, barons Carew.

In Carlow, De Bigod, Mowbray, and Howard, dukes of Norfolk, were lords of Carlow ; Butler, barons of Tullyophelim, and viscounts of Tullow ; Carew, barons of Idrone ; O'Cavanagh, barons of Balian ; Cheever, viscounts Mountleinster ; Fane, barons of Carlow ; Ogle, viscounts of Carlow ; and Dawson, viscounts of Carlow ; Knight, earls of Carlow ; the celebrated Duke of Wharton, Lord Lieutenant of Ireland in the reign of Queen Anne, was created Marquis of Carlow.

In Wicklow, Howard, earls of Wicklow ; Stuart, earls of Blessington ; and Boyle, viscounts Blessington ; Wingfield, viscounts Powerscourt ; Maynard, barons Maynard ; the family of Cole, barons of Ranelagh ; and Jones, viscounts Ranelagh ; Butler, barons of Arklow ; Eustace, viscounts of Baltinglass ; and the Ropers, viscounts of Baltinglass ; Stradford, barons of Baltinglass and earls of Aldborough ; Proby, earls of Carysfort ; Brabazon, earls of Meath ; Berkeley, barons of Rathdown ; and the family of Monk, earls of Rathdown ; the earls Fitzwilliam in England have extensive possessions in Wicklow.

Wexford was formed into a County in the reign of King John, and was, as already stated, part of the ancient territory of Hy-Cinsellagh ; it was called by the Irish writers "The County of Lough Garman," as already mentioned. It was also called *Contae Riavach* (signifying the grey county), from some peculiar *greyish* appearance of the country ; but which Camden incorrectly states to have meant the "rough county." It got the name of "Wexford" from the town of Wexford, which was called by the Danes, "Weisford," signifying the *western haven* : a name given to it by the Danish colonies who possessed that city in the tenth and eleventh centuries. The greater part of Wexford was in former times also sometimes called "The County of Ferns," from (as stated by Spenser) the city of *Ferns*, which was the capital of the MacMurroughs, kings of Leinster. In the tenth century, the Danes of Wexford worked the silver mines situated at Clonmines, in the county Wexford ; and in that city had a mint where they struck several coins.

Carlow was formed into a County in the reign of King John ; it was called by the Irish writers *Cathairloch* and *Ceatharloch*, anglicised "Caherlough," now "Carlow ;" and the name is said to have been derived from the Irish "Cathair," *a city*, and "loch," *a lake* : thus signifying the City of the Lake ; as it is stated that there was in former times a lake adjoining the place where the town of Carlow now stands ; but there is no lake there at present.

Wicklow was formed into a County in the reign of King James the First ; its name being derived from the town of Wicklow, which, it is said, was called by the Danes "*Wykinlow* or *Wykinlough*," signifying the "Harbour of Ships ;" it was called by the Irish Cilmantan. According to O'Flaherty, the name of "Wicklow" was derived from the Irish *Buidhe Cloch*, signifying the yellow stone or rock ; and probably so called from the *yellow* colour of its granite rocks. Wicklow was in ancient times covered with extensive forests ; and the oak woods of Shillelagh, on the borders of Wicklow and Wexford, were celebrated in former times. The gold mines of Wicklow, celebrated in history, were situated in the mountain of Croghan Kinselagh, near Arklow ; and pieces of solid golden ore of various sizes were found in the rivulets : one of which pieces was twenty-three ounces in weight.

---

2. OSSORY,* 3. OFFALEY, 4. LEIX.

Or, Kilkenny, King's, and Queen's Counties.

(a) THE IRISH CHIEFS AND CLANS.

THE following accounts of the Irish chiefs and clans of Ossory, Offaley, and Leix, have been collected from the Topographies of O'Heeran, O'Dugan, O'Brien,

---

* *Ossory, Offaley, and Leix :* An account of the ancient history and inhabitants of what constituted ancient Leinster has been given in the Chapter on "Hy Kinselagh ;" in this chapter is given the history and topography of the territories comprised in Kilkenny, King's and Queen's Counties, with their chiefs and clans, and the possessions of each in ancient and modern times.

Ossory comprised almost the whole of the present county of Kilkenny, with a small part of the south of Tipperary, and also that portion of the Queen's County now called the barony of Upper Ossory ; and the name of this ancient principality, which was also called the "Kingdom of Ossory," is still retained in that of the diocese of Ossory. Ancient Ossory, according to some accounts, extended through the whole country between the rivers Nore and Suir ; being bounded on the north and east by the Nore, and on the west and south by the Suir ; and was sometimes subject to the kings of Leinster, but mostly to the kings of Munster. It is stated by O'Halloran, MacGeoghagan, and others, that Conaire Mor or Conary the Great, who was Monarch of Ireland at the commencement of the Christian era (of the race of the Clan-na-Deaga of Munster, a branch of the Heremonians of Ulster), having made war on the people of Leinster, to punish them for having killed his father, Edersceol, Monarch of Ireland, imposed on them a tribute called Eric-ui-Edersceoil or the Fine of Edersceol ; to be paid annually every first day of November, and consisting of three hundred cows, three hundred steeds, three hundred goldhandled swords, and three hundred purple cloaks. This tribute was sometimes paid to the Monarchs of Ireland, and sometimes to the kings of Munster ; and its levying led to many fierce battles for a long period. Conary the Great separated Ossory from Leinster ; and, having added it to Munster, gave it to a prince of his own race, named Aongus, and freed it from all dues to the King of Munster, except the honour of composing their body guards : hence, Aongus was called Amhas Righ, signifying the king's guard ; and from this circumstance, according to O'Halloran, the territory got the name of "Amhas-Righ," afterwards changed to *Osraighe*, and anglicised "Ossory."

Offaley or *Ophaley*, in Irish, "Hy-Failge," derived its name from Ross Failge or Ross of the

O'Halloran, and others :—1. **Mac Giolla Padruig*** or **MacGillpatrick,** anglicised "Fitz-patrick," princes of Ossory. From the reign of Henry the Eighth down to that of George the Second, the Fitzpatricks were created barons of Castletown, barons of Gowran, and earls of Upper Ossory. 2. **O'Cearbhaill** or **O'Carroll,** and O'Donchadha or O'Donoghoe, chiefs of the barony of Gowran and Sliogh Liag, which is probably the barony of "Shillelogher," both in Kilkenny. These O'Carrolls, it is thought, were a branch of the O'Carrolls, princes of Ely; and the O'Donoghoes, a branch of the O'Donoghoes, princes of Cashel. 3. **O'Conchobhair** or **O'Connor,** princes of Hy-Failge or Offaley, had a fortress at the green mound of Cruachan or Croghan, a beautiful hill situated in the parish of Croghan, within a few miles of Philipstown, on the borders of the King's County and Westmeath. The O'Connors, princes of Offaley, usually denominated "O'Connors Failey," took their name from Conchobhar, prince of Hy-Failge. who is mentioned in the Annals of the Four Masters, at A.D. 1014; and had their chief fortress at Dangan (now called Philipstown, in the King's County), and several castles in other parts of that county and in Kildare. They maintained their independence and large possessions down to the reign of Elizabeth, after which their estates were confiscated. 4. **O'Mordha** or **O'Moore,** princes of Laoighis or Leix, were

Rings, King of Leinster, son of Cahir Mor, Monarch of Ireland in the second century. The territory of Hy-Failge possessed by the posterity of Ross Failge, comprised almost the whole of the present King's County, with some adjoining parts of Kildare and Queen's County; and afterwards, under the C'Connors (who were the head family of the descendants of Ross Failge, and styled princes of Offaley), this territory appears to have comprised the present baronies of Warrenstown and Coolestown, and the greater part of Philipstown, and part of Geashill, all in the King's County, with the barony of Tine-hinch, in the Queen's County, and those of East and West "Offaley," in Kildare ; in which the ancient name of this principality is still retained.

Leix.—In the latter end of the first century, the people of Munster made war on Cucorb, King of Leinster, and conquered that province as far as the hill of Maistean, now Mullaghmast, in the county Kildare ; but Cucorb having appointed as commander-in-chief of his forces, Lugaid Laighis, a famous warrior, who was grandson to the renowned hero Conall Cearnach or Conall the Victorious, chief of the Red Branch Knights of Ulster, both armies fought two terrific battles, about A.D. 90 : one at Athrodan, now Athy, in Kildare, and the other at Cainthine on Magh Riada, now the plain or heath of Mary-borough, in the Queen's County ; in which the men of Leinster were victorious, having routed the Munster troops from the hill of Maistean across the river Bearbha (now the "Barrow"). and pursued the remnant of their forces as far as Slieve Dala mountain or Ballach Mór, in Ossory, near Borris in Ossory, on the borders of Tipperary and Queen's County. Being thus reinstated in his Kingdom of Leinster, chiefly through the valour of Lugaid Laighis, Cucorb conferred on him a territory, which he named *Laoighise* or the "Seven districts of Laighis :" a name anglicised "Leise" or "Leix," and still retained in the name "Abbeyleix." This territory was possessed by Lugaid Laighis and his posterity, who were styled princes of Leix ; and his descendants, on the introduction of sirnames, took the name O'Mordha or O'Morra (anglicised "O'Moore"), and for many centuries held their rank as princes of Leix. The territory of Leix, under the O'Moores, comprised the present baronies of Maryboro', Cullinagh, Ballyadams, Stradbally, and part of Portnehinch, In the Queen's County ; together with Athy, and the adjoining country in Kildare, now the baronies of Narragh and Rheban. The other parts of the Queen's County, as already shown, formed parts of other principalities : the barony of Upper Ossory belonged to Ossory ; Tinehinch, to Offaley ; part of Portnehinch, to O'Dempsey of Clan Maliere ; and the barony of Slievemargy was part of Hy-Kinselagh.

The territories of Ossory, Offaley, and Leix, are connected with many of the earliest events recorded in Irish history: according to our ancient annalists a great battle was fought between the Nemedians and Fomorians at Sliabh Bladhma, now the "Slievebloom" mountains, on the borders of the King's and Queen's Counties. Heremon and Heber Fionn, sons of Milesius, having contended for the sovereignty of Ireland, fought a great battle at Geisiol, now "Geashill," in the King's County ; in which the forces of Heber were defeated, and he himself slain ; by which Heremon became the first sole Milesian Monarch of Ireland. Heremon had his chief residence and fortress at Airgiodros, near the river Feoir, now the "Nore ;" and this royal residence was also called Rath Beathach, and is now known as "Rathbeagh," near Freshford, in the county Kilkenny. Heremon died at Rathbeagh, and was buried in a sepulchral mound which still remains. It appears that other kings of Ireland in early times also resided there ; for it is recorded that Ruraighe Mór, who was the 86th Monarch of Ireland, died at Airgiodros. Conmaol or Conmalius (No. 38. page 63), son of Heber Fionn, was the first Monarch of Ireland of the race of Heber ; he fought many great battles for the crown with the race of Heremon, particularly a great battle at Geashill, where Palpa, a son of Heremon, was slain.

Kilkenny was, out of the greater part of Ossory, formed into a county, in the reign of King John ; and so called from its chief town ; the name of which, in Irish Cill Chainnigh (signifying the Church of Canice or Kenny), was derived from Cainneach, a celebrated saint who founded the first church there in the latter end of the sixth century.

King's and Queen's Counties.—The greater part of the principality of Leix, with parts of Ossory and Offaley, were formed into the Queen's County ; and the greater part of the principality of Hy-Falgia or Offaley, with parts of Ely O'Carroll and of the ancient Kingdom of Meath, was formed into the King's County—both in the sixteenth century, A.D. 1557, by the Earl of Sussex, lord deputy in the reign of Philip and Mary, after whom they were called the King's and Queen's Counties ; and hence the chief town of the King's County got the name of "Philipstown," and that of the Queen's County "Maryboro'."

* *Giolla Padruig :* Some of the descendants of this Giolla Padruig (or Padraig) have anglicised their name *Stapleton.*

marshals and treasurers of, Leinster; and had their chief fortress at Dunamase, a few miles from Maryboro', erected on a rock situated on a hill: a place of almost impregnable strength, of which some massive ruins still remain. Like other independent princes, as the O'Reillys of Brefney, the O'Tooles of Wicklow, etc,, the O'Moores coined their own money; and it is stated in Sir Charles Coote's "Survey of the Queen's County," that some of the silver coins of the O'Moores were in his time extant. 5. **O'Diomosaigh** or **O'Dempsey**, lords of Clan Maoilughra or "Clanmaliere," were a branch of the race of Cahir Mór, and of the same descent as the O'Connors Failey; and were sometimes styled princes and lords of Clanmaliere and Offaley. The O'Dempseys had their chief castle at Geashill in the King's County, and, among many others in that county, had one in the barony of Offaley in Kildare, and one at Ballybrittas, in the barony of Portnehinch, in the Queen's County. 6. **O'Duinn, O'Dunn,** or **O'Dunne,** chiefs of Hy-Riagain [O'Regan], now the barony of Tinehinch in the Queen's County; some of the O'Dunns have changed the name to *Doyne*. 7. **O'Riagain** or **O'Regan** were, it appears, the ancient chiefs of Hy-Riagain, and who gave its name to that territory; which is still retained in the name of the parish of "Oregon" or Rosenallis, in the barony of Tinehinch. Of the ancient clan of the O'Regans was Maurice Regan, secretary to Dermod MacMorrough, king of Leinster; and who wrote an account of the Anglo-Norman invasion under Strongbow and his followers, which is published in Harris's *Hibernica*. 8. **O'Brogharain** (anglicised Broghan, and Brougham) are given by O'Dugan as chiefs of the same territory as O'Dunn and O'Dempsey. 9. **O'Haongusa** or **O'Hennesy,** chiefs of Clar Colgan; and O'Haimirgin, chiefs of Tuath Geisille: the districts of these two chiefs appear from O'Dugan to have been situated about Geashill and Croghan, in the baronies of Geashill and Philipstown, in the King's County. Another O'Hennessy is mentioned by O'Dugan as chief of Galinga Beag [Beg], now the parish of Gallen, in the barony of Garrycastle. 10. **O'Maolchein** (anglicised Whitehead), chiefs of Tuath Damhuighe, signifying the Land of the Oxen, or of the two plains: a district which appears to have adjoined that of O'Hennesy. 11. **O'Maolmuaidh** or **O'Molloy,** princes of Fear Ceall or the territory comprised in the present baronies of Eglish or "Fearcall," Ballycowan, and Ballyboy, in the King's County; and formed originally a part of the ancient kingdom of Meath. The O'Molloys were of the southern Hy-Niall race or Clan Colman. 12. **The O'Carrolls,** princes of Ely O'Carroll, possessed, as already mentioned, the barony of Lower Ormond in Tipperary, and those of Clonlisk and Ballybritt in the King's County; and had their chief castle at Birr or Parsonstown. 13. **MacCochlain** or **Coghlan,** princes of Dealbhna Earthra [Delvin Ahra], or the present barony of Garrycastle in the King's County; and O'Maollughach, chiefs of the Brogha, a district which appears to have adjoined MacCoghlan's territory, and was probably part of the barony of Garrycastle, in the King's County, and of Clonlonan in Westmeath. The MacCoghlans were of the race of the Dalcassians, same as the O'Briens, kings of Munster. 14. **O'Sionnaigh** or **Fox,** a lord of Teffia or Westmeath. O'Dugan in his Topography gives O'Catharnaigh as head prince of Teffia: hence the name Sionnaigh has been rendered "Catharnaigh" [Kearney]. The chief branch of this family took the name of Sionnach O'Catharnaigh, and, the word "sionnach" signifying *a fox*, the family name became "Fox;" and the head chief was generally designated An Sionnach or The Fox. They were of the race of the southern Hy-Niall; and their territory was called Muintir Tadhgain, which contained parts of the baronies of Rathconrath and Clonlonan in Westmeath, with part of the barony of Kilcourcy in the King's County. In the reign of Queen Elizabeth the Foxes got the title of lords of Kilcourcy. 15. **MacAmhalgaidh** (MacAuley, Magauley, or MacGawley), chiefs of Calraidhe-an-Chala or Calry of the Ports: a territory which comprised the present parish of Ballyloughloe, in the barony of Clonlonan in Westmeath. The "ports" here alluded to were those of the Shannon, to which this parish extends. 16. **O'Gormain** (anglicised MacGorman, O'Gorman, and Gorman), chiefs of Crioch mBairce, now the barony of Slievemargue in the Queen's County. The O'Gormans were of the race of Daire Barach, son of Cahir Mór, Monarch of Ireland in the second century; and some of them settled in the county Clare, where they had large possessions. 17. **O'Duibh** or **O'Duff,** chiefs of Hy-Criomthan: a district about Dun Masc or "Dunamase," which comprised the greater part of the two baronies of Maryboro' in the Queen's County. 18. **MacFiodhbhuidhe,** MacAodhbhuidhe [mac-ee-boy], or "MacEvoy," chiefs of Tuath-Fiodhbhuidhe: a district or territory which appears to have been situated in the barony of Stradbally, in the Queen's County. The MacEvoys were of the Clan Colla of Ulster; and also possessed a territory in Teffia, called *Ui Mac Uais* (signifying the

descendants of King Colla Uais), now the barony of "Moygoish" in the county Westmeath. Some of this family have anglicised the name "MacVeigh" and "MacVeagh."
19. **O'Ceallaigh** or **O'Kelly**, chiefs of Magh Druchtain and of Gailine : territories situated in the baronies of Stradbally and Ballyadams, in the Queen's County, along the river Barrow. 20. **O'Caollaidhe** or **Keely**, chief of Crioch O'Muighe, situated along the Barrow, now probably the parish of "Tullowmoy," in the barony of Ballyadams, Queen's County. 21. **O'Leathlabhair** (O'Lawlor, or Lalor) took their name from "Lethlobhar," No. 104 on the "Lawlor" of Monaghan pedigree, who was their ancestor. The Lawlors are therefore of the Clan Colla ; and in ancient times had extensive possessions in Leix, chiefly in the barony of Stradbally, Queen's County. 22. **O'Dubhlaine** (or Delany, Delaune, Delane), chiefs of Tuath-an-Toraidh ; and a clan of note in the barony of Upper Ossory, Queen's County, and also in Kilkenny. 23. **O'Bracnain** or **O'Brenan**, chiefs of Hy-Duach or Idoagh, now the barony of Fassadining, in Kilkenny. 24. **MacEracin** (Bruen or Breen), and O'Broith (O'Brit or O'Berth), chiefs of Magh-Seadna. 25. **O'Caibhdeanaich**, chiefs of Magh Arbh [Moy Arve] and Clar Coill. The plain of Moy Arve comprised the present barony of Cranagh, in Kilkenny. 26. **O'Gloiairn** or **MacGloiairn**, anglicised MacLairn or MacLaren, chiefs of Cullain : the name of which territory is still retained in that of the parish of "Cullan," barony of Kells, county Kilkenny. 27. **O'Calloaidhe** or **Keely**, chiefs of Hy-Bearchon [Ibercon], an ancient barony (according to Seward) now joined to that of Ida in the county Kilkenny ; and the name is partially preserved in that of the parish of "Rosbercon," in the barony of Ida. 28. **O'Bruadair** (O'Broderick or O'Broder), chiefs of Hy-n-Eirc, now the barony of "Iverk," in the county Kilkenny. 29. **O'Shee** of Kilkenny were some of the O'Seaghdhas, chiefs in Munster. 30. **Q'Ryan** and **O'Felan** were ancient families of note in Kilkenny, as well as in Carlow, Tipperary, and Waterford. 31. **Tighe** of Kilkenny were of the ancient Irish clan of the O'Teiges, who were chiefs of note in Wicklow and Wexford. 32. **Flood** of Kilkenny are of Irish descent, though supposed to be of English origin ; as many of the ancient clans of the Maoltuiles and of the MacThellighs (MacTullys or Tullys) changed the name to "Flood"—thus translating the name from the Irish "Tuile," which signifies a flood. 33. **MacCoscry** or **Cosgrave**, ancient clans in Wicklow and Queen's County, changed their name to "Lestrange" or "L'Estrange." On the map of Ortelius, the O'Mooneys are placed in the Queen's County ; and the O'Dowlings and O'Niochals or Nicholls are mentioned by some writers as clans in the Queen's County. O'Beehan or Behan were a clan in the King's and Queen's Counties.

(b) The New Settlers in Ossory, Offaley, and Leix.

As already explained, the daughter of Dermod MacMurrough, King of Leinster, having been married to Richard de Clare, earl of Pembroke, commonly called Strongbow, the kingdom of Leinster was conferred on Strongbow by King Dermod ; and William Marshall, earl of Pembroke, having married Isabella, daughter of Strongbow, by his wife Eva, the inheritance of the kingdom of Leinster passed to the family of the Marshalls, earls of Pembroke, and was possessed by the five sons of William Marshall, who became in succession earls of Pembroke and lords of Leinster ; and on the extinction of the male line of the Marshalls, the counties of Leinster were divided amongst the daughters of the said William Marshall, earl of Pembroke ; and their descendants in the thirteenth and fourteenth centuries (see Hanmer's "Chronicle," Baron Finglas's "Breviate of Ireland," and Harris's "Hibernica") : Joanna, the eldest daughter of the said William Marshall, had, on the partition of Leinster, Wexford allotted to her as her portion ; and being married to Warren de Montcheney, an English baron, he, in right of his wife, became lord of Wexford, which afterwards passed by intermarriage to the De Valences, earls of Pembroke, and lords of Wexford ; and, in succession, to the family of Hastings, earls of Abergavenny ; and to the Talbots, earls of Shrewsbury, Waterford, and Wexford. Matilda or Maud, another daughter of William Marshall, earl of Pembroke, had the county Carlow allotted to her ; and she married Hugh Bigod, earl of Norfolk : this family became lords of Carlow, which title, together with the county Carlow, afterwards passed in succession, by intermarriages, to the Mowbrays and Howards, earls of Norfolk. Sibilla, another of the daughters, got the county Kildare, and was married to William Ferrars, earl of

Ferrers and Derby, who became lord of Kildare ; a title which passed by inter-marriage to the De Veseys. The family of the Fitzgeralds afterwards became earls of Kildare. Isabel, another daughter of William Marshall, earl of Pembroke, had for her portion the county Kilkenny, and was married to Gilbert de Clare, earl of Gloucester and Hereford ; and, leaving no issue, the county Kilkenny, after his decease, fell to his three sisters, and passed by intermarriage chiefly to the family of De Spencers, barons De Spencer, in England, and afterwards became possessed mostly by the Butlers, earls of Ormond. Eva, the fifth daughter of William Marshall, had, as her portion, Leix and the manor of Dunamase or "O'Moore's Country," comprising the greater part of the present Queen's County ; and having married William de Bruse, lord of Gower and Brecknock in Wales, he became, in right of his wife, lord of Leix ; and one of his daughters being married to Roger Mortimer, lord of Wigmore in Wales, Leix passed to the family of Mortimer, who were earls of March in England. The King's Connty, as already stated, was formed out of parts of Offaley, Ely O'Carroll, and the kingdom of ¡Meath ; and in the grant of Meath given by King Henry the Second to Hugh de Lacy, a great part of the present King's County was possessed by De Lacy, who built in that county the castle of Durrow, where he was slain by one of the Irish galloglasses, as mentioned in the Annals of the Four Masters, at A.D. 1186. The Fitzgeralds, earls of Kildare and barons of Offaley, became possessed of a great part of the King's County ; and the family of De Hose or Hussey had part of Ely O'Carroll, and the country about Birr.

The following have been the chief families since the English invasion in Kilkenny, King's, and Queen's Counties.

In Kilkenny : Butler, Grace, Walsh, Fitzgerald, Roth, Archer, Cantwell, Shortall, Purcell, Power, Morris, Dalton or D'Alton, Stapleton, Wandesford, Lawless, Langrish, Bryan, Ponsonby, etc. The Butlers became the chief possessors of the county Kilkenny, as earls of Ormond and Ossory, dukes of Ormond, earls of Kilkenny and Gowran, viscounts of Galmoy, and various other titles derived from their exten-sive estates in this county and in Tipperary. "The Graces :" An account has already been given of Maurice Fitzgerald, a celebrated Anglo-Norman Chief who came over with Strongbow, and was ancestor of the earls of Kildare and Desmond. William Fitzgerald, brother of Maurice, was lord of Carew in Wales ; and the descendants of one of his sons took the name of De Carew, and from them, it is said, are descended the Carews of Ireland—great families in Cork, Wexford, and Carlow. From another of the sons of William Fitzgerald, were descended the Gerards, families of note in Ireland. The eldest son of William Fitzgerald, called Raymond Fitzwilliam, got the name of "Raymond le Gros," from his *great size* and strength ; he was one of the most valiant of the Anglo-Norman commanders ; was married to Basilia de Clare, sister of Strongbow; held the office of standard bearer of Leinster; and was for some time chief Governor of Ireland. Raymond died about A.D. 1184, and was buried in the Abbey of Molana, on the island of Darinis, on the river Blackwater, in the bay of Youghal. Maurice, the eldest son of Raymond le Gros, was ancestor of the great family of the Fitzmaurices, earls of Kerry. Raymond had another son called Hamon le Gros, and his descendants took the name of "le Gros," or "le Gras," afterwards changed to *Grace.* The Graces were created barons of Courtown, and held an exten-sive territory in the county Kilkenny, called "Graces' Country ;" but, in the wars of the Revolution, the Graces lost their hereditary estates : John Grace, the last baron of Courtown, having forfeited thirty thousand acres of land in Kilkenny for his adherence to King James the Second. "The Walshes :" This family was, by the Irish, called Branaghs, from "Breatnach," which signifies *a Briton:* as they originally came from Wales with Strongbow and his followers, They therefore got extensive possessions in Waterford, Kilkenny, Wexford, and Carlow ; and held the office of seneschals of Leinster, under the successors of Strongbow. The Butlers, viscounts of Galmoy ; the Graces, Walshes, Roths, and Shees, lost their extensive estates in Kil-kenny, in the war of the Revolution. The Bourkes, a branch of the Bourkes of Con-naught, settled in Kilkenny and Tipperary ; and some of them in Kilkenny took the name of *Gaul,* from "Gall," the name by which the Irish then called Englishmen ; and from them "Gaulstown" got its name. The Purcells were also numerous and respect-able in Kilkenny and Tipperary ; and, in the latter county, had the title of barons of Loughmoe.

In the Queen's County: The following were the chief families of English descent : After Leix had been formed into a county, the following seven families were the chief

English settlers in the reigns of Queen Mary and Elizabeth, and were called the seven tribes ; namely, Cosby, Barrington, Bowen, Rush, Hartpole, Hetherington, and Hovendon ; and in the reign of Charles the First, Villiers, Duke of Buckingham, having got extensive grants of land in the Queen's County, his lands were formed into the " Manor of Villiers," and passed to the present dukes of Buckingham ; and after the Cromwellian wars and the Revolution, the families of Parnell, Pole, Pigot,* Prior, Coote, Cowley, Dawson, Despard, Vesey, Staples, Brown, Johnson,'Trench, Weldon, and Walpole, got extensive possessions.

In King's County ; Fitzgerald, Digby, Hussey, and Fitzsimon, were the chief families before the reign of Elizabeth ; and some of the Fitzimons took the Irish name of " MacRuddery," from the Irish *MacRidire,* which signifies the Son of the Knight. In aftertimes, the families of Armstrong, Drought, Bury, Parsons, Molesworth, Lestrange, and Westenra, were the chief new settlers.

(c) THE MODERN NOBILITY IN OSSORY, OFFALEY AND LEIX.

The following have been the noble families in Kilkenny, King's and Queen's Counties, since the reign of King John :—

In Kilkenny : Marshall, earls of Pembroke ; De Clare, earls of Gloucester and Hertford ; and De Spencer, as above mentioned, were all lords of Kilkenny ; Butler, earls of Ormond and Ossory, and marquises and dukes of Ormond, earls of Kilkenny, earls of Gowran, earls of Glengall, earls of Carrick, viscounts of Galmoy, viscounts Mountgarrett, and barons of Kells ; Butler, earls of Ossory ; Fitzpatrick, barons of Gowran and earls of Ossory ; Grace, barons of Courtown ; Fitzgerald, barons of Burntchurch ; Wandesford, earls of Castlecomer ; De Montmorency,† viscounts Montmorres and viscounts Frankfort ; Flower, barons of Castle Durrow and viscounts Ashbrook ; Ponsonby, earls of Besborough, and viscounts Duncannon ; Agar, barons of Callan, viscounts of Clifden, and barons of Dover ; Cuffe, viscounts Castlecuffe, and barons of Desart.

In Queen's County : Marshall, earls of Pembroke ; De Bruce and Mortimer, as above mentioned, were lords of Leix ; Fitzpatrick, barons of Castletown, barons of Gowran, and earls of Upper Ossory ; Butler, barons of Cloughgrennan ; Coote, earls of Mountrath ; Moylneux, viscounts of Maryborough and earls of Sefton, in England ; Dawson, earls of Portarlington ; De Vesey, barons of Knapton and viscounts De Vesey or De Vesci.

In King's County : Fitzgerald, barons of Offaley and earls of Kildare ; Digby, barons of Geashill, and earls Digby, in England ; O'Carroll, barons of Ely ; O'Sionnagh or Fox, barons of Kilcourcey ; O'Dempsey, barons of Philipstown and viscounts of Clanmaliere ; Lambert, barons of Kilcourcey and earls of Cavan ; Blundell, barons of Edenderry ; the family of Parsons, at Birr or Parsonstown, earls of Ross and barons of Oxmantown ; Molesworth, barons of Philipstown ; Moore, barons of Tullamore ; Bury, barons of Tullamore and earls of Charleville ; Toler, earls of Norbury and viscounts Glandine ; Westenra, barons of Rossmore.

VI.—THE ANCIENT KINGDOM OF CONNAUGHT.‡

RODERICK O'CONNOR, the last Milesian Monarch of Ireland, after having reigned twenty years, abdicated the throne, A.D. 1186, and, after a religious seclusion of thirteen

* *Pigot :* According to some authorities, it was in the reign of Queen Elizabeth that the "Pigott" family came to the Queen's County.

† *Montmorency :* In p. 135, Vol. I., of the "De la Ponce MSS.," are given twenty-seven generations of this family : commencing with Bouchard I., who d. A.D. 984, and ending with Hervey, who d. 1840.

‡ *Connaught :* According to Keating and O'Flaherty, Connaught derived its name either from "Con," one of the chief Druids of the Tua-de-Danans, or from Conn Ceadcatha (Conn of the Hundred Battles), Monarch of Ireland, in the second century, and of the line of Heremon (see No. 80, page 358), whose posterity possessed the country ; the word *iacht* or *iocht,* signifying children or posterity, and

years in the monastery of Cong, in the county Mayo, died, A.D. 1198, in the 82nd year
of his age ; and was buried in Clonmacnoise, in the same sepulchre with his father,
Torlogh O'Connor, the 181st Monarch of Ireland.   In the chronological poem on the
Christian Kings of Ireland, written in the twelfth century, is the following stanza :—

> " Ocht m-Bliadhna agus deich Ruadri an Ri,
>   Mac Toirdhealbhaidh an t-Ard Ri,
>   Flaith na n-Eirend : gan fhell,
>   Ri deighneach deig Eirenn."

Anglicised—

> " Eighteen years the Monarch Roderick,
>   Son of Torlogh, supreme sovereign,
>   Ireland's undisputed ruler,
>   Was fair Erin's latest king."
>
>   —CONNELLAN.

According to the Four Masters, Roderick O'Connor, reigned as Monarch for
twenty years : from A.D. 1166 to A.D. 1186.

1.—MAYO AND SLIGO.

(a) THE IRISH CHIEFS AND CLANS.

THE following chiefs and clans and the territories they possessed in the twelfth
century, in the present counties of Sligo and Mayo, have been collected from O'Dugan

---

hence " Coniacht," the ancient name of Connaught, means the territory possessed by the posterity of
Conn.
   The ancient kingdom of Connaught comprised the present counties of Galway, Mayo, Sligo, Roscommon, and Leitrim, together with Clare, now in Munster, and Cavan, now a part of Ulster ; and was
divided into *Tuaisceart Conacht* or North Connaught, *Deisceart Conacht* or South Connaught, and *Iar
Conacht* or West Connaught.   North Connaught was also called *Iachtar Conacht* or Lower Connaught ;
as was South Connaught called *Uachtar Conacht* or Upper Connaught.
   North Connaught is connected with some of the earliest events in Irish history.   According to our
ancient annalists, it was in the time of Partholan or Bartholinus, who planted the first colony in Ireland,
that the lakes called Lough Conn and Lough Mask in Mayo, and Lough Gara in Sligo, on the borders of
Roscommon, suddenly burst forth ; and in South Connaught, according to O'Flaherty, the lakes called
Lough Cime (now Lough Hackett), Lough Riadh or Loughrea, and some other lakes in the county Galway,
and also the river Suck between Roscommon and Galway, first began to flow in the time of Heremon,
Monarch of Ireland, No. 37, page 351 ; and Lough Key in Moylurg, near Boyle in the county Roscommon,
first sprang out in the reign of the Monarch Tiernmas, No. 41, page 352.   On the arrival of the colony
of the Firvolgians in Ireland, a division of them landed on the north-western coast of Connaught, in one
of the bays, now called Blacksod or the Broadhaven.   These Firvolgians were named *Fir-Domhnan* or
Damnonians: and the country where they landed was called *Iarras*, or *Iarras Domhnan*, (from "iar,"
the *west*, and " ros," a *promontory* or peninsula, signifying the western promontory or peninsula of the
Damnonians) : a term exactly corresponding with the topographical features of the country ; and to the
present day the name has been retained in that of the half barony of " Erris." in the county Mayo.
When the Tua-de-Danans, who conquered the Firvolgians, first invaded Ireland, they landed in Ulster,
and proceeded thence to *Slieve-an-Iarain* (or the Iron Mountain), in Brefney, and thenceforward into
the territory of Connaught.   The Firvolgians having collected their forces to oppose their progress, a
desperate battle was fought between them at a place called *Magh Tuireadh* or the Plain of the Tower,
in which the Firvolgians were totally defeated—ten thousand of them being slain, together with
Eochad, son of Eirc their king, who was buried on the sea-shore : a cairn of large stones being erected
over him as a sepulchral monument, which remains to this day.   This place is on the strand, near Bally-
sodare in the county of Sligo, and was called *Traigh-an-Chairn* or the Strand of the Cairn.   After a
few more battles, the De-Danans became possessors of Ireland, which they ruled until the arrival of
the Milesians, who conquered them ; and in their turn became masters of Ireland.   The Firvolgians,
having assisted the Milesians in the conquest of the Tua-de-Danans, were, in consequence, restored by
the Milesians to a great part of their former possessions, particularly in Connaught ; in which province
they were ruled by their own kings of the Firvolgian race down to the third century, when the Monarch
Cormac Mac Art, of the Heremon line, brought them under subjection, and annexed Connaught to his
kingdom.   The Firvolgians appear to have been an athletic race ; and the "Clan-na-Morna" of Connaught,
under their Firvolgian chief, Goll, son of Morna, are celebrated in the Ossianic poems and ancient annals
as famous warriors in the third century.   Many of the Firvolgian race are still to be found in Connaught,
but blended by blood and intermarriages with the Milesians.   The Tua-de-Danans were originally
Scythians, who had settled some time in Greece, and afterwards migrated to Scandinavia or the countries now forming Norway, Sweden, and Denmark.   From Scandinavia (the " Fomoria" of the ancient
Irish) the De-Danans came to North Britain where they settled colonies, and thence passed into Ireland.
It appears that the Danans were a highly civilized people, skilled in the arts and sciences : hence they

and other authorities :—1. **O'Maolcluiche** or **Mulclohy** (*cloch* : Irish, *a stone*), chief of Cairbre, now the barony of Carbery, in the county Sligo. This name has been anglicised "Stone" and "Stoney." 2. **MacDiarmada** or **MacDermott**, chief of Tir Oliolla, now the barony of Tirerill, in the county Sligo. The MacDermotts were also princes of Moylurg, in the county Roscommon, in South Connaught. They afterwards became princes of Coolavin, as successors to the O'Garas, lords of Coolavin ; and to the present day, as the only family of the Milesian Clans who have preserved their ancient titles, retain the title of "Prince of Coolavin." (See the "MacDermott" pedigree.) 3. **MacDonchaidh** or **MacDonogh**, a branch of the MacDermotts, afterwards chiefs of Tirerill and of Corran, now the barony of "Corran" in Sligo. O'Donchathaigh is given by O'Dugan as a chief in Corran ; this name has been anglicised O'Donogh. 4. **O'Dubhalen** or **O'Devlin**, another chief in Corran. 5. **O'Headhra** or **O'Hara**, chief of Luighne, now the barony of "Lieney" in the county Sligo ; but Lieney anciently comprised part of the baronies of Costello and Gallen in Mayo. The O'Haras were descended from Olioll Olum, King of Munster in the third century. In the reigns of Queen Anne and George the First, the O'Haras were created "Barons of Tirawley and Kilmain," in the county Mayo. 6. **O'Gadhra or O'Gara**, given by O'Dugan as chief of Lieney, but in aftertimes Lord of *Cuil-O'bh-fionn*, now the barony of "Coolavin," was of the same stock as the O'Haras and O'Briens, kings of Thomond. 7. **O'Ciernachain** or **Kernighan** and **O'Huathmharain** (O'Horan or O'Haran), other chiefs in Lieney. 8. **O'Muiredhaigh** or **O'Murray**, chief of Ceara, now the barony of "Carra," in the county Mayo ; and also chief of the Lagan, a district in the northern part of the barony of Tirawley, in Mayo. 9. **O'Tighearnaigh** or **O'Tierney**, a chief in Carra. 10. **O'Gormog** (modernized O'Gorman), another chief in Carra. 11. **O'Maille** or **O'Malley**, chief of Umhall, which O'Dugan states was divided into two territories. This territory, whose name is sometimes mentioned as Umalia and Hy-Malia, comprised the present baronies of Murrisk and "Burrishoole," in the

were considered as *magicians*. O'Brien, in his learned work on the "Round Towers of Ireland," considers that these beautiful structures were built by the Tua-de-Danans, for purposes connected with pagan worship and astronomical observations : an opinion very probable when it is considered that they were highly skilled in architecture and other arts, from their long residence in Greece and intercourse with the Phœnicians. It is stated that Orbsen, a chief descended from the Danans and Fomorians, was a famous merchant, and carried on a commercial intercourse between Ireland and Britain ; and that he was killed by Uillinn of the Red Brows, another De-Danan chief, in a battle called, from that circumstance, *Magh Uillinn* or the Plain of Uillinn, now the barony of "Moycullen," [in the county Galway. In South Connaught, the territory which forms the present county Clare was taken from Connaught in the latter part of the third century, and added to part of Limerick, under the name of *Tuadh-Mumhain* or North Munster (a word anglicised "Thomond") ; of which the O'Briens, of the Dalcassian race, became Kings.

Cormac Mac Art, the celebrated Monarch of Ireland in the second century, was born in Corran at the place called Ath-Cormac or the Ford of Cormac, near Keis-Corran (now "Keash") in the county Sligo ; and hence he was called "Cormac of Corran."

The territory of North Connaught is connected in a remarkable manner with the mission of St. Patrick to Ireland : Mullagh Farry (in Irish *Forrach-mhac-nAmhailgaidh*), now "Mullafarry," near Killala, in the barony of Tyrawley, and county Mayo, is the place where St. Patrick converted to Christianity the king or prince of that territory (Enda Crom) and his seven sons ; and baptized twelve thousand persons in the water of a well called *Tobar Enadharc*. And Croagh Patrick mountain also in Mayo, was long celebrated for the miracles it is said the saint performed there. The See of Killala was founded by St. Patrick.

At Carn Amhalgaidh or "Carnawley," supposed to be the hill of Mullaghcarn (where King Awley was buried), the chiefs of the O'Dowds were inaugurated as princes of Hy-Fiachra ; while, according to other accounts they were inaugurated on the hill of Ardnaree, near]Ballina. This principality of Northern Hy-Fiachra comprised the present counties of Mayo and Sligo, and a portion of Galway ; while the territory of Hy-Fiachra, in the county Galway was called the Southern Hy-Fiachra or Hy-Fiachra Aidhne : so named after Eogan Aidhne, son of Dathi, the last pagan Monarch of Ireland, who was killed by lightning at the foot of the Alps, A.D. 429. This territory of Hy-Fiachra Aidhne was co-extensive with the present diocese of Kilmacduagh ; and was possessed by the descendants of Eoghan Aidhne, the principal of whom were—O'Heyne or Hynes, O'Clery, and O'Shaughnessy. According to O'Dugan and MacFirbis, fourteen of the race of Hy-Fiachra were kings of Connaught : some of whom had their chief residence in Aidhne, in Galway ; others at Ceara, now the barony of "Carra" in Mayo ; and some on the plain of the *Muaidhe* or the (river) Moy, in Sligo. O'Dubhda or O'Dowd were head chiefs of the northern Hy-Fiachra, and their territory comprised nearly the whole of the present county Sligo, with the greater part of Mayo. Many of the O'Dowds, even down to modern times, were remarkable for their great strength and stature. (See the "O'Dowd" pedigree.)

Cruaghan or Croaghan, near Elphin in the county Roscommon, became the capital of Connaught and the residence of its ancient kings ; and the estates of Connaught held conventions there to make laws and inaugurate their kings. At Cruaghan was the burial place of the pagan kings of Connaught, called Reilig na Riogh or The Cemetery of the kings ; here Dathi, the last pagan Monarch of Ireland, was buried ; and a large red pillar-stone erected over his grave remains to this day. A poem, giving an account of the kings and queens buried at Cruaghan, was composed by Torna Eigeas or Torna, the learned, chief county Mayo. The O'Malleys are of the same descent as the O'Connors, Kings of Connaught; and seem to have been great mariners. Of them O'Dugan says :—

> "A good man yet there never was
> Of the O'Malleys, who was not a *mariner;*
> Of every weather ye are prophets;
> A tribute of brotherly affection and of friendship."

Of this family was the celebrated heroine Graine-Ni-Mhaille [Grana Wale] or Grace O'Malley, widow of O'Flaherty, wife of Rickard an Iarain Bourke, and daughter of the chief "O'Malley" (see the "Bourkes," Lords Viscounts Mayo, pedigree); who, in the reign of Elizabeth, commanded her fleet in person, performed many remarkable exploits against the English. 12. O'Talcharain, chief of Conmaicne Cuile, now the barony of Kilmain, co. Mayo. The following chiefs and clans, not given in O'Dugan, have been collected from other sources :—1. O'Caithniadh (or O'Catney), chief of Iorras, now the barony of "Erris," in Mayo. 2. Q'Ceallachain or O'Callaghan, chiefs in Erris; this family was not of the O'Callaghans of Munster. 3. O'Caomhain (see the "Cowan" pedigree), a senior branch of the O'Dowd family, and chiefs of some districts on the borders of Sligo and Mayo, in the baronies of Tireragh, Corran, and Costello. 4. O'Gaibhtheachain or O'Gaughan; and O'Maoilfhiona or O'Molina, chiefs of Calraighe Moy Heleog—a district comprising the parish of "Crossmolina," in the barony of Tyrawley, and county Mayo. 5. O'Gairmiallaigh or O'Garvaly, and O'Dorchaidhe or O'Dorchy, chiefs of Partraigh or Partry; an ancient territory at the Partry Mountains in Mayo, the situation of which the present parish of "Party" determines (see the "Darcy" pedigree). 6. O'Lachtnain or Loughnan (by some of the family anglicised "Loftus"), chiefs of the territory called "The Two Bacs," now the parish of *Backs,* situated between Lough Conn and the river Moy, in Mayo. 7. O'Maol-

bard to the Monarch Niall of the Nine Hostages, in the fourth century, of the commencement of which the following is a translation:

> "Under thee lies the fair king of the men of Fail,
> Dathi, son of Fiachra, man of fame:
> O! Cruacha (Cruaghan), thou hast this concealed
> From the Galls and the Gaels."

The "Gaels" here mean the Irish themselves; and the "Galls" mean all foreigners, as the Danes, the Britons, etc. In the first line of the quotation Ireland is called Fail, as Inis Fail (signifying Insula Fatalis or the Island of Destiny): a name given to Ireland by the Tua-de-Danans, from a remarkable stone called the Lia Fail (signifying Lapis Fatalis, Saxum Fatale) or Stone of Destiny, which they brought with them into Ireland. This Lia Fail is believed to be the stone or pillar on which Jacob rested; and sitting on which the ancient kings, both of the De Danan and Milesian race in Ireland, were crowned at Tara. This stone was sent to Scotland in the sixth century by the Monarch Murcheartach Mor Mac-Earca, for the coronation purpose of his brother Fergus Mor MacEarca, the founder of the Scottish Monarchy in Scotland; and was used for many centuries at the coronation of the Scottish kings, and kept at the Abbey of Scone. When King Edward the First invaded Scotland, he brought with him that Lia Fail to England, and placed it under the coronation chair in Westminster Abbey, where it still remains; though it has been erroneously stated in some modern publications, that the large pillar stone which stands on the mound or rath at Tara is the Stone of Destiny: an assertion at variance with the statements of O'Flaherty, the O'Connors, and all other learned antiquarians. Three of the De Danan queens, who gave their names to Ireland, namely, Eire (from which the name "Eirin" or "Erin" is derived), Fodhla, and Banba, together with their husbands, Mac Coill, Mac Cecht, and Mac Greine, the three Tua-de-Danan Kings slain at the time of the Milesian conquest of Ireland, were buried at Cruachan in Connaught. Among the Milesian kings and queens interred there, were Hugony the Great, Monarch of Ireland (No. 59, p. 354); his daughter, the princess Muireasc; and his son, Cobthach Caolbhreagh; Bresnar Lothar (No. 73, p. 356); Maud (the famous queen of Connaught), Deirbhre, and Clothra—all sisters of Bresnar Lothar, and daughters of Eochy Feidlioch; Conn of the Hundred Battles and the other sons of Felim Rachtmar, the 108th Monarch of Ireland; and other kings, descendants of Conn of the Hundred Battles, with the exception of his son Art, the 112th Monarch (who directed that he should be buried at Trevet in Meath), and of Art's son Cormac, the famous Monarch of Ireland in the 3rd century, who was buried at Ros-na-Riogh (now Rosnaree or Rosnari), near Slane in the county Meath. According to the "Book of Ballymote," this King Cormac, who had some knowledge of Christianity, gave orders that he, too, should not be buried at Brugh Boine (which was the cemetery of most of the pagan kings of Meath), but at Ros-na-Riogh; and that his face should be towards the rising sun! Brugh Boine (which signifies the "town or fortress of the Boyne") was a great cemetery of the pagan kings of Ireland, and, according to some antiquaries, was situated near Trim; but, according to others, more probably at the place now called Stackallen; between Navan and Slane in Meath. In various parts of the ancient kingdom of Meath, in the counties of Meath, Westmeath, and Dublin, are many sepulchral mounds (usually called "moats"), of a circular form, and having the appearance of hillocks: these are the sepulchres of kings, queens, and warriors of the pagan times. There are several of these mounds of great size, particularly on the banks of the Boyne, between Drogheda and Slane; and one of them, at Newgrange, is of immense extent, covering an area of two acres; is about eighty feet in height; and foghmair, anglicised "Milford;" and O'Maolbrennain, anglicised "Mulrennin," chiefs of Hy-Eachach Muaidhe, a district extending along the western bank of the river "Moy," between Ballina and Killala. 8. O'Mongan or O'Mangan, chiefs of Breach Magh—a district in the parish of Kilmore Moy, on the eastern bank of the Moy, in the co. Sligo. 9. O'Conniallain or O'Connellan, chief of Bun-ui-Conniallan, now "Bonny-connellan"—a district in the barony of Kilmain, county Mayo; and also of Cloon-connellan, in the barony of Kilmain. 10. O'Ceirin or O'Kearns, chiefs of Ciarraighe Loch-na-Nairneadh—a territory in the barony of Costello, county Mayo, comprising the parishes of Aghamore, Bekan, and Knock.

The other clans in Mayo and Sligo were : O'Bannen, O'Brogan, Mac Conbain, O'Bean (ban : Irish, white), some of whom have anglicised the name "White" and "Whyte;" O'Beolan or O'Boland ; O'Beirne, some of whom have anglicised their name "Barnes;" O'Flatelly, O'Crean, O'Carey, O'Conachtain or O'Conaty of Cabrach or Cabra in Tireragh; O'Flanelly, O'Coolaghan, O'Burns, O'Hughes; O'Huada or Heady, O'Fuada or Fodey (fuadach : Irish, an elopement), and O'Tapa or Tappy (tapadh : Irish, haste)—these three last sirnames have been anglicised "Swift;" O'Loingsy or O'Lynch ; O'Maolmoicheirghe (moch : Irish, early), anglicised "Early" and "Eardly;" O'Mulrooney or Rooney, O'Moran, O'Muldoon, O'Meehan, O'Caffrey or Caffrey, O'Finnegan, O'Morrisey, O'Morris or O'Morrison; MacGeraghty, anglicised "Gar-rett;" O'Spillane, O'Donnell, and MacSweeney.

(b) THE NEW SETTLERS IN MAYO AND SLIGO.

In the 12th century John de Courcy made some attempts with his Anglo-Norman forces towards the conquest of Connaught, but did not succeed to any extent. The De Burgos or Bourkes, in the reign of King John, obtained grants in various parts of Connaught ; and, for a long period, carried on fierce contests with the O'Connors,

was surrounded by a circle of huge stones standing upright, many of which still remain. The interior of this mound is formed of a vast heap of stones of various sizes; and a passage, vaulted over with great flags, leads to the interior, where there is a large chamber or dome, and in it have been found sepulchral urns, and remains of human bones. Cairns or huge heaps of stones, many of which still remain on hills and mountains in various parts of Ireland, were also in pagan times erected as sepul-chres over kings and chiefs.

In the "Books" of Armagh and Ballymote, and other ancient records, are given some curious ac-counts of the customs used in the interment of the ancient kings and chiefs : Laoghaire (or Leary), Monarch of Ireland in the fifth century, was buried in the rampart or rath called Rath Leary, at Tara, with his military weapons and armour on him ; his face turned southwards, bidding defiance, as it were, to his enemies the men of Leinster. And Owen Beul, a king of Connaught in the sixth century, who was mortally wounded at the battle of Sligeach (or Sligo), fought with the people of Ulster, gave directions that he should be buried with his red javelin in his hand, and his face towards Ulster, as in defiance of his enemies ; but the Ulstermen came with a strong force and raised the body of the king, and buried it near Lough Gill, with the face downwards, that it might not be the cause of making them "fly" before the Conacians. Near Lough Gill in Sligo are two great cairns still remaining, at which place was probably an ancient cemetery of some of the kings of Connaught; and another arge one, near Cong, in the county Mayo. There are still some remains of Reilig-na-Riogh at Cruaghan or Cro-aghan in the county Roscommon, consisting of a circular area of about two hundred feet in diameter, surrounded with some remains of an ancient stone ditch ; and in the interior are heaps of rude stones piled upon each other, as stated in "Weld's Survey of Roscommon." Dun Aengus or the Fortress of Aengus. erected on the largest of the Arran Islands, off the coast of Galway, and situated on a tremen-dous cliff overhanging the sea, consists of a stone work of immense strength of Cyclopean architecture, composed of large stones without mortar or cement. It is of a circular form, and capable of containing within its area two hundred cows. According to O'Flaherty, it was erected by Aengus or Conchobhar, two of the Firvolgian kings of Connaught, before the Christian era ; and was also called the Dun of Concovar or Connor.

After the introduction of Christianity, the Irish kings and chiefs were buried in the abbeys, churches, and cathedrals : the Monarch Brian Boru, killed at the battle of Clontarf, was, it is said, buried in the cathedral of Armagh; the kings of Connaught, in the abbeys of Clonmacnoise, Cong, Knockmoy, Roscommon, etc.

It is stated by O'Flaherty, that six of the sons of Brian, king of Connaught, the ancestor of the Hy-Briuin, were converted and baptized by St. Patrick, together with many of the people, on the plain of Moyseola in Roscommon ; and that the saint erected a church, called Domhnach Mór or the "great church," on the banks of Lough Sealga, now Lough Hacket ; and that on three pillar stones which, for the purpose of pagan worship, had been raised there in the ages of idolatry, he had the name of Christ inscribed in three languages : [on one of them, "Iesus;" on another, "Soter;" and on the third, "Salvator." Ono, a grandson of Brian, king of Connaught, made a present to St. Patrick of his palace, called Imleach Ona, where the saint founded the episcopal see of Oilfinn or "Elphin," which obtained the name from a spring well the saint had sunk there, and on the margin of which was erected a large stone : thus from "Oil," which means a stone or rock, and "finn," which signifies fair or clear, the

3 H

kings of Connaught, and various chiefs. They made considerable conquests in the country, and were styled lords of Connaught ; but it appears that in the fourteenth century, several chiefs of the Bourkes renounced their allegiance to the English Government, and some of them took the sirname of "MacWilliam ;" and, adopting the Irish language and dress, identified themselves with the ancient Irish in customs and manners. One of them took the name of Mac William *Oughter* or Mac William the Upper, who was located in Galway, the *upper* part of Connaught ; and another, Mac William *Eighter*, or Mac William the Lower, who was located in Mayo, or the *lower* part. Some branches of the Bourkes took the sirnames of MacDavid, Mac-Philbin, MacGibbon, from their respective ancestors. (See the "Bourke" pedigree.)

From Richard or Rickard de Burgo, a great portion of the county Galway got the name of *Clanrickard*, which, according to Ware, comprised the baronies of Clare, Dunkellin, Loughrea, Kiltartan, Athenry, and Leitrim. The De Burgos became the most powerful family in Connaught, and were its chief governors under the kings of England. They were styled lords of Connaught, and also became earls of Ulster ; but, on the death of William de Burgo, earl of Ulster, in the fourteenth century, and the marriage of his daughter Elizabeth, to Lionel, Duke of Clarence, son of King Edward the Third, his titles passed into the Royal Family of England.

Ulick Burke, the progenitor of the marquises of Clanrickard, had great possessions in Galway and Roscommon ; and Sir Edmund Bourke, called "Albanach," had large possessions in Mayo, and was ancestor of the earls of Mayo.

Mayo : The other families who settled in Mayo, were the following :—De Angulo or Nangle, who took the Irish surname "MacCostello," and from whom the barony of "Costello" derived its name. De Exter, who took the name of "MacJordan," and were styled lords of Athleathan, in the barony of Gallen. Barrett, some of whom took the sirname of "MacWatten ;" and "MacAndrew." Staunton, in Carra—some of whom took the name of "MacAveely." Lawless, Cusack, Lynot, Prendergast, and Fitzmaurice ; Bermingham, who changed their name to "MacFeorais ;" Blake, Dillon, Bingham, etc. The MacPhilips are placed on the map of Ortelius in the barony of Costello ; their principal seat is at Cloonmore, and they are a branch of the Bourkes who took the name of "MacPhilip."

Mayo, according to some accounts, was formed into a county, as early as the reign of Edward the Third ; but not altogether reduced to English rule till the reign of Queen Elizabeth. In Speed's "Theatre of Great Britain," published, A.D. 1676, Mayo is stated to be "replenished both with pleasure and fertility, abundantly rich in cattle, deer, hawks, and plenty of honey." Mayo derives its name from "magh," a *plain* and " eo," a *yew tree*, signifying the Plain of the Yew Trees.

In Sligo, the Anglo-Normans under the Bourkes and the Fitzgeralds (earls of Kildare) made some settlements, and had frequent contests with the O'Connors ; and

---

name Oilfinn or Elphin was derived, and which meant the rock of the limpid water. O'Flaherty states that this stone continued there till his own time, A.D. 1675.

A king of Connaught in the latter end of the seventh century, named Muireadhach Muilleathan, who died A.D. 700, and a descendant of the above named Brian, son of Eochy Moyvone, was the ancestor of the Siol Muireadhaigh ; which became the chief branch of the Hy-Briune race, and possessed the greater part of Connaught, but were chiefly located in the territory now forming the county Roscommon : hence the term "Siol Murray" was applied to that territory. The O'Connors who became kings of Connaught were the head chiefs of Siol Murray ; and took their name from Conchobhar or Connor, who was a king of Connaught in the tenth century. The grandson of this Conchobhar, Tadhg an Eich Geal or Teige of the White Steed, who was king of Connaught in the beginning of the eleventh century, and who died A.D. 1030, was the first who took the sirname of "O'Connor." In the tenth century, as mentioned in the Annals of the Four Masters, two or three of the O'Rourkes are styled kings of Connaught ; but, with these exceptions, the ancestors of the O'Connors of the race of Hy-Briune and Siol Murray, and the O'Connors themselves, held the sovereignty of Connaught from the fifth to the fifteenth century ; and two of them became Monarchs of Ireland, in the twelfth century, namely, Torlogh O'Connor, called Toirdhealbhach Mór or Torlogh the Great, who is called by the annalists the "Augustus of Western Europe ;" and his son, Roderick O'Connor, who was the last Milesian Monarch of Ireland. This Torlogh O'Connor died at Dunmore, in Galway, A.D. 1156, in the 68th year of his age, and was buried at Clonmacnoise. And Roderick O'Connor, after having reigned eighteen years, abdicated the throne, A.D. 1184, in consequence of the Anglo-Norman invasion ; and, after a religious seclusion of thirteen years in Cong Abbey, in the county Mayo, died A.D. 1198, in the 82nd year of his age, and was buried in Clonmacnoise in the same sepulchre with his father. In the "Memoirs" of Charles O'Connor of Belenagar, it is said, that in the latter end of the fourteenth century the two head chiefs of the O'Connors, namely, Torlogh Roe and Torlogh Don, having contended for the lordship of Siol Murray, agreed to divide the territory between them. The families descended from Torlogh Don called themselves the O'Connors "Don" or the Brown O'Connors ; while the descendants of Torlogh Roe called themselves the O'Connors "Roe" or the Red O'Connors. Another branch of the O'Connors got great possessions in the county Sligo, and were styled the O'Connors "Sligo."—CONNELLAN.

with the O'Donnells (princes of Tirconnell), who had extended their power over a great part of Sligo. Sligo derives its name from the river *Sligeach* ("Slig," *a shell*), and was formed into a county, A.D. 1565, in the reign of Queen Elizabeth, by the lord deputy Sir Henry Sydney.

(c) Modern Nobility in Mayo and Sligo.

The following have been the noble families in Mayo and Sligo since the reign of King James the First.

Mayo : Bourke, viscounts Clanmorris and earls of Mayo. Browne, barons of Kilmain, barons of Westport, and barons of Oranmore. Bingham, barons of Castlebar ; and Saville, barons of Castlebar. Dillon, barons of Costello-Gallen, and viscounts Dillon. O'Hara, barons of Tyrawley and Kilmain.

Sligo : Taaffe, barons of Ballymote, and viscounts of Corran. Coote, barons of Collooney. Scudamore, viscounts of Sligo. And Browne, marquises of Sligo.

2.—ROSCOMMON AND GALWAY.

(a) The Irish Chiefs and Clans.

The following chiefs and clans in Roscommon and Galway, and the territories possessed by them in the twelfth century, have been collected from O'Dugan's Topography and other sources :—1. **MacDiarmada** or **MacDermott**, princes of Moylurg, Tir-Oilill, Tir-Tuathail, Arteach, and Clan Cuain. Moylurg comprised the plains of Boyle, in the county Roscommon ; Tir-Oilill, now the barony of "Tirerill" in Sligo ; Arteach, a district in Roscommon near Lough Gara, on the borders of Sligo and Mayo ; Clan Cuain was a district in the barony of Carra, near Castlebar, comprising the present parishes of Islandeady, Turlough, and Breaffy. The MacDermotts were hereditary marshals of Connaught, the duties attached to which were to raise and regulate the military forces, and to prepare them for battle, as commanders-in-chief ; also to preside at the inauguration of the O'Connors as kings of Connaught, and to proclaim their election. The MacDermotts derive their descent from Teige of the White Steed, king of Connaught in the eleventh century ; and are a branch of the O'Connors. This Teige had a son named Maolruanaidh, the progenitor of the Mac-Dermotts : hence their tribe name was *Clan Maolruanaidh* or Clan Mulrooney. Diarmaid (*dia :* Irish, *a god*, and *armaid*, of *arms*, and signifying a great warrior), grandson of Mulrooney, who died, A.D. 1165, was the head of the clan ; and from him they took the name of "MacDermott." The MacDermotts had their chief fortress at the Rock of Lough Key, on an island in Lough Key, near Boyle ; and are the only Milesian family who have preserved their title of Prince, namely, "Hereditary Prince of Coolavin :" a title by which the MacDermott is to this day recognised in the county Sligo. The principal families of the MacDermotts in Connaught are—The Mac-Dermott of Coolavin, and MacDermott Roe of Alderford in the county Roscommon. The following were, according to O'Dugan, the ancient chiefs of Moylurg before the time of the MacDermotts :—

> "The ancient chiefs of Moylurg of abundance :
>   MacEoach (or MacKeogh) ; MacMaoin (or MacMaine), the great.
>   And MacRiabhaidh (or Magreevy) the efficient forces."

2. **O'Ceallaigh** or **O'Kelly.** This name is derived from Ceallach, a celebrated chief of the ninth century, who is the ancestor of the O'Kellys, princes of Hy-Maine. These O'Kellys are a branch of the Clan Colla of Orgiall in Ulster, and of the same descent as the MacMahons, lords of Monaghan ; Maguires, lords of Fermanagh ; O'Hanlons, lords of Orior in Armagh, etc. In the fourth century, Main Mór or Main the Great, a chief of the Clan Colla, conquered a colony of the Firbolgs in Connaught ; and the territory so conquered, which was possessed by his posterity, was after him called Hy-Maine (signifying the territory possessed by the descendants of Main), which has been Latinized "Hy-Mania" and "I-Mania." This extensive territory comprised,

according to O'Flaherty and others, a great part of South Connaught in the present county Galway, and was afterwards extended beyond the river Suck to the Shannon, in the south of Roscommon. It included the baronies of Ballymoe, Tiaquin, Killian, and Kilcollan, with part of Clonmacnoon, in Galway ; and the barony of Athlone in Roscommon. The O'Kellys were styled princes of Hy-Maine, and their territory was called "O'Kelly's Country."

According to the "Dissertations" of Charles O'Connor, the O'Kellys held the office of high treasurers of Connaught, and the MacDermotts that of marshals. Tadhg or Teige O'Kelly, one of the commanders of the Connaught contingent of Brian Boru's army at the battle of Clontarf, was of this ancient family. The O'Kellys had castles at Aughrim, Garbally, Gallagh, Monivea, Moylough, Mullaghmore, and Aghrane (now Castlekelly), in the county Galway ; and at Athlone, Athleague, Corbeg, Galy, and Skrine, in the county Roscommon. The chiefs of the O'Kellys, according to some accounts, were inaugurated at Clontuskert, about five miles from Eyrecourt in the county Galway, and held their rank as princes of Hy-Maine down to the reign of Queen Elizabeth. 3. **MacOireachtaigh** or **MacGeraghty**, of the same stock as the O'Connors of Connaught. In the Annals of the Four Masters, at A.D. 1278, MacOiraghty is mentioned as head chief of Siol Murray, a term applied to the central parts of the county Roscommon ; and, in the sixteenth century, when deprived of their territories, some of the clan Geraghty settled in Mayo and Sligo, and gave their name to the island of *Innis Murray*, off the coast of Sligo, on account of their former title as head chiefs of Siol Murray, as in the Annals above mentioned. 4. **O'Fionnachta** or **O'Finaghty**, chiefs of Clan Conmaigh, and of Clan Murchada, districts in the two half baronies of Ballymoe in the counties of Galway and Roscommon, in O'Kelly's principality of Hy-Maine. The O'Finaghtys here mentioned were of the Clan Colla ; and two distinct chiefs of them are given by O'Dugan : one of them, Finaghty of "Clan Murrogh of the Champions ;" and the other, Finaghty of the "Clan Conway." O'Finaghty (modernized "Finnerty"), chiefs of Clan Conway, had their castle at Dunamon, near the river Suck, in the county Roscommon. It is stated in some old authorities, that the O'Finaghtys had the privilege of drinking the first cup at every royal feast. 5. **O'Fallamhain** or **O'Fallon** were chiefs of Clan Uadach, a district in the barony of Athlone, in the county Roscommon, comprising the parishes of Cam and Dysart, and had a castle at Miltown. The O'Fallons were originally chiefs in Westmeath, near Athlone. 6. **O'Birn** or **O'Beirne**, chiefs of Muintir O'Mannachain, a territory along the Shannon in the parish of Ballintobber, in Roscommon, extending nearly to Elphin. 7. **O'Mannachain** or **O'Monaghan**, was also chief on the same territory as O'Beirne. These O'Beirnes are of a distinct race from the O'Byrnes of Wicklow. 8. **O'Hainlidhe**, **O'Hanley**, or **Henley**, chiefs of Cineal Dobhtha, a large district in the barony of Ballintobber, along the Shannon. It formed part of the Three Tuatha or the Three Districts. 9. **MacBranain** or **MacBrennan**, sometimes anglicised O'Brennan ; and O'Mailmichil, anglicised "Mitchell." The O'Brennans and Mitchells were chiefs of Corca Achlann, a large district adjoining Cineal-Dobtha, in the barony of Roscommon. This district formed part of the "Tuatha" in which was situated the Slieve Baun Mountain. 10. **O'Flannagain** or **Flanagan**, chiefs of Clan Cathail, a territory in the barony of Roscommon, north of Elphin. O'Maolmordha, O'Morra, or O'Moore, O'Carthaidh or O'Carthy, and O'Mughroin or O'Moran, were also subordinate chiefs of Clan Cathail (*Cathal* and *Serlus ;* Irish, *Charles ;* Span. *Carlos*), or Clan Charles. 11. **O'Maolbrennain**, anglicised "Mulrenan," chiefs of Clan Conchobhair or Clan Connor, a district near Cruachan or Croaghan, in the barony and county of Roscommon. 12. **O'Cathalain**, chief of Clan Fogartaigh [Fogarty] ; and O'Maonaigh or O'Mooney, chiefs of Clan Murthuile. Clan Fogarty and Clan Murthuile were districts in Ballintubber, county Roscommon. 13. **O'Conceannain** or **O'Concannon**, chiefs of Hy-Diarmada, a district on the borders of Roscommon and Galway, in the baronies of Athlone and Ballymoe. 14. **MacMurchada**, **MacMurrough** or **Murphy**, chiefs of Tomaltaigh in Roscommon, of which MacOiraghta was head chief. 15. **O'Floinn** or **O'Flynn**, chiefs of Siol Maolruain, a large district in the barony of Ballintubber, county Roscommon ; in which lay Slieve Ui Fhloinn or O'Flynn's Mountain, which comprised the parishes of Kilkeeran and Kiltullagh, and part of the parish of Ballynakill, in the barony of Ballymoe, county Galway. O'Maolmuaidh or O'Mulmay, was a subordinate chief over Clan Taidhg or Clan Teige in the same district. 16. **O'Rothlain** (O'Rowland, O'Roland, and O'Rollin), chiefs of Coill Fothaidh, a district on the borders of Roscommon and Mayo. 17. **O'Sgaithgil** or **Scahil**, chiefs of Corca Mogha, a district which comprised the parish of Kilkeeran, in the barony of Killian, county Galway. O'Broin, anglicised "Burns," was chief of Lough Gealgosa, a district adjoining Corca Mogha. 18. O'Talcharain (Taleran or Taleyrand), chiefs of Conmaicne Cuile, a district in the barony of Clare, county Galway. 19. O'Cadhla, O'Cawley, or Kealy, chiefs of Conmaicne Mara (or Connemara), now the barony of Ballynahinch, in the county Galway. 20. MacConroi, anglicised "King," chiefs of Gno Mór; and O'Haidhnidh or O'Heany, chiefs of Gno Beag : districts which lay along the western banks of Lough Corrib, in the barony of Moycullen, and county of Galway, in the direction of Galway Bay. 21. MacAodha or MacHugh, chiefs of Clan Cosgraidh, a district on the eastern side of Lough Corrib. 22. O'Flaithbheartaigh or O'Flaherty, chiefs of Muintir Murchadha, now the barony of Clare, county Galway. In the thirteenth century the O'Flahertys were expelled from this territory by the English ; and, having settled on the other side of Lough Corrib, they got extensive possessions there in the barony of Moycullen, and were styled lords of Iar Conacht or West Connaught. They also had the chief naval command about Lough Corrib, on some of the islands of which they had castles. 23. O'Heidhin or O'Heyne, anglicised "Hynes," was styled Prince of South Hy-Fiachra, a district co-extensive with the diocese of Kilmacduagh ; and comprised the barony of Kiltartan, and parts of the baronies of Dunkellin and Loughrea, in the county Galway. 24. O'Seachnasaigh, Cineal-Aodha O'Shaughnessey, O'Shannesy, chiefs of Cineal-Aodha (or Cineal-Hugh), a district in the barony of Kiltartan, county Galway. Cineal-Hugh was sometimes called Cineal-Hugh of Echty, a mountainous district on the borders of Galway and Clare. O'Cathail or O'Cahil was also a chief of Cineal-Hugh. 25. MacGiolla Ceallaigh or MacGilkelly, anglicised "Kilkelly," chiefs in South Fiachra. 26. O'Cleirigh or O'Clery, anglicised "Clarke," chiefs in Hy-Fiachra Aidhne, same as MacGilkelly. This family took the name "Cleirigh" from Cleireach, one of their celebrated chiefs in the tenth century ; and a branch of them having settled in Donegal, became bards and historians to the O'Donnells, princes of Tirconnell, and were the authors of the Annals of the Four Masters, etc. Other branches of the O'Clerys settled in Brefney O'Reilly or the county Cavan. 27. O'Duibhgiolla or O'Diffely, chiefs of Cineal-Cinngamhna [Cean Gamhna] ; Mac-Fiachra, chiefs of Oga Peathra ; O'Cathain or O'Cahan, chiefs of Cineal-Sedna ; and O'Maghna, chiefs of Ceanridhe, all chiefs in Aidhne or South Hy-Fiachra : all these chiefs were descended from Guaire Aidhne, a king of Connaught in the seventh century. 28. O'Madagain or O'Madadhain, anglicised "Madden," chief of Siol Anmchadha or Silancha ; a name derived from "Anmchadh," a descendant of Colla-da-Chrioch. This territory comprised the present barony of Longford in the county Galway, and the parish of Lusmagh, on the Leinster side of the river Shannon, in the King's County. The O'Maddens'are a branch of the Clan Colla, and of the same descent as the O'Kellys, princes of Hy-Maine ; and took their name from Madud an Mór, one of their ancient chiefs. 29. O'Hullachain or O'Hoolaghan, sometimes anglicised "O'Coolaghan" and MacCoolaghan, chiefs of Siol Anmchadha. 30. O'Maolalaidh or O'Mullally, anglicised "Lally." 31. O'Neachtain or O'Naghten, anglicised "Norton." The O'Naghtens and O'Mullallys are given by O'Dugan as the two chiefs of Maonmuighe or Maenmoy : an extensive plain comprising a great part of the present baronies of Loughrea and Leitrim in the county Galway. The O'Naughtens and O'Mullallys are branches of the Clan Colla. When dispossessed of their territories, the O'Mullallys settled at Tullachna-Dala near Tuam, where they had a castle : and the head of the family having afterwards removed to France, a descendant of his became celebrated as an orator and a statesman, at the time of the French Revolution, and was known as "Count Lally Tollendal :" taking his title from the ancient territory in Ireland, Tullach-na-Dala, above mentioned. Several of the O'Lallys were celebrated commanders in the Irish Brigade in France ; and one of them was created "Marquis de Lally Tollendal," and a peer of France, by Napoleon the First. 32. O'Connaill or O'Connell, chiefs of the territory from the river Grian, on the borders of Clare, to the plain of Maenmoy : comprising parts of the barony of Leitrim in Galway, and of Tullagh in Clare. These O'Connells and the MacEgans were marshals of the forces to the O'Kellys, princes of Hy-Maine ; and of the same descent as the O'Kellys, namely that of the Clan Colla. 33. MacEideadhain or MacAodhagain (anglicised "MacEgan") were chiefs of Clan Diarmada, a district in the barony of Leitrim, county Galway ; and had a castle at Dun Doighre, now "Duniry." The MacEgans were Brehons in Connaught, and also in Ormond ; and many of them eminent literary men. 34. MacGiolla Fionnagain or O'Finnegan, sometimes rendered "Finucane ;" and O'Cionaoith or O'Kenny, chiefs of Clan

Iaitheamhaim or Flaitheamhain [or Fleming], called also Muintir Cionaith, a district in the barony of Moycarnon, county Roscommon. Of the O'Finnegan family was Mathias Finucane, one of the Judges of the Common Pleas in Ireland, who died A.D. 1814. 35. **O'Domhnallain** or **O'Donnelan**, chiefs of Clan Breasail, a district in the barony of Leitrim, and county Galway. 36. **O'Donchadha** or **O'Donoghoe**, chiefs of Clan Cormaic, a district in Maenmoy in Galway, already defined. 37. **O'Duibhghind**, chiefs of the Twelve Ballys or Townlands of Duibhghind, a district near Loughrea, in the county Galway. 38. **O'Docomlain**, chiefs of Eidhnigh ; and O'Gabhrain or O'Gauran, chiefs of Dal Druithne, districts about Loughrea. 39. **O'Maolbrighde** or **O'Mul-bride**, chiefs of Magh Finn and of Bredagh, a district in the barony of Athlone, county Roscommon, east of the river Suck. 40. **O'Mainnin, O'Mannin, O'Mannion, or O'Man-ning**, chiefs of Sodhan : a large territory in the barony of Tiaquin, made into six divisions, called "The Six Sodhans." The O'Mannins or O'Mannings had their chief residence at the castle of Clogher, barony of Tiaquin, county Galway, and after-wards, at Menlough, in the parish of Killascobe in the same barony. The other chiefs given by O'Dugan on the "Six Sodhans" were Mac-an-Bhaird, MacWard or Ward ; O'Sguira or Scurry ; O'Lennain or Lennon ; O'Casain or Cashin ; O'Gialla or O'Gial-lain, rendered Gilly, and Geallan ; and O'Maigin or Magin. 41. **O'Cathail, or Cahill, O'Mughroin or Moran, O'Maolruanaidh, Mulrooney, or Rooney**, the three chiefs of Crumthan or Cruffan, a district comprising the barony of Killian, and part of Ballymoe in the county Galway. 42. **O'Laodog or O'Laodhaigh**, anglicised "O'Leahy," chiefs of Caladh, a district in the barony of Kilconnell, county Galway.

The following chiefs and clans not given by O'Dugan are collected from other sources :—43. **O'Daly** (who were a branch of the O'Donnells, princes of Tirconnell) had large possessions in the counties of Galway and Roscommon. The O'Dalys, it appears, settled in Connaught as early as the twelfth century. 44. **O'Coindealbhain, O'Con-ghiollain, O'Conniallain, O'Connollain, O'Connellan**, princes of Hy-Leary in the tenth and eleventh centuries ; but branches of this family in the twelfth and thirteenth centuries, settled in the counties of Roscommon, Galway, and Mayo. Pedigrees of this ancient clan are given in the "Books" of Leacan and Ballymote ; and also in the "Genealogical Book" of the O'Clerys. 45. **O'Halloran**, chiefs of Clan Fargal, a large district on the east side of the river of Galway, near Lough Corrib. 46. **O'Callanan** and **O'Canavan**, whom O'Dugan mentions as hereditary physicians in Galway. 47. **O'Dubhthaigh or O'Duffy**, families of note in Galway and Roscommon. 48. **O'Brien**, a branch of the O'Briens of Thomond in the county Clare, and lords of the Isles of Arran, off the coast of Galway. 49. **MacCnaimhin or MacNevin**, according to the "Book of Leacan," chiefs of a district called Crannog MacCnaimhin or Crannagh MacNevin, in the parish of Tynagh, barony of Leitrim, and county of Galway. This name "MacCnaimhin" (*cnaimh :* Irish, a *bone*), has been anglicised "Bone" and "Bonas." 50. **MacEochaidh, MacKeogh, or Keogh** (a branch of the O'Kellys, princes of Hy-Maine), chiefs of Omhanach, now "Onagh," in the parish of Taghmaconnell, in the barony of Athlone, county Roscommon. 51. **MacGiolladuibh or MacGillduff**, anglicised "Kilduff," chiefs of Caladh, along with the O'Leahys, in the barony of Kilconnell, county Galway. 52. **O'Lorcan or O'Larkin** ; O'Gebenaigh or Gevenny, Gebney, and Gibney ; O'Aireach-tain, anglicised "Harrington ;" O'Fahy, O'Fay or O'Foy ; O'Laidins or Laydon, and O'Horan or Horan, all clans in Hy-Maine, in the county Galway. 53. **O'Cobthaigh or O'Coffey**, a branch of the O'Kellys, princes of Hy-Maine ; and chiefs of a large district in the barony of Clonmacnoon, county Galway. 54. **MacManus** ; Keon, MacKeon, or MacEwen ; O'Common or Cummins, and O'Ronan or Ronayne, clans in the county Roscommon.

(b) THE NEW SETTLERS IN GALWAY.

In the twelfth and thirteenth centuries several new families settled in the town of Galway, and other parts of that county ; the principal of whom were Athy, Ber-mingham, Blake, Bodkin, Browne, Blundel, Deane, Dillon, Darcy, French, De Jorse, Kirwan, Lynch, Lawless, Morris, Martin, White, etc. The De Jorses came from Wales to Galway in the reign of Edward the First, and having formed an alliance with the O'Flahertys, chiefs of West Connaught, got large possessions in Connemara in the barony of Ross; and towards the borders of Mayo a territory which is called "Joyces' Country." These De Jorses changed their name to "Joyce."

(c) The Modern Nobility in Galway and Roscommon.

The following have been the noble families in Galway and Roscommon since the reign of King James the First:—

In Galway : De Burg or Burke, earls and marquises of Clanrickard ; Bourke, viscounts of Galway, and barons of Brittas ; Bermingham, barons of Athenry : Butler and Gore, earls of Arran ; De Massue and Moncton, viscounts of Galway ; Le Poer Trench, earls of Clancarty, viscounts Dunloe, and barons of Kilconnell ; Vereker, viscounts of Gort ; Dillon, barons of Clonbrock; French, barons French ; Browne, barons of Oranmore ; Blake, barons of Wallscourt ; Trench, barons of Ashtown.

In Roscommon : Dillon, earls of Roscommon ; Wilmot and De Ginkle, earls of Athlone ; King, viscounts Lorton ; Coote, barons of Castlecoote ; Crofton, barons Croftou ; Mahon, barons Hartland ; and Sandford, barons of Mountsandford.

In the reign of Elizabeth, the Lord Deputy Sir Henry Sydney, A.D. 1565, formed Galway into a county; which took its name from the chief town, called in Irish *Gaillimh* [Galliv], anglicised "Galway." And in the same reign the same Lord Deputy formed Roscommon into a county, which took its name from the town of Roscommon, which in Irish is *Ros-Comain* (signifying the Wood of Coman), and was so called from St. Coman, who founded an abbey there in the sixth century.

5.—ANCIENT IRISH SIRNAMES.

As many of the ancient Irish sirnames are not recorded in O'Clery's, or in Mac-Firbis's Genealogies, or in the *Linea Antiqua*, or in the Betham Genealogical Collections, we have collected from "The Topographical Poems of O'Dugan and O'Heerin," "The Tribes and Customs of Hy-Fiachra," and other works published by the Celtic and Archæological Societies in Ireland, the following Irish family names, and the modern anglicised forms which they assumed :

The Name		*Has been modernized.*
Clan Shane (a Sept of the O'Farrells)	...	Shaen.
MacAindris ...	...	Andrews, MacAndrew, Anderson.
MacBlosky ...	...	MacClosky, Closky.
MacBrehon ...	...	Judge.
MacCarrghanma	...	Carron, MacCarron, MacCarroon, MacCarhon, and Carson.
MacCionnaith	...	MacKenna (of the Meath Hy-Niall).
MacConboirne	...	Bourns.
MacConin ...	...	Kennyon, Canning.
MacCoshy ...	...	Foote ("cos :" Irish, *the foot*).
MacCrossan ...	...	Crosby, Crosbie.
MacFinnbhair	...	Maginver, Gaynor.
MacGallogly ...	...	Ingoldsby.
MacGilla Sinin	...	Synan.
MacGillicuskly	...	Cuskley.
MacGilla Kenny	...	Kilkenny.
MacGilla tSamhais ...		MacIltavish, MacTavish.
MacGillimore	...	Merryman.
MacGiolla Phoil	...	MacGilfoyle, Gilfoyle, Paul.
MacGuiggan ...	...	Maguiggan, Goodwin, Godwin.
MacGunshenan	...	Magunshinan, Nugent, Leonard.

The Name		Has been Modernized.
MacInogly	... ...	Ingoldsby (See " MacGallogly.")
MacLaighid	... ...	Lye, Leigh.
MacLave	... ...	Hand (" lamh :" Irish, *a hand*).
MacMahon	... ...	Mathews, Fitzursula.
MacMurchada (of		
Ulster)	... ...	MacMorrow, MacMurray, Morell.
MacNamee	... ...	Meath, Mee.
MacNebo	... ...	Victory, Victoria.
MacOscar	... ...	Cosgrave, Costello.
MacPartholain	...	Bat, Bats, Batson, Bateson.
MacReachtagain	...	Rafter.
MacSimoin	... ...	Sims, Simmes, Simpson, Simkins, Simcocks, Simon.
MacSpallane	... ...	Spenser.
Mac Speallain		Spenser.
MacTaidhg	...	MacTague, MacTeig, Montague, Montagu.
MacTyre	... ...	Wolf, Wolfe.
MacUaithnin	...	MacHoneen, Green, Greene, Tonyson, Tennyson.
MacUalhairg	...	MacGolderick, Goderich, Golding, Goulding, Waller.
Mag Aedha	... ...	Magee.
Magilsinan	... ...	Magilsitnan.
Muintir Ceallaigh	...	O'Kelly and Kelly, in Londonderry.
Muintir Lideadha	...	O'Liddy and Liddy.
Murtagh	... ...	Mortimer.
O'h-Aichir	... ...	O'Hehir, Hehir.
O'Aimirgin	... ...	Mergin, Bergin.
O'Banain	... ...	Banan.
O'Barrain	... ...	Barrington.
O'Beirne	... ...	Briun.
O'Brachain	... ...	Brahan.
O'Breadhdha	...	Bray. (of Imokilly, co. Cork.)
O'Breen	... ...	O'Brien.
O'Brien	... ...	Brine.
O'Breithe	... ...	Broghie, Brophy.
O'Bruadair	...	Broder, Broderick, Bradner, Brothers.
O'Byrne	... ...	Leycester, Lester, Lyster, Warren.
O'Cain* [O'Koin]	...	Coyne, Koin, Kain, Kean, Keane.
O'Caolloaidhe	...	Cayley, Kaely, Keely.
O'Ceadfhada	...	Keating, Keatinge.
O'Cearnachain	...	Kernaghan.
O'Ceathaigh	...	Keaty, Keating.
O'Ceirin	... ...	Kerrin.
O'Ciardha	... ...	Carey, Keary.
O'Ciarmhaic	...	Kirby, Berwick.
O'Cindellain	...	Cunningham.
O'Cinnfhaelaidh	...	Kinealy.
O'Clumain	... ...	Coalman.
O'Coilen	... ...	Collins, Collings.
O'Coilligh†	... ...	Wood, Woods.
O'Conagan	... ...	Conyngham.
O'Conaing‡	... ...	Gunning.
O'Conaill	... ...	Connell, O'Connell.
O'Conaighain	...	Conway.
O'Connowe	... ...	Conway.
O'Conor	... ...	Conyers.
O'Cornain	... ...	Corbett.
O'Cribbain	... ...	Corbett, Cribban.

* *O'Cain :* Quite distinct from " O'Cahan."

† *O'Coilligh :* See also No. 103 on the " O'Mealla" pedigree, p. 689, *ante.*

‡ *O'Conaing :* The chief of this family was seated at *Caislean Ui Chonaing,* now " Castle Connell" in the county Limerick.

The Name		Has been Modernized.
O'Dowling	... ...	Du Laing, Laing.
O'Drum	... ...	Drum, Drummond.
O'Duibhdiorma	...	Diarmid, MacDermott.
O'Duibhraic	... ...	Durack.
O'Duineadhaigh	...	Doney, Denny.
O'Echtighearn	...	Ahern.
O'Faelchoin	... ...	Wolfe. (See also " Mac'l'yre.")
O'Fearceallaighe	...	Farrelly.
O'Feehily	... ...	Pickley, O'Feely.
O'Finntighearn	...	Finneran.
O'Flaithri	... ...	Flattery.
O'Fodhladha	...	Foley (of Waterford.)
O'Fraechain	... ...	French, Ffrench, Frenshe.*
O'Gaoithin	... ...	Gehan, Gihson, Gettins.
O'Gathlaoich	...	Gately, Keightley, Catley.
O'Gormog	... ...	Gorman.
O'Gowan	... ...	Smith.
O'Griobhtha	...	Griffy, Griffin.
O'h-Aghmaill	...	Hamill.
O'h-Aidith	... ...	Hatty, Hetty.
O'h-Ailche	... ...	Halley, Ally.
O'Haughey	... ...	Haugh, Hoy, Hoey, Hawe, Howe.
O'Hay ...	... ...	Hay, Hughes.
O'Hease	..	Hussey, Oswell.
O'h-Eitegein	...	Magettigan.
O'h-Eochagain	...	Haughion.
O'h-Eoghain	...	O'Howen, Owens.
O'h-Heraghty	...	MacGeraghty, Harrington.
O'Hooneen	...	Greene. (See " MacUaithnin.")
O'h-Iomhair†	...	Howard, Ivers.
O'h-Ir‡	...	O'Hir, O'Hayer, O'Hare, Hare.
O'Hurley	...	Harley.
O'Labhradha	...	Lavery.
O'Lahiff	... ...	Guthrie.
O'Lairgnen	...	Largan, Lorigan, Legge.
O'Laodhog	...	Lee.
O'Laoghain	...	Lane.
O'Lochain	...	Loughan, Duck.
O'Lorcain	...	Larkin, Larcom.
O'Luain	...	Loane, Lamb.
O'Luane	...	Lamb.
O'Kelaghan	...	Callaghan.
O'Maoilbloghain	...	Mullowne, Mullowney, Malony.
O'Maoilcallain	...	Mulhollan, Mulholland.
O'Maoileoin	...	Malone.
O'Maoilgaoithe	...	Mulgeehy, Wynn, and Wynne.
O'Marcachain	...	Markam, Horseman, Ryder, Ryding.
O'Mearadhaigh	...	O'Meara, O'Mara.
O'Mellain	...	Mellan, Millan, Mellon.
O'Mordha	...	O'More.
O'Mughroin	...	Moran.
O'Mulclohy	...	Stone, Stoney.
O'Mulfaver	...	Palmer.

*Frenshe: A friend informs me that he has met this sirname variously written, as follows :— Freynsce, Freynsh, Freynsshe, Frainche, Freinche, Frensche, Frenshe, Frensch, Frense, ffrench, and French.

† O'h-Iomhair : Among the peasantry in Ireland this sirname is anglicised Howard ; but, among the gentry, Ivers.

‡ O h-Ir : This sirname is derived from Slioght Ir, a branch of the " Reynolds" Family. (See No. 118, p. 345, ante.)

The Name		*Has been Modernised.*
O'Mulfover	... ...	Milford.
O'Mullaville	... ...	Lavelle.
O'Mulrian	... ...	Murrian, Ryan.
O'Mulrony	... ...	Moroni (of the county Clare.)
O'Mulligan	... ...	Baldwin.
O'Muineog	... ...	Monaghan.
O'Murgally	... ...	Morley.
O'Murphy	... ...	Morphie.
O'Neill	... ...	Neele, Neely.
O'Rourke	... ...	Rooke.
O'Seagha	... ...	O'Shea.
O'Sedna	... ...	Shade.
O'Seisnain	... ...	Sexton.
O'Sewell*	... ...	Walker, Sewell.
O'Shaughnessy	...	Sandys.
O'Sullivan	...	Silvan, Silvers.
O'Sumaghain	... ...	Somers.
O'Tackney	... ...	Tackit.
O'Taichligh	... ...	Tully, Tilly.
O'Tiompain	... ...	Tenpenny.
O'Trehy†	... ...	Foote. (See " MacCoshy.")
O'Tuathlain	... ...	Tolan, Toland, Thulis.
O'Turrain	... ...	Troy.
O'h-Uisgin	... ...	O'Hiskeen, O'Histeen, Hastings.
O'h-Uallachain	... ...	MacUallachain, MacCuolahan, Cuolahan, Nolan.‡

6.—CELTIC FAMILIES.

IN page 412¾ of MacFirbis's "Irish Genealogies" the following Celtic names are designated *Maghaidh Saxonta* (" magadh :" Irish, *mocking, jeering*); meaning that it was only in *jest* these names were said to be of *Saxon* origin :

1. Auchinlek	15. Gordon	29. Lindesay
2. Barclay	16. Grakane	30. Little
3. Barde	17. Gray	31. Lundie
4. Biset	18. Guthrie	32. Murray
5. Blaire	19. Haliday	33. Newbigging
6. Boyd	20. Hay	34. Oliphant
7. Cambell	21. Ireland	35. Ramsay
8. Cleland	22. Jardan	36. Ruther
9. Crawfurd	23. Johnston	37. Ruthven
10. Currie	24. Kar	38. Scot
11. Dasse	25. Keith	39. Scrimager
12. Dowglas	26. Killpatrick	40. Sebon
13. Dun	27. Lawder	41. Tints
14. Foorde	28. Lennox	42. Wallace.

* *O'Sewell :* This sirname in Irish is *O'Siubhail* (Siubhal :" Irish, *walking ;* Heb., "shubh," *to walk;* "shebhila," *a path*).

† *O'Trehy :* In Irish this sirname would be *O'Treathain* (" treathan :" Irish, another word for *foot*).

‡ *Nolan :* This is not the *Nolan* or *Nowlan* family, which, at the time of the Cromwellian Settlement of Ireland, was transplanted from the county Waterford to the county Galway.

7.—GREEN WERE THE FIELDS.

THIS poem was first published under the title of "*Catholic Lamentation.*" It is one of George Nugent Reynolds's Poems, and was composed, A.D. 1792. It was meant to describe the affliction of a poor Irish peasant—one of the *old* race—who was turned out of his small farm, for sectarian reasons. Others of the Poems by George Nugent Reynolds, bearing on the poor "Irish Exile," are given in Volume II. of this Edition.

I.

Green were the fields where my forefathers dwelt, O ;
 Erin Mavourneen, slán leat gò bragh !
Tho' our farm was small yet comforts we felt, O ;
 Erin Mavourneen, slán leat gò bragh !
At length came the day when our lease did expire,
And fain would I live where before lived my sire,
But ah ! well-a-day, I was forced to retire ;
 Erin Mavourneen, slán leat gò bragh !

II.

Though the laws I obeyed, no protection I found, O ;
 Erin Mavourneen, slán leat gò bragh !
With what grief I beheld my cot burned to the ground, O ;
 Erin Mavourneen, slán leat gò bragh !
Forced from my home—yea from where I was born—
To range the wide world—poor, helpless, forlorn ;
I look back with regret, and my heart-strings are torn ;
 Erin Mavourneen, slán leat gò bragh !

III.

With principles pure, patriotic, and firm,
 Erin Mavourneen, slán leat gò bragh !
To my country attached and a friend to reform,
 Erin Mavourneen, slán leat gò bragh !
I supported old Ireland,—was ready to die for it ;
If her foes e'er prevailed, I was well known to sigh for it ;
But my Faith I preserved, and am now forced to fly for it;
 Erin Mavourneen, slán leat gò bragh !

IV.

But hark ! I hear sounds, and my heart is strong beating,
 Erin Mavourneen, slán leat gò bragh !
Loud cries for redress, and avaunt on retreating ;
 Erin Mavourneen, slán leat gò bragh !
We have numbers,—and numbers do constitute power,
Let us will to be free, and we're free from that hour ;
Of Hibernia's brave sons, oh, we feel we're the flower,
 Buadh leat Mavourneen, Erin gò Bragh !

ERRATUM.

O'ROURKE. (No. 3.)

Of Innismagrath, County Leitrim.

THE Owen O'ROURKE, to whom Hardiman refers in his *Memoir of Carolan,*
Vol. I., pp. liii. and lxii., was not Owen (No. 128), son of Tiernan Bán, as
some readers might suppose from reading pp. 752-753, *supra;* but his
younger son Owen, brother of Hugh, who is No. 129 on that pedigree.
The said younger son Owen, who "lived on the banks of Lough Allen,"
is the man whose name appears on the *souvenir* referred to in Note,
p. 752; his father Owen (No. 128) lived in the parish of Drumlease.

INDEX OF SIRNAMES.

3 I

INDEX OF SIRNAMES.

3 K

3 L

*O'CONNELL.
(See page 184, *supra*.)

It may be well here to observe that :
No. 14, Daniel, son of John, had by
his wife Mary O'Donoghue twenty-two

children, who lived to be adults ; the eldest son of whom was Maurice.

No. 15, Morgan, was the second son. He had four sons and five daughters ; the sons were—1. Daniel, 2. John, 3. Maurice, 4. James.

No. 16. Daniel, "The Liberator," had four sons and three daughters ; the sons were—1. Maurice, 2. Morgan, 3. John, 4. Daniel.

No. 17. Maurice, eldest son of "The Liberator."

No. 18. Daniel O'Connell, of Derrynane Abbey, co. Kerry : eldest son of Maurice (No. 17), and living in 1887.

(See the "O'Connell" pedigree in Vol. II.)

3 M

*This is the anglicised form of the Irish sirname *O'Seasnain.*—See No. 93, p. 155, *ante.*

	PAGE
Snow	449
Sobieski	332
Somers	573, 827, 858
Somerset	162
Somerville	832
Soople	488
Southwell	480, 806
Spaine	261, 494
Sparks	115
Sparling	620
Speed	850
Spellan	261, 777
Spellman	261
Spelman	777
Spence	116
Spencer	125, 310, 527, 810
Spenser	799, 840, 856
Spillane	371, 777
Spillers	777
Spilman	261
Spollen	261, 777
Sporle	117
Spratt	294
Spring	810
Springkiel	811
Stack	617, 810
Stackpole	810
Stackpool	242
Stackpoole	386, 658
Stafford	76, 838
Stanhope	479, 734
Staniburst	834
Stanley	247, 478
Staples	845
Stapleton	188, 841
Staunton	803, 820
Steele	453
Steinagel	526
Stevens	286
Stevenson	394, 630
Stewart	69, 92, 262, 457, 530, 561, 774,
	821, 823, 824, 825
—— of America	265
—— of Castlestewart	266
Stirling	658
St. Jean	151
St. John	120, 676
St. Lawrence	253
St. Leger	165, 577, 810, 815
Stock	335
Stockton	76
Stokes	258
Stone	76, 151, 857
Stonebraker	586
Stoney	151, 857
Storange	304
Stoughton	164
Stowell	626
Strachan	456
Stradford	839
Stritch	465, 806
Strong	304, 815

	PAGE
Strongbow	795
Stronge	304, 473, 834
Stroude	806
Stuart	69, 92, 162, 262, 263, 566, 629,
	726, 774, 815, 839
Sugrue	147, 334
Sullivan	266, 269, 508, 667, 680
Summers	573, 827
Suple	488
Supple	488, 810
Sutton	259, 478, 838
Swain	558
Swaine	79
Swan	603
Swayne	558
Sweeney	526, 558, 561, 769
Sweeny	558, 561
Sweetman	803, 834
Sweney	558
—— of Connaught	778
—— of U. S. America	779
Swift	526, 849
Swiggan	558
Swiney	558
Swiny	779
Swords	117, 334
Swyney	558
Swyny, of Cork	779
Sydney	722
Symes	579
Symmers	153
Synan	855
Synge	72, 219
Synnott	694
Synott	691
TAAFFE	165, 380, 816, 851
Tabb	410
Tabuteau	251
Tackit	858
Talbot	244, 371, 727, 737, 815, 826, 834
Talty	406, 634
Tamany	267
Tarkert	824
Tarpy	372
Tate	217
Tatlock	780
Tatlow	780
Tatly	780
Tavney	267
Taylor	76, 77, 615, 643, 832, 834
Teeling	661
Teighe, of Kilkenny	781
Temple	619, 745
Tenison	788
Tennyson	856
Tenpenny	858
Terrie	511, 825
Territt	458
Terry	810
Tew	834
Teyssier	739

THE END.